Garage Sale & Flea Market Annual

FIFTEENTH EDITION

CASHING IN ON TODAY'S LUCRATIVE COLLECTIBLES MARKET

CURRENT VALUES ON:

TODAY'S COLLECTIBLES
TOMORROW'S ANTIQUES

COLLECTOR BOOKS
A Division of Schroeder Publishing Co., Inc.

Front cover: Darth Vader, loose, $15.00; Precious Moments figurine, Let's Keep Our Eyes On The Goal, 549975, $45.00; Tomatoes, ceramic, from $15.00 to $18.00; Snow White and the Seven Dwarfs toy top, $150.00; Socony-Vacuum, Mobil, fiberglass, $3,500.00; Indianapolis 500 yearbook, 1984, $15.00; ART parrot with large yellow cabochon, $55.00; Blue crackle glass pitcher, Pilgrim, from $45.00 to $50.00; Enesco head vase, E-9013 (a.k.a. Ruth), 7", $1,200.00; Amber Glo platter, #3899, Casual, 13½", from $35.00 to $40.00; Coca-Cola tray, 1940, NM, $400.00.

Back cover: Kay Finch — Pup shaker, #4617, $425.00 and Puss shaker, #54, $425.00; Hippopotamus with bow figurine, $400.00; Puss shaker, $450.00; Camel figurine, #464, $395.00; Owl figurine, $75.00.

Cover design by Beth Summers
Book design by Heather Carvell, Terri Hunter,
and Lisa Henderson

COLLECTOR BOOKS
P.O. Box 3009
Paducah, Kentucky 42002-3009

www.collectorbooks.com

Copyright © 2007 Schroeder Publishing Company

The current values in this book should be used only as a guide. They are not intended to set prices, which vary from one section of the country to another. Auction prices as well as dealer prices vary greatly and are affected by condition as well as demand. Neither the editors nor the publisher assumes responsibility for any losses that might be incurred as a result of consulting this guide.

Searching for a Publisher?

We are always looking for people knowledgeable within their fields. If you feel that there is a real need for a book on your collectible subject and have a large comprehensive collection, contact Collector Books.

Proudly printed and bound in the
United States of America

A Word From the Editor

It's been a good hunting season, from a garage-saler's perspective, though I will agree with some of you who feel that the likelihood of finding bona fide antiques out there isn't as good as it once was. There are, after all, legions of us out there on any given day of the weekend, and competition has become fierce. And no matter how well you plan your strategy or how early you get started, at best, you can be first at only a few sales! Add to that the fact that most of those who hold garage sales are young marrieds trying to sell baby and toddler clothes and unwanted wedding gifts, and you realize the cards may not be stacked in your favor. As the old adage goes, 'you have to kiss a lot of frogs to find your prince,' and the only way to find your 'prince' in this case is to get up, get out, and get around to as many sales as you possibly can work into any given day. The really great items we all hope to find may be more elusive nowadays, but if we retrain our thinking and diversify our intent, there are any number of collectibles out there — we may just have to look a little harder!

I tend to direct my thinking toward those of us who like to dabble a bit in buying to sell. We've been collectors all our married life, and since we were never especially 'rich,' we've often sold garage sale or flea market bargains to fund our own collections. But whether you shop with the intent to keep your treasures or like us look for underpriced goodies that you can sell at a profit, we want to open your eyes to collectibles you may not yet be aware of that may be right in front of you. Unless you're looking for them specifically, you may pass them by unnoticed.

We always search for developing trends and see that every edition contains information on fresh categories of collectibles. New for this edition are linens — vintage tablecloths, tea towels, and printed feed bags, all very marketable, but things many garage sale buyers will overlook. (Watch for vintage handkerchiefs and aprons as well.) Also featured for the first time are discontinued china patterns by Sanyo that sold through Target as well as other mega stores. These sell quickly on eBay as well as other Internet outlets; serving pieces from some of these lines do very well. Another new section is Robinson Ransbottom, and other dealers tell us that their blue-sponged kitchenware items are beginning to move very well for them.

Besides the new categories, we've expanded the information on many other lines which as garage-sale shoppers you're most likely to be finding. Armed with determination and this book as your guide, we promise you that your garage sale hunts can be just as successful as ours have been this year.

Some subjects you may want to concentrate on in glassware are Wexford, Avon Cape Cod, Indiana carnival glass, Fenton, Moon and Star, Early American Prescut, Golden Foliage, Pyrex, Corning Ware, Tiara, Princess House, Anchor Hocking/Fire-King, Kentucky Derby glasses, and kitchen items such as reamers, measuring cups, and salt and pepper shakers. These subjects are all found in this edition, and you'll spend your time wisely if you'll study them well enough to know which items in these categories are the more valuable. For instance, in Early American Prescut, though most of it sells for well under $10.00 per item, the individual salt and pepper shakers are bringing $40.00 on eBay. I learned this the hard way, when I passed them up not long ago for a mere 50¢. I hadn't done my homework, so I totally disregarded them, as they're not at all impressive. I did

have the presence of mind to buy the egg plate (it books for $30.00), the five-part relish tray ($30.00), and a stack of 6¾" plates with the cup ring (they book at $55.00 each). In Wexford, I found the complete punch set still in the box, original recipe booklet and cup hooks included, for only $3.00 (a late-in-the-morning price reduction had been taken), and I sold it on eBay for $55.00 plus formidable postage. At a garage sale in the country, we bought three Fire-King bowls with Gay Fad fruit at $8.00 for all. These book from $15.00 to $30.00 apiece, depending, of course, on size.

In ceramics watch for Sears kitchenware items, Lefton, restaurant china, Josef, Moss Rose, Mood Indigo, Enesco, Avon's Mrs. Albee, discontinued Pfaltzgraff lines, teapots, teabag holders, and salt and pepper shakers. The Sears lines have themes like Neil the Frog, Merry Mushrooms, and Country Kitchen, all of which were accessorized with towels, woodenware, cookware, and plastic items. The appeal that made them so popular during the 1970s is still working for them today, and good examples are selling for well over their original prices. You often see Lefton items on your garage sale/flea market rounds, and though prices are down from a few years ago, their Green Holly is still selling strong (I collect that myself), and the little Kewpie shelf-sitters I paid $1.00 for this summer just sold at our mall for $25.00. Dog and cat figurines appeal to pet lovers, clowns are popular, so are the Chintz and Heritage pieces. Birthday angels are very collectible, and Lefton made some of the nicer ones. A Zodiac Virgo angel (#K8650) recently closed on eBay with an amazing winning bid of $100.00. We've found lots of Pfaltzgraff, and though it's heavy and doesn't do well on eBay due to postage charges, if you do flea markets or have a mall booth, their Village and Yorktown lines are popular sellers. Mood Indigo is a fun line and very affordable, and in Enesco, lady's head vases are big ticket items. Teapots, cookie jars, and salt and pepper shakers can be found at nearly any sale, and some of them are well worth picking up. You'll just need to put a little time into your study to know which to buy and which to pass up.

Coca-Cola, Coppercraft, Syroco, Guardian ware, Fisher-Price and Little Tykes toys, Wilton cake pans, and, of course, jewelry finish off our list of suggested reading. With a little legwork, awareness, and perseverance, the things we've mentioned are easy to find, and though fairly contemporary, still are fun to collect, and can be profitable as well.

Good buys and rare finds are still out there, and thankfully so are collectors. The marketplace is alive and well, and if we can judge it by what's going on in our little town, it's not only alive but thriving. Within the past few months, two antique shops and a large mall have been added to the four shops that were already in business here, and just about any day of the week if we happen to drive through town, we're pleasantly surprised to notice how foot traffic has increased. (All but one are located on the square.) Like many small towns, one by one we've seen many stores close, so it's great to see it busy again.

We've rented a booth in the mall now, and though we're just getting started, it's been a positive, eye-opening experience, one that has restored our faith in the 'system'! Many of us tend to have tunnel vision when it comes to buying/selling antiques and collectibles. But garage sale and flea market buying can open you up to diversification, and that's the key to being successful. Except for a very few pieces of good Fiesta and Roseville, we filled our booth and a case with our garage sale finds — just bargains, nothing we personally collect or even have an interest in for the most part. It was near the end of the month, so in just a few days, we received our first 'paycheck.' It was just a few dollars short of $150.00, but what was amazing was the fact that the merchandise that sold cost us a mere $7.50. Here's what we sold: the pair of Lefton Kewpies I mentioned earlier, a mallard duck TV lamp with two matching planters (a $2.00 purchase), a Boyd jadeite toothpick holder, an Eric Staufer figurine, a Monmouth pitcher (another $2.00 purchase), and a Guardian Ware coaster (which I bought for 10¢ and sold for $5.00). About a week into the second month, we had to restock our tables, and our check this time went over the $1,000.00 mark. It's easy to see that the other dealers are also doing well. Besides 'smalls,' furniture is selling well — oak pieces from early in the century in particular. (I'm sure interest varies in every area of the country, but here in rural Indiana, this type of furniture is very much in demand.) So knowing that we had a place to sell it, the first weekend after we moved into the mall, we found a rather primitive, hand-built birchwood mirrored dresser with some simple applied carvings for $150.00. Within the week, it had sold, bringing us a fast profit of $100.00.

Yes, it is true that the market has changed, and admittedly, garage sale treasures are becoming more and more difficult to come by, but it's still very possible to do well at buying and selling, whether you do it on a small scale for enjoyment as we do, or whether you are a serious dealer. We enjoy the challenge, though, and we go mentally prepared. We know when we arrive at a sale later than a few minutes after it opens, an earlier shopper will more than likely have scooped up the best items. But time spent in research gives us an edge the not-so-knowing competition won't have. Being familiar with a wide range of antiques and collectibles is absolutely necessary. It's easy to spot items you yourself like, but through study, some of the more

esoteric collectibles that really hold no appeal for you personally will catch your trained eye. The key is knowledge. In this guide, we'll suggest references for in-depth study, all written by by today's leading experts. We concentrate on items from the 1940s on, since that's where the market's activity is strongest today. We'll list websites, clubs, tradepapers, and newsletters related to many specific areas; we recommend all of them very highly. There is much knowledge to be gleaned by networking through clubs with collectors whose interests are similar to yours.

An exclusive feature of this book is the section called Special Interests. It contains the addresses of authors, collectors, and dealers sorted by specific collectible categories. Not only are these people potential buyers, but under most circumstances, they'll be willing to help you with questions that remain after you've made a honest attempt at your own research. Just remember if you do write one of our people, you will have to include an SASE if you want a response. And if you call, please consider the differences in time zones. But first, please, read the text. Then go to your library; you should be able to find most of the books we reference. Check them out for study — they're all wonderful. Buy the ones you find particularly helpful or interesting. Good books soon pay for themselves many times over.

If you'd like to collect some nice pieces to decorate your home, as more and more people are doing, or if you're interested in becoming a dealer but find there's no room in the budget for extra spending, we'll show you how to earn extra money by holding your own garage sale. And we'll give you some timely pointers on how to set up at your first flea market.

Remember that our prices in no way reflect what you will be paying at garage sales. Our values are well established and generally accepted by seasoned collectors and authorities; they have been checked over before publication by people well versed in their particular fields.

How to Hold Your Own Garage Sale

Just as we promised we would, here are our suggestions for holding your own garage sale. If you're toying with the idea of getting involved in the business of buying and selling antiques and collectibles but find yourself short of any extra cash to back your venture, this is the way we always recommend you get started. Everyone has items they no longer use; get rid of them! Use them to your advantage. Here's how.

Get Organized. Gather up your merchandise. Though there's not a lot of money in selling clothing, this is the perfect time to unload things you're not using. Kids' clothing does best, since it's usually outgrown before it's worn out, and there's lots of budget-minded parents who realize this and think it makes good sense to invest as little as possible in their own children's wardrobes. Everything should of course be clean and relatively unwrinkled to sell at all, and try to get the better items on hangers.

Leave no stone unturned. Clean out the attic, the basement, the garage — then your parents' attic, basement, and garage. If you're really into it, bake cookies, make some crafts. Divide your house

plants; pot the starts in attractive little containers — ladies love 'em. Discarded and outgrown toys sell well. Framed prints and silk flower arrangements you no longer use, recipe books and paperbacks, tapes, records, and that kitchen appliance that's more trouble to store than it's worth can be turned into cash to get you off and running!

After you've gathered up your merchandise, you'll need to price it. Realistically, clothing will bring at the most about 15% to 25% of what you had to pay for it, if it's still in excellent, ready-to-wear shape and basically still in style. There's tons of used clothing out there, and no one is going to buy much of anything with buttons missing or otherwise showing signs of wear. If you have good brand-name clothing that has been worn very little, you would probably do better by taking it to a resale or consignment shop. They normally price things at about one-third of retail, with their cut being 30% of that. Not much difference money-wise, but the garage-sale shopper that passes up that $150.00 suit you're asking $25.00 for will probably give $50.00 for it at the consignment shop, simply because like department stores, many have dressing rooms with mirrors so you can try things on and check them for fit before you buy. Even at $25.00, the suit is no bargain if it doesn't fit when you get it home.

Remember that garage-sale buyers expect to find low prices. Depending on how long you plan on staying open, you'll have one day, possibly two to move everything. If you start out too high, you'll probably be stuck with lots of leftover merchandise, most of which you've already decided is worthless to you. The majority of your better buyers will hit early on; make prices attractive to them and you'll do all right. If you come up with some 'low-end' collectibles — fast-food toys, character glasses, played-with action figures, etc. — don't expect to get much out of them at a garage sale. Your competition down the block may underprice you. But if you have a few things you think have good resale potential, offer them at about half of 'book' price. If they don't sell at your garage sale, take them to a flea market or a consignment shop. You'll probably find they sell better on that level, since people expect to find prices higher there than at garage sales.

You can use pressure-sensitive labels or masking tape for price tags on many items. But *please* do not use either of these on things where damage is likely to occur when they are removed. For instance (as one reader pointed out), on boxes containing toys, board games, puzzles, etc.; on record labels or album covers; or on ceramics or glass with gold trim or unfired, painted decoration. Unless a friend or a neighbor is going in on the sale with you, price tags won't have to be removed; the profit will all be yours. Of course, you'll have to keep tabs if others are involved. You can use a sheet of paper divided into columns, one for each of you, and write the amount of each sale down under the appropriate person's name, or remove the tags and restick them on a piece of poster board, one for each seller. I've even seen people use straight pins to attach small paper price tags which they remove and separate into plastic butter tubs. When several go together to have a sale, the extra help is nice, but don't let things get out of hand. Your sale can get *too* big. Things become too congested, and it's hard to display so much merchandise to good advantage.

Advertise. Place your ad in your local paper or on your town's cable TV information channel. It's important to make your ad interesting and upbeat. Though most sales usually start early on Friday or Saturday mornings, some people are now holding their sales in the early evening, and they seem to be having good crowds. This gives people with day jobs an opportunity to attend. You *might* want to hold your sale for two days, but you'll do 90% of your selling during the first two or three hours, and a two-day sale can really drag on. Make signs — smaller ones for street corners near your home to help direct passers-by, and a large one for your yard. You might even want to make another saying 'Clothing ½-Price after 12:00.' (It'll cut way down on leftovers that you'll otherwise have to dispose of yourself.) Be sure that you use a wide-tipped felt marker and print in letters big enough that the signs can be read from the street. Put the smaller signs up a few days in advance unless you're expecting rain. (If you are, you might want to include a rain date in your advertising unless your sale will be held under roof.) Make sure you have lots of boxes and bags and plenty of change. If you price your items in increments of 25¢, you won't need anything but a few rolls of quarters, maybe ten or fifteen ones, and a few five-dollar bills. Then on the day of the sale, put the large sign up in a prominent place out front with some balloons to attract the crowd. Take a deep breath, brace yourself, and raise the garage door!

What to Do with What's Left. After the sale, pack up any good collectibles that didn't sell. Think about that consignment shop or setting up at a flea market. (We'll talk about that later on.) Sort out the better items of clothing for Goodwill or a similar charity, unless your city has someone who will take your leftovers and sell them on consignment. This is a fairly new concept, but some of the larger cities have such 'bargain centers.'

Learning to Become a Successful Bargain Hunter

Let me assure you, anyone who takes the time to become an informed, experienced bargain hunter will be successful. There is enough good merchandise out there to make it well worthwhile, at all levels. Once you learn what to look for, what has good resale potential, and what price these items will probably bring for you, you'll be equipped and ready for any hunting trip. You'll be the one to find treasures. They are out there!

Garage sales are absolutely wonderful for finding bargains. But you'll have to get up early! Even non-collectors can spot quality merchandise, and at those low garage sale prices (low unless of course held by an owner who's done his homework) those items will be the first to move.

In order for you to be a successful garage sale shopper, you have to learn how to get yourself organized. It's important to conserve your time. The sales you hit during the first early-morning hour will prove to be the best nine times out of ten, so you must have a plan before you ever leave home. Plot your course. Your local paper will have a section on garage sale ads, and local cable TV channels may also carry garage sale advertising. Most people hold their sales on the weekend, but some may start earlier in the week, so be sure to turn to the 'Garage Sales' ads daily. Write them down and try to organize them by areas — northwest, northeast, etc. At first, you'll probably need your city map, but you'll be surprised at how quickly the streets will become familiar to you. Upper middle-class neighborhoods generally have the best sales and the best merchandise, so concentrate on those areas, though sales in older areas may offer older items. (Here's where you have to interpret those sale ads.) When you've decided where you want to start, go early! If the ad says 8:00, be there at 7:00. This may seem rude and pushy, but if you can bring yourself to do it, it will pay off. And chances are when you get there an hour early, you'll not be their first customer. If they're obviously not ready for business, just politely inquire if you may look. If you're charming and their nerves aren't completely frayed from trying to get things ready, chances are they won't mind.

Competition can be fierce during those important early morning hours. Learn to scan the tables quickly, then move to the area that looks the most promising. Don't be afraid to ask for a better price if you feel it's too high, but most people have already priced garage sale merchandise so that it will sell. Keep a notebook to jot down items you didn't buy the first time around but think you might be interested in if the price were reduced later on. After going through dozens of sales (I've done as many as 30 or so in one morning), you won't remember where you saw what! Often by noon, at least by mid-afternoon, veteran garage sale buyers are finished with their rounds and attendance becomes very thin. Owners are usually much more receptive to the idea of lowering their prices, so it may pay you to make a second pass. In fact, some people find it advantageous to go to the better sales on the last day as well as the first. They'll make an offer for everything that's left, and since most of the time the owner is about ready to *pay* someone to take it at that point, they can usually name their price. Although most of the collectibles will normally be gone at this point, there are nearly always some useable household items and several pieces of good, serviceable clothing left. The household items will sell at flea markets or consignment shops, and if there are worthwhile clothing items, take them to a resale boutique. They'll either charge the 30% commission fee or buy the items outright for about half of the amount they feel they can ask, a new practice some resale shops are beginning to follow. Because they want only clothing that is in style, in season, and like new, their prices may be a little higher than other shops, so half of that asking price is a good deal.

Tag sales are common in the larger cities. They are normally held in lieu of an auction, when estates are being dispersed, or when families are moving. Sometimes only a few buyers are admitted at one time, and as one leaves another is allowed to take his place. So just as is true with garage sales, the early bird gets the goodies. Really serious shoppers begin to arrive as much as an hour or two before the scheduled opening time. I know of one who will spend the night in his van and camp on the 'doorstep' if he thinks the sale is especially promising. And he can tell you fantastic success stories! But since it's customary to have tag sale items appraised before values are set, be prepared to pay higher prices. That's not to say, though, that you won't find bargains here. If you think an item is overpriced, leave a bid. Just don't forget to follow through on it, since if it doesn't sell at their asking price, they may end up holding it for you. It's a good idea to check back on the last day of the sale. Often the prices on unsold items may have been drastically reduced.

Auctions can go either way. Depending on the crowd and what items are for sale, you can sometimes spend all day and never be able to buy anything anywhere near 'book' price. Better items often go high. On the other hand, there are often 'sleepers' that can be bought cheaply enough to resell at a good profit. Toys, dolls, Hummels, Royal Doultons, banks, cut glass, and other 'high-profile' collectibles usually sell well, but white ironstone, dinnerware sets from the '20s through the '50s, silver-plated hollow ware, books, records, and linens, for instance, often pass relatively unnoticed by the majority of the buyers.

If there is a consignment auction house in your area, check it out. These are usually operated by local auctioneers, and the sales they hold in-house often involve low-income estates. You won't find something every time, so try to investigate the merchandise ahead of schedule to see if it's going to be worth your time to attend. Competition is probably less at one of these than in any of the other types of sales we've mentioned, and wonderful buys have been made from time to time.

Flea markets are often wonderful places to find bargains. I don't like the small ones — not that I don't find anything there, but I've learned to move through them so fast (to get ahead of the crowd), I don't get my 'fix'; I just leave wanting more. If you've never been to a large flea market, you don't know what you're missing. Even if you're not a born-again collector, I guarantee you will love it. And they're excellent places to study the market. You'll be able to see where the buying activity is; you can check and compare prices, talk with dealers and collectors, and do hands-on inspections. I've found that if I first study a particular subject by reading a book or a magazine article, this type of exposure to that collectible really 'locks in' what I have learned.

Because there are many types of flea market dealers, there are plenty of bargains. The casual, once-in-a-while dealer may not always keep up with changing market values. Some of them simply price their items by what they themselves had to pay for it. Just as being early at garage sales is important, here it's a must. If you've ever been in line waiting for a flea market to open, you know that cars are often backed up for several blocks, and people will be standing in line waiting to be admitted hours before the gate opens. Browsers? Window shoppers? Not likely. Competition! So if you're going to have a chance at all, you'd better be in line yourself. Take a partner and split up on the first pass so that you can cover the grounds more quickly. It's a common sight to see the serious buyers conversing with their partners via walkie-talkies, and if you like to discuss possible purchases with each other before you actually buy, this is a good way to do it.

Learn to bargain with dealers. Their prices are usually negotiable, and most will come down by 10% to 20%. Be polite and fair, and you can expect the same treatment in return. Unpriced items are harder to deal for. I have no problem offering to give $8.00 if an item is marked $10.00, but it's difficult for me to have to ask the price and then make a counter offer. So I'll just say 'This isn't marked. Will you take...?' I'm not an aggressive barterer, so this works for me.

There are so many reproductions on the flea market level (and at malls and co-ops), that you need to be suspicious of anything that looks too new! Some fields of collecting have been especially hard hit. Whenever a collectible becomes so much in demand that prices are high, reproductions are bound to make an appearance. For instance, Black Americana, Nippon, Roseville, banks, toys of all types, teddy bears, lamps, glassware, doorstops, cookie jars, prints, advertising items, and many other fields have been especially vulnerable. Learn to check for telltale signs — paint that is too bright, joints that don't fit, variations in sizes or colors, creases in paper that you can see but not feel, and so on. Remember that zip codes have been used only since 1963, and this can sometimes help you date an item in question. Check glassware for areas of wavy irregularities often seen in new glass. A publication we would highly recommend to you is called *Antique and Collector Reproduction News*, a monthly report of 'Fakes, Frauds, and Facts.' To subscribe, call 1-515-274-5886. You can find them on the web at repronews.com. Rates are very reasonable compared to the money you may save by learning to recognize reproductions.

Antique malls and co-ops should be visited on a regular basis. Many mall dealers restock day after day, and traffic and buying competition is usually fierce. As a rule, you won't often find great bargains here; what you do save on is time. And if time is what you're short of, you'll be able to see lots of good merchandise under one roof, on display by people who've already done the leg work and invested *their* time, hence the higher prices. But there are always underpriced items as well, and if you've taken the time to do your homework, you'll be able to spot them right away.

Unless the dealer who rents the booth happens to be there, though, mall and co-op prices are usually firm. But often times they'll run sales — '20% off everything in booth #101.' If you have a dealer's license, and you really should get one, most will give you a courtesy 10% discount on items over $10.00, unless you want to pay with a credit card.

Antique shows are exciting to visit, but obviously if a dealer is paying several hundred dollars to set up for a three-day show, he's going to be asking top price to offset expenses. So even though bargains will be few, the merchandise is usually superior, and you may be able to find that special item you've been looking for.

Mail order buying is not only very easy, but most of the time economical as well. Many people will place an ad in 'For Sale' sections of tradepapers. Some will describe and price their merchandise in their ad, while others offer lists of items they have in exchange for an SASE (stamped, self-addressed envelope). You're out no gas or food expenses, their overhead is minimal so their prices are usually very reasonable, so it works out great for both buyer and seller. I've made lots of good buys this way, and I've always been fairly and honestly dealt with. You may want to send a money order or cashier's check to save time, otherwise (especially on transactions involving larger sums of money) the seller might want to wait until your personal check clears.

Goodwill stores and re-sale shops are usually listed in the telephone book. When you travel, it will pay you to check them out. If there's one in your area, visit it often. You never know what may turn up there.

Internet shopping is still at the hub of most of the buying/selling activity today. Set-price online malls are expanding as many dealers find that auction prices are very often too soft to accept, and scores of long-time antiques and collectibles dealers now have wonderful websites. Buyers often voice the opinion that they are more confident when trading with these well-established sellers than they are some of the part-time vendors more often encountered on eBay and similar sites. Still, there is no doubt that there are many bargains to be had on eBay, and it will continue to be a big factor in the marketplace. But where you could basically sell anything via eBay a couple of years ago, now to attract a buyer, you may very often have to relist your item with a lower reserve, and you'll find some things won't sell at all.

What's Hot on Today's Market

As anyone who has been involved in this hobby is well aware, today's market is quite different than it was several years ago. The better examples in the well-established fields continue to appreciate, but as we all know, those are seldom found on our garage sale and flea market rounds. So lets focus here on the glassware, pottery, toys, etc., that this venue generally has to offer. Because there is such a plethora of this type of merchandise still available, applying the simple law of supply and demand, it only reasons that values will soften somewhat. At the same time, eBay is a great place to turn your finds into cash fast, and those lower prices are enticing new collectors, so the future looks good, and values can only go up.

Look for trends; ferret them out. To do this, you'll have to spend some time in study. Attend shows, talk to dealers and fellow collectors. Read tradepapers and magazines, and check out the 'antiques and collectibles' isles of your bookstore. Watch for new books on any subject. Sometimes that's all it takes to get one off and running.

For the most part, the areas we reported as 'hot' last year still are, but there are some new categories worth listing this year — pay special attention to them.

Linens! Vintage aprons, brightly patterned tablecloths, and tea towels, are doing very well. If you Google for vintage tablecloths, you'll see that those with especially interesting and colorful designs are bringing very high prices. Those with states themes are selling very well, and towels with Black Americana designs bring top dollar. Aprons that have been handmade and commercially made ones with original tags are among the best.

Dolls will always be hot, and Barbie dolls are still stealing the spotlight. There seems to be no end to books on Barbie collectibles, and vintage Barbie dolls continue to do well in holding value. In fact, the high-end Barbie doll are inching up and up. Values for loose Liddle Kiddles may have softened, but MIB items still find a ready market at very good prices. Shirley Temple dolls and related memorabilia, Madame Alexander dolls, Nancy Ann Storybook dolls, and Knickerbocker Raggedy Ann and Andy dolls are strong on the market. Strawberry Shortcake is doing very well, especially the earlier editions. Watch for Mattel talkers (Chatty Cathy among them), Dawn dolls, Ideal dolls, and celebrity dolls. Steiff teddy bears and animals are always good.

American dinnerware continues to do well. Lines that reflect the mid-century high-style concept by designers such as Zeisel, Schreckengost, and Russel Wright top the list, but more traditional lines by chinaware companies like Hall and Homer Laughlin are close behind. Lu-Ray by Taylor, Smith and Taylor; many of the popular lines by Metlox, Franciscan, Vernon Kilns, and the Royal China company; the Western lines by Wallace; the lovely hand-painted patterns by Blue Ridge; and the charming primitive lines of Watt, Purinton, and Pennsbury are all very collectible. Although eBay has caused Fiesta collectors to be reluctant to pay high book for anything other than mint condition items with no factory flaws or signs of wear, except for very common items, Fiesta remains a good seller, and discontinued colors from Post86 Fiesta are sometimes prefered over vintage. There is a lot of interest in the lines made by Bauer. Marcrest made stoneware in a brown glossy glaze in a pattern called Daisy and Dot, and evidence strongly suggests this is well worth picking up. Top-marked restaurant ware with logos of railroads, hotels, or branches of the military is often being bought not only as nostalgic souvenirs but for actual use in the home.

Among ceramic items, several companies' wares are basically

strong; though prices may be down from their high of a few years ago, interest is still there. That group would include the wonderful figurines by Ceramic Arts Studios, Kay Finch, Brayton Laguna, Will-George, Florence Ceramics, Max Weil, Hedi Schoop, and Howard Pierce. High-style designs made by Glidden, Sascha Brastoff, and Royal Arden Hickman appeal to those whose tastes run toward mid-century modern. There are several more designers, each of whom conveyed diversified personal vision through their creations: Dorothy Kindell, Matthew Adams, Brad Keeler, and the Cleminsons, among others; watch for items that carry these signatures, as they continue to be popular. You often see small pieces of Noritake and Nippon on garage sale tables at prices that allow for a good profit margin.

Roseville, Weller, and Rookwood — probably the giants among the American pottery companies produced wonderful vases and pots that will never go out of favor. Of course, there are many others. Hull, Shawnee, Haeger, McCoy, Brush, Cowan, Muncie, Van Briggle, and Abingdon are marks to watch for. If you find a piece of pottery with the mark of any manufacturer, American or otherwise, you would do well to buy it up at garage sale prices.

Novelty ceramics have fallen off in value over the past few years, but already some are making a comeback. Lefton items often have crossover collector appeal; for example Christmas, animal figurines, and cups and saucers. Holt Howard prices have declined as a whole, but those powerhouse Pixies are more than holding their own. Good head vases, string holders, reamers, cookie jars, and clothes sprinkler bottles continually sell at respectable prices. The Royal Copley line of figurines, planters, wall pockets, etc., are well done and very collectible, and Hagen-Renaker figures often bring spectacular prices. Sears ceramics from the 1970s — Neil the Frog, Merry Mushrooms, and Country Kitchen items are drawing lots of interest.

In glassware, Depression glass, carnival glass, and of course, elegant glass ever endure. Kitchen glass finds a ready market, Anchor Hocking's Fire-King in particular. You'll often see good Fenton at garage sales; L.G. Wright, Blenko, and Westmoreland are certainly worth your time and investment. Colored glassware, especially Jadeite, ruby red, forest green, and Delphite Blue have been favorites for years and are still good choices. Crackle glass by Blenko and other companies is very collectible.

Costume jewelry signed by noted designers can sell for prices as dazzling a their appearance. Watch for names such as Trifari, Hattie Carnegie, Napier, Coro, Haskell, and Lisner. Well done unmarked rhinestone jewelry continues to have worth, and Bakelite/Catalin plastics often sell in the same price range as fine jewelry. Even unsigned high quality jewelry can turn a good profit for you. Quality cuff links and those with a particularly interesting design are well worth buying.

In furniture, '50s Modern is a popular look, and Mission/Arts and Crafts dominates the scene. Signed pieces from either genre can be worth hundreds of dollars, but even unsigned items if well made in good condition are well worth your attention.

In the advertising field, character collectibles maintain a high profile. Our advertising category features some of the most popular stars of the advertising world — Mr. Peanut, Elsie the Cow, Old Crow, Poppin' Fresh, Mr. Bib, and Campbell Kids. Coca-Cola items are plentiful, and there are thousands of collectors for them. They may prefer vintage items, but even interesting post-1950s Coke

memorabilia sells well. Pepsi-Cola, Hires, Orange Crush, Nehi, and 7-Up have their own devotees.

In addition to those we've already mentioned, here are other areas where you'll see considerable interest right now:

American Indian relics

American pottery (besides those we mentioned in the previous paragraphs), anything of quality that is marked or has good lines

Automobilia

Bottles, especially dairy bottles, figurals, barber bottles, and soda bottles with painted labels

Black Americana

Cast-iron figural items such as bookends, doorstops, doorknockers, trivets, and bottle openers

Breweriana

Cat and dog collectibles — especially Shafford black cats

Children's books, especially Little Golden Books, Dick and Jane readers, Big Little Books, and series books

Christmas ornaments and lighting

Clocks, especially motion clocks by Haddon, Mastercrafters, Spartus, Lux, and United

Clothing, hats, and accessories, anything vintage, preferably from the forties through the seventies; vintage denims in particular

Cookbooks

Compacts and ladies' purse accessories

Corning ware and Visions cookware

Czechoslovakian glass and pottery

Fishing tackle and lures — rods and reels, tackle boxes, catalogs and vintage advertisements

Fountain pens

Furniture by Heywood-Wakefield and all well-known Fifties Modern designers

Gas station memorabilia

Glass candlesticks

Golf collectibles

Granite ware

Guardian ware

Halloween collectibles

John Deere collectibles

Ladies' fine handkerchiefs

Lamps, especially Aladdin, those with 1950s styling, motion lamps, and TV lamps

LP records with great or interesting covers, including jazz

Lunch boxes

Made in Japan ceramics

Marbles

Model kits — Aurora, Monogram, MPC, and Revel

Musical instruments — vintage guitars are sizzling!

Paintings and prints

Patriotic and homefront collectibles, especially sweetheart jewelry

Perfume bottles — watch for those marked Czechoslovakia

Photographica — from cameras to hand-painted photographs

Pocketknives

Pyrex with colorful designs and solid-color treatments

Quilts

Racing collectibles, especially NASCAR

Radios — character and novelty related, transistor, and
those made of colorful Bakelite and Catalin

Railroadiana

Salt and pepper shakers

Sewing collectibles and buttons; Singer Featherweight
sewing machines

Silver-plated flatware

Singer Featherweight sewing machines

Soda pop memorabilia

Sports collectibles

Tins for everthing from spices to tobacco

Toothpick holders

Wall pockets

Watches — character related, advertising, and of course the
better American- and European-made examples

Wicker furniture

Zippo lighters

8mm boxed films with great graphics on the boxes, especially
horror films

For right now, at least, these areas are sluggish: ashtrays, Beanie Babies, bubble bath containers, California Raisins, fast-food items, Norman Rockwell items, Jim Beam bottles, Avon bottles, collector plates, and brown-drip dinnerware. There are always exceptions, however. In every field, there are rarities that are always desirable, and we all need to be aware of them, if we're going to take full advantage of all the opportunities garage sale and flea market shopping have to offer. Remember, the most important factor to consider when buying any of these items for resale is condition. If they show more than just a little wear or are damaged more than a minimal amount, don't waste you're time on them at any price. Today's collectors are more discerning than ever, thanks again to the Internet and the preponderance of supply over demand. Condition is all-important.

How to Evaluate Your Holdings

When viewed in its entirety, granted, the antiques and collectibles market can be overwhelming. But in each line of glassware, any type of pottery or toys, or any other field I could mention, there are examples that are more desirable than others, and these are the ones you need to be able to recognize. If you're a novice, it will probably be best at first to choose a few areas that you find most interesting and learn just what particular examples or types of items are most in demand within that field. Concentrate on the top 25%. This is where you'll do 75% of your business. Do your homework. Quality sells. Obviously no one can be an expert in everything, but gradually you can begin to broaden your knowledge. As an added feature of our guide, information on clubs and newsletters, always a wonderful source of up-to-date information on any subject, is contained in each category when available. (Advisors' names are listed as well. We highly recommend that you exhaust all other resources before you contact them with your inquiries. Their role is simply to check over our data before we go to press to make sure it is as accurate as we and they can possibly make it for you; they do not agree to answer readers' questions, though some may. If you do write, you must send them an SASE. If you call, please take the time zones into consideration. Some of our advisors are professionals and may charge an appraisal fee, so be sure to ask. Please, do *not* be offended if they do not respond to your contacts, they are under no obligation to do so.)

There are many fields other than those we've already mentioned that are strong and have been for a long time. It's impossible to list them all. But we've left very little out of this book; at least we've tried to represent each category to some extent and where at all possible to refer you to a source of further information. It's up to you to read, observe the market, and become acquainted with it to the point that you feel confident enough to become a part of today's antiques and collectibles industry.

The thousands of current values found in this book will increase your awareness of today's wonderful world of buying, selling, and collecting antiques and collectibles. Use it to educate yourself to the point that you'll be the one with the foresight to know what and how to buy as well as where and how to turn those sleepers into cold, hard cash.

In addition to this one, there are several other very fine price guides on the market. One of the best is *Schroeder's Antiques Price Guide*; another is *The Flea Market Trader*. Both are published by Collector Books. *The Antique Trader Antiques and Collectibles Price Guide, Warman's Antiques and Their Prices,* and *Kovel's Antiques and Collectibles Price List* are others. You may want to invest in a copy of each. Where you decide to sell will have a direct bearing on how you price your merchandise, and nothing will affect an item's worth more than condition.

If you're not familiar with using a price guide, here's a few tips that may help you. When convenient and reasonable, antiques will be sorted by manufacturer. This is especially true of pottery and most glassware. If you don't find the item you're looking for under manufacturer, look under a broader heading, for instance, cat collectibles, napkin dolls, cookie jars, etc. And don't forget to use the index. Most guides of this type have very comprehensive indexes — a real boon to the novice collector. If you don't find the exact item you're trying to price, look for something similar. For instance, if it's a McCoy rabbit planter you're researching, go through the McCoy section and see what price range other animal planters are in. (There are exceptions, however, and if an item is especially rare and desirable, this will not apply. Here's where you need a comprehensive McCoy book.) Or if you have a frame-tray puzzle with Snow White and the Seven Dwarfs, see what other Disney frame-trays are priced at. Just be careful not to compare apples to oranges. Age is important as well. You can judge the value of a 7" Roseville Magnolia vase that's not listed in any of your guides; just look at the price given for one a little larger or smaller and adjust it up or down. Pricing collectibles is certainly not a science; the bottom line is simply where the buyer and the seller finally agree to do business. Circumstances dictate sale price, and we can only make suggestions, which we base on current sales, market observations, and the expert opinions of our advisors.

Once you've found 'book' price, decide how much less you can take for it. 'Book' price represents a high average retail. A collectible will often change hands many times, and obviously it will not always be sold at book price. How quickly do you want to realize a profit? Will you be patient enough to hold out for top dollar, or would you rather price your merchandise lower so it will turn over more quickly? Just as there are both types of dealers, there are two types of collectors. Many are bargain hunters. They shop around — do the legwork themselves. On the other hand, there are those who are willing to pay whatever the asking price is to avoid spending precious time searching out pieces they especially want, but they represent the minority. You'll often see tradepaper ads listing good merchandise (from that top 25% we mentioned before) at prices well above book value. This is a good example of a dealer who knows that his merchandise is good enough to entice the buyer who is able to pay a little more and doesn't mind waiting for him (or her) to come along, and that's his prerogative.

Don't neglect to access the condition of the item you want to sell. This is especially important in online and mail order selling. Most people, especially inexperienced buyers and sellers, have a tendency to overlook some flaws and to overrate merchandise. Mint condition means that an item is complete and undamaged — in effect, just as it looked the day it was made. Glassware, china, and pottery may often be found today in wonderful mint condition. Check for signs of wear, though, since even wear will downgrade value. (Looking 'good considering its age' is like coming close

in horseshoes — it doesn't really count!) Remember that when a buyer doesn't have the option of seeing for himself, your written description is all he has to go by. Save yourself the hassle of costly and time-consuming returns by making sure the condition of your merchandise is accurately and completely described. Unless a toy is still in its original box and has never been played with, you seldom see one in mint condition. Paper collectibles are almost never found without some deterioration or damage. Most price guides will list values that apply to glass and ceramics that are mint (unless another condition is specifically indicated within some descriptions). Other items are usually evaluated on the assumption that they are in the best as-found condition common to that area of collecting, for instance magazines are simply never found in mint condition. Grade your merchandise as though you were the buyer, not the seller. You'll be building a reputation that will go a long way toward contributing to your success. If it's glassware or pottery you're assessing, an item in less than excellent condition will be mighty hard to sell at any price. Just as a guideline (a basis to begin your evaluation, though other things will factor in), use a scale of one to five with good being a one, excellent being a three, and mint being a five. As an example, a beer tray worth $250.00 in mint condition would then be worth $150.00 if excellent and $50.00 if only good. Remember, the first rule of buying (for resale or investment) is 'Don't put your money in damaged goods.' And the second rule should be be, 'If you do sell damaged items, indicate 'as is' on the price tag, and don't price the item as though it were mint.' The Golden Rule applies just as well to us as antique dealers as it does to any other interaction. Some shops and co-ops have poor lighting, and damage can be easily missed by a perspective buyer — your honesty will be greatly appreciated. If you include identification on your tags as well, be sure it's accurate. If you're not positive, say so. Better yet, let the buyer decide.

Deciding Where To Best Sell Your Merchandise

Personal transactions are just one of many options. Overhead and expenses will vary with each and must be factored into your final pricing. If you have some especially nice items and can contact a collector willing to pay top dollar, that's obviously the best of the lot. Or you may decide to sell to a dealer who may be willing to pay you only half of book. Either way, your expenses won't amount to much more than a little gas or a phone call.

Internet auctions may be your preferred venue. Look at completed auctions for sales results of similar items to decide. Unless you have a digital camera, factor in the cost of photography (sales of items with no photograph suffer), image hosting, and listing fees. Remember that the cost of boxes and bubble wrap must also be considered, not to mention the time spent actually listing the item, answering e-mail questions, contacting the buyer with the winning bid, leaving feedback, etc.

Internet selling works. In fact, I know some dealers who have quit doing shows and simply work out of their home. No more unpacking, travel expenses, or inconvenience of any kind to endure. You may sell through a set-price online mall or an auction. If you

choose the auction (eBay is the most widely used right now), you can put a 'reserve' on everything you sell, a safeguard that protects the seller and prevents an item from going at an unreasonably low figure should there be few bidders.

Classified ads are another way to get a good price for your more valuable merchandise without investing much money or time. Place a 'For Sale' ad or run a mail bid in one of the collector magazines or newsletters, several of which are listed in the back of this book. Many people have had excellent results this way. If you have several items and the cost of listing them all is prohibitive, simply place an ad saying (for instance) 'Several pieces of Royal Copley (or whatever) for sale, send SASE for list. Be sure to give your correct address and phone number.

When you're making out your list or talking with a prospective buyer by phone or by e-mail, try to draw a picture with words. Describe any damage in full; it's much better than having a disgruntled customer to deal with later, and you'll be on your way to establishing yourself as a reputable dealer. Better yet, send photographs. Seeing the item exactly as it is will often help the prospective buyer make up his or her mind. If you use regular mail, send an SASE along and ask that your photos be returned to you, so that you can send them out again, if need be. A less expensive alternative is to have your item photocopied. This works great for many smaller items, not just flat shapes but things with some dimension as well. It's wonderful for hard-to-describe dinnerware patterns or for showing their trademarks. Of course, the easiest way to communicate and send photos is through e-mail, and digital cameras make the process so convenient. If at all possible, invest in one!

If you've made that 'buy of a lifetime' or an item you've hung onto for a few years has turned out to be a scarce, highly sought collectible, you should be able to get top dollar for your prize. If you decide to take it online, you'll want to start your auction with a high but reasonable reserve. Should the item fail to meet reserve, relist it with one that is lower than the original. The final bid the first time around will give you a good idea of where it may go the second time.

Be sure to let your buyer know what form of payment you prefer. Some dealers will not ship merchandise until personal checks have cleared. This delay may make the buyer a bit unhappy. So you may want to request a money order or a cashier's check. Nowadays there are several hassle-free ways to make transactions online, and though Pay Pal is by far the most familiar, there are are other alternatives. Check them out through your favorite search engine.

Be very careful about how you pack your merchandise for shipment. Breakables need to be well protected. There are several things you can use. Plastic bubble wrap is excellent and adds very little weight to your packages. Or use scraps of foam rubber such as carpet padding (check with a carpet-laying service or confiscate some from family and friends who are getting new carpet installed). I've received items wrapped in pieces of egg-crate type mattress pads (watch for these at garage sales!). If there is a computer business near you, check their dumpsters for discarded foam wrapping and other protective packaging. It's best not to let newspaper come in direct contact with your merchandise, since the newsprint may stain certain surfaces. After you've wrapped them well, you'll need boxes. Find smaller boxes (one or several, whatever best fits your needs) that you can fit into a larger one with several inches of space between them. First pack your well-wrapped items snugly into the smaller box, using crushed newspaper to keep them from shifting. Place it into the larger box, using more crushed paper underneath and along the sides, so that it will not move during transit. Remember, if it arrives broken, it's still your merchandise, even though you have received payment.

You may want to insure the shipment; check with your carrier. Some have automatic insurance up to a specified amount.

After you've mailed your box, it's good to follow it up with a phone call or an e-mail after a few days. Make sure it arrived in good condition and that your customer is pleased with the merchandise. Most people who sell by mail or the Internet allow a 10-day return privilege, providing their original price tag is still intact. For this purpose, you can simply initial a gummed label or use one of those pre-printed return address labels that most of us have around the house.

For very large or heavy items such as furniture or slot machines, ask your buyer for his preferred method of shipment. If the distance involved is not too great, he may even want to pick it up himself.

Flea market selling can either be lots of fun, or it can turn out to be one of the worst experiences of your life. Obviously you will have to deal with whatever weather conditions prevail, so be sure to listen to weather reports so that you can dress accordingly. You'll see some inventive shelters you might want to copy. Even a simple patio umbrella will offer respite from the blazing sun or a sudden downpour. I've recently been seeing stands catering just to the needs of the flea market dealer — how's that for being enterprising! Not only do they carry specific items the dealers might want, but they've even had framework and tarpaulins, and they'll erect shelters right on the spot!

Be sure to have plastic table covering in case of rain and some large clips to hold it down if there's much wind. The type of clip you'll need depends on how your table is made, so be sure to try them out before you actually get caught in a storm. Glass can blow over, paper items can be ruined, and very quickly your career as a flea market dealer may be cut short for lack of merchandise!

Price your things, allowing yourself a little bargaining room. Unless you want to collect tax separately on each sale (for this you'd need lots of small change), mentally calculate the amount and add this on as well. Sell the item 'tax included.' Everybody does.

Take snacks, drinks, paper bags, plenty of change, and somebody who can relieve you occasionally. Collectors are some of the nicest people around. I guarantee that you'll enjoy this chance to meet and talk them, and often you can make valuable contacts that may help you locate items you're especially looking for yourself.

Auction houses are listed in the back of this book. If you have an item you feel might be worth selling at auction, be sure to contact one of them. Many have appraisal services; some are free while others charge a fee, dependent on number of items and time spent. We suggest you first make a telephone inquiry before you send in a formal request.

In Summation

As any collector will tell you, becoming involved in the antiques and collectibles field can be not only an enjoyable social experience but a profitable one as well. Whether you're strictly a collector, or a part- or full-time dealer, you no doubt already know that today's market is a collector's market. But even those of us who buy to resell can do quite well, as long as we familiarize ourselves with emerging trends and are willing to make the extra effort to do our research, attend shows, and network with others. Knowlege is the key, and the time you invest in gaining it will pay off. Keep an open mind and develop good instincts. The rewards will be well worth your efforts. We hope you enjoy the hunt for today's collectibles, tomorrow's antiques!

Abbreviations

dia — diameter
ea — each
EX — excellent
G — good condition
gal — gallon
H — high
L — long, length
lg — large
M — mint condition
med — medium
MIB — mint in (original) box
MIP — mint in package
MOC — mint on card
NM — near mint
NRFB — never removed from box
oz — ounce
pc — piece
pr — pair
pt — pint
qt — quart
sm — small
sq — square
VG — very good
w/ — with
(+) — has been reproduced

Note: When no condition is noted within our description lines, assume that the value we give is for mint condition items.

Abingdon Pottery

You may find smaller pieces of Abingdon around, but it's not common to find many larger items. This company operated in Abingdon, Illinois, from 1934 until 1950, making not only nice vases and figural pieces but some kitchen items as well. Their cookie jars are very well done and popular with collectors. They sometimes used floral decals and gold to decorate their wares, and a highly decorated item is worth a minimum of 25% more than the same shape with no decoration. Some of their glazes also add extra value. If you find a piece in black, bronze, or red, you can add 25% to those as well. Note that if you talk by phone about Abingdon to a collector, be sure to mention the mold number on the base.

For more information we recommend *Abingdon Pottery Artware, 1934 – 50, Stepchild of the Great Depression,* by Joe Paradis (Schiffer).

See also Cookie Jars.

Club: Abingdon Pottery Collectors Club
Elaine Westover, Membership and Treasurer
210 Knox Hwy. 5, Abingdon, IL 61410; 309-462-3267

Ashtray, New Mode, #456, 5¾" dia	$32.50
Bookends, Dolphin, #443, 8", pr	$70.00
Bowl, Shell, #533, 12" L	$25.00
Candleholders, Ribbed, #688, 1¾", pr	$30.00
Candleholders, Rope, #323, 3¾" dia, pr	$46.00
Cigarette box, Trix, #348, 3¾x4¾"	$58.00
Cornucopia, low, #643, 9½" L	$48.00
Figurine, Peacock, #416, 7"	$65.00
Flowerpot, La Fleur, #151, 5"	$18.00
Jardiniere, La Fleur, #P8, 7"	$28.00

Jardiniere, white with blue birds, #468, 7½", $50.00.

Sculpture, Fruit Girl, #3904, 10"	$260.00
String holder, Mouse, #712D, 8½"	$175.00
Vase, Bird, #468D, 7½"	$70.00
Vase, Cactus, #616D, 6½"	$72.50
Vase, Chinese Terrace, #698, 6"	$48.00
Vase, Classic, #118, 10"	$32.50
Vase, Fluted, #550, 11"	$32.50
Vase, Morning Glory, #390, 10"	$60.00
Vase, Sang, #304, 9½"	$60.00
Vase, Swedish, #314, 8¼"	$90.00
Vase, What Not, #A1, 3¾"	$68.00

Wall mask, Male, #378M, 4"	$185.00
Wall pocket, Butterfly, #601D, 8½"	$125.00
Window box, Han, #498, 14½" L	$22.50

Vase, #177, 10", $65.00.

Adams, Matthew

In the 1950s a trading post located in Alaska contacted Sascha Brastoff to design a line of decorative ceramics with depictions of Eskimos, Alaskan scenes, or with animals indigenous to that area. These items were intended to target the tourist trade.

Brastoff selected Matthew Adams as the designer. These earlier examples have the Sascha B mark on the front, and the pattern number often appears on the back.

After the Alaska series became successful, Matthew Adams left Brastoff's studio and opened his own. (In all, Mr. Adams was employed by Brastoff for three years.) Pieces made in his studio are all signed Matthew Adams in script on the front. Some carry the word Alaska as well.

Mr. Adams was born in 1915. Presently his studio is located in Los Angeles, but he is no longer working.

Advisor: Marty Webster (See Directory, California Pottery)

Ashtray, cabin on stilts on green, #F1, free-form, 5¼x5x6½"	$25.00
Ashtray, hooded; glacier on black, #194P, footed, 6½x4", from $45 to	$50.00
Ashtray, totem on white, #191C, 3¼x6x7¾"	$35.00
Bowl, igloo & Eskimo girl on green, #190, 10½"	$85.00
Bowl, sheep on green, #108, free-form, 8¼x6¾"	$40.00
Bowl, walrus, shaped rim, 6x13", from $140 to	$160.00
Charger, walrus on blue, marked Alaska, 18"	$150.00
Covered dish, glacier on black, #145, 4x7½"	$45.00
Cup & saucer, Eskimo	$45.00
Ginger jar, walrus on blue, w/lid, 6½"	$90.00
Lighter, cabin on stilts on blue & white, #183C, 4¼"	$50.00
Lighter, ram, 3½"	$35.00
Mug, coffee; dogsled on blue & white, #112B, 4"	$40.00

Pitcher, Eskimo w/spear, 11½" $130.00
Plate, Eskimo w/spear on blue, #161, 11½", from $95 to..$115.00
Plate, Eskimo w/spear on blue, 7½", from $45 to...............$55.00
Plate, moose standing in water, #161, 11½", from $100 to $120.00
Tile, igloo & dogsled on blue, marked Alaska, 9¾x8½".....$135.00
Tray, igloo & Eskimo w/fishing net on green, #123, 15¼x11¾" .$150.00
Tray, polar bear, #0122, 12½x12½", from $100 to $125.00
Vase, chicken wire on brown & white, conical, 11" $60.00
Vase, Eskimo w/spear, cylindrical, 12x5"............................$135.00
Vase, walrus on blue, #115A, 10" $100.00
Vase, walrus on green, #195, 9" $85.00

Dish, Eskimo child, 3x12x21", from $235.00 to $250.00.
(Photo courtesy popartcandy)

Advertising Character Collectibles

The advertising field holds a special fascination for many of today's collectors. It's vast and varied, so its appeal is universal; but the characters of the ad world are its stars right now. Nearly every fast-food restaurant and manufacturer of a consumer product has a character logo. Keep your eyes open on your garage sale outings; it's not at all uncommon to find the cloth and plush dolls, plastic banks and mugs, bendies, etc., such as we've listed here. Unless noted otherwise, our values are for items in near mint to mint condition.

See also Breweriana; Bubble Bath Containers; Character Clocks and Watches; Character and Promotional Drinking Glasses; Coca-Cola Collectibles; Novelty Radios; Novelty Telephones; Pez Candy Containers; Pin-Back Buttons; Salt and Pepper Shakers; Soda Pop Memorabilia.

Aunt Jemima

One of the most widely recognized ad characters of them all, Aunt Jemima has decorated bags and boxes of pancake flour for more than 90 years. In fact, the original milling company carried her name, but by 1926 it had become part of the Quaker Oats Company. She and Uncle Mose were produced in plastic by the F&F Mold and Die Works in the 1950s, and the salt and pepper shakers, syrup pitchers, cookie jars, etc., they made are perhaps the most sought-after of the hundreds of items available today. (Watch for reproductions.) Age is a big worth-assessing factor for memorabilia such as we've listed below, of course, but so is condition. In the following listings, when

no condition is noted, all values are for examples in excellent condition, except glass and ceramic items, in which case values are for mint condition items. Watch for very chipped or worn paint on the F&F products, and avoid buying soiled cloth dolls.

Advisor: Judy Posner (See Directory, Advertising)

Box, Pancake Flour, cardboard, VG, $125.00.

Butter pat, color portrait on white ceramic, 3"....................$15.00
Button, Aunt Jemima Breakfast Club, made to clip to pencil, ⅞" dia..$18.00
Cake decoration/candleholder, nursery rhyme characters, plastic, F&F, 1950s, 6 for $50.00
Cookbook, Aunt Jemima Morning to Midnight Cook Book, Follett, Blume illustrations, 1969, 118 pages+index.................$20.00
Cookie jar, figural, plastic, F&F..................................$400.00
Creamer, Aunt Jemima face, ceramic, Japan, 4" $40.00
Hand fan, portrait, Aunt Jemima Eat a Better Breakfast, wooden handle, from $15 to....................................$20.00
Magazine ad, Aunt Jemima Pancakes, full color, McCall's 1962 March issue, 13¼x9¾"..$18.00
Pancake mix shaker, yellow plastic w/white lid, Perfect Pancakes in 10 Minutes, 1948, 8½x3½" dia $35.00
Pancake mold, aluminum, 4 shapes on disk shape, 8" dia.$65.00
Place mat, Aunt Jemima's Restaurant at Disneyland, Story of Aunt Jemima, paper, 1955, 9¾x13¾" $45.00
Plate, Aunt Jemima Days Are Here..., paper, 9¼" dia $30.00
Plate, Aunt Jemima's Kitchen Restaurant, Wellsville China, 1950s-60s, 7⅜"...$80.00
Recipe box, hard plastic w/molded face on front, Fosta Product, Made in USA, 3¾x5¼x3".....................................$150.00
Sack, Aunt Jemima Corn Meal, printed paper, 1960s-70s, 11½x8½"...$22.00
Sack, Aunt Jemima Hominy Grits, printed paper, ca 1960s-70s, 11½x8½"...$22.00
Salt & pepper shakers, Aunt Jemima & Uncle Mose, plastic, F&F, 5½", pr from $55 to $65.00

Sheet music, Carolina Mammy, Aunt Jemima on cover, 6-page, 1911 ....**$29.00**
Spice jar, figural, plastic, F&F, 4" **$50.00**
Syrup pitcher, figural, plastic, F&F, 5½" **$75.00**
Table card, Aunt Jemima Restaurant die-cut, Folk's It's a Treat..., dated 1953, 3x4¾" **$35.00**
Tin container, Aunt Jemima Pancakes, Quaker Limited Edition, 1983, 5⅞x5¼" dia **$15.00**
Tin container, Aunt Jemima's Special Cake & Pastry Flour, paper label, minor rust & stains, 5x4" dia, G **$25.00**

Big Boy and Friends

Bob's Big Boy, home of the nationally famous Big Boy, the original double-deck hamburger, was founded by Robert C. 'Bob' Wian in Glendale, California, in 1938. He'd just graduated from high school, and he had a dream. With the $300.00 realized from the sale of the car he so treasured, he bought a run-down building and enough basic equipment to open his business. Through much hard work and ingenuity, Bob turned his little restaurant into a multimillion-dollar empire. Not only does he have the double-decker burger to his credit, but car hops and drive-in restaurants were his creations as well.

With business beginning to flourish, Bob felt he needed a symbol — something that people would recognize. One day in walked a chubby lad of six, his sagging trousers held up by reluctant suspenders. Bob took one look at him and named him Big Boy, and that was it! It was a natural name for his double-decker hamburger — descriptive, catchy, and easy to remember. An artist worked out the drawings, and Bob's Pantry was renamed Bob's Big Boy.

The enterprise grew fast, and Bob added location after location. In 1969 when he sold out to the Marriott Corporation, he had 185 restaurants in California, with franchises such as Elias' Big Boy, Frisch's Big Boy, and Shoney's Big Boy in other states. The Big Boy burger and logo was recognized by virtually every man, woman, and child in America, and Bob retired knowing he had made a significant contribution to millions of people everywhere.

Since Big Boy has been in business for over 60 years, you'll find many items and numerous variations. Some, such as the large statues, china, and some menus, have been reproduced. If you're in doubt, consult an experienced collector for help. Many items of jewelry, clothing, and kids promotions were put out over the years, too numerous to itemize separately. Values range from $5.00 up to $1,500.00.

Advisor: Steve Soelberg (See Directory, Advertising)

Ashtray, Big Boy enameling on clear glass, 3¾" dia..............**$15.00**
Bank, Big Boy w/no shirt, holds hamburger in left hand, hard plastic, 8" **$45.00**
Bank, vinyl figure, Taiwan, 8¾" **$20.00**
Comic book, Adventures of Big Boy, #1, NM **$300.00**
Comic book, Adventures of Big Boy, #2-#5, NM, ea............**$50.00**
Comic book, Adventures of Big Boy, #6-#10, NM, ea.........**$35.00**
Comic book, Adventures of Big Boy, #11-#100, NM, ea.....**$25.00**
Comic book, Adventures of Big Boy, #101-#250, NM, ea...**$20.00**
Doll, Dakin, complete w/hamburger & shoes, NM **$100.00**

Matchbook cover, Big Boy figural hamburger, Home of the Big Boy Double Decker **$15.00**
Menu, Big Boy die-cut, lists 14 locations, printed 1964, 13x10½" **$80.00**
Nodder, Big Boy, 1960s original, minimum value..............**$400.00**
Pocket mirror, Bob's Famous Home of the Big Boy, red, white & black enameling **$17.50**
Rotary phone dialer, plastic figural, Stays in Your Dial by Itself, MOC...**$20.00**
Salt & pepper shakers, Big Boy & Dolly (girlfriend), multicolor on white, ceramic, EBR limited edition, 2-pc set **$70.00**
Salt & pepper shakers, boy w/thumbs tucked in suspenders, multicolor on white, ceramic, Japan, 1940s, 4", pr, $150 to.**$175.00**
Wristwatch, Big Boy & Dolly in winter scenes along strap, 1990s, MIP **$15.00**

Bank, Twin Winton, copyright 56, Made in USA, 8", $125.00.
(Photo courtesy Joyce and Fred Roerig)

Campbell Kids

The introduction of the world's first canned soup was announced in 1897. Later improvements in the manufacturing process created an evolutionary condensed soup. The Campbell's® Soup Company is now the primary beneficiary of this early entrepreneurial achievement. Easily identified by their red and white advertising, the company has been built on a tradition of skillful product marketing through five generations of consumers. Now a household name for all ages, Campbell's Soups have grown to dominate 80% of the canned soup market.

The first Campbell's licensed advertising products were character collectibles offered in 1910 — composition dolls with heads made from a combination of glue and sawdust. They were made by the E.I. Horsman Company and sold for $1.00 each. They were the result of a gifted illustrator, their creator, Grace Drayton, who in 1904 gave life to the chubby-faced cherub 'Campbell's Kids.'

In 1994 the Campbell's Soup Kids celebrated their ninetieth birthday. They have been revised a number of times to maintain a likeness to modern-day children. Over the years hundreds of licensees have been commissioned to produce collectibles and novelty items with the Campbell's logo in a red and white theme.

Licensed advertising reached a peak from 1954 through 1956 with 34 licensed manufacturers. Unusual items included baby carriages, toy vacuums, games, and apparel. Many of the more valuable Campbell's advertising collectibles were made during this period. In 1956 a Campbell's Kid doll was produced from latex rubber. Called 'Magic Skin,' it proved to be the most popular mail-in premium ever produced. Campbell's received more than 560,000 requests for this special girl chef doll.

Bean pot, Kids on dark brown stoneware, unmarked **$95.00**
Bell, kids on milk glass, Christmas 1984, Fenton, 7" **$45.00**
Children's dishes, plastic, Chilton, 1992, 42 pcs, serves 4, MIB. **$32.00**
Doll, boy dressed as Charlie Chaplin, 1995, M in Campbell's Soup can **$45.00**
Doll, boy dressed as pirate, porcelain, w/crate & soup cans, Danbury Mint, 1995, w/certificate of authenticity, MIB **$70.00**
Doll, cloth, girl tennis player, 1985, M w/tag **$30.00**

Doll, composition, five-piece body, Horsman (unmarked), 12", EX, $180.00. (Photo courtesy McMasters Harris Auction Co.)

Dolls, vinyl, boy & girl, original red & white outfits, 1960s-70s, 10", pr **$35.00**
Dolls, vinyl, dressed as bride & groom, 1994, 10", pr **$90.00**
Figurine, Souper Steady, girl gymnast, made for 1984 summer olympics, Roman Ceramics, 4" **$60.00**
Kaleidoscope, metal soup can form, 1981, EX **$40.00**
Mug, plastic face figural, yellow-orange hair, Trademark Campbell Soup Company Campbell Kid, 2⅝x3¼" **$75.00**
Mugs, Kid dressed as nurse, fireman, policeman, etc, multicolor on white, ceramic, 1993, 6 for **$35.00**
Plate, Campbell's Tomato Soup, kids in garden, Danbury Mint, 1993, limited edition **$35.00**
Salt & pepper shakers, figural, palstic, F&F, pr from $25 to **$35.00**
Squeak figure, boy dressed as chef, vinyl w/silent squeaker, 1958, 8" **$70.00**

Teapot, Kids heads & torsos on stove, multicolor on white, ceramic **$32.50**
Toy, pedal tractor w/boy, replica of 1950s item made by Xonex, diecast limited edition, 1998, 3½" L, M in can **$37.50**
Tumblers, etched figures on clear, 12-oz, 5½", 6 for **$30.00**
Utensil holder, girl marching w/wooden spoon in reserve on white ceramic, CSC copyright mark, 5¾x4⅜" **$12.50**

Salt and pepper shakers, range size, recent, MIB, $15.00. (Photo courtesy Helene Guarnaccia)

Cap'n Crunch

Cap'n Crunch was the creation of Jay Ward, whom you will no doubt remember was also the creator of the Rocky and Bullwinkle show. The Cap'n hails from the '60s and was one of the first heroes of the presweetened cereal crowd. Jean LaFoote was the villain always scheming to steal the Cap'n's cereal.

Action figure, Cap'n Crunch, w/Crunch-a-scope, treasure chest & map, plastic, 1st edition, 5½", MIB **$22.50**
Bank, Cap'n Crunch figural, plastic, painted multicolor **$15.00**
Comic books, Picture Pirates, I'm Dreaming of a Wide Isthmus & Fountain of Youth, 1963, complete set of 3 .... **$25.00**
Doll, Cap'n Crunch, stuffed cloth, 1992, 18", MIP **$38.00**
Figure, Cap'n Crunch, PVC, 1980s, sm **$2.50**
Hand puppets, Cap'n Crunch & Seadog, printed figure on white plastic, pr **$12.00**

Mug, Anchor Hocking, $85.00.

Ring, Brunhilde 'spin' top, blue plastic, premium **$17.50**

Ring, Captain (blue) stands atop red ring, all plastic, 2" **$15.00**
T-shirt, Cap'n Crunch on white cotton, never worn **$20.00**
Toy, Cap'n Crunch & Seadog Sea Cycle, plastic, powered by rubber band, complete w/instructions **$12.00**

Wacky Wobbler, Cap'n Crunch, Funko, MIB, $15.00.

Whistle, yellow & orange plastic (or all blue), premium, 3", from $25 to **$35.00**

Charlie Tuna

Poor Charlie is never quite good enough for the Star-Kist folks to can, though he yearns for them to catch him; but since the early 1970s he's done a terrific job working for them as the company logo. A dapper blue-fin tuna in sunglasses and a beret, he's appeared in magazines, done TV commercials, modeled for items as diverse as lamps and banks, but still they deny him his dream. 'Sorry, Charlie.'

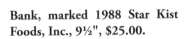

Bank, marked 1988 Star Kist Foods, Inc., 9½", $25.00.

Alarm clock, Robert Shaws, 1969 ....**$30.00**
Beach towel, Dundee Mills, 1974 ....**$35.00**

Bracelet, gold-tone chain w/emb Charlie on 1¼" charm, marked SKF **$15.00**
Figure, vinyl, 1973, 7", from $35 to **$40.00**
Radio, figural plastic, 1970s, working, 3x6" **$40.00**
T-shirt, Charlie on blue cotton, printed both sides, short sleeves, never worn **$25.00**
Telephone, figural, stands w/arms akimbo, marked 1987 Star-Kist Foods Inc, from $25 to **$35.00**
Tumbler, gold Charlie in circle of blue green on clear glass, 3½", set of 8, MIB **$20.00**
Wristwatch, character & Sorry Charlie on dial, Sheffield, Swiss.**$45.00**
Wristwatch, Charlie on dial, Star-Kist..., blue band, Timex, c 1977, EX, from $15 to **$20.00**

Colonel Sanders

There's nothing fictional about the Colonel — he was a very real guy, who built an empire on the strength of his fried chicken recipe with 'eleven herbs and spices.' In the 1930s, the Colonel operated a small cafe in Corbin, Kentucky. As the years went by, he developed a chain of restaurants which he sold in the mid-1960s. But even after the sale, the new company continued to use the image of the handsome southern gentlemen as their logo. The Colonel died in 1980.

Bank, figural (holding bucket of chicken), plastic, dated 1977, 7½", M **$15.00**
Bobble head, plastic, Our Colonel on base, Topps, 1967, MIB.**$115.00**

Cookbook, 20 Favorite Recipes of Col. Harland Sanders, 1964, paperback, NM, $12.00.
(Photo courtesy Frank Daniels)

Lamp shade, resembles cookie jar, 1969 ....**$75.00**
Lapel pin, face embossed on gold-tone metal **$10.00**
Magazine ad, Colonel in Santa hat holding bucket of fried chicken **$18.00**
Mask & membership card kit, to punch out of heavy card stock, copyright 1965, 8½x11" sheet **$15.00**
Record, Christmas w/Colonel Sanders, RCA Special Products LP, 1967 ....**$12.50**
Stamp, Wanted for (portrait) Fowl Deeds, 2¾x2¼", EX **$6.50**
Tumbler, Harland Sanders Court & Cafe, blue lettering on clear glass, Libbey, ca 1955 ....**$22.00**
Wacky Wobbler, figural nodder, Funko, retired, MIB, from $20 to **$25.00**

Elsie the Cow and Family

She's the most widely recognized cow in the world; everyone knows Elsie, Borden's mascot. Since the mid-1930s, she's been seen on booklets and posters; modeled for mugs, creamers, dolls, etc.;

and appeared on TV, in magazines, and at grocery stores to promote their products. Her husband is Elmer (who once sold Elmer's Glue for the same company), and her twins are best known as Beulah and Beauregard, though they've been renamed in recent years (now they're Bea and Beaumister). Elsie was retired in the 1960s, but due to public demand was soon reinstated to her rightful position and continues today to promote the company's dairy products.

Advisor: Lee Garmon (See Directory, Advertising)

Banner, Elsie at top, If It's Borden It's Got..., red lettering on white silk, yellow fringe, 36x24"...$35.00
Bottle, Elsie in red & yellow pyro on clear, 1-gal $35.00
Charm, Elsie in relief, plastic promotional giveaway, 1950s, ¾" dia $15.00
Creamer, Elsie full figure, white w/red & yellow details, porcelain, Borden mark, 5¾x5¾" **$35.00**
Creamer & sugar bowl, Elsie & Elmer, he has removable hat lid, brown tones, plastic **$135.00**

Handkerchief, from $35.00 to $40.00. (Photo courtesy Helene Guarnaccia & Barbara Guggenheim)

Magazine ad, Elsie & family, Borden, full-page color, 1948 .**$15.00**
Mug, Elsie face in yellow flower on white, ceramic, Borden.**$35.00**
Pencil, mechanical; floaty game in top: try to put daisy collar over Elsie's head, Progressive Products, 5¼" **$60.00**
Pin-back button, Beulah (Elsie's daughter) head & shoulders figural, 2¼x1½", EX **$50.00**
Placemat, Elsie & family, For Over 125 Years Folks Have Known..., paper, 11x16½" **$18.00**
Playing cards, Elsie pointing to glass of milk, set of 5 mounted on heavy cardboard stock, c Borden **$18.00**
Postcard, Elsie & Beauregard in Person, from tour..............**$18.00**
Poster, Be Sure To Vote, Elsie w/elephant & donkey, Starlac milk powder ad, 1956, 32x24"..**$35.00**
Punch bowl, Elsie, Elmer, Beaulah & Beauregard portraits on white, ceramic, Universal...Oven Proof, Borden, 10¼" **$160.00**
Salt & pepper shakers, Beulah & Beauregard, multicolor ceramic, Japan, 1950s, 3½", 2-pc set..**$75.00**
Salt & pepper shakers, Elsie & Elmer, multicolor on white, ceramic, 1940s, 4", pr...**$85.00**

Sherbet/sundae, Elsie logo enameled on clear glass w/fluted edge, footed, 4½", 6 for **$50.00**
Sign, Elsie in center of lg sunflower, painted aluminum, Borden, 24" dia..**$175.00**
Toy, Beauregard riding rocking horse, painted rubber, Borden, 5x3⅜" **$40.00**

Sign, embossed self-framed image, 17½x17½", $140.00. (Photo courtesy Buffalo Bay Auction Co.)

Green Giant

The Jolly Green Giant has been a well-known ad fixture since the 1950s (some research indicates an earlier date); he was originally devised to represent a strain of European peas much larger than the average-size peas Americans had been accustomed to. At any rate, when Minnesota Valley Canning changed its name to Green Giant, he was their obvious choice. Rather a terse individual himself, by 1974 he was joined by Little Green Sprout, with the lively eyes and more talkative personality.

In addition to a variety of toys and other memorabilia already on the market, in 1988 Benjamin Medwin put out a line of Little Green Sprout items. Some of these are listed below.

Radio, Little Sprout, ca 1970s, NM, $25.00.

Alarm clock, Little Sprout, talking, Pillsbury, 1985, MIP, from $30 to **$40.00**
Bank, Little Sprout, composition, musical, 8½" **$50.00**
Cookie jar, Little Green Sprout, Pillsbury, Taiwan, 1988, 12x7", from $40 to **$50.00**
Doll, Green Giant, cloth, 1966, 6" **$20.00**
Doll, vinyl w/brown hair, open/close eyes, Green Giant print on dress, Green Giant Co label, 1950s, 18", MIB..............**$85.00**

Figure, Little Sprout, stuffed felt, 12" **$15.00**
Figure, Little Sprout, vinyl, 1970s, 6½", EX **$8.00**
Figure, Little Sprout, vinyl, 1970s, 6½", M in mailer **$15.00**
Gumball machine, Little Sprout, metal & green glass, Pillsbury, 13" **$45.00**
Jump rope, Little Sprout handles, MIP **$20.00**
Kite, Jolly Green Giant, plastic, 1960s, 42x48", from $20 to . **$30.00**
Lamp, Little Sprout figure holds 3 balloons (light up), touch base to turn on & off, 1985, 14x8" **$25.00**
Napkin holder, Little Sprout, Benjamin Medwin **$15.00**
Pin, Little Sprout, pewter-like metal, 1½" **$5.00**
Popsicle set, Little Sprout, 4 compartments hold liquid, 4 figural tops w/sticks, green & yellow plastic, from $15 to **$20.00**
Puzzle, Planting Time in the Valley, 1,000 pcs in can, 1981 .. **$15.00**
Record, sketch of Green Giant ea side, Fo Fum Fie Fee/New Happy Birthday Song, Green Giant's 20th Birthday, 1949, 7" . **$25.00**
Sheet music, Fred Waring's New Happy Birthday Song, Green Giant & Niblets, 1950 .... **$25.00**
Truck, freight; white painted metal w/Green Giant Brands on trailer, Tonka, 1950, VG **$190.00**

Joe Camel and the Hard Pack

Joe Camel, the ultimate 'cool character,' was only on the scene for a few years as a comic character. The all-around Renaissance beast, he dated beautiful women, drove fast motorcycles and cars, lazed on the beach, played pool, hung around with his pals (the Hard Pack), and dressed formally for dinner and the theatre. He was 'done in' by the anti-cigarette lobby because he smoked. Now reduced to a real camel, his comic strip human persona is avidly collected by both women and men, most of whom don't smoke. Prices have been steadily rising as more and more people come to appreciate him as the great icon he is.

Advisors: C.J. Russell and Pamela E. Apkarian-Russell (See Directory, Halloween)

Alarm clock, plastic pyramid w/Joe among pyramids, battery-operated, 4½x5" **$30.00**

Ashtray, Pool Table, MIB, from $15.00 to $18.00. (Photo courtesy Pamela E. Apkarian-Russell)

Baseball cap, blue tie-dyed nylon w/embossed image on front.. **$6.00**
Baseball cap, leather, purple crown w/black trim, NM **$20.00**

Belt buckle, Joe w/pyramids in background, Smooth Character, brass, MIB **$50.00**
Calendar, Joe on his back, various scenes ea month, 1993 ..... **$7.00**
Canister, golf ball; Joe playing golf, 1994, G **$15.00**
Car, Action Joe Smokin' Joe Dragster, 1/24 scale, 1995, in acrylic case, MIB **$50.00**
Cigarette lighter, Joe Camel on gold-tone, butane **$22.00**
Clock, Joe leaning on lg Camel cigarette package, yellow background, sq, 1991, 15¾" **$60.00**
Dartboard, Joe in blue jacket holding dart, regulation boar bristle, double doors, 25½x30x3½" **$300.00**
Door chime, Joe on front, battery-operated, 1989, 8½x5½", MIP. **$15.00**
Ice bucket, clear plastic w/multicolor scenes, clear lid, w/4 tumblers **$35.00**
Mug, Joe in beach chair, Wish You Were Here, The Fridge Cools Like Ice 1991 RJRTC (for freezer), plastic, 4x3½" **$12.00**
Mug, Joe's portrait on blue plastic, 75th Birthday, RJRTC, 1988 .... **$10.00**
Pin-back button, Joe wearing white wig, 3" **$8.00**
Plate, Joe playing pool, 1995 RJRTC limited edition **$60.00**
Salt & pepper shakers, Joe in tuxedo, 1 in white, 2nd in black, plastic, pr **$22.50**
Shot glass set, Joe Camel's Band, 1 member on ea, etched cobalt glass, set of 5 .... **$70.00**
Stein, Joe playing accordion, ceramic **$65.00**
Switch plate, Joe shooting pool, single **$18.00**
Tumbler, Joe Camel & Hard Pack, clear plastic, 4½x3½" **$10.00**
Tumbler, Joe's Place w/Joe on clear plastic, Made in USA, 1994, 4½" **$12.00**

M&M Candy Men

Everyone recognizes the familiar M&M guys. Today you'll find collectibles of every sort — planters, telephones, dispensers, plush dolls, and scores of other items. Some of the dispensers are harder to find than others, for instance the red skier and the yellow basketball player. In addition to the plain peanut-shaped dispensers, there are others that are more unusual, such as the Rock 'n Roll Cafe and the M&M guys in their recliners. Together they make a darling collection, and the colors are dazzling.

Toppers for M&M packaging first appeared about 1988; since then other M&M items have been introduced that portray the clever antics of these colorful characters. Toppers have been issued for seasonal holidays as well as Olympic events.

Alarm clock/radio, M&Ms Wakeup Call, Red (plain) pops out when alarm sounds, uses 9-volt battery **$45.00**
Basket, M&M guys in relief on white, ceramic, lilac ceramic bow on handle, 6½" **$10.00**
Camera, Yellow giving peace sign about to press button, M&M border print on ea photo, 35mm, built-in flash **$35.00**
Candy dish, figures in hearse (Halloween theme), top opens to reveal candy, ceramic, M (w/sealed candy), from $40 to **$50.00**
Candy dish, Red (plain) driving motorcycle & Yellow (plain) sitting behind, sidecar holds candy, Mars, 2002 .... **$40.00**
Candy dish, Red riding motorcycle, lid at back of seat, ceramic, w/tag **$28.00**

Cookie jar, all M&M characters on lavender, ceramic.......... $30.00
Cookie jar, M&M guys stirring cookie dough on white, brown lid, ceramic, Mars.. $85.00

Cookie jar, Mars, 1982, 8", $75.00.

Cookie jar, Red (plain) leaning against brown M&Ms bag, ceramic, 9".. $30.00
Cuckoo clock, Red at top opens door on the hour, Yellow dangles from bottom, battery-operated, MIB, from $65 to $85.00
Dispenser, Blue (peanut shape) waving, 3½"........................ $45.00
Dispenser, Green (plain) as hiker, hard to find, 7" $35.00
Dispenser, Green (plain) w/pitcher's glove & ball, wearing yellow baseball cap, limited edition, 10", MIP........................ $70.00

Dispenser, Hot Rod, blue car, $45.00.

Dispenser, Red pilots biplane w/Yellow atop wing, spin propeller & candy dispenses from bottom wing, 12x11"................... $35.00
Dispenser, Red w/checkered flag, push down flag & candy dispenses into tire cup $35.00
Dispenser, Yellow (peanut) & Red (plain) waving, Melts in Your Mouth Not in Your hand on base $30.00
Dispenser, Yellow (plain) as golfer, MIB.............................. $50.00
Easter basket, Yellow (plain) peeking from edge, head covered w/lavender eggshell, ceramic, multicolor pastels $35.00
Lamp, Yellow (plain) w/lampshade on head, voice activated on/off switch, Official Licensed Product, MIB $35.00
Sign, M&M Lover Parking Only, All Others Will Be Towed, plain figure, blue & white painted metal, 18x12"................... $25.00
Telephone, Red & Green sit by M&M Dial, Blue in handstand holds up yellow receiver, talking type........................... $60.00
Topper, Red on motorcycle $100.00

Michelin Man (Bibendum or Mr. Bib)

Perhaps one of the oldest character logos around today, Mr. Bib actually originated in the late 1800s, inspired by a stack of tires that

one of the company founders thought suggested the figure of a man. Over the years his image has changed considerably, but the Michelin Tire Man continues today to represent his company in many countries around the world.

Ashtray, Mr Bib at side of black Bakelite tray, 5x5"............ $140.00
Ashtray, Mr Bib at side of green ceramic tray, labeled Michelin on Bib's chest $110.00
Ashtray, Mr Bib at side of yellow & blue tire-shaped tray, 4 rests, ceramic $135.00
Belt buckle, metal, round w/Michelin & running Mr Bib ... $35.00
Business card holder, Mr Bib kneeling down & holding stack of tires, painted resin, holds up to 25 cards, 3x5x2½" $15.00
Clock, Mr Bib waving left of clock, black, white, blue & yellow, sits on counter or hangs, 10x21".. $90.00
Doll, Mr Bib, cloth, Chase Bag Co, 1967, 21" $45.00
Figure, Mr Bib, plastic, 12".. $75.00
Figure, Mr Bib, poly resin, recent reproduction of 1920s statue, 32x16" $275.00
Figure, Mr Bib holding baby, rubber, 7" $125.00
Hood ornament/basket, Mr Bib, bronze (original was pewter), reproduction, 3¾" $90.00
Key chain, silver metal, ring enclosing running Mr Bib, 1960s. $20.00
Mug, coffee; Mr Bib running w/black tire on white glass, Miller Tire Service, Fire-King.. $110.00
Ramp walker, Mr Bib, wind-up, MIB.................................. $25.00
Shirt, Mr Bib on yellow jersey w/blue shoulders & sleeves, Michelin, Louis Garneau, never worn $35.00
Sign, Mr Bib w/tire, painted tin, sq, 24" $55.00

Sign, porcelain, blue background, made in France, 15x18", minimum value, $750.00.

Mr. Peanut

The trademark character for the Planters Peanuts Company, Mr. Peanut, has been around since 1916. His appearance has changed a little from the original version, becoming more stylized in 1961. Today he's still a common sight on Planters' advertising and product containers.

Mr. Peanut has been modeled as banks, salt and pepper shakers, whistles, and many other novelty items. His image has decorated T-shirts, beach towels, playing cards, sports equipment, etc.

Today Mr. Peanut has his own 'fan club,' Peanut Pals, the collector's organization for those who especially enjoy the Planters Peanuts area of advertising.

Advisors: Judith and Robert Walthall (See Directory, Advertising)

Club: Peanut Pals
Judith Walthall, Founder
P.O. Box 4465, Huntsville, AL 35815; 205-881-9198
www.peanutpals.org
Dues: Primary member, $20 per year; Associate member (16 years old and over), $10 per year; Under 16 years old, $3 per year. Bimonthly newsletter, annual directory and convention news sent to members. Sample newsletter: $2. For membership write: 246 Old Line Ave., Laurel, MD 20724

Ashtray, bisque, shell-shape w/3 peanuts behind Mr Peanut figure **$75.00**
Bank, plastic, Mr Peanut, common colors, 1970s, 9" **$25.00**
Bank, plastic, Mr Peanut, yellow, Souvenir of Atlantic City decal, 1970s, 9" **$250.00**

Blotter, early, 6½" long, EX, $190.00. (Photo courtesy Wm. Morford Auctions)

Box, Salted Cashews, cardboard w/peanut graphics, held 24 5¢ bags **$295.00**
Costume, hard plastic Mr Peanut torso w/arm holes, 47", VG+ . **$250.00**
Doll, Mr Peanut, stuffed cloth, Chase Bag Co, 1970, 18", NM **$25.00**
Doll, Mr Peanut, wood w/painted features, 8½", VG+ **$150.00**
Fan, Mr Peanut driving peanut-shaped car, advertising on back, 1940s, 5¼x8", EX (watch for reproductions) **$225.00**
Figure, Mr Peanut, painted pot metal, 1930s, 7", EXIB **$450.00**
Jar, Barrel, peanut finial, paper label, 1935, 12¼" **$250.00**
Jar, Football, peanut finial lid, 1931, 8½", EX **$225.00**
Nodder, Mr Peanut on spring, clayware, LEGO, 6½", NM.**$150.00**
Nut spoon, plastic, Mr Peanut finial, common colors, from $3 to **$4.00**
Peanut Butter tin, Homogenized, key-wind lid, Mr Peanut/peanuts, 2-lb **$230.00**
Pedal car, plastic, yellow w/blue advertising stripe, Kingsbury Toys, 41", VG **$75.00**
Race car, plastic, Mr Peanut driving, w/trigger, 1950s, 5¼"..**$350.00**
Salad fork & spoon set, wood w/ceramic figural handles, MIB... **$135.00**
Thermometer, plastic key w/tassel, 8", M in mailer **$800.00**
Tin, Egyptian design, 1919, rare, 2x6" dia....................**$1,000.00**
Trolley card, When Guests Drop In, maid serving, 1950, 11x21" **$400.00**
Whistle, plastic Mr Peanut figure, common, 2½" **$5.00**

Old Crow

Old Crow whiskey items are popular with collectors primarily because of the dapper crow dressed in a tuxedo, top hat, spectacles, and cane, that was used by the company for promotional purposes from the early 1950s until the early 1970s. Though many collectibles carry only the whiskey's name, in 1985, the 150th anniversary of Old Crow, the realistic crow that had been used prior to 1950 re-emerged.

Advisors: Judith and Robert Walthall (See Directory, Advertising)

Ashtray, Bakelite, 3½" dia, ...**$25.00**
Bar light, coach light w/Old Crow figure in center, marked, 12".**$35.00**
Bottle pourer, Old Crow plastic figure, sm......................**$5.00**
Dice, I Buy, You Buy, Old Crow on 1, ½", set of 2.............**$45.00**
Display figure, Old Crow, hard vinyl, ca 1956, 13½" **$35.00**
Display statue, Old Crow, plastic, Advertising Novelty Mfg Co, 1960s, 32" **$125.00**
Figure, Old Crow, brass, on round footed base, 11"............**$85.00**
Figure, Old Crow, composition, name embossed on base, 1940s, 27½", VG **$450.00**
Figure, Old Crow, plastic, lights up, missing glasses, 30" **$65.00**
Figure, Old Crow, plastic, 8½"...**$15.00**

Football, black print on orange vinyl, 9" L, VG, $20.00. (Photo courtesy Judith and Robert Walthall)

Lamp, figural Old Crow chalkware base, Old Crow 86 Proof... on base, 1940s-50s, 16½" overall **$60.00**
Paperweight, clear glass w/red & black rectangular center featuring Old Crow & Finest Name in Bourbon, 3x4"................**$25.00**
Paperweight, historical scene under glass, on base, 2½x3x4¼" ..**$28.00**
Pitcher, ceramic, 'Broken Leg' decor, NM..........................**$100.00**
Pitcher, Jim Beam, maroon w/white logo, ceramic, 1999, M .**$35.00**
Shot glass, Old Crow & crow fired on in black...................**$20.00**
Swizzle sticks, black plastic w/figural Old Crow top & Old Crow in white letters, set of 20 ....**$10.00**
Thermometer, round dial, 1950s, 9x13" **$150.00**
Thermometer, Taste the Greatness of Historic..., painted metal, red, white & black, 1950s, 13x6" **$95.00**

Poppin' Fresh (Pillsbury Doughboy) and Family

Who could be more lovable than the chubby blue-eyed Doughboy with the infectious giggle introduced by the Pillsbury

Company in 1965. Wearing nothing but a neck scarf and a chef's hat, he single-handedly promoted the company's famous biscuits in a tube until about 1969. It was then that the company changed his name to 'Poppin' Fresh' and soon after presented him with a sweet-faced, bonnet-attired mate named Poppie. Before long, they had created a whole family for him. Many premiums such as dolls, salt and pepper shakers, and cookie jars have been produced over the years. In 1988 the Benjamin Medwin Co. made several items for Pillsbury; some of these white ceramic Doughboy items are listed below. Also offered in 1988, the Poppin' Fresh Line featured the plump little fellow holding a plate of cookies; trim colors were mauve pink and blue. The Funfetti line was produced in 1992, again featuring Poppin' Fresh, this time alongside a cupcake topped with Funfetti icing (at that time a fairly new Pillsbury product), and again the producer was Benjamin Medwin.

Alarm clock, Poppin' Fresh & numbers in blue on round white case, TCP, Made in Germany, 1986, EX **$25.00**

Bank, Benjamin Medwin, marked 1988, The Pillsbury Co., 8", $25.00.

Beanie, Poppin' Fresh, 2 different styles, M, ea from $10 to ... **$20.00**
Bookends, Poppin' Fresh stands before flat back w/Pillsbury logo, resin, MIB **$45.00**
Bowls, mixing; clear w/checkerboard design & Poppin' Fresh logo, Anchor Ovenware, stacking set of 3 .... **$38.00**
Canister, Poppin' Fresh on clear glass, w/locking lid, from $12 to **$18.00**
Cookie jar, Poppin' Fresh figural, ceramic, 1997, 12" **$27.50**
Creamer & sugar bowl, Poppin' Fresh & Poppie as handles, 1988 .... **$15.00**
Doll, Poppin' Fresh, plush, push tummy & he giggles, 16" .. **$25.00**
Doll, Poppin' Fresh, plush, 25th Birthday on scarf, 1990, 12".. **$15.00**
Dolls, Poppin' & Poppie Fresh, terry cloth, 1972, pr **$60.00**
Figure, Poppin' Fresh, vinyl, 1970s, w/sand, 7" **$15.00**
Figures, Grandmommer & Grandpopper, vinyl, Pillsbury, 1974, 5", pr **$50.00**
Finger puppets, Poppin' Fresh & His Pals (Flapjack & Popper), Pillsbury Playthings, 1974, MIB **$45.00**
Frisbee, Poppin' Fresh on white plastic **$10.00**
Jacket, blue nylon shell w/polyester lining, from 1996 Lovin Connection, Poppin' Fresh on back **$55.00**
Jar, clear glass w/enameled label showing Poppin' Fresh, red & white checkerboard border & word Goodies, ca 1990, 10" **$30.00**

Jellybean machine, clear plastic Poppin' Fresh in chef's hat as top, blue base, 1996, 12", MIB **$60.00**
Lotion/soap dispenser, Poppin' Fresh figural, ceramic, Benjamin Medwin, 1997, 7¾" **$20.00**
Measuring cup, Poppin' Fresh on clear glass, red pyro measurements, 2-cup **$15.00**
Mug, Poppin' Fresh figural, ceramic, Pillsbury, 1985, 5¼" ... **$15.00**
Napkin holder, Poppin' Fresh in relief on front, ceramic, Pillsbury, 2002 .... **$15.00**
Party kit, party for 8 in a Pillsbury 'flour' sack, w/plates, cups, napkins, hats, etc, 1987, MIP **$30.00**
Playhouse, w/Bun Bun, Poppie Fresh, Popper & Poppin' Fresh dolls, Pillsbury Playthings, 1974, from $120 to **$135.00**
Radio, Poppin' Fresh figure, w/headphones, MIB, from $60 to **$75.00**
Recipe/salt box, painted wood, Poppin' Fresh among pink polka dots, NM **$85.00**
Salt & pepper shakers, Poppin' Fresh & Poppie, ceramic, 1988, 4½", pr **$15.00**
Spoon rest, Poppin' Fresh, white w/blue details, ceramic, 8", EX **$12.00**
Teapot, Poppin' Fresh figural, ceramic, Benjamin Medwin, 1997, 9" **$20.00**
Toaster cover, blue background w/Poppin' Fresh holding up a cookie, lace trim **$32.00**
Utensil holder, Poppin' Fresh figural, flour sack container behind, Benjamin Medwin, 1988, 7¾" **$20.00**
Vases, Poppin' Fresh by red pepper (or celery, ear of corn, or eggplant), ceramic, set of 4, MIB **$75.00**

Cookie cutters, Poppin' Fresh and Poppie, $35.00 for the pair.

Reddy Kilowatt

Reddy was developed during the late 1920s and became very well known during the 1950s. His job was to promote electric power companies all over the United States, which he did with aplomb! Reddy memorabilia is highly collectible today. On Reddy's 65th birthday (1992), a special 'one-time-only' line of commemoratives was issued. This line consisted of approximately 30 different items issued in crystal, gold, pewter, silver, etc. All items were limited editions and quite costly. Because of high collector demand, new merchandise is flooding the market. Watch for items such as a round mirror, a small hand-held game with movable squares, a ring-toss game, etc., marked 'Made in China.'

Apron, Reddy in garden w/She Loves Me, plastic, EX **$30.00**
Ashtray, Reddy dressed as cowboy, red on clear glass, 4½" dia .**$20.00**
Ashtray, Reddy in red & white on clear glass, 6-sided **$15.00**
Bowl, oatmeal; Reddy in red on white, ceramic, Syracuse, 5".**$70.00**
Charm, Reddy figural, red & gold enameling, 1" **$25.00**
Cookie cutter, Reddy's head only, red plastic, 1950s **$12.00**
Cup, coffee; clear glass w/red Reddy image & Reddy for Safety.**$25.00**
Earrings, Reddy figural, brass w/red enameling, 1", pr **$25.00**
Figure, red & white plastic Reddy on black outlet switch-plate base, lg head, mk MCMLXI, 6", NM, minimum value **$150.00**
Figure, Reddy painted wood die-cut, registered trademark on foot, 1940s-50s, 17", VG **$160.00**
Lighter, Reddy & Gulf States Utilites, Zippo, code date 1973, NM **$75.00**
Measuring tape, Go Total Electric & Reddy figure in red enamel on brushed silver, Zippo, 1½" sq, NM **$15.00**
Paperweight, Reddy's face in red & white on blue plug, encased in heavy clear glass, ¾x4¼x3" **$45.00**
Patch, die-cut cloth, 7¼", NM **$30.00**
Pin, Reddy figural, Trade Mark Your Favorite Pin-Up on original paper backing, copyright 1955 ....**$15.00**
Playing cards, Reddy Kilowatt Servant of the Century, double deck, MIB **$30.00**
Saucer, Reddy on pale green w/gold rim, 6⅛" **$30.00**
Sign, Washington Water Power Co (Reddy) Electric Service Is Cheap, porcelain, 12x12", VG **$235.00**

Stick pin, enameled metal, 1",
$20.00. (Photo courtesy Lee Garmon)

Table setting, Reddy on white, Syracuse China, 9" plate+6⅜" plate+cup & saucer **$150.00**
Wacky Wobbler, Reddy figural, Funko, MIB **$50.00**
Wristwatch, reclining Reddy on face, Amazing Time, wind-up mechanism, leather band, 1972 ....**$110.00**
Wristwatch, 1930s, VG **$250.00**

Smokey Bear

The fiftieth anniversary of Smokey Bear, the fire-prevention spokesbear for the State Foresters, Ad Council, and US Forest Service, was celebrated in 1994. After ruling out other mascots (including Bambi), by 1944 it had been decided that a bear was best suited for the job, and Smokey was born. When a little cub was rescued from a fire in a New Mexico national forest in 1950, Smokey's role intensified. Over the years his appearance has evolved from one a little more menacing to the lovable bear we know today.

The original act to protect the Smokey Bear image was enacted in 1974. The character name in the 'Smokey Bear Act' is Smokey Bear. Until the early 1960s, when his name appeared on items such as sheet music and Little Golden Books, it was 'Smokey *the* Bear.' Generally, from that time on, he became known as simply Smokey Bear.

Ash bucket, Smokey Says: Use Your Ash Tray, metal clip-on, 1982, 4", from $30 to **$35.00**
Ashtray, Smokey figural, ceramic, Smokey - Prevent Forest Fires, 4" **$95.00**
Ashtray, Smokey says Snuffit, plastic w/suction cup to fit in car, EX **$55.00**
Ashtrays, anodized aluminum w/embossed Smokey portrait, 4" dia, 4 for **$20.00**
Bandana, 4 printed games (word search, find hazards in picture, unscramble words, forest maze), w/answer key, 21x21" ...**$20.00**
Bank, Smokey stands by tree stump, Let Smokey Bank on You Too, red plastic, 1960s, 5" **$50.00**

Banks, ceramic, unmarked, 6", each from $40.00 to $45.00.

Baseball cards, Smokey Bear's Fire Prevention Team, 1987, 4x6", 3 for..**$18.00**
Belt buckle, Forest Fire Fighter & face embossed on brass plate **$25.00**
Book, Smokey Bear Presents: A Story Book of the Forest, Trees & Animals, H Rossoll illustrations, 1968, 16-page, EX.....**$22.00**
Button, fold-tab; I'm Helping Smokey Prevent Forest Fires, tin, Green Duck Co, Chicago, NM..................................**$15.00**
Cookie jar, Smokey figural, ceramic, Norcrest, 10", NM ...**$210.00**
Decal, Smokey's Friends Don't Play w/Matches, Smokey's face, 5¼" dia..**$35.00**
Doll, Bear Ranger, button eyes, Ideal, VG **$40.00**
Doll, Smokey, brown plush, complete w/belt, badge & hat, Knickerbocker, 22" **$75.00**
Figurine, Smokey in rocker w/cubs, Lefton **$30.00**
Flag, Only You Can Prevent Wildfires, & Smokey face on white cloth, 36x60" w/3-section pole, extends from 66" to 99" **$60.00**
Flashlight, Smokey's face w/hat lights up, Hong Kong British Empire, Ashton...**$35.00**
Garden figure, hard plastic, w/stake for anchor, Art Line, 1960s, 14", VG..**$20.00**
Garden sign, Prevent Forest Fires, Smokey by sign, plastic, spike to hold in ground, Hong Kong, 1977, 12x8" **$35.00**

House slippers, plush Smokey & hat, Authorized by Forest Service USDA, 1960s, child's...**$20.00**

Leaf dish, Smokey w/forest friends before smiling evergreen trees on white porcelain, 4½" **$27.50**

Lunch box, metal, 1970s, from $225 to........................**$300.00**

Lunch box, vinyl, Smokey & forest friends, 1960s, EX......**$165.00**

Mug, milk glass w/brown Smokey head & Help Prevent, 1960s .**$18.00**

Music box, Smokey in bed sleeping w/2 cubs, hat on bedpost, plays Brahms Lullaby, Lefton, 1996, 3½x5".........................**$70.00**

Plaque, Prevent Forest Fires, Smokey w/shovel, Norcrest, 5¼x4¼" **$85.00**

Playset, Camping the Smokey Bear Way, Tonka, 1970s, EXIB.**$65.00**

Plush toy, Smokey, name on belt, badge on chest, Knickerbocker, 24"..**$20.00**

Plush toy, Smokey, yellow plastic hat marked Smokey, Ideal, 20". **$20.00**

Poster, ..& Please Make People Careful..., Smokey on knees praying as creatures watch, Hansen, 1948, 1-sheet, VG............**$40.00**

Poster, Be Sure They're Dead Out, campfires, cigarettes, etc, 1951, 18½x13" **$45.00**

Poster, Please Help People Be More Careful, Smokey standing by burnt forest, 1952, 18¾x13⅛" **$60.00**

Ruler, Smokey image on front & 6" ruler on back, plastic, 1962, 8" **$18.00**

Salt & pepper shakers, Smokey's face & ranger hat, multicolor ceramic, 2-pc set **$25.00**

Sheet, Smokey in the forest w/his friends, 1970s, twin size ..**$15.00**

Shirt, Smokey patches on yellow Aramid fire-resistant material, long sleeves, 1960s, never worn **$27.50**

Sweatshirt, Smokey's face, Only You Can..., 50th Anniversary, Jerzees, never worn...**$22.50**

Thermos bottle, NM, $65.00.

Wristwatch, Smokey's face on dial, Remember Only You..., black woven band...**$20.00**

Tony the Tiger

Kellogg's introduced Tony the Tiger in 1953, and since then he's appeared on every box of their Frosted Flakes. In his deep, rich voice, he's convinced us all that they are indeed 'Gr-r-reat'!

Bank, Tony figural, plastic, 9¼" **$37.50**

Cap, striped plush w/Tony's face on front, tail on back, 1960s, NM **$35.00**

Cereal cup and spoon, Houston Harvest Gift Products, 2001, $12.00. (Photo courtesy ss396hsh)

Cookie jar/cereal keeper, Tony's head, plastic, 7½x8x6½".....**$35.00**

Creamer & sugar bowl, Tony head & Toucan Sam, multicolor on white, ceramic, Kellogg's, 2002 only, 4½x4" **$22.50**

Doll, plastic, Cereal Celebrities, Fun4All, 1998, 4½", MIB .**$13.50**

Doll, Talking Tony, touch his hand to hear They're Great, 1998, 16", MIB...**$22.50**

Doll, Tony, plush w/pink bandana, Kellogg's, 1970, 12½" ...**$25.00**

Duffle bag, Feeling Great & Tony, multicolor on blue nylon, adjustable shoulder strap, 18" L **$27.50**

Game card, Tony Tiger Pocket Billiards, 1977, 3x2" **$47.50**

Mug, Tony's head, F&F, 1964 ....**$12.00**

Mug, white w/Tony image, tiger-tail handle w/3-D Tony, Houston Harvest, 5½"..**$15.00**

Pitcher, Tony & Friends, Kellogg's & rising sun on back, multicolor on white, ceramic, 6¾" **$60.00**

Postcard, Tony fishing out of boat w/whale beside him, Having a Whale of a Time... on side, ca 1966, used..................**$20.00**

Spoon, Tony figural handle, ca 1965 ....**$13.50**

Wacky Wobbler, Tony, Funko, MIB.................................**$25.00**

Wristwatch, Tony's face on dial, gold numbers, Kellogg, leather strap **$22.50**

Wristwatch, Tony's face on dial, no numbers, sm link band, Kellogg **$27.50**

Miscellaneous Characters

Alka Seltzer, bank, Pron-Tito (Mexican version of Speedy), coin slot on head, 1950s, 5½" **$110.00**

Alka Seltzer, bank, Speedy figural, 1950s, 5½", VG **$45.00**

Bosco Chocolate Syrup, jar, Bosco the Clown head topper, hat removes to place straw, 7½" **$14.00**

Bucky Bradford, doll, vinyl, It's Yum Yum Time on front, squeaker, 9"..**$35.00**

Del Monte, plush figures, Country Yumkins, Brawny Bear, Country Strawberry, Reddie Tomato, 1988, set of 7, M.............**$20.00**

Domino's Pizza, figure, Noid, plastic w/suction cup, 6¼", MIP.**$15.00**

Domino's Pizza, T-shirt, Noid on white, white cotton, 1980s, never worn **$17.50**

Dutch Boy National Lead Company, paperweight, embossed Dutch boy on heavy metal, 3⅝" dia............ **$40.00**

Dutch Boy Paints, lamp, Dutch Boy figural, painted composition, 12", from $75 to............ **$135.00**

Energizer Batteries, bobble head Energizer Bunny, Bobbledreams USA, 12", MIB............ **$70.00**

Energizer Batteries, plush doll, Energizer Bunny, 10", MIP .**$35.00**

Energizer Batteries, plush doll, Energizer Bunny, 1995, 23" .**$20.00**

Eskimo Pie, doll, cloth Eskimo boy, 1970s, 15", MIP **$15.00**

Flour Fred, spice shaker for Spillers Flour, hard plastic figural, 9" **$38.00**

Hamburger Helper, clock, Helping Hand, uses AA battery, Made in Hong Kong, 1980s, 6½" **$40.00**

Hamburger Helper, wall clock, Helping hand on face, uses A battery, 9" dia, EX **$20.00**

Hawaiian Punch, board game, Punchy on lid of box, Mattel, 1978, EXIB............ **$12.50**

Hawaiian Punch, doll, Punchy, plastic & cloth talker, Fun 4 All Corp, Made in China, 15", MIB **$22.50**

Hawaiian Punch, lapel pin, Punchy, enamel on metal, 1970s, ¾" **$22.50**

Hawaiian Punch, wristwatch, Punchy on face, black cloth band, 1963 .... **$20.00**

Icee, bank, Icee Bear w/drink in front of him, rubber, 7½x5".**$25.00**

Kool-Aid, pitcher, frosted smiling face on clear glass............ **$45.00**

Kool-Aid, pitcher & mugs, plastic, F&F, Goofy Grape 8⅜" pitcher+6 fruit character mugs **$225.00**

Little Caesar's Pizza, figure, Pizza Pizza Man holding glass dish, free-standing, 12" **$20.00**

Mack Bulldog, tie clip, enameled image on gold-tone metal, metal clip on back, ½x1¾" **$15.00**

McDonald's, doll, Ronald McDonald, w/whistle attached, Hasbro, 1978, 20", MIB **$45.00**

McDonald's, figurine, Ronald seated on bench w/child & holding yellow umbrella, painted porcelain, 6x3½" **$58.00**

McDonald's, T-shirt, Ronald McDonald Says Hello, Ronald w/children on blue, never worn **$32.50**

Mr Bubble, bath toy, Mr Bubble, pink plastic, 1997, 4", EX ..**$10.00**

Mr Bubble, T-shirt, Mr Bubble on white cotton, Jerzees, never worn **$12.50**

Nabisco, toy, Buffalo Bee Breakfast Buddy, plastic, made to hang on the rim of cereal bowl, 2¼" **$30.00**

Nabisco, toys, Munchy & Crunchy Moon Men, plastic, made to attach to spoons, 1960s, 2", 2½", pr............ **$75.00**

Pedro, mug, South of the Border (roadside attraction), ceramic, 1950s, 4" **$39.00**

Raid, doll, Raid Bug, green plush, Dakin, 1987, 17" **$12.50**

Raid, doll, Raid Bug, stuffed cloth, 1970s, 14", MIP..........**$35.00**

Raid, robot, Raid Bug, plastic, remote control, w/instruction manual, MIB **$160.00**

RCA, figure, Nipper, painted plaster reproduction, made in USA, 14½" **$110.00**

RCA, figurine, Nipper, clear glass, Fenton, 3"............ **$50.00**

Sambo's Restaurant, dolls, Sambo & Tiger, cloth, Dakin, 1960s, pr **$110.00**

Sambo's Restaurant, souvenir menu, Sambo & Tiger on cover, 1960s-70s, opens to 6¾x14½" **$30.00**

Snuggle Fabric Softener, doll, Snuggle Bear, plush, Gund, 11".**$20.00**

Snuggle Fabric Softener, doll, Snuggle Bear, Russ, 1985, 15", M w/tags **$25.00**

Squirt, tray, Squirt Boy & bottle on white w/yellow rim, tin litho, oval, 1960s, 14½" **$35.00**

Taco Bell, bobble head, chihuahua dog, w/collar, 7x3½" **$15.00**

Tastee-Freeze Ice Cream, doll, Miss Tastee-Freeze, hard plastic, 1960s, 7" **$15.00**

Tyson Chicken, doll, Chicken Quick, stuffed cloth, sitting, 6".**$15.00**

Vlasic Pickles, doll, stork, plush white fur, plastic eyes, red bow, white glasses, Trudy Toys, 1989, 24" **$15.00**

Westinghouse Tuff Guy, plaque, Tuff Guy Club 20th Anniversary 1936-57, pottery, 4⅜" **$22.50**

Pepto-Bismol '24 Hour Bug,' vinyl figure, 7", $40.00.

Advertising Tins

One of the hottest areas of tin collecting today is spice tins, but if those don't appeal to you, consider automotive products, cleaners, cosmetics, guns, medical, fishing, sewing, or sample sizes. Besides the aesthetics factor, condition and age also help determine price. The values suggested below represent what you might pay in an antique store for tins, but what makes this sort of collecting so much fun is that you'll find them much cheaper at garage sales, Goodwill Stores, and flea markets. Unless coded otherwise, our values are for tins in near-mint to mint condition. For more information see *Modern Collectible Tins* by Linda McPherson (Collector Books).

Black Cat Cigarette Tobacco, yellow, green & black graphics, Canada, 4" H............ **$20.00**

Borden's Meadow Brand Malted Milk, red, white & blue, screw-on lid, sq, 10¼x5¼", EX............ **$38.00**

Butter-Nut Drip Grind Coffee, key-wind lid, 3¾x5" dia, EX.**$30.00**

CD Kenny Tea Dealer & Coffee Roaster, some staining & fading, 7½x11½x8", G............ **$60.00**

Charles Cookies, brown & tan, ca 1950s, 5¼x8½", EX............ **$35.00**

Chocolate Cream Coffee, brown on tan, 4x5½" dia, EX......**$50.00**

Cook's Cocoa, 2 cocoa recipes on side, brown, tan & red, sq, 6" **$32.00**

Cornease 'King of Corn Killers,' black lettering on yellow, ½x1⅜" dia, VG **$22.50**

Curad Battle Ribbon Plastic Bandages, shows red, blue, green & yellow band-aids, hinged lid, 1950s, 4x3⅜x1⅝", EX........ **$27.50**

Dutch Maid Herring, Dutch girl on light blue, multicolor lettering, AM Smith Co, 5x7¼" dia, EX+........ **$125.00**

Edgeworth Smoking Tobacco Extra-High Grade, Larus & Bro... Richmond VA, blue w/silver, hinged lid, tall & sq........ **$35.00**

Everfresh Coffee, steaming cup, red, white black, Koenig Coffee Co, key-wind, 3½x5" dia, EX........ **$75.00**

Gold Dust Cleanser, twins on red, w/contents, holds 14-oz, unopened........ **$110.00**

Golden Virginia Hand Rolling Tobacco, insert coin in groove in corner & twist, 1x4½x3½"........ **$18.00**

Grand Union Cloves, brown, orange & cream, 4⅛x2¼x1³⁄₁₆", EX........ **$20.00**

Hershey's Instant Cocoa Mix, shows hot cup & cold glass of product on yellow, pry-off lid, EX+........ **$45.00**

Kroger Coffee, red, white & blue, key-wind, 3½x5" dia, EX. **$35.00**

Life Savers, multicolor bands resembling roll of product form pail, slip lead, metal handle, 12½x4¾"........ **$110.00**

Mac's Super Gloss Car Wash, Scotsman, yellow & black, 4½x3⅜" dia........ **$45.00**

Mennen Quinsana, black lettering on white w/light blue at top & bottom, square, 5x1½x1½"........ **$32.00**

Mineral Compound for Horses, black horse on orange, Mineral Remedy Co, sq, 3⅝x2⅛x2⅛"........ **$30.00**

Monarch Cocoa, lion's portrait ea side, Reid Murdoch & Co, 1930s, 6"........ **$68.00**

Nabisco Premium Saltines, multicolor on white w/red triangle in corner, 1963, EX+........ **$15.00**

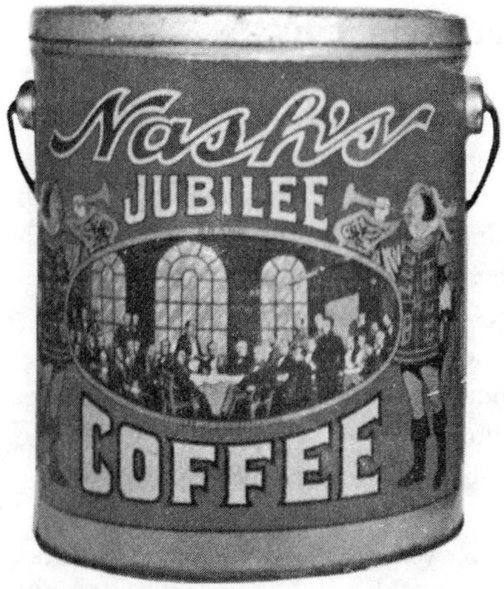

Nash's Jubilee Coffee, five-pound, 8¾x7½", EX, $95.00.

Old Dutch Potato Chips, red, green & cream, slip lid, 11½x7½", EX........ **$35.00**

Old Smoky Peanut Brittle, line of hillbilly dancers circle container, brown on tan, slip lid, 5¼x4⅛" dia, EX........ **$125.00**

Partola Antiseptic Mint Candy Laxative Tablets, black & white, held 6 candies, 1⅞x1¹⁄₁₆", EX+........ **$20.00**

Peter Pan Smooth Peanut Butter, girl in green outfit, 4-color litho, key-wind lid, 1940s-50s, 4½x4" dia, EX........ **$65.00**

Pikes Peak Brand Pure Lard, Nuckoll's Packing Co, multicolor pail w/original lid & wire bail, EX........ **$100.00**

Purity Highest Quality Fruit Cake, girl in gingham dress & high-button shoes & holly border on brown, 1920s-30s, VG+........ **$100.00**

Rawleigh's Medicated Ointment for Minor Injuries, Douglas Congdon-Martin, held 5-oz, 3½" dia........ **$15.00**

Red Dot Cigars, girl in red dot on white, Liberty Can Co, sq, ca 1920-30, 5½x4¾x4¾", EX........ **$185.00**

Rose Kist Popcorn, Um-m-m-m Good!, red, white & black, directions & recipes on side & back, 10⅞x2⅝" dia, NM... **$115.00**

Scotch Cellophane Tape, plaid, held tape roll, ca 1939-46, ¾x3" dia, EX........ **$12.50**

Shedd's Peanut Butter, elves, giraffe holds towel for elephant, other animals, pail form, 6½", EX........ **$65.00**

Spry Pure Vegetable Shortening, baker w/hat & tray of donuts, green & white, EX........ **$8.00**

SS Pierce Sahib Orange Pekoe Tea, brown, tan, green & white, sq, unopened, 4½x3½"........ **$100.00**

Tender Foam Shampoo, Stanhome, bunny graphics, VG........ **$7.50**

Tetley Orange Pekoe & Pekoe Tea Bags w/elephant, blue, brown & white, held 36 tea bags, 2⅛x5¼x3¼", EX........ **$20.00**

Thomas Wood Coffee, historical locations: Bunker Hill Monument, Boston Harbor, King's Chapel, etc, wooden finial, EX.. **$15.00**

Wool-O-Lene Cold Water Fluff Soap, multicolor pastels, triangular, 1958, 5x3½", EX........ **$22.50**

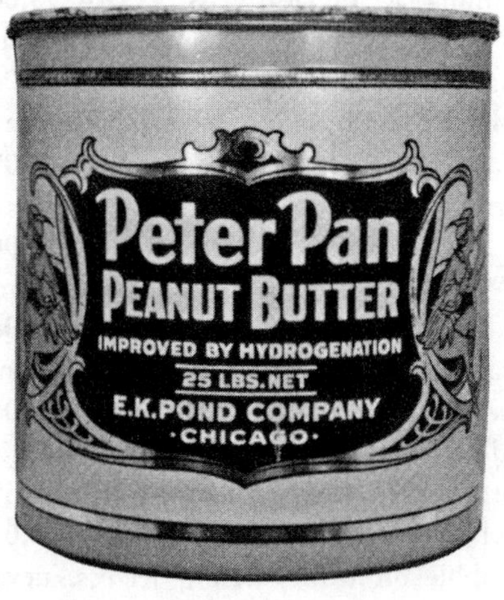

Peter Pan Peanut Butter, 25-pound store bin, 10x10", EX+, $200.00.

Airline Memorabilia

Even before the Wright brothers' historic flight shortly after the turn of the century, people have been fascinated with flying. What better way to enjoy the evolution and history of this amazing transportation industry than to collect its memorabilia. Today just about any item ever used or made for a commercial (non-military) airline is collectible, especially dishes, glassware, silver serving pieces and flatware, wings and badges worn by the crew, playing cards, and junior wings given to passengers. Advertising items such as timetables and large travel agency plane models are also widely collected. The earlier, the better! Anything pre-war is good; items from before the 1930s are rare and very valuable.

Unless noted otherwise, our values are for items in mint condition. See also Restaurant China. For more information we recommend *Restaurant China* by Barbara J. Conroy (Collector Books).

Advisor: Dick Wallin (See Directory, Airline)

Clubs and Newsletters: World Airline Historical Society
P.O. Box 101, Covington, LA 70434

Website: www.airlinecollectibles.com

Badge, hat; Braniff International Airways, red & blue enameling on gold, wings at side, 1½x3½".......................................**$200.00**

Bag, British Airways, zipper closure, 4 metal feet, strap handle, Sims Trading Co, Hong Kong, 14½x12x4½" **$25.00**

Bag, Canadian Pacific Airlines Serving 5 Continents, vinyl w/zipper closure, strap handle, 1960s-70s, 6½x14½", EX **$30.00**

Bag, Singapore Airlines, Affairs To Remember, zipper closure, shoulder strap, 13x14" **$30.00**

Bank, Southwest Airlines, comic airplane, multicolor, ceramic, 7¼" L, MIP..**$50.00**

Book, Pan Am Jet Flight Story Book, Once I Had a Monster, Tell-A-Tales, copyright 1969, EX..**$20.00**

Booklet, Air India, Foolishly Yours, man removes outer garment for lady to walk over, 1963, 36 pages, 6¼x4½", EX **$20.00**

Booklet, Know Your Airlines, Shell BP Aviation, 1950s, 7½x5¾", EX **$20.00**

Brochure, BOAC, Europe Is for Fun!, 1965, 16 pages+cover, VG.**$10.00**

Brochure, Pan Am Airlines, Welcome to Miami, 1930s, EX.**$15.00**

Certificate, Pan Am Airlines, Jupiter Rex equator crossing, Nandi to Honolulu flight, 1959, 13¼x11", EX **$20.00**

Cup and saucer, Air Zimbabwe (Africa), $25.00. (Photo courtesy Richard Wallin)

Fan, Pan American Presidential Service...Six Continents, printed paper, wooden sticks **$22.50**

Fan, Thai International Airlines, Royal Orchid Service on silk, purple wooden sticks & ribs, silk tassel, open: 13" **$25.00**

Jigsaw puzzle, Lufthansa Airlines, Boeing 707-320 pictured, 20 pcs, 1960s, unopened..**$20.00**

Menu cover, Pan Am, Brazilian Clipper arriving in Rio de Janeiro, 1984, 11x8½" **$25.00**

Model, Continental Airlines B727 airplane, painted mahogany, 18" w/13" wingspan **$110.00**

Model, Eastern Airlines Douglas DC-9, Air Jet Advanced Models, 7" w/5⅝" wingspan **$55.00**

Mug, American Airlines, Willie Mays commemorative, 1970, Lewis Bros Ceramics, 5" **$15.00**

Mug, coffee; Delta Airlines logo on front, pedestal foot, Mayer.**$7.50**

Mug, Northwest Airlines, black logo on fired-on yellow, black at rim, stackable, Fire-King..**$15.00**

Pin-back button, Pan Am 747, plane graphics, blue on white, 2" **$10.00**

Postcard, American Airlines, Douglas DC-7 main cabin interior, full color, 1950s, EX **$7.00**

Postcard, Lufthansa, Boeing 747 Jet Airliner, divided back, unused **$7.00**

Postcard, TWA, St Peter's, Vatican City, Rome, Kodachrome on linen, divided back, EX...**$8.00**

Poster, Delta Airlines, Houston, oil worker in hard hat, heavy stock, 28x22" **$45.00**

Poster, Delta Airlines, Washington, judge w/gavel, heavy stock, 22x22½" **$40.00**

Poster, Hughes Airwest, San Diego, surfer on lg blue wave, 37x24" **$90.00**

Poster, TWA Airlines, Las Vegas, queen (playing card), 1960s, 39x25", EX **$48.00**

Poster, United Airlines, Hawaii, girl (flowers in hair) in water up to bossom, 28x22", EX **$70.00**

Poster, United Airlines, San Francisco, cable car scene, Stan Galli, 1950s, 1-sheet, in black frame.............................**$150.00**

Questionnaire, British Commonwealth Pacific Airlines, passenger survey to mail in, 1940s, EX...................................**$10.00**

Salt and pepper shakers, British Airways original Concord Pattern, Royal Doulton, $35.00 for the pair. (Photo courtesy Richard Wallin)

Scarf, McDonnell Douglas, printed planes on polyester, Mr Blackwell Exclusive, 43x13½" **$20.00**

Sewing/manicure kit, KLM Airlines First Class, gold embossed logo on brown leather, triangular, complete, NM **$50.00**

Shot glass, Eastern Airlines, white logo on clear glass **$5.00**

Sticker, United Airlines, Hawaii, oceanside scene, 1940s, 3¼x4½" ..**$20.00**

Windsock, Piedmont Airlines, red, white & blue fabric w/speedbird logo, 30" L, EX+ **$30.00**

Wings, Braniff Airlines, enamel on silver, Sterling, ¾" **$42.50**

Wings, KLM Airlines Junior Skipper, multicolor enamel on gold-tone metal, 2½" **$30.00**

Wings, Piedmont Airlines Pilot, blue & white enameling on metal, EX **$150.00**
Wings, TAL Airlines Pilot, gold wire & brocade, 4" **$40.00**
Wings, United Airlines Junior Stewardess, red & blue enameling .. **$12.50**

Akro Agate

The Akro Agate Company operated in West Virginia from 1914 until 1951, and in addition to their famous marbles they made children's dishes as well as many types of novelties — flowerpots, powder jars with Scottie dogs on top, candlesticks, and ashtrays, for instance — in many colors and patterns. Though some of their glassware was made in solid colors, their most popular products were made of the same swirled colors as their marbles. Though many pieces are not marked, you will find some that are marked with their distinctive logo: a crow flying through the letter 'A' holding an Aggie in its beak and one in each claw. Some novelty items may instead carry one of these trademarks: 'JV Co, Inc,' 'Braun & Corwin,' 'NYC Vogue Merc Co USA,' 'Hamilton Match Co,' and 'Mexicali Pickwick Cosmetic Corp.'

Color is a very important worth-assessing factor. Some pieces may be common in one color but rare in others. Occasionally an item will have exceptionally good multicolors, and this would make it more valuable than an example with only average color.

Recently boxed sets of marbles have increased dramatically. When buying either marbles or juvenile tea sets in original boxes, be sure the box contains its original contents. For more information we recommend *The Complete Line of the Akro Agate Co.* by our advisors, Roger and Claudia Hardy.

Advisors: Roger and Claudia Hardy (See Directory, Akro Agate)

Club: Akro Agate Collectors Club
Clarksburg Crow newsletter
Claudia and Roger Hardy
10 Bailey St., Clarksburg, WV 26301-2524
304-624-7600 (days) or 304-624-4523 (evenings)
Dues $25.00; Canadian and foreign, $35.00. US checks or money orders only

Concentric Rib, creamer, dark green or white, 1⁵⁄₁₆" **$15.00**
Concentric Rib, creamer, yellow or med blue, 1⁵⁄₁₆" **$12.00**
Concentric Rib, plate, light blue, 3¼" **$18.00**
Concentric Rib, sugar bowl, canary yellow or med blue, ¹⁵⁄₁₆" .. **$15.00**
Concentric Rib, teapot, orange, 2⅜" **$60.00**
Concentric Ring, cereal, lg, light or med blue, 3⅜" **$28.00**
Concentric Ring, pitcher, blue transparent, 2⅞" **$75.00**
Concentric Ring, plate, purple, 3⁵⁄₁₆" **$45.00**
Concentric Ring, sugar bowl, blue/white marbleized, 1⁹⁄₁₆" ... **$125.00**
Concentric Ring, tumbler, blue transparent, 2" **$32.00**
Interior Panel, cereal, dark greeen, 16 panels, 3⅜" **$30.00**
Interior Panel, cup, lemon & oxblood, lg, 1½" **$72.00**
Interior Panel, plate, dark green lustre, 18 panels, 3⁵⁄₁₆" **$10.00**
Interior Panel, sugar bowl, topaz transparent, 18 panels, 1⁵⁄₁₆" **$75.00**
Interior Panel, teapot, royal blue, 16 panels, 2¾" **$45.00**
Miss America, cup, red transparent, 1⁹⁄₁₆" **$175.00**
Miss America, plate, red onyx, 4½" **$60.00**
Miss America, saucer, green transparent, 3⅝" **$40.00**
Miss America, teapot, white w/decal, 2½" **$100.00**
Octagonal, cup, canary yellow, open handle, 1¼" **$32.00**
Octagonal, cup, turquoise or light blue, 1½" **$40.00**
Octagonal, pitcher, lt blue, open handle, 3" **$55.00**
Octagonal, teapot, lemon & oxblood, closed handles, 3⅝" ... **$175.00**
Octagonal, tumbler, orange, 2" **$30.00**

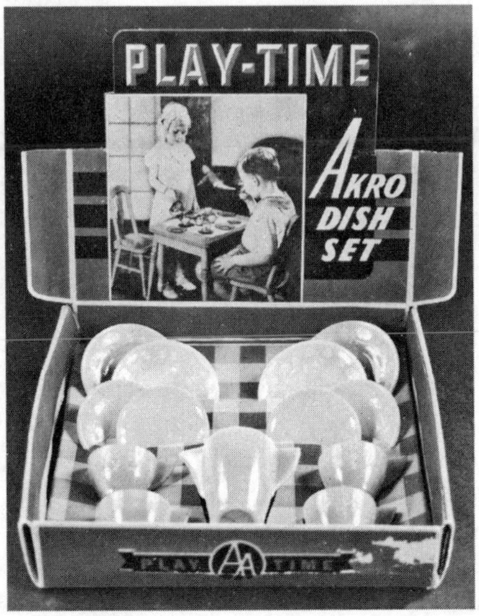

Raised Daisy, 13-piece boxed set, $300.00.
(Photo courtesy Roger and Claudia Hardy)

Raised Daisy, creamer, dark ivory, 1⁵⁄₁₆" **$100.00**
Raised Daisy, cup, dark green, 1⁵⁄₁₆" **$40.00**
Raised Daisy, plate, dark turquoise or dark blue, 3" **$28.00**
Raised Daisy, teapot, dark green, no lid, 2⅜" **$40.00**
Raised Daisy, tumbler, plain, dark or light yellow, 2" **$75.00**
Stacked Disc, creamer, dark green or white, 1⁵⁄₁₆" **$15.00**
Stacked Disc, cup, pink or dark ivory, 1⁵⁄₁₆" **$100.00**
Stacked Disc, plate, med or dark blue, 2¾" **$7.00**
Stacked Disc, teapot, purple or orange, 2⅜" **$60.00**
Stacked Disc, tumbler, pink, dark ivory or canary yellow, 2" **$10.00**
Stacked Disc & Interior Panel, cereal, white or yellow, 3⅜" . **$52.00**
Stacked Disc & Interior Panel, creamer, blue transparent, 1⅜" **$65.00**
Stacked Disc & Interior Panel, pitcher, med or royal blue, 2⅞" . **$125.00**
Stacked Disc & Interior Panel, sugar bowl, med or royal blue, 1⅜" . **$20.00**
Stacked Disc & Interior Panel, tumbler, white or ivory, 2" .. **$75.00**
Stippled Band, cup, green or topaz transparent, 1¼", from $18 to **$19.00**
Stippled Band, saucer, topaz transparent, 2¾" **$6.00**
Stippled Band, sugar bowl, green or topaz transparent, 1¼" **$85.00**
Stippled Band, tumbler, azure blue, 2⅛" **$200.00**

Miscellaneous

Ashtray, marbleized, sq, 5", from $60 to **$90.00**
Bell, dark green (forest green) **$450.00**
Candlestick, Inkwell Type 1, amber, ea **$20.00**
Flowerpot, #1311, 4" **$195.00**
Jardiniere, bell shaped, solid colors, 4¾", from $60 to **$100.00**
Marble, Brick (oxblood swirled w/black or white), ⅝-1", from $40 to **$100.00**

Marble, Brushed Transparent Ribbon (clear glass base), ⅝-⅞", from $1 to **$5.00**

Marble, Helmet (3-color patch & 1 ribbon opaque), ⅝-¾", from $10 to **$25.00**

Marble, Pee Wee Oxblood Snake, scarce, under ¼", from $60 to **$90.00**

Marble, Sparkler (multicolor strands & transparent base), ⅝-¾", from $15 to **$60.00**

Marble, Transparent Oxblood Spiral (corkscrew), ⅝-1¹⁄₁₆", from $75 to **$125.00**

Marble, Tri-Onyx 'Popeye' (3-color corkscrew on triple base), navy, yellow & white, ⅝-¾", from $15 to **$35.00**

Planter, Lily, ivory, 5¼", from $35 to **$40.00**

Tray, Victory Safety, 6" **$400.00**

Vase, Grecian Urn, Niagara Falls, 5-sided foot, 3¼" **$35.00**

Vivaudou, apothecary jar, pink.. **$95.00**

Vase, #312, blue, $125.00; Bowl, orange, footed, from $400.00 to $450.00; Candlesticks, orange, $325.00 for the pair. (Photo courtesy Roger and Claudia Hardy)

Aluminum

The aluminum items which have become today's collectibles range from early brite-cut giftware and old kitchen wares to furniture and hammered aluminum cooking pans. But the most collectible, right now, at least, is the giftware of the 1930s through the 1950s.

There were probably several hundred makers of aluminum accessories and giftware with each developing their preferred method of manufacturing. Some pieces were cast; other products were hammered with patterns created by either an intaglio method or repoussé. Machine embossing was utilized by some makers; many used faux hammering, and lightweight items were often decorated with pressed designs.

As early as the 1940s, collectors began to seek out aluminum, sometimes to add to the few pieces received as wedding gifts. By the late 1970s and early 1980s, aluminum giftware was found in abundance at almost any flea market, and prices of $1.00 or less were normal. As more shoppers became enthralled with the appearance of this lustrous metal and its patterns, prices began to rise and have not yet peaked for the products of some companies. A few highly prized pieces have brought prices of four or five hundred dollars and occasionally even more.

One of the first to manufacture this type of ware was Wendell August Forge, when during the late 1920s they expanded their line of decorative wrought iron and began to use aluminum, at first making small items as gifts for their customers. Very soon they were involved in a growing industry estimated at one point to be comprised of several hundred companies, among them Arthur Armour, the Continental Silver Company, Everlast, Buenilum, Rodney Kent, and Palmer-Smith. Few of the many original companies survived the WWII scarcity of aluminum.

During the 1960s, anodized (colored) aluminum became very popular. It's being bought up today by the younger generations who are attracted to its neon colors and clean lines. Watch for items with strong color and little if any sign of wear — very important factors to consider when assessing value. Because it was prone to scratching and denting, mint condition examples are few and far between.

Prices differ greatly from one region to another, sometimes without regard to quality or condition, so be sure to examine each item carefully before you buy.

Unless otherwise noted, our values are for items in at least near mint condition. See also Kitchen.

Advisor: Dannie Woodard (See Directory, Aluminum)

Notebook cover, tree, Wendell August Forge, $250.00. (Photo courtesy Everett Grist)

Basket, hammered, twisted handle (fixed), Cromwell Hand Wrought Aluminum, 10½" dia **$17.50**

Beverage set, Chrysanthemum, Continental Hand Wrought Silverlook, 10½" pot w/hinged lid+creamer & sugar bowl+tray **$85.00**

Bowl, leaf shape, stem hdl, Bruce Fox, 8¾x16¼" **$55.00**

Butler's tray w/stand, 4 different leaves, Hand Forged Everlast Metal, 27½x17½" on X-style base **$165.00**

Calling card case, engraved name & embossed floral decor, hinged rectangle.. **$28.00**

Candlesticks, daffodil blossom w/2 leaves, Bruce Fox, 10⅜x3", pr......$110.00

Casserole, embossed floral decor, flower finial on lid, 1½-qt Pyrex insert, Everlast, EX......$50.00

Casserole, hammered, open handles, Hand Forged Everlast Metal, w/lid, 6½x11½"......$22.50

Casserole carrier, carries 9" Pyrex glass bowl, aluminum lid w/rose finial, Rodney Kent #440, 10½x8½"+bowl......$30.00

Cheese/butter dish, beaded rim, coiled finial on lid, Buenilum, 3½x6½"......$15.00

Coasters, wild geese in flight, pr......$10.00

Cups, hammered, Buenilum, 4¾x3", 4 for......$25.00

Ice bucket, hammered w/etched tulips, tulip finial, side handles, w/liner insert, Rodney Kent, 7½x9"......$26.00

Lazy Suzan, 4 glass inserts, center bowl w/chrome lid, Kromex, 13½" dia......$20.00

Nut server, fluted 6-sided bowl w/pedestal foot, embossed floral band, center holds nutcracker & 6 picks, VG+......$25.00

Percolator, Chrysanthemum, clear Lucite handle, 15", +14" Chrysanthemum tray......$275.00

Punch bowl, hammered, embossed floral inside, footed, World Hand Forged, 6¾x13¼", +6 hooks, 6 cups & ladle......$165.00

Silent butler, tulip design on lid, Hand Wrought Creations By Rodney Kent #439, 13" L......$25.00

Tidbit tray, double, embossed roses, center handle, Farber & Shlevin, 4x8½x5"......$22.50

Tidbit tray, stacking set of 3, curved spacers attached w/screws, Regal Silver, 10x11" dia......$20.00

Tray, apple-blossom form, Bruce Fox, 12x10"......$65.00

Tray, berries & leaves embossed, etched & braided edge, basket-like handle, Wrought Farberware, 8" dia......$30.00

Tray, berries & pears embossed along rim, Everlast, 15½"......$25.00

Tray, butterflies, 6-scallop rim, sm fancy feet, Arthur Armour, 18⅜" dia, EX......$95.00

Tray, butterfly shape w/many embossed details, marked AC (Arthur Court?), 20" W......$75.00

Tray, dogwood flowers, ribbon-shaped handles, Hand Wrought Creation by Rodney Kent, 13¼x10¼"......$50.00

Tray, fish form, Bruce Fox, 22½x7"......$85.00

Tray, duck hunter, bird dog, and ducks, LA Hand Forged, $85.00. (Photo courtesy Everett Grist)

Tray, flamingos, palm trees & seashore, 1950s, 17½" dia......$19.00

Tray, hammered w/embossed fruit, openwork handles, 13" (across handles)......$18.00

Tray, lobster, hammered figural, Bruce Cox #370, 15½x10½"......$90.00

Tray, mixed floral bouquets embossed, scalloped edge, 12⅜" dia, EX+......$12.50

Tray, stylized leaf shape w/twisted tubular handle, Buenilum, 15x5½"......$15.00

Tray, 4-leaf clover form w/3-D lobster hdl, Bruce Fox, 10"......$70.00

Wastebasket, Bittersweet, Wendel August Forge, #900, 10½x10", EX+......$85.00

Anodized (Colored)

Bowls, cereal; various colors, Bascal, 5¼", 6 for......$40.00

Canister set, copper-tone w/white plastic lid, West Bend, graduated set of 5, EX......$35.00

Coasters, various colors, embossed oak leaves & acorns, West Bend, set of 4......$15.00

Cream pitcher, pink, Color Craft, 4¾"......$15.00

Pitcher, light beige, black plastic handle, ice lip, Regal Ware, 1950s, 7½x5¼", EX+......$27.50

Pitcher, magenta, Sunburst Made in Italy, 7¾", EX......$25.00

Pitcher, red, ice lip, 64-oz, 7", from $20 to......$30.00

Sherbets, various color bases, clear ruffled glass inserts, 3½", 8 for...$70.00

Tallstirs, various colors, RJ Walthes Co, 1960s, 7⅞", set of 6, MIB......$30.00

Tongs, brass trim, Lurelle Guild design, Kensington USA, 6¼"...$110.00

Tray, gold, geometric floral w/scalloped edge, unmarked, 13¾" dia......$10.00

Tumblers, various colors, Perma Hues, 5½", 4 for......$20.00

Tumblers, various colors, Sunburst, 3½", 6 forr......$28.00

Tumblers, various colors, West Bend, 14-oz, 5½", set of 8, MIB w/instructions for care......$45.00

American Bisque

This was a West Virginia company that operated there from 1919 until 1982, producing a wide variety of figural planters and banks, cookie jars, kitchenware, and vases. It has a look all its own; most of the decoration done by the airbrushing method, and some pieces were gold trimmed. Collectors often identify American Bisque items by the 'wedges' or dry-footed cleats on the bottom of the ware. The most valuable pieces are those modeled after characters like Popeye and the Flintstones.

See also Cookie Jars.

Bank, Cinderella, Walt Disney, 1950, 6½"......$98.00

Bank, Fatsy Pig, pink ears & cheeks, blue overalls, 6x4"......$40.00

Bank, Humpty Dumpty, Alice in Philcoland (promotional item), 6"......$85.00

Bank, Mr Pig, yellow pants, 6¼"......$30.00

Bank, Polka Dot Pig, 5"......$30.00

Pitcher, chick, green body, gold trim, 6"......$60.00

Pitcher, Donald Duck, gold trim, c Walt Disney, 1944-48, scarce, 6¼"......$145.00

Pitcher, Dumbo, trunk forms spout, C Walt Disney, 6".......**$85.00**

Pitcher, flowers on brown wooden barrel design, ice lip, 5¾"....**$30.00**

Pitcher, pig, multicolor pastels, 5"................................**$45.00**

Pitcher, wild rose, pink w/green leaves on white swirled body, 5¾"..**$22.00**

Planter, bear cubs (2) hugging tree trunk, brown & yellow tones.**$30.00**

Planter, bear on log, 6x6"...**$20.00**

Planter, crying kitten, pink & black, yellow bunny at side, planter behind, 5½"..**$25.00**

Planter, Davy Crockett, 5x6", $25.00.

Planter, girl holds pot of tulips, stands before Dutch shoe, multicolor pastels **$20.00**

Planter, Mickey Mouse w/flower, holds lg bag in left hand, c USA Walt Disney, 6¾"...**$85.00**

Planter, panther (brown) crouched on green base, lg yellow flower forms planter, 4¾x6¼x2"..**$30.00**

Sugar bowl, Polka Dot Pig, NM cold paint.........................**$35.00**

Teapot, wild rose, pink w/green leaves in white swirled body, flower finial **$30.00**

Anchor Hocking/Fire-King

From the 1930s until the 1970s, Anchor Hocking (Lancaster, Ohio), produced a wide and varied assortment of glassware including kitchen, restaurant ware, and tableware for the home. Fire-King was their trade name for glassware capable of withstanding high oven temperatures without breakage. So confident were they in the durability of this glassware that they guaranteed it for two years against breakage caused by heat.

Many colors were produced over the years. Blues are always popular with collectors, and Anchor Hocking made two, Turquoise Blue and Azurite (light sky blue). They also made pink, Forest Green, Ruby Red, gold-trimmed lines, and some with fired-on colors. Jade-ite was a soft opaque green glass that was very popular from the 1940s until well into the 1960s. (See the Jade-ite category for more information.) During the late 1960s they made Soreno in Avocado Green to tie in with home-decorating trends.

Bubble (made from the '30s through the '60s) was produced in just about every color Anchor Hocking ever made. It is especially collectible in Ruby Red. You may also hear this pattern referred to as Provencial or Bull's Eye.

Alice was a mid-'40s to '50s line. It was made in Jade-ite as well as white that was sometimes trimmed with blue or red. Cups and saucers were given away in boxes of Mother's Oats, but plates had to be purchased (so they're scarce today).

In the early 1950s they produced a 'laurel leaf' design in peach and 'Gray Laurel' lustres (the gray is scarce), followed later in the decade and into the 1960s with several lines of white glass decorated with decals — Honeysuckle, Fleurette, Primrose, and Game Bird, to name only a few.

One of their most expensive lines of dinnerware today is Philbe in Sapphire Blue, clear glass with a blue tint. It was made during the late 1930s. Values range from about $50.00 for a 6" plate to $1,500.00 for the cookie jar.

If you'd like to learn more about this type of very collectible glassware, we recommend *Anchor Hocking's Fire-King and More, Second Edition,* by Gene and Cathy Florence (Collector Books).

Note: Values for Rainbow apply only to items with the color layer in pristine mint condition. Only items identified by pattern names are listed here; for miscellaneous glassware items by Anchor Hocking/Fire-King, see Kitchen Collectibles, Glassware. See also Early American Prescut; Jade-ite.

Philbe, blue: cup, $175.00; saucer, $75.00. (Photo courtesy Gene and Cathy Florence)

Alice, cup, Vitrock w/red trim...**$18.00**

Alice, plate, Jade-ite, 9½"...**$26.00**

Alice, saucer, Vitrock w/blue trim **$4.00**

Anniversary Rose, bowl, vegetable; white w/decals, 8¼".......**$25.00**

Anniversary Rose, cup, snack; white w/decals, 5-oz...............**$5.00**

Anniversary Rose, platter, white w/decals, 9x12".................**$25.00**

Anniversary Rose, saucer, white w/decals, 5¾" **$2.50**

Anniversary Rose, tray, snack; white w/decals, 6x11" **$8.00**

Blue Mosaic, bowl, vegetable; white w/decals, 8¼" **$20.00**

Blue Mosaic, creamer, white w/decals.................................**$8.00**

Blue Mosaic, plate, dinner; white w/decals, 10" **$9.00**

Blue Mosaic, sugar bowl, white w/decals.............................**$8.00**

Bubble, bowl, berry; Sapphire Blue, 4" **$18.00**

Bubble, candlesticks, crystal iridescent, pr.........................**$16.00**

Bubble, plate, bread & butter; Forest Green, 6¾" **$18.00**

Bubble, saucer, white..**$2.00**

Bubble, tidbit, Royal Ruby, 2-tier **$75.00**

Classic, bowl, white, deep, 5¼" **$7.50**

Classic, plate, Royal Ruby, 14½".......................................**$40.00**

Classic, plate, snack; crystal, 6½x10¾"..............................**$5.00**

Fish Scale, bowl, cereal; ivory w/red, deep, 5½" **$18.00**

Fish Scale, cup, ivory w/blue, 8-oz...................................**$28.00**

Fish Scale, plate, salad; ivory, 7⅜" **$8.00**

Fleurette, bowl, chili; white w/decals, 5" **$22.00**

Fleurette, sugar bowl lid, white w/decals **$5.00**

Fleurette, tumbler, water; white w/decals, 9½-oz, 4⅛" **$125.00**

Forest Green, ashtray, hexagonal, 5¾" **$8.00**

Forest Green, cocktail, 3½-oz $10.00
Forest Green, punch bowl $22.50
Forest Green, vase, bud; 9" $10.00
Forget-Me-Not, creamer, white w/decals $10.00
Forget-Me-Not, custard, white w/decals $8.00
Forget-Me-Not, mug, white w/decals, 8-oz $18.00
Forget-Me-Not, platter, white w/decals, 9x12" $22.00
Harvest, bowl, vegetable; white w/decals, 8¼" $16.00
Harvest, creamer, white w/decals $7.00
Harvest, plate, dinner; white w/decals, 10" $6.00
Harvest, saucer, white w/decals, 5¾" $2.00
Harvest, sugar bowl, white w/decals $7.00
Hobnail, cookie jar, Milk White, w/lid $25.00
Hobnail, jardiniere, coral, green & yellow (fired-on), 4½" ... $10.00
Hobnail, pitcher, Milk White, 72-oz $18.00
Hobnail, vase, coral, green & yellow (fired-on), 9½" $20.00
Homestead, bowl, dessert; white w/decals, 4⅝" $5.00
Homestead, creamer, white w/decals $5.00
Homestead, platter, white w/decals, 9x12" $20.00
Homestead, sugar bowl, white w/decals $5.00
Jane Ray, bowl, dessert; ivory, 4⅞" $14.00
Jane Ray, bowl, oatmeal; Jade-ite, 5⅞" $16.00
Jane Ray, bowl, soup; Jade-ite, flat rimmed, 9" $295.00
Jane Ray, plate, dinner; Vitrock, 9⅛" $18.00
Jane Ray, saucer, demitasse; Vitrock $20.00
Lace Edge, cake plate, Milk White, 13" $15.00
Lace Edge, compote, Milk White, 3½x7" $6.00
Laurel, bowl, vegetable; peach lustre, 8¼" $10.00
Laurel, creamer, white, footed $15.00
Laurel, plate, serving; gray, 11" $16.00
Meadow Green, bowl, mixing; white w/decals, 2-qt $8.00
Meadow Green, casserole, white w/decals, w/crystal lid, 2-qt . $9.00
Meadow Green, loaf pan, white w/decals, 5x9" $6.50
Meadow Green, mug, white w/decals, 8-oz $3.00
Philbe, bowl, cereal; crystal, 5½" $18.00
Philbe, bowl, salad; green or pink, 7¼" $80.00
Philbe, pitcher, juice; blue, 36-oz, 6" $895.00
Philbe, plate, salver; blue, 11⅝" $95.00
Philbe, sherbet, crystal, 3¾" $100.00
Philbe, tumbler, iced tea; green or pink, footed, 15-oz, 6½" ... $85.00
Primrose, egg plate, white w/decal $175.00
Primrose, gravy boat, white w/decal $295.00
Primrose, mug, white w/decal $95.00
Primrose, plate, dinner; white w/decal, 9⅛" $7.00
Primrose, vase, white w/decal $165.00
Rainbow, bowl, fruit; pastels, 6" $25.00
Rainbow, jug, primary colors, 64-oz $65.00
Rainbow, salt & pepper shakers, primary colors, pr $25.00
Rainbow, tumbler, table; pastels, 9-oz $15.00
Royal Ruby, ashtray, leaf, 4½" $5.00
Royal Ruby, bottle, milk; Borden's $400.00
Royal Ruby, lamp $35.00
Royal Ruby, plate, 13¾" $25.00
Royal Ruby, sugar bowl, footed $7.50
Royal Ruby, tumbler, water; 9-oz $6.50
Sheaves of Wheat, bowl, dessert; Jade-ite, 4½" $55.00
Sheaves of Wheat, cup, crystal $5.00

Sheaves of Wheat, saucer, Jade-ite $15.00
Sheaves of Wheat, tumbler, juice; crystal, 6-oz $14.00
Shell, bowl, vegetable; Milk White, round, 8½" $12.00
Shell, cup, demitasse; Aurora Shell, 3¼-oz $25.00
Shell, plate, dinner; Lustre Shell, 10" $7.00
Shell, plate, snack; Golden Shell, w/indent, 10" $6.00
Shell, sugar bowl lid, Jade-ite $45.00
Soreno, ashtray, aquamarine, 4¼" $5.00
Soreno, cup, Avocado or Milk White, 7-oz $2.00
Soreno, plate, snack; crystal, w/indent, 10" $3.00
Soreno, tumbler, water; Honey Gold, 12-oz $3.50
Swirl, bowl, cereal; Azur-ite, 5⅞" $18.00
Swirl, cup, Jade-ite, 8-oz $30.00
Swirl, platter, ivory, 9x12" $18.00
Three Bands, bowl, fruit; burgundy, 4⅞" $110.00
Three Bands, cup, Jade-ite, 8-oz $50.00
Three Bands, saucer, ivory, 5¾" $5.00
Turquoise Blue, bowl, vegetable; 8" $25.00
Turquoise Blue, creamer $8.00
Turquoise Blue, mug, 8-oz $18.00
Turquoise Blue, plate, 7¼" $12.00
Turquoise Blue, sugar bowl $8.00
Wheat, bowl, chili; white w/decals, 5" $23.00
Wheat, cake pan, white w/decals, sq, 8" $10.00
Wheat, cup, white w/decals, 8-oz $4.00
Wheat, mug, white w/decals $30.00
Wheat, tumbler, juice; white w/decals, 5-oz $6.00

Primrose, salt shaker, $275.00 for the pair. (Photo courtesy Gene and Cathy Florence)

Angels

Birthday

Manufactured by many import companies primarily in the 1950s and 1960s, birthday angels are relatively easy to find, although completing a set can be a real challenge. Pricing is determined by the following factors: 1) Condition. 2) Company — look for Lefton, Napco, Norcrest, and Enesco marks or labels. Unmarked or unknown sets can be of less value. However, if two collectors are looking for the same item to complete their collection prices can go high on the Internet. 3) Details — the added touches of flowers, bows, gold trim, 'coconut' trim, rhinestones, etc. More detail means more value. 4) Quality of workmanship involved, detail, and accuracy of painting. 5) Age. 6) As a rule boy angels will usually bring more than girls as far fewer were sold. It is difficult to identify the manufacturer by the design because so many companies used similar designs. In addition to birthday months, angels were made to represent age and days of the week. They often adorned the top of birthday cakes.

Advisors: Jim and Kaye Whitaker (See Directory Angels; no appraisals please)

Arnart, Kewpies, in choir robes, w/rhinestones, 4½", ea from $12 to **$15.00**

Enesco, angels on round base w/flower of the month, gold trim, ea from $15 to **$18.00**

High Mountain Quality, colored hair, 7", ea from $30 to **$32.00**

Japan, J-6736, June bride w/veil & rose bouquet, 5¼".........**$32.00**

Japan (fine quality), months or days of the week, 4½", ea from $20 to **$25.00**

Josef, black eyes, Japan: #1, #2, and #3, from $25.00 to $30.00 each. (Photo courtesy Jim and Kaye Whitaker)

Kelvin, C-230, holding flower of the month, 4½", ea from $15 to..**$20.00**

Kelvin, C-250, holding flower of the month, 4½", ea from $15 to..**$20.00**

Lefton, #AR-1987, w/ponytail, 4", ea from $18 to **$22.00**

Lefton, #130, Kewpie, 4½", ea from $35 to........................**$40.00**

Lefton, #489, holding basket of flowers, 4", ea from $25 to...**$35.00**

Lefton, #556, boy of the month, 5½", ea from $25 to.........**$30.00**

Lefton, #574, day of the week series (like #8281 but not as ornate), ea from $25 to **$28.00**

Lefton, #627, day of the week series, 3½", ea from $28 to...**$32.00**

Lefton, #985, flower girl of the month, 5", ea from $30 to **$35.00**

Lefton, #1323, angel of the month, bisque, ea from $18 to.**$22.00**

Lefton, #1411, angel of the month, 4", ea from $28 to **$32.00**

Lefton, #1987, angel of the month, ea from $30 to.............**$35.00**

Lefton, #1987J, w/rhinestones, 4½", ea from $30 to **$40.00**

Lefton, #2600, birthstone on skirt, 3¼", ea from $25 to **$30.00**

Lefton, #3332, w/basket of flowers, bisque, 4", ea from $25 to.**$30.00**

Lefton, #4883, in yellow w/January ribbon across white apron, 1985, 3"...**$25.00**

Lefton, #5146, birthstone on skirt, 4½", ea from $22 to **$28.00**

Lefton, #6224, applied flower/birthstone on skirt, 4½", ea from $20 to **$30.00**

Lefton, #6883, day of the week & months in sq frame, 3¼x4", ea from $28 to **$32.00**

Lefton, #6949, day of the week series in oval frame, 5", ea from $28 to **$32.00**

Lefton, #6985, musical, sm, ea from $40 to......................**$45.00**

Lefton, #8281, day of the week series, applied roses, ea from $30 to **$35.00**

Mahana Importing, #1194, angel of the month series, white hair, 5", ea from $20 to **$22.00**

Mahana Importing, #1294, angel of the month, white hair, 5", ea from $20 to **$22.00**

Mahana Importing, #1600, Pal Angel, month series of both boy & girl, 4", ea from $15 to **$20.00**

Napco, #1307E, bell of the month, 3½", from $30.00 to $40.00. (Photo courtesy Judy Ferguson)

Napco, A-1360-1372, angel of the month, ea from $20 to ..**$30.00**

Napco, A-1917-1929, boy angel of the month, ea from $20 to..**$25.00**

Napco, A-4307, angel of the month, sm, ea from $22 to.....**$25.00**

Napco, C-1361-1373, angel of the month, ea from $20 to..**$25.00**

Napco, C-1921-1933, boy angel of the month, ea from $20 to .**$25.00**

Napco, S-1291, day of the week 'Belle,' ea from $22 to.......**$25.00**

Napco, S-1361-1372, angel of the month, ea from $20 to ..**$25.00**

Napco, S-1392, angel of the month in oval frame, ea from $25 to **$30.00**

Napco, S-401-413, angel of the month, ea from $20 to **$25.00**

Napco, S-429, day of the week angel (also available as planters), ea from $25 to **$30.00**

Napco, X-8371, Christmas angels w/instrument, 3¾", ea....**$26.00**

Norcrest, F-015, angel of the month on round base w/raised pattern on dress, 4", ea from $18 to................................**$22.00**

Norcrest, F-23, day of the week angel, 4½", ea from $18 to...**$22.00**

Norcrest, F-120, angel of the month, 4½", ea from $18 to ..**$22.00**

Norcrest, F-167, bell of the month, 2¾", ea from $8 to **$12.00**

Norcrest, F-210, day of the week angel, 4½", ea from $18 to.**$22.00**

Norcrest, F-340, angel of the month, 5", ea from $20 to.....**$25.00**

Norcrest, F-535, angel of the month, 4½", ea from $20 to..**$25.00**

Norcrest, F-755, girl angel w/mask & jack-o'-lantern pumpkin, 4"...**$30.00**

Relco, angel of the month, 4¼", ea from $15 to **$18.00**

Relco, angel of the month, 6", ea from $18 to **$22.00**

Sanmyro, blond girl angel w/yellow flower, pink streaked gown, March on yellow ribbon, 4"...**$23.00**

Schmid, boy angel sitting w/gift, label, 1950s, 3½".............**$29.00**

SR, angel of the month, w/birthstone & 'trait' of the month (i.e. April - innocence), ea from $20 to **$25.00**

TMJ, angel of the month, w/flower, ea from $20 to **$25.00**

Ucagco, angel of the month, white hair, 5¾", from $12 to ..**$15.00**

Wales, angel w/long white gloves, white hair, Made in Japan, 6⅜", ea from $25 to **$28.00**

Zodiac

These china figurines were made and imported by the same companies as the birthday angels. Because they were not as popular as birthday angels fewer were made so they are more difficult to find. Examples tend to be more individualized due to each sign having a specific characteristic associated with it.

Japan, angel wearing pastel dress, applied pink rose on head, stands on cloud base w/stars, 4½", ea from $15 to **$20.00**

Japan, angel wearing pastel dress w/rhinestones on gold stars, applied pink rose on head, 4", ea from $20 to **$25.00**

Josef, angel holding tablet w/sign written & shown in gold, ea from $30 to **$45.00**

Josef, no wings, sign written in cursive on dress, 4", ea from $40 to **$55.00**

Lefton, K-8650, angel w/applied flowers & gold stars, 4" when standing, ea from $40 to **$45.00**

Napco, A-2646, angel wearing gold crown, applied 'coconut' gold trim on hem, 5", ea from $25 to **$30.00**

Napco, S-980, 'Your Lucky Star Guardian Angel,' 4", ea from $22 to **$28.00**

Napco, S-1259, 'Your Lucky Star Guardian Angel' planter series, 4", ea from $30 to **$35.00**

Semco, angel w/gold wings, applied roses & pleated ruffle on front edge of dress, 5", ea from $20 to...................................**$25.00**

Miscellaneous

Japan, Christmas boy & girl angel, he w/revolving musical base, 10", pr **$45.00**

Japan, nurse angel w/Red Cross hat, Get Well on base, 3¾"...**$34.00**

Napco, A-1917, New Year's Boy..**$30.00**

Napco, A-1926, September boy angel w/pencils & schoolbag.**$35.00**

Napco, A-5577, angel w/lyre, 7½" **$35.00**

Napco, C-1918, Valentine boy w/card stands beside mailbox, 4¼"...**$35.00**

Napco, C-6362, boy angel w/football, 4½" **$30.00**

Napco, C-7361, angel w/iron, 4¾" **$35.00**

Napco, S-1703, girl angel w/wreath & candy cane, 7¾", from $25 to **$35.00**

Napco, S-542F, devil boy in red w/long spear looks at sleeping angel, 4"...**$35.00**

Napco, X-5974, Christmas angel w/presents, 4" **$35.00**

Napco, X-6963, Christmas girl w/gold bells.......................**$20.00**

Norcrest, F-299, angel w/instrument, all white, plain, 7½"..**$12.50**

Aprons

America's heartland offers a wide variety of aprons, ranging from those once worn for kitchen duty or general household chores to fancier styles designed for cocktail parties. Today they can be found in an endless array of styles and in fabrics ranging from feed sacks to fine silk with applied rhinestones. Some were embroidered or pieced, some were even constructed of nice handkerchiefs. Aprons were given and received as gifts; often they were cherished and saved. Some of these are now surfacing in today's market. You may find some in unused condition with the original tags still attached.

Condition is important when assessing the value of vintage aprons. Unless very old, pass up those that are stained and torn. Hand-sewn examples are worth more than machine- or commercial-made aprons, and if they retain the tags from their original maker, you can double their price. Some labels themselves are collectible. Children's and young ladies' dress aprons command very high prices, as often they were recycled into quilt patches and dust cloths.

Perhaps no other area of Americana evokes as much nostalgia as vintage aprons. Our advisor's favorite, he says, is a grandmother's that has become stained from cookie baking and worn soft from use. He recommends tying them onto your old caned dining chair or, as he does, to the grandfather clock in his kitchen, giving the impression that the wearer is only temporarily absent.

Advisor: Darrell Thomas (See Directory, Aprons)

Adult's bib type, red and white organdy with embroidery and lace, tie back, 1940s, from $35.00 to $45.00. (Photo courtesy LaRee Johnson Bruton)

Adult's bib type, blue cotton chambray w/lg faded rose pattern, red-orange trim, from $30 to **$45.00**

Adult's bib type, canvas, Johns Manville/Iverson-Larson Lumber Co, early 1960s, from $25 to...**$35.00**

Adult's bib type, ladies wearing aqua, green, chartreuse & blue aprons, 1960s..**$25.00**

Adult's bib type, pastel blue dots w/painted decal of elephant holding a basket, flowers surround...**$25.00**

Adult's bib type, pink cotton w/white openwork, 1930s-40s, from $35 to **$40.00**

Adult's bib type, polka dots w/lg Bakelite buttons, various sizes buttons used to make a border, unique, 1930s-40s **$75.00**

Adult's bib type, sm tulips on turquoise, Dutch girls between lg tulips on bottom, 1930s, from $15 to..........................**$20.00**

Adult's bib type, white cotton w/mint green trim, puppy & kitten at bottom, 1930s, from $40 to **$50.00**

Adult's pinafore-type, cream w/pink, green, blue & yellow floral sprays, shoulder straps become aprons strings **$25.00**

Adult's shoulder type, pink and white checked cotton with organdy trim, black embroidery, and applied flower, 1930s – 1940s, from $30.00 to $40.00. (Photo courtesy LaRee Johnson Bruton)

Adult's shoulder type, white cotton w/yellow rose pattern, organdy neck ruffle, 1930s, from $20 to **$25.00**

Adult's smock type, green w/sm white daisies, lg hot pink cats, black trim, 1960s, from $20 to **$30.00**

Adult's smock-type, black floral cotton w/red pockets & ties, 4 lg red buttons on back, 1960, from $15 to **$20.00**

Adult's tea type, ivory cotton w/2 lg blue geese embroidered on front, wings are pockets, from $25 to **$33.00**

Adult's tea type, red & navy cotton w/green paisley & rose pattern, ruffled hem, 1930s, from $20 to...................................**$30.00**

Adult's waist type, black cotton canvas, Red Cross issued, drawstring pouch, early 1900s, from $45 to......................................**$65.00**

Adult's waist type, Black mammy w/green Humpty Dumpty bandana, reverses to green, 1940s-50s, from $35 to...........**$40.00**

Adult's waist type, blue & white crocheted, scalloped edge w/floral pattern, from $15 to **$20.00**

Adult's waist type, blue & white gingham alternating w/sm floral pattern cotton, sheer fabric panels in between, 1940s ...**$12.00**

Adult's waist type, cotton floral pattern on red organdy, red rickrack, from $14 to **$18.00**

Adult's waist type, cream cotton & blue calico w/embroidered flower, 1940s, from $15 to..**$25.00**

Adult's waist type, fox hunt equestrian scene on white cotton, red rickrack, from $45 to...**$55.00**

Adult's waist type, milk chocolate, w/brown & pink circles around bottom that form 3 lg pockets, 1940s.........................**$25.00**

Adult's waist type, patchwork w/white rickrack, 1930s, from $18 to **$25.00**

Adult's waist type, pink lotus flower w/green leaves & ties, embroidered details, from $12 to...**$18.00**

Adult's waist type, sheer black fabric w/white lace detail, 1950s, from $15 to **$20.00**

Adult's waist type, white & red striped w/poodle on pocket, white rickrack, from $25 to **$30.00**

Adult's waist type, white cotton muslin w/yellow & green hand embroidery, silk lace trim, 1940s, from $25 to **$35.00**

Adult's waist type, white cotton w/embroidered bluebird & flower design in blue, pink, orange & green, blue trim...........**$25.00**

Adult's waist type, white cotton w/lace heart insert along sides, lace trim, 1920s, from $40 to **$50.00**

Adult's waist type, white cotton w/multicolored Tyrolean pattern embroidery on bottom, 1950s, from $7 to **$10.00**

Adult's waist type, white fluer-de-lis pattern on pink, blue trim, from $12 to **$16.00**

Adult's waist type, white organdy w/yellow roses appliqués, from $10 to **$20.00**

Adult's waist type, yellow w/navy & yellow plaid ties, deep pockets, yellow rickrack, from $10 to **$20.00**

Adult waist type, made from tablecloth, Aprons by Annie J WI, very nice (unused oddity, great use of fabrics), 1940s **$65.00**

Child's bib type, cream feed-sack material & cotton muslin w/purple & pink flowers, from $20 to......................................**$25.00**

Child's pinafore type, white cotton w/hand-embroidered bunny rabbit w/carrots on pockets, from $30 to **$45.00**

Child's shoulder type, white feed-sack material w/girl in pink & blue bonnet, from $30 to **$45.00**

Child's smock type, green, blue, orange & brown circus print, from $25 to **$30.00**

Child's waist type, green & white cotton w/frog pattern, 1950s, from $25 to **$35.00**

Child's waist type, made from dish towels, brightly colored morning glories, 1 pocket, 1940s **$35.00**

Child's waist type, pink & white gingham, 1950s, from $45 to... **$50.00**

Child's waist type, red & white gingham w/gray, black & white Scottie pup & dish, black trim, from $40 to................**$50.00**

Child's waist type, yellow & turquoise cotton, 3 pockets w/raccoons, elephants & kangaroos, ties are drawstring...................**$15.00**

Pattern, Disney style w/Snow White, w/rhinestones from dwarfs' diamond mine, apple pocket, uncut, 1940s, M, from $75 to **$95.00**

Pattern, fancy serving/cocktail waist style w/matching tea towel, uncut, mailed in 1935, M...**$45.00**

Ashtrays

Ashtrays, especially for cigarettes, did not become widely used in the United States much before the turn of the century. The first examples were simply receptacles made to hold ashes for pipes, cigars, and cigarettes. Later, rests were incorporated into the design. Ashtrays were made in a variety of materials. Some were purely functional, while others advertised or entertained, and some stopped just short of being works of art. They were made to accommodate smokers in homes, businesses, or wherever they might be. Today their prices range from a few dollars to hundreds. Since today so many people buy and sell on eBay and other Internet auction sites, there is much more exposure to ashtray collecting. Also these auction prices must be considered when determining the value of an item. Many of the very fine ashtrays from the turn of the century do not command the same price as they did in the early 1990s unless the maker's name is widely known. And now, in the twenty-first century, many of the old ashtrays are actually antiques. This may contribute to the continued fluctuation of prices in this still new collectibles field. For further information see *Collector's Guide to Ashtrays, Second Edition, Identification and Values,* by Nancy Wanvig.

See also specific glass companies and potteries; Japan Ceramics; Disney; Tire Ashtrays; World's Fairs.

Advisor: Nancy Wanvig (See Directory, Ashtrays)

Advertising, Aqua Velva, glass w/blue decal on bottom, 3¾".. **$7.00**
Advertising, Galleries Lafayette, cobalt blue center w/gold emblem, gold name on rim, Limoges, 4" **$8.00**
Advertising, General Electric, blue ceramic w/dark green motor figural, GE logo raised in center, 5⅜" **$55.00**
Advertising, Hennessy Cognac, Limoges, cream w/gold letters, 4" **$9.00**
Advertising, Hotel Peabody Memphis, black plastic w/match holder, 1930s, 7" **$12.00**
Advertising, JC Penney Co, white ceramic, yellow & black letters, 5¼" **$25.00**
Advertising, Lakeland College, ceramic w/black picture of building in center, Old Main, 1960s, 7½" **$5.00**
Advertising, Martini & Rossi, white ceramic w/black & red logo, name only on side, 4½" **$9.00**
Advertising, Oxford University, chrome w/enameled seal in blue, yellow & silver, 4" **$20.00**
Advertising, Polar Ware, enamelware w/black letters & picture of bear, 1928, 4¾" **$60.00**

Advertising, Rod and Gun Club, Bad Hersfeld, marked Royal Bayreuth, 9", $35.00. (Photo courtesy Nancy Wanvig)

Advertising, Schlitz, tan ceramic w/brown logo & picture, 5¼". **$20.00**
Advertising, US Pump-Western Land Roller Pumps, green ceramic w/gray pump figural, ¼x7⅞" **$35.00**
Bone china, Napoleon Ivy, green edge/ivy in center, Wedgwood, 1955, 4¼" **$15.00**
Brass, long-earred rabbit beside tray on pedestal, China, 3½". **$30.00**
Ceramic, wine floral on aqua, triangular, Moorcroft, 5½"....**$65.00**
Glass, amber, Daisy & Button, fan form, 4" **$10.00**
Glass, amethyst, w/golf ball stem, Cambridge, 3½" **$70.00**
Glass, cobalt cloverleaf, Tiffin, 4¾" **$28.00**

Glass, cobalt stretch, Depression type, 3 rests, 4 snufferetttes, Fenton, 1927, 4⅞" **$28.00**
Glass, crystal, duck, Duncan & Miller, 5x7" **$40.00**
Glass, crystal, duck w/1 rest in tail, LE Smith, 4½" **$8.00**
Glass, crystal w/nude stem, Cambridge, 6½" **$175.00**
Glass, Dutch boy & girl, match-holder center, Hazel Atlas, 1920, 5¾" **$28.00**
Glass, Lily of the Valley, embossed & frosted flower stem, Duncan & Miller, 7" **$35.00**
Glass, Mayfair, crystal, rose embossed in center, sq, Fostoria, 3⅞" **$11.00**
Glass, Mayfair, frosted, Fostoria, 3⅞" **$9.00**
Glass, milk glass w/matchbox holder, oval, 3 rests, 5" **$14.00**
Glass, ruby dish on 3 sm legs, New Martinsville, 4" **$10.00**
Glass, ruby English Hobnail, smooth hobs, sq, Westmoreland, 1920-40, 4½" **$30.00**
Glass, Trojan, topaz yellow, Fostoria, 1929-44, 3⅞" **$27.00**
Glass, Versailles, blue, etching around rim only, 1 rest, Fostoria, 1928-44, 4" **$20.00**
Glass, windmill scene, fired-on orange, 3 wide rests, 5¼" **$25.00**
Marble, off-white w/gray markings, 7" **$17.00**
Marble, yellow w/gray markings, heavy, sq, 4½" **$18.00**
Metal, 1939 calendar, thin sheet metal, 4¼" **$18.00**
Novelty, black bowling-pin shape, plastic w/black glass ashtray, 8⅜" **$9.00**
Novelty, black top hat, glass, 2 rests, 2⅛" **$9.00**
Novelty, Cubs, ceramic, bats & ball in relief in center, 4⅛". **$25.00**
Novelty, Indian w/tepee, ceramic, smoke comes out top of tepee, 4¼" **$25.00**
Novelty, Jerusalem, solid brass w/some enameling, cut-out camels around upper rim, 3⅝" **$8.00**
Novelty, Leaning Tower of Pisa, Italy, silver finish on pot metal, 4¼" **$15.00**

Novelty, lion head, ceramic, Japan, 3½" long, $45.00. (Photo courtesy Nancy Wanvig)

Novelty, Moon Mullins nodder, ceramic, luster, Germany, 4⅝".**$120.00**
Novelty, Niagara Falls, Canada, bronze-plated pot metal, 5". **$10.00**
Novelty, San Pietro, Rome, cathedral & Pope figural, pot metal, 2⅛" **$20.00**
Novelty, Ziggy watering thankful flower, ceramic, 1982, 5"...**$7.00**
Pewter, Prairie dogs holding up tray, American, 3¾" **$35.00**
Plastic, red w/black base, cigarette lighter in center, 7½"......**$20.00**
Plastic, yellow, chrome-plated rim, Japan, 2⅞" **$7.00**

Pottery, man on horse, cream w/green edge, sq, Spode, 4½" . **$20.00**

Soapstone, gray, elephant figural on back rim, 4¼" **$35.00**

Soapstone, green, leaf-shape, China, 4¾" **$12.00**

Wood, gnome smoking pipe, copper ashtray, 8" **$50.00**

Autographs

'Philography' is an extremely popular hobby, one that is very diversified. Autographs of sports figures, movie stars, entertainers, and politicians from our lifetime may bring several hundred dollars, depending on rarity and application, while John Adams' simple signature on a document from 1800, for instance, might bring thousands. A signature on a card or cut from a letter or document is the least valuable type of autograph. A handwritten letter is generally the most valuable, since in addition to the signature you get the message as well. Depending upon what it reveals about the personality who penned it, content can be very important and can make a major difference in value.

Many times a polite request accompanied by an SASE to a famous person will result in receipt of a signed photo or a short handwritten note that might in several years be worth a tidy sum!

Obviously as new collectors enter the field, the law of supply and demand will drive the prices for autographs upward, especially when the personality is deceased. There are forgeries around, so before you decide to invest in expensive autographs, get to know your dealers.

Over the years many celebrities in all fields have periodically employed secretaries to sign their letters and photos. They have also sent out photos with preprinted or rubber stamped signatures as time doesn't always permit them to personally respond to fan mail. With today's advanced printing, even many long-time collectors have been fooled with a mechanically produced signature. The letters 'COA' in our descriptions stand for 'Certificate of authenticity.'

Newspaper: *Autograph Times*
2303 N 44th St., #225,
Phoenix, AZ 85008; 602-947-3112 or fax: 602-947-8363

Andrews, Julie; signed photo, color, COA, 8x10" **$45.00**

Bennett, Joan; signed photo, black & white, 5x7" **$40.00**

Bogart, Humphrey; signed postcard, black & white, 3½x5½" .**$375.00**

Bonds, Barry; signed baseball card, 2001 .... **$60.00**

Burton, Richard; signature from album, COA, 2¾x3" **$40.00**

Cash, Johnny; signature on black & white photograph in booklet, 1960s-70s **$85.00**

Cher, signed photo, color, COA, 8x10" **$23.00**

Clift, Montgomery; signed album page, 3x5" **$40.00**

Connery, Sean; ink signature on color photo, as James Bond in Goldfinger, 8x10" **$85.00**

Connors, Chuck; inscribed signed black & white photo, as Rifleman, dated 1986, 8x10 .... **$45.00**

Crawford, Joan; signed postcard, 5¼x3½" **$55.00**

DeCarlo, Yvonne; signed black & white photo, 5x7" **$40.00**

Dressen, Chuck; signed baseball card, 1961 .... **$150.00**

Durante, Jimmy; signed letter w/black & white photo, 11x14" **$40.00**

Ford, Harrison; signed photo, as Indiana Jones, COA, 8x10" ... **$70.00**

Gordon, Jeff; signed color photo, COA, 8x10" **$35.00**

Hanks, Tom; signed color photo, as Forrest Gump, COA, 8x10" **$65.00**

Hepburn, Audrey; signed color photo, 8x10" **$100.00**

Hepburn, Katherine; blue ink signed card, 2½x6" **$50.00**

Heston, Charlton; signed black & white photo, Planet of the Apes, COA, 8x10" **$35.00**

Johnson, Van; red ink signed black & white photo, 8x10"...**$15.00**

Jones, Tom; signed color photo, COA, 8x10" **$15.00**

Kelly, Gene; signed movie photo, Cover Girl, 5x7" **$50.00**

Loren, Sophia; ink signature w/color photograph, matted & framed **$65.00**

Lugosi, Bela; signed cardboard-type album page, 2½x4⅛" .**$150.00**

Madonna, blue ink signature on color photo, COA, 8x10" ..**$125.00**

Marx, Groucho; signature clipped contract in frame w/early black & white photo **$70.00**

McCartney, Paul; signed poster, COA **$250.00**

Nelson, Ricky; signed black & white photo, 8x10" **$85.00**

Peck, Gregory; signed black & white head shot photo, 4x6" ..**$40.00**

Presley, Elvis; signature on wall plaque w/vinyl record Heartbreak Hotel, #7 of 90, sealed & never opened **$200.00**

Rockwell, Norman; signed painting, Christmas at Stockbridge, 12½x31½" **$95.00**

Rogers, Ginger; signed black & white photo, 3¼x6" **$45.00**

Rogers, Will; signed pastel sepia photo, 8x10" **$95.00**

Sheridan, Ann; white ink signature on black & white photo, 1940s, 5x7" **$40.00**

Sinatra, Frank; signed record album, This Is Sinatra **$200.00**

Starr, Ringo; signature w/color photo, matted, COA, 12x16" ... **$75.00**

Stewart, James; signed black & white photo, Harvey, COA, 8x10" **$85.00**

Taylor, Elizabeth; signed photo, w/Montgomery Clift, A Place in The Sun, frame w/biography plaque, 8x10" **$100.00**

Temple, Shirley; signed black & white photo, 10½x13½" **$70.00**

The Three Stooges, black and white publicity photo signed by all three, photo copyrighted 1963, 8½x10", NM, minimum value, $1,500.00. (Photo courtesy Early American History Auctions)

Wayne, John; signed $1 bill, 1935 .... **$200.00**

Welch, Raquel; signed color photo, 8x10" **$20.00**

Young, Loretta; signed Life magazine article, 10 pictures in various poses, 10x14" **$35.00**

Automobilia

Automobilia remains a specialized field, attracting antique collectors and old car buffs alike. It is a field that encompasses auto-related advertising and accessories like hood ornaments, gear shift and steering wheel knobs, sales brochures, and catalogs. Memorabilia from the high-performance, sporty automobiles of the sixties is very popular with baby boomers. Unusual items have been setting auction records as the market for automobilia heats up. Note: Badges vary according to gold content — 10k or sterling silver examples are higher than average. Dealership booklets (Ford, Chevy, etc.) generally run about $2.00 to $3.00 per page, and because many reproductions are available, very few owner's manuals sell for more than $10.00. Also it should be mentioned here that there are many reproduction clocks and signs out there. Any 'Guard' badges with round Ford logos are fake. Buyers beware. Our values are for items in excellent to near-mint condition unless noted otherwise.

See also License Plates; Tire Ashtrays.

Advisor: Leonard Needham (See Directory, Automobilia)

Emblem sign, Chevrolet, die-cut Masonite, chain hung, 1950s, 9½x21", EX, $350.00. (Photo courtesy B.J. Summers)

Booklet, color & upholstery; Oldsmobile, 1941, G $220.00
Booklet, sales; Buick, 1938, 32 pages, VG $48.00
Bowl, soup; white w/dark blue & green Ford logo, rimmed, Shenango China, 6½", EX $48.00
Brochure, Chevrolet Chevelle, 1965, 16 pages $10.00
Brochure, Oldsmobile Sports Cars, 1964, 6 pages $10.00
Display, Proto Tools drill bits; wood & press board, 1950s, 24", VG $140.00
Emblem, body; Buick, 3 die-cast chrome frame shields w/red, white & blue plastic inserts, 1960s-70s, 2¼x3⅜" $40.00
Emblem, body; Chevrolet, chrome script, 1955-56, 12x1", VG $55.00
Emblem, body; Chevrolet, chrome w/red accent, 1949, 14" ... $48.00
Emblem, body; Oldsmobile, oval, 2⅝x1⅝" $20.00
Emblem, hood; Buick, blue & white enameled porcelain, 1910s-20s, 4⅞x3" $28.00
Emblem, hood; Chevrolet, chrome bird, 1950, VG $80.00
Emblem, hood; Chevrolet Monte Carlo, knight's helmet w/red scroll work, mounting attachments, 1977, 3½x2½" $38.00
Emblem, hood; Dodge Ram, chrome, 1953, marked DG 1347253, 11", G $100.00
Emblem, hood; Ford, chrome, 4¾x4¾" $30.00

Emblem, nose; Dodge truck, chrome w/red behind Dodge logo, 1946, G- $61.00
Emblem, radiator; Oldsmobile Boyce Moto Meter, 3½x5½" .. $80.00
Emblem, radiator; Plymouth Dodge, winged girl holding tire, #194572, 1920s-30s $50.00
Fender skirts, Oldsmobile 88, mounting brackets, 1955, G... $200.00
Fire extinguisher, Ford Model A, brass, mounting attachments, 1930s $225.00
Gear shift knob, Lucite picture of child wearing lg brimmed hat in a red robe w/basket, 2¼x3" $18.00
Gum machine, Ford, Ford logo sticker fired on globe, original lock & key, #060221 .... $158.00
Hubcap, Chevrolet, wire wheel w/Chevy bow tie embossed on 3-pronged spinner, mid-1960s, 14" $150.00
Hubcaps, Ford, Thunderbird, chrome, 1957-59, set of 4, VG $100.00
Keychain, Oldsmobile rocket, 1950s, 3" $16.00
Lamp, kerosene; Buick, brass w/blue, red & clear glass, marked Model 805-D, 1900s, VG $100.00
Manual, service; Oldsmobile Super 88 F85, 1962, G........... $45.00
Manual, shop; Chevrolet, 1939, 277 pages, 11x8", G.......... $25.00
Manual, shop; Ford & Mercury, 1965 .... $15.00
Seat belt buckle, Oldsmobile; solid brass, signed LCI, 2x3½". $21.00
Sign, Buick, wood, red & white w/pointing hand, 1920s, 34x8½x1" $315.00
Sign, Genuine Ford Parts, porcelain, dark navy blue & white, 17x24" $536.00

Sign, Pontiac, Authorized Service, porcelain, 41½" diameter, EX, $225.00. (Photo courtesy B.J. Summers and Wayne Priddy)

Speedometer, Chevrolet, 1946, chrome & light tan metal bezel, black face w/white numbers, 5¼", G $14.50
Valve covers, Ford, big block FE, B cam & 3" stands, heavy aluminum $92.00

Autumn Leaf Dinnerware

A familiar dinnerware pattern to just about all of us, Autumn Leaf was designed by Hall China for the Jewel Tea Company who offered it to their customers as premiums. In fact, some people erroneously refer to the pattern as 'Jewel Tea.' First made in 1933, it continued in production until 1978. Pieces with this date in the backstamp are from the overstock that was in the company's warehouse when production was suspended. There are matching tumblers and stemware made by the Libbey Glass Company, and a set of enameled cookware that came out in 1979. You'll find blankets, tablecloths, metal canisters, clocks, playing cards, and many other items designed around the Autumn Leaf pattern. All are collectible.

Since 1984 the Hall company has been making special items for the National Autumn Leaf Collectors Club. These pieces are designated as such by the 'Club' marking that is accompanied by the date of issue. Limited edition items (also by Hall) are being sold by China Specialties, a company in Ohio; but once you become familiar with the old pieces, these are easy to identify, since the molds have been redesigned or were not previously used for Autumn Leaf production.

For further study, we recommend *The Collector's Encyclopedia of Hall China* by Margaret and Kenn Whitmyer. For information on company products, see Jewel Tea.

Club: National Autumn Leaf Collectors

Newsletter: *Autumn Leaf*
Bill Swanson, President NALCC
807 Roaring Springs Dr.
Allen, TX 75002-2112; 972-727-5527
bescome@nalcc.org

Baker, cake; Heatflow clear glass, Mary Dunbar, 1½-qt	**$85.00**
Bean pot, handles, 2½-qt	**$250.00**
Blanket, Autumn Leaf color, Vellux, full size	**$175.00**
Bowl, cereal; 6", from $8 to	**$12.00**
Bowl, fruit; 5½"	**$6.00**
Bowl, refrigerator; metal w/plastic lids, 3 for $250 to	**$325.00**
Bread cover set, plastic, 8-pc, 7 assorted covers in pouch	**$100.00**

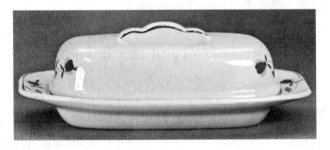

Butter dish, regular, one quarter pound, from $240.00 to $290.00.

Butter dish, sq top, rare, ¼-lb	**$2,000.00**
Cake safe, metal, motif on top or sides, 5", ea from $25 to	**$50.00**
Candleholder, Chamber, club gift, 1991, ea	**$125.00**
Clock, electric	**$550.00**
Coffeepot, Jewel's Best, 30-cup	**$600.00**
Cookie jar, Tootsie, Rayed	**$310.00**
Creamer & sugar bowl, Rayed, 1930s style	**$80.00**
Flatware, silver plated, ea	**$35.00**
Hot pad, metal, oval, 10¾", from $12 to	**$15.00**
Jug, batter; Sundial (bowl), rare	**$5,500.00**

Loaf pan, Mary Dunbar, from $90 to	**$125.00**
Napkin, ecru muslin, sq, 16"	**$50.00**
Pie plate, Heatflow, clear glass, Mary Dunbar, from $45 to	**$60.00**
Place mat, paper, scalloped, set of 8, from $150 to	**$325.00**
Plate, 9"	**$12.00**
Platter, oval, 13½", from $20 to	**$28.00**
Pressure cooker, Mary Dunbar, metal	**$225.00**
Saucer, regular, Ruffled D, from $1 to	**$3.00**
Tablecloth, muslin, 56x81"	**$300.00**
Teapot, Newport, dated 1978, from $200 to	**$250.00**
Tidbit tray, 3-tier	**$100.00**
Tin, fruitcake; white or tan	**$10.00**
Toaster cover, plastic, Mary Dunbar	**$50.00**
Toy, Jewel Truck, orange & white, from $200 to	**$225.00**
Tray, glass, wood handle	**$140.00**
Tumbler, Brockway, 9-oz, 13-oz or 16-oz, ea	**$45.00**
Tumbler, Libbey, gold frost etched, flat or footed, 10-oz, ea.	**$65.00**
Vase, bud; regular decal, 6"	**$350.00**
Vase, Edgewater, club pc, 626 made, 1987	**$550.00**
Warmer, oval, from $150 to	**$225.00**

Cake stand, metal base, from $225.00 to $275.00.

Avon

You'll find Avon bottles everywhere you go! But it's not just the bottles that are collectible — so are items of jewelry, awards, magazine ads, catalogs, and product samples. Of course, the better items are the older ones (they've been called Avon since 1939 — California Perfume Company before that), and if you can find the mint in the box, all the better.

Very popular with today's collectors are the Mrs. Albee figurines. They're remarkably detailed and portray the 'first Avon lady' in elegant period fashions. They're awarded yearly to Avon's most successful representatives.

For more information we recommend *Hastin's Avon Collector's Price Guide* by Bud Hastin.

See also Cape Cod.

Bell, Humming bird, etched pattern on crystal, 5¼", MIB	**$17.50**
Bell, Tapestry Collection, milk glass w/peach trim, dove finial, 5x3"	**$20.00**

Bowl, Hummingbird, etched pattern on crystal, 1980s, 4¼x25½x8¼".....................$35.00

Bottle, racing car, Wild Country After Shave Sure Winner, blue glass, MIB, 7", $35.00. (Photo courtesy Monsen and Baer)

Cake plate, Hummingbird, etched pattern on crystal, pedestal foot, MIB..........................$45.00

Decanter, Rosepoint, bell form, contains Roses Roses cologne, 1977, 4-oz, 8", MIB.............................$8.00

Decanter set, Jeweled Loop, clear decanter w/emerald green stopper, 2 goblets (ea w/green stem & foot), on green tray........$30.00

Doll, Girl Scout, Tender Memories, 1995, 14", MIB, from $25 to........................$30.00

Figurine, Enjoying the Night Before Christmas, porcelain, Christmas Memories, 1983.......................$15.00

Figurine, girl about to blow on dandelion, porcelain, 1982, 5½".$8.00

Figurine, magnolia & bud on stem w/leaves, pastel tones, ceramic, 1986, 3½x6½"........................$20.00

Figurine, Scarlett O'Hara, white ruffled dress, porcelain, 1983, 4½"...........................$36.00

Goblet, wine; Hummingbird, etched pattern on crystal, tall foot, 8¼", 4 for........................$40.00

Mrs Albee figurine, 1978, holding parasol & sample case, from $65 to........................$85.00

Mrs Albee figurine, 1979, standing w/satchel over arm, from $40 to........................$50.00

Mrs Albee figurine, 1980, dressed in yellow & holding bottle, from $$0 to........................$50.00

Mrs Albee figurine, 1982, seated in chair, from $30 to........$40.00

Mrs Albee figurine, 1985, working at desk, from $35 to......$50.00

Mrs Albee figurine, 1986, 100th Anniversary commemorative, from $35 to........................$50.00

Mrs Albee figurine, 1996, standing w/hand to hat, from $40 to..$50.00

Mrs Albee figurine, 2005, stands w/flowers, pedestal at side, from $45 to........................$60.00

Mrs Albee figurine/music box, dressed as bride, plays Somewhere My Love........................$90.00

Pitcher, water; Hummingbird, etched pattern on crystal, 7⅞".$35.00

Planter, A Mother's Love, mother duck w/2 ducklings under wing, white, ceramic, 1984.......................$8.00

Plate, A Mother's Love, gold trim, Mother's Day 2000, 5", MIB.$35.00

Plate, Christmas on the Farm, Wedgwood, 1973, 8¾".........$16.00

Plate, Gene Kelly from Singing in the Rain, 8", w/musical stand, MIB...........................$30.00

Plate, Hummingbird, etched pattern on crystal, 10", MIB ..$20.00

Plate, I Baked It Myself w/Love, red hearts along rim, 1982...$75.00

Plate, Trimming the Tree w/Friends, Christmas 2004, 8¼", MIB $22.50

Platter, George & Martha Washington, dark blue glass, 9¼x6½" .$30.00

Pot Pal, ET (alien), porcelain, hangs from flowerpot, 1982, 2x2¾x1½"..........................$25.00

Salt & pepper shakers, Hummingbird, etched pattern on crystal, metal tops, pr.......................$17.50

Vase, Hummingbird, etched pattern on crystal, 7½x4¼" $25.00

Mrs. Albee figurine, 1990, M, from $45.00 to $55.00.

Barbie Doll and Her Friends

Barbie was first introduced in 1959, and soon Mattel found themselves producing not only dolls but tiny garments, fashion accessories, houses, cars, horses, books, and games as well. Today's Barbie collectors want them all. Though the early Barbie dolls are very hard to find, there are many of her successors still around. The trend today is toward Barbie exclusives — Holiday Barbie dolls and Bob Mackie dolls are all very 'hot' items. So are special-event Barbie dolls.

When buying the older dolls, you'll need to do lots of studying and comparisons to learn to distinguish one Barbie from another, but this is the key to making sound buys and good investments. Remember, though, collectors are sticklers concerning condition; compared to a doll mint in the box (or package), they'll often give an additional 20% if it has never been opened (or as collectors say 'never removed from box,' indicated in our lines by 'NRFB' or 'NRFP')! As a general rule, a mint-in-the-box doll is worth from 50% to 100% more than one mint, no box. The same doll, played with and in only good condition, is worth half as much (or less than that). If you want a good source for study, refer to one of these fine books: *Barbie Doll Fashion, Vol. I, Vol. II,* and *Vol. III,* by Sarah Sink Eames; *Collector's Encyclopedia of Barbie Doll Exclusives, Collector's Encyclopedia of Barbie Doll Collector's Editions,* and *Barbie Doll Around the Woeld* by J. Michael Augustyniak; *The Barbie Doll Years, 6th Edition,* by Patrick C. and Joyce L. Olds; *Barbie, The First 30 Years, 1959 Through 1989,* by Stefanie Deutsch; and *Schroeder's Collectible Toys, Antique to Modern.* (All are published by Collector Books.)

Dolls

Allan, 1965, bendable legs, MIB $300.00
Barbie, #4, 1960, blond or burnette hair, original swimsuit, M, ea
    from $450 to $400.00
Barbie, #6, brunette hair, MIB, from $525 to $600.00
Barbie, American Airline Stewardess, 1963, NRFB $700.00
Barbie, American Girl, 1964, red hair, replica swimsuit, NM . $600.00
Barbie, Bay Watch (Black or white), 1995, NRFB $20.00
Barbie, Calvin Klein, 1996, Bloomingdale's, NRFB............$40.00
Barbie, Color-Magic, 1966, blond or brunette hair, original swim-
    suit, hair band & belt, NM, ea $750.00

Barbie, Color Magic, 1966, red hair, MIB, from $1,200.00 to $1,400.00. (Photo courtesy McMasters Doll Auction)

Barbie, Enchanted Evening, 1993, Sears, NRFB.................$75.00
Barbie, Fabulus Fur, 1986, NRFB.......................................$65.00
Barbie, French Lady, 1997, Great Eras Collection, NRFB ...$50.00
Barbie, Holiday, 1988, NRFB..$500.00
Barbie, Miss America, 1972, Kellogg Co, NRFB $175.00
Barbie, Queen of Hearts, 1994, Bob Mackie, NRFB $250.00
Barbie, Teen Speeder, 1973, NRFB.....................................$30.00
Brad, 1970, darker skin, bendable legs, NRFB..................$225.00
Chris, 1967, any hair color, MIB $200.00
Christie, Fashion Photo, 1978, MIB $95.00
Christie, Golden Dream, 1980, MIB $50.00
Francie, Malibu, 1971, NRFB...$75.00
Francie, Twist 'n Turn, 1966, brunette hair, original swimsuit,
    EX $150.00
Ginger, Growing Up, 1977, MIB..$100.00
Kelly, Quick Curl, 1972, NRFB $175.00
Ken, Army, 1993, Stars 'n Stripes, NRFB $35.00
Ken, Dream Date, 1983, NRFB $30.00

Ken, Hawaiian, 1979, MIB..$45.00
Ken, Jewel Secrets, 1987, NRFB $40.00
Ken, King Arthur, 1964, NRFB..$500.00
Ken, Party Time, 1977, NRFB $35.00

Ken, Roller Skating, 1981, MIB, $50.00. (Photo courtesy Beth Summers)

Ken, Sun Lovin' Malibu, 1979, NRFB................................$35.00
Ken, Tin Man, 1995, Hollywood Legends Series, NRFB $60.00
Ken, 1961, flocked hair, straight legs, MIB, ea..................$125.00
Midge, Japanese, brunette hair, straight legs, original swimsuit, rare,
    NM...$1,250.00
Midge, 1963, blond or red hair, bendable legs, MIB, ea..........$500.00
Midge, 30th Anniversary, 1992, porcelain, MIB $175.00
Nikki, Animal Lovin', 1989, NRFB....................................$30.00
PJ, Deluxe Quick Curl, 1976, MIB $65.00
PJ, Fashion Photo, 1978, MIB..$95.00
PJ, Talking, 1970, original outfit & beads, M, from $175 to... $250.00
Ricky, 1965, original outfit & shoes, NM...........................$75.00
Skipper, Deluxe Quick Curl, 1975, NRFB $125.00
Skipper, Dream Date, 1990, NRFB $25.00
Skipper, Music Lovin', 1985, NRFB....................................$75.00
Skipper, Super Teen, 1980, NRFB.......................................$35.00
Skooter, 1965, blond hair, bendable legs, MIB $225.00
Teresa, California Dream, 1988, MIB $30.00
Tutti, 1974, blond hair, original outfit, EX $60.00
Whitney, Style Magic, 1989, NRFB.....................................$35.00

Accessories

Case, Barbie, 1963, pink vinyl, Bubble-Cut Barbie wearing Solo in
    the Spotlight, rare, NM, from $75 to $85.00
Case, Midge, 1963, blue vinyl, Midge wearing Movie Date, rare,
    NM, from $100 to...$125.00
Furniture, Barbie & Skipper Deluxe Dream House, Sears Exclusive,
    1965, MIB, minimum value $175.00
Furniture, Barbie Dream Glow Vanity, 1986, MIB $20.00
Furniture, Barbie Fashion Wraps Boutique, 1989, MIB.......$35.00
Furniture, Barbie Glamour Home, 1985, MIB $125.00

Furniture, Barby & the Rockers Dance Cafe, 1987, MIB $50.00
Furniture, Go-Together Chair, Ottoman & End Table, MIB . $100.00
Furniture, Ice Capades Skating Rink, 1989, MIB $70.00
Furniture, Living Pretty Cooking Center, 1988, MIB $25.00
Furniture, Pink Sparkles Armoire, 1990, NRFB $25.00
Furniture, Workout Center, 1985, MIB............................$30.00
Gift set, Army Barbie & Ken, 1993, Stars 'n Stripes, MIB...$60.00
Gift Set, Ballerina Barbie on Tour, 1976, MIB.................$175.00
Gift Set, Barbie Beautiful Blues, Sears Exclusive, 1967, MIB $3,000.00
Gift set, Barbie Loves Elvis, 1996, NRFB $75.00
Gift set, Hollywood Hair Barbie, #10928, 1993, MIB $35.00
Gift set, Loving You Barbie, 1984, MIB.........................$75.00
Gift set, Stacey & Butterfly Pony, 1993, NRFB.................$30.00
Gift set, Talking Barbie Golden Groove Set, Sears Exclusive, 1969, MIB $1,500.00
Outfit, Barbie, After Five, #934, 1962, NRFP $450.00
Outfit, Barbie, Busy Morning, #981, 1960, NRFP............$415.00
Outfit, Barbie, City Fun, #5717, 1983, NRFP $10.00
Outfit, Barbie, Evening Outfit, #2221, 1978, NRFP...........$30.00
Outfit, Barbie, Glamour Group, #1510, 1970, NRFP.......$350.00
Outfit, Barbie, Knit Separates, #1602, 1964, NRFP $140.00
Outfit, Barbie, Make Mine Midi, #1861, 1969, NRFP $300.00
Outfit, Francie, Clam Diggers, #1258, 1966, NRFP $185.00
Outfit, Francie, Merry-Go-Rounders, #1230, NRFB........$375.00
Outfit, Francie, Wedding Whirl, #1244, 1970-71 & 1974, complete, M $275.00
Outfit, Francie & Casey, Culotte-Wot?, #1214, 1968-69, MIB . $300.00
Outfit, Ken, Baseball, #9168, 1976, NRFP......................$70.00
Outfit, Ken, Date w/Barbie, #5824, 1983, NRFP $10.00
Outfit, Ken, Groom, #9596, 1976, NRFP........................$15.00
Outfit, Ken, Mr Astronaut, #1415, 1965, NRFP $725.00
Outfit, Ken, Yachtsman, #789, complete, NM $225.00
Outfit, Ken & Brad, Way Out West, #1720, 1962, NRFP..$75.00
Outfit, Skipper, All Over Felt, #3476, NRFP $150.00
Outfit, Skipper, Budding Beauty, #1731, 1970, NRFP........$70.00
Outfit, Skipper, Hearts 'n Flowers, #1945, 1967, NRFB...$300.00

Outfit, Tutti, Birthday Beauties, #3617, 1968 – 1969, NRFB, $125.00. (Photo courtesy Sarah Sink Eames)

Vehicle, Allan's Roadster, 1964, aqua, MIB $500.00
Vehicle, Barbie & Ken Dune Buggy, Irwin, pink, 1970, MIB . $250.00
Vehicle, Barbie Travelin' Trailer, MIB $40.00
Vehicle, California Dream Beach Taxi, 1988, MIB $35.00
Vehicle, Ken's Classy Corvette, 1976, yellow, MIB............$75.00
Vehicle, Sunsailer, 1975, NRFB $55.00
Vehicle, Western Star Traveler Motorhome, 1982, MIB.......$50.00
Vehicle, Ken's Hot Rod, Sears Exclusive, red, 1964, MIB ..$900.00
Vehicle, 1957 Belair Chevy, 1990, 2nd edition, pink, MIB.$125.00

Vehicle, Skipper, Beach Buggy, 1964, rare, MIB, $500.00.

Miscellaneous

Ballerina Dress-Ups, Coloforms, 1977, complete, EXIB $15.00
Barbie Beauty Kit, 1961, complete, M.............................$125.00
Barbie Nurse Kit, 1962, MIB..$300.00
Booklet, World of Barbie Fashion, 1968, M $10.00
Christie Quick Curl Beauty Center, Sears Exclusive, 1982, MIB $35.00
Diary, black vinyl w/metal clasp & key, image of Barbie in long gown & fur stole, EX $100.00

Jigsaw puzzle, Crystal Barbie and Ken, Western Publishing #4609-43, 1987, NRFB, $8.00. (Photo courtesy Beth Summers)

Ornament, Holiday Barbie, Hallmark, 1993, 1st edition, MIB..$75.00
Paper Dolls, Barbie Country Camper, Whitman, #1990, 1973, uncut, M...$30.00

Umbrella, Barbie, 1962, several variations, EX, ea **$65.00**
Wristwatch, Barbie & Ken, Bradley, 1963, MIB **$200.00**

Barware

During the 1990s, the cocktail shaker emerged as a hot new collectible. These micro skyscrapers are now being saved for the enjoyment of future generations, much like the 1930s buildings saved from destruction by landmarks preservation committees of today.

Cocktail shakers — the words just conjure up visions of glamour and elegance. Seven hard shakes over your right shoulder and you can travel back in time, back to the glamor of Hollywood movie sets with Fred Astaire and Ginger Rogers and luxurious hotel lounges with gleaming chrome; back to the world of F. Scott Fitzgerald and *The Great Gatsby*; or watch *The Thin Man* movie showing William Powell instruct a bartender on the proper way to shake a martini — the reveries are endless.

An original American art form, cocktail shakers reflect the changing nature of various styles of art, design, and architecture of the era between WWI and WWII. We see the graceful lines of Art Nouveau in the early '20s being replaced by the rage for jagged geometric modern design. The geometric cubism of Picasso that influenced so many designers of the '20s was replaced with the craze for streamline design of '30s. Cocktail shakers of the early '30s were taking the shape of the new deity of American architecture, the skyscraper, thus giving the appearance of movement and speed in a slow economy.

Cocktail shakers served to penetrate the gloom of depression, ready to propel us into the future of prosperity like some Buck Rogers rocket ship — both perfect symbols of generative power, of our perpetration into better times ahead.

Cocktail shakers and architecture took on the aerodynamically sleek industrial design of the automobile and airship. It was as Norman Bel Geddes said: 'a quest for speed.' All sharp edges and corners were rounded off. This trend was the theme of the day, as even the sharp notes of jazz turned into swing.

Cocktail shakers have all the classic qualifications of a premium collectible. They are easily found at auctions, antique and second-hand shops, flea markets, and sales. They can be had in all price ranges. They require little study to identify one manufacturer or period from another, and lastly they are not easily reproduced.

The sleek streamline cocktail shakers of modern design are valued by collectors of today. Those made by Revere, Chase, and Manning-Bowman have taken the lead in this race. Also commanding high prices are those shakers of unusual design such as penguins, zeppelins, dumbbells, bowling pins, town crier bells, airplanes, even ladies' legs. They're all out there, waiting to be found, waiting to be recalled to life, to hear the clank of ice cubes, and to again become the symbol of elegance.

For more information we recommend *Vintage Bar Ware, An Identification and Value Guide*, by Stephen Visakay.

Advisor: Stephen Visakay (See Directory, Barware)

Bar tools, gold-plated w/black Bakelite handles, double jigger, cherry spoon & zester/strainer, 1950s, set................................**$20.00**

Coasters, tin, petunias, morning glories & tulips on white, set of 12, ca 1950s, 3⅛" **$18.00**

Cocktail set, Holiday, #90064, shaker, four cocktails and tray, Chase Brass & Copper Co., designed by Howard Reichenbach and Harry Layton, from $100.00 to $125.00. (Photo courtesy Stephen Visakay)

Cocktail set, stainless steel, pitcher, zester/strainer & clear blown glass stirrer, Harold Leonard Co, Norway, 1950s.........**$26.00**

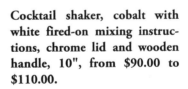

Cocktail shaker, cobalt with white fired-on mixing instructions, chrome lid and wooden handle, 10", from $90.00 to $110.00.

Decanter, brass w/cut-out anchors & wheels, glass insert, James Bliss, 5¼x7" **$55.00**
Decanter, frosted art glass w/polished pontil, signed Robert Mc Laudler, ca 1940s-50s, 17x5½" **$175.00**
Decanter label, silver-plated w/shell & leaf border, marked Sherry, Made in England, 2½x1½" **$13.00**

Ice bucket, walnut, Vermillion Inc, 8¼x7¼" **$22.00**
Ice crusher, chrome w/turquoise enamel, hand crank, wall mount Swing-A-Way Model #1809, 1960s, 8" **$30.00**
Jigger/pourer, silver-plated Art Nouveau, double-sided, scalloped shell design handle, 1920s-30s, 5¾x5" **$24.00**
Shaker, drink recipes printed on clear glass, 7" **$18.00**
Shaker, fired-on White Polar bear & blue icicle pattern, aluminum cap, Hazel-Atlas, 1950s, 9¾x4" **$54.00**
Shaker, silver-plated w/copper screw cap, pouring spout w/strainer, marked Currier & Roby, ca 1911, 5½" **$87.00**
Shaker set, Art Deco chrome shaker w/red Bakelite handle, 4 5x3" goblets & 17½x10½" tray **$65.00**
Shot set, 6 glasses w/black polka-dot design on metal tray, 1950s **$88.00**
Shot set, 8 glasses in metal frame, cowgirl w/cowboy on reverse, 1950s, glasses: 6⅜x2½", tray: 16x8x3½" **$70.00**
Stein, beer; courting scene on 1 side, mountain scene on reverse, paper label CMC Japan on bottom, sm, 2⅞x2⅞" **$22.00**
Swizzle sticks, bowling pins & ball, plastic & glass, ca 1940s-50s, 6" **$75.00**
Tallstirs, blue, gold, green, pink, purple, & red aluminum, leaf-design, Ray J Walthes Co, 1950s, 7⅞", set of 8 .... **$35.00**
Tray, red metal w/Gay Nineties graphic & 7 bar recipes, Hazel Atlas, 1950s, 13" dia **$25.00**
Tumbler, rocks; owl design in black & 22k gold, Courock of Monterey, 12-oz, 3½x3¼", set of 4 .... **$28.00**
Tumblers, highball; Art Deco gold bands on clear glass, 1940s, set of 6 .... **$84.00**

Bauer Pottery

The Bauer Pottery Company is one of the best known of the California pottery companies and is noted for both its artware and its dinnerware. Over the past ten years, Bauer pottery has become particularly collectible, and prices have risen accordingly. Bauer actually began operations in Kentucky in 1885, but in 1910 they moved to Los Angeles where they continued in business until they closed in 1962. The company produced several popular dinnerware lines, including La Linda, Monterey, and Brusche Al Fresco. Most popular (and most significant) was the Ringware line begun in 1932, which preceded Fiesta as a popular solid-color, everyday dinnerware. The earliest pieces are unmarked, although to collectors they are unmistakable, due in part to their distinctive glazes, which have an almost primitive charm due to their drips, glaze misses, and color variations.

Another dinnerware line popular with collectors is Speckleware, a term that refers to a 1950s-era speckled glaze used on several different kinds of pottery other than dinnerware, including vases, flowerpots, and kitchenware. Though not as popular as Ringware, it holds its value well and is usually available at much lower prices than Ring. Keep an eye out for other flowerpots and mixing bowls, as they are common garage-sale items.

Artware by Bauer is not so easy to find any more, but it is worth seeking out because of its high values. So-called oil jars sell for upwards of $1,500.00, and Rebekah vases routinely fetch $400.00 or more. Matt Carlton is one of the most desirable designers of handmade ware.

Colors are particularly important in pricing Bauer pottery, especially Ringware. Burgundy, cobalt blue, delph blue, and ivory are generally higher than other colors. (If no specific color is indicated in the descriptions, our values are mid range.) Black and white glazes on Ringware items are worth as much as twice the prices listed here. Common colors in dinnerware are orange-red, jade green, and Chinese yellow.

Caution: A new Bauer line has been produced, using original items as models, with an emphasis on pieces from the 1930s and 1940s.

For more information we recommend *Collector's Encyclopedia of California Pottery* and *California Pottery Scrapbook* by Jack Chipman.

Art Pottery, #2000 Hi-Fire, and Matt Carlton

Flower bowl, turquoise, deep, Hi-Fire, #211, 6" **$45.00**
Jar, Carnation, green, #1, 14", minimum value............... **$1,800.00**
Jardiniere, green matt, embossed filigree, 10", minimum value.. **$750.00**

Pumpkin bowl by Tracy Irwin, matt black, 6½x10", minimum value, $150.00. (Photo courtesy Jack Chipman)

Rose bowl, Monterey Blue, Hi-Fire, 4" **$5.00**
Vase, Chinese Yellow, signature style, M Carlton, 12", minimum value **$1,500.00**
Vase, garden; Fred Johnson, Hi-Fire, 18", minimum value... **$750.00**

Brusche

Al Fresco, bowl, fruit; burgundy, 5" **$10.00**
Al Fresco, creamer, jumbo; olive green **$18.00**
Al Fresco, cup, burgundy **$10.00**
Al Fresco, French casserole, Dubonnet, 2-qt **$100.00**
Al Fresco, pitcher, gray, 2-pt.. **$40.00**
Al Fresco, plate, dinner; gray, 10" **$12.00**
Al Fresco, platter, speckled pink, rectangular, 12⅝" **$22.50**
Contempo, bowl, deep soup/cereal; Pumpkin, 5¼" **$15.00**
Contempo, cup & saucer, Spicy Green **$12.00**
Contempo, mug, Pumpkin, short, 8-oz **$15.00**

Cal-Art and Garden Pottery

Flowerpot, Swirl, gray gloss, drilled, 6" **$25.00**
Flowerpot, Swirl, olive green, 6" **$55.00**
Flowerpot, Swirl, white matt, 3" **$25.00**

Flowerpot, Swirl, yellow, 4"......................................$25.00
Jardiniere, Swirl #6, glossy, 6", from $50 to $60.00
Jardiniere, Swirl #12, speckled pink, 12"................$125.00
Oil jar, speckled blue, 16", minimum value $500.00
Sand jar, speckled white, 20"....................................$250.00
Spanish pot, #4, speckled colors, 4", from $18 to $25.00
Spanish pot, turquoise, 8"..$80.00
Swan, black gloss, Ray Murray, 3x9", minimum value $200.00
Vase, burgundy, Robot midget, 4" $35.00

Vase, 'flat'; blue with overdrip, 4½", minimum value $50.00.
(Photo courtesy Jack Chipman)

Gloss Pastel Kitchenware (aka GPK)

Bowl, mixing; #18, light brown $30.00
Bowl, mixing; #24, all colors, from $30 to............$40.00
Bowl, vegetable; oval, 10" $45.00
Cookie jar (aka Beehive), all colors, from $95 to $150.00
Pitcher, all colors, 1½-pt $25.00

Monterey

Bowl, batter..$90.00
Bowl, fruit; footed, 12", from $150 to $225.00
Custard baking set, 6 cups in metal frame..............$275.00
Ramekin..$30.00
Refrigerator beverage dispenser, w/lid.....................$300.00

Monterey Moderne and Related Kitchenware

Bowl, salad; low, 8½" $35.00
Casserole, speckled beige, w/lid, 1½-qt $30.00
Coffee server, chartreuse & brown, open.................$48.00
Cookie jar, olive green, 8"...$85.00
Pitcher, speckled yellow, 5½"....................................$22.00
Plate, dinner; 10½" $20.00
Platter, chartreuse, rectangular, 12" $25.00
3-Tier serving piece $45.00

Plainware

Bowl, mixing; #3, colors other than yellow, 2-gal, minimum value $350.00
Coffee server, w/lid, from $75 to $100.00
Creamer, yellow, individual, handmade by Matt Carlton $95.00

Mug, handmade, 4", from $100 to $150.00
Pitcher, Dutch; orange-red, Carlton, 12", from $300 to $350.00
Pudding dish, #6, 10¼", from $80 to.....................$120.00

Ringware (Ring)

Bowl, mixing; #24, cobalt, double ring....................$90.00
Bowl, salad; light blue, low, 9".................................$60.00
Carafe, orange-red w/copper raffia-wrapped handle $120.00
Cigarette jar, minimum value...................................$750.00
Cookie jar, Delph Blue, no lid.................................$110.00
Cookie jar, Delph Blue, w/lid..................................$350.00
Cup, punch; Chinese Yellow $60.00
Cup & saucer, cobalt..$50.00
Plate, dessert; Chinese Yellow, 6½"..........................$15.00
Plate, dinner; orange-red, 9½".................................$30.00
Plate, salad; cobalt, 7½"...$30.00

Spice jar, cobalt, from $100.00 to $150.00. (Photo courtesy Jack Chipman)

Sugar bowl, from $75 to $100.00
Tumbler, cobalt, no handle, 12-oz...........................$50.00
Tumbler set, Chinese Yellow, w/handles, set of 6, 12-oz, minimum value $180.00

Speckled Kitchenware

Candleholder, votive, brown, ea $15.00
Casserole, pink, frame, 1½-qt...................................$40.00
Pitcher, pelican, yellow, 20-oz $35.00
Pitcher, pelican, blue, 20-oz.....................................$45.00
Pitcher, yellow, Brusche style, 1-pt..........................$35.00

Miscellaneous

Baker, tuna; burgundy, Chicken of the Sea, w/original stand..$45.00
Candlestick/bud vase, early stoneware, 8"................$300.00
Cookie jar, fish; speckled green, Cemar turned Bauer $75.00
Jar, oil; Jade Green, 16", minimum value.................$850.00

Beanie Babies

Ty Beanie Babies were first introduced in 1994. By 1996, they had become widely collected. Crazed collectors swarmed stores for the newest releases, and prices soared for many Beanie Babies through the year 2000, when the hype subsided. However, Beanie Babies continue to be favorites among collectors, and Ty regularly issues new animals. You will still find value in the rare and exclusive Beanies, as well as some of the regular retired issues.

Values given are for Beanie Babies with mint or near-mint condition swing or tush tags. Many counterfeits exist on the market, and it is important to be familiar with swing and tush tags. Removing tags from the more current Beanie Babies or having ripped, creased, or damaged tags decreases the value of the animal. However, most of the rarer 1994, 1995, and 1996 issues are still quite valuable without a swing tag, due to their scarcity. For more information on these tags, see *Ty Beanies & More*, a collector magazine published every other month which contains photos and details on all Beanie Baby tags.

This is just a sampling of the Beanie Babies on the market. Unless otherwise indicated, all Beanie Babies listed are retired and no longer being procuced by Ty, Inc. All current and more common retired Beanie Babies are valued at $7.00 to $10.00, and you will not see them listed here. There are also foreign Beanie Babies produced exclusively in Canada and in Europe that are not listed here; these range in value from $10.00 to $100.00. You'll need to have your Beanie Baby professionally authenticated if you are unsure whether it is one of the rarer, more valuable Beanie Babies listed below. All listings here are for retired Beanie Babies, unless otherwise noted.

Advisor: Amy Sullivan (See Directory, Beanie Babies)

Key:
— style number

Cubbie the Bear, #4010, brown, from $10.00 to $15.00. (Photo courtesy Amy Sullivan)

Ally the Alligator, #4032 .... $20.00
Baldy the Eagle, #4074, from $5 to $10.00
Beak the Wiwi, #4211 .... $10.00
Bessie the Cow, #4009, brown $15.00
Blackie the Bear, #4011 .... $10.00
Blizzard the Tiger, #4163 .... $10.00
Bones the Dog, #4001, brown $10.00
Bongo the Monkey, #4067, 2nd issue, tan tail, from $10 to ... $15.00
Bronty the Brontosaurus, #4085, blue, minimum value $100.00
Brownie the Bear, #4010, w/swing tag, minimum value $200.00
Bubbles the Fish, #4078, yellow & black $10.00
Bumble the Bee, #4045, minimum value $50.00
Caw the Crow, #4071, minimum value $50.00
Chilly the Polar Bear, #4012, minimum value $200.00

Chops the Lamb, #4019 .... $20.00
Coral the Fish, #4079, tie-dyed $10.00
Curly the Bear, #4052, brown, from $5 to $10.00
Daisy the Cow, #4006, black & white $15.00
Derby the Horse, #4008, 2nd issue, coarse mane & tail $10.00
Digger the Crab, #4027, 1st issue, orange, minimum value . $50.00
Digger the Crab, #4027, 2nd issue, red, minimum value $10.00
Doodle the Rooster, #4171, tie-tyed $10.00
Flash the Dolphin, #4021, minimum value $15.00
Flashy the Peacock, #4339 .... $10.00
Flip the Cat, #4012, white $10.00
Floppity the Bunny, lavender, from $7 to $9.00
Flutter the Butterfly, #4043, minimum value $50.00
Garcia the Bear, #4051, tie-died, minimum value $20.00
Glory the Bear, #4188, from $8 to $10.00
Goldie the Goldfish, #4023 .... $10.00
Grunt the Razorback Pig, #4092, red, minimum value $20.00
Happy the Hippo, #4061, gray, minimum value $50.00
Happy the Hippo, #4061, 2nd issue, mint green, from $7 to .. $9.00

Hippity the Bunny, #4119, mint green, from $7.00 to $9.00. (Photo courtesy Amy Sullivan)

Holiday Teddy (1997), #4200, from $8 to $10.00
Holiday Teddy (1998), #4204 .... $10.00
Holiday Teddy (1999), #4257 .... $10.00
Holiday Teddy (2000), #4332 .... $10.00
Holiday Teddy (2001), #4395 .... $10.00
Holiday Teddy (2002), #4564 .... $10.00
Hoppity the Bunny, #4117, pink, from $7 to $9.00
Humphrey the Camel, #4060, minimum value $100.00
Inch the Worm, #4044, felt antennae $20.00
Inch the Worm, #4044, yarn antennae, from $7 to $10.00
Inky the Octopus, #4028, 3rd issue, pink, from $6 to $15.00
Kiwi the Toucan, #4070, minimum value $30.00
Lefty the Donkey, #4087, gray $20.00
Legs the Frog, #4020 .... $10.00
Libearty the Bear, #4057, minimum value $50.00
Lizzy the Lizzard, #4033, tie-dyed, minimum value $50.00
Lizzy the Lizzard, #4033, 2nd issue, blue, from $10 to ... $20.00
Lucky the Ladybug, #4040, 3rd issue, 11 spots, from $10 to . $15.00
Magic the Dragon, #4088, from $10 to $20.00
Manny the Manatee, #4081, minimum value $20.00
Millennium the Bear, #4226, from $10 to $12.00
Nectar the Hummingbird, #4361, from $10 to $20.00
Nuts the Squirrel, #4114 .... $10.00

Patti the Platypus, #4025, 2nd issue, purple, from $10 to ... **$20.00**
Peanut the Elephant, #4062, light blue, from $7 to **$15.00**
Peking the Panda Bear, #4013, minimum value **$100.00**
Pinchers the Lobster, #4026 .... **$15.00**
Quackers the Duck, #4024, 1st issue, no wings **$450.00**
Quackers the Duck, #4024, 2nd issue, w/wings, from $10 to .. **$20.00**
Radar the Bat, #4019, black, minimum value **$30.00**
Rex the Tyrannosaurus, #4086, minimum value **$100.00**
Righty the Elephant, #4085, gray **$20.00**
Ringo the Raccoon, #4014, from $10 to.............................. **$15.00**
Rover the Dog, #4101, red, from $10 to.............................. **$15.00**
Sammy the Bear, #4215, tie-tyed **$10.00**
Seamore the Seal, #4029, white, minimum value................ **$20.00**
Slither the Snake, #4031, minimum value **$200.00**
Snowball the Snowman, #4201, from $10 to **$12.00**
Snowgirl the Snowgirl, #4333, from $10 to **$12.00**
Spangle the Bear, #4245, blue face, from $10 to **$20.00**
Sparky the Dalmatian, #4100, minimum value................... **$15.00**
Splash the Whale, #4022, minimum value **$15.00**
Spooky the Ghost, #4090, orange ribbon, minimum value.. **$10.00**
Spot the Dog, #4000, w/spot **$30.00**
Squealer the Pig, #4005 .... **$10.00**
Sting the Stingray, #4077, tie-dyed, minimum value........... **$20.00**
Tabasco the Bull, #4002, red feet, minimum value **$20.00**
Tank the Armadillo, #4031, no shell, 7 lines on back, minimum
   value **$40.00**
Teddy Bear, #4050, brown, new face, from $15 to............... **$30.00**
The Beginning Bear, #4267, w/silver stars.......................... **$10.00**
The End Bear, #4265, black.. **$10.00**
Trap the Mouse, #4042, minimum value **$100.00**
Tusk the Walrus, #4076, minimum value **$20.00**
Valentino the Bear, #4058, white w/red heart **$10.00**
Velvet the Panther, #4064, minimum value **$10.00**
Web the Spider, #4141, black, minimum value.................. **$100.00**

Hoot the Owl, #4073, $10.00. (Photo courtesy Amy Sullivan)

Beatles Collectibles

Possibly triggered by John Lennon's death in 1980, Beatles fans (recognizing that their dreams of the band ever reuniting were gone along with him) began to collect vintage memorabilia of all types. Recently some of the original Beatles material has sold at auction with high-dollar results. Handwritten song lyrics, Lennon's auto-

graphed high school textbook, and even the legal agreement that was drafted at the time the group disbanded are among the one-of-a-kind multi-thousand dollar sales recorded.

Unless you plan on attending sales of this caliber, you'll be more apt to find the commercially produced memorabilia that literally flooded the market during the '60s and beyond when the Fab Four from Liverpool made their unprecedented impact on the entertainment world. A word about their 45 rpm records: they sold in such mass quantities that unless the record is a 'promotional' (made to send to radio stations or for jukebox distribution), they have very little value. Once a record has lost much of its original gloss due to wear and handling, becomes scratched, or has writing on the label, its value is minimal. Even in near-mint condition, $4.00 to $6.00 is plenty to pay for a 45 rpm (much less if it's worn), unless the original picture sleeve is present. (An exception is the white-labeled Swan recording of 'She Loves You/I'll Get You'.) A Beatles' picture sleeve is usually valued at $30.00 to $40.00, except for the rare 'Can't Buy Me Love,' which is worth ten times that amount. (Beware of reproductions!) Albums of any top recording star or group from the '50s and '60s are becoming very collectible, and the Beatles' are among the most popular. Just be very critical of condition! An album must be in at least excellent condition to bring a decent price. Unless another code is given in the descriptions that follow, values are for items in near mint to mint condition.

See also Celebrity Dolls; Magazines; Movie Posters; Records; Sheet Music.

Advisor: Bojo/Bob Gottuso (See Directory, Character and Personality Collectibles)

Newsletter: *Beatlefan*
P.O. Box 33515
Decatur, GA 30033
Send SASE for information

Air mattress, UK by Lilo, inflatable vinyl, 1964................. **$900.00**
Badge, I've Got My Beatles Movie Ticket Have You? w/center portrait, cardboard w/string, 1964, 3¾" dia, EX+ **$40.00**
Coin, silver w/ad, UK, 1966.. **$250.00**
Colorforms Cartoon Kit, 1966, complete, MIB............. **$1,000.00**

Comb, Lido, various colors with sticker attached to front, has been reproduced, 14" long, from $200.00 to $300.00. (Photo courtesy Barbara Crawford, Hollis Lamon, and Michael Stern)

Concert book, 1964, USA, 12x12" **$40.00**
Decals, black & orange on yellow, unused, set of 11 .... **$90.00**
Drum, black outline of Ringo's head, hand & signature, w/stand, New Beat, 14" dia, EX.. **$750.00**
Figures, cartoon series, painted resin, 1985, set of 4, 6" **$150.00**
Figures, Swingers Music Set, 4" versions of the 8" mascot nodders, set of 4, MOC (sealed), from $125 to **$150.00**

Game board, Flip Your Wig, Milton Bradley, complete, 1960s,
EX+ **$175.00**
Guitar, Four Pop, head images of group & name...............**$575.00**
Key chain, Love Songs promo, record shape w/logo, EX......**$15.00**
Magazine, Life, Paul & Linda on cover, 1971 ....**$20.00**
Magazine, The Original Beatles Book, 1964 ....**$30.00**
Money clip, apple cutout, Apple Records.........................**$275.00**
Nesting dolls, hand-painted wood w/Sgt Pepper costumes, EX ..**$50.00**
Pennant, I Love the Beatles, felt, 29", EX.........................**$175.00**
Pin-back button, I'm a Beatles Fan, 4 head shots w/center ban-
ner, black & white on red, Nems Ent Ltd/Green Duck, 4",
EX+.. **$35.00**
Poster, Ringo for President, 1964 ....**$200.00**
Purse, black vinyl clutch-type w/white printed photo & names,
original leather strap, rare, EX....................................**$375.00**
Scrapbook, The Beatles Scrap Book, 4 head images, Whitman/
Nems, 1964, unused, 13½x11", EX..........................**$75.00**
Socks, ironed-on emblems on white, w/black & white cardboard
package insert, 1964, rare, pr **$600.00**
Spatter toy, 16", rare, MIP **$250.00**
Squirt gun, 1960s, yellow plastic submarine, 6", EX...........**$40.00**
Thimble, Fenton, baked-on image, 1990s, EX...................**$15.00**
Wallet, red vinyl w/black & white group portrait & signatures,
Standard Plastic, 1964, EX+ **$90.00**
Watercolor set, Yellow Submarine, 4 6x8" pictures to paint,
Craftmaster, MIB...**$150.00**

Comic book, Dell Giant, from $75.00 to $125.00;
Magazine, 1964, from $20.00 to $25.00. (Photo courtesy
Barbara Crawford, Hollis Lamon, and Michael Stern)

Beatrix Potter Figures

Since 1902 when *The Tale of Peter Rabbit* was published by
Fredrick Warne & Company, generations have enjoyed the adven-
tures of Beatrix Potter's characters. Beswick issued 10 characters in
1947 that included Peter Rabbit, Benjamin Bunny, Squirrel Nutkin,
Jemima Puddleduck, Timmy Tiptoes, Tom Kitten, Mrs. Tittlemouse,
Mrs. Tiggywinkle, Little Pig Robinson, and Samuel Whiskers. The
line grew until it included figures from other stories. Duchess
(P1355) was issued in 1955 with two feet that were easily broken.
Later issues featured the Duchess on a base and holding a pie. This
was the first figure to be discontinued in 1967. Color variations on

pieces indicate issue dates as do the different backstamps that were
used. Backstamps have changed several times since the first figures
were issued. There are three basic styles: Beswick brown, Beswick
gold, and Royal Albert — with many variations on each of these.
Unless stated otherwise, figures listed here are Beswick brown.

**Tom Kitten With Butterfly,
BP-3c, 1981, from $225.00
to $265.00.**

Amiable Guinea Pig, B3...**$300.00**
Anna Maria, B3a...**$450.00**
Apple Dappley-Bottle Out..**$250.00**
Aunt Petitoes, B3 ....**$125.00**
Babbity Bumble, B6...**$250.00**
Benjamin Ate Lettuce Leaf, B6a..**$50.00**
Benjamin Bunny, BP2...**$150.00**
Benjamin Bunny, ears out, B3..**$195.00**
Cecily Parsley, B3 ....**$95.00**
Cicely Parsley, head down, bright blue dress (1st version), BP3B,
4" **$75.00**
Foxy Whiskered Gentleman, F Warne & Co Ltd Beswick England,
4½" **$90.00**
Gentleman Mouse Made a Bow, B6a **$200.00**
Goody & Timmy Tiptoes, C3..**$275.00**
Hunca Munca, BP2 ....**$68.00**
Hunca Munca Sweeping, B3..**$75.00**
Jemima & Foxy Gentleman, B6..**$95.00**
Jemima Puddleduck, BP2, from $75 to.................................**$85.00**
Jeremy Fisher, BP6, copyright 1989, MIB.............................**$60.00**
Lady Mouse Made Curtsy, B6...**$85.00**
Little Black Rabbit, F Warne & Co 1977 Beswick England, 4".**$110.00**
Little Pig Robinson Spying, B6..**$150.00**
Miss Moppet, 3B..**$55.00**
Mr Jackson, B6..**$65.00**
Mrs Flopsy Bunny, BP-2..**$95.00**
Mrs Rabbit, BP-2...**$250.00**
Mrs Rabbit & Peter, B6...**$80.00**
Mrs Rabbit Cooking, B6...**$65.00**
Mrs Tiggy Winkle, B3...**$55.00**
Mrs Tittlemouse, 3B **$45.00**
Old Mr Brown, B3 ....**$60.00**
Peter & the Red Handkerchief, B6 ....**$65.00**
Peter Rabbit Digging, F Warne & Co 2000, 4¾" **$95.00**
Pickles, F Warne & Co Ltd...Beswick England, 4½".........**$230.00**

Pigling Bland, BP-3b, c 1956, 4¼" $165.00
Pigling Eats Porridge, B6 ....$195.00
Poorly Peter Rabbit, B3...$75.00
Rebecca Puddleduck, B6..$45.00
Sally Henny Penny, Warne & Co Ltd, 1974, 4" $75.00
Samuel Whiskers, B3 ....$45.00
Sir Isaac Newton, BP3b $200.00
Squirrel Nutkin..$65.00
Susan, Frederick Warne PLC 1983 Beswick England, 4½" ...$175.00
Tabitha Twitchett, F Warne & Co Ltd Copyright Beswick England,
    3¾"...$70.00
Tabitha Twitchit & Miss Moppet, B3 ....$150.00
Thomasina Tittlemouse, B3 ....$110.00
Timmy Tiptoes, 1948, 3½"..$90.00
Tom Thumb, BP6, F Worn & Co 1987, 1989 Royal Albert Ltd,
    3¼" $90.00
Tommy Brock, lg eye patch, B3..$65.00
Tommy Brock, spade out, BP-3, 3½", MIB, from $150 to ..$175.00

Ribby and the Patty Pan, BS-6a, 1991, 3¼", from $75.00 to $90.00.

Bellaire, Marc

Marc Bellaire, originally Donald Edmund Fleischman, was born in Toledo, Ohio, in 1925. He studied at the Toledo Museum of Art under Ernest Spring while employed as a designer for the Libbey Glass Company. During World War II while serving in the Navy, he traveled extensively throughout the Pacific, resulting in his enriched sense of design and color.

Marc settled in California in the 1950s where his work attracted the attention of national buyers and agencies who persuaded him to create ceramic lines of his own, employing hand-decorated techniques throughout. As a result, he founded a studio in Culver City. There he produced high quality ceramics often decorated with ultra-modern figures or geometric patterns and executed with a distinctive flair. His most famous pattern was Mardi Gras, decorated with slim dancers on spattered or striped colors of black, blue, pink, and white. Other major patterns were Jamaica, Balinese, Beachcomber, Friendly Island, Cave Painting, Hawaiian, Bird Isle, Oriental, Jungle Dancer, and Kashmir. (Kashmir usually has the name Ingle on the front and Bellaire on the back.)

It is to be noted that Marc was employed by Sascha Brastoff during the '50s. Many believe that he was hired for his creative imagination and style.

During the period 1951 – 1956, Marc was named one of the top ten artware designers by *Giftwares Magazine*. After 1956 he taught and lectured on art, design, and ceramic decorating techniques from coast to coast. Many of his pieces were one of a kind, and his work was commissioned throughout the United States.

During the 1970s he worked from his studio in Marin County, California. He eventually moved to Palm Springs where he set up his final studio/gallery. There he produced large pieces with a Southwest style. Mr. Bellaire died in 1994.

For more information we recommend *California Pottery Scrapbook* and *Collector's Encyclopedia of California Pottery, 2nd Edition* by Jack Chipman (Collector Books).

Advisor: Marty Webster (See Directory, California Pottery)

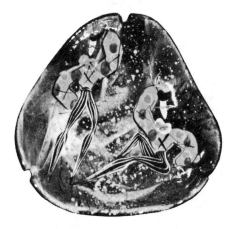

Ashtray, Mardi Gras, from $50.00 to $65.00.

Ashtray, Balinese Dancers on pink, free-form, 1½x6x6".......$38.00
Ashtray, clown on gray, marked Ingle, free-form, footed,
    3½x15½x9"..$65.00
Ashtray, Mardi Gras on mottled black, free-form, footed, 8½x13".$45.00
Candelabra, pink & white mottled, 5 cups on cowbell-shaped base
    w/leaf design $120.00
Candlestick, Asian man on off-white abstract, 10⅜" ea from $100
    to $120.00
Dish, African Dancer on pink, free-form, 5½x11½" $65.00
Dish, Balinese Dancers, boomerang shape, #B73-10, 12" $50.00
Dish, fruit design, 5x5"...$30.00
Dish, horse head, pink sponged on white, footed, 3x10x5¾" ... $30.00
Dish, white w/stylized trees, free-form, marked Original on back,
    3½x9" $65.00
Dish, Zulu Dancer on pink, free-form, 16" $90.00
Figurine, bird, white w/blue, brown & black, 6¼x9¾" $60.00
Plate, African Tribal, stylized, 5¾".....................................$22.00
Plate, lady w/long eyelashes & dangling earrings, 1957, 10½" ..$40.00

Bells

Bell collectors claim that bells rank second only to the wheel as being useful to mankind. Down through the ages bells have awakened people in the morning, called them to meals and prayers, and readied them to retire at night. We have heard them called rising bells, Angelus Bells (for deaths), noon bells, Town Crier bells (for important announcements), and curfew bells. Souvenir bells are often the first type collected, with interest spreading to other contemporaries, then on to old, more valuable bells. As far as limited edition bells are concerned, the fewer made per bell, the better. (For example, a bell made in an edition of 25,000 will not appreciate as much as one from an edition of 5,000.)

Bisque, mermaid holding a conch shell to her ear, ocean waves around bottom, 4¼x2¼", EX...**$23.00**

Bone china, San Remo pattern, floral pattern at base, Coalport Made in England, 1960s, 4" **$45.00**

Bone china, Susie Cooper Wedgwood design, silver lustre floral & leaf pattern, Made in England...Lustre, 4¼" **$80.00**

Bone china, white w/blue & sage green, red accents, marked Danbury Mint **$20.00**

Brass, Art Deco lady figural, 3⅛x2" **$70.00**

Brass, bird figural on handle, 6½" **$20.00**

Brass, counter type, thumb pulls down clapper, ca 1880, 4½x2¾" **$225.00**

Brass, counter type, thumb pulls down clapper, ornate leafy base, 1880s, 4x3½" **$235.00**

Brass, desk/servant; turtle w/etched bird & flower design on shell, wind key on bottom, 5½x2½x2"..................................**$225.00**

Brass, dragon heads w/emb angel, German writing, pull chain, wall mount, 6¾x3¾" **$70.00**

Brass, Dutch children (2) figural, double, 2x2⅛" **$26.00**

Brass, embossed spirals, openwork on handle, 5¼x2⅞"........**$55.00**

Brass, forged rivets hold leather strap handle, ca 1900, 2⅞x3¼" (+strap) **$100.00**

Brass, hotel-desk call bell, windup w/eagle finial, 1900s, 8½x2¾" **$70.00**

Brass, Kewpie figural handle, 5½x2½" **$165.00**

Brass, lady in hoop skirt, ca late 1940s, 3⅛x3x2"..............**$50.00**

Brass, lady w/fan (Elizabethan), high collar & hoop skirt, 1940s, 4x2¼x2⅛" **$65.00**

Brass, school, turned wooden handle, 5½" **$85.00**

Brass, school, turned wooden handle, 7x3¾" **$120.00**

Brass, school, turned wooden handle, 9½" **$150.00**

Brass, sleigh, 11 bells on leather strap, 19th Century **$325.00**

Brass, sleigh/horse, embossed frame, 7½x2½" (across bell).**$165.00**

Brass, Stanley & Patterson Faraday Signal (on plate), Patent 1916, 11x7x3" **$68.00**

Brass w/ornate cast-iron back plate, wire pull cord, Pat 1872, 3¾" dia...**$62.50**

Bronze, temple type w/dragon handle, Japan, 7½x4⅞" **$450.00**

Cast iron, cat on base, curling tail supports hanging bell, 13x8½x4" **$65.00**

Cast iron, counter type, Nouveau decor, 3 cherub feet, cogged wheels inside, 4⅞" dia...**$250.00**

Cast iron, longhorn steer head, horns are frame, 11" **$100.00**

Ceramic, pink & gold w/flowers in relief, 6¾x4" **$49.00**

Ceramic, rooster standing atop green bell, 5¼" **$14.00**

Ceramic, white open-weave design w/blue, pink & yellow applied flowers **$28.00**

Chrome, child's pedal car, in triangular frame, 1940s-50s, 4½x4" overall **$60.00**

Chrome dome w/red Bakelite & sterling silver handle, Art Deco styling, 3½x1¾" **$125.00**

Faience, French lady in traditional costume, France, 6¾x3¼". **$195.00**

Glass, cranberry with Mary Gregory-type decoration, Bohemian, 5½", from $45.00 to $60.00.

Glass, crystal, diamond & fan pattern, paneled prism pattern handle, Lenox label, 6½" **$25.00**

Glass, crystal, frosted hearts around base, recent, 7x4½" **$24.00**

Glass, crystal w/frosted nude handle, Cristallerie de Champagne... Bayel, 6¾" **$85.00**

Glass, crystal w/gold bands at bottom of handle & base, labels w/1979 & B1467 imprinted, 7½" **$45.00**

Glass, crystal w/pewter handle of boy on knees, praying, 1977 Franklin Mint, 5x2¾" **$75.00**

Glass, crystal w/pink ribbon spirals & mica speckles alternating w/ white crosshatch bands, 4¼x3" **$48.00**

Lustre, embossed fruit band, multicolor on white w/black trim on blue lustre, 4¼x3" **$65.00**

Majolica, lady in French costume, tin-glazed faience, hand signed France, 6¾x3¼" **$197.00**

Metal, Blum's Genuine Kentucky No 2 Cow Bell original label, 6¼x4¾" **$70.00**

Metal, counter/desk, mounted on 3½" sq stepped plinth, 1890, 5" **$145.00**

Metal, inscribed 1938-45 RAF Benevolent Fund, images of Churchill & FDR, 6" **$100.00**

Nickel over brass, desk/counter; dome shape w/plunger on top, 1800s-1900s, 2¾x3¼" **$30.00**

Pewter, repoussé vines & floral pattern, braided etched handle, 4".**$24.00**

Porcelain, colonial lady holding black purse, multicolor, Japan, 5" **$35.00**

Porcelain, dove handle, Avon Tapestry Collection, 5x3".......**$25.00**

Porcelain, Easter Girl, dangling blue egg, signed Marjorie Sarnat 1992-Enesco Corp, 5½x2⅞" **$21.00**

Porcelain, lady in white dress w/pink flowers, gold trim, hand painted, Japan, 4½" **$25.00**

Porcelain, purple w/embossed fruit design around center, gold trim & handle, 4¼x3" **$65.00**

Pottery, blue marble w/white horse, Kentucky souvenir, signed KSS, 5¾" **$15.00**

Pressed/cut/etched glass w/hobstars, whirlwinds & crosshatching, 10x4¾" **$100.00**

Wood, covered bridge carving painted in brown, green & blue, musical mechanism in bell plays Try To Remember, 5x2" **$18.00**

Black Americana

There are many avenues one might pursue in the broad field of Black Americana and many reasons that might entice one to become a collector. For the more serious, there are documents such as bills of sale for slaves, broadsides, and other historical artifacts. But by and far, most collectors enjoy attractive advertising pieces, novelties and kitchenware items, toys and dolls, and Black celebrity memorabilia.

It's estimated that there are at least 50,000 collectors around the country today that specialize in this field. There are large auctions devoted entirely to the sale of Black Americana. The items they feature may be as common as a homemade pot holder or a magazine or as rare as a Lux Dixie Boy clock or a Mammy cookie jar that might go for several thousand dollars. In fact, many of the cookie jars have become so valuable that they're being reproduced; so are salt and pepper shakers, so beware.

See also Advertising, Aunt Jemima; Condiment Sets; Cookie Jars; Postcards; Salt and Pepper Shakers; Sheet Music; String Holders.

Advisor: Judy Posner (See Directory, Black Americana)

Face mask, die-cut embossed lithograph, 12" wide, $95.00. (Photo courtesy Jackson's International Auctioneers & Appraisers of Fine Art & Antiques)

Advertising, Green River Whiskey good luck token, gold-tone metal w/man & horse, The Whiskey...Green River..., 1¼" **$25.00**

Bell, porcelain, figural girl knelt in prayer, Japan, 1950s, 3¾" . **$35.00**

Book, His Eye Is on the Sparrow: An Autobiography by Ethel Waters w/Charles Samuels, 1951, dust jacket, 8¾x6". **$35.00**

Book, Little Black Sambo, Kellogg's Story Book of Games, 1931, EX **$60.00**

Bookmark, sterling silver, Johnny Griffin Sambo face, marked 925, early 1900s, 3", G **$275.00**

Bowl, boy w/green hat, Brownie Downing Ceramics, 1962, 6⅜". **$35.00**

Card, Happy Birthday, 8 Years Old, boy playing banjo on paddlewheel boat w/Captain & children, ca 1950s, 6x4", EX. **$22.00**

Dish towel, grandpa plays banjo as children dance on white, 23x15" **$52.00**

Doll, knit, hand-crafted, Golligwog, red vest & tails, yellow bow tie & blue pants, 1950s-60s, 13", EX **$39.00**

Figurine, baby (w/hair) wrapped in blanket, hand-carved wood, 1930s, 4x1¾" **$45.00**

Figurine, baby girl, heavy pottery, hollow bottom, 1950s, 4½". **$35.00**

Figurine, boy attacked by goose, bisque, Germany, 1940s or earlier, 4⅜" **$149.00**

Figurine, boy riding an alligator, ceramic, 3½x5", VG **$20.00**

Figurine, boy w/fruit cart, ceramic, 1960s, 5½x7" **$50.00**

Figurine, minstrel w/palm tree, chenille on wooden base, Japan, 1940s-50s, 3¾", EX **$18.00**

Game, Adventures of Little Black Sambo, Cadaco-Ellis, 1945, 19⅝x19¾" **$45.00**

Menu, Club Plantation, autographed by the Ink Spots, 13", $65.00.

Mug, child's, boy in sombrero, Brownie Downing ceramics, 1962, 3½" **$25.00**

Mug, Muscle Moe, reddish clay w/dark brown glaze, handle is arm w/bottle in hand, Made in Japan, 1940s-50s, 5x5½" **$75.00**

Mug, Sambo's Restaurant, pottery, USA, 1970s, 3¼" **$24.00**

Paper dolls, Oh Susanna, w/punch-outs, coloring book & record, 1950, M..**$55.00**

Pincushion, wood w/Mammy cutout, original red cushion, 2 thread spools, Brevard HC, 1940s-50s, 6x5¾x2" **$55.00**

Postcard, A Busy Line, boy & girl talking on telephone w/Cupid sitting on line, 1900s, unposted, EX..........................**$15.00**

Pot holder, bust of little girl w/pink bows, hand-painted wood, 4¾x4¾" **$45.00**

Salt & pepper shakers, bust of natives, pottery, red Japan mark, 1950s, 4", pr..**$45.00**

Salt & pepper shakers, girl w/head to the ground, pottery, Hi Nosey on bottom, 1940s-50s, EX, pr **$85.00**

Salt & pepper shakers, Mammy w/mixing bowl, bisque pottery, foil labels, Taiwan, 1977, EX, pr **$32.00**

Sheet music, Hear Dem Bells, couple singing to church steeple, in 10x13" gold-painted wooden frame, 1880s..................**$40.00**

Syrup pitcher, Aunt Jemima, plastic, head tilts back for pouring, F&F, 1950s, 5½" **$65.00**

Syrup pitcher, Mammy, Made in Japan, 3½-oz, 3¼"..........**$35.00**

Tablecloth, little girl taking laundry off line as raindrops fall, ivory cotton embroidered in Royal Blue, 1940s, 33x17"........**$45.00**

Wall plaque, boy w/red umbrella, incised 350 on bottom, 8".**$45.00**

Wall pocket, lady's head, ceramic w/metal coil necklace, Horton, 1950s...**$35.00**

Pincushion, velvet and cotton, roll represents watermelon, pink-headed pins used to represent seeds, 4½", from $40.00 to $50.00.

Black Cats

Kitchenware, bookends, vases, and many other items designed as black cats were made in Japan during the 1950s and exported to the United States where they were sold by various distributors who often specified certain characteristics they wanted in their own line of cats. Common to all these lines were the red clay used in their production and the medium used in their decoration — their features were applied over the glaze with 'cold (unfired) paint.' The most collectible is a line marked (or labeled) Shafford. Shafford cats are plump and pleasant looking. They have green eyes with black pupils; white eyeliner, eyelashes, and whiskers; and red bow ties. The same design with yellow eyes was marketed by Royal, and another fairly easy-to-find 'breed' is a line by Wales with yellow eyes and gold whiskers. You'll find various other labels as well. Some collectors buy only Shafford, while others like them all.

When you evaluate your black cats, be critical of their paint. Even though no chips or cracks are present, if half of the paint is missing, you have a half-price item (if that). Collectors are very critical. These are readily available on Internet auctions, and unless pristine, they realize prices much lower than ours. Remember this when using the following values which are given for cats with near-mint to mint paint.

Advisor: Peggy Way (See Directory Black Cats)

Ashtray, flat face, Shafford, hard-to-find size, 3¾"..............**$30.00**

Ashtray, flat face, Shafford, 4¾", from $18 to **$25.00**

Ashtray, head shape, not Shafford, several variants, ea from $15 to...**$20.00**

Ashtray, head shape, Shafford, #109, 3", from $20 to **$30.00**

Bank, seated, coin slot in top of head, Shafford, from $125 to...**$150.00**

Bank, upright, Shafford features, marked Tommy, 2-part, minimum value **$100.00**

Biscuit jar, embossed white cat face w/blue eyes, wicker handle, 6", from $30 to **$45.00**

Biscuit jar, embossed yellow-eyed cat, wicker handle, Wales .**$125.00**

Bonbon, flat face, wicker handle, Shafford, scarce, from $50 to...**$75.00**

Cigarette lighter, Shafford, 5½", from $175 to..................**$200.00**

Cigarette lighter, sm cat stands on book by table lamp.........**$30.00**

Condiment set, upright, embossed faces w/yellow eyes, 2 bottles & shakers pr in wire frame...**$95.00**

Cookie jar, head form, Shafford **$75.00**

Cookie jar, head w/fierce look, yellow eyes, brown-black glaze, red clay, Wales, scarce, lg...**$150.00**

Creamer, Shafford, 5½", from $20 to...................................**$30.00**

Creamer, upraised left paw is spout, yellow eyes, gold trim, 6½x6" **$25.00**

Creamer & sugar bowl, embossed white cat face w/blue eyes, from $15 to **$20.00**

Creamer & sugar bowl, head lids are shakers, yellow eyes, 5⅜".**$50.00**

Cruets, O eyes for Oil, V eyes for vinegar, Shafford, from $65.00 to $75.00.

Decanter, long cat w/red fish in mouth as stopper **$65.00**

Decanter, upright cat holds bottle w/cork stopper, Shafford, from $50 to **$65.00**

Decanter, upright cat holds bottle w/cork stopper & 6 cat-face cups, Shafford, from $95 to **$125.00**

Decanter set, upright, yellow eyes, 6 plain wines..................**$35.00**

Demitasse coffeepot, tail handle, bow finial, Shafford #58/811, 7½", from $100 to **$150.00**

Egg cup, cat face on bowl, pedestal foot, Shafford, from $25 to .**$35.00**

Grease jar, sm head, Shafford #58/807, from $125 to........**$150.00**

Measuring cups, 4 sizes on wood wall rack w/painted cat face, Shafford, rare **$450.00**

Mug, embossed cat face, cat on handle w/cat's head above rim, Shafford, scarce, 3", from $25 to **$50.00**

Mug, embossed cat face, cat on handle w/cat's head below rim, Shafford, rare, 4", from $50 to....................................**$75.00**

Oil & vinegar set, embossed white cat face w/blue eyes, from $15 to **$20.00**

Oil & vinegar set, 2 cats hugging (1-pc, 2 heads), Royal Sealy or Tico, from $50 to **$60.00**

Paperweight, head on stepped chrome base, open mouth, yellow eyes, rare **$75.00**

Pincushion, cushion on back, tongue measure **$25.00**

Pitcher, squatting cat, pour through mouth, Shafford, rare, cream size, 4½" **$75.00**

Pitcher, squatting cat, pour through mouth, Shafford, rare, cream size, 5" **$90.00**

Pitcher, squatting cat, pour through mouth, Shafford, very rare, cream size, 5½" **$250.00**

Pitcher, upright cat, pours from ear spout, Shafford, 18-oz or 24-oz, (6" or 6½"), from $130 to **$150.00**

Planter, upright, Shafford, from $25 to **$35.00**

Planter, 2 cats in overturned top hat, 4½x3½x3¾" **$125.00**

Pot holder caddy, 'teapot' cat, 3 hooks, Shafford #873, minimum value **$150.00**

Salad set, conjoined cruet, shakers pr, fork, spoon & funnel, complete w/wooden rack, Royal Sealy, from $500 to **$650.00**

Salt & pepper shakers, embossed white cat face w/blue eyes, pr from $15 to **$20.00**

Salt & pepper shakers, range; upright, Shafford, 5", pr **$65.00**

Salt & pepper shakers, round-bodied 'teapot' cats, Shafford, pr from $60 to **$75.00**

Salt & pepper shakers, upright, Shafford, 3¾", pr from $22 to. **$28.00**

Shaker, long & crouching (shaker ea end), Shafford, 10", from $30 to **$50.00**

Spice set, triangular, 3 round tiers (8 in all), in wood wall mount, rare, from $500 to **$750.00**

Spice set, 4 cat shakers hook onto wireware cat-face rack, Shafford #58-806, from $450 to **$600.00**

Spice set, 6 pcs in wood frame, yellow eyes, Wales, from $60 to **$75.00**

Spice set, 6 sq shakers in wood frame, Shafford, from $75 to . **$150.00**

Spice set, 9 pcs in wood frame, yellow eyes, Wales, from $75 to **$100.00**

Sugar bowl, Shafford, from $20 to **$30.00**

Teakettle, embossed cat face, yellow eyes, wire handle, Wales, 4x7", from $45 to **$60.00**

Teapot, ball-shaped body, head lid, paw spout, tail handle, Shafford #542, 2-cup, 4" **$30.00**

Teapot, ball-shaped body, head lid, paw spout, tail handle, Shafford #543, 3-cup, 4½" **$35.00**

Teapot, ball-shaped body, head lid, paw spout, tail handle, Shafford #545, 5-cup, 6½" **$45.00**

Teapot, cat face w/double spout, woven handle, scarce, 5", from $150 to **$250.00**

Teapot, embossed white cat face w/blue eyes, kettle style, wire handle **$40.00**

Teapot, upright, head lid, rare 8", minimum value **$200.00**

Teapot/teakettle, cat head w/yellow 'straw' hat, blue & white eyes, C superimposed over N (Napco?) mark **$30.00**

Thermometer, yellow eyes, red ears, front paws resting on thermometer, 6" **$25.00**

Toothpick holder, cat w/arched back beside vase, from $10 to.. **$12.00**

Utensil set w/cat-shape wall hanger, w/strainer, dipper & funnel, Shafford #5149, from $300 to **$500.00**

Utensil: strainer, dipper or funnel, wood handles, Shafford, ea individual pc **$75.00**

Wall pocket, 'teapot' cat, Shafford #4122, minimum value... **$150.00**

Tea set, mother cat as pot, kittens as creamer and sugar bowl, $65.00.

Blair Ceramics

After graduating from the Cleveland School of Art in the 1930s, William H. Blair became an employee of the Purinton Pottery Company in Wellsville, Ohio, and later in Shippenville, Pennsylvania. His sister Dorothy was married to Bernard Purinton (founder of the Purinton Pottery Company). Bill Blair was responsible for designing most of Purinton's early lines, including both of their most recognized patterns, Apple and Intaglio. In 1946 he left the Purinton Pottery Company and opened his own pottery, Blair Ceramics, in Ozark, Missouri. William Blair designed his dinnerware line with a modernistic look utilizing square and rectangular shapes, with many items accented by twisted rope handles. Gay Plaid, Blair's signature pattern, features large bold stripes of dark green, chartreuse, and brown on ivory slip. Other patterns such as Spiced Pear, Leaves, Yellow and Gray Plaid, Bamboo, and Rick Rack, were produced in smaller quantities. The two most elusive patterns, Bird and Brick, were manufactured from red clay, and their shapes were rounded. Both Bird and Brick are intaglio-style designs, meaning that the motif is etched into the pottery. Blair Ceramics was sold by Neiman-Marcus and several other fine department stores in New York and Chicago. The pottery closed in 1955 after a devastating fire caused by lightning striking some of the machinery.

Almost all items produced by Blair Ceramics (except for the smaller pieces) were marked 'Blair, Decorated by Hand.' Although this appears to be a signature, it is only a facsimile that was applied with an ink stamp. A few experimental plates and tumblers have surfaced that are signed with Mr. Blair's personal signature, 'William H. Blair' or simply 'Blair.' These pieces are rare and command premium prices.

Advisor: Joe McManus (See Directory, Dinnerware)

Club/Newsletter: *Purinton News & Views*
P.O. Box 153
Connellsville, PA 15425

A quarterly newsletter devoted to enthusiasts of Purinton Pottery and Blair Ceramics

Bamboo, bowl, onion soup; w/lid, from $20 to **$25.00**
Bamboo, coffee server, from $45 to.........................**$50.00**
Bamboo, creamer, from $14 to **$18.00**
Bamboo, cup & saucer, from $10 to **$15.00**
Bamboo, pitcher, water; 7½", from $40 to.................**$45.00**
Bamboo, plate, sq, 8", from $10 to.........................**$14.00**
Bamboo, plate/server, rectangular, from $15 to.................**$18.00**
Bamboo, sugar bowl, w/lid, from $18 to......................**$20.00**
Brick, cup & saucer, from $9 to...........................**$12.00**
Brick, plate, dessert; 6½" **$8.00**
Brick, plate, dinner; from $12 to **$15.00**
Brick, platter, sq, 10", from $15 to **$18.00**
Brick, syrup jug, from $45 to...............................**$50.00**
Gay Plaid, beer mug, from $45 to..........................**$55.00**
Gay Plaid, bowl, cereal; from $8 to.........................**$10.00**
Gay Plaid, bowl, soup; triangular, w/handle, from $15 to....**$20.00**
Gay Plaid, bowl, soup; w/lid, from $20 to....**$25.00**
Gay Plaid, bowl, sq, 2¾x7¾" **$15.00**

Gay Plaid, bowl, square, 6½", $8.00.

Gay Plaid, bowl, teardrop shape, 8¾" **$16.00**
Gay Plaid, bowl, teardrop shape, 10" **$20.00**
Gay Plaid, canisters, set of 4 from $250 to.................**$300.00**
Gay Plaid, casserole, individual, w/lid, from $30 to **$40.00**
Gay Plaid, cookie jar, round, wooden lid, from $100 to **$120.00**
Gay Plaid, creamer, from $14 to **$18.00**
Gay Plaid, creamer & sugar bowl, mini, from $40 to **$50.00**
Gay Plaid, cup & saucer, from $9 to........................**$12.00**
Gay Plaid, mug, from $15 to **$18.00**
Gay Plaid, pitcher, twisted handle, 6", from $25 to **$30.00**
Gay Plaid, pitcher, water; w/ice lip, from $50 to.............**$65.00**
Gay Plaid, plate, dinner; from $12 to **$15.00**
Gay Plaid, platter, sq, 10", from $15 to **$18.00**
Gay Plaid, salt & pepper shakers, conical, tall, pr from $50 to.. **$60.00**
Gay Plaid, salt & pepper shakers, sq, 1¾", pr from $15 to ..**$20.00**
Gay Plaid, sugar bowl, w/lid, from $20 to **$25.00**
Gay Plaid, tumbler, tall, from $15 to **$20.00**
Gay Plaid, water cooler, 5-gal, rare, minimum value **$200.00**
Leaves, bowl, dessert; from $6 to **$9.00**
Leaves, bowl, lg, from $12 to **$15.00**
Leaves, coffeepot, w/lid, 8", from $45 to **$55.00**

Leaves, creamer & sugar bowl, mini, from $30 to **$35.00**
Leaves, cup & saucer, from $10 to **$14.00**
Leaves, nut dish, from $10 to.............................**$15.00**
Leaves, pitcher, ice lip, from $75 to **$85.00**
Leaves, plate, dinner; from $12 to **$15.00**
Leaves, tumbler, from $15 to **$18.00**
Primitive Bird, beer mug, from $90 to.....................**$100.00**
Primitive Bird, bowl, divided vegetable; from $35 to **$45.00**
Primitive Bird, bowl, serving; lg..........................**$65.00**
Primitive Bird, celery dish, from $20 to **$25.00**
Primitive Bird, cup & saucer, from $30 to **$40.00**
Primitive Bird, pitcher, 10½", from $450 to................**$500.00**
Primitive Bird, plate, dessert; 6½", from $20 to **$30.00**
Primitive Bird, plate, dinner; from $40 to..................**$50.00**
Primitive Bird, salt & pepper shakers, pr from $25 to.........**$30.00**
Specialty pc, dinner plate, Amish couple, signed William H Blair, minimum value.................**$350.00**
Spiced Pear, bowl, cereal; from $15 to.....................**$20.00**
Spiced Pear, pitcher, ice lip, from $125 to.................**$150.00**
Spiced Pear, plate, dinner; from $20 to **$25.00**
Spiced Pear, tumbler, from $20 to.........................**$25.00**
Yellow & Gray Plaid, creamer, from $15 to **$20.00**
Yellow & Gray Plaid, plate, dinner; sq, from $12 to **$15.00**
Yellow & Gray Plaid, salt & pepper shakers, 1¾", pr from $10 to.................**$12.00**
Yellow & Gray Plaid, sugar bowl, w/lid, from $18 to.........**$22.00**

Leaves, casserole, individual, with lid, from $20.00 to $25.00.

Blenko

The Blenko Glass Company is still operating in Milton, West Virginia, where they began production in 1921 (at that time known as Eureka Art Glass). Though at first they made only stained glass, primarily for making church windows, the depression of the late 1920s and the lack of church construction that resulted caused them to diversify. They hired local workers whom they trained in glassblowing and began producing decorative items for the home — decanters, bowls, candleholders, and the like. The company changed its name to Blenko in 1930. Over the years they have become famous for their brilliant colors, unique forms, and unusual techniques, including crackle glass, bubble glass, Venetian type glass, and mouth-blown cathedral glass from which they made reproductions of Colonial Williamsburg glassware. Most items found today are unmarked, since except for a short time (1950 – 1960) when the ware carried an etched signature, only paper labels were used.

See also Crackle Glass.

Advisor: Stan and Arlene Weitman (See Directory, Crackle Glass)

Bottle, light blue, 3 individual bubble-shape sections that fit together to form 1 pc, w/stopper, 14".......................................**$185.00**

Bottle, olive green, dimpled texture, fluted neck, original label, 7¾x3", from $75 to **$100.00**

Bowl, blue, ruffled, #3716, marked, 1959-60, 11x5", from $40 to...**$65.00**

Bowl, console; Forest Green, foil label, 4x11", from $75 to..**$100.00**

Bowl, crystal crackle w/blue foot, 1950s, 7", from $125 to ..**$150.00**

Bowl, light blue crackle, scalloped rim, 1960s, 2½x5½", from $55 to **$65.00**

Bowl, red to clear to blue at bottom, Wayne Husted, 5½x6", from $50 to **$75.00**

Bowl, salad; amber, foil label, #6143M, 1961, 9", from $60 to ..**$85.00**

Bowl, Sea Green, scalloped, 1950s-60s, 3x11¾" **$35.00**

Bowl, sea green crackle, applied decor at rim, 1950s-60s, 2½x4½", from $60 to **$80.00**

Candleholder, cobalt, foil label, 4x5½", ea **$75.00**

Candlesticks, crystal w/green twisted center, Joel Myers, ca 1960s, 6¾x2¼", pr from $75 to...**$100.00**

Compote, amethyst, clear foot, 12½x14½x8", from $85 to..**$110.00**

Compote, orange w/applied pedestal base, floral pattern, 10½x5½", from $50 to **$75.00**

Cruet, amberina crackle w/applied handle, 1950s, 6½x4¼", from $75 to **$100.00**

Cruet, cranberry flash crackle, w/crystal 2-ball stopper & handle, 6½", from $55 to...**$75.00**

Decanter, amber, #6935, signed Myers, 13½", from $150.00 to $200.00.

Decanter, amber w/flame stopper, #37, 13¾", from $125 to ..**$150.00**

Decanter, teal blue, ribbed w/clear flame stopper, 1950s, 14", from $135 to **$165.00**

Fruit, apple, cobalt crackle, 1950s-60s, 4½", from $75 to..**$100.00**

Goblet, amethyst crackle, very long stem, attributed, 1960s, 13½", from $175 to **$200.00**

Ice bucket, black top hat, 10½x11⅝x7¼" **$42.00**

Jug, amberina crackle w/gold drop-over handle, 1940-50s, 8¼", from $125 to **$150.00**

Ladle, green crackle, 1950s-60s, #925L, 13½", from $75 to.**$125.00**

Paperweight, apple, tangerine w/green leaves, foil label, 4x4" .**$40.00**

Paperweight, clear w/twisted blue center amid controlled bubbles, original foil sticker, 4¼x2¼" **$50.00**

Paperweight, crystal, 3 owls, original sticker, 4¼x3½".........**$40.00**

Pitcher, clear crackle with applied blue spiral and handle, 1960s, 12⅔", from $150.00 to $250.00. (Photo courtesy Stan and Arlene Weitman)

Pitcher, crystal crackle w/green drop-over handle, cylindrical, 1940s, 10", from $100 to...**$125.00**

Pitcher, emerald green crackle along bottom, bulbous, smooth rim, crescent-shaped pontil, 6x6½", EX **$40.00**

Pitcher, green crackle, bulbous, sm, 4x4¼" **$30.00**

Pitcher, olive green crackle w/pulled-back handle, ruffled rim, 1960s, 8¼", from $110 to...**$125.00**

Vase, amethyst crackle, double neck, late 1940s-50s, 4", from $60 to **$85.00**

Vase, crystal, stylized sun face design, oval foot, Wayne Husted, 1962, 10x9½", from $125 to **$150.00**

Vase, crystal crackle w/applied blue serpentine at neck, foil label, 7x5½", from $75 to **$100.00**

Vase, floor; charcoal, flared base w/faint ribbing along sides, Wayne Husted, 1954, 21", from $175 to **$225.00**

Vase, olive green, cylinder, John Nickerson, 11½x4½", from $125 to **$150.00**

Vase, purple w/yellow serpentine at neck, 15", from $150 to..**$175.00**

Vase, tangerine, round w/3-leaf clover design on front, #6322, 1963, 6½x6", EX, from $75 to **$100.00**

Vase, tangerine w/yellow foot, lg, ca 1950s-60s, 18x8" **$260.00**

Vase, teal crackle, double-crimped ruffled neck, footed, ca 1950s, 8", from $75 to **$100.00**

Vase, yellow crackle, cylindrical, 1940s-50s, 13½", from $125 to **$150.00**

Block Pottery

Richard Block founded his pottery in Los Angeles, California, sometime around 1940, and during that decade produced figural novelties and decorative items for the home. His product was marked Block Pottery, California, often with a copyright date.

Figurine, Betty w/wide polka-dot hat, holding pot, 7½" **$15.00**
Flower holder, Boston terrier, white w/bug on side, blue bowl, 4½" **$30.00**
Flower holder, lady in green & white dress w/matching hat, 7½" ..**$25.00**
Head vase, lady w/blue hat & blue collar, dated, 6" **$35.00**
Planter, baby shoe, 3x5" **$12.00**
Planter, Bonzo dog, eyes closed, flower decor, 4x3½x3" **$10.00**
Planter, dog w/lg blue eyes, 4" **$30.00**
Planter, Heidi, girl holding basket at side, 6½" **$18.00**
Planter, spaniel-type dog w/eyes closed, 5" **$10.00**
Planter vase, deer & fawn beside tree trunk, hand painted w/flower decor, 6" **$20.00**
Vase, Daisy, girl in wide-brimmed hat (forms rim of vase), 7x4" **$30.00**
Vase/planter, highchair shape, blue & pink decor w/flower motif on tray table, 6", EX **$15.00**
Wall pocket, white circle w/raised blue flowers & green leaves, #2, 5¾" **$15.00**
Wall pocket, white elephant w/yellow tusks, hand-painted floral around body, 4¼" **$15.00**
Wall pocket, yellow flowers on stems in relief on white, 5½", pr..**$35.00**

Blue Danube

A modern-day interpretation of the early Meissen Blue Onion pattern, Blue Danube is an extensive line of quality dinnerware that has been produced in Japan since the early 1950s and distributed by Lipper International of Wallingford, Connecticut. It is said that the original design was inspired by a pattern created during the Yuan Dynasty (1260 – 1368) in China. This variation is attributed to the German artist Kandleva. The flowers depicted in this blue-on-white dinnerware represent the ancient Chinese symbols of good fortune and happiness. The original design, with some variations, made its way to Eastern Europe where it has been produced for about 200 years. It is regarded today as one of the world's most famous patterns.

At least 125 items have at one time or another been made available by the Lipper company, making it the most complete line of dinnerware now available in the United States. Collectors tend to pay higher prices for items with the earlier banner mark (1951 to 1976), and reticulated (openweave) pieces bring a premium. Unusual serving or decorative items generally command high prices as well. The more common items that are still being produced sell for less than retail on the secondary market.

The banner logo includes the words 'Reg US Pat Off' along with the pattern name. In 1976 the logo was redesigned and the pattern name within a rectangular box with an 'R' in circle to the right of it was adopted. Very similar lines of dinnerware have been produced by other companies, but these two marks are the indication of genuine Lipper Blue Danube. Among the copycats you may encounter are Mascot and Vienna Woods — there are probably others. Some of our listings will indicate the mark, others will have a range. Items with the rectangular mark should be valued at 25% to 40% less than the same item with the banner mark. When our values are ranged, use the lower end to evaluate items with the rectangular mark.

Advisor: Lori Simnioniw (See Directory, Dinnerware)

Cake plate/bonbon tray, pierced handles, rectangular mark, from $45.00 to $55.00. (From the collection of Elaine France)

Ashtray, sq, 7x7", from $25 to **$35.00**
Ashtray, triangular, rests in ea corner, banner mark, 7" **$22.00**
Ashtray, 3¾" **$8.00**
Au gratin, 6½", from $12 to **$20.00**
Au gratin, 7⅜" dia...**$55.00**
Bell, 6", from $20 to **$25.00**
Biscuit jar, 9", from $65 to **$75.00**
Bone dish/side salad, crescent shape, banner mark, 6¾".......**$25.00**
Bone dish/side salad, crescent shape, banner mark, 9", from $35 to **$50.00**
Bowl, basketweave, scalloped rim, 9" **$60.00**
Bowl, cereal; banner mark, 6" **$20.00**
Bowl, cereal; rectangular mark, 6"............................**$12.00**
Bowl, cream soup; w/handles, 5" wide (across handles) w/saucer, rectangular mark **$40.00**
Bowl, dessert; banner mark, 5½", from $10 to..................**$14.00**
Bowl, divided vegetable; oval, banner mark, 11x7½", from $65 to...**$85.00**
Bowl, divided vegetable; oval, rectangular mark, 11x7½", from $35 to...**$48.00**
Bowl, heart shape, 2¼x8½"...................................**$65.00**
Bowl, lattice edge, banner mark, 8" **$35.00**
Bowl, lattice edge, banner mark, 9", from $40 to **$50.00**
Bowl, lattice edge, open handles, oval, 7¾" L, from $35 to .**$45.00**
Bowl, low pedestal skirted base, shaped rim, banner mark, 2x9x12", from $65 to **$70.00**
Bowl, onion soup; tab handles, w/lid, 2" H **$40.00**
Bowl, rice; conical, 2x4½", from $25 to........................**$30.00**
Bowl, rounded diamond shape, ¾" H foot ring, banner mark, 12" L, from $85 to **$110.00**
Bowl, rounded diamond shape, ¾" H foot ring, rectangular mark, 12" L, from $65 to **$80.00**

Bowl, salad; rectangular mark, 3x10" **$50.00**

Bowl, soup; banner mark, 8½", from $15 to...................... **$20.00**

Bowl, soup; coupe shape, rectangular mark, 7½" **$15.00**

Bowl, spaghetti; 9", rectangular mark, from $20 to............ **$30.00**

Bowl, spaghetti; 12", from $50 to **$60.00**

Bowl, triangular, 9½" **$42.00**

Bowl, vegetable; oval, banner mark, 10" L, from $40 to **$50.00**

Bowl, vegetable; round, banner mark, 9" **$45.00**

Bowl, vegetable; round, rectangular mark, 9" **$35.00**

Bowl, vegetable; round, w/lid, 5⅜x8", from $100 to.......... **$125.00**

Bowl, vegetable; round w/lid & handles, rectangular mark, 4¾x11x8" **$75.00**

Bowl, wedding; w/lid, footed, sq, rectangular mark, 8½x5", from $60 to **$80.00**

Box, white lacquerware, gold label w/rectangular logo, 2¼x4½".**$30.00**

Butter dish, banner mark, ¼-lb, from $50 to **$60.00**

Butter dish, rectangular, w/handles, 1-lb **$140.00**

Butter dish, round, rectangular mark, 8½", from $55 to...... **$65.00**

Cache pot, w/handles, 8x8" **$45.00**

Cake breaker, long tines **$30.00**

Cake knife, from $20 to **$30.00**

Cake pedestal, lattice edge, rectangular mark, 5x10", from $65 to **$75.00**

Cake pedestal, 4x10" **$55.00**

Cake server, ornate semicircular blade, 9x3¼" **$30.00**

Candelabrum, 5-light, 12x11" **$225.00**

Candleholders, sq base, w/handle, rectangular mark, 2½", pr ... **$25.00**

Candlesticks, rectangular mark, 6½", pr............................. **$40.00**

Candy dish, open, 8", from $28 to **$32.00**

Candy dish, w/lid, 7½" **$75.00**

Candy/nut dish, 3-section w/'Y' handles, rectangular mark, 7x10½" **$40.00**

Casserole, French; stick handle, w/lid, banner mark, 7" dia .**$85.00**

Casserole, individual; banner mark, 6" across handles, from $25 to **$30.00**

Casserole, individual; rectangle mark, 6" across handles, from $18 to **$22.00**

Casserole, oval, w/lid, banner mark under handle, 9" L **$55.00**

Casserole, round, w/lid, banner mark, 7¼" **$55.00**

Casserole, round, w/lid, banner mark, 8¾" **$70.00**

Chamberstick, Old Fashioned, 4x6" dia............................. **$25.00**

Cheese board, wooden, w/6" dia tile & glass dome, from $35 to ..**$50.00**

Cheese knife, 9", from $20 to **$30.00**

Chop plate, banner mark, 12", from $50 to......................... **$65.00**

Chop plate, banner mark, 14", from $60 to......................... **$70.00**

Chop plate, banner mark, 16", from $75 to......................... **$85.00**

Chop plate, rectangular mark, 12" **$45.00**

Coasters, 3½", set of 8, from $40 to **$50.00**

Coffee mug, banner mark, 3¼", from $20 to **$25.00**

Coffee mug, rectangular mark, 3¼" **$15.00**

Coffee mug, rectangular mark, 4" **$22.00**

Coffeepot, 6", from $45 to **$55.00**

Coffeepot, 7½", from $50 to.. **$60.00**

Coffeepot, 8½", from $60 to.. **$70.00**

Coffeepot, 10" **$115.00**

Compote, 4", from $65 to **$75.00**

Compote, 13", from $85 to **$100.00**

Condiment bowl, 2½" deep, w/saucer, 6¾", from $22 to **$28.00**

Cookie jar, rectangular mark, 8½", from $65 to.................. **$75.00**

Creamer, scroll-decorated spout (like coffeepot), rectangular mark, 2¾x4½" **$18.00**

Creamer & sugar bowl, 'Y' handles, bulbous, 4¾", 3½", from $38 to **$42.00**

Cruet, banner mark, 8" **$85.00**

Cruets, oil & vinegar, ea 6", on wooden tray w/banner mark .**$75.00**

Cup & saucer, 'Y' handle, scalloped rims, rectangular mark... **$6.00**

Cup & saucer, demitasse; 2x2⅝", from $15 to.................... **$18.00**

Cup & saucer, Irish coffee; cylindrical cup, banner mark, 3¼" . **$12.00**

Cutting board, 14x9½", +stainless steel knife **$45.00**

Dish, embossed flowers on bottom, w/handle, no mark, 5¾x4", from $20 to **$30.00**

Dish, lattice rim, braided handles, banner mark, 7½x5" **$40.00**

Dish, leaf shape, banner mark, ¾x4" **$25.00**

Dish, rim w/5 openweave sections alternating w/5 solid medallions, rectangular mark, 2¼x8" **$38.00**

Dish, shell shape, 9x9½" **$45.00**

Egg cup, double; rectangular mark, set of 8 .... **$50.00**

Flowerpot, w/undertray, 3½", from $40 to.......................... **$45.00**

Fork, serving; 7½" **$35.00**

Ginger jar, rectangular mark, 5" **$35.00**

Ginger jar, rectangular mark, 7" **$50.00**

Goblet, clear glass w/Blue Danube design, 7¼", set of 12, from $80 to **$100.00**

Gravy boat, banner mark, 3¼"x5½", w/5½" L undertray..... **$70.00**

Gravy boat, banner mark, 10" long, $50.00. (From the collection of Elaine France)

Gravy boat, double spout, w/undertray, rectangular mark, 7" L, from $35 to **$40.00**

Gravy boat, w/attached undertray, 3x8" L........................... **$40.00**

Hurricane lamp, glass mushroom globe.............................. **$75.00**

Ice bucket, plastic, from $25 to **$30.00**

Ice cream scoop, cutting blade, no mark **$50.00**

Inkstand, 2 lidded inserts, shaped base, banner mark, 9" L ..**$300.00**

Jam pot, straight sides, w/lid & underplate, rectangular mark, 4x3" **$40.00**

Jar, slender w/flare at rim, w/lid, banner mark, 7"............... **$55.00**

Jar, slender w/flare at rim, w/lid, banner mark, 9"............... **$70.00**

Mug, soup; 2⅞x4½", set of 4, from $55 to **$70.00**

Mustard/mayonnaise, footed, lg handles, w/lid, rectangular mark, 5x7", from $65 to $90.00

Napkin rack, scalloped back, 3½x6½" L $165.00

Napkin rings, set of 4............$30.00

Napkins, Sunnyweave, set of 4, from $25 to $30.00

Pie plate, 9"............$35.00

Pitcher, milk; 'Y' handle, 5¼", from $25 to $30.00

Pitcher, syrup; tall & slim, banner mark, 5½x5½x3"............$25.00

Pitcher, waisted neck w/wide spout, scroll handle, banner mark, 6½"............$60.00

Pitcher, waisted neck w/wide spout, scroll handle, rectangular mark, 5¼", from $18 to $22.00

Pitcher, water; waisted neck w/lg pouring spout, scroll handle, banner mark, 8"............$125.00

Plate, banner mark, 8½", from $10 to $15.00

Plate, banner mark, 10¼", from $15 to $20.00

Plate, bread & butter; 6¾"............$6.00

Plate, collector; from $40 to $48.00

Plate, cookie; 10", from $38 to $42.00

Plate, deviled egg; from $80 to $90.00

Plate, lattice rim, banner mark, 8" $50.00

Plate, lattice rim, banner mark, 10"............$60.00

Plate, triangular, 9¾" L $35.00

Platter, banner mark, 12x8½"............$65.00

Platter, banner mark, 14x10"............$85.00

Platter, banner mark, 16½" L, from $75 to $90.00

Platter, banner mark, 18½x13½", from $200 to............$240.00

Platter, rectangular mark, 12x8½", from $40 to $50.00

Platter, rectangular mark, 14x10", from $50 to $65.00

Quiche dish, straight sides, white interior w/sm pattern in center, banner mark............$50.00

Reamer, 2-pc, from $35 to $40.00

Relish, rectangular mark, 7¾", from $25 to $35.00

Relish, 2-part, rectangular mark, 7¼", from $25 to............$35.00

Rolling pin, 16" L, from $75 to $95.00

Salad servers, fork, 11¼", & spoon, 11½", pr $70.00

Salt & pepper shakers, cylindrical, rectangular mark, 3½", pr ...$35.00

Salt & pepper shakers, dome top w/bud finial, bulbous bottom, banner mark, 5", pr $40.00

Salt box, wooden lid, 4¾x4¾", from $55 to $65.00

Server, 3-part w/'Y' handle, 11" L............$52.00

Snack plate & cup, banner mark, from $25 to $30.00

Soap dish, from $10 to $14.00

Souffle, 7½", from $40 to $50.00

Soup ladle, Lucky, 10"............$75.00

Spice rack, 8 jars in wooden rack, from $85 to $110.00

Spooner, 4¾x4"............$50.00

Sugar bowl, ovoid, w/lid, rectangular mark, 4x5"............$22.00

Sugar bowl, w/lid, mini, from $20 to $25.00

Sugar bowl, wide bowl w/'Y' handles, dome lid, banner mark, 4x8"............$50.00

Sugar bowl, wide bowl w/'Y' handles, rectangular mark, scarce, 5x6"............$35.00

Sweetmeat dish, 7½", from $35 to $42.00

Tablecloth, oval, 80x62", EX............$50.00

Tablecloth, 70x50", +4 napkins, unused $95.00

Tablecloth, 100x60", EX............$65.00

Tazza, attached pedestal foot, banner mark, 4½x15", from $85 to............$95.00

Tazza, lattice edge, ped foot, banner mark, 4x8"............$65.00

Tea tile/trivet, 6", from $15 to $20.00

Teakettle, enamel, wooden handle, w/fold-down metal sides, 9x9½"............$25.00

Teapot, 'Y' handle, rectangular mark, 3⅜"............$45.00

Teapot, 'Y' handle, rectangular mark, 6½"............$60.00

Tidbit tray, 1-tier, banner mark, from $25 to............$30.00

Tidbit tray, 2-tier, banner mark, from $45 to............$55.00

Tidbit tray, 3-tier, banner mark, from $60 to............$75.00

Toothbrush holder, from $15 to $18.00

Tray, oblong, 10¼", from $40 to............$45.00

Tray, rectangular, closed handles, slightly scalloped, rectangular mark, 14½x7"............$70.00

Tray, rectangular, pierced handles, 14½"............$105.00

Tray, sq w/pierced handles, rectangular mark, 10"............$50.00

Tray, sq w/2 open handles, 2 handle-like closed-in devices on opposing sides, banner mark, 12½"............$125.00

Tray, sq w/2 open handles, 2 handle-like closed-in devices on opposing sides, banner mark, 15½"............$225.00

Tray, 5-sided, 12", from $40 to............$50.00

Tumbler, china, 3⅜", from $8 to............$10.00

Tumbler, glass, 4"............$8.00

Tumbler, glass, 7½", set of 6............$60.00

Tureen, w/handles & lid, banner mark, 10x12" L, on 13x9½" tray............$200.00

Undertray, for soup tureen, from $50 to $55.00

Vase, bud; 6"............$30.00

Vase, waisted neck, rectangular mark, 9", from $50 to............$60.00

Vase, 10"............$68.00

Blue Garland

During the 1960s and 1970s, this dinnerware was offered as premiums through grocery stores. Its ornate handles, platinum trim, and the scalloped rims on the flat items and the bases of the hollow ware pieces when combined with the 'Haviland' backstamp suggested to most supermarket shoppers that they were getting high quality dinnerware for very little. And indeed the line was of good quality, but the company that produced it had no connection at all to the famous Haviland company of Limoges, France, who produced fine china there for almost 100 years. The mark is Johann Haviland, taken from the name of the founding company that later became Philip Rosenthal and Co. This was a German manufacturer who produced chinaware for export to the United States from the mid-1930s until well into the 1980s. Today's dinnerware collectors find the delicate wreath-like blue flowers and the lovely shapes very appealing.

This line may also be found with the Thailand – Johann Haviland backstamp, a later issue. Our values are for the dinnerware with the Bavarian backstamp. The Thailand line will usually sell for at least 30% less.

Bell, 5½x3¼"............$40.00

Bowl, coupe soup; 7⅝"............$12.00

Bowl, fruit; 5⅛" **$5.00**
Bowl, oval, 11¼", from $60 to **$75.00**
Bowl, vegetable; round, 8½" **$35.00**
Butter dish, ¼-lb, from $35 to **$50.00**
Butter pat/coaster, 3½" **$5.00**
Candleholder, 2½x6", ea **$35.00**
Candlesticks, 1-light, 4", pr from $35 to **$45.00**
Casserole, metal, stick handle, w/lid, 3-qt, 8¼", from $35 to . **$50.00**
Casserole, metal, tab handles, w/lid, 3-qt, from $20 to **$28.00**
Casserole, metal, w/lid, 4-qt, 9¾", from $40 to **$50.00**
Casserole, w/lid, 1½-qt, 5x8", from $50 to **$60.00**
Casserole, w/lid, 2½-qt, 6x9" **$60.00**
Casserole/soup tureen, 11" wide **$50.00**
Clock plate **$25.00**
Coffeepot, 11" **$45.00**
Creamer, 9-oz, 4¼" **$15.00**
Cup & saucer, flat or footed **$5.00**
Fondue pot, w/lid, from $50 to **$65.00**
Goblet, glass, 6¾", set of 6 .... **$40.00**
Gravy boat, w/attached or separate underplate, 10" L, from $20
    to **$30.00**
Nut dish, footed, w/handles **$30.00**
Plate, dinner; 10" **$7.00**
Plate, salad; 7¾" **$6.00**

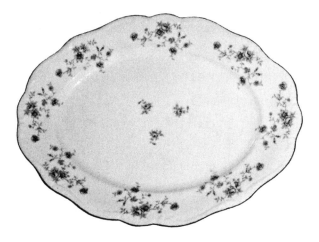

Platter, 12⅞", $30.00.

Platter, oval, 14½" **$40.00**
Roaster, metal, oval, 13", from $50 to **$75.00**
Salt & pepper shakers, 4", pr **$22.00**
Saucepan, metal, w/lid, 1½-qt, 2 styles, ea from $30 to **$40.00**
Skillet, metal, w/lid, 8½", from $35 to **$45.00**
Sugar bowl, w/lid, 5½x7" **$18.00**
Teapot, 7¾" **$60.00**
Tray, tidbit; 2-tier **$35.00**
Tray, tidbit; 3-tier **$40.00**

Blue Ridge Dinnerware

Blue Ridge has long been popular with collectors, and prices are already well established, but that's not to say there aren't a few good buys left around. There are! It was made by a company called Southern Potteries, who operated in Erwin, Tennessee, from sometime in the latter '30s until the mid-'50s. They made many hundreds of patterns, all hand decorated. Some collectors prefer to match up patterns, while others like to mix them together for a more eclectic table setting.

One of the patterns most popular with collectors (and one of the most costly) is called French Peasant. It's very much like Quimper with simple depictions of a little peasant man with his staff and a lady. But they also made many lovely floral patterns, and it's around these where most of the buying and selling activity is centered. You'll find roosters, plaids, and simple textured designs, and some vases in addition to the dinnerware.

Very few pieces of dinnerware are marked except for the 'china' or porcelain pieces which usually are. Watch for a similar type of ware often confused with Blue Ridge that is sometimes (though not always) marked Italy.

The values suggested below are for the better patterns. To evaluate the French Peasant line, double these figures; for the simple plaids and textures, deduct 25% to 50%, depending on their appeal.

If you'd like to learn more, we recommend *The Collector's Encyclopedia of Blue Ridge Dinnerware*, by Betty and Bill Newbound.

Advisors: Bill and Betty Newbound (See Directory, Dinnerware

Newsletter: *National Blue Ridge Newsletter*
Norma Lilly
144 Highland Dr., Blountsville, TN 37617

Cake tray, Verna, maple leaf shape with handles, from $60.00 to $65.00.
(Photo courtesy Betty and Bill Newbound)

Ashtray, advertising; railroad, from $60 to **$70.00**
Basket, aluminum edge, 10", from $30 to **$35.00**
Bowl, fruit; 5¼", from $7 to **$10.00**
Bowl, mixing; med, from $20 to **$25.00**
Box, Sherman Lily, from $700 to **$900.00**
Butter dish, from $35 to **$45.00**
Carafe, w/lid, from $100 to **$150.00**
Casserole, w/lid, from $45 to **$50.00**
Coffeepot, ovoid shape, from $150 to **$175.00**
Creamer, Colonial, open, lg, from $18 to **$25.00**
Creamer, Fifties shape, from $15 to **$20.00**
Cup, dessert; glass, from $10 to **$14.00**
Cup & saucer, Holiday, from $50 to **$75.00**

Cup & saucer, Turkey & Acorn, from $75 to **$100.00**
Custard cup, from $18 to.. **$22.00**
Deviled egg dish, from $60 to.. **$75.00**
Dish, baking; divided, 8x13", from $25 to **$30.00**
Gravy tray, from $50 to.. **$70.00**
Jug, character, Pioneer Woman, from $450 to **$550.00**
Lazy Susan, wooden base, from $50 to **$60.00**
Pie baker, from $35 to **$45.00**
Pitcher, Antique, china, 5", from $85 to **$100.00**
Plate, Christmas Tree, from $75 to.................................... **$85.00**
Plate, dinner; 10½", from $20 to **$25.00**
Plate, round, 6", from $8 to **$10.00**
Plate, Square Dance, 14", from $350 to............................ **$400.00**
Plate, 11½-12", from $50 to **$65.00**
Ramekin, w/lid, 7½", from $30 to **$35.00**
Salad fork, china, from $45 to **$50.00**
Salad fork, earthenware, from $50 to **$60.00**
Salt & pepper shakers, Bud Top, pr from $75 to................ **$85.00**
Salt & pepper shakers, range, pr from $40 to...................... **$45.00**
Sugar bowl, Rope Handle, w/lid, from $15 to **$18.00**
Teapot, Charm House, from $300 to.................................... **$350.00**
Teapot, Piecrust, from $150 to.. **$200.00**
Teapot, Skyline, from $110 to.. **$125.00**
Tray, snack; Martha, from $150 to...................................... **$175.00**
Tumbler, juice; glass, from $12 to **$15.00**
Vase, boot, 8", from $80 to.. **$95.00**
Vase, bud; from $225 to **$250.00**
Vase, handled, china, from $95 to.. **$100.00**

Chocolate set, French Peasant: pot, $225.00; creamer and sugar bowl, pedestal feet, $125.00. (Photo courtesy Betty and Bill Newbound)

Blue Willow Dinnerware and Accessories

Blue Willow dinnerware has been made since the 1700s, first by English potters, then Japanese, and finally American companies as well. Tinware, glassware, even paper 'go-withs' have been produced over the years — some fairly recently, due to on-going demand. It was originally copied from the early blue and white wares made in Nanking and Canton in China. Once in awhile you'll see some pieces in black, pink, red, or even multicolor.

Obviously the most expensive will be the early English wares,

easily identified by their backstamps. You'll be most likely to find pieces made by Royal or Homer Laughlin, and even though comparatively recent, they're still collectible, and their prices are very affordable.

For further study we recommend *Gaston's Blue Willow* by Mary Frank Gaston (Collector Books).

See also Royal China.

Advisor: Mary Frank Gaston

Baking dish, oven proof, Japan, 2½x5" **$40.00**
Biscuit jar, metal handle, unmarked Japan, 6", from $150 to.. **$175.00**
Bone dish, kidney shape, Bourne & Leigh, 6¼", from $45 to .. **$55.00**
Bowl, chestnut; reticulated lattice sides, handles, unmarked English, 10"..**$1,000.00**
Bowl, lug soup; Homer Laughlin, from $25 to **$30.00**
Bowl & pitcher, Wedgwood...**$1,200.00**

Butter dish, Japan, one quarter pound, from $60.00 to $75.00.
(Photo courtesy Mary Frank Gaston)

Butter dish, Royal China, ¼-lb **$45.00**
Casserole, Empress, w/lid, Homer Laughlin, from $70 to....**$75.00**
Cheese dish, sq plate w/canted corners, sq lid, Biltshaw & Robinson **$250.00**
Coffeepot, Booth's, gold trim, Real Old Willow, 8½" **$210.00**
Cup, chili; Japan, 3½x4" **$50.00**
Cup & saucer, Royal China **$6.00**
Dish, child's, Ridgway, w/lid, 5" **$175.00**
Gravy boat, Wood & Sons, 7" L.. **$65.00**
Horseradish dish, Doulton, 5½" **$65.00**
Jug, batter; frosted glass, Hazel-Atlas, 10" **$100.00**
Ladle, unmarked, 7" L, from $140 to **$160.00**
Lamp, kerosene; ceramic shade, Japan, 11½", from $125 to.**$150.00**
Matchsafe, slotted cylinder w/saucer base, Shenango China Co, 2" **$80.00**
Mustard pot, barrel shape, unmarked, 2½", from $65 to **$75.00**
Pie plate, Royal China, 10" **$30.00**
Pitcher, milk; Homer Laughlin, 5".....................................**$45.00**
Pitcher, w/lid, Japan, 11" **$125.00**
Plate, dinner; Imperial, 9¾" **$27.00**
Platter, Allerton's, 16x12".. **$275.00**
Relish tray, Booth's center pattern, Bow-Knot border, Wood & Sons, 9"..**$30.00**
Salt & pepper shakers, Royal China, pr.............................. **$25.00**
Sugar bowl, rope & anchor finial, unmarked, 6", from $45 to . **$55.00**
Teapot, Two Temples II, butterfly border, Malkin mark: MIE, 3½" **$125.00**

Toast rack, Grimwades, 6", from $80 to **$100.00**
Tureen, soup; Traditional center, Ridgeway's, 1912-27 mark,
    7¾x11"...**$450.00**
Waste bowl, Doulton, 3½x6½", from $125 to **$150.00**

Salad fork and spoon, ceramic and silver plate, no mark, 11½", from $200.00 to $225.00 for the pair. (Photo courtesy Mary Frank Gaston)

Bookends

You'll find bookends in various types of material and designs. The more inventive their modeling, the higher the price. Also consider the material. Cast-iron examples, especially if in original polychrome paint, are bringing very high prices right now. Brass and copper are good as well, though elements of design may override the factor of materials altogether. If they are signed by the designer or marked by the manufacturer, you can boost the price. Those with a decidedly Art Deco appearance are often good sellers. The consistent volume of common to moderately uncommon bookends that are selling on line has given the impression that some are more easily available than once thought. Hence, some examples have not accrued in value. See *Collector's Guide to Bookends* by Louis Kuritzky (Collector Books) for more information.

Advisor: Louis Kuritzky (See Directory, Bookends)

Club: Bookend Collector Club
Louis Kuritzky
4510 NW 175h Pl. 7
Gainesville, FL 32605; 352-377-3193
Quarterly full-color newsletter: $25 per year

Flapping Flamingos, gray metal, Jennings Bros. #3024, 6½", $125.00. (Photo courtesy Louis Kuritzky)

Airedales, bronze, EB Parsons Gorham Co Founders, ca 1920,
    5½" **$1,500.00**

Athens, cast iron, Bradley & Hubbard, ca 1925, 4½" **$90.00**
Buffalo, gray metal, Ronson, LV Aronson 1923, 4¼" **$250.00**
Classic Polar Bear, gray metal, Ronson, ca 1930, 6½" **$325.00**
Dutch Pair, gray metal, polychrome, Ronson, company paper tag
    #16510, ca 1925, 5½" **$125.00**
Elephants, bronze-clad, ca 1925, 5" **$125.00**
Flower, copper, Roycroft, shopmark, ca 1925, 5¼" **$350.00**
Girl Posing, gray metal, Dodge, company paper tag, ca 1947,
    7".. $175.00

Horse on Arc, metal, Dodge, ca 1947, 5½", $95.00. (Photo courtesy Louis Kuritzky)

Hunters, bronze, Laboy Trauy, ca 1930, 8¾" **$1,000.00**
Lady Godiva, glass, Haley, ca 1940, 6" **$125.00**
Lady Reading, plaster-filled plastic, ca 1935, 7" **$200.00**
Lincoln, cast iron, ca 1925, 7" **$65.00**
Miles Standish, gray metal, ca 1930, 7" **$125.00**

Minerva, iron, Judd, ca 1925, 5¾", $100.00. (Photo courtesy Louis Kuritzky)

Nashville Surgical Supply Co, B&B Bakelite, B&B Remembrance St
    Paul Patent #2284849, ca 1930, 4¾"............................**$50.00**
Nude With Tambourine Backarching, bronze-clad, Armor Bronze,
    company paper tag, ca 1927, 6½" **$450.00**
Pink Lady, chalk on polished stone base, JB Hirsch, JBH, ca 1943,
    5½" **$125.00**
Spunky Spaniel, gray metal, ca 1930, 5" **$100.00**
St Francis, pottery, Rookwood, XLV #6883, ca 1945, 7¼" ...**$500.00**
Ten Commandments, gray metal, Ronson, LV Aronson 1922,
    3¾" **$175.00**
Up to Her Neck in Geese, glass, ca 1950, 7½" **$75.00**

Wedding Children, gray metal, Nuart, shopmark, ca 1930, 5½". **$90.00**
Wrestlers, cast iron, 5¼"......................................**$100.00**
Young Boy, bronze, Gorham, B Johnson, ca 1920, 8".....**$3,000.00**

Books

Books have always fueled the imagination. Before television lured us out of the library into the TV room, everyone enjoyed reading the latest novels. Western, horror, and science fiction themes are still popular to this day — especially those by such authors as Louis L'Amour, Steven King, and Ray Bradbury, to name but a few. Edgar Rice Burrough's Tarzan series and Frank L. Baum's Wizard of Oz books are regarded as classics among today's collectors. A first edition of a popular author's first book (especially if it's signed) is avidly sought after, so is a book that 'ties in' with a movie or television program.

Dick and Jane readers are fast becoming collectible. If you went to first grade sometime during the 1930s until the mid-1970s, you probably read about their adventures. These books were used allover the United States and in military base schools over the entire world. They were published here as well as in Canada, the Philippine Islands, Australia, and New Zealand; there were special editions for the Roman Catholic parochial schools and the Seventh Day Adventists', and even today they're in use in some Mennonite and Amish schools.

On the whole, ex-library copies and book club issues (unless they are limited editions) have very low resale values.

Big Little Books

The Whitman Publishing Company started it all in 1933 when they published a book whose format was entirely different from any other's. It was very small, easily held in a child's hand, but over an inch in thickness. There was a cartoon-like drawing on the right-hand page, and the text was printed on the left. The idea was so well accepted that very soon other publishers — Saalfield, Van Wiseman, Lynn, World Syndicate, and Goldsmith — cashed in on the idea as well. The first Big Little Book hero was Dick Tracy, but soon every radio cowboy, cartoon character, lawman, and space explorer was immortalized in his own adventure series.

When it became apparent that the pre-teen of the '50s preferred the comic-book format, Big Little Books were finally phased out; but many were saved in boxes and stored in attics, so there's still a wonderful supply of them around. You need to watch condition carefully when you're buying or selling.

Newsletter: *Big Little Times*
Big Little Book Collectors Club of America
Larry Lowery
P.O. Box 1242, Danville, CA 94526; 415-837-2086

Beasts of Tarzan, #1410, 1937, EX+ **$50.00**
Blonde & Dagwood in Some Fun, #703-10, 1949, EX+ **$35.00**
Buck Jones in Ride 'Em Cowboy, #116, 1937, EX+ **$75.00**
Captain Midnight & the Secret Squadron, #1488, 1941, NM **$65.00**

Cinderella, #711-10, 1950, VG **$20.00**
Donald Duck Up in the Air, #1486, 1945, VG+ **$35.00**
Flame Boy & the Indians' Secret, #1464, 1938, EX............**$40.00**
Gene Autry & the Gun-Smoke Reckoning, #1434, 1943, EX+ .**$50.00**
John Carter of Mars, #1402, 1940, NM **$150.00**
Kayo & Moon Mullins & the One Man Gang, #1415, 1939, EX+ **$40.00**
Little Lord Fauntleroy, #1598, 1936, VG+...........................**$35.00**
Mickey Mouse & the Bat Bandit, #1153, 1935, VG...........**$25.00**

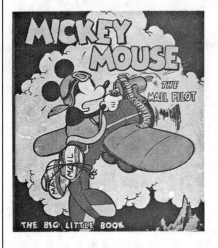

Mickey Mouse the Mail Pilot, **#731, copyright 1933, EX+, $65.00.**

Mother Goose (576 Pages of), #725, 1934, G **$50.00**
New Adventures of Tarzan, #1180, 1935, EX+ **$50.00**
Porky Pig All Pictures Comics, #1408, 1942, EX+...............**$45.00**
Red Ryder Acting Sheriff, #702-10, 1949, NM **$45.00**
Scrappy, #112, 1934, very scarce, VG+ **$60.00**
Smilin' Jack & the Stratosphere Ascent, #1152, 1927, VG+ ...**$25.00**
Tarzan & the the Jewels of Opar, #1495, 1941, VG **$25.00**
Texas Kid, #1429, c 1937, VG...**$20.00**
Tim McCoy in the Westerner, #1193, 1938, EX **$35.00**

Tom Mix Plays a Lone Hand, **#1173, copyright 1935, EX, 4½x5", $35.00.**

Wing of the USA, #1407, c 1940, EX **$35.00**

Children's Miscellaneous Books

Adventures of Andy Panda, Dell Fast Action, NM..............**$75.00**
Andy Panda's Rescue, Tiny-Tot-Tale #2942, 1949, EX........**$20.00**
Assignment in Space With Rig Foster, #1576, G+ **$7.00**

Baby's Day, by Annette Edwards, Treasure Books #859, illustrated by Priscilla Pointer, hardback, 1953, EX+ **$8.00**

Batman - Three Villians of Doom, Signet, 1966, 160 pages, EX+ **$20.00**

Beverly Hillbillies in the Saga of Wildcat Creek, Whitman, 1963, NM...**$15.00**

Big Golden Animal ABC, #10457, last printing, 1954, NM..**$18.00**

Billy & His Steam Roller, Wonder Book, #557, 1951, EX+.**$14.00**

Black Beauty, Whitman, #1604, 1955, NM.......................**$12.00**

Black Beauty, Wonder Book, #595, 1952, EX.....................**$8.00**

Bugs Bunny Party Best, Whitman, Tell-a-Tale, 1976, EX+.....**$6.00**

Building a Skyscraper, Louise L Kozak, Rand McNally, Start Right series, Paul frame illustrations, hardback, 1973, EX........**$6.00**

Bullwinkle Book, Golden Press #5954, head shape, 1976, EX..**$25.00**

Butter Battle Book, Dr Seuss, Random House, 1984, M.....**$10.00**

Charlie Brown's All-Stars, Charles M Schulz, Signet Books, 1966, EX **$5.00**

Choo Choo Train, Wonder Book, #718, 1958, EX+...........**$12.00**

Crusader Rabbit in Bubble Trouble, Tip-Top-Tales #2468, 1960, EX **$45.00**

Dale Evans Prayer Book for Children, Big Golden Book, 1956, VG+...**$10.00**

Deputy Dawg & the Space Man, Wonder Book, #773, 1961, unused, M **$35.00**

Disney on Parade, Mary Poppins cover, 1973, 12x8½", EX.**$28.00**

Disney Storybook Collection, Disney Press, 1st edition, 1998, EX **$18.00**

Donald Duck Takes It on the Chin, Dell Fast-Action, softcover, 1941, EX **$75.00**

Dopey He Don't Talk None, Whitman #955, 1938, NM+ ..**$150.00**

Emerald City of Oz, Rand McNally Jr edition #301, 1939, EX.. **$45.00**

F Troop in The Great Indian Uprising, #1544, hardback, 1967, VG+...**$12.00**

Felix on Television, A Flip-It Book, Irwin Shapiro, Wonder Book, #716, 1956, NM **$30.00**

Felix the Cat, Treasure Book, #872, 1953, EX+ **$35.00**

Flash Gordon, Treasure Books #906, illustrated by Alex Berger, hardback, 1956, NM **$30.00**

Flintstones at the Circus, Tell-a-Tale #2552, 1963, NM **$25.00**

Gingerbread Man, Whitman Tell-a-Tale, 1953, VG.............**$12.00**

Hector Heathcoate & the Knights, Wonder Book, #840, EX...**$28.00**

Helen Keller, The Story of My Life, Helen Keller, softcover, 1969, VG..**$10.00**

Here's to You Charlie Brown, Charles Schulz, hardback, 1978, EX+ **$8.00**

Hop on Pop, Dr Seuss, Random House Beginner Books, 1990s, M **$6.00**

House That Jack Built, Whitman Tell-a-Tale, 1960, EX+ **$15.00**

House That Popeye Built, Wonder Book, #750, 1960, EX ..**$25.00**

Hungry Lion, Whitman Tell-a-Tale, 1960, VG+ **$12.00**

It's a Dog's Life Charlie Brown, Holt Rinehart Winston, 1967, NM..**$6.00**

Jetsons in the Birthday Surprise, Tip-Top-Tales #2471, 1964, EX+ **$25.00**

Jungle Book, Giant Classic #11299, 1964, EX....................**$35.00**

King Leonardo & the Royal Contest, Tip-Top-Tales #2472, 1962, EX+..**$32.00**

Lassie Come Home, Eric Knight, 1st edition of reissue, 1978, EX+ **$18.00**

Let's Have a Farm, by Jeffery Victor, Capitol Publishing, landscape scene w/changes w/ea turn of page, 1940s, EX+ **$65.00**

Let's Play, Whitman Tell-a-Tale, 1952, EX **$15.00**

Little Deer, Naomi Zimmerman, Rand McNally, Jr Elf Series, illustrated by Marge Opitz, hardback, 1956, EX+ **$15.00**

Little Lulu & the Magic Paints, Golden Press #10498, 1974, EX **$40.00**

Little Red Bicycle, Whitman Tell-a-Tale, 1953, EX+...........**$10.00**

Little Tiger, Mabel Watts, Rand McNally Jr Elf #8097, 1962, EX+ **$10.00**

Magilla Gorilla & the Super Kite, Wonder Book, #707, 1976, EX+ **$12.00**

Mighty Mouse Dinky Learns To Fly, Wonder Book, #677, 1953, unused, M **$35.00**

Munsters & the Great Camera Caper, Whitman, 1965, VG+ ..**$18.00**

My First Golden Dictionary, Golden Press #10417, A edition, 1963, NM..**$12.00**

My Many Colored Days, Dr Seuss, A Knof, 1996, NM+ **$12.00**

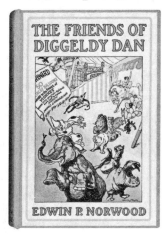

The Friends of Diggeldy Dan, Edwin Norwood, Little Brown, paste-on-pictorial cover, 240 pages, eight color illustrations by A. Conway Peyton, 1922, EX, $45.00. (Photo courtesy Diane McClure Jones and Rosemary Jones)

Gene Autry & the Golden Ladder Gang, 1950, EX............**$18.00**

Nils, **Ingri and Edgar Parin d'Aulaire, Doubleday first edition, oversize picture book, color covers, 1948, $55.00. (Add $10.00 for same-as-cover dust jacket.)** (Photo courtesy Diane McLure Jones and Rosemary Jones)

On a Torn-Away World, #2348, 1930s, EX+ (w/dust jacket) .**$25.00**

Pastoral, Harper & Bros/WDP, hardback, 1940, EX............**$50.00**

Pecos Bill, Wonder Book, #767, 1961, EX.........................**$10.00**

Peter Pan, Wonder Book, #597, EX+ **$14.00**

Peter Rabbit & Reddy Fox, Wonder Book, #611, 1954, NM . **$25.00**

Play It Again Charlie Brown, Charles M Schulz, Times Mirror/ World Publishing, 1st edition, hardback, 1971, EX+ **$5.00**

Puss 'n Boots Pop Ups With Moving Figures, Artia Prague, 1973, EX **$20.00**

Raggedy Ann & Andy & the Camel With the Wrinkled Knees, Johnny Gruelle, Bobbs-Merrill, hardback, 1960, EX+ .. **$15.00**

Raggedy Ann Stories, by Johnny Gruelle, Bobbs-Merrill, 1960, hardback, EX **$12.00**

Rocky & Bullwinkle Off to Hollywood, Whitman Tip-Top Tales, #2494, 1961, EX+ **$32.00**

Rolling Wheels, Wonder Book, #762, 1950, EX+ **$20.00**

Scalawag the Monkey, by Ruth Dixon, Rand McNally, photographs by Rie Gaddis, hardback, 1952, EX **$15.00**

Sgt Preston & Yukon King, MH Comfort, Rand McNally, 1955, NM+ **$10.00**

Shirley Temple's Favorite Poems, Saalfield #1720, 1936, EX+ . **$30.00**

Stories From Fantasia, Random House/WDP, hardback, 1940, EX **$50.00**

Strawberry Shortcake & the Fake Cake Surprise, Little Pop-Up, 1982, NM **$10.00**

Thimble Theatre Starring Popeye, Whitman, hardcover, 1935, VG **$30.00**

Three Little Pigs, Rand McNally, Jr Elf series, illustrated by Ruth Bendel, hardback, 1956, NM **$15.00**

Tinder Box, Stephen Dave Inc, 5 mechanical pages animated by Julian Wehr, c 1945, EX **$85.00**

Tom Sawyer, Whitman, #1603, 1955, NM **$12.00**

Ugly Duckling & Other Stories, Tower Books, NY, 1930, EX+ . **$28.00**

Uncle Wiggly & the Apple Dumpling, by Howard R Gais, Platt & Munk #3600A, illustrated by George Carlson, 1939, EX+ **$18.00**

Who Goes There? Wonder Book, #779, 1961, EX+ **$25.00**

Winnie the Pooh A Tight Squeeze, Big Golden Book, 1974, EX+ **$12.00**

Yip & Yap, by Ruth Dixon, Rand McNally #8690, Tip-Top Elf series, photos by Harry W Frees, hardback, 1958, VG+ **$15.00**

Your Friend the Policeman, Ding Dong School Book, by Miss Frances, Rand McNally, illustrated by William Neebe, 1953, EX+ . **$8.00**

Juvenile Series Books

Peggy Stewart at School, Gabrielle E Jackson, Macmillan, hardcover, 1912, EX in dust jacket **$30.00**

Adventure Girls in the Air, Clair Bank, Burt, hardcover, 1920, in dust jacket, EX **$25.00**

Air Service Boys Over Enemy's Lines, Charles Amory Beach, hardcover, 1st edition, 1918, VG **$17.50**

Alfred Hitchcock & 3 Investigators in Mystery of Green Ghost, Robert Arthur/Harry Kane, hardcover, 1965, EX **$10.00**

Andy Blake's Secret Service, Leo Edwards, Grosset & Dunlap, illustrated by Bert Salg, ca 1928-30, VG **$10.00**

Betsy Hale Succeeds, Mary Pemberton Ginther, Winston, illustrated by author, hardcover, ca 1920s, EX **$35.00**

Blue Birds at Happy Hills, Lillian Elizabeth Roy, Burt, blue pictorial hardcover, ca 1930s, EX in dust jacket **$30.00**

Campfire Girl's Adventure, Jane L Stewart, hardcover, 4th in series, VG w/dust jacket **$15.00**

Campfire Girls on the March, Jane L Stewart, blue hardcover w/girl, G **$12.00**

Cherry Ames at Spencer, Julie Tatham, Grosset & Dunlap, hardcover, 1949, EX w/dust jacket **$22.50**

Cherry Ames Senior Nurse, Helen Wells, Grosset & Dunlap, hardcover, 1944, EX w/dust jacket **$12.50**

Cherry Ames Student Nurse, Helen Wells, hardcover, VG w/dust jacket **$10.00**

Chicken Little Jane, Lily Munsel Ritchie, Britton, hardcover, 1918, EX **$30.00**

Chip Hilton & Championship Ball, Clair Bee, Grosset & Dunlap, hardcover, 1948, EX **$8.00**

Christopher Cool in Department of Danger, Jack Lancer, Grosset & Dunlap, hardcover, 1967, EX in dust jacket **$8.00**

Connie Morgan With the Forest Rangers, James Hendryx, Putnam & Doubleday, 1st edition, hardcover, 1925, EX **$100.00**

Daddy Takes Us Fishing, Howard Garis, Donohue, sm hardcover w/paste-on-pictorial, 1st edition, 1920s, EX **$35.00**

Dangerous Deeds (Aviator Series), Capt Frank Cobb, hardcover, 1927, w/dust jacket, VG+ **$35.00**

Donna Parker in Hollywood, Marcia Martin, Whitman #1576, hardcover, 1961, EX **$5.00**

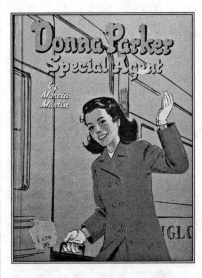

Donna Parker Special Agent, **Marcia Martin, copyright 1957, EX+, $20.00.** (Photo courtesy Harry and Jody Whitworth)

Dorothy at Oak Knowe, Evelyn Raymond, Chatterton-Peck, impressed illustration on hardcover, 1907-13, EX in dust jacket **$20.00**

Eight Cousins, Louisa May Alcott, Grosset & Dunlap, hardcover, 1927, VG in dust jacket **$20.00**

Emma in Love, Honor Arundel, Nelson, 1st American edition, 1970, EX in dust jacket **$25.00**

For the Honor of the School, Ralph Henry Barbour, Appleton, hardcover, 1900, VG **$45.00**

Girl of the Limberlost, Gene Stratton Porter, Grosset & Dunlap, green hardcover, 1949, VG **$10.00**

Girl Scouts at Penguin Pass, Mildred Wirt, Cupples & Leon, hardcover, 1950, EX in dust jacket **$30.00**

Hardy Boys, House on the Cliff, Franklin W Dixon, Applewood Books, hardcover, 1991 printing, VG **$12.00**

Hardy Boys, Secret of the Caves, Franklin W Dixon, Grosset & Dunlap, hardcover, 1954 printing, EX.....................$30.00

Hardy Boys, Tower Treasure, Franklin W Dison, Grosset & Dunlap, glossy picture hardcover, EX $5.00

Heidi Grows Up, Johanna Spyri, Jean Coquillot, Grosset & Dunlap, hardcover, 1938 printing, EX.....................$10.00

Hunniwell Boys' Victory, Levi Wyman, Burt, hardcover, 1929, EX in dust jacket.....................$20.00

Ike & Mama & the Once-a-Year Suit, Carol Snyder, Howard McCann, sm hardcover, 1978, VG $10.00

Joy & Gypsy Joe, Dorothy Whitehill, Grosset & Dunlap, hardcover, ca 1930s, VG $10.00

Judy Bolton & Invisible Chimes, Margaret Sutton, Grosset & Dunlap, hardcover, 1932, EX in dust jacket.....................$17.50

Judy Bolton & the Mystic Ball, Margaret Sutton, Grosset & Dunlap, hardcover, 1934, VG in dust jacket.....................$30.00

Just Jennifer, Janet Lambert, Dutton, 1st edition, 1945, EX in dust jacket $150.00

Kathy Martin Assignment in Alaska, Josephine James, William Plummer illustrations, hardcover, 1961, G.....................$7.50

Kay Tracy & Message in the Sand Dunes, Frances K Judd, Bantam, softcover, 1980, EX.....................$4.50

Kay Tracy & the Double Disguise, Frances K Judd, Garden City, red hardcover, 1952 printing, EX.....................$10.00

Kid From Tomkinville, John R Tunis, Morrow, 1st edition, hardcover, 1940 EX in dust jacket $50.00

Lakewood Boys on the Lazy S, Levi Wyman, Burt, hardcover, 1920s, VG.....................$10.00

Let's Play Fireman, Edith Lowe, Whitman, illustrated by Ruth Newton, sm, 1939, VG.....................$25.00

Linda Craig & Mystery of Horseshoe Canyon, Ann Sheldon, Wanderer, softcover, 1963, EX.....................$6.00

Linda Goes on a Cruise, Nancy Dudley, Coward-McCann, illustrated by Sofia, hardcover, 1958, EX in dust jacket.....................$20.00

Loraine and the Little People of Summer, Elizabeth Gordon, Rand McNally, color illustrated paper-over cover, illustrated by James McCracken (four books in series), 1930s, EX+, $35.00.

Madge Morton's Victory, Amy Chalmers, Altemus, hardcover w/ paste-on-pictorial, ca 1930s, VG.....................$10.00

Maggie Muggins & the Cottontail, Thomas Allen, 1st edition, hardcover, 1960, EX in dust jacket $30.00

Mary Jane in Scotland, Clara Ingram Judson, CL Wren illustrator, green hardcover, 1927 edition, EX.....................$12.50

Meadow-Brook Girls in the Hills, Janet Aldridge, hardcover, 1914, VG w/dust jacket.....................$12.00

Mystery Boys & Captain Kidd's Message, Van Powell, hardcover, 1931, VG.....................$12.50

Mystery Boys & the Inca Gold, A Van Buren Powell, Burt & World, ca 1930, 280+ pages, VG.....................$15.00

New Boys at Oakdale, Morgan Scott, Hurst, hardcover, 1911-13, 300+ pages, VG $30.00

Obadiah the Bold, Brinton Turkle, Dutton, 1st edition, illustrated by author, oblong hardcover, 1970s, EX in dust jacket .$75.00

On the Blockade, Lee & Shepard, blue & gray cloth-over-board cover w/gold, 1890, VG.....................$40.00

Outdoor Girls at Bluff Point, Laura Lee Hope, Grosset & Dunlap, hardcover, 1920, EX $7.50

Patty Lou & White Gold Ranch, Basil Miller, hardcover, 1943, EX in dust jacket $12.00

Penny Parker & Ghost Beyond the Gate, Mildred A Wirt, hardcover, 1943, EX in dust jacket $80.00

Penrod & Sam, Booth Tarkington, Doubleday, illustrated by Worth Brehm, hardcover, 1914, EX in dust jacket.....................$35.00

Renfrew of the Royal Mounted, Laurie Erskine, Appleton, hardcover, 1922-41, VG $15.00

Return of Tarzan, Edgar Rice Burroughs, thick green hardcover, 1915, G $10.00

Rick & Ruddy Out West, Howard Garis, Milton Bradley, tan hardcover, 1920s, VG $15.00

Rick Brant & Pirates of Shan, John Blaine, Grosset & Dunlap, hardcover, EX $20.00

Rover Boys in the Mountains, Arthur M Winfield, Grosset & Dunlap, red hardcover, 1929, EX $10.00

Sue Barton Nurse, Helen Dore Boylston, Little Brown Co, hardcover, 1936, EX in dust jacket $60.00

Sue Barton Rural Nurse, Helen Dore Boylston, softcover, 1967 printing, EX.....................$30.00

Tarzan & the Jewels of Opar, Edgar Rice Burrows, light blue hardcover, 1918, VG $17.50

Ted Jones, Fortune Hunter, Perilous Adventures With a Chinese Pearl Trader, Frank Gee Patchin, Atlemus, hardcover, 1928.....................$15.00

Ted Scott Over the Rockies w/the Air Mail, Franklin W Dixon, Grosset & Dunlap, tan hardcover, 1927, VG.....................$15.00

This Is Espie Sanchez, Terry Dunnahoo, Dutton, hardcover, 1976, VG.....................$10.00

Under the Lilacs, Golden Days Series, Louisa M Alcott, Donahue, hardcover, VG.....................$12.50

Winds of March, Lenora Mattingly Weber, Crowell, 1st edition, hardcover, 1965, VG.....................$50.00

Little Golden Books

Everyone has had a few of these books in their lifetime; some we've read to our own children so many times that we still know them word for word, and today they're appearing in antique malls and shops everywhere. The first were printed in 1942. These are recognizable by their blue paper spines (later ones had gold foil). Until the early 1970s, they were numbered consecutively; after that they were unnumbered.

First editions of the titles having a 25¢ or 29¢ cover price can be identified by either a notation on the first or second pages, or a letter on the bottom right corner of the last page (A for 1, B for 2, etc.). If these are absent, you probably have a first edition.

Condition is extremely important. To qualify as mint, these books must look just as good as they looked the day they were purchased. Naturally, having been used by children, many show signs of wear. If your book is only lightly soiled, the cover has no tears or scrapes, the inside pages have only small creases or folded corners, and the spine is still strong, it will be worth about half as much as one in mint condition. Additional damage would of course lessen the value even more. A missing cover makes it worthless.

A series number containing an 'A' refers to an activity book, while a 'D' number identifies a Disney story.

For more information we recommend *Collecting Little Golden Books* by Steve Santi (who provided us with our narrative material).

Brave Little Tailor, A edition, 1953, EX+ **$15.00**
Chicken Little, #413, A edition, 1960, EX **$8.00**
Colors Are Nice, #207-1, L edition, 1979, EX+ **$3.50**
Doctor Dan the Bandage Man, #111, A edition, 1950, VG ... **$10.00**
Emerald City of Oz, #151, A edition, 1952, EX **$40.00**
Hansel & Gretel, #17, A edition, 1943, EX **$25.00**
Heroes of the Bible, #236, A edition, 1955, EX **$20.00**
Howdy Doody & Clarabell, A edition, 1951, EX+ **$35.00**

Huckleberry Hound Builds a House, **#376, copyright 1959, NM, from $12.00 to $18.00.**

I'm an Indian Today, #425, A edition, 1961, EX+ **$20.00**
Kitten's Surprise, A edition, 1951, EX+ **$15.00**
Lippy the Lion & Hardy Har Har, #508, A edition, 1963, NM **$35.00**
My Little Golden Dictionary, #90, A edition, 1949, NM **$16.00**
Night Before Christmas, L edition, 3rd cover variation w/Santa stepping out of fireplace, 1949, EX+ **$12.00**
Riddles Riddles from A to Z, #490, F edition, 1974, NM **$4.00**
Three Little Kittens, #1, O edition, 1942, VG **$15.00**

Top Cat, #453, A edition, 1962, EX **$35.00**
We Help Daddy, #468, A edition, 1962, NM **$20.00**

Yogi Bear, A Christmas Visit, **#432, A edition, copyright 1961, NM, from $9.00 to $12.00.**

Movie and TV Tie-Ins

Battlestar Galactica, Scholastic Book Services, over 100 photos from movie, softcover, 1978, EX **$5.00**
Beatles Yellow Submarine, Max Wilt & the Beatles, Signet Q3632, paperback, 1968, EX **$12.50**
City on the Edge of Forever, Harlan Ellison, Star Trek tie-in, Bantam Books Paperback Original, 1st edition, 1977, EX **$12.00**
Devil in the Dark, Star Trek Fotonovel 9, Gene Coone, Bantam, First Paperback Edition, photos from TV show, EX **$10.00**
Don McNeil Breakfast Club Yearbook, 1947, EX **$25.00**
Getaway, Jim Thompson, Bantam, paperback, EX **$6.00**
Gone With the Wind Cook Book, Scarlett at Tara in scene from picture on cover, Pebeco Tooth Past promo, ca 1940, EX **$90.00**
Journey to Beloved, Oprah Winfrey, hardback w/black & white photos from movie, 1998, NM **$25.00**

Land of the Lost, Dinosaur Adventure, **Whitman, 1975, EX, from $15.00 to $20.00.**

Leave It to Beaver, Beverly Cleary, Berkley, 1st paperback edition, NM **$20.00**
Little Minister, Five Star Library & RKO-Radio Pictures, Katharine Hepburn on cover, 1935, EX **$25.00**
Love Story, Erich Segal, paperback, Ryan O'Neal & Ali McGraw on cover, 1971, EX **$6.00**

Mystery in Dracula's Castle, Scolastic, paperback, Johnny Whitaker on cover, 1973, EX $4.00

Nanny, Evelyn Piper, paperback, Bette Davis & William Dix on cover, 1965, EX $8.00

One Flew Over the Cuckoo's Nest, Ken Kesey, Signet Paperback edition, Jack Nicholson on cover, G $5.00

Robin & the 7 Hoods, Jack Pearl, paperback w/Frank Sinatra, Sammy Davis Jr & Dean Martin on cover, EX $7.50

Star Wars Episode I, The Phantom Menace Movie Storybook, Random House, 1999, NM $8.00

Star Wars Return of the Jedi Read-Along Book, w/33⅓ rpm record, Buena Vista Records, 1983, NM $15.00

Subterraneans, Jack Kerouac, paperback, Avon T-390, EX e-in, EX $15.00

True Grit, Charles Portis, Signet, John Wayne on front cover, EX $8.00

The Mod Squad, **Pyramid Books, #1 – #5, 1968 – 1970, EX, from $8.00 to $10.00 each.** (Photo courtesy Greg Davis and Bill Morgan)

Boru, Sorcha

This studio was one of many that operated in California during the middle of the twentieth century. Sorcha Boru Ceramics produced colorful slip-decorated figurines, salt and pepper shakers, vases, wall pockets, and flower bowls in San Carlos, from 1938 until 1955. Most items carry a hand-incised cypher, 'S.B.C.'

Salt and pepper shakers, bride and groom, from $85.00 to $100.00 for the pair. (Photocourtesy Helene Guarnaccia)

Cookie jar/canister, cable car, people on ea corner, 3x5x2¼" .. $35.00
Cup, 3 dinosaur handles $75.00
Figurine, baby sitting on blanket w/seashell held to ear, 5" .. $50.00
Salt & pepper shakers, bears, med blue, standing: 2¾", sitting: 2¼". $35.00
Salt & pepper shakers, King & Queen, pr from $95 to $130.00
Salt & pepper shakers, lamb, 1940s, 2¼", 2½", pr.............. $15.00
Salt & pepper shakers, monkeys, seated, stylized, pr $50.00
Salt & pepper shakers, pig (1 pink, 1 white), pr.................. $85.00
Sugar shaker, lady figure, 6" $110.00
Vase, dancing girls, 5½" $48.00

Bottle Openers

A figural bottle opener is one where the cap lifter is an actual feature of the subject being portrayed — for instance, the bill of a pelican or the mouth of a four-eyed man. Most are made of painted cast iron or aluminum; others were chrome or brass plated. Some of the major bottle-opener producers were Wilton, John Wright, L&L, and Gadzik. They have been reproduced, so beware of any examples with 'new' paint. Condition of the paint is an important consideration when it comes to evaluating a vintage opener.

For more information, read *Figural Bottle Openers, Identification Guide,* by the Figural Bottle Opener Collectors. Several of the examples we list sold recently at a major auction in the east; though they are seldom seen outside mature collections, we've included some of them along with the more common ones.

Advisor: Charlie Reynolds (See Directory, Bottle Openers)

Club: Figural Bottle Opener Collectors
Mary Link
1774 N 675 E., Kewanna, IN 46949; 219-946-4614
marylind@pwrtc.com

Newsletter: Just for Openers
John Stanley, Editor
P.O. Box 64, Chapel Hill, NC 27514
www.just-for-openers.org

Elephant, painted cast iron, marked WHR, 3¾", EX, from $40.00 to $50.00.

Alligator, F-136, painted cast iron, 6", VG $70.00
Alligator w/head up, painted cast iron, John Wright, 2½x5⅛", EX $250.00

Amish boy, F-31, painted cast iron, 4x2", VG $80.00

Bear, cast iron, wall mount, 3½x3", VG $15.00

Bear head, painted cast iron, wall mount, John Wright, 3¾x3⅛", EX $195.00

Billy goat, painted cast iron, John Wright, 2¾x2¾", EX $85.00

Black caddy, painted nickel plate, 1950s, 5¾x1⅞", VG...... $840.00

Black girl w/grass skirt clinging to signpost, painted cast iron, 4⅞x1½", VG $615.00

Boy winking (head only), painted cast iron, wall mount, Wilton Prod, very rare, 3¾x3⅝", VG $2,000.00

Bulldog, painted cast iron, Wilton, #4, 4⅛x3¾", EX $300.00

Canada goose, painted cast iron, head down, Wilton Products, 1¾x3⅝", VG $140.00

Cathy Coed, painted cast iron, standing w/books, signed Gadzik Phil, EX $500.00

Clown, painted cast iron, wall mount, Wilton, 4x4", VG $85.00

Cockatoo, painted cast iron, John Wright, 3¼x2⅞", EX $225.00

Cowboy drunk by cactus, painted cast iron, John Wright, Woodstock NY on front of base, 3¾x2⅝", EX $165.00

Cowboy in chaps, painted cast iron, Wilton Products, 4½x2¾", NM.. $450.00

Cowboy w/guitar, painted cast iron, John Wright, 4¾x3⅛", EX+ $165.00

Cowboy w/guitar, painted cast iron, unmarked, 4¾x3¼", G.. $55.00

Cowgirl w/lasso, painted cast iron, 4¾x3", EX.................... $30.00

Dolphin, cast iron w/sea blue enamel finish, 6½x3", VG $20.00

Duck, painted wood, 4½", EX $32.00

Duck's head, metal w/pewter-type finish, marked Ducky, Kirby Beard & Co, Paris, 1920, 4¾x2¼", NM $185.00

Elephant, painted cast iron, flat figural, 3x2½", VG............. $55.00

Elephant, painted cast iron, walking, Wilton, 2½x3¼", EX .$35.00

Fish, mother-of-pearl, jointed, Mexican, 5¾", NM........... $100.00

Fish w/tail up, painted cast iron, John Wright, 2⁵⁄₁₆x4⅝", EX..... $170.00

Flamingo, painted cast iron, EX....................................... $22.00

Foundry man, painted cast iron, John Wright, 3½x8⅝", EX .. $140.00

Freddy Frosh, painted cast iron, L&L Fabors, 4x2", EX..... $400.00

Gentleman clinging to signpost in high wind, painted cast iron, souvenir of Mackinaw City $40.00

Gray squirrel, painted cast iron, John Wright, 2x2⅞", EX.. $225.00

Handy Hans, painted cast iron, L&L Fabors, 2⅞x2⅜", NM .. $390.00

Karate Man, F-250, cast iron, NM, $95.00. (Photo courtesy Charlie Reynolds)

Key, brass, made in India, 5½" $16.00

Lobster, metal, 4⁵⁄₁₆x2⅛" $15.00

Man sitting on barrel, painted wood, w/corkscrew, 5½", VG... $20.00

Mermaid w/arms up, solid brass, Thailand, 5⅜x1⅞", EX..... $25.00

Monkey, painted cast iron, brown, John Wright, 2⅝x2¹¹⁄₁₆", NM. **$500.00**

Monkey, painted cast iron, John Wright, G **$120.00**

Moose, painted cast iron, wall mount, 4½x3½" **$50.00**

Neck tie, silver-plated w/diagonal stripes, pry-off & screw top features, Princess House, 6¾x1¾" **$55.00**

Paddy the Pledgemaster, painted cast iron, Gaedzik Phila, 3⅞x2¼", G **$250.00**

Palm tree, painted cast iron, Wilton Products, 4⁹⁄₁₆x2⅝", EX. **$500.00**

Parrot, painted cast iron, on perch, John Wright, 5x3", NM .. **$85.00**

Parrot, painted cast iron, 3½" **$50.00**

Pelican, painted cast iron, Wilton Products, 3⅜x3¾", VG. **$390.00**

Pheasant, painted cast iron, John Wright, 2¼x3⅞", EX **$335.00**

Pixie (Lincoln Imp) on mushroom, cast brass, Great Britain, 5".. **$30.00**

Sammy Samoa, painted cast iron, L&L Favors, 4⁵⁄₁₆x2", VG .. **$400.00**

Saw fish, painted cast iron, Wilton Products, 2¹⁄₁₆x5¾", EX.... **$670.00**

Schlitz beer bottle, wood, 1940s, 4½" **$25.00**

Sea gull, painted cast iron, John Wright, 3¼x2¾", EX....... **$195.00**

Sea gull, painted cast iron, unmarked, 3x2¼", EX **$35.00**

Sea horse, painted cast iron, John Wright, 4¼x2¼", NM... **$195.00**

Springer spaniel, painted enamel over metal, Scott Products Inc, 3½x6", EX **$63.00**

Squirrel, cast metal w/bronze finish, 2x2¾", NM................ **$50.00**

Toucan, painted cast iron, facing left, John Wright, 3⅜x2⅞", NM **$140.00**

Trout, painted cast iron, Wilton Products, 1⅝x4⅞", NM ..**$280.00**

Boyd's Crystal Art Glass

After the Degenhart glass studio closed (see the Degenhart section for information), it was bought out by the Boyd family, who added many of their own designs to the molds the acquired from the Degenharts, and other defunct glasshouses. They are located in Cambridge, Ohio, and the glass they've been pressing in more than 350 colors they've developed since they opened in 1978 and is marked with their 'B in diamond' logo. All the work is done by hand, and each piece is made in a selected color in limited amounts — a production run lasts only about 12 weeks or less. Items in satin glass or an exceptional slag are especially collectible, so are those with hand-painted details, commanding as much as 30% more.

Beware: Boyd's has recently reissued some of the closed issues, confusing the pricing structure as well as collectors.

Boyd Taxi, Royal Plum Carnival, 1995, 3¼" long, $20.00.

Airplane, Aqua Diamond **$25.00**

Bunny Salt, Columbia Green **$18.00**

Bunny Salt, Spring Surprise, #98, 1997 .... **$18.00**

Chick Salt, Cornsilk, #46, 1983.. **$28.00**

Chick Salt, Dawn, 1980...**$135.00**
Chick Salt, Ebony, #57, 1984, from $25 to **$30.00**
Chick Salt, Heatherbloom, #60, 1984 ....**$24.00**
Chick Salt, Molasses, #50, 1983 ....**$28.00**
Chick Salt, Peanut Butter, #30, 1980 ....**$30.00**
Chick Salt, Peridot, #61, 1984 ....**$22.50**
Chick Salt, Persimmon, #13, 1980 ....**$30.00**
Chick Salt, Pink Champagne, #11, 1979 ....**$30.00**
Daisy & Button Top Hat, Autumn Splendor **$20.00**
Gypsy Pot, Cobalt Blue..**$16.00**
Heart Jewel Box, Blue Valor **$20.00**
Hen on Nest Covered Dish, Heather, #10, 1980, 5"............**$30.00**
Hen on Nest Covered Dish, Platinum Carnival, #56, 1984, 5"...**$30.00**
JB Scottie Dog, Budding Pink #27 ....**$115.00**
JB Scottie Dog, Crystal, #11, 1984 ....**$130.00**
JB Scottie Dog, Olympic White, #9, 1984 ....**$38.00**
JB Scottie Dog, Royal Plum Carnival.................................**$70.00**
Jeremy Frog, Vaseline Carnival, 1978................................**$24.00**
Joey Horse, Alice Blue, #82, 1983.....................................**$40.00**
Joey Horse, Chocolate Slag, 1980 ....**$36.00**
Joey Horse, Crown Tuscan Carnival, #71, 1990.................**$40.00**
Joey Horse, English Yew, 1983...**$44.00**
Joey Horse, Flame, 1980 ....**$20.00**
Joey Horse, Fur Green, #13, 1981 ....**$24.00**
Joey Horse, Olde Ivory Slag, #11, 1981 ....**$35.00**
Joey Horse, Olympic White Carnival, 1984........................**$48.00**
Joey Horse, Purple Amethyst, #6, 1980 ....**$24.00**
Joey Horse, Violet Slate, #30, 1984...................................**$40.00**
Joey Horse, Willow Blue, #82, 1980...................................**$24.00**
Joey Horse, Zack Boyd Slag, #7, 1980 ....**$30.00**
Kitten on Pillow, Firefly, #38, 1980 ....**$30.00**
Leaf Flower Candy Dish, Chocolate, #9, 1980 ....**$32.00**
Olivia Colonial Doll, Amberina Slag, 1964..........................**$25.00**
Owl, Bermuda (dark opaque red), signed Bernard F Boyd...**$15.00**
Owl, Candy Swirl, #23, 1980 ....**$15.00**
Owl, Fur Green, 1980s **$12.00**
Pooche, Blackberry Slag, #154 ....**$13.00**
Pooche, Cobalt Blue Swirl, #162..**$14.00**
Pooche, Toffee Slag, #127 ....**$13.50**
Pooche, Tomato Creame, #1, 1978....................................**$30.00**

Bunny Salt, Blue Flame, 2003, 2x2½", $18.00.

Boyds Bears and Friends

The Bearstone Collection figures were originally designed by Gary M. Lowenthal in 1993. Soon to follow in 1994, the Folkstone collection was introduced. Over the years, many lines have been added, inclucding Dollstones, Purrstones, Faeries, Angels, Treasure Boxes, and porcelain dolls. Many collectors pursue with diligence many of the older pieces, which were produced in smaller editions.

Counterfeits do exist. All original pieces will have a bear paw (Bearstones), a star (Folkstones), or shoe (Dollstones) imprinted somewhere on the piece. Also, each piece is hand numbered with the edition number on the bottom — example: 1E/3103. Boxes for first and second editions are marked with a *red* dot (first edition) or *blue* dot (second edition). This way collectors know which edition they are purchasing without having to open the box.

First editions are the most collected, but there are cases when a second or third edition may be more valuable due to a smaller edition size. Some limited editions or special editions will also have the month of issue instead of a numbered edition.

For further information we recommend the Boyds value guide by Bangzoom, currently available with 2004 values.

Advisor: Christine Cregar (See Directory Boyds Bears)

Bearstone, Norman Doinuttin', Sorry Girls, 1-E #3848, retired, $34.00.

Bearstone, Abby T Bearymuch...Yours Truly, #22742, 2001, 4¾", MIB...**$20.00**
Bearstone, Amy & Mark...The Perfect Match, #2277926, to be retired, 2004, 4¼", MIB...**$18.00**
Bearstone, Bubbles Bearsall...It's Good To Be Retired, #2277929, to be retired, 2004, 4", MIB.........................**$25.00**
Bearstone, Doug & Jill...A Day To Remember, #2277930, to be retired, 4¾"...**$25.00**
Bearstone, Flash McBear & the Sitting, #227721, 1999, 4½", MIB **$37.00**
Bearstone, Gypsy Rose...Surprise!, #228332, 2000, 5¼", MIB.**$32.00**
Bearstone, Justina...the Message Bearer, #2273, 1996, 3", MIB...**$18.00**
Bearstone, Martha Bloomengrow...Thime To Garden, #227748, 2001, 4¼", MIB...**$38.00**
Bearstone, Nick & Rudy...Hide & Seek, #228445PAW, 2004, 3¼", MIB...**$20.00**
Bearstone, Stonewall...the Rebel, #228302, 1997, MIB.......**$68.00**
Bearstone, Wilson...the Perfesser, #2222, 1994, MIB...........**$92.00**
Dollstone, Alyssa...Secret Garden, #3582, 1993, MIB **$22.00**
Dollstone, Cheryl w/Ashley...Nighty Night, #3544, 1999, 3¼", MIB **$25.00**

Dollstone, Jessica & Timmy...Animal Hospital, #3532, MIB, (January, $76; February, $55), all others **$40.00**

Dollstone, Maggie...Grandmom's Helper, #3578, 2002, 5¼", MIB **$26.00**

Dollstone, Rebecca w/Elliot...Birthday, #3509, 1996, MIB . **$40.00**

Dollstone, Shelby...Asleep in Teddy's Arms, #3527, 1998, MIB.. **$28.00**

Folkstone, Edna B Sungoddess...Life's a Beach, #28255, 2002, 6½", MIB **$22.00**

Folkstone, Laverne B Bowler...Strikes & Spares, #28248, 1999, 7", MIB **$26.00**

Folkstone, Ludwig Puffenhuff...Ornament Maker, #28005, 2000, 6½", MIB **$35.00**

Folkstone, Salem...Give Thanks, #2867, 1999, 7¼", MIB ... **$31.00**

Purrstone, Kandace Purrshop...Hidden Surprises, #371054, 2000, 4", MIB **$25.00**

Purrstone, Sabrina & Boo...Purrfect Treats, #81010, 2000, MIB. **$31.00**

Purrstone, Mario Fenderbender...1 Down, 8 To Go, #371009, 2000, 4¾", MIB **$23.00**

Shoe Box Bear, Alvin Elfbeary, #3245, 2003, 4", MIB........ **$15.00**

Shoe Box Bear, Cinderellie, #3240, 2003, 4¼", MIB.......... **$17.00**

Shoe Box Bear, Flutterby Bear, posable, #3255, 2005, 4¼", MIB.. **$16.00**

Shoe Box Bear, Nicholas 'Uncle Nick' Grizberg, #3205, 1997, MIB **$39.00**

Shoe Box Bear, Scarecrow, #3259, 2005, MIB **$15.00**

Shoe Box Bear, Zinnia Goodwish...Feel Better Soon, #3235, 2002, 4¼", MIB **$17.00**

Wee Folkstone, Dentinata Fairiefloss..the Tooth Faerie, #36102, 1997, MIB.. **$35.00**

Wee Folkstone, Flossie Faerie Floss, The Tooth Faerie, 1-E #361201, $28.00.

Wee Folkstone, Ms Picklesencream...Heaven's Lil' Blessing, #36202, 1999, 4¼", MIB **$25.00**

Wee Folkstone, Sudsie Faeriesock...Mischief Maker, #36306, 2000, 3¾", MIB **$26.00**

Wee Follkstone, Felicity Angelbliss...the Bride's Angel, #36103, 1999, 4", MIB **$29.00**

Brastoff, Sascha

Who could have predicted when Sascha Brastoff joined the Army's Air Force in 1942 that he was to become a well-known artist!

It was during his service with the Air Force that he became interested in costume and scenery design, performing, creating Christmas displays and murals, and drawing war bond posters.

After Sascha's stint in the Armed Forces, he decided to follow his dream of producing ceramics and in 1947 opened a small operation in West Los Angeles, California. Just six years later, along with Nelson Rockefeller and several other businessmen with extensive knowledge of mass production techniques, he built a pottery on Olympic Boulevard in Los Angeles.

Brastoff designed all the products while supervising approximately 150 people. His talents were so great they enabled him to move with ease from one decade to another and successfully change motifs, mediums, and designs as warranted. Unusual and varying materials were used over the years. He created a Western line that was popular in the 1940s and early 1950s. Just before the poodle craze hit the nation in the 1950s, he had the forsight to introduce his poodle line. The same was true for smoking accessories, and he designed elegant, hand-painted dinnerware as well. He was not modest when it came to his creations. He knew he was talented and was willing to try any new endeavor which was usually a huge success.

Items with the Sascha Brastoff full signature are always popular, and generally they command the highest prices. He modeled obelisks; one with a lid and a full signature would be regarded as a highly desirable example of his work. Though values for his dinnerware are generally lower than for his other productions, it has its own following. The Merbaby design is always high on collectors' lists.

The 1940 Clay Club pieces were signed either with a full signature or 'Sascha.' In 1947 Sascha hired a large group of artists to hand decorate his designs, and 'Sascha B' became the standard mark. Following the opening of his studio in 1953, a chanticleer, the name Sascha Brastoff, the copyright symbol, and a hand-written style number (all in gold) were used on the bottom, with 'Sascha B.' on the front or topside of the item. (Be careful not to confuse this mark with a full signature, California, U.S.A.). Costume designs at 20th Century Fox (1946 – 1947) were signed 'Sascha'; war bonds and posters also carried the signature 'Sascha' and 'Pvt.' or 'Sgt. Brastoff.'

After Brastoff left his company in 1962, the mark became an 'R' in a circle (registered trademark symbol) with a style number, all handwritten. The chanticleer may also accompany this mark. Brastoff died on February 4, 1993. For additional information consult *Collector's Encyclopedia of California Pottery, Second Edition,* and *California Pottery Scrapbook* by Jack Chipman. Both are available from Collector Books.

Advisor: Lonnie Wells (See Directory, Sascha Brastoff)

Ahtray, Rooftops, #D3, 5¾x5¾" **$40.00**

Ashtray, Puddle Dog, hooded, #H6, 7x6" dia **$35.00**

Ashtray, Star Steed on blue, #03B, 8x8" **$55.00**

Bowl, Sungay, #S-52, 5x6x12" **$50.00**

Bowl, Winrock, white w/platinum band, 6" **$30.00**

Box, flowers, #021, 2x5x8" **$65.00**

Candleholder, blue-green resin w/diamond-shaped designs, 6x4x4", ea **$65.00**

Charger, mermaid, fluted edge, 1¼x15"............................... **$75.00**

Creamer & sugar bowl, Roman Coin, 1950s **$55.00**

Figurine, bird, orange resin, squat, 6" **$225.00**

Figurine, cat, green resin, 10".............................$425.00
Figurine, foo dog, black w/gold, 8x16" $465.00
Figurine, octopus, gr resin, 9" $350.00
Figurine, owl, green resin, 14" $495.00
Figurine, owl, orange resin, 7½" $150.00
Figurine, pelican, amber resin, 10".......................$425.00
Figurine, pelican, green resin, 10½" $425.00
Figurine, seal, blue resin, 4x9" $375.00
Figurine, seal, green resin, 10½" $120.00
Mug, mosaic band in pastels on brown pottery, 4" $60.00
Necklace, leaping fish, 2x4", on 24" chain.................$175.00
Pendant, Butterfly Girl, gold, 5".........................$85.00
Plate, Deco figure w/4 'moons' above, enameled copper, 7¾". $225.00
Plate, fish shape, green, yellow & black, 10½x10¾"..........$110.00
Plate, Winrock, white w/platinum rim, 11" $30.00
Teapot, Roman Coin on dove gray, 1950s, 5¾x6½" $55.00
Tile, circus tent, mc on blk, 9x7".........................$265.00
Tray, nude on gray w/darker border, 5⅝x5⅝"................$40.00
Vase, blue resin w/embossed grapes, 7⅝" $35.00
Vase, cylindrical, gold, notched rim, ca 1960, 13¼" $125.00
Wall mask, man w/4 horned headpiece, 12¾" $190.00

Dish, Hawaiian boy with guitar, 10", $85.00. (Photo courtesy Steve Conti, A. Dewayne Bethany, and Bill Seay)

Brayton Laguna

This company's products have proven to be highly collectible for those who appreciate their well-made, diversified items, some bordering on the whimsical. Durlin Brayton founded Brayton Laguna Pottery in 1927. The marriage between Durlin and Ellen (Webb) Webster Grieve a few years later created a partnership that brought together two talented people with vision and knowledge so broad that they were able to create many unique lines. At the height of Brayton's business success, the company employed over 125 workers and 20 designers.

Durlin's personally created items command a high price. Such items are hand-turned, and those that were made from 1927 to 1930 are often incised 'Laguna Pottery' in Durlin's handwriting. These include cups, saucers, plates of assorted sizes, ashtrays, etc., glazed in eggplant, lettuce green, purple, and deep blue as well as other colors. Brayton Laguna's children's series (created by Lietta J. Dodd) has always

been favored among collectors. However, many lines such as Calasia (artware), Blackamoors, sculpture, and the Hillbilly line are picking up large followings of their own. The sculptures, Indian and Peruvian pieces including voodoo figures, matadors, and drummers, among others, were designed by Carol Safholm. Andy Anderson created the Hillbilly series, most notably the highly successful shotgun wedding group. He also created the calf, bull, and cow set, which is virtually always found in the purple glaze, though very rarely other colors have been reported as well. Webton Ware is a good line for those who want inexpensive pottery and a Brayton Laguna mark. These pieces depict farmland and country-type themes such as farmers planting, women cooking, etc. Some items — wall pockets, for instance — may be found with only a flower motif; wall hangings of women and men are popular, yet hard to find in this or any of Brayton's lines. Predominantly, the background of Webton Ware is white, and it's decorated with various pastel glazes including yellow, green, pink, and blue.

More than 10 marks plus a paper label were used during Brayton's history. On items too small for a full mark, designers would simply incise their initials. Webb Brayton died in 1948, and Durlin died just three years later. Struggling with and finally succumbing to the effect of the influx of foreign pottery on the American market, Brayton Laguna finally closed in 1968.

For further study, read *Collector's Encyclopedia of California Pottery, Second Edition,* and *California Pottery Scrapbook* by Jack Chipman (Collector Books).

See also Cookie Jars.

Advisor: Lee Garmon (See Directory, Elvis Presley Memorabilia)

Figurine, lady from Gay 90s line, titled 'Bob's First Lady,' Bringhurst design, $125.00. (Photo courtesy Jack Chipman)

Bank, Mammy in white w/blue trim, slot in back, 6¾" $20.00
Dish, turquoise interior w/brushed brown exterior, oval, marked 41-25, 1¾x13¾x9¼"..$20.00
Figurine, Anna, seated child, 4", from $115 to $130.00
Figurine, Blackamoor in green w/gold bowl, 8¼" $70.00
Figurine, borzoi, blue, 9½x14".................................$70.00
Figurine, corset, ca 1938-42, 4½" $35.00
Figurine, Dorothy, seated child, 4".............................$145.00

FIgurine, fairy princess baby, 3½x2½", from $75 to............**$85.00**
Figurine, Gay Nineties men (3) singing at bar, 8½x7½".......**$95.00**
Figurine, horse pulling carrige w/loving couple, tired driver, 11x8x4"...**$225.00**
Figurine, lady w/basket in right hand, left hand on hip, 8½", from $35 to...**$45.00**
Figurine, lady w/dog at ea side, dated 1943, 10½", from $55 to **$65.00**
Figurine, maestro at piano, 4" w/6x6½" piano, from $90 to...**$150.00**
Figurine, peasant lady w/2 baskets, 7¾", from $85 to........**$100.00**
Figurine, pheasant, shaded brown, 8¼x9¾"........................**$45.00**
Figurine, pheasant, stylized, marked 41-47, 17"..................**$65.00**
Figurine, Pluto sniffing, 3⅜x6x 3½", from $80 to **$90.00**
Figurine, swan preening, bright aqua w/yellow feet & bill, dated 1939, 3½x7", from $70 to..**$85.00**
Figurines, Black sailors playing dice, complete w/dice, ca 1940s.. **$220.00**
Figurines, Orientals, blue/green w/brown hands & face, 15 1 /2", pr from $90 to **$125.00**
Figurines, Peruvian dancing couple, 9½" male, 8½" female..**$175.00**
Planter, Blackamoor, in pink & yellow w/much gold, beside white cornucopia vase, 10"..**$85.00**
Planter, bunny in blue jacket & yellow open sack on back, 8½".**$30.00**
Planter, bunny in pink dress w/vase opening in front, 6".....**$30.00**
Planter, green, 3-tiered, 6¾", 4⅝" & 3" tiers, 9".................**$45.00**
Planter, lady w/wolfhounds, blue dress, white dogs, 10½"...**$90.00**
Planter, Matilda, lady in wine & yellow w/2 planter baskets, 7⅝"..**$75.00**
Planter, Sally, marked Sally #8, 7", from $25 to..................**$30.00**
Salt & pepper shakers, Mammy & Chef, 5¾", pr...............**$45.00**

Vases, early, handmade by Durlin Brayton with incised marks: flowerpot, $150.00; vase, 5½", minimum value, $250.00; bud vase with entwined snake, 8", minimum value, $350.00. **(Photo courtesy Jack Chipman)**

Breweriana

Breweriana refers to items produced by breweries which are intended for immediate use and discard, such as beer cans and bottles, as well as countless items designed for long-term use while promoting a particular brand. Desirable collectibles include metal, cardboard, and neon signs; serving trays; glassware; tap handles; mirrors; coasters; and other paper goods.

Breweriana is generally divided into two broad categories: pre- and postprohibition. Preprohibition breweries were numerous and distributed advertising trays, calendars, etched glassware, and other items. Because American breweries were founded by European brewmasters, preprohibition advertising often depicted themes from that region. Brewery scenes, pretty women, and children were also common.

Competition was intense among the breweries that survived prohibition. The introduction of canned beer in 1935, the postwar technology boom, and the advent of television in the late 1940s produced countless new ways to advertise beer. Moving signs, can openers, enameled glasses, and neon are prolific examples of post-prohibition breweriana.

A better understanding of the development of the product as well as advertising practices of companies helps in evaluating the variety of breweriana items that may be found. For example, 'chalks' are figural advertising pieces which were made for display in taverns or wherever beer was sold. Popular in the 1940s and 1950s, they were painted and glazed to resemble carnival prizes. Breweries realized in addition to food shopping, women generally assumed the role of cook — what better way to persuade women to buy a particular beer than a cookbook? Before the advent of the bottle cap in the early 1900s, beer bottles were sealed with a porcelain stopper or cork. Opening a corked bottle required a corkscrew which often had a brewery logo.

Prior to the advent of refrigeration, beer was often served at room temperature. A mug or glass was often half warm beer and half foam. A 1" by 8" flat piece of plastic was used to scrape foam from the glass. These foam scrapers came in various colors and bore the logo of the beer on tap.

Before prohibition, beer logos were applied to glassware by etching the glass with acid. These etched glasses often had ornate designs that included a replica of the actual brewery or a bust of the brewery's founder. After prohibition, enameling became popular and glasses were generally 'painted' with less ornate designs. Mugs featuring beer advertising date back to the 1800s in America; preprohibition versions were generally made of pottery or glass. Ceramic mugs became popular after prohibition and remain widely produced today.

Tap handles are a prominent way to advertise a particular brand wherever tap beer is sold. Unlike today's ornate handles, 'ball knobs' were prominent prior to the 1960s. They were about the size of a billiard ball with a flat face that featured a colorful beer logo.

Unless noted otherwise, values are for items in excellent condition. See also Barware.

Club: Beer Can Collectors of America
747 Merus Ct., Fenton, MO 63026
Annual dues: $27; although the club's roots are in beer can collecting, this organization offers a bimonthly breweriana magazine featuring many regional events and sponsors an annual convention; www.bcca.com.

Ashtray, Hamm's Beer & Hamm's Bear in blue on milk glass, triangular, 4½"...**$265.00**
Bag, Falstaff Beer, red plaid insulated vinyl, 12x11x7", NM...**$20.00**
Beer bottle, Excelsior Lager Bier (sic), Valentine Blatz Bottling... embossed on clear glass, original closure, 9¼"..............**$55.00**
Beer bottle, F Anthoni & Sons Delaware Ohio embossed on dark amber w/seed bubbles, 12"..**$55.00**

Beer bottle, Falstaff embossed on green glass, Lemp, St Louis MO **$17.50**

Beer bottle, Great Falls Beer, Great Falls MT, paper label w/1941 punched code on amber glass, ½-gal **$75.00**

Beer bottle, MC Beer, Mound City Brewing Co, New Athens IL, paper label (VG) on amber glass, 1950s.......................**$50.00**

Beer bottle, Oldbru Beer label, top label: Keep 'Em Flying Buy US War Bonds & Stamps on amber glass, unopened, 1939..**$65.00**

Beer bottle, Red Fox Ale label on amber glass, Largay Brewing Co, Waterbury CT, unopened, 1950s, 7" **$55.00**

Beer bottle, Schroeder's BWB Co, St Louis MO, dark green, blob top, 9½"...**$60.00**

Beer bottle, Storz Triumph Beer label on amber glass, Storz Brewing Co, Omaha NE, 1936, 64-oz, 14" **$42.50**

Beer bottle, Zoller's Draught Beer label on amber glass, Zoller Brewing Co, Davenport IA, 64-oz, 14" **$50.00**

Beer can, Big Cat Malt Liquor, cat leaping, flat top (bottom opened), Pabst Brewing, Los Angeles CA **$45.00**

Beer can, Burger Bohemian Beer, Burger Brewing Co, Cincinnati OH, cone top **$175.00**

Beer can, Drewry's Extra Dry, Mountie & blue shield on white, flat top, Drewry's Ltd, South Bend IN, ½-qt, VG.............**$32.50**

Beer can, Famous Dallas Malt Liquor, Walter Brewing Co, Pueblo CO, flat top **$90.00**

Beer can, Fort Pitt Specialty Beer, cone top, plain gold cap, Pittsburgh PA...**$75.00**

Beer can, Grand Prize Beer, red, white & gold, Golf Brewing, Houston TX, flat top, VG **$50.00**

Beer can, Meister Brau Fiesta Series, flat top, Peter Hand Brewing Co, Chicago IL, 1955, VG **$80.00**

Beer can, Neuweiler's Pilsener Beer, crowntainer, LFN Sons, Allentown PA, Internal Revenue Tax Paid, 1946, NM..**$38.00**

Beer can, Old Export, cone top, Cumberland Brewing Co, Cumberland MD...**$60.00**

Beer can, Pabst Blue Ribbon Beer, red, white & blue, flat top, stamped S41477 on bottom....................................**$50.00**

Beer can, Ruppert Beer, flat top (opened from bottom), New York NY, NM **$40.00**

Beer can, Schmidt Beer, snowmobilers, flat top, NM..........**$35.00**

Beer glass, GB, Good Beer Griesedieck Bros Beer, red pyro on clear glass, gold rim, 3¼" **$45.00**

Beer glass, Iroquois Beer & buffalo etched on clear glass, 3½". **$45.00**

Beer glass, Jack Daniels Amber Lager & factory, multicolor enameling on clear glass, 3¼" **$55.00**

Beer glass, Lone Star Brewing, San Antonio Texas etched on clear, faded gold rim, 3½x2⅜" **$155.00**

Beer glass, Olympia Beer, It's the Water, Olympia Brewing Co... Washington etched on clear, 3½x2⅜" **$110.00**

Beer glass, Pabst Blue Ribbon etched on clear glass, Pabst Brewing Co, Milwaukee WI, 3½" **$65.00**

Beer glass, Schlitz & world trademark etched on clear, Schlitz Brewing, Milwaukee WI, 3½"...................................**$55.00**

Belt buckle, Lone Star Beer embossed on brass, opener on back, c 1975 Bergamot Brass Works, 2¾x3¾" **$55.00**

Belt buckle, Schlitz in relief on solid brass............................**$35.00**

Bottle stopper, man lifts stein & opens mouth, lever on his back, carved & painted wood, Anri, 5" **$20.00**

Coaster, Remove the Shadow, Buy Victory Bonds, soldier/Nazi, Blue Top Brewing Co, Kitchener Ontario, 4¼" **$57.50**

Cooler, Budweiser, red & white steel w/styrene insulation, plastic liner, 1950s, 11x17x12", MIB **$170.00**

Display figure, Labatt's Pilsener Beer, vinyl, 1960s, 10", NM, $100.00. (Photo courtesy gasolinealleyantiques.com)

Mug, Grain Belt Beer on clear glass w/gold-flashed top, 4⅜x3½". **$125.00**

Opener, Compliments of Maier Brewing Co, Drink Select Beer, Pat Feb 19, 1901, light rust, 3x1" **$37.50**

Opener, S-K Lager Beer, enamel on metal, 2½" L (when closed), EX **$50.00**

Opener, Schlitz in cursive enclosed in rectangle, solid brass, 5¼x2½" **$35.00**

Opener, Yoerg's Beer, Cave Aged, Vaughan Chicago, 3½x1½" .. **$55.00**

Pitcher, Falstaff Beer, red pyro on clear glass, 8¼" **$20.00**

Sign, Budweiser, beveled-edge stamped tin on cardboard, easel back and hanging chain, 12x14", $250.00. (Courtesy Buffalo Bay Auction Co.)

Sign, Guinness Extra Stout, Brewers Since 1759, leaded & beveled glass, ca 1950s, 18x16" **$165.00**

Sign, Hanley Beer & Ale Tastes Like a Million!, girl in bikini, cardboard w/easel back, 17x13" **$185.00**

Sign, Miller High Life on Tap, neon, GHN Neon, 1984...**$115.00**

Sign, Pabst, neon, red lettering on blue ribbon shape, 1960s-70s **$120.00**

Sign, Red Top Beer, red top on white, tin litho, #B-104, 21x14½" **$165.00**

Sign, Rheingold Beer, light-up counter type, 1940s, 10x12" ...**$250.00**

Sign, Royal Bohemian Beer, blue & white tin litho, 1950s, 29½x32½", NM $225.00

Sign, Schlitz, The Beer That Made Milwaukee Famous, red & white, lights up, 1949, 12x17" $40.00

Sign, Schmidt's of Philadelphia Beer As Beer Should Be, foaming glass on black, tin litho, 1950s, 29½" dia $115.00

Statue, bartender w/4 drinks on arm, lg Pabst Beer bottle at side, Enjoy Old Time Flavor, painted metal, 15" $135.00

Statue, boxer in ring w/bottle, Pabst Blue Ribbon at Popular Prices, 1940s, 15x12x7", from $65 to.....................................$80.00

Statue, Canadian Mountie stands by sm bottle of Drewry's Beer, painted composition, Drewry's LTD, 1950s, 7"............$75.00

Statue, Senorita, Miller High Life, painted composition, ca 1950s, 15"..$80.00

Stein, Budweiser, Birch Trees, CS-50 Holiday series, ceramic, Ceramarte, 1981, 6⅜" $170.00

Stein, Budweiser Bud Man, ceramic, Ceramarte, #CS1, 1975, from $300 to $325.00

Stein, Budweiser CS18 Bud label, ceramic, Ceramarte, 1976, 6" $185.00

Stein, Edelweiss, clear glass w/Edelweiss in porcelain on pewter lid, 6½" $645.00

Stein, Falstaff shield on front, Sir John embossed on both stein w/ bottle in hand, ceramic, Germany, 1940s, 9½" $75.00

Stein, Schuler's Cafe German Kitchen Cincinnati on pewter lid, clear glass, 7x4½" $345.00

Tap handle, Beisenbrau & man w/stein inlay, 2½x2", VG ...$85.00

Tap handle, Budweiser Bud Man, w/mounting stem, 9½", MIB $160.00

Tap handle, Dos Equis (XX) Special Lager, painted wood w/gold-plated top, 10" $70.00

Tap handle, Olde Heurich Brewing Senate, turned wood w/Lucite finial $95.00

Tap handle, Shiner Bock Beer Brewed w/an Attitude, ram's head finial $55.00

Tap knob, Anheuser Busch, St Louis, Bakelite w/porcelain face, 2⅜x1⅞" $65.00

Tap knob, Bull Dog Beer, red enamel lettering on white, 1950s, 2" $70.00

Tap knob, Chief Oshkosh Beer, enamel on chrome, 1940s, 2½" . $80.00

Tap knob, Coors, cowboy boot w/spur $70.00

Tap knob, Esslingers Premium, red & white enameling on chrome, ca 1941, 2¾" $55.00

Tap knob, Iroquois Beer, Indian chief on ball form, 1930s, 2½".$85.00

Tap knob, Schmidt Beer, red & white on chrome, Robbins of Attleboro MA, 2¼" $55.00

Tap knob, Utica Club XXX Pale Cream Ale, red, white & black enameling $60.00

Thermometer, Auto City Brewing Co, mercury-filled tube, printed on wood, 15x4", VG...$185.00

Thermometer, Stegmaier Gold Medal Beer, c 1953 Stegmaier Brewing Wilkes-Barre PA, 9" dia $30.00

Tray, Beverwick Lager Beer, Victorian brunette w/pink roses drinks from glass, copyright 1911, 13", VG $75.00

Tray, Corona Extra, Spaniard drinking beer from footed glass, 1950s, 13" dia...$65.00

Tray, Dow Old Stock Ale, painted porcelain, 13" dia..........$45.00

Tray, Falstaff Beer, smiling man being served by maid, castle beyond, 24" dia, VG $50.00

Tray, Good Old Esslinger's Beer, redcap waiter w/glasses & bottle on tray, 1950s-60s, lg...$80.00

Tray, Hampden Brewing Co, waiter w/2 beers on tray on black, tin litho, ca 1934, 12½" $125.00

Tray, Hull's Ale Lager on faux wood-grain background, Hull Brewing Co, New Haven CT, 1930s, 13" dia $110.00

Tray, Iroquois Indian Head Beer, tin litho, New York, G, $55.00. (Photo courtesy B.J. Summers)

Tray, Narranganset Chief, Dr Seuss art, 12" dia, VG............$95.00

Tray, Old Export Beer, Cumberland Brewing Co, Electro-Chemical Engraving Co NY, 4⅛", M $135.00

Tray, Pabst, man pouring from bottle, American Can Co, #536, 13¼x10½" $100.00

Tray, Valley Forge Beer, waitress w/tray, Maxwell Parrish design, Adam Scheidt Brewing, 13¼x10½", VG......................$60.00

Breyer Horses

Breyer horses have been popular children's playthings since they were introduced in 1952, and you'll see several at any large flea market. Garage sales are good sources as well. The earlier horses had a glossy finish, but after 1968 a matt finish came into use. You'll find smaller domestic animals too. They are evaluated by condition, rarity, and desirability; some of the better examples may be worth a minimum of $150.00. Our values are for average condition; examples in mint condition are worth from 10% to 15% more.

For more information and listings, see *Schroeder's Collectible Toys, Antique to Modern* (Collector Books).

Adios, Clayton Quarter Horse, dappled palomino, Stablemates scale, 1995 – 1996, $25.00. (Photo courtesy Carol Karbowiak Gilbert)

Andalusian Foal (#3060FO), Cloud's Legacy, smutty palomino w/ white mane & tail, star, 2003 .... **$28.00**

Andalusian Foal (#3060FO), Precious Beauty & Foal Gift Set, bay blanket appaloosa w/black points, socks, 1996-97 .... **$6.00**

Andalusian Mare (#3060MA), Bay Andalusian, dark bay w/black points, stripe, 3 socks, 2003.............................. **$12.00**

Andalusian Mare (#3060MA), Classic Andalusian Family, dapple gray w/darker points, socks, 1979-93............................. **$11.00**

Andalusian Stallion (#3060ST), Spirit Kiger Mustang Family, Action, buckskin w/black points, Wal-Mart, 2002-current **$19.00**

Arabian Foal (#3055FO), alabaster w/light gray mane, tail & hooves, 1973-82 .... **$12.00**

Arabian Foal (#3055FO), Drinkers of the Winds, rose gray w/darker gray points, right hind sock, Toys R Us, 1993 .... **$10.00**

Arabian Mare (#3055MA), Arabian Mare & Foal Set, light bay w/black points, dappling, front socks/hind stockings, 1997-98....... **$11.00**

Arabian Mare (#3055MA), Collector's Arabian Family Set, black w/broad blaze, front socks, JC Penney, 1988-90 .... **$16.00**

Black Beauty (#3040BB), Black Beauty Family, black w/star, right front stocking, 1980-93 .... **$11.00**

Black Beauty (#3040BB), Quarter Horse, sorrel w/lighter mane & tail, gray hooves, 2002 .... **$13.00**

Black Stallion (#3030), King of the Wind Set, red bay w/black points, white spot on right hind ankle, 1990-93........... **$12.00**

Bucking Bronco (#190), Dakota Bucking Bronco, palomino w/ white mane & tail, dappling, shaded muzzle, hind socks, 1995-96 .... **$16.00**

Bucking Bronco (#190), gray w/darker mane & tail, bald face, stockings, 1961-67.. **$43.00**

Cutting Horse (#491), Cutting Horse & Calf Set, chestnut w/darker mane & tail, hind socks, 2004 .... **$31.00**

Duchess (#3040DU), Lady Roxanna, King of the Wind Set, alabaster w/gray mane & tail, darker hooves, 1990-93 .... **$11.00**

Fighting Sombra (#4811ME), Runaway, Mustang Kiger, cocoa dun w/brown points, left hind sock, BLM Adopt-a-Horse, 1997 .... **$17.00**

Five-Gaiter, sorrel, 1953 – 1986, Traditional scale, $45.00.

Ginger (#3040GI), Black Beauty Family, chestnut w/darker mane, tail & hooves, stripe & snip, 1980-93.......................... **$12.00**

Hobo (#625), Hobo the Mustang of Lazy Heart Ranch, buckskin w/black mane & tail, shading, 1975-80 .... **$32.00**

Jet Run (#3035JR), US Olympic Team, light chestnut w/darker mane & tail, front socks, Sears Wish Book, 1987........ **$16.00**

Johar (#3030JO), The Black Stallion Returns Set, alabaster w/gray mane, tail & hooves, 1983-93............................ **$12.00**

Keen (#3035KE), Liver Chestnut Appaloosa Sporthorse, liver chestnut blanket appaloosa w/darker points, socks, 1998 ..... **$11.00**

Keen (#3035KE), Olympic Team Set, gray w/lighter lower legs, gray hooves, Sears Wish Book, 1987 .... **$16.00**

Kelso (#601), dark bay/brown w/black points, w/ or w/o right hind sock, 1975-90.. **$17.00**

Kelso (#601), Ladies of the Bluegrass, red chestnut w/blaze, left front sock, QVC, 2002.. **$20.00**

Lipizzan Stallion (#620), alabaster w/lightly shaded mane & tail, pink/natural hooves, 1975-80 .... **$21.00**

Lipizzan Stallion (#620), Pegasus, alabaster w/pink hooves, wings fit in slots on back, 1984-87................................ **$29.00**

Man O' War (#602), red chestnut w/darker mane & tail, w/stripe or star, 1975-90.. **$17.00**

Merrylegs (#3040ML), Martin's Dominique Champion Miniature Horse, semigloss black, 3 socks, 1994-95..................... **$14.00**

Midnight Tango (US Equestrian Team Set), dapple gray, 1980 – 1981, Classic scale, $15.00. (Photo courtesy Carol Karbowiak Gilbert)

Might Tango (#3035MT), US Olympic Team Set, bay w/black points, hind socks, Sears Wish Book, 1987.................. **$15.00**

Mustang Foal (#3065FO), Cloud's Legacy, grulla w/black mane & tail, star, shaded leg joints w/bars, 2004-current **$28.00**

Mustang Foal (#3065FO), Mustang Family, grulla w/chestnut mane & tail, knee & hock stripes, hind socks, JC Penney, 1992. **$9.00**

Mustang Mare (#3065MA), Mustang Family, chestnut pinto w/ chestnut mane & tail, gray hooves, Sears Wish Book, 1976-90.. **$12.00**

Polo Pony, (#626), bay w/black points, early ones w/socks, molded woodgrain base, 1976-82............................ **$29.00**

Quarter Horse Foal (#3045FO), Dapple Gray Mare & Bay Foal Set, red bay w/black points, Wal-Mart, 2002........................ **$7.00**

Quarter Horse Foal (#3045FO), palomino w/white mane & tail, socks, gray hooves, 1975-82........................ **$11.00**

Quarter Horse Mare (#3045MA), bay w/black points, socks, gray hooves, 1974-93 .... **$12.00**

Quarter Horse Stallion (#3045ST), Quarter Horse Family, dark chestnut/bay w/darker points, hind sock, JC Penney, 1991 .... **$16.00**

Rearing Stallion (#180), bay w/black mane & tail, bald face, stockings, hooves, 1965-80 .... **$17.00**

Rearing Stallion (#180), Promises, dark bay pinto w/bay & black mane & tail, white hind legs, fronts socks, 1994-95 ..... **$15.00**

Ruffian (#606), dark bay w/black points, star, left hind sock, 1977-90 .... **$16.00**

Sagr (#3030SA), Arabian Stallion, black w/high stockings, 2003-current **$12.00**

Sagr (#3030SA), Bay Arabian w/black points, left front sock, 1998 .... **$12.00**

Silky Sullivan (#00387), Ladies of the Bluegrass, dark gray w/black points, blaze, 3 socks, QVC, 2002 .... **$20.00**

Silky Sullivan (#603), T Bone, black roan w/black points, gray speckles, 1991-92 .... **$13.00**

Swaps (#604), chestnut w/darker mane & tail, star, hind sock & light hoof w/3 dark hooves, 1975-90 .... **$17.00**

Terrang (#605), Ambrosia, palomino w/white mane & tail, shaded, front socks & hind stockings, 1997 .... **$13.00**

Terrang (#605), dark brown w/darker mane & tail, lighter hind leg, 1975-90 .... **$17.00**

Wahoo King (#466), Roping Horse & Calf Set, bay w/black points, hind socks, 2000 .... **$16.00**

Other Animals

Bear (Bear Family), black, adult, 1964-76 .... **$45.00**

Benji, matt/semigloss shaded tan, 1978-79 .... **$62.50**

Calf (Ayrshire), dark red & white pinto pattern, 1972-73 ... **$55.00**

Cow (Jersey), dark tan, 1972-73 .... **$88.00**

Kitten (calico), 1966-73 .... **$88.00**

Labrador, black, yellow or chocolate, 1999-current, ea.......... **$6.00**

Moose, Traditional scale, 1996-95, up to **$25.00**

Mountain goat, alabaster, 1998-current............................. **$25.00**

Poodle, glossy black w/collar of various colors, 1958-68 ...... **$50.00**

St. Bernard, 1972–1980, $40.00. (Photo courtesy Carol Karbowiak Gilbert)

St Bernard (Brandy), golden brown & white w/shaded head, 1995-96 .... **$20.00**

Texas longhorn, dark chestnut pinto, 1990-95..................... **$28.00**

Zebra (Damara), 2000-current.. **$30.00**

British Royal Commemoratives

While seasoned collectors may prefer the older pieces using circa 1840 (Queen Victoria's reign) as their starting point, even pres-ent-day souvenirs make a good inexpensive beginning collection. Ceramic items, glassware, metalware, and paper goods have been issued on the occasion of weddings, royal tours, birthdays, christenings, and many other celebrations. Food tins are fairly easy to find, and range in price from about $30.00 to around $75.00 for those made since the 1950s.

We've all seen that items related to Princess Diana have appreciated rapidly since her untimely and tragic demise, and in fact collections are being built exclusively from memorabilia marketed both before and after her death. For more information, we recommend *British Royal Commemoratives* by Audrey Zeder.

Advisor: Audrey Zeder (See Directory, British Royalty Commemoratives)

Album, Royal Family in Panini, completely filled, 1984 ...... **$50.00**

Bank, Charles & Diana 1981 wedding portrait, blue, Adams, round, 3" **$50.00**

Beaker, George V jubilee, sepia portrait, multicolored official design, 4" **$55.00**

Bell, Queen Elizabeth II, ceramic w/wooden handle **$40.00**

Booklet, Charles/Diana wedding, Royal Betrothal, Pitkins, 8-page fold-out **$35.00**

Bookmark, Elizabeth II 2002 jubilee, leather w/gold portrait & decoration **$10.00**

Bowl, George VI coronation, multicolored portrait/decor, scalloped rim, 5½" **$45.00**

Box, Princess Diana and Prince Charles, Crummles, 2½" diameter, from $35.00 to $45.00. (Photo courtesy James Williamson)

Bust, Elizabeth II coronation, white bisque, rose dress, Foley, 6" **$125.00**

Compote, Elizabeth II 1959 Canada visit, multicolored decoration, Paragon **$110.00**

Cup & saucer, Edward VII coronation, portrait/decor on turquoise **$165.00**

Cup & saucer, Elizabeth II 2002 jubilee, multicolored portrait & decoration on bone china... **$30.00**

Doll, Prince Philip, vinyl, blue uniform, Nisbit, ca 1950, 8½"...**$150.00**

Doll, Prince William birth, cloth, Nottingham lace gown, 3", MIB **$50.00**

Egg cup, Elizabeth II '02 jubilee, black silhouette, footed **$15.00**

Figure, Princess Diana, hand painted, dark blue dress, 1997, 11¾" **$85.00**

Jewelry, Elizabeth II coronation, crown earrings, MOC....... **$25.00**

Jewelry, Princess Diana 1997 earrings, multicolored portrait, silver-plated..$25.00
Jewelry, Queen Victoria coin, gold bezel w/extended ring....$35.00
Magazine, Daily Mail, Princess Diana memorial, 9-6-97 .....$30.00
Magazine, Hello, Charles & Harry in South Africa, 11-15-97.. $12.00
Magazine, Illustrated London News, Charles/Diana 10th wedding anniversary, pastel portrait cover, 10-page article...........$35.00
Magazine, Illustrated London News, Elizabeth II coronation, coronation week, double number, 1953.............................$35.00
Medal, Victoria coronation, profile & coronation scene, pierced, 2"..$160.00
Mug, Charles/Diana engagement, black line portrait, ear handle, Carlton $75.00
Mug, Edward VII coronation, blue & green portrait, barrel shape, CTM $165.00
Mug, Elizabeth II 2002 jubilee, multicolor portrait on bone china...$20.00
Mug, Prince Henry 1984 birthday, multicolored decor, miniature, 1½"..$35.00
Newspaper, Di Badly Injured, News of the World, 8-31-97. $60.00
Novelty, Elizabeth II coronation pocketknife, multicolored decor, 5x2½"..$45.00
Photograph, Princess Diana 1987 at London gala, black & white, 6x8"...$50.00
Pin-back button, Prince of Wales, black & white portrait, 1936, ¾"..$30.00
Plate, Elizabeth II 1959 Canada visit, multicolored decor, Paragon, 10½"...$125.00
Plate, Princess Diana memorial, portrait on iridized pressed glass, 3½"...$35.00

Plate, Princess Elizabeth, marked Paragon, 5", $50.00. (Photo courtesy James Williamson)

Plate, Queen Elizabeth coronation, #1609, 9" $40.00
Playing cards, Charles/Diana wedding, multicolored portrait & decor, double pack, unused..................................$55.00
Postcard, Charles & Diana wedding, multicolored portrait, line of descent, 32x23"..$35.00
Poster, Princess Diana 1998, Dresses for Humanity, multicolored, 21x34"...$45.00
Print, Princess Diana memorial, artist signed Heiner, 11x16". $50.00

Spoon, multicolored portrait w/tiara, silver-plated, ca 1982.$25.00
Tea caddy, Elizabeth II coronation, embossed+inscribed, copper/brass, Purity Tips..$75.00
Textile, Charles & Diana wedding, tea towel, multicolored portrait, Irish linen $35.00
Textile, Queen Mother 100 birthday, tea towel, multicolored portrait $15.00
Thimble, Elizabeth II '02 jubilee, young queen portrait, multicolored decor..$6.00
Tin, Elizabeth II '77 jubilee, light blue w/multicolored portrait, Jameson, 9" dia...$35.00
Tin, Elizabeth II coronation, multicolored portrait, round, flat, Daintee, 2x4"..$30.00
Trinket box, Charles & Diana wedding, heart shape, 2¼x1¾" . $30.00

Brock of California

This was the trade name of the B.J. Brock Company, located in Lawndale, California. They operated from 1947 until 1980, and some of the dinnerware lines they produced have become desirable collectibles. One of the most common themes revolved around country living, farmhouses, barns, chickens, and cows. Patterns were Rooster, California Farmhouse, and California Rustic. Shapes echoed the same concept — there were skillets, milk cans, and flatirons fashioned into sugar bowls, creamers, and salt and pepper shakers. The company marketed a three-piece children's set as well. Also look for their '50s modern line called Manzanita, with pink and charcoal branches on platinum. With the interest in this style of dinnerware on the increase, this should be one to watch.

California Farmhouse, bowl, cereal; barn & hay wagon, yellow border, 6½" $6.00
California Farmhouse, butter dish, flatiron shape, yellow border, 9" $40.00
California Farmhouse, coal bucket, yellow border, 1¾x3"....$20.00
California Farmhouse, deviled egg plate, yellow border, 13", from $30 to $35.00
California Farmhouse, egg cup, rooster on fence, yellow border, 3⅜" $15.00
California Farmhouse, lazy Susan, yellow border, 5 pcs on wooden tray, 14½" dia $65.00
California Farmhouse, pitcher, milk; yellow border, 7½" $25.00
California Farmhouse, plate, yellow border, 10"....................$8.00
California Farmhouse, plate, yellow border, 6⅜" $4.00
California Farmhouse, relish jar, yellow border, w/lid..........$22.00
California Farmhouse, server, 2-part, yellow border, 11" L, from $15 to $20.00
California Farmhouse, sugar bowl, yellow border, w/lid.......$22.00
California Farmhouse, tid-bit tray, yellow border, w/center handle $35.00
California Rustic, bowl, fruit/dessert; 5" $7.00
California Rustic, cup & saucer, flat................................$10.00
California Rustic, plate, bread & butter; 6½"........................$4.00
California Wildflower, bowl, coral border, 8¾", from $14 to.. $18.00
California Wildflower, plate, coral border, 11" $7.00
California Wildflower, platter, coral border, rectangular, 17" L. $30.00

Chanticleer, chafing dish, brown border, stick handle, w/metal warmer base $35.00
Chanticleer, cheese & cracker set, brown border $40.00
Chanticleer, creamer, brown border.............................$12.00
Chanticleer, cup, brown border.................................$8.00
Chanticleer, cup & saucer, brown border $12.50
Chanticleer, gravy boat, brown border $35.00
Chanticleer, lazy Susan, brown border.........................$50.00
Chanticleer, mug, brown border, barrel form $10.00
Chanticleer, plate, bread & butter; brown border, 6¾" $5.00
Chanticleer, plate, brown border, 10½" $15.00
Country Lane, bowl, divided vegetable; brown border, 11" L, from $25 to $30.00
Country Lane, creamer, brown border, stick handle, from $9 to.. $12.00
Country Lane, gravy boat, brown border, from $18 to $22.00
Country Lane, plate, chop; brown border, 14" dia, from $25 to.. $35.00
Country Lane, salt & pepper shakers, brown border, pr, from $15 to $18.00
Country Modern, bowl, yellow border, footed, 6½".............$14.00
Country Modern, candlestick, yellow border, 2¼", ea...........$9.00
Country Modern, cup & saucer, yellow border, flat, from $7 to $10.00
Country Modern, mug, yellow border, 3¼" $15.00

Forever Yours, carafe, 7½", from $25.00 to $30.00. (Photo courtesy Robin Young)

Forever Yours, carafe, aqua border, w/stopper, 5" $16.00
Forever Yours, condiment set: mustard, relish, onion jars w/lids & plastic spoons, aqua borders, in black metal stand $125.00
Forever Yours, creamer & sugar bowl, aqua border, w/lid, 8-oz $18.00
Forever Yours, cup & saucer, aqua border $12.00
Forever Yours, plate, aqua border, 10"........................$12.00
Forever Yours, salt & pepper shakers, aqua border, w/handles, 2⅝", pr...$12.00
Forever Yours, tray, aqua border, 13" dia.....................$25.00
Harvest, bowl, coupe soup; brown border.......................$8.00
Harvest, bowl, vegetable; brown border, 9" $24.00
Harvest, plate, brown border, 10" $10.00
Harvest, plate, chop; brown border, 13", from $22 to $25.00
Harvest, sugar bowl, brown border, w/lid, 4", from $12 to..$15.00
Manzanita, pink & coral branches on platinum, 10" $25.00

Manzanita, plate, pink & coral branches on platinum, 8"......**$8.00**
Manzanita, saucer, pink & coral branches on platinum..........**$4.00**

Bubble Bath Containers

Most bubble bath containers were made in the 1960s. The Colgate-Palmolive Company produced the majority of them — they're the ones marked 'Soaky' — and these seem to be the most collectible. Each character's name is right on the bottle. Other companies followed suit; Purex also made a line, so did Avon. Be sure to check for paint loss, and look carefully for cracks in the brittle plastic heads of the Soakies. Our values are for examples in excellent to near mint condition.

For more information, we recommend *Schroeder's Collectible Toys, Antique to Modern* (Collector Books).

Advisors: Matt and Lisa Adams (See Directory, Bubble Bath Containers)

Alvin (Chipmunks), red sweater w/white A, w/puppet, Colgate-Palmolive, neck tag & contents, M $50.00
Anastasia, Kid Care, 1997, NM $8.00

Aristocrats, Avon, 1970s, NMIB, $28.00. (Photo courtesy whatacharacter.com)

Baloo Bear, Colgate-Palmolive, 1966, NM...........................$20.00
Batman, blue & gray, 1992, 12", EX $5.00
Bear, Tubby Time, 1960s, NM.......................................$35.00
Cecil (Beany & Cecil), Purex, 1962, NM $40.00
Creature From the Black Lagoon, Colgate-Palmolive, 1960s, NM, A7, from $100 to..$150.00
Dopey, purple, yellow & red, Colgate-Palmolive, 1960s, NM .. $20.00
Florence, girl w/red skirt, blue shirt & hair bow, holding flower, Grosvenor, Magic Roundabout series, 1993, 8", EX $10.00
Garfield lying in tub, Kid Care, NM $10.00
GI Joe (Drill Instructor), DuCair Bioescence, 1980s, NM...$15.00
Gravel truck, orange & gray w/movable wheels, Colgate-Palmolive, 1960s, EX...$20.00
Huckleberry Hound & Yogi Bear, Milvern (Purex), 1960s, MIB (sealed)..$75.00

Lamb Chop (Shari Lewis) holding duck, Kid Care, w/tag, M .. **$8.00**
Little Mermaid w/tail up, Kid Care, 1991, NM.................. **$10.00**
Mickey Mouse as Band Leader, Colgate-Palmolive, 1960s, NM **$25.00**
Minnie Mouse w/legs crossed, red skirt, pie-eyed, topper, Prelude/UK, 1994, NM... **$15.00**
Mr Met, New York Mets mascot, white & light blue uniform, Let's Go Mets on bottom, 10", EX **$110.00**
Mr Robottle, Avon, 1971, MIB **$20.00**
Nala (Lion King) on pink base, Centura/Canada, 1994, M. **$20.00**
Oil Truck, Colgate-Palmolive, green & gray w/movable wheels, VG **$35.00**
Olive Oyl sitting w/hands clasped, Damascar/Italy, 1995, NM **$35.00**
Oscar the Grouch taking a bath in trash can w/I Hate Baths sign, Grosvenor/UK, 1994, NM **$25.00**
Paddington Bear, topper, Grosvenor/UK, 1989, EX (EX window box) **$20.00**
Pocahontas standing on rock about to dive, Grosvenor/UK, 1995, NM.. **$20.00**
Pumbaa (Lion King), Prelude/UK, 1994, M...................... **$20.00**
Quick Draw McGraw, several variations, Purex, 1960s, NM, ea.. **$30.00**
Rainbow Brite, Hallmark, 1995, NM **$10.00**
Robin squatting on eagle-head statue, Damascar/Italy, 1995, M **$35.00**
Rupert Bear in yellow airplane, topper, UK, 1995, M.......... **$20.00**

Secret Squirrel, Purex, 1966, MIP, from $75.00 to $85.00. (Photo courtesy Greg Moore and Joe Pizzo)

Skeletor (Masters of the Universe), Ducair Bioescence, NM... **$15.00**
Spouty Whale, blue, Roclar (Purex), original card, M **$20.00**
Sylvester & Tweety, Warner Bros, 1977, 9½", VG................. **$5.00**
Tasmanian Devil w/mouth open wide, movable arms, Prelude/UK, 1995, M... **$25.00**
Tom & Jerry sitting in drum, Damascar/Italy, 1995, NM.... **$35.00**
Tweety Bird in blue robe w/white towel, Prelude/UK, 1995, NM **$35.00**
Two-Face (Batman), topper, Prelude/UK, 1995, NM **$15.00**
USS Enterprise (Star Trek), Euromark/UK, 1994, NM....... **$30.00**
Wile E Coyote w/rocket backpack, Prelude/UK, 1995, NM .. **$35.00**
Wilma Flintstone standing on turtle shell, Damascar/Italy, 1993, M **$35.00**
Winnie the Pooh on black base, Boots/UK, M **$35.00**

Yogi Bear standing on green base w/purple grass, Damascar/Italy, 1994, M.. **$35.00**
101 Dalmatians, father w/pup on head & 1 between legs, Grosvenor/UK, 1994, NM.. **$35.00**
101 Dalmatians, pups on pillow w/red sunglasses, topper, Grosvenor/UK, 1994, M.. **$15.00**

Snow White, Colgate-Palmolive, 1960s, movable arms, NM, $35.00.

Butter Pats

Butter pats were used extensively in Victorian times, but even up until the 1970s, they were included in commercial table service. Though most were made of vitrified or fine china, a variety of materials — ironstone, sterling, and fine porcelain, for instance — were used as well. You'll find they range from very ornate styles to the very simple. They were made by nearly all major dinnerware manufacturers both here and abroad. Just be careful not to confuse them with small plates intended for other uses, such as nut and sauce dishes, salt dips, coasters, or children's toy dishes.

Indian Tree, Copeland Spode, $18.00. (From the collection of Dorothy Crowder)

Alliance, green transfer, Staffordshire, ca 1795 .... **$12.00**
Apple Blossom on white porcelain, scalloped edge w/gold, Theodore Haviland **$15.00**
Argyle, flow blue, no gold, Grindley, ca 1896 .... **$50.00**
Argyle, flow blue w/gold trim, Grindley, 3¼" **$72.50**
Beeston, floral chintz on black, Royal Winton, sq, 3¼" **$40.00**

Begonia, majolica, multicolor leaf form, 3½", NM $65.00

Begonia leaf, green, majolica, Edge Malkin & Co, ca 1900, 3x3", NM.. $45.00

Blackberry on Basketweave, majolica, 1890s, 3⅜" $110.00

Blue Adam, D&RGW Railroad, Syracuse China Co, 1930s-40s, 3", from $30 to $35.00

Blue Fluted, full lace, porcelain, Royal Copenhagen, #1004, 2⅞" $30.00

Blue Jay, signed HA Pausch, Royal Cauldon, 3⅞" $12.00

Bramble, light green transfer w/gold trim on white ironstone, Alfred Meakin Co, 3" $20.00

Briar Rose, Donatello shape, Rosenthal, 3" $18.00

Briar Rose, floral border, Copeland Spode England, ca 1940, 3½" $14.00

Butterfly & meadow grasses w/painted accents on white, scalloped, sq, Haviland Limoges, ca 1900, 2¾" $40.00

Butterfly center w/flowers on rim, clear pressed glass, American, 19th century, 3¼" $75.00

California Poppy, Santa Fe, no back stamp, 3" $30.00

Cambridge, flow blue, New Wharf Pottery, 2¾", NM $30.00

Country Life, horse & rider pink transfer, Myotts, 3⅛" $26.00

Daisies transfer w/gold, H Alcock, 1910-35 mark, 3¼" $12.00

Fern & roses, gray-blue transfer, straight sides, rounded ends, unmarked.. $20.00

Floral border & rim, blue transferware, unmarked, 3¼" $15.00

Floral on white w/silver border, Schnarzenhammer crest, Bavaria Germany, 4½" $10.00

Florals & detailed scenic reserve, brown transfer, EM&Co, 3" . $17.50

Flowers, mixed bouquet on white w/gold trim, reticulated rim, Schumann, Ausberg Germany, 4" $25.00

Flowers hand painted along border, gold trim, Hand Painted Nippon $75.00

Geranium, majolica green & brown leaf form, old-style Etruscan, 3¼" $65.00

Gold bands (2) on white bone china, Crown Staffordshire, 1930s, 3½" $22.50

Grace, flow blue, WH Grindley, 1897, 3" $75.00

Haddon Hall (floral pattern), gold trim, Minton, 3½", NM .. $24.00

Hyde Park, pink floral pattern, NY Central Lines, Haviland-Limoges, sq $125.00

Kalundborg Kirke (church), blue & white, Royal Copenhagen bee-hive mark, ca 1980, 3¼" $8.00

Kansas City MO souvenir, Victorian scene on white china, Occupied Japan, 3⅛" $15.00

Kelvin, flow blue w/gold, Alfred Meakin, 3⅛" $65.00

Kingfisher on white china, 5-sided, Guild Craft Ltd, 1970s, 3x3½x5" $10.00

Landscape w/gazebo & trees, building reserves in floral border, blue transfer, JD Crouse Canastota, 4¼", NM $48.00

Little Black Sambo (w/umbrella) transfer on shiny white, unmarked, 3" $60.00

Maple leaf, majolica, green w/brown edge on tan, Etruscan . $95.00

Mascotte, clear non-flint pressed glass, Ripley & Co or US Glass, 2¾" $18.00

Mimbreno, Santa Fe Dining Car Service, flaw, 3⅜" $45.00

Mission pattern for Missouri Pacific Railroad, Adobe Ware line of Syracuse China, 3" $115.00

Morning Glory on Napkin w/cobalt trim, majolica, unmarked, 3¼" $60.00

Multicolor chintz floral w/gold trim, Staffordshire England, 3⅞" $26.00

Niagara Falls souvenir, view w/in red band, scalloped white rim, Occupied Japan, 3⅛" $24.00

Orchard, Ansley, gold trim, $20.00.

Orchids on slender stems on white china w/gold rim, Austria, 3" $24.00

Pansy, majolica, Etruscan multicolor petals $140.00

Patrician, embossed scrolls w/red leaves along rim, Made in England, 3¼" $13.00

Peacock pattern, Chicaco, Milwaukee, St Paul & Pacific RR, Econo-Rim, Syracuse, 3" $140.00

Pine cones on white, Chepco China, 3⅛" $28.00

Pink floral transfer, Campania Cunard Steamship, T&R Boote, 3", NM $60.00

Prince Edward Island souvenir w/lady-slipper flower, gold trim, Bone China, Made in England, 1⅞" $8.00

Queen Anne's Lace, brown transfer, gold rim, Adamantine China, 3½" $12.00

Rose, lg yellow flower on white w/gold rim, Thomas R Germany 3287/1 .... $20.00

Rose Briar, Copeland Spode England, 3½" $15.00

Roses, dark to light pink on white porcelain w/gold trim, Theodore Haviland, 3" $28.00

Roses, multicolor pastels on white w/green rim, Paragon China, 4⅛" $15.00

Roses, red & white on white bone china, Hammersley Fine Bone China, Princess House Exclusive, 3½" $10.00

Somerset, floral chintz w/gold, sq, Royal Winton, 1930s, 4".. $37.50

St Louis, flow blue, Johnson Brothers England, ca 1900, 3"... $95.00

Swallow flying among flowered branches on shaded pink ground, unmarked, ca 1930s, 3½" $28.00

Sweet Pea, floral chintz, Royal Winton, 4", NM $27.50

Traveler, CMSt&P (Milwaukee Road) Railroad, unmarked Syracuse... $50.00

Tulip Time, brown & green transfer, Johnson Brothers, ca 1913, 4" $20.00

USBF (United States Bureau of Fisheries), red, white & blue logo, Buffalo China, 3½" $135.00

Victorian lady's portrait, elegant clothes & plumed hat, hand painted on white porcelain, sq, 2¼" $47.50

Violets & Daisies, CB&Q Railroad, Shenango China, ca 1930-50, 3⅛" **$28.00**

Violets & green leaves hand painted on border w/gold trim, Racine PR Bavaria, 1930s, 3⅛" **$60.00**

Virginia, flow Blue, Maddocks, 3" **$48.00**

Buttons

Collectors refer to buttons made before 1918 as 'old,' those from 1918 on they call 'modern.' Age is an important consideration, but some modern buttons are very collectible too. You might find some still in your Grandmother's button jar, and nearly any flea market around will have some interesting examples.

Some things you'll want to look for to determine the age of a button is the material it is made of, the quality of its workmanship, the type of its decoration, and how it was constructed. Early metal buttons were usually made in one piece of steel, copper, or brass. Old glass buttons will have irregularities on the back, while the newer ones will be very smooth. 'Picture' buttons with animals and people as their subjects were popular in the last quarter of the nineteenth century. Many were quite large and very fancy. As a rule, those are the most valuable to collectors.

For more information, refer to *Antique and Collectible Buttons Vol. 1* and *Vol. 2*, by Debra J. Wisniewski (Collector Books).

Aurora borealis, late 1950s-early 1960s, sm...........................**$3.00**

Bakelite, imitation tortoise shell, carved flower, med.............**$3.00**

Bakelite, knife, spoon & fork, red, 3-pc set, from $200 to.**$300.00**

Bakelite, w/black glass center & gold lustre, for lady's coat, lg, from $8 to **$10.00**

Brass, stork scene enameling, med..**$40.00**

Celluloid, old seaman, gray tint w/black lacquered rim, steel back w/self-shank, lg **$95.00**

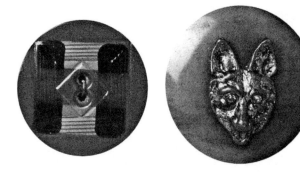

Celluloid, various styles, from $3.00 to $8.00. (Photo courtesy Debra Wisniewski)

Glass, black w/gold-lustre leaf, 1940s-60s, from $2 to **$5.00**

Glass, black w/gunmetal lustre, modern, lg.............................**$8.00**

Glass, blue w/embossed decor & sm amount of gold enameling, modern, med, from $2 to **$4.00**

Glass, blue w/silver enameling in Art Deco style, 1930s, lg, from $4 to **$6.00**

Glass, candy-striped moonglow, modern, from $3 to.............**$6.00**

Glass, faceted amethyst ball w/white overlay & rhinestone center **$12.00**

Glass, green, faceted, w/paperweight top, 6-sided **$18.00**

Glass, green moonglow heart shape, modern, sm, from $2 to ..**$4.00**

Glass, transparent colored or clear, Germany, Austria or Czechoslovakia, 1930s-40s, med or lg, ea from $1 to......**$3.00**

Glass, white moonglow w/aurora lustre, 1960s, sm...............**$3.00**

Glass ball, metal loop shank or metal loop shank & plate, from $4 to **$8.00**

Milk glass w/blue enameled flower, modern, 1930s-60s, sm to med, from $2 to **$4.00**

Pearl, gray w/engraved & painted flower design **$18.00**

Picture type, barn swallow w/babies, pierced windows on barn, mirrored liner showing through, white metal, lg **$22.00**

Picture type, bird, brass w/faceted steel border & tiny steel eye, med..**$18.00**

Picture type, castle on a rocky promontory, lg, 1½" **$15.00**

Picture type, Cleopatra w/asp, lg...**$15.00**

Picture type, deer in woods, lg **$20.00**

Picture type, fly in spider's web, stamped and tinted brass, steel back and wire shank, minimum value, $40.00. (Photo courtesy Debra Wisniewski)

Picture type, gargoyle heads, pierced border, lg **$15.00**

Picture type, Henry of Navarre **$32.00**

Picture type, Lucy & Edgar (operatic characters), 1¾".........**$25.00**

Picture type, Mars (god of war), lg..**$10.00**

Picture type, Mary Tudor, lg **$12.00**

Picture type, putto & lady at well, lg **$18.00**

Picture type, rabbit learning ABCs, white metal sm.............**$15.00**

Picture type, sailboat in a shell, 1-pc, stamped & painted brass, lg **$20.00**

Plastic, autumn leaves, self-shank, set of 6...........................**$15.00**

Plastic, bird on a limb, red w/painted trim (reissues have no paint), self-shank, set of 6.......................................**$22.00**

Plastic, Disney animal w/rhinestone eye, self-shank, set of 3..**$8.00**

Rhinestones, claw set in silver-plated mounting, early 1900s, from $15 to **$24.00**

Rhinestones, cup-set stones, sm..**$5.00**

Rhinestones set in plastic, 1930-50s, lg, from $7 to............**$10.00**

Satsuma, bamboo w/gold, 1940s-50s, sm to med, ea **$18.00**

Shell, carved geometric pattern, sew through 4 holes, lg, from $6 to **$12.00**

Wooden, rolling pin shape, realistic, from $3 to **$8.00**

California Raisins

Since they starred in their first TV commercial in 1986, the California Raisins have attained stardom through movies, tapes, videos, and magazine ads. Today we see them everywhere on the secondary market — PVC figures, radios, banks, posters — and they're very collectible. The PVC figures were introduced in 1987. Originally there were four, all issued for retail sales — a singer, two conga dancers, and a saxophone player. Before the year was out, Hardee's, the fast-food chain, came out with the same characters, though on a slightly smaller scale. A fifth character, Blue Surfboard (horizontal), was created, and three 5½" Bendees with flat pancake-style bodies appeared.

In 1988 the ranks had grown to 21: Blue Surfboard (vertical), Red Guitar, Lady Dancer, Blue/Green Sunglasses, Guy Winking, Candy Cane, Santa Raisin, Bass Player, Drummer, Tambourine Lady (there were two styles), Lady Valentine, Boy Singer, Girl Singer, Hip Guitar Player, Sax Player with Beret, and four Graduates (styled like the original four, but on yellow pedestals and wearing graduation caps). And Hardee's issued an additional six: Blue Guitar, Trumpet Player, Roller Skater, Skateboard, Boom Box, and Yellow Surfboard.

Still eight more characters came out in 1989: Male in Beach Chair, Green Trunks with Surfboard, Hula Skirt, Girl Sitting on Sand, Piano Player, AC, Mom, and Michael Raisin. They made two movies and thereafter were joined by their fruit and vegetable friends, Rudy Bagaman, Lick Broccoli, Banana White, Leonard Limabean, and Cecil Thyme. Hardee's added four more characters in 1991: Anita Break, Alotta Style, Buster, and Benny.

All Raisins are dated with these exceptions: those issued in 1989 (only the Beach Scene characters are dated, and they're actually dated 1988) and those issued by Hardee's in 1991.

For more information we recommend *Schroeder's Collectible Toys, Antique to Modern* (Collector Books).

Beach Theme Edition, boy with surfboard, brown base, CALRAB-Applause, 1988, M, $10.00. (Photo courtesy Larry DeAngelo)

Beach Theme Edition, male in beach chair, orange sunglasses, brown base, CALRAB-Applause, 1988, M **$20.00**

Christmas Issue, candy cane or red hat, CALRAB, 1988, M, ea **$7.50**

Commercial Issue (1st), hitchhiker winking (Winky), CALRAB, 1988, M **$5.00**

Commercial Issue (1st), Sunglasses II, aqua glasses & sneakers, eyes not visible, CALRAB, 1988, M **$4.00**

Commercial Issue (2nd), female tambourine player (Ms Delicious), yellow shoes, CALRAB-Applause, 1988, M **$15.00**

Commercial Issue (3rd), female singer w/microphone, yellow shoes & bracelet, CALRAB-Applause, 1988, M **$12.00**

Commercial Issue (3rd), Hip Band Guitarist (Jimi Hendrix), headband, yellow guitar, CALRAB-Applause, 1988, M **$15.00**

Commercial Issue (3rd), saxophone player, black beret, blue eyelids, CALRAB-Applause, 1988, M **$15.00**

Hardee's 1st Promotion, male singer w/microphone, right hand pointing up, CALRAB, 1987, M **$3.00**

Hardee's 2nd Promotion, Captain Toonz, blue boom box, yellow glasses & sneakers, Applause, 1988, sm, M, from $1 to.. **$3.00**

Hardee's 2nd Promotion, FF Strings, blue guitar & orange sneakers, Applause, 1988, sm, M, from $1 to **$3.00**

Key Chains (Graduate), male singer w/microphone, right hand pointing up, CALRAB-Applause, 1988, M **$85.00**

Key Chains (Graduate), male w/hands up & thumbs touching forehead, CALRAB-Applause, 1988, M **$85.00**

Key Chains (1st), male in sunglasses, index finger touching face, CALRAB, 1987, M **$5.00**

Meet the Raisins 1st Edition, Lick Broccoli, green & black w/red & orange guitar, Applause-Claymation, 1989, M **$20.00**

Meet the Raisins 1st Edition, piano player, blue piano, red hair, green sneakers, Applause-Claymation, 1989, M **$35.00**

Meet the Raisins 1st Edition, Ruby Bagaman w/cigar, purple shirt & flipflops, Applause-Claymation, 1989, M **$20.00**

Meet the Raisins 2nd Edition, Lenny Lima Bean, purple shirt, CALRAB-Applause, 1989, M **$175.00**

Post Raisin Bran Issue, Graduate, sunglasses, yellow base, CALRAB-Claymation, 1988, from $45 to **$65.00**

Post Raisin Bran Issue, Graduate saxophone player, yellow base, CALRAB-Claymation, 1988, from $45 to **$65.00**

Special Lovers Edition, Valentine Girl & Boy holding hearts, CALRAB-Applause, 1988, M, ea **$8.00**

Unknown Promotion, male w/blue surfboard, board connected to foot, CALRAB, 1988, M **$40.00**

Unknown Promotion, male w/blue surfboard in right hand, board not connected to foot, CALRAB, 1987, M **$75.00**

Hardee's Second Promotion, Waves Weaver II, yellow surfboard not connected to foot, 1988, M, $2.00. (Photo courtesy Larry DeAngelo)

Miscellaneous

Auto Sun Shield, roll-away type, suction cup mounting, 16¾x51", MIP (sealed) **$15.00**

Autograph book, rainbow-colored pages, Autumn Rose/CALRAB 988, MIP (sealed) **$12.00**

Bank, figure standing w/Sun-Maid Raisins box, CALRAB, 1987, 7", MIB **$8.00**

Beach towel, singer w/3 musicians, blue, 58x29", EX **$12.00**

Belt, yellow w/purple characters, Lee, EX..................... **$10.00**

Card Game, CALRAB, 1987, MIP **$6.00**

Cassette tape, Christmas w/the California Raisins, 1988, M . **$15.00**

Chalkboard, w/eraser, Rose Art/CALRAB 1988, MIP **$20.00**

Computer game, Box Office, MIB (sealed) **$20.00**

Costume, w/white gloves, CALRAB, 1987, 33", EX............ **$10.00**

Crayon-By-Number Set, Rose Art, 1988, MIB **$40.00**

Fan Club Kit, w/watch, ID card, button & bumper sticker,
 M **$35.00**

Fingertronic Puppet, male or female, Bendy Toys/CALRAB 1988,
 MIB **$25.00**

Inflatable figure, vinyl, Imperial Toy, 1987, 42", MIB **$50.00**

Key chains, various plastic figures, NM, C3, ea **$6.00**

Pin-back, California Raisins for President, 1¾" dia, M **$8.00**

Pin-back, Soft Toys Are Here, Grapevine Tour '88, worn by Hardee's
 employees, 3¾x3", EX **$10.00**

Puffy Stick-Ons, 1987, MIP **$8.00**

Radio, AM/FM, figure w/poseable arms & legs, MIB........ **$150.00**

Record, Rudolph the Red Nosed Reindeer, 45 rpm, Atlantic, NM
 (w/sleeve) **$12.00**

Record, When a Man Loves a Woman/Sweet, Delicious & Marvelous,
 Buddy Miles lead vocals, NM+ (w/sleeve)...................... **$20.00**

Sandwich Stage, slice of bread shaped stage w/3 figures, Del Monte
 mail-in, EX **$25.00**

Sheet, Raisins doing their line dance, cotton, CALRAB 1988,
 64x84", EX **$8.00**

Suspenders, yellow w/purple figures & red I Heard It Through the
 Grapevine, EX **$20.00**

Wall clock, female raisins w/tambourines, battery-op, 8½" dia,
 M **$35.00**

Watch, figural, Applause, 1988, MIP **$5.00**

Camark Pottery

Camark Pottery was manufactured in CAMden, ARKansas, from 1927 to the early 1960s. The pottery was founded by Samuel J. 'Jack' Carnes, a native of east-central Ohio familiar with Ohio's fame for pottery production. Camark's first wares were made from Arkansas clays shipped by Carnes to John B. Lessell in Ohio in early to mid-1926. Lessell was one of the associates responsible for early art pottery making. These art wares consisted of Lessell's lustre and iridescent finishes based on similar ideas he pioneered at Weller and other potteries. The variations made for Camark included versions of Weller's Marengo, LaSa, and Lamar. These 1926 pieces were signed only with the 'Lessell' signature. When Camark began operations in the spring of 1927, the company had many talented, experienced workers including Lessell's wife and step-daughter (Lessell himself died unexpectedly in December 1926), the Sebaugh family, Frank Long, Alfred Tetzschner, and Boris Trifonoff. This group produced a wide range of art pottery finished in glazes of many types, including lustre and iridescent (signed LeCamark), Modernistic/Futuristic, crackles, and combination glaze effects such as drips. Art pottery manufacture continued until the early 1930s when emphasis changed to industrial castware (molded wares) with single-color, primarily matt glazes.

In the 1940s Camark introduced its Hand Painted line by Ernst Lechner. This line included the popular Iris, Rose, and Tulip patterns. Concurrent with the Hand Painted Series (which was made until the early 1950s), Camark continued mass production of industrial castware — simple, sometimes nondescript pottery and novelty items with primarily glossy pastel glazes — until the early 1960s.

Some of Camark's designs and glazes are easily confused with those of other companies. For instance, Lessell decorated and signed a line in his lustre and iridescent finishes using porcelain (not pottery) blanks purchased from the Fraunfelter China Company. Camark produced a variety of combination glazes including the popular drip glazes (green over pink and green over mustard/brown) closely resembling Muncie's — but Muncie's clay is generally white while Camark used a cream-colored clay for its drip-glaze pieces. Muncie's are marked with a letter/number combination, and the bottoms are usually smeared with the base color. Camark's bottoms have a more uniform color application.

In the listings that follow, the term '1st block letter' refers to the die-stamped CAMARK mark. These block-style letters were ³⁄₁₆" high and were used circa 1928 to the early 1930s, while the '2nd block letter' mark was stamped in ⅛" letters and used for a brief time in the early to mid-1930s.

Advisor: Tony Freyaldenhoven (See Directory, Camark)

Newsletter: *Camark Pottery News Bulletin*
Colony Publishing, owner: Letitia Landers
P.O. Box 203
Camden, AR 71711
870-836-3022; fax: 870-836-0127
One-year subscription $30.00

Advertising sign, 6⅜", from $250.00 to $300.00. (Photo courtesy David Edwin Gifford)

Ashtray, yellow, incurvate scalloped rim, embossed ribs, 1st block
 letter **$15.00**

Bank, seated pig w/bow tie, white, w/accents, 6¾" **$160.00**

Basket, orange, unmarked, 3¾", from $10 to...................... **$15.00**

Basket, Orange Green Overflow, marked, 6", from $60 to... **$80.00**

Basket, pastel green matt, 1st block letter, 5¾", from $40 to . **$60.00**

Basket, white, embossed rings, 1st block letter, 5¾", from $40 to **$60.00**

Bowl, Azurite Blue, sm angle handles, sticker, unmarked, 5", from $140 to **$160.00**

Bowl, yellow to blue matt, 2x6¼" **$250.00**

Box, frosted green, sticker, 2¼x4¼", from $60 to **$80.00**

Candlestick, blue & white stipple, Arkansas die stamp, 1¼"...**$50.00**

Candlesticks, Ivory, flower form, unmarked, 1x3" dia, pr **$30.00**

Candlesticks, Lechner's Bas Relief Iris, hand painted, #269 USA, 5¼", pr **$70.00**

Candlesticks, pineapple form, brown & green, USA R-51, 3½", pr **$40.00**

Charger, blue & white stipple, 1st block letter, 13¼", from $200 to **$250.00**

Creamer, Lechner's Festoon of Roses, hand painted, w/lid, #653 USA, 5½" **$80.00**

Dealer sign, black lettering on yellow, unmarked, 6"..........**$300.00**

Figurine, cat, black, tail up, unmarked, 12½" **$200.00**

Figurine, horse, ivory, marked Harry Lee Gibson, ink stamp, 9x8¼" **$250.00**

Fishbowl, Wistful Kitten, Emerald Green, w/original bowl, unmarked, 8¾" **$80.00**

Flower bowl, yellow to blue matt, ink stamp, 5¼" **$200.00**

Flower frog, Rose Green Overflow, 1st block letter, ¾x3" dia, from $20 to **$30.00**

Ginger jar, desert scene w/palms, Lessell, signed LeCamark, 8¾" **$500.00**

Humidor, brown stipple, 1st block letter, 6½", from $120 to .**$140.00**

Humidor, Rose Green Overflow, 1st block letter, 7¼", from $180 to **$200.00**

Lamp base, river scenic, gray-blue, Lessell, 8" **$400.00**

Pig bottle, bright orange, 1st block letter, 3x9", from $200 to **$250.00**

Pitcher, Barcelona/Spano Ware, Sea Green, unmarked, 8½", from $180 to **$200.00**

Pitcher, Celestial Blue, parrot handle, ink stamp, 6½", from $160 to **$180.00**

Pitcher, lemonade; lemons & leaves on cream, 7¾" **$55.00**

Sugar jar, Autumn (brown), 1st block letter, 8"...................**$80.00**

Vase, Aztec Red mottle, bulbous, Arkansas die stamp, 10".**$350.00**

Vase, Aztec Red mottle, shouldered, bulbous, unmarked, 5", from $160 to **$180.00**

Vase, black/white combination, ring handles, unmarked, 4½", from $120 to **$140.00**

Vase, brown stipple, flared cylinder, unmarked, 10"...........**$200.00**

Vase, bud; 3 intertwining twigs, black gloss, 5¾" **$35.00**

Vase, Celestial Blue w/black overflow, flared cylinder, ink stamp, 10¾" **$300.00**

Vase, green crackle, swollen, gold stamp, 12¼" **$500.00**

Vase, Rose Green Overflow, ring handles, 1st inventory sticker, 6¼" **$100.00**

Vase, Rose Green Overflow, 4-ruffle rim, unmarked, 6¼", from $80 to **$100.00**

Vase, Sea Green, unmarked, 4½" **$35.00**

Vase, white crackle, pinched sides, unmarked, 9½" **$350.00**

Vase, Yellow Green Overflow, 1st block letter, 5" **$350.00**

Wall pocket, Iris (hand painted/bas-relief), Lechner, 9" **$250.00**

Cambridge Glassware

If you're looking for a 'safe' place to put your investment dollars, Cambridge glass is one of your better options. But as with any commodity, in order to make a good investment, knowledge of the product and its market is required. There are two books we would recommend for your study, *Colors in Cambridge Glass,* put out by the National Cambridge Collectors Club, and *The Collector's Encyclopedia of Elegant Glass* by Gene and Cathy Florence.

The Cambridge Glass Company (located in Cambridge, Ohio) made fine quality glassware from just after the turn of the century until 1958. They made thousands of different items in hundreds of various patterns and colors. Values hinge on rarity of shape and color. Of the various marks they used, the 'C in triangle' is the most common. In addition to their tableware, they also produced flower frogs representing ladies and children and models of animals and birds that are very valuable today. To learn more about them, you'll want to read *Glass Animals, Second Edition,* by Dick and Pat Spencer (Collector Books).

See also Glass Animals and Related Items.

Club: National Cambridge Collectors, Inc.
P.O. Box 416
Cambridge, OH 43725-0416
www.cambridgeglass.org
Master membership $20.00; associate members $3.00.

Achilles, bowl, crystal, flared, 4-toed, #3900/62, 12"..........**$75.00**

Achilles, crystal, candy box, #3900/165 ....**$135.00**

Achilles, crystal, claret, #3121, 4½-oz **$65.00**

Achilles, crystal, cup, demi; #3400/69................................**$65.00**

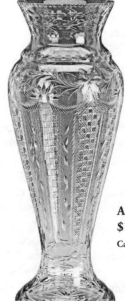

Achilles, crystal, floor vase, 18", $1,100.00. (Photo courtesy Gene and Cathy Florence)

Achilles, crystal, plate, luncheon; #3900/22, 8½"................**$16.00**

Achilles, crystal, tumbler, juice; footed, #3121, 5-oz...........**$35.00**

Achilles, crystal, vase, floral, footed, #278, 11" **$225.00**

Adonis, crystal, candlestick, #627, ea $35.00
Adonis, crystal, compote, blown, #3500, 5⅜" $75.00
Adonis, crystal, decanter, #1321, 28-oz.....................$295.00
Adonis, crystal, mayonnaise, 2-pc, #3900/11 ....$35.00
Adonis, crystal, plate, bread; #3500, 6" $12.00
Adonis, crystal, salt & pepper shakers, pr...................$85.00
Apple Blossom, amber or yellow, butter dish, 5½" $395.00
Apple Blossom, crystal, cocktail, #3130, 3-oz $18.00
Apple Blossom, crystal, plate, bread & butter; 6".............$8.00
Apple Blossom, pink or green, ice bucket......................$235.00
Apple Blossom, pink or green, vase, 5" $145.00
Candlelight, crystal, bonbon, footed, handles, #3900/130, 7" .. $40.00
Candlelight, crystal, candy box, 3-part, #3500/57 ....$165.00
Candlelight, crystal, compote, cheese; #3900/135, 5".........$45.00
Candlelight, crystal, tumbler, iced tea; #3776, 12-oz $45.00
Caprice, blue or pink, creamer, lg, #41 ....$25.00
Caprice, blue or pink, fruit cocktail, footed, #7, 4½-oz........$75.00
Caprice, blue or pink, oil cruet, w/stopper, #100, 5-oz $235.00
Caprice, blue or pink, tumbler, tea; flat, #310, 12-oz.........$120.00
Caprice, crystal, bowl, fruit; #18, 5" $30.00
Caprice, crystal, compote, low foot, #130, 7" $35.00
Caprice, crystal, plate, cabaret; 4-footed, #33, 14" $40.00
Caprice, crystal, vase, crimped top, #345, 5½" $90.00

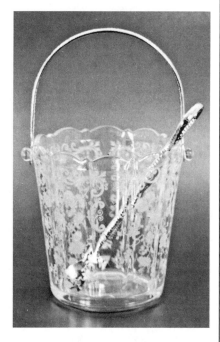

Chantilly, crystal, ice bucket, $125.00.

Cleo, amber, green, pink or yellow, bowl, vegetable; w/lid, 9". $295.00
Cleo, amber, green, pink or yellow, candy dish, tall $225.00
Cleo, amber, green, pink or yellow, creamer, ewer style, 6"..$125.00
Cleo, amber, green, pink or yellow, platter, #1079, 15" $225.00
Cleo, amber, green, pink or yellow, syrup pitcher, w/glass lid.. $250.00
Cleo, blue, bowl, celery; oval, #1083, 11"........................$125.00
Cleo, blue, bowl, fruit; 5½" $40.00
Cleo, blue, gravy boat, 2-spout, #917 ....$185.00
Cleo, blue, pitcher, w/lid, #3077, 63-oz...........................$895.00
Cleo, blue, tumbler, footed, #3022, 12-oz $95.00
Cleo, blue, wine, footed, #3077, 3½-oz $95.00
Daffodil, crystal, bonbon, #1181 ....$30.00

Daffodil, crystal, jug, #3400/140 ....$295.00
Daffodil, crystal, plate, salad; 8½"..................................$18.00
Daffodil, crystal, relish, 3-part, #214, 10" $65.00
Diane, crystal, bottle, bitters $195.00
Diane, crystal, bowl, cream soup; w/liner, #3400................$55.00
Diane, crystal, bowl, oval, 4-footed, 12" $80.00
Diane, crystal, bowl, pickle; 9½" $40.00
Diane, crystal, butter dish, round...................................$165.00
Diane, crystal, cabinet flask...$295.00
Diane, crystal, cigarette urn..$75.00
Diane, crystal, cordial, #1066, 1-oz $60.00
Diane, crystal, cup $20.00
Diane, crystal, decanter, lg, footed $225.00
Diane, crystal, hurricane lamp, candlestick base................$195.00
Diane, crystal, pitcher, martini $795.00
Diane, crystal, platter, 13½"...$110.00
Diane, crystal, saucer..$6.00
Diane, crystal, tumbler, old-fashioned; 7-oz.......................$55.00
Diane, crystal, vase, flower; 11" $115.00
Diane, crystal, vase, keyhole base, 9" $95.00
Elaine, crystal, basket, upturned sides, handles, 6" $30.00
Elaine, crystal, cup $22.00
Elaine, crystal, hat, 9"...$395.00
Elaine, crystal, pitcher, #3900/115, 78-oz..........................$250.00
Elaine, crystal, sugar bowl, individual $22.00
Elaine, crystal, tumbler, tea; footed, #3500, 12-oz $40.00
Elaine, crystal, tumbler, water; footed, #1402, 9-oz $25.00
Elaine, crystal, vase, footed, 6" $75.00
Gloria, crystal, bowl, cranberry; 3½" $40.00
Gloria, crystal, bowl, nut; 4-footed, individual, 3" $65.00
Gloria, crystal, butter dish, handles................................$225.00
Gloria, crystal, compote, low, 7" $40.00
Gloria, crystal, mayonnaise, w/liner & ladle $45.00
Gloria, crystal, pitcher, ball shape, 80-oz..........................$295.00
Gloria, crystal, plate, dinner; 9½" $65.00
Gloria, crystal, plate, sandwich; tab handles, 11½" $60.00
Gloria, crystal, salt & pepper shakers, short, pr...................$45.00
Gloria, crystal, saucer, round.......................................$4.00
Gloria, crystal, tray, sandwich; center handle, 11"................$35.00
Gloria, crystal, tumbler, footed, #3120, 5-oz......................$22.00
Gloria, crystal, vase, 11"..$125.00
Gloria, green, pink, or yellow, sugar bowl, tall, footed $35.00
Gloria, green, pink or yellow, bowl, cereal; sq, 6"................$55.00
Gloria, green, pink or yellow, cordial, #3120, 1-oz.............$175.00
Gloria, green, pink or yellow, creamer, tall, footed $35.00
Gloria, green, pink or yellow, cup, sq, 4-footed..................$100.00
Gloria, green, pink or yellow, ice pail, metal handle, w/tongs, #3400/851 ....$195.00
Gloria, green, pink or yellow, plate, bread & butter; sq........$15.00
Gloria, green, pink or yellow, platter, 11½".......................$150.00
Gloria, green, pink or yellow, tray, relish; center handle, 4-part $65.00
Gloria, green, pink or yellow, tumbler, high foot, #3035, 12-oz .$55.00
Gloria, green, pink or yellow, tumbler, juice; #3135, 5-oz....$40.00
Gloria, green, pink or yellow, vase, keyhole base, 10"........$165.00
Imperial Hunt Scene, colors, compote, #3085, 5½"............$60.00
Imperial Hunt Scene, colors, creamer, flat.........................$60.00
Imperial Hunt Scene, colors, humidor $595.00

Imperial Hunt Scene, colors, parfait, #3085, 5½-oz.............$75.00
Imperial Hunt Scene, colors, salt & pepper shakers, #396, pr. $295.00
Imperial Hunt Scene, colors, saucer, #1481 ....$15.00
Imperial Hunt Scene, crystal, bowl, 8" $40.00
Imperial Hunt Scene, crystal, candlestick, 2-light, keyhole, ea. $35.00
Imperial Hunt Scene, crystal, cup, #933/481 ....$50.00
Imperial Hunt Scene, crystal, pitcher, w/lid, #711, 76-oz ..$195.00
Imperial Hunt Scene, crystal, plate, #244, 10½" $20.00
Imperial Hunt Scene, crystal, plate, #554, 7"....................$20.00
Imperial Hunt Scene, crystal, tumbler, flat, tall, #1402, 15-oz. $35.00
Marjorie, crystal, bottle, oil & vinegar; 6-oz....................$350.00
Marjorie, crystal, compote, jelly; #2090, 5" $70.00
Marjorie, crystal, decanter, #7606, 28-oz $400.00
Marjorie, crystal, finger bowl, #7606 ....$40.00
Marjorie, crystal, jug, #104, 30-oz $265.00
Marjorie, crystal, nappy, #4111, 4" $30.00
Marjorie, crystal, stem, cocktail; #3750, 3½-oz..................$25.00
Marjorie, crystal, syrup, #106, 8" $300.00
Marjorie, crystal, tumbler, #8858, 5-oz...........................$15.00
Marjorie, crystal, tumbler, tea; #7606, 12-oz $22.00
Mt Vernon, amber or crystal, ashtray, #68, 4" $12.00
Mt Vernon, amber or crystal, bottle, cologne; w/stopper, #1340, 2½-
    oz..$45.00
Mt Vernon, amber or crystal, bowl, salad; #120, 10½" $25.00
Mt Vernon, amber or crystal, box, sq, #17, 4" $32.50
Mt Vernon, amber or crystal, cake stand, footed, #150, 10½". $35.00
Mt Vernon, amber or crystal, pitcher, #91, 86-oz $130.00
Mt Vernon, amber or crystal, relish, 3-handled, 3-part, #103,
    8" $20.00
Mt Vernon, amber or crystal, tray, sweetmeat; handles, 4-part,
    8½" $8.00
Portia, crystal, basket, handles, 7" $350.00
Portia, crystal, bowl, bonbon; handles, #3400/180, 5¼".....$30.00
Portia, crystal, bowl, relish; 2-part, 7" $35.00
Portia, crystal, candy box, round.................................$135.00
Portia, crystal, cocktail shaker, w/glass stopper $195.00
Portia, crystal, creamer, footed, #3400/68 ....$20.00
Portia, crystal, decanter, sherry; footed, w/stopper, 29-oz...$265.00
Portia, crystal, oil cruet, loop handle, w/stopper, 6-oz........$125.00
Portia, crystal, plate, bread & butter; 6½" $7.50
Portia, crystal, puff box, ball shape, 3½" $225.00
Portia, crystal, tumbler, juice; footed, #3122, 5-oz.............$25.00
Portia, crystal, vase, #1242, 10" $70.00
Rosalie, amber or crystal, claret, #7606, 4½-oz $25.00
Rosalie, amber or crystal, platter, 15".........................$100.00
Rosalie, amber or crystal, sugar shaker $225.00
Rosalie, blue, green or pink, bottle, French dressing..........$210.00
Rosalie, blue, green or pink, bowl, cranberry; 3½" $50.00
Rosalie, blue, green or pink, plate, cheese & cracker; 11" $80.00
Rosalie, blue, green or pink, tray, wafer.........................$140.00
Rose Point, crystal, ashtray, sq, #721, 2½" $35.00
Rose Point, crystal, bell, dinner; #3121..........................$150.00
Rose Point, crystal, bowl, fancy rim, 4-footed, #3400/136, 6". $165.00
Rose Point, crystal, bowl, nut; footed, #3400/71, 3"............$75.00
Rose Point, crystal, candelabrum, 3-light, #1338, ea............$95.00
Rose Point, crystal, cocktail shaker, w/glass stopper, #101, 32-
    oz...$295.00

Rose Point, crystal, creamer, flat, #944............................$165.00

**Rose Point, crystal, divided relish with center handle, 7½"
diameter, $150.00.**

Rose Point, crystal, honey dish, w/lid, #3500/139 ....$425.00
Rose Point, crystal, ice bucket, chrome handle, #3900/671 .$195.00
Rose Point, crystal, pitcher, #3900/118, 32-oz..................$400.00
Rose Point, crystal, plate, torte; #3500/38, 13".................$185.00
Rose Point, crystal, sherry, plain foot, #7966, 2-oz $125.00
Rose Point, crystal, tray, round, #3500/67, 12" $210.00
Rose Point, crystal, urn, w/lid, #3500/42, 12" $795.00
Rose Point, crystal, vase, sweet pea; #629.......................$395.00
Tally Ho, amber or crystal, ash well, center handle, 2-pc $20.00
Tally Ho, amber or crystal, bowl, grapefruit; flat rim, 6½"...$20.00
Tally Ho, amber or crystal, coaster, 4".........................$10.00
Tally Ho, amber or crystal, creamer, footed......................$12.50
Tally Ho, Carmen Royal, plate, dinner; 10½".....................$125.00
Tally Ho, Carmen Royal, tumbler, tall, 10-oz $45.00
Tally Ho, Carmen Royal, vase, footed, 12" $225.00
Tally Ho, Carmen Royal, wine, high stem, 3-oz....................$35.00
Tally Ho, Forest Green, decanter, 34-oz $65.00
Tally Ho, Forest Green, goblet, cocktail; #1402 ....$16.00
Tally Ho, Forest Green, mug, punch; 6-oz $15.00
Valencia, crystal, bowl, cereal; #3500/37, 6" $30.00
Valencia, crystal, candy dish, #3500/103.........................$165.00
Valencia, crystal, cigarette holder, footed, #1066..............$65.00
Valencia, crystal, claret, #3500, 4½-oz..........................$40.00
Valencia, crystal, cup, #3500/1..................................$20.00
Valencia, crystal, oyster cocktail, #1402 ....$18.00
Valencia, crystal, pitcher, Doulton shape, #3400/141, 80-oz.$395.00
Valencia, crystal, salt & pepper shakers, #3400/18, pr $65.00
Valencia, crystal, sugar basket, #3500/13 ....$175.00
Valencia, crystal, sugar bowl, #3500/14 ....$16.00
Valencia, crystal, tumbler, footed, #3500, 13-oz.................$25.00
Wildflower, bowl, bonbon; #3900/130, handles, 7"............$35.00
Wildflower, crystal, basket, footed, handles, #3400/1182,6" ..$35.00
Wildflower, crystal, bowl, celery & relish; 3-part, #3900/126,
    12" $55.00
Wildflower, crystal, candlestick, #3121, 7", ea $110.00

Wildflower, crystal, cocktail icer, #968, 2-pc.........................$75.00
Wildflower, crystal, compote, blown, #3121, 5⅜" $65.00
Wildflower, crystal, creamer, #3900/41 ....$20.00
Wildflower, crystal, hat, #1704, 5"....................................$295.00
Wildflower, crystal, oil cruet, w/stopper, #3900/100, 6-oz.$135.00
Wildflower, crystal, plate, footed, handles, #3900/161, 8" ...$18.00
Wildflower, crystal, plate, service; 4-footed, #3900/26, 12" .$55.00

Wildflower, crystal, salt and pepper shakers, $50.00 for the pair. (Photo courtesy Gene and Cathy Florence)

Wildflower, crystal, sugar bowl, #3400/68 ....$20.00
Wildflower, crystal, tumbler, tea; #3121, 12-oz....................$35.00
Wildflower, crystal, vase, bud; #1528, 10" $110.00
Wildflower, crystal, water goblet, #3121, 10-oz $37.50

Cameras

Camera collecting as a hobby can provide both enjoyment and potential profit if a careful selection is made. The large number of older cameras that have been offered for sale on the Internet continues to create a good buyer's market, and excellent cameras can often be purchased that offer great potential for future increases in value. The faster than expected growth of the digital camera technology and popularity has also strongly affected the film camera market, except for the rare collectible categories. There is currently no 'collectible' market for the digital cameras, and sales of used ones are not good, due to the difficulty of checking out one of these cameras and the complexity of the associated software and computer adapters necessary for their use. The use of digital cameras for first-time photographers is increasing rapidly and will continue to have a drastic effect on the prices of regular film cameras.

Buying at garage sales, flea markets, auctions, or estate sales are ways to add to collections, although it is rare to find an expensive classic camera offered through these outlets. However, buying at such sales to resell to dealers or collectors can be profitable if one is careful to buy quality items, not common cameras that sell for very little at best, especially when they show wear. A very old camera is not necessarily valuable, as value depends on availability and quality.

Knowing how to check out a camera or to judge quality will pay off when building a collection or when buying for resale. Another factor to consider on many older film cameras is the growing difficulty in finding the prescribed batteries for them. Many of them used 1.35 volt mercury batteries which are illegal now and no longer available. Conversions to many of the cameras are possible but expensive and often impracticable. Some of the other types of camera batteries are beginning to disappear from the market.

Some very general guidelines follow; but for the serious buyer who intends to concentrate on cameras, there are several reference books that can be obtained. Most are rather expensive, but some provide good descriptions and/or price guidelines.

There are many distinct types of cameras to consider: large format (such as Graflex and large view cameras), medium format, early folding and box styles, 35mm single-lens-reflex (SLR), 35mm range finders, twin-lens-reflex (TLR), miniature or sub-miniature, novelty, and other types — including the more recent 'point-and-shoot' styles, Polaroids, and movie cameras. Though there is a growing interest in certain types, we would caution you against buying common Polaroids and movie cameras for resale, as there is very little market for them at this time. In these categories, buy only those that are like new and still in their original boxes to attract collectors.

Most folding and box-type cameras were produced before the 1930s and today make good collector items. Most have fairly low values because they were made in vast numbers. Many of the more expensive classics were manufactured in the 1930 – 1955 period and include primarily the Rangefinder type of camera and those with the first built-in light meters. The most prized of these are of German or Japanese manufacture, valued because of their innovative designs and great optics. The key to collecting these types of cameras is to find a mint-condition example or one still in the original box. In camera collecting, quality is the most important aspect.

This updated listing includes only a few of the various categories and models of cameras from the many thousands available and gives current average retail prices for working models with average wear. Note that cameras in mint condition or like new with their original boxes may be valued much higher, while very worn examples with defects (scratches, dents, torn covers, poor optics, nonworking meters or rangefinders, torn bellows, corroded battery compartments, etc.) would be valued far less. A dealer, when buying for resale, will pay only a percentage of these values, as he must consider his expenses for refurbishing, cleaning, etc., as well as sales expenses. Again, remember that quality is the key to value, and prices on some cameras vary widely according to condition. Also be aware that many of the great classic cameras, even in very poor condition, are valued for their parts and often have good value if bargains can be found. Look also for camera lenses alone, some of which are very valuable.

Typical collector favorites are old Alpa, Canon, Contax, Nikon, Leica, Rolleiflex, some Zeiss-Ikon models, Exakta, and certain Voigtlander models. For information about these makes as well as models by other manufacturers, please consult the advisor.

Advisor: C.E. Cataldo (See Directory, Cameras)

Agfa, Billy, 1930s $15.00
Agfa, box type, 1930-50, from $5 to...................................$20.00
Agfa, Isolette $20.00

Agfa, Karat-35, 1940 .... $35.00
Agfa, Optima, 1960s, from $15 to.................. $35.00
Aires, 35III, 1958, from $15 to...................... $35.00
Alpa, Standard, 1946-52, Swiss, from $700 to $1,500.00
Ansco, Cadet.. $5.00
Ansco, Folding, Nr 1 to Nr 10, ea from $5 to $30.00
Ansco, Memar, 1954-58.................................. $20.00
Ansco, Memo, 1927 type, from $60 to............. $80.00
Ansco, Speedex, Standard, 1950..................... $15.00
Argoflex, Seventy-five, TLR, 1949-58 .... $7.00
Argus A2F, 1940, from $10 to $20.00
Argus C3, Black brick type, 1940-50 .... $8.00
Asahi Pentax, Original, 1957 .... $200.00
Asahiflex I, 1st Japanese SLR $500.00
Baldi, by Balda-Werk, 1930s $30.00
Bell & Howell Dial 35, from $25 to $40.00
Bell & Howell Foton, 1948, from $500 to $700.00
Bosley B2 .... $20.00
Braun Paxette I, 1952, from $20 to $30.00
Burke & James Cub, 1914 .... $20.00
Canon A-1, from $70 to $130.00
Canon AE-IP, from $70 to $125.00
Canon AE-1, from $40 to $80.00
Canon F-1, from $150 to $225.00
Canon IIB, 1949-53 .... $225.00
Canon III.. $250.00
Canon IV SB, rangefinder w/50/fl.8 lens, 1952-55, from $250 to... $350.00
Canon J, 1939-44, from $3,000 to $5,000.00
Canon L-1, 1956-57 .... $400.00

Conley, 4x5 Folding Plate, 1905, from $90 to $140.00
Contax II or III, 1936, from $200 to.............. $400.00
Contessa 35, 1950-55, from $100 to $150.00
Detrola Model D, Detroit Corp, 1938-40 .... $20.00
Eastman Folding Brownie Six-20.................... $12.00
Eastman Kodak Baby Brownie, Bakelite, from $5 to ... $10.00
Eastman Kodak Bantam, Art Deco, 1935-38 .... $35.00
Eastman Kodak Medalist, 1941-48, from $100 to $175.00
Eastman Kodak Retina II, from $45 to............ $60.00
Eastman Kodak Retina IIa, from $55 to $75.00
Eastman Kodak Retina IIIC, from $250 to....... $325.00
Eastman Kodak Retina IIIc, from $90 to......... $150.00
Eastman Kodak Retinette, various models, ea from $15 to .. $40.00
Eastman Kodak Signet 35 .... $35.00
Eastman Kodak Signet 80 .... $50.00
Eastman Kodak 35, 1940-51, from $20 to $40.00
Eastman Premo, many models exist, ea from $30 to $200.00
Eastman View Camera, early 1900s, from $100 to $200.00
Edinex, by Wirgen $30.00
Exakta II, 1949-50, from $100 to $130.00
Exakta VX, 1951, from $75 to......................... $85.00
FED 1, USSR, postwar, from $30 to $50.00
FED 1, USSR, prewar, from $70 to $100.00
Fujica AX-3, from $45 to................................ $75.00
Fujica AX-5.. $115.00
Graflex Pacemaker Crown Graphic, various sizes, ea from $80 to.. $150.00
Graflex Speed Graphic, various sizes, ea from $60 to $200.00
Hasselblad 1000F, 1952-57, from $300 to....... $500.00
Herbert-George, Donald Duck, 1946 .... $25.00

Canon P, 1958 – 1961, from $250.00 to $350.00.
(Photo courtesy C.E. Cataldo)

Canon Rangefinder IIF, ca 1954, from $200 to $300.00
Canon S-II, Seiki-Kogaku, 1946-47, from $500 to........... $800.00
Canon S-II, 1947-49.................................... $375.00
Canon T-50, from $30 to................................ $50.00
Canon TL, from $30 to $50.00
Canon TX, from $30 to $40.00
Canon VT, 1956-57, from $200 to.................. $300.00
Canon 7, 1961-64, from $200 to $400.00
Canonet QL1, from $25 to.............................. $40.00
Compass Camera, 1938, from $1,000 to $1,300.00

Kodak Jiffy Vest Pocket, 1935 – 1941, from $20.00 to $35.00. (Photo courtesy C.E. Cataldo)

Kodak No 2 Folding Pocket Brownie, 1904-07 .... $25.00
Konica Autoreflex TC, various models, ea from $40 to........ $70.00
Konica FS-1 .... $50.00
Konica III Rangefinder, 1956-59, from $90 to $110.00
Kowa H, 1963-67 .... $25.00
Leica II, 1963-67, from $200 to $400.00
Leica IID, 1932-38, from $200 to $400.00
Leica IIIF, 1950-56, from $200 to $400.00

Leica M3, 1954-56, from $400 to **$900.00**
Mamiya-Sekor 500TL, 1966......................**$20.00**
Mamiyaflex TLR, 1951, from $70 to **$100.00**
Minolta Autocord, TLR, from $75 to **$100.00**
Minolta HiMatic Series, various models, ea from $10 to **$25.00**
Minolta SR-7 ....**$40.00**
Minolta SRT-101, from $40 to **$65.00**
Minolta SRT-202, from $50 to **$90.00**
Minolta X-700, from $75 to **$135.00**
Minolta XD-11, 1977......................**$130.00**
Minolta XG-1m XG-7, XG-9, XG-A, ea from $35 to.........**$80.00**
Minolta 35, early rangefinder models, 1947-50, ea from $250 to......................**$400.00**
Minolta-16, mini, various models, ea from $15 to..............**$30.00**
Minox B, spy camera **$125.00**
Miranda Automex II, 1963 ....**$70.00**
Nikkormat (Nikon), various models, ea from $70 to **$150.00**
Nikon EM, from $45 to **$75.00**
Nikon F, various finders & meters, ea from $125 to **$225.00**
Nikon FG **$100.00**
Nikon FM......................**$150.00**
Nikon S Rangefinder, 1951-54, from $450 to **$800.00**
Nikon SP Rangefinder, 1958-60, from $1500 to **$2,000.00**
Nikon S2 Rangefinder, 1954-58, from $700 to **$1,000.00**
Olympus OM-1, from $90 to **$120.00**
Olympus OM-10, from $40 to **$60.00**
Olympus Pen EE, compact half-frame **$35.00**
Olympus Pen F, compact half-frame SLR, from $100 to....**$200.00**
Pax M3, 1957 ....**$30.00**
Pentax K-1000, from $50 to **$90.00**
Pentax ME, from $50 to **$75.00**
Pentax Spotmatic, many models, ea from $40 to **$100.00**
Petri FT, FT-1000, FT-EE & similar models, ea from $35 to ... **$70.00**
Petri-7, 1961 ....**$20.00**
Plaubel-Makina II, 1933-39......................**$200.00**
Polaroid, most models, ea from $5 to......................**$10.00**
Polaroid SX-70, from $20 to......................**$35.00**
Polaroid 110, 110A, 110B, ea from $20 to **$40.00**
Polaroid 180, 185, 190, 195, ea from $100 to..................**$250.00**
Praktica FX, 1952-57......................**$30.00**
Praktica Super TL......................**$40.00**
Realist Stereo, 3.5 lens......................**$80.00**
Regula, King, fixed lens, various models, ea **$25.00**
Regula, King, interchangeable lens, various models, ea **$60.00**
Ricoh Diacord 1, TLR, built-in meter, 1958......................**$65.00**
Ricoh Singlex, 1965, from $50 to **$70.00**
Rollei 35, mini, Germany, 1966-70, from $150 to **$250.00**
Rollei 35, mini, Singapore, from $80 to............................**$150.00**
Rolleicord II, 1936-50, from $70 to **$90.00**
Rolleiflex Automat, 1937 model **$125.00**
Rolleiflex SL35M, 1978, from $75 to **$100.00**
Rolleiflex 3.5E......................**$300.00**
Samoca 35, 1950s **$25.00**
Seroco 4x5, Folding Plate, Sears, 1901, from $90 to.......**$135.00**
Spartus Press Flash, 1939-50......................**$10.00**
Taron 35, 1955 ....**$25.00**
Tessina, mini, from $300 to **$500.00**

Topcon Super D, 1963-74 ....**$125.00**
Topcon Uni......................**$35.00**
Tower 45, Sears, w/Nickkor lens **$200.00**
Tower 50, Sears, w/Cassar lens **$20.00**
Univex-A, Univ Camera Co, 1933......................**$25.00**
Voigtlander Bessa, various folding models, 1931-49, ea from $15 to **$35.00**
Voigtlander Bessa, w/rangefinder, 1936......................**$140.00**
Voigtlander Vitessa L, 1954, from $150 to **$200.00**

Voigtlander Vitessa T, 1957, from $150.00 to $200.00.
(Photo courtesy C.E. Cataldo)

Voigtlander Vito II, 1950......................**$40.00**
Yashica A, TLR **$35.00**
Yashica Electro-35, 1966......................**$25.00**
Yashica FX-70......................**$60.00**
Yashicamat 124G, TLR, from $125 to......................**$200.00**
Zeiss Baldur Box Tengor, Frontar lens, 1935, from $35 to.**$150.00**
Zeiss Ikon Juwell, 1927-39 ....**$500.00**
Zeiss Ikon Nettar, Folding Roll Film, various sizes, ea from $25 to **$35.00**
Zeiss Ikon Super Ikonta B, 1937-56 ....**$150.00**
Zenit A, USSR, from $20 to......................**$35.00**
Zorki, USSR, 1950-56, from $20 to......................**$40.00**
Zorki-4, USSR, Rangefinder, 1957-73......................**$50.00**

Candlewick Glassware

This is a beautifully simple, very diverse line of glassware made by the Imperial Glass Company of Bellaire, Ohio, from 1936 to 1982. (The factory closed in 1984.) From all explored written material found so far, it is known that Mr. Earl W. Newton brought back a piece of the French Cannonball pattern upon returning from a trip. The first Candlewick mold was derived using that piece of glass as a reference. As for the name Candlewick, it was introduced at a Wheeling, West Virginia, centennial celebration in August of 1936, appearing on a brochure showing the crafting of 'Candlewick Quilts' and promoting the new Candlewick line.

Imperial did cuttings on Candlewick; several major patterns

are Floral, Valley Lily, Starlight, Princess, DuBarry, and Dots. Remember, these are *cuts* and should not be confused with etchings. (Cuts that were left unpolished were called Gray Cut — an example of this is the Dot cut.) The most popular Candlewick etching was Rose of Sharon (Wild Rose). All cutting was done on a wheel, while etching utilized etching paper and acid. Many collectors confuse these two processes. Imperial also used gold, silver, platinum, and hand painting to decorate Candlewick, and they made several items in colors.

With over 740 pieces in all, Imperial's Candlewick line was one of the leading tableware patterns in the country. Due to its popularity with collectors today, it is still number one and has the distinction of being the only single line of glassware ever to have had two books written about it, a national newsletter, and over 15 collector clubs across the USA devoted to it exclusively.

There are reproductions on the market today — some are coming in from foreign countries. Look-alikes are often mistakenly labeled Candlewick, so if you're going to collect this pattern, you need to be well informed. Most collectors use the company mold numbers to help identify all the variations and sizes. The *Imperial Glass Encyclopedia, Vol. 1*, has a very good chapter on Candlewick. Also reference *Candlewick, The Jewel of Imperial*, by Mary Wetzel-Tomalka; *Elegant Glassware of the Depression Era* by Gene and Cathy Florence (Collector Books), and *Candlewick and Decorated Candlewick* by Myrna and Bob Garrison.

Advisor: National Imperial Glass Collectors Society, Inc.

Club: National Imperial Glass Collectors Society, Inc.
P.O. Box 534
Bellaire, Ohio 43906
Membership $18.00 per year plus $3.00 for each associate
www.imperialglass.org

Ashtray, eagle, #1776/1, 6½"	$55.00
Ashtray, matchbook holder center, #400/60, 6"	$165.00
Basket, beaded handle, #400/273, 5"	$265.00
Bell, #400/108, 5"	$95.00
Bottle, bitters; w/tube, #400/117, 4-oz	$75.00
Bowl, boullion; handles, #400/126	$50.00
Bowl, round, #400/5F, 8"	$37.50

Cake stand, high foot, 11", $75.00.

Calendar, desk; 1947	$250.00
Candleholder, flat, #400/280, 3½", ea	$40.00
Candleholder, urn, holders on circle center bead, #400/129R , 6", ea	$185.00
Candy box, sq, w/round lid, #400/245, 6½"	$350.00
Cigarette box, w/lid, #400/134	$35.00
Clock, round, 4"	$295.00
Coaster, #400/78, 4"	$10.00
Condiment set, 4-pc, #400/1769	$80.00
Cruet, w/stopper, etched Oil, #400/121	$75.00
Cup, after dinner; #400/77	$20.00
Decanter, cordial; w/stopper, #400/82/2, 15-oz	$495.00
Deviled egg server, center handle, #400/154, 12"	$130.00
Finger bowl, footed, #3400	$35.00
Fork & spoon, #400/75, set	$35.00
Goblet, brandy; #3800	$60.00
Goblet, tea; #4000, 12-oz	$35.00
Goblet, wine; #3800, 4-oz	$30.00
Hurricane lamp, candle base, 2-pc, #400/79	$135.00
Jam set, 5-pc: oval tray w/2 marmalade jars w/ladles, #400/1589	$120.00
Knife, butter; #4000	$500.00
Ladle, mayonnaise; 3-knob, #400/165	$12.00
Lamp shade	$85.00
Mirror, standing; round, 4½"	$150.00
Pitcher, #400/24, 80-oz	$165.00
Pitcher, juice/cocktail; #400/19, 40-oz	$215.00
Plate, bread/butter; #400/1D, 6"	$8.00
Plate, canape; w/off-center indent, #400/36, 6"	$18.00
Plate, cupped edge, #400/20V, 17"	$95.00
Plate, luncheon; $400/7D, 9"	$15.00
Plate, salad; #400/3D, 7"	$9.00
Platter, 400/131/D, 16"	$245.00
Punch set, 15-pc: bowl on 18" plate, 12 cups & ladle, #400/20	$300.00
Salad set, buffet; 4-pc: lg, round tray, divided bowl & 2 spoons, #400/17	$135.00
Salt & pepper shakers, #400/167	$16.00
Strawberry set, 2-pc: 7" plate & sugar dip bowl, #400/83	$50.00
Sugar bowl, domed foot, #400/18	$135.00
Teacup, #400/35	$8.00
Tidbit server, 2-tier, cupped, #400/2701	$60.00
Tray, lemon; center handle, #400/221, 5½"	$35.00
Tray, relish; 5 sections, #400/102, 13"	$65.00
Tumbler, juice; #3800, 15-oz	$30.00
Tumbler, parfait; #3400, 6-oz	$70.00
Vase, bud; footed, #400/186, 7"	$310.00
Vase, fan, w/bead handles, #400/87F, 8"	$35.00
Vase, footed, #400/193, 10"	$295.00

Candy Containers

Most of us can recall buying these glass toys as a child, since they were made well into the 1960s. We were fascinated by the variety of their shapes then, just as collectors are today. Looking back, it couldn't have been we were buying them for the candy, though perhaps as a child those tiny sugary balls flavored more with the coloring agent than anything else were enough to satisfy our 'sweet tooth.'

Glass candy containers have been around since our country's centennial celebration in 1876 when the first two, the Liberty Bell and the Independence Hall, were introduced. Since then they have been made in hundreds of styles, and some of them have become very expensive. The leading manufacturers were in the east — Westmoreland, Victory Glass, J.H. Millstein, Crosetti, L.E. Smith, Jack Stough, T.H. Stough, and West Bros. made perhaps 90% of them — and collectors report finding many in the Pennsylvania area. Most are clear, but you'll find them in various other colors as well.

If you're going to deal in candy containers of either the vintage glass variety or modern plastics, you'll need a book that will show you all the variations available. Vintage candy container buffs will find *Collector's Guide to Candy Containers* by Douglas M. Dezso, J. Leon Poirier, and Rose D. Poirier to be a wonderful source of pictures and information. D&P numbers in our listings refer to that book. Published by Collector Books, it is a must for beginners as well as seasoned collectors. Another good reference is *The Compleat American Glass Candy Containers Handbook* by Eilkelberner and Agadjaninian (revised by Adele Bowden).

Because of their popularity and considerable worth, many of the original glass containers have been reproduced. Beware of any questionable glassware that has a slick or oily touch. Among those that have been produced are Amber Pistol, Auto, Carpet Sweeper, Chicken on Nest, Display Case, Dog, Drum Mug, Fire Engine, Independence Hall, Jackie Coogan, Kewpie, Mail Box, Mantel Clock, Mule and Waterwagon, Peter Rabbit, Piano, Rabbit Pushing Wheelbarrow, Rocking Horse, Safe, Santa, Santa's Boot, Station Wagon, and Uncle Sam's Hat. Others are possible.

Plastic parts were incorporated into candy containers as early as the 1940s, and by 1960 virtually all were made entirely of this inexpensive, colorful, and versatile material. Children were soon clamoring for these new all-plastic containers, many of which seemed as much a toy as a mere candy container. Today most of these are imported from China and Mexico. Shapes vary from vehicles of all sorts to cartoon, movie, and TV characters, TV sets and telephones, to holiday decorations and household items. Collector interest is apparent in shops and malls as well as on the Internet.

Our values are given for candy containers that are undamaged, in good original paint, and complete (with all original parts and closure). Repaired or repainted containers are worth much less.

See also Christmas; Easter; Halloween.

Club/Newsletter: *The Candy Gram*
Candy Container Collectors of America
Jo Anna Baldwin, Membership Chairperson
P.O. Box 2871
Anderson, IN 46108
gmja59@insightbb.com
www.candycontainer.org

Plastic

Candy Soda Fountain, dispenses 'candy sodas,' Par Beverage Corp, 1950, 5x4", M (torn box) **$70.00**

Cowboy boot w/embossed floral decor, brown, 4½x4½" **$10.00**

Harry (and the Hendersons), made for Topps Chewing Gum Inc., 1987, 2⅜", from $5.00 to $7.00. (Photo courtesy Jack Brush and William Miller)

Heart shape, To My Valentine, red w/white painted bow, E Rosen Plastics, 1940s-50s, 2½x2" **$20.00**
Hillbilly clown, red hat & blue pants, hole in ea hand for lollipops, Rosbro, 5" **$22.00**
Mickey Mouse as magician, multicolor paint, move his arm w/top hat & find hole for candy, Disney **$15.00**
Minnie Mouse face, black paint on clear, 5½x5½" **$35.00**
Peanut shape, light brown, 12" L **$17.50**
Rooster, yellow w/multicolor details, sticker: Buy Genuine Jaw Teasers Refills, 1960s?, 8½x6" **$24.00**
Snowman on silver-colored skis, backpack holds candy, 1950s, 5x4", EX **$30.00**
Tugboat on wheels, clown figurehead on front, red, Tico, 1940s, 2½x4½" **$30.00**

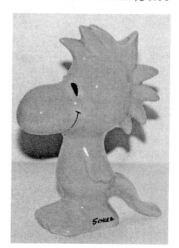

Woodstock, copyright 1965, 1972, United Features Syndicate Inc., 6", $30.00. (Photo courtesy Jack Brush and William Miller)

Ziggy, I've Got the Red Hots for You!, Ziggy-shaped box, 1990, 7¼x4¾x1¼", EX **$32.00**

Vintage

Airplane, Army Bomber; marked JH Millstein Co, D&P 76/E&A 6/L 328 .... **$40.00**
Airplane, Patent 113053, tin propeller, D&P/81/E&A 4 ..... **$85.00**
Blimp, heavy glass, D&P 88 .... **$200.00**

Boat, Uruguay; anchor each side of bow, D&P 105............$200.00

Bureau, slide-on closure, real mirror, D&P 294/E&A 112/L 125 .... $200.00

Camel, Shriner's; clear or amber glass, sitting, D&P 4 ....$35.00

Car, Miniature Streamlined; D&P 173/E&A 33/L 377 (+) .$25.00

Cheery Cholly Clown, cardboard suit & shoes, composition head, D&P 194/L 530 ....$300.00

Clock, Betty Barker Time Teacher; D&P 478 ....$150.00

Dirigible, Mu-Mu; Bakelite closure, D&P 90 ....$150.00

Elephant, GOP, original paint, D&P 43/E&A 206/L 31 ...$250.00

Flapper, paper face glued inside, D&P 203/E&A 227 ....$65.00

Gas Pump, 23¢ To-Day; D&P 439/E&A 240/L 316........$375.00

Gun, Sm Revolver, grip w/diamond embossing, D&P 398/E&A 253 ....$30.00

Horn, 3-Valve; gilt valves, D&P 455/E&A 312/L 281 ......$175.00

Lamp, Kerosene w/Swizzle Stick; D&P 333.......................$75.00

Lamppost, glass globe/pewter stand, D&P 341/L 553 ....$90.00

Lantern on Stand, shaker closure, ruby stain, D&P 358/L 571 ..$50.00

Locomotive, Stough's Musical Toy; D&P 506/E&A 476 .....$40.00

Nurser, Waisted; Crosetti, D&P 125/E&A 548/L 71 ....$25.00

Pencil, Kiddies Candy, w/box, D&P 217 ....$50.00

Play Packs, Toy Assortment, Christmas; D&P 469 ....$125.00

Rabbit Running on a Log, gilded, D&P #62, from $300.00 to $400.00. (Photo courtesy Poirier, Poirier, and Dezso)

Racer, Plastic; clear w/green wheels, D&P 472 ....$30.00

Safe, Dime; CD Kenney, D&P 312/E&A 661/L 268........$100.00

Santa Claus Leaving Chimney, Victory Glass; D&P 281/E&A 673/ L 102 ....$150.00

Tank, 2 Cannons; D&P 413/E&A 723 ....$35.00

Tomahawk & Gun, wooden handle, cardboard head, glass gun, D&P 416...$50.00

Village Drug Store, w/liner, D&P 137/E&A 10 ....$135.00

Wheelbarrow, Victory Glass, tin snap-on closure, D&P 534/E&A 843 ....$95.00

Miscellaneous

Bulldog, composition, cream w/orange hat, Germany, 4", VG ..$100.00

Cabin cruiser, clear glass, 1950s, 5" L $20.00

Cat in shoe, composition & gesso w/multicolor paint, repaired, 4" $175.00

Collie, papier-maché, glass eyes, sm repair, 4¾x7" $145.00

George Washington bust, composition, bottom plug, 4-6"...$150.00

Hen on nest, papier-maché, Drake Process Pat May 29 1919, 6½x6½" $50.00

Irish man's bust, composition, w/plug, Germany, 5-6".......$150.00

Pig sleeping, papier-maché, pink flocking, 5⅝"...................$90.00

Watermelon w/face, molded cardboard w/celluloid body, Austria, 4¼" $125.00

Cape Cod by Avon

You can't walk through any flea market or mall now without seeing a good supply of this lovely ruby red glassware. It was made by Wheaton Glass Co. and sold by Avon from 1975 until it was discontinued in 1993. A gradual phasing-out process lasted for approximately two years. The small cruet and tall candlesticks, for instance, were filled originally with one or the other of their fragrances, the wine and water goblets were filled with scented candle wax, and the dessert bowl with guest soap. Many 'campaigns' featured accessory tableware items such as plates, cake stands, and a water pitcher. Though still plentiful, dealers tell us that interest in this glassware is on the increase, and we expect values to climb as supplies diminish.

For more information we recommend *Avon's Cape Cod*, by Debbie and Randy Coe.

Advisor: Debbie Coe (See Directory, Cape Cod)

Bell, Hostess; marked Christmas 1979, 6½" $18.00

Bell, Hostess; unmarked, 1979-80, 6½"...............................$17.50

Bowl, dessert; 1979-80, 6½" $10.00

Bowl, rimmed soup; 1991, 7½" $22.00

Bowl, vegetable; marked Centennial Edition 1886-1986, 8¾". $30.00

Box, trinket; heart form, w/lid, 1989-90, 4" $15.00

Butter dish, 1983-84, ¼-lb, 7" L, from $20 to......................$22.00

Cake knife, red plastic handle, wedge-shaped blade, Regent Sheffield, 1981-84, 8" $18.00

Cake plate, pedestal foot, 1991, 3½x10¾" dia $48.00

Candleholder, hurricane type, clear chimney, 1985, ea.........$39.50

Candlesticks, 8¾", pr $25.00

Candy dish, 1987-90, 3½x6" $19.50

Christmas ornament, 6-sided, marked Christmas 1990, 3¼" .$12.50

Creamer, footed, 1981-84, 4" $10.00

Cruet, oil; w/stopper, 1957-80, 5-oz $12.50

Cup & saucer, 15th Anniversary, marked 1975-90 on cup, 7-oz...$20.00

Cup & saucer, 1990-93, 7-oz...$15.00

Decanter, 9¾"..$18.00

Goblet, claret; 1992, 5-oz, 5¼", from $10 to........................$14.00

Goblet, saucer champagne; 1991, 8-oz, 5¼" $14.00

Goblet, water; 1976-90, 9-oz..$9.00

Goblet, wine; 1976-90, 3-oz...$2.00

Mug, pedestal foot, 1982-84, 5-oz, 5", from $8 to $12.00

Napkin ring, 1989-90, 1¾"...$10.00

Pie plate/server, 1992-93, 10¾" dia, from $20 to.................$25.00

Pitcher, water; footed, 1984-85, 60-oz, from $40 to $45.00

Plate, bread & butter; 1992-93, 5½"......................................$8.00

Plate, dessert; 1980-90, 7½"...$7.50

Plate, dinner; 1982 – 1990, 11", from $20.00 to $25.00.

Platter, oval, 1986, 13"..$48.00
Relish, rectangular, 2-part, 1985-96, 9½" $15.00
Salt & pepper shakers, unmarked, 1978-80, pr..................$12.00
Sauce bowl, footed, 1988, 8" L.......................................$28.00
Sugar bowl, footed, 1980-83, 3½", from $7 to $10.00
Tidbit tray, 2-tiered (7" & 10" dia), 1987, 9¾", from $30 to ... $40.00
Tumbler, straight-sided, footed, 1988, 8-oz, 3½" $10.00
Tumbler, straight-sided, 1990, 12-oz, 5½" $14.00
Vase, footed, 1985, 8", from $15 to $20.00

Cardinal China Company

This was the name of a distributing company who had their merchandise made to order and sold it through a chain of showrooms and outlet stores in several states from the late 1940s through the 1950s. (Although they made some of their own pottery early on, we have yet to find out just what they themselves produced.) They used their company name to mark cookie jars (some of which were made by the American Bisque Company), novelty wares, and kitchen items, many of which you'll see as you make your flea market rounds. *The Ultimate Collector's Encyclopedia of Cookie Jars* by Joyce and Fred Roerig (Collector Books) shows a page of their jars, and more can be seen in *American Bisque* by Mary Jane Giacomini (Schiffer).

See also Cookie Jars.

Measuring spoon holder, flowerpot base, with spoons, $12.00; spoon rest, flower form, $6.00; salt and pepper shakers, Chinese man and lady, green and yellow, $20.00 for the pair.

Bowl, lettuce-leaf shape, green, 6¼"..............................$6.00
Cake plate, gold-plated, marked Cardinal China Co Warranted 228 Made in USA, 10¼" $10.00
Cake server, gold-plated, marked Cardinal China Co Warranted 22k Made in USA...$6.00
Cake stand, I Knew You Were Coming So I Baked a Cake, pink roses & baby's breath, gold trim, w/music box, 4x10¼" dia ..$30.00
Candleholder, beehive shape, gr, 5x5", ea...................$12.00
Celery dish, celery-stalk form, marked $17.00
Cheese dish, cheese wedges (various types) in white, rectangular, 5x3¾" $8.00
Corn holder, corn husks, marked Corn Husks by Cardinal China, 8¾", 4 for..$24.00
Corn serving dish, ear of corn, 11½" $12.50
Cracker server, Cracker & Bar Hound, dachshund figural, 10" L..$30.00
Crock, Stinky Stuff on front, skunk finial, 5" $20.00
Crumber set, airbrushed leaves, wood-handled brush w/plastic bristles, 2-pc..$12.50
Dresser dish, Doxie-dog, from $15 to $18.00
Egg dish, rooster decor, 2 rests in side, 6" $25.00
Egg timer, windmill, 4½" $45.00
Flower holder, turquoise on white, doughnut shape, 7" $8.00
Gravy boat, dark green, double-spout, 2¾x6" dia, 7½" to tip of handle..$12.00
Gravy boat, roses, 2⅝x7¾" $10.00
Gravy boat, sunflower yellow, double-spouted, 6¾" L.........$18.00
Gravy server, turquoise, double-spout, single 2" handle, 3 sm feet, embossed mark $15.00
Gravy/grease separator, yellow, 7¼" L $15.00
Measuring spoon holder, cottage w/peaked roof, 5½" $50.00
Measuring spoon holder, flowerpot, plain (not basketweave) base..$10.00
Measuring spoon holder, flowerpot, plain (not basketweave) base, w/plastic spoons as flowers.............................$15.00
Measuring spoon holder, flowerpot w/basketweave base, w/ spoons..$12.00
Measuring spoon holder, Measure Boy...............................$25.00
Measuring spoon holder, Measure Boy, w/cups & spoons....$50.00
Measuring spoon holder, windowsill-planter shape w/plastic spoons as flowers $15.00
Ring holder, elephant figural, shamrock, flat back w/hole for hanging $12.00
Scissors holder, nest w/chicken figural.............................$22.00
Shrimp boats, 4¾" L w/cardboard sail on wooden pole, various colors, set of 4, from $65 to $75.00
Spoon rest, double sunflower form, 6x5½", from $7 to $10.00
Spoon rest, rooster on white, triangular, 1950s $15.00
Switch plate, bluebirds, Good Morning/Good Night, 5¼x4". $22.00
Teabag holder, single 5-petal flower face...........................$6.00
Teapot, Bar-B-Que; 3-D picnic on top w/embossed hamburgers/hot dogs/etc on side, blue trim on spout & handle, 5x9"....$25.00

Carnival Chalkware

From about 1910 until sometime in the 1950s, winners of carnival games everywhere in the United States were awarded chalkware figures of Kewpie dolls, the Lone Ranger, Hula girls, comic characters, etc. The assortment was vast and varied. The earliest were made of plaster with a pink cast. They ranged in size from about 5" up to 16".

They were easily chipped, so when it came time for the carnival to pick up and move on, they had to be carefully wrapped and packed away, a time consuming, tedious chore. When stuffed animals became available, concessionists found that they could simply throw them into a box without fear of damage, and so ended an era.

Today the most valuable of these statues are those modeled after Disney characters, movie stars, and comic book heroes.

Chalkware figures are featured in *The Carnival Chalk Prize, Vols. I* and *II,* and *A Price Guide to Chalkware/Plaster Carnival Prizes,* all written by Thomas G. Morris. Along with photos, descriptions, and values, Mr. Morris has also included a fascinating history of carnival life in America.

Our values are for examples in excellent to near-mint condition.

Alice the Goon, from Popeye, 1930-40, 10" $165.00
Bellhop girl w/hand on hip, 1930s, 14¼" $75.00
Boy, w/top hat/tux/cane/spats, 1930s, 8" $45.00
Bulldog, sitting, 1925-35, 10¼" $65.00
Cat & goldfish bowl (clear glass), 1930-40, 9½" $47.50

Charlie McCarthy, J.Y. Jenkins, May 3, 1935, 15", $90.00. (Photo courtesy Tom Morris)

Charlie McCarthy, seated, 1930-40, 9½" $55.00
Dog sitting upright w/flower, 1935-45, 10¾" $30.00
Donald Duck, head bank, Disney, 1940-50, 10½" $80.00
Elephant sitting upright trumpeting, bank, 1955, 12½" $67.50
Felix the Cat, 1922-40, 12½" $245.00
Frenchie, Jenkins, 1924, rare, 15" $195.00
Girl reading, bust, 1910-25, 12x8½" $65.00
Indian chief on horseback, 1930-50, 11", from $50 to........$60.00
Kewpie, jointed arms, mohair wig, 1920s, 12½"................$165.00
Lighthouse, 1935-40, 12¼" $45.00
Little Sheba, original feathers, hand painted, 1920s, 13" ...$165.00
Lone Ranger, 16" $85.00
Mae West, w/lg hat & parasol, 1930-40, 14"....................$125.00
Maggie & Jiggs, 1920-35, 8¼" & 9½", pr.........................$265.00
Ming Toy, Jenkins, 1924, 13"...$185.00
Monkey sitting upright scratching head, bank, 1940-50, 12¼" ..$47.50
Navy WAVE, marked Remember Pearl Harbor, 1944, 13" ..$65.00
Nude bust, lamp, Art Deco style, 1930-40, 8½" $135.00

Paul Revere, 1935-45, 14½"..$25.00
Piano baby, 1910-25, 10½"..$120.00
Pinocchio standing w/arms down to side, 1940-50, 11½" ...$95.00

Pinocchio, 14½", $110.00. (Photo courtesy Tom Morris)

Popeye, saluting, 1930-40, 11½".......................................$115.00
Sailor girl, Jenkins, 1934, 13½" $80.00
Sitting lady, pink chalk, hand painted, ca 1920, 6½" $65.00
Snow White standing w/hands clasped, 1930s, 13½"..........$95.00

Cash Family, Clinchfield Artware

Some smaller East Tennessee potteries are beginning to attract collector attention. Clinchfild Artware produced by the Cash family of Erwin is one of them. The pottery was started in 1945 when the family first utilized a small building behind their home where they made three pottery pieces: a rolling-pin planter, a small elephant-shaped pitcher, and a buttermilk jug. Eventually they hired local artists to hand paint their wares. Cash products are sometimes confused with those made by the better-known Blue Ridge Pottery, due to the fact that many of the area's artisans worked first at one local company then another, and as a result, a style emerged that was typical of them all. Molds were passed around as local companies liquidated, adding to the confusion. But Cash's production was limited to specialty and souvenir pieces; the company never made any dinnerware.

Creamer & sugar bowl, blue leaves w/silver spots, blue sponging on
    handles, rim & foot, w/lid, 5", 4¾" $50.00
Jug, Little Brown Jug on white shoulders, brown body, 4¼x2½"
    dia $25.00
Mug, sunflowers on cream w/brown sponging on rim & handle..$24.00
Piggy bank, lg blue rose & buds w/green leaves on white, unmarked,
    4½x6½" $25.00
Pitcher, blue clovers on white, Jane shape, 7½" $45.00
Pitcher, blue leaves w/silver spots, blue sponging on handle, rim &
    foot, 9" $55.00
Pitcher, chartreuse & gray-green flowers, Buttermilk shape,
    8½" $60.00

Pitcher, cows & sponge painting, blue on white, 7x5", from $30 to **$40.00**

Pitcher, fruit painted & in relief, brown trim at rim & handle, 7¼" **$48.00**

Pitcher, Indian chief (head) figural, Hand Painted 1945, 7". **$115.00**

Pitcher, orange & brown flowers w/green leaves on Dixie shape, 3" **$20.00**

Pitcher, orange daisies w/orange sponging on handle, rim & foot, Buttermilk shape, 4¼" **$20.00**

Pitcher, pig drawing in blue on white, dated 1945, 8½", EX..**$65.00**

Pitcher, red & green leaves w/purple berries, 5" **$15.00**

Pitcher, red roses w/buds & green leaves, sponging at rim, handle & base, 6-sided Buttermilk shape, 7½" **$55.00**

Pitcher, rhododendrons on white, 6" **$45.00**

Pitcher, roses (lg) red w/green & lavender leaves, 4½x3¾" ...**$40.00**

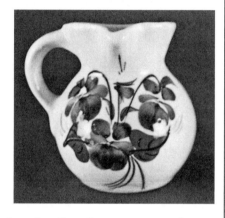

Pitcher, violets, three-spouted, 3", $22.00.
(Photo courtesy Bill and Betty Newbound)

Vase, blue flowers on urn form, handles, 9", NM **$50.00**

Vase, lady's high-button shoe, yellow flowers & laces, green leaves on white, 6" **$25.00**

Vase, lady's Victorian boot, blue floral design w/green leaves on white, 9⅝x9" **$36.00**

Vase, man's boot, yellow flowers w/green leaves, 8" **$30.00**

Wall pocket, Dutch Girl/Cherokee Betsy, cobalt & white, 7½x3½" **$45.00**

Wall pockets, flatiron shapes w/apples, pears & leaves, 5¾x4x4", pr **$35.00**

Wash set, windmill, tree & mountain scene on 11¾" pitcher, similar scene on scalloped 16¾" bowl.................................**$75.00**

Wash set, yellow roses & buds w/green leaves, ornate handle on 11¾" pitcher, matching 17" bowl, NM **$55.00**

Washbowl, blue petals w/silver spots, dated 1945, 3¾x16" ..**$50.00**

Cat Collectibles

Cat collectibles remain popular as cats continue to dominate the world of household pets. Cat memorabilia can be found in almost all categories, and this allows for collections to grow rapidly! Most cat lovers/collectors are attracted to all items and to all breeds, though some do specialize. Popular categories include Siamese, black cats, Kitty Cucumber, Kliban, cookie jars, teapots, books, plates, postcards, and Louis Wain.

Because cats are found throughout the field of collectibles and antiques, there is some 'crossover' competition among collectors.

For example: Chessie, the C&O Railroad cat, is collected by railroad and advertising buffs; Felix the Cat, board games, puppets, and Steiff cats are sought by toy collectors. A Weller cat complements a Weller pottery collection just as a Royal Doulton Flambé cat fits into a Flambé porcelain collection.

Since about 1970 the array and quality of cat items have made the hobby explode. And, looking back, the first half of the twentieth century offered a somewhat limited selection of cats — there were those from the later Victorian era, Louis Wain cats, Felix the Cat, the postcard rage, and the kitchen-item black cats of the 1950s. But prior to 1890, cat items were few and far between, so a true antique cat (100 years old or more) is scarce, much sought after, and when found in mint condition, pricey. Examples of such early items would be original fine art, porcelains, and bronzes.

There are several 'cat' books available on today's market; if you want to see great photos representing various aspects of 'cat' collecting, you'll enjoy *Cat Collectibles* by Pauline Flick, *Antique Cats for Collectors* by Katharine Morrison McClinton, *American Cat-alogue* by Bruce Johnson, and *The Cat Made Me Buy It* and *The Black Cat Made Me Buy It*, both by Muncaster and Yanow.

See also Black Cats; Character Collectibles; Cookie Jars; Holt Howard; Lefton.

Club: International Cat Collector's Club
Contact: Peggy Way
CatCollectors@earthlink.net
www.CatCollectors.com

Figurines, brass, Made in Korea on paper label, 4¾", $12.00 for the pair. (Photo courtesy Marilyn Dipboye)

Book, Cat's Eyes-1st Edition, Anthony Taber, hardcover w/dust jacket, 1978, 12x9½" **$25.00**

Box, cat on cushioned footrest, sleepy look, porcelain, Limoges France, 2⅛" **$92.50**

Figurine, Bastet the Egyptian Cat, black porcelain w/gold trim, Lenox, 1995, 6" **$38.00**

Figurine, Carousel Cat, Tobin Fraley...Designs, ceramic w/brass base, 7x6½ **$42.50**

Figurine, cat, clear crystal w/sm round base, flexible metal tail & whiskers, Swarovsky, 1⅞", MIB (w/papers) **$45.00**

Figurine, cat w/tail curled around body, pink alabaster, Franklin Mint, 2⅞", w/original pamphlet **$120.00**

Figurine, First Kiss, 2 white cats, Lenox, MIB **$50.00**

Figurine, Hannibal & Hagar (cats playing), pastels, Royal Copenhagen 3-line mark, sm..$50.00

Figurine, kitten begging, clear crystal w/green crystal eyes & black crystal nose, Swarovski, 1991 (retired), 1½".............$150.00

Figurine, Morning Stretch, cat stretching w/tail up, lead crystal, Lenox, 1998, 8x9¼", MIB...$45.00

Figurine, Motherly Love, mother cat w/kitten, white porcelain w/ lavender & blue jewels, gold trim, Lenox, 1995, 4¾"...$48.00

Figurine, Persian, ceramic, Made in Japan, ca 1950, 5x4"....$10.00

Figurine, Silent Persuit, western mountain lion, Nick Bibby, Danbury Mint, 8x7½"...$45.00

Mug, fat black & white cat on rug, Warren Kimble, 3¼x3½" .$12.00

Ornament, angel w/gold & glitter wings, Walnut Ridge, 1995, 5½"..$25.00

Ornament, kitten perched in planter, mold-blown, hand painted, silver lined, Christopher Radco......................................$37.50

Pin, cat w/tail hanging down, sterling silver, Beau Sterling, black velveteen pouch, 1"..$10.00

Pitcher, Art Deco cat, hand-painted purple w/blue & gold tail, ceramic $30.00

Planter, kitten, gray & white w/pink bow & gold trim, Shafer 23k Gold, 3½x6"...$48.00

Plate, Cat Nap, 9th issue of Litter Rascals, Bradford Exchange, 1998, MIB...$40.00

Plate, Fairweather Felines, 2 cats w/umbrella, Laurel Burch, Franklin Mint, 8"..$50.00

Plate, Happy Cat, Warren Kimble, Lenox, 1994, 8⅛" $42.00

Plate, My Kitty, blond girl w/Siamese kitten, Margaret Keane, Sone China, Dave Grossman Design, Japan, 1977 ....$40.00

Plate, Scent of Mischief, Siamese on dresser top, Daphine Baxter, Franklin Mint $48.00

Plate, Welcome Cat, Warren Kimble, Lenox, 1995, 8⅛".......$50.00

Salt & pepper shakers, Ma & Pa couple, hand painted, ceramic, Otagiri, 4"..$40.00

Shelf sitter, striped kitten, ceramic, Made in Japan, #H58A83, 8½"..$72.00

Teapot, brown cat in blue dress holding tray w/teapot, teacup & cookies, 7" $13.00

Teapot, 5 Cat Faces on turquoise ceramic, Laurel Burch, 1998, 6¾"...$52.50

Tile, Lowell Herrero, kitten w/yarn, 1992, 4½x4½"............$18.00

Towel, kitchen; embroidered kitten doing chores, days of week below, cotton, set of 7...$40.00

Character Cats

Cat in the Hat, book, Cat in the Hat, 1st edition, dust jacket, hardcover, Random House, 1957, 61 pages, 9¼x6¾" $39.00

Cat in the Hat, booster step stool, painted wood, 6" step w/round back, 12" H, MIB...$45.00

Cat in the hat, doll, stuffed cloth, Manhattan Toy Co, 52", NM. $70.00

Cat in the Hat, doorstop, Cat holding purple & white striped umbrella, iron, rare..$25.00

Cat in the Hat, figurine, Cat holding folded blue umbrella, mounted on onyx w/24k gold accents, 119/950, Ron Lee, 6" $58.00

Cat in the Hat, frame, Cat w/Thing 1 & 2, Fun-in-a-Box, hand-painted resin, 3x3" photo, Vandor, 6"........................$25.00

Cat in the Hat, Jack-in-the-box, plays For He's a Jolly Good Fellow, 1970, 5½x5¼"..$33.00

Cat in the Hat, lamp, Cat, Conrad & Sally w/her cupcake, poly-resin base, 14¾", MIB...$40.00

Cat in the Hat, lunch box, World of Dr Seuss, metal, Aladdin Industries, 1970s..$200.00

Cat in the Hat, ornament, Cat holding presents, blown glass, hand-painted, #98-SUS-01, Christopher Radko, 7½", MIB ..$58.00

Cat in the Hat, pin-back button, I Love Reading, red & black on white, Dr Seuss Enterprises, 1996..............................$57.50

Cat in the Hat, rattle, Thing 1 & 2 hugging each other, red w/blue hair, cloth, 6x7" $15.00

Cat in the Hat, talking storybook, *Friends of Dr. Seuss*, Mattel, 1970, NM, $100.00.

Cat in the Hat, wastebasket, blue w/Cat's head, 10x8¾"......$15.00

Chessie, belt buckle, railroad scene w/Chessie emblem in center Ohio, pewter, 1984 safety award, 3½x2½"..................$15.00

Chessie, button, cuff-size, Chessie sleeping, gold, Waterbury Co's Inc Conn, ⅝"...$12.00

Chessie, calendar print, Chessie sleeping, Chessie As We Found Her, framed, 1937, 13¼x11¾" $33.00

Chessie, calendar print, military theme, signed, framed, 1946, 12x13"...$200.00

Chessie, cup & saucer, demitasse; sleeping cat on white china, 1983 commemorative $15.00

Chessie, handkerchief, cat & kittens printed on white cotton, Chessie Peake & Kittens, 14x14"............................$22.50

Chessie, pin-back button, Chessie sleeping, metal w/porcelain coating, round, Whitehead & Hoag, paper backing, 1½" ...$12.00

Chessie, pocket mirror, Peake-Chessie's Old Man, 3x2", EX..$9.00

Chessie, scarf, sleeping cats on white, printed silk, Lady Heritage, 1940s, 30x30½"...$32.00

Chessie, trading cards, set of 8 Chessie & Peake in various poses, VG...$7.50

Felix the Cat, board game, Down on the Farm, Fishing & Road Race, double-sided board, Built Rite, 1956, 11x11" $68.00

Felix the Cat, children's record, 78 rpm, Peter Pan Records, #536, 1962 ....$15.00

Felix the Cat, egg cup, Felix w/arms outstretched, Good Morning, Confectionery Company, Ltd, 2½x1¾" $37.50

Felix the Cat, figure, stuffed plush, name on yellow shirt, Determined, 1983, 16"..$15.00

Felix the Cat, figure, stuffed plush, You're My Catnip on red satin shirt, Applause, 1989, 16½", w/hang tag **$12.00**

Felix the Cat, lighter, Felix bent over looking through legs, Ronson Wind 11 .... **$22.00**

Felix the Cat, On Television a Flip It Book, Irwin Shapiro, illustrated by Joe Oriolo, hardcover, 1956, 6½x8", G **$27.00**

Felix the Cat, pencil box, green, Felix w/pencil & books, American Pencil Co, New York, #3509, 8½x11¾" **$25.00**

Felix the Cat, postcard, Clara Bow & Felix both winking, sepia tint, 3½x5¼" **$35.00**

Felix the Cat, postcard, Felix & white cat w/bow on front, I'm Surprised at You, Felix, 3½x5½" **$40.00**

Felix the Cat, sand pail, tin litho w/red wooden handle, 6x7" dia **$90.00**

Felix the Cat, squeeze toy, Felix standing w/legs together, arms out & down at sides, Eastern Moulded Prod, 1962, 6" **$45.00**

Felix the Cat, T-shirt, Felix w/bubble pipe on black, never worn . **$20.00**

Figaro, pin, Figaro, back view, looking hover his shoulder **$6.00**

Figaro, plush toy, 9½" **$11.00**

Garfield, alarm clock, yellow, round w/Garfield in middle, bells on top, windup, Sunbeam, 1978, MIB **$30.00**

Garfield, Arlene (his girlfriend) figure, stuffed plush, pink w/red felt lips, lg plastic eyes, Dakin, 1974, 7" **$10.00**

Garfield, autograph, Garfield & Odie in corner w/Thanks! Jim Davis above, matted & framed, 11x13" **$160.00**

Garfield, bank, Garfield as hobo w/tooth missing & holding hat w/slot, 8" **$20.00**

Garfield, bank, Garfield standing, w/red bow tie, ceramic, Japan/ King Features, 1980s, 5¾" **$85.00**

Garfield, bank, Garfield w/hands crossed in front, plastic, 4", from $5 to **$8.00**

Garfield, cookie jar, Garfield on cookie, Enesco **$325.00**

Garfield, cookie jar, Garfield sleeping w/Pookie teddy bear on back, hand-painted ceramic, 9x9½x9½" **$35.00**

Garfield, figurine, Garfield in nurse's uniform holding needle, Nurses Call the Shots, porcelain, Enesco, 1981, 3¼" **$23.00**

Garfield, figurine, Garfield w/arm & head bandaged, Yeah, But You Should See the Other Truck, porcelain, Enesco, 4" **$9.00**

Garfield, figurine, Garfield dressed as devil w/pitchfork, Red Hot Lover, plastic, 2¼" **$3.50**

Garfield, mug, Garfield in blue & orange jersey holding Go Team pennant, I'm a Bears Fan-Atic, Enesco, NFL, 3½x3¼" . **$15.00**

Garfield, ornament, Garfield popping out of Macy's bag, 2003, MIB.. **$8.00**

Garfield, pencil sharpener, Garfield napping, plastic, 2⅝x2" .. **$4.50**

Garfield, plush toy, Garfield as snowman w/green & red striped scarf & black top hat, 1981, 11", G.. **$12.00**

Garfield, plush toy, Garfield in stocking cap w/Odie & mini Christmas book attached, Limited Edition, Macy's **$18.00**

Garfield, plush toy, Garfield in various outfits, Dakin, 1980s, 10" **$12.00**

Garfield, salt & pepper shakers, Garfield as farmer, Arlene as wife in polka-dots, Enesco, 1978, MIB........................... **$80.00**

Garfield, teapot, Garfield crouching, Floyd mouse finial, hand-painted ceramic, 29-oz, 6½x2½" **$25.00**

Garfield, telephone, Garfield napping, opens eyes when phone rings, Tyco, ca 1980 .... **$25.00**

Garfield, tin, catching snowflake on tongue, red velvet ribbon attached, 2¾x2" **$6.00**

Garfield, tumbler, Garfield drinking w/beverage coming out of ears, Goosh, glass, United Feature Syndicate, 1978, 5x2" **$15.00**

Garfield, wristwatch, Garfield's face, Armitron, w/original box . **$25.00**

Garfield, 3-ring binder, Garfield pulling Odie's tongue, That's My Air You're Breathing, vinyl, Mead, 1994 .... **$20.00**

Kitty Cucumber, figurine, Albert & Kitty in hot-air balloon, floral trim, Just Married on basket, Schmid, 1989, 6x3½" **$18.50**

Kitty Cucumber, figurine, Albert painting eggs, Schmid, 1985, 3x2" **$25.00**

Kitty Cucumber, figurine, Albert w/flowers & Kitty in red & white dancing, Schmid, 1990 B Shackman **$20.00**

Kitty Cucumber, figurine, Ellie in pink dress w/blue & white scarf holding bell, Schmid, 1985 B Shackman, 4" **$50.00**

Kitty Cucumber, figurine, Jr Buster & Priscilla, painted porcelain, B Shackman, 3x5" **$25.00**

Kitty Cucumber, figurine, Kitty wearing reindeer costume pulling sleigh full of toys, Schmid, 1988 B Shackman **$15.00**

Kitty Cucumber, figurine, Party Dress Kitty, pink dress & hat, pewter, Frances Wilson, Hantel, jointed miniature............. **$55.00**

Kitty Cucumber, music box, Kitty looking into a fishbowl, porcelain, Oh What a Beautiful Morning, #330-136, box, 1988 .... **$25.00**

Kitty Cucumber, music box, Kitty sitting on top of world, bisque porcelain, Schmid, 1990 B Shackman, 6½" **$30.00**

Kitty Cucumber, music box, 3 cats at tea table, plays Tea for Two, Schmidt, 1985 .... **$57.50**

Kitty Cucumber, ornament, Kitty dressed as an angel in pink reading blue book, porcelain, 1986 B Schackman, 1¾x2¾" **$60.00**

Kitty Cucumber, paper doll book, Kitty Cucumber Goes to School, Merrimack, 1985, EX **$6.50**

Kitty Cucumber, plate, Kitty, Ginger & Priscilla, Ring Around the Posie, #267, 1989, original box w/certificate, 7" **$25.00**

Kitty Cucumber, thimble, Cinderella, porcelain, Schmid, 1992, 1⅞x1½" **$8.00**

Kitty Cucumber, toothbrush holder, Kitty on pedestal w/yellow ducks, arms outstretched, mounts to wall, Schmid, 1989.......... **$23.50**

Kliban, apron, playing guitar, I Love To Eat Them Mousies..., 34"+neck strap.. **$40.00**

Kliban, bank, black & white cat w/red shoes, Sigma, 1970s, 6", from $45 to **$60.00**

Kliban, book, B Kliban Catcalendar Cats, calendar pictures from 1977-81, Workman Publishing, hardcover.................... **$30.00**

Kliban, bookends, cats resting on bookshelves & coming out, Sigma, 8x4⅜x5½", EX.. **$45.00**

Kliban, canister, 3 cats coming out of white trousers w/black shoes, red scarf in pocket, paper label, 1970s, 8", from $70 to **$80.00**

Kliban, comforter, cat in red sneakers on white, twin size, EX. **$45.00**

Kliban, cookie jar, cat w/red kiss on cheek, Sigma, 1970s-80s, paper label, 8", M.. **$152.50**

Kliban, creamer, cat w/red bow tie on tail, mouth is spout, Sigma, 7x3x4½", from $38 to **$48.00**

Kliban, mug, cat face, black & white w/red bow tie, tail forms handle, signed, 1970s-80s, 4¼x3½x5¾" **$25.00**

Kliban, mug, front & back views, cat in red sneakers bottom, signed, Gift Creations, 1989, original box **$58.00**

Kliban, plate, cats dressed in winter attire sipping tea, Afternoon Tea, Danbury Mint, limited edition, 8" $45.00

Kliban, plush toy, cat w/gray & black stripes holds heart that says San Francisco, hang tag, Fiesta......................................$15.00

Kliban, sheet, cats eating ice cream, wearing Hawaiian shirt or playing guitar, 1980s, flat, twin size, 86x78" $50.00

Kliban, sheets, cats w/red kisses on cheeks, 4-pc, queen size, EX.. $45.00

Kliban, soap dish, cat whose tummy forms body of dish, Sigma.$50.00

Kliban, T-shirt, Surf the Net, drawing of internet surfing cat, gray, never worn...$20.00

Kliban, teapot, cat w/white beard in Santa hat, red bow on tail, 1980s, 8x8", EX...$140.00

Mr Jinks, figure, soft rubber, standing w/hands on hips, Bucky, 1970s, 8½", EX+...$75.00

Mr Jinks, figure, stuffed plush cat w/vinyl face, black & white w/pink bow tie & buttons, Knickerbocker, 1959, 13", VG.........$50.00

Pink Panther, bank, bright pink & red plastic cat dressed as golfer on yellow container, 1970s, 9x4½", EX $50.00

Pink Panther, candleholder, panther in his pajamas, multicolor ceramic, UAC Geoffrey, 5x3½", ea $25.00

Pink Panther, figurine, panther dressed as conductor, musical wind-up $40.00

Pink Panther, golf club cover, plush w/knit panther head, MIP ..$55.00

Pink Panther, gumball machine, transparent pink plastic head on yellow base, Tarrson Co, 1970s, 8" $30.00

Pink Panther, music box, Happy Landings, panther dressed as Santa on rooftop, Royal Orleans, 1983, 7x4½" $70.00

Pink Panther, toy, Pink Panther 1-Man Band, battery operated, plays drums & 2 cymbals, Illco Toys, 1970s, MIB.................$90.00

Pink Panther, trinket box, panther finial, pink & white ceramic, Royal Orleans, 1981, 6½" L $40.00

Kliban, candy jar/canister, Sigma, 8", from $70.00 to $80.00.

Cat-Tail Dinnerware

Cat-Tail was a dinnerware pattern popular during the late 1920s until sometime in the 1940s. So popular, in fact, that ovenware, glassware, tinware — even a kitchen table was made to coordinate with it. The dinnerware was made primarily by Universal Potteries of Cambridge, Ohio, though a catalog from Hall China circa 1927 shows a three-piece coffee service, and others may have produced it as well. It was sold for years by Sears Roebuck and Company, and some items bear a mark that includes their name.

The pattern is unmistakable: a cluster of red cattails (usually six, sometimes one or two) with black stems on creamy white. Shapes certainly vary; Universal used at least three of their standard mold designs, Camwood, Old Holland, Laurella, and possibly others. Some Cat-Tail pieces are marked Wheelock on the bottom. (Wheelock was a department store in Peoria, Illinois.)

If you're trying to decorate a '40s vintage kitchen, no other design could afford you more to work with. To see many of the pieces that are available and to learn more about the line, read *The Collector's Encyclopedia of American Dinnerware* by Jo Cunningham (Collector Books).

Advisors: Barbara and Ken Brooks (See Directory, Dinnerware)

Giant cookie jar, 9", minimum value, $125.00 to $150.00.

Bowl, footed, 9½" $20.00
Bowl, mixing; 8" $23.00
Bowl, Old Holland shape, Wheelock, 6" $7.00
Bowl, salad; lg $25.00
Bowl, sauce; Camwood, Ivory, 5¼" $6.00
Bowl, soup; flat rim, 7¾" $15.00
Bowl, soup; tab handles, 8"..$17.50
Bowl, straight sides, 6¼" $12.00
Bowl, vegetable; oval, 9" $27.50
Bowl, vegetable; Universal, 8¾" $25.00
Bowl, w/lid, part of ice box set, 4" $20.00
Bowl, w/lid, part of ice box set, 5" $25.00
Bowl, w/lid, part of ice box set, 6" $28.00
Bowl, 3x4" $15.00
Bread box, tinware, 12x13½", VG $50.00
Butter dish, 1-lb...$100.00
Butter dish, ¼-lb, 3½x6x3¼", NM $55.00
Cake keeper, w/copper-colored lid & knob, 5¼x11½", EX+ .$65.00
Cake plate, Mt Vernon...$25.00
Canister set, tin, 4-pc $60.00
Casserole, paneled sides & lid, 6½x8½" $35.00
Casserole, w/lid, 3¾x7", from $25 to..................................$30.00
Casserole, w/lid, 4¼x8¼"..$55.00

Coffeepot, electric, Westinghouse, 13", from $300 to........**$350.00**
Coffeepot, 3-pc **$70.00**
Cracker jar, barrel shape, 8¼" **$175.00**
Creamer, from $18 to **$25.00**
Creamer & sugar bowl, w/lid, Camwood Ivory, 3¾x5¼" **$45.00**
Custard cup...**$9.00**
Gravy boat, from $18 to **$25.00**
Gravy boat, w/underplate, marked Sears & Roebuck, from $35
    to...**$40.00**
Jug, ball; ceramic-topped cork stopper **$37.50**
Jug, 1-qt, 6" **$25.00**
Match holder, tinware **$45.00**
Pickle dish/gravy boat liner **$20.00**
Pie plate, from $25 to **$30.00**
Pie server, hole in handle for hanging, marked.................**$25.00**
Pitcher, batter; shaped like syrup pitcher **$85.00**
Pitcher, clear glass w/Cat-Tail pattern, ribbed neck & base, 9", from
    $20 to **$25.00**
Pitcher, ice lip, ball shape, 8", from $45 to **$60.00**
Pitcher, milk/utility; straight sides, 5x6"........................**$35.00**

Pitcher, milk; 7½", $35.00. (Photo courtesy Barbara and Ken Brooks)

Pitcher, utility; straight paned sides, w/lid, 6½" **$35.00**
Plate, dinner; Laurella shape, from $15 to.........................**$20.00**
Plate, luncheon; 9", from $7 to..**$8.50**
Plate, salad or dessert; round, from $5 to **$6.50**
Plate, sq, 7¾" **$7.00**
Plate, tab handles, 11"...**$30.00**
Platter, oval, tab handles, Camwood Ivory, 14½" **$35.00**
Platter, oval, tab handles, 13⅜" **$30.00**
Platter, oval, 11½", from $15 to...**$20.00**
Relish tray, Cat-Tail pattern repeated 4 times at rim, oval, 9x5"..**$50.00**
Salad set (fork, spoon & bowl), from $50 to.......................**$60.00**
Salt & pepper shakers, barrel shape, 2 cattails w/leaves, red ring
    around top rim, EX, pr...**$45.00**
Salt & pepper shakers, footed cylinder w/4 vertical recessed panels,
    4½", pr **$35.00**
Salt & pepper shakers, Salt or Pepper, glass, 4", pr.............**$35.00**
Salt & pepper shakers, wider ribbed bottom, 4½", pr **$50.00**

Saucer, Old Holland shape, marked Wheelock, from $4 to....**$6.00**
Scale, metal **$45.00**
Shaker set (salt, pepper, flour & sugar shakers), glass, on red metal
    tray, made by Tipp, from $70 to..................................**$85.00**
Stack set, 3-pc, w/lid, from $40 to.....................................**$50.00**
Sugar bowl, w/lid, from $20 to...**$25.00**
Syrup, red top **$70.00**
Tablecloth..**$90.00**
Teapot, 7x8"...**$40.00**
Tidbit tray, 2-tier, 6" & 7", from $100 to...........................**$120.00**
Tray, for batter set **$75.00**
Tumbler, juice; glass, 3¾", from $18 to..............................**$25.00**
Tumbler, marked Universal Potteries, scarce, from $65 to....**$70.00**
Tumbler, water; glass..**$35.00**
Waste can, step-on, tinware...**$45.00**

Catalin/Bakelite Napkin Rings

Bakelite (developed in 1910) and Catalin (1930s) are very simi-lar materials — identical, in fact, in chemical composition. Both are phenol resin, and both were made in the same wonderful colors that found favor in American kitchens from the 1930s until the 1950s. In particular, figural napkin rings made of this material have become very collectible. Those most desirable will have an inlaid eye or some other feature of a second color.

Scottie, no inlaid eyes, various colors, from $35.00 to $45.00 each.

Band, lathe-turned, amber, red or green, 1¾" **$8.00**
Band, plain, amber, red or green, 2", ea **$6.00**
Band, plain, green, 1", set of 12...**$85.00**
Band, plain colors, 2", set of 6, MIB....................................**$60.00**
Bird, no inlaid eyes..**$35.00**
Bird, no inlaid eyes, green w/brown beak, from $35 to........**$45.00**
Camel, inlaid eye rod **$90.00**
Camel, no inlaid eyes...**$70.00**
Chicken, no inlaid eyes **$30.00**
Chicken, no inlaid eyes, amber w/green beak, from $35 to..**$45.00**
Donald Duck, w/decal, from $120 to **$150.00**
Duck, inlaid eye rod, from $65 to...**$75.00**
Duck, no inlaid eyes...**$30.00**
Elephant, ball on head **$120.00**
Elephant, inlaid eye rod **$80.00**
Elephant, no inlaid eyes, on wheels.....................................**$65.00**
Fish, inlaid eye rod **$60.00**
Fish, no inlaid eyes...**$40.00**
Mickey Mouse, no decal **$80.00**
Mickey Mouse, w/decal, from $135 to..................................**$150.00**

Popeye, no decal, no inlaid eyes, from $45 to **$55.00**
Rabbit, inlaid eye rod **$40.00**
Rabbit, no inlaid eyes **$30.00**
Rocking horse, inlaid eye rod **$50.00**
Rocking horse, no inlaid eyes **$40.00**
Rooster, inlaid eye rods, from $60 to **$75.00**
Rooster, no inlaid eyes **$50.00**
Schnauzer, sitting, inlaid eye rods **$65.00**
Schnauzer, sitting, no inlaid eye rods **$35.00**
Scottie, no inlaid eyes, on wheels **$80.00**
Scottie, seated, no inlaid eyes, from $45 to **$60.00**
Scottie, standing, inlaid eye rods, from $60 to **$70.00**
Squirrel, standing over ring, inlaid eyes, rare **$180.00**

Ceramic Arts Studios

Although most figural ceramic firms of the 1940s and 1950s were located on the West Coast, one of the most popular had its base of operations in Madison, Wisconsin. Ceramic Arts Studio was founded in 1940 as a collaboration between entrepreneur Reuben Sand and potter Lawrence Rabbitt. Early ware consisted of hand-thrown pots by Rabbitt, but CAS came into its own with the 1941 arrival of Betty Harrington. A self-taught artist, Harrington served as the Studio's principal designer until it closed in 1955. Her imagination and skill quickly brought Ceramic Arts Studio to the forefront of firms specializing in decorative ceramics. During its peak production period in the 1940s, CAS turned out more than 500,000 figurines annually.

Harrington's themes were wide ranging, from ethnic and theatrical subjects, to fantasy characters, animals, and even figural representations of such abstractions as fire and water. While the majority of the Studio's designs were by Harrington, CAS also released a limited line of realistic and modernistic animal figures by 'Rebus' (Ulle Cohen). In addition to traditional figurines, the Studio responded to market demand with such innovations as salt-and-pepper pairs, head vases, banks, bells, shelf-sitters, and candleholders. Metal display shelves for CAS pieces were produced by Jon-San Creations, a nearby Reuben Sand operation. Most Jon-San designs were produced by Ceramic Art Studio's head decorator Zona Liberace, stepmother of the famed artist.

Betty Harrington carved her own master molds, so the finished products are remarkably similar to her initial sketches. CAS figurines are prized for their vivid colors, characteristic high-gloss glaze, lifelike poses, detailed decoration, and skill of execution. Unlike many ceramics of the period, CAS pieces today show little evidence of crazing.

Most Ceramic Arts Studio pieces are marked, although in pairs only one piece may have a marking. While there are variants, including early paper stickers, one common base stamp reads 'Ceramic Arts Studio, Madison, Wis.' (The initials 'BH' which appear on many pieces do not indicate that the piece was personally decorated by Betty Harrington. This is simply a design indicator.)

In the absence of a base stamp, a sure indicator of a CAS piece is the decorator 'color marking' found at the drain hole on the base. Each studio decorator had a separate color code for identification purposes, and almost any authentic CAS piece will display these tick marks.

Following the Madison's studio's close in 1955, Reuben Sand briefly moved his base of operations to Japan. While perhaps a dozen master molds from Madison were also utilized in Japan, most of the Japanese designs were original ones and do not correlate to those produced in Madison. Additionally, about 20 master molds and copyrights were sold to Mahana Imports, which created its own CAS variations, and a number of molds and copyrights were sold to Coventry Ware for a line of home hobbyware. Pieces produced by these companies have their own individual stampings or labels. While these may incorporate the Ceramic Arts Studio name, the vastly different stylings and skill of execution are readily apparent to even the most casual observer, easily differentiating them from authentic Madison products. When the CAS building was demolished in 1959, all remaining molds were destroyed. Betty Harrington's artistic career continued after the studio's demise; and her later work, including a series of nudes and abstract figurals, are especially prized by collectors. Mrs. Harrington died in 1997. Her last assignment, the limited-edition *M'amselle* series, was commissioned for the Ceramic Arts Studio Collectors Association Convention in 1996.

For more information we recommend *Ceramic Arts Studio: The Legacy of Betty Harrington* written by Donald-Brian Johnson (our advisor for this category), Timothy J. Holthaus, and James E. Petzold (Schiffer Publishing, 2003). Mr. Johnson encourages collectors to e-mail him with any new information concerning company history and/or production.

See also Clubs and Newsletters.

Advisor: Donald-Brian Johnson (See Directory, Ceramic Arts Studio)

Club/Newsletter: CAS Collectors
206 Grove St.
Rockton, IL 61702
www.cascollectors.com
Publishes quarterly newsletter, hosts annual convention. Family membership: $25 per year. Ceramic Arts Studio history website: www.ceramicartsstudio.com

Bank, Mr & Mrs Blankety Blank, 4½", pr from $240 to ... **$280.00**
Bank, Tony the Barber (blade bank), 4¾", from $75 to **$100.00**

Bells: Summer Belle, 5¼", from $100.00 to $120.00; Lillibelle, 6½", from $75.00 to $85.00; and Winter Belle, 5¼", from $75.00 to $85.00.

Candleholders, Triad Girls, left/right: 7", center: 5", 3-pc set, from $250 to **$340.00**
Figurine, Adonis & Aphrodite, 9", 7", pr from $500 to **$700.00**

Figurine, Alice & March Hare (White Rabbit), 4½", 6", pr from $350 to **$450.00**

Figurine, All Children's Orchestra, 5" boys/4½" girls, 5-pc, $700 to **$800.00**

Figurine, Bear Mother & Cub, realistic, 3¼", 2¼", pr, $320 to . **$380.00**

Figurine, Bird of Paradise, A&B, 3", pr from $360 to........**$440.00**

Figurine, Butch & Billy (boxer dogs), snugglers, 3", pr from $120 to **$160.00**

Figurine, Chinese Girl w/umbrella, very rare, 5½", from $400 to **$500.00**

Figurine, Cinderella & Prince, 6½", pr from $60 to **$80.00**

Figurine, Comedy & Tragedy, 10", pr from $160 to..........**$200.00**

Figurine, Daisy Donkey, 4¾", from $85 to **$110.00**

Figurine, Donkey Mother & Young Donkey, 3¼", 3", pr from $320 to **$380.00**

Figurine, Egyptian Man & Woman, rare, 9½", pr from $1,400 to **$1,500.00**

Figurine, Frisky & Balky Colts, 3¾", pr from $200 to.......**$250.00**

Figurine, Guitar Man on stool, rare, 6½", from $500 to....**$600.00**

Figurine, Harem Trio, Sultan & 2 harem girls, from $320 to . **$395.00**

Figurine, Leopards A&B, fighting, 3½", 6¼" L, pr from $180 to **$250.00**

Figurine, Lightning & Thunder stallions, 5¾", pr from $300 to ..**$350.00**

Figurine, Love Trio, Lover Boy, Willing & Bashful Girls, 3-pc, from $300 to **$375.00**

Figurine, Madonna w/golden halo, 9½", from $350 to......**$450.00**

Figurine, Mermaid Trio, 4" mother/3" & 2½" babies, 3-pc, from $475 to **$550.00**

Figurine, Pekingese dog, 3", from $85 to **$100.00**

Figurine, Peter Pan & Wendy, 5¼", pr from $220 to.........**$270.00**

Figurine, Pioneer Sam & Suzie, 5½", 5", pr from $80 to...**$100.00**

Figurine, Rhumba Man & Woman, 7¼", 7", pr from $80 to. **$120.00**

Figurine, Square Dance Boy & Girl, 6½", 6", pr from $200 to **$250.00**

Figurine, Tom Cat standing, 5", from $75 to......................**$95.00**

Figurine, tortoise w/hat crawling, 2½" L, from $150 to.....**$175.00**

Figurine, Winter Willie, 4", from $90 to **$120.00**

Figurines, Mother Horse & Spring Colt, 4¼", 3½", pr from $425 to **$475.00**

Figurines, Temple Dancers, 7", 6¾", pr from $900 to **$1,000.00**

Figurines, Wing-Sang & Lu-Tang, 6", pr from $90 to.......**$110.00**

Head vase, Mei-Ling, 5", from $150 to **$175.00**

Head vase, Svea & Sven, 6", 5¾", from $350 to...........**$400.00**

Head vases, African Man & Woman, 8", pr from $250 to.**$300.00**

Honey pot, w/bee, 4", from $150 to...............................**$175.00**

Lamps, Fire Man & Woman, by Moss, 17½", pr from $700 to .**$750.00**

Mug, Barbershop Quartet (1949), 3½", from $650 to.......**$750.00**

Pitcher, Pine Cone, mini, 3¾", from $65 to **$85.00**

Plaque, Jack Be Nimble, 5", from $400 to......................**$450.00**

Plaques, Comedy & Tragedy masks, 5¼", pr from $180 to.**$220.00**

Plaques, Dutch Boy & Girl, 8½", 8", pr from $120 to **$150.00**

Plaques, Greg & Grace, 9½", 9", pr from $50 to **$70.00**

Plaques, striped mother fish & baby, 5", 3", pr from $900 to..**$1,000.00**

Salt & pepper shakers, bear & cub, snuggle, 4¼", 2¼", pr from $40 to **$60.00**

Salt & pepper shakers, boy & girl in chairs (4 pcs), 1", 1½", set from $240 to **$320.00**

Salt & pepper shakers, Calico Cat & Gingham Dog, 3", 2¾", pr from $90 to **$100.00**

Salt & pepper shakers, fish up on tails, 3½", pr from $100 to . **$150.00**

Salt & pepper shakers, kitten & creamer, 3", 2½", pr from $140 to **$180.00**

Salt & pepper shakers, Sambo & Tiger, 3½", 5" L, from $500 to **$575.00**

Salt & pepper shakers, Wee Scottish Boy & Girl, 3¼", 3", pr from $70 to **$80.00**

Shelf sitter, collie mother, 5", from $75 to **$100.00**

Shelf sitter, Willy, ball down, 4½", from $220 to **$250.00**

Shelf sitters, Dutch Boy & Girl, 4½", pr from $50 to..........**$70.00**

Shelf sitters, Maurice & Michelle, 7", pr from $130 to......**$150.00**

Shelf sitters, Young Love Couple (kissing boy & girl), 4¼", pr from $150 to **$200.00**

Teapot, mini, applied swan, 3", from $60 to......................**$65.00**

Vase, Flying Duck, round, 2½", from $75 to......................**$85.00**

Figurines, Minnehaha, 6½", from $260.00 to $290.00; Hiawatha, 4½", from $220.00 to $250.00. (Photo courtesy Helene Guarnaccia)

Character and Promotional Drinking Glasses

In any household, especially those with children, I would venture to say, you should find a few of these glasses. Put out by fast-food restaurant chains or by a company promoting a product, they have for years been commonplace. But now, instead of glass, the giveaways are nearly always plastic. If a glass is offered at all, you'll usually have to pay 99¢ for it.

Some are worth more than others. Among the common ones are Camp Snoopy, B.C. Ice Age, Garfield, McDonald's, Smurfs, and Coca-Cola. The better glasses are those with super heroes, characters from Star Trek and '30s movies such as 'Wizard of Oz,' sports personalities, and cartoon characters by Walter Lantz and Walt Disney. Some of these carry a copyright date, and that's all it is. It's not the date of manufacture.

Many collectors are having a good time looking for these glasses. If you want to learn more about them, we recommend *Tomart's Price Guide to Character and Promotional Drinking Glasses* by Carol

Markowski, and *Collectible Drinking Glasses, Identification and Values*, by our advisors Mark Chase and Michael Kelly.

There are some terms used in the descriptions that may be confusing. 'Brockway' style refers to a thick, heavy glass that tapers in from top to bottom. 'Federal' style, on the other hand, is thinner, and the top and bottom diameters are the same.

Advisors: Mark Chase and Michael Kelly (See Directory, Character and Promotional Drinking Glasses)

Newsletter: *Collector Glass News*
P.O. Box 308
Slippery Rock, PA 16057; 724-946-2838; fax: 724-946-9012
cgn@glassnews.com
www.glassnews.com

Al Capp, Dogpatch USA, ruby glass, oval portraits of Daisy or Lil' Abner, ea from $15 to **$20.00**

Al Capp, Shmoos, USF, 1949, Federal, 3 different sizes (3½", 4¾", 5¼"), from $10 to...**$20.00**

Al Capp, 1975, footed, Daisy Mae, Li'l Abner, Mammy, Pappy, Sadie, ea from $35 to...**$50.00**

Animal Crackers, Chicago Tribune/NY News Syndicate, 1978, Louis, scarce...**$25.00**

Arby's, Actor Series, 1979, 6 different, smoked-colored glass w/black & white images, silver trim, numbered, ea from $3-.......**$5.00**

Arby's, Bicentennial Cartoon Characters Series, 1976, 10 different, 5", ea from $8 to **$15.00**

Archies, Welch's, 1971 & 1973, many variations in ea series, ea from $3 to...**$5.00**

Battlestar Galactica, Universal Studios, 1979, 4 different, ea from $7 to **$10.00**

Beverly Hillbillies, CBS promotion, 1963, rare, NM **$200.00**

Bozo the Clown, Capital Records, 1965, Bozo on 3 sides only, from $8 to **$10.00**

Burger King, Collector Series, 1979, 5 different Burger King characters featuring Burger Thing, etc, ea from $3 to **$5.00**

California Raisins, Applause, 1989, juice, 12-oz, 16-oz, ea from $4 to **$6.00**

Cinderella, Disney/Libbey, 1950s-60s, set of 8...................**$120.00**

Dick Tracy, 1940s, frosted, eight different characters, 3" or 5", from $50.00 to $75.00 each. (Photo courtesy Collector Glass News)

Disney Characters, 1936, Clarabelle, Donald, F Bunny, Horace, Mickey, Minnie, Pluto, 4¼" or 4¾", ea from $30 to **$50.00**

Donald Duck, Donald Duck Cola, 1960s-70s, from $10 to .. **$15.00**

ET, Pizza Hut, 1982, footed, 4 different, from $2 to **$4.00**

Flintstones, Welch's, 1962 (6 different), 1963 (2 different), 1964 (6 different), ea from $4 to...**$6.00**

Hanna-Barbera, 1960s, jam glasses featuring Cindy Bear, Flintstones, Huck, Quick Draw, Yogi Bear, rare, ea from $60 to......**$90.00**

Harvey Cartoon Characters, Pepsi, 1970s, static pose, Baby Huey, Casper, Hot Stuff, Wendy, ea from $12 to **$15.00**

Hopalong Cassidy, milk glass w/black graphics, Breakfast Milk, Lunch Milk, Dinner Milk, ea from $15 to **$20.00**

Indiana Jones & the Temple of Doom, 7-Up (w/4 different sponsers), 1984, set of 4, from $8 to **$15.00**

James Bond 007, 1985, 4 different, ea from $10 to **$15.00**

Jungle Book, Disney/Canada, 1966, 6 different, numbered, 6½", ea from $20 to **$40.00**

Jungle Book, Disney/Pepsi, 1970s, Mowgli, unmarked, from $15 to **$20.00**

Leonardo TTV Collector Series, Pepsi, Underdog, Go-Go Gophers, Simon Bar Sinister, Sweet Polly, 6", ea from $10 to......**$15.00**

Little Mermaid, 1991, 3 different sizes, ea from $6 to **$10.00**

Masters of the Universe, Mattel, 1983, He-Man, Man-at-Arms, Skeletor, Teels, ea from $5 to **$10.00**

McDonald's, McDonaldland Action Series or Collector Series, 1970s, 6 different ea series, ea from $2 to......................**$3.00**

Mickey Mouse, Happy Birthday, Pepsi, 1978, Donald, Goofy, Mickey, Minnie, Pluto, Uncle Scrooge, ea from $5 to **$7.00**

Mickey Mouse, Pizza Hut, 1980, milk glass mug, Fantasia, MM Club, Steamboat Willie, Today, ea from $2 to **$5.00**

Mickey Mouse Club, 4 different w/filmstrip bands top & bottom, ea from $10 to **$20.00**

Pac-Man, Bally Midway Mfg/Libbey, 1982, 6" flare top, 5⅜" flare top or mug, from $2 to...**$4.00**

PAT Ward, Pepsi, late 1970s, action pose, Bullwinkle w/balloons, Dudley in canoe, Rocky in circus, 5", ea from $5 to.....**$10.00**

PAT Ward, Pepsi, late 1970s, Dudley Do-Right (black lettering), 6", from $10 to **$15.00**

PAT Ward, Pepsi, late 1970s, static pose, Boris & Natasha, 6", from $15 to **$20.00**

PAT Ward, Pepsi, late 1970s, static pose, Dudley Do-Right, 5", from $10 to **$15.00**

PAT Ward, Pepsi, late 1970s, static pose, Rocky, 5", from $15 to ..**$20.00**

PAT Ward, Pepsi, late 1970s, static pose, Snidley Whiplash, 5", from $8 to **$10.00**

Peanuts Character, footed, Snoopy sitting on lemon or Snoopy sitting on lg red apple, ea from $2 to.............................**$3.00**

Peanuts Characters, McDonald's, 1983, Camp Snoopy, white plastic w/Lucy or Snoopy, ea from $5 to.............................**$8.00**

Peanuts Characters, plastic, I Got It! I Got It!, I Have a Strange Team, Let's Break for Lunch!, ea from $3 to **$5.00**

Popeye, Coca-Cola, 1975, Kollect-A-Set, any character, ea from $3 to **$5.00**

Popeye, Popeye's Famous Fried Chicken, 1978, Sports Scenes, Brutus, Olive Oyl, Swee' Pea, ea from $10 to **$15.00**

Rescuers, Pepsi, 1977, Brockway tumbler, Bernard, Bianca, Brutus & Nero, Evinrude, Orville, Penny, ea from $5 to **$10.00**

Super Heroes, DC Comics or NPP/Pepsi Super (Moon) Series, 1976, Aquaman, Flash, Superman, ea $12 to...............**$20.00**

Super Heroes, DC Comics/Pepsi, 1978, Brockway, flat bottom, Batman, Robin, Wonder Woman (red boots), ea from $8 to **$15.00**

Super Heroes, DC Comics/Pepsi Super (Moon) Series, 1976, Green Arrow, from $20 to **$30.00**

Universal Monsters, Universal Studio, 1980, footed, Creature, Dracula, Frankenstein, Mummy, Mutant, Wolfman, ea from $125 to **$150.00**

Walter Lantz, Pepsi, 1970s, Cuddles, from $40 to **$60.00**

Warner Bros, Marriott's Great America, 1989, Bugs, Porky, Sylvester, Taz, ea from $7 to...................................... **$10.00**

Warner Bros, Pepsi, 1973, Federal 16-oz tumbler, Speedy Gonzales, black lettering, from $6 to **$10.00**

Warner Bros., Pepsi, 1976, Interaction, Foghorn Leghorn and Henry Hawk, from $10.00 to $15.00.

Wizard of Oz, Swift's, 1950s-60s, fluted bottom, Glinda, from $15 to **$25.00**

Ziggy, Number Series, 1-8, ea from $4 to **$8.00**

Ziggy, 7-Up Collector Series, 1977, Here's to Good Friends, 4 different, ea from $3 to **$5.00**

Character Banks

Since the invention of money there have been banks, and saving it has always been considered a virtue. What better way to entice children to save than to give them a bank styled after the likeness of one of their favorite characters! Always a popular collectible, mechanical and still banks have been made of nearly any conceivable material. Cast-iron and tin banks are often worth thousands of dollars. The ones listed here were made in the past 50 years or so, when ceramics and plastics were the materials of choice. Still, some of the higher-end examples can be quite pricey!

See also Advertising Character Collectibles; Cowboy Collectibles; Star Wars.

Alvin (Alvin & the Chipmunks), vinyl figure holding harmonica, CBS Toys, 9", 1984, NM **$20.00**

Andy Panda, composition figure, Crown Toy, 1940s, 5", EX. **$85.00**

Annie, ceramic figure w/dog, Applause, 1982, 6½x6¾", NM. **$20.00**

Astro Boy, ceramic figure, 10", MIB **$60.00**

Bamm-Bamm, plastic figure sitting on turtle, 1960s, 11", NM+. **$50.00**

Barney (Dinosaur), vinyl figure seated in chair w/mug, blanket & book, 1992, 7", M **$10.00**

Barney Rubble, vinyl figure standing on 'rock' base, 1994, 6", M **$12.00**

Bart Simpson, vinyl figure seated on yellow block, Street Kids, 1990, 6½", NM+ **$10.00**

Batman, plastic waist-length figure w/arms crossed, 7½", EX+ . **$20.00**

Bert (Sesame Street), vinyl figure w/lg head, hands in front, shoes protruding from under shirt, NY Vinyl, 1971, 13", EX........ **$25.00**

Betty Boop, red plastic coin sorter w/Betty Boop graphics, drop a coin & she winks, Mag-Nif, 1986, 8", MIB **$18.00**

Big Bird, ceramic train engine w/Big Bird as engineer & Big Bird embossed on sides, 6", NM **$20.00**

Bionic Woman, vinyl figure in jogging suit running on 'rocky' base, Animals Plus, 1976, 10", EX+ **$25.00**

Bozo the Clown, vinyl bust figure w/big smile, 1987, 5", NM. **$20.00**

Bullwinkle, vinyl figure standing against tree trunk waving, Play Pal Plastics, 1973, 12", EX+ **$65.00**

Casper the Friendly Ghost, ceramic figure w/arms up, Japan, 6", NM... **$50.00**

Cecil (Beany & Cecil), plastic head, NM...................... **$35.00**

Cookie Monster, vinyl figure standing holding cookie jar, Illco, 1980s, 9½", NM+ **$15.00**

Cool Cat, image on yellow on sq metal box, Warner Bros, 4x4x1", EX+ **$22.00**

Daffy Duck, ceramic figure hugging money bag embossed w/dollar symbol, Good Co, 1989, 6", NM+............................. **$40.00**

Dark Wing Duck, vinyl figure holding onto safe, Happiness Express, 1990s, 7", NM+ **$10.00**

Darth Vader, ceramic head, black Lucasfilm LTD, 1996, 6¼", NM **$50.00**

Disney, 2nd National Duck Bank, litho tin building w/Donald as teller & Mickey & Minnie customers, 6½", EX.......... **$200.00**

Donald Duck, composition figure looking up w/hand in fist, 7", NM.. **$22.00**

Donald Duck, vinyl head form w/red bow tie, Play Pal, 1971, EX+ **$25.00**

Dumbo, vinyl figure seated upright, gray w/orange hat & gray, white & red collar, Play Pal, 1970s, 8", EX+ **$25.00**

Fred Flintstone, plastic figure standing next to safe, MIB..... **$35.00**

Heckle (Heckel & Jeckle), painted wood figure, w/hang tag, EX.. **$150.00**

Howdy Doody, flocked plastic figure in wide stance on base w/name on label, Straco, 1976, 9", EX+................................ **$35.00**

Huckleberry Hound, plastic figure, 1960, 10", EX **$20.00**

Joker (Batman), plastic, Mego, 1970s, NM.......................... **$50.00**

Mickey Mouse, composition figure seated on stool looking & pointing upward, WDP, 8", EX................................... **$25.00**

Miss Piggy, ceramic figure, Sigma, NM.............................. **$50.00**

Mister Magoo, yellow vinyl figure w/black & blue trim, Renzi, 1960, 17", M... **$150.00**

Mr Bluster (Howdy Doody), flocked plastic figure, Mr Bluster Savings Bank, Strauss, 1979s, EX+................................ **$35.00**

Pebbles Flintstone, vinyl figure sleeping in chair, Homecraft, 1979s, NM... **$30.00**

Pinocchio, vinyl bust w/eyes looking upward, lg bow tie, Play Pal, 1970s, 10", NM **$28.00**

Planet of the Apes, General Urus, molded plastic, Apac Productions, 1967, 18", $25.00.

Pluto, composition figure sitting upright looking up w/mouth open, WDP, 6½", NM **$25.00**

Quick Draw McGraw, plastic figure, orange, blue & white, Looney Tunes, 1960s, 10", EX+ **$35.00**

Raggedy Andy, ceramic, no mark, 7½", $40.00. (Photo courtesy Jim and Beverly Mangus)

Raggedy Ann, vinyl figure in brown felt jumper, molded blouse & shoes, Royalty, 1974, 9", NM **$35.00**

Roadrunner, composition figure, VG+ **$25.00**

Schroeder (Peanuts), ceramic figure, 7", M **$100.00**

Scooby-Doo, vinyl figure seated on haunches, 1980s, 6", EX+. **$20.00**

She-Ra Princess of Power, vinyl head, HG Toys/Hong Kong, MIB...**$10.00**

Snoopy, ceramic figure sitting on bright red strawberry, Japan, 1968, NM...**$35.00**

Snoopy, composition figure on rainbow, NM **$25.00**

Spider-Man, red plastic bust figure, Renzi, 1979, 15", EX...**$20.00**

Tasmanian Devil, Looney Tunes, Applause, 1980s, NM+ **$75.00**

Tom (Tom & Jerry), ceramic figure resting atop hamburger, Gorham, 1980s, 5", M..**$50.00**

Topo Gigio, nodder figure w/pineapple, M........................**$125.00**

Winnie the Pooh, ceramic figure seated licking his chops w/Pooh's Honey Bank between legs, Enesco/WDP, 1960, NM+ .**$30.00**

Woodstock, yellow ceramic figure, signed Schulz, 1970s, 6", M.**$40.00**

Woody Woodpecker, ceramic figure popping out of tree trunk, Applause, 1980s, 7", MIB...**$40.00**

Woody Woodpecker, plastic figure standing w/head turned to side, 1 hand on hip & other pointing up, Imco, 1977, 10", NM **$50.00**

Yogi Bear, vinyl figure standing on grassy base w/flowers, 1980s, 6", NM...**$22.00**

Ziggy, ceramic figure atop lg red heart, Don't Break My Heart, 6½", M...**$45.00**

Character Clocks and Watches

There is a great deal of interest in the comic character clocks and watches produced from about 1930 into the 1950s and beyond. They're in rather short supply simply because they were made for children to wear (and play with). They were cheaply made with pin-lever movements, not worth an expensive repair job, and many were simply thrown away. The original packaging that today may be worth more than the watch itself was usually ripped apart by an excited child and promptly relegated to the wastebasket.

Condition is very important in assessing value. Unless a watch is in like-new condition, it is not mint. Rust, fading, scratching, or wear of any kind will sharply lessen its value, and the same is true of the box itself. Good, excellent, and mint watches can be evaluated on a scale of one to five, with excellent being a three, good a one, and mint a five. In other words, a watch worth $25.00 in good condition would be worth five times that amount if it were mint ($125.00). Beware of dealers who substitute a generic watch box for the original. Remember that these too were designed to appeal to children and (99% of the time) were printed with colorful graphics.

Some of these watches have been reproduced, so be on guard. For more information, we recommend *Schroeder's Collectible Toys, Antique to Modern* (Collector Books).

Clocks

Batman & Robin Talking Alarm Clock, molded plastic, Batman: Time To Wake Our Friend Robin, Janex, 1974, EX **$60.00**

Batman running along Robin who is in Batmobile, skyline beyond, plastic, Janex, 1974, EX **$65.00**

Mickey & Friends, musical w/alarm, white case, Bradley, 1968, NM...**$175.00**

Mickey & Goofy on face, red base, alarm type, Disney, Bradley, 1970s, 5x4" dia, NM **$75.00**

Mickey Mouse as astronaut on blue face, motion alarm w/single bell, Disney, Lorus, 1984, NM...**$60.00**

Mickey Mouse on face, yellow w/brass bells, Phinney Walker, 1960s, 4x2½", NM **$55.00**

Mickey Mouse The Brave Little Tailor on face, dark red w/brass bells, Bradley, 1970s, MIB **$100.00**

Mickey Mouse Train Engineer, talking alarm, Mickey on orange train w/black & white face, Bradley, 1970s, M **$120.00**

Mighty Mouse, travel alarm, yellow w/brass trim, Territoons, 1970s, 3" dia, EX..**$90.00**

Minnie Mouse on face, purple w/2 white bells, Disney, Bradley, 1970s, 7x4", EX...**$50.00**

Peter Pan, green w/brass bells, Phinney Walker, 1960s, NM. **$90.00**

Snoopy Cuckoo Clock, Japan, 1983, Snoopy golfing, Woodstock is cuckoo bird, NM, from $150.00 to $175.00. (Photo courtesy Andrea Podey and Derrick Bang)

Snoopy (w/Woodstock) Rock Around the Clock, motion alarm, Salton, 1960s, 7x4" dia, MIB **$65.00**

Winnie the Pooh on face, mustard yellow w/orange bells, Bradley, 1970s, 4x2½" dia, EX..**$90.00**

Pocket Watches

Captain Marvel, full figure on face, round chrome case, plastic strap, Fawcett, 1948, EXIB..**$750.00**

Cinderella, Disney, US Time, EX.....................................**$45.00**

Don Winslow of the Navy, New Haven, 1939, EX.........**$1,600.00**

Mickey Mouse, arms & hands point out minutes & hours, gold-tone case w/stainless steel back, Lorus, 1⅜"+12" chain **$15.00**

Mickey Mouse, arms & hands point to hours & minutes, Bradley, Made in USA, EX...**$25.00**

Mickey Mouse on face, round chrome case, Ingersoll, 1930s, NMIB w/Mickey fob...**$1,750.00**

Mickey Mouse w/flag in background, Cast Exclusive Limited Edition, Disney, NM **$25.00**

Roy Rogers w/sm image of Roy on trigger in background, stopwatch feature, Bradley, EX **$600.00**

Toy Story's Woody, Fossil limited edition, 1996, MIB **$125.00**

Wizard of Oz, 4 characters on face, silver-tone case, Westclock, 1980s, MIB...**$75.00**

Wristwatches

Aladdin, characters fly over city on dial, Disney Store limited edition, 1993, MIB **$75.00**

Aladdin & Jafar, dual face pivots on band, Disney, 1998, MIB .**$125.00**

Bedknobs & Broomsticks Fossil, underwater magic bed scene on face, Collector Club limited edition, 1995, MIB **$125.00**

Bullwinkle, head on brushed silver face, 17-jewel movement, 1972 Jay Ward Prod, leather band, NM..............................**$235.00**

Charlie Tuna, 1971 and 1972 versions, Starkist premiums, EX, $35.00 each.

Dudley Do Right w/earing Mountie hat, 17-jewel movement, 1972 Jay Ward, black leather band, NM..............................**$215.00**

Goofy, arms & hands point to hours & minutes, Helbros, Walt Disney Productions, black leather band, EX **$515.00**

Lion King, Circle of Life motion type, Times, 1994, MIP...**$50.00**

Mulan, chrome case, leather band, Disney Fantasma, 1998, MIB...**$75.00**

Nightmare Before Christmas, Jack Skellington, Disney, 1993, MIB **$110.00**

Roger Rabbit, silhouette, gold bezel, leather band, Disney, 1988, NM...**$75.00**

Snoopy on orange face, orange vinyl wrist band, Determined, 1960s, MIB...**$300.00**

Snoopy on red face, stainless steel case, red plastic wrist band, Hong Kong, EX...**$25.00**

Toy Story characters on rectangular face, Fossil, Disney, 1996, M **$110.00**

Character Collectibles

Any popular personality, whether factual or fictional, has been promoted through the retail market to some degree. Depending on the extent of their fame, we may be deluged with this merchandise for weeks, months, even years. It's no wonder, then, that the secondary market abounds with these items or that there is such wide-spread collector demand for them today. There are rarities in any field, but for the beginning collector, many nice items are readily available at prices most can afford. Disney characters, Western heroes, TV and movie personalities, super heroes, comic book characters, and sports greats are the most sought after.

For more information, we recommend *Toys of the Sixties* and *Superhero Collectibles: A Pictorial Price Guide,* both by Bill Bruegman. *Schroeder's Collectible Toys, Antique to Modern,* published by Collector Books, contains an extensive listing of character collectibles with current market values.

See also Advertising Characters; Beatles Collectibles; Bubble Bath Containers; California Raisins; Cat Collectibles; Character and Promotional Drinking Glasses; Character Watches; Coloring Books; Cookie Jars; Cowboy Character Collectibles; Disney Collectibles; Dolls, Celebrity; Elvis Presley Memorabilia; Movie Posters; Paper Dolls; Pez Candy Containers; Pin-Back Buttons; Puzzles; Rock 'n Roll Memorabilia; Shirley Temple; Star Wars; Toys; Vandor.

Barney, lamp, plasic, Happiness Express, 1992, NM, $20.00. (Photo courtesy whatacharacter. com)

Addams Family, candy dispenser, Gomez figure singing, plastic, Bee Int'l, 5", MIP **$8.00**

Alf, figure, Stick Around Alf, stuffed plush, suction-cup hands, Coleco, 1988, 7½", MIB **$22.00**

Alf, figure, stuffed plush, 19", Coleco, 1986, VG **$22.00**

Alvin & the Chipmunks, figure, Alvin, stuffed plush, lg yellow A on red sweater, red hat, CBS Toys, 1983, 12", NM **$15.00**

Alvin & the Chipmunks, harmonica, red plastic triangular shape w/Alvin decal, Dairy Queen, 1984, NM **$6.00**

Alvin & the Chipmunks, jack-in-the-box, plastic w/Alvin pop-up figure & graphics, CBS Toys, 1983, 9", NM **$35.00**

Alvin & the Chipmunks, ornament, 3 on sled, embossed resin, 4", Adler, MIP **$6.00**

Annie (Movie), wallet, white vinyl w/name & image of Annie & Sandy, Henry Gordy Int'l, 1981, 3½", MIP (sealed) **$12.00**

Archies, game, Ring Toss, features Jughead stand-up figure, Ja-Ru, 1987, NRFP **$10.00**

Astro (Jetsons), figure, stuffed plush, tan w/green collar, felt tongue, plastic eyes, Nanco, 1989, 10½", M **$10.00**

Baba Looey, figure, stuffed plush & vinyl, light green w/orange vinyl sombrero, Knickerbocker, 1959, 16", EX **$50.00**

Babe, figure, stuffed plush, pink w/felt pouch holding 3 piglets, 1 green foot pad & 1 red, Equity Toys, 1998, 13", NM .. **$12.00**

Bamm-Bamm (Flintstones), figure, stuffed cloth, felt hair, hat & outfit, Knickerbocker, 1970s, 8", MIB **$45.00**

Bamm-Bamm (Flintstones), ornament, hollow plastic figure, 1976, 3¼", EX+ **$6.00**

Bamm-Bamm (Flintstones), push-button puppet, Arco, 5", 1976, EX+ **$30.00**

Bamm-Bamm (Flintstones), push-button puppet, Kohner, 1960s, NM+ **$35.00**

Banana Splits, Kut-Up Kit, Larami, 1970s, MOC (sealed) .. **$20.00**

Barney, figure, vinyl, in baseball shirt catching baseball in glove, 1990s, 5¼", NM+ **$10.00**

Barney, nightlight, plastic figure hot-air balloon, Happiness Express, 1992, 8½", NM **$18.00**

Barney (Flintstones), figure, stuffed cloth & vinyl, green-painted hair, furry outfit, Knickerbocker, 12", EX **$75.00**

Barney (Flintstones), figure, stuffed cloth & vinyl, green-painted hair, furry outfit, Knickerbocker, 16½", EX **$100.00**

Barney (Flintstones), figure, vinyl, standing w/arms at sides, swivel head, green hair & toenails, 1960, 10", EX **$75.00**

Barney (Flintstones), magnet, figure on roller skates w/glass of water, decal on vinyl, 1970s, NRFP **$8.00**

Barney (Flintstones), marionette, stuffed cloth w/furry outfit, Knickerbocker, 1962, 12", NM **$35.00**

Barney (Flintstones), nightlight, plastic figure, Leviton, 1975, 4", MOC **$15.00**

Batman, figure, hard vinyl, jointed, blue shorts, gloves & boots, turquoise cape, yellow belt, Presents, 1988, 15", M **$40.00**

Batman, flowerpot, white ceramic w/Batman motif on both sides, 1970s, 3", M **$18.00**

Batman, hand puppet, body image & name printed on vinyl w/ molded vinyl head, Ideal, 1966, EX+ **$75.00**

Batman, Print Putty, Colorforms, 1966, MOC **$150.00**

Batman, Sliding Puzzle, color image of Batman on white plastic sliding tiles, American Publishing, 1977, MOC **$18.00**

Batman & Robin, scissors, Chemtoy, 1973, MOC **$25.00**

Betty (Flintstones), figure, plastic, standing w/arms behind head in green dress, Imperial, 1976, 3", NM **$10.00**

Betty Boop, Fancy Rings, set of 9, Ja-Ru, 1990s, MOC **$8.00**

Betty Boop, figure, stuffed cloth, in bathing suit w/chest banner, Ace Novelty, 1989, 13", NM **$15.00**

Betty Boop, Play Set, includes watch, makeup case, lipstick & eye shadow kit, Ja-Ru, 1994, MOC **$8.00**

Boo Boo, figure, stuffed cloth w/print face, felt hair & bow tie, Knickerbocker, 1973, 7", MIB **$50.00**

Bozo the Clown, Bozo's Pocket Watch, plastic, 2", MIP **$12.00**

Bozo the Clown, figure, stuffed cloth, fuzzy hair, plastic eyes, Novelty, 1989, 7½", NM+ **$15.00**

Bozo the Clown, gumball machine, plastic Bozo figure waving & hugging clear gum globe on base, Leaf Inc, 1994, 10", MIB.. **$28.00**

Bozo the Clown, Super Magnet, plastic horseshoe shape, Laurie Import Ltd, 1976, 9½", MIP **$15.00**

Broom Hilda, Spurt Stick, vinyl window stick-on reads Next Time Bring Your Wife, Meyercord, 1975, 14", MIP **$10.00**

Bugs Bunny, figure, flocked plastic, gray & white, Lucky Bell, 1988, 6", NRFP **$10.00**

Bugs Bunny, figure, inflatable vinyl, gray & white w/black accents, 1970s, 12", NM **$10.00**

Bugs Bunny, figure, stuffed plush & vinyl, toothy smile, Mattel, 1960s, 15", EX **$25.00**

Bugs Bunny, finger puppet, as Uncle Sam, cloth body w/vinyl head, 1978, 5", NM+ **$15.00**

Bugs Bunny, mug, vinyl head form, gray & white w/red mouth, toothy grin, Promotional Partners, 1992, 4", EX+ **$5.00**

Bugs Bunny, pencil holder/sharpener, Bugs standing & eating carrot, composition, Holiday Fair, 1970, 6", NM **$18.00**

Bullwinkle (Rocky & Friends), figure, bendable rubber, green sweater w/red B, Jesco, 1991, 7", MOC **$12.00**

Captain Kangaroo, pull-string talking doll, Mattel, 1967, EX, $55.00.

Casper the Friendly Ghost, figure, squeeze vinyl, name on chest banner, Sutton, 1972, 7", EX+ **$28.00**

Charlie Brown (Peanuts), figure, stuffed terry cloth pillow type w/ printed image front & back, 7½x1", NM **$8.00**

Charlie Brown (Peanuts), squeeze toy, holding bowl of dog food, Con Agra, 1990s, 5½", NM+ **$8.00**

Cindy Bear, figure, stuffed cloth w/print face, felt hair, cloth skirt, Knickerbocker, 1973, 6", NRFB **$60.00**

Clarabell (Howdy Doody), push-button puppet, wooden bead figure, Kohner #188, 6", VG **$140.00**

Curious George, figure, stuffed plush, name on red shirt, Gund, 1990, 8", M **$10.00**

Curious George, jack-in-the-box, litho metal, Schylling, 1995, EX .**$25.00**

Daffy Duck, figure, bisque, on flowery grassy base w/1 hand on head & 1 to mouth, Price, 1979, 6", M **$28.00**

Daffy Duck, figure, stuffed plush, vinyl w/collar, Mighty Star, 1971, 15", NM **$10.00**

Daffy Duck, figure, stuffed-cloth pillow-type w/printed image & name, 1970s, 16", NM **$15.00**

Dennis the Menace, figure, stuffed cloth, printed features, cloth outfit, Determined, 1976, 8", NM+ **$15.00**

Dennis the Menace, figure, stuffed cloth, stitched nose & mouth, plastic eyes, cloth outfit, Nanco, 11", NM **$8.00**

Dennis the Menace, figure, stuffed cloth & vinyl, cloth outfit, Presents, 1987, w/hand tag, 9", NM+ **$30.00**

Dick Tracy, hand puppet, Joe Jitsu, printed cloth body w/vinyl head, 1960s, EX+ **$30.00**

Dick Tracy, magnifying glass, plastic w/attched vinyl case, Larami, 1970s, MOC **$18.00**

Dracula, figure, bendable rubber, JusToys, 1991, MOC **$10.00**

Dracula, figure, vinyl, jointed arms, cloth cape, Presents, 1991, 13", M **$30.00**

Droopy Dog, hand puppet, cloth & plush body w/molded vinyl head, Turner Ent/MGM, 1989, 12", EX+ **$12.00**

Eddie Munster (Munsters), doll, stuffed cloth w/vinyl head & limbs, black cloth outfit, Presents, 9", NM+ **$40.00**

Elmer Fudd, mug, ceramic head form in green hat & shoulders w/ peach trim, Applause, 1989, 5", M **$12.00**

Elroy (Jetsons), figure, stuffed cloth & vinyl, Applause, 1990, 5½", NM+ **$15.00**

ET, charm bracelet, enameled metal, Aviva, 1982, MOC (Elliot & ET graphics) **$6.00**

ET, Finger Light, vinyl finger that glows when pressed, battery-operated, Knickerbocker, 1982, MOC **$10.00**

Fat Albert, figure, stuffed cloth & vinyl, Hey Hey Hey! I'm a 'Cosby Kid' on shirt, Remco, 1985, 22", MIB **$75.00**

Flintstones, figure, Bamm-Bamm, vinyl, standing holding club on gray rock base, 1994, 5½", NM **$12.00**

Flintstones, Magnetic Stickers, package of 3, 1970s, NRFP.**$20.00**

Flipper, figure, stuffed plush, gray & white w/blue sailor's vest, white sailor's hat, Knickerbocker, 1976, 17" L, NM **$35.00**

Flub-A-Dub (Howdy Doody), push-button puppet, wood, Kohner, 1950s, 5", NM (G box) **$175.00**

Foghorn Leghorn, Bake a Craft Stained Glass Kit, Road Champos, 1991, MOC (sealed) **$12.00**

Fonz, transistor figural radio, Sutton Associates, 1974, EX, from $50.00 to $75.00. (Photo courtesy Greg Davis and Bill Morgan)

General Halftrack (Beetle Bailey), doll, stuffed cloth w/vinyl head, hands & shoes, green jumpsuit, Toy Works, 15", NM ..**$20.00**

Ghostbusters, gumball machine, vinyl ghost in 'No' symbol atop plastic dispenser, Superior Toy, 1986, 7", NM **$12.00**

Ghostbusters, Streamer Kite, features the 'No' symbol & Slimer, Spectra Star, 1989, MIP **$12.00**

Gomez (Adams Family), figure, stuffed cloth w/pink cloth outfit, plastic eyes, w/book, Ace Novelty, 1993, 13", NM+ **$15.00**

Grandpa (Munster), figure, stuffed cloth body w/vinyl head, black cloth outfit, Presents, 1990s, 11", M **$35.00**

Grandpa (Munsters), doll, stuffed cloth & vinyl, black cloth 'vampire' outfit, Toy Works, 15", NM+ **$18.00**

Grandpa (Munsters), figure, stuffed cloth & vinyl, black cloth outfit, Presents, 1990s, 8", M **$30.00**

Grinch (Dr Seuss), figure, stuffed plush, green w/red collar, yellow plastic eyes, Macy's, 1997, 30", EX+ **$35.00**

Gumby, figure, bendable rubber, Jesco, ca 1980-90, 6", NM. **$8.00**

Gumby, figure, bendable rubber, red w/black, Jesco, 9½", NM ..**$12.00**

Gumby, figure, cloth-covered wire upper body w/bean-stuffed lower body, Sher-Stuff/Perma, 1982, 14", EX **$15.00**

Gumby, figure, PVC, in brown bomber-type jacket w/white collar, Applause, 1989, 3", NM+ **$6.00**

Gumby, figure, stuffed cloth, wearing sheriff's badge, Trendmasters, 1995, 13", NM+ **$15.00**

Gumby, figure, stuffed plush, Ace Novelty, 1988, 6½", NM. **$10.00**

Gumby, figure, stuffed vinyl, painted features, Good Stuff, 1990s, 7", EX+ **$12.00**

Gumby, hand puppet, cloth body w/vinyl head, Lakeside, 1965, NM **$25.00**

Gumby (or Pokey), windup figure, vinyl, Lakeside, 1966, 4", EX, ea **$45.00**

Gumby & Pokey, paint set, 6 watercolors w/accessories, Henry/Gordy Int'l, 1988, MOC **$12.00**

Herman Munster (Munsters), figure, stuffed cloth w/vinyl head & shoes, brown cloth suit, Toy Factory, 16", M **$18.00**

Herman Munster (Munsters), hand puppet, cloth body w/vinyl head & hands, Mattel, 12", 1964, VG **$50.00**

Hi (Hi & Lois), figure, stuffed cloth w/vinyl head & hands, cloth outfit, brown flocked shoes, Presents, 1985, 16", NM+. **$32.00**

Howdy Doody, bath mitt, terry cloth w/printed image & name, 1950s-60s, 8", EX...**$15.00**

Howdy Doody, finger puppet, full-hand type, foam rubber & cardboard, Bendy Toys, 10½x5", NM **$22.00**

Howdy Doody, marionette, composition w/cloth jeans & plaid shirt, blue neckerchief, boots, 16", VG+ **$100.00**

Howdy Doody, push-button puppet, wood, Kohner #180, 6", VG+ **$75.00**

Howdy Doody, squeeze toy, in airplane w/smiling face, yellow rubber, 4½x5½", EX..**$175.00**

Howdy Doody, ventriloquist doll, stuffed body w/vinyl head & hands, Goldberger, 1970s, 11", NMIB **$65.00**

Huckleberry Hound, figure, Flintstone Inflatables, inflatable vinyl, MIP **$28.00**

Huckleberry Hound, figure, squeeze rubber, standing w/black cane & top hat in hand, Dell, 6", NRFP **$50.00**

Huckleberry Hound, figure, stuffed plush w/rubber face, red & white, Knickerbocker, 1959, 18", EX+ **$35.00**

Huckleberry Hound, figure, vinyl w/jointed arms, red w/top hat & tie, Knixies by Knickerbocker, 6", NM **$40.00**

Huckleberry Hound, flashlight, plastic w/molded face, Laurie Import Ltd, 1976, 7", unused, MIP **$15.00**

Huckleberry Hound, sticker, puffy vinyl figure standing w/arms at sides, 1977, 7", MIP **$10.00**

Incredible Hulk, figure, bendable rubber, Just Toys, 1989, 6", EX+ **$8.00**

Incredible Hulk, figure, vinyl w/jointed limbs, Toy Biz, 1991, 14", EX **$25.00**

Inspector Gadget, figure, in trenchcoat, squeeze vinyl, Jujasa, 1983, 6½", MIP...**$50.00**

Inspector Gadget, toy telephone, half-figure atop red & blue phone, HG Toys, 1980s, 10", NM **$30.00**

Jetsons, fast-food toy, any character in space car, Wendy's, 1989, NM+, ea from $5 to **$6.00**

Jetsons, nightlight, Orbity, Elroy & Astro in bed sleeping, bisque, Giftique, 1980s, 6" L, M **$35.00**

Jetsons, ornament/clock, Astro Multi-Function Countdown Clock, vinyl, digital, Radio Shack, 1999, 3¾", MIB **$18.00**

Judy Jetson (Jetsons), figure, vinyl w/2-tone pink cloth outfit, Applause, 10", NM+...**$15.00**

Kermit the Frog (Muppets), figure, stuffed cloth, red & green plaid cloth vest, red bow tie, Eden Toys, 25", NM+ **$22.00**

Kermit the Frog (Muppets), figure, stuffed plush w/cloth outfit, plastic eyes, black & white plaid pants, Nanco, 14", M.......**$10.00**

Kermit the Frog (Muppets), figure, stuffed plush w/felt collar, Hasbro, 1985, 19", NM+ **$22.00**

Knight Rider, KITT Dashboard, Illco, battery-operated, NMIB, $65.00.

Laurel & Hardy, figure, either, bendable rubber, Lakeside, 1967, 6", EX+, ea **$25.00**

Laurel & Hardy, roly poly, either, vinyl, red, white & blue, chimes, 1970s, 11", VG+, ea **$30.00**

Laverne & Shirley, Paint-by-Numbers, acrylic paint set, Hasbro, 1981, unused, MIP (sealed) **$20.00**

Lily Munster (Munsters), figure, stuffed cloth & vinyl, white gown w/black trim, Presents, 11", NM **$40.00**

Little Audrey, carrying case, Around the World With..., w/graphics on white vinyl hat-box shape w/handle, 1960s, EX.......**$55.00**

Little Bill, figure, stuffed cloth w/vinyl head, Hey Hey Hey! I'm a 'Cosby Kid,' Remco, 1985, 22", MIB.......................**$75.00**

Little Lulu, Cooking Set, plastic, Larami, 1974, unused, MOC (sealed)...**$15.00**

Magilla Gorilla, figure, stuffed (hard) ribbed cloth w/pink shorts, Playtime Toys, 1979, 7½", NM+ **$20.00**

Magilla Gorilla, figure, stuffed plush, Nanco, 1990, 8½", NM+..**$10.00**

Magilla Gorilla, stuffed felt w/vinyl head, Ideal, 1960s, 7½", EX+ **$55.00**

Man From Uncle, Secret Print Putty, USA, 1965, MOC...**$100.00**

Margaret (Dennis the Menace), figure, stuffed cloth & vinyl, synthetic hair, cloth outfit, Presents, 1987, 10", NM **$30.00**

Marvin Martian, figure, vinyl, jointed arms, 1990s, w/hang tag, 8¼", NM+ **$15.00**

Marvin Martian, ice machine, plastic, Saltan, 1990s, 12", NM+ **$20.00**

Marvin Martian, push puppet, wood, 1990s, 4½", NM **$18.00**

Mighty Mouse, Merry-Pack, complete collection of 20 games & toys, die-cut litho cardboard, CBS TV Ent, 1956, unused, EX+ **$75.00**

Mister Magoo, figure, stuffed cloth w/vinyl head, all yellow w/shiny hat, shirt & feet, Cuddle Wit, 13", NM+ **$18.00**

Mister Magoo, figure, stuffed cloth w/vinyl head & hat, felt outfit w/3 plastic buttons, Ideal, 1960s, 16", NM **$100.00**

Mrs Buxles (Beetle Bailey), figure, stuffed cloth, vinyl head, red cloth dress, red shoes, Sugar Loaf, 15", 1990s, NM **$20.00**

Muppets, kaleidoscope, cardboard & metal w/lithoed Muppet characters, Hallmark, 1981, 9" L, EX+ **$30.00**

Olive Oyl (Popeye), bookmark, figure w/tennis racket, plastic, Industries, 1980, 5", NRFC (marked Popeye & Pals) ... **$12.00**

Pac-Man, figure, stuffed plush, yellow w/open red mouth, 1980s, 17", NM **$15.00**

Partridge Family Bus, Remco, MIB, $150.00.

Peanuts, bulletin board, brown cork w/images of the Peanuts gang amidst a musical staff & Schroeder at piano, 18x23", NM **$12.00**

Peanuts, megaphone, litho tin w/images of Snoopy w/megaphone, Lucy & Charlie Brown, Chein, 1970, 6", VG+ **$25.00**

Peanuts, Snoopy Fun Flashlight, plastic Snoopy figure as Flying Ace, squeeze to light, Garrity, 1980s, 4", MOC **$15.00**

Pearl Pureheart (Mighty Mouse), figure, stuffed cloth w/red cloth jacket, yellow hair, A&A Plush, Inc, 1990s, 15", NM+ . **$12.00**

Pebble (Flintstones), figure, squeeze vinyl, Sanitoy, 6", 1979, NM **$25.00**

Pebbles (Flintstones), doll, vinyl w/cloth outfit, Knickerbocker, 1970s, 4½", EX....................................... **$10.00**

Pebbles (Flintstones), figure, printed stuffed cloth, brown felt hair, cloth outfit, Knickerbocker, 1970s, 7", EX **$15.00**

Pepe Le Pew, figure, stuffed vinyl, Ace Novelty, 1997, 8", NM . **$8.00**

Pixie (Pixie & Dixie), figure, vinyl w/jointed head & arms, Knixie by Knickerbocker, 1962, 6", NM **$40.00**

Pixie & Dixie, bop bag, infatable vinyl, reversible images, Kestral, 18", M **$50.00**

Pixie & Dixie, squeeze toy, characters on cheese wedge, rubber, Dell, 1960s, 5½", EX+..................................... **$40.00**

Pokey (Gumby & Pokey), figure, foam-stuffed bendy, red w/black, Sher-Stuff, 1983, 12", NM **$22.00**

Popeye, Hip-Pop Ball, solid rubber, Ja-Ru, 1981, 2", NRFP . **$10.00**

Popeye, Pocket Puzzles, 4 dexterity puzzles on 1 card, Ja-Ru, 1989, NRFC **$12.00**

Popeye, Popeye Comics Department Stamp Set, StamperKraft #4007, complete, EX **$75.00**

Popeye, Stuffed Foam Toy, Cribmates, 1979, 6", NRFP **$22.00**

Porky Pig, figure, squeeze vinyl, standing waving in turquoise jacket, orange bow tie, Reliance, 1978, NM **$20.00**

Prickles (Gumby & Pokey), figure, rubber yellow dinosaur w/jointed arms, 1980s, NM.. **$6.00**

Ren & Stempy, Talking Ren Hoek, stuffed cloth w/vinyl head, Mattel, 1992, 10", MIP.. **$25.00**

RH Pufnstuf, figure, bean-stuffed plush, cloth outfit, Street Players, 1999, 12", NM+..................................... **$10.00**

Road Runner, figure, rubber, Arby's, 1988, 3", NM+............ **$8.00**

Rocky (Rocky & Friends), figure, stuffed plush, Wallace Berrie, 1982, 12", NM+.. **$20.00**

Rocky & Friends, wallet, brown vinyl w/Bullwinkle & Rocky lettered above image w/white stars, stitched trim, Larami, MOC **$25.00**

Schroeder (Peanuts), figure, vinyl w/orange Beethoven sweater & black cloth pants, 1970s, 7½", EX+ **$35.00**

Tasmanian Devil, figure, bendable foam rubber, Bendy Toys, 1988, 7½", MIP.. **$25.00**

Tasmanian Devil, wall plaque, scowling image on multicolor plastic popcorn-type material, 1973, M **$12.00**

Three Little Pigs, bank, tin litho, Chein, #538, NM, $145.00.
(Photo courtesy Smith House Toy & Auction Company)

Top Dog (Peanuts), magic slate, various images of Snoopy, Child Art Productions, 1970s, M (sealed) **$15.00**

Tweety Bird, figure, flocked plastic, dressed as sheriff, Lucky Bell, 1989, 3", NM+... **$8.00**

Wile E Coyote, mug, ceramic head form, Applause, 1989, 4", M **$15.00**

Woodstock (Peanuts), Flying Trapeze Toy, plastic, Aviva, NM .. **$25.00**

Cherished Teddies

Cherished teddies were designed by artist Patricia Hillman for Enesco. They debuted in 1992 and have proved to be one of the most popular collectibles for the Enesco company. The Cherished Teddies are made from cast resin and are highly detailed. On the bottom of each figurine (room permitting), you'll find their name and a saying as well as a date.

Advisors: Debbie and Randy Coe

Figurine, Abigail in a basket with a kitten, Inside We're All the Same, 1992, $8.50. (Photo courtesy Debbie and Randy Coe)

Figurine, Arthur holding a sailboat, August, 1993 .... **$7.50**
Figurine, baby laying in a cradle, Cradled w/Love, 1992........ **$6.50**
Figurine, Betsy, crawling baby, First Step To Love, 1993 .... **$7.50**
Figurine, Chantel & fawn, 2 angels, We're Kindred Spirits, 1999. **$9.50**
Figurine, Dennis, barbeque cook, You Put the Spice in My Life, 1999 national event pc.. **$8.50**
Figurine, Father in blue suit, A Father Is the Bearer of Strength, 1995 .... **$8.50**
Figurine, Freda & Tina, tea party on a blanket, Our Friendship Is a Perfect Blend, 1992.. **$12.50**
Figurine, Jacki, green bow in hair, Hugs & Kisses, 1991........ **$8.50**
Figurine, Karen, orange bow in hair, Best Buddy, 1991 .... **$8.50**
Figurine, Kyle writing a letter, Even Though We Are Far Apart, You'll Always Have a Place in My Heart, 1998.......................... **$9.50**
Figurine, Lance, old-time pilot, Come Fly w/Me, 1998 national event pc **$9.50**
Figurine, Little Jack Horner, I'm Plum Happy You're My Friend, 1993 .... **$14.50**
Figurine, Logon, has on overalls, hat & tie, Love Is a Bear Necessity, 1996 .... **$9.50**
Figurine, Nolan holding a string of blocks that spell NOEL, A String of Good Things, 1996 .... **$9.50**
Figurine, Sara, white bow in hair, Love Ya.............................. **$8.50**

Picture frame, bear sitting by kitten, A Friend Is Forever, 1992. **$5.00**
Vase, 2 bears by heart vase, Love Bears All Things, 1996 .... **$9.50**

Figurine, Judy and Diane talking on phone, Always Remember I'm Just a Phone Call Away, 2001, $12.50. (Photo courtesy Debbie and Randy Coe)

Christmas Collectibles

Christmas is nearly everybody's favorite holiday, and it's a season when we all seem to want to get back to time-honored traditions. The stuffing and fruit cakes are made like Grandma always made them, we go caroling and sing the old songs that were written two 200 years ago, and the same Santa that brought gifts to the children in a time long forgotten still comes to our house and yours every Christmas Eve.

So for reasons of nostalgia, there are thousands of collectors interested in Christmas memorabilia. Some early Santa figures are rare and may be very expensive, especially when dressed in a color other than red. Blown glass ornaments and Christmas tree bulbs were made in shapes of fruits and vegetables, houses, Disney characters, animals, and birds. There are Dresden ornaments and candy containers from Germany, some of which were made prior to the 1870s, that have been lovingly preserved and handed down from generation to generation. They were made of cardboard that sparkled with gold and silver trim.

Artificial trees made of feathers were produced as early as 1850 and as late as 1950. Some were white, others blue, though most were green, and some had red berries or clips to hold candles. There were little bottle-brush trees, trees with cellophane needles, and trees from the '60s made of aluminum.

Collectible Christmas items are not necessarily old, expensive, or hard to find. Things produced in your lifetime have value as well. To learn more about this field, we recommend *Pictorial Guide to Christmas Ornaments and Collectibles* by George Johnson (Collector Books).

Bank, Rudolph, plastic, battery-operated, USA, ca 1960, 5¼" . **$35.00**
Bulb, canary, clear glass w/exhaust tip beak, 4¾", from $30 to . **$40.00**
Bulb, elephant sitting on a ball, milk glass, Japan, 2¾", from $30 to **$40.00**
Bulb, frog, milk glass, Japan, ca 1925-55, 2¼", from $10 to. **$15.00**

Bulb, Kewpie doll w/no clothes, milk glass, Japan, ca 1925, 3", from $75 to **$100.00**

Bulb, Paramount metal star, 3¼", from $6 to **$7.00**

Bulb, rose, clear glass, marked Watt on base insulator, Austria, ca 1920, 1½", from $25 to.................................**$35.00**

Bulb, Santa head in chimney, milk glass, Japan, from $15 to..**$20.00**

Bulb, smiling sitting dog, clear glass, German, ca 1925, 2½", from $125 to...**$150.00**

Bulb, walnut w/exhaust tip, clear glass, Europe, ca 1915, 1½", from $30 to..**$40.00**

Candelabrum, 3-socket red candles w/poinsettia flower at base, wreath around center candle, Mirostar Corp, ca 1950 ....**$50.00**

Candelabrum, 9-socket blue bubble lights on stair-step base, Royal Electric Co, #790, 1948................................**$150.00**

Candy container, boy skater, plastic, Rosbro Plastics, Providence, RI, ca 1955, 5", from $15 to **$20.00**

Candy container, colored paper cornucopia w/Santa lithograph, marked Germany 1930s, 9¾", from $60 to **$80.00**

Candy container, lady's high boot, cardboard covered w/pink satin, 1950s, 5½", from $35 to **$45.00**

Candy container, little boy whispering into Santa's ear on printed box, American, 4¼", from $10 to **$12.00**

Candy containers: Santa, chenille strips form suit, crepe paper bag, marked Germany, late 1930s, 9", EX, from $60.00 to $75.00; Santa in nightcap, Western Germany, 7", MIB, from $45.00 to $55.00. (Photo courtesy George Johnson)

Candy container, snowman w/candy cane, plastic, Reliable Plastics, Canada, ca 1950, 5", from $35 to **$45.00**

Decoration, chimney w/bubble light & sm Santa, battery-operated, Japan, ca 1960 ....**$40.00**

Decoration, Christmas Eve Capers, boy & girl on stairs w/Santa coming down chimney, Glolite Corp, #1530, ca 1948 ....**$125.00**

Decoration, Glo-rious Angel, Glolite Corp, #537, ca 1955, 7½".**$25.00**

Decoration, Hi-Ho Santa, plastic Santa riding reindeer, Raylite Electric Co, #93, ca 1958, 10"................................**$40.00**

Decoration, Navtivity Scene, Royal Electric Co, #900, ca 1954, 13½" **$65.00**

Decoration, Santa on snow shoes, Gem Electric Co, #639, USA, ca 1952, 6" **$65.00**

Decoration, Santa on train, ceramic, Japan, ca 1960 ....**$30.00**

Decoration, Santa w/light bulb eyes, ca 1930, 26" **$150.00**

Decoration, Sno-Man Winter Scene, #516, snowman behind red gate w/snow-covered tree background, ca 1953, 8".......**$85.00**

Decoration, snowman holding bubble light, Royal Electric Co, #945, 1950, 11½" **$55.00**

Decoration, Twas the Night Before Christmas, 3 carolers standing at door, Glolite Corp, #1512, ca 1949 ....**$50.00**

Flashlight, Santa head, battery-operated, Hong Kong, 1960 .**$20.00**

Lamp, blinking Merry Xmas, ca 1965, USA, 12" **$20.00**

Lamp, white & gold Christmas tree, ca 1940, 16½" **$50.00**

Lanterns, battery-operated, Japan, 5", MIB: snowman globe, $50.00; Santa globe, $65.00.

Lighting set, Fairymark Liliput Xmas Lights, #12355, 16-socket, Japan, ca 1930, MIB..**$30.00**

Lighting set, Flame-lites, Noma of Canada, #715, 15-socket, ca 1960, MIB..**$35.00**

Lighting set, Glimmer Lites, New York Merchandising Co, #1015, 15-socket, ca 1950, MIB..**$20.00**

Lighting set, Heavenly Twinkle Star Set, Noma Electric Co, #2221, 20-socket, 1961, MIB..**$20.00**

Lighting set, Mazda Fairy-Lights, British Thomson-Houston Co Ltd, 12-socket, England, ca 1955, MIB.........................**$40.00**

Lighting set, Twinkle Lites, Radiant Glass Fibers Co Inc, #30, 20-socket, ca 1950, MIB..**$30.00**

Motion Lamp, Santa, Cartwright Co, ca 1940, 9½" **$175.00**

Motion lamp, White Christmas, Econolite Corp, 1953, 12".**$300.00**

Novelty lighting, Cross Light, Raylite Electric Co, ca 1949, 5", MIB..**$15.00**

Novelty lighting, Flying Saucer Lites, Noma of Canada, #JS22, set of 10, ca 1962, MIB **$250.00**

Novelty lighting, Krystal Star Lamps, set of 10, Japan, ca 1935, MIB..**$100.00**

Novelty lighting, ornament set, Germany, center light in round ornament, ca 1955, MIB **$200.00**

Novelty lighting, Pep-Mint Stik Set, Leo Pollock Co, #X3402, ca 1942, MIB..**$125.00**

Ornament, alligator, free-blown glass, Czechoslovakia, 7", from $300 to **$325.00**

Ornament, angel w/cornucopia, paper, Littauer & Boysen, ca 1900, 4½", from $75 to..**$90.00**

Ornament, bird embossed on egg, mold-blown glass, lg, 3½", from $30 to **$50.00**

Ornament, butterfly, velour, Germany, 5", from $50 to.......**$75.00**

Ornament, cardboard house, Czechoslovakia, 2", from $10 to **$12.00**

Ornament, cat in a bag, mold-blown glass, Germany, 1985, sm, 3½", from $100 to...**$125.00**

Ornament, chalet house w/angel & deer, plastic, marked Western Germany, 2¼", from $5 to.............................**$6.00**

Ornament, child-like angel on cloud w/white pine trees, plastic, Germany, 2¾", from $8 to.............................**$9.00**

Ornament, dancing bear, mold-blown glass, Germany, 1950s, 3⅛", from $50 to **$60.00**

Ornament, flamingo, free-blown glass w/annealed legs, Germany, 1920s-30s, 6½", from $60 to............................**$80.00**

Ornament, glass ball w/Santa inside, Germany, miniature, 2½", from $50 to **$75.00**

Ornament, glass basket w/fabric flowers, 4¾", from $100 to.**$125.00**

Ornament, gold angel in gold ring, plastic, USA, ca 1950, from $4 to **$5.00**

Ornament, hummingbird w/spun-glass wings, miniature, 1½", from $30 to **$40.00**

Ornament, hunting dog, Russia, 3¼", from $60 to.............**$70.00**

Ornament, nativity w/translucent back, plastic, Hong Kong, ca 1970, from $2 to **$3.00**

Ornament, oyster shell w/pearl, Italy, 1950s, 2½", from $75 to..**$90.00**

Ornament, Raphael Angel in Dresden sunburst, spun-glass rosette, lg, 6¾", from $55 to **$65.00**

Ornament, rooster, cotton, Russian, 4", from $40 to...........**$50.00**

Ornament, Santa w/spun-glass skirt, 6½", from $50 to **$75.00**

Ornament, sitting sheepdog, mold-blown glass, 3", from $30 to **$40.00**

Ornament, star, frosted cardboard covered w/Venetian Dew, Czechoslovakia, ca 1920-30, 3", from $15 to **$20.00**

Ornament, star, Russia, 2½", from $40 to **$50.00**

Ornament, 2 kittens in basket, mold-blown glass, Czechoslovakia, 1980s, sm, 2", from $60 to.................................**$75.00**

Sign, Merry Christmas, WH Fayle & Co, USA, ca 1925, 11" . **$50.00**

Tree, Crysta-Lite plastic w/clear edges, Royal Electric, ca 1955, 10", from $45 to **$55.00**

Tree, plastic in pot, marked Rosbro Plastics Providence RI, ca 1950, 6", from $18 to...**$22.00**

Tree, shredded rayon, flat back, 8 sockets, USA, ca 1950, 14½", from $100 to **$125.00**

Tree stand, cast iron, 4-leg, 2 candelabra base sockets, USA, ca 1930, 12" **$60.00**

Tree stand, metal, automatic, 5 candelabra base sockets, Noma Electric Co, #174, 1940, 19".........................**$20.00**

Tree stand, metal, rotating Santa scene, USA, ca 1960, 18" . **$200.00**

Tree stand, plastic, Santa face & bells on yellow, Noma of Canada, #175, 1951, 14"...**$30.00**

Tree topper, blown-glass spike wrapped in glass beads & rods, Czechoslovakia, ca 1930s, from $35 to **$45.00**

Tree topper, Celestial Light Top, Bradford Novelty Co Inc, #35, ca 1960 ....**$40.00**

Tree topper, Electric Chimes, 3 angel figures holding chimes, M Propp Co, #3000, ca 1928.........................**$100.00**

Tree topper, Heavenly Reflecting Light, angel on cloud, Bradford Novelty Co Inc, #20, ca 1955.........................**$25.00**

Tree topper, Metal Star, Glolite Corp, #426, 1941.............**$15.00**

Tree topper, star w/red center & trim, plastic, Glolite Corp, #430, ca 1955 ....**$10.00**

Wall hanging, cellophane bell spray, ca 1941, 9".................**$50.00**

Wall hanging, chenille 1-light cross, Peerless Electric Co, #510, ca 1960, 12"...**$20.00**

Wall hanging, church in winter scene, Merry Christmas, oval, Made in Germany, ca 1930-55, 12½", from $35 to...............**$45.00**

Wall hanging, plastic Rudolph, Burwood Products, 1953 ..**$300.00**

Wall hanging, plastic Santa face, Noma Electric Co, #551, ca 1948, 15"..**$15.00**

Wall hanging, Vinylite Star of Bethlehem, Noma Electric Co, #460, 1959, 29"...**$25.00**

Wall hanging, 3 candles w/halos, Germany, ca 1930-55, 6½x9", from $25 to **$35.00**

Wreath, cast iron w/candle light in center, ca 1930...........**$125.00**

Wreath, red cellophane w/plastic Santa figural in center, Goodlite, ca 1955 ....**$30.00**

Wreath, red w/Merry Xmas silver bell in center, Leo Pollock Corp, #63, 1935 ....**$50.00**

Toy, Santa Claus, Little Folk from Sunnyslope, latex rubber squeaker, 1950s, NMIB, $30.00. (Photo courtesy Linda Baker)

Christmas Pins

Once thought of as mere holiday novelties, Christmas pins are now considered tiny prizes among costume jewelry and Christmas collectors. Hollycraft, Weiss, Lisner, and other famous costume jewelry designers created beautiful examples. Rhinestones, colored 'jewels', and lovely enameling make Christmas pins tiny works of art, and what used to be purchased for a few dollars now may command as much as one hundred dollars, especially if signed. Pins are plentiful and prices vary. Buyers should be aware that many fakes and repros are out there. Many 'vintage looking' pins are actually brand new and retail for less than $10.00. Know your dealer, and if you are unsure, let it pass.

Assume that the pins we describe below are all Christmas trees unless noted otherwise; our line length is very limited, and we have tried to include as much pertinent information as possible.

Anthony Attruia, tree, black 'diamonds' w/24k gold pears, partridges & gold star on top, 2¾x1¾", from $110 to **$150.00**

Beegee McBride, Christmas Morning, tree, prong-set clear & green rhinestones in frame, green & clear in center, 2x3¾"....**$65.00**

Bettina Von Walhof, Bow Tree, bright blue diamond cuts outlined by clear prong-set round stones, bow at base is trembler, 5x3", $185.00.

(Photo courtesy Jill Gallina)

Bettina Von Walhof, Santa w/red, green & clear crystals holding branch w/green sack, 6x3⅝", from $375 to **$450.00**

BG Small, Winter Wonderland tree w/blue & clear rhinestones & 6 milk glass flowers, 2¾x1¾" **$45.00**

Dominique, tree, teal miniature baguettes, 2½x2" from $65 to **$85.00**

Dorothy Bauer, Christmas Ole tree, multicolor stones & rhine stones in silver, limited edition, 4x2¾" **$413.00**

Eisenberg, angel outlined in clear rhinestones w/frosted glass face, 2x1¾" from $18 to **$25.00**

Eisenberg, tree, emerald green navettes w/red stone inset on star, rhinestone stem, 3x1¾", from $75 to **$85.00**

Hobè, candy cane, alternating, prong-set red & clear crystals w/green jeweled bow, 4½x2" **$290.00**

Hobè, tree, brushed antique gold w/sm glued-on multicolor stones, 2¾", from $25 to..**$35.00**

Hollycraft, tree, red enamel bows w/red & green stones on gold frame, 2¼x1½", from $95 to **$115.00**

Ian St Gielar, orange Czech glass flower petals w/black onyx centers, 2½x1⅞", from $150 to **$200.00**

Ian St Gielar, tree, fuchsia beaded flowers w/crystal centers, beads & pearls form basket below, 5x3½", from $400 to..........**$450.00**

James Avery, tree, sterling, various animals w/message of peace below, 1⅝x1⅜", from $60 to **$75.00**

Jewelart, wreath, sterling silver, 1¾", from $35 to **$45.00**

Kirks Folly, Crystal Snowman, dangling aurora borealis crystals in many shapes & sizes, 4½x1¼" **$71.50**

Lia, tree, Lucite flowers over enameled green petals w/purple cabochon stones in center, 2x1⅛", from $45 to **$60.00**

Marcel Boucher, tree, red, green & turquoise sm stones in gold frame, 1¾x1¼", from $75 to **$95.00**

Radko, Regal Reindeer, sterling silver, limited edition, 2⅝x3⅜", from $175 to **$200.00**

RJ Graziano, tree, gold-plated leaves w/scattered clear rhinestones, 2¾x2" **$95.00**

Terri Friedman, tree, red, white & blue baguettes, rounds & teardrops, 2⅜x1½"..**$28.00**

Unsigned, cactus tree w/glued-on jingle bells & foil gifts, clear stone star on top, 3½x3", from $35 to **$45.00**

Unsigned, enameled Santa w/flag & green bag, 2½x1½" **$16.00**

Unsigned, polar bear, silver w/pavè crystals, 2⅛x1⅝", from $35 to **$45.00**

Unsigned, red poinsettia tree in metal basket, 2x2", from $15 to.**$20.00**

Unsigned, tree, brass w/clear tones, teddy bear, toy soldier & rocking horse at bottom, 1⅞x1⅜", from $25 to **$35.00**

Unsigned, tree, dark blue round stones in sq settings w/5 aurora borealis disks & angel on top, 2¼x3", from $95 to.....**$110.00**

Unsigned, tree, gold w/prong-set stones & dangling gold chains on bottom, 3x2¾", from $45 to.......................................**$60.00**

Von Walhof, tree, green, red, & white beads on wire frame w/4 faux holly berries, topped w/gold star, 4½x2½" **$485.00**

Weiss, red enameled poinsettia w/jeweled center, 2x2", from $45 to **$75.00**

Unsigned, trees, ca 1960s – 1970s, 2¼", from $25.00 to $35.00 each. (Photo courtesy Jill Gallina)

Cigarette Lighters

Collectors of tobacciana tell us that cigarette lighters are definitely hot! Look for novel designs (figurals, Deco styling, and so forth), unusual mechanisms (flint and fuel, flint and gas, battery, etc.), those made by companies now defunct, advertising lighters, and quality lighters made by Dunhill, Evans, Colibri, Zippo, and Ronson. For more information we recommend *Collector's Guide to Cigarette Lighters* by James Flanagan (Collector Books).

Newsletter: *On the Lighter Side*
Judith Sanders
P.O. Box 1733
Quitman, TX 75783; 903-763-2795
SASE for information

Advertising, Coors, plastic bowling pin, KEM, ca early 1950s, 2⅞x⅞", from $20 to **$25.00**

Advertising, Guinness, metal beer bottle, Ireland, ca mid-1960s, 2½x¾", from $15 to $20.00

Advertising, Mindy's Rigging Specialist, enamel on chromium, Barlow, ca early 1960s, 2¼x1½", from $15 to..............$20.00

Advertising, Paducah Sash & Door Co., by Dundee, 1950s – 1960s, 2x2x⅜", EX, $45.00. (Photo courtesy B.J. Summers)

Advertising, Valiant Steel, enamel on chromium, Barlow, ca 1965, 2¼x1½", from $10 to $20.00

Advertising, Willie the Kool penguin, painted metal, table lighter, ca mid-1930s, 4x1½", from $100 to $125.00

Advertising, ZEP cleaner, metal oil drum, ca 1950s, 2¼x1¼", from $15 to $25.00

Cheesecake, pinup girl, enamel on chromium, Realite, ca 1950s, 1⅞x1⅝", from $25 to $30.00

Cheesecake, Varga Girl, pewter on chromium, Zippo lighter in tin gift box, ca 1993, 2¼x1½", from $40 to.......................$50.00

Decorative, apple, gold-toned brass, Evans, ca mid-1950s, 3x2¼", from $40 to $60.00

Decorative, chromium nude on plastic base, Dunhill, ca 1935, 5x3", from $70 to $100.00

Decorative, lamppost w/chain, brass, ca 1929, 9½x3", from $75 to $100.00

Decorative, pipe, chromium w/etched wood base, Albert, ca 1950s, 2⅜x4½", from $25 to $40.00

Decorative, Statue of Liberty, butane, ca mid-1950s, 7½x3½", from $90 to $115.00

Figural, duck, ceramic, Evans, ca mid-1950s, 2¼x6½", from $25 to $30.00

Figural, horse, painted ceramic, Japan, ca 1955, 5½x5½", from $15 to $25.00

Figural, penguin, gold- & silver-plated, 1960s, 2x⅞", from $40 to..$70.00

Figural, Scottie dog, white painted metal, lighter on back, Strikalite, ca late 1930s, 2½x3", from $25 to.............................$40.00

Figural, swan, chromium table, Japan, ca early 1960s, 3x3¾", from $10 to $20.00

Figural, wolf, brass, head hinged to reveal table lighter, ca 1912, 2½x1½", from $60 to $100.00

Gun, cannon shape, brass, Negbaur, ca 1939, 3⅛x8", from $50 to $75.00

Gun, pistol shape w/mother-of-pearl grips, chromium, Japan, ca early 1950s, 1½x2", from $25 to $40.00

Gun, spark pistol shape, metal, Ronson, ca 1915, 3x4¾", from $200 to $300.00

Miniature, brass, Japan, mid-1950s, 1⅛x⅝", from $5 to......$10.00

Miniature, chromium, lift-arm type, mother-of-pearl band, New York by Aladdin, ca mid-1950s, ⅞x¾", w/gift box, $40 to $60.00

Novelty, boot, metal, lever on back opens lighter, ca 1920s, 1¾x2⅝", from $80 to $125.00

Novelty, Coca-Cola truck, turn spare wheel in back & flame comes out of the roof, Japan, ca 1990s, 1¾x3⅜", $10 to.........$15.00

Novelty, cowboy boot, Evans, ca 1948, 5x5", from $40 to...$60.00

Novelty, fire extinguisher, butane, handle pulls down to light, Japan, ca 1990s, 3x1¼", from $10 to $15.00

Novelty, Lucky Key, brass, ca mid-1960s, 1¾x⅜", from $25 to ..$40.00

Novelty, Model T Ford, lighter behind seat, painted metal, 1960, 3⅛" long, from $15.00 to $25.00. (Photo courtesy James Flanagan)

Novelty, stein, ceramic, Germany, ca 1958, 3¾x1⅝", from $45 to...$60.00

Novelty, twin bullets, blue-painted metal, New Method, ca 1930s, 2¼x1⅛", from $20 to $35.00

Occupied Japan, belt buckle, chromium, ca 1940s, 1¼x1⅞", from $150 to $200.00

Occupied Japan, chromium lizard-covered pocket type, lift arm, ca late 1940s, 1½x1", from $50 to $75.00

Occupied Japan, lighthouse, silver-plated, ca 1948, 4¼x1½", from $60 to $90.00

Occupied Japan, owl, silver-plated w/glass eyes, ca 1948, 3x2", from $90 to $110.00

Occupied Japan, rocket ship, chromium, squeeze fins together to light, ca 1949, 2x5⅛", from $80 to............................$110.00

Occupied Japan, typewriter, press space bar down to light, ca 1948, 1¾x3½", from $175 to $200.00

Pocket, brass w/leather band, Evans, ca late 1940s, 2½x1½", from $25 to $40.00

Pocket, brass w/plaid band, Evans, ca late 1930s, 1½x1½", from $25 to $30.00

Pocket, chromium w/Delft ceramic inlay scene of mountain, river & trees, Evans, ca mid-1930s, 2x1½", from $50 to...........$70.00

Pocket, chromium w/red leather insert band, Evans, ca 1934, 2x1½", from $25 to $40.00

Pocket, chromium w/turqoise band, Sport, w/gift box, Ronson, ca 1956, 2x1¾", from $35 to $60.00

Pocket, submarine, brass, ca 1918, 1½x3¼", from $100 to ..$150.00

Pocket, violin, brass, striker lighter, ca 1920s, 2½x¾", from $200 to $300.00

Table, alarm clock, chrome, push bell to light, Japan, ca 1950s, 2½x1⅞", from $70 to $90.00

Table, bulldog in Lucite cube, Evans, ca mid-1950s, 3¼x1⅞", from $30 to $40.00

Table, chromium & tortoise Lucite, Thornes, ca late 1940s, 3¾x1¾", from $50 to $75.00

Table, chromium & wood, butane, Japan, ca 1970s, 3x2⅛", from $10 to **$15.00**

Table, deer hoof, brass-finished, 1960s, 3¼x5¼", from $100 to...**$125.00**

Table, egg shape on leaf pedestal, turquoise, Evans, mid-1950s, 2½x3", from $60 to **$75.00**

Table, golf bag on cart, chrome & red paint, pull handle on cart to light, Japan, ca late 1960s, 5¼x4", from $50 to **$75.00**

Cleminson Pottery

One of the several small potteries that operated in California during the middle of the century, Cleminson was a family-operated enterprise that made kitchenware, decorative items, and novelties that are beginning to attract a considerable amount of interest. At the height of their productivity, they employed 150 workers, so as you make your rounds, you'll be very likely to see a piece or two offered for sale just about anywhere you go. Prices are not high; this may be a 'sleeper.'

They marked their ware fairly consistently with a circular ink stamp that contains the name 'Cleminson.' But even if you find an unmarked piece, with just a little experience you'll easily be able to recognize their very distinctive glaze colors. They're all strong, yet grayed-down, dusty tones. They made a line of bird-shaped tableware items that they marketed as 'Distlefink' and several plaques and wall pockets that are decorated with mottoes and Pennsylvania Dutch-type hearts and flowers.

In Jack Chipman's *The Collector's Encyclopedia of California Pottery, Second Edition,* you'll find a chapter devoted to Cleminson Pottery. Roerig's *The Ultimate Collector's Encyclopedia of Cookie Jars* has additional information. (Both of these books are published by Collector Books.)

See also Clothes Sprinkler Bottles; Cookie Jars.

Salt box, 6½x5¾", from $40.00 to $45.00.

Ashtray, folksy fruit pattern, 1960s $20.00
Ashtray, You're the Big Wheel, 8".........................$15.00
Bank, baby in blue diaper w/pink flowers, Bonds for Baby, 7x4". $30.00
Butter dish, Distlefink, bird form, 4½x6½"..................$40.00
Cheese dish, lady figural, 6½x7½", from $65 to $80.00
Cleanser shaker, Katrina, 6¼", from $40 to $50.00

Creamer, rooster figure, 5½", from $40 to $58.00
Creamer & sugar bowl, Pennsylvania Dutch decor $18.00
Darning egg, girl figure, Darn It on apron, pink ribbon, feet painted on bottom, 1940s, 5", from $50 to.............................$65.00
Figurine, Granvilee, gremlin figure, white w/green shoes & hat, flower wreath around neck, 3¼", from $100 to $115.00
Figurine, Italian man in green jacket w/yellow & blue polka-dot scarf, holding pink basket w/one arm raised, 4½", NM $18.00
Gravy boat, Distlefink, bird figure, 5¾x6" $35.00
Head vase, girl w/curly blond hair & freckles, red lips, 4"....$50.00
Jam jar, white w/green polka-dots, lid w/strawberry finial, 4½" ..$15.00
Mug, anthropomorphic cabbage, Head of the House, 5½" ..$42.00
Pitcher, honey; Queen Bee, 5½", from $75 to $90.00
Pitcher, watering can shape, white w/floral decoration, 5", from $35 to $40.00
Plaque, Family Tree, flowers hanging from tree w/child, light blue background, from $60 to $75.00
Plaque, God Bless Our Mortgaged Home, house w/trees, 6⅝". $15.00
Razor blade bank, bell-shaped, man's face on front getting ready to shave, 3¾x3¼", from $30 to $40.00
Ring holder, hand coming out of yellow & green floral decor, 3", from $15 to $18.00
Ring holder, worm in apple...$60.00
Salt & pepper shakers, bowling pin shape, 5⅝", pr $40.00
Salt & pepper shakers, French artist w/palette, 6¼", pr........$55.00
Salt & pepper shakers, kangaroo mother w/baby in pouch, 6¼x2¼" baby, pr $45.00
Salt & pepper shakers, white w/burgundy pink trim w/green leaf, 6", pr $13.00
Spoon rest, white w/musical notes, Whistle While You Work, original tag, 8" $35.00
String holder, heart shape w/verse $45.00
Tea bag holder, teapot shape, 3x4¼" $15.00
Wall pocket, Antoine, 7¼" $75.00
Wall pocket, brown teapot w/floral border around verse, A Penny Saved Is a Penny Earned, green mark, 8x5", from $35 to...........$45.00
Wall pocket, cream & green, square, Welcome, Good Friends... Family Cheer, 7x8" $15.00
Wall pocket, Home Sweet Home w/in wood-like frame, from $28 to $33.00

Wall pockets: Mortgage, 7⅛", from $20.00 to $25.00; Kitchen, 7x8½", from $25.00 to $30.00. (Photo courtesy Bill and Betty Newbound)

Clothes Sprinkler Bottles

In the days before perma-press, the process of getting wrinkles out of laundered clothing involved first sprinkling each piece with water, rolling it tightly to distribute the moisture, and packing it all down in a laundry basket until ironing day. Thank goodness those days are over!

To sprinkle the water, you could simply dip your fingers in a basin and 'fling' the water around, or you could take a plain old bottle with a screw-on cap, pierce the cap a few times, and be in business. Figural ceramic bottles were first introduced in the late 1920s and are found in the forms of a variety of subjects ranging from cute animals to people who actually did the ironing. Maybe these figural bottles were made to add a little cheer to this dreary job. Anyway, since no one irons any more, today they simply represent a little bit of history, and collectors now take an interest in them. Prices are already fairly high, but there still may be a bargain or two out there!

See also Kitchen Prayer Ladies.

Advisor: Larry Pogue (See Directory, String Holders)

Clothespin, face with stenciled eyes and airbrushed cheeks, ceramic, marked Cardinal, $400.00.

Cat, marble eyes, ceramic, American Bisque	$400.00
Cat, marble eyes, ceramic, marked Cardinal USA, 8½"	$255.00
Cat, variety of designs & colors, handmade ceramic, from $75 to	$125.00
Chinese man, removable head, ceramic, from $250 to	$400.00
Chinese man, Sprinkle Plenty, white, green & brown, holding iron, ceramic, 8½", from $125 to	$175.00
Chinese man, Sprinkle Plenty, yellow & green, ceramic, Cardinal China Co	$85.00
Chinese man, towel over arm, ceramic, from $300 to	$350.00
Chinese man, variety of designs & colors, handmade, ceramic, from $50 to	$150.00
Chinese man, white & aqua w/paper shirt tag, ceramic, California Cleminsons, from $75 to	$100.00
Chinese man w/removable head, ceramic, from $250 to	$400.00

Clothespin, hand decorated, ceramic, from $250 to	$400.00
Clothespin, red, yellow & green plastic, from $20 to	$40.00
Clothespin, yellow w/face, ceramic, 1940s-50s, 7¾"	$275.00
Dearie Is Weary, ceramic, Enesco, from $350 to	$500.00
Dutch boy, green & white, ceramic	$275.00
Dutch girl, white w/green & pink trim, wetter-downer, ceramic, from $175 to	$250.00
Elephant, pink & gray, ceramic	$165.00
Elephant, trunk forms handle, ceramic, American Bisque, extremely rare, minimum value	$700.00
Emperor, variety of designs & colors, handmade ceramic, from $150 to	$200.00

Fireman, California Cleminsons, ceramic, very rare, 6¼", minimum value, $3,000.00. (Photo courtesy Larry Pogue)

Iron, blue flowers, ceramic, from $100 to	$150.00
Iron, green ivy, ceramic, from $95 to	$125.00
Iron, green plastic, from $35 to	$75.00
Iron, lady cleaning, ceramic	$125.00
Iron, lady ironing, ceramic	$95.00
Iron, man & woman farmer, ceramic, from $200 to	$275.00
Iron, souvenir of Aquarena Springs, San Marcos TX, ceramic, from $200 to	$300.00
Iron, souvenir of Florida, pink flamingo, ceramic	$300.00
Iron, white w/black rooster decoration, black stripe on handle, ceramic w/metal lid, VG Japan sticker, 6½"	$100.00
Iron, Wonder Cave - San Marcos TX, white w/green, brown & black scene	$300.00
Lady w/embossed apron, cobalt glass, metal sprinkler cap, 7".	$60.00
Mammy, ceramic	$450.00
Mary Maid, all colors, plastic, Reliance, from $20 to	$35.00
Mary Poppins, ceramic, Cleminsons, from $300 to	$450.00
Myrtle (Black), ceramic, Pfaltzgraff, from $275 to	$375.00
Myrtle (white), ceramic, Pfaltzgraff, from $250 to	$350.00
Peasant woman, w/laundry poem on label, ceramic, from $200 to	$300.00
Poodle, gray, pink or white, ceramic, from $200 to	$300.00

Rooster, green, tan & red detailing over white, ceramic, Sierra Vista.. **$125.00**

Clothing and Accessories

Watch a 'golden oldie' movie, and you can't help admiring the clothes — what style, what glamour, what fun! Due in part to the popularity of old movie classics and great new movies with retro themes, there's a growing fascination with the fabulous styles of the past — and there's no better way to step into the romance and glamour of those eras than with an exciting piece of vintage clothing!

'OOOhhh, it don't mean a thing, if it ain't got that S-W-I-N-G!' In 1935, Benny Goodman, 'King of Swing,' ushered in the swing era from Los Angeles's Polmar Ballroom. After playing two standard sets, he switched to swing, and the crowd went crazy! Swing era gals' clothing featured short full or pleated skirts, wide padded shoulders and natural waistlines. Guys, check out those wild, wide ties that were worn with 'gangster-look' zoot suits!

Clothes of the 1940s though the 1970s are not as delicate as their Victorian and Edwardian counterparts; they're easier to find and much more affordable! Remember, the more indicative of its period, the more desirable the item. Look for pieces with glitz and glamour — also young, trendy pieces that were expensive to begin with. Look for designer pieces and designer look-alikes. Although famous designer labels are hard to find, you may be lucky enough to run across one! American designers like Adrian, Claire McMardell, Charles James, Mainboucher, Hattie Carnegie, Norell, Pauline Trigere, and Mollie Parnis came to the fore during World War II. The '50s were the decade of Christian Dior; others included Balenciaga, Balmain, Chanel, Jacques Heim, Nona Ricci, Ann Fogarty, Oleg Cassini, and Adele Simpson. In the '60s and '70s, Mary Quant, Betsey Johnson, Givenchy, Yves St. Laurent, Oscar de la Renta, Galanos, Pierre Cardin, Rudi Gernreich, Paco Rabanne, Courreges, Arnold Scassi, Geoffrey Beene, Emilio Pucci, Zandra Rhodes, and Jessica McClintock (Gunne Sax) were some of the names that made fashion headlines.

Pucci, Lilli Ann of Calfornia, Eisenberg, and Adele Simpson designs continue to be especially sought after. Look for lingerie — '30s and '40s lace/hook corsets, and '50s pointy 'bullet' bras (like the ones in the Old Maidenform Dream ads). For both men and women, '70s disco platform shoes (the wilder, the better); cowboy shirts and jackets, also fringed 'hippie' items. For men, look for bowling shirts, '50s 'Kramer' shirts, and '40s and '50s wild ties, especially those by Salvadore Dali.

Levi jeans and jackets made circa 1971 and before have a cult following, especially in Japan. Among the most sought-after denim Levi items are jeans with a capitol 'E' on a *red* tab or back pocket. The small 'e' jeans are also collectible; these were made during the late 1960s and until 1970 (with two rows of single stitching inside the back pocket). Worth watching for as well are the 'red line' styles of the '80s (these have double-stitched back pockets). Other characteristics to look for in vintage Levis are visible rivets inside the jeans and single pockets and silver-colored buttons on jackets with vertical pleats. From the same era, Lee, Wrangler, Bluebell, J.C. Penney, Oxhide, Big Yanks, James Dean, Doublewear, and Big Smith denims are collectible as well.

As with any collectible, condition is of the utmost importance.

'Deadstock' is a term that refers to a top-grade item that has never been worn or washed and still has its original tags. Number 1 grade must have no holes larger than a pinhole. A torn belt loop is permissible if no hole is created. There may be a few light stains and light fading. The crotch area must have no visible wear and the crotch seam must have no holes. And lastly, the item must not have been altered. Unless another condition is noted within the lines, values in the listing here are for items in number 1 grade. There are also other grades for items that have more defects.

While some collectors buy with the intent of preserving their clothing and simply enjoy having it, many buy it to wear. If you do wear it, be very careful how you clean it. Fabrics may become fragile with age.

For more information, refer to *Vintage Hats and Bonnets, 1770 – 1970, Identifications and Values,* by Sue Langley; *Vintage Fashions for Women, the 1950s & '60s,* by Kristina Harris (Schiffer); *Clothing and Accessories From the '40s, '50s and '60s,* by Jan Lindenberger (Schiffer); *Vintage Denim* by David Little; *Fashion Footwear, 1800 – 1970* by Desire Smith; *Plastic Handbags* by Kate E. Dooner; *Fit To Be Tied, Vintage Ties of the '40s and Early '50s,* by Rod Dyer and Ron Spark; and *The Hawaiian Shirt* by H. Thomas Steele. For more information about denim clothing and vintage footwear see *How to Identify Vintage Apparel for Fun and Profit,* which is available from Flying Deuce Auction & Antiques (see Auction Houses).

Prices are a compilation of shows, shops, and Internet auctions. They are retail values and apply to items in excellent condition. Note: Extraordinary items bring extraordinary prices!

Advisors: Ken Weber, Clothing (www.vintagemartini.com); Flying Duce Auctions, Vintage Denim (See Directory, Clothing and Accessories)

Newsletter: *Costume Society of America*
55 Edgewater Dr., P.O. Box 73
Earleville, MD 21919
1-800-CSA-9447 or Fax: 410-275-8936
www.costumesocietyamerica.com

Newsletter (on-line): *The Vintage Connection*
Editor: Kristina Harris
www.geocities.com/vintage connection
damefashion@aol.com

1940s Day Wear

Bra top, checked seersucker, gathered at center w/loop, ties at back of neck & across back **$28.00**
Dress, floral rayon, rounded neck w/diamond panel at gathered waist, slight bustle effect, short sleeves, zipper............**$125.00**
Dress, floral rayon, shawl collar, button front, shoulder yoke, long sleeves, cloth belt w/slide buckle, gored skirt.................**$88.00**
Dress, printed jersey knit, V neck w/sm drape, flat-front bodice, short sleeves, slim skirt, zipper **$68.00**
Dress, printed linen/rayon blend, scoop neckline, raised yoke, sash belt, short sleeves, pleated skirt, 2-pc **$85.00**
Dress, red 2-pc sweater type w/white angora trim, elbow-length sleeves w/cuffs, ribbed skirt..**$88.00**

Shorts, cotton/rayon windowpane, button & loop closures down both sides...$35.00

Suit, aubergine wool, wide notched lapels, double breasted, fitted jacket w/long sleeves, metal buttons, slim skirt...........$165.00

Suit, brown & gray pinstripe, fluted V neck, gold buttons, peplum, gored skirt w/gathered back, Helen of California........$155.00

Suit, burgundy wool gabardine, platter collar, covered buttons, princess seams, sack back, slim skirt, Gilbert Original.......$155.00

Suit, green linen, sm notched collar, covered buttons, silver studs decor, ¾-length sleeves, Lombardi label.....................$145.00

Suit, med gray wool w/pink & chartreuse windowpane pattern, wide collar, covered button, slim skirt w/kick pleat.............$165.00

Suit, printed muslin, shawl collar, 6 sm brass buttons, ¾-length cuffs, gored skirt..$110.00

Suit, wheat-colored gabardine, sm notched collar, covered butons, slim skirt w/center front slit.......................................$145.00

Suit jacket, black wool gabardine, spread collar w/notched under-collar, diamond panels, long sleeves, Neiman Marcus...$98.00

Suit jacket, navy gabardine wool, spread collar & button front, patch pockets, decorative stitching, cuffs, fully lined.............$68.00

Sweater, nylon, pale beige w/multicolor fleck, rounded neckline, short sleeves, ribbed bottom, Tish-u-Knit label............$45.00

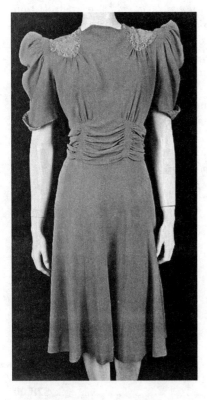

Dress, pink silk crepe, bias-cut bodice, lace appliqués, and rouched cummerbund, $85.00. (Photo courtesy Vintage Martini)

1940s Ladies' Coats and Jackets

Coat, brown & black tweed wool, flared out round neck, cuffed ¾-length sleeves, no label, 42" L.......................................$70.00

Coat, navy blue wool, single lg button, diagonal pocket......$85.00

Coat, navy gabardine wool, petal lapels, long sleeves, fully lined, 3 lg buttons...$125.00

Coat, navy gabardine wool, spread lapels, single decorative button, set-in sleeves w/cuffs, fully lined...................................$85.00

Jacket, navy wool w/velvet appliqué on collar & pocket flaps, 8 buttons, dart fitted, cap sleeves, silk lined.........................$75.00

Jacket, red linen, long sleeves w/narrow cuffs, V neck.........$58.00

1940s Ladies' Evening Wear

Ball gown, silver metallic satin brocade, attached petticoat, $225.00. (Photo courtesy Vintage Martini)

Cocktail suit, black wool gabardine, pointed collar, 4 covered buttons, black & green beading, long sleeves, fully lined..$185.00

Dress, aqua lace long-sleeved bodice over beige crepe chemise w/grosgrain ribbon at top, black wool gathered skirt......$175.00

Dress, black crepe, plunging V neck, rouching at shoulders & side seams, short bias sleeves & peplum, slim skirt, sashes...$75.00

Dress, black crepe, rounded neck, flat-front bodice, short sleeves, tiered ruffled apron w/sequins, sash ties........................$90.00

Dress, black crepe-back satin, round neck w/heavy jet beading, faux pockets, elbow-length sleeves w/rouching...................$145.00

Dress, black rayon crepe, scooped neck w/side notch & fold-back wings, black floral beading, long sleeves, slim skirt.....$110.00

Dress, gold leaf pattern on red chiffon, Mandarin collar, button front, ¾-length sleeves, full gathered skirt....................$98.00

Dress, green taffeta & tulle, snap-off straps, bustier bodice w/V neck w/fold-over collar, gathered skirt w/crinoline.............$185.00

Dress, purple chiffon w/velvet bow pattern, V neck w/sunburst pleats, short bias sleeves, cloth belt, slim skirt, +slip...$195.00

Dress, rose taffeta & tulle, bustier bodice w/gathers, metal dots & rhinestones, attached net shawl, full length................$225.00

1940s Lingerie

Crinoline, fuchsia net, grosgrain waistband w/snap closure, 2 tiers of ruffles..$22.00

Dressing gown, creamy silk charmeuse, V neck w/crochet lace, floral embroidery, bias cut w/sashes, ties in back...................$48.00

Dressing gown, peach floral rayon satin, sweetheart neckline, sm collar, zipper, puff elbow-length sleeves, sm train **$65.00**

Nightgown, candlelight satin, sq neck w/inset lace across chest, gathers above raised waistline, short sleeves w/lace **$75.00**

Nightgown, ivory silk charmeuse, V neck w/white crochet lace, floral embroidery, bias cut w/sashes that tie in back **$48.00**

Nightgown, pale green silk charmeuse w/scooped neck, center front slit, ivory lace inserts & appliqués, bias cap sleeves **$95.00**

Peignoir, black & pink nylon, triple spaghetti straps, lacy bust, full gathered skirt, short puff sleeves on robe...................... **$58.00**

Slip, peach rayon, fitted bodice, raised waistline, adjustable shoulder straps... **$24.00**

Slip, peach rayon, wide shoulder straps, darts at bust, flared skirt, side snap closures **$28.00**

1940s Ladies' Accessories

Hat, black felt, flat top w/narrow rise, button crown, bow in yellow netting, felt riser under brim hugs back of head............ **$65.00**

Hat, black felt, upturned brim w/cone-shaped crown, pin-tuck wings stand on top of crown, flat head ring **$58.00**

Hat, black felt ring w/petal-cut edges, net top, Astelle label . **$45.00**

Hat, black felt w/purple & fuchsia velvet scrunched across front & sides, cutouts in back, black silk netting, 22" **$48.00**

Hat, black wool felt, swooping brim, black faille crown gathered into button top, lg pink satin bow...................... **$110.00**

Hat, brown felt, tall crown, chip straw open floral design covers curved brim, bow at back, Gude's label......................... **$45.00**

Hat, brown furled felt in tricorn shape, brown silk netting, lg gold appliqué, sm flap hugs nape... **$58.00**

Hat, brown jersey knit turban, fabric gathered through loop top, narrow rise w/loop at center front................................. **$35.00**

Hat, chip straw w/brown & red raffia, floppy brim, tall crown, velvet piping, bow at center back **$85.00**

Hat, green velveteen, center front knot w/pleating around sides & back **$32.00**

Hat, ivory felt, curved brim, diagonal cut crown, twisted felt band, lg white plumes on lift, 20" **$75.00**

Hat, pink woven chip straw w/black ribbon trim & beaded appliqué & bows, crownless, Helen Stafford label **$48.00**

Hat, sculpted brown felt, turned-back brim w/sm crown, brown jersey knit scarf pleated at top falls from the back........ **$85.00**

Hat, sm straw base w/lg curved white feathers, black velvet ribbon & bows, single white silk rose at back, G Beigel................ **$85.00**

Hat, spoon-shaped straw w/wire base covered in satin flowers, black ribbon tails, black netting **$65.00**

Shoes, red leather slip-on pumps, sweetheart-cut piped instep, vented toe tips, chunky 2½" heel **$48.00**

Shoes, yellow patent leather, open-toe sandals w/mesh cutouts, side buckle ankle straps, 2" shunky heel.................. **$40.00**

Turban, black jersey knit, pleating across front & sides, flat on top.. **$40.00**

1950s Ladies' Daywear

Dress, batik-printed cotton, halter strap extends from midriff yoke & makes bust shelf, gathered skirt, back zipper............. **$85.00**

Dress, blue & white printed cotton halter type, V neck w/wide midriff yoke & gathers, crystal buttons, full skirt............... **$85.00**

Dress, floral cotton piqué, bustier style w/wide pleated straps, gathered skirt, cloth belt, bolero jacket, Gay Gibson **$78.00**

Dress, green polished cotton w/diagonal windowpane, spread collar, white buttons, short sleeves w/wing cuffs, cloth belt..... **$65.00**

Dress, navy polka-dot crepe bodice w/V neck that ties at base, crepe skirt w/taffeta underskirt & ruffle, cap sleeves............... **$65.00**

Dress, printed cotton, navy ribbon straps, flared skirt, back buttons, w/matching bolero double-breasted jacket **$85.00**

Dress, printed cotton, plunging neck, narrow straps, lg bow across bust & at back of skirt, Neiman Marcus **$85.00**

Dress, printed cotton, scooped neck, pin-tuck bust yoke, short raglan sleeves, sm front bow, gathered skirt...................... **$85.00**

Dress, printed cotton peasant style, V neck, short puffed sleeves, wide sash ties, full pleated skirt **$58.00**

Dress, printed cotton w/wavy pattern, spread collar, rhinestone buttons, short sleeves, A-line skirt w/lg patch pockets........ **$58.00**

Skirt, quilted cotton circle style, waist sash ties in back, side zipper.. **$65.00**

Suit, grape linen, rounded collar w/sm lapels, decorative loop & lg button on front, ¾-length sleeves, slim skirt **$145.00**

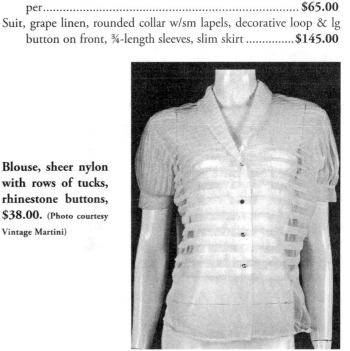

Blouse, sheer nylon with rows of tucks, rhinestone buttons, $38.00. (Photo courtesy Vintage Martini)

1950s Ladies' Coats and Jackets

Coat, black cashmere, boxy, platter collar, open front, ¾-length raglan sleeves, satin lined, Neiman Marcus **$115.00**

Coat, brown wool bouclé w/beige wide fur collar, dart shaping, label missing... **$65.00**

Coat, chocolate brown synthetic blend w/animal fur collar, raglan sleeves, slash pockets, no label...................................... **$45.00**

Coat, heavy black faille, open front, ¾-length sleeves w/cuffs, 2 inset pockets, pink iridescent lining.................................... **$85.00**

Coat, raspberry wool, front slip-in pockts w/diagonal flaps, 3-button front, notched collar, lined............................... **$35.00**

Coat, royal blue wool blend, set-in sleeves, high/wide short lapels, slip-in pockets, 3-button front **$32.50**

Jacket, gold-tan deerskin suede, straight sides, rounded collar, rayon lining **$50.00**

Jacket, rayon brocade print, 4-button, w/slide slits, unlined.**$30.00**

Rain coat, green printed nylon acetate, fully lined, big buttons, 2 lg front pockets **$28.00**

1950s Ladies' Cocktail and Evening Wear

Blouse, sheer white silk w/gold metallic & black stripes, gold collar, short sleeves, sm gold buttons **$48.00**

Dress, black crepe V neck w/inset at chest, layered white organza Bertha-style collar w/black trim, kick-pleated skirt........**$78.00**

Dress, black silk organza, rounded neck w/sheer black souffle yoke, rows of black lace on skirt, taffeta petticoat.................**$135.00**

Dress, black velvet bodice w/scooped neck, darted, sleeveless, tiered lace skirt w/velvet waistband, 2-pc **$98.00**

Dress, blue netting over pink taffeta, bustier bodice, strapless, net ruffles, net skirt, ribbon decoration............................**$110.00**

Dress, brown silk jersey & lace, strapless bodice gathered down sides, taffeta flounce w/attached crinoline, lace shrug...........**$250.00**

Dress, cocktail; red taffeta w/peach floss embroidery, scooped neck, fitted bodice, short sleeves, gored skirt w/pleats **$85.00**

Dress, green silk jacquard w/floral pattern, mink fur trim at base of neck, ¾-length sleeves, full pleated skirt........................**$85.00**

Dress, ivory lace Empire bodice w/sq neck & short raglan sleeves, black velvet midriff & skirt, rhinestone trim..............**$160.00**

Dress, silvery champagne satin with gold cord braidwork, $85.00. (Photo courtesy Vintage Martini)

Dress, upper portion is black tulle w/black linen/rhinestone collar & long sleeves, black linen bodice w/slim skirt.................**$85.00**

Dress, white lace, net & taffeta, strapless, full net skirt w/rows of lace, matching bolero w/long sleeves **$180.00**

Dress, white netting w/silver mylar stripes encased in net & sewn on, bustier bodice w/bust shelf, spaghetti straps................**$225.00**

1950s Lingerie

Bra, black floral lace, elastic bottom, satin straps, hook & eye closures, Neiman Marcus tags..**$22.00**

Bra, white cotton, narrow straps, single hook closure..........**$18.00**

Bra, white netting & organza w/black floral lace overlay, wire supports, pink rosette in center, strapless............................**$28.00**

Bustier & petticoat combination, dark red w/embroidered floral pattern, boned, padded cups, zipper front **$98.00**

Crinoline, white net, full skirt.......................................**$28.00**

Crinoline, white net w/red bows & bells along front ruffle..**$28.00**

Hat, turban, stretched pleated teal satin at base, Miss Alice .**$32.00**

Hoop, white netting, double hoop at bottom, hook & eye closure at waist..**$35.00**

Pajamas, printed nylon, Mandarin collar, button front, short sleeves, wide-leg pants **$58.00**

Pajamas, white & pink windowpane cotton, Oxford nightshirt w/elbow-length sleeves, elastic waist band & legs on bloomers **$58.00**

Purse, box style w/gold frame, black felt front, felt handle, lg rhinestone sunburst, 1 pocket **$55.00**

Shoes, tooled leather wedgies, ankle strap & side buckle, 2¼" wedge..**$45.00**

Slip, ivory acetate, narrow shoulder straps, fitted bodice, lace-trimmed flounce, side zipper.......................................**$30.00**

1950s Ladies' Accessories

Handbag, floral motif, Margaret Smith, $85.00.
(Photo courtesy Vintage Martini)

Shoes, black velvety suede, pointed toes w/oval decor of gathered lace, 3" chunky heels, Hill & Dale................................**$32.00**

Shoes, brown leather, stitched cutwork instep, spiked stacked wood heels, pointed toes, Naturalizer **$40.00**

Shoes, gray suede pumps w/spike 3" heels, pointed toes **$40.00**

1960s – 1970s Ladies' Day Wear

Cardigan, gold mohair wool & nylon loopy boucle knit, ¾-length raglan sleeves w/band trim, 1960s..............................**$30.00**

Cardigan, striped polyester doubleknit, V neck, long sleeves, 1960s $20.00

Dress, blue and gold Hawaiian print rayon, sarong-style skirt, has matching bolero jacket, Mahilini Made in Hawaii label, $265.00. (Photo courtesy Vintage Martini)

Dress, soft blue synthetic knit shift w/Empire look, blue pinstriping, matching long-sleeved cardigan sweater, 1960s **$36.00**

Sweater, blue & white V-striped bouckle knit, sleeveless round neck, rib knit waist, extended shoulders **$20.00**

Sweater set, white acrylic knit w/red & blue stripes, V neck short sleeve w/matching long-sleeved cardigan, 1970s **$20.00**

Swimsuit, green geometric nylon & spandex 1-pc, V neck, molded bra, front buttons & loops, boy legs, 1970s **$65.00**

Swimsuit, Hawaiian print polyester 1-pc w/princess seaming, pleated flounce skirt, Catalina label, 1970s **$40.00**

Swimwear, print tapestry cotton blend Hawaiian print bikini top, 3-button closure down back, fully lined, 1970s **$15.00**

1960s – 1970s Ladies' Coats and Jackets

Cape, ivory wool, platter collar w/loop band, inset pockets, arm holes in side seams, lined, 1960s **$65.00**

Coat, bright red textured wool w/drop-set black rabbit collar, ¾-sleeves, lg buttons, Neiman Marcus, 1960s **$58.00**

Coat, brown sherpa-lined suede leather, brown sheepskin shawl collar, wrap-style front, 2 patch pockets, matching belt **$70.00**

Coat, brown suede, rounded neckline w/no collar, button front, inset pockets, acetate lining, 39" L **$30.00**

Coat, smooth leather, w/brown shawl collar, clutch front, 2 lower patch pockets, acetate lining **$75.00**

Jacket, crushed red vinyl w/wet look, patch pockets, self belt, gold-tone buttons, Miss Holly **$70.00**

Jacket, ivory lamb's wool w/beads & sequins, long sleeves.... **$80.00**

Jacket, shiny navy wet-look nylon w/white topstitching, silver-tone snaps, front belt, patch pockets **$35.00**

Jacket, red soft leather, toggle closure, hooded, fleece lining, car length.. **$80.00**

Jacket, suede leather poncho w/fold-over collar, shaped neck, twist-latch closure at center front, caplet sleeves **$75.00**

1960s – 1970s Ladies' Evening Wear

Dress, green polyester w/Empire waist, sheer short sleeves, floor-length train, home sewn (nicely made) **$30.00**

Dress, lavender silk georgette w/Empire waistline, lace trim, long sleeves w/lace trim, full length...................................... **$30.00**

Dress, orange linen, Empire waist, scoop neck, floral sheer sleeves w/cuffs, matching lined vest, full length...................... **$35.00**

Dress, pale pink silk w/flocked fleur-de-lis, long sleeves, round neck, fitted bodice, 57" L, matching 16" sq cape **$40.00**

Dress, silver stretchy metallic polyester, Empire waist, gold & silver trim, sleeveless, floor length **$35.00**

Mini, gold sequins piped in gold braid, $65.00. (Photo courtesy Vintage Martini)

Pants, shocking pink silk shantung, 38" palazzo style w/elastic waist **$30.00**

Shirt, silver metallic lurex w/white rayon fringe, taffeta lining, scoop neck, sleeveless, back zipper **$27.50**

Suit, black & emerald green metallic doubleknit, shell top, jewel-neck ¾-sleeve jacket, flared skirt, 3-pc **$50.00**

1960s – 1970s Ladies' Accessories

Boot, brown leather mod ankle style, sq toe & buckle detail, Kraus **$26.00**

Bustier, black lace & spandex, underware, padded cups, Hollywood Vassarette **$35.00**

Peignoir, pink-gray rayon satin, V neck w/fluted collar, midriff yoke, long sleeves w/cuffs, pink sash tie................................. **$65.00**

Robe, golden yellow acetate w/floral embroidery, frog closures **$20.00**

Shoes, alligator leather pumps, 3½" stiletto heels, pointed toes, Evins... **$50.00**

Shoes, beige leather, vented toe & instep, 2½" stacked wood heel, Florsheim... **$35.00**

Shoes, black leather stilletos w/pointed toes, 3½" heel, side cutouts w/T straps, Palizzio $30.00

Shoes, black suede & leather w/burnished gold patent trim, 2½" heels, slightly rounded toes, Personality $25.00

Shoes, black vinyl, vented toes, ankle straps, 3" chunky heels, Young Modes, 1960s...$30.00

Shoes, coral fabric-covered pumps w/rounded toes, 2½" hills, Life Stride $20.00

Shoes, gold leather wedgies w/clear acrylic slide toe, Gepetto .$20.00

Shoes, gold metallic leather, pointed toes, 3" spiked heels, French Room Originals $30.00

Shoes, ivory vinyl slip-on ankle boots w/rubber soles, 1½" heels .$40.00

Shoes, tan cotton canvas casual lace-ups w/rope trim, crepe sole, 1¼" wedge heel, Beacon $30.00

Shoes, white vinyl sandals w/wild beaded vamp straps, 2" block heels, Tommi of Hawaii, 1970s, unused $40.00

Slip, ivory nylon, midriff yoke comes to a point at V neck, lace border at top, appliquè at center of bust $22.00

Slip, white nylon, lace along top & at hem, adjustable shoulder straps, Lorraine $20.00

Slip, white nylon, lace bodice & border at hem, adjustable straps, w/original Vanity Fair tags $20.00

Hat, natural straw with silk flowers, Miss Dior, from $55.00 to $75.00. (Photo courtesy La Ree Johnson Bruton)

1940s – 1970s Men's Wear

Boxer shorts, printed cotton, yoke front w/snap closures, elastic at sides of waistband, 1950s...$28.00

Cardigan, blue, white & black knit w/checkered front, solid sleeves & back, V neck, Penney's label, 1960s $38.00

Cardigan, green wool knit w/olive suede panels on front, in set pockets, long knit sleeves w/wide wrist band $65.00

Coat, golden tan suede w/shirred lamb lining, patchwork design w/lg leather buttons, 2 patch pockets, 1970s $138.00

Coat, soft brown leather w/wide collar, belt, leather buttons, satin lining, 1970s...$85.00

Jacket, black velveteen, wide notched lapels, 2-button front, long sleeves, silk lining, 1970s, Eminio Pucci label $345.00

Jacket, dark red silk, shawl collar, single button, long sleeves w/single button decor, Harry J Rook label, 1950s $165.00

Jacket, sports; green-gray wool w/faint windowpane, sm collar w/ notched lapels, single button, 3 patch pockets, 1940s...$95.00

Overcoat, dove gray brushed wool, raglan sleeves w/turned-back cuffs, Maybrook label, 1950s $65.00

Shirt, batik-patterned heavy cotton, wide spread collar, button front, short sleeves, 1960s..$65.00

Shirt, black, red & gray cotton stripes, spread collar w/button front, long sleeves w/button cuffs, patch pocket, 1960s..........$65.00

Shirt, blue & white plaid cotton, spread collar, button front, long sleeves w/button cuffs, patch pocket, 1960s...................$35.00

Shirt, blue silk, spread collar, striped front, 2 patch pockets, long sleeves w/button cuffs, Schiaparelli, 1950s...................$145.00

Shirt, bowling; yellow & black rayon, embroidered name on pocket, 1950s...$125.00

Shirt, green & rust patterned polyester, button front, lg pointed collar, long sleeves w/button cuffs, 1970s $28.00

Shirt, green polished cotton w/white stripe on left front, spread collar, button front, short sleeves w/cuffs...........................$65.00

Shirt, kelly green open-weave knit, long pointed button-down collar, button front, short sleeves, Catalino logo, 1960s $58.00

Shirt, light green cotton w/nub texture, spread collar, button front, 2 patch pockets, short sleeves w/faux cuff $45.00

Shirt, orange polyester/cotton blend, pointed collar, patch pocket, long sleeves w/2-button cuff, Van Heusen, 1970s........$22.00

Shirt, red & white windowpane cotton w/red appliqué border on short sleeves & patch pocket, 1940s............................$58.00

Shirt, tan linen blend w/knit front, spread collar, piping at center front, short sleeves, button pleats at back, 1950s $85.00

Shirt, Western, cotton with rodeo print, snap front, $145.00. (Photo courtesy Vintage Martini)

Shirt, Western; patterned yoke w/piping, curved inset pockets, snap closures, long sleeves w/embroidered cuffs, 1950s.......$135.00

Shirt, work; yellow gabardine, 2 chest pockets, long sleeves w/button cuffs, Mark Twain Sportsman label, 1950s...................$50.00

Suit, dark blue silk blend, 2-button front w/stitching around collar & pocket flaps, Lanvin Paris label, 1981 ....$185.00

Suit, hunting; red & black plaid wool, button closures, game pocket, fully lined coat, Woolrich label **$150.00**

Swim trunks, black & white knit honeycomb, wide waistband w/ drawstring, Brent label, 1950s....................................... **$25.00**

Swim trunks, Hawaiian print on blue, side button closure, Hawaiian label, 1950s... **$58.00**

Swim trunks, textured wool stretch knit, high waist, matching belt w/brass buckle, sm inset pocket, 1940s-50s **$35.00**

Top coat, beige tweed wool w/windowpane threads, lg leather buttons, Towne-Clad label, 1940s **$100.00**

Vintage Demim

Bib overalls, Lee Jelt Denim House tag, long L buttons, sanforized, deadstock, 46x33" **$75.00**

Bib overalls, Oshkosh, low back, deadstock, 44x34" **$50.00**

Jacket, Lee 101J, indigo, minor wear, 1950s **$120.00**

Jacket, Lee 91B, lg, deadstock **$200.00**

Jacket, Levi 3rd Edition, lg label, red tag missing.............. **$200.00**

Jacket, Levi 506E, 1-pocket, buckle back, redline, size 40.. **$860.00**

Jacket, Levi 557XX, dark indigo, ca early 1960s **$265.00**

Jacket, Levi 70505E, red tab, dark blue, size 38, from $60 to. **$75.00**

Jacket, Sledge's, pleated front, strap buckle back, 1 front pocket, cuffed sleeves, ca 1940s **$115.00**

Jacket, Wrangler Blue Bell, 1st model, side buckles, elastic inside at shoulders, pleated, 2-pocket, dark indigo **$300.00**

Jeans, Lee, 200 series, zipper fly, straight legs, R/MR on pocket flag, dark indigo, ca 1980s.. **$30.00**

Jeans, Levi Cargo, 2 patch pockets w/snap closure on front/2 on back, 1970s.. **$275.00**

Jeans, Levi 501E, button fly, redline, #8 on back of top button, tag embroidered on both sides, 38x31" **$400.00**

Jeans, Levi 501E, single stitch, button fly, redline, ca 1966-68. **$575.00**

Jeans, Levi 501E (on red tab), single stitch, red line selvage, excellent color, no damage, $350.00.

Jeans, Levi 501E, single stitch on back & sm pocket, button fly, V-stitch, no back tag, #14 on back of top button, VG....**$800.00**

Jeans, Levi 501E, zipper fly, single stitch, #8 on back of top button, rivets not hidden, dark indigo, NM **$325.00**

Jeans, Levi 501XX, V-stitch, 5-button fly, blue/white salvage, leather patch, 1949-50, never washed................................**$2,850.00**

Jeans, Levi 501XX E, button fly, redline, #4 top button, single stitched, good hedge, 32x29", G.............................**$135.00**

Jeans, Levi 504ZXX E, zipper fly, single stitched, offset belt loop, V-stitch, no # on back of top button, redline, G.........**$300.00**

Jeans, Levi 516, flare legs, dark indigo **$185.00**

Jeans, Wrangler Super Slim (Like Levi 606), deadstock w/flashers, 32x32" **$25.00**

Overall shorts, lady's, orange double-stitched seams, bodice w/thick straps that cross in back, metal snaps, ca 1970s...........**$225.00**

Overalls, Osh Kosh Union Made Vestbak, button fly, sanforized, clover buttons, single-stitched back pockets, 1940s.....**$100.00**

Shirt, Remco, heavy w/fine stripes in indigo blue, red & white, ca 1940s, deadstock.. **$165.00**

Shirt, Western; Wrangler Blue Bell, W-stitched pockets, dark indigo... **$650.00**

Tote bag, Levi E, 13x15", VG **$20.00**

Coca-Cola Collectibles

Coca-Cola was introduced to the public in 1886. Immediately an advertising campaign began that over the years and continuing to the present day has literally saturated our lives with a never-ending variety of items. Some of the earlier calendars and trays have been known to bring prices well into the four figures. Because of these heady prices and the extremely widespread collector demand for good Coke items, reproductions are everywhere, so beware! Some of the items that have been reproduced are pocket mirrors (from 1905, 1906, 1908 – 11, 1916, and 1920), trays (from 1899, 1910, 1913 – 14, 1917, 1920, 1923, 1926, 1934, and 1937), tip trays (from 1907, 1909, 1910, 1913 – 14, 1917, and 1920), knives, cartons, bottles, clocks, and trade cards. In recent years, these items have been produced and marketed: an 8" brass 'button,' a 27" brass bottle-shaped thermometer, cast-iron toys and bottle-shaped door pulls, Yes Girl posters, a 12" 'button' sign (with one round hole), a rectangular paperweight, a 1949-style cooler radio, and there are others. Look for a date line.

In addition to reproductions, 'fantasy' items have also been made, the difference being that a 'fantasy' never existed as an original. Don't be deceived. Belt buckles are 'fantasies.' So are glass doorknobs with an etched trademark, bottle-shaped knives, pocketknives, (supposedly from the 1933 World's Fair), a metal letter opener stamped 'Coca-Cola 5¢,' a cardboard sign with the 1911 lady with fur (9"x11"), and celluloid vanity pieces (a mirror, brush, etc.).

When the company celebrated its 100th anniversary in 1986, many 'centennial' items were issued. They all carry the '100th Anniversary' logo. Many of them are collectible in their own right, and some are already expensive.

If you'd really like to study this subject, we recommend these books: *Goldstein's Coca-Cola Collectibles* by Sheldon Goldstein; *Collector's Guide to Coca-Cola Items, Vols. I* and *II*, by Al Wilson; *Petretti's Coca-Cola Collectibles Price Guide* by Allan Petretti; *Coca-Cola Commemorative Bottles* by Bob and Debra Henrich; *B.J.*

Summers' Guide to Coca-Cola; and *Collectible Soda Pop Memorabilia* (both by B.J. Summers).

Advisor: Craig Stifter (See Directory, Soda Pop Collectibles)

Club: Coca-Cola Collectors Club
PMB 609, 4780 Ashform Dunwoody Rd, Suite A9166
Atlanta, GA 30338
Annual dues: $30

Clock, metal with reverse-painted glass, Lunch With Us painted on face, lights up, 9x20", EX, $800.00.

Ashtray, ceramic & plastic, Drink Coca-Cola red logo in bowl, miniature bottle on edge, Canadian bottler, 1950s, EX.....**$250.00**

Banner, canvas, Coca-Cola Brings You Edgar Bergen w/Charlie McCarthy..., truck mounted, 1950s, 60x42", EX **$1,100.00**

Banner, vinyl & canvas, Drink Coca-Cola Ice Cold, fishtail logo in center, 1960s, 8x14", EX **$200.00**

Border, Enjoy Coco-Cola Classic, corrugated paper, EX **$35.00**

Bottle, glass, Tri-State...Boy Scouts of America, green commemorative, straight sides, 1953, EX.............................**$265.00**

Bottle, perfume; glass, hobbleskirt, w/stopper, 1930s, miniature, EX **$85.00**

Bottle, plastic, hobbleskirt bottle, lg, 1953, 20", EX..........**$375.00**

Bottle, pre-mix; glass, green, used in early bottling process, 1920s, 2¼x7¾", EX **$95.00**

Bottle, rubber, displays advertising, 1940s, 43", VG **$850.00**

Bottle, water; glass, Compliments Coca-Cola Bottling Co, green w/advertising on front, EX, from $125 to...................**$145.00**

Bottle topper, cardboard, Coca-Cola...Good w/food, 6-pack w/food in basket, 1950s, 8x7", NM..**$550.00**

Bottle topper, cardboard, Daddy - Here It Is..., redhead w/tray, 3-D, 1920s, 11½x14", NM...............................**$2,600.00**

Bottle topper, cardboard, King Size Ice Cold..., bottle in snow, string for use as a hanger, 1960s, EX, from $100 to **$175.00**

Bottle topper, paper, Regular Size Coca-Cola, Santa's elves peering around carton, 9x11¾", EX, from $45 to **$55.00**

Button, metal, Coca-Cola, white lettering over bottle on redbackground, 1950s, 48", EX..**$600.00**

Button, metal, hand holding bottle, 1950s, 16", NM..........**$25.00**

Calendar, pocket; 1943, Here's to Our GI Joes, 2 girls toasting Coke bottles, all months shown on front, EX **$70.00**

Calendar, 1935, Out Fishin', boy on stump holding a Coke bottle, Norman Rockwell, framed, paper, 24x12", M **$875.00**

Calendar, 1949, girl in red hat drinking from Coke bottle, double-month, paper, M..**$400.00**

Calendar, 1962, Enjoy...New Feeling, young couple dancing, man has a Coke bottle in his hand, M..................................**$95.00**

Carrier, cardboard, Coca-Cola...6 for 24¢, for 6-pack, 1939, EX.. **$95.00**

Carrier, polished aluminum, Coca-Cola embossed, rounded corners, holds 24 bottles, 1940-50s, EX...............................**$140.00**

Carrier, wood, Pause...Go Refreshed, wire handle w/wood grip, holds 6 bottles, 1930s, EX **$375.00**

Carrier, wood, Refresh Yourself...Drink Coca-Cola in Bottles, holds 24 bottles, dovetailed joints, 1920s, EX **$295.00**

Clock, desk; leather, Drink Coca-Cola in Bottles, gold lettering & 2 gold hobble-skirt bottles, rare, 1910, 4⅓x6", EX.....**$1,500.00**

Clock, metal & glass, Drink Coca-Cola, fishtail logo on green background, 1960s, EX..**$325.00**

Cooler, picnic; metal, Drink Coca-Cola in Bottles, lg logo in red on front, wire handles, opener on side, hinged top, G **$135.00**

Cooler, picnic; metal, Drink Coca-Cola white on red decal, round shape w/zinc liner inside, 1940s, 8x9", VG.................**$250.00**

Cooler, store; metal & wood, Serve Yourself...Pay the Clerk, original Starr opener, zinc lining, EX, 32x29x2¼" **$1,600.00**

Creamer, white w/red & black lettering, Drink Coca-Cola, 1930s, VG...**$350.00**

Decal, vinyl, Drink...Pay Cashier, 1960s, 13x6", EX............**$10.00**

Display, cardboard, Bartender on Duty..., 1950-60s, 14x12", NM **$375.00**

Display, cardboard, Buy the Case...Plus Deposit, black background w/yellow & white lettering, EX, from $65 to................**$95.00**

Fan, bamboo, Keep Cool, Drink Coca-Cola, Oriental scene on one side, advertisement on other, VG..............................**$235.00**

Fan, cardboard, Buy by the Carton, solid back, Memphis TN bottler, 1930s, EX...**$195.00**

Glass, flare shape, Drink Coca-Cola, etched syrup line, 1910s, EX **$500.00**

Glass, pewter, bell shape, Coca-Cola, scarce, 1930s, EX.....**$375.00**

Ice pick, metal & wood, Drink Coca-Cola in Bottles, black lettering on handle, 1920-30s, EX....................................**$50.00**

Lighter, metal, Enjoy Coca-Cola logo in white diamond on front of red can shape, 1960s, EX, from $45 to........................**$65.00**

Lighter, metal, hobble-skirt bottle, pocket size, 1950s, M....**$45.00**

Magazine ad, Even the Bubbles Tastes Better, boy drinking from a hobble-skirt bottle, bubbles all around, 1956, VG........**$15.00**

Magazine ad, So Easy...Carton, sm girl on grocery counter holding pack, insert of Mom putting in fridge, 1949, 7x10", VG **$10.00**

Menu board, metal, Specials...Refresh Yourself, bottle w/straw in lower right hand corner, wall hung, 1930s, VG **$325.00**

Menu board, plywood, Drink...Menu, double rack of menu stripes, bottle in center, Kay Displays, 1930s, 36x26", VG.....**$550.00**

Mirror, pocket; cardboard, Drink Coca-Cola in Bottles, folds into shape of cat's head, 1920s, EX **$95.00**

Mirror, pocket; celluloid, Drink Delicious Coca-Cola, featuring Hamilton King Coca-Cola girl, 1911, 1¾x2¾" **$195.00**

Opener, metal, wall-mounted w/corkscrew, 1920s, EX **$85.00**

Opener, metal & plastic, 50th Anniversary Coca-Cola in Bottles, EX **$60.00**

Plate, sandwich; white, Coca-Cola...Good w/Food, Wellsville China Co, 1940-50s, 7½", VG................................**$750.00**

Poster, cardboard, Accepted Home Refreshment, couple w/Coke & popcorn by fireplace, 1942, VG, from $425 to...........**$450.00**

Poster, cardboard, America's Favorite Moment, couple dining in a booth, 1940s, 36x20", EX, from $295 to **$395.00**

Poster, cardboard, Bacon & Tomato, sandwich w/Coke glass in corner, 1930-40s, 21x14", EX **$200.00**

Poster, cardboard, Be Really Refreshed, die-cut, double-sided pretty girl holding glass of Coke, 1960s, 13x17", EX............**$425.00**

Poster, cardboard, Coke...Friendly Circle, people in pool w/floating cooler, 1955, 36x20", EX...**$375.00**

Poster, cardboard, Entertain Your Thirst, 2 ballerinas resting, 1942, 16x27", EX **$600.00**

Poster, cardboard, Refreshing New Feeling, couple laying on beach w/bottles of Coke, truck size, 1960s, 67x32", NM **$125.00**

Radio, plastic, hobble-skirt, AM-FM, 1970s, EX.................**$45.00**

Radio, plastic, vending machine w/left-hand see-through door, 1960s, G **$165.00**

Score card, paper, Ice-Cold Coca-Cola, St Louis stadium vendor, EX **$30.00**

Sheet music, The Coca-Cola Girl, couple toasting w/2 glasses of Coke, paper, framed & under glass, 1927, EX............**$395.00**

Sign, paper, Drink...& Refreshing, hot dog w/hobble-skirt bottle, flat mount, 1950s, EX **$195.00**

Sign, porcelain, Delicious Refreshing, green lettering, w/hobble-skirt bottle in center, flat mount, 1950s, 24 , EX...............**$325.00**

Sign, porcelain, Drink Coca-Cola Here, flange, 1940s, NM .**$850.00**

Thermometer, desk; metal, Drink Coca-Cola, scale measurement in Celsius & Fahrenheit, 1940s, VG **$55.00**

Thermometer, wall; cardboard, Drink Coca-Cola, retailers reference for settings of air temperature, 1960s, VG **$75.00**

Thermometer, wall; metal & glass, Enjoy Coca-Cola, round, dial type, 1960s, 12", EX..**$155.00**

Thermometer, wall; porcelain, Drink...No Season, silhouette of girl drinking on bottom, Canada, 1942, 5¾x18", VG **$475.00**

Thermometer, wall; wooden, Drink Coca-Cola in Bottles..., VO Colson Co, Paris IL, vertical, 1910s, VG **$725.00**

Tray, 1933, Francis Dee, 10½x13¼", NM..........................**$900.00**

Tray, 1934, Weismuller & O'Sullivan, 10½x13¼", NM..**$1,400.00**

Sign, easel-backed standup, Santa, 1944, 54", EX, $400.00. (Photo courtesy Craig Stifter)

Sign, metal, ...Ice Cold Sold Here, round, red w/green border, flat mount, 1933, 20", G **$225.00**

Sign, metal, Coca-Cola in white lettering, die-cut bottle, 1951, 6", G **$550.00**

Sign, metal, Coca-Cola...Good Taste, logo on horizontal fishtail, flange, 1960s, VG **$225.00**

Sign, metal, die-cut bottle, embossed Coca-Cola, flat mount, 36", G **$350.00**

Sign, metal, Drink...Refreshing New Feeling, bottle w/fishtail logo on striped background, flat mount, 1960s, 32x12", VG.....**$275.00**

Sign, metal & wire, Drink...Wherever You Go, tropical island scene, seashell attached, flat mount, 1960s, 14x18", EX **$275.00**

Tray, 1936, Hostess, 13¼x10½", NM, $750.00. (Photo courtesy Gary Metz)

Tray, 1937, Running Girl, 10½x13¼", NM......................**$450.00**

Tray, 1939, Springboard Girl, 10½x13¼", NM..................**$375.00**

Tray, 1941, Ice Skater, 10½x13¼", NM **$475.00**

Tray, 1950s, Girl w/Wind in Hair, screen background, 10½x13¼", M..**$100.00**

Tray, 1955, Menu Girl, 10½x13¼", M **$65.00**

Coloring and Activity Books

Coloring and activity books representing familiar movie and TV stars of the 1950s and 1960s are fun to collect, though naturally unused examples are hard to find. Condition is very important, of course, so learn to judge their values accordingly. Unused books are worth as much as 50% to 75% more than one only partially colored.

A-Team Storybook/Coloring Book, Peter Pan, 1984, The Maltese Cow, unused, EX **$5.00**

Adventures of Batman, Whitman, 1966, some use, EX+......**$25.00**

Anastasia Coloring & Water Paint Book, Golden Books, 1997, M **$5.00**

Annette Coloring Box, Whitman, 1962, complete w/all 256 pgs, no crayons, some use, EX+IB...**$50.00**

Baby Lamb Chop & Friends Paint w/Water, Golden Book, 1993, M..**$5.00**

Batman Forever Coloring & Activity Book, Golden Books, 1995, unused, EX **$5.00**

Batman Paint-by-Number, Whitman, 1966, EX+ **$25.00**

Bewitched Coloring Book, Treasure Books, 1965, NM......**$125.00**

Bewitched Fun & Activity Book, Grossett & Dunlap Treasure Books #8908, 1965, M **$30.00**

Big Jim, Whitman, 1975, some use, EX+.............................**$20.00**

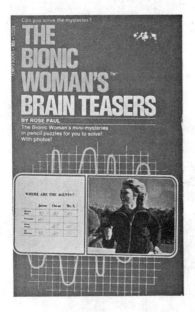

Bionic Woman, Brain Teasers, Temp Books, 1976, NM, from $10.00 to $15.00. (Photo courtesy Greg Davis and Bill Morgan)

Blondie Paint Book, Whitman, 1947, unused, NM+.........**$175.00**

Buffalo Bill Jr, Whitman #1316, 1956, some use, NM........**$15.00**

Bugs Bunny Book To Color, 1951, some use, VG................**$20.00**

Calling Dr Kildare for Fun & Games, Lowe #3092, 1960s, unused, EX **$50.00**

Captain Gallant, Lowe #2505, 1956, NM **$85.00**

Captain Kangaroo, 1960, some coloring, EX+ **$30.00**

Chilly Willy Paint Book, Whitman #2946, 1960, some use, EX+. **$35.00**

Crusader Rabbit, A Story Coloring Book, Treasure Books #298, 1957, some use, EX **$65.00**

Davy Crockett Punch-Out Book, Whitman #1943, 1955, M..**$75.00**

Donna Reed Coloring Book, Saalfield, 1964, M..................**$30.00**

Donny & Marie Osmond Coloring Book, Whitman, 1977, M **$25.00**

Dukes of Hazzard New Adventure Coloring & Activity Book, Modern Promotions, 1981, M.......................................**$35.00**

Fantastic Four, Whitman, 1977, some use, EX **$20.00**

Flash Gordon Coloring Book, Whitman, 1952, some use, VG ..**$30.00**

Flipper, Watkins-Strathmore #1851, 1965, some use, VG....**$20.00**

Gene Autry Coloring Book, Whitman #1124, 1950, some use, VG+..**$15.00**

Gene Autry Cowboy Paint Book, Merrill, 1940, some use, EX+.. **$50.00**

Gilligan's Island Coloring Book, Whitman, 1965, M.........**$100.00**

Goofy Dots, 1952, some use, EX+.....................................**$20.00**

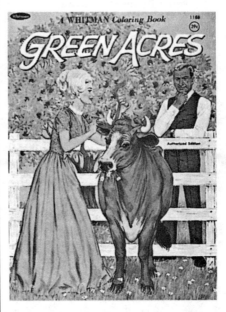

Green Acres, coloring book, Whitman, 1967, unused, EX, $30.00. (Photo courtesy Greg Davis and Bill Morgan)

Howdy Doody Coloring Book, Whitman #1188, 1956, some use, VG..**$15.00**

Howdy Doody Fun Book, Whitman #2187, 1950s, some use, VG **$20.00**

HR Pufnstuf Coloring Book, Whitman 1970, M **$75.00**

Incredible Hulk, Whitman, 1977, M...................................**$25.00**

Jonny Quest Paint w/Water Book, Landolls, 1994, NM......**$50.00**

Jurassic Park - The Lost World Paint w/Water, Landolls, 1997, M..**$5.00**

Knight Rider Activity Book, Modern Publishing, 1983, unused, EX+ **$8.00**

Land of the Lost Coloring & Activity Book, Whitman #1271, 1975, M...**$30.00**

Land of the Lost Coloring Book, Whitman #1045, 1975, M.**$30.00**

Lassie Coloring Book, Whitman #1151-2, 1982, unused, EX..**$15.00**

Little Lulu, Whitman #1663, 1974, M................................**$45.00**

Love Bug, Disney/Hunt's Ketchup promo, 1969, some use, EX.**$22.00**

Lucille Ball & Desi Arnez Coloring Book, Whitman #2079, 1953, some use, EX+ **$75.00**

Mickey Mouse Club Old McDonald Had a Farm Coloring Book, 1955, some use, EX...**$25.00**

Mr Ed Coloring Book, Whitman #1135, 1963, some use, EX. **$50.00**

Peanuts Featuring Linus Coloring Book, Artcraft #4650, 1972, some use, EX **$10.00**

Planet of the Apes, Saalfield, 1974, some use, EX...............**$10.00**

Popeye Paint w/Water Book, Whitman, 1981, unused, NM..**$10.00**

Ramar of the Jungle, Saalfield #1029, 1955, unused, NM...**$65.00**

Rambo Coloring & Activity Book, Modern Publishing, 1985, some use, EX+ **$6.00**

Range Rider Coloring Book, Lowe #2506, 1956, M............**$45.00**

Rango Texas Ranger Coloring Book, Artcraft #9675, M......**$40.00**

Ripcord Pictures To Color, Saalfield #9629, 1963, unused, NM...**$38.00**

Roy Rogers' Double-R-Bar Ranch Coloring & Many Things To Do, Whitman #1035, 1955, some use, VG **$25.00**

Roy Rogers Rodeo Sticker Fun w/Dale Evans, Trigger & Bullet, Whitman, some use, EX+ **$50.00**

Sergeant Preston Coloring Book, Whitman, 1957, some use, NM **$25.00**

Sesame Street Coloring Book, Whitman, 1975, unused, EX ..**$10.00**

Sgt Preston Coloring Book, Whitman #2946, 1953, unused, EX .**$35.00**

Sid & Marty Krofft's Kaleidoscope Puppets Punch-out Book, As Presented by the Coca-Cola Co, 1968, unpunched, EX+.**$50.00**

Six Million Dollar Man Dot-to-Dot, #C2412, 1977, unused, NM+ **$35.00**

Spider-Man Coloring Book, Marvel, 1983, The Arms of Dr Octopus, some use, EX+...**$15.00**

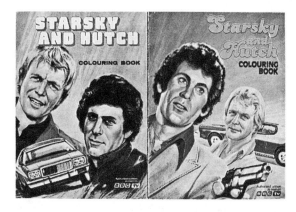

Starsky and Hutch, coloring books, Stafford Pemberton, 1977 – 1978, NM, from $75.00 to $100.00 each. (Photo courtesy Greg Davis and Bill Morgan)

Superman Sticker Book, Whitman, 1977, unused, EX **$18.00**

Superman to the Rescue, Whitman #1001, 1964, some use, EX+... **$30.00**

Three Stooges Funny Coloring Book, Lowe #2855, 1959, VG ..**$50.00**

TV Roundup of Western Heroes..., Saalfield Artcraft #7819, 1961, unused, NM **$40.00**

Universal Monsters Paint 'n Marker Book, Golden Book, 1991, unused, NM+ **$10.00**

Wally Walrus, Saalfield #4547, 1962, unused, NM+............**$55.00**

Who Framed Roger Rabbit Paint & Water Book, Golden #1702, unused, NM+ **$25.00**

Winnie the Pooh Trace & Color Book, Whitman, 1976, unused, EX **$12.00**

Wizard of Oz (Tales of) Coloring Book, Whitman, 1962, from cartoon TV show, unused, NM+ **$25.00**

Wonderbug, Whitman, 1978, M **$35.00**

Comic Books

Though just about everyone can remember having stacks and stacks of comic books as a child, few of us ever saved them for more than a few months. At 10¢ a copy, new ones quickly replaced the old, well-read ones. We'd trade them with our friends, but very soon, out they went. If we didn't throw them away, Mother did. So even though they were printed in huge amounts, few survive, and today they're very desirable collectibles.

Factors that make a comic book valuable are condition (as with all paper collectibles, extremely important), content, and rarity, but not necessarily age. In fact, comics printed between 1950 and the late 1970s are most in demand by collectors who prefer those they had as children to the earlier comics. They look for issues where the hero is first introduced, and they insist on quality. Condition is first and foremost when it comes to assessing worth. Compared to a book in excellent condition, a mint issue might bring six to eight times more, while one in only good condition would be worth less than half the price. We've listed some of the more collectible (and expensive) comics, but many are worth very little. You'll really need to check your bookstore for a good reference book before you actively get involved in the comic book market.

Adventure Into Mystery, Atlas Comics, #2, VG **$40.00**

Alice in Wonderland, Dell Publishing, #331, 1951, EX.......**$45.00**

Alvin, Dell, #28, 1973, VG...**$7.50**

Andy Griffith, Dell Four-Color #1252, VG **$75.00**

Annie, Marvel Comics Group, Treasury Edition, NM **$20.00**

Avengers, Marvel, #1, 1963, EX....................................**$500.00**

Avengers, Marvel Giant Size, #2, 1974, EX.........................**$15.00**

Barney Google & Snuffy Smith, Charlton Comics, #2, 1970, EX+ **$12.50**

Batman & Robin Adventures, DC Comics, #1, 1995, NM...**$3.00**

Beany & Cecil, Dell, #2, 1962, rare, EX............................**$35.00**

Bear Country, Dell Publishing, Disney, Four Color, #758, 1956, VG **$40.00**

Black Condor, DC Comics, #10, 1993, NM **$3.00**

Blazing Combat, Warren Publishing, #4, 1966, EX **$32.00**

Bomba the Jungle Boy, National Periodical Publishing, #6, 1968, VG **$9.00**

Brave Old World, DC Comics, #4, 2000, M.......................**$2.50**

Bugs Bunny Christmas Funnies, Dell, #7, NM...................**$60.00**

Buz Sawyer, Standard Comics, #3, 1949, EX.....................**$75.00**

Captain America, Marvel Comics, #12, 1997, NM **$4.00**

Captain Easy, 1939, VG, $47.50.

Captain Nice, Gold Key, #1, 1967, VG **$15.00**

Chain Gang War, DC Comics, #1, 1993, NM **$3.00**

Christian Heroes of Today, David C Cook, 1964, NM........**$20.00**

Cisco Kid, Dell, #17, VG..**$20.00**

Combat, Atlas Comics, #2, 1952, VG $25.00
Congo Bill, DC Comics, #4, 2000, NM............................$3.00
Cupid, Marvel Comics, #1, 1949, VG..............................$28.00

Daredevil, Marvel Comics #1, 1964, G, minimum value, $150.00. (Photo courtesy Bill Bruegman)

Darkman, Marvel Comics, #1, 1993, NM............................$4.00
Death Valley, Charlton Comics, #7, 1955, EX....................$35.00
Dennis the Menace, Marvel, #1, 1981, NM/M $15.00
Destroyer, Marvel Comics, #1, 1989, NM/M......................$4.00
Dick Tracy, Blackthorne Publishing, #13, NM.......................$7.00
Disney's Aladdin, Marvel Comics, #2, 1994, NM/M.............$3.00
Dixie Dugan, Prize Publicatons, #4, 1954, EX....................$45.00
Double Dragon, Marvel Comics, #1, 1991, NM/M $2.50
Double Trouble w/Goober, Dell Four Color, #417, 1953, EX. $30.00
Ella Cinders, United Features Syndicate, #1, 1948, VG.......$28.00
Emergency Doctor, Charlton Comics, #1, 1963, EX+ $22.50
Fables, DC Comics, #1, 2002, NM $8.00
Fantastic Voyages of Sinbad, Gold Key, #1, 1965, VG.........$15.00
Flash Gordon, Dell Four Color, #173, G.............................$17.50
Flash Gordon, Dell Four-Color, #175, 1967, NM.............$130.00
George of the Jungle, Gold Key, #1, 1979, EX $95.00
Gotham Girls, DC Comics, #1, 1992, NM/M......................$2.00
Green Lantern Annual, DC Comics, 1998 reprint, NM/M...$5.00
Hopalong Cassidy, National Periodical Publications, #92, EX. $80.00
Hunchback of Notre Dame, Dell Four-Color, #854, 1957, EX $40.00
Hunchback of Notre Dame, Classic Comics, #15, 1964, NM . $15.00
Iron Man, Marvel Comics, #13, 1997, NM/M.....................$3.00
John Carter of Mars, Gold Key, #1, 1964, VG $20.00
Journey to the Center of the Earth, Dell Four Color, #1060, 1959/60, VG+ $45.00
Kiss, Image Comics, #1, 1997, NM....................................$10.00
Kookie, Dell Publishing, #2, 1962, EX...............................$55.00
Lidsville, Gold Key, #1, 1972, EX.......................................$35.00
Lone Ranger, Dell, #37, EX+ $45.00
Maggie the Cat, Image Comics, #2, 1966, NM/M.................$2.50
Martha Washington Saves the World, Dark Horse Comics, #1, 1957, NM $3.00

Mary Poppins, Gold Key, 1964, EX....................................$15.00
Maverick, Dell Four Color, #980, EX.................................$65.00
Mod Squad, Dell, #1, 1969, NM/M....................................$50.00
Mod Wheels, Gold Key, #1, 1971, EX................................$28.00
Movie Comics, King Kong, Whitman Treasury, 1978, EX...$35.00
Nick Halliday, Argo, #1, 1956, VG.....................................$17.50
OK Comics, United Features Syndicate, #2, 1940, EX......$475.00
Outlaws of the West, Charlton, #15, VG+.........................$15.00
Owl, Gold Key, #2, 1968, EX...$35.00
Phantom, DC Comics, #13, 1990, NM/M $3.00
Picture Stories From the Bible, DC Comics, #1, 1947, EX ..$175.00
Prize Mystery, Key Publications, #2, 1955, EX $45.00
Race for the Moon, Harvey Publications, #2, 1958, EX $85.00
Raggedy Ann & Andy, Dell #2, 1946, VG...........................$35.00
Restless Gun, Dell Four-Color, #1146, VG........................$25.00
Return to Jurassic Park, Topps, #1, 1995, NM/M.................$3.00
Sabrina the Teen-Age Witch, Archie Publications, #2, 1971, EX..$100.00
Safest Place in the World, Dark Horse Comics, #1, 1993, NM/M $3.00
Scooby Doo, Marvel, #1, 1977, NM+ $25.00
Secret Wars II, Marvel Comics Group, #1, 1993, NM/M......$4.00
Son of Satan, Marvel Comics Group, #1, 1975, NM/M......$25.00
Spooky Spooktown, Harvey Publications, #2, 1962, EX......$50.00
Star Trek, Gold Key, #2, 1968, M.....................................$150.00
Steve Canyon Comics, Harvey Publications, #1, 1948, EX ..$140.00
Superman, National Periodical Publishing/DC Comics, #123, 1958, EX $215.00
Tainted, DC Comics, #1, 1955, NM/M $5.00
Tales To Astonish, Atlas #22, 1961, VG............................$35.00
Teen-Age Brides, Harvey/Home Comics, #1, 1953, VG......$35.00
Tex Ritter Western, Fawcett, #2, 1954, EX $60.00
Thunderbolt, Charlton Comics, #51, 1966, NM/M............$30.00
Top Cat, Gold Key, #5, 1963, NM......................................$45.00
True Bride's Experiences, Harvey Publications, #8, 1954, EX. $50.00
Voyage to the Bottom of the Sea, Gold Key, #6, 1966, EX..$15.00
Walt Disney's Picnic Party, Dell Giant, #8, 1957, VG+........$50.00
Woody Woodpecker Back to School, Dell Giant, #1, 1952, EX..$25.00

Compacts and Purse Accessories

When 'liberated' women entered the work force after WWI, cosmetics, previously frowned upon, became more acceptable, and as a result the market was engulfed with compacts of all types and designs. Some went so far as to incorporate timepieces, cigarette compartments, coin holders, and money clips. All types of materials were used — mother-of-pearl, petit-point, cloisonnè, celluloid, and leather among them. There were figural compacts, those with wonderful Art Deco designs, souvenir compacts, and some with advertising messages.

Carryalls were popular from the 1930s to the 1950s. They were made by compact manufacturers and were usually carried with evening wear. They contained compartments for powder, rouge, and lipstick, often held a comb and mirror, and some were designed with a space for cigarettes and a lighter. Other features might have included a timepiece, a tissue holder, a place for coins or stamps, and some even had music boxes. In addition to compacts and carryalls, solid perfumes and lipsticks are becoming popular collectibles as well.

For further study, we recommend *The Estée Lauder Solid Perfume Compact Collection* and *Vintage and Contemporary Purse Accessories*, by Roselyn Gerson.

Newsletter: The Compacts Collector Chronicle
Powder Puff
P.O. Box 40
Lynbrook, NY 11563
Subscription: $25 (4 issues, USA or Canada) per year

Allwyn, floral enameling on copper, blue enameled reverse & lid ground, foil label: Black Eyed Susans, 3 2½x½" **$55.00**

Atomette, brushed gold-tone w/crystal poodle, 2¾", from $90 to **$120.00**

Bliss Bros, mock tortoiseshell enameled case, signed BBCO, sq, 2¾x¼", from $65 to **$75.00**

Dorothy Gray, silver-tone round hat shape, raised dome center w/ bow & flowers, 3⅞", from $125 to............................**$175.00**

Eisenberg Original, brushed gold-tone w/applied lg emerald-colored stones, mirror & powder well inside, sq, 3x3" **$200.00**

Estée Lauder, 'On Your Toes,' gold-tone, 2000, 2¼", $55.00. (Photo courtesy Roselyn Gerson)

Estée Lauder, polished gold-tone roulette wheel w/rhinestones, red & black enameled numbers, sm pearl on 7, 3", $60 to. **$85.00**

Evans, black suede covering on gold-tone, rigid wrist handle, sq, signed, 5½x3⅛x1", from $150 to................................**$175.00**

Evans, silver-tone charm/photograph compact, lid decorated w/9 charms in high relief, sq, 2½", from $75 to **$95.00**

Hingeco, sterling silver heart-shaped cartouche on lid monogrammed w/initials RG, 2½x2½", from $125 to **$175.00**

K&K, brass-colored basket w/embossed swinging handle, satin-finished metal interior, 2⅛x1¼", from $80 to **$120.00**

Max Factor, gold-tone round, lid decorated w/fishes & centered green cabochon stone, 2", from $55 to **$75.00**

Mondaine, red leather embossed w/Art Deco green & ivory floral & linear zigzag, gold-tone trim, book shape, 2¾x2x½" **$75.00**

Rex Fifth Ave, blue champlevé enamel lid w/leaf design & embossed floral border, gold-tone mesh case, 2¾x½", $50 to **$65.00**

Rex Fifth Ave, green enameled case w/white enameled floral motif, 4x⅜", from $50 to **$60.00**

Ritz, brushed gold-tone w/embossed umbrellas & raindrops, 3⅞x⅜", from $65 to **$75.00**

Riviera, gold-tone link-mesh case, signed, 2¾x2¼x⅝", from $45 to **$50.00**

Stratton, mother-of-pearl lid decorated w/musical notes & G clef, gold trim, music box, 3¼x2¾x¾", from $150 to **$175.00**

Unmarked, black plastic guitar w/plastic strings, 2x5½", from $175 to **$225.00**

Unmarked, dark green marbleized Bakelite w/pink carved Bakelite roses & painted green leaves, plastic link chain, 2½" ..**$200.00**

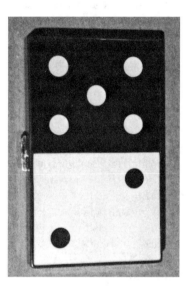

Unmarked, gold-tone with black and white dice motif, $125.00. (Photo courtesy Roselyn Gerson)

Voluptè, white enamel w/red, white & blue drum major & 2 marching musicians, 3¼x3", from $85 to **$95.00**

Wadsworth, gold-tone matchbook w/black striker & 2 applied matches, engraved Ruth From Vic, 2½x3¾" **$375.00**

Wadsworth, gold-tone vanity table w/interior & exterior mirrors, collapsible cabriole legs, 3x2", from $150 to...............**$275.00**

Wadsworth, polished gold-tone sq w/decorative framed round mirror on lid, 3", from $45 to..**$55.00**

Zell, brushed gold-tone w/cast pewter scroll on lid in high relief, maroon enamel reverse, 4x⅜", from $50 to **$65.00**

Zell, silver plated w/embossed fruit motif in gold-tone w/colored washed lacquer, 3⅞x⅜", from $65 to **$75.00**

Cookbooks and Recipe Leaflets

Cookbook collecting is not new! Perhaps one of the finest books ever written on the subject goes back to just after the turn of the century when Elizabeth Robins Pennell published *My Cookery Books*, an edition limited to 330 copies; it had tipped-in photographs and was printed on luxurious, uncut paper. Mrs. Pennell, who spent much of her adult life traveling in Europe, wrote a weekly column on food and cooking for the *Pall Mall Gazette,* and as a result, reviewed many books on cookery. Her book was a compilation of titles from her extensive collection which was later donated to the Library of Congress. That this book was reprinted in 1983 is an indication that interest in cookbook collecting is strong and ongoing.

Books on food and beverages, if not bestsellers, are at the least generally popular. Cookbooks published by societies, lodges, churches, and similar organizations offer insight into regional food preferences and contain many recipes not found in other sources. Very early examples are unusually practical, often stressing religious observances and sometimes offering medical advice. Recipes were simple combinations of basic elements. Cookbooks and cooking guides of World Wars I and II stressed conservation of food. In sharp contrast are the more modern cookbooks often authored by doctors, dietitians, cooks, and domestic scientists, calling for more diversified materials and innovative combinations with exotic seasonings. Food manufacturers' cookbooks abound. By comparing early cookbooks to more recent publications, the fascinating evolution in cookery and food preparation is readily apparent.

Because this field is so large and varied, we recommend that you choose the field you find most interesting and specialize. Will you collect hardbound or softcover? Some collectors zero in on one particular food company's literature — for instance, Gold Medal Flour and Betty Crocker, the Pillsbury Flour Company's Pillsbury Bake-Offs, and Jell-O. Others look for more general publications on chocolate, spices and extracts, baking powers, or favored appliances. Fund-raising, regional, and political cookbooks are other types to consider.

For more information we recommend *Collector's Guide to Cookbooks* by Frank Daniels (Collector Books).

Our suggested values are based on cookbooks in near mint condition; remember to adjust prices up or down to evaluate examples in other conditions.

Hardbound

ABC of Casseroles, Peter Pauper Press, 1954, 61 pages, w/dust jacket **$5.00**

All About Home Baking, General Foods, 1933, 144 pages **$6.00**

American Cookery Book, Jennie June, J Baumann & Co, 1878, 399 pages **$75.00**

Baker's Weekly Revised Recipes, American Trade Pub, 1924, 294 pages **$30.00**

Ballet Cook Book, Tanaquil Le Clercq, Stein & Day, 1966, 416 pages, w/dust jacket **$175.00**

Better Homes & Gardens New Cook Book, Better Homes & Gardens, 1968, ring binder, 400 pages..........................**$20.00**

Bible Cook Book, Marian Maeve O'Brien, Bethany Press, 1958.. **$10.00**

Book of Hors d'Oeuvres, Lucy Allen, Bramhall House, 1941, 141 pages, w/dust jacket **$12.00**

Breakfast, Dinner, Tea; D Appleton & Co, 1865, 351 pages .**$300.00**

Century Cook Book, Mary Ronald, The Century Co, 1895, 587 pages **$15.00**

Common Sense in the Household, Marion Harland, Scribner's, 1881, 546 pages..**$100.00**

Dessert Cook Book, Better Homes & Gardens, Meredith, 1960, 160 pages..**$3.00**

Dora's Cook Book, Dora Fairfield, Hunter, Ross, 1888, 311 pages...**$75.00**

Electric Refrigerator Recipes, Alice Bradley, General Electric, 1927, 136 pages **$15.00**

Family Harvest, Jane Moss Snow, Bobbs-Merrill, 1976, 221 pages, w/dust jacket..**$6.00**

Fondue Magic, Anita Prichard, Heathside Press, 1969, 192 pages...**$4.00**

Golden Age Cook-Book, Henrietta Latham Dwight, Alliance Publishing, 1898, 178 pages **$45.00**

Helen Corbitt Cooks For Looks, Helen Corbitt, Houghton Mifflin, 1967, 115 pages, w/dust jacket **$8.00**

In the Kitchen, Elizabeth S Miller, Lee & Shepard, 1875, 568 pages...**$50.00**

Jolly Times Cook Book, Marjorie Noble Osborn, Rand McNally, 1934, 64 pages..**$15.00**

Joy of Cooking, by Irma S. Rombauer, published by Bobbs-Merrill Co., 1943, 884 pages, $50.00. (Photo courtesy Frank Daniels)

Keep It Short & Simple Cookbook, Ruth H Brent, Holt, Rinehart & Winston, 1972, 180 pages.........................**$3.00**

Laurel's Kitchen, Laurel Robertson et al, Nilgin Press, 1981, 508 pages, w/dust jacket **$9.00**

Mother Maybelle's Cook Book, June Carter Cash, Wynwood Press, 1989, 192 pages..**$100.00**

National Foods Cookbook, Beatrice Trum Hunter, Simon & Schuster, 1961, 296 pages...................................**$5.00**

Our Home Cyclopedia, Frank S Burton, Mercantile Publishing, 1889, 400 pages..**$200.00**

Quick & Easy Gourmet Recipes, Hyla O'Connor, Vollrath Co, 1968, 128 pages...**$5.00**

Rare Old Receipts, Jacqueline Harrison Smith, John C Winston Co, 1906, 30 pages..**$25.00**

Savory Stews, Mary Savage, Doubleday, 1969, 230 pages, w/dust jacket..**$5.00**

Slenderella Cook Book, Myra Waldo, GP Putnamn's Sons, 1957, 335 pages, w/dust jacket **$6.00**

Tempting Kosher Dishes, Manischewitz Co, 1930, 156 pages. **$125.00**

Thousand Ways To Please a Husband, Louise Bennett Weaver & Helen Cowles LeCron, Britton Publishing, 1917, 479 pages **$90.00**

White House Cook Book, FL Gillette, LP Miller & Co, 1889, 521 pages, silver cover...**$150.00**

World Famous Chefs' Cook Book, Ford Naylor, Otto Naylor Corporation, 1941, 637 pages **$50.00**

Young Housekeeper's Friend, Mrs Mary Hooker Cornelius, Brown, Taggard & Chase, 1859, 200 pages............................**$200.00**

Young Wife's Own Cook Book, Mrs Jane Warren, Grand Union Tea Company, 1890, 124 pages.............................**$40.00**

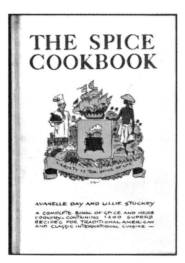

Spice Cookbook, by Avanell Day and Lillie Stuckey, published by Grosset & Dunlap, 1968, 623 pages, $12.00. (Photo courtesy Frank Daniels)

Paperback

Adventures in Good Cooking, Duncan Hines, 1955, 26th printing..**$3.00**

Book of Merry Eating, M17, McCall's, 1965, 64 pages **$3.00**

Dollars in Doughnuts, Procter & Gamble, 1933, 81 pages..**$12.00**

Ice Creams: Frozen Without Stirring, Leaflet #49, USDA, 1930, 8 pages **$12.00**

Jell-O Pudding Idea Book, General Foods, 1968, 44 pages....**$3.00**

Newman's Own 22 Favorite Recipes, Ursula Hotchner, Klein's Printing Co, 1990, 16 pages **$3.00**

Quantity Recipes for Quality Foods, Evaporated Milk Association, 1948, 63 pages, brown cover..**$8.00**

Sunkist Recipes: Oranges-Lemons, Alice Bradley, California Fruit Growers Exchange, 1916, 64 pages...............................**$20.00**

US Navy Cook-Book, Division of Naval Militia Affairs, 1908, 62 pages **$20.00**

Walton Family Cook Book, Sylvia Resnick, Bantam Books, 1975, 148 pages **$50.00**

500-Plus Ideas for Freezing & Canning, Elizabeth Henley, Bruce-Royal Publishing, 1964, 128 pages **$5.00**

641 Tested Recipes From the Sealtest Kitchens, National Dairy Products Corp, 1954, 256 pages **$5.00**

Recipe Leaflets and Pamphlets

Casserole Cookery w/Protein-Rich Cheese, Kraft, 1946.........**$1.00**

Certo Recipes for Making Perfect Jams, Jellies & Marmalades, Pectin Sales Co, 1922 ....**$3.00**

Creative Cookery, Martha Logan, Swift & Co, 1960, 31 pages...**$3.00**

Easy Hospitality, Marni Wood, Coca-Cola Co, 1951, 48 pages **$5.00**

Festive Christmas Foods, Brown & Bigelow, 1958, 16 pages .**$1.00**

Flavor Touches, Kraft, 1944...**$3.00**

Happy Eatings Make Christmas Greetings, Borden Co, 1956..**$3.00**

I'm Getting Scarce, Baker's Coconut, 1943 ....**$3.00**

Jell-O, America's Most Famous Dessert, Genessee Foods, 1902, 4 pages **$50.00**

Makamix Recipes, Jel Sert Co, 1930s....................................**$2.00**

Mary Poppins Cook Book, C&H Frosting Sugar, Walt Disney Co, 1963, 25 pages..**$40.00**

New Delicacies, Kraft, 1946..**$3.00**

Omelette Originals, Irena Kirshman, Potpourri Press, 1970, 47 pages **$3.00**

Recipes & Menus for Buffet Entertaining, Daisy Dean, Tree Sweet Products, 1960, 3rd edition, 24 pages......................**$3.00**

Salads: Tossed & Otherwise, Kraft, 1946 ....**$3.00**

Square Meals...Speedy Meals..., Kraft, 1945.........................**$3.00**

Tempting Banana Recipes, United Fruit Co, 1958................**$3.00**

Trail Cookery, Girl Scouts of America, Kellogg Co, 1945, 30 pages **$15.00**

Vermont Recipes, Maltex Company, 1950s...........................**$1.00**

Where There's Fire, There's Smoke, Florida Department of Natural Resources, 1970s..**$1.00**

Your Favourite Recipes, Robin Hood Flour, 1960s, 31 pages.**$3.00**

12 Pies Husbands Like Best, Aunt Jenny, Lever Brothers Co, 1952, 21 pages..**$6.00**

Pillsbury's Best Butter Cookie Cookbook, Vol. III, 1961, 24 pages, 6x5", $4.50. (Photo courtesy Frank Daniels)

Cookie Cutters

In recent years, cookie cutters have come into their own as worthy kitchen collectibles. Prices on many have risen astronomically, but a practiced eye can still sort out a good bargain. Advertising cutters and product premiums, especially in plastic, can still be found without too much effort. Aluminum cutters with painted wood handles are usually worth several dollars each, if in good condition. Red and green are the usual handle colors, but other colors are more highly prized by many. Hallmark plastic cookie cutters, especially those with painted backs, are always worth considering, if in good condition.

Be wary of modern tin cutters being sold for antique. Many present-day tinsmiths chemically antique their cutters, especially if done in a primitive style. These are often sold by others as 'very old.' Look closely because most tinsmiths today sign and date these cutters.

Apple, copper, w/curved handle, Cape Cod Copper Works, 6x6" **$25.00**
Bald eagle w/wings slightly spread, tin, flat back, 2½x3" **$40.00**
Barnaby Bunny, white plastic, Hallmark, 1975, 5" **$10.00**

Betsy McCall, molded metal, McCall Pub. Co., Hong Kong, 1971, 8", $30.00.

Bird, tin, flat back, 3¾x3½" **$55.00**
Bridge shapes (diamond, heart, club, spade), aluminum, 2", set of 4 .... **$17.50**
Bugs Bunny, red plastic, 1978, 6" **$6.00**
Crow, tin, strap handle, 2⅝x5¾" **$95.00**
Donatello (Teenage Mutant Ninja Turtle), green plastic, solid crescent handle, 1977 .... **$5.00**

Dragon, green plastic, Hallmark, 1979, $30.00.

Gingerbread lady, tin, brace handle at waist, 7½x5" **$10.00**
Gingerbread man, aluminum w/green strap handle, 6x2" **$10.00**
Gingerbread man, clear plastic, Hallmark, 3 attached tabs to fit through greeting card, ca 1963-64 .... **$60.00**
Heart in hand, tin, flat back, dark patina, 5½x4½" **$55.00**
Horse running, tin, flat back, light rust/dark patina, 3¼x4¾" . **$55.00**
James the Red Engine (from Thomas the Tank), blue plastic.. **$30.00**
Lady in long dress, tin, flat back, 5½x2¾" **$50.00**
Martha Stewart Easter Eggs, copper, complete set of 13, MIB. **$145.00**

Martha Stewart Hearts, copper, open backs, complete set of 13, from 1x1" to 3½x5", M (no box) **$170.00**
Martha Stewart Seashore set, crab, starfish, 3 shells of varied shapes, retired, M (no box) **$55.00**
Peacock w/tail spread, tin, flat back, 4x4" **$120.00**
Pear w/2 leaves & stem, tin, handle w/rolled edge, 3x1½" ... **$40.00**
Pennsylvania Dutch man standing (portly), pointed cap, tin, flat back, 6x2½" **$60.00**
Porky Pig, red plastic, 1950s, 5" **$5.00**
Pumpkin face, orange plastic, Hallmark, MIP...................... **$5.00**
Rabbit, copper, flat back, 8", MIP **$45.00**
Rabbit w/ears back (primitive style), tin, flat back, 4¼x6¼" . **$100.00**
Razorback hog, tin, flat back, 2½x4¼" **$50.00**
Roller type w/6 varied shapes, tin w/wooden handle, light rust... **$45.00**
Rooster crowing, tin, flat back, EX patina, 4¼x3½" **$40.00**
Sailor boy (resembles Cracker Jack boy), tin, flat back, 9¼x4¼" .**$85.00**
Santa holding tree, tin, flat back, Germ 14?, 8½" (cuts 6" cookie) **$220.00**
Santa w/pack, aluminum w/green wooden handle, original Santa paper litho on back, 3 4/8" **$35.00**
Santa w/pack, tin, open back w/X reinforcement, ca 1940-50, 8" **$15.00**
Sesame Street characters (Ernie, Bert, Big Bird, Cookie Monster, Elmo & Zoe), yellow plastic, 1996, set of 6.................. **$36.00**
Sheep standing, tin, flat back, 4½x5½" **$25.00**
Star, aluminum w/red painted handle, 1950s, 3x3" **$30.00**
Swan w/wings raised, tin, flat back, 5½x5½" **$35.00**
Thistle flower, tin, flat back, 4½x2½" **$145.00**
Turkey, copper, w/handle, Cape Cod Copper Works, 8", MIP. **$55.00**

Cookie Jars

This is an area that for years saw an explosion of interest that resulted in some very high prices. Though the market has drastically cooled off, some of the rare jars still sell for upwards of $1,000.00. Even a common jar from a good manufacturer will fall into the $40.00 to $100.00 price range. At the top of the list are the Black-theme jars, then come the cartoon characters such as Popeye, Howdy Doody, or the Flintstones — in fact, any kind of a figural jar from an American pottery is collectible.

The American Bisque company was one of the largest producers of these jars from 1930 until the 1970s. Many of their jars have no marks at all; those that do are simply marked 'USA,' sometimes with a mold number. But their airbrushed colors are easy to spot, and collectors look for the molded-in wedge-shaped pads on their bases — these say 'American Bisque' to cookie jar buffs about as clearly as if they were marked.

The Brush Pottery (Ohio, 1946 – 1971) made cookie jars that were decorated with the airbrush in many of the same colors used by American Bisque. These jars tend to hold their values, and the rare ones continue to climb in price. McCoy was probably the leader in cookie jar production. Even some of their very late jars bring high prices. Abingdon, Shawnee, and Red Wing all manufactured cookie jars, and there are lots of wonderful jars by many other companies. Joyce and Fred Roerig's book *The Ultimate*

Collector's Encyclopedia of Cookie Jars, covers them all beautifully. It is published by Collector Books.

Warning! The marketplace abounds with reproductions these days. Roger Jensen of Rockwood, Tennessee, is making a line of cookie jars as well as planters, salt and pepper shakers, and many other items which for years he marked McCoy. Because it was believed the 'real' McCoys had never registered their trademark, he was able to receive federal approval to begin using this mark in 1992. Though he added '#93' to some of his pieces, the vast majority of his wares are undated. He used old molds, and novice collectors are being fooled into buying the new for 'old' prices. Here are some of his reproductions that you should be aware of: McCoy Mammy, Mammy With Cauliflower, Clown Bust, Dalmatians, Indian Head, Touring Car, and Rocking Horse; Hull Little Red Riding Hood; Pearl China Mammy; and the Mosaic Tile Mammy. Within the past few years, though, one of the last owners of the McCoy Pottery Company was able to make a successful appeal to end what they regarded as the fradulent use of their mark (it seems that they at last had it registered), so some of the later Jensen reproductions have been marked 'Brush-McCoy' (though this mark was never used on an authentic cookie jar) and 'B.J. Hull.' Besides these forgeries, several Brush jars have been reproduced as well (see Roerig's books for more information), and there are others. Some reproductions are being made in Taiwan and China, however there are also jars being reproduced here in the States.

Cookie jars from California are getting their fair share of attention right now, and then some! We've included several from companies such as Brayton Laguna, Treasure Craft, Vallona Starr, and Twin Winton. Roerig's books have information on all of these. Advisor Mike Ellis is the author of *Collector's Guide to Don Winton Designs*; and another of our advisors, Bernice Stamper, has written *Vallona Starr Ceramics*, which we're sure you will enjoy. *The Collector's Encyclopedia of Metlox Potteries* by Carl Gibbs provides information not only on their artware and dinnerware lines, but covers cookie jar production as well. Carl is our advisor for Metlox cookie jars.

See also Fitz & Floyd; Vandor.

Advisors: Jim and Beverly Mangus, Shawnee (See Directory, Shawnee); Mike Ellis, Twin Winton (See Directory, Twin Winton); Carl Gibbs, Metlox (See Directory, Metlox); George A. Higby, Treasure Craft (See Directory, Treasure Craft)

Newsletter: *Cookie Jarrin' With Joyce*
1501 Maple Ridge Rd.
Walterboro, SC 29488

A Little Company, Blanket Couple, c 87, 12" **$150.00**
A Little Company, Edmund, c 1992, 19" **$125.00**
A Little Company, Grandmother w/Child, limited edition, 1992, 13" **$150.00**
A Little Company, Italian Couple, c 1991 ....**$150.00**
Abingdon, Bo Peep, #694 ....**$235.00**
Abingdon, Choo Choo (Locomotive), #651 ....**$145.00**
Abingdon, Clock, #653, 1949................................**$90.00**
Abingdon, Daisy, #677, 1949 ....**$45.00**

Abingdon, Fat Boy, #495 ....**$250.00**
Abingdon, Hippo, #588, decor, 1942 ....**$250.00**
Abingdon, Hobby Horse, #602.........................**$185.00**
Abingdon, Humpty Dumpty, #663, decor.........**$200.00**
Abingdon, Jack-in-the-Box, #611.....................**$275.00**
Abingdon, Little Girl, #693, from $60 to **$75.00**

Abingdon, Little Old Lady, #471, with decoration, from $400.00 to $425.00. (Photo courtesy Ermagene Westfall)

Abingdon, Miss Muffet, #622..........................**$205.00**
Abingdon, Money Bag, #588 ....**$65.00**
Abingdon, Mother Goose, #695 ....**$295.00**
Abingdon, Pineapple, #664...............................**$65.00**
Abingdon, Pumpkin, #674, 1949, minimum value............**$300.00**
Abingdon, Three Bears, #696, from $90 to........**$100.00**
Abingdon, Wigwam, #665...............................**$200.00**
Abingdon, Windmill, #678, from $200 to..........**$225.00**
American Bisque, Baby Elephant, no mark, from $175 to .**$200.00**
American Bisque, Bow Bear, white bear w/black ears & paws & blue bow, USA, from $65 to..............................**$75.00**
American Bisque, Carousel, USA, from $40 to **$50.00**
American Bisque, Clown, blue & pink costume, hands on belly, USA, 1959, from $50 to..............................**$60.00**
American Bisque, Cookie Girl, jar w/Cookie spelled across girl's face, pink bows in hair, USA, #202, from $55 to.................**$65.00**
American Bisque, Cookie Sack, #201, from $30 to.............**$40.00**
American Bisque, Cowboy Boots, USA 742, from $75 to....**$85.00**
American Bisque, Dancing Elephant, no mark, from $150 to .**$175.00**
American Bisque, Dutch Girl, blue dress w/tulips on front, USA, 1958, from $75 to **$100.00**
American Bisque, Flower Jar, blue flower in center & on lid, USA, from $25 to **$35.00**
American Bisque, French Poodle, burgundy w/black bow tie, USA, from $100 to **$125.00**
American Bisque, Grandma, white & pink apron w/dots over yellow dress, USA, 1958, from $70 to **$80.00**
American Bisque, Jack-in-Box, USA, 1958, from $125 to .**$150.00**
American Bisque, Magic Bunny, rabbit coming out of yellow top hat, USA, 1959, from $100 to......................**$125.00**

American Bisque, Potbellied Stove, black w/glowing red inside, USA, from $35 to...$45.00

American Bisque, Puppy, puppy w/shoestring in mouth atop quilted base, USA, 1959, from $125 to.................................$135.00

American Bisque, Rooster, heavy gold trim, from $125 to.$150.00

American Bisque, Schoolhouse, bell in lid, USA, from $35 to.. $45.00

American Bisque, Seal on Igloo, USA, from $275 to.........$295.00

American Bisque, Spool of Thread, thimble finial, USA, from $100 to...$125.00

American Bisque, Treasure Chest, USA, 1959, from $70 to.$80.00

American Bisque, Yarn Doll, gold trim, no mark, from $300 to.. $325.00

Benjamin & Medwin, Pillsbury Best Flour Sack, Taiwan, 1993, from $35 to...$45.00

Benjamin & Medwin, Snoopy Doghouse, c '58 '66 UFS, Taiwan, from $35 to..$40.00

Brush, Antique Touring Car, from $950 to.....................$1,100.00

Brush, Boy w/Balloons, minimum value..........................$850.00

Brush, Chick in Nest, #W38 (+), from $325 to................$425.00

Brush, Cinderella Pumpkin, #W32 (+)...........................$225.00

Brush, Circus Horse, green (+)..$800.00

Brush, Clown, yellow pants, #W22..................................$200.00

Brush, Clown Bust, #W49..$275.00

Brush, Cookie House, #W31, from $75 to........................$100.00

Brush, Covered Wagon, dog finial, #W30, minimum value (+).$500.00

Brush, Cow w/Cat on Back, brown, #W10 (+)..................$150.00

Brush, Cow w/Cat on Back, purple, minimum value (+)...$950.00

Brush, Davy Crockett, no gold, USA (+)..........................$300.00

Brush, Dog & Basket...$300.00

Brush, Donkey Cart, ears down, gray, #W33, from $350 to...$450.00

Brush, Donkey Cart, ears up, #W33, minimum value.......$750.00

Brush, Elephant w/Ice Cream Cone, #W18 (+).................$500.00

Brush, Elephant w/Monkey on Book, minimum value...$5,000.00

Brush, Fish, #W52 (+), from $450 to..............................$500.00

Brush, Formal Pig, gold trim, #W7 Brush USA (+)...........$425.00

Brush, Formal Pig, no gold, green hat & coat (+), from $275 to... $325.00

Brush, Gas Lamp, #K1...$75.00

Brush, Granny, pink apron, blue dots on skirt, #W19, from $250 to...$300.00

Brush, Granny, plain skirt, minimum value (+)................$300.00

Brush, Happy Bunny, white, #W25.................................$200.00

Brush, Hen on Basket, no mark......................................$125.00

Brush, Humpty Dumpty, w/beany & bow tie (+), from $225 to... $275.00

Brush, Humpty Dumpty, w/peaked hat & shoes, #W29....$200.00

Brush, Laughing Hippo, #W27 (+), from $700 to.............$800.00

Brush, Little Angel (+)...$725.00

Brush, Little Boy Blue, gold trim, #K25, sm, from $700 to.$800.00

Brush, Little Girl, #017 (+), from $500 to........................$550.00

Brush, Night Owl, #W40, from $85 to.............................$125.00

Brush, Old Clock, #W20...$125.00

Brush, Old Shoe, #W23 (+)...$100.00

Brush, Panda, #W21 (+)...$225.00

Brush, Peter Pan, gold trim, lg (+)..................................$800.00

Brush, Raggedy Ann, #W16, from $450 to.......................$500.00

Brush, Sitting Pig, #W37 (+) from $350 to.......................$425.00

Brush, Smiling Bear, #W46 (+).......................................$300.00

Brush, Squirrel on Log, #W26, from $80 to......................$100.00

Brush, Stylized Owl...$325.00

Brush, Teddy Bear, feet apart...$250.00

Brush, Treasure Chest, #W28...$150.00

California Originals, Beaver, green tie, #2625, from $30 to.$35.00

California Originals, Christmas Tree, no mark, from $125 to.$200.00

California Originals, Lion, brushed-on gold mane, no mark, from $25 to..$30.00

California Originals, Mouse With Cookie Bag, from $30.00 to $35.00. (Photo courtesy Ermagene Westfall)

California Originals, Mushrooms on Stump, #2956, from $25 to..$30.00

California Originals, Upside Down Turtle, #2627 USA, from $40 to..$50.00

California Originals, White Rabbit, blue hat & collar, paper label, from $40 to...$50.00

Clay Art, Cabbage Bunny, 1992, from $35 to...................$45.00

Clay Art, Catfish, 1990, from $35 to...............................$45.00

Clay Art, Humpty Dumpty, 1991.....................................$125.00

Clay Art, Pig Watermelon, 8½", from $30 to....................$35.00

Clay Art, Stacked Animals, polka-dot hen on pink on black & white cow, 1991, from $30 to...$35.00

Clay Art, Wizard of Oz, hand-painted, paper label, 1990, from $125 to..$150.00

De Forest, Monk, Thou Shalt Not Steal around bottom of robe, c 1964, from $50 to...$60.00

De Forest of California, Barrel, #553, from $15 to.............$20.00

De Forest of California, Dachshund, #518, begging, from $50 to..$60.00

De Forest of California, Owl, green w/black glass, cap, #5537-5545, from $25 to...$30.00

De Forest of California, Snappy Gingerbread Boy, c #6, USA, from $100 to...$125.00

Dept 56, Mirage Cactus, from $30 to...............................$35.00

Dept 56, Mrs Kringle, holding tray of goodies, Christmas tree on apron, paper label, Japan, from $50 to........................$60.00

Dept 56, Short-Order Toaster, Japan, from $30 to.............$40.00

Dept 56, Witch, red hair, holding broom, no mark, from $60 to **$80.00**

Disney, Alice in Wonderland, looking-glass lid, no mark, rare, minimum value **$500.00**

Disney, Birthday Cake, Mickey's 50th, from $500 to.........**$550.00**

Disney, Donald Duck, reaching into cookie jar, $80 to........**$90.00**

Disney, Goofy, from $50 to...**$60.00**

Disney, Mary Poppins, scarce, minimum value **$1,000.00**

Disney, Mickey Mouse, music box in lid, Japan, from $450 to..**$500.00**

Disney, Pinocchio, minimum value...................................**$700.00**

Disney, The Incredibles, Made in China, Pixar, from $40 to . **$50.00**

Disney, Thumper, Made in USA, from $125 to.................**$150.00**

Disney, Winnie the Pooh, Made in Japan, 1982, from $200 to.**$225.00**

Doranne of California, Basset Hound, from $35.00 to $45.00. (Photo courtesy Ermagene Westfall)

Doranne of California, Cow on Moon, #J 2 USA, late 1950s, from $275 to **$325.00**

Doranne of California, Cow With Can of Milk, #C J107, 1984, from $50 to **$60.00**

Doranne of California, Dragon, USA, from $225 to **$250.00**

Doranne of California, Green Pepper, #C J 30 USA, from $30 to..**$35.00**

Doranne of California, Hound Dog, #J 1 USA, from $35 to ... **$45.00**

Doranne of California, Jeep, #C J 115, from $100 to........**$125.00**

Doranne of California, Mother Goose, #C J 16 USA, late 1960s, from $225 to **$250.00**

Doranne of California, Shoe House, USA, from $30 to.......**$35.00**

Enesco, Bulldog, green jacket w/red collar, from $35 to.......**$40.00**

Enesco, Mammy (Gone With The Wind), paper label.........**$95.00**

Enesco, Sweet Pickles Alligator, gold foil lablel, 1981, from $90 to **$110.00**

Hirsch, Gingerbread House, no mark, from $35 to **$45.00**

Hirsch, Planet, Cookie Planet in white lettering on brown, rocket finial, from $75 to **$85.00**

Hirsch, Smiling Bear w/Badge, no mark, from $40 to **$50.00**

Lefton, Bloomer Girl, #3966, 10"...................................**$275.00**

Lefton, Bossie Cow, #6594, from $125 to **$150.00**

Lefton, Chef Boy, #396, from $200 to.............................**$225.00**

Lefton, Dutch Girl, #2697, from $35 to...........................**$40.00**

Lefton, French Girl, #1174, from $275 to **$300.00**

Lefton, Pear 'n Apple, #4335, from $35 to **$45.00**

Lefton, Pennsylvania Dutch, #3702, from $150 to **$200.00**

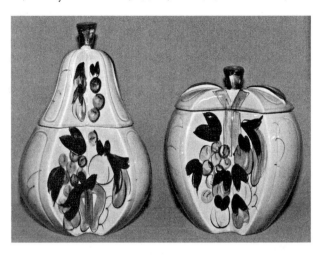

Los Angeles, Pear or Apple, from $25.00 to $35.00. (Photo courtesy Ermagene Westfall)

Maddux of California, Bear, #2101, from $75 to.................**$85.00**

Maddux of California, Beatrix Potter Rabbit, marked, from $75 to **$85.00**

Maddux of California, Cat, marked, from $75 to **$85.00**

Maddux of California, Grapes Cylinder, #8412, from $25 to.**$35.00**

Maddux of California, Queen, #210, from $50 to...............**$60.00**

Maddux of California, Shopping Cat or Shopping Rabbit (aka Beatrix Potter Rabbit), from $75.00 to $85.00. (Photo courtesy Ermagene Westfall)

Maddux of California, Squirrel Hiker, #2110, from $175 to.**$200.00**

McCoy, Animal Crackers **$100.00**

McCoy, Apollo Age...**$600.00**

McCoy, Apple, 1950-64..**$50.00**

McCoy, Apples on Basketweave **$70.00**

McCoy, Asparagus..**$50.00**

McCoy, Astronauts................................$650.00
McCoy, Bananas $95.00
McCoy, Barnum's Animals $150.00
McCoy, Barrel, Cookies sign on lid..................$75.00
McCoy, Baseball Boy.............................$95.00
McCoy, Basket of Eggs............................$40.00
McCoy, Basket of Poatoes $40.00
McCoy, Bear, cookie in vest, no 'Cookies'...........$85.00
McCoy, Betsy Baker (+) $125.00
McCoy, Black Kettle, w/immovable bail, hand-painted flowers ..$40.00
McCoy, Black Lantern $65.00
McCoy, Blue Willow Pitcher........................$75.00
McCoy, Bobby Baker $65.00
McCoy, Bugs Bunny $125.00
McCoy, Burlap Bag, red bird on lid $50.00
McCoy, Caboose $95.00
McCoy, Cat on Coal Scuttle $125.00
McCoy, Chairman of the Board (+) $550.00
McCoy, Chef Head $150.00
McCoy, Chilly Willy $65.00
McCoy, Chipmunk $125.00
McCoy, Christmas Tree $450.00
McCoy, Churn, 2 bands............................$35.00
McCoy, Circus Horse, black.........................$195.00
McCoy, Clown Bust (+) $75.00
McCoy, Clown in Barrel, yellow, blue or green $85.00
McCoy, Clyde Dog $95.00
McCoy, Coalby Cat $250.00
McCoy, Coca-Cola Can $100.00
McCoy, Coca-Cola Jug $85.00
McCoy, Coffee Grinder............................$45.00
McCoy, Coffee Mug...............................$45.00
McCoy, Colonial Fireplace $85.00
McCoy, Cookie Bank, 1961..........................$125.00
McCoy, Cookie Barrel, from $35 to...................$45.00
McCoy, Cookie Boy...............................$225.00
McCoy, Cookie Cabin $80.00
McCoy, Cookie Jug, double loop $35.00
McCoy, Cookie Jug, w/cork stopper, brown & white...........$40.00
McCoy, Cookie Log, squirrel finial $45.00
McCoy, Cookie Mug..............................$45.00
McCoy, Cookie Pot, 1964 ....$40.00
McCoy, Cookie Safe $65.00
McCoy, Cookstove, black or white....................$35.00
McCoy, Corn, row of standing ears, yellow or white, 1977..$85.00
McCoy, Corn, single ear...........................$150.00
McCoy, Covered Wagon $95.00
McCoy, Cylinder, w/red flowers $45.00
McCoy, Dalmatians in Rocking Chair (+)..............$150.00
McCoy, Davy Crockett (+)..........................$400.00
McCoy, Dog in Doghouse $150.00
McCoy, Dog on Basketweave $75.00
McCoy, Drum, red...............................$90.00
McCoy, Duck on Basketweave $75.00
McCoy, Dutch Boy...............................$65.00
McCoy, Dutch Girl, boy on reverse, rare...............$250.00
McCoy, Dutch Treat Barn $50.00

McCoy, Eagle on Basket, from $35 to.................$50.00
McCoy, Early American Chest, (Chiffoniere).............$65.00
McCoy, Elephant $150.00
McCoy, Elephant w/Split Trunk, rare, minimum value......$200.00
McCoy, Engine, black $125.00
McCoy, Flowerpot, plastic flower on top...............$350.00
McCoy, Football Boy (+)...........................$125.00
McCoy, Forbidden Fruit $90.00
McCoy, Fortune Cookies $50.00
McCoy, Freddy Gleep (+), minimum value...............$350.00
McCoy, Friendship 7..............................$150.00
McCoy, Frog on Stump............................$75.00
McCoy, Frontier Family $55.00
McCoy, Fruit in Bushel Basket.......................$85.00
McCoy, Gingerbread Boy...........................$75.00
McCoy, Globe...................................$195.00
McCoy, Grandfather Clock $75.00
McCoy, Granny $120.00
McCoy, Hamm's Bear (+)...........................$225.00
McCoy, Happy Face..............................$80.00
McCoy, Hen on Nest.............................$95.00
McCoy, Hillbilly Bear, rare, minimum value (+) $900.00
McCoy, Hobby Horse, brown underglaze (+).............$150.00
McCoy, Hocus Rabbit.............................$45.00
McCoy, Honey Bear, rustic glaze.....................$80.00
McCoy, Hot Air Balloon...........................$40.00
McCoy, Ice Cream Cone...........................$45.00
McCoy, Indian, brown (+).........................$250.00
McCoy, Indian, majolica $350.00
McCoy, Jack-O'-Lantern $500.00
McCoy, Kangaroo, blue $250.00
McCoy, Keebler Tree House $70.00
McCoy, Kettle, bronze, 1961 ....$40.00
McCoy, Kissing Penguins $100.00
McCoy, Kitten on Basketweave $90.00
McCoy, Kittens (2) on Low Basket $600.00
McCoy, Kittens on Ball of Yarn......................$85.00
McCoy, Koala Bear $85.00
McCoy, Kookie Kettle, black........................$35.00
McCoy, Lamb on Basketweave $90.00
McCoy, Lemon $75.00
McCoy, Leprechaun, minimum value (+)...............$1,800.00
McCoy, Liberty Bell $75.00
McCoy, Little Clown $75.00
McCoy, Lollipops................................$80.00
McCoy, Mac Dog $95.00
McCoy, Mammy, Cookies on base, white w/cold paint (+) ..$150.00
McCoy, Mammy w/Cauliflower, G paint, minimum value (+). $1,100.00
McCoy, Milk Can, Spirit of '76 ....$45.00
McCoy, Modern..................................$65.00
McCoy, Monk...................................$50.00
McCoy, Mother Goose $95.00
McCoy, Mouse on Clock $40.00
McCoy, Mr & Mrs Owl $90.00
McCoy, Mushroom on Stump $55.00
McCoy, Nursery, decal of Humpty Dumpty, from $70 to....$80.00
McCoy, Oaken Bucket, from $25 to $45.00

McCoy, Orange..$55.00
McCoy, Owl, brown $70.00
McCoy, Pear, 1952..$85.00
McCoy, Pears on Basketweave.......................$70.00
McCoy, Penguin, yellow or aqua...................$95.00
McCoy, Pepper, yellow....................................$40.00
McCoy, Picnic Basket......................................$75.00
McCoy, Pig, winking......................................$250.00

McCoy, Pillsbury Dough Boy, from $40.00 to $50.00.

McCoy, Pine Cones on Basketweave $70.00
McCoy, Pineapple $80.00
McCoy, Pineapple, Modern $90.00
McCoy, Pirate's Chest $95.00
McCoy, Popeye, cylinder......................................$150.00
McCoy, Potbelly Stove, black $30.00
McCoy, Puppy, w/sign $85.00
McCoy, Quaker Oats, rare, minimum value $700.00
McCoy, Raggedy Ann $110.00
McCoy, Red Barn, cow in door, rare, minimum value $150.00
McCoy, Rooster, white, 1970-74..........................$60.00
McCoy, Rooster, 1955-57 ....$95.00
McCoy, Round w/hand-painted leaves..................$40.00
McCoy, Sad Clown $85.00
McCoy, Snoopy on Doghouse (+), marked United Features
    Syndicate $150.00
McCoy, Snow Bear..$75.00
McCoy, Spaniel in Doghouse, bird finial $250.00
McCoy, Stagecoach, minimum value....................$650.00
McCoy, Strawberry, 1955-57 ....$65.00
McCoy, Strawberry, 1971-75 ....$45.00
McCoy, Teapot, 1972..$60.00
McCoy, Tepee, slant top.......................................$250.00
McCoy, Tepee, straight top (+).............................$200.00
McCoy, Thinking Puppy, #0272 ....$40.00
McCoy, Tilt Pitcher, black w/roses $50.00
McCoy, Timmy Tortoise $45.00
McCoy, Tomato $60.00
McCoy, Touring Car $75.00

McCoy, Traffic Light..$50.00
McCoy, Tudor Cookie House $95.00
McCoy, Tulip on Flowerpot $100.00
McCoy, Turkey, green, rare color......................$250.00
McCoy, Turkey, natural colors..........................$250.00
McCoy, Upside Down Bear, panda $50.00
McCoy, WC Fields...$150.00
McCoy, Wedding Jar..$90.00
McCoy, Windmill $100.00
McCoy, Wishing Well $40.00
McCoy, Woodsy Owl..$175.00
McCoy, Wren House, side lid $125.00
McCoy, Yellow Mouse (head)............................$45.00
McCoy, Yosemite Sam, cylinder $125.00
Metlox, Ali Cat, from $175 to $200.00
Metlox, Ballerina Bear, from $100 to................$125.00
Metlox, Barrel (aka Apple Barrel), Red Apple lid, 3¾-qt, 11", from
    $65 to $75.00
Metlox, Basket, white w/basket lid, from $35 to.................$45.00
Metlox, Basket (aka Cookie Basket), Natural; w/cookie lid, 10½",
    from $35 to $45.00
Metlox, Beau Bear, from $60 to $75.00
Metlox, Bubbles Hippo, yellow & green, minimum value .$350.00
Metlox, Bucky Beaver, from $125 to..................$150.00
Metlox, Chicken (Mother Hen), white, from $100 to $125.00
Metlox, Children of the World, 2-qt, from $125 to..........$150.00

Metlox, Circus Bear, rare, from $175.00 to $225.00. (Photo courtesy Joyce and Fred Roerig)

Metlox, Clown, yellow, 3-qt, from $125 to........................$150.00
Metlox, Cub Scout, from $475 to $500.00
Metlox, Daisy Cookie Canister, 3½-qt, from $125 to........$150.00
Metlox, Daisy Topiary Cookie Jar, 3½-qt, from $125 to....$150.00
Metlox, Debutante, blue or pink dress, minimum value $400.00
Metlox, Drummer Boy, 2½-qt, from $425 to $450.00
Metlox, Egg Basket, from $175 to $200.00

Metlox, Ferdinand Calf, minimum value $900.00
Metlox, Flamingo, minimum value................................$350.00
Metlox, Gingham Dog, blue, from $175 to $200.00
Metlox, Granada Green, 3-qt, from $35 to $45.00
Metlox, Grape, from $200 to...$250.00
Metlox, Green w/Daisy lid, from $35 to $45.00
Metlox, Happy the Clown, minimum value.....................$350.00
Metlox, Hen & Chick, minimum value............................$350.00
Metlox, Jolly Chef, blue & black eyes, 11", from $375 to..$400.00
Metlox, Kangaroo, 11¼", minimum value $1,000.00
Metlox, Lamb, white, from $275 to $300.00
Metlox, Lighthouse, from $275 to $300.00
Metlox, Loveland, from $65 to $75.00
Metlox, Lucy Goose, from $125 to $150.00
Metlox, Mediereé, beige, gold, green or orange, ea from $35
    to $45.00
Metlox, Merry-Go-Round, from $250 to....................$275.00
Metlox, Noah's Ark, color glazed, from $225 to.............$250.00
Metlox, Owl, blue, 2½-qt, from $125 to $150.00
Metlox, Pear, green or yellow, from $125 to.................$150.00
Metlox, Rabbit on Cabbage, 3-qt, 10", from $125 to........$150.00
Metlox, Red Apple, 3½-qt, 9½", from $75 to $85.00
Metlox, Rex-Tyrannosaurus Rex, aqua, French Blue, rose or yellow,
    ea from $150 to $175.00
Metlox, Salty Pelican, from $200 to $225.00
Metlox, Scrub Woman Mammy, minimum value $1,500.00
Metlox, Slenderella Pig, from $125 to $150.00
Metlox, Space Rocket, 12⅞", minimum value..................$750.00
Napco, Spaceship, space-man finial................................$900.00
North American Ceramics, Airplane, movable propeller $300.00
Omnibus, Cabbage Patch Rabbit, c OCI, paper label, from $25
    to $35.00
Omnibus, Humpty Dumpty, c OCI, paper label, from $40 to. $50.00
Pan American Art, Bartender $175.00
Pfaltzgraff Pottery Co, Derby Dan $250.00
Pitman-Dreitzer & Co, Albert Apple, from $90 to $115.00
Red Wing, Carousel, unmarked, from $725 to $775.00
RedWing, Friar Tuck, green, marked, from $250 to $300.00
Red Wing, Grapes, green, from $150 to $175.00
Red Wing, King of Tarts, multicolored, marked (+), from $850
    to... $950.00
Red Wing, King of Tarts, white, unmarked, minimum value . $500.00
Red Wing, Peasant design, embossed & painted figures on brown,
    tall, from $90 to $125.00
Red Wing, Pierre (chef), blue, from $175 to $225.00
Regal, Cat, from $425 to $475.00
Regal, Churn Boy $250.00
Regal, Clown, green collar, from $500 to $600.00
Regal, Davy Crockett, from $525 to............................$575.00
Regal, Diaper Pin Pig, from $400 to...........................$500.00
Regal, Dutch Girl, from $650 to.................................$750.00
Regal, FiFi Poodle, minimum value $500.00
Regal, Fisherman, from $650 to...................................$720.00
Regal, French Chef, from $475 to................................$525.00
Regal, Goldilocks (+), from $200 to............................$300.00
Regal, Harpo Marx $1,080.00
Regal, Hubert Lion, minimum value $1,000.00

Regal, Little Miss Muffet, from $200 to............................$275.00
Regal, Majorette, from $400 to.....................................$500.00
Regal, Oriental Lady w/Baskets, from $725 to..................$775.00
Regal, Peek-a-Boo (+), from $925 to...............................$975.00
Regal, Quaker Oats, from $100 to.................................$125.00
Regal, Rocking Horse, from $275 to..............................$325.00
Regal, Three Bears...$175.00
Regal, Toby Cookies, no mark, from $675 to $725.00
Regal, Tulip, from $200 to...$225.00
Regal, Uncle Mistletoe...$765.00
Robinson Ransbottom, Bud, Army Man, brown, 1942-43, 12",
    from $150 to $175.00
Robinson Ransbottom, Doughboy Head, thinning paint/stains .$75.00
Robinson Ransbottom, Doughgirl Head, thinning paint/stains..$75.00
Robinson Ransbottom, Dutch Girl, gold trim, 1956, 12", from
    $250 to $275.00
Robinson Ransbottom, Frosty the Snowman, from $325 to.$375.00
Robinson Ransbottom, Hootie Owl, from $100 to...........$125.00
Robinson Ransbottom, Jack, sailor in black, EX $200.00
Robinson Ransbottom, Log w/Squirrel, from $250 to $350.00
Robinson Ransbottom, Sheriff Pig, gold trim, from $175 to.$200.00

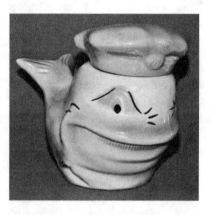

Robinson Ransbottom, Whale, from $1,000.00 to $1,075.00. (Photo courtesy Ermagene Westfall)

Sailor Elephant, Treasure Craft, from $30 to........................$40.00
Shawnee, Basketweave, decal, USA, 7½", from $125 ....$150.00
Shawnee, Drum Major, USA 10, 10", from $575 to..........$600.00
Shawnee, Dutch Boy (Happy), double-striped pants, USA, from
    $550 to $600.00
Shawnee, Great Northern Boy, Great Northern USA 1025, from
    $475 to $500.00
Shawnee, Great Northern Girl, dark green, Great Northern USA
    1026, from $475 to $500.00
Shawnee, Jack Tar, gold trim, black hair, USA, 12", from $1,100
    to $1,150.00
Shawnee, Jumbo Elephant, red or blue bow tie, cold paint, USA,
    12", from $200 to...$250.00
Shawnee, Little Chef, caramel, USA, 8½", from $17 to $200.00
Shawnee, Muggsy, green bow, rare, from $1,600 to $1,800.00
Shawnee, Pennsylvania Dutch, USA, 8¼", from $275 to...$300.00
Shawnee, Puss 'n Boots, gold & decals, long tail, marked Puss 'n
    Boots, 10¼" $640.00
Shawnee, Smiley the Pig, green neckerchief, USA, from $180 to.$200.00
Shawnee, Winnie the Pig, blue collar, USA, from $375 to.$425.00
Sierra Vista, Circus Wagon, white w/lion peering through cage, c
    1957, from $65 to $75.00

Sierra Vista, Elephant, gray, sitting w/trunk in the air, from $60 to **$70.00**

Sierra Vista, Poodle, gray w/pink bow tie, c 1956, from $100 to ..**$125.00**

Sierra Vista, Rooster, brown, from $30 to **$40.00**

Sierra Vista, Squirrel, red jacket w/green collar, holding a nut, from $50 to **$60.00**

Sierra Vista, Stagecoach, brown, c 1956, from $150 to **$175.00**

Sierra Vista, Dog on Drum, from $40 to **$50.00**

Sierra Vista, Train, smiling face, from $50 to **$60.00**

Sigma, Beaver Fireman **$250.00**

Sigma, Fat Cat **$275.00**

Sigma, Mrs Tiggy-Winkle...**$300.00**

Sigma, Popcorn Vendor, paper label, from $325 to...........**$350.00**

Sigma, Rag Doll **$175.00**

Star Jars Cowardly Lion, from $250 to **$300.00**

Taiwan, Harley-Davidson Gas Tank, from $75 to.............**$100.00**

Terrace Ceramics, Corn, yellow & green, #4299, USA, from $35 to **$45.00**

Treasure Craft, Bart Simpson, USA mark only, from $100 to. **$110.00**

Treasure Craft, Baseball Bunny, LA Dodgers, from $30 to...**$35.00**

Treasure Craft, Birdhouse, light green w/blue trim, bird finial on roof, from $35 to **$45.00**

Treasure Craft, Coffeepot, brown w/gold, c Made in USA, from $20 to **$25.00**

Treasure Craft, Conestoga, wood stain, from $32 to **$36.00**

Treasure Craft, Cookiesaurus, from $32 to........................**$38.00**

Treasure Craft, Cookieville **$45.00**

Treasure Craft, Cowboy, from $40 to **$45.00**

Treasure Craft, Cowboy Boot, c USA, from $30 to.............**$35.00**

Treasure Craft, Dale Evans, McMe Prod, limited edition, from $145 to **$165.00**

Treasure Craft, Disney Channel, cylinder, from $80 to........**$90.00**

Treasure Craft, Duck Decoy, from $35 to **$45.00**

Treasure Craft, Eight Ball, Made in USA, from $45 to **$55.00**

Treasure Craft, Elmer, elm tree, Rose Petal Place, minimum value **$500.00**

Treasure Craft, Famous Amos, cookie bag, from $65 to.......**$75.00**

Treasure Craft, Goofy, from $80 to **$90.00**

Treasure Craft, Grandfather Clock, white w/key finial, Made in USA, from $35 to... **$45.00**

Treasure Craft, Hobo, Made in USA, from $35 to..............**$45.00**

Treasure Craft, Ice Wagon, from $32 to **$38.00**

Treasure Craft, Jukebox, 1st version, from $55 to **$65.00**

Treasure Craft, Mouse, yellow outfit w/white hat, c USA, from $35 to **$45.00**

Treasure Craft, Nick at Night Television, Nickelodeon **$600.00**

Treasure Craft, Noah's Ark, Don Winton design, from $30 to . **$35.00**

Treasure Craft, Owl, Made in USA, from $30 to.................**$40.00**

Treasure Craft, Pirate Bust, Made in USA, from $225 to...**$275.00**

Treasure Craft, Puppy, blue hat & yellow neckerchief, c USA, from $35 to **$45.00**

Treasure Craft, Radio, Made in USA, from $35 to..............**$45.00**

Treasure Craft, Rocking Horse, Made in USA, from $35 to . **$45.00**

Treasure Craft, Seymour J Snailsworth, green snail in dark green sweater w/beige shell, Rose-Petal Place, from $325 to.**$375.00**

Treasure Craft, Soccer Ball, c Made in USA, from $25 to....**$35.00**

Treasure Craft, Spaniel, 1961, from $30 to **$35.00**

Treasure Craft, Sugar With Button Eyes, from $40.00 to $50.00. (Photo courtesy Ermagene Westfall)

Treasure Craft, Toucan, from $35 to **$40.00**

Treasure Craft, Trolley, Made in USA, from $40 to.............**$50.00**

Treasure Craft, Tug Boat, from $60 to **$70.00**

Tulip Time, 2-qt, from $65 to..**$85.00**

Twin Winton, Bear, TW-84, 7x12" **$50.00**

Twin Winton, Cable Car, TW-98, 7x12" **$75.00**

Twin Winton, Cookie Barn, TW-41, 8x12" **$80.00**

Twin Winton, Cow, TW-69, 8½x13½" **$75.00**

Twin Winton, Dinosaur, TW-51, 8x13" **$350.00**

Twin Winton, Duck, TW-79, 9x12" **$150.00**

Twin Winton, Dumbo, 12" **$250.00**

Twin Winton, Elf Bakery, 8¾x12" **$90.00**

Twin Winton, Foo Dog, TW-51, 8x12" **$400.00**

Twin Winton, Frog, TW-73, 8x9" **$350.00**

Twin Winton, Gorilla, TW-39, 8x12" **$350.00**

Twin Winton, Hippo, TW-67, 7x11" **$400.00**

Twin Winton, Howard Johnson's, 10x12"........................**$3,000.00**

Twin Winton, Noah's Ark, TW-94, 9½x10" **$75.00**

Twin Winton, Pirate Fox, TW-46, 8½x11" **$85.00**

Twin Winton, Poodle, TW-64, 7½x13" **$85.00**

Twin Winton, Stove, TW-65, 8x13" **$75.00**

Twin Winton, Teddy Bear, TW-53, 8x10" **$85.00**

Twin Winton, Walrus, TW-63, 10x11".............................**$375.00**

Warner Bros, Animaniacs Chocolate Cookies, TM & C94, Made in China, from $75 to... **$95.00**

Warner Bros, Foghorn-Leghorn, TM & 1993 Warner Bros Inc... Taiwan, from $125 to.. **$150.00**

Warner Bros, Michael Jordan & Bugs Bunny Space Jam, TM & c 1996 Warner Bros, from $125 to............................. **$150.00**

Warner Bros, Olympic Torch **$95.00**

Warner Bros, Porky Pig, in green chair, 1975....................**$110.00**

Coors Rosebud Dinnerware

Golden, Colorado, was the site for both the Coors Brewing Company and the Coors Porcelain Company, each founded by the same man, Adolph Coors. The pottery's inception was in 1910, and in the early years they manufactured various ceramic products such as industrial needs, dinnerware, vases, and figurines; but their most famous line and the one we want to tell you about is 'Rosebud.'

The Rosebud 'Cook 'n Serve' line was introduced in 1934. It's very easy to spot, and after you've once seen a piece, you'll be able to recognize it instantly. It was made in solid colors — rose, blue, green, yellow, ivory, and orange. The rose bud and leaves are embossed and hand painted in contrasting colors. There are nearly 50 different pieces to collect, and bargains can still be found; but prices are accelerating, due to increased collector interest. For more information we recommend *Coors Rosebud Pottery* by Robert Schneider.

Note: Yellow and white tends to craze and stain. Our prices are for pieces with minimal crazing and no staining. To evaluate pieces in blue, add 10% to the prices below; add 15% for items in ivory. Rosebud is prone to have factory flaws, and the color on the rosebuds may be of poor quality. When either of these factors are present, deduct 10%.

Advisor: Rick Spencer (See Directory, Silverplated Flatware)

Apple baker, w/lid	$45.00
Baker, lg	$40.00
Baker, tab handles, 7"	$20.00
Bean pot, handles, lg	$70.00

Bowl, batter; large, $65.00.

Bowl, batter; sm	$30.00
Bowl, cream soup; 4"	$22.00
Bowl, mixing; 6-pt	$50.00
Bowl, oatmeal	$22.00
Cake plate, 11"	$30.00
Casserole, Dutch; 1¾-pt	$50.00
Casserole, French, 3¾-pt	$45.00
Casserole, triple service, lg, 7-pt	$55.00
Honey pot, no spoon	$80.00
Loaf pan	$40.00
Pitcher, w/lid, lg	$150.00
Pitcher, water; no stopper	$70.00
Pitcher, water; w/stopper	$120.00
Plate, bread; 7¼"	$8.00
Plate, dinner; 9¼"	$23.00
Ramekin	$45.00
Salt & pepper shakers, round, pr	$25.00

Saucer, 5½"	$5.00
Shirred-egg dish	$25.00
Sugar shaker	$60.00
Teapot, 6-cup	$125.00

Platter, 12x9", $38.00.

Coppercraft Guild

During the 1960s and 1970s, the Coppercraft Guild Company of Taunton, Massachusetts, produced a variety of copper and copper-tone items which were sold through the home party plan. Though copper items such as picture frames, flowerpots, teapots, candleholders, trays, etc., were their mainstay, they also made molded wall decorations such as mirror-image pairs of birds on branches and large floral-relief plaques that they finished in metallic copper-tone paint. Some of their pictures were a combination of the copper-tone composition molds mounted on a sheet copper background. When uncompromised by chemical damage or abuse, the finish they used on their copper items has proven remarkably enduring, and many of these pieces still look new today. Collectors are beginning to take notice. Unless otherwise described, the items listed below are made of copper.

Clock, copper face with embossed acorns and oak leaves, from $15.00 to $20.00.

Bank, bell shape, slot on side, wooden handle, 8½x3⅛", from $15 ..... **$20.00**

Bowl, embossed w/floral on sides, 1½x11", from $25 to......**$35.00**

Bowl, salad/fruit; footed, 4¼x9"..**$55.00**

Bread tray, 12x6¾"...**$20.00**

Butter dish, rectangular w/scalloped base, ¼-lb...................**$27.50**

Candelabrum, 4-arm, 5-light, MIB......................................**$40.00**

Candleholder, brass finger loop, 6½" dia or 4" dia, ea.........**$15.00**

Candleholder, leaf shape, wall hanging, ring at bottom, 13x7", ea..**$15.00**

Candleholders, hurricane lamp shape w/glass globes, 9½" (w/globe), pr..**$30.00**

Candlesticks, tapered bottom, 4x3¾", pr from $15 to.........**$20.00**

Coffee set, tall pot w/stick handle, creamer & sugar bowl on rectangular tray, from $35 to...**$45.00**

Creamer & sugar bowl, 2¾", pr..**$15.00**

Fondue pot, w/lid & metal warming stand, 5½" dia, from $25 to...**$30.00**

Gravy boat, w/stand...**$27.50**

Ice bucket, w/liner, ornate handles, 8", from $25 to...........**$35.00**

Leaf dish, 9x6"...**$22.00**

Mirror, copper paint on pressed molded plastic, eagle finial, 21x15"...**$48.00**

Mirror, copper paint on pressed molded plastic, 22x9½".....**$35.00**

Napkin holder, 4⅜x7", from $15 to.....................................**$20.00**

Napkin rings, floral engraving around band, 1½x1½", MIB, from $18 to..**$22.00**

Piggy bank, all brass, including, ears, feet & tail, 5", MIB...**$25.00**

Planter, applied brass figure of lady at spinning wheel, 10" long, from $9.00 to $12.00.

Planter, pot hangs from 3 brass chains suspended from simple hanger...**$18.00**

Punch set, 12" bowl & 6 3" cups on 18" dia tray.................**$60.00**

Salad servers, 12½", 12¼"...**$25.00**

Salt & pepper shakers, tapered bottoms, S&P shape in holes on top, 3", pr..**$15.00**

Stein, 5x3¼"..**$15.00**

Teapot, w/bail handle, Solid Copper Made in USA, 4x5⅛"..**$20.00**

Wall decoration, fruit in relief, copper paint on pressed plastic, #7221/#7222, 20¼x5¾", pr.......................................**$15.00**

Wall decoration, owls on tree limb in relief, copper paint on pressed molded plastic, 11x9½"......................................**$20.00**

Wall decoration, Raggedy Ann & Andy by well, copper paint on press molded plastic, c Bobbs-Merrill, 1977, 13x14¾"..**$15.00**

Wall decoration, sailing ship, copper paint on press molded plastic, c MCMLXII, 21x27½"...**$37.50**

Wall decoration, Traveler's Rest, stagecoach before Riverside Inn, copper paint on pressed molded plastic, 10x14"...........**$20.00**

Wall plaque, acorns & leaves surround lady w/2 children & sm dog, copper paint on pressed molded plastic, 13" dia...........**$20.00**

Corkscrews

When the corkscrew was actually developed remains uncertain (the first patent was issued in 1795), but it most likely evolved from the worm on a ramrod or cleaning rod used to draw wadding from a gun barrel and found to be equally effective in the sometimes difficult task of removing corks from wine bottles. Inventors scurried to develop a better product, and as a result, thousands of variations have been made and marketed. This abundance and diversification invariably came to attract collectors, whose ranks are burgeoning. Many of today's collectors concentrate their attention on one particular type — those with advertising, a specific patent, or figural pullers, for instance.

Our advisor has written a very informative book, *Bull's Pocket Guide to Corkscrews* (Schiffer), with hundreds and full-color illustrations and current values.

Advisor: Donald A. Bull (See Directory, Corkscrews)

Richard Recknagle's 1899 German Patent, from $250.00 to $300.00; Cotter pin in shank above worm (impractical design), from $80.00 to $100.00. (Photo courtesy Donald A. Bull)

Advertising, Columbia Brewing Co w/William Williamson's 1897 American patent bell, from $30 to................................**$50.00**

Advertising, North Brewing Co imprinted on barrel shape, wooden handle, twisted wire worm, from $30 to.......................**$40.00**

Barrel, chrome, closed w/handle marked ITALY, from $30 to.**$40.00**

Double-lever, Clown, Italian aluminum, 1950s-60s, rare, from $150 to...**$200.00**

Figural, Bar Bum, aluminum, from $40 to **$50.00**

Figural, cast fish swallowing worm, marked JB, from $50 to .. **$60.00**

Figural, cat playing fiddle, brass, 2-finger pull, English, from $15 to **$50.00**

Figural, doves w/grapes, Denmark, from $125 to **$150.00**

Figural, French champagne bottle w/hollow back, folding worm, cap lifter & champagne cork puller, from $75 to **$100.00**

Figural, seal, copper, wood ball removes to reveal corkscrew, from $75 to **$100.00**

Figural, smoking sailor's head, carved wood, from $70 to **$90.00**

Finger pull, metal, heart-shaped handle, from $75 to......... **$100.00**

Key, brass, Holland, from $20 to **$30.00**

Picnic, sterling sheath w/cap lifter, Muller & Schmidt, Solingen, Germany, from $75 to **$125.00**

Pocket folder, Indian head in headdress, carved & painted wood, from $40 to **$50.00**

Prong puller, San Bri, black metal w/plastic sheath, from $30 to **$40.00**

Roundlet, nickel-plated, threaded case, from $150 to **$250.00**

Silver, corkscrew hidden in handle, from $75 to **$125.00**

T-handle, clawfoot handle w/bulbed shank, from $100 to . **$125.00**

T-handle, wood, direct pull, from $10 to **$75.00**

T-handle, wood w/brush, from $50 to **$60.00**

2-finger pull, plastic, horse heads form handle, amber, from $90 to **$100.00**

Corning Ware

Corning Ware was a high-fired glassware capable of going from freezer to oven or range top without fear of breakage. The first to hit the market was the Blue Cornflower line, which was made from 1958 until late in the 1970s in a very extensive range of cooking and serving items, some of which were electric. Lids were made of clear glass, and from 1958 until 1962, the handle was shaped like a bar, tapering on each side. Collectors refer to this type as the 'fin' handle. After 1962 the 'fin' handle was replaced with a simple knob.

Spice O' Life (introduced in 1982 and discontinued in 1987) brought a French flair to the market, as nearly each item carried a French inscription beneath the colorful design of vegetables and herbs. It was the company's second-best seller after Blue Cornflower.

Floral Bouquet (introduced in 1971), Country Festival (1975), Blue Heather (1976), and Wildflower (1977) are just a few of the many other lines of freezer-to-range cookware that were made of this space-age material. To learn more about them, we recommend *The Complete Guide to Corning Ware and Visions Cookware* by Kyle Coroneos (Collector Books). The author urges collectors to be critical of condition. Because the market has been relatively untapped until recently, you should be able to find mint-condition examples — possibly even some sill unused and in their original boxes.

Black Starburst, percolator, 1959-62, 6-cup, from $15 to **$20.00**

Black Trefoil, chafing dish, 1961, 2½-qt, from $10 to.......... **$12.00**

Black Trefoil, percolator, 1963-65, 9-cup, from $20 to **$25.00**

Blue Cornflower, broil & serve platter, 1961-71, 16", from $8 to **$10.00**

Blue Cornflower, cake dish, 1968-71, 8" dia, from $15 to... **$20.00**

Blue Cornflower, cake/utility dish, sq, 1968-?, 8", from $12 to .. **$15.00**

Blue Cornflower, chicken fryer, w/clear knob lid, 1966-71, 10", from $15 to **$20.00**

Blue Cornflower, double boiler, 1961-65, 2½-qt bowl w/2-qt insert, from $20 to **$25.00**

Blue Cornflower, drip coffeemaker, uses filter, 1960-75, 6-cup, from $8 to **$10.00**

Blue Cornflower, drip coffeemaker, 1965-71, 4-cup, from $15 to **$20.00**

Blue Cornflower, electromatic percolator, 1961-66, 10-cup, from $25 to **$30.00**

Blue Cornflower, electromatic skillet, 1961-71, 10", from $35 to **$40.00**

Blue Cornflower, Menu-ette, 1966-?, w/clear knob lid, 1-pt, from $6 to **$8.00**

Blue Cornflower, party buffet w/candle warmer & clear knob lid, 1961-72, 1¾-qt, from $8 to.. **$10.00**

Blue Cornflower, petite pan, 1971-?, 1¾-cup, from $2 to...... **$4.00**

Blue Cornflower, petite pan, 1971-87, 2¾-cup, from $3 to ... **$5.00**

Blue Cornflower, range-top saucepan, 1980-?, w/clear knob lid, 1-qt, from $15 to **$20.00**

Blue Cornflower, range-top saucepot, 1980-?, w/clear knob lid, 5-qt, from $40 to **$50.00**

Blue Cornflower, royal buffet w/candle warmer, 1961-72, 2½-qt, from $12 to **$15.00**

Blue Cornflower, saucepan, 1957-71, 1½-qt, w/fin or clear knob lid, from $6 to **$8.00**

Blue Cornflower, saucepan, 1972-87, 5-qt, from $40 to...... **$50.00**

Blue Cornflower, skillet, w/clear knob lid, 1957-71, 9", from $10 to **$12.00**

Blue Cornflower, teakettle, 1964-?, 2-qt (8-cup), from $12 to. **$15.00**

Butterscotch, Dutch oven, 1969, 1970, 4-qt, from $10 to... **$12.00**

Butterscotch, party buffet w/candle warmer, 1969, w/clear lid & green knob, 1¾-qt, from $12 to.................................. **$15.00**

Country Festival, baking dish, w/clear knob lid, 1975-76, 1½-qt, from $6 to **$8.00**

Country Festival, cake dish, sq, 1975-76, 8", from $12 to... **$15.00**

Country Festival, saucepan, w/clear knob lid, 1975-76, 5-qt, from $35 to **$40.00**

Country Festival, skillet, w/clear knob lid, 1975-76, 8", from $12 to **$15.00**

Country Festival, teapot, 1975-76, 6-cup, from $15 to........ **$20.00**

Harvest Gold, saucepan, w/clear knob lid, 1971, 1¾-qt, from $12 to **$15.00**

Harvest Gold, saucepan, w/clear knob lid, 1971, 1-qt, from $10 to **$12.00**

Merry Mushroom, saucepan, w/clear knob lid, 1971-?, 8½-qt, from $5 to **$7.00**

Merry Mushroom, teapot, 1971-?, 6-cup, from $12 to **$15.00**

Nature's Bounty, deluxe skillet w/serving cradle, w/clear knob lid, 1971, 10", from $15 to.. **$20.00**

Nature's Bounty, saucepot w/serving cradle, w/clear knob lid, 1971, from $15 to **$20.00**

Platinum Filigree, electromatic percolator, 1966-68, 6-cup, from $15 to **$20.00**

Platinum Filigree, party buffet w/candle warmer, w/clear knob lid, 1966, 1¾-qt, from $8 to.. **$10.00**

Renaissance, percolator, 1970, 9-cup, from $20 to..............**$25.00**

Shadow Iris, casserole, 1986-1993, w/clear knob lid, 1½-qt, from $12 to **$15.00**

Shadow Iris, skillet, 1988-?, open, 7", from $10 to **$12.00**

Spice O' Life, loaf dish, 1974-?, 2-qt, from $10 to............**$12.00**

Spice O' Life, open roaster, 1974-75, 13", from $12 to.......**$15.00**

Spice O' Life, saucepan, w/clear knob lid, 1972-83, 4-qt, from $20 to **$25.00**

Spice O' Life, saucepan, w/clear knob lid, 1972-87, 1½-qt, from $10 to **$12.00**

Spice O' Life, teapot, 1972-87, 6-cup, from $12 to **$15.00**

Wildflower, open roaster, 1978-84, 14x11½", from $12 to..**$15.00**

Wildflower, petite pan, w/clear knob lid, 1974-84, 1½-cup, from $2 to **$4.00**

Wildflower, saucepot, w/clear knob lid, 1978-84, 5-qt, from $50 to **$60.00**

Wildflower, teapot, 1977-84, 6-cup, from $10 to **$12.00**

Merry Mushroom, covered saucepan, 1971 – ?, from $3.00 to $5.00. (Photo courtesy Klyle Coroneos)

Cottage Ware

Made by several companies, cottage ware is a line of ceramic table and kitchen accessories, each piece styled as a cozy cottage with a thatched roof. At least four English potteries made the ware, and you'll find pieces marked 'Japan' as well as 'Occupied Japan.' You'll also find pieces styled as windmills and water wheels. The pieces preferred by collectors are marked 'Price Brothers' and 'Occupied Japan.' They're compatible in coloring as well as in styling, and values run about the same. Items marked simply 'Japan' are worth considerably less.

Bank, double slot, Price Brothers, 4½x3½x5", from $60 to..**$70.00**

Bell, Price Brothers, minimum value, from $50 to **$60.00**

Biscuit jar, wicker handle, Maruhon Ware, Occupied Japan, 6½", $65 to **$80.00**

Biscuit jar, wicker handle, Price Bros, 6½", from $65 to **$75.00**

Bowl, salad; Price Brothers, 4x9", from $65 to.....................**$75.00**

Butter dish, cottage interior (fireplace), Japan, 6¾x5" **$60.00**

Butter dish, oval, Burlington Ware, 6" **$60.00**

Butter dish, Price Brothers/Kensington, from $50 to **$65.00**

Butter dish, round, Beswick, England, 3½x6", from $75 to.**$85.00**

Butter dish, sq green base, Old England by Rubian Art Pottery Grimwades, 7½" L...**$85.00**

Butter pat, embossed cottage, rectangular, Occupied Japan..**$20.00**

Cheese dish, Staffordshire Croft Hand Made..., 3¾x7"........**$50.00**

Chocolate pot, Price Brothers, 9½", from $60 to **$80.00**

Condiment set, mustard, 2½" shakers on 5" handled leaf tray, Price Brothers **$75.00**

Condiment set, mustard pot, salt & pepper, tray, row arrangement, Price Brothers/Kensington, 6"........................**$50.00**

Condiment set, mustard pot, salt & pepper shakers in row arrangement on tray, Price Brothers, 7¾", from $50 to...........**$65.00**

Condiment set, 3-part cottage on shaped tray w/applied bush, Price Brothers, 4½", from $75 to.........................**$85.00**

Cookie jar, pink, brown & green, sq, Japan, 8½x5½" **$65.00**

Cookie jar, windmill, wicker handle, Price Brothers...........**$125.00**

Cookie jar/canister, cylindrical, Price Brothers, 8½x5", from $65 to **$80.00**

Cookie/biscuit jar, Occupied Japan, 6½", from $65 to.........**$80.00**

Cookie/biscuit jar, Price Brothers, 6½", from $65 to **$80.00**

Covered dish, Occupied Japan, sm....................................**$40.00**

Creamer, windmill, Occupied Japan, 2⅝" **$30.00**

Creamer & sugar bowl, Price Brothers, 2½x4½", from $40 to . **$50.00**

Cup and saucer, 2½", 4½", from $40.00 to $50.00; Chocolate cup and saucer, 3¾", 5⅜", $35.00. (Both are made by Price Brothers.)

Demitasse pot, Price Brothers, 6x6¼", from $80 to **$110.00**

Egg cup set, Price Brothers, 4 on 6" sq tray, from $55 to.....**$65.00**

Egg cup set, 4 (double) on 5½" sq tray, from $55 to...........**$65.00**

Gravy boat & tray, Price Brothers, rare, from $200 to **$250.00**

Grease jar, Occupied Japan, from $25 to............................**$38.00**

Hot water pot, Westminster, England, 8¼x4" **$50.00**

Marmalade, Price Brothers, 4", from $35 to **$45.00**

Marmalade & jelly, 2 conjoined houses, Price Brothers, 5x7", from $65 to **$85.00**

Mug, Price Brothers, 3⅞", from $20 to...............................**$25.00**

Mug, Price Brothers, 4½", from $25 to...............................**$35.00**

Pin tray, Price Brothers, 4" dia...**$30.00**

Pitcher, embossed cottage, lg flower on handle, Price Brothers/Kensington, lg, from $80 to.......................................**$100.00**

Pitcher, tankard; round, 7 windows on front, Price Brothers, 7½", from $65 to **$85.00**

Pitcher, tendril applied to angular handle, Price, 8x7", from $65 to **$75.00**

Plate, 7", from $9 to $12.00
Platter, oval, Price Brothers, 11¾x7½", from $45 to $65.00
Reamer, Japan $150.00
Sugar cube box/butter dish, roof as lid, Price Brothers, 4x3x6½" L,
   from $55 to $70.00
Tea set, Japan, child's, serves 4............................$165.00
Teapot, Keele Street, w/creamer & sugar bowl, from $75 to .$95.00
Teapot, Occupied Japan, 6½", from $45 to.....................$55.00
Teapot, Price Brothers/Kensington, scarce size, 5x4½x3½", from $50
   to $65.00
Teapot, Price Brothers/Kensington, 6½x5¾x4", from $50 to..$65.00
Teapot, Ye Olde Fireside, Occupied Japan, 9x5", from $60 to.$75.00
Toast rack, 3-slot, Price Brothers, 3½", from $65 to $75.00
Toast rack, 4-slot, Price Brothers, 5½", from $65 to $85.00
Tumbler, Occupied Japan, 3½", set of 6.......................$65.00

Cow Creamers

Cow creamers (and milk pitchers) have been around since before the nineteenth century, but, of course, those are rare. By the early 1900s, they were becoming quite commonplace. In many of these older ones, the cow was standing on a platform (base) and very often had a lid. Not all cows on platforms are old, however, but it is a good indication of age. Examples from before WWII often were produced in England, Germany, and Japan.

Over the last 50 years there has been a slow revival of interest in these little cream dispensers, including the plastic Moo cows, made by Whirley Industries, U.S.A, that were used in cafes during the '50s. With the current popularity of anything cow-shaped, manufacturers have expanded the concept, and some creamers now are made with matching sugar bowls. If you want to collect only vintage examples, nowadays you'll have to check closely to make sure they're not new.

Germany, Delft, pre-1890, 10½" long, $300.00.

American, yellow ware body w/mottled brown, clear glaze w/crackle,
   free-standing, late 19th Century, 5⅜x10⅛"....................$95.00
Canada, brown & white w/blue flowers around neck, 5½x7½" ...$10.00
Czechoslovakia, bright orange w/black tail handle, seated, ceramic,
   pre-WWII, 4⅞x5½" $37.50
Czechoslovakia, orange splash over cream, w/black accents on ears &
   handle, seated, 3x4¾" $35.00

Czechoslovakia, orange w/black tail, seated, 4½"................$20.00
Delft, blue windmill scenes on white, 4½x7½" $45.00
England, blue calico & chintz transferware, Royal Crownford Co,
   recumbent, 3½x7¼"..$95.00
France, gold, free standing, tail over back as handle, 4½x6½" ..$37.00
Germany, brown & white w/black hooves, tail over back as handle,
   free-standing, 3¼x5⅛".......................................$50.00
Germany, gray w/muscular detail (shield marking underneath), free-
   standing, 5x7"..$10.00
Japan, multicolored pastels, yellow bell around neck, 4½x6"..$25.00
Japan, purple, brass bell around neck, label: Kenmar Japan,
   4x6"..$13.00
Japan, purple w/sm brass bell, label: Lugenes, 5x6½"..........$37.50
Japan, white w/floral design, recumbent, 1940s, 7½" L $10.00
Japan, yellow & orange floral design on sides, recumbent, label:
   Lenwile Ardalt Art Ware Japan #7254, 3½x6" $27.00
Jell-O premium, white w/decaled cherry, lemon, grape, lime &
   orange,4½x6½" $135.00
Unmarked, brown & white w/pink udders, tail over back as handle,
   free-standing, 7x3¾x2¼" $20.00
Unmarked, Delft w/windmill scene on 1 side, flowers on other, free-
   standing, 4x6½" $15.00
Unmarked, gold & white, free-standing, tail over back as handle,
   7½" L..$25.00
Unmarked, white, tail over back as handle, free-standing,
   4½x7"...$39.00

Unmarked, hand-painted decoration, 5½x8", from $40.00 to $45.00. (Photo courtesy Shirley Green)

Cowboy Character Memorabilia

When we come across what is now termed cowboy character toys and memorabilia, it rekindles warm memories of childhood days for those of us who once 'rode the range' (often our backyards) with these gallant heroes. Today we can really appreciate them for the positive role models they were. They sat tall in the saddle; reminded us never to tell an un-truth; to respect 'women-folk' as well as our elders, animal life, our flag, our country, and our teachers; to eat all the cereal placed before us in order to build strong bodies; to worship God; and have (above all else) strong values that couldn't be compromised. They were Gene, Roy, and Tex, along with a couple of dozen other names, who rode beautiful steeds such as Champion, Trigger, and White Flash.

They rode into a final sunset on the silver screen only to return and ride into our homes via television in the 1950s. The next decade found us caught up in more western adventures such as Bonanza, Wagon Train, The Rifleman, and many others. These set the stage for a second wave of toys, games, and western outfits.

Annie Oakley was one of only a couple of cowgirls in the corral; Wild Bill Elliott used to drawl, 'I'm a peaceable man'; Ben Cartwright, Adam, Hoss, and Little Joe provided us with thrills and laughter. Some of the earliest collectibles are represented by Roy's and Gene's 1920s predecessors — Buck Jones, Hoot Gibson, Tom Mix, and Ken Maynard. There were so many others, all of whom were very real to us in the 1930s – 1960s, just as their memories and values remain very real to us today.

Remember that few items of cowboy memorabilia have survived to the present in mint condition. When found, mint or near-mint items bring hefty prices, and they continue to escalate every year.

For more information we recommend these books: *Roy Rogers, Singing Cowboy Stars, Silver Screen Cowboys, Hollywood Cowboy Heroes*, and *Western Comics: A Comprehensive Reference*, all by Robert W. Phillips. Another good book is *Collector's Guide to Hopalong Cassidy Memorabilia* by Joseph J. Caro.

See also Toys, Guns; Toys, Rings.

Club/Newsletter: The Old Cowboy Picture Show (TOCPS)
George F. Coan and Leo Pando
P.O. Box 66
Camden, SC 29020
cowboy50@camden.net
www.cowboyshow.com
Subscription by donation

Club/Newsletter: Cowboy Collector
Joseph J. Caro, Publisher
P.O. Box 7486
Long Beach, CA 90807
Hoppycnn@aol.com

Club/Newsletter: Hopalong Cassidy Fan Club International
Hopalong Cassidy Newsletter
Laura Bates, Editor
6310 Friendship Dr.
New Concord, OH 43762-9708
LBates1205@cs.com

Club/Newsletter: The Lone Ranger Fan Club
The Silver Bullet
P.O. Box 1493
Longmont, CO 80502
theloneranger@worldnet.att.net
Membership ($30/US, $40/outside the US) includes newsletter, color photo, certificate, card, and silver bullet

Bat Masterson, cane, chrome-covered plastic handle w/name embossed across top, 1958, EX+ **$35.00**
Dale Evans, washcloth mitt, terry cloth w/color image of Dale, inscribed name & Queen of the West, EX **$25.00**

Daniel Boone, figure, painted plastic w/soft vinyl head, fur cap & powder horn, American Tradition Co, 1964, 5½", NM **$50.00**
Davy Crockett, binoculars, plastic, Harrison, MIB **$175.00**
Davy Crockett, Frontierland Pencil Case, brown vinyl holster w/ gun-shaped pencil case, 1950s, 8", VG **$50.00**
Davy Crockett, guitar, plastic w/yarn strap, multicolored paper litho label, windup to play music, Mattel, 14", EX **$50.00**
Davy Crockett, marionette, composition w/cloth outfit, 'Coonskin' cap, guitar & gun, Peter Puppet Playthings, 14", EX.. **$150.00**
Davy Crockett, pin, die-cast metal rectangle w/scalloped border, crossed swords embossed on front, NMOC **$65.00**
Davy Crockett, tie clip, copper-tone metal w/embossed image of musket & powder horn w/name, sq, 1950s, M **$18.00**
Davy Crockett, Woodburning Set, Frontier..., ATF/USA, MIB. **$175.00**
Gene Autry, figure, ceramic, caricature-style figure standing on horseshoe base w/faux signature, 1950s, 8½", EX... **$400.00**
Gene Autry, flashlight, Cowboy Lariat, EXIB **$100.00**
Gene Autry, wallet, leather w/zipper closure, image of Gene & Champion, Aristocrat, 1950s, VGIB **$75.00**
Gunsmoke, slippers, black vinyl w/yellow & red image of Matt, Chester & Doc, Columbia, 1959, NM+IB **$200.00**
Hopalong Cassidy, coin, front w/embossed image of Hoppy, back marked Good Luck From Hoppy, 1¼" dia, VG **$15.00**
Hopalong Cassidy, Crayon & Stencil Set, Transogram, 1950s, complete, some use, EXIB **$50.00**
Johnny Ringo, hand puppet, Laura (girlfriend), cloth body w/vinyl head, felt hands, Tops in Toys, 1959-60, 10", EX+ **$40.00**
Lone Ranger, guitar, heavy cardboard w/wooden neck, Jefferson, 1950s, 28½" L, EX **$100.00**
Lone Ranger, Hi-Yo Silver the Lone Ranger Target Game, Marx, EXIB, A **$65.00**
Lone Ranger, neck scarf & concho slide, purple silky material w/ images of Lone Ranger & Silver, 1940s-50s, EX **$50.00**
Lone Ranger, ring-toss, die-cut cardboard, complete, Rosebud Art, MIB **$250.00**
Lone Ranger, soap figure set, Lone Ranger, Tonto & Silver, Kerk, 1939, 4", VG **$50.00**
Lone Ranger, Target, litho tin w/metal support, Marx, TLR Inc, 1930s, 9½" sq, EX **$50.00**

Lone Ranger, tote bag, embossed white design on red vinyl, 1950s, EX, $175.00. (Photo courtesy Lee Felbinger)

Maverick, Oil Painting by Numbers, Hasbro, 1958, complete, partially used, EXIB **$75.00**

Red Rider, gloves, Playmates, brown, red & blue cloth, tag w/premium offers, Wells Lamont Corp & SS, 1950s, NM..**$30.00**

Rin-Tin-Tin, figure, Rinny, painted plaster w/black & bronze-tone finish, rhinestone eyes, 1939, 11x8x4", EX...................**$75.00**

Roy Rogers, bank, metal boot form w/copper finish, Almar Metal Arts Co, 1950s, 5½", EX **$75.00**

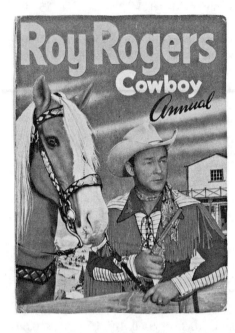

Roy Rogers, Cowboy Annual #6, British, 1956, $30.00.

Roy Rogers, flashlight, Signal Siren, tin, Usalite, 7", MIB..**$150.00**

Roy Rogers, lamp base, painted plaster figure of Roy on rearing Trigger on round base, Plasto, 1950s, 10½", EX+.......**$100.00**

Roy Rogers, postcard, image of Roy on rearing Trigger, acknowledges contest entry, Quaker Oats, 1948, NM **$50.00**

Roy Rogers, pull toy, horsedrawn covered wagon, paper litho on wood, removable cloth cover, NN Hill, 20", EX.........**$250.00**

Roy Rogers, scarf, red & gold silky material w/vignette graphics, King of the Cowboys, 1950s, 25x25", EX **$75.00**

Roy Rogers, telescope, plastic, H George, 9", MIB............**$200.00**

Roy Rogers, wagon train, plastic stagecoach w/driver & horses leading 3 litho tin wagons, windup, 14" L, VG, A............**$135.00**

Roy Rogers & Dale Evans, school tablets, Frontiers Inc, 1950s, 10x8", unused, EX, ea **$25.00**

Zorro, accessory set w/mask, whip, lariat & ring, Shimmel/WDP, M (w/24" L card picturing Guy Williams) **$150.00**

Zorro, hand puppet, vinyl head w/cloth body, felt hat, Gund/WDP, 1950s, EX+ **$75.00**

Zorro, Oil Painting By Numbers, Hassenfeld Bros, 1960s, complete, VGIB..**$65.00**

Zorro, tote bag, red vinyl, EX **$275.00**

Cracker Jack Toys

In 1869 Frederick Rueckheim left Hamburg, Germany, bound for Chicago, where he planned to work on a farm for his uncle. But farm life did not appeal to Mr. Rueckheim, and after the Chicago fire, he moved there and helped clear the debris. With another man whose popcorn and confectionary business had been destroyed in the fire, Mr. Rueckheim started a business with one molasses kettle and one hand popper. The following year, Mr. Rueckheim bought out his original partner and sent for his brother, Louis. The two brothers formed Rueckheim & Bro. and quickly prospered as they continued expanding their confectionary line to include new products. It was not until 1896 that the first lot of Cracker Jack was produced — and then only as an adjunct to their growing line. Cracker Jack was sold in bulk form until 1899 when H.G. Eckstein, an old friend, invented the wax-sealed package, which allowed them to ship it further and thus sell it more easily. Demand for Cracker Jack soared, and it quickly became the main product of the factory. Today millions of boxes are produced — each with a prize in every box.

The idea of prizes came along during the time of bulk packaging; it was devised as a method to stimulate sales. Later, as the wax-sealed package was introduced, a prize was given (more or less) with each package. Next, the prize was added into the package, but still not every package received a prize. It was not until the 1920s that 'a prize in every package' became a reality. Initially, the prizes were put in with the confection, but the company feared this might pose a problem, should it inadvertently be mistaken for the popcorn. To avoid this, the prize was put in a separate compartment and, finally, into its own protective wrapper. Thousands of prizes have been used over the years, and it is still true today that there is 'a prize in every package.' Prizes have ranged from the practical girl's bracelet and pencils to tricks, games, disguises, and stick-anywhere patches. To learn more about the subject, you'll want to read *Cracker Jack Toys, The Complete Unofficial Guide for Collectors*, and *Cracker Jack, The Unauthorized Guide to Advertising Collectibles*, both by our advisor, Larry White.

Note: Words printed in upper case lettering actually appear on the toy.

Advisor: Larry White (See Directory, Cracker Jack)

Kangaroo punch-out, $9.50; fish plate, $7.50, comic character standup Herby, $87.50, tankard charm, $55.00. (Photo courtesy Larry White)

A-MAZE PUZZLE, plastic/paper/dexterity game, about 1" sq ...**$5.00**

Alphabet letter standup, metal, K - Kite, I - Iron, etc, ea ...**$145.00**

ALWAYS ON TOP, tin top..$60.00

Angelus Marshmallows, tape measure, celluloid, image of marshmallow tin on back, 1½", NM...$75.00

ANIMANIACS STICKER MADNESS, paper, any of 24 ....$.50

ANIMATED JUNBLE BOOK, paper, pop-up book..........$95.00

Astronaut, plastic, CJ CO, 1 of 10....................................$12.50

Aviation wings, metal, CRACKER JACK AIR CORPS.......$55.00

BADGE FUN, paper, B Series 75, any of 21 ....$2.00

Baseball card, paper, 1914, 1 of 144, typical $75.00

Baseball card, plastic, CJ CO, any of 11 ....$5.00

BIKE STICKER, paper, series ID 1380, any $2.50

BIRDS TO COLOR, paper, paint books, ea $75.00

Book, paper, CHILDREN'S NOTES, about 2" high, early.$90.00

Booklet, paper, HUB A DUB-DUB, JACK AND JILL, etc, ea.$40.00

Bookmark, plastic, set #40, any of 14 ....$3.50

Box prize, paper, insert separator w/game, etc, any of 40 .....$21.00

Boy eating Cracker Jack, paper, mechanical prize, about 3"..$325.00

BREAKFAST SET, agateware in matchbox..........................$27.50

Button, metal, US ARMY QUARTERMASTER, gold or silver wash..$12.50

BUTTON CLIP-ON, plastic, series 1375, any....................$8.50

Ceramic figure, FAS JAPAN, various comic characters, painted .$25.00

Ceramic figure, JAPAN, 2-3", various, some paint, ea $9.50

Charm, pot metal, horse, cat, dog, rabbit, etc, ea..................$5.50

Clamshell w/water flowers inside, about 1½" $25.00

Comb, plastic, marked, thick, Canadian $12.50

Compass, paper & metal, balance on needlepoint, 1½" dia .$97.50

Coupon, paper, The Cracker Jack Embroidery Outfit..........$55.00

CRACKER JACK BANK, metal, book shape....................$325.00

CRACKER JACK clicker/screamer $55.00

CRACKER JACK NURSERY GAMES, paper book, about 3".$127.50

CRACKER JACK PUZZLE BOOK, paper, series 3..........$115.00

CRACKER JACK RIDDLES, paper book w/jester on cover .$15.50

Decal, plastic/paper, Z-1138, bunny, bear, etc, ea............$20.00

Dirigible, metal w/celluloid 'blimp,' charm.........................$65.00

DRAWING STENCILS, paper, rabbit, flower, etc, ea.........$27.50

Eraser boy, paper, Jack at blackboard writes/erases slogan...$325.00

FELT PATCH, felt on paper, series ID 1383, any color or design ..$4.50

Finger puppet, C Cloud, 1937, one of four, $30.00 each. (Photo courtesy Harriet Joyce)

Fish plaque, plastic, grouper, salmon, etc, ea.....................$17.50

FLICK-A-WINK, paper, marked, game $25.00

Fortune teller, celluloid Sailor Jack in paper envelope, various colors...$75.00

Frog, paper w/jumping mechanism, about 3" $95.00

FROG CHIRPER, metal, copyright 1946 Cloudcrest $40.00

GLOW IN THE DARK STICKERS, paper, 1972 copyright.$5.50

GOOFY ZOO, paper, wheeled zoo animal poses.................$35.00

Handy Andy, paper, any of 12, ea $67.50

Hat, Me for Cracker Jack, paper $425.00

Hat, paper, ME FOR CRACKER JACK $375.00

Hoe, metal w/wood handle, about 6" L $9.50

HOLD UP TO LIGHT, plastic, astronaut, egg, etc, ea $15.00

JIG-SAW PUZZLE, paper, 6 sections, boy fishing, etc, ea.....$8.50

MAGICARD, paper, D SERIES #44, ANY OF 15 ....$7.50

Match shooter, metal, hand gun, rifle, machine gun, japanned, ea..$27.50

MINUTE MOVIES, paper flip book of moving animal, any of 12 ....$15.00

NURSERY RHYMES AND RIDDLES, paper, booklet....$125.00

Palm puzzle, paper & celluloid, cow over moon, etc, ea.......$95.00

Paper dolls, paper, JANE AND JIMMY CUT OUT TWINS..$145.00

Patch, FELT PATCH, felt on paper, series ID 1383, any color or design, ea $4.50

PENCIL HOLDER, paper, about 2x4"..............................$90.00

PHONEY PENNY 1¢, metal w/gold wash..........................$30.00

Postcard, paper, CJR-1 miniature of 1908 designs, any of 12 .$2.50

Postcard, paper, Cracker Jack Bears, 1908, any of 16 ....$19.50

Put...Take, metal spinner, about 1½" $27.00

RIDDLE BOOK, paper, series 1335, any of 18....................$3.50

Riddle card, paper, Cracker Jack Riddles, any of 20 ....$9.50

RING TOSS, paper, game, Makatoy.....................................$24.00

Sailboat, plastic put-together...$5.50

Scale, metal, gold bottom, red pans.....................................$35.50

SCORE COUNTER, paper, baseball game counter $195.00

SEND A MESSAGE BY DOT & DASH, paper, game.......$19.50

Serving tray, plastic, 5 fishes, thick, Canadian.....................$10.00

SMITTY, vacuform plastic, 1 of various comic characters....$12.50

Stand-up, plastic, marked NOSCO, various figures, ea.........$1.50

Stand-up, plastic 3-D, Sailor Jack, 2000 copyright.................$2.50

Stand-up, tin litho metal, OFFICER, about 3"...................$19.50

SUPER SLATE, paper & plastic, B SERIES 49, any of 30....$3.50

SWINGING FROG, paper, 1 of 4 (monkey, parrot, skeleton) ..$40.00

TAG ALONGS, plastic, SERIES #72, any of 15 ....$5.00

TATTOOS, paper, SERIES Z-1366, any of 9........................$.75

TELE-VIZ, paper, wheel prize about 2" sq $125.00

Telescope, plastic, POKEMON, series CJ #20, any of 24 ......$2.50

Top, TWO TOPPERS, metal w/wood dowel, Jack & Angelus...$65.00

Traffic sign, plastic, CJ CO, STOP, NARROW BRIDGE, etc, ea..$7.50

TRANSFER FUN, paper, B SERIES 35, any of 20..............$7.50

Truck, Express, litho tin $74.50

TWIG AND SPRIG, paper, booklet, any title.....................$97.50

Visor, paper, marked, about 6½" across.............................$145.00

Whistle, metal, airplane shape w/eagle design $39.00

Whistle, metal, SIMPLEX FLUTE......................................$6.75

Whistle, paper, BLOW FOR MORE w/PRIZE box pictured ..$49.50

Whistle, plastic, 2-tube, about 3" L, any 2-color...................$2.75

WORDS OF WISDOM, paper, book, about 3x5"...........$275.00

WRITE MOVIE STAR'S NAME HERE, paper, movie star card $27.50

YOU'RE IT, metal, singer pointing spinner.........................$9.50
ZEPHYR, metal, TOOTSIETOY, about 2½".....................$20.00
Zodiac coin, plastic, 1 of 12..$5.00

Crackle Glass

At the height of productivity from the 1930s through the 1970s, nearly 500 companies created crackle glass. As pieces stayed in production for several years, dating an item may be difficult. Some colors, such as ruby red, amberina, cobalt, and cranberry, were more expensive to produce. Smoke gray was made for a short time, and because quantities are scarce, prices tend to be higher than on some of the other colors, amethyst, green, and amber included. Crackle glass is still being produced today by the Blenko Glass Company, and it is being imported from Taiwan and China as well. For further information on other glass companies and values we recommend *Crackle Glass from Around the World* by Stan and Arlene Weitman.

See also Blenko.

Advisors: Stan and Arlene Weitman (See Directory, Crackle Glass)

Decanter, topaz, Rainbow, 1953, 11", from $100.00 to $125.00.
(Photo courtesy Stan and Arlene Weitman)

Ashtray, dark topaz, Viking, 1944-70, 7¾", from $35 to $45.00
Basket, blue w/crystal handle, tall, Pilgrim, 1949-69, 5¼", from $75 to $100.00
Basket, ruby, twisted crystal handle, Hamon/Kanawha, 1960s-70s, 5¼", from $75 to..$100.00
Bowl, amber w/applied serpentine around middle, flared rim, Kanawha, 1957-87, 2¾x4½", from $50 to....................$55.00
Candlesticks, blue, Rainbow, 1940s-60s, 6", pr from $150 to . $175.00
Candy dish, green, scalloped rim, Bischoff, 1942-63, 3x3½", from $55 to $75.00

Compote, tangerine, footed, Blenko, 1950s, 6x6", from $100 to $125.00
Creamer, blue, drop-over handle, Rainbow, 3", from $40 to ..$50.00
Creamer, emerald green, drop-over handle, Pilgrim, 1949-69, 3", from $40 to $50.00
Creamer & sugar bowl, blue, creamer has blue drop-over handle, Pilgrim, 1949-69, 3½", pr, from $100 to....................$125.00
Creamer & sugar bowl, gold, gold drop-over handle, Kanawha, 1957-87, 3½", from $100 to..$125.00
Cruet, sea green, no handle, green ball stopper, Pilgrim, 1949-69, from $85 to $100.00
Cup, amberina, drop-over handle, Kanawha, 1957-87, 2¼", from $40 to $50.00
Decanter, amber w/enameled floral design, amber stopper, Czechoslovakian, 1920s, 7", from $150 to.................$250.00
Decanter, crystal w/green medallion, green stopper, unknown manufacturer, late 1950s, 8¼", from $150 to $200.00
Fruit, pear, amethyst, Blenko, 1950-60, 5", from $100 to .$125.00
Lamp shade, hurricane; light pink, Kanawha, 1957-87, 7", from $100 to $125.00
Perfume bottle, pale blue, metal atomizer, unknown manufacturer & date, 4½", from $50 to $75.00
Pitcher, blue, clear pulled-back handle, teardrop shape, Pilgrim, 7", from $80 to $90.00
Pitcher, blue, pulled-back handle, Hamon, 1960s, 5½", from $60 to $70.00
Pitcher, chartreuse, drop-over handle, Pilgrim, 1960s, 6½", from $65 to $75.00
Pitcher, cobalt, clear pulled-back handle, Hamon, 1940s-70s, 5¾", from $85 to $100.00

Pitcher, crystal with aquamarine handle, Kanawha, 1957 – 1987, from $75.00 to $85.00. (Photo courtesy Stan and Arlene Weitman)

Pitcher, green, double drop-over handle, Jamestown, 1950s, from $60 to $85.00
Pitcher, ruby, drop-over handle, Pilgrim, 1949-69, 3¼", from $50 to $55.00

Pitcher, satin amberina, pulled-back handle, waisted, Kanawha, 1957-87, 6½", from $75 to..$85.00

Salt & pepper shakers, amethyst, unknown manufacturer & date, 3¼", pr from $80 to $100.00

Syrup pitcher, amberina, amberina pulled-back handle, Kanawha, 1957-87, 7¼", from $75 to..$100.00

Tumbler, crytal w/applied green snake, unknown manufacturer, 1920s, 8", from $85 to $110.00

Tumbler, topaz, unknown manufacturer, 6¾", from $50 to . $60.00

Vase, green w/applied serpentine at neck, Kanawha, 1957-87, 3½", from $55 to $60.00

Vase, lemon lime, pinched body, strawberry pontil mark on bottom, Pilgrim, 1949-69, 5", from $45 to...............................$55.00

Vase, orange, scalloped rim, Rainbow, 1940s-60s, 5", from $50 to...$55.00

Vase, smoke gray, scalloped rim, Rainbow, 1940-1960s, from $75 to..$80.00

Cuff Links

Cuff link collecting continues to be one of the fastest growing hobbies. Few collectibles are as affordable, available, and easy to store. Cuff links can often be found at garage sales, thrift shops, and flea markets for reasonable prices.

People collect cuff links for many reasons. Besides being a functional and interesting wearable, cuff links are educational. The design, shape, size, and materials used often relate to events, places, and products, and they typically reflect the period of their manufacture: examples are Art Deco, Victorian, Art Nouveau, Modern, etc. They offer the chance for the 'big find' which appeals to all collectors. Sometimes pairs purchased for small amounts turn out to be worth substantial sums.

Unless otherwise noted, the following listings apply to cuff links in excellent to mint condition. The higher end of the suggested range of values represents average retail prices asked in antique shops.

Advisor: Gene Klompus (See Directory, Cuff Links)

Club/Newsletter: The National Cuff Link Society
The Link
Eugene R. Klompus
P.O. Box 5970
Vernon Hills, IL 60061
847-816-0035; fax: 847-816-7466.
genek@justcufflinks.com
www.justcufflinks.com
Also related items

American Indian chief (lg side)/brave (on sm end), 14k gold, 4.8 grams $315.00

Barbell style, 18k yellow gold ball & smaller silver ball, Tiffany mark on silver cross-bar..$175.00

Baseball batter, catcher & umpire in relief on silver 1" sq, F&S Sterling $55.00

Black enamel Victorian design on gold-filled rectangle, ¾x½". $50.00

Black onyx w/.10ct diamond set on 14k yellow gold mount, 4.6 grams $145.00

Bloodstone circles set in 14k yellow gold, Long's Boston... Northshore..$110.00

Bright blue butterfly wings encased in clear diamond shape on silver back, Sterling, ¾"..$50.00

Budweiser Clydesdale horses, 18 karat gold, limited edition, M, $3,000.00. (Photo courtesy Gene Klompus)

Comedy & Tragedy Masks, 14k yellow gold, Avedon, 14.1 grams $185.00

Copper w/verdigris & silver overlay, Arts & Crafts rectangle design, double-sided $210.00

Devil's face, carved antique ivory, stained details, silver chain, 1" $200.00

Embossed geometric pattern on 14k gold squares, undistinguishable logo, #585, 16.5 grams $145.00

Engraved flowers on 10k yellow gold, ⅝x¾", 8 grams..........$55.00

Gold (14k) w/lg jade stone, rectangular, ¾" $130.00

Gold (14k) w/mother-of-pearl, double-sided, ½".................$70.00

Gold-filled oval w/fine scrolling on gold chain attached to black satin glass oval, Victorian mourning type $130.00

Gold-tone palm tree w/green & brown enameling, 1x⅞".....$50.00

Green glass w/starburst center on gold-tone metal, Swank, 1x¾" $55.00

Horse's head, yellow gold w/diamond eyes (4 eyes, 2 points each), 26.4 grams, ¾"..$260.00

Jasperware, eagle (detailed) in white on blue oval, Wedgwood England, ¾x½" $47.50

Jockey's cap, sterling silver, GJ (Georg Jensen), ½" $385.00

Knight in armour on horse, gold-tone metal w/black enameling...$60.00

Navajo silver & turquoise made of recycled conchos, 1930s-401, 1x1¼" $110.00

Onyx ovals mounted on 14k gold backs, Tiffany & Co, ca 1900..$300.00

Orange moonstone set in 925S sterling silver, Georg Jensen, ¾x½", MIB $130.00

Red & white celluloid, snap type, 1920s.............................$65.00

Repoussè Nouveau floral on 18k gold, 4.8 grams...............$120.00

Reverse-painted 50's-style nude in gold-wash oval frame, 1x⅞" ..$75.00

Roulette wheel (working!) enameled on gold-tone metal, 1950s, 1" $55.00

Round-cut .10 carat total-weight sapphire on 14k yellow gold rayed oval, 1930s $185.00
Shield, cross banner & 2 dragons, multicolor enamel on gold-plated body, marked MP, ¾" $55.00
Silver alloy, LV (Louis Vuitton) monogram, hinged bar creates clasp $90.00
Silver Comedy & Tragedy masks, Silver Mexico on shaft, ¾x½" . $45.00
Silver w/black enameling, 8-sided Art Deco shape, MIB (box marked NJ Meyers...NY) $115.00
Silver w/engraved Atlas symbol, Tiffany & Co, MIB $110.00
Silver w/green enamel over French guilloche design, David Anderson Sterling, 1x½" $88.00
Silver w/lg cobalt blue stone w/green swirls, oval bark marked Sterling, ½x⅜" $190.00
Silver w/orange enamel, designed in guilloche manner, double-sided, 1950s, MIB $160.00
Silver w/shiny red & white enamel, rectangles on rectangles, marked Sterling $85.00
Silver w/yellow enamel, double-sided ovals, marked Silver, ¾x7/16" $55.00
Silver w/2 smooth 14k gold bands, David Yurman Thoroughbred Collection, M in Yurman pouch $285.00
Silver X w/blue crystal stones, A Michael $50.00
Silver-tone metal w/red Bakelite spinning dice, 1950s $45.00
St Christopher in relief, sterling silver, 1950s, w/matching tie clasp, 30 grams $60.00
Star design on 24k gold w/black enameling, ¾" dia $115.00
Sterling w/amber stone, rectangular, marked Sterling Denmark, 11/16x13/16" $50.00
Vice President of the United States, Walter Mondale, given as gift to his staff, MIB $100.00
Zuni sun god, onyx/white shell/coral/turquoise inlay in sterling silver, full bonnet surrounds face, ¾" dia $95.00
10mm pearl set into solid 18k gold toggle mounts, 26.2 grams . $160.00

Huckleberry Hound, three-piece set with tie bar, 1959, M on original card, G, $85.00. (Photo courtesy Gene Klompus)

Cup and Saucer Sets

Lovely cups and saucers are often available at garage sales and flea markets, and prices are generally quite reasonable. If limited space is a consideration, you might enjoy starting a collection, since they're easy to display en masse on a shelf or one at a time as a romantic accent on a coffee table. English manufacturers have produced endless bone china cups and saucers that are both decorative and functional. American manufacturers were just about as prolific as were the Japanese. Collecting examples from many companies and countries is a wonderful way to study the various ceramic manufacturers. Our advisors have written *Collectible Cups and Saucers, Identification and Values, Books I, II,* and *III* (Collector Books), with hundreds of color photos organized by six collectible categories: cabinet cups, nineteenth and twentieth century dinnerware, English tablewares, miniatures, Japanese, and glass cups and saucers.

Advisors: Jim and Susan Harran (See Directory, Cups and Saucers)

Breakfast, white & yellow w/portrait of lady sitting in grass, Rosenthal, 1901-1933, 4½x2¼", 6½", from $60 to $75.00
Coffee, blue w/gold & blue hand-painted floral & leaf design, tapered cup, signed Dorothy C Thorpe, California, $50 to $75.00
Coffee, cobalt ground w/floral cartouches & gilt stylized flowers, Swaine & Co, 1900-1920, from $30 to $45.00

Coffee, coral and white, Aynsley, 1930s, $35.00. (Photo courtesy Jim and Susan Harran)

Coffee, ivory w/transfers of children, footed cup w/loop handle, Haviland, 1938-present, from $40 to $55.00
Demitasse, beige w/courting scene transfers, flared can w/4 gilt curved feet, Retsch, 1953-present, from $40 to $55.00
Demitasse, cobalt w/gilt flowers, tapered cup, Bareuther, 1930s-1950s, from $30 to $45.00
Demitasse, cream, Belleek, 6-sided tapered cup, Lenox, 1906-24, 2¼x2½", from $45 to $60.00
Demitasse, hand-painted pink flowers w/gold leaves & stems, round cup w/gold handle, Stouffer, 1930s, from $75 to $95.00
Demitasse, heavy silver overlay on blue, Freiberg, 1926-45, 2½x1¾", 4⅔", from $145 to $175.00
Demitasse, ivory w/Rich Blue Onion pattern, scalloped cup w/entwined leaf handle, Meissen, 1950s, 2½x1¾, 4¼" ... $190.00
Demitasse, multicolored birds & bowls of fruits on black w/etched gold bands, Hutschenreuther, 1925-41, 2x2¼", 4½" $90.00
Demitasse, peach w/heavy gold beads, portrait medallion of lady w/pearls, Dresden, 1888-1916, 2⅛x2", 4¼", $400 to . $450.00

Demitasse, silver overlay on white, 6-paneled, Fraureuth, 1898-1935, from $100 to **$125.00**

Demitasse, white w/underglaze bluebird painting, blue rim, Tirschenreuth, 1930-1950s, from $40 to **$45.00**

Demitasse, white wreath & beads on Wedgewood blue ground, Pompadour shape, Rosenthal, 1925-41, from $40 to....**$55.00**

Miniature coffee, beige w/floral transfer, can cup w/sq handle, Palissy, 1960, from $50 to..**$60.00**

Miniature mustache, white w/burgundy band, man w/mustache on flared cup, unmarked, 1930-50s, from $100 to **$125.00**

Miniature tea, Autumn pattern from Brambley Hedge series, footed cup, Royal Doulton, 1990, 1⅞x1½", 3", from $35 to...**$45.00**

Miniature tea, green w/applied flowers & gold, round cup, leaf-shaped saucer, Noritaki, 1930s, from $75 to..............**$100.00**

Miniature tea, turquoise & gold w/rose inside cup, Crown Staffordshire, 1950s, 1½x1", 2⅓", from $60 to.............**$75.00**

Miniature tea, white w/Green Willow pattern, Coalport, 1960-70, from $75 to **$100.00**

Tea, blue & white windmill scene, gold trim, cup w/angular handle, Embassy Ware, 1950s, from $35 to **$45.00**

Tea, gold w/multicolored flowers, Embassy Ware, 1950s, from $70 to **$90.00**

Tea, ivory w/thistle pattern, swirled cup w/kicked loop handle, Adderleys Ltd, 1950-62, from $40 to **$45.00**

Tea, white w/purple pansies, gold trim, squarish cup w/4 feet, Crown Dorset, 1920-37, from $40 to..............................**$45.00**

Teacup, Art Nouveau red peonies & gold, footed cup, Limoges, 1891-96, from $40 to **$50.00**

Teacup, black w/gold trim, scalloped & footed cup w/gold interior, Pickard, 1925-38, from $60 to **$75.00**

Teacup, cream w/aqua border of gold warriors on horseback, R Wachter, 1930s, from $35 to **$45.00**

Teacup, cream w/cobalt band & gold flowers, tapered cup, Golden Crown, 1955-1980s, from $35 to.............................**$45.00**

Teacup, ivory w/floral bouquets, gold scrolls on rim, cup w/squarish handle, footed, Onodaga, 1960-66, from $40 to **$45.00**

Teacup, ivory w/gilt decoration, tapered, molded cup, ruffled foot, Edelstein, 1934-present, from $25 to............................**$30.00**

Teacup, light green, gold trim, flowers inside cup, footed, Tirschenreuth, 1950s, from $30 to **$40.00**

Teacup, peach & yellow flowers w/silver leaves on cream, low footed cup, Shonwald Porcelain, 1930s, from $40 to...............**$45.00**

Teacup, pink w/flowerpots & garland of roses, gold trim, Royal Bayreuth, 1916-30s, 4x2¼", 5⅔", from $40 to.............**$55.00**

Teacup, robins egg blue w/cartouches of roses, footed cup, loop handle, Furstenberg, 1950s, from $40 to **$45.00**

Czechoslovakian Glass and Ceramics

Established as a country in 1918, Czechoslovakia is rich in the natural resources needed for production of glassware as well as pottery. Over the years it has produced vast amounts of both. Anywhere you go, from flea markets to fine antique shops, you'll find several examples of their lovely pressed and cut glass scent bottles, Deco vases, lamps, kitchenware, tableware, and figurines.

More than 35 marks have been recorded; some are ink stamped, some etched, and some molded in. Paper labels have also been used.

Club: Czechoslovakian Collectors Guild International
P.O. Box 901395
Kansas City, MO 64190
888-910-0988
cgi@kc.net

Ceramics

Teapot, lady figural, 8", $185.00. (Photo courtesy Ruth A. Forsythe)

Bowl, Art Deco daisies, hand-painted multicolor w/red floral border, Ditmar Urbach..., 1940s, 9" **$35.00**

Bowl, basket-weave base w/fruit & nuts forming lid, multicolor, Erphila, 4½x7⅛" **$30.00**

Canisters, cherub reserve on white w/blue, French titles (Sucre (Sugar), etc, Urbach mark, graduated set of 6 ....**$485.00**

Canisters, man & lady in reserve w/blue trim on white porcelain, Victoria, set of 4 w/salt box **$275.00**

Creamer, moose in tree, antlers form rim, shaded multicolors, 1930s, 3¼x5" **$25.00**

Creamer & sugar bowl, white lustre w/orange trim, orange finial on lid, Made in Czechoslovakia, 3½" **$40.00**

Figurine, Scottish terrier puppies (3) in a row, taupe-tray, Erphila, 2x3" **$45.00**

Flower frog, bird on stump, red, blue & green, red stamped mark, 5" **$40.00**

Flower holder, bird perched on top of a 2-sided holder, multicolor, orange mark, 5½x3½" **$26.00**

Gravy boat, bird of paradise transfer w/orange lustre trim, 1930s, 3¾x6" **$28.00**

Gravy boat, Bohemian tulips w/gold trim, attached undertray, Baronet **$95.00**

Invalid feeder, Victoria pattern, gold trim, 5¼" from spout to rim...**$110.00**

Jug, toby; sailor holding pipe, #886, Ebeling & Reuss, 5½".**$55.00**

Mug, toby-style head & shoulders of man in blue, gray white beard, heavy eyelids, triangle mark, ca 1930, 6⅜" **$100.00**

Nut/mint dish, white w/gold interior, triangular, rolled rim, single handle, 1¼x4¾x4¼" **$30.00**

Pitcher, Art Deco flowers on ivory, orange rim & handle, Hand Painted Ditmar Urbach..., 4x3" **$42.00**

Pitcher, diamond pattern in gold & blue lustre w/black outlines on white, 4½" **$20.00**

Pitcher, milk; flame design, black angular handle, #681, Bern. **$80.00**

Pitcher, parrot, flowing multicolor, #30, Made in Czechoslovakia, 5x4" **$35.00**

Planter, buggy shape, multicolor w/flower decor, Eichwald I, 1930s, 10½x18½x9" **$950.00**

Plate, lady in plumed hat, blue rim w/gold trim, early mark, 9¾" **$45.00**

Plate, maidens & cherubs, signed Kauffman, Tiffany finish, gold trim, Epiag Royal Czechoslovakia, 10½" **$165.00**

Sugar bowl, flower bouquet on white w/gold, w/lid, RKG Czechoslovakia, ca 1928-39 ....**$35.00**

Teapot, fruit transfer on white, Fine Bohemian China, Belfor Czechoslovakia, 6½" **$45.00**

Tidbit server, fruit transfer, 2-tier w/gold-tone metal handle, MZ Czechoslovakia **$25.00**

Tidbit tray, Chelsea pattern, 2-tier, center handle, Erphila Czechoslovakia, 9½" sq **$68.00**

Vase, Art Deco geometrics, hand-painted multicolor, sq foot, 1930s-30s, 8⅝x6⅛" **$195.00**

Vase, floral on tan shaded to white, angle handles w/molded cherries, Made in Czechoslovakia, 5½" **$30.00**

Vase, lg pink rose on brown to ivory, handles, Made in Czechoslovakia, 5¼" **$35.00**

Vase, nautilus shell, white, Erphila, 1940s-50s, 5⅞x5½x2½", pr .. **$25.00**

Vase, peacock figural, tail spread wide, 1930s, 6x4¼" **$295.00**

Vase, white lustreware urn style w/ornate handles, cobalt trim, Made in Czechoslovakia, 5½x4½" **$35.00**

Wall pocket, bird perched before birdhouse, multicolor, 5½x4½x3½" **$55.00**

Wall pocket, multicolor floral on yellow, 13", $65.00. (Photo courtesy Bill and Betty Newbound)

Glassware

Basket, bright pink w/applied clear flowers & foliage, black rim & handle (simple), 7½x6" **$95.00**

Basket, multicolor mottle w/aventurine w/embossed diamond pattern, ruffled rim, clear thorn handle, 6x4¾" **$85.00**

Basket, white opaque w/simple arched dark orange handle, ruffled rim, 6¾x6¾" **$200.00**

Bottle, black w/random red threads, fan-shaped matching stopper, 5¾x3¾" **$350.00**

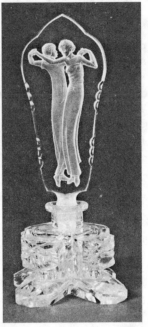

Bottle, dancing ladies intaglio in stopper, base cut with four feet, signed, $485.00. (Photo courtesy Monsen & Baer)

Bottle, scent; black opaque w/cuttings, stepped sides, crystal faceted stopper, 5⅞" **$250.00**

Bottle, scent; burgundy-red w/floral cutting to clear, w/original atomizer bulb & tassel, 5x3" **$135.00**

Bottle, scent; clear w/applied brass filigree & red glass jewels, ornamented lid, 2¼x1¾" **$135.00**

Bottle, scent; crystal frost w/hand-painted decor, tall foot, atomizer, 6½" **$175.00**

Bottle, scent; crystal w/cuttings, flared shoulders, fan-shaped stopper, 3⅝" **$175.00**

Bottle, scent; Hobnail, cranberry opal, bulbous, 5½" **$225.00**

Bottle, scent; light apple green, pyramidal shape w/heavily faceted corners, faceted clear ball stopper, 2½" **$75.00**

Bottle, scent; pink, conical w/jeweled stopper, 7¼" **$115.00**

Bottle, scent; pink pyramidal base w/cuttings, frosted floral stopper, 6⅛" **$235.00**

Bottle, scent; pink w/Deco-style cuttings, clear faceted stopper, 2⅜" **$65.00**

Bottle, scent; white satin w/red serpentine, green stem, red finial & disk foot, 7¾" **$40.00**

Bowl, crystal, geometric cuttings, stars on facets, scalloped rim, 3-footed, 3⅛x7¼" **$50.00**

Bowl/vase, black w/bright yellow interior, wide flared rim, 4½x10" **$250.00**

Box, crystal, geometric cuttings, sq, etched mark, 2½x3" **$15.00**

Candy jar, orange/red/yellow canes floating in clear, cobalt disk foot, 8½" **$225.00**

Jar, dresser; reverse-painted cottage scene on lid, yellow background, label, 3x2¾" **$35.00**

Vase, autumn-colored mottle w/hand-painted white flowers, sm gold accents, white cased, slim neck, 4" $25.00

Vase, bud; orange w/silver overlay bird & flowers, 8⅜x2⅜" . $50.00

Vase, cobalt w/multicolor pink-lavender canes at base, flared cylinder, 10" $375.00

Vase, green cased, hand-painted floral decor w/white trim, stick form, 8½x2½" $150.00

Vase, green multicolor mottle, flared rim, shaped stem & foot, 10¼" $150.00

Vase, lavender-blue, putti among flower garlands in relief, 3⅛x2" $175.00

Vase, light cranberry w/controlled bubbles, black rim, 5¼" .. $175.00

Vase, orange & black swirls, gourd shape, 10x7" $125.00

Vase, orange w/black & white hand-painted scroll beading, waisted cylinder, 8¼x3" $60.00

Vase, orange w/hand-painted bird & flowers, black foot & rim, 6½x2⅜" $50.00

Vase, red-orange w/black overlay foot, 9½x5" $135.00

Vase, white cased w/clear, embossed ribs, applied amber serpentine, 12" $55.00

Vase, white w/pink interior, scalloped/ruffled rim, ball form, etched mark, 6" $50.00

Dakin

Dakin has been in the toy-making business since the 1950s and has made several lines of stuffed and vinyl dolls and animals, and collectors love 'em all! But the Dakins that garner the most interest are the licensed characters and advertising figures made from 1968 through the 1970s. Originally there were seven Warner Brothers characters, each with a hard plastic body and a soft vinyl head, all under 10" tall. The line was very successful and eventually expanded to include more than 50 cartoon characters and several more that were advertising related. In addition to the figures, there are banks that were made in two sizes. Some Dakins are quite scarce and may sell for over $100.00 (a few even higher), though most will be in the $30.00 to $60.00 range. Dakin is now owned by Applause, Inc.

Condition is very important, and if you find one still in the original box, add about 50% to its value. Figures in the colorful 'Cartoon Theatre' boxes command higher prices than those that came in a clear plastic bag or package (MIP). More Dakins are listed in *Schroeder's Collectible Toys, Antique to Modern*, published by Collector Books.

Animal (Muppet Babies), hand puppet, plush w/plastic eyes, 10", NM $10.00

Barney Rubble, vinyl, felt outfit, 7" or 8", 1970, NM, ea.... $45.00

Bozo the Clown, vinyl, jointed, 7½", 1974, NM $28.00

Bugs Bunny, stuffed plush, lying down w/carrot, Fun Farm, 1978, 8" L, EX $25.00

Bugs Bunny, vinyl, Goofy Gram, Happy Birthday, 1971, 12", NM $38.00

Bugs Bunny, vinyl, standing w/carrot, swivel head, 10", EX+ . $20.00

Bugs Bunny, vinyl, standing w/legs apart & hand on hip w/carrot, solid orange, 1976, 6", NM $20.00

Daffy Duck, vinyl, standing w/legs together & feet spread, hand on hip, 1960s-70s, 9", NM.................................. $20.00

Elmer Fudd, vinyl w/black cloth jacket, yellow pants, red vinyl shoes & hat, 8", NM+ $25.00

Elmer Fudd, vinyl w/cloth hunting outfit & gun, vinyl boots, 1968, 7", NM+ $100.00

Elroy (Jetsons), stuffed cloth w/printed features, fuzzy yellow hair, w/beanie, 1986, 12", EX+................................ $12.00

Foghorn Leghorn, vinyl, jointed, 1970, EX+ $55.00

Laurel & Hardy, either, squeeze vinyl, 1970s, 5½", EX, ea . $30.00

Laurel & Hardy, either, vinyl w/cloth shirts, 1970s, 8", w/hang tags, MIP, ea.. $50.00

Merlin the Magic Mouse, 1974, EX+, from $20.00 to $25.00.

Odie (Garfield), stuffed plush, as rabbit w/orange carrot, 1980s, 10", M.. $15.00

Odie (Garfield), stuffed plush, Fun Farm, 1983, 14", NM+... $12.00

Pepe Le Pew, vinyl, Goofy Gram, You're a Real Stinker, 1971, 9", EX+ $75.00

Porky Pig, squeeze vinyl, black cloth cape, white bow tie, 1969, 8", MIP (Looney Tunes bag) $35.00

Porky Pig, squeeze vinyl, standing w/arms down a palms forward, black jacket, 1960s, 5", NM $20.00

Porky Pig, stuffed plush, seated w/legs apart, felt hat, felt features, 1975, 8", EX+ $15.00

Decanters

The first company to make figural ceramic decanters was the James Beam Distilling Company. Until mid-1992 they produced hundreds of varieties in their own US-based china factory. They first issued their bottles in the mid-'50s, and over the course of the next 25 years, more than 20 other companies followed their example. Among the more prominent of these were Brooks, Hoffman, Lionstone, McCormick, Old Commonwealth, Ski Country, and Wild Turkey. In 1975, Beam introduced the 'Wheel Series,' cars, trains, and fire engines with wheels that actually revolved. The popularity of this series resulted in a heightened interest in decanter collecting.

There are various sizes. The smallest (called miniatures) hold two ounces, and there are some that hold a gallon! A full decanter is worth no more than an empty one, and the absence of the tax stamp doesn't lower its value either. Just be sure that all the labels are intact and that there are no cracks or chips. You might want to empty your decanters as a safety precaution (many collectors do) rather than risk the possibility of the inner glaze breaking down and allowing the contents to leak into the porous ceramic body.

All of the decanters we've listed are fifths unless we've specified 'miniature' within the description.

See also Elvis Presley Collectibles.

Advisor: Roy Willis (See Directory Decanters)

Beam, '57 Bel Air Convertible, red, 1990 ....$96.00
Beam, '69 Camero, yellow w/black top, 1988 ....$90.00
Beam, Armadillo, 1981 ....$18.00
Beam, Baseball '100 Years,' 1969.....................................$30.00
Beam, Bluegill, 1974...$28.00
Beam, Cadillac, '59 Convertible, green, 1992 ....$125.00
Beam, Cardinal (male), 1968 ....$28.00
Beam, Centennial, Santa Fe, 1960 ....$85.00

Beam, Chevrolet, 1953 Corvette, 1989, $175.00.

Beam, Chevrolet, '57 Hot Rod, yellow, 1987......................$95.00
Beam, Chevrolet, '63 Stingray, black, 1987.......................$100.00
Beam, Chevrolet, '86 Pace Car Convertible, yellow, 1990..$105.00
Beam, Chicago Fire, 1971...$28.00
Beam, Circus Wagon, 1979..$30.00
Beam, Convention, Houston (#9), Poodle on Rocket, 1979 ..$26.00
Beam, Convention, Jim Beam Guitar (membership), white, 2004 ....$45.00
Beam, Convention, San Antonio (#29), Alamo, 1999 ....$55.00
Beam, D-Day, 1984...$20.00

Beam, Dodge, '70 Hot Rod, yellow, 1992 ....$55.00
Beam, Donkey (Political), New York City, 1976 ....$20.00
Beam, Ducks Unlimited, #3 Mallard Hen, 1977 ....$45.00
Beam, Ducks Unlimited, #9 American Widgeon Pair, 1983...$65.00
Beam, Fire Truck 1930 Ford Model A, 1983 ....$225.00
Beam, Ford, '56 Thunderbirds, yellow, 1986 ....$110.00
Beam, George Washington, 1986..$18.00
Beam, Grant Train, Baggage Car, 1982..............................$65.00
Beam, Harold's Club Covered Wagon, blue, 1969 ....$10.00
Beam, Harold's Club Covered Wagon, 1974.......................$35.00
Beam, JB Turner Locomotive, 1982..................................$120.00
Beam, Model A Ford, Woodie Wagon, green, 1984 ....$100.00
Beam, Noel Candle w/Music Box, 1986 ....$145.00
Beam, Shriner, Moila w/Sword, 1972 ....$20.00

Beam, Siamese Cat, 1967, $10.00.

Beam, St Bernard, 1979 ....$35.00
Beam, Texas Jack Rabbit, 1971 ....$15.00
Beam, Volkswagen, bl, 1973 ....$70.00
Brooks, Duesenberg, 1971 ....$35.00
Brooks, Greensboro Open - 40th, 1977 ....$25.00
Brooks, Indy Car, Norton #3, 1982....................................$80.00
Brooks, Iowa Farmers Elevator, 1978 ....$30.00
Brooks, Kentucky Long Rifle, 1978 ....$95.00
Brooks, Macaw, 1980..$52.00
Brooks, Owl #5, Great Gray, 1982.....................................$30.00
Brooks, Razorback Hog #2, 1979 ....$33.00
Brooks, Riverboat, Delta Belle, 1969 ....$16.00
Brooks, Saddle, silver, 1972...$28.00
Brooks, Shrine, King Tut Guard, 1979................................$20.00
Brooks, Snow Leopard, 19880 ....$39.00
Brooks, Stan Laurel, 1978..$38.00
Brooks, Totem Pole #2, 1973...$20.00
Brooks, Washington Salmon, 1971 ....$26.00

Cyrus Noble, Bear & Cubs #2, 1978 ....$75.00
Cyrus Noble, Buffalo & Bow & Calf #2, 1977 ....$63.00
Cyrus Noble, Burro, 1973...$55.00
Cyrus Noble, Gambler, 1974 ....$50.00
Cyrus Noble, Landlady, 1977 ....$35.00
Cyrus Noble, Mt Sheep #1, 1978 ....$85.00
Cyrus Noble, Penguin Family, 1978 ....$50.00
Double Springs, Bicentennial Series, Iowa, 1976 ....$52.00
Double Springs, Buick 1913 Touring Car, 1972 ....$40.00
Double Springs, Rolls Royce 1912, 1971 ....$50.00
Dugs Nevada Miniatures, Arizona Charlie - Horse, 1990 ....$29.00
Dugs Nevada Miniatures, Carol's Stardust, 1981 ....$72.00
Dugs Nevada Miniatures, Chicken Ranch, 1979 ....$120.00
Dugs Nevada Miniatures, Old Bridge Ranch, 1984 ....$23.00
Dugs Nevada Miniatures, Valley of the Dolls, 1988 ....$50.00
Famous First, '53 Corvette, 1975, 500 ML.......................$95.00
Famous First, Bell - St Paul, 1970 ....$20.00
Famous First, Bennie Bow Wow, 1973, 200 ML.................$15.00
Famous First, Butterfly, 1971, mini................................$12.00
Famous First, Corvette, '63 Stingray, red, 1977 ....$80.00
Famous First, Lockheed, USAF Transport, 1982.................$79.00
Famous First, Porsche Targa, 1979 ....$69.00
Famous First, Squirrel, 1981, mini.................................$35.00
Famous First, Visigoth, 1979, mini.................................$22.00
Famous First, Winnie Mae Plane, 1972, mini.....................$52.00
Garnier, Aladdin's Lamp, 1963.......................................$40.00
Garnier, Alfa Romeo - 1913, 1969 ....$25.00

Garnier, Cardinal, 1969, $15.00.

Garnier, Cocker Spaniel, 1970 ....$19.00
Garnier, Ski Boot $20.00
Garnier, SS Queen Mary, 1970 ....$27.00
Grenadier, Africa Rifle Corps British Soldier, 1970.............$35.00
Grenadier, American Thoroughbred, 1978.........................$60.00
Grenadier, Fire Chief, 1973..$100.00
Grenadier, Napoleon, 1969 ....$32.00
Grenadier, Pontiac Trans Am, 1979.................................$50.00
Grenadier, San Carlos Mission, 1977 ....$22.00
Grenadier, Texas Ranger, 1979, mini..............................$15.00

Grenadier, 1st Georgia Regiment Bicentennial Soldier, 1976..$20.00
Grenadier, 1st Pennsylvania Revolutionary Soldier, 1970 .....$29.00
Grenadier, 1st Regiment Virginia Civil War Soldier, 1974, mini..$16.00
Hoffman, AJ Foyte #2, 1972...$125.00
Hoffman, Androcles & the Lion, 1978 ....$22.00
Hoffman, Band Street Swinger, Accordion Player, 1978, mini..$15.00
Hoffman, Beagle, 1978, mini...$26.00
Hoffman, Bear & Cub, 1978 ....$65.00
Hoffman, Blue Jay Pair, 1979 ....$35.00
Hoffman, Children of the World, Spain, 1979, 8-oz...........$26.00
Hoffman, Eagle - Open Wing, 1979................................$20.00
Hoffman, Mallards - Closed Wing, 1982...........................$24.00
Hoffman, Mare & Colt, 1979...$45.00
Hoffman, Merganser (decoy), 1978 ....$20.00
Hoffman, Mr Lucky Series #1, Cobbler, 1973 ....$26.00
Hoffman, Mr Lucky Series #2, Dancer, 1974 ....$35.00
Hoffman, Mr Lucky Series #3, School Teacher, 1976 ....$30.00
Hoffman, Mr Lucky Series #4, Tailor, 1979.......................$30.00
Hoffman, Mr Lucky Series #5, Farmer, 1980.....................$30.00
Hoffman, Panda, 1976...$50.00
Hoffman, Pointer (dog), 1979 ....$52.00
Hoffman, Rodeo Series (Belt Buckles), Bareback Riding, 1979....$30.00
Hoffman, Russell CM Series #2, Stage Robber, 1978 ....$48.00
Hoffman, Springer Spaniel, 1979....................................$58.00
Hoffman, Suzie Siamese, 1981, 50ml...............................$15.00
Hoffman, Wolf & Raccoon, 1978.....................................$50.00
Jack Daniels, 125th Anniversary, 1990.............................$50.00
Jack Daniels, 1904 St Louis World's Fair, 1996...................$25.00
Kontinental, Dentist, 1978 ....$30.00
Kontinental, Saddle Maker, 1977....................................$28.00
Lionstone, Afghan Dog, 1977 ....$25.00
Lionstone, Bartender, 1969...$30.00
Lionstone, Basketball Players, 1974 ....$56.00
Lionstone, Betsy Ross, 1975 ....$26.00
Lionstone, Buccaneer, 1973 ....$27.00
Lionstone, Buffalo, 1977, mini $20.00
Lionstone, Canvasback Duck, w/base, 1981 ....$40.00
Lionstone, Country Doctor, 1969....................................$22.00
Lionstone, Eastern Bluebird, 1972 ....$24.00
Lionstone, Falcon, 1973..$30.00
Lionstone, Fireman #8, Alarm Box, 1983 ....$115.00
Lionstone, Lucky Buck, 1975 ....$32.00
Lionstone, Monkey Business #1 (clown), 1978...................$40.00
Lionstone, Olsonite Eagle #6, 1973 ....$100.00
Lionstone, Roadrunner, 1979, mini $14.00
Lionstone, Snow Goose, w/base, 1981 ....$55.00
Lionstone, Tattooed Lady, 1973 ....$25.00
Lionstone, Valley Forge, 1975 ....$30.00
McCormick, Ben Franklin, 1975 ....$25.00
McCormick, Black Bart, 1974 ....$35.00
McCormick, Brahma Bull, 1973.......................................$33.00
McCormick, Buffalo Bill, 1979 ....$59.00
McCormick, Cable Car, 1969 ....$32.00
McCormick, Centurion, 1969 ....$29.00
McCormick, Hank Williams Sr, 1980................................$140.00
McCormick, Pirate #12, 1972, ½-pt $19.00
McCormick, Robert E Lee, 1978, mini $23.00

McCormick, Spirit of St Louis, 1969, 1-pt $125.00
McCormick, Spirit of 76, 1976.. $49.00
McCormick, Thelma Lu $30.00
McCormick, Thomas Jefferson, 1975 .... $25.00
McCormick, US Marshall, 1979.. $42.00
McCormick, Weary Willie, 1981 .... $100.00
OBR, Balloon, 1969 .... $19.00
OBR, Pierce Arrow, 1969 .... $45.00
OBR, WC Fields, Top Hat, 1976 .... $65.00
Old Bardstown, Bull Dog, 1980 .... $155.00
Old Bardstown, Stanley Steamer, 1978 .... $53.00
Old Bardstown, Wildcat #3, 1979 .... $155.00
Old Commonwealth, Auburn Tiger Fooball Mascot, 1979.. $43.00
Old Commonwealth, Birds of Ireland, 1993..................... $35.00
Old Commonwealth, Fireman (modern), #2 Nozzleman, 1983. $73.00
Old Commonwealth, Fireman #1, Cumberland Valley, 1976. $112.00
Old Commonwealth, Miner #5, Shooter, 1983, mini.......... $21.00
Old Commonwealth, Virginia University, 1980.................. $29.00
Old Commonwealth, Waterfowler #1, 1978 .... $56.00
Old Commonwealth, Western Boot, 1982.......................... $29.00

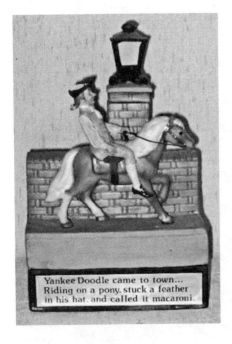

Old Commonwealth, Yankee Doodle with Music, 1982, $30.00.

Old Fitzgerald, Candelite, glass, 1955 .... $15.00
Old Fitzgerald, Eagle, glass, 1973....................................... $7.00
Old Mr Boston, Clown Head, 1973 .... $17.00
Old Mr Boston, Fire Engine, 1974 .... $36.00
Old Mr Boston, Nebraska #1, gold, 1970.......................... $59.00
Old Mr Boston, Ship Lantern, 1974.................................... $18.00
Pace Setter, Corvette Stingray, dark blue, 1975 .... $29.00
Pace Setter, John Deer Tractor #1, 1982............................ $149.00
Pace Setter, Mack Pumper.. $150.00
Pacesetter, Case Tractor, mini $35.00
Ski Country, Alaskan Walrus, 1985, mini $27.00
Ski Country, Badger, 1981... $31.00
Ski Country, Birth of Freedom, 1976, mini $85.00
Ski Country, Brown Trout, 1976, mini $58.00
Ski Country, Jaguar, 1983 .... $180.00

Ski Country, Labrador w/Pheasant, 1978, mini $40.00
Ski Country, Mallard Drake, 1973..................................... $72.00
Ski Country, Mountain Eagle, 1973 .... $195.00
Ski Country, Peacock, 1973 .... $115.00
Ski Country, Rainbow Dancer, 1984 .... $98.00
Ski Country, Rhino, black, 1993, mini $59.00
Ski Country, Rocky Mountain Sheep, 1981 .... $79.00
Ski Country, State Theater, 2001 .... $48.00
Ski Country, Tom Thumb, 1974.. $38.00
Ski Country, Turkey, 1976... $138.00
Ski Country, White Tail Deer, 1982, mini $55.00
Ski Country, Whooping Crane, 1984 .... $63.00
Ski Country, Wood Duck, 1974, mini $156.00
Wild Turkey, Series #1, #2 Female, on Log, 1972.............. $149.00
Wild Turkey, Series #1, #4 w/Poult, 1974 .... $60.00

Wild Turkey, Series #1, #6 Striding, 1983, mini, $30.00.

Wild Turkey, Series #2, #3 Lore, 1981 .... $44.00
Wild Turkey, Series #3, #3 Turkey Fighting, 1983 .... $149.00
Wild Turkey, Series #3, #6 Turkey & Poults, 1984, mini $45.00
Wild Turkey, Series #3, #10 Turkey & Coyote, 1986........... $95.00
Wild Turkey, Series #3, #12 Turkey & Skunk, 1986 .... $125.00

DeForest of California

This family-run company (operated by Jack and Margaret DeForest and sons) was located in California; from the early 1950s until 1970 they produced the type of novelty ceramic kitchenware and giftware items that state has become known for. A favored theme was their onion-head jars, bowls, ashtray, etc., all designed with various comical expressions. Some of their cookie jars were finished in a brown wood-tone glaze and were very similar to many produced by Twin Winton.

See also Cookie Jars.

Ashtray, orange, gold & green free-form, #168 & #8168, 11¼x7¼" $18.00
Ashtray, red drips on round tray w/3 rests in center, #243, 8½" dia $12.00

Bowl, centerpiece; orange coral-like oval in center on shaded green, #855, 2x14½x5¾" **$25.00**

Cheese keeper, cheese wedge w/smiling face, 4x5" **$15.00**

Chip & dip set, pig's head condiment w/Go Ahead Make a Pig... on lid, 4 trays form circle on turntable, from $75 to **$95.00**

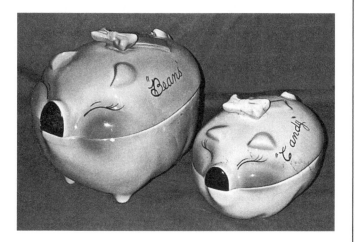

Covered bowls, pig figural, ca 1959, large, $80.00; small, $40.00.

(Photo courtesy Fred and Joyce Roerig)

Figure vase, Lizzy, hand up to brim of lg hat, vase behind & to right, 8½" **$60.00**

Figurine, angel 'Noel,' head bowed, hands clasped, 6¼x3½" .. **$70.00**

Figurine planter, Lucky elephant, 4¼x5½x2" **$20.00**

Figurine planter, Mickey, kitten plays w/ball under right front paw, 4" **$50.00**

Jar, garlic head, smiling face, 4½", from $20 to **$25.00**

Jar, man's face w/lg mustache, Mustard on yellow hat lid **$20.00**

Jar, May O'Naise, smiling face w/hat cover, 4¾x4", from $50 to **$65.00**

Jar, onion head, tears on cheeks, leaves on lid, from $20 to . **$25.00**

Jar, Perky (pig's face), black nose & blue bow, Mustard written on top, 1956, 3x4½x3", from $35 to **$45.00**

Jar, Perky (pig's face), Go Ahead Make a Pig of Yourself! on forehead, dated 1957, 4", from $35 to **$45.00**

Jar, relish; hamburger w/smiling face, olive finial, Relish on top of bun, 1956, 3½x4¼" **$20.00**

Jar, Swiss cheese quarter w/smiling face, Cheezy on lid, 4x5x3¼" ..**$35.00**

Lazy Susan, 4 shell like bowls surround center jar w/lid, multicolor pastels, on wooden tray **$25.00**

Nut dish, peanut shape w/squirrel finial, 5x8" **$17.50**

Pitcher, Perky (pig's face), 7½", from $55 to **$65.00**

Planter, caterpillar/inch worm, green w/black top hat, #323 ... **$25.00**

Plaque, fish, pink & purple striped w/gold highlights, 11x8½", from $28 to **$35.00**

Plaques, fish, pink w/gold trim, 5x6½" & 2 babies: 4x3½", set of 3, from $35 to **$45.00**

Salt & pepper shakers, Perky (pig's head), 3", pr **$40.00**

Spoon rest, flower on milk-can shape, avocado green, #3278 . **$17.50**

Tidbit, 3 gold shell shapes w/touches of olive green & orange, center metal handle, #FL35, ... **$17.50**

Tray, pineapple shape, brown/orange & gold, 1¼x7¼x3½" . **$12.00**

Tureen, rooster figural, w/lid & ladle, 11½x12" **$165.00**

Degenhart Glass

John and Elizabeth Degenhart owned and operated the Crystal Art Glass Factory in Cambridge, Ohio. From 1947 until John died in 1964, they produced some fine glassware. John was well known for his superior paperweights, but the glassware that collectors love today was made after 1964, when Elizabeth restructured the company, creating many lovely moulds and scores of colors. She hired Zack Boyd, who had previously worked for Cambridge Glass, and between the two of them, they developed almost 150 unique and original color formulas.

Complying with provisions she had made before her death, close personal friends at Island Mould and Machine Company in Wheeling, West Virginia, took Elizabeth's moulds and removed the familiar 'D in a heart' trademark from them. She had requested that ten of her moulds be donated to the Degenhart Museum, where they remain today. Zack Boyd eventually bought the Degenhart factory and acquired the remaining moulds. He has added his own logo to them and is continuing to press glass very similar to Mrs. Degenhart's.

For more information, we recommend *Degenhart Glass and Paperweights* by Gene and Cathy Florence, published by the Degenhart Paperweight and Glass Museum, Inc., Cambridge, Ohio.

Club: Friends of Degenhart
Degenhart Paperweight and Glass Museum
P.O. Box 186, Cambridge, OH 43725
614-432-2626
Individual membership: $5 per year; Membership includes newsletter, *Heartbeat*, a quarterly publication and free admission to the museum.

Elizabeth Degenhart Portrait Plate, Amber, 5½", $20.00.

Bicentennial Bell, Charcoal **$12.00**
Bird Salt, Bittersweet **$20.00**
Bird Toothpick Holder, Butter Nut **$15.00**
Bird Toothpick Holder, Caramel Slag **$25.00**
Buzz Saw Wine, Crystal **$20.00**
Daisy & Button Toothpick Holder, Amberina **$30.00**

Forget-Me-Not Toothpick Holder, Amberina........................$15.00
Forget-Me-Not Toothpick Holder, Misty Green..................$23.00
Gypsy Pot, Amethyst...$15.00
Heart Jewel Box, Crown Tuscan....................................$25.00
Heart Jewel Box, Vaseline...$20.00
Heart Toothpick Holder, Blue Opal...............................$15.00
Hen Covered Dish, Sapphire Blue $25.00
Hobo Baby Shoe, Caramel Custard Slag $20.00
Liberty Bell, Lemonade Opalescent................................$20.00
Owl, Antique Blue w/White (faint swirls)...........................$22.00
Owl, Apple Green $20.00
Owl, Bloody Mary, #4, from $12 to $25.00
Owl, Cambridge Pink..$30.00
Owl, Caramel Dark...$24.00
Owl, Elizabeth's Lime Ice #1..$25.00
Owl, Green Maverick Variant $20.00
Owl, Nile Green Opal..$27.00
Owl, Old Lavender $18.00
Owl, Sapphire Blue...$15.00
Owl, Violet #3 (dark purple)..$20.00
Paperweight, The Lord Is My Shepherd..., 2¼x3"..............$88.00
Paperweight, 4 light blue flowers in clear, John Degenhart (unsigned),
  3"...$30.00
Pooch, Brown Gray Slag..$20.00
Pooch, Dark Toffee Slag..$25.00
Pooch, Lemon Opalescent..$30.00
Pooch, Lime Ice $15.00
Pooch, Tomato Gray-Ivory Slag Mix $30.00
Priscilla, Amethyst w/Heathbloom $22.00
Priscilla, Bernard Boyd's Ebony $22.00
Priscilla, Bluebell...$55.00
Priscilla, Powder Blue Slag..$17.50
Priscilla, Willow Blue, 1976..$22.50
Puss in Boot, Bloody Mary Tomato Slag.........................$15.00
Robin Covered Dish, Amethyst, 5" $40.00
Skate Boot, Amethyst..$25.00
Turkey Covered Dish, Sapphire Blue, 5" $30.00

deLee Art Pottery

Jimmie Lee Adair Kohl founded her company in 1937, and it continued to operate until 1958. She was the inspiration, artist, and owner of the company for the 21 years it was in business. The name deLee means 'of or by Lee' and is taken from the French language. She trained as an artist at the San Diego Art Institute and UCLA where she also earned an art education degree. She taught art and ceramics at Belmont High School in Los Angeles while getting her ceramic business started. On September 9, 1999, at the age of 93, Jimmie Lee died after having lived a long and wonderfully creative life.

The deLee line included children, adults, animals, birds, and specialty items such as cookie jars, banks, wall pockets, and several licensed Walter Lantz characters. Skunks were a favorite subject, and more of her pieces were modeled as skunks than any other single animal. Her figurines are distinctive in their design, charm, and excellent hand painting; when carefully studied, they can be easily recognized. Jimmie Lee modeled almost all the pieces — more than 350 in all.

The beautiful deLee colors were mixed by her and remained essentially the same for 20 years. The same figurine may be found painted in different colors and patterns. Figurines were sold wholesale only. Buyers could select from a catalog or visit the deLee booth in New York and Los Angeles Gift Marts. All figurines left the factory with name and logo stickers. The round Art Deco logo sticker is silver with the words 'deLee Art, California, Hand Decorated.' Many of the figures are incised 'deLee Art' on the bottom.

The factory was located in Los Angeles during its 21 years of production and in Cuernavaca, Mexico, for four years during WWII. Production continued until 1958, when Japanese copies of her figures caused sales to decline. For further study we recommend *deLee Art* by Joanne and Ralph Schaefer and John Humphries.

Advisors: Joanne and Ralph Schaefer (See Directory, deLee)

Figurine, angel girl, blue ribbon in hair, flowers along hem of dress,
  7"...$70.00
Figurine, blond girl stands w/hands in muff, round balls form hair
  curls, 5¼" $280.00
Figurine, boy sitting cross-legged, resting head on right hand,
  1939...$185.00
Figurine, Can Can lady, ivory, pinks & green w/gold, fine detail,
  13½x9½"...$295.00
Figurine, Dapper Dan w/cane & top hat, 7".......................$80.00
Figurine, Jimmy Aviator, Deco-style sticker, 5½", from $85 to..$100.00
Figurine, June, girl w/black hair holding bouquet in both hands,
  4½"..$165.00
Figurine, Rye, lamb standing w/eyes downcast, 4½" $135.00
Figurine, Skippy, white dog w/blue collar, sticker, 3½x3½" .$75.00
Figurine, Stinkie & Phew, skunks, 4", 4½", pr $35.00

Figurine, Tops the giraffe, 7½", from $50.00 to $60.00.
(Photo courtesy Joanne and Ralph Schaefer and John Humphries)

Figurine, Trixie, cat standing on hind legs...........................$135.00
Figurines, blond twin babies (nude), 3½", pr.....................$200.00
Figurines, Leilani & Maui (Hawaiian boy & girl), both seated, 9",
  pr $340.00
Figurines, Mandy & Moe (Black boy & girl), brown, blue & white,
  6", 4½", pr $215.00
Figurines, Winkums, girl w/applied curls sits w/doll, 3" $240.00

Flower holder, blond girl stands by open basket, white w/multicolor flowers on skirt (dainty, sm), 6" $70.00

Flower holder, boy w/vase on shoulder, flowered shirt, white bib pants, 7" $185.00

Flower holder, Buddy, blond boy holds container on shoulder. $175.00

Flower holder, Butch, WWII sailor boy, 5¾" $165.00

Flower holder, Irene, blond girl w/opening in apron, lavender flower trim, 7¼x5" $35.00

Flower holder, Johnny, boy w/bouquet, brown jacket, NM ..$115.00

Flower holder, lady in pink floral dress, plumed hat, opening behind, 10" $165.00

Flower holder, Lou, girl in pink w/hands up to chin, opening behind, 8x4½" $85.00

Flower holder, Mary & her lamb, 6½x3½" $85.00

Flower holder, Pedro playing guitar, brown & blue tones, holder behind, 1944, 8" $120.00

Flower holder, Sally, blond in peach, green & pink, opening in back, deeLee (sic) mark, 7" $170.00

Flower holder, Sis, blond girl w/braids holding jar, peach & green, 1942, 6¾" $170.00

Flower holders, boy holding hat (dated 1949) & blond girl w/nosegay in both hands, 7¾", pr $120.00

Planter, pony w/pink mane & tail, blue flowers on white body, opening on back, 6½x5½" $25.00

Vase, girl leans over edge of flower form, pastels on white, 5x3½" $215.00

Vase, lady w/flowered bonnet (opening there), holds skirt in right hand, flower decor, 7¾" $39.00

Wall hanger, mallard duck, 7x7", from $35.00 to $50.00. (Photo courtesy Joanne and Ralph Schaefer and John Humphries)

Wall pocket, teakettle, black w/cherries & green leaves applied to front, 6¼x6¾" $30.00

Delft

Collectors have been in love with the quaint blue and white Delftware for many years. It was originally made in the Dutch city of Delft (hence its name), but eventually it was also produced in England and Germany. Antique Delft can be very expensive, but even items made in the twentieth century are very collectible and much less pricey. Thousands of Delft pieces are being imported every year from the Netherlands, ranging from souvenir grade to excellent quality ware made under the Royal Delft label. All of our examples are from more recent production, such as you might find at garage sales and flea markets. In the listings that follow, items are blue and white unless noted otherwise.

Canister, Rice, windmill scene, Germany, 1930s, 8" $35.00

Charger, couple in horsedrawn sleigh, Royal Sphinx Maastricht Delfts, 16" $95.00

Charger, floral pattern w/bird, multicolor, Royal Porceleyne Fles, 1968, 11¾" $170.00

Charger, florals, Royal Porceleyne Fles, 1965, 14¼" $315.00

Charger, Spring, couple in horsedrawn buggy, Boch Delfts, 15½" $125.00

Coffee grinder, windmill reserve among flowers, metal frame marked PeDe, mounts to wall, 13½x5x6¾", EX $85.00

Cup & saucer, demitasse; Hand Painted Delft Blue DALC #28. $25.00

Ewer, fishing boats, flowers & geometrical patterns, De Porceleyne Fles, #2274, 9" $70.00

Ewer, ships on water scene & lg florals, artist signed, Royal Porceleyne Fles, ca 1916, 9½x5½" $100.00

Ginger jar, floral panels, Boch Freres Delfts mark, 13⅝x7¾" . $115.00

Ginger jar, floral reserves, animal finial, Petrus Regout, 18".. $100.00

Jar, floral, bulbous body, marked H Bl - CU - Delft - 1456, 20th C, 11½x5¾" $140.00

Plate, Borman, Lovell, Anderson, First Men Around the Moon, 1968, 7" $30.00

Plate, De Eerste Austronauten 1961, Porceleyne Fles, 7¼" .. $90.00

Plate, De Hand Moet Uit de Mouw (The Hand Must Come Out of Sleeve), Royal Porceleyne Fles, 1928, 10" $175.00

Plate, Den Vaderland Ghetrouwe (Faithful to the Fatherland), Royal Porceleyne Fles, ca 1917, 7¼" $300.00

Plate, floral, De Porceleyne Fles, 4½" $35.00

Plate, floral, scalloped rim, Royal Porceleyne Fles, 1963, 8". $60.00

Plate, flower-filled urn, De Porceleyne Fles, 1966, 7", from $35.00 to $45.00. (Photo courtesy Jim and Marsha Fleeners)

Plate, lady at clothesline, signed CS, Royal Porceleyn Fles, 1939, 9" $200.00

Plate, man w/scythe, Royal Porceleyne Fles, 10" $100.00

Plate, Pander Postjager airplane, Royal Porceleyne Fles, 1934, 7¼", NM...$175.00

Plate, Sputnik, Marcelius de Bruijn, Royal Delft Porceleyne Fles, 1957, 7⅜"...$90.00

Platter, fish, Made in Holland, #1379, ca 1935-49, 9½x5"..$85.00

Platter, flower basket & flowers, canted corners, 2 factories in back rim, Royal Delft, 1975, 15¾x10¼"............................$265.00

Tea caddy, Dutch sailing barges in reserves, De Porceleyne Fles, 1938...$85.00

Tray, Dutch water scene w/boats, canted corners, Royal Porceleyne Fles, 1x6x4⅜"..$65.00

Vase, bud; floral, urn style, marked AVK, 7¼".....................$35.00

Vase, Dutch windmill reserve & flowers, amphora shape, Quo Vadis, 1946-69, 7"..$50.00

Vase, floral, baluster, Porceleyne Fles, 1968, 5¾x3¾"..........$50.00

Vase, floral, De Porceleyne Fles, 1951, 3½x2¼"................$30.00

Vase, floral, 8-sided, slim neck, Royal Porceleyne Fles, 1976, 13"..$130.00

Vase, Liberation of Holland 1945 commemorative, Royal Porceleyne Fles, 1946, 8¼"...$180.00

Vase, scenic reserves & lg flowers, spherical, Royal Porceleyne Fles, ca 1944, 6⅞x5½".......................................$250.00

Vase, windmill reserve/flowers, sm handles, Royal Delft De Porceleyne Fles, ca 1910, 14"...................................$325.00

Vase/bottle, floral, Royal Porceleyne Fles, #39, 1953, 10½".$140.00

Wall pocket, lg flowers, resembles handled vase, unmarked Holland, 3½x4"..$27.50

Vase, floral, De Porceleyne Fles, with handle, 1986, 9", from $200.00 to $235.00. (Photo courtesy Jim and Marsha Fleeners)

Department 56 Inc.

In 1976, Department 56 Inc. introduced a line of six handcrafted buildings; this original Snow Village proved to be very successful, and soon the company added not only more buildings but acces-sories as well. Other villages were added in the 1980s including the Dicken's Series, New England, Alpine, Christmas in the City, and Bethlehem. During that decade they also introduced their popular Snow Babies line; these are very collectible today. Offerings in the '90s included the North Pole, Disney Parks, and Seasons Bay.

Alpine Village, Josef Engel Farmhouse, 1987, MIB............$395.00

Christmas in the City, Sutton Place Brownstones, 1987-89, MIB..$350.00

Christmas Story, Ralphie's House, MIB..............................$85.00

Dickens Village, Brick Abbey, #6549-8, MIB, $90.00.

Dickens Village, Buckingham Palace, 4-pc set w/Household Guard, MIB..$110.00

Dickens Village, Chesterton Manor, 1987, EXIB..............$325.00

Dickens Village, Ramsford Palace.....................................$95.00

Dickens Village, Tower of London, MIB..............................$120.00

Dickens Village, Twelve Drummers Drumming, retired 2000, MIB, from $235 to...$275.00

Dickens Village, Victoria Station, MIB, from $75 to.........$100.00

Elvis Presley's Graceland, MIB..$100.00

Halloween, Creepy's Pet Store, MIB..................................$100.00

Halloween, Dr Lunatic's Laboratory, MIB.........................$100.00

Halloween, Ghostly Carousel, retired, MIB.......................$185.00

Halloween, Haunted Barn, MIB, from $135 to..................$175.00

Halloween, Haunted Mansion, green roof (no snow), retired, MIB, from $325 to...$350.00

Halloween, Scaredy Cat Ferris Wheel, #53208, MIB.........$115.00

Merry Makers, Merrily-We-Roll-Along Carolers & Gabriel the Goat, 1994-96, 13" L, MIB, from $275 to.........................$325.00

New England Village, Smythe Woolen Mill, 1987, MIB...$385.00

Season's Bay, Mystic Ledge Lighthouse, MIB.....................$110.00

Snow Village, Crystal Theater, limited edition, 1998, M (no box)..$160.00

Snow Village, Jingle Belle Houseboat, 1991, MIB, from $150 to.$175.00

Snow Village, Manchester Square, #58301, 1997-2000, MIB.$115.00

Snow Village, Mansion w/green roof, 1998-2000, MIB.....$350.00

Snow Village, McDonald's, MIB, from $100 to **$135.00**
Snow Village, Mickey's Dining Car, #50784, 1986-87, MIB, from $300 to **$375.00**
Snow Village, Shelly's Diner, MIB..**$90.00**
Snow Village, Starbucks Coffee Shop, #54859, 1995, MIB, from $100 to **$125.00**
Snow Village, Stardust Drive-In Theatre, MIB....................**$95.00**
Snowbabies, And Toto Too?, 1991, MIB.............................**$90.00**
Snowbabies, Cinderella, baby w/glass slipper & 2 on pumpkin coach, set of 3 ....**$125.00**
Snowbabies, Climbing on Tree, 1987, MIB **$375.00**
Snowbabies, Jack Frost Through the Frosty Forest, MIB, from $150 to **$185.00**
Snowbabies, Jack Frost Touch of Winter Magic, #68543, 1994-99, MIB, from $75 to **$90.00**

Snowbabies, Polar Express, retired 1992, 6" long, $65.00.

Depression Glass

Since the early '60s, this has been a very active area of collecting. Interest is still very strong, and although values have long been established, except for some of the rarer items, Depression glass is still relatively inexpensive. Some of the patterns and colors that were entirely avoided by the early wave of collectors are now becoming popular, and it's very easy to reassemble a nice table setting of one of these lines today.

Most of this glass was manufactured during the Depression years. It was inexpensive, mass-produced, and available in a wide assortment of colors. The same type of glassware was still being made to some extent during the '50s and '60s, and today the term 'Depression glass' has been expanded to include the later patterns as well.

Some things have been reproduced, and the slight variation in patterns and colors can be very difficult to detect. For instance, the Sharon butter dish has been reissued in original colors of pink and green (as well as others that were not original); and several pieces of Cherry Blossom, Madrid, Avocado, Mayfair, and Miss America have also been reproduced. Some pieces you'll see in 'antique' malls and flea markets today have been recently made in dark uncharacteristic carnival colors, which, of course, are easy to spot.

For further study, Gene and Cathy Florence have written several informative books on the subject, and we recommend them all: *Elegant Glassware of the Depression Era; Glass Candlesticks of the Depression Era, Vols. 1* and *2; Kitchen Glassware of the Depression Years; Florences' Glassware Pattern Identification Guides, Vols. I – IV; Pocket Guide to Depression Glass;* and *Collector's Encyclopedia of Depression Glass* (Collector Books).

See also Anchor Hocking and other specific companies.

Adam, pink or green, pitcher, 8", $45.00.

American Pioneer, green, candlesticks, 6½", pr **$135.00**
American Pioneer, green, candy jar, w/lid, 1-lb **$110.00**
American Pioneer, green, cup..**$12.00**
American Pioneer, green, goblet, wine; 3-oz, 4" **$55.00**
American Pioneer, green, plate, 6" **$15.00**
American Pioneer, green, saucer **$5.00**
American Pioneer, green, sherbet, 4¾"...............................**$45.00**
American Pioneer, pink, bowl, console; 10¾" **$60.00**
American Pioneer, pink, creamer, 2¾" **$25.00**
American Pioneer, pink, lamp, tall; 8½" **$135.00**
American Pioneer, pink, plate, w/handles, 11½"................**$30.00**
American Pioneer, pink, sugar bowl, 3½" **$20.00**
American Pioneer, pink, tumbler, juice; 5-oz **$40.00**
American Pioneer, pink, vase, crimped edge, 7" **$120.00**
Anniversary, crystal, cake plate, w/cover **$10.00**
Anniversary, crystal, candy jar, w/lid **$30.00**
Anniversary, crystal, creamer, footed...................................**$5.00**
Anniversary, crystal, cup..**$4.00**
Anniversary, crystal, saucer..**$1.00**
Anniversary, crystal, vase, 6½" **$30.00**
Anniversary, pink, bowl, berry; 4⅞" **$10.00**
Anniversary, pink, butter dish **$60.00**
Anniversary, pink, plate, dinner; 9" **$15.00**
Anniversary, pink, plate, sherbet; 6¼" **$4.00**
Anniversary, pink, sugar bowl..**$10.00**
Anniversary, pink, vase, wall pinup **$38.00**

Beehive, crystal, bowl, utility; 19¾-oz.................................$12.50
Beehive, crystal, creamer, 9½-oz...................................$5.00
Beehive, crystal, sugar bowl, 11½-oz.............................$5.00
Beehive, crystal, sugar bowl lid.......................................$4.00
Beehive, crystal, tray, serving; 12¼"............................$12.00
Beehive, pink, bowl, berry; 4⅞"......................................$5.00
Beehive, pink, butter dish, 6"..$35.00
Beehive, pink, goblet, tea; footed, 15-oz.....................$12.50
Beehive, pink, pitcher, w/ice lip, 84-oz.......................$35.00
Beehive, pink, sherbet, flat, 3¾".....................................$6.00
Block Optic, green, bowl, salad; 7¼"..........................$155.00
Block Optic, green, candy jar, w/lid, 6¼"......................$70.00
Block Optic, green, pitcher, bulbous; 54-oz, 7⅝".........$95.00
Block Optic, green, plate, dinner; 9"............................$27.50
Block Optic, green, sandwich server, center handle.............$75.00
Block Optic, green, sherbet, 6-oz, 4¾"...........................$16.00
Block Optic, green, tumbler, footed, 9-oz......................$20.00
Block Optic, green, vase, blown, 5¾"..........................$365.00
Block Optic, pink, bowl, cereal; 5¼"...............................$30.00
Block Optic, pink, creamer, cone-shaped.........................$15.00
Block Optic, pink, goblet, cocktail; 4"............................$40.00
Block Optic, pink, pitcher, 80-oz, 8"............................$150.00

Block Optic, pink, pitcher, 8½", $38.00.

Block Optic, pink, plate, luncheon; 8"..............................$8.00
Block Optic, pink, salt & pepper shakers, footed, pr...........$95.00
Block Optic, pink, sherbet, 6-oz, 4¾"..............................$17.00
Block Optic, pink, tumbler, flat, 10-oz............................$18.00
Bowknot, green, bowl, berry; 4½"...................................$28.00
Bowknot, green, cup...$12.00
Bowknot, green, tumbler, 10-oz, 5"................................$28.00
Camellia, crystal, bowl, 5"...$5.00
Camellia, crystal, creamer, footed....................................$7.50
Camellia, crystal, plate, luncheon; 8⅜"...........................$10.00
Camellia, crystal, tidbit, 2-tier..$20.00
Circle, green, bowl, 4½"...$17.50
Circle, green, goblet, wine; 4½".......................................$15.00
Circle, green, pitcher, 60-oz..$75.00

Circle, green, plate, sandwich; 10"..................................$14.00
Circle, green, tumbler, tea; 10-oz, 5"...............................$20.00
Circle, pink, creamer..$25.00
Circle, pink, plate, luncheon; 8¼"...................................$10.00
Circle, pink, saucer, w/cup ring...$3.00
Circle, pink, sherbet, 3⅛"...$10.00
Circle, pink, sugar bowl..$25.00
Colonial Fluted, green, bowl, berry; 4".............................$15.00
Colonial Fluted, green, cup...$9.00
Colonial Fluted, green, plate, sherbet; 6"...........................$4.00

Coronation (Banded Rib), pink, pitcher, 68-ounce, 7¾", $695.00. (Photo courtesy Gene and Cathy Florence)

Cremax, ivory, cup...$4.00
Cremax, ivory, plate, bread & butter; 6¼"..........................$2.00
Cremax, ivory, sugar bowl...$5.00
Dewdrop, crystal, bowl, 4¾"..$7.00
Dewdrop, crystal, butter dish...$27.50
Dewdrop, crystal, pitcher, flat..$50.00
Dewdrop, crystal, tumbler, water; 9-oz.............................$20.00
Diana, amber, candy jar, w/lid, round...............................$40.00
Diana, amber, plate, sandwich; 11¾"................................$10.00
Diana, amber, salt & pepper shakers, pr..........................$115.00
Diana, amber, sugar bowl, oval..$8.00
Diana, pink, ashtray, 3½"..$3.50
Diana, pink, bowl, salad; 9"..$20.00
Diana, pink, creamer, oval...$15.00
Diana, pink, plate, dinner; 9½"...$18.00
Diana, pink, sherbet..$10.00
Doric & Pansy, pink, bowl, handles, 9"..............................$20.00
Doric & Pansy, pink, plate, sherbet; 6"...............................$8.00
Doric & Pansy, Ultra Marine, bowl, berry; lg, 8"................$95.00
Doric & Pansy, Ultra Marine, tray, handles, 10".................$38.00
Doric & Pansy Pretty Polly Party Dishes, pink, creamer......$35.00
Doric & Pansy Pretty Polly Party Dishes, pink, plate............$8.00
Ellipse, all colors, bowl, vegetable; handles......................$30.00
Ellipse, all colors, creamer...$12.50

Ellipse, all colors, cup	$10.00
Ellipse, all colors, jug, 24-oz	$40.00
Ellipse, all colors, plate, 8½"	$8.00
Ellipse, all colors, saucer	$2.00
Ellipse, all colors, sugar bowl	$12.50
Ellipse, all colors, tumbler, juice; 5-oz	$8.00
Ellipse, all colors, tumbler, tea; 12-oz	$12.50
Ellipse, all colors, tumbler, water; 9-oz	$10.00
Flora & Diamond Band, pink, pitcher, 42-oz, 8"	$115.00
Floral, green, bowl, vegetable; w/lid, 8"	$75.00
Floral, green, compote, 9"	$995.00
Floral, green, pitcher, lemonade; 48-oz, 10¼"	$285.00
Floral, green, plate, sherbet, 6"	$9.00
Floral, green, platter, oval; 10¾"	$28.00
Floral, green, sugar bowl	$12.00
Floral, pink, bowl, cream soup; 5½"	$750.00
Floral, pink, candy jar, w/lid	$43.00
Floral, pink, lamp	$325.00
Floral, pink, plate, dinner; 9"	$20.00
Floral, pink, sugar bowl	$10.00
Floral, pink, tumbler, water; footed, 7-oz, 4¾"	$22.00
Floral & Diamond Band, green, butter dish	$130.00
Floral & Diamond Band, green, creamer, sm	$12.00
Floral & Diamond Band, green, tumbler, iced tea; 5"	$50.00
Floral & Diamond Band, pink, compote, tall, 5½"	$20.00
Floral & Diamond Band, pink, plate, luncheon; 8"	$45.00
Floral & Diamond Band, pink, tumbler, water; 4"	$25.00
Florentine #1, cobalt, bowl, berry; 5"	$25.00
Florentine #1, cobalt, bowl, cream soup; 5"	$65.00
Florentine #1, cobalt, creamer	$65.00
Florentine #1, cobalt, cup, ruffled	$85.00
Florentine #1, cobalt, pitcher, footed, 36-oz, 6½"	$895.00
Florentine #1, cobalt, saucer	$17.00
Florentine #1, cobalt, sugar bowl, ruffled	$70.00
Florentine #1, green, butter dish	$125.00
Florentine #1, green, compote, ruffled, 3½"	$40.00
Florentine #1, green, plate, dinner; 10"	$22.00
Florentine #1, green, plate, grill; 10"	$14.00
Florentine #1, green, platter, oval; 11½"	$28.00
Florentine #1, green, sugar bowl	$9.50
Florentine #1, green, tumbler, water; footed, 10-oz, 4¾"	$22.00
Florentine #1, yellow, ashtray, 3¾"	$22.00
Florentine #1, yellow, bowl, berry; lg, 8½"	$35.00
Florentine #1, yellow, plate, salad; 8½"	$14.00
Florentine #1, yellow, plate, sherbet; 6"	$7.00
Florentine #1, yellow, sherbet, footed, 3-oz	$15.00
Florentine #1, yellow, tumbler, juice; footed, 5-oz, 3¾"	$28.00
Florentine #2, green, bowl, flat, 9"	$27.50
Florentine #2, green, butter dish	$110.00
Florentine #2, green, creamer	$9.00
Florentine #2, green, plate, grill; 10¼"	$14.00
Florentine #2, green, sugar bowl	$10.00
Florentine #2, pink, bowl, cream soup; 4¾"	$16.00
Florentine #2, pink, candy dish, w/lid	$145.00
Florentine #2, pink, compote, ruffled, 3½"	$45.00
Florentine #2, pink, pitcher, 76-oz, 8¼"	$225.00
Florentine #2, pink, plate, salad; 8½"	$8.50
Florentine #2, yellow, gravy boat	$65.00
Florentine #2, yellow, plate, dinner; 10"	$15.00
Florentine #2, yellow, tumbler, juice; 5-oz, 3⅜"	$22.00
Florentine #2, yellow, tumbler, tea; 12-oz, 5"	$55.00
Florentine #2, yellow, vase, 6"	$60.00
Fortune, crystal or pink, bowl, dessert; 4½"	$10.00
Fortune, crystal or pink, candy dish, flat, w/lid	$30.00
Fortune, crystal or pink, cup	$12.00
Fortune, crystal or pink, plate, luncheon; 8"	$30.00
Fortune, crystal or pink, saucer	$5.00
Fortune, crystal or pink, tumbler, juice; 5-oz, 3½"	$12.50
Georgian, green, bowl, berry; 4½"	$9.00
Georgian, green, bowl, vegetable; oval, 9"	$60.00
Georgian, green, butter dish	$85.00
Georgian, green, creamer, footed, 4"	$18.00
Georgian, green, cup	$10.00
Georgian, green, plate, center design only, 9¼"	$20.00
Georgian, green, plate, luncheon; 8"	$11.00
Georgian, green, platter, closed handles, 11½"	$65.00
Georgian, green, saucer	$3.00
Georgian, green, sugar bowl, footed, 4"	$18.00
Georgian, green, tumbler, flat, 9-oz, 4"	$65.00
Harp, crystal, cup	$28.00
Harp, crystal, plate, 7"	$15.00
Harp, crystal, vase, 6"	$24.00
Hex Optic, pink or green, bowl, mixing; 9"	$28.00
Hex Optic, pink or green, butter dish, rectangular, 1-lb	$95.00
Hex Optic, pink or green, ice bucket, metal handle	$32.00
Hex Optic, pink or green, pitcher, footed, 48-oz, 9"	$45.00
Hex Optic, pink or green, plate, luncheon; 8"	$5.50
Hex Optic, pink or green, platter, round, 11"	$15.00
Hex Optic, pink or green, salt & pepper shakers, pr	$30.00
Hex Optic, pink or green, sugar shaker	$250.00
Hex Optic, pink or green, tumbler, footed, 7"	$10.00
Hex Optic, pink or green, tumbler, 12-oz, 5"	$7.00
Homespun, pink, bowl, cereal; 5"	$32.00
Homespun, pink, platter, closed handles, 13"	$20.00
Homespun, pink, sugar bowl, footed	$10.00
Homespun, pink, tumbler, 6-oz, 3⅞"	$22.00
Iris & Herringbone, crystal, bowl, soup; 7½"	$155.00
Iris & Herringbone, crystal, butter dish	$47.50
Iris & Herringbone, crystal, goblet, cocktail; 4-oz, 4½"	$22.00
Iris & Herringbone, crystal, plate, luncheon; 8"	$100.00
Iris & Herringbone, crystal, tumbler, footed, 6"	$18.00
Iris & Herringbone, crystal, vase, 9"	$30.00
Iris & Herringbone, iridescent, bowl, salad; ruffled, 9½"	$13.00
Iris & Herringbone, iridescent, cup	$14.00
Iris & Herringbone, iridescent, goblet, 4-oz, 5½"	$495.00
Iris & Herringbone, iridescent, saucer	$9.00
Iris & Herringbone, iridescent, sherbet, footed, 4"	$295.00
Jubilee, pink, creamer	$32.00
Jubilee, pink, plate, sandwich; 13½"	$75.00
Jubilee, pink, sugar bowl	$35.00
Jubilee, pink, tumbler, water; 10-oz, 6"	$75.00
Jubilee, pink, vase, 12"	$250.00
Jubilee, yellow, bowl, fruit; handles, 9"	$125.00
Jubilee, yellow, cheese & cracker set	$225.00

Jubilee, yellow, cordial, 1-oz, 4" $300.00
Jubilee, yellow, plate, luncheon; 8¾" $10.00
Laurel, ivory, bowl, vegetable; oval, 9¾" $28.00
Laurel, ivory, plate, dinner; 9⅛" $13.00
Laurel, ivory, salt & pepper shakers, pr $50.00
Laurel, ivory, saucer $3.50
Laurel, ivory, tumbler, flat, 12-oz, 5" $55.00
Laurel, jade, bowl, 11" $60.00
Laurel, jade, creamer, short $25.00
Laurel, jade, platter, oval, 10¾" $55.00
Laurel, jade, sherbet $22.00
Laurel, jade, sugar bowl, short $25.00
Lincoln Inn, blue or red, ashtray $17.50
Lincoln Inn, blue or red, bonbon, oval, handles $16.00
Lincoln Inn, blue or red, compote $30.00
Lincoln Inn, blue or red, plate, 8" $15.00
Lincoln Inn, blue or red, tumbler, footed, 5-oz $30.00
Manhattan, crystal, cup $20.00
Manhattan, crystal, plate, dinner; 10¼" $22.00
Manhattan, crystal, vase, 8" $25.00
Manhattan, pink, bowl, cereal; 5¼" $200.00
Manhattan, pink, cup $300.00
Manhattan, pink, tumbler, footed, 10-oz $24.00
Miss America, crystal, cake plate, footed, 12" $26.00
Miss America, crystal, goblet, juice; 5-oz, 4¾" $25.00
Miss America, crystal, plate, grill; 10¼" $11.00
Miss America, crystal, relish dish, round, divided, 11¾" $22.00
Miss America, pink, bowl, vegetable; oval, 10" $45.00
Miss America, pink, compote, 5" $32.00
Miss America, pink, goblet, juice; 5-oz, 4¾" $110.00
Miss America, pink, salt & pepper shakers, pr $67.50
Miss America, pink, tumbler, iced tea; 14-oz, 5¾" $115.00
Miss America, pitcher, w/ice lip, 65-oz, 8½" $225.00
Moderntone, amethyst, bowl, cream soup; ruffled, 5" $33.00
Moderntone, amethyst, cup $12.00
Moderntone, amethyst, plate, salad; 6¾" $10.00
Moderntone, amethyst, platter, oval, 12" $50.00
Moderntone, amethyst, tumbler, 12-oz $90.00
Moonstone, opalescent, bowl, flat, 7¾" $12.00
Moonstone, opalescent, candleholders, pr $20.00
Moonstone, opalescent, cigarette jar, w/lid $23.00
Moonstone, opalescent, plate, luncheon; 8" $12.00
Moonstone, opalescent, vase, bud; 5½" $18.00
Mt Pleasant, black, amethyst or cobalt, creamer $20.00
Mt Pleasant, black, amethyst or cobalt, plate, grill; 9" $20.00
Mt Pleasant, black, amethyst or cobalt, saucer $3.00
Mt Pleasant, black, amethyst or cobalt, tumbler, footed $25.00
Mt Pleasant, black, amethyst or cobalt, vase, 7¼" $33.00
National, crystal, ashtray, sm $3.00
National, crystal, bowl, berry; 4½" $4.00
National, crystal, candy dish, footed, w/lid $22.50
National, crystal, marmalade $15.00
National, crystal, pitcher, milk; 20-oz $17.50
National, crystal, vase, 9" $20.00
New Century, green, decanter, w/stopper $75.00
New Century, green, plate, breakfast; 7⅛" $13.00
New Century, green, sugar bowl $12.00

New Century, green, tumbler, 10-oz, 5" $22.00

No. 610 (Pyramid), pink or green, pickle bowl, with handles, 9½" long, $35.00.

No 610 (Pyramid), pink, pitcher $395.00
No 610 (Pyramid), pink, tumbler, footed, 11-oz $70.00
No 610 (Pyramid), yellow, creamer $40.00
No 610 (Pyramid), yellow, ice tub lid $700.00
No 610 (Pyramid), yellow, sugar bowl $40.00
No 612 (Horseshoe), green, bowl, berry; 4½" $30.00
No 612 (Horseshoe), green, candy dish in metal frame, decorated lid
  only $225.00

No. 612 (Horseshoe), green or yellow, sandwich plate, 11½", $30.00. (Photo courtesy Gene and Cathy Florence)

No 612 (Horseshoe), yellow, plate, salad; 8⅜" $13.00
No 612 (Horseshoe), yellow, tumbler, footed, 12-oz $195.00
No 616 (Vernon), green or yellow, cup $16.00
No 616 (Vernon), green or yellow, saucer $4.00
No 616 (Vernon), green or yellow, sugar bowl, footed $28.00
No 622 (Pretzel), crystal, bowl, olive; leaf shape; 7" $5.00
No 622 (Pretzel), crystal, pitcher, 39-oz $450.00
No 622 (Pretzel), crystal, plate, sandwich; 11½" $12.00
No 622 (Pretzel), crystal, tumbler, water; 9-oz $45.00
Normandie, amber, pitcher, 80-oz, 8" $85.00
Normandie, amber, platter, 11¾" $22.00
Normandie, amber, sugar lid $110.00
Normandie, pink, bowl, cereal; 6½" $60.00
Normandie, pink, plate, dinner; 11" $150.00

Normandie, pink, salt & pepper shakers, pr........................$90.00
Old Cafe, pink, bowl, cereal; 5½"................................$32.00
Old Cafe, pink, cup...$12.00
Old Cafe, pink, pitcher, 36-oz, 6"............................$150.00
Old Cafe, pink, plate, sherbet; 6".............................$10.00
Old Cafe, pink, tumbler, water; 4".............................$25.00
Old Cafe, red, bowl, berry; tab handles, 3¾"....................$9.00
Old Cafe, red, cup...$12.00
Old Cafe, red, tumbler, juice; 3".............................$22.00
Old Cafe, red, tumbler, water; 4".............................$35.00
Old Colony, pink, bowl, 3 legs, 10½"..........................$275.00
Old Colony, pink, plate, grill; 10½"..........................$26.00
Old Colony, pink, plate, salad; 7¼"...........................$28.00
Old Colony, pink, sherbet, footed............................$120.00
Old Colony, pink, sugar bowl..................................$30.00
Oyster & Pearl, pink, bowl, heart-shaped, handle, 5¼".......$15.00
Oyster & Pearl, pink, candleholders, 3½", pr $40.00
Oyster & Pearl, pink, relish dish, oblong, 10¼" $18.00
Oyster & Pearl, red, bowl, deep, handles, 6½"...............$27.50
Oyster & Pearl, red, bowl, fruit; deep, 10½".................$60.00
Oyster & Pearl, red, plate, sandwich; 13½"...................$55.00
Park Ave, crystal, ashtray, sq, 3½"............................$5.00
Park Ave, crystal, bowl, vegetable; 8½" $10.00
Park Ave, crystal, candleholder, 5", ea $10.00
Park Ave, crystal, tumbler, iced tea; 12-oz, 5⅛" $7.00
Park Ave, yellow, bowl, dessert; 5"............................$7.00
Park Ave, yellow, tumbler, juice; 4½-oz, 3½" $8.00
Park Ave, yellow, tumbler, 10-oz, 4¾".........................$10.00
Parrot, amber, bowl, berry; 5"................................$23.00
Parrot, amber, cup..$42.50
Parrot, amber, hot plate, 5".................................$995.00
Parrot, amber, saucer...$18.00
Parrot, green, bowl, berry; 5"................................$30.00
Parrot, green, butter dish...................................$425.00
Parrot, green, pitcher, 80-oz, 8½" $3,000.00
Parrot, green, sherbet, high, 4¼"...........................$1,450.00
Patrician, amber, bowl, berry; 5".............................$14.00
Patrician, amber, pitcher, 75-oz, 8".........................$125.00
Patrician, amber, plate, dinner; 10½".........................$9.00
Patrician, amber, sugar bowl...................................$9.00
Patrician, green, bowl, berry; lg, 8½".......................$40.00
Patrician, green, butter dish................................$110.00
Patrician, green, plate, luncheon; 9".........................$16.00
Patrick, pink, candlesticks, pr..............................$195.00
Patrick, pink, mayonnaise, 3-pc $195.00
Patrick, pink, plate, salad; 7½".............................$25.00
Patrick, pink, sherbet, 4¾"..................................$38.00
Patrick, yellow, bowl, fruit; handles, 9" $145.00
Patrick, yellow, cup..$35.00
Patrick, yellow, goblet, water; 10-oz, 6" $70.00
Patrick, yellow, saucer.......................................$12.00
Primo, yellow & green, cake plate, 3-footed, 10" $50.00
Primo, yellow & green, saucer..................................$3.00
Primo, yellow & green, tumbler, 9-oz, 5¾" $20.00
Princess, green, bowl, salad; octagonal, 9"..................$42.00
Princess, green, pitcher, 37-oz, 6"..........................$65.00
Princess, green, platter, closed handles, 12"................$32.00

Princess, green, sugar bowl..................................$10.00
Princess, green, vase, 8"....................................$43.00
Princess, pink, bowl, berry; 4½".............................$34.00
Princess, pink, creamer, oval................................$20.00
Princess, pink, plate, dinner; 9½"...........................$28.00
Princess, pink, salt & pepper shakers, 4½", pr $60.00
Princess, pink, tumbler, iced tea; 13-oz, 5¼" $45.00
Raindrops, green, bowl, berry; 7½"...........................$60.00
Raindrops, green, bowl, cereal; 6" $12.50
Raindrops, green, creamer.....................................$9.00
Raindrops, green, cup...$7.00
Raindrops, green, plate, sherbet; 6"..........................$3.00
Raindrops, green, saucer......................................$2.00
Raindrops, green, tumbler, 4-oz, 3"...........................$5.00
Raindrops, green, tumbler, 14-oz, 5⅜"........................$14.00
Ribbon, black, bowl, flared, 9"..............................$45.00
Ribbon, black, plate, luncheon; 8"...........................$14.00
Ribbon, green, bowl, cereal; 5"..............................$50.00
Ribbon, green, cup..$5.00
Ribbon, green, plate, sherbet; 6¼"............................$4.00
Ribbon, green, saucer...$2.50
Ripple, all colors, bowl, berry; shallow, 5"................$15.00
Ripple, all colors, creamer...................................$7.00
Ripple, all colors, cup.......................................$3.50
Ripple, all colors, plate, salad; 6⅞".........................$4.00
Ripple, all colors, sugar bowl................................$7.00
Ripple, all colors, tidbit, 3-tier...........................$35.00
Ripple, all colors, tumbler, 20-oz, 6¼" $10.00

Rock Crystal, colors other than clear or red: wine, three-ounce, $33.00; pitcher with lid, $295.00.

Rock Crystal, crystal, plate, dinner; scalloped, lg center design, 10½"..$50.00
Rock Crystal, crystal, salt cellar...........................$60.00
Rock Crystal, crystal, stemware, cordial; footed, 1-oz..........$25.00
Rock Crystal, crystal, sugar bowl, w/lid, footed, 10-oz.........$55.00
Rock Crystal, crystal, tumbler, juice; 5-oz $22.00
Rock Crystal, red, plate, cake; scalloped, sm center design...$60.00
Rock Crystal, red, sandwich server, center handle $145.00
Rock Crystal, red, saucer....................................$20.00

Rock Crystal, red, stemware, champagne; footed, 6-oz **$35.00**
Rock Crystal, red, tumbler, whiskey; 2½-oz **$50.00**
Rock Crystal, red, vase, footed, 11" **$225.00**
Romanesque, all colors, candlesticks, 2½", pr **$30.00**
Romanseque, all colors, cake plate, 11½x2¾" **$45.00**
Rose Cameo, green, bowl, cereal; 5" **$24.00**
Rose Cameo, green, bowl, straight sides, 6" **$32.00**
Rose Cameo, green, tumbler, footed, 2 styles, 5", ea **$25.00**
Roulette, green, plate, sandwich; 12" **$18.00**
Roulette, green, tumbler, old-fashioned; 7½-oz, 3¼" **$50.00**
Roulette, pink, bowl, fruit; 9" **$25.00**
Roulette, pink, tumbler, juice; 5-oz, 3¼" **$28.00**
Round Robin, green, cup, footed **$6.00**
Round Robin, green, saucer **$2.00**
Round Robin, iridescent, bowl, berry; 4" **$9.00**
Round Robin, iridescent, plate, luncheon; 8" **$4.00**
Round Robin, iridescent, sugar bowl **$9.00**
Roxana, yellow, bowl, berry; 5" **$16.00**
Roxana, yellow, tumbler, 9-oz, 4" **$23.00**
Royal Lace, blue, bowl, berry; 5" **$75.00**
Royal Lace, blue, bowl, rolled edge, 3 legs, 10" **$650.00**
Royal Lace, blue, butter dish **$695.00**
Royal Lace, blue, plate, dinner; 9⅞" **$50.00**
Royal Lace, blue, tumbler, 12-oz, 5⅜" **$132.00**

Royal Lace, green, cookie jar, $100.00.

Royal Lace, pink, bowl, cream soup; 4¾" **$32.00**
Royal Lace, pink, bowl, vegetable; oval, 11" **$35.00**
Royal Lace, pink, cup **$20.00**
Royal Lace, pink, nut dish **$550.00**
Royal Lace, pink, pitcher, 96-oz, 8½" **$150.00**
Sandwich, crystal, bowl, cereal; 6¾" **$50.00**
Sandwich, crystal, cookie jar **$40.00**
Sandwich, crystal, custard cup **$3.00**
Sandwich, crystal, plate, dessert; 7" **$8.00**
Sandwich, crystal, plate, sandwich; 12" **$35.00**
Sandwich, crystal, tumbler, juice; 5-oz **$4.00**
Sandwich, green, bowl, scalloped, 6½" **$85.00**
Sandwich, green, creamer **$30.00**
Sandwich, green, pitcher, ice lip, ½-gal **$495.00**

Sandwich, green, plate, dinner; 9" **$130.00**
Sandwich, green, saucer **$22.50**
Sandwich, green, sugar bowl, w/lid **$25.00**
Sandwich, green, tumbler, water; 9-oz **$5.00**
Sandwich, pink, bowl, console; 9" **$40.00**
Sandwich, pink, candlesticks, 3½", pr **$45.00**
Sandwich, pink, creamer, flat **$45.00**
Sandwich, pink, plate, dinner; 10½" **$18.00**
Sandwich, pink, sandwich server, center handle **$27.50**
Sandwich, pink, sugar bowl, flat **$45.00**
Sierra, green, bowl, cereal; 5½" **$20.00**
Sierra, green, bowl, vegetable; oval, 9½" **$160.00**
Sierra, green, pitcher, 32-oz, 6½" **$170.00**
Sierra, green, platter, oval, 11" **$80.00**
Sierra, green, sugar bowl **$30.00**
Sierra, green, tumbler, footed, 9-oz, 4½" **$100.00**
Starlight, crystal, creamer, oval **$7.00**
Starlight, crystal, plate, luncheon; 8½" **$5.00**
Starlight, crystal, salt & pepper shakers, pr **$28.00**
Starlight, pink, bowl, cereal; 5½" **$14.00**
Starlight, pink, bowl, closed handles, 8½" **$20.00**
Starlight, pink, plate, sandwich; 13" **$20.00**
Sunburst, crystal, bowl, 10¾" **$25.00**
Sunburst, crystal, creamer, footed **$10.00**
Sunburst, crystal, plate, sandwich; 11¾" **$20.00**
Sunburst, crystal, tumbler, flat, 9-oz, 4" **$35.00**
Thistle, green, bowl, fruit; lg, 10¼" **$350.00**
Thistle, green, cake plate, heavy, 13" **$235.00**
Thistle, green, plate, grill; 10¼" **$35.00**
Thistle, green, saucer **$12.00**
Thistle, pink, bowl, cereal; 5½" **$35.00**
Thistle, pink, cup, thin **$28.00**
Thistle, pink, plate, luncheon; 8" **$20.00**
Thousand Line, crystal, bowl, vegetable; 8" **$12.00**
Thousand Line, crystal, candy dish, w/lid **$20.00**
Thousand Line, crystal, plate, luncheon; 8" **$11.00**
Thousand Line, crystal, vase, bud **$13.00**
Thousand Line, cyrstal, tray, sandwich; 12½" **$14.00**
Tulip, amethyst or blue, candy dish, w/lid **$195.00**
Tulip, amethyst or blue, decanter, w/stopper **$495.00**
Tulip, amethyst or blue, plate, 6" **$11.00**
Tulip, amethyst or blue, tumbler, whiskey **$35.00**
Tulip, crystal or green, bowl, oval, oblong, 13¼" **$95.00**
Tulip, crystal or green, creamer **$18.00**
Tulip, crystal or green, saucer **$6.00**
Tulip, crystal or green, tumbler, juice **$22.00**
US Scroll, black, creamer **$10.00**
US Scroll, black, plate, 7½" **$8.00**
US Scroll, black, saucer **$3.00**
US Scroll, pink or green, cup **$6.00**
US Scroll, pink or green, plate, 8½" **$9.00**
US Scroll, pink or green, sugar bowl **$7.50**
US Swirl, green, bowl, berry; 4⅜" **$6.00**
US Swirl, green, creamer **$20.00**
US Swirl, green, salt & pepper shakers, pr **$65.00**
US Swirl, green, vase, 6½" **$30.00**
US Swirl, pink, compote, 5¼" **$30.00**

US Swirl, pink, pitcher, 48-oz, 8" $90.00
US Swirl, pink, plate, sherbet; 6⅛" $2.50
US Swirl, pink, sugar bowl, w/lid...................................$45.00
Victory, blue, bowl, console; 12"...................................$65.00
Victory, blue, bowl, soup; flat, 8½".................................$70.00
Victory, blue, cup...$30.00
Victory, blue, goblet, 7-oz, 5" $95.00
Victory, blue, plate, bread & butter; 6"............................$16.00
Victory, blue, plate, dinner; 9"....................................$55.00
Victory, blue, sherbet, footed $26.00
Victory, blue, sugar bowl...$50.00
Victory, pink, bonbon, 7"...$11.00
Victory, pink, bowl, cereal; 6½" $14.00
Victory, pink, bowl, rolled edge, 11"...............................$30.00
Victory, pink, candlesticks, 3", pr.................................$35.00
Victory, pink, creamer..$15.00
Victory, pink, gravy boat, w/platter................................$250.00
Victory, pink, plate, salad; 7".....................................$7.00
Victory, pink, platter, 12"...$30.00
Victory, pink, saucer...$4.00
Vitrock, white, bowl, berry; 4".....................................$4.00
Vitrock, white, creamer, oval.......................................$6.00
Vitrock, white, plate, salad; 7¼"...................................$4.00
Vitrock, white, platter, 11½".......................................$30.00
Vitrock, white, saucer..$2.50
Vitrock, white, sugar bowl, oval....................................$6.00
Waterford, crystal, ashtray...$7.50
Waterford, crystal, bowl, berry; lg, 8¼" $14.00
Waterford, crystal, pitcher, juice; tilted, 24-oz...................$24.00
Waterford, crystal, plate, dinner; 9⅝"..............................$11.00
Waterford, crystal, sugar bowl......................................$5.00
Waterford, crystal, tumbler, footed, 10-oz, 4⅞"....................$10.00
Waterford, pink, bowl, cereal; 5½" $35.00
Waterford, pink, butter dish..$225.00
Waterford, pink, creamer, oval $15.00
Waterford, pink, cup..$12.00
Waterford, pink, pitcher, ice lip, tilted, 80-oz...................$165.00
Waterford, pink, plate, sherbet; 6" $7.00
Windsor, crystal, ashtray, 5¾"......................................$13.50
Windsor, crystal, bowl, boat shape, 7x11¾"..........................$25.00
Windsor, crystal, cup...$3.00
Windsor, crystal, pitcher, 52-oz, 6¾"...............................$20.00
Windsor, crystal, plate, sherbet; 6"................................$2.50
Windsor, crystal, platter, oval, 11½"...............................$8.00
Windsor, crystal, tray, sq, 4" $5.00
Windsor, crystal, tumbler, 12-oz, 5"................................$10.00
Windsor, pink, bowl, cream soup; 5" $30.00
Windsor, pink, butter dish..$65.00
Windsor, pink, candlesticks, 3", pr.................................$110.00
Windsor, pink, pitcher, 16-oz, 4½"..................................$195.00
Windsor, pink, plate, dinner; 9"....................................$22.00
Windsor, pink, relish platter, divided, 11½" $250.00
Windsor, pink, salt & pepper shakers, pr............................$45.00
Windsor, pink, sugar bowl, w/lid....................................$30.00
Windsor, pink, tray, 4⅛x9"..$10.00
Windsor, pink, tumbler, 5-oz, 3¼" $22.00
Yorktown, crystal or yellow, bowl, berry; #2905, 5½"...........$4.00

Yorktown, crystal or yellow, celery tray, #2907, 10" $9.00
Yorktown, crystal or yellow, creamer, #2908........................$4.00
Yorktown, crystal or yellow, cup, #2910............................$3.00
Yorktown, crystal or yellow, mug, 5⁵⁄₁₆"...........................$17.50
Yorktown, crystal or yellow, plate, #2903, 8¼" $4.00
Yorktown, crystal or yellow, sugar bowl, w/lid, #2909...........$7.50
Yorktown, crystal or yellow, vase, 8"..............................$16.00

Sandwich, crystal, candlesticks, 3½", $15.00 for the pair.

Disney Collectibles

The largest and most popular area in character collectibles is without doubt Disneyana. There are clubs, newsletters, and special shows that are centered around this hobby. Every aspect of the retail market has been thoroughly saturated with Disney-related merchandise over the years, and today collectors are able to find many good examples at garage sales and flea markets.

Disney memorabilia from the late 1920s and 1930s was marked either 'Walt E. Disney' or 'Walt Disney Enterprises.' After about 1940 the name was changed to 'Walt Disney Productions.' This mark was in use until 1984 when the 'Walt Disney Company' mark was introduced, and this last mark has remained in use up to the present time. Some of the earlier items have become very expensive, though many are still within the reach of the average collector.

During the '30s, Mickey Mouse, Donald Duck, Snow White and the Seven Dwarfs, and the Three Little Pigs (along with all their friends and cohorts) dominated the Disney scene. The last of the '30s characters was Pinocchio, and some 'purists' prefer to stop their collections with him.

The '40s and '50s brought many new characters with them — Alice in Wonderland, Bambi, Dumbo, Lady and the Tramp, and Peter Pan were some of the major personalities featured in Disney's films of this era.

Even today, thanks to the re-releases of many of the old movies and the popularity of Disney's vacation 'kingdoms,' toy stores and department stores alike are full of quality items with the potential of soon becoming collectibles.

If you'd like to learn more about this fascinating field, we recommend *Schroeder's Collectible Toys, Antique to Modern* (Collector Books).

See also Character and Promotional Drinking Glasses; Character Banks; Character Watches; Cowboy Character Memorabilia; Dolls, Mattel; Enesco; Games; Hagen-Renaker; Pin-Back Buttons; Puzzles; Salt and Pepper Shakers; Toys; Valentines; Wade.

Advisor: Judy Posner (See Directory, Character and Personality Collectibles)

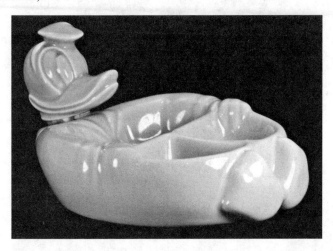

Donald Duck, hot water feeding dish, WDE, 1940s, M, 100.00.

Alice in Wonderland, figure, hard plastic, standing on round base waving, WDP, 1960s, sold w/wristwatch, 5", EX..........$35.00
Alice in Wonderland, makeup kit, cardboard box w/metal closure & handle, Hasbro/WDP, 1950s, 11x6x4", NM $50.00
Ariel (Little Mermaid), jewelry box, musical, 5x6", NM+....$20.00
Baloo (Jungle Book), figure, beanbag type, 8", EX.................$5.00
Bambi, push-button puppet, Kohner, 1960s, EX.................$25.00
Belle (Beauty & the Beast), tea set, 12-pc white china set w/decal head images of Belle, Schmid, MIB $75.00
Bianca (Rescuers Down Under), figure, beanbag type, 8", NM+ $5.00
Buzz Light Year (Toy Story), figure, beanbag type, Kellogg's premium, 5", MIP..$5.00
Captain Hook, figure, plastic, 8", NM+................................$20.00
Captain Hook, hand puppet, cloth w/vinyl head, Gund, 1950s, EX+ $50.00
Chip (Chip 'n Dale Rescue Ranger) figure, plush, brown coat w/fur trim, beige hat, w/tag, 10", EX $8.00
Cinderella, figure, blue satin dress w/lace trim, 7", NM+.....$10.00
Dale (Chip 'n Dale), figure, PVC, cereal premium, sm, MIP...$4.00
Donald Duck, bank, Second National Duck Bank, litho tin w/images of Donald, Mickey & Minnie, Chein, NMIB $150.00
Donald Duck, birthday party kit, Donald Duck on box, Rendoll Paper Co, 1940s, some use, incomplete o/w VGIB.......$55.00
Donald Duck, bracelet, enameled image on white heart on gold- & silver-tone flexible band, 1940s, EX.........................$55.00

Donald Duck, camera, black plastic, Herbert George Co, 2½x4½", EX (w/partial box) $95.00
Donald Duck, egg cup, ceramic, embossed painted image of Donald's head on side of footed cup, vintage, 4", VG...$65.00
Donald Duck, figure, celluloid, roly-poly figure w/push-down head causing squeaking noises, 1930s, 6⅓", EX................$330.00
Donald Duck, figure, ceramic, pirate w/hands on hips, WDP, 1970s, 3½", EX...$30.00
Donald Duck, handkerchief, setting sail w/3 nephews, 1950s, 8¼" sq, EX...$28.00
Dopey (Snow White), marionette, wood w/painted compo head, cloth & felt outfit, Peter Puppet Playthings, 1950s, 12", VG..$100.00
Fates (Hercules), figure, beanbag type, 5", EX $5.00
Ferdinand the Bull, figure, bisque, 3½", NM+....................$50.00
Figaro the Cat (Pinocchio), mask, paper, Gillette Razor Blue Blades premium, 1939, 8x9", EX..$25.00
Flit the Bird (Pocahontas), figure, cloth, Mattel, 1995, 9", EX.$5.00
Geppetto (Pinocchio), figure, wood fiber, sitting on box w/chin in hand, Multiproducts, 1940s, 5x3x3", EX.....................$45.00

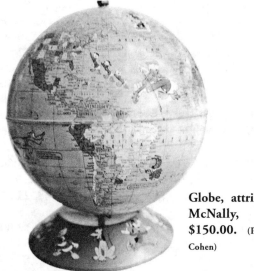

Globe, attributed to Rand McNally, 1950s, NM, $150.00. (Photo courtesy Joel Cohen)

Goofy, figure, cloth, holding Christmas cake (Merry Christmas-1999), 7", EX $5.00
Goofy, figure, stuffed, Jacob Marley (Mickey's Christmas Carol, issued by Hardee's, 1984, 6", EX $5.00
Hercules, figure, cloth, Mattel, 5", EX.................................$5.00
Iago the Parrot (Aladdin), figure, cloth, 6", EX....................$5.00
Jessica (Who Framed Roger Rabbit), figure, ceramic, leaning against fire hydrant, 5½", EX $30.00
Jessica (Who Framed Roger Rabbit), license plate, NM+.....$15.00
Jiminy Cricket, figure, injection-molded wax made by novelty machines at Disneyland or 1964 World's Fair, 5", NM.$30.00
Jiminy Cricket, hand puppet, 1st version, Gund, 1950s, EX+.$50.00
Lady (Lady & the Tramp), figure, plush roly-poly style w/vinyl face, felt feet, Gund, 1950s, 8½", EX $35.00
Mary Poppins, figure, bendable, Gund, 12", EX+..............$40.00
Mickey, Donald & Pluto, grow chart, Ready Set Grow!, Hallmark/Disney, 1970s, EX (w/original envelope) $18.00

Mickey, Minnie & Pluto, figure set, lead, unpainted, Home Foundry Mfg, 1930s, 5", NM...**$50.00**

Mickey, pillow cover, Mickey w/flower, black, gray & yellow on white cloth, Vogue Needlecraft, 1930s, 17x15", EX......**$50.00**

Mickey & Minnie Mouse, Colorforms Sew-ons, 6 unused cards, 1970s, EXIB **$30.00**

Mickey Mouse, bank, head, ceramic, 1950s, 6", EX+ **$50.00**

Mickey Mouse, Dexterity Puzzle, rectangular box w/image of Mickey on skis, complete w/18 balls, 1930s, 4x6", NM.........**$175.00**

Mickey Mouse, drum, painted wood w/paper top & bottom, w/drum stick, Nobel & Cooley/Borgfeldt, 1930s, 6½" dia, NM **$225.00**

Mickey Mouse, egg cup, porcelain, figural w/painted detail, 1930s, 3", EX..**$125.00**

Mickey Mouse, figure, bisque, standing w/hand on hip, other arm articulated, red shorts, yellow feet, 5", G+ **$225.00**

Mickey Mouse, figure, ceramic, Santa Mickey hugging lg candy cane, Royal Orleans/WDP, older, 4¼", MIB................**$25.00**

Mickey Mouse, figure, rubber, Seiberling, 1930s, 6½", VG+..**$75.00**

Mickey Mouse, figure, stuffed, vinyl head, hands & feet, red pants, Applause #8528, 1981, 10½", EX+ **$15.00**

Mickey Mouse, figure, wood, red body w/Mickey Mouse decal, black arms & legs w/yellow hands & feet, 5", VG **$220.00**

Mickey Mouse, flute, litho tin w/images of Mickey conducting barnyard animals, SFC/Italy, 1930s, 10", VG **$115.00**

Mickey Mouse, lamp, figure waving, other hand on hip, on base w/name, ceramic, w/shade, Dan Brechner, 1961, 15", EX.**$165.00**

Mickey Mouse, mask, canvas, pie-eyed, 1930s, 8½x11", EX..**$55.00**

Mickey Mouse, pin, enameled figure playing soccer, gold-tone trim, 1", EX...**$15.00**

Mickey Mouse, ring, plastic, flashes from Mickey Mouse Club to Mickey Mouse Memeber & WDP, premium, EX **$24.00**

Mickey Mouse, Weebles, Magic Kingdom, Romper Room, 1974, complete, EXIB, from $100.00 to $125.00.
(Photo courtesy June Moon)

Mickey Mouse Club Boy, ceramic, standing on round base wearing ears, Twinton, 1970s, rare, 6¾", EX **$125.00**

Minnie Mouse, figure, bisque, looking at nest of Easter eggs & hen while holding basket, WDP, 3", EX.............................**$40.00**

Minnie Mouse, figure, ceramic, cheerleader w/red hair bow & '50s skirt w/Pluto silhouette, Japan, 1987, 4½", EX **$28.00**

Minnie Mouse, figure, ceramic, playing parade drum while looking up, multicolored, Ucago, 3", EX...................................**$30.00**

Minnie Mouse, hand puppet, printed cloth body w/name on waist of dress, vinyl head, Gund, EX **$25.00**

Minnie Mouse, hat holder, 2-sided die-cut wood figure of Minnie on round base, 1930s, 14", EX **$200.00**

Mushu the Dragon (Mulan), figure, cloth, red, 12", EX........**$8.00**

Peter Pan, figure, Ideal, 1950s, 18", EX+ **$95.00**

Peter Pan, hand puppet, rubber, Oak, 1950s, EX+...............**$40.00**

Pinocchio, bank, head form, vinyl, Play Pal, 1970s, 10", NM+..**$25.00**

Pinocchio, bank, painted composition, leaning against tree stump, WDE, 1950s, 5½", NM **$75.00**

Pinocchio, figure, plush, cloth mask face w/painted features, wooden arms & legs, cloth outfit, 1940, 15", EX **$165.00**

Pluto, figure, ceramic, rump in air holding up left front paw, 1940s, 2¼" L, EX **$100.00**

Pluto, hand puppet, WDP, 1970s, G **$10.00**

Pluto, lamp, figure & shade w/Disney characters, ceramic, 1950s, about 16", EX..**$175.00**

Queen of Hearts (Alice in Wonderland), figure, beanbag type, red & black cape, Disney Store, 9", M...................................**$10.00**

Simba (Lion King), figure, cloth w/rubber head, young version, Applause, 6x7" L, VG+..**$8.50**

Sleeping Beauty, figure, squeeze rubber, w/rabbit, Dell, 1959, 5", EX **$40.00**

Snow White & the Seven Dwarfs, bracelet, 8 enameled metal charm figures on chain, WD, 1938, 7", VG+ **$50.00**

Snow White & the Seven Dwarfs, pencil box, Venuz, 1x3x8" L, VG...**$50.00**

Snow White & the Seven Dwarfs, phonograph, litho tin, PortoFonic, 14" dia, VG **$185.00**

Three Little Pigs, light switch plate, minstrel images, plastic, EX.**$15.00**

Three Little Pigs, toothbrush holder, wood plaque w/painted image showing 3 Pigs from back, Dibble Studio, 1938, EX..**$125.00**

Toy Story, posters to color, Golden Books, 1996, unused, MIP...**$5.00**

Winnie the Pooh, bank, ceramic, Pooh's Honey Bank on pot between Pooh's legs, Enesco/WDP, 1964, 6", EX" **$85.00**

Winnie the Pooh, jack-in-the-box, Carnival Toys, 1960s, EX+.**$25.00**

Winnie the Pooh, magic slate, Western Publishing, 1965, unused, NM+..**$50.00**

Woody (Toy Story), doll, Think Way, stuffed-cloth talker with vinyl head and hands, MIB, $45.00.

101 Dalmatians, egg coloring, Sunhill, MIP (sealed) **$5.00**

101 Dalmatians, Lucky, figure, squeeze vinyl, sitting upright w/head & ear cocked, Dell, from original movie, 7", EX **$25.00**

Dog Collectibles

Dog lovers appreciate the many items, old and new, that are modeled after or decorated with their favorite breeds. They pursue, some avidly, all with dedication, specific items for a particular accumulation or a range of objects, from matchbook covers to bronzes.

Perhaps the Scottish terrier is one of the most highly sought-out breeds of dogs among collectors; at any rate, Scottie devotees are more organized than most. Both the Aberdeen and West Highland terriers were used commercially; often the two are found together in things such as magnets, Black & White Scotch Whiskey advertisements, jewelry, and playing cards, for instance. They became a favorite of the advertising world in the 1930s and 1940s, partly as a result of the public popularity of Franklin Roosevelt's dog, Fala.

Poodles were the breed of the 1950s, and today items from those years are cherished collectibles. Trendsetter teeny-boppers wore poodle skirts, and the 5-&-10¢ stores were full of pink poodle figurines with 'coleslaw' fur. For a look back at these years, we recommend *Poodle Collectibles of the '50s and '60s* by Elaine Butler (L-W Books).

Many of the earlier collectibles are especially prized, making them expensive and difficult to find. Prices listed here may vary as they are dependent on supply and demand, location, and dealer assessment.

Club: Heart of America Scottish Terrier Club
Julia Dahn
P.O. Box 204
Old Monroe, MO 63369

Collie, salt and pepper shakers, excellent quality, from $25.00 to $35.00. (Photo courtesy Helene Guarnaccia)

Bonzo, figurine, brown & white, ceramic, Made in Germany, #3732, 3½x2½" **$70.00**

Borzoi, figurine, reclining, brown & white, porcelain, Austria, 1920s, 5¼x11½" **$75.00**

Boxer, figurine, head only, realistic brown & black tones, Inarco foil label, 6" **$22.50**

Boxer, planter, seated beside sq brown form marked Pal, ceramic, Japan, 6x4½" **$25.00**

Cocker spaniel, figurine, painted ceramic, Japan, 3½x4½" .. **$25.00**

Cocker spaniel, Miss Trixie, ceramic, Bar Hound Collection, Enesco, 5½" **$50.00**

Cocker spaniel, paperweight, cast iron, brown paint, Hubley, 2¼x3½" **$85.00**

Cocker spaniel puppy, lg eyes, gray & white spots on white ceramic, Japan mark, 5¼" **$20.00**

Dachshund, figurine, rhinestone eyes, matt finish, #3213, 5", $20.00. (Photo courtesy Loretta DeLozier)

Dalmatian, pill box, painted metal w/magnetic lock, 1½x3" ... **$18.00**

Dalmatian puppy, figurine, white w/sm black spots, ceramic, Homco, 2¾x2¼" **$30.00**

English setter, plaque, on point in grassy meadow, brown, cream & tan on chalkware oval, 10½x13¾" **$25.00**

English setter, tray, brass w/embossed dog's portrait, 5" dia.. **$25.00**

Fox terrier, handkerchief, from $30.00 to $35.00. (Photo courtesy Helene Guarnaccia and Barbara Guggenheim)

German shepherd, head vase, realistic coloring, ceramic, #E1847, 6" **$35.00**

Hound, decanter, It's a Dog's Life, music box in base, porcelain figural, ice bag cap w/cork stopper, 13" **$25.00**

Irish setter, ceramic, red-brown, seated, Japan label, 6" **$25.00**

Irish setter, figurine, Ivan the Orator, Bar Hound Collection by Enesco **$150.00**

Irish wolfhound, plate, signed KM Ciullohundley, Laurelwood limited edition, 8½" **$47.00**

King Charles spaniel, figurine, brown to cream, very realistic, attributed to Lefton, 4½x3¾" **$45.00**

Mastiff, figurine, recumbent, white, porcelain, T Karner, Nymphenburg Germany, 9" L **$250.00**

Pekinese, postcard, portrait of Princess, signed Zula Kenyon, 1907, EX **$15.00**

Pekinese w/pup, planter, life-like, ceramic, Relpo #2014......**$25.00**

Poodle, figurine, female w/fancy flowered hat, pink, blue & gold details on white ceramic w/spaghetti, 4⅝x4" **$65.00**

Poodle, figurine, playing clarinet w/rhinestone keys, white ceramic w/multicolor details, much spaghetti, 5¾x3" **$85.00**

Poodle, figurine, recumbent w/legs stretched out, white ceramic w/painted features, Enesco, 3x4½" **$24.00**

Poodle, figurine, standing w/black cat-eye glasses w/rhinestones, white w/turquoise bow tie, ceramic w/spaghetti, 5x5" ..**$65.00**

Poodle, figurine, white ceramic w/much spaghetti, Giftcraft Japan label, 5" **$20.00**

Poodle, nodder, stands as head nods, white ceramic w/red collar, knobby tufts (no spaghetti), 2x3¼" **$50.00**

Poodle, purse, white beaded, Walborg replica by Robin Piccone **$225.00**

Poodle, planter, spaghetti fur, 8" long, $35.00.

Poodles, figurine, mother w/2 pups joined by chains, white ceramic w/spaghetti, blue eyes, gold trim, Japan, 1950s.............**$65.00**

Puppy by shoe, planter, green & brown, pottery, Sylvac #1903, 3½x5½" **$55.00**

Schnauzer, figurine, gray tones, realistic features, ceramic, Napcoware sticker, #9854, 7½x7" **$50.00**

Scottie, creamer, clear glass w/etched details, ca 1930s-40s, 3¼x5¾x2" **$32.00**

Scottie, figurine, celluloid w/hand-painted eyes & nose, 1930s, 2¾x3½" **$60.00**

Scottie, figurine, white w/pink collar, celluloid, 2½x3¾"......**$75.00**

Scottie; lamp, boudoir; dog seated on black base, pink frosted glass shade w/stenciled Scottie, 11x5" **$100.00**

Scottie, planter, opening in back, brown tones on white, ceramic, 5½x5" **$15.00**

Scottie, plaque, jumping to look over fence, painted chalkware, 5¾x3⅛" **$55.00**

Scottie, powder jar, marigold iridescent glass, 5x3⅞" **$35.00**

Scottie, table lighter, Deco style, black w/red nose, original silver cap, ca 1930, 3¾" **$20.00**

Scottie, wall pocket, standing before red picket fence, ceramic, Japan, 5¼x3½" **$15.00**

Scottie dog, paperweight, cast iron, original brown paint, unmarked, 2¾x4" **$35.00**

Sealyham terrier, solid bronze, detailed male, marked Austria, 3" L **$95.00**

Skye terrier, shaded bisque, Germany #686, 2x2½" **$20.00**

Skye terrier puppies (2), print, Arthur Wardle, 8x10"+simple frame **$35.00**

Spaniel, figurine, howling, brown & white, ceramic, Walker Pottery of California, 1940s, 3½" **$20.00**

Spaniel, print, artist signed, under convex glass, Bilderback's Inc of Detroit, 6" dia **$60.00**

Spaniel puppy, figurine, painted ceramic, illegible silver label, 2" **$20.00**

Springer spaniel, tray, tin litho w/red edge, 13½x10½", EX.**$25.00**

Terrier, creamer, dog's head, white w/gray markings, red collar w/ gold bell, ceramic, 3¾x4¼" **$50.00**

Wire-fox terrier, book, Teddy the Terrier, Rand McNally Elf Book #8308, 1959 ....**$55.00**

Wire-haired terrier, figurine, playful pose, painted ceramic, Japan mark w/3-leaf clover, 3½x6½" **$25.00**

Dollhouse Furniture

Some of the mass-produced dollhouse furniture you're apt to see on the market today was made by Renwal and Acme during the 1940s and Ideal in the 1960s. All three of these companies used hard plastic for their furniture lines and imprinted most pieces with their names. Strombecker furniture was made of wood, and although it was not marked, it has a certain recognizable style to it. Remember that if you're lucky enough to find doll furniture complete in the original box, you'll want to preserve the carton as well.

Advisor: Judith Mosholder (See Directory Dollhouse Furniture)

Arcade, dresser with mirror, cast iron, 6½", EX, $220.00.

Acme/Thomas, cat for dog sled..**$8.00**

Acme/Thomas, doll, baby in diaper, Thomas, 2" **$4.00**

Acme/Thomas, doll, girl, hard plastic, yellow dress, Thomas, 3½" **$20.00**

Acme/Thomas, seesaw, blue w/yellow horse heads **$6.00**
Allied/Pyro, bed, red w/white spread.................................... **$10.00**
Allied/Pyro, cupboard, corner; aqua...................................... **$8.00**
Allied/Pyro, sofa, yellow, unmarked **$8.00**
Allied/Pyro, vanity, aqua, blue or pink, ea.............................. **$4.00**
Arcade, bathtub, painted cast iron, ivory.............................**$125.00**
Arcade, icebox (Leonard), painted cast iron, white, 6", VG ..**$185.00**
Blue Box, chest, 4-drawer, light brown.................................... **$4.00**
Blue Box, stove, avocado w/silver top...................................... **$3.00**
Casablanca, vanity w/mirror, brown..................................... **$12.00**
Cheerio, any hard plastic piece, ea **$4.00**
Commonwealth, rake, any color, ea **$4.00**
Donna Lee, chair, kitchen; white **$3.00**
Fisher-Price, cradle, white **$5.00**
Fisher-Price, refrigerator, white w/yellow............................... **$5.00**
Grand Rapids, dresser w/mirror, decals on drawers **$12.00**
Hasbro, kitchen sink or stove, ea... **$2.00**
Ideal, bench, lawn; blue **$18.00**
Ideal, buffet, red.. **$15.00**
Ideal, doll, baby, painted diaper **$10.00**
Ideal, hamper, blue.. **$6.00**
Ideal, highchair, collapsible, blue or pink, ea........................ **$25.00**
Ideal, Petite Princess, bed, #4416-4, blue or pink, MIB, ea.. **$30.00**
Ideal, piano w/bench, caramel swirl **$35.00**
Ideal, potty chair, pink, complete.. **$15.00**
Ideal, sewing machine, dark marbleized brown or dark marbleized
   maroon, ea.. **$20.00**
Ideal, toilet, ivory w/black handle **$20.00**
Ideal Petite Princess, cabinet, Treasure Trove #4418-09, MIB. **$12.00**
Ideal Petite Princess, clock, grandfather; #4423-0 .... **$10.00**
Ideal Petite Princess, dressing table, #4417-2, blue, complete . **$20.00**
Ideal Petite Princess, lamp, table; Heirloom #4428-9............. **$5.00**

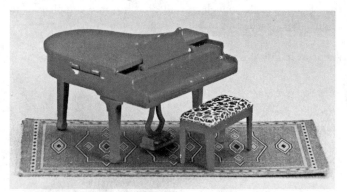

Ideal Petite Princess, piano with bench and rug, EX, $20.00.

Ideal Petite Princess, planter, Salon #4440-4 .... **$15.00**
Ideal Petite Princess, sofa, #4407-3, beige/gold, MIB.......... **$25.00**
Ideal Petite Princess, tea cart, rolling, #4424-8, MIB **$20.00**
Ideal Petite Princess, telephone, Fantasy #4432-1................. **$8.00**
Ideal Young Decorator, bathtub, corner; blue w/yellow........ **$35.00**
Ideal Young Decorator, playpen, pink **$45.00**
Ideal Young Decorator, stove, white **$55.00**
Irwin, broom, any color, ea **$5.00**
Irwin, hoe, orange... **$3.00**
Irwin Interior Decorator, bathtub, light green...................... **$5.00**

Jaydon, hamper, red **$5.00**
Jaydon, nightstand, pink.. **$4.00**

Jaydon, piano with bench, $15.00; living room chair, $19.00; chest of drawers, $5.00; dining chair, $1.00. (Photo courtesy Judith Mosholder)

Jaydon, toilet, ivory w/red lid.. **$10.00**
JP Co, chair, brown.. **$1.00**
JP Co, hutch, brown... **$4.00**
Kage, refrigerator, white w/black & red trim......................... **$8.00**
Kage, table, coffee; walnut **$3.00**
Lundby, fireplace, 3¼x2¾" or 2¾x4¼", ea........................... **$15.00**
Marvi, Ferris wheel, multicolored... **$15.00**
Marx, hard plastic, swimimng pool (red), ¾" scale **$10.00**
Marx, soft plastic, ¾" scale, floor lamp, bright yellow or light yellow,
   ea **$6.00**
Marx Little Hostess, dresser, double; ivory **$8.00**
Marx Little Hostess, lowboy, red **$12.00**
Mattel Littles, armoire.. **$8.00**
Mattel Littles, sofa & Hedy doll, MIB **$15.00**
Nancy Forbes, buffet, walnut **$3.00**
Nancy Forbes, lamp, table; gold **$3.00**
Plasco, bathtub, any color, ea **$4.00**
Plasco, chair, kitchen; any color, ea **$2.00**
Plasco, clock, grandfather; light brown swirl or dark brown, card-
   board face, ea... **$15.00**
Plasco, highboy, tan... **$8.00**
Plasco, vanity bench, any color, ea **$3.00**
Reliable, bathtub, ivory w/blue trim..................................... **$15.00**
Reliable, radio, floor; rust... **$15.00**
Reliable, table, kitchen; ivory **$12.00**
Renewal, baby bath, blue or pink, duck decal, ea................. **$15.00**
Renwal, china closet, brown or reddish brown, stenciled, ea... **$15.00**
Renwal, clock, mantel; ivory or red, ea................................ **$10.00**
Renwal, desk, teacher's; blue **$25.00**
Renwal, doll, mother, metal trivets, rose dress..................... **$25.00**
Renwal, hamper, ivory.. **$2.00**
Renwal, highboy, opening doors, brown **$8.00**
Renwal, ironing board, blue or pink **$7.00**
Renwal, kiddie car, blue w/red & yellow.............................. **$55.00**
Renwal, lamp, table; yellow w/ivory shade **$10.00**
Renwal, piano, marbleized brown **$35.00**
Renwal, scale, ivory or red, ea **$10.00**

Renwal, server, brown **$6.00**
Renwal, table, cocktail; reddish brown **$8.00**
Renwal, table, folding; gold.. **$20.00**
Renwal, washing machine, blue w/pink or pink w/blue, both w/bear
    decal, ea **$30.00**
Sounds Like Home, hair dryer, blue................................... **$5.00**
Sounds Like Home, sink, electronic **$12.00**
Strombecker, nightstand, light green or pink, ¾" scale, ea **$6.00**
Strombecker, sofa, green flocked, 1950s, 1" scale **$25.00**
Strombecker, television, paper screen, ivory, 1961, ¾" scale. **$20.00**
Superior, dustpan, red, ¾" scale **$8.00**
Tomy-Smaller Homes, armoire, no hangers **$10.00**
Tomy-Smaller Homes, bed, canopy.................................. **$15.00**
Tomy-Smaller Homes, checkerboard................................. **$5.00**
Tomy-Smaller Homes, diary... **$10.00**
Tomy-Smaller Homes, plant, tall..................................... **$8.00**
Tomy-Smaller Homes, towel **$5.00**
Tomy-Smaller Homes, vanity **$15.00**
Tootsietoy, lamp, table; blue.. **$45.00**
Tootsietoy, piano bench, yellow w/tan seat......................... **$15.00**
Tootsietoy, tea cart, dark brown **$22.00**

Dolls

Doll collecting is one of the most popular hobbies in the United States. Since many of the antique dolls are so expensive, modern dolls have come into their own and can be had at prices within the range of most budgets. Today's thrift-shop owners know the extent of 'doll mania,' though, so you'll seldom find a bargain there. But if you're willing to spend the time, garage sales can be a good source for your doll buying. Granted most will be in a 'well loved' condition, but as long as they're priced right, many can be re-dressed, rewigged, and cleaned up. Swap meets and flea markets may sometimes yield a good example or two, often at lower-than-book prices.

Modern dolls, those from 1935 to the present, are made of rubber, composition, magic skin, synthetic rubber, and many types of plastic. Most of these materials do not stand up well to age, so be objective when you buy, especially if you're buying with an eye to the future. Doll repair is an art best left to professionals, but if yours is only dirty, you can probably do it yourself. If you need to clean a composition doll, do it very carefully. Use only baby oil and follow up with a soft dry cloth to remove any residue. Most types of wigs can be shampooed with wig shampoo and lukewarm water. Be careful not to matt the hair as you shampoo, and follow up with hair conditioner or fabric softener. Comb gently and set while wet, using small soft rubber or metal curlers. Never use a curling iron or heated rollers.

In our listings, unless a condition is noted in the descriptions, values are for dolls in excellent condition.

For further study, we recommend these books: *Collector's Guide to Dolls of the 1960s and 1970s* by Cindy Sabulis; *Doll Values, Antique to Modern, 9th Edition,* by Linda Edward; *Horsman Dolls* by Don Jensen; *American Character Dolls* by Judith Izen; *and Collector's Encyclopedia of American Composition Dolls, 1900 – 1950, Vols. I and II,* by Ursula R. Metz. All these references are published by Collector Books.

See also Barbie and Friends; Shirley Temple; Toys (Action Figures); and GI Joe.

Magazine: *Doll Castle News*
37 Belvidere Ave., P.O. Box 247
Washington, NJ 07882
908-689-7042 or fax: 908-689-6320

Newsletter: *Doll News*
United Federation of Doll Clubs
10900 North Pomona Ave.
Kansas City, MO 64153
816-891-7040
www.ufdc.org

Annalee

Barbara 'Annalee' Davis was born in Concord, New Hampshire, on February, 11, 1915. She started dabbling at doll-making at an early age, often giving her creations to friends. She married Charles 'Chip' Thorndike in 1941 and moved to Meredith, New Hampshire, where they started a chicken farm and sold used auto parts. By the early 1950s, with the chicken farm failing, Annalee started crafting her dolls on the kitchen table to help make ends meet. She designed her dolls by looking into the mirror, drawing faces as she saw them, and making the clothes from scraps of material.

The dolls she developed are made of wool felt with hand-painted features and flexible wire frameworks. The earlier dolls from the 1950s had a long white red-embroidered tag with no date. From 1959 to 1964, the tags stayed the same except there was a date in the upper right-hand corner. From 1965 to 1970, this same tag was folded in half and sewn into the seam of the doll. In 1970 a transition period began. The company changed its tag to a satiny white tag with a date preceded by a copyright symbol in the upper right-hand corner. In 1975 they made another change to a long white cotton strip with a copyright date. In 1982 the white tag was folded over, making it shorter. Many people mistake the copyright date as the date the doll was made — not so! It wasn't until 1986 that they finally began to date the tags with the year of manufacture, making it much easier for collectors to identify their dolls. Besides the red-lettered white Annalee tags, numerous others were used in the 1990s, but all reflect the year the doll was actually made.

Annalee's signature can increase a doll's value by as much as $300.00, sometimes more. Annalee died in April 2002, but she had personally signed no dolls for several years. Chuck (her son) and Karen Thorndike are now signing them.

Remember, these dolls are made of wool felt. To protect them, store them with moth balls, and avoid exposing them to too much sunlight, since they will fade. Our advisor has been a collector for almost 20 years and a secondary market dealer since 1988. Most of these dolls have been in her collection at one time or another. She recommends 'If you like it, buy it, love it, treat it with care, and you'll have it to enjoy for many years to come.'

Unless noted otherwise, our values are suggested for dolls in very good to excellent condition, not personally autographed by Annalee herself.

Advisor: Jane Holt (See Directory, Dolls)

Newsletter: *The Club News*
Annalee Doll Society
P.O. Box 1137, 50 Reservoir Rd., Meredith, NH 03253-1137

1963, Go-Go girl, 10" $85.00
1972, fireman mouse, w/ladder, 7" $25.00
1975, tennis player mouse, holding metal racket, made several years..$15.00
1976, Colonial drummer boy, w/blue tricorn hat, 10".........$75.00
1976, scarecrow, patchwork blue denim, produced 1 year, rare, 29" $200.00
1979, Santa & Mrs Claus, outdoor, made many years, 30", M, pr..$125.00
1980, Easter Parade boy rabbit, purple & white gingham vest w/pink jacket & hat, 18" $40.00
1980, hobo clown, red & & white seersucker pants w/yellow clown feet & black derby hat, 18"...........................$60.00
1981, angel sitting on cotton cloud, original tag, made several years, 6"..$15.00
1982, country girl, pink & white gingham dress w/strawberries, red hair in pigtails w/red ribbons, 7"...............$30.00
1982, monk, white beard, brown cap, robe & sandals w/white cord belt, 30"..$125.00
1982, Santa scene, 1-year production, rare, 22" $200.00
1983, Christmas boy w/snowball, made several years, 7" $15.00
1983, workshop elf, comes in several colors, has blue & white striped apron, 10"...$30.00
1984, duck on sled, green & white striped scarf w/green, pink & yellow hat, 5" $15.00
1984 or 1985, birthday boy or girl, 7", ea...........................$25.00
1985, graduation mouse, (girl in white gown, boy in blue gown), 7", ea $25.00

1986, Fishing Bear, 10", $50.00. (Photo courtesy Bette Todd)

1988, Pilgrim mouse, 7" $25.00

1989, Tacky Tourist mouse wearing Hawaiian shirt & blue & green hat, w/yellow hatbox & brown suitcase, 7" $25.00
1991, waiter mouse, black sleeveless coat & bow tie, holding silver tray w/champagne in ice bucket, 7" $25.00
1992, schoolgirl, blue jeans w/pink shoes, holding apple w/school books beside her, Society doll, produced 1 year, 7".......$35.00
1993, leprechaun, green suit & hat, holding pot of gold, 10" .$25.00
1994, Sweetheart Girl, white dress w/red ribbons & shoes, holding heart-shape valentine I Love You, #039094, 7" $25.00
1995, Christmas Window Shopper, ostrich w/glasses in red & green plaid, green hat & scarf, holding empty bag, 10"..........$43.00
1996, hiker mouse, green jacket w/brown hat, red sleeping bag on backpack, holding stick, 3" $20.00
1996, man & woman carollers, 10", pr.............................$30.00
1997, Autumn Angel, yellow dress w/red scarf, floral decor in hair, 10"..$20.00
1997, clown mouse, polkadot shirt w/1 blue shoe & 1 orange shoe, holding balloons, 7"...$20.00
1997, Trick-or-Treat boy, red plaid shirt w/blue overalls & white hat, carrying trick-or-treat bag, 7".........................$25.00

Betsy McCall

The tiny 8" Betsy McCall doll was manufactured by the American Character Doll Company from 1957 through 1963. She was made from high-quality hard plastic with a bisque-like finish and hand-painted features. Betsy came in four hair colors — tosca, red, blond, and brunette. She had blue sleep eyes, molded lashes, a winsome smile, and a fully jointed body with bendable knees. On her back there is an identification circle which reads McCall Corp. The basic doll wore a sheer chemise, white taffeta panties, nylon socks, and Mary Jane-style shoes, and could be purchased for $2.25.

There were two different materials used for tiny Betsy's hair. The first was a soft mohair sewn into fine mesh. Later the rubber skullcap was rooted with saran which was more suitable for washing and combing.

Betsy McCall had an extensive wardrobe with nearly 100 outfits, each of which could be purchased separately. They were made from wonderful fabrics such as velvet, taffeta, felt, and even real mink. Each ensemble came with the appropriate footwear and was priced under $3.00. Since none of Betsy's clothing was tagged, it is often difficult to identify other than by its square snap closures (although these were used by other companies as well).

Betsy McCall is a highly collectible doll today but she is getting more difficult to locate in fine contition. Prices continue to rise for this beautiful clotheshorse and her many accessories. For further information we recommend *Betsy McCall, A Collector's Guide,* by Marci Van Ausdall.

Advisor: Marci Van Ausdall (See Directory, Dolls)

Club: *Betsy McCall Fan Club*
Subscription $16 per year or $4 for sample copy

Accessories, shoes, American Character, for 14" doll, VG, pr .$50.00
American Character, hard plastic, rooted hair, jointed knees, white nylon chemise, 1957, 8", MIB...............................$400.00

American Character, vinyl, rooted hair, 1958, all original, 14"...**$350.00**

American Character, vinyl w/jointed limbs & waist, rooted hair, original clothing, ca 1960s, 22" **$250.00**

American Character, 36", vinyl, Patti Playpal-style body, frosted hair, 1959 ....**$325.00**

Clothes, Betsy McCall Ski Outfit, 8", MOC **$250.00**

Clothes, Brunchtime Outfit, 8" **$125.00**

Clothes, panties, white, 8", EX **$25.00**

Figure, Heirloom Tradition, porcelain (12 made in all), MIB, ea **$35.00**

Ideal, hard plastic, Toni body, rooted hair, original outfit, 14" . **$225.00**

Ideal, vinyl head, hard plastic Toni Walker body, marked McCall/Ideal Doll/P-90), MIB, $400.00. (Photo courtesy McMasters Harris Auction Company)

Paper doll book, Saalfield, 1966, uncut, from $25 to..........**$35.00**

Pretty Pac carrying case, vinyl, vintage, empty, from $25 to.**$75.00**

Record album, Betsy McCall Sing Along Party, EX..............**$50.00**

Rothchild, rigid vinyl body w/rooted hair, 1996, 14", MIB.**$75.00**

Celebrity Dolls

Celebrity and character dolls have been widely collected for many years, but they've lately shown a significant increase in demand. Except for rarer examples, most of these dolls are still fairly easy to find at doll shows, toy auctions, and flea markets, and the majority are priced under $100.00. These are the dolls that bring back memories of childhood TV shows, popular songs, favorite movies, and familiar characters. Mego, Mattel, Remco, and Hasbro are among the largest manufacturers.

Condition is a very important worth-assessing factor, and if the doll is still in the original box, so much the better! Should the box be unopened (NRFB), the value is further enhanced. Using mint in box as a standard, deduct 30% to 35% for one that is mint (no box). Increase the price for 'never removed from box' examples by about 40%. Values for dolls in only good or poorer condition drop at a rapid pace. For more information we recommend *Collector's Guide to Celebrity Dolls* by David Sporgeon (Collector Books).

See also Elvis Presley Memorabilia.

Andy Gibb, Ideal, 1979, 7½", MIB **$65.00**

Audrey Hepburn (Breakfast at Tiffany's), Mattel, 1998, 11½", MIB **$75.00**

Betty Grable, blond Dynel hair, International Doll Co, 1940s, w/ tag, 19", NM, minimum value **$400.00**

Brooke Shields, Prom Party, LJN, 1982, rare, 11½", MIB.**$150.00**

Cher, Growing Hair, Mego, 1976, MIB, from $65.00 to $85.00. (Photo courtesy Cindy Sabulis)

Cheryl Ladd, Mattel, 1978, 11½", MIB **$75.00**

Dick Clark, Juro, 1958, 26½", VG **$150.00**

Dick Van Dyke as Mr Potts, Chitty Chitty Bang Bang, cloth, 1969, EX **$85.00**

Elizabeth Taylor (Butterfield 8), Tri-Star, 1982, 11½", MIB.**$150.00**

Ellie May (Beverly Hillbillies), complete w/wardrobe, Unique Art, 1964, 12", MIB **$400.00**

Farrah Fawcett, white jumpsuit, blond hair, Mego, 1975, EX .**$25.00**

Florence Griffith Joyner, LJN, 1989, 11½", MIB **$50.00**

Fonz (Happy Days), stuffed print cloth, Samet & Wells, 1976, 16", M...**$50.00**

Gene Simmons (KISS), Mego, 1977, 12", EX **$40.00**

Glenn Close as Cruella DeVille (1001 Dalmatians) The Great Villians Series, Mattel, 1996, M (EX box) **$50.00**

Harold Lloyd, lithoed stuffed cloth, standing w/hands in pockets, 1920s, 12", EX **$100.00**

James Cagney, Effanbee, pinstripe suit & hat, 1987, 16", MIB .**$125.00**

Kate Jackson, Mattel, 1978, 11½", MIB............................**$85.00**

Kelly Rowland, Destiny's Child, 2001 Grammy Award outfit, Mattel, MIB...**$20.00**

KISS, Mego, 1978, any from group, 12½", MIB, ea **$350.00**

Leann Rimes (Country Music Stars), Exclusive Premiere, 1998, 9", MIB...**$30.00**

Lucille Ball, LA at Last, Mattel, M (EX box) **$35.00**

Marilyn Monroe, white sequin dress, Celebrity Series by World Dolls, 1983, MIB **$45.00**

Nicole Boebeck (Olympic Ice Skater), Playmates, 1998, 11½", MIB **$25.00**

Punky Brewster, Galoob, 1984, 18", MIB...........................$75.00

Queen Elizabeth, Effanbee, long white satin gown, 1980s, 14", MIB...$75.00

Robert Crippen (Astronaut), Kenner, 1997, 12", MIB........$45.00

Shirley Temple, Armand Marseille, bisque, jointed, white red polka-dotted dress, 22", VGIB...$135.00

Suzanne Sommers, Chrissy of Three's Company, Mego, 1978, MIB, from $45.00 to $60.00. (Photo courtesy Cindy Sabulis)

Three Stooges, any character, Presents, 1988, 14", M, ea.....$65.00

Welcome Back Kotter, any character, Mattel, 1976, 9½", MOC, ea $75.00

Wizard of Oz, any character, Largo, 1989, 14", MIB, ea.....$45.00

Chatty Cathy and Other Mattel Talkers

One of the largest manufacturers of modern dolls is the Mattel company, the famous maker of the Barbie doll. But besides Barbie, there are many other types of Mattel dolls that have their own devotees, and we've tried to list a sampling of several of their more collectible lines.

Next to Barbie, the all-time favorite doll was Mattel's Chatty Cathy. She was first made in the 1960s, in blond and brunette variations, and much of her success can be attributed to that fact that she could talk! By pulling the string on her back, she could respond with 11 different phrases. The line was expanded and soon included Chatty Baby, Tiny Chatty Baby and Tiny Chatty Brother (the twins), Charmin' Chatty, and finally Singing Chatty. They all sold successfully for five years, and although Mattel reintroduced the line in 1969 (smaller and with a restyled face), it was not well received.

In 1960 Mattel introduced their first line of talking dolls. They decided to take the talking doll's success even further by introducing a new line — cartoon characters that the young TV viewers were already familiar with.

Below you will find a list of the more popular dolls and animals available. Most MIB (mint-in-box) toys found today are mute, but this should not detract from the listed price. If the doll still talks, you may consider adding a few more dollars to the price. (See the Celebrity Doll narrative for information that will help you evaluate dolls in less than mint condition.)

Baby Beans, beanbag w/vinyl head, 1971-75, 12", VG........$40.00

Baby Say 'n See, eyes & lips move, white dress pink yoke, 17", VG $20.00

Baby Secret, cloth body w/vinyl head, red hair, whispers 11 phrases, moves lips, 18", VG...$15.00

Baby Small Talk, in Nursery Rhyme outfit, says 8 phrases in infant voice, 10¾", VG...$20.00

Baby Small Talk, says 8 phrases in infant voice, 10¾", EX.$55.00

Captain Kangaroo, 1967, 19", MIB.................................$150.00

Captain Kangaroo, 1967, 19", VG......................................$10.00

Charmin' Chatty, hard vinyl w/soft vinyl head, smiling, 5 records to play in left side slot, 24", VG......................$55.00

Chatty Baby, red pinafore over rompers, 1962-64, 18", G...$20.00

Chatty Baby, 1970 – 1971 restyle but marked copyright 1969, Made in Mexico, MIB, from $65.00 to $85.00. (Photo courtesy Cindy Sabulis/Mark A. Salyers)

Drowsy, stuffed body, vinyl head, sleeper, pull-string activated, 1965-74, 15½", MIB..$200.00

Herman Munster, cloth, 1965, 21", VG $25.00

Scooba Doo, striped top w/gold necklace, pull-string activated, 1964, 23", EX, minimum value.................................$75.00

Shrinkin' Violette, cloth, yarn hair, pull-string activated, 1964-65, 16", VG...$50.00

Sister Belle, cloth w/vinyl head, 1961-63, 16", EX.............$75.00

Tatters, cloth, rag clothes, 1965-67, 19", EX.....................$125.00

Teachy Keen, cloth w/vinyl head, ponytail, accessories: buttons, zippers & comb, 1966-70, 16", EX...................................$30.00

Tiny Chatty Baby, blue romper, striped panties, bib w/name, 15½", VG..$90.00

Tiny Chatty Baby, nude, VG $20.00

Tiny Chatty Brother, blue & white suit & cap, hair parted on side, 1963-64, 15½", EX..$75.00

Tiny Chatty Brother, nude, 1963-64, 15½", VG.................$20.00

Dawn Dolls by Topper

Made by Deluxe Topper in the 1970s, this 6" fashion doll and her friends were sold individually as regular or dancing dolls. There were also various series, including modeling agencies, flower fantasies, and majorettes. They're becoming highly collectible, especially when mint in the box. They were issued already dressed in clothes of the highest style, or you could buy additional outfits, many complete with matching shoes and accessories. To evaluate loose dolls in good to very good condition, deduct about 75% to 80% from our NRFB values.

Advisor: Dawn Diaz (See Directory, Dolls)

Doll, Dancing Angie, NRFB	**$50.00**
Doll, Dancing Dawn, NRFB	**$50.00**

Doll, Dancing Dawn, Topper, 1970, MIB, from $35.00 to $45.00.
(Photo courtesy Cindy Sabulis)

Doll, Dancing Gary, NRFB	**$50.00**
Doll, Dancing Jessica, NRFB	**$50.00**
Doll, Dancing Ron, NRFB	**$50.00**
Doll, Dancing Van, NRFB	**$80.00**
Doll, Daphne, Dawn Model Agency, green & silver dress, NRFB	**$100.00**
Doll, Dawn, Head to Toe, silver or pink mini dress, NRFB, from $65 to	**$80.00**
Doll, Dawn Majorette, NRFB	**$75.00**
Doll, Denise, Dawn Model Agency, NRFB	**$100.00**
Doll, Dinah, Dawn Model Agency, NRFB	**$100.00**
Doll, Gary, NRFB	**$50.00**
Doll, Jessica, NRFB	**$50.00**
Doll, Kip Majorette, NRFB	**$65.00**
Doll, Longlocks, NRFB	**$50.00**
Doll, loose, knees w/green oxidation from metal inside from $5 to	**$15.00**
Doll, Ron, NRFB	**$50.00**
Outfit, Green Slink, #0716, NRFB	**$25.00**

Fisher-Price

Though you're more familiar with the lithographed plastic toys this company has made for years, they also made dolls as well. The earlier dolls that were made in the 1970s had stuffed cloth bodies and vinyl heads, hands, and feet. Some had battery-operated voice boxes. In 1981 they introduced Kermit the Frog and Miss Piggy and a line of clothing for each.

Our values are for dolls in excellent to near mint condition, not including original boxes.

Doll, Audrey, #203, 1974-76	**$25.00**
Doll, Baby Ann, #204, 1974-76	**$25.00**
Doll, Billie, #242, 1970-80	**$10.00**
Doll, Honey, #208, 1977-80	**$20.00**
Doll, Joey, #206, 1975-76	**$25.00**
Doll, Mary, #200, 1974-77	**$25.00**
Doll, Muffy, #241, 1979-80, M	**$10.00**
Doll, My Baby Sleep, #207, 1979-80	**$25.00**
Doll, My Friend Becky #218, 1982-84	**$20.00**
Doll, My Friend Christie, #8210, 1990, from $40 to	**$75.00**
Doll, My Friend Mandy, #216, 1984 only	**$35.00**
Doll, My Friend Nicky, #3206, 1985	**$30.00**

Doll, Natalie, #202, 1973, MIB, from $50.00 to $75.00.
(Photo courtesy Cindy Sabulis)

Doll, Natalie, #202, 1974-76	**$25.00**
Outfit, Aerobics, #4110, 1985	**$10.00**
Outfit, Let's Go Camping, #222, 1978-79	**$10.00**
Outfit, Party Dress Outfit & pattern, #221, 1978-79	**$10.00**
Outfit, Rainy Day Slicker, #219, 1978-80	**$10.00**
Outfit, Valentine Party Dress, #238, 1984-85	**$10.00**

Hasbro

Hasbro is probably best known for their GI Joe dolls, but they made many other lines that are collectible, though on a lesser scale. Among them are the Jem dolls that were introduced in 1985, paralelling the popular Saturday morning TV show. This line consisted of the members of the show's rock band, The Holograms, as well as members of the cast. Their clothes makeup, and hairdos were wonderfully exotic, and their faces were beautifully modeled. The Jem line was discontinued in 1987. They also made Dolly Darlings, little 4" dolls that came packaged inside round plastic hatbox cases, boxes with cellophane fronts, or in a bubble with cardboard backing. Some had rooted hair, while others had hair that was simply molded. Other lines were Flower Darlings, 3½" dolls that came with fragrant pin-on flowers; Storykins, 3½" plastic dolls representing characters such as Mother Hubbard, Cinderella, Snow White, and Pinocchio; World of Love dolls; Leggy dolls (10"); and many others.

Jem/Jerrica, flashing star earrings, blond hair, 12", MIB, $92.00. (Photo courtesy Cornelia Ford)

Aimee, original maxi-length dress, 1972, 18", M, from $25 to. **$40.00**
Aja (Jem), original outfit, 1986, M **$35.00**
Aja (Jem), original outfit, 1986, MIB, from $80 to **$100.00**
Banee (Jem), original outfit, MIB **$55.00**
Clash (Jem), original outfit, MIB, from $40 to....................**$60.00**
Danse (Jem), original outfit, MIB, from $80 to.................**$100.00**
Dolly Darling, molded hair, original clothes, no accessories, 1965, 4", from $7 to.......................................**$12.00**
Dolly Darling, rooted hair, original clothes, no accessories, 1967, 4", from $15 to **$45.00**
Flower Darling, rooted hair, original outfit, 3½", stands inside plastic flower pin, 1968, from $20 to **$25.00**
Flying Nun Dolly Darling, all original, 1967, 4", MIB, from $75 to **$120.00**

Goldilocks Storykin, w/accessories & 33⅓ rpm LP record, 1967, MIP, from $85 to......................................**$100.00**
Jem Rock 'n Curl, 1986, MIB, from $70 to **$80.00**
Kate (Leggy), red rooted hair, re-dressed, 1972, 10", from $20 to **$25.00**
Kimber (Jem), original outfit, 1985, MIB, from $80 to.....**$100.00**
Little Miss No Name, teardrop on cheek, burlap dress, 1965, 15", EX/NM, from $90 to **$125.00**
Love (World of Love), long rooted hair, original clothes & headband, 1971, 9", MIB, from $35 to **$40.00**
Peteena, poodle face & doll body, in Twinkle Toes ballerina outfit, 1966, 9", EX, from $25 to.................................**$35.00**
Rio (Jem), original outfit, 1985, MIB, from $40 to............**$45.00**

Storykins, Cinderella, mail-order premium (also sold in stores), complete, in box as shown, from $25.00 to $35.00. (Photo courtesy Robin Englehart, vintagelane.com/photo by Nancy Jean Mong)

Storykins, w/accessory & 33⅓ rpm record, 1967, complete loose set, from $15 to **$45.00**
Sweet Cookie, blond rooted hair, blue eyes, freckles, jointed elbows, re-dressed, 1972, 18", from $15 to **$20.00**

Holly Hobbie

In the late 1960s a young homemaker and mother, Holly Hobbie, approached the American Greeting Company with some charming country-styled drawings of children as proposed designs for greeting cards. Her concepts were well received by the company, and since that time thousands of Holly Holly items have been produced. Nearly all are marked HH, H. Hobbie, or Holly Hobbie. Unless another code is mentioned in the line, assume that our values are for items in at least near-mint condition.

Ashtray, Happiness Is Having Someone To Care For, girl carrying cat, sm butterfly on side...**$25.00**
Book, Holly Hobbie's Nursery Rhymes, American Greetings, Ottenheimer Publishers Inc, 1977, 45 pages, EX..........**$20.00**
Book bag, 2 girls on bike, Holly standing in front, vinyl, plastic handle & latch, 9x12"...**$36.00**
Clock, alarm; Holly Hobbie in blue & white w/plaid apron, American Greetings, 1972, 6" **$22.00**
Doll, Amy, Knickerbocker, 10", MIB...............................**$38.00**
Doll, Amy, Knickerbocker, 16", EX **$20.00**
Doll, Grandma Holly, Knickerbocker, 16", EX...................**$45.00**
Doll, Grandma Holly, Knickerbocker, 24", EX...................**$30.00**

Doll, Heather, Knickerbocker, 27", MIB $56.00
Doll, Holly Hobbie, Knickerbocker, 1970s, 26", EX, from $40 to..$55.00
Doll, Holly Hobbie, 25th Anniversary, 1993, 12", MIB......$25.00

Dollhouse, M, $300.00. (Photo courtesy Helen McCale)

Figurine, girl holding blue flowers w/lg 16 in front, American Greetings, hand-painted bisque, 6½x3½" $25.00
Figurine, Sweet Dreams, girl asleep while holding book & sitting on bench, miniature, pewter, Limited Edition $17.00
Music box, Be Glad You're You, That's a Nice Thing To Be, girl holding dish of milk w/2 cats below, ceramic, 1974.............$30.00
Plate, Thoughtfulness Is to Friendship What Sunshine Is to Flowers, girl sitting in flower patch, 1972...................................$14.00
Purse, house shape w/dimensional Holly Hobbie prints in ea window, wood, blue felt lining, 8x6x10" $25.00
Record player, Holly Hobbie & Robby, Model SP-29, EX...$37.00
Salt & pepper shakers, A True Friend Is the Best Possession, Holly carrying cat, Made in Japan, 1974 ....$30.00
Tea set, Friends Are Fun, Holly & friend having tea w/doll, child's-size service for 4, MIB $23.00
Toothbrush holder, girl holding flowers, floral decor on top, porcelain, Made in Japan, 1973...$22.00
Tray, Start Each Day in a Happy Way, girl holding flowers, metal, 1972, MIP $17.00
Trinket box, piano shape, Happiness Is Having Someone To Care For, porcelain, Sands, Made in Japan $30.00
Wristwatch, It's Time To Be Happy, girl holding flowers on face, yellow band, Bradley, 1972, MIB.....................................$18.00

Ideal Dolls

The Ideal Toy Company made many popular dolls such as Shirley Temple, Betsy Wetsy, Miss Revlon, Toni, and Patti Playpal. Ideal's doll production was so enormous that since 1907 over 700 different dolls have been 'brought to life,' made from materials such as composition, latex rubber, hard plastic, and vinyl.

Since Ideal dolls were mass produced, most are still accessible and affordable. Collectors often find these dolls at garage sales and flea markets. However, some Ideal dolls are highly desirable

and command high prices — into the thousands of dollars. These sought-after dolls include the Samantha doll, variations of the Shirley Temple doll, certain dolls in the Patti Playpal family, and some Captain Action dolls.

The listing given here is only a sampling of Ideal dolls made from 1907 to 1989. This listing reports current, realistic selling prices at doll shows and through mail order. Please remember these values are for dolls in excellent condition with original clothing.

For more information please refer to *Collector's Guide to Ideal Dolls: Identification and Values, Third Edition,* by Judith Izen (Collector Books).

See also Advertising Characters; Shirley Temple; and Dolls' sub-categories: Betsy McCall, Celebrity Dolls, and Tammy.

Club: Ideal Collectors Club
Judith Izen
P.O. Box 623, Lexington, MA 02173
jizen@rcn.com

Betsy Wetsy, vinyl with hard plastic head, complete with clothing, glass bottle, rattle, etc., 15", NRFB, $450.00. (Photo courtesy McMasters Harris Auction Company)

Buster Brown, cloth body w/tin eyes, red outfit, 1929, 16", EX. **$300.00**
Charlie McCarthy, hand puppet, painted tuxedo, wire monocle, 1938-39, 8", VG...**$15.00**
Cracker Jack Boy w/package of Cracker Jack, sailor suit & cap, 1917, 14", EX...**$375.00**
Dennis the Menace, cloth, overalls w/striped shirt, Hank Ketcham, 1976, 14", EX..**$20.00**
Dorothy Hamill, vinyl head w/plastic posable body, ice rink on stand w/skates, 1978, 11½", VG...**$20.00**
Evel Knievel, plastic, helmet & stuntcycle, 1974-77, 7", EX ..**$25.00**
Howdy Doody, ventriloquist doll operated by pull string, hard plastic head, cloth body, cowboy outfit, 1950-53, 24", EX....**$250.00**
Jiminy Cricket, wood segmented body, yellow suit w/black coat, wooden umbrella, 1940, 9", VG.................................**$125.00**
Miss Ideal, vinyl, rooted nylon hair, jointed, original dress, comb & beauty kit, 1961, 25", EX...**$375.00**
Scarecrow, character from Wizard of Oz, yarn hair, 1939, 17", VG **$250.00**
Snow White, cloth body, black human hair wig, red & white dress w/caricatures of 7 Dwarfs on bottom, 1938, 16", EX.**$550.00**

Soozie Smiles, cloth body, 2 faces:smiling & crying, original romper & hat, 1923, 15½" $400.00

Stormer, original outfit & accessories, 1985, M $96.00

Tickletoes, cloth body w/rubber arms & legs, squeaker in ea leg, original dress & bonnet, 1928-39, 14", EX $250.00

Liddle Kiddles

These tiny little dolls ranging from ¾" to 4" tall were made by Mattel from 1966 until 1979. They all had poseable bodies and rooted hair that could be restyled, and they came with accessories of many types. Some represented storybook characters, some were flowers in perfume bottles, some were made to be worn as jewelry, and there were even spacemen 'Kiddles.'

Serious collectors prefer examples that are still in their original packaging and for them will often pay a minimum of 30% (to as much as 100%) over the price of a doll in excellent condition with all her original accessories. A doll whose accessories are missing is worth from 65% to 70% less. For more information, we recommend *Schroeder's Collectible Toys, Antique to Modern* (Collector Books).

Advisor: Dawn Diaz (See Directory, Dolls)

Animiddle, Kiddles, MIP, ea $75.00
Babe Biddle, #3505, complete, M $75.00
Baby Rockaway, #3819, MIP $100.00
Blue Funny Bunny, #3532, MIP $65.00
Chitty-Chitty Bang-Bang Kiddles, #3597, MOC $150.00
Chocolottie's House, #2501, MIP $25.00
Florence Niddle, #3507, complete, M $75.00
Flower Ring Kiddle, #3741, MIP $50.00
Frosty Mint Kone, #3653, complete, M $60.00
Greta Griddle, #3508, complete, M $75.00
Heart Charm Bracelet Kiddle, #3747, MIP $50.00
Heart Ring Kiddle, #3744, MIP $50.00

Heather Hiddlehorse, complete, NM, from $75.00 to $100.00. (Photo courtesy Cindy Sabulis)

Hot Dog Stand, #5002, complete, M $25.00
Jewelry Kiddles, #3735 & #5166 Treasure Box, M, ea $25.00
Kampy Kiddle, #3753, complete, M $150.00

King & Queen of Hearts, #3784, MIP $150.00
Lenore Limousine, #3743, complete, M $50.00
Lolli-Grape, #3656, complete, M $60.00
Lorelei Locket, #3717, 1967, MIP $75.00
Lucky Lion, #3635, complete, M $25.00
Luvvy Duvvy Kiddle, #3596, MIP $50.00
Nappytime Baby, #3818, complete, M $45.00
Pink Funny Bunny, #3532, MIP $65.00
Robin Hood & Maid Marian, #3735, MIP $150.00
Sizzly Friddle, MIP $300.00
Tiny Tiger, #3636, MIP $75.00
Vanilla Lilly, #2819, MIP $25.00
Violet Kologne, #3713, MIP $60.00
Windy Fliddle, #3514, complete, M $75.00

Littlechap Family

In 1964 Remco Industries created a family of four fashion dolls that represented an upper-middle class American family. The Littlechaps family consisted of the father, Dr. John Littlechap, his wife, Lisa, and their two children, teenage daughter Judy and pre-teen Libby. Interest in these dolls is on the rise as more and more collectors discover the exceptional quality of these fashion dolls and their clothing.

Advisor: Cindy Sabulis (See Directory, Dolls)

Carrying case, EX $40.00
Doll, Dr John, MIB $50.00

Doll, Judy, EX, $25.00; in complete football outfit, EX, $40.00. (Photo courtesy Cindy Sabulis)

Doll, Judy, MIB $75.00
Doll, Lisa, MIB $65.00
Outfit, Dr John's all-weather coat, NRFB $35.00
Outfit, Dr John's business suit, NRFB $40.00

Outfit, Dr John's golf outfit, NRFB	$40.00
Outfit, Dr John's medical outfit, NRFB	$45.00
Outfit, Judy's dance dress, NRFB	$55.00
Outfit, Judy's football outfit, NRFB	$75.00
Outfit, Judy's nightshirt, NRFB	$25.00
Outfit, Judy's party dress, NRFB	$55.00
Outfit, Judy's 3-piece suit, NRFB	$55.00
Outfit, Libby's Levis & sweatshirt, NRFB	$45.00
Outfit, Libby's plaid reefer coat, NRFB	$40.00
Outfit, Libby's Ya Ya dress, NRFB	$40.00
Outfit, Libby's 3-piece blazer outfit, NRFB	$45.00
Outfit, Lisa's basic black dress, NRFB	$50.00
Outfit, Lisa's formal evening ensemble, NRFB	$75.00
Outfit, Lisa's lingerie, NRFB	$25.00
Playset, Dr John's Office, complete, EX	$85.00
Playset, Family Room, complete, EX	$85.00

Madame Alexander

This company was founded in 1923 by Beatrice Alexander. The first doll they produced was Alice in Wonderland, made entirely of cloth with an oil-painted face. With the help of her three sisters, the company prospered, and by the 1960s, there were over 600 employees busy making Madame Alexander dolls. They're still in business today. If you'd like to learn more about these lovely dolls, refer to *Collector's Encyclopedia of Madame Alexander Dolls, 1948 – 1965,* and *Madame Alexander's Collector Dolls Price Guide* by Linda Crowsey. Both are published by Collector Books.

Our values are for perfect dolls. Prices for those made before 1973 will not include the original box; but for those made since that time, the box must be present to warrant the values given below.

Alice in Wonderland, hard plastic, blue w/lace trim, organdy pinafore, 1995, 8"	$65.00
Anne of Green Gables, #260418, hard plastic, puff-sleeve dress, 1994, 8"	$95.00
Baby Genius, cloth, 1930s, 11"	$425.00
Baseball boy, red & white baseball outfit, 1997, #16313, 8"	$50.00
Charlene, cloth & vinyl, 1991-92 only, 18"	$100.00
Cherub, vinyl, 1960-61, 12"	$250.00
Chloe, #25345, pink gingham dress, 2000, 14"	$60.00
Cissy Bride, porcelain portrait doll, #52011, 1994 only, 21"	$350.00
Dancing Clara, #34305, pink dress, holding nutcracker, 2002, 8"	$85.00
Dionne Quints, hard plastic, 75th Anniversary set w/carousel, #12230, 1998, complete, 8"	$450.00
Emily, cloth/felt, 1930s	$600.00
French Flowergirl, #610, hard plastic, 1956 only (Wendy Ann), 8", minimum value	$800.00
Geranium, vinyl toddler, red organdy dress & bonnet, 1953 only, 9"	$100.00
Giselle, #22050, aqua tutu, 1998, 16"	$110.00
Hiawatha, #720, Americana Series, hard plastic, 1967-69 (Wendy Ann), 8"	$375.00
Indian girl, hard plastic, bent knees, Wendy Ann, #721, 1966 only, 8"	$400.00
Jessica, cloth/vinyl, 1990 only, 18"	$100.00

Kathy, hard plastic, braids, Maggie, 1949-51, from 15" to 18", from $550 to	$750.00
Little Women, plastic & vinyl, Nancy Drew, 1969-82, 12", ea.	$65.00
Lucy Ricardo, gingham dress w/bottle & spoon, 1950s, 9"	$110.00
Muffin, cloth, 1966 only, 19"	$100.00
Natasha, #2255, brown & paisley brocade, Jacqueline, 1989-90, 21"	$325.00
Off to Class, #35645, blue plaid dress, book bag & books, 2003, 8"	$75.00

Party Maid, Alexander-Kins, 8", MIB, $550.00.
(Photo courtesy McMasters Harris Auction Company)

Pumpkin, cloth/vinyl, 1967-76, 22"	$125.00
Queen of Storyland, #26025, long white gown, limited to 2,600, 2000, 10"	$100.00
Rebecca, plastic & vinyl, Classic Series, 2-tiered pink skirt, Mary Ann, #1485, 1968-69, 14"	$150.00
Rosebud, cloth/vinyl, 1952-53, from 16" to 19"	$150.00
Smiley, cloth & vinyl, Happy, 1971 only, 20"	$250.00
Sweet Sixteen, #21060, pink silk dress, lace stole, 1997, 10"	$90.00
Tommy, hard plastic, Lissy, 1962 only, 12"	$800.00
Train Journey, #486, hard plastic, white wool jacket & hat, red plaid dress, 1955, 8"	$550.00
Victorian Catherine, #90010, porcelain, elaborate gown, 16"	$200.00
White Rabbit, cloth/felt, 1940s, from 14" to 17", from $500 to	$750.00
Yellow Daffodil, #25620, long white & yellow gown, 2000, 10"	$90.00
Zorina Ballerina, composition, extra makeup, 1937-38 (Wendy Ann), 17", M, minimum value	$1,900.00

Nancy Ann Storybook Dolls

This company was in business as early as 1936, producing painted bisque dolls with mohair wigs and painted eyes. Later they made hard plastic 8" Muffie and Miss Nancy Ann Style Show dolls. Debby

(11") and Lori Ann (7½") had vinyl heads and hard plastic bodies. In the 1950s and 1960s, they produced a 10½" Miss Nancy Ann and Little Miss Nancy Ann, both vinyl high-wheeled fashion-type dolls. Some of the listings that follow contain more than one number. The first number is their original stock number, the second is the number that was assigned to them after 1940, when the company began to print pamphlets to go with each doll.

For more information we recommend *Encyclopedia of Bisque Nancy Ann Storybook Dolls* by Elaine M. Pardee and Jackie Robertson.

Alice Through the Looking Glass (#125), frozen legs, plastic arms, NA mold, blue floral dress w/white apron, #125 .... **$45.00**

Anne at the Garden Gate (#29), frozen legs, white dress w/red trim, #129 .... **$55.00**

Beauty (from Beauty & the Beast), frozen legs, blonde hair, lavender w/white polka dots, #156 .... **$45.00**

Cinderella (#23), jointed legs, brown hair, peach dress w/black lace, blue ribbon w/rosebuds in hair, #155 .... **$1,500.00**

Goldilocks, frozen leg, yellow dress w/blue apron, blue ribbon in hair, #128 .... **$65.00**

Goose Girl, frozen legs, red cotton w/floral print, blue bodice & Dutch-style hat, #169 .... **$55.00**

Little Betty Blue Wore Her Holiday Shoe, jointed legs, pudgy tummy, blue dress w/red ribbon, #109 .... **$135.00**

Lucy Locket (#115), frozen legs, plastic arms, floral print dress, blue hat, #124 or #134 .... **$45.00**

Mary Had a Little Lamb (#20), jointed legs, pudgy tummy, taffeta rose print, feather on pink felt hat, #152 .... **$250.00**

Regina, frozen legs, flocked taffeta dress, organdy half-slip, #255, $125.00. (Photo courtesy Elaine M. Pardee and Jackie Robertson)

Ring Around The Rosy, jointed legs, pudgy tummy, brown hair, red dress, purple flower in hair #159................................. **$200.00**

Rose Red (#17), jointed leg, Dusty Rose layered net skirt w/satin bodice, satin cap w/rose net, silver slippers, #151 .... **$900.00**

Roses Are Red Violets Are Blue (#123), frozen legs, pink taffeta dress w/floral apron, #113 .... **$55.00**

Snow White (#16), jointed legs, ivory layered netting w/3 pearls on taffeta bodice, ivory cap w/netting, #150 .... **$800.00**

Sugar & Spice & Everything Nice, frozen legs, brown plaid w/white apron, red ribbon in hair, #158..................................... **$55.00**

Raggedy Ann and Andy

Raggedy Ann dolls have been made since the early part of the twentieth century, and over the years many companies have produced their own versions. They were created originally by Johnny Gruelle, and though these early dolls are practically nonexistent, they're easily identified by the mark, 'Patented Sept. 7, 1915.' P.F. Volland made them from 1920 to 1934; theirs were very similar in appearance to the originals. The Mollye Doll Outfitters were the first to print the now-familiar red heart on her chest, and they added a black outline around her nose. These dolls carry the handwritten inscription 'Raggedy Ann and Andy Doll/Manufactured by Mollye Doll Outfitters.' Georgene Averill made them ca 1938 to 1950, sewing their label into the seam of the dolls. Knickerbocker dolls (1963 to 1982) also carry a company label. The Applause Toy Company made these dolls for two years in the early 1980s, and they were finally taken over by Hasbro, the current producer, in 1983.

Unless noted otherwise, our values are for dolls in excellent/near-mint condition. If your doll has been played with but is still in good condition with a few minor flaws (as most are), you'll need deduct 75% from these prices.

Georgene Novelties, Raggedy Ann and Andy, tin eyes, 1930s, some fading and soil, $375.00 for the pair. (Photo courtesy Patsy Moyer/Debbie Crume)

Applause, Ann & Andy, musical, cloth w/yarn hair, head rotates when music plays, 1986, 7", ea...................................... **$60.00**

Applause, Raggedy Ann & Andy, sleeping bag dolls, original tags, 8", ea **$25.00**

Applause, Raggedy Ann & Andy, 1986, 12", ea.................**$25.00**

Applause, Raggedy Ann & Andy babies, 5", ea...................**$25.00**

Applause, Raggedy Ann or Andy, 75th Anniversary edition, 1992, 19", M, pr..**$175.00**

Georgene, Beloved Belindy, 1938-50 ....**$1,250.00**

Georgene, Raggedy Ann, no heart or tag, 50"...................**$650.00**

Georgene Novelties, Raggedy Andy, cloth w/yarn hair, 1938-45, 19", M.. **$350.00**

Georgene Novelties, Raggedy Ann, cloth w/yarn hair, 1946-63, 22" **$165.00**

Kenner, Raggedy Ann & Andy, cloth, Black, original box, 9", set..**$30.00**

Knickerbocker, Andy, printed features, yarn hair, original paper tag, 31"..**$125.00**

Knickerbocker, Arthur dog, Made in Taiwan **$275.00**

Knickerbocker, Bedtime Raggedy Ann & Andy, I Love You on chest, 15", ea...**$30.00**

Knickerbocker, Raggedy Ann, pajama bag doll, cloth w/yarn hair, 1960s, 27", NM **$80.00**

Knickerbocker, Raggedy Ann & Andy, vinyl, original box, 1973, 3½" **$30.00**

Knickerbocker, Raggedy Ann & Andy, 1976, 5", ea **$25.00**

Knickerbocker, Raggedy Ann & Andy Embracables, original box, 1973, 7", set...**$45.00**

Reliable, Raggedy Ann & Andy, 19", ea.......................**$275.00**

Strawberry Shortcake and Friends

Strawberry Shortcake came on the market with a bang around 1980. The line included everything to attract small girls — swimsuits, bed linens, blankets, anklets, underclothing, coats, shoes, sleeping bags, dolls and accessories, games, and many other delightful items. Strawberry Shortcake and her friends were short lived, lasting only until the mid-1980s.

Note: Out-of-the-box, played-with dolls should be valued at as much as 75% less than mint-in-box dolls (much less if they show wear).

Online Club: Strawberryland Town Square

Big Berry Trolley, 1982, M, $45.00.

Bedspread & sham, print resembling quilt squares, twin size, EX.. **$60.00**

Berry Happy Home Fun Room, 1984, MIB.....................**$400.00**

Big Berry Trolley, 1982, EX **$35.00**

Bookcase, American Greetings, 1982, 40x20x9", NM **$80.00**

Charm bracelet, gold-tone links w/4 charms, vintage, M **$30.00**

Crib set, padded headboard, 3-sided bumper, 45" sq quilt w/pink chenille border, 11x11" pillow, complete, NM **$175.00**

Doll, Angel Cake, 6", MIB.....................................**$25.00**

Doll, Angel Cake w/Soufflè, Strawberryland Miniatues, EX ..**$8.00**

Doll, Apple Dumpling w/Tea Time Turtle, 1983, 6", MIB..**$40.00**

Doll, Baby Strawberry Shortcake Blow Kiss, 1982, 13½", MIB, from $125 to...**$140.00**

Doll, Berry Baby Orange Blossom, 6", MIB **$30.00**

Doll, Butter Cookie w/Jelly Bear, 6", 1981, MIB.................**$35.00**

Doll, Cherry Cuddler w/Gooseberry, flying airplaine, MIB .**$75.00**

Doll, Cherry Cuddler w/Gooseberry, Strawberryland Miniatures, MIP **$30.00**

Doll, Lemon Meringue w/Frappe, Strawberryland Miniatures, NM **$15.00**

Doll, Lime Chiffon w/Parfait Parrot, 2nd Issue, 1981, MIB...**$25.00**

Doll, Merry Berry Worm, MIB, from $25 to.....................**$35.00**

Doll, Mint Tulip w/Berrykin, 1985, NM.........................**$200.00**

Doll, Peach Blush and Melonie lamb, NM, 110.00.

Doll, Peach Blush w/Melonie Bell, Strawberryland Miniatures, EX+..**$85.00**

Doll, Peach Blush w/Melonie Belle, Party Pleasers, MIB....**$100.00**

Doll, Plum Puddin' Party Pleaser w/Elderberry Owl, Strawberryland Miniatures, MIB **$85.00**

Doll, Plum Puddin' Party Pleaser w/Elderberry Owl, MIB, from $160 to...**$180.00**

Doll, rag; Cherry Cuddler, 1983, 15", VG.........................**$35.00**

Doll, Raspberry Tart, 1980, 6", MIB **$40.00**

Doll, Raspberry Tart Sweet Sleeper, sleep eyes, w/Rhubarb pet, 1984, MIB **$55.00**

Doll, Raspberry Tart w/Rhubarb on seesaw, Strawberryland Miniatures, NM...**$18.00**

Doll, Sour Grapes, 1982, MIB......................................$50.00

Doll, Sour Grapes w/Dregs, Strawberryland Miniatures, MIP .. $25.00

Doll, Strawberry Shortcake, Party Pleaser, w/Custard, MIB . $50.00

Doll, Strawberry Shortcake Berry Princess, 1985, MIB......$135.00

Dollhouse Furniture, attic, 6-pc, rare, M $150.00

Dollhouse Furniture, bathroom, 5-pc, rare, M....................$65.00

Dollhouse Furniture, bedroom, 7-pc, rare, M $90.00

Dollhouse Furniture, kitchen, 11-pc, rare, M......................$100.00

Dollhouse Furniture, living room, 6-pc, rare, M $85.00

Figurine, Strawberry Shortcake, ceramic, 5", EX...................$8.00

Game, Strawberry Shortcake Rescues Fig Boot, 1984, complete,
    VGIB $35.00

Ice skates, EX..$35.00

Latch hook rug kit, partially completed, rug: 20x27", EXIB .. $40.00

Motorized bicycle, EX..$95.00

Mug, Angel Cake, Good Friends Are a Special Blessing, American
    Greetings, 1983 ....$50.00

Mug, Strawberry in yellow on milk glass, Anchor Hocking.. $85.00

Pillow doll, Huckleberry Pie, 9", EX................................$10.00

Plush figure, Rhubarb Monkey (mouse), 1980s, 6", EX.......$50.00

Sleeping bag, EX..$25.00

Stickers, vinyl, American Greetings, 1-sheet, MIP................$35.00

Storybook Play Case, M...$35.00

Stroller, Coleco, 1981, M...$85.00

Telephone, Strawberry Shortcake figure, battery-operated, EX.. $85.00

Tammy and Friends

In 1962 the Ideal Novelty and Toy Company introduced their teenage Tammy doll. Slightly pudgy and not quite as sophisticated-looking as some of the teen fashion dolls on the market at the time, Tammy's innocent charm captivated consumers. Her extensive wardrobe and numerous accessories added to her popularity with children. Tammy had a car, a house, and her own catamaran. In addition, a large number of companies obtained licenses to issue products using the 'Tammy' name. Everything from paper dolls to nurses' kits were made with Tammy's image on them. Her success was not confined to the United States; she was also successful in Canada and several other European countries.

Advisor: Cindy Sabulis (See Directory, Dolls)

Accessory Pak, baseball, catcher's mask, mitt & ball, unknown #,
    NRFP $35.00

Accessory Pak, Misty Hair Color Kit, #9828-5, MIB..........$75.00

Accessory Pak, pizza, princess phone, Tammy's Telephone Directory,
    white sandals, #9184-80, NRFP $25.00

Accessory Pak, plate of crackers, juice, glasses, sandals & newspaper,
    #9179-3, NRFP..$30.00

Accessory Pak, poodle on leash, red vinyl purse & white sneakers,
    #9186-80, NRFP..$25.00

Case, Misty, Dutch door-type, black, EX...........................$30.00

Case, Misty & Tammy, double telephone, green or pink, ea... $25.00

Case, Misty & Tammy, hatbox style, EX............................$30.00

Case, Pepper, hatbox style, turqoise, EX...........................$40.00

Case, Tammy Beau & Arrow, hatbox style, blue or red, EX. $40.00

Case, Tammy Model Miss, red or black, EX $25.00

Doll, Glamour Misty the Miss Clairol Doll, MIB.............$150.00

Doll, Pepper, MIB...$65.00

Doll, Pepper ('carrot'-colored hair), MIB $75.00

Doll, Pepper (Canadian version), MIB $75.00

Doll, Pos'n Dodi, M (decorated box) $150.00

Doll, Pos'n Misty & Her Telephone Booth, MIB..............$125.00

Doll, Pos'n Salty, MIB...$125.00

Doll, Pos'n Ted, MIB...$100.00

Doll, Tammy, straight legs, marked Ideal Toy Corp. BS-12", on her head, EX, from $25.00 to $40.00; outfit, EX, from $30.00 to $45.00. (Photo courtesy Cindy Sabulis)

Doll, Ted, MIB $50.00

Outfit, Dad & Ted, sports car coat & cap, #9467-2, NRFP...$20.00

Outfit, Dad & Ted, sweater, shorts & socks, #9476-3, MIP...$25.00

Outfit, Pepper, Flower Girl, #9332-8, complete, M.............$50.00

Outfit, Pepper, Miss Gadabout, #9331-0, MIP...................$50.00

Outfit, Pepper & Dodi, Light & Lacy, #9305-4, MIP.........$45.00

Outfit, Tammy, Beach Party, #9056-3 or #9906-9, complete,
    M $45.00

Outfit, Tammy, Jet Set, #9155-3 or #9943-2, MIP..............$75.00

Outfit, Tammy, Opening Night, #9954-9, MIP $100.00

Outfit, Tammy's Mom, Evening in Paris, #9421-9, complete,
    M $40.00

Outfit, Tammy's Mom, Lazy Days, #9418-5, MIP..............$50.00

Pak Clothing, afternoon dress & shoes, #9345-2, NRFP.....$45.00

Pak Clothing, pedal pushers, orange juice, newspaper & hanger,
    #9224-7, NRFP...$30.00

Pak Clothing, sheath dress, black belt, shoes & hanger, #9243-7,
    NRFP $45.00

Pak Clothing, sweater, scarf & hanger, #9244-5, NRFP $25.00

Pepper's Pony, MIB $250.00

Tammy Bubble Bath Set, NRFB....................................$75.00

Tammy Dress-Up Kit, Colorforms, 1964, complete, MIB...$30.00

Tammy's Bed, Dress & Chair, MIB.................................$85.00

Tammy's Ideal House, M, minimum value........................$100.00

Tammy's Magic Mirror Fashion Show, Winthrop-Atkins,
    NRFB $50.00

Tressy

Tressy was American Character's answer to Barbie. This 11½" fashion doll was made from 1963 to 1967. Tressy had a unique feature — her hair 'grew' by pushing a button on her stomach. She and her little sister, Cricket, had numerous fashions and accessories.

Unless other wise noted, our values are for loose mint-condition items.

Advisor: Cindy Sabulis (See Directory, Dolls)

Apartment...$350.00
Case, Tressy..$30.00

Doll, Posing Tressy, possibly re-dressed, with extra #25900 Hootenanny outfit inside a cardboard Tressy carrying case; gift set complete with NRFC outfit, from $125.00 to $200.00. (Photo courtesy Cindy Sabulis, Janet Lawrence, and Mike Lawrence)

Doll, Pre-Teen Tressy...$30.00
Doll, Tressy & her Hi-Fashion Cosmetics, MIB.................$145.00
Doll, Tressy in Miss America Character outfit......................$65.00
Doll, Tressy w/Magic Make-up Face.................................$25.00
Gift Pak w/Doll & Clothing, NRFB, minimum value.......$100.00
Hair or Cosmetic Accessory Kits, ea, minimum value.........$50.00
Hat Shoppe..$150.00
Outfits, MOC, ea from $40 to $65.00
Outfits, NRFB, ea minimum value...................................$65.00

Uneeda Doll Co., Inc.

The Uneeda Doll Company was located in New York City and began making composition dolls about 1917. Later a transition was made to plastics and vinyl.

Baby Dollikin, hard plastic w/vinyl head, jointed body, drinks & wets, 1960, 21", MIB $200.00
Baby Trix, hard plastic & vinyl, 1965, 19", NM $25.00
Bareskin Baby, hard plastic & vinyl, 1968, 12½", NM........$20.00

Blabby, hard plastic & vinyl, 1962, 14", NM $25.00
Coquette, hard plastic & vinyl, Black, 1963, 16", NM.......$36.00
Coquette, hard plastic & vinyl, 1963, 16", NM $20.00

L'il Agatha Bride, vinyl head, light-weight plastic limbs and torso, copyright 1967, 9¾", MIB, $20.00. (Photo courtesy Cindy Sabulis)

Maggie Meg w/Hair That Grows, hard plastic & vinyl, rooted hair & sleep eyes, 16", NM...$45.00
Pollyana, made for Disney, 1960, 17", MIB.....................$130.00
Suzette, hard plastic & vinyl, 12", M $65.00
Tiny Teen, 6-pc hard plastic & vinyl, rooted hair, pierced ears, 1957-59, 10½", EX $40.00

Vogue Dolls, Inc.

Vogue Dolls Incorporated is one of America's most popular manufacturer of dolls. In the early 1920s through the mid-1940s, Vogue imported lovely dolls of bisque and composition, dressing them in the fashionable designs hand sewn by Vogue's founder, Jennie Graves. In the late '40s through the early '50s, they became famous for their wonderful hard plastic dolls, most notably the 8" Ginny doll. This adorable toddler doll skyrocketed into nationwide attention in the early '50s as lines of fans stretched around the block during store promotions, and Ginny dolls sold out regularly. A Far-Away-Lands Ginny was added in the late '50s, sold well through the '70s, and is still popular with collectors today. In fact, a modern-day version of Ginny is currently being sold by the Vogue Doll Company, Inc.

Many wonderful dolls followed through the years, including unique hard-plastic, vinyl, and soft-body dolls. These dolls include teenage dolls Jill, Jan, and Jeff; Ginnette, the 8" baby doll; Miss Ginny; and the famous vinyl and soft-bodied dolls by noted artist and designer E. Wilkin. It is not uncommon for these highly collectible dolls to turn up at garage sales and flea markets.

Over the years, Vogue developed the well-deserved reputation as 'The Fashion Leaders in Doll Society' based on their fine quality sewing and on the wide variety of outfits designed for their dolls to wear. These outfits included frilly dress-up doll clothes as well as action-oriented sports outfits. The company was among the first in the doll industry to develop the concept of marketing and selling separate outfits for their dolls, many of which were 'matching' for their special doll lines. The very early Vogue outfits are most sought after, and later outfits are highly collectible as well. It is wise for collectors to become aware of Vogue's unique styles, designs, and construction methods in order to 'spot' these authentic Vogue 'prizes' on collecting outings.

Values here are only a general guide. For further information we recommend *Collector's Encyclopedia of Vogue Dolls* by Judith Izen and Carol Stover (Collector Books).

Baby Dear, Redesigned; vinyl & cloth, original outfit, 1964-80, 12", M...$150.00

Cowboy and Cowgirl, hard plastic with painted features, 1959, EX, $225.00 each. (Photo courtesy McMasters Harris Auction Company)

Ginnette, vinyl, painted eyes, open mouth, original outfit, 1955-56 & 1959, 8", M..$150.00
Ginny, Coronation Queen, hard plastic, straight-leg walker, 1954, 8", M, minimum value $800.00
Ginny, hard plastic w/vinyl head, bent-knee walker, original outfit, 1963-65, 8", M...$150.00
Ginny, Queen of Hearts, hard plastic strung, open & closed eyes, original outfit, 1950, 8", M, minimum value $500.00
Ginny, vinyl, jointed arms, straight legs, rooted hair, original outfit, 1965-72, 8", M...$100.00
Jan, Loveable or Sweetheart, vinyl, original outfit, 1959-60, 10½", MIB, ea...$60.00
Jan, vinyl, straight legs, open & closed eyes, swivel waist, original outfit, 1959-60, 10½", M...............................$75.00
Jill, All New; vinyl, rooted hair, high heels, original outfit, 1962, 10½", EX...$76.00
Jill, All New; vinyl, rooted hair, high heels, original outfit, 1962, 10½", M..$175.00
Jill, hard plastic, nude, 10½", VG, minimum value $50.00
Jill, hard plastic, open & closed eyes, bent-knee walker, basic original outfit, 1957, 10½", M.................................$150.00
Jill, Sweetheart, vinyl, rooted hair, high heels, original outfit, 1963, M..$175.00
Jimmy, vinyl, jointed, painted eyes, open mouth, original outfit, 1958, 8", M...$100.00

Li'l Imp, hard plastic & vinyl, bent-knee walker, original outfit, 1959-60, 11", M...$150.00
Li'l Lovable Imp, vinyl, straight legs, open & closed eyes, original outfit, 1964-65, 11", M......................................$65.00
Littlest Angel, hard plastic & vinyl, bent-knee walker, original outfit, 1961-63, 10½", M...$65.00
Miss Ginny, vinyl, sm open & closed eyes, closed mouth, original outfit, 1962-64, 16", M..$80.00
Sunshine Baby, composition, molded hair, original outfit, 1943-47, 8", M..$400.00
Toddles, Alpine Boy, composition, painted eyes, original outfit, 1944-46, 8", M, from $250 to....................................$300.00
Toddles, composition, molded hair, military original outfit, 1937-48, 8", M, minimum value $325.00

Door Knockers

Though many of the door knockers you'll see on the market today are of the painted cast-iron variety (similar in design to doorstop figures), they're also found in brass and other metals. Most are modeled as people, animals, and birds, and baskets of flowers are common. All items listed are cast iron unless noted otherwise, and values reflect excellent condition.

Advisor: Craig Dinner (See Directory, Door Knockers)

Club: Cast Iron Collectors Club
Contact: Dan Morphy Auctions
morphyauctions.com or 717 335-3455)

Aberdeen Terrier (titled at bottom), facing right, cast brass, ca 1920, 4x6" $85.00
Alsatian Wolf Dog (German shepherd), brass, 5x4" $50.00
Basket of daffodils, blue bow at top, 4½x2½" $300.00
Black Mammy w/wicker laundry basket of clothes on her head, arms & chest comprise the clapper, 7" (new record value)..$2,500.00
Black shoeshine man walking on cobblestone road, brass, 3⅛". $65.00
Bloodhound's head, brass, English, ca 1940, 3¼x2¼" $85.00
Bluebell flower, VG $150.00
Castle fortress against embossed woods, CJO, rare, NM....$330.00
Cat w/arched back, MIB.......................................$275.00
Centurion in relief, black paint, figurative back plate, 4½x2¼" .$100.00
Collie (titled base), brass, unmarked, 2½x2"......................$46.00

Colonial lady, Waverly Studios, white dress, repainted backplate, 4", VG, $50.00. (Photo courtesy Bertoia Auctions)

Colonial man medallion, Waverly Studios, 4½", M..........$195.00

Eagle w/wings wide, brass, EX detail, G age & patina, 5¼x4" . **$85.00**
Flower basket, Hubley #205, rare......................**$175.00**
Flower basket, Judd, 4", NM..........................**$165.00**
Flower basket, multicolor flowers in white basket, Hubley, 4x3" **$150.00**
Girl w/basket knocking at door, Hubley, 3⅝"....................**$550.00**

Grandpa Bunny, brown with red coat, black detailing, white trousers, 4", M, $500.00. (Photo courtesy Bertoia Auctions)

Ivy basket, light & dark green in yellow basket, white backplate, 4½x2½"..**$145.00**
Ivy pot, Hubley #3-23, 4½"..........................**$160.00**
Kewpie doll, brass, #A-74, 7x2½" backplate **$110.00**
Lady in flower garden collecting clippings, brass, 3"..........**$225.00**
Lady w/bonnet, flowing hair, painted cast iron, CJO, 4¾"...**$260.00**
Lion head, ring in mouth, brass, 6¼"................................**$75.00**
Masonic symbol of hand w/gavel entertwined w/letter G, backplate is sq & compass, brass, 6⅛x5½"......................**$85.00**
Morning Glory, green leaves form backplate, Judd #608, 3¼". **$175.00**
Owl, old dark repaint, oval backplate, 4¾x3"....................**$200.00**
Parrot among leaves on oval back plate, 4¾x3".................**$150.00**
Parrot perched on branch, multicolor paint on cast iron, Hubley, 4¾", NM...**$275.00**
Peace dove, w/olive branch in beak, 4x2¾"........................**$290.00**
Rabbit, running, brass, 4".................................**$140.00**
Rooster w/branch, oval backplate, 4½x3"........................**$200.00**
Sir Thomas Wikeham, w/3 children at feet, brass, 19th C, 6x1¾"...**$55.00**
Spaniels (2) sitting side by side, brass, 1930s, 3½x2¼"........**$85.00**
Spider & web, 3½x1⅞"...............................**$1,000.00**
Tulip, wide frame, aluminum, 8x5¼"..............................**$140.00**
Woodpecker, red head w/black & white feathers, backplate is tree, brown & green w/pink flowers (paint worn), 3¾"........**$85.00**
Zinnias, marked Pat Pend LVL, rare, 3¾x2½"..................**$300.00**

Doorstops

There are three important factors to consider when buying doorstops — rarity, desirability, and condition. Desirability is often a more important issue than rarity, especially if the doorstop is well designed and detailed. Subject matter often overlaps into other areas, and if they appeal to collectors of Black Americana and advertising, for instance, this tends to drive prices upward. Most doorstops are made of painted cast iron, and value is directly related to the condi-

tion of the paint. If there is little paint left or if the figure has been repainted or is rusty, unless the price has been significantly reduced, pass it by.

Be aware that Hubley, one of the largest doorstop manufacturers, sold many of their molds to the John Wright Company who makes them today. Watch for seams that do not fit properly, grainy texture, and too-bright paint. Watch for reproductions!

The doorstops we've listed here are all of the painted cast-iron variety unless another type of material is mentioned in the description. Values are suggested for original examples without damage and in near-mint paint and should be reduced equivalent to the amount of wear apparent. Recent auctions report even higher prices realized for examples in pristine condition.

Club: Doorstop Collectors of America
Jeanie Bertoia
2413 Madison Ave.
Vineland, NJ 08361; 609-692-4092
Membership $20.00 per year, includes 2 *Doorstoppers* newsletters and convention. Send two-stamp SASE for sample.

Aunt Jemima, wedge back, 7½x3¾", EX..........................**$385.00**

Bathing Beauties, signed Fish, Hubley, 11x5", EX, $700.00. (Photo courtesy Bertoia Auctions)

Bobby Blake w/teddy bear, Grace Dayton design, Hubley, 9½". **$250.00**
Cape Cod cottage, Eastern Specialty, 5¾x8¾"..................**$495.00**
Cat sleeping, red bow at neck, National Foundry, 3⅜x9⅝"..**$660.00**
Cocker spaniel, full figure, embossed details, Hubley, 11" L.**$770.00**
Cottage w/fence, flowers growing along walls & door, National Foundry, 7¼", EX....................................**$140.00**
Cottage w/flowers along walls & surrounding doorway, Hubley, 5½x7½"...**$110.00**
Delphiniums, roses & forget-me-nots in vase w/blue ribbon, Hubley, 9"...**$415.00**
Duck, stylized, yellow on green base, wedge back, 5x3¾"..**$415.00**
Elephant on stair base, B&H 7798, 10½".......................**$330.00**
Geese (3), Fred Everett design, Hubley, 8x8"....................**$415.00**
German shepherd, embossed harness, heavy green base, 7⅞x9", EX...**$140.00**

187

Girl on racehorse jumping hurdle, flat back, 7x7"............$550.00

Heron perched by sea, EX details, Albany Foundry, 7½x5⅛", EX $440.00

Hunchback cat, startled look, 10⅝x7½", EX..................$385.00

Kitten reclining, bow at neck, National Foundry, 4x8⅛"...$1,050.00

Koala on log base, #5 copy 1930 Taylor Cook, 4⅞x8⅜", EX. $880.00

Pansy bowl, Hubley, 7x6½" $165.00

Parlour maid, signed & designed by Fish, Hubley, 9½x3½". $1,875.00

Pekinese, very lifelike, Hubley, 9x14½", VG+ $1,875.00

Persian kitten w/tail curled around body, Hubley, 8½x6½"..$275.00

Pheasant, realistic painting, Fred Everett, Hubley, 8½x7½"..$470.00

Rabbit eating carrot, green base w/cast bushes, 5½"...........$440.00

Roses in classic style vase, Hubley, 8¾x7⅞" $880.00

Scottie seated, wearing red collar, hollow casting, Hubley, 11x15"...$990.00

Ship, 10x12", EX, $275.00; Nautical scene, B&H, 11x5", EX, $140.00. (Photo courtesy Bertoia Auctions)

Stork, stylized, comic pose, wedge back, 5x3¾" $415.00

Tropical woman w/hands supporting fruit basket on head, 12x6¼", NM..$1,100.00

Tulips in pot, National Foundry, 8¼x7" $550.00

Twin cats, 1 in dress, 2nd in jumper, Hubley, #73, 7x5¼" ...$525.00

Windmill in field, National Foundry #10, 6¾x6⅞", EX ...$195.00

Dragonware

Dragonware is the name given to Japanese-made ceramics decorated with a fierce slipwork dragon. Sometimes cups have lithophanes in the bottom. It was often sold through gift shops at popular tourist attractions and may be imprinted with names such as Chinatown, San Francisco; Rock City; or Washington D.C. It's still being made, but collectors prefer vintage items, which have much more detail in the dragon. Background color is another clue you can use to determine age. New colors include green, lavender, yellow, pink, blue, pearl, orange, and blue-black. Though some of the same colors may be found in vintage ware, compared to the new, background colors of older pieces are flat rather than glossy.

Club: Dragonware Club
c/o Suzi Hibbard
849 Vintage Ave.
Fairfield, CA 94585
Dragon_Ware@hotmail.com
www.Dragonware.com
Inquiries must be accompanied with LSASE; contributions welcome

Vase, marked ENDO, Japan, 3½", $30.00.

Ashtray, blue, 3¾", from $8 to..................................$12.00

Candlesticks, black, Made in Japan, pr from $50 to $125.00

Condiment set, black, salt & pepper shakers, mustard w/spoon, & tray (5 pcs), from $40 to..............................$75.00

Cup & saucer, child's, green, D China, from $10 to...........$20.00

Cup & saucer, coffee; black cloud, HP Betsons, from $20 to. $25.00

Cup & saucer, demitasse; double nude lithophane, gray, Nikoniko China, from $75 to......................................$125.00

Cup & saucer, demitasse; goggle eyes, red & black, Castle mark, from $30 to $35.00

Cup & saucer, demitasse; orange cloud, Made in Occupied Japan, from $20 to $25.00

Ginger jar, blue cloud, Lego Made in Japan, 5", from $35 to. $50.00

Incense burner, gray, Hand Painted Made in Japan, 3½", from $35 to $45.00

Mustard jar, gray, w/spoon, 3½", 3 pcs, from $15 to $40.00

Pitcher, yellow, Made in Japan, miniature, 2⅞", from $15 to. $25.00

Saki cups, yellow, whistling, set of 6, from $30 to................$45.00

Saki set, blue cloud, w/plate, 7 pcs, from $50 to...............$100.00

Salt & pepper shakers, gray, Made in Japan, pr from $10 to...$25.00

Salt & pepper shakers, orange, pagoda style, Japan, 4", pr from $15 to $40.00

Table lighter, black, from $50 to $75.00

Tea set, demitasse; white pearl, Japan, 17 pcs, from $75 to...$125.00

Tea set, gray, gold trim, 1940s-50s, 7½" teapot, w/creamer & sugar bowl..$65.00

Tea set, gray, sq, Noritake, teapot, creamer & sugar bowl, w/lid, from $75 to $125.00

Tidbit tray, gray, Nippon, 9x6½", from $100 to $175.00

Vase, gray, yellow or orange, 4¼", set of 3, from $30 to $60.00

Wall pocket, blue & orange lustre, Japan flower mark, 7", from $25 to $50.00

Duncan and Miller Glassware

Although the roots of the company can be traced back as far as 1865 when George Duncan went into business in Pittsburgh, Pennsylvania, the majority of the glassware that collectors are interested in was produced during the twentieth century. The firm became known as Duncan and Miller in 1900. They were bought out by the United States Glass Company who continued to produce many of the same designs through a separate operation which they called the Duncan and Miller Division.

In addition to crystal, they made some of their wares in a wide assortment of colors including ruby, milk glass, some opalescent glass, and a black opaque glass they called Ebony. Some of their pieces were decorated by cutting or etching. They also made a line of animals and bird figures. For information on these, see *Glass Animals* by Dick and Pat Spencer (Collector Books).

See also Glass Animals and Related Items.

Canterbury, crystal, ashtray, club, 5" $12.00
Canterbury, crystal, basket, crimped, handled, 3x4"............$30.00
Canterbury, crystal, bowl, salad; shallow, 2¾x15" $42.00
Canterbury, crystal, candlestick, 6", ea................................$25.00
Canterbury, crystal, cup $8.00

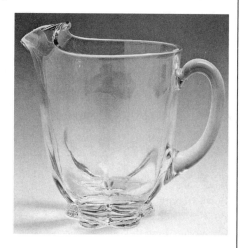

Canterbury, crystal, pitcher, 64-ounce, $265.00. (Photo courtesy Gene and Cathy Florence)

Canterbury, crystal, plate, cracker; w/ring, handles, 11".......$20.00
Canterbury, crystal, rose bowl, 6"..$25.00
Canterbury, crystal, top hat, 3"..$20.00
Canterbury, crystal, tumbler, ice cream; footed, #5115, 5-oz, 2½" $10.00
Canterbury, crystal, vase, flared, 12" $80.00
Caribbean, blue, bowl, grapefruit; footed, handles, 7¼" $50.00
Caribbean, blue, ladle, punch..$100.00
Caribbean, blue, saucer $8.00
Caribbean, blue, teacup...$65.00
Caribbean, blue, tumbler, shot glass; 2-oz, 2¼" $65.00
Caribbean, crystal, bowl, epergne; flared edge, 9½" $37.50

Caribbean, crystal, creamer $14.00
Caribbean, crystal, ice bucket, 6½" $75.00
Caribbean, crystal, plate, bread & butter; 6¼" $5.00
Caribbean, crystal, vase, footed, 10" $55.00
First Love, crystal, basket, oval handle, #115, 10x4¼x7" ...$200.00
First Love, crystal, bowl, olive; oval, #115, 2½x6" $25.00
First Love, crystal, candelabra, 2-light, #41, ea....................$35.00
First Love, crystal, carafe, water; w/stopper, #5200 ....$195.00
First Love, crystal, claret, #5111½, 4½-oz, 6" $45.00
First Love, crystal, honey dish, #91, 3x5".............................$30.00
First Love, crystal, lamp, hurricane; w/prisms, #115, 15"...$165.00
First Love, crystal, nappy, w/bottom star, #25, 1x5".............$20.00
First Love, crystal, plate, #111, 11" $20.00
First Love, crystal, urn, sq foot, ring handle, 5½" $65.00
Lily of the Valley, crystal, candlestick, double, 5", ea............$60.00
Lily of the Valley, crystal, cordial..$80.00
Lily of the Valley, crystal, mayonnaise $30.00

Lily of the Valley, crystal, plate, 9", $45.00. (Photo courtesy Gene and Cathy Florence)

Lily of the Valley, crystal, relish, 3-part $25.00
Lily of the Valley, crystal, tumbler, water; footed.................$25.00
Mardi Gras, crystal, bottle, bitters $75.00
Mardi Gras, crystal, plate, 6"...$9.00
Mardi Gras, crystal, stem, goblet..$45.00
Mardi Gras, crystal, vase, ball form, 4" $40.00
Nautical, blue, cocktail shaker, fish design $195.00
Nautical, blue, marmalade...$75.00
Nautical, blue, relish, 7-part, 12"..$75.00
Nautical, blue, sugar bowl..$45.00
Nautical, crystal, ashtray, 3" $8.00
Nautical, crystal, decanter $225.00
Nautical, crystal, plate, 10" $25.00
Nautical, crystal, tumbler, orange juice; footed $15.00
Nautical, opalescent, candy jar, w/lid $695.00
Nautical, opalescent, compote, 7" $595.00
Nautical, opalescent, decanter $695.00
Nautical, opalescent, ice bucket..$300.00
Plaza, amber or crystal, bowl, console; flared, 14"................$35.00
Plaza, amber or crystal, parfait $12.00
Plaza, amber or crystal, plate, salad; 7½" $4.00
Plaza, amber or crystal, saucer champagne $8.00
Plaza, amber or crystal, vase, 8"..$30.00
Plaza, green or pink, bowl, cereal; 6¼" $20.00

Plaza, green or pink, candy dish, round, 4½"........................$40.00
Plaza, green or pink, cocktail...$20.00
Plaza, green or pink, mustard, w/slotted lid $30.00
Plaza, green or pink, tumbler, whiskey; flat.......................$15.00
Puritan, any color, bowl, cream soup; handles....................$20.00
Puritan, any color, bowl, vegetable; oval, 9".....................$55.00
Puritan, any color, bowl, 5"..$12.50
Puritan, any color, candlestick, ea $26.00
Puritan, any color, pitcher...$135.00
Puritan, any color, plate, dinner; 10" $20.00
Puritan, any color, saucer, demitasse................................$5.00
Puritan, any color, tumbler, tea; flat...............................$22.00
Puritan, any color, vase...$65.00
Purtian, any color, sugar bowl..$17.50
Sandwich, crystal, bonbon, heart shape, ring handled, 5" $15.00
Sandwich, crystal, bowl, fruit salad; 6"............................$12.00
Sandwich, crystal, candy box, footed, 8½"........................$80.00
Sandwich, crystal, compote, 2¼".....................................$15.00
Sandwich, crystal, condiment set: 2 cruets, 3¾" salt & pepper shakers & 4-part tray $125.00
Sandwich, crystal, plate, dessert; 7"..................................$9.00
Sandwich, crystal, salad dressing set: 2 ladles, 5" footed mayonnaise & 13" plate w/ring...$75.00
Sandwich, crystal, sundae, flared rim, 5-oz, 3½"................$10.00
Sandwich, crystal, syrup pitcher, 13-oz $55.00
Sandwich, crystal, tray, oil/vinegar; 8"............................$22.00
Sandwich, crystal, vase, hat shape, 4"..............................$25.00
Spiral Flutes, amber, green or pink, bowl, almond; 2"..........$12.00
Spiral Flutes, amber, green or pink, bowl, cereal; sm flange, 6½" $30.00
Spiral Flutes, amber, green or pink, cup.............................$9.00
Spiral Flutes, amber, green or pink, pie plate, 6" $3.00
Spiral Flutes, amber, green or pink, platter, 13" $55.00
Spiral Flutes, amber, green or pink, seafood sauce cup, 2½x3".. $22.00
Tear Drop, crystal, bonbon, 4-handled, 6"..........................$12.00
Tear Drop, crystal, bowl, flower; crimped, 11½"..................$35.00
Tear Drop, crystal, cake salver, footed, 13"........................$55.00
Tear Drop, crystal, candy basket, oval, handles, 5½x7½".....$85.00
Tear Drop, crystal, celery, 3-part, 12"..............................$25.00
Tear Drop, crystal, creamer, 8-oz.....................................$8.00
Tear Drop, crystal, lazy Susan, 18"..................................$65.00
Tear Drop, crystal, olive dish, 2-part, 6" $15.00
Tear Drop, crystal, teacup, 6-oz.......................................$6.00
Tear Drop, pitcher, milk; 16-oz, 5"...................................$55.00
Terrace, amber or crystal, ashtray, sq, 3½".........................$17.50
Terrace, amber or crystal, candlestick, 2-light, bobeche & prisms, 7x9¼", ea..$100.00
Terrace, amber or crystal, finger bowl, #5111½, 4¼"............$30.00
Terrace, amber or crystal, pitcher....................................$325.00
Terrace, amber or crystal, plate, 8½"................................$20.00
Terrace, amber or crystal, relish, 4-part, 9"........................$35.00
Terrace, amber or crystal, saucer, sq...................................$6.00
Terrace, amber or crystal, sugar lid..................................$12.50
Terrace, amber or crystal, tumbler, juice; footed, #5111½, 5-oz, 5¼"..$20.00
Terrace, amber or crystal, vase, footed, 10" $115.00
Terrace, cobalt or red, cake plate, crystal top, footed, 13" ..$210.00

Terrace, cobalt or red, cocktail shaker, w/metal lid $225.00
Terrace, cobalt or red, compote, w/lid, 5½x8¾" $425.00
Terrace, cobalt or red, creamer, 10-oz, 3"..........................$38.00
Terrace, cobalt or red, finger bowl, #5111½, 4¼" $75.00
Terrace, cobalt or red, plate, torte; 13¼"..........................$195.00
Terrace, cobalt or red, saucer champagne, #5111½, 5-oz, 5" ..$50.00
Terrace, cobalt or red, sugar bowl, 10-oz, 3" $35.00
Terrace, cobalt or red, tumbler, shot, 2-oz.........................$40.00
Terrace, cobalt or red, urn, 4½x10½"...............................$425.00

Tear Drop, crystal, relish, two-part, 7½", $22.50. (Photo courtesy Gene and Cathy Florence)

Early American Prescut

This was a line of inexpensive but good quality glassware made during the 1960s and 1970s by Anchor Hocking. It was marketed through dime-stores and houseware stores, and as is obvious judging from the plentiful supplies available at today's garage sale and flea markets, it sold very well. If you like it, now's the time to buy! For more information, refer to Gene and Cathy Florence's book called *Collectible Glassware from the 40s, 50s, and 60s* (Collector Books).

Ashtray, #718-G, 7¾" $12.00
Bowl, console; #797, 9" $14.00
Bowl, dessert; #765, 5⅜" $5.00
Bowl, salad; #788, 10¾" $12.00
Bowl, smooth rim, #726, 4¼" $22.00
Bowl, 3-toed, sm..$6.00
Cake plate, footed, #706, 13½".......................................$30.00
Candlestick, double; #784, 7x5⅝", ea from $20 to............$25.00
Candy dish, w/lid, #792, 7¼x5½".....................................$12.00
Deviled egg plate...$30.00
Dish, oval, 8½"...$7.50
Lazy Susan, #700/713, 9-pc..$40.00
Pitcher, sq, 40-oz, from $32 to..$38.00
Plate, snack; #780, 10"...$10.00
Plate, 11"..$12.00
Punch set, 15-pc...$35.00
Relish, oval, 2-part, #778, 8½" $8.00
Salt & pepper shakers, individual, 2¼", pr........................$40.00
Salt & pepper shakers, plastic lids, #725, 4¼", pr................$5.00
Tray, hostess; #750, 6½x12", from $8 to...........................$10.00

Tumbler, #731, 10-oz, 4½" **$3.00**
Tumbler, iced tea; #732, 15-oz, 6", from $15 to **$20.00**
Tumbler, juice; #730, 5-oz, 4" **$3.00**
Vase, #741, 8½" **$7.00**

Relish tray, five-part, 13½", $30.00. (Photo courtesy Gene and Cathy Florence)

Easter Collectibles

The egg (a symbol of new life) and the bunny rabbit have long been part of Easter festivities; and since early in the twentieth century, Easter has been a full-blown commercial event. Postcards, candy containers, toys, and decorations have been made in infinite varieties. In the early 1900s many holiday items were made of papièr-machè and composition and imported to this country from Germany. Rabbits were made of mohair, felt, and velveteen, often filled with straw, cotton, and cellulose.

Bank, bunny in blue dress & bonnet w/yellow glasses holding yellow rabbit, plastic, Knickerbocker, 1950s, 11" **$15.00**
Bank, pink chick w/blue bonnet, apron & egg basket, plastic, Knickerbocker, 9" **$60.00**
Basket, bunny pops up & squeaks, pink & blue plastic windup, Made in Japan, 1960s, 9" **$46.00**
Booklet, An Easter Crown, F Schuyler Matthews, religious poetry, Boston L Prang & Co, 8 pages, 1886, 6x5 .... **$30.00**
Candy container, boy & girl in mushroom house w/Easter egg & yellow chicks, papier-maché, 1950s, 5x6½x4" **$30.00**
Candy container, bunny, clear plastic, separates into 2 halves, 1950s, Irwin, Made in USA, 6" **$32.00**
Candy container, mama hen & chicks off to market, papier-maché, liner stamped w/ducks & bunnies, 1950s, 5x6", G **$42.00**
Candy container, spring scene w/white lamb pulling a cart of colorful Easter eggs, papier-maché, West Germany, 7½x12". **$30.00**
Candy dish, white bunny standing next to open & decorated Easter egg, Enesco Imports Corp, 1984, 4x5" **$15.00**
Decoration, egg, cream-white fold-out honeycomb paper w/pink ribbons, bows & flowers, 18½x10" **$60.00**
Egg cup, white bunny holding cup decorated w/pink flowers, 1981, Avon, 5½" **$25.00**
Figurine, Easter Bunny Mouse, mouse in aqua bunny costume holding decorated eggs in basket, Wee Forest Folk M-082 .... **$48.00**

Pitcher, white bunny holding pink & purple tulips w/Easter egg, ceramic, Made in China, 8x7" **$40.00**
Planter, white bunny in top hat & topcoat w/carrot standing next to blue barrel, porcelain, 7¼x5x2½" **$30.00**
Plate, Bunnykins getting ready for Easter parade, Royal Doulton Bunnykins, 8", EX **$33.00**
Platter, rabbit shape, hand-painted details on white, ceramic, 1½x11" **$23.00**
Postcard, Loving Easter Greetings, baby riding Easter egg being pulled by yellow chicks, Mabel Lucie Attwell, postmark **$52.00**
Postcard, Rose O'Neill Kewpies Easter, Kewpies climbing on big blue egg, signed, 1923, EX **$50.00**
Rattle, rabbit wearing red coat carrying doctor's bag, celluloid, Japan, 4½" **$72.00**
Rattle, yellow rabbit in red overalls, plastic, 1950s, Made in USA, Irwin, 6" **$15.00**
Rattle, yellow rooster wearing red top hat, plastic, embossed, Irwin Plastics, ca 1950s, 3½x2½" **$18.00**
Salt & paper shakers, yellow chicks, ceramic, unmarked, 2½", pr **$13.00**
Salt & pepper shakers, white lamb w/rhinestone eyes, ceramic, 2½x3", pr **$23.00**
Salt & pepper shakers, yellow chick w/red bow tie, egg resting on back, ceramic, Japan, 3½x4½", 2-pc set **$15.00**

Toy, Easter Bunny Delivery Cart, tin litho, Chein #511, $225.00. (Photo courtesy Smith House)

Toy, lamb w/purple bow, stuffed fabric w/gold felt lining under ears, eyes roll around, 1940s-50s, 9x8" **$17.00**
Toy, yellow rabbit on red wheels, plastic, marked Lucky #115 Hong Kong, 3x5x1" **$48.00**

Egg Cups

Egg cups were once commonplace kitchen articles that were often put to daily use. These small egg holders were commonly made in a variety of shapes from ceramics, glass, metals, minerals, treen, and plastic. They were used as early as ancient Rome and were very common on Victorian tables. Many were styled like whimsical animals or made in other shapes that would specifically appeal to children. Some were commemorative or sold as souvenirs. Still others were part of extensive china or silver services.

Recent trends in US dietary patterns have caused egg cups to follow butter pats and salt dishes into relative obscurity. Yet today in other parts of the world, especially Europe, many people still eat soft-boiled eggs as part of their daily ritual, so the larger china companies in those locations continue to produce egg cups.

Though many are inexpensive, some are very pricey. Sought-after categories (or cross-collectibles) include Art Deco, art pottery, Black memorabilia, chintz, golliwogs, majolica, personalities, pre-Victorian, railroad, and steamship. Single egg cups with pedestal bases are the most common, but shapes vary to include buckets, doubles, figurals, hoops, and sets of many types.

Pocillovists, as egg cup collectors are known, are increasing in numbers every day. For more extensive listings we recommend *Egg Cups: An Illustrated History and Price Guide,* by Brenda C. Blake (Antique Publications); and *Schroeder's Antiques Price Guide* (Collector Books).

Unless noted otherwise, our values are for ceramic egg cups in mint condition.

Advisor: Brenda C. Blake (See Directory, Egg Cups)

Newsletter: *Egg Cup Collector's Corner*
Dr. Joan George, Editor
67 Stevens Ave., Old Bridge, NJ 08857
Subscription $18 per year for four issues; sample copies available at $5 each

Bucket, British Airways, blue border, silver stripes, Royal Doulton $16.00
Bucket, Holly Hobby, ca 1978...$14.00
Bucket, Raffles Hotel, maroon bands, Churchill, 1990s.......$12.00
Double, Boston City Hospital, floral transfer, Jones McDuffee & Stratton..$80.00
Double, Caesar's Palace, brown logo, 1990s $15.00

Double, Dresden Flowers, Schumann, from $65.00 to $75.00.

Double, Eastern Steamship Line, 1920s.............................$80.00
Double, Frost Flowers, Eva Zeisel, Hall, 1950s $35.00
Double, Luckenbach Lines...$40.00
Double, Mr Snowman w/hat, Royal Doulton $90.00
Double, Peasant, yellow & green, floral panels, HB Quimper .. $45.00
Double, Prairie Mountain Wildflower, South Pacific, 1940s.$350.00
Double, Riviera, Hugh Casson..$75.00
Double, Rooster, Pennsbury...$28.00
Figural, Bear, whistler, lustre, foreign $95.00
Figural, Betty Boop, lustreware figural face w/earrings, Japan, 1930s..$275.00
Figural, chicken, milk glass, John E Kemple $15.00
Figural, duck, blue, Fanny Farmer, 1930s $25.00
Figural, hen, Keele St Pottery..$16.00
Figural, Humpty Dumpty on brick wall, Mansell $85.00
Figural, Margaret Thatcher, Spitting Image, 1982...............$50.00
Figural, Miss Priss, Lefton $30.00
Figural, Oriole, Goebel, 1989 ....$20.00
Figural, Prince Charles, Spitting Image, 1982 ....$70.00
Figural, Ronald Reagan, Spitting Image, 1982 ....$100.00
Figural, swan, lustre, Japan, 1930s $15.00
Figural, Swee' Pea, yellow, KFS, 1980 ....$60.00

Figural, Teen-agers, Napco, from $18.00 to $22.00 for the pair. (Photo courtesy Helene Guarnaccia)

Figural, Volkswagon, Devon Ceramics, 1959 ....$20.00
Figural bellhop, pillbox hat, smoking cigarette, Art Deco, Made in France $75.00
Set, majolica basket w/6 egg cups, leaf pattern, 1880s........$500.00
Set, monkeys (3) on tray, Goebel, 1961 ....$60.00
Set, 4 single mini cups in metal dollhouse stand, England, 1998..$20.00
Set, 6 tulip cups in chrome stand, English $70.00
Single, Anne of Green Gables, Crown Ashton, 1990s..........$10.00
Single, Apple, Franciscan...$32.00
Single, Bakelite, on 3 prongs, England, 1940s $12.00
Single, Bluebird, Lefton, Japan...$60.00
Single, Channel Tunnel 1988-94, 1994 ....$16.00
Single, Crocus, Clarice Cliff..$200.00
Single, Denver & Rio Grande, recent $15.00
Single, Donald Duck, Good Morning series $16.00
Single, Ford Motor Co, logo, 1960s...................................$38.00
Single, Harriman Blue, Union Pacific $135.00
Single, Messena, Baccarat, 1970s......................................$45.00
Single, Plymouth Rock, Plymouth MA, Germany, ca 1900 .$40.00

Single, purple slag, vertical ribs $70.00

Single, Queen Victoria, '1837' coronation, pink lustre, ca 1890s $450.00

Single, Real Old Willow, Booth $40.00

Single, Sea Gull, Bing & Grondahl $22.00

Single, Winged Streamliner, UP, Scammell $70.00

Single, World's Fair, St Louis 1904, transfer scene, 1904....$100.00

Single, Beatrix Potter, Grimwades, minimum value, $200.00.

Egg Timers

Egg timers were largely imported from Japan and Germany during the 1930s and 1940s to help you produce the perfect three-minute egg. They were highly functional and consisted of two parts: a little glass tube filled with sand and a figural base to which it was attached. They were made in the likenesses of clowns, Black children, chefs, and animals of every type, and in almost every type of material. Because of their whimisical nature, they are highly sought after by today's collectors!

Because of the very nature of the thin glass tubes that held the sand, they were easily damaged, so many egg timers you find today will be missing the tube. But don't hesitate to buy an otherwise good example for that reason only — tubes can be easily replaced; just buy a new inexpensive egg timer from your local grocery store.

Our values are for complete timers with tubes intact.

Advisor: Larry Pogue, L&J Antiques and Collectibles (See Directory, String Holders)

Bunny standing on hind quarters, timer in right paw w/left ear bent, 3" $55.00

Chicken holding timer in front w/both wings, embossed Germany $125.00

Coffeepot, long spout & wooden handle, black finial, 8½" .$35.00

Duck, yellow w/green hat, red umbrella closed under right wing, timer under left..$85.00

Dutch boy & girl kissing in front of windmill, E-6101, 4⅜" .$75.00

Elf stands beside stump w/recipe holder atop, timer beside stump, 5½"..$55.00

Friar Tucks (2) in brown hold timer between them, Goebel, 3¼" $125.00

Girl in black hat & pants, white shirt w/red trim, red shoes, holding timer in right hand, Germany, 4¾" $125.00

Lighthouse, blue, cream & orange lustre, German, 4½" $85.00

Mrs Santa Claus, timer sits in bag next to her.....................$75.00

Newspaper boy, Japan, 3¾" $40.00

Penguin, chalkware, England, 3¾", from $25 to.................$40.00

Sailor w/sailboat, German, 4" $50.00

Telephone, black glaze on clay, Japan, 2" $35.00

Veggi man or woman, bisque, Japan, 4½", ea $95.00

Welsh woman, German, 4½" $50.00

Dog, standing and holding a flower, lustre, marked Germany, $125.00. (Photo courtesy Larry Pogue)

Elvis Presley Memorabilia

Since he burst upon the '50s scene wailing 'Heartbreak Hotel,' Elvis has been the undisputed 'king of rock 'n roll.' The fans that stood outside his dressing room for hours on end, screamed themselves hoarse as he sang, or simply danced till they dropped to his music are grown-up collectors today. Many of their children remember his comeback performances, and I'd venture to say that even their grandchildren know Elvis on a first-name basis.

There has never been a promotion in the realm of entertainment to equal the manufacture and sale of Elvis merchandise. By the latter part of 1956, there were already hundreds of items that appeared in every department store, drugstore, specialty shop, and music store in the country. There were bubble gum cards, pin-back buttons, handkerchiefs, dolls, guitars, billfolds, photograph albums, and scores of other items. You could even buy sideburns from a coin-operated machine. Look for the mark 'Elvis Presley Enterprises' (along with a 1956 or 1957 copyright date); you'll know you've found a gold mine. Items that carry the 'Boxcar' mark are from 1974 to 1977, when Elvis's legendary manager, Colonel Tom Parker, promoted another line of merchandise to augment their incomes during the declining years. Upon his death in 1977 and until 1981, the trademark became 'Boxcar Enterprises, Inc., Lic. by Factors ETC. Bear, DE.' The 'Elvis Presley Enterprises, Inc.' trademark reverted back to Graceland in 1982, which re-opened to the public in 1983.

Due to the very nature of his career, paper items are usually a large part of any 'Elvis' collection. He appeared on the cover of countless magazines. These along with ticket stubs, movie posters, lobby cards, and photographs of all types are sought after today, especially those from before the mid-'60s.

Though you sometimes see Elvis 45s with $10.00 to $15.00 price tags, unless the record is in near mint to mint condition, this is just not realistic, since they sold in such volume. In fact, the picture sleeve itself (if it's in good condition) will be worth more than the record. The exceptions are, of course, the early Sun label records (he cut five in all) that collectors often pay in excess of $500.00 for. In fact, a near-mint copy of 'That's All Right' (his very first Sun recording) realized $2,800.00 at an auction held a few years ago! And some of the colored vinyls, promotional records, and EPs and LPs with covers and jackets in excellent condition are certainly worth researching further. For instance, though his *Moody Blue* album with the blue vinyl record can often be had for under $25.00 (depending on condition), if you find one of the rare ones with the black record you can figure on about ten times that amount! For a thorough listing of his records as well as the sleeves, refer to *Official Price Guide to Elvis Presley Records and Memorabilia* by Jerry Osborne.

For more general information and an emphasis on the early items, refer to *Elvis Collectibles* and *Best of Elvis Collectibles* by Rosalind Cranor, P.O. Box 859, Blacksburg, VA 24063 ($19.95+$1.75 postage each volume). Also available: *Elvis Presley Memorabilia* by Sean O'Neal (Schiffer).

Unless noted otherwise, values are for items in near-mint to mint condition. See also Magazines; Movie Posters; Pin-back Buttons; Records.

Advisor: Lee Garmon (See Directory, Elvis Presley Memorabilia)

Belt buckle, Elvis in script over guitar shape, w/loop & hook, 1970s, EX **$30.00**
Bust, Elvis in white w/microphone, Clay Art, 1987, 14x9x7". **$150.00**
Bust, white porcelain, Elvis Presley 1935-1977, Goebel, from $50 to **$60.00**
Charm necklace, portrait of Elvis in red shirt on dogtag w/chain, 1956, EX **$55.00**
Christmas tree, porcelain tabletop type, lights up, plays Blue Christmas, Bradford Exchange, 13" **$115.00**
Collector's plate, '68 Comeback Special, 1990 Limited Edition..**$55.00**
Collector's plate, Jailhouse Rock, Solid Gold Elvis series, Bradford Exchange, 1996..**$50.00**
Decanter, McCormick, Aloha Elvis, plays Blue Hawaii, 750 ml, from $150 TO **$200.00**
Decanter, McCormick, Elvis '55, plays Loving You, 750 ml...**$75.00**
Decanter, McCormick, Elvis '55 Mini, plays Loving You, 50 ml **$45.00**
Decanter, McCormick, Elvis '68, plays Can't Help Falling in Love, 750 ml **$80.00**
Decanter, McCormick, Elvis '68 Mini, plays Can't Help Falling in Love, 50 ml..**$45.00**
Decanter, McCormick, Elvis '77, plays Love Me Tender, 750 ml **$95.00**
Decanter, McCormick, Elvis '77 Mini, plays Love Me Tender, 50 ml, from $45 to **$55.00**
Decanter, McCormick, Elvis & Gates of Graceland, plays Welcome to My World, 750 ml, from $150 to..........................**$200.00**

Decanter, McCormick, Elvis & Rising Sun, plays Green Grass of Home, 750 ml **$495.00**
Decanter, McCormick, Elvis & Rising Sun Mini, plays Green Green Grass of Home, 50 ml, from $250 to **$275.00**

Decanter, McCormick, Elvis Bust, no music box, 750 ml, $75.00. (Photo courtesy Lee Garmon)

Decanter, McCormick, Elvis Designer I Gold, plays Are You Lonesome Tonight, 750 ml, from $200 to..................**$250.00**
Decanter, McCormick, Elvis Designer I Gold Mini, plays Are you Lonesome Tonight, 50 ml, from $165 to....................**$190.00**
Decanter, McCormick, Elvis Designer I Silver Mini, plays Are You Lonesome Tonight, 50 ml, from $175 to....................**$225.00**
Decanter, McCormick, Elvis Designer I White (Joy), Plays Are You Lonesome Tonight, 750 ml..**$150.00**
Decanter, McCormick, Elvis Designer I White Mini, plays Are You Lonesome Tonight, 50 ml..**$85.00**
Decanter, McCormick, Elvis Designer II Gold, plays It's Now or Never, 750 ml, from $225 to....................................**$250.00**
Decanter, McCormick, Elvis Designer II White (Love), plays It's Now or Never, 750 ml..**$125.00**
Decanter, McCormick, Elvis Designer III Gold, plays Crying in the Chapel, 750 ml, from $250 to....................................**$300.00**
Decanter, McCormick, Elvis Designer III White (Reverence), 750 ml..**$250.00**
Decanter, McCormick, Elvis Gold Tribute, plays My Way, 750 ml..**$160.00**
Decanter, McCormick, Elvis Gold Tribute Mini, plays My Way, 50 ml, from $125 to **$150.00**
Decanter, McCormick, Elvis Hound Dog, plays Hound Dog, 750 ml..**$650.00**
Decanter, McCormick, Elvis Karate, plays Don't Be Cruel, 750 ml.. **$350.00**
Decanter, McCormick, Elvis Karate Mini, plays Don't Be Cruel, 50 ml..**$125.00**
Decanter, McCormick, Elvis Memories, cassette player base, lighted top, extremely rare, 750 ml......................................**$750.00**
Decanter, McCormick, Elvis on Stage Mini, play's Can't Help Falling in Love, 50 ml (decanter only)....................................**$195.00**

Decanter, McCormick, Elvis on Stage Mini (w/separate stage designed to hold decanter), 50 ml................................$450.00

Decanter, McCormick, Elvis Season's Greetings, plays White Christmas, 375 ml $195.00

Decanter, McCormick, Elvis Silver, plays How Great Thou Art, 750 ml $175.00

Decanter, McCormick, Elvis Silver Mini, plays How Great Thou Art, 50 ml, from $100 to $120.00

Decanter, McCormick, Elvis Teddy Bear, plays Let Me Be Your Teddy Bear, 750 ml................................$695.00

Decanter, McCormick, Elvis 50th Anniversary, plays I Want You, I Need You..., 750 ml, from $500 to $535.00

Decanter, McCormick, Elvis 50th Anniversary Mini, plays I Want You, I Need You..., 50 ml $250.00

Decanter, McCormick, Sgt Elvis, plays GI Blues, 750 ml, from $300 to $340.00

Decanter, McCormick, Sgt Elvis Mini, plays GI Blues, 50 ml, from $100 to $120.00

Doll, '68 Special, black jumpsuit, Hasbro, 1993, 12", MIB. $25.00

Doll, Aloha From Hawaii jumpsuit, Danbury Mint, 19", on stand, M................................$75.00

Doll, Burning Love, white jumpsuit w/flames, World Doll, 1984, 21", MIB $70.00

Doll, Celebrity Collection, black vinyl jumpsuit, World Doll, 1984, 21", MIB $75.00

Doll, porcelain w/poseable leather body, gold lamè jumpsuit & gold medallion, World Doll, 1984, 21", MIB................................$125.00

Doll, The Army Years, Mattel, 1999 Collector Series, 2nd in series, MIB................................$65.00

Doll, vinyl 'magic skin,' original clothes, Elvis Presley Enterprises c 1957, 18", extremely rare, EX, from $900 to...........$1,200.00

Dolls, Barbie Loves Elvis Gift Set (2 dolls), Mattel, 1996, MIB................................ $45.00

Figurine, painted chalkware, ESCO $280.00

Hat, wide printed band w/black brim & top, Magnet Hat & Cap Corp, 1956, w/tag................................$135.00

Magazine, Las Vegas Hilton NOW, Elvis cover, 11x8½", EX . $60.00

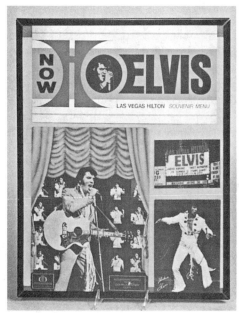

Menu from Las Vegas Hilton, Elvis Now, $50.00. (Photo courtesy Joe Hilton and Greg Moore)

Model, 1955 Cadillac Fleetwood, Frankln Mint, 1:24 scale, 2¾x9½x3½", MIB $85.00

Painting on velvet in Aloha Hawaii jumpsuit, in wooden frame, 26x48" $55.00

Pin-back button, Elvis Summer Festival, color portrait on white, 1971 ....$55.00

Pin-back button, flasher, portrait closeup & w/guitar, black & white, copyright 1956, 2½", EX................................$35.00

Plate, The King, Remembering Elvis Collection, Nate Giorgio, 1995, MIB $50.00

Poster, Double Trouble, 1967, 6-sheet, 81x41", EX...........$240.00

Poster, Easy Come Easy Go, 3 scenes from movie & Elvis in scuba gear, 41x28", EX................................$110.00

Poster, Girl Happy, Elvis dancing on yellow background, 1-sheet, folds/pin pricks, otherwise EX $60.00

Poster, Kissin Cousins, 1-sheet, folds & pin pricks otherwise EX................................ $60.00

Reel-to-reel, Girls, Girls, Girls, from $40.00 to $45.00.

Scrapbook, Elvis Presley Solid Gold Memories, 218 pages, Ballentine Books of NY, 1977, EX $55.00

Scrapbook, pink vinyl, Elvis singing to hound dog, string holds it together, 1950s, 14x12", EX................................$165.00

Sheet music book, Elvis Presley Album of Juke Box Favorites No 1 USA, 26 pages, 15 songs, 1955, very rare, EX $60.00

Straw holder, silhouette on clear glass, chrome-colored lid, Elvis Presley Enterprises Inc, 1977 ....$30.00

Suitcase, printed vinyl (?) cover, pink Bakelite handle, 6½x12¼x8¾", EX $235.00

T-shirt, Elvis w/guitar before lg green record on white, Allison, 1956, some fading & stains, VG................................$360.00

Thimble, Elvis Presley's Graceland, heart cap, pewter, Nicholas Gish, 1"................................$50.00

Ticket stub, San Antonio concert, April 18, 1972, EX.......$100.00

Tour program, photo cover, 12-page, 13 black & white photos, 1956, 11x8½", EX................................$55.00

Wallet, red vinyl, Elvis Presley Enterprises, dated 1956, missing clasp................................$110.00

Enesco

Enesco is a company that imports and distributes ceramic novelty items made in Japan. Some of their more popular lines are the Human Beans, Partners in Crime Christmas ornaments, Eggbert, Dutch Kids, and Mother in the Kitchen (also referred to as Kitchen Prayer Ladies, see also that category). Prices are climbing steadily.

See also Cats, Character; Cookie Jars.

Bookends, Dear God kids (boy & girl), 4x5" $38.00
Candle climbers, Rag Tag Teddies (panda bears), 1985, 3", pr . $8.00
Creamer, character face on orange, E-0309, 3", NM $90.00
Creamer & sugar bowl, Chip & Dale figural, pr $85.00
Figurine, Birthday Girl (17th birthday), Growing Up Girls, 1982, 6⅞" $45.00
Figurine, brunette bride, Growing Up Girls series, musical, retired, MIB $125.00
Figurine, Clydesdale, dark brown, E-4235, 5½x6½" $35.00
Figurine, Esadora, Coral Kingdom mermaid, limited edition, 7", MIB $115.00
Figurine, Evangelista, Coral Kingdom maid, 6" $90.00
Figurine, How I Love Jesus, Jonathan & David, 1977, 5" $50.00

Figurine, Human Bean, Love the Jingle, $20.00.

(Photo courtesy Joyce and Fred Roerig)

Figurine, Kewpie bride, for Jesco, 1993, 4¼", EX $45.00
Figurine, Kewpie taking bath w/duck, for Jesco, 1991, 4x2¾" . $55.00
Figurine, Kewpie wearing Santa hat, for Jesco, 1993, 4" $35.00
Figurine, Love Begins w/Friendship, boy & girl, Memories of Yesterday, 1994, 5½x4¾" $60.00
Figurine, Love Covers All, 1984, 4½x4¾x3⅛" $20.00
Figurine, Miss Trixie Bar Hound, Collie, foil label, 6" $65.00
Figurine, mother & baby, brunette version, Growing Up Girls series, MIB $60.00
Figurine, mustang, pinto paint, Japan sticker, 6x6½" $65.00
Figurine, owls (4) perched on branch, Aman, 6½x8½x5¾" . $50.00
Figurine, Sledding Hill from It's a Wonderful Life, 4x5x5", MIB $80.00
Figurine, Spring Is Upon Us, Cream & Cocoa, bunny w/robin, 3½", 1995, MIB $45.00
Figurine, Trimming the Tree, father lifts son, Treasured Memories, E-6412, 1984 .... $55.00
Figurine, unicorn w/butterfly resting on its back, recumbent, 1985, 7x11" $38.00

Figurine, We'd Do Anything for You Dear, Memories of Yesterday, 1995, 5", MIB $40.00
Figurine, West Highland terrier, Kathy Wise Purebred Pets, 1984, 4½x3½" $32.00
Frame, The Purr-fect Grandma, grandma in rocker holding cat, Jonathan & David, 1981 .... $12.50
Jack-in-the-box, Dorothy from the Wizard of Oz, 50th Anniversary limited edition, 1988, MIB $110.00
Juice set, Good Morning Sunshine, chickens, tulips & daisies, 6" pitcher+4 3½" tumblers $30.00
Mug, Memories of Yesterday, 3½" $10.00
Napkin holder, anthropomorphic bunch of grapes, E-0301, .. $38.00
Ornament, Fido, sm puppy, Mabel Lucie Attwell Memories of Yesterday, 1995, 2", MIB $75.00

Planter, lady and flowers, 1979, 7½", $125.00.

(Photo courtesy David Barron)

Planter, lady in green & white w/purple flowers on skirt which is held wide, opening behind, 1960s, 5½x4¾x3½" $30.00
Salt & pepper shakers, dinosaur, wooden corks, labels, 2½x4", pr $45.00
Salt & pepper shakers, Dutch boy (& girl) on wooden shoe, E-5186, 1950-60s, 2¾", pr $18.00
Salt & pepper shakers, horses, brown w/white spots, black manes & tails, stickers, 3¾", pr $75.00
Salt & pepper shakers, pig in overalls, pastels, pr $45.00
Salt & pepper shakers, pixie on mushroom, 4", pr $30.00
Salt & pepper shakers, potato form, 3", pr $17.50
Salt & pepper shakers, red keg (1 marked Bar & Grill, 2nd marked Free Lunch), 2½", pr $10.00
Salt & pepper shakers, swans (2) on base, silver paint, 3-pc set $12.50
Salt & pepper shakes, mouse & wedge of cheese, 2-pc set ... $10.00
Tabletop fountain, Friends of a Feather, Indian girl & wolf pup at edge of pool by waterfall, 1998, 11x9x7" $70.00
Teapot, Holiday Bungalow, plays multiple songs, illuminated, 1993, 12x8", MIB $85.00
Trinket box, yellow roses on white, 2½x3" dia $15.00
Trinket box, Your No Bunny Til Some Bunny Loves You, bunny & butterfly finial, 4x4x4" $15.00

Vase, You're the Sweetest Rose in the Bunch, girl smelling Rose, 4-sided, Kim Anderson, 4½x3½".......................................$37.50

Watering can, frogs singing on white, Suzy Spafford, Suzy's Zoo 1976, 5¾"...$55.00

Fans, Electric

Vintage fans can be fascinating collectibles with various complex working parts and styling varying from the very basic to the most wonderful Art Deco designs. Values hinge on age, style, condition, and manufacturer. To qualify as excellent, a fan must retain its original paint (with only a few blemishes). It must be clean and polished, the original cord must be present, and it must be in good working order with no replacement parts.

AC Gilbert #2017-D, 4 blades, wire cage, black paint, Deco styling, 1930s-40s, 13".....................................$65.00

Dominion #2017, 4-blade, turquoise paint, oscillator.........$25.00

Emerson, 4 blades, 17½" cage, 3-speed oscillator, can be used on floor or mounted to wall, 21" $125.00

Emerson #21666, 6 blades, brass cage, patent date 1899, 3-speed oscillator, 18" $400.00

Emerson #456122, 6 blades, 14" cage, oscillator, original paint, very heavy, 15½" $775.00

Eskimo #20, 4 blades, brass cage, 2 speeds, cord needs replaced, 13"..$40.00

General Electric, 4 brass blades, 12" brass cage, logo in center, cord needs replaced, 20" $175.00

Menominee, 4 8" blades, 9" brass cage, 3-speed, original black paint, 12"..$375.00

Wagner #5260, 10" blades, ca. 1931, EX, $25.00. (Photo courtesy John M. Witt)

Western Electric Style No W-134168, 4 6" brass blades, no cage, last patent date Oct 9, '06, 12" $165.00

Wizard, Bersted Mfg Co of Fostoria OH, 4 blades, spider-web cage, 3-speed oscillator, original paint......................................$45.00

Wizard, 4 10" blades, wire cage w/blue center, blue Deco-style base, single speed, 13" $30.00

Zero, 4 10" turquoise blades, brass cage, 1940s, 13"............$30.00

Fenton Glass

Located in Williamstown, West Virginia, the Fenton company is still producing glassware just as they have since the early part of the century. Nearly all fine department stores and gift shops carry an extensive line of their beautiful products, many of which rival examples of finest antique glassware. The fact that even some of their fairly recent glassware has collectible value attests to its fine quality.

Over the years they have made many lovely colors in scores of lines, several of which are very extensive. Paper labels were used exclusively until 1970. Since then some pieces have been made with a stamped-in logo.

Numbers in the descriptions correspond with catalog numbers used by the company. Collectors use them as a means of identification as to shape and size. If you'd like to learn more about the subject, we recommend *Fenton Glass, The Second Twenty-Five Years,* and *Fenton Glass, The Third Twenty-Five Years,* by William Heacock; *Fenton Glass, The 1980s,* by James Measell; *Fenton Art Glass, 1907 – 1939, Fenton Art Glass Patterns, 1939 – 1980; Fenton Art Glass Colors and Hand-Decorated Patterns, 1939 – 1980;* and *Fenton Art Glass Hobnail Pattern;* all by Margaret and Kenn Whitmyer; and *Fenton Glass Made for Other Companies, 1907 – 1980,* and *Fenton Glass Made for Other Companies, 1970 – 2005,* by Carrie and Gerald Domitz.

Club: Fenton Art Glass Collectors of America, Inc.

Newsletter: Butterfly Net
P.O. Box 384, 702 W. 5th St.
Williamstown, WV 26187
Full membership $20 per year; $5 for each associate membership; children under 12 free

Club: Pacific Northwest Fenton Association
P.O. Box 881
Tillamook, OR 97141, 503-842-4815
jhirley@oregoncoast.com
www.glasscastle.com/pnwfa.htm
Subscription: $23 per year; includes quarterly newsletter and exclusive piece of Fenton glass

Baskets

Aqua Crest, #192, 1942-43, 10½", from $160 to.............$180.00

Basket, cranberry, #CV214, 1998, 6x4½", from $70 to.......$80.00

Block & Star, milk glass, #5637-MI, 1955-56, from $30 to...$35.00

Blue overlay, #192, 1943-48, 10½", from $100 to.............$120.00

Cactus, milk glass, #3430-MI, 1959-60, from $45 to..........$55.00

Emerald Crest, #203, 1952-55, 7", from $120 to $140.00

Gold overlay, #711, 1949, 7", from $65 to $75.00

Grape, custard satin, 3-toed, #8438-CU, 1978-80+, from $27 to...$32.00

Hobnail, blue opalescent, #3834, 1940-55, 4½", from $40 to . $50.00

Hobnail, Gold Pearl, 1992, #3335, 8", from $45 to $55.00

Hobnail, orange, crimped edge, 1952-57, 7½x7", from $90 to.$110.00

Hobnail, Wisteria opalescent, #3834, 1942-44, 4½", from $90 to...$110.00

Lily of the Valley, blue opalescent, #8437-BO, 1979-90+, from $37 to $40.00

Persian Medallion, amethyst carnival, #8238-CN, 1972-75, from $75 to $85.00

Poppy, Lime Sherbet, #9138-LS, 1973-78, 7", from $57 to.$65.00

Rose satin, #7437-RS, 1975-78, from $45 to.....................$55.00

Silver Crest, #1523, 13", from $165.00 to $185.00. (Photo courtesy Margaret and Kenn Whitmyer)

Silver Crest w/Violets in the Snow, #6436-DV, 1968-808+, sm, from $65 to $85.00

Spiral Optic, French opalescent, #1923, 1939, 6", from $50 to..$55.00

Spiral Optic Hobnail, cranberry opalescent, #CV186, 1997, 6x5½", from $90 to $110.00

Threaded Diamond Optic, Rosalene, #8435-RE, 1976-78, from $130 to $150.00

Bells

Bride & Broom, Crystal Velvet, #9168-VE, 1977-80+, from $18 to $22.00

Bride & Groom, white satin, #9168-WS, 1977-79, from $20 to...$25.00

Daisy & Button, custard satin, #1966-CU, 1972-80+, from $20 to $22.00

Fabergé, lavender satin, #8466-LN, 1978-79, from $60 to ..$80.00

Hobnail, blue opal, #2667, 1978-81, 6", from $40 to $45.00

Hobnail, ruby, #2667, 1972-85, 6", from $30 to................$40.00

Medallion, bluebirds on custard satin, #8267-BC, 1977-080, from $32 to $37.00

Medallion, butterflies on milk glass, #8267-BY, 1977-79, from $27 to $32.00

Medallion, chocolate roses on cameo satin, #8276-DR, 1979-80+, from $25 to $30.00

Medallion, Silver Crest w/Violets in the Snow, #8267-DV, 1978-80+, from $55 to $60.00

Patriot's, Patriot Red, #8467-PR, 1975-76, from $30 to $35.00

Threaded Diamond Optic, Colonial Amber, #8435-CA, 1977-79, 7", from $22 to..$27.00

Threaded Diamond Optic, Wisteria, #8465-WT, 1977-79, 7", from $30 to $35.00

Violets in the Snow on Spanish Lace, #3567DV, 1974-80+, from $50 to $60.00

Crystal Velvet, #9465, 1980, from $20.00 to $27.00. (Photo courtesy Margaret and Kenn Whitmyer)

Carnival Glass

Note: Carnival glass items listed here were made after 1970.

Bonbon, amethyst, butterfly handle, #8230-CN, 1973-75, from $18 to $22.00

Bowl, Hearts & Flowers, amethyst, cupped, #8229-CN, 1971-74, from $50 to $60.00

Candle bowl, Orange Tree, amethyst, #9173-CN, 1973-74, from $28 to $32.00

Candy box, Pagoda, ruby, #8201-RN, 1976-78, from $80 to... $90.00

Compote, Jefferson, Independence Blue, #8476-IB, 1974-75, from $160 to $165.00

Compote, Pinwheel, ruby, #8227-RN, 1976-78, from $30 to. $35.00

Plate, American Craftsmen series, 1977, 8", from $12.00 to $15.00. (Photo courtesy Margaret and Kenn Whitmyer)

Plate, Christ Church, Alexandria Virginia, amethyst, Christmas series, #8280-CN, 1980, from $12 to............................$14.00

Plate, Glassmaker, amethyst, #9115-CN, 1970, from $18 to .$20.00

Plate, Madonna on the Rose Hedge, ruby, #9379-RN, 1979, from $30 to **$35.00**

Plate, Persian Medallion, amethyst, #8219-CN, 1971-73, from $35 to **$40.00**

Toothpick holder, Strawberry, orange, #8295-CO, 1971-74, from $22 to **$25.00**

Vase, Independence Blue, #91255-IB, 1976-77, 8", from $32 to **$37.00**

Crests

Apple Blossom, cake plate, #7213-AB, 1960-61, from $180 to. **$200.00**

Apple Blossom, vase, #7262-AB, 1960-61, 12", from $250 to .. **$280.00**

Aqua, bowl, #203, 1941-43, 4½", from $22 to **$27.00**

Aqua, candleholder, #680, 1949-51, ea from $55 to **$65.00**

Aqua, epergne set, #1522, 1941-43, 4-pc, from $300 to **$325.00**

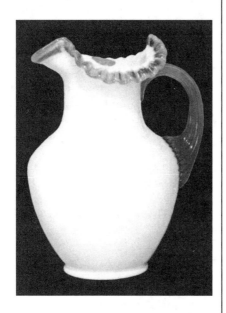

Aqua, pitcher/jug, #1353, 70-ounce, from $400.00 to $450.00. (Photo courtesy Margaret and Kenn Whitmyer)

Aqua, top hat, #1924, 1942-43, 5", from $55 to **$65.00**

Aqua, vase, tulip; triangular, #192, 1942-43, 6", from $55 to. **$60.00**

Black, plate, #7219-BC, 1970s, 6", from $14 to **$16.00**

Black Rose, vase, #7256-BR, 1953-55, 6", from $145 to... **$165.00**

Blue Ridge, top hat, #1921, ca 1939, 10", from $200 to... **$250.00**

Crystal, bottle, #192, ca 1942, 7", from $125 to **$150.00**

Crystal, candy jar, footed, #206, ca 1942, from $140 to.... **$175.00**

Crystal, vase, tulip; triangular, #1924, ca 1942, 5", from $50 to **$60.00**

Emerald, nut dish, footed, #7229-EC, 1949-56, from $35 to. **$40.00**

Emerald, planter, 2-tier, #680, 1949-54, from $100 to **$125.00**

Flame, tidbit, 2-tier, 1963, from $125 to **$135.00**

Gold, bottle, cologne; squat, #192, from $55 to **$65.00**

Gold, bowl, double crimped, #1522, 10", from $55 to **$60.00**

Gold, tidbit, 2-tier, #7294-GC, 1963-65, from $65 to **$85.00**

Peach, bowl, 8-pointed, #1522, 1940-41, 10", from $75 to... **$85.00**

Peach, vase, triangular, #1925, 1940-43, 6½", from $25 to. **$28.00**

Ruby Snowcrest, vase, #4516, 1950-54, 8½", from $75 to.. **$85.00**

Silver, bottle, #192, 1943-49, 5½", from $50 to **$60.00**

Silver, compote, low foot, #7329SC, 1954-78, from $25 to... **$28.00**

Silver, plate, #680, 1948-60, 12", from $40 to **$45.00**

Silver, sugar bowl, #680, 1948-67, from $25 to **$30.00**

Silver, vase, double crimped, #186, 1943-67, 8", from $25 to .. **$30.00**

Silver Rose, bonbon, #7225-SR, 1956-58, 5½", from $20 to. **$25.00**

Silver w/Spanish Lace, #3551-SC, 1968-80+, 8", from $50 to . **$60.00**

Silver w/Violets in the Snow, top hat, #7292-DV, 1968-70, 5", from $50 to **$60.00**

Peach, vase, Roses and Bows decoration, #7256, 6", from $140.00 to $160.00. (Photo courtesy Margaret and Kenn Whitmyer)

Figurals and Novelties

Slipper candy box, Blue Marble, 1974, 5¼" long, from $40.00 to $50.00. (Photo courtesy Margaret and Kenn Whitmyer)

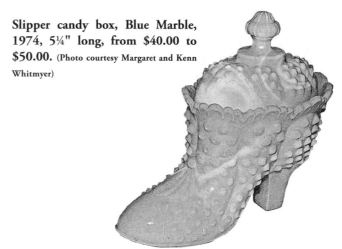

Bird, black, #5196-BK, 1953-55, from $45 to **$55.00**

Bird, Happiness; lavender satin, #5197-LN, 1977-79, from $70 to **$80.00**

Boot, Daisy & Button, carnival, 1990-CN, 1970-75, from $20 to **$22.00**

Bootee, Daisy & Button, green pastel, #1994-GP, 1954-55, from $30 to **$35.00**

Bunny, custard satin, #5162-CU, 1978-80+, from $25 to ... **$30.00**

Butterfly, milk glass, #5170-MI, 1970-71, from $10 to **$12.00**

Chick, milk glass, #5185, 1953-56, from $22 to **$27.00**

Eagle paperweight, Valley Forge White, #8470-VW, 1976-77, from $18 to **$22.00**

Frog, Lime Sherbet, #5166-LS, 1979-80, from $40 to......... **$50.00**

Hen on basket, blue pastel, #5183-BP, 1954-55, from $75 to. **$85.00**

Hen on basket, milk glass, #5182-YM, 1953-55, lg, from $150 to **$175.00**

Hen on nest, blue marble, #5186-MB, 1971-73, sm, from $45 to **$55.00**

Leaf ashtray, Daisy & Button, Colonial Amber, #1976-CA, 1968-70, from $8 to **$10.00**

Madonna prayer light, blue satin, #5107-BA, 1978-80+, from $35 to **$40.00**

Owl fairy lamp, Lime Sherbet, #5108-LS, 1973-80, from $28 to **$32.00**

Swan, custard satin, #5161-CU, 1978-80+, from $18 to **$22.00**

Witch's kettle, Burred Hobnail, blue opal, #489, from $25 to **$30.00**

Hobnail

Vase, Jack-in-the-pulpit, cranberry, made for Levay, 1988, from $70.00 to $80.00. (Photo courtesy Margaret and Kenn Whitmyer)

Bonbon, cranberry, star-shaped rim, #3921, 1953-57, 2¾x5", from $75 to **$90.00**

Bowl, dessert; blue opalescent, sq, #3828, 1951-55, from $25 to **$28.00**

Bowl, topaz opal, footed, double crimped, #3731, 1959-60, 10", from $125 to **$150.00**

Cake plate, French opalescent, #3913, 1941-44, 13", from $80 to **$95.00**

Candleholder, cornucopia; French opal, #3874, 1943-54, ea from $40 to **$45.00**

Compote, blue marble, double crimped, footed, #3628, 1970-74, 6", from $27 to **$30.00**

Creamer & sugar bowl, crystal, #3606, 1968-69, w/lid, from $8 to **$12.00**

Epergne, rose pastel, 3-lily, #3800, 1954-55, 5-pc, from $150 to **$200.00**

Goblet, milk glass, #A-016, 6", from $20 to **$25.00**

Honey jar, milk glass, #3886, 1953-60, from $95 to **$120.00**

Pitcher, champagne, #3366, 2000-2001, 5½", from $40 to.**$45.00**

Pitcher, cranberry, #3360, 1981, 11", from $300 to **$325.00**

Puff box, French opalescent, wooden lid, 1930s, from $22 to **$27.00**

Relish, milk glass, 3-compartment, chrome handle, #3607, 1970-85, from $22 to **$25.00**

Spoon holder, milk glass, #3612, 1967-69, from $85 to **$110.00**

Vase, ruby, double crimped, #3853, 1972-85, 3", from $14 to. **$16.00**

Lamps

Ball, Poppy, milk glass, #9108-MI, 1967-74, 21½", from $160 to **$180.00**

Boudoir, blue pastel, electric, #7392-BP, 1954-55, from $95 to **$125.00**

Courting, blue opaque overlay, electric, #1691-OB, 1962-63, from $100 to **$125.00**

Currier & Ives, crystal velvet, #8400-VE, 1980, 11", from $200 to **$225.00**

Fairy, Persian Medallion, custard, #8408-CU, 1974-80+, from $40 to **$45.00**

Gone-with-the-Wind, Burmese, #9101-BR, 1976-78, 24", from $340 to **$375.00**

Hurricane, chocolate roses on cameo satin, #7311-DR, 1979-80+, 11", from $145 to **$175.00**

Student, Hobnail, cranberry, #1150, 2002-2003, 18", from $175 to **$200.00**

Student, Poppy, milk glass, #9107-MI, 1967-80+, 20", from $125 to **$145.00**

Student, Poppy, ruby iridescent, #9107, 1977-78, 20", from $225 to **$250.00**

Student, Thumbprint, ruby overlay, #1410-RO, 1967-75, 20", from $250 to **$290.00**

Table, Coin Dot, Cranberry, from $300.00 to $350.00. (Photo courtesy Margaret and Kenn Whitmyer)

Table, Coin Dot, Honey Amber, #1406-HA, 1977-78, 20", from $150 to **$175.00**

Miscellaneous

Atomizer, Pearls, cranberry, #CS300-1, from $160.00 to $180.00. (Photo courtesy Margaret and Kenn Whitmyer)

Candleholder, Horizon, Jamestown Blue, w/insert, #8175, 5", ea from $12 to **$15.00**
Candy box, Medallion, butterflies on milk glass, #8288-BY, 1977-79, from $75 to **$85.00**
Candy jar, Swirled Feather, blue satin, #2083-BA, 1953-55, from $350 to **$450.00**
Compote, blue roses on blue satin, footed, #7249-BL, 1978-80+, from $50 to **$60.00**

Compote, Jefferson, Chocolate, #8476, 1976 – 1977, from $110.00 to $130.00. (Photo courtesy Margaret and Kenn Whitmyer)

Cruet, Fern, satin blue, #1863-BA, 1952-54, from $250 to .**$300.00**
Cruet, Hanging Heart on custard iridescent, #8969-CI, from $125 to **$150.00**
Puff box, Swirled Feather, French satin, 1953-55, from $100 to. **$140.00**
Temple jar, chocolate roses on cameo satin, #7488-DR, 1979-80+, from $40 to **$50.00**
Vase, bud; bluebirds on custard satin, #9056-BC, 1977-80, from $30 to **$35.00**

Vase, bud; Christmas Holly, white on ruby, #9056-RH, 1976-78, 10", from $22 to **$27.00**
Vase, Cardinals in Winter on milk glass, #7252-CW, 1978-79, 7", from $45 to **$55.00**
Vase, Christmas Holly on custard satin, #7254-CH, 1978-79, 4½", from $20 to **$25.00**
Vase, Hanging Heart on turquoise iridescent, #8954-TH, 4", from $75 to **$85.00**
Vase, tulip; daisies on cameo satin, #7255-CD, 1979-80+, from $80 to **$95.00**

Fiesta

Fiesta is a line of solid-color dinnerware made by the Homer Laughlin China Company of Newell, West Virginia. It was introduced in 1936 and was immediately accepted by the American public. The line was varied. There were more than 50 items offered, and the color assortment included red (orange-red), cobalt, light green, and yellow. Within a short time, ivory and turquoise were added. (All these are referred to as 'original colors.')

As tastes changed during the production years, old colors were retired and new ones added. The colors collectors refer to as '50s colors are dark green, rose, chartreuse, and gray, and today these are very desirable. Medium green was introduced in 1959 at a time when some of the old standard shapes were being discontinued. Today, medium green pieces are the most expensive. The majority of pieces are marked. Plates were stamped, and molded pieces usually had an indented mark.

In 1986 Homer Laughlin reintroduced Fiesta, but in colors different than the old line: white, black, cobalt, rose (bright pink), and apricot. Many of the pieces had been restyled, and the only problem collectors have had with the new colors is with the cobalt. But if you'll compare it with the old, you'll see that it is darker. Turquoise, periwinkle blue, yellow, and Seamist green were added next, and though the turquoise is close, it is a little greener than the original. Lilac and persimmon were later made for sale exclusively through Bloomingdale's department stores. Production was limited on lilac (not every item was made in it), and once it was discontinued, collectors were clamoring for it, often paying several times the original price. Sapphire blue, a color approximating the old cobalt, was introduced in 1996 — also a Bloomingdale's exclusive, and the selection was limited. Then came Chartreuse (a little more vivid than the chartreuse of the '50s); Gray was next, then Juniper (a rich teal). Several colors have followed: Cinnabar (maroon), a strong yellow called Sunflower; a dark bluish-purple they've aptly named Plum; Shamrock (similar to the coveted medium green); Tangerine (pale orange), Scarlet (described by some as lipstick red), Peacock (a vivid '50s turquoise), and lastly Heather.

Items that have not been restyled are being made from the original molds. This means that you may find pieces with the old mark in the new colors (since the mark is an integral part of the mold). When an item has been restyled, new molds had to be created, and these will have the new mark. So will any piece marked with the ink stamp. The new ink mark is a script 'FIESTA' (all letters upper case), while the old is 'Fiesta.' Compare a few, the difference is obvious. Just don't be fooled into thinking you've found a rare cobalt juice pitcher or individual sugar and creamer set, they just weren't made in the old line. And if you find a piece with a letter H below the mark, you'll know that piece is new.

Because Fiesta is in good supply on eBay, more than ever before, condition has become a major factor in determining value. Unless an item is free from signs of wear, smoothly glazed, and has no distracting manufacturing flaws, it will not bring 'book' price. Some of the description lines that follow simply give a range for 'original colors.' When that is the case, use from the lower end to mid-range to evaluate yellow, turquoise, and light green; use from mid-range to the higher end to evaluate red, cobalt, and ivory.

For more information we recommend *The Collector's Encyclopedia of Fiesta, 10th Edition,* by Sharon and Bob Huxford (Collector Books).

Newsletter: *Fiesta Collector's Quarterly*
China Specialties, Inc.
Box 471, Valley City, OH 44280
$12 (4 issues) per year
www.chinaspecialties.com/fiesta.html

Club: Homer Laughlin China Collector's Association (HLCCA)
P.O. Box 26021
Crystal City, VA 22215-6021
info@hlcca.org
Dues $25.00 single, $40.00 couple; includes magazine

Ashtray, '50s colors, from $55 to.........................**$75.00**
Ashtray, original colors, from $35 to...................**$60.00**
Bowl, covered onion soup; red, cobalt or ivory, from $600 to. **$675.00**
Bowl, covered onion soup; yellow or light green, from $525
    to **$625.00**
Bowl, cream soup; '50s colors, from $60 to **$75.00**
Bowl, cream soup; med green, minimum value..............**$4,000.00**
Bowl, cream soup; original colors, from $30 to....................**$60.00**
Bowl, dessert; 6", '50s colors, from $35 to............**$45.00**
Bowl, dessert; 6", med green, from $650 to **$700.00**
Bowl, dessert; 6", original colors, from $30 to **$50.00**
Bowl, footed salad; red, cobalt, ivory, or turquoise, from $350
    to...**$475.00**
Bowl, footed salad; yellow or light green, from $275 to.....**$375.00**
Bowl, fruit; 4¾", '50s colors, from $30 to **$35.00**
Bowl, fruit; 4¾", med green, minimum value..................**$550.00**
Bowl, fruit; 4¾", original colors, from $20 to.....................**$30.00**
Bowl, fruit; 5½", '50s colors, from $35 to **$40.00**
Bowl, fruit; 5½", med green, from $65 to...........................**$70.00**
Bowl, fruit; 5½", original colors, from $20 to.....................**$30.00**
Bowl, fruit; 11¾", original colors, from $225 to...............**$300.00**
Bowl, individual salad; med green, 7½", from $100 to......**$120.00**
Bowl, individual salad; red, turquoise, or yellow, 7½", from $80
    to **$90.00**
Bowl, mixing; #1, original colors, from $220 to **$300.00**
Bowl, mixing; #2, original colors, from $100 to **$150.00**
Bowl, mixing; #3, original colors, from $110 to **$150.00**
Bowl, mixing; #4, original colors, from $110 to **$185.00**
Bowl, mixing; #5, original colors, from $175 to **$235.00**
Bowl, mixing; #6, original colors, from $230 to **$300.00**

Bowl, mixing; #7, original colors, from $325 to **$500.00**
Bowl, nappy; 8½", '50s colors, from $50 to.......................**$60.00**
Bowl, nappy; 8½", med green...**$150.00**
Bowl, nappy; 8½", original colors, from $30 to **$50.00**
Bowl, nappy; 9½", original colors, from $55 to **$70.00**
Bowl, Tom & Jerry; ivory w/gold letters, from $250 to......**$260.00**
Bowl, unlisted salad; red, cobalt, or ivory, minimum value... **$2,000.00**
Bowl, unlisted salad; yellow, from $80 to **$100.00**
Bowl lid, for mixing bowl #1-#3, any color, from $600 to.**$750.00**
Bowl lid, for mixing bowl #4, any color, minimum value..**$1,000.00**
Candleholders, bulb; original colors, pr from $80 to **$130.00**

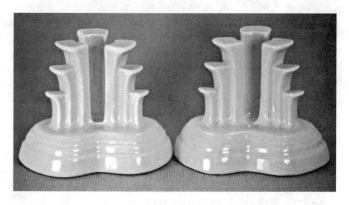

Candleholders, tripod; original colors, from $450.00 to $700.00 for the pair.

Carafe, original colors, from $250 to **$300.00**
Casserole, French; standard colors other than yellow, no established
    value
Casserole, French; yellow, from $250 to............................**$300.00**
Casserole, med green, minimum value.................................**$1,000.00**
Casserole, original colors, from $150 to............................**$200.00**
Casserole, '50s colors, from $250 to...................................**$275.00**
Coffeepot, demitasse; original colors other than turquoise, from
    $350 to **$600.00**
Coffeepot, demitasse; turquoise, minimum value...............**$750.00**
Coffeepot, original colors, from $180 to............................**$265.00**
Coffeepot, '50s colors, from $300 to...................................**$350.00**
Compote, sweets; original colors, from $95 to **$135.00**
Compote, 12", original colors, from $160 to **$200.00**
Creamer, individual; red, minimum value.........................**$325.00**
Creamer, individual; yellow, from $60 to **$80.00**
Creamer, regular; '50s colors, from $35 to **$45.00**
Creamer, regular; med green, from $90 to **$120.00**
Creamer, regular; original colors, from $20 to **$30.00**
Creamer, stick-handled; original colors, from $45 to **$65.00**
Cup, demitasse; '50s colors, from $325 to **$400.00**
Cup, demitasse; original colors, from $70 to.....................**$100.00**
Cup, see teacup
Egg cup, '50s colors, from $140 to **$160.00**
Egg cup, original colors, from $55 to.................................**$70.00**
Marmalade, original colors, from $350 to...........................**$400.00**
Mug, Tom & Jerry; '50s colors, from $80 to......................**$90.00**
Mug, Tom & Jerry; ivory w/gold letters, from $55 to **$65.00**
Mug, Tom & Jerry; original colors, from $50 to **$80.00**

Mustard, original colors, from $240.00 to $300.00.

Pitcher, disk juice; gray, minimum value $2,000.00
Pitcher, disk juice; Harlequin yellow, from $65 to $75.00
Pitcher, disk juice; red, from $550 to $650.00
Pitcher, disk juice; yellow, from $45 to $50.00
Pitcher, disk water; '50s colors, from $200 to $275.00
Pitcher, disk water; med green, minimum value.............$1,500.00
Pitcher, disk water; original colors, from $100 to..............$175.00
Pitcher, ice; original colors, from $110 to $145.00
Pitcher, jug, 2-pt; '50s colors, from $120 to......................$140.00
Pitcher, jug, 2-pt; original colors, from $70 to $105.00
Plate, cake; original colors, from $1,000 to....................$1,200.00
Plate, calendar; 9-10", ea, from $45 to..............................$55.00
Plate, chop; 13", '50s colors, from $90 to $95.00
Plate, chop; 13", original colors, from $40 to $55.00
Plate, chop; 15", '50s colors, from $135 to......................$150.00
Plate, chop; 15", original colors, from $70 to $100.00
Plate, compartment; 10½", '50s colors, from $60 to $70.00
Plate, compartment; 10½", original colors, from $35 to.....$45.00
Plate, compartment; 12", original colors, from $40 to........$60.00
Plate, deep; '50s colors, from $50 to $55.00
Plate, deep; med green, from $130 to $145.00
Plate, deep; original colors, from $35 to $60.00
Plate, 6", '50s colors, from $7 to..$10.00
Plate, 6", med green, from $30 to $45.00
Plate, 6", original colors, from $4 to....................................$7.00
Plate, 7", '50s colors, from $10 to......................................$12.00
Plate, 7", med green, from $30 to $45.00
Plate, 7", original colors, from $7 to..................................$10.00
Plate, 9", '50s colors, from $20 to......................................$25.00
Plate, 9", med green, from $60 to $75.00
Plate, 9", original colors, from $10 to................................$20.00
Plate, 10", '50s colors, from $45 to....................................$50.00
Plate, 10", med green, minimum value $125.00
Plate, 10", original colors, from $30 to $45.00
Platter, '50s colors, from $50 to $60.00
Platter, med green, from $175 to $225.00
Platter, original colors, from $40 to $55.00
Relish tray, gold decor, complete, from $220 to................$250.00
Relish tray base, original colors, from $80 to $100.00
Relish tray center insert, original colors, from $50 to..........$70.00

Relish tray side insert, original colors, from $45 to $60.00
Salt & pepper shakers, '50s colors, pr from $40 to..............$45.00
Salt & pepper shakers, med green, pr from $200 to..........$225.00
Salt & pepper shakers, original colors, pr from $22 to.........$30.00
Sauce boat, '50s colors, from $60 to $75.00
Sauce boat, med green, from $200 to................................$225.00
Sauce boat, original colors, from $40 to............................$70.00
Saucer, demitasse; '50s colors, from $70 to......................$100.00
Saucer, demitasse; original colors, from $15 to....................$20.00
Saucer, med green, from $10 to $15.00
Saucer, original colors, from $2 to..$3.00
Saucer, '50s colors, from $3 to $5.00
Sugar bowl, individual; turquoise, from $400 to................$500.00
Sugar bowl, individual; yellow, from $125 to....................$175.00
Sugar bowl, w/lid, '50s colors, 3¼x3½", from $70 to..........$80.00
Sugar bowl, w/lid, med green, 3¼x3½", from $225 to......$250.00
Sugar bowl, w/lid, original colors, 3¼x3½", from $50 to $75.00

Syrup, original colors, from $325.00 to $475.00.

Teacup, '50s colors, from $35 to $40.00
Teacup, med green, from $60 to $75.00
Teacup, original colors, from $15 to $40.00
Teapot, lg; original colors, from $250 to $350.00
Teapot, med; '50s colors, from $250 to............................$300.00
Teapot, med; med green, minimum value......................$1,500.00
Teapot, med; original colors, from $150 to $250.00
Tray, figure-8; cobalt, from $90 to $100.00
Tray, figure-8; turquoise, from $350 to $400.00
Tray, figure-8; yellow, from $500 to $600.00
Tray, utility; original colors, from $40 to............................$50.00
Tumbler, juice; chartreuse or dark green, minimum value..$750.00
Tumbler, juice; original colors, from $40 to $50.00
Tumbler, juice; rose, from $55 to $60.00
Tumbler, water; original colors, from $70 to......................$90.00
Vase, bud; original colors, from $75 to $125.00
Vase, 8", original colors, from $600 to..............................$800.00

Vase, 10", original colors, from $700 to **$1,100.00**
Vase, 12", red, cobalt, ivory, or turquoise, from $1,400 to ..**$1,900.00**
Vase, 12", yellow or light green, from $1,100 to **$1,500.00**

Kitchen Kraft

Bowl, mixing; 6" **$60.00**
Bowl, mixing; 8" **$80.00**
Bowl, mixing; 10", from $100 to **$110.00**
Cake plate **$35.00**
Cake server, from $150 to **$175.00**
Casserole, individual; from $150 to **$160.00**
Casserole, 7½" **$75.00**
Casserole, 8½" **$85.00**

Covered jar, large, from $350.00 to $375.00.

Covered jar, med; from $275 to **$300.00**
Covered jar, sm; from $300 to **$325.00**
Covered jug, lg, from $275 to **$300.00**
Covered jug, sm, from $300 to **$320.00**
Fork, from $150 to **$160.00**
Metal frame for platter **$15.00**
Pie plate, Spruce Green **$150.00**
Pie plate, 9" or 10" (other than Spruce Green) **$40.00**
Platter, from $60 to **$75.00**
Platter, Spruce Green..**$150.00**
Salt & pepper shakers, pr from $120 to **$150.00**
Spoon, from $150 to...**$200.00**
Spoon, ivory, 12", from $400 to **$500.00**
Stacking refrigerator lid, ivory, from $200 to **$225.00**
Stacking refrigerator lid, other than ivory, from $90 to......**$110.00**
Stacking refrigerator unit, ivory, from $200 to **$210.00**
Stacking refrigerator unit, other than ivory, from $50 to......**$60.00**

New Fiesta — Post86

Bowl, chili; lilac, 18-oz, from $40 to...................................**$50.00**
Bowl, mixing; chartreuse, 44-oz, from $25 to **$30.00**
Bowl, stacking cereal; apricot, 6½", from $15 to **$18.00**
Candlestick, pyramid; chartreuse, ea from $28 to **$32.00**
Cup, jumbo; sapphire, 18-oz, from $22 to...........................**$28.00**
Cup & saucer, AD; sapphire, from $22 to **$28.00**
Hostess set, apricot, 4-pc, from $18 to.................................**$22.00**
Pie baker, lilac, deep dish, 10¼", from $60 to **$75.00**

Pitcher, disk; apricot, mini, from $25 to **$30.00**
Plate, chop; apricot, 11¾", from $25 to **$30.00**
Plate, chop; chartreuse, 11¾", from $30 to........................**$35.00**
Plate, salad; sapphire, 7", from $15 to **$22.00**
Salt & pepper shakers, apricot, 2¼", pr from $22 to **$28.00**
Sugar caddy, lilac, from $45 to...**$50.00**
Teapot, chartreuse, 2-cup, from $30 to...............................**$40.00**
Tumbler, sapphire, from $25 to **$30.00**
Vase, bud; apricot, 6", from $15 to **$20.00**

Individual creamer and sugar on figure-eight tray, apricot, from $35.00 to $45.00.

Finch, Kay

Wonderful ceramic figurines signed by sculptor-artist-decorator Kay Finch are among the many that were produced in California during the middle of the last century. She modeled her line of animals and birds with much expression and favored soft color combinations often with vibrant pastel accents. Some of her models were quite large, but generally they range in size from 12" down to a tiny 2". She made several animal 'family groups' and some human subjects as well. After her death a few years ago, prices for her work began to climb.

She used a variety of marks and labels, and though most pieces are marked, some of the smaller animals are not; but you should be able to recognize her work with ease, once you've seen a few marked pieces.

For more information, we recommend *Kay Finch Ceramics, Her Enchanted World,* by Mike Nickel and Cindy Horvath (Schiffer); and *The Collector's Encyclopedia of California Pottery, Second Edition,* by Jack Chipman (Collector Books). Please note: Prices below are for near-mint condition items (allowing for moderate crazing, which is normal) decorated in multiple colors, not solid glazes. Chips and cracks drastically reduce values.

Advisors: Mike Nickel and Cindy Horvath (See Directory, Kay Finch)

Ashtray, Swan, #4958, 4½" **$25.00**
Bank, Lion, #5921, 8" **$300.00**
Box, heart; #B5051, bird on lid, 2½" **$40.00**
Brooch, Afghan head, 2x3" **$200.00**
Candlesticks, turkey figures, #5794, 3¾", pr **$150.00**

Figurine, Afghan Dog, sitting, #5553, 5¼" **$450.00**
Figurine, bull, #621, 6½" **$200.00**
Figurine, Cockatoo, #5401, 15" **$400.00**
Figurine, Cubby & Tubby, playful bears, #3837, #4848, 4¼", pr **$250.00**
Figurine, Dickey Bird, Mr & Mrs, #4905a, #4905b, ea **$100.00**
Figurine, Donkey standing, Florentine White, #839, 9½" .**$150.00**
Figurine, Hoot, owl, #187, 8½" **$125.00**
Figurine, Littlest Angel, #4803, 2½" **$100.00**
Figurine, Mama Quail, #5984, 7" **$350.00**
Figurine, Mermaid, #161, 6½" **$200.00**
Figurine, Mouse, rare, 3" **$350.00**
Figurine, Mumbo, sitting elephant, #4840, 4½" **$100.00**
Figurine, Pajama Girl, #5002, 5½" **$250.00**

Figurine, Peanuts, #191, $175.00.

Figurine, Piggy Wiggy, #5408, 1x1½" **$100.00**
Figurine, Scandi Boy & Girl, #126, #127, 5¼", pr **$75.00**
Figurine, Seababy, #162, 2½x3½" **$125.00**
Figurine, Skunks, #4774/#4775, 4¼", 3", pr **$550.00**

Figurine, Sleepy Bear, #5004, 4½", $125.00.

Figurine, Turkey, #5843, 4½" **$75.00**
Figurine, Windblown Afghan, pewter-like glaze, #5757, 6x6" . **$550.00**
Figurine, Yorkie Pups, #170 & #171, pr **$400.00**
Planter, Animal Book series, #B5145, 6½", ea **$50.00**

Plaque, Baby Fish, 2¼x3" **$50.00**
Plaque, Starfish, #5790, 9" **$125.00**
Salt & pepper shakers, stallion heads, 5", pr **$100.00**
Salt shaker, kitchen; Puss, cat, #4616, 6" **$275.00**
String holder, dog w/bow over left ear, wall mount, 4½x4" ..**$400.00**
Tumbler, Afghan design (embossed), marked Kay & Brayden, 6" **$250.00**
Tureen, Turkey, #5361, platinum/gray, w/ladle, 9" **$250.00**
Vase, Elephant, #B5155, 6" **$75.00**
Vase, South Sea Girl, #4912, 8¼" **$125.00**
Wall pocket, Girl & Boy, #5501, 10", ea **$350.00**

Fishbowl Ornaments

Prior to World War II, every dime store had its bowl of small goldfish. Nearby were stacks of goldfish bowls — small, medium, and large. Accompanying them were displays of ceramic ornaments for these bowls, many in the shape of Oriental pagodas or European-style castles. The fish died, the owners lost interest, and the glass containers along with their charming ornaments were either thrown out or relegated to the attic. In addition to pagodas and castles, other ornaments included bridges, lighthouses, colonnades, mermaids, and fish. Note that figurals such as mermaids are difficult to find.

Many fishbowl ornaments were produced in Japan between 1921 and 1941, and again after 1947. The older Japanese items often show clean, crisp mold designs with visible detail of the item's features. Others were made in Germany and some by potteries in the United States. Aquarium pieces made in America are not common. Those produced in recent years are usually of Chinese origin and are more crude, less colorful, and less detailed in appearance. In general, the more detail and more colorful, the older the piece. A few more examples are shown in *Collector's Encyclopedia to Made in Japan Ceramics* by Carole Bess White (Collector Books).

Advisor: Carole Bess White (See Directory, Japan Ceramics)

Arch w/lion on top, red, white & blue, 2 bubbler holes, Japan, 3½x3¼x1½" **$95.00**
Bathing beauty on shell, cinnamon & white lustre, red Japan mark, 3", from $40 to **$60.00**
Bathing beauty on turtle, multicolor on white, 2½", from $20 to **$30.00**
Boy riding dolphin on wave, multicolored matt glazes, 3¾", from $20 to **$40.00**
Bridge, brown & green, arched footbridge style, Japan, 3¼x7x2½" .**$55.00**
Castle, multicolored glossy glazes, no mark, 4½", from $20 to. **$25.00**
Castle towers w/3 arches, tan lustre towers w/red arches on green & white rocks, 5¼" **$22.00**
Castle-like tower connected to brige that reaches wooded hillside, multicolor **$50.00**
Coral, shiny orange w/shadow of black sea diver, red mark, 3½", from $18 to **$28.00**
Diver holding dagger, white suit & helmet, blue gloves, brown boots & black airpack, 4¾" **$22.00**
Diver spearing fish, hole at back of head to attach an air hose, top has bubbler hole, Japan, 5½" **$48.00**

Doorway, stone entry w/open aqua wood-look door, 2" **$15.00**

Fish, multicolored, black Japan mark, 2½", from $15 to **$25.00**

Frogs on lily pad before sign: Welcome to Our Pad, multicolor, 3¾x5x3½" **$16.00**

Houses (2) & tree above sm bridge w/hole for fish to swim through, multicolor, Japan, 3½x2⅜x1⅛" **$50.00**

Houses & cave, top has bubbler hole, Japan, 3½"................ **$15.00**

Lighthouse, orange, yellow & brown, 2x2½" **$16.00**

Lighthouse, tan, black, brown & green, 6½x4" **$26.00**

Mermaid, sitting w/shell in hand, multicolor, unmarked Japan, 4½x4" **$30.00**

Mermaid on snail, multicolor, Japan, 4", from $45 to **$65.00**

Mermaid on 2 seashells, multicolor, 3½" **$40.00**

Nude on starfish, painted bisque, 4½", from $75 to **$125.00**

Octopus, pink & brown, black Japan mark, 4" **$35.00**

Pagoda, red, white, blue & green, Japan, 2x2½" **$25.00**

Pagoda, triple roof, blue, brown & yellow, 4" **$27.50**

Pagoda, 6 roof lines, green, yellow & brown, Japan, 6½"..... **$50.00**

Ruins among rocks, aqua, green & brown, Japan, 4x4" **$15.00**

Sailing ship, multicolor, green Japan mark, 4"..................... **$20.00**

Sand castle, 2 openings for fish to swim through, Japan, 3x3½" .**$18.00**

Sign on tree trunk, No Fishing, brown, black & white, 2¼x4" ..**$12.00**

Sunken ship wreckage, pastels, unmarked, 2x8¼x4⅛" **$50.00**

Thatched house, brown tones, holes for fish to swim through, Hand Decorated Japan, 5x6¾" **$60.00**

Torii gate, multicolor, 3¾", from $25 to **$35.00**

Towers w/gateway, brown & green, 3 openings, bubbler in roof, from $35 to **$45.00**

Windmill w/house on mountainside, hole for fish to swim through, multicolor, Japan, 1940s, from $35 to **$40.00**

Castles: tan lustre on green and white rocks, Japan, 5", from $20.00 to $25.00; 3¾", from $18.00 to $25.00. (Photo courtesy Carole Bess White)

Fisher-Price

Probably no other toy manufacturer is as well known among kids of today as Fisher-Price. Since the 1930s they've produced wonderful toys made of wood covered with vividly lithographed paper. Plastic parts weren't used until 1949, and this can sometimes help you date your finds. These toys were made for play, so very few older examples have survived in condition good enough to attract collectors. Watch for missing parts and avoid those that are dirty. Edge wear and some paint dulling is normal and to be expected. Our values are for toys with minimum signs of such wear. Mint condition examples will bring considerably higher prices, of course, and if the original box is present, add from 20% to 40% more.

For more information we recommend *Fisher-Price, A Historical, Rarity Value Guide* by John J. Murray and Bruce R. Fox (Books Americana); and *Schroeder's Collectible Toys, Antique to Modern*, published by Collector Books.

Advisor: Brad Cassity (See Directory, Toys)

Club: Fisher-Price Collector's Club
Jeanne Kennedy
1442 N Ogden, Mesa, AZ 85205
Monthly newsletter with information and ads; send SASE for more information

Museum: Toy Town Museum
636 Girard Ave., PO Box 238
East Aurora, NY 14052
Monday through Saturday, 10-4.

#172, Roly Raccoon, waddles side to side, tail bobs, 1980 – 1982, $5.00. (Photo courtesy Brad Cassity)

#5, Bunny Cart, 1948-49..**$50.00**

#7, Doggy Racer, 1942-43 ....**$150.00**

#14, Ducky Daddles, 1941 ....**$85.00**

#28, Bunny Egg Cart, 1950..**$50.00**

#112, Picture Disk Camera, w/5 picture disks, 1968-71 ......**$20.00**

#118, Tumble Tower Game, w/10 marbles, 1972-75 .... **$5.00**

#121, Happy Hopper, 1969-76..**$10.00**

#124, Roller Chime, 1961-62 & Easter 1963 ....**$25.00**

#125, Music Box Iron, aqua w/yellow handle, 1966 ....**$40.00**

#131, Toy Wagon, 1951-54 ....**$200.00**

#132, Molly Moo Cow, 1972-78 ....**$10.00**

#138, Jack-in-the-Box Puppet, 1970-73.............................**$20.00**

#140, Katy Kackler, 1954-56 & Easter 1957 ....**$75.00**

#142, Three Men in a Tub, w/bell, 1970-73 ....**$10.00**

#145, Husky Dump Truck, 1961-62 & Easter 1963............**$30.00**

#150, Teddy Tooter, 1940-41 ....**$400.00**
#155, Jack & Jill TV Radio, wood & plastic, 1968-70 ....**$25.00**
#166, Piggy Bank, pink plastic, 1981-82 ....**$10.00**
#183, Play Family Fun Jet, 1st version, 1970 ....**$15.00**
#198, Band Wagon, 1940-41 ....**$300.00**
#215, Fisher-Price Choo-Choo, engine w/3 cars, 1955-57 ...**$75.00**
#300, Scoop Loader, 1975-77 ....**$10.00**
#301, Shovel Digger, 1975-77 ....**$15.00**
#314, Queen Buzzy Bee, 1956-58 ....**$20.00**
#322, Adventure People Dune Buster, 1979-82 ....**$10.00**
#331, Husky Farm Set, 1981-83 ....**$20.00**
#345, Boat Rig, 1981-84 ....**$10.00**
#353, Adventure People Scuba Divers, 1976-81 ....**$15.00**
#402, Duck Cart, 1943.....................................**$250.00**
#445, Nosey Pup, 1956-58 & Easter 1959 ....**$50.00**
#472, Jingle Giraffe, 1956.................................**$200.00**

#476, Cookie Pig, 1966 – 1970, squeals, tail spins, from $30.00 to $40.00. (Photo courtesy Brad Cassity)

#512, Bunny Drummer, 1942 ....**$225.00**
#550, Toy Lunch Kit, red, white & green plastic barn shape, no litho, 1957 ....**$40.00**
#569, Basic Hardboard Puzzle, Airport, 1975 ....**$10.00**
#615, Tow Truck, 1960-61 & Easter 1962...............**$65.00**
#634, Tiny Teddy, 1955-57................................**$50.00**
#674, Sports Car, 1958-60................................**$75.00**
#694, Suzie Seal, 1979-80................................**$10.00**
#703, Bunny Engine, 1954-56..........................**$100.00**
#719, Cuddly Cub, 1973-77...............................**$5.00**
#728, Pound & Saw Bench, 1966-67 ....**$25.00**
#732, Happy Whistlers, 1977-79..........................**$5.00**
#741, Teddy Zilo, 1967 ....**$35.00**
#749, Egg Truck, 1947 ....**$225.00**
#760, Peek-A-Boo Block, 1970-79.........................**$5.00**
#772, Pocket Radio, Jack & Jill, 1974-76 ....**$15.00**
#777, Squeaky the Clown, 1958-59.....................**$225.00**
#780, Snoopy Sniffer, 1955-57 & Easter 1958 ....**$65.00**
#786, Perky Penguin, 1973-75...........................**$15.00**
#793, Jolly Jumper, 1963-64 & Easter 1965.............**$40.00**

#794, Big Bill Pelican, w/cardboard fish, 1961-63 ....**$75.00**
#808, Pop 'n Ring, 1956-58 & Easter 1959 ....**$75.00**
#810, Timber Toter, 1957 & Easter 1958 ....**$85.00**
#875, Looky Push Car, 1962-65 & Easter 1966 ....**$45.00**
#902, Junior Circus, 1963-70 ....**$225.00**
#909, Play Family Rooms, Sears only, 1972 ....**$200.00**
#929, Play Family Nursery School, 1978-79.................**$30.00**

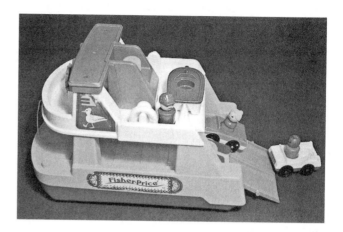

#932, Ferry Boat, eight-piece playset, 1970 – 1980, $30.00. (Photo courtesy Brad Cassity)

#937, Play Family Sesame Street Clubhouse, 1977-79 ....**$70.00**
#961, Woodsey's Store, complete, 1980-81 ....**$30.00**
#972, Fisher-Price Cash Register, 1960-72....................**$40.00**
#985, Play Family Houseboat, complete, 1972-76..............**$40.00**
#992, Play Family Car & Camper, 1980-84 ....**$35.00**
#2155, McDonald's Happy Meal, 1989-90.....................**$15.00**
#2361, Little People Fire Truck, 1989-90 ....**$10.00**
#2504, Little People Garage, 1986, rare **$55.00**
#2550, Little People School, 1988-89 ....**$20.00**
#2552, McDonald's Restaurant, 1st version, 1990 ....**$65.00**
#2582, Little People Floating Marina, 1988-90 ....**$15.00**
#2712, Pick-Up & Peek Puzzle, Haunted House, 1985-88..**$15.00**
#4521, Dozer Loader, 1985-86..............................**$15.00**
#4551, Pontiac Firebird, 1985 ....**$20.00**
#4581, Power Dump Truck, 1985-86 ....**$20.00**
#6550, Buzzy Bee, ToyFest limited edition of 5,000, 1987...**$120.00**
#6575, Toot-Toot, ToyFest limited edition of 4,800, 1989 ..**$65.00**
#6592, Teddy Bear Parade, ToyFest limited edition of 5,000, 1981 ....**$50.00**
#6599, Molly Bell Cow, ToyFest limited edtion of 5,000, 1992 .**$150.00**

Fishing Lures

There have been literally thousands of lures made since the turn of the century. Some have bordered on the ridiculous, and some have turned out to be just as good as the manufacturers claimed. In lieu of buying outright from a dealer, try some of the older stores in your area — you just might turn up a good old lure. Go through any old tackle boxes that might be around, and when the water level is low, check out the river banks.

If you have to limit your collection, you might want to concentrate just on wooden lures, or you might decide to try to locate one of every lure made by a particular company. Whatever you decide, try to find examples with good original paint and hardware. Though many lures are still very reasonable, we have included some of the more expensive examples as well to give you an indication of the type you'll want to fully research if you think you've found a similar model. For such information, we recommend *Fishing Lure Collectibles, An Encyclopedia of the Early Years* by Dudley Murphy and Rick Edmisten; *Fishing Lure Collectibles, An Encyclopedia of the Modern Era,* by Dudley Murphy and Deanie Murphy; *Field Guide to Fishing Lures* and *Modern Fishing Lure Collectibles, Vols. 1 – 5,* by Russell E. Lewis; *Spring-Loaded Fish Hooks, Traps & Lures* by William Blauser & Timothy Mierzwa; *Captain John's Fishing Tackle Price Guide* by John A. Kolbeck. All are published by Collector Books.

Advisor: Dave Hoover (See Directory, Fishing Lures)

Club: NFLCC Tackle Collectors
Drew Reese, contact
197 Scottsdale Circle
Reeds Spring, MO 65737; 417-338-4427
Send SASE for more information about membership and their publications: *The National Fishing Lure Collector's Club Magazine* and *The NFLCC Gazette*

Cheek Chub, Surf Popper #7500, thru-wire w/painted eyes, 2 treble hooks, 1955-59, 7¼", from $90 to $100.00
Creek Chub, Castrola #3100, spinner on wire shaft, 3 treble hooks, 1927-1941, 3⅝", from $85 to $100.00
Creek Chub, Deluxe Wagtail Cub #800, red & silver finish, fluted tail, 2 treble hooks, 1921-53, 2¾", from $100 to $120.00
Creek Chub, Fintail Shiner #2100, metal dorsal & pectoral fins, 2 treble hooks, 1924-37, 4", from $250 to $300.00

Creek Chub, Injured Minnow #1500, 3¾" long, from $20.00 to $35.00. (Photo courtesy Dudley and Deannie Murphy)

Creek Chub, River Scamp #4300, lead weight, 2 treble hooks, 1934-53, 2½", from $25 to $35.00
Creek Chub, Snook Plunker #7100, glass eyes, thru-wire construction, 1952-64, 5", from $75 to...$90.00
Creek Chub, Surface Dingbat #5400, green w/yellow hair, curved grooved lip, 2 double hooks, 1939-55, 1¾", from $45 to. $55.00

Creek Chub, The Seven Thousand #7000, Western Auto sable, 2 treble hooks, 1950-54, 2¾", from $60 to $75.00
Creek Chub, Wee Dee #4800, yellow w/green back, 3 single hooks, 1936-46, 2½", from $250 to $325.00
Creek Chub, Wiggler #100, reinforced lip w/screw-on head, 2 treble hooks, 1906-1964, 3½", from $50 to $60.00
Heddon, Commando #2020, weedless plastic w/spinning tail, single hook, introduced 1968, 4¼", from $10 to $15.00
Heddon, Dowagiac Minnow #150, cream & red w/painted eyes, surface hardware, 1904 to mid-50's, 3⅝", from $100 to....$125.00
Heddon, Drop Zara, dressed dropper, 2 treble hooks, 1980, 4¼", from $10 to $15.00

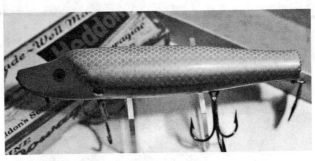

Heddon, Flaptail, #7050PAS, Allen Stripey color, painted eyes, late 1940s – early 1950s, original box, $65.00. (Photo courtesy Russell Lewis)

Heddon, Jointed Giant Vamp #7350, green w/painted eyes, jointed body, introduced 1937, 6¾", from $40 to $50.00
Heddon, King Spoon #290, red w/red feather, single hook, 1937, 2¾", from $25 to...$35.00
Heddon, Meadow Mouse #F4000, surface hardware, leather ears, 2 treble hooks, 1955, 2¾", from $20 to $30.00
Heddon, Midgit Digit #B-110, wood, brown w/black stripes, red face, 2 treble hooks, 1941-47, 1½", from $55 to..........$75.00
Heddon, Salmon River-Runt #8850, scooped lip, teddy bear glass eyes, 2 treble hooks, 1939, 5", from $80 to $100.00
Heddon, Tiny Runt #350, black w/red underbelly, painted eyes, 2 treble hooks, 1952-93, 1⅞", from $10 to $15.00
Heddon, Wounded Spook #9140, plastic, 2 propellers, 2 treble hooks, 1970, 3¼", from $10 to $15.00
Paw Paw, Bullhead #3500, brown flock, rare, 1930s-40s, 3⅞", from $125 to $180.00
Paw Paw, Croaker #71, real frog skin over wood, 2 side treble hooks, 1940, from $275 to $325.00
Paw Paw, Feather Tail Minnow #1200, green & yellow w/red stripes, red feather tail, 1940s, 2½", from $50 to.....................$60.00
Paw Paw, Flap Jack Phantom #3400, based on the Helin Flatfish, 1941, 3⅝", from $15 to $20.00
Paw Paw, Flyrod Centipede, yellow w/black splatters, 1 treble hook, 1946, 1½", from $30 to $40.00
Paw Paw, Frog, beady-eyed, frog shape wooden body w/hair for legs, 1940, 1⅜", from $40 to $50.00
Paw Paw, Hair Mouse, deer-skin covering w/hair left on, 1 propeller, 1 treble hook, 1938, 2½", from $175 to.....................$225.00
Paw Paw, Nature Mouse #50, white suede w/long tail, 1 sm treble hook, 1940s, 1⅞", from $30 to $36.00

Paw Paw, Platypuss #3500, black w/yellow & red scales, flat-nose, 4 treble hooks, 1941, 3¾", from $50 to **$60.00**

Paw Paw, Seagram's Lucky 7, silver #7 w/red crown, 1 treble hook, 1953, 3", from $15 to.................................... **$20.00**

Paw Paw, Weedless Wow #75, frog w/rubber legs, 1 double hook, 1960, 1¾", from $40 to **$50.00**

Paw Paw, Wing Wobler #3-P, white spoon w/red wings, 1 treble hook, 1938, 3½", from $20 to............................ **$25.00**

Paw Paw, Wounded Trout Caster, rainbow trout color, 2 propellers, 2 treble hooks, 1941, 3⅝", from $180 to **$240.00**

Paw Paw, 5-Hook Torpedo, 2 propellers, 5 treble hooks, 1938, 4", from $250 to **$300.00**

Pflueger, Fan-Tail Squid, yellow w/red head, celluloid plastic, 1940, 2¼", from $15 to....................................... **$20.00**

Pflueger, Harp Spinner, paper pattern of frog attached, 1937, 1³⁄₁₆" blade, from $10 to... **$15.00**

Pflueger, Kidney Pearl Bait #600, genuine salt-water pearl blade, 1 treble hook, 1940, 2¹⁄₁₆" blade, from $15 to **$20.00**

Pflueger, Musky Mustang, black & silver, multiple attachment line tie, 3 treble hooks, 1940, 7¼", from $200 to **$225.00**

Pflueger, Salamo Spoon #1500, polished finish w/dressed treble hook, 1948, 4½", from $10 to................................ **$15.00**

Pflueger, The Watusi, yellow & black jointed body, 2 treble hooks, 1965, 2⅝", from $10 to **$15.00**

Pflueger, Woopee Spinner #2300, spring-loaded device beneath bucktail to keep tension on pork rind, 1948, 4¾", $15 to...... **$25.00**

Shakespeare, Glo Lite Mouse #6570, white w/black head, glow-in-the-dark, 2 treble hooks, 1940, 2¾", from $10 to **$15.00**

Shakespeare, Grumpy #6602, cream w/red head w/metal lip, 2 treble hooks, 1941, 1¾", from $5 to **$10.00**

Shakespeare, Jim Dandy Floater, yellow w/black stripes, 3 treble hooks, 2 propellers, 1936, 3¾", from $60 to **$80.00**

Shakespeare, Sardinia #621, white speckled body w/glass eyes, 2 treble hooks, 1936, 3", from $120 to......................... **$180.00**

Shakespeare, Sea Witch #6531, pearlized finish w/glass eyes, 2 treble hooks, 1940, 3⅞", from $20 to **$25.00**

Shakespeare, Slim Jim #6552, reddish green w/pressed eye, 3 treble hooks, 2 propellers, 1937, 4¼", from $25 to **$35.00**

Shakespeare, Striped Bass Wobbler, lg cream body w/blue head, 2 treble hooks, 1940, rare, 6", from $100 to.................. **$150.00**

Shakespeare, Tarpalunge #6640, jointed body w/belly hook hanger, 2 lg single hooks, 1938, 5¾", from $175 to **$200.00**

South Bend, Bass-Obite #1973, greenish yellow plastic w/molded eye, hook-mounting screw, 1938-42, 3¾", from $40 to......... **$50.00**

South Bend, King Andy #975, red & yellow w/nickel-plated back strip, tack eyes, 2 treble hooks, 1951-53, 4⅝", $40 to..**$50.00**

South Bend, Lunge-Oreno #966, yellow w/red dots, thru-wire construction w/2 steel propellers, 1932-42, 7¼", $200 to **$225.00**

South Bend, Panatella Minnow #913, white w/red nose, 3 belly-mounted treble hooks, 1912-42, 4½", from $40 to......**$50.00**

South Bend, Rock Hopper #675, red scales w/yellow underbelly, long nose, 1959, 2⅛", from $10 to............................ **$15.00**

South Bend, Tex-Oreno Sinker #995, flush-fitting metal weight beneath head, 2 treble hooks, 1938-39, 2¾" from $70 to.............. **$90.00**

South Bend, Vacuum Bait #1, red w/yellow eye detail, 3 treble hooks, 1921-38, 2½", from $175 to **$225.00**

South Bend, Wee-Nipper #T912, gray, 2 treble hooks, 2 propellers, 1952-53, 2⅜", from $10 to **$15.00**

South Bend, Wiz-Oreno #967, yellow w/green scales, extended spinnered belly hook, tail clip, 1925-29, 3", from $60 to....**$75.00**

South Bend, Spin-I-Oreno, carved eye, 1950s, from $15.00 to $20.00. (Photo courtesy Russell Lewis)

Fitz & Floyd

If you've ever visited a Fitz & Floyd outlet store, you know why collectors find this company's products so exciting. Steven Speilberg has nothing on their designers when it comes to imagination. Much of their production is related to holidays, and they've especially outdone themselves with their Christmas lines. But there are wonderful themes taken from nature featuring foxes, deer, birds, or rabbits, and others that are outrageously and deliberately humorous. Not only is the concept outstanding, so is the quality.

See also Cookie Jars.

Advisor: Susan Robson (See Directory Fitz & Floyd)

Cookie jar, Kitty Witches, 2002, 12½", from $30 to.......... **$35.00**
Cookie jar, Owl, c MCMLXXVII FF, from $40 to **$50.00**
Cookie jar, Pumpkin & Ghosts, 1999, 9x10", from $35 to . **$50.00**

Cookie jar, Santa and Reindeer in Biplane, 1986, $450.00. (Photo courtesy Fred and Joyce Roerig)

Cookie jar, Santa & Reindeer in Rolls Royce, 1986, 15" ...**$400.00**
Cookie jar, Santa & Reindeer on Harley Motorcycle, 1986, 15" ..**$400.00**
Dracula, candy jar, 1987, 8" **$100.00**
Dracula, mug, 1987 .... **$35.00**

Dinosaur, toothbrush holder, 1986, $25.00.
(Photo courtesy Sharon Robson)

Dracula, pitcher, 1987, 10".................................$150.00
Fables & Fairy Tales Collectors Teapot Series, Bremen Town
 Musicians, 1993..$150.00
Fables & Fairy Tales Collectors Teapot Series, Little Red Riding
 Hood, 1993 ....$150.00
Fables & Fairy Tales Collectors Teapot Series, Old Woman in a Shoe,
 1993 ....$150.00
Fables & Fairy Tales Collectors Teapot Series, 3 Little Pigs,
 1993 ....$150.00
Halloween, bowl, serving; witch, 1987.................$125.00
Halloween, chip & dip, pumpkin & ghost, 1987 ....$85.00
Halloween, pitcher, pumpkin & black cat, 1987.........$100.00
Halloween Harvest, candy jar, owl & cart, 1996, 7¼".......$200.00
Halloween Harvest, candy jar, white cat, 1996.........$450.00
Halloween Harvest, cookie jar, owl, 1996, 11" $450.00
Halloween Harvest, cookie jar, witch (boo inside), 1987 ...$125.00
Halloween Harvest, platter, 1996, 19" $95.00
Halloween Harvest, teapot, tree trunk w/ghosts, 1996.......$200.00
Halloween Hoedown, canape plate, witch, 1993.........$50.00
Halloween Hoedown, candy bowl, witch, 1993, 12" $150.00
Halloween Hoedown, cookie jar, witch, 1993, 12" $200.00
Halloween Hoedown, creamer & sugar bowl, w/spoon, 1993 ..$75.00
Halloween Hoedown, teapot, witch, 1993, 9" $145.00
Harvest Farm, bookends, Gretta & Sheila, 1994.........$130.00
Harvest Farm, cookie jar, Piggly Pig, 1994............$200.00
Harvest Farm, pitcher, Rapunzel Rabbit, 1994 ....$150.00
Harvest Farm, teapot, Prudence Pig, 1994 ....$150.00
Harvest Farm, tray, sectioned, 1994 ....$150.00
Harvest Farm, tureen, Henrietta Hen, w/ladle & liner, 1994 .$400.00
Hummingbird Collection, condiment server, 3-part, 1987, 12" .$65.00
Hummingbird Collection, teapot, 1987, 7½" $75.00
Hummingbird Collection, vase, 1987, 14" $45.00
Important Women Teapot Series, Betsy Ross, 1993 ....$150.00
Important Women Teapot Series, Cleopatra, 1993.........$165.00
Important Women Teapot Series, Queen Victoria, 1993....$150.00
MacDonald's County Fair, box, pig, 1995...............$100.00
MacDonald's County Fair, cookie jar, cow, 1995 ....$200.00
MacDonald's County Fair, cookie jar, duck, 1995.........$200.00
MacDonald's County Fair, pitcher, country store, 1995.....$135.00
MacDonald's County Fair, platter, oval, 1995 ....$150.00
MacDonald's County Fair, teapot, boy pig, 1995.........$125.00
Paint Party, cookie jar, Hedda Gobbler (turkey), 1995.....$350.00
Paint Party, teapot, bear & squirrels, 1995 ....$200.00
Pilgrim's Progress, candleholders, 1991, pr............$150.00

Pilgrim's Progress, creamer & sugar bowl, 1991 ....$100.00
Pilgrim's Progress, gravy boat w/underplate, 1991............$200.00
Pilgrim's Progress, pitcher, female pilgrim, 1991, 10".........$220.00
Pilgrim's Progress, pitcher, male pilgrim, 1991, 8" $200.00
Pilgrim's Progress, platter, 1991, 18" $175.00
Pilgrim's Progress, teapot, turkey, 1991, 8½"...............$185.00
Pilgrim's Progress, tureen, w/ladle & round undertray, 1991...$400.00
Polka Dot Witch, cookie jar, 11" $150.00
Polka Dot Witch, mug, cauldron w/witch & broom............$25.00
Polka Dot Witch, mug, witch face $30.00
Polka Dot Witch, string holder $125.00
Rub A Dub, bowl, Cat Nap, 1978, 8" $50.00
Rub A Dub, soap dish, bubble-bath woman, w/lid, 1978 ....$45.00
Rub A Dub, string holder, Cat-Snip, 1978 ....$50.00
Rub A Dub, string holder, kangaroo, 1978 ....$150.00

Flashlights

The flashlight was invented in 1898 and has been produced by the Eveready Company for these past 105 years. Eveready dominated the flash light market for most of this period, but more than 125 other U.S. flashlight companies have come and gone, providing competition along the way. Add to that number more than 35 known foreign flashlight manufacturers, and you end up with over 1,000 different models of flashlights to collect. They come in a wide variety of styles, shapes, and sizes. The flashlight field includes tubular, lanterns, figural, novelty, litho, etc. At present over 45 different categories of flashlights have been identified as collectible. For further information we recommend *Flashlights, Early Flashlight Makers of the First 100 Years of Eveready*, by Bill Utley.

Unless otherwise noted, our values are for examples in excellent plus to near-mint condition.

Advisor: Bill Utley (See Directory, Flashlights)

Newsletter: *Flashlight Collectors of America*
Bill Utley
P.O. Box 4095
Tustin, CA 92781
714-730-1252

Armax, lantern type w/Winchester 6-volt battery, 10½x10½",
 EX $35.00
Armax, nickel over brass, last copyright date: March 30, 1926, non-
 working, 7" $235.00
Bantam, cream paint on metal base w/bluebird decal, plastic flip top,
 Pat 2-2412313, EX.....................................$40.00
Bond Electric Co, black body, built-on adjustable stand, beveled
 glass lens, 2-cell, working..............................$45.00
Chase Bomb, nickel body, hang from wrist or place on table, uses 2
 C-cell batteries, #22001, ca 1933-42, 3½" dia, EX.......$45.00
Eveready, black paint on brass body, holds 3 D-cell batteries, #2642,
 ca 1925, 9½x3¼" dia, EX................................$45.00
Eveready, brass, sliding on/off switch, Pat Dec 12, 1912, 3x1⅜x¾",
 EX $25.00

Eveready, ribbed battery tube, Shriner symbols, Islam Temple San Francisco 1922, Pat Jan 9, 1917, working.....................$40.00

Eveready by Daylo, chrome-plated, 1920s, 3½x2½x1½", EX w/ instructions $27.50

Flasher, red plastic dog figural, eyes light up, Flasher Is Your Best Friend... on base, 1940s, 5½x5¼", EX $30.00

General Electric, radio/flashlight combination w/squeeze light, AM stations, Japan, ca 1950s, EX $27.50

Homart, brass body, thick curved lens, takes 2 D-cell batteries, 7⅜", EX $32.00

Hong Kong British Empire, Aladdin-lamp shape, Bakelite plastic, 2 C batteries, ca 1950s, EX...$20.00

Kel-lite, gold anodized aluminum, Don Keller design w/white switch & black tail cap...$75.00

Ox Power Chief Spotlight, metal telescoping case, 3-way switch, Made in Hong Kong, 6⅞-9", NMIB $10.00

Ray-O-Vac, brass w/black enameling, ca 1930-31, 6¾", EX ..$22.50

Red Head, USA Lite, Pat Dec 20, 1921, ca 1936, sm dent, otherwise EX $465.00

Winchester, silver-tone, 5 D cells, glass lens, 3½" dia face, 14½" L $40.00

Eveready, ca 1920s, 7½", any model shown, $35.00. (Photo courtesy Bill Utley)

Florence Ceramics

During the 1940s Florence Ward began modeling tiny ceramic children as a hobby at her home in Pasadena, California. She was so happy with the results that she expanded, hired decorators, and moved into a larger building where for two decades she produced the lovely line of figurines, wall plaques, busts, etc., that have become so popular today. The 'Florence Collection' featured authentically detailed models of such couples as Louis XV and Madame Pompadour, Pinkie and Blue Boy, and Rhett and Scarlett. Nearly all of the Florence figures have names which are written on their bases.

Many figures are decorated with 22k gold and lace. Real lace was cut to fit, dipped in a liquid material called slip, and fired. During the firing it burned away, leaving only hardened ceramic lace trim. The amount of lace work that was used is one of the factors that needs to be considered when evaluating a 'Florence.' Size is another. Though most of the figures you'll find today are singles, a few were made as groups, and once in awhile you'll find a lady seated on a divan. The more complex, the more expensive.

There are Florence figurines that are very rare and unusual, i.e., Mark Anthony, Cleopatra, Story Hour, Grandmother and I, Carmen, Dear Ruth, Spring and Fall Reverie, Clocks, and many others. These may be found with a high price; however, there are bargains still to be had.

Our wide range of values reflects the amounts of detailing and lace work present. If you'd like to learn more about the subject, we recommend *The Complete Book of Florence, A Labor of Love,* by Barbara and Jerry Kline, our advisors for this category, and Margaret Wehrspaun. (Ordering information may be found in the Directory.) Other references include *The Collector's Encyclopedia of California Pottery, Second Edition,* by Jack Chipman; and *The Florence Collectibles, An Era of Elegance,* by Doug Foland.

Advisors: Jerry and Barbara Kline (See Directory, Florence Ceramics)

Club: Florence Ceramics Collectors Club (FCCS)
Jerry Kline
PO Box 468
Bennington, VT 05201
802-442-3336
www.sweetpea.net
sweetpea@sweetpea.net and florenceCeramics@aol.com

Louis XV and Madame Pompadour, 12", $800.00 for the pair.

Amelia, 8¼" $275.00

Baby, flower holder, from $75 to......................................$100.00

Blossom Girl, flower holder $125.00

Blue Boy, 11¾", from $400 to..$450.00

Butch, 5½", from $175 to $200.00

Cindy, 8", from $425 to $475.00

Claudia, 8¼", from $250 to..$275.00

Darleen, 8¼", from $825 to $900.00

Delia, yellow, hand showing, 7¼", from $325 to $375.00

Eve, 8½", from $375 to $425.00

Gary, 8½", from $150 to $170.00

Halloween Child, 4", from $600 to $700.00

Jennifer, 7¾", from $450 to $500.00

John Alden, 9¼", from $250 to $275.00

Joy, child, 6", from $175 to $200.00

Kathy, white dress w/pink & blue flowers, flower holder, 7", from $60 to $70.00

Lillian, 7¼" $150.00

Louise, 7½", from $125 to...................................$140.00

Madonna, 10½", from $500 to $550.00

Marie Antoinette, 10", from $375 to $400.00

Mary, seated, 7½", from $650 to $700.00

Masquerade, rare, 8¼", from $800 to $900.00

Master David, rare, 8", from $500 to........................$550.00

Memories, Grandmother with book, 6½", $250.00.

Nita, 8", from $500 to......................................$550.00

Oriental couple, in aqua & white, 7¾", pr from $125 to ..$140.00

Pamela, 7¼", from $350 to..................................$400.00

Pinkie, white dress w/pink belt & hat w/ribbon, 11½", from $400 to $450.00

Rhett, beige w/green trim, 9", from $325 to.................$375.00

Scarlett, beige dress w/green trim, brown hair, 9", from $200 to $250.00

Story Hour w/Boy & Girl, 8", from $1,100 to $1,250.00

Sue Ellen, 8¼", from $160 to $175.00

Summer, 6¼", from $400 to $450.00

Victor, 9¼", from $275 to $325.00

Vivian, lamp, 10", from $550 to $650.00

Yvonne, plain, 8¾", from $425 to $500.00

Flower Frogs

Flower frogs reached their peak of popularity in the United States in the 1920s and 1930s. During that nearly every pottery and glasshouse in the United States produced some type of flower frog. At the same time numbers of ceramic flower frogs were being imported from Germany and Japan. Dining tables and sideboards were adorned with flowers sparingly placed around dancing ladies, birds, and aquatic animals in shallow bowls.

In the 1930s garden clubs began holding competitions in cut flower arranging. The pottery and glass flower frogs proved inadequate for the task and a new wave of metal flower frogs entered the market. Some were simple mesh, hairpin, and needle holders; but many were fanciful creations of loops, spirals, and crimped wires.

German and Japanese imports ceased during World War II, and only a very few American pottery and glass companies continued to produce flower frogs into the 1940s and 1950s. Metal flower frog production followed a similar decline; particularly after the water soluble florist foam, Oasis, was invented in 1954. For further information we recommend *Flower Frogs for Collectors* (Schiffer) by our advisor, Bonnie Bull.

Advisor: Bonnie Bull (See Directory, Flower Frogs)

Bird w/long beak stands on blue base w/7 openings, multicolor, ceramic, Made in Japan, 4½x3⅜" $28.00

Amber glass w/14 holes & 3 sm raised feet, 1½x4" dia........$30.00

Bird, lustre and shiny glazes, Japan, 7", from $50.00 to $75.00. (Photo courtesy Carole Bess White)

Bird, orange & green on blue lustre base w/6 openings, ceramic, Japan...$18.00

Bird on branch, multicolor, ceramic, Japan, 5½x3¼" $20.00

Bird perched on arched piece on ring w/4 openings, multicolor, ceramic, Made in Czechoslovakia, 4¼" dia $42.50

Birds (2) on stepped tree-trunk base, blue & orange lustre, 7 holes in base, ceramic, Japan, 5½x2¾" $20.00

Bluebird perched on peach lustre base w/6 holes, ceramic, Made in Japan, 2½x1¼" $30.00

Draped lady, amber glass, Cambridge, 8½".....................$150.00

Draped lady, light emerald glass, Cambridge, 8½" $160.00

Fish (2) w/6 flower tubes, marked w/Oriental characters in oval, 4½" L, VG $105.00

Fish in C-like position resting lower body on base, majolica-like, Jamieson's Capistrano Calif mark, 6¼x7½" $28.00

Frog, jade green opaque glass, Northwood, 4" L...............$110.00

Frog, marked Hand Painted Japan, 5", from $45.00 to $55.00. (Photo courtesy Bonnie Bull)

Frog on lily pad w/bloom, cast metal, 2¼x3½", VG............$75.00

Green vaseline glass w/13 holes, Depression era, 4½" dia, NM ..$30.00

Mermaid on flower-topped base, glossy white w/pastel flowers (openings in centers), porcelain, 1940s-50s, 7"..........$175.00

Nude dancing, glossy white w/creamy-tan scarf, left leg raised, ceramic, Germany, 7½" $90.00

Nude lady dancing w/long rope of flowers on rocky base, white w/multicolor details, ceramic, Germany, ca 1930s, 7¼" .$125.00

Nude lady dancing w/scarf, pastels on white porcelain, Germany, 1930s, 7½" $185.00

Nude lady sitting on tree stump, green frosted glass, drape across lower body, ribbed base, 7x3¼" $150.00

Nude on rock, Muskota, pottery, Weller, 8"......................$700.00

Nude sitting on base, creamy white, ceramic, Yanko Ware Made in Japan, 7¼x4¾x4½" $30.00

Nude standing w/scarf behind her, white porcelain, Germany Sp 493, 5"..$115.00

Parakeet on stump, bright multicolor glazes, ceramic, Made in Czechoslovakia, #48, 5"...$30.00

Parakeet perched on limb across 2 stumps, majolica-like glazes, 3 holes to place flowers, Japan, 3½" $30.00

Parrot on base w/openings & single red tulip, multicolor lustre, Made in Japan mark $22.00

Parrot on stump, multicolor details on white porcelain, Germany, 6"..$40.00

Sailboat, white matt, 8 openings along body, Made in California, USA, #43...$35.00

Sailing ship in rough sea, vaseline glass, 12 holes, 10x6½" dia (base) $200.00

Seminude dancer w/long drape, head up, 21 holes in base, white, ceramic, Made in Japan mark, 7"...................$58.00

Silver-plated lotus shape w/pointed petals, 2-pc, Reed & Barton . $25.00

Snail w/openings on back, ivory gloss, ceramic, Shawnee (unmarked), 4x5"..$27.50

Sun-colored amethyst glass, 16 openings, 1½x3½" dia $55.00

Swan w/wings raised, white satin glaze, pottery, signed AA, Van Briggle, 8½x8¼x4" $75.00

Turtle, green glass, 7 holes, Westmoreland, 4½" L............$100.00

Turtle, heavy pot metal w/needle base insert, 4½" L, VG $50.00

Two Kids, amber glass, Cambridge, 9¼"..........................$275.00

Fostoria

This was one of the major glassware producers of the twentieth century. They were located first in Fostoria, Ohio, but by the 1890s had moved to Moundsville, West Virginia. By the late 1930s they were recognized as the largest producers of handmade glass in the world. Their glassware is plentiful today and, considering its quality, not terribly expensive.

Though the company went out of business in the mid-'80s, the Lancaster Colony Company continues to use some of the old molds — herein is the problem. The ever-popular American and Coin Glass patterns are currently in production, and even experts have trouble distinguishing the old from the new. Before you invest in either line, talk to dealers. Ask them to show you some of their old pieces. Most will be happy to help out a novice collector. Read *Elegant Glassware of the Depression Era* by Gene and Cathy Florence and *The Fostoria Value Guide* by Milbra Long and Emily Seate.

You'll be seeing a lot of inferior 'American' at flea markets and (sadly) antique malls. It's often priced as though it is American, but in fact it is not. It's been produced since the 1950s by Indiana Glass who calls it 'Whitehall.' Watch for pitchers with only two mold lines, they're everywhere. (Fostoria's had three.) Remember that Fostoria was handmade, so their pieces were fire polished. This means that if the piece you're examining has sharp, noticeable mold lines, be leery. There are other differences to watch for as well. Fostoria's footed pieces were designed with a 'toe,' while Whitehall feet have a squared peg-like appearance. The rays are sharper and narrower on the genuine Fostoria pieces, and the glass itself has more sparkle and life. And if it weren't complicated enough, the Home Interior Company sells 'American'-like vases, covered bowls, and a footed candy dish that were produced in a foreign country, but at least they've marked theirs.

Coin Glass was originally produced in crystal, red, blue, emerald green, olive green, and amber. It's being reproduced today in crystal, green (darker than the original), blue (a lighter hue), and red. Though the green and blue are 'off' enough to be pretty obvious, the red is very close. Beware. Here are some (probably not all) of the items currently in production: bowl, 8" diameter; bowl, 9" oval; candlesticks, 4½"; candy jar with lid, 6¼"; creamer and sugar bowl; footed comport; wedding bowl, 8¼". Know your dealer!

Numbers included in our descriptions were company-assigned stock numbers that collectors use as a means to distinguish variations in stems and shapes.

See also Glass Animals and Related Items.

Newsletter/Club: *Facets of Fostoria*
Fostoria Glass Society of America
P.O. Box 826, Moundsville, WV 26041
Membership: $12.50 per year

Alexis, crystal, egg cup $12.50

Alexis, crystal, nappy, 8" $22.50

Alexis, crystal, nut bowl $15.00

Alexis, crystal, pitcher, ice; 64-oz........................$85.00
Alexis, crystal, spooner $30.00
American, crystal, ashtray, oval, 5½"...................$20.00
American, crystal, bottle, cordial; w/stopper, 9-oz, 7¼" $90.00
American, crystal, bowl, bonbon; 3-footed, 8" $17.50
American, crystal, candy box, triangular, 3-part $90.00
American, crystal, spooner, 3¾" $35.00

American, crystal, vase, 9", $45.00.

American, crystal, vase, swung; 14"....................$250.00
American Beauty, crystal, pitcher, 48-oz, 8" $195.00
Baroque, blue, bowl, pickle; 8" $32.50
Baroque, blue, tray, oval, 12½" $85.00

Baroque, blue, vases: 6½", $125.00; 7", $165.00. (Photo courtesy Gene and Cathy Florence)

Baroque, crystal, bowl, punch; footed, 1½-gal, 8¼x13¼" ..$400.00
Baroque, crystal, plate, torte; 14" $28.00
Baroque, yellow, ashtray $15.00
Baroque, yellow, sugar bowl, footed, 3½" $20.00
Brocade, #287 Grape, blue, candy box, 3-part, #2331 ....$185.00
Brocade, #287 Grape, green, tray, round, fleur-de-lis handle, #2387 ....$90.00
Brocade, #287 Grape, orchid, vase, #4100, 8" $135.00

Brocade, #289 Paradise, green or orchid, compote, stacked disk stem, footed, #2362, 11" **$100.00**
Brocade, #290 Oakleaf, crystal, bowl, mint; #2394, 4½" $30.00
Brocade, #290 Oakleaf, green or rose, candlestick, scroll, #2395, 3", ea **$65.00**
Brocade, #72 Oakwood, azure or orchid, tumbler, footed, #877, 9-oz.....**$85.00**
Brocade, #73 Palm Leaf, green or rose, cake plate, #2375, 10" ..**$155.00**
Coin, amber, ashtray, #1372/124, 10" $25.00
Coin, amber, cruet, w/stopper, #1372/531, 7-oz...............$65.00
Coin, crystal, candleholders, #1372/326, 8", pr...............$50.00
Coin, crystal, tumbler, #1372/73, 9-oz, 4¼" $22.00
Coin, green, bowl, #1372/179, 8" $70.00
Coin, green, nappy, #1372/495, 4½".....................$22.00
Coin, ruby, candy jar, w/lid, #1372/347, 6⁵⁄₁₆" $50.00
Coin, ruby, vase, bud; #1372/799, 8" $45.00
Colony, crystal, ashtray, sq, 2⅞" $12.00
Colony, crystal, bowl, almond; footed, 2¾" $20.00
Colony, crystal, butter dish, ¼-lb $45.00
Colony, crystal, compote, low foot, 4" $17.50
Colony, crystal, crystal, bowl, olive; oblong, 7" ..$14.00
Colony, crystal, goblet, 9-oz, 5¼"........................$15.00
Colony, crystal, ice bucket, plain edge................$225.00
Colony, crystal, pitcher, milk; 16-oz....................$65.00
Colony, crystal, plate, dinner; 9"..........................$25.00
Colony, crystal, salt & pepper shakers, 3⅝", pr.................$28.00
Colony, crystal, tumbler, tea; 12-oz, 4⅞" $40.00
Colony, crystal, vase, cornucopia; 9".....................$80.00
Fairfax No 2375, amber, baker, oval, 9" $16.00
Fairfax No 2375, amber, oil cruet, footed $85.00
Fairfax No 2375, amber, sugar pail $35.00
Fairfax No 2375, amber, whipped cream pail.........$35.00
Fairfax No 2375, green or topaz, bowl, dessert; handles, lg..$30.00
Fairfax No 2375, green or topaz, cigarette box.....................$25.00
Fairfax No 2375, green or topaz, creamer, footed................$10.00
Fairfax No 2375, green or topaz, platter, oval, 12"...............$45.00
Fairfax No 2375, rose, blue or orchid, creamer, footed........$15.00
Fairfax No 2375, rose, blue or orchid, lemon dish, handles, 6¾" $95.00
Fairfax No 2375, rose, blue or orchid, plate, chop; 13"...........$30.00
Fairfax No 2375, rose, blue or orchid, sauceboat.................$50.00
Fuchsia, crystal, bowl, #2395, 10" $95.00
Fuchsia, crystal, lemon dish, #2470 ....$32.00
Fuchsia, crystal, parfait, footed, #6004, 5½-oz, 6" $85.00
Fuchsia, crystal, plate, luncheon; #2440, 8" $22.00
Fuchsia, crystal, saucer, #2440 ....$7.50
Fuchsia, crystal, sugar bowl, footed, #2440 ....$30.00
Fuchsia, crystal, tumbler, #833, 8-oz....................$22.00
Fuchsia, Wisteria, bowl, #2470, 12" $175.00
Fuchsia, Wisteria, compote, tall, #2470, 6"..........$150.00
Fuchsia, Wisteria, cordial, #6004, ¾-oz................$195.00
Fuchsia, Wisteria, tumbler, footed, #6004, 12-oz....$75.00
Glacier, crystal, bowl, fruit; 5" $15.00
Glacier, crystal, creamer, footed..........................$15.00
Glacier, crystal, cup...$10.00
Glacier, crystal, decanter, rectangular $100.00
Glacier, crystal, plate, torte; 11".........................$35.00

Glacier, crystal, rose bowl, 5" $40.00
Glacier, crystal, salt dip $18.00
Glacier, crystal, sherbet, 5½-oz, 3½" $11.00
Glacier, crystal, tray, condiment; 8½" $60.00
Glacier, crystal, tumbler, whiskey; 2-oz, 2¼" $10.00

Hermitage, amber, green, or topaz, pitcher, three-pint, $100.00. (Photo courtesy Gene and Cathy Florence)

Hermitage, Wisteria, pitcher, #2449, 3-pt.....................$595.00
June, blue or rose, bottle, salad dressing; #2083 or #2375, ea . $995.00
June, blue or rose, creamer, footed, #2375½ $28.00
June, blue or rose, goblet, claret; 4-oz, 6" $165.00
June, blue or rose, pitcher, footed, #5000 ....$695.00
June, blue or rose, platter, #2375, 12" $125.00
June, blue or rose, sauceboat $295.00
June, crystal, bowl, soup; 7" $65.00
June, crystal, ice dish $35.00
June, crystal, plate, bread & butter; 6" $7.00
June, crystal, saucer, after dinner $6.00
June, crystal, vase, fan shape, footed, 8½" $90.00
June, topaz, bowl, Grecian, 10" $95.00
June, topaz, oil cruet, footed $350.00
June, topaz, plate, canape $30.00
June, topaz, tumbler, water; 9-oz, 5¼" $25.00
June, topaz, whipped cream pail...................................$175.00
Kashmir, blue, ashtray...$30.00
Kashmir, blue, bowl, pickle; 8½" $30.00
Kashmir, blue, candy dish, w/lid, #2430 ....$165.00
Kashmir, blue, creamer, footed $23.00
Kashmir, blue, pitcher, footed......................................$495.00
Kashmir, blue, plate, dinner; 10" $75.00
Kashmir, green or yellow, cup, #2350½.........................$15.00
Kashmir, green or yellow, plate, bread & butter; 6" $6.00
Kashmir, green or yellow, plate, grill; 10" $35.00
Kashmir, green or yellow, saucer, sq, #2419 ....$5.00
Kashmir, green or yellow, sherbet, tall, #5099, 6-oz $17.50
Kashmir, green or yellow, sugar bowl, footed $20.00
Kashmir, green or yellow, tumbler, footed, 12-oz $25.00
Kashmir, green or yellow, vase, 8" $125.00
Lafayette, burgundy, cake plate, oval, handles, 10½" $65.00
Lafayette, crystal or amber, bowl, olive; 6½" $18.00
Lafayette, Empire Green, creamer, footed, 4½" $40.00
Lafayette, Regal Blue, cup $35.00
Lafayette, rose, green or topaz, plate, torte; 13" $50.00
Lafayette, Wisteria, sugar bowl, footed, 3⅝" $45.00
Narcissus, crystal, cocktail, #3408, 3-oz $18.00
Narcissus, crystal, plate, luncheon; #1519, 8" $16.00

Narcissus, crystal, salt & pepper shakers, #1519, pr $75.00
Narcissus, crystal, tumbler, juice; footed, #3408, 5-oz.........$24.00
Navarre, crystal, bowl, tricornered, #2496, 4⅝" $22.00

Navarre, crystal, console bowl, 10½", $95.00.

Navarre, crystal, mayonnaise, 3-pc, #2375 ....$65.00
Navarre, crystal, plate, salad; #2440, 7½" $14.00
Navarre, crystal, syrup, metal cut-off top, #2586, 5½".......$450.00
Navarre, crystal, tidbit, turned-up edge, 3-footed, #2496, 8¼". $28.00
Navarre, crystal, tumbler, juice; footed, #6106, 5-oz, 4⅝" ...$22.00
Navarre, crystal, vase, #4128, 5" $135.00
New Garland, amber or topaz, bowl, baker; 10" $35.00
New Garland, amber or topaz, pitcher, footed $250.00
New Garland, amber or topaz, vase, 8" $75.00
New Garland, rose, cordial, #6002................................$40.00
New Garland, rose, cup, after dinner; #2419 ....$25.00
New Garland, rose, relish dish, 8½" $18.00
Pioneer, amber, crystal or green, butter dish...................$75.00
Pioneer, amber, crystal or green, plate, 10" $17.50
Pioneer, blue, bowl, bouillon; flat $14.00
Pioneer, blue, platter, 15" $35.00
Pioneer, Ebony, ashtray, 3¾" $18.00
Pioneer, Ebony, saucer..$4.00
Pioneer, rose or topaz, compote, 8" $30.00
Pioneer, rose or topaz, egg cup $25.00
Priscilla, amber or green, creamer....................................$9.00
Priscilla, amber or green, cup $9.00
Priscilla, amber or green, custard, footed, handles $8.00
Priscilla, amber or green, pitcher, footed, 48-oz $125.00
Priscilla, amber or green, saucer $2.00
Priscilla, blue, ashtray, sq, 3" $12.50
Priscilla, blue, plate, 8"...$15.00
Priscilla, blue, sugar bowl $15.00
Priscilla, blue, tumbler, footed.......................................$22.50
Rogene, crystal, creamer, flat, #1851..............................$30.00
Rogene, crystal, decanter, cut neck, #300, qt $90.00
Rogene, crystal, mayonnaise ladle $22.50
Rogene, crystal, plate, w/cut star, 11" $27.50
Rogene, crystal, plate, 5"..$6.00
Rogene, crystal, saucer champagne, #5082, 5-oz.................$15.00
Rogene, crystal, sugar bowl, flat, #1851..........................$30.00
Rogene, crystal, tumbler, table; flat, #4076 ....$14.00
Rogene, crystal, vase, rolled edge, 8½" $100.00
Royal, amber or green, bowl, bouillon; flat, #2350 ....$15.00

Royal, amber or green, bowl, soup; #2350, 7¾" $32.00
Royal, amber or green, butter dish, #2350 .... $325.00
Royal, amber or green, candlestick, #2324, 4", ea $22.00
Royal, amber or green, cocktail, #869, 3-oz $20.00
Royal, amber or green, creamer, flat $18.00
Royal, amber or green, ice bucket, #2378 .... $65.00
Royal, amber or green, plate, salad; #2350, 7½" $4.00
Royal, amber or green, saucer, demitasse; #2350 .... $8.00
Royal, amber or green, sugar lid, #2350½ $135.00
Royal, amber or green, vase, flared, #2292 .... $110.00
Seville, amber, ashtray, #2350, 4" $17.50
Seville, amber, bowl, baker; oval, #2350, 9" $25.00
Seville, amber, cup, flat, #2350 .... $10.00
Seville, amber, platter, #2350, 15" $85.00
Seville, amber, urn, #2324, sm $75.00
Seville, green, bowl, bouillon; flat, #2350 .... $13.50
Seville, green, candy jar, w/lid, flat, 3-part, #2331 .... $95.00

Versaille, Azure, water goblet, 8", $40.00. (Photo courtesy Gene and Cathy Florence)

Seville, green, grapefruit bowl, $45.00. (Photo courtesy Gene and Cathy Florence)

Seville, green, pitcher, footed, #5084 .... $295.00
Seville, green, tray, center handle, #2287 .... $30.00
Sunray, crystal, ashtray, sq $12.00
Sunray, crystal, bowl, onion soup; w/lid $45.00
Sunray, crystal, bowl, rolled edge, 13" $40.00
Sunray, crystal, butter dish, ¼-lb $35.00
Sunray, crystal, cigarette box, oblong $25.00
Sunray, crystal, decanter, w/stopper, 18-oz $70.00
Sunray, crystal, nappy, tricornered, handles $15.00
Sunray, crystal, pitcher, cereal; 16-oz $50.00
Sunray, crystal, plate, torte; 15" $50.00
Sunray, crystal, tray, condiment; cloverleaf, 8½" $45.00
Sunray, crystal, vase, crimped, 6" $40.00
Trojan, rose, bowl, lemon; #2375 .... $24.00
Trojan, rose, cake plate, handles, #2375, 10" $65.00
Trojan, rose, celery, #2375, 11½" $38.00
Trojan, rose, mayonnaise ladle $30.00
Trojan, rose, vase, #4105, 8" $275.00
Trojan, topaz, ashtray, lg, #2350 .... $28.00
Trojan, topaz, bowl, fruit; #2375, 5" $22.00
Trojan, topaz, bowl, grapefruit; #5282½ $45.00
Trojan, topaz, plate, chop; #2375, 13" $65.00
Trojan, topaz, sugar bowl, tea; #2375½ $40.00
Trojan, topaz, whipped cream pail, #2378 .... $115.00

Versailles, blue, ashtray, #2350 .... $35.00
Versailles, blue, cheese & cracker set, #2375 or #2368 ...... $125.00
Versailles, blue, ice dish, #2451 .... $65.00
Versailles, blue, plate, canape; #2375, 6" $35.00
Versailles, green, bottle, salad dressing; crystal glass top, #2083 .... $695.00
Versailles, green, bowl, cereal; #2375, 6½" $55.00
Versailles, green, salt & pepper shakers, footed, #2375, pr . $150.00
Versailles, green, vase, fan shape, footed, #2385, 8½" $295.00
Versailles, pink or yellow, creamer, tea; #2375½ $40.00
Versailles, pink or yellow, pitcher, #5000 .... $395.00
Versailles, pink or yellow, relish, 2-part, #2375, 8½" $38.00
Versailles, pink or yellow, tray, service & lemon $250.00
Vesper, amber, butter dish, #2350 .... $850.00
Vesper, amber, cheese, footed, #2368 .... $25.00
Vesper, amber, plate, center handle, #2287, 11" $35.00
Vesper, amber, sherbet, tall, #5093 .... $18.00
Vesper, blue, bowl, bouillon; footed, #2350 .... $36.00
Vesper, blue, candy jar, footed, w/lid, 3-part, #2331 .... $295.00
Vesper, blue, tumbler, footed, #5100, 9-oz $50.00
Vesper, blue, vanity set, combination cologne/powder & stopper $425.00
Vesper, green, bowl, soup; shallow, #2350, 7¾" $30.00
Vesper, green, compote, 8" $55.00
Vesper, green, cup, after dinner; #2350 .... $42.00
Vesper, green, urn, lg $115.00
Woodland, crystal, compote, 5" $25.00
Woodland, crystal, finger bowl, #766, 4½" $75.00
Woodland, crystal, jelly bowl, w/lid, #825 .... $25.00
Woodland, crystal, marmalade, w/lid, #4089 .... $37.50
Woodland, crystal, night bottle, #1697, 23-oz $65.00
Woodland, crystal, oil cruet, w/stopper, #1465, 7-oz $50.00
Woodland, crystal, pitcher, #300, 65-oz $175.00
Woodland, crystal, plate, luncheon; #2238, 8¼" $8.00
Woodland, crystal, salt & pepper shakers, #2022, pr $40.00
Woodland, crystal, sweetmeat, #766 .... $25.00

Woodland, crystal, syrup, w/cut-off top, #2194, 8-oz **$95.00**
Woodland, crystal, tumbler, tea; #889, 5½" **$14.00**
Woodland, crystal, wine, 2¾-oz **$14.00**

Franciscan Dinnerware

Franciscan is a trade name of Gladding McBean, used on their dinnerware lines from the mid-1930s until it closed its Los Angeles-based plant in 1984. They were the first to market 'starter sets' (four-place settings), a practice that today is commonplace.

Two of their earliest lines were El Patio (simply styled, made in bright solid colors) and Coronado (with swirled borders and pastel glazes). In the late '30s, they made the first of many hand-painted dinnerware lines. Some of the best known are Apple, Desert Rose, and Ivy. From 1941 to 1977, 'Masterpiece' (true porcelain) china was produced in more than 170 patterns.

Many marks were used, most included the Franciscan name. An 'F' in a square with 'Made in U.S.A.' below it dates from 1938, and a double-line script 'F' was used in more recent years.

For other hand-painted patterns not listed below, we recommend the following general guide for comparable pieces (based on current Desert Rose values).

Daisy .... -20%
October .... -20%
Cafe Royal .... Same as Desert Rose
Forget-Me-Not .... Same as Desert Rose
Meadow Rose .... Same as Desert Rose
Strawberry Fair .... Same as Desert Rose
Strawberry Time .... Same as Desert Rose
Fresh Fruit .... Same as Desert Rose
Bountiful .... Same as Desert Rose
Desert Rose .... Base-Line Values
Apple .... +10%
Ivy .... +20%
Poppy .... +50%
Original (small) Fruit .... +50%
Wild Flower .... 200% or more!

Advisors: Mick and Lorna Chase, Fiesta Plus (See Directory, Dinnerware)

Coronado

Bowl, cream soup; w/underplate, from $25 to **$40.00**
Bowl, nut cup; from $8 to **$12.00**
Bowl, serving, 8½" dia, from $10 to.................................**$17.00**
Bowl, serving; oval, 10½", from $20 to **$33.00**
Cup & saucer, demitasse; from $20 to **$32.00**
Fast-stand gravy, from $25 to...**$35.00**
Pitcher, 1½-qt, from $25 to..**$45.00**
Plate, chop; 14" dia, from $20 to.....................................**$30.00**
Plate, 7½", from $7 to...**$10.00**
Plate, 9½", from $10 to...**$15.00**
Plate, 10½", from $12 to...**$18.00**
Platter, oval, 13", from $24 to..**$36.00**

Relish dish, oval, from $12 to **$25.00**
Vase, 5¼" **$65.00**

Teapot, from $45.00 to $75.00; demitasse pot, from $100.00 to $150.00; butter dish, from $30.00 to $40.00; sugar bowl with lid, from $15.00 to $20.00; creamer, from $10.00 to $15.00.

Desert Rose

Ashtray, individual **$15.00**
Bell, Danbury Mint **$95.00**
Bowl, cereal; 6" **$15.00**
Bowl, mixing; lg **$175.00**
Bowl, rimmed soup **$25.00**
Box, cigarette **$95.00**
Box, round **$165.00**
Casserole, 2½-qt, minimum value....................................**$295.00**
Coffeepot, individual, from $300 to **$395.00**
Compote, low **$125.00**
Mug, barrel form, 12-oz...**$45.00**
Plate, chop; 12" **$50.00**
Plate, divided; child's..**$195.00**
Plate, 8½" **$12.00**
Plate, 10½" **$18.00**
Salt & pepper shakers, rose bud, pr..................................**$22.50**

Salt and pepper shakers, tall, $45.00 for the pair; syrup pitcher, $75.00.

Tea canister **$295.00**
Teacup & saucer...**$10.00**

Tidbit tray, 2-tier..$95.00
Tile, sq $50.00
Tumbler, 10-oz...$30.00

Starburst

Ashtray, individual $20.00
Bowl, crescent salad; 9½" L, from $50 to $60.00
Bowl, fruit; individual..$15.00
Bowl, vegetable; 8½"..$45.00
Canister/jar, w/lid, from $150 to $225.00
Cruet, vinegar/oil; ea from $80 to.....................$110.00
Mug, tall, 5", from $80 to.....................................$90.00
Pitcher, water; 10"...$135.00
Plate, luncheon; 9½", from $25 to.......................$35.00
Platter, 15" $65.00

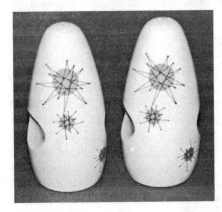

Salt and pepper shakers, $50.00 for the pair.

Snack/TV tray w/cup rest, 12½", from $80 to..................$110.00
Teapot, 5½x8½", from $175 to $225.00

Frankoma

John Frank opened a studio pottery in Norman, Oklahoma, in 1933, creating bowls, vases, etc., which bore the ink-stamped marks 'Frank Pottery' or 'Frank Potteries.' At this time, only a few hundred pieces were produced. Within a year, Mr. Frank had incorporated. Though not everything was marked, he continued to use these marks for two years. Items thus marked are not easy to find and command high prices. In 1935 the pot and leopard mark was introduced.

The Frank family moved to Sapulpa, Oklahoma, in 1938. In November of that year, a fire destroyed everything. The pot and leopard mark was never re-created, and today collectors avidly search for items with this mark. The rarest of all Frankoma marks is 'First Kiln a Sapulpa 6-7-38,' which was applied to only about 100 pieces fired on that date.

Grace Lee Frank worked beside her husband, creating many limited edition Madonna plates, Christmas cards, advertising items, birds, etc. She died in 1996.

Clay is important in determining when a piece was made. Ada clay, used through 1954, is creamy beige in color. In 1955 they changed over to a red brick shale from Sapulpa. Today most clay has a pinkish-red cast, though the pinkish cast is sometimes so muted that a novice might mistake it for Ada clay.

Rutile glazes were created early in the pottery's history; these give the ware a two-tone color treatment. However the US government closed the rutile mines in 1970, and Frank found it necessary to buy this material from Australia. The newer rutile produced different results, especially noticeable with their Woodland Moss glaze.

Upon John Frank's death in 1973, their daughter Joniece became president. Though the pottery burned again in 1983, the building was quickly rebuilt. Due to so many setbacks, however, the company found it necessary to file Chapter 11 in order to remain in control and stay in business.

Mr. Richard Bernstein purchased Frankoma in 1991. Sometime in 2001, Mr. Bernstein began to put the word out that Frankoma Pottery Company was for sale. It did not sell and because of declining sales, he closed the doors on December 23, 2004. The company sold July 1, 2005, to another pottery company owned by Det and Crystal Merryman of Las Vegas, Nevada. They took possession the next day and began bringing life back into the Frankoma Pottery once more. Today they are producing pottery from the Frankoma molds as well as their own pottery molds, which goes by the name of 'Merrymac Collection,' a collection of whimsical dogs.

Frank purchased Synar Ceramics of Muskogee, Oklahoma, in 1958; in late 1959, the name was changed to Gracetone Pottery in honor of Grace Lee Frank. Until supplies were exhausted, they continued to produce Synar's white clay line in glazes such as 'Alligator,' 'Woodpine,' 'White Satin,' 'Ebony,' 'Wintergreen,' and a black and white straw combination. At the Frankoma pottery, an 'F' was added to the stock number on items made at both locations. New glazes were Aqua, Pink Champagne, Cinnamon Toast, and Black, known as Gunmetal. Gracetone was sold in 1962 to Mr. Taylor, who had been a long-time family friend and manager of the pottery. Taylor continued operations until 1967. The only dinnerware pattern produced there was 'Orbit,' which is today hard to find. Other Gracetone pieces are becoming scarce as well.

If you'd like to learn more, we recommend *Frankoma Treasures* and *Frankoma and Other Oklahoma Potteries* by Phyllis Bess Boone.

Advisor: Phyllis Bess Boone (See Directory, Frankoma)

Club/Newsletter: Frankoma Family Collectors Association
c/o Nancy Littrell
P.O. Box 32571, Oklahoma City, OK 73123-0771
Membership dues: $35; includes newsletter and annual convention

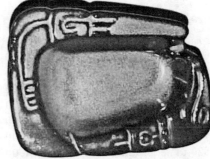

Christmas card, 1961, $50.00.

Ashtray, peach Glow, Sapulpa clay, #479.............................$25.00
Bean pot, Wagon Wheel, Prairie Green, horseshoe handles, #94W $55.00

Bookends, Charger Horse, Prairie Green, #420, 7" **$225.00**

Bowl, cereal; Plainsman, Desert Gold, Sapulpa clay, #5XL **$8.00**

Bowl, Plainsman, Prairie Green, 10⅝x18¾" **$50.00**

Candleholder, Oral Roberts, Desert Gold, Sapulpa clay, 1971, ea from $12 to **$18.00**

Christmas card, 1949, from $60 to **$70.00**

Christmas card, 1950-51, from $125 to **$150.00**

Christmas card, 1952, from $125 to **$140.00**

Christmas card, 1957 .... **$65.00**

Christmas card, 1958-61 .... **$50.00**

Christmas card, 1962-71 .... **$40.00**

Christmas card, 1972 .... **$35.00**

Christmas card, 1973-75 .... **$30.00**

Christmas card, 1976-83 .... **$25.00**

Cookie jar, Prairie Green, Sapulpa clay, #25K **$65.00**

Creamer & sugar bowl, Plainsman, Ada clay, #51/#5B **$35.00**

Decanter, Prairie Green, #7JH, w/lid, 10¼" **$55.00**

Flower frog, cross on base, Prairie Green, Sapulpa clay, 6½", from $75 to **$90.00**

Leaf dish, Dark Brown Satin, #226 .... **$12.00**

Mini pitcher, Spiral, Ivory, Ada clay, 2", from $75 to **$85.00**

Mug, Donkey, plum, 1983 .... **$35.00**

Mug, Elephant, black, 1997 .... **$30.00**

Mug, Elephant or Donkey, 1973-76, from $30 to **$40.00**

Mug, Elephant or Donkey, 1977-90, from $20 to **$30.00**

Mug, Mayan-Aztec, Prairie Green, 16-oz **$22.50**

Napkin rings, Butterfly, Sapulpa clay, #263, 4 for **$20.00**

Pitcher, batter; Desert Gold, Ada clay, #553, mini, from $20 to **$25.00**

Plate, dinner; Wagon wheel, Prairie Green, 10", from $22 to ... **$25.00**

Plate, Oklahoma State, Desert Gold **$25.00**

Plate, salad; Westwind, White Sand, 7" **$7.50**

Sculpture, greyhound, Autumn Yellow, 1983 limited edition, #827, from $200 to **$225.00**

Sculpture, Indian Bowl Maker, Prairie Green, Sapulpa clay, 6", $90.00. (If marked 'Taylor,' from $2,500.00 to $3,000.00.)

Sculpture, Pony Tail Girl, Desert Gold, Sapulpa clay, #106, from $90 to **$100.00**

Sculpture, Trojan Horse, Desert Gold, Ada clay, 2½", from $175 to **$185.00**

Trivet, Horseshoe, Desert Sand, 3-footed, #5TR, 6", from $22 to **$25.00**

Vase, bud; Snail, black, Ada clay, #31, from $45 to **$60.00**

Vase, collector; V-2, 1970, 12", from $80 to **$90.00**

Vase, collector; V-6, from $80 to **$90.00**

Vase, collector; V-8, w/stopper, 13" **$75.00**

Vase, collector; V-14, from $75 to **$80.00**

Vase, Mountain Haze, angle handles, Sapulpa clay, #20 .... **$25.00**

Vase, Ram's Head, Verde Bronze, Ada clay, 338, 5⅝x5⅛", from $65 to **$85.00**

Wall pocket, Woodland Moss, Sapulpa clay, #190, from $85 to **$95.00**

Wall vase, Phoebe, Black Onyx, #730, 1948-49, from $85 to .. **$95.00**

Freeman-McFarlin

This California-based company was the result of a union between Gerald McFarlin and Maynard Anthony Freeman, formed in the early 1950s and resulting in the production of a successful line of molded ceramic sculptures (predominately birds and animals, though human figures were also made) as well decorative items such as vases, flowerpots, bowls, etc. Anthony was the chief designer, and some of the items you fine today bear his name. Glazes ranged from woodtones and solid colors to gold leaf, sometimes in combination. The most collectible of the Freeman-McFarlin figures were designed by Kay Finch, who sold some of her molds to the company in the early 1960s. The company produced these popular sculptures in their own glazes without Kay's trademark curlicues, making them easy for today's collectors to distinguish from her original work. This line was so successful that in the mid-'60s the company hired Kay herself, and until the late '70s, she designed numerous new and original animal models. Most were larger and more realistically detailed than the work she did in her own studio. She worked for the company until 1980. Her pieces are signed.

In addition to the signatures already mentioned, you may find pieces incised 'Jack White' or 'Hetrick,' both free-lance designers affiliated with the company. Other marks include paper labels and an impressed mark 'F.McF, Calif USA,' often with a date.

For more information we recommend, *Collector's Encyclopedia of California Pottery* and *California Pottery Scrapbook* by Jack Chipman (Collector Books).

Figurine, reclining cat, gold leaf, #833, from $95.00. (Photo courtesy Jack Chipman)

Box, antique gold, Anthony, #585 USA, w/lid, 3½x6½" dia..**$42.50**

Figurine, cat, marked Anthony, #175 USA, 9"..................**$42.50**

Figurine, cat grooming itself, brown woodgrain glaze, signed Anthony, USA #198, 6x8x4" **$50.00**

Figurine, cow, purple w/gold trim, 3¾x4" **$20.00**

Figurine, German shepherd, recumbent, realistic coloring, 2x5"..**$42.50**

Figurine, goldfish, gold, Anthony, #348, paper label, 13" L. **$35.00**

Figurine, koala bear, gold, USA, 1970s, 5x9" **$20.00**

Figurine, mouse sitting, gray gloss w/black eyes, 6".............**$25.00**

Figurine, mushrooms, bright orange, 8x10", 5½x7½", pr....**$25.00**

Figurine, parrot on tall perch, cream w/brown accents, Anthony, 11" **$110.00**

Figurine, Siamese cat reclining, Anthony, #177, gold sticker, NM **$50.00**

Figurine, Siamese kitten, head up, blue eyes, 4x4" **$40.00**

Figurine, Virgin Mary, gold, Anthony, 1960s, 20x3" **$65.00**

Figurines, cats sitting, gold, Anthony, #137 USA/illegible, 12¾", 12", pr...**$75.00**

Figurines, ducks standing & sitting, #125/#126, 1970s, 8x5", 5x5", pr...**$35.00**

Figurines, kittens standing & sitting, Anthony, #123/#124, 7¼", 10x7", pr...**$45.00**

Nodder, Siamese-like cat, brown tones, sm **$42.50**

Planter/dresser caddy, hound dog, brown tones w/white at neck & mouth, paper label...**$20.00**

Planter/dresser caddy, St Bernard w/keg under his neck, brown & yellow tones, 4¾x7"..**$20.00**

Plaque, blond mermaid child w/2 separate gold bubbles, 5", 3-pc set **$75.00**

Plaque/wall pocket set, lg fish (wall pocket) & 2 babies, 3-pc set **$45.00**

Soap dish, mermaid beside scalloped shell, blond hair, 8½x8".. **$60.00**

Vase, green, gold & teal mottle, Deco shape, USA Calif #548, 4¼x3⅝"..**$20.00**

Vase, green w/gold & brown ridges, flared foot, w/label, 10½x5" **$20.00**

Furniture

A piece of furniture can often be difficult to date, since many seventeenth- and eighteenth-century styles have been reproduced. Even a piece made early in the twentieth century now has enough age on it that it may be impossible for a novice to distinguish it from the antique. Sometimes cabinetmakers may have trouble identifying specific types of wood, since so much variation can occur within the same species; so although it is usually helpful to try to determine what kind of wood a piece has been made of, results are sometimes inconclusive. Construction methods are usually the best clues. Watch for evidence of twentieth century tools — automatic routers, lathes, carvers, and spray guns.

For further information we recommend *Early American Furniture* by John W. Obbard, *Heywood-Wakefield Modern Furniture* by Steve Rouland and Roger Rouland; and *The Market Place Guide to American Oak Furniture* by Peter S. Blundell. All are published by Collector Books.

Armchair, quartersawn oak, vase splat, claw feet, needlepoint seat, early 1900s, 38" **$195.00**

Armchair rocker, dark oak Mission style w/leather back & seat, 39" **$325.00**

Armchair rocker, natural wicker w/apron, upholstered seat cushion, Bar Harbor, 35x29½x36" **$350.00**

Armchair rocker, painted steel w/minor rust, EX **$90.00**

Armoire, oak w/geometric Deco design on front, zebrawood inlay below hat door, Bakelite knobs, 1930s, 60x36x19".....**$275.00**

Bed, dark oak w/applied decorations, tall arched headboard, low footboard, refinished, full size **$695.00**

Bed, dark oak w/pineapple-like finials, twin size **$375.00**

Bed, mahogany w/applied maple strips, Paul Frankl for Johnston Furniture, 32x42" headboard..**$375.00**

Bed, oak Louis XV style, ca 1940, full size, 45" H headboard . **$900.00**

Bed frame, painted iron, simple style w/4 brass knobs, 59x78x54", EX **$325.00**

Bench, white painted wicker, w/arms & apron, cushion seat, 25x40" **$200.00**

Bench, white wicker, tight weave w/apron, low arms, very sturdy, 1920s, 22½x47x20" **$400.00**

Birdcage, painted wicker, 6-sided, wooden handle/hook, 17x16", EX **$55.00**

Bookcase, mahogany Duncan Phyfe style, open w/4 shelves, 1930s, 48x23x12" **$295.00**

Buffet, ribbon mahogany, 2 doors & 2 drawers, 6 legs, 1930s, restored, 38"(+backsplash)x60x19" **$600.00**

Cabinet, corner; bird's-eye maple, 2-shelf, 1-pane door, wall hanging, 27x21x10" **$275.00**

Cabinet, corner; pine, double 1-pane doors over double panel doors, 1910s, 81x38"..**$600.00**

Chair, desk; chestnut w/swivel base, arrow back, early 1900s, original finish, 38"..**$150.00**

Chair, dining; green upholstery, chrome X-bases, Knoll, 33½x22", 4 for..**$475.00**

Chair, Egg, by Fritz Hansen, white vinyl upholstery, 1979, reupholstered, 42", VG, $1,500.00. (Photo courtesy Treadway Gallery)

Chair, ice cream; bentwood back, round seat, recent paint...**$95.00**

Chair, side; mahogany Hepplewhite style, reupholstered seat, 37½", pr..**$400.00**

Chair, side; oak w/pressed back w/carved crest, woven seat, 42" **$65.00**

Chair, side; oak w/vase splat, saddle seat, curved front legs, cross bars, 20th Century..**$135.00**

Chair, side; rosewood Louis XV style w/rush seat, pr **$350.00**

Chair side; 3-slat ladder-back w/slat seat, yellow paint, 35" . **$65.00**

Chest, walnut veneer, Paul Frankl style (50s Modern), multi-drawer w/open spaces, 37x28x14" **$150.00**

Daybed, black-painted wrought-iron frame w/curlicues, made from 1930s bed, quality upholstery, 31x74x48" **$800.00**

Daybed, Old Hickory, 77" long, $1,200.00. (Photo courtesy Treadway Gallery)

Desk, corner; oak, simple rustic style, single drawer, 1940s, 29x43x31", +matching 34" oak chair.........................**$355.00**

Desk, golden oak, kidney shape w/2 pedestals, center drawer, Deco style, refinished **$850.00**

Desk, golden oak, single drawer, solid end & back panels, 32x48x28" **$325.00**

Desk, gray Formica top over single pedestal, chrome pulls, black metal legs, Forever Modern, 1950s, 29x46x21" **$375.00**

Desk, Heywood-Wakefield, birch with wheat finish, 50" long, $650.00. (Photo courtesy Jackson's International Auctioneers & Appraisers of Fine Art & Antiques)

Desk, quartersawn oak, drawer interiors are metal, restored, 30x60x34" **$495.00**

Desk, roll-top; walnut Eastlake style w/brass rail, fitted interior, 45x27x18" **$950.00**

Dresser, oak w/serpentine front, 2 short drawers over 2 long drawers, carved frame w/swivel mirror **$695.00**

Dresser, quartersawn oak w//2 bowfront drawers, serpentine top, 1900s, 29x31x21" **$325.00**

Footstool, dark wood w/needlepoint upholstered top, 13½x18" dia **$75.00**

Footstool, maple w/4 turned legs w/stretchers, plank top, 12x13½" dia..**$25.00**

Living room set, 2-cushion couch w/rolled arms+2 wingback armchairs+hassock, 1940s-50s.......................**$800.00**

Loveseat, rolled arms, loose/overstuffed back & seat cushions, floral upholstery, Ralph Lauren, 60x32x37" **$200.00**

Magazine basket, white painted wicker, curlicures ea corner, open-work, center handle...**$100.00**

Nightstand, bird's-eye maple, mid-century design ebonized base w/scroll design, LA Period Furniture, 26x16x14", pr ..**$500.00**

Ottoman, black leather woven seat, mortise & tenon construction, 17x23x23" **$100.00**

Shelf, painted wicker, 2 wooden shelves, woven top, sides & back in diamond pattern, 18x18x6"............................**$30.00**

Sideboard, oak w/recessed top w/2 panel doors, 2 drawers over 2 panel doors on base, 1930s, 49x48x18" **$425.00**

Sofa, 2-pc sectional w/fold-out bed, original upholstery, 1950s, 30x60x34"..**$300.00**

Stand, cherry & bird's-eye maple Sheraton, 1 drawer, 31x19x19". **$500.00**

Stand, plant; quartersawn tiger oak, round top, sq base, 26x10½" **$125.00**

Stand, plant; walnut, turned pedestal w/applied ornamental brackets, 3-footed, 13½" dia **$110.00**

Stand, sewing; oak & oak veneer Martha Washington style, 3 drawers, refinished, 1930s **$225.00**

Stand, sewing; white painted wicker, tight weave, hinged top, lower shelf, 27½x15x11" **$150.00**

Stool, kitchen; painted wood w/4 legs, hand-painted flowers on seat, 1950s **$45.00**

Stool, oak swivel type w/laced cane seat, 22x13½" dia.......**$150.00**

Stool, oak turned legs & stretchers, woven rope seat, 11x14".. **$135.00**

Stool, piano; oak w/metal leg caps & glass ball feet, adjusts & swivels **$145.00**

Stool, quartersawn oak, swivels (does not tilt), w/foot rest, restored, 45" **$295.00**

Stool, upholstered triangle top, 3 wrought-iron legs, 1950s, 17x14", set of 4 ....**$130.00**

Table, bedside; mahogany Louis XVI style, 2 paneled drawers, marble top, carved apron, 26x20x13", pr...................**$425.00**

Table, cocktail; dark wood/glass top, Deco style w/brass & amber Bakelite details, 21x36x16" **$350.00**

Table, dining; oak Versailles marquetry top, Deco style w/2 leaves, 1930s, 30x98x40" (extended) **$450.00**

Table, dining; white laminate top on steel pedestal shaft w/star-shaped base, Jacobsen/Hansen, 1950s, 28x45" dia......**$275.00**

Table, occasional; mahogany Duncan-Phyfe style w/pie-crust edge, 1930s, 19x29x20" **$135.00**

Table, occasional; mahogany w/turned ball legs, 17x18x14".**$175.00**

Table, parlor; bird's-eye maple, drawer, shelf w/spindles at sides, early 20th Century, 30x30x20" **$235.00**

Table, phone, white paint, glass knob drawer, 26x14x14" ..**$100.00**

Table, side; oak, French Louis XIII style, twisted legs, X-stretcher, 30x20x19" **$650.00**

Table, side; walnut stain, 2-tiered cloverleaf shape, 1950s, 27½" **$150.00**

Table, sofa; oak Chippendale style w/inlay top, cabriole legs, claw & ball feet, carved skirt, 1930s, 20x35x22"................**$255.00**

Table, white painted wicker, tight weave apron, slatted lower shelf, 27x18x18" **$60.00**

Tables, nesting; mahogany veneer w/over-painted sides, largest 23x30x16", set of 3..**$100.00**

Tea cart, mahogany w/2 drop leaves, lower shelf, on castors .**$600.00**

Tea cart, natural wicker, 2 shelves, galley top, flatware caddy handle, 31x35x25" **$550.00**

Trunk, camel-back, oak slats, replaced leather handles, late 19th Century, 24x30x19" **$275.00**

Trunk, pine w/oak cross boards, flat top, restored, 1900s...**$300.00**

Trunk, white painted wicker w/tight weave, upholstered top, 13x30x13" **$200.00**

Washstand, oak w/serpentine top, long drawer over 2 short drwers, flat panel door, refinished, 30x33x20" **$350.00**

Games

Games from the 1870s to the 1970s and beyond are fun to collect. Many of the earlier games are beautifully lithographed. Some of their boxes were designed by well-known artists and illustrators, and many times these old games are appreciated more for their artwork than for their entertainment value. Some represent a historical event or a specific era in the social development of our country. Characters from the early days of radio, television, and movies have been featured in hundreds of games designed for children and adults alike.

If you're going to collect games, be sure that they're reasonably clean, free of water damage, and complete. Most have playing instructions printed inside the lid or on a separate piece of paper that include an inventory list. Check the contents and remember that the condition of the box is very important too.

If you'd like to learn more about games, we recommend *Schroeder's Collectible Toys, Antique to Modern* (Collector Books).

Club: Association of Game and Puzzle Collectors
PMB 321, 197 M Boston Post Road West
Marlborough, MA 01752

Chutes and Ladders, Milton Bradley, 1956, MIB, from $25.00 to $30.00. (Photo courtesy Rick Polizzi)

Addams Family, Ideal, 1965, EXIB **$50.00**

Advance to Boardwalk, Parker Bros, 1985, NMIB...............**$15.00**

Alien, Kenner, 1979, EXIB **$25.00**

Ally Slooper, Milton Bradley, 1907, EXIB **$50.00**

Atom Ant Saves the Day, Transogram, 1966, NMIB **$50.00**

Auto Racing Game, Milton Bradley, VGIB, A **$125.00**

B-17 Queen of the Skies, Avalon Hill, 1983, NMIB **$15.00**

Barbie's Little Sister Skipper Game, Mattel, 1964, NMIB....**$45.00**

Bermuda Triangle, 1976, EXIB **$25.00**

Blondie, Parker Bros, 1970s, NMIB....................................**$12.00**

Boris Karloff's Monster Game, Gems, 1965, VGIB **$75.00**

Branded, Milton Bradley, 1966, EXIB **$25.00**

Bugaloos, Milton Bradley, 1971, EXIB **$30.00**

Buy & Sell, Whitman, 1953, EXIB **$10.00**

Cabbage Patch Kids, Parker Bros, 1984, EXIB.....................**$8.00**

Captain Kangaroo TV Lotto, Ideal, 1961, EXIB..................**$25.00**

Careers, Park Bros, 1965, NMIB **$20.00**

Chutes & Ladders, Milton Bradley, 1956, NMIB................**$20.00**

Clean Sweep, Schaper, 1960s, NMIB..................................**$25.00**

Clue, Parker Bros, 1972, NMIB **$10.00**

Combat Card Game, Milton Bradley, EXIB **$20.00**

Conflict, Parker Bros, 1960, EXIB **$50.00**

Dating Game, Hasbro, 1967, EXIB **$15.00**

Dennis the Menace Baseball Game, MTP, 1960, NMIB......**$45.00**

Dick Tracy Crime Stopper Game, Ideal, 1963, MIB............**$40.00**

Diner's Club Credit Card Game, Ideal, 1961, NMIB **$40.00**

Disney's True Life Electric Quiz Game, 1952, VGIB **$25.00**

Don't Spill the Beans, 1967, EXIB......................................**$30.00**

Dream House, Milton Bradley, 1968, EXIB **$40.00**

Electric Sports Car Race, Tudor, 1959, NMIB.....................**$75.00**

Ensign O'Toole USS Appleby Game, Hasboro, 1968, NMIB.. **$30.00**

Escort Game of Guys & Gals, Parker Bros, 1955, unused, MIB **$30.00**

Eye Guess, 1966, EXIB..**$25.00**

Family Ties, Apple Street, 1986, EXIB................................**$15.00**

Fantastic Voyage, Milton Bradley, 1968, NMIB..................**$30.00**

Felix the Cat Target, Lido, 1960s, EXIB **$25.00**

Flying Nun Marble Maze Game, Milton Bradley, 1967, NMIB.**$45.00**

Fonz Hanging Out at Arnold's Card Game, Milton Bradley, 1976, MIB...**$30.00**

Game of Coney Island, Selchow & Righter, 1956, EXIB.....**$55.00**

Gene Autry Bandit Trail Game, Kenton, EXIB...................**$200.00**

George of the Jungle, Parker Bros, 1968, NMIB..................**$110.00**

Great Obstacle Race Game, Spear's, VGIB..........................**$30.00**

Gumby & Pokey Playful Trails, 1968, NMIB **$25.00**

Hardy Boys Treasure, Parker Bros, 1960, VGIB **$45.00**

High Gear, Mattel, 1953, NMIB **$40.00**

Howdy Doody Bean Bag Game, Parker Bros, 1950s, EXIB.**$75.00**

Huckleberry Hound Spin-O-Game, 1959, EXIB.................**$90.00**

Identipops, Playvalue, 1969, VGIB **$200.00**

Indiana Jones in the Raiders of the Lost Ark, Kenner, 1981, NMIB **$25.00**

Intrigue, Milton Bradley, 1954, NMIB................................**$40.00**

Jack & Jill, Milton Bradley, VGIB.......................................**$100.00**

Jackie Gleason & Away We Go! TV fun Game, Transogram, 1956, EX **$55.00**

James Bond 007 Thunderball, Milton Bradley, 1965, NMIB.**$45.00**

Jeopardy, Milton Bradley, 1964, EXIB **$25.00**

Jetson's Fun Pad, Milton Bradley, 1963, NMIB **$80.00**

Joker's Wild, Milton Bradley, 1973, NMIB.........................**$15.00**

Jungle Book, Parker Bros, 1966, NMIB.................$45.00

KerPlunk, Ideal, 1967, MIB, $20.00. (Photo courtesy Rick Polizzi)

King Kong, Milton Bradley, 1966, NMIB...........................$35.00

Lame Duck, Parker Bros, 1928, VGIB.......................$125.00

Letter Carrier, McLoughlin, VGIB.................................$275.00

Little Rascals Clubhouse Bingo, Gabriel, 1958, EXIB.........$50.00

Lone Ranger Game, Milton Bradley, 1938, EXIB................$50.00

Lone Ranger Silver Bullets, Whiting, 1956, MIB..............$150.00

Lucy Tea Party Game, Milton Bradley, 1971, EXIB............$45.00

Madame Planchette Horoscope Game, SelRight, 1967, NMIB..$25.00

Man From UNCLE the Pinball Game, 1966, EX..............$110.00

Margie The Game of Woopie, Milton Bradley, 1961, NMIB.$25.00

McKeever & the Colonel Bamboozle Game of Hide & Seek, Milton Bradley, 1962, NMIB.................................$30.00

Merry Game of Fibber McGee & the Wistful Vista Mystery, VGIB..$55.00

Mickey Mouse Kiddy Keno, Jaymar, 1950s-60s, NMIB......$20.00

Mighty Mouse, Milton Bradley, 1978, NMIB....................$30.00

Mind Maze, Parker Bros, 1970, NMIB...........................$20.00

Mission Impossible, Ideal, 1967, EXIB.........................$120.00

Mr Green Jeans Animal Yummy Card Game, Fairchild, 1950s, VG+IB...$24.00

Murder She Wrote, Warren, 1985, VGIB........................$10.00

Nancy & Sluggo Game, 1944, rare, NMIB......................$100.00

Neck & Neck, Yaquinto, 1981, MIB................................$25.00

Newlywed Game, Hasbro, 1st Edition, 1967, NMIB..........$25.00

No Time for Sergeants, Ideal, 1964, EXIB......................$25.00

Our Game Tipple-Topple Game, All-Fair, c 1930, EXIB.....$40.00

Overland Trail, Transogram, 1960, NMIB.......................$90.00

Partridge Family, Milton Bradley, 1974, NMIB.................$45.00

Perry Mason, Case of the Missing Suspect, Transogram, 1959, NMIB...$40.00

Pink Panther, Warren, 1977, NMIB...............................$25.00

Pirate Ship, Lowe, 1940, EXIB.....................................$30.00

Popeye Pipe Toss Game, Rosebud Art #17, 1935, MIB.....$100.00

PT Boat 109, Ideal, 1963, VGIB...................................$45.00

Quick McGraw ED-U Cards, 1961, NMIB......................$10.00

Rat Patrol, Transogram, 1966, NMIB............................$90.00

Rebel, Ideal, 1961, NMIB..$75.00

Rin-Tin-Tin (Adventures of), Transogram, 1955, EXIB......$50.00

Rondezvous, Create, 1965, NMIB.................................$25.00

Scarlett O'Hara - One of Her Problems Marble Game, Marietta Games/MGM, 1939, EXIB.............................$75.00

Shopping, John Ladell, 1973, NMIB..............................$20.00

Star Trek, Milton Bradley, 1979, EXIB...........................$45.00

Superboy Game, Hasbro, 1960s, EX..............................$50.00

Tales of Wells Fargo, Milton Bradley, 1959, EXIB.............$85.00

To Tell the Truth, Lowell, 1957, EXIB............................$20.00

Town & Country Traffic, Ranger Steel, 1940s, EXIB.........$50.00

Turn Over, Milton Bradley, EXIB..................................$75.00

Uncle Sam's Mail, Milton Bradley, GIB, A......................$90.00

Uncle Wiggily, Parker Bros, 1979, NMIB.......................$25.00

Untouchables, Marx, 1950s, NMIB...............................$220.00

Virginian, Transogram, 1962, EXIB..............................$100.00

Wagon Train, Milton Bradley, 1960, EXIB......................$50.00

Walt Disney's Fantasyland, Parker Bros, 1950, MIB..........$50.00

Walter Johnson Baseball Game, VGIB............................$200.00

Wink Tennis, Transogram, 1956, NMIB..........................$15.00

World's Fair Ed-U Cards, 1965, NMIB...........................$15.00

Wyatt Earp, Transogram, 1958, EXIB............................$70.00

Yogi Bear Rummy Ed-U Cards, 1961, MIB (sealed)...........$15.00

You Don't Say, Milton Bradley, 1963, EXIB.....................$20.00

Young America Target, Parker Bros, VGIB.......................$275.00

Zorro, Parker Bros/Walt Disney, 1966, EXIB...................$55.00

Swahili, Milton Bradley, 1968, MIB, $25.00. (Photo courtesy Rick Polizzi)

Gas Station Collectibles

Items used and/or sold by gas stations are included in this very specialized area of advertising collectibles. Those with an interest in this field tend to specialize in memorabilia from a specific gas station like Texaco or Signal. This is a very regional market, with items from small companies that are no longer in business bringing the best prices. For instance, memorabilia decorated with Gulf's distinctive 'orange ball' logo may sell more readily in Pittsburgh than in Los Angeles. Gas station giveaways like plastic gas pump salt and pepper sets and license plate attachments are gaining in popularity with collectors. If you're interested in learning more about these types of collectibles, we recommend *Petroleum Collectibles Monthly* (see address below) and *Value Guide to Gas Station Memorabilia* by B.J. Summers and Wayne Priddy (Collector Books).

See also Ashtrays; Automobilia.

Advisor: Scott Benjamin (See Directory Gas Station Collectibles)

Newsletter: *Petroleum Collectibles Monthly*
Scott Benjamin and Wayne Henderson, Publishers
PO Box 556, LaGrange, OH 44050-0556
440-355-6608
Subscription: $35.95 per year in US, Canada: $44.50; International: $71.95 (Samples: $5)
www.pcmpublishing.com or www.gasglobes.com

Banner, A Wonderful Change for Spring, Golfpride HD..., lady w/new hat, 32x84" $165.00
Banner, Change to Gulfpride Oil, Don't Let Winter Scare You, girl w/jack-o'-lantern, 32x84" $225.00
Blotter, Gulf Gasoline, There Is More Power..., attendant pumping gas into early car, 4x6", EX $65.00
Blotter, Gulf Oil, Harper's Ferry, 1920s $40.00
Blotter, Sure Glad I Put In Marathon Endurance Oil, man looking at very low barometer, unused felt back, EX $15.00
Bottle, oil; clear glass w/Gargoyle Mobiloil A embossed on metal funnel top w/cap, ca 1926, 14⅝" $65.00
Bottle, oil; Standard Oil Sohio Valve Oil, red, white & black label on brown glass, 16 Fl Oz $20.00
Bottle, oil; Sunoco painted label on clear glass, Master Mfg Co spout & cap, EX $85.00
Calendar, 1942, Esso advertising, 1941 Christmas message on front sheet, M in wrapper $45.00
Calendar, 1944, Marathon, The Ohio Oil Co, runner logo, complete, 28x14", EX $20.00
Can, gas; Gulfpride, blue, white & orange, 5-gal, VG $85.00
Can, Mobilgrease #8, cone top, metal, 1940s, full, 7-oz, EX .. $20.00
Can, oil; Esso Humble 997 Motor Oil, Humble Oil Refining Co, Houston TX, 1-qt, EX $45.00
Can, oil; Gulfpride HD Select, empty, 1-qt, EX $45.00
Can, oil; Mobiloil triangle, prewar, G $125.00
Can, oil; Phillips 66 Premium Motor Oil, red, white & black, unopened, 1-qt, EX $25.00
Can, Sinclair Opaline Motor Oil, marked Patent Pending May 10, 1927, 5-gal, 8½x14½" dia, EX $115.00
Can, Texado Home Lubricant, 1960s, 4-oz, EX $25.00
Can oil; Conoco, red, white & black on green painted metal, 5-gal, EX $50.00
Clock, Cities Service, green neon, 15" dia, NM $70.00
Clock, Sinclair Dino Gasoline, green dinosaur logo, green neon light along edge of face, metal frame, 15" dia, NM $85.00
Gas globe, Atlantic White Flash, red, white & blue, screw base w/gill glass frame, ca 1932 .... $650.00
Gas globe, Crownzoil, milk glass inserts on gill frame, ca 1933, NM $600.00
Gas globe, Gulf, red, white & blue, 1-pc, ca 1930, EX $950.00
Gas globe, Mobile Regular, sm flying horse, new Capco frame, ca 1962, EX $350.00

Gas globe, Mobilgas, red Pegasus flying, wide glass frame, 1930s-40s, EX $500.00
Gas globe, Red Star Gasoline, red, white & black, metal frame, 1920s, 15", EX $1,850.00
Gas globe, Regular Tresler Comet, red, white & blue, wide glass frame, ca 1955, EX $650.00
Gas globe, Sinclair Dino Gasoline, red & green on white, gill body, 13½", NM $200.00

Gas globe, Super Crown Extra, Standard Oil of Kentucky, three-piece, plastic band with glass lens globe, 1950s, $200.00. (Photo courtesy B.J. Summers and Wayne Priddy)

Gas globe, Texaco Black T, screw-on base, 1930s, EX $500.00
Gas globe, White Rose Ethyl, wide glass frame, ca 1936, scarce, EX $750.00
Hat, attendant's; blue cloth w/Pennzoil logo on sides, folds flat w/no bill, unused, EX $25.00

Hat, Mobiloil, summer uniform, $175.00. (Photo courtesy B.J. Summers and Wayne Priddy)

Kit, Gulf Tube Repair #10, patches & glue in multicolor tin can, EX $32.50
Letter opener, Globe Oil Co, Remember the Globe Oil Co, 8", EX $125.00
Map, Gulf Oil, Florida w/inset map of Cuba, 1954, VG+ ... $14.00

Map, Phillips 66, Highways of Indiana, 1932, EX...............$35.00

Map, Shell Oil, California, 1948, EX.........................$8.00

Map, Texaco, New York, Long Island & New Jersey, 1937, EX..$15.00

Map holder, Gulf Oil, 1950s, 18x9x5", EX, w/15 vintage maps $125.00

Oil bottle, Esso embossed on clear, Esso marked funnel top, EX.$245.00

Padlock, Philgas on front, Phillips 66 on back, 2¼x1½", w/key, EX...$20.00

Pennant, Firestone, blue letters on orange felt, 8x28", EX....$45.00

Photo, Phillips 66 station, black & white, 1930s-early 1940s, 5x7", EX $25.00

Pocketknife, Texaco, single blade, corkscrew & bottle opener, 5" open, EX...$100.00

Postcard, Texaco Tire Service, black, white & red, 1935, 3¼x5½", EX $80.00

Sign, Conoco, red & white triangle w/name in middle, enamel over metal, 7½x8⅝", EX.................................$75.00

Sign, Firestone, double-sided, signed Grace Brite 'N' Grace Sign & MFG Co 28, 1950s, 9½x48", EX...........................$345.00

Sign, Full Serve Island, double-sided, plastic w/aluminum frame, lights up, 1960s-70s, 25x25x6½", EX...................$150.00

Sign, Goodyear, red and white painted tin, 12x22", $350.00.
(Photo courtesy B.J. Summers and Wayne Priddy)

Sign, Grant Battery Cables, tin litho, w/7 hangers for cables, ca 1950, 7x13½", EX....................................$60.00

Sign, Ladies, blue lettering on white, porcelain, mounts to wall, EX $60.00

Sign, Pennzoil, black & red & yellow paint on metal oval, 18x31", VG..$275.00

Sign, Phillips 66, red, white & black shield shape, aluminum back, lights up, 48x48x6", EX.............................$285.00

Sign, Shell, plastic, mounts to pump, sq, EX $90.00

Sign, Sinclair HC Gasoline, red, white & green on porcelain, double-sided, round, VG.................................$335.00

Sign, STP, red, white & blue paint on metal rectangle, 11x16", EX $235.00

Sign, Texaco Fire Chief Gasoline, fireman's helmet, painted metal, 1963, 18x12", EX....................................$90.00

Soap, Dino Soap, Sinclair dinosaur figural, 6", 1960s, NMIB $30.00

Spark plugs, Phillips 66, M in red & white box, set of 4......$32.00

Spout, oil; Garboyle Mobiloil 'E', sm dents, 1920s.............$20.00

Thermometer, Gulf, red, white & blue on tin, 27x6¼", EX..$95.00

Thermometer, Sunoco logo on white painted metal, 36x8", EX...$50.00

Tin, shock absorber fluid M-1046-S; Canco Co, paper label, 2x3x6⅛", EX..$47.00

Tire gauge, Schrader Balloon, Model 'A' Ford, w/leather pouch, 1923, G $40.00

Towel, driving graphics, It Pays To Farm w/Texaco Products, Startex, 29x16", NM...$40.00

Toy helmet, Texaco Fire Chief, 1960s, MIB.................$125.00

Tumblers, Mobil, Pegasus (red) on clear glass, 5", M, 6 for..$50.00

Yardstick, Burt Chevy Center, 1960s-70s, 36" collapses to 19", NM...$5.00

Gay Fad Glassware

What started out as a home-based 'one-woman' operation in the late 1930s within only a few years had grown into a substantial company requiring much larger facilities and a staff of decorators. The company was founded by Fran Taylor. Originally they decorated kitchenware items but later found instant success with the glassware they created, most of which utilized frosted backgrounds and multicolored designs such as tulips, state themes, Christmas motifs, etc. Some pieces were decorated with 22-karat gold and sterling silver. In addition to the frosted glass which collectors quickly learn to associate with this company, they also became famous for their 'bentware' — quirky cocktail glasses whose stems were actually bent.

Some of their more collectible lines are 'Beau Brummel' — martini glasses with straight or bent stems featuring a funny-faced drinker wearing a plaid bow tie; 'Gay Nineties' — various designs such as can-can girls and singing bartenders; '48 States' — maps with highlighted places of interest; 'Rich Man, Poor Man' (or Beggar Man, Thief, etc.); 'Bartender' (self-explanatory); 'Currier & Ives' — made to coordinate with the line by Royal China; 'Zombies' — extra tall and slim with various designs including roses, giraffes, and flamingos; and the sterling silver- and 22-karat gold-trimmed crystal glassware.

Until you learn to spot it a mile away (which you soon will), look for an interlocking 'G' and 'F' or 'Gay Fad,' the latter mark indicating pieces from the late 1950s to the early 1960s. The frosted glassware itself has the feel of satin and is of very good quality. It can be distinguished from other manufacturers' wares simply by checking the bottom — Gay Fad's are frosted; generally other manufacturers' are not. Hand-painted details are another good clue. (You may find similar glassware signed 'Briard'; this is not Gay Fad.)

This Ohio-based company was sold in 1963 and closed altogether in 1965. Be careful of condition. If the frosting has darkened or the paint is worn or faded, it's best to wait for a better example.

Advisor: Donna S. McGrady (See the Directory, Gay Fad)

Ashtray, Trout Flies, clear $8.00

Bent tray, Phoenix Bird, clear, signed Gay Fad, 13¾" dia $20.00

Bent tray, Stylized Cats, clear, signed Gay Fad, 11½" dia.....$30.00

Beverage set, Apple, frosted, 86-oz ball pitcher+6 13-oz round-bottom tumblers $130.00

Beverage set, Colonial Homestead, frosted, 85-oz pitcher & 6 12-oz tumblers $80.00

Beverage set, Magnolia, clear, 86-oz pitcher & 6 13-oz tumblers . **$75.00**

Canister set, Red Rose, red lids, white interior, 3-pc **$60.00**

Chip 'n dip, Horace the Horse w/cart, knife tail, 3 bowls, double old-fashioned glass as head, signed Gay Fad..................**$48.00**

Cocktail set, Poodle, metal frame 'body' w/martini mixer, double old-fashioned glass as head & 4 5-oz glasses, signed......**$60.00**

Cocktail shaker, Ballerina Shoes, red metal screw-top lid, frosted, 32-oz, 7"..**$25.00**

Cocktail shaker, full-figure ballerina, frosted, 28-oz, 9"........**$40.00**

Cruet set, Oil & Vinegar, Cherry, clear.................................**$14.00**

Decanter set, Gay '90s, Scotch, Rye, Gin & Bourbon, frosted or white inside..**$85.00**

Goblet, Bow Pete, Hoffman Beer, 16-oz **$15.00**

Ice tub, Gay '90s, frosted **$21.00**

Juice set, Tommy Tomato, frosted, 36-oz pitcher & 6 4-oz tumblers..**$40.00**

Luncheon set, Fantasia Hawaiian flower, 1-place setting (sq plate, cup & saucer) **$16.00**

Martini mixer, 'A Jug of Wine...,' w/glass stirring rod, clear, signed Gay Fad, 10⅝" **$25.00**

Mix-A-Salad set, Ivy, 22-oz shaker w/plastic top, garlic press, measuring spoon, recipe book, MIB **$75.00**

Mug, Notre Dame, frosted, 16-oz **$15.00**

Mug set, minstrels w/different song on ea mug, frosted, 16-oz, 8-pc **$115.00**

Mug set, toasts from a different country on ea mug, frosted, 12-pc **$120.00**

Pilsner set, Gay 90s, portraits: Mama, Papa, Victoria, Rupert, Aunt Aggie, Uncle Bertie, Gramps & Horace, frosted, 8-pc ..**$80.00**

Pitcher, Currier & Ives, blue & white, frosted, 86-oz...........**$90.00**

Pitcher, juice; Ada Orange, frosted, 36-oz **$20.00**

Pitcher, Magnolia, with six matching tumblers (one shown), seven-piece set, $75.00. (Photo courtesy Donna McGrady)

Pitcher, martini; cardinal & pine sprig, frosted, w/glass stirrer, 42-oz..**$38.00**

Pitcher, Musical Notes, frosted, 86-oz................................**$55.00**

Pitcher, Rosemaling (tulips), white inside, 32-oz.................**$28.00**

Plate, Fruits, lace edge, Hazel Atlas, 8½" **$17.50**

Punch set, pink veiling, bowl & 8 cups in white metal frame. **$65.00**

Range set, Rooster, salt, pepper, sugar & flower shakers, frosted w/ red metal lids, 8-oz, 4-pc **$120.00**

Salad set, Fruits, frosted, lg bowl, 2 cruets, salt & pepper shakers, 5-pc..**$55.00**

Salad set, Outlined Fruits, lg bowl, 2 cruets, salt & pepper shakers, frosted, 5-pc..**$60.00**

Salt & pepper shakers, Morning Glory, frosted w/red plastic tops, pr...**$16.00**

Stem, bent cocktail, Beau Brummel, clear, signed Gay Fad, 3½-oz..**$10.00**

Stem, bent cocktail, Souvenir of My Bender, frosted, 3-oz...**$10.00**

Syrup pitcher, Rosemaling (tulips), frosted, 11½-oz.............**$30.00**

Tea & toast, Magnolia, sq plate w/cup indent & cup, clear..**$15.00**

Tom & Jerry set, Christmas bells, milk white, marked GF, bowl & 6 cups...**$70.00**

Tumbler, Bob White, brown, turquoise & gold on clear, signed Gay Fad, 10-oz...**$12.00**

Tumbler, Christmas Greetings From Gay Fad, frosted, 4-oz.**$17.00**

Tumbler, Hors D'oeuvres, clear, 14-oz **$10.00**

Tumbler, Kentucky state map (1 of 48), pink, yellow or lime, frosted, marked GF, 10-oz **$8.00**

Tumbler, Oregon state map on pink picket fence, clear, marked GF **$8.00**

Tumbler, Pegasus, gold & pink on black, 12-oz **$11.00**

Tumbler, Say When, frosted, 4-oz..**$8.00**

Tumbler, Zombie, flamingo, frosted, marked GF, 14-oz......**$20.00**

Tumbler, Zombie, giraffe, frosted, marked GF, 14-oz...........**$14.00**

Tumbler, 1948 Derby Winner Citation, frosted, 14-oz........**$50.00**

Tumblers, angels preparing for Christmas, frosted, 12-oz, set of 8...**$72.00**

Tumblers, Dickens Christmas Carol characters, frosted, 12-oz, set of 8...**$48.00**

Tumblers, Famous Fighters (John L Sullivan & the others), frosted, 16-oz, set of 8..**$85.00**

Tumblers, French Poodle, clear, 17-oz, set of 8 in original box.. **$96.00**

Tumblers, Game Birds & Animals, clear, 12-oz, set of 8, MIB. **$65.00**

Tumblers, Ohio Presidents, frosted, 12-oz, set of 8 ....**$55.00**

Tumblers, Rich Man, Poor Man (nursery rhyme), frosted, marked GF, 16-oz, set of 8..**$80.00**

Tumblers, Sports Cars, white inside, 12-oz, set of 8.............**$45.00**

Vanity set, butterflies in meadow, pink inside, 5-pc **$60.00**

Vase, Red Poppy, clear, footed, 10" **$24.00**

Waffle set, Blue Willow, 48-oz waffle batter jug & 11-oz syrup jug, frosted, pr **$125.00**

Waffle set, Little Black Sambo, frosted, 48-oz waffle batter jug, 11½-oz syrup jug..**$250.00**

Waffle set, Peach Blossoms, 48-oz waffle batter jug & 11½-oz syrup jug, frosted...**$52.00**

Waffle set, Red Poppy, frosted, 48-oz waffle batter jug, 11½-oz syrup jug...**$25.00**

Wine set, Grapes, decanter & 4 2½-oz stemmed wines, clear, 5-pc **$40.00**

Geisha Girl China

The late nineteenth century saw a rise in the popularity of Oriental wares in the US and Europe. Japan rose to meet the demands of this flourishing ceramics marketplace with a flurry of growth in potteries and decorating centers. These created items for export which would appeal to Western tastes and integrate into Western dining and decorating cultures, which were distinct from those of Japan. One example of the wares introduced into this marketplace was Geisha Girl porcelain.

Hundreds of different patterns and manufacturers' marks have been uncovered on Geisha Girl porcelain tea and dinnerware sets, dresser accessories, decorative items, etc., which were produced well into the twentieth century. They all share in common colorful decorations featuring kimono-clad ladies and children involved in everyday activities. These scenes are set against a backdrop of lush flora, distinctive Japanese architecture, and majestic landscapes. Most Geisha Girl porcelain designs were laid on by means of a stencil, generally red or black. This appears as an outline on the ceramic body. Details are then completed by hand-painted washes in a myriad of colors. A minority of the wares were wholly hand painted.

Most Geisha Girl porcelain has a colorful border or edging with handles, finials, spouts, and feet similarly adorned. The most common border color is red which can range from orange to red-orange to a deep brick red. Among the earliest border colors were red, maroon, cobalt blue, light (apple) green, and Nile green. Pine green, blue-green, and turquoise made their appearance circa 1917, and a light cobalt or Delft blue appeared around 1920. Other colors (e.g. tan, yellow, brown, and gold) can also be found. Borders were often enhanced with gilded lace or floral decoration. The use of gold for this purpose diminished somewhat around 1910 to 1915 when some decorators used economic initiative (fewer firings required) to move the gold to just inside the border or replace the gold with white or yellow enamels. Wares with both border styles continued to be produced into the twentieth century. Exquisite examples with multicolor borders as well as ornate rims decorated with florals and geometrics can also be found.

Due to the number of different producers, the quality of Geisha ware ranges from crude to finely detailed. Geisha Girl porcelain was sold in sets and open stock in outlets ranging from the five-and-ten to fancy department stores. It was creatively used for store premiums, containers for store products, fair souvenirs, and resort memorabilia. The fineness of detailing, amount of gold highlights, border color, scarcity of form and, of course, condition all play a role in establishing the market value of a given item. Some patterns are scarcer than others, but most Geisha ware collectors seem not to focus on particular patterns.

The heyday of Geisha Girl porcelain was from 1910 through the 1930s. Production continued until the World War II era. During the 'Occupied' period, a small amount of wholly hand-painted examples were made, often with a black and gold border. The Oriental import stores and catalogs from the 1960s and 1970s featured some examples of Geisha Girl porcelain, many of which were produced in Hong Kong. These are recognized by the very white porcelain, sparse detail coloring, and lack of gold decoration. The 1990s has seen a resurgence of reproductions with a faux Nippon mark. These items are supposed to represent high quality Geisha ware, but in reality they are a blur of Geisha and Satsuma-style characteristics. They are too busy in design, too heavily enameled, and bear a variety of faux Nippon marks. Once you've been introduced to a few of these reproductions, you'll be able to recognize them easily.

Note: Colors mentioned in the following listings refer to borders.

Advisor: Elyce Litts (See Directory, Geisha Girl China)

Berry set, Dragon Boat, cobalt w/gold, master & 5 individual bowls...**$85.00**
Berry set, Garden Bench, red & pine green border w/gold, 10" master bowl & 4 5½" individual bowls.............................**$35.00**
Bonbon dish, Battledore, mum shaped, olive green.............**$22.00**
Bowl, Bamboo Trellis w/gold, red border, red & gold leaves on exterior, 3x9¾" **$35.00**
Bowl, Carp, red w/gold, 6" **$18.00**
Bowl, Cherry Blossoms, red-orange border, 7½".................**$30.00**
Bowl, Footbridge B, red border w/gold buds, scalloped rim, 3x9½" **$35.00**
Bowl, Parasol C, flower groupings on exterior, red border, Made in Japan, 2x7½" **$17.50**
Bowl, Parasol Modern, red border, incurvate rim, Japan, 2x6" .**$15.00**
Bowl, Pointing Q, flower & butterfly border on reticulated rim, 2x7½", EX...**$20.00**
Celery set, apple green border, orange & blue background w/white dots, 11½" master & 4 3½" individual salts **$45.00**
Cocoa pot, Basket A, 4 ladies gather shells at river, apple green border, 8" **$55.00**
Cracker jar, Baskets of Mums, melon ribs, 3-footed, red w/ gold...**$50.00**
Cracker jar, Spider Puppet, footed & lobed, cobalt w/gold border...**$65.00**
Creamer, Chrysanthemum Garden, red, toy size.................**$15.00**
Creamer, Porch, red-orange, modern.................................**$10.00**
Cup & saucer, child's; Mother & Son A, diapered border, 1½x3¾", 4¼"...**$12.50**
Egg cup, double; Child Reaching for Butterfly, red w/gold..**$13.00**

Hair receiver, Spider Puppet (rare pattern), hand-painted roses, blue and gold border, $40.00. (Photo courtesy Elyce Litts)

Hatpin holder, Rendezvous, vines & leaves, Kutani mark **$55.00**
Jar, sachet; Fan C, red w/gold, handles, footed, 6½" **$75.00**

Jar, water; Meeting A, red border, unmarked, mini, 2⅛" $14.00

Leaf dish, Gardening, blue w/gold border (some wear), 6¾x5½" .. $28.00

Mustard pot, blue-green w/white polka-dot border, 3x4" handle to handle $25.00

Nut dish, master; Feather Fan, footed, Nippon $48.00

Pitcher, Processional, red w/multicolored geometrics, gold handle & border, 4½" $25.00

Plate, Butterfly Dancers (rare pattern), red w/gold, 7" $35.00

Plate, Fort Dearborn Brand advertising, Gardening, red border w/ gold buds, early 1900s, 4¾" $15.00

Plate, River's Edge, Made in Japan, gold edge, 7¾" $10.00

Plate, River's Edge, red & gold border, Japanese mark, 7¼". $12.00

Plate, Wait for Me, floriate shape, red-orange w/gold buds, 8¾" $26.00

Plate, Writing A, scalloped cobalt border w/gold lacing, Japan, 7⅜" $26.00

Platter, Boat Festival, scalloped blue w/gold-laced interior border, pierced handles, Cherry Blossom mark, 11" $35.00

Platter, Parasol C, red border, pierced handles, EX $28.00

Powder jar, Chinese Coin, wear to gold, Terazawa zo mark, 4½" dia $20.00

Powder jar, Court Lady, cobalt border w/gold, 2¼x4½" dia ... $35.00

Relish, Paper Carp, fluted edge, cut-out handles, red border .. $20.00

Relish, scenic & ladies w/parasols reserves, red w/gold-laced border, oval, pierced handles, 9¼x5" $24.00

Roll tray, Bird Cage, red border, $35.00. (Photo courtesy Elyce Litts)

Salt & papper shakers, Parasol H, hand painted, red & gold border, pink flower frame, NM, pr $16.00

Salt & pepper shakers, Garden Bench, red border, unmarked, 3½", pr $15.00

Tea set, River's Edge, blue border, Made in Japan, teapot, creamer & sugar bowl w/lid, NM $35.00

Tea set, Torii, geometric yellow & green border, Hand Painted Made in Japan, 5" pot & creamer & sugar bowl w/lid $45.00

Teacup & saucer, Blue Hoo, red-orange border $14.00

Teacup & saucer, Cloud B, red-orange w/yellow $14.00

Teacup & saucer, Geisha in Sampan A, gold trim $15.00

Teapot, Bamboo Trellis, lobed body, red border, 4½" $25.00

Teapot, Kite A, brown w/gold $28.00

Toothbrush holder, Flute, red-orange border, 4" $25.00

Vase, Cloud A, cobalt w/gold-drip neck & rim, 5½" $30.00

Vase, Parasol variation, red border & foot rim, 3¾" $12.00

GI Joe

The first GI Joe was introduced by Hasbro in 1964. He was 12" tall, and you could buy him with blond, auburn, black, or brown hair in four basic variations: Action Sailor, Action Marine, Action Soldier, and Action Pilot. There was also a Black doll as well as representatives of many other nations. By 1967 GI Joe could talk, all the better to converse with the female nurse who was first issued that year. The Adventure Team series (1970 – 1976) included Black Adventurer, Talking Astronaut, Sea Adventurer, Talking Team Commander, Land Adventurer, and several variations. At this point, their hands were made of rubber, making it easier for them to grasp the many guns, tools, and other accessories that Hasbro had devised. Playsets, vehicles, and clothing completed the package, and there were kid-size items designed specifically for the kids themselves. The 12" dolls were discontinued by 1976.

Brought out by popular demand, Hasbro's 3¾" GI Joes hit the market in 1982. Needless to say, they were very well accepted. In fact, these smaller GI Joes are thought to be the most successful line of action figures ever made. Loose figures (those removed from the original packaging) are very common, and even if you can locate the accessories that they came out with, most are worth only about $3.00 to $10.00. It's the mint-in-package items that most interest collectors, and they pay a huge premium for the package. There's an extensive line of accessories that goes with the smaller line as well. Many more are listed in *Schroeder's Collectible Toys, Antique to Modern*, published by Collector Books.

12" Figures and Accessories

Accessory, Adventure Team Headquarters, EX (G box) $150.00

Accessory, Astronaut Suit, multi-pocket, w/side tabs, EX ... $400.00

Accessory, Belt, Action Man, brown web, EX $3.00

Accessory, canteen & cover, British, EX $35.00

Accessory, Desert Explorer Action Outfit, Adventure Team, #8205, M (EX card), $65.00. (Photo courtesy Cotswold Collectibles Inc.)

Accessory, fatigue pants, Action Soldier, #7504, green M (NM card) $250.00

Accessory, first aid pouch, green cloth, w/snap closure, EX .. $50.00

Accessory, flag, Army, EX $35.00

Accessory, flame thrower, green, EX......................$35.00
Accessory, geiger counter, Volcano Jumper, yellow, EX..........$7.00
Accessory, handgun (.45), Action Man, EX....................$5.00
Accessory, hunting rifle, Action Man.....................$10.00
Accessory, jacket & trousers, Airborne MP, green, VG.........$85.00
Accessory, life vest, orange, padded, 1960s.........................$29.00
Accessory, parachute pack, Sky Dive to Danger, EX+.........$125.00
Accessory, pup tent, Marine, EX.....................$25.00

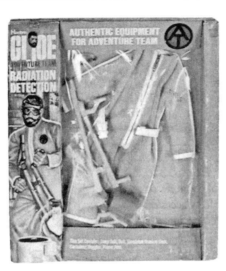

Accessory, Radiation Detection, #7341A, M (VG+ card), $175.00. (Photo courtesy Cotswold Collectibles Inc.)

Accessory, rockblaster, Sonic Blaster, EX................................$5.00
Accessory, shorts, Australian, EX.....................$27.00
Accessory, stethoscope, Medic, EX.....................$19.00
Accessory, survival life raft, #7802, MIB.....................$100.00
Accessory, tripod, Combat Engineer, w/plumb & bob, EX+.$250.00
Accessory, trousers, Capture of Pygmy Gorilla, camo, EX......$6.00
Accessory, uniform, State Trooper, w/accessories, NM.......$500.00
Accessory, White Tiger Hunt, NMIB.....................$100.00
Figure, Action Marine, Demolition, EX, C6.....................$325.00
Figure, Action Marine, Talking, #7790, NM.....................$200.00
Figure, Action Marine, 30th Anniversary, 1994, NRFB.......$50.00
Figure, Action Pilot, #7800, M (EX box).....................$400.00
Figure, Action Sailor, Breeches Buoy Set, EX.....................$200.00
Figure, Action Sailor, Deep Sea Diver, NM.....................$300.00
Figure, Action Sailor, Landing Signal Officer, NM...........$200.00
Figure, Action Soldier, Deep Freeze Set, EX.....................$175.00
Figure, Action Soldier, Green Beret, EX.....................$115.00
Figure, Action Soldier, Military Police, VG+.....................$260.00
Figure, Action Soldier, Ski Patrol, EX.....................$315.00
Figure, Action Soldier, West Point Cadet, NM.................$325.00
Figure, Adventure Team Adventurer (Black), Hidden Treasure, EX.....................$130.00
Figure, Adventure Team Air Adventurer, Aerial Recon, EX...$175.00
Figure, Adventure Team Eagle Eye Land Commander, #7276, MIP.....................$80.00
Figure, Adventure Team Land Adventurer, Winter Rescue, EX..$175.00
Figure, Adventure Team Man of Action, #7500, VGIB......$200.00
Figure, Adventure Team Man of Action, Photo Recon, EX..$98.00
Figure, Adventure Team Sea Adventurer, #7281, VG+.........$70.00
Figure, German Soldier, near complete, EX.....................$150.00
Vehicle, ATV, yellow, EX, from $50 to.....................$75.00

Vehicle, Big Trapper, cardboard set & side panels, EX, from $175 to.....................$200.00
Vehicle, Crash Crew Truck, M.....................$1,200.00
Vehicle, Escape Car, #7360, MIB, from $50 to....................$75.00
Vehicle, Iron Knight Tank, M.....................$135.00

Vehicle, Jet Helicopter, Irwin, #5395, EX (EX box), $175.00. (Photo courtesy Cotswold Collectibles, Inc.)

Vehicle, Sandstorm Jeep, green, EXIB.....................$275.00
Vehicle, Trouble Shooter ATV, orange w/tracks, EX...........$210.00

3¾" Figures and Accessories

Accessory, Ammo Dump Unit, 1985, #6129-1, MIP...........$30.00
Accessory, Cobra Terror Dome, 1986, #6003, MIP...........$325.00

Accessory, Thunderclap, 1989, MIB, $115.00.

Figure, Astro Viper, 1988, MOC.....................$30.00
Figure, Barbecue, 1985, EX.....................$25.00
Figure, Baroness, 1984, MOC.....................$160.00
Figure, Bazooka, 1985, EX.....................$25.00
Figure, Chuckles, 1987, MOC.....................$24.00
Figure, Cobra, 1983, MOC.....................$100.00
Figure, Croc Master, 1987, NM.....................$12.00

Figure, Dial-Tone, 1986, MOC $45.00
Figure, Dr Mindbender, 1986, NM $18.00
Figure, Falcon, 1987, NM...$17.00
Figure, Frostbite, 1985, MOC $18.00
Figure, Grunt, 1982, NM $30.00
Figure, Hardball, 1988, NM $12.00
Figure, Jinx, 1987, MOC $28.00
Figure, Ken Masters, 1993, MOC $10.00
Figure, Leatherneck, 1986, MOC $50.00
Figure, Major Bludd, 1983, MIP $55.00

Figure, Mercer, 1987, MOC, $20.00.

Figure, Ninja Force Banzai, 1993, MOC $15.00
Figure, Pedacon Star Brigade, 1994, MOC $16.00
Figure, Ranger-Viper, 1990, MOC $19.00
Figure, Ripper, 1985, EX $12.00
Figure, Shipwreck, 1985, MOC..$100.00
Figure, Spirit, 1984, MOC $80.00
Figure, Tunnel Rat, 1987, MOC.......................................$38.00

Figure, Voltar, MOC, $30.00. (Photo courtesy Old Tyme Toy Store)

Figure, Zap, 1982, MOC...$90.00
Vehicle, Battlefield Robot Radar Rat, 1989, MIP................$25.00
Vehicle, Dragon Fly XH-1, #4025, w/Wild Bill, MIP........$135.00
Vehicle, LCV Recon Sled, 1986, #6067, EX......................$14.00
Vehicle, Motorized Battle Wagon, 1991, MIP....................$30.00
Vehicle, Sky Patrol Sky Raven Set, 1990, MIB..................$95.00
Vehicle, Tiger Cat w/Frostbite, 1988, EX..........................$20.00
Vehicle, Tiger Force Tiger Shark, 1988, MIP $30.00

Gilner

Gilner Potteries was a California company in Culver City. Founded by Beryl Gilner, the company produced decorative items that were marketed across the country to dime stores and gift shops. Their specialty lines included figurines, floral ware, and a number of other items including cookie jars and decorative home accessories. Today their Pixie line continues to be increasingly popular with collectors. Other ceramic items made by Gilner Potters are also gaining in popularity. Gilner Potteries ceased operations in 1957 when competition from imports made it to difficult to continue in business and recover from the effects of a major plant fire.

Nearly all items listed below contain the original company identification names and numbers as found in Gilner Potteries' wholesale catalogs. Original 1950 colors for Pixies include green, chartreuse, maroon, red, and some yellow. Pink and turquoise indicate the 1955+ period of production. Price ranges are for items in very good to excellent condition, free of chips or stained unglazed parts, and have no repairs to re-attach broken arms, legs, etc.

If you collect Pixies or want to learn more about them or Gilner Potteries, we suggest the 'Pixie Watch' website (See Directory, Pixies)

In the listings below HP was as an abbreviation for 'Happy People' (boy Pixies) and MM was used for 'Merry Maids' (girl Pixies). Letters after the hyphen refer to poses.

Advisor: Carol Power (See Directory, Gilner Potteries)

Ashtray, Native ('Happy Cannibal') girl sits on side of bamboo-patterned tray, 4½x5¾", from $25 to $30.00
Creamer & sugar bowl, M-128, yellow apples, red HP Pixie as handle on sugar bowl, from $75 to $80.00
Dish, serving; green Pixie sitting in center of chartreuse 4-leaf clover, marked 1951, from $20 to...$22.00
Figurine, HP-108-B, red 'Sweetheart' Pixie standing slightly bent at waist, lips puckered, 4¼", from $35 to $40.00
Figurine, HP-108-N, maroon Pixie standing on head, 4½", from $35 to $40.00
Figurine, HP-109-F, chartreuse Pixie laying on stomach w/head in hands, 2⅜x4½", from $15 to...$20.00
Figurine, MM-109-B, chartreuse 'Sweetheart' Pixie standing slightly bent at waist, lips puckered, 4¼", from $35 to $40.00
Mighty Maurice Hotpad Holder, M-16, red Pixie shelf sitter w/ upstretched arms, closed fists, 6½x3½", $50 to $60.00
Planter, M-100, maroon HP Pixie sitting on side of sm chartreuse log, from $15 to..$20.00
Planter, M-133, pink HP Pixie seated on lg turquoise 'Happy Shoe' sprinkled w/'Pixie dust,' 4x6", from $35 to...................$45.00

Planter, M-133, red HP Pixie seated on lg chartreuse 'Happy Shoe,' 4x6", from $25 to **$30.00**

Planter, M-134, lg green 'Playmate' HP Pixie sitting on edge of stump, 7½x5", from $30 to **$40.00**

Planter, M-401, green Pixie kneeling in front of fish riding wave (facing right or left), ea from $35 to **$40.00**

Planter, M-410, 2 red Pixies sitting on brim of green straw hat, from $30 to **$35.00**

Planter, Native ('Happy Cannibal'), boy sitting in yellow & brown canoe, 8½", from $30 to... **$32.00**

Planter, red fire engine w/green HP Pixie sitting at wheel, 5¾x3½", from $80 to **$100.00**

Salt & pepper shakers, M-122, chartreuse Pixies (1 HP & 1 MM) sitting w/crossed legs, pr from $25 to **$30.00**

Shelf sitter, M-108-E, green Pixie w/outstretched arms & open hands, from $35 to **$40.00**

TV lamp, L-300, Double Fish, black, marked Gilner, 9x10½", from $45 to **$55.00**

Versatile Happy, M-127, red HP Pixie slotted in rear to fit on rim of drinking glass, from $75 to.. **$85.00**

Wall pocket, Cutie Fruities, M-150, red Pixie w/leafy hat sitting on sm strawberry, 5x5", from $50 to.................................... **$60.00**

Wall pocket, Cutie Fruities, M-150, sm strawberry (no Pixie), 5x5", from $20 to **$25.00**

Wall pocket, Mother's Pets, M-117, red Pixie sitting on lg chartreuse grape cluster, 7½x6¼", from $50 to **$60.00**

Wall pocket, Mother's Pets, M-119, maroon Pixie sitting in center of lg pumpkin (hard to find), from $60 to........................ **$65.00**

Willie the Waterer, M-161, red, green or chartreuse Pixie on watering can, 6½x3½x2½", from $75 to **$85.00**

Figurine, chartreuse Pixie standing on leaf, 4", $55.00.

Glass Animals and Related Items

In addition to their dinnerware lines, many important American glass manufacturers — Heisey, Imperial, Cambridge, Fostoria, Paden City, and Tiffin among them — also made many exquisite figurines of animals, birds, fish, and insects. Some were designed as bookends, candleholders, and vases. As these companies went out of business, their molds were often bought by other still-active manufacturers who used them to produce their own products. This can be very confusing to the collector. To help you sort out the facts, we recommend *Glass Animals* by Dick and Pat Spencer (Collector Books).

See also Fenton; Westmoreland.

Cambridge

Buddha, lamp base, light emerald green, 1920s, from $475 to .. **$500.00**

Cat, bottle, crystal, 22-oz, 11", from $45 to **$50.00**

Moth, crystal satin, 2¼" W, from $25 to **$30.00**

Rose Lady, flower frog, light emerald, 9¾", from $250 to . **$275.00**

Scottie, bookend, crystal, hollow, 6½", ea from $125 to.... **$150.00**

Sea gull, flower holder, crystal, 8", from $65 to **$75.00**

Duncan and Miller

Bird of Paradise, crystal, 8½x13", from $650 to **$750.00**

Duck, ashtray, Pall Mall line, black, 4" L, from $125 to **$150.00**

Goose, crystal, fat, 6½x6", from $250 to **$300.00**

Sailfish, Pall Mall Line, crystal, 1940s, 5", from $200 to ... **$250.00**

Tropical fish, candleholder, crystal frosted, 5", ea from $550 to . **$600.00**

Fostoria

Duckling, cobalt, head down, ca 1965-70, 1½", from $20 to . **$25.00**

Eagle, bookend, crystal, 1940-43, 7", ea from $100 to **$125.00**

Elephant, bookend, crystal, 1940-43, 6½", ea from $100 to. **$125.00**

Frog, lemon, #2821/420, 1971-73, 1⅞x3½", from $30 to .. **$35.00**

Madonna, Silver Mist, ca 1978, 4", from $25 to **$30.00**

Mermaid, crystal, 1950-58, 10⅛", from $140 to **$160.00**

Owl, crystal, 1980-90s, mini, 2½", from $10 to.................. **$12.00**

Rabbit, Mama; Lemon, #2821/628, 1971-73, 2x4", from $35 to.. **$40.00**

Rearing horse bookends, crystal, 1937 – 1938, 7¾", from $60.00 to $70.00 each. (Photo courtesy Lee Garmon and Dick Spencer)

Heisey

Duckling, crystal, standing, 1947-49, 2½x1¾", from $225 to .. **$250.00**

Elephant, Papa; crystal, 1944-53, 5x6½", from $450 to **$475.00**

Fish, candlesticks, crystal, 1941-48, 5x4", pr from $350 to..**$400.00**
Goose, cordial w/figural stem, crystal, 1-oz, from $200 to.**$225.00**
Goose, crystal, wings up, 1942-53, 6½x7½", from $100 to.**$125.00**

Plug Horse, crystal, 1941 – 1946, 4x4", from $100.00 to $125.00.

Pouter pigeon, crystal, 1947-49, 6½x7½", from $1,000 to..**$1,200.00**
Ram's head, stopper, crystal, 1940s, from $300 to **$325.00**

Imperial

Colt (kicking, balking or standing), Horizon Blue, 1979, set of 3 from $90 to **$120.00**
Dolphin, candlestick, vaseline, 1970s, 10½", ea from $125 to **$150.00**
Dragon, candleholder, crystal frosted, ca 1949, 6¾x6¾", ea from $150 to **$175.00**
Egret, crystal satin, ca 1949, 9½", from $450 to...............**$550.00**
Elephant, Eminent; milk glass, 1980s, 4", from $375 to....**$425.00**
Hen, charcoal satin, made from Heisey mold, 1980, 4½", from $150 to **$200.00**

Scolding Bird, frosted, signed Evans, 1949, 5", from $175.00 to $200.00.

Scottie dog, bookend, caramel slag, 1982-85, 6½", ea from $100 to **$150.00**
Servants (man & lady), candleholder, crystal frost, Cathay Line, ca 1949, 9", ea from $250 to **$275.00**

L.E. Smith

Camel, cobalt, recumbent, 4½x6", from $65 to...................**$75.00**
Cock, Fighting; amberina, 1960s, 9", from $45 to..............**$65.00**
Horse, Rearing; bookend, Almond Nouveau, 8", ea from $55 to **$60.00**
King Fish, aquarium, green, 7¼x15", from $400 to **$450.00**
Owl on stump, crystal frosted w/hand-painted rose, 3½", from $14 to **$17.00**
Scottie dog, black, 5", from $50 to **$75.00**
Sparrow, yellow satin, head down, 3½", from $20 to..........**$25.00**
Swan, milk glass, #15, 1930s, 4½" L, from $20 to **$25.00**

New Martinsville

Eagle, crystal, #509, 1938, 8", from $65 to **$75.00**

Elephant bookend, crystal, 1990s, 5½", each from $70.00 to $90.00.

Elephant, incense burner, green w/decor, 1940, 6", from $350 to...**$400.00**
German shepherd, pink, oval base, #733, 6", from $125 to .**$150.00**
Horse, Rearing; bookend, crystal satin, 1940s, 7½x5½", ea from $70 to **$80.00**
Porpoise on wave, crystal, 1940s, 6", from $350 to............**$400.00**

Paden City

Bunny (Cotton Tail), dispenser, frosted blue, ears up, from $250 to **$300.00**
Dragon Swan, pale blue, ca 1940, 6½x10" **$550.00**
Goose, pale blue, ca 1940, 5", from $100 to.....................**$150.00**
Pelican, crystal, early 1940s, 10", from $650 to **$750.00**
Pheasant, Chinese; cobalt, ca 1940, 13½" L, from $225 to..**$250.00**

Tiffin

Dancing girl, puff box, pink satin, #9313, ca 1924, 6" H, from $150 to **$175.00**
Dog, in center of pin holder/ashtray, green, 1920s-30s, 3½x4" dia, from $35 to **$40.00**

Goose, crystal, head down, 1940s, 5x11½", from $350 to. **$400.00**

Lovebirds, lamp, orange w/green heads, 10½", from $450 to. **$550.00**

Pheasant, pale blue, turned head, 1940, 12" L, from $200 to. **$225.00**

Pheasant, paperweight, crystal, controlled bubbles, 12" L, from $250 to **$275.00**

Viking

Angelfish, crystal, #1303, 6½", from $65 to **$75.00**

Basset hound, crystal satin, #7965, ca 1980-81, 6" L, from $15 to **$20.00**

Duck, fighting; crystal, head down, #6712, ca 1967, 2½", from $45 to **$50.00**

Horse, amber, #1302, ca 1957, 11½", from $100 to **$125.00**

Horse head, crystal satin, 1980s, 5½" W, from $20 to.........**$25.00**

Mushroom, paperweight, med green, #6942, ca 1971, lg, from $40 to **$45.00**

Rabbit, pink, #7908, 1980s, 2", from $25 to......................**$30.00**

Rooster, orange, 9½", from $40.00 to $50.00. (Photo courtesy Lee Garmon and Dick Spencer)

Squirrel, crystal satin, ca 1980-81, 5x4¾", from $15 to.......**$20.00**

Swan, blue, Epic Line, #1324, 1960s-70s, 7" L, from $20 to. **$30.00**

Swan, yellow mist, paper label, 6" **$25.00**

Miscellaneous

Blenko, fish, vase, crystal w/green details, 1960s, 13x15", from $100 to **$150.00**

Co-Operative Flint Glass, elephant, amber, flower-frog back, ca 1930, 4½x7", from $350 to..**$400.00**

Dalzell-Viking, horse rearing, bookend, lavender ice, ca 1993, 7½", ea from $100 to **$125.00**

Federal, Mopey dog, crystal, #2565, 3½", from $5 to..........**$10.00**

Greensburg, elephant, ashtray, black, 1920s, 6½" dia, from $35 to **$45.00**

Kanawha, donkey, amber, 4¾x4", from $20 to....................**$25.00**

KR Haley, horse & rider, bookend, crystal, 6x6", ea from $45 to **$55.00**

Mosser, collie, crystal, #193, 1980s, 3", from $10 to **$15.00**

Pilgrim, cat, crystal & cobalt combination w/ruby collar, 7", from $35 to **$40.00**

Pilgrim, porpoise, crystal, #904, ca 1972, 6x9", from $25 to . **$35.00**

Pilgrim, sailboat, amber, #987, ca 1976-77, 6¼x8", from $15 to **$25.00**

Steuben, fish, vase, lavender, blown, swirl optic, #6421, 1920s, 12¾", from $400 to..**$450.00**

Unknown, pigeon, relish, yellow, 13" L, from $25 to **$35.00**

Unknown, rooster, crystal, 9½x10½", from $65 to..............**$75.00**

Glass Baskets

Glassmakers have produced lovely glass baskets in as many colors as there are styles and sizes. All were conceived with aesthetics in mind, and collectors are drawn to them, possibly more than to any other glass novelty, just because of the care taken by the manufacturer to make them attractive.

Czechoslovakia, multicolored swirl, etched mark, from $75.00 to $150.00. (Photo courtesy Carole Bess White)

Dugan/Diamond Glass, basketweave, marigold carnival, 7½", from $35 to **$55.00**

Duncan/Duncan Miller, paneled w/light floral cutting, crystal, attributed, 9¾", from $50 to **$75.00**

Duncan/Duncan Miller, pressed flower pattern, amber, slim w/ flared, scalloped rim, 10", from $65 to **$85.00**

Duncan/Duncan Miller, Souvenir Roseburg in red letters on clam-broth, gold on handle, 5", from $35 to......................**$45.00**

Duncan/Duncan Miller, Tavern, crystal, PAT'D molded in bottom, 11¾", from $65 to..**$85.00**

Heisey, Banded Picket, Moongleam, #461, 10½", from $375 to..**$425.00**

Heisey, Double Rib & Panel, crystal w/light cutting, #417, 8¼", from $190 to **$225.00**

Heisey, Recessed Panel, white satin, #465, 11", from $225 to. **$250.00**

Imperial, Daisy, caramel slag, IG logo molded in base, #40, 10", from $80 to **$95.00**

Imperial, Monticello, marigold carnival, #698, 10", from $100 to **$125.00**

Indiana, Garland w/ruby flash on crystal, crystal handle, 10½", from $40 to **$45.00**

Italy, multicolor millefiori, flared rim, striped handle, unmarked, ca 1973, 7½", from $55 to **$75.00**

Kanawha, Hobnail, milk glass opal, attributed, 7½", from $12 to **$20.00**

Kanawha, orange crackle, clear handle, 4½", from $15 to ... **$25.00**

LG Wright, Daisy & Button, yellow vaseline, 7½", from $65 to. **$75.00**

New Martinsville, Janice, crystal w/red handle, 8½", from $125 to **$135.00**

Tiffin, emerald green satin, smooth rim, #9574, 10½", from $85 to **$125.00**

Tiffin, favor type, sky blue satin, rope handle, #310, 3¼", from $35 to **$55.00**

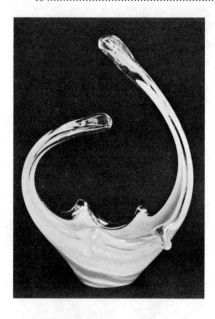

Unknown maker, green and white slag, 9", from $20.00 to $35.00. (Photo courtesy Carole Bess White)

Unmarked, blue cased w/milk glass, clear blue handle, 4¼", from $20 to **$25.00**

Unmarked, emerald green w/silver overlay, 10", from $200 to. **$250.00**

Unmarked, pink opaque w/crystal crest, foot & rigaree, 10¼", from $50 to **$75.00**

Viking, amber, scalloped rim, sm foot, 7½", from $15 to **$25.00**

Viking, ruby w/4 folds to rim, crystal handle, Viking Hand Made label, 6½", from $20 to **$40.00**

Westmoreland, English Hobnail, milk glass, newer rim (not flared out), 9", from $10 to **$20.00**

Westmoreland, orange w/black fired-on enamel at rim & foot, clear handle, 9½", from $45 to **$55.00**

Westmoreland, pink mist satin w/daisy decal, #750, 1970s-80s, 6½", from $20 to **$30.00**

Westmoreland, white satin w/floral decal, 6½", from $20 to.. **$30.00**

Glass Candlesticks

If you collect glass candlesticks, you'll need to get copies of *Glass Candlesticks of the Depression Era, Vols. 1* and *2,* by noted glass authorities, Gene and Cathy Florence. Candlesticks are organized by color, and they're shown large enough that you can see important details necessary to help you make a proper identification. Also available are *The Glass Candlestick Book, Vol. 1, 2,* and *3* by Tom Felt and Elaine and Rich Stoer. All are published by Collector Books.

Values suggested below are for a single candlestick, not a pair.

Anchor Hocking, Bedford, #280, crystal, Anchor mark inside candle cup, 5½", from $5 to **$8.00**

Anchor Hocking, Hurricane #1000, flashed pink, 7" (w/shade) .**$15.00**

Anchor Hocking, Oyster & Pearl #A881, pink, ca 1938-40, from $15 to **$20.00**

Anchor Hocking, Oyster & Pearl #881, pink & Vitrock, 3¼" ...**$12.50**

Anchor Hocking, Queen Mary #982, Royal Ruby, 4"........**$100.00**

Beaumont, Triple Candle, crystal satin, 4" **$40.00**

Blenko, #692, Olive Green, 8-pointed star, candleblock, 1969, 4⅜", from $10 to **$15.00**

Bryce Brothers, Aquarius, amber, 4½" **$15.00**

Bryce Brothers, Aquarius, crystal w/amethyst, 1950, 4½x4⅜", from $15 to **$20.00**

Cambridge, Caprice #72, Smoke, 2-light, 6" **$250.00**

Cambridge, Cherub #1191 (figural), crystal, 6" **$150.00**

Cambridge, Colonial #2657, crystal, hexagonal base, 1910-1920, 7x4", from $25 to **$30.00**

Cambridge, Corinth #3900/68, crystal, 5"........................... **$22.50**

Cambridge, Daisy Design (also known as Red Sunflower) #2760, crystal, 1910-1920, 9", from $55 to **$65.00**

Cambridge, Decagon #646, Royal Blue w/gold wildflower, 5" ..**$400.00**

Cambridge, pattern #647, Heatherbloom, 2-light, 5½" **$75.00**

Cambridge, Pristine #500 w/Wildflower etch, crystal, 6½"..**$65.00**

Cambridge, Sonata #1957/121, Carmen, 5⅜" **$45.00**

Cambridge, Tally Ho #1402/80 w/Elaine etch #762, crystal, 6" **$65.00**

Central Glass, Harding #2000, Orchid, 3⅛" **$30.00**

Dalzell Viking, Princess Plaza #5515, black w/pink inserts, 3-light, 6¾" **$25.00**

Dell, Tulip, amethyst, 1946, 5¼", from $30 to **$35.00**

Diamond Glass, Gothic #716, black, 3-light, 3½" **$25.00**

Dritz-Traum, Chateau #9648, crystal, round base, 3¼x3⅜", from $12 to **$15.00**

Diamond, Flounce, pink, 3¼", $22.00. (Photo courtesy Gene and Cathy Florence)

Duncan & Miller, Canterbury #115, crystal, 6"................... **$25.00**

Duncan & Miller, Deco, ebony w/gold encrusted & etched base, ca 1930, 6x4¾", from $45 to... **$50.00**

Duncan & Miller, Quilted Diamond #44, amber, 3¾"........ **$25.00**

Duncan & Miller, Ripple (also known as Rings) #101, cobalt, low, 1927-30s, 3x4⅜", from $50 to **$60.00**

Duncan & Miller, Venetian #5, cobalt, 6" **$75.00**

Fenton, Hobnail #3870, milk glass, ring handle, 3¼".........**$25.00**

Fenton, Ming/Cornucopia #950, rose pink, 5½" **$30.00**

Fenton, Princess #315, Chinese Yellow, 1924-25, 3-3½", 4¾" dia base, from $50 to **$65.00**

Fostoria, Coronation, crystal, 6" **$30.00**

Fostoria, Fairfax #2375, Acanthus etch #282, amber, 3" **$35.00**

Fostoria, Heirloom #1515/311, blue opalescent, 9" **$75.00**

Fostoria, Palm Leaf Brocade #2394, rose w/Mother-of-Pearl iridescence w/gold, 1¾" **$35.00**

Fostoria, Scroll #2395, Ebony, 3⅜" **$25.00**

Fostoria, Spiral Optic #2372, green, 1½" **$20.00**

Fostoria, Sunray #2510, crystal, 3¼" **$18.00**

Fostoria, Versailles #2375 w/#278 etch, topaz, 3¼" **$30.00**

Fostoria, Wistar #2620, crystal, 4" **$18.00**

Hazel-Atlas, Star #930, Moroccan Amethyst, 1¼" **$50.00**

Heisey, Crystolite #1502, crystal, candleblock, 1941-55, 2¼x1⅝x3⅜", from $15 to **$20.00**

Heisey, Crystolite #1503, crystal, 2-light, 6" **$50.00**

Heisey, Empress, crystal, 1938-42, 3½x4⁵⁄₁₆", from $25 to ..**$30.00**

Heisey, Four Leaf #1552, crystal, 1½" **$30.00**

Heisey, Old Sandwich #1404, Moonleam, 1931-37, 6x4¼", from $130 to **$145.00**

Heisey, Queen Ann, crystal, footed, handles, 1938-44, from $30 to...**$35.00**

Heisey, Thumbprint & Panel #1433, Flamingo, 2-light, 5½" .**$65.00**

Imperial, Double Heart #753, crystal, 3-light, 6½" **$45.00**

Imperial, Empire Dolphin #779, Viennese Blue, 5" **$25.00**

Imperial, Hobnail #643, Dewdrop Opalescent, ca 1966, 2x4½", from $25 to **$30.00**

Imperial, Hoffman House #46, Antique Blue, ground bottom rim, 1966-71, 4¾" dia, from $16 to **$20.00**

Imperial, Provencial, #1506, Heather, 1960-62, 2½x3¼", from $25 to **$30.00**

Indiana, Coronation, crystal w/silver overlay, early 1950s, 4½x3½", from $20 to **$25.00**

Indiana, Harvest #2970, milk glass, 4"............................**$8.00**

Indiana, Wedgwood, crystal w/fired-on orange, black trim on round base & cup, 8⅛x4⅛", from $12 to **$17.50**

Indiana, Wild Rose & Leaves, marigold carnival, 2¼" **$5.00**

Indiana, Willow/Oleander #1008, crystal, 4"............................**$18.00**

Indiana, Willow/Oleander #1008, Terrace Green, 4" **$45.00**

Jefferson, Chippendale #T335, crystal, 5-sided scalloped base w/ribbed column, 1910-1918, 8½x4⅜", from $35 to **$40.00**

Libbey, Worthington #4084, cobalt, round base w/6 panels, 1994, 4x3½", from $6 to............................**$8.00**

McKee, Brocade #200, rose pink, octagonal base, 2⅞" **$20.00**

McKee, Cinderella, blue opaque, Victorian-style chamberstick, 4½x4½", from $25 to............................**$35.00**

McKee, Crucifix, Opaque Blue, sm, gold-painted Christ figural, hexagonal base, ca 1899-1920s, 9x3¾", from $140 to.......**$180.00**

Morgantown, Spindle #1205, Peacock Blue, Fostoria design, mid-1960s, 10x2¾", from $35 to **$50.00**

New Martinsville, #220 (Largo Line), crystal, 5¼" **$18.00**

New Martinsville, Christina #821, crystal, 1940s, 5⅝x3¾", from $25 to **$30.00**

New Martinsville, Diamond Thumbprint #7202, crystal, 4x6", from $15 to............................**$20.00**

New Martinsville, Epic, #1199, Amethyst, ca 1957, 5", from $20 to **$25.00**

New Martinsville, Janice (flame) #4585, Colonial Blue, 5½" ..**$75.00**

New Martinsville, Princess Plaza, ruby, ca 1955 – 1960s, 4¾", from $50.00 to $65.00. (Photo courtesy Gene and Cathy Florence)

Paden City, Crow's Foot #890, ruby, 2-light, 5¼"...............**$50.00**

Paden City, Party Line #191, amber, 4¼" **$10.00**

Paden City, Party Line #192, green, 3½" **$15.00**

Smith (LE), Dominion #1641, crystal, octagonal base, 1986-87, 7¾x3¾"............................**$16.00**

US Glass, Hobnail #518, Plum, 3½"............................**$25.00**

United States Glass, King's Crown, US-166 No. 4016-18, ca 1952 – 1962, from $70.00 to $90.00. (Photo courtesy Gene and Cathy Florence)

US Glass/Tiffin, Twisted, blue satin, 9" **$25.00**

Westmoreland, Ball Stem, #1050, crystal, ca 1924-1930s, 9", from $25 to **$35.00**

Westmoreland, Della Robbia #1058, Green Mist, 3¼" **$35.00**

Westmoreland, Lotus #1921, amber, 4" **$15.00**

Westmoreland, Lotus #1921, green satin, leaf base w/twisted column, tulip candle-cup, 1926, 9x5¾", from $65 to.......**$75.00**

Westmoreland, Mt Vernon #1017, Antique Topaz, hexagonal base w/ribbed column, 8½x4⅝", from $50 to......................**$60.00**
Westmoreland, Ring & Petal #1875, milk glass, 3½"...........**$12.50**

Glass Knives

Popular during the Depression years, glass knives were made in many of the same colors as the glass dinnerware of the era — pink, green, light blue, crystal, and more rarely, amber or white (originally called opal). Some were hand painted with flowers or fruit. The earliest boxes had poems printed on their tops explaining the knife's qualities in the pre-stainless steel days: 'No metal to tarnish when cutting your fruit, and so it is certain this glass knife will suit.' Eventually, a tissue flyer was packed with each knife, which elaborated even more on the knife's usefulness. 'It is keen as a razor, ideal for slicing tomatoes, oranges, lemons, grapefruit and especially constructed for separating the meaty parts of grapefruit from its rind...' Boxes add interest by helping identify distributors as well as commercial names of the knives.

When originally sold, the blades were ground to a sharp cutting edge, but due to everyday usage, the blades eventually became nicked. Collectors will accept reground, resharpened blades as long as the original shape has been maintained.

Documented US glass companies that made glass knives are the Akro Agate Co., Cameron Glass Corp., Houze Glass Corp., Imperial Glass Corp., Jeannette Glass Co., and Westmoreland Glass Co.

Internet final-bid auction prices indicate what a person is willing to pay to add a new or different piece to a personal collection and may not necessarily reflect any price guide values.

Aer-Flo, green, 7½", from $70 to...**$75.00**

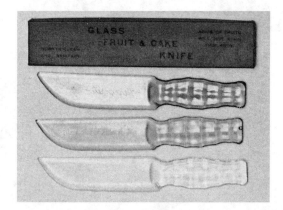

Block, crystal, from $15.00 to $22.00; green, $35.00; pink, $30.00; box, $5.00. (Photo courtesy Gene and Cathy Florence)

Buffalo Knife (BK Co), crystal, 9¼", from $15 to **$18.00**
Candlewick, crystal, 8½", from $500 to **$550.00**
Durex, 3-Leaf, pink, 9¼", from $32 to................................**$35.00**
Durex 3-Leaf, blue, 8½", from $38 to **$45.00**
Durex 3-Leaf, crystal, 8½", from $10 to **$15.00**
Durex 3-Leaf, green, 9¼", from $35 to...............................**$40.00**
Durex 5-Leaf, crystal, 8½" or 9¼", from $10 to **$15.00**
Durex 5-Leaf, green, 8½", from $35 to...............................**$40.00**

Durex 5-Leaf, pink (light or dark), 9¼", from $25 to..........**$35.00**

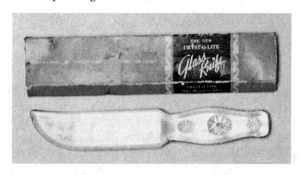

Pinwheel, crystal, $10.00; box, $5.00. (Photo courtesy Gene and Cathy Florence)

Plain handle, green, 8½", from $35 to...............................**$40.00**
Rose spray, amber, 8½", from $275 to **$295.00**
Stonex, crystal, 8¼", from $30 to **$40.00**
3-Star, blue, 8½", from $30 to..**$35.00**
3-Star, crystal, 9¼", from $10 to..**$15.00**
3-Star, pink (light or dark), 9¼", from $32 to **$35.00**

Golden Foliage

In 1935 Libbey Glass was purchased by Owens-Illinois but continued to operate under the Libbey Glass name. After World War II, the company turned to making tableware and still does today. Golden Foliage is just one of the many patterns made during the 1950s. It is a line of crystal glassware with a satin band that features a golden maple leaf as well as other varieties. The satin band is trimmed in gold, above and below. Since this gold seems to have easily worn off, be careful to find mint pieces for your collection. This pattern was made in silver as well.

Advisor: Debbie Coe (See Directory, Cape Cod)

Decanter, 12", $12.50. (Photo courtesy Randy and Debbie Coe)

Bowl, 2x3¾" **$5.00**
Creamer & sugar bowl **$12.50**
Creamer & sugar bowl, in metal frame **$14.50**
Goblet, cocktail; 4-oz **$6.00**
Goblet, cordial; 1-oz **$8.50**
Goblet, pilsner; 11-oz **$9.50**
Goblet, sherbet; 6½-oz **$5.00**
Goblet, water; 9-oz **$8.50**
Ice bucket **$15.00**
Ice tub, in metal 3-footed frame **$19.50**
Pitcher, cocktail; slim, 10½x3", w/glass stir rod ... **$45.00**
Pitcher, 5¼", w/metal frame **$16.50**
Salad dressing set, includes 3 bowls (4") & brass-finished caddy . **$19.50**
Tumbler, beverage; 12½-oz **$8.50**
Tumbler, cooler; tall & slim, 14-oz **$9.50**
Tumbler, iced tea; flared sides, 15-oz **$6.50**
Tumbler, juice; 6-oz **$5.00**
Tumbler, old-fashioned; 9-oz **$6.00**
Tumbler, shot glass, 2-oz **$6.50**
Tumbler, water; 10-oz **$8.50**
Tumblers, beverage; 12½-oz, set of 8 in metal frame **$60.00**

Granite Ware

Though it really wasn't as durable as its name suggests, there's still a lot of granite ware around today, though much of it is now in collections. You may even be able to find a bargain. The popularity of the 'country' look in home decorating and the exposure it's had in some of the leading decorating magazines has caused granite ware prices, especially on rare items, to soar in recent years.

It's made from a variety of metals coated with enameling of various colors, some solid, others swirled. It's color, form, and, of course, condition that dictates value. Swirls of cobalt and white, purple and white, green and white, and brown and white are unusual, but even solid gray items such as a hanging salt box or a chamberstick can be expensive because pieces like those are rare. Decorated examples are uncommon — so are children's pieces and salesman's samples.

Unless otherwise noted, our values reflect the worth of items in at least near mint condition. To evaluate items with wear and chipping, be sure to drastically reduce these values in proportion to the amount of damage.

For further information, we recommend *The Collector's Encyclopedia of Granite Ware* by Helen Greguire (Collector Books).

Bean pot, solid blue w/white interior, perforated lid, seamless, 7¾" **$125.00**
Boiler, rice/farina; blue & white lg swirl, black trim, seamless, 6½" **$485.00**
Bowl, blue & white lg mottle, white interior, US Standard...label, 2½x6" **$125.00**
Bowl, mixing; yellow & white lg swirl w/black trim, 1950s, 6x12¼" **$50.00**
Bowl, vegetable; brown & white lg swirl, white interior, oval, 1½x7½x9" **$295.00**
Bread pan, blue & white lg mottle, white interior, oblong, 3x4¾x9¾" **$345.00**

Bucket, gray med mottle, riveted ears, wire bail, 5x4¾" **$115.00**
Bucket, green to moss green, white interior, Shamrock Enameled... label, 7¼" **$275.00**
Bucket, slop; blue & white med mottle, black wood bail, 9½" .. **$225.00**
Candlestick, red w/black trim, shell form, finger ring, 1½x5¾" . **$145.00**
Chamber pot, blue & white lg mottled, blue trim & handles, seamless, 8" dia, G+ **$135.00**
Coffee basket, solid light gray, stemmed, 4¾x2⅜" dia, VG.. **$45.00**
Coffeepot, gray lg mottle, seamed, 9½", VG **$195.00**
Coffeepot, light blue & white med swirl, white interior, black trim, 6¾x4½" **$160.00**
Cup, yellow & white lg mottle w/black trim, 1960s, 2x3⅛" .. **$45.00**
Cupsidor, white w/cobalt trim, 2-pc, marked Sweden, 2⅜x8" .. **$95.00**
Double boiler, blue & white mottle, gray interior w/blue flecks/black trim, 8½", VG **$250.00**
Double boiler, cream w/green trim & handles, Belle shape, seamless, 6½" **$75.00**
Dustpan, solid red, 13⅜x10½" **$265.00**
Egg cup, white w/green trim, 2x2" **$95.00**
Funnel, blue & white med mottle, gray interior, squatty, seamed, 4¾", VG **$130.00**
Funnel, white w/black trim & handle, squatty, 4¾x7½", G+ . **$45.00**
Grater, cream w/green handle, flat, 1x4½x6½" **$130.00**
Kettle, cream w/green trim, 16 ribs, w/lid, 6x7⅜", NM **$40.00**
Ladle, soup; gray sm mottle, riveted handle, 7¾" L, G+ **$75.00**
Lady finger pan, gray lg mottle, Agate...L&G Mfg..., ½x11½x6" .. **$395.00**
Milk can, white w/green trim & handle, wooden bail, marked Savory Ware, 6¼" **$95.00**
Mold, lobster; solid blue w/white interior, handles, 3¾x7x10", G+ **$165.00**

Muffin pan, cobalt blue with white mottle, $425.00; sugar bowl, cobalt blue with white mottle, $495.00. (Photo courtesy Helen Greguire)

Muffin pan, solid red w/cream interior, 11-cup, Griswold mark, 11⅛" L **$145.00**
Mug, light gray & white lg marbleized, white interior, seamless, 4⅛", VG **$75.00**
Pail, water; white w/blue scallop design, white interior, Bonny Blue, 9½", VG **$160.00**

Pan, pink & white lg mottle, cobalt trim, white interior, handles, 8¼"..$235.00

Paperweight, light gray on cast iron, Your Warm Friend...Furnaces, 2½", VG...$175.00

Pitcher, milk; brown & white med mottle, black handle, Onyx Ware, 5½", G+..$135.00

Pitcher, molasses; solid white, dark blue handle/trim, 5½x3½" .$145.00

Pitcher, solid mauve rose w/white interior, black trim, Poland, 3x3⅝", VG $35.00

Pitcher, water; mauve rose w/white interior, black trim, seamless, 9¼"...$135.00

Plate, light blue & white med swirl, ¾x10", VG..................$75.00

Platter, blue & white med mottle, white interior, blue trim, oval, 20½", VG...$195.00

Pudding pan, lg gray mottle, La Fayette Quality...label, 5¼" ..$50.00

Roaster, blue & white fine mottle, white interior, black trim, seamless, 16½" $150.00

Roaster, cream & green, oval, embossed Savory, 8x10⅝x17", G+....$85.00

Saucepan, red-orange w/white interior, black trim/handle, 1960s, 6" dia, VG...$20.00

Scoop, solid white, seamless, 2¾x9¼", VG........................$95.00

Scoop, spice; solid red w/gold bands & trim, white interior, 4¼" L $185.00

Strainer, tea; gray med mottle, perforated bottom, 4x⅞"......$95.00

Teakettle, dark gray relish, seamed, aluminum whistle, 4⅝", VG $130.00

Teakettle, red w/black interior, bottom, trim & handle, seamless, 7½"...$100.00

Teakettle for oil stove, gray medium mottle, $500.00. (Photo courtesy Helen Greguire)

Teapot, blue & white chicken wire w/white interior, 5¾x4⅝"...$165.00

Tray, blue & white lg swirl, white interior, black trim, oblong, 15⅝"..$595.00

Vegetable dish, white w/cobalt trim, oblong, 1½x6¼x4⅝" ..$35.00

Washbasin, blue & white lg swirl, eyelet for hanging, 3⅝x13¾" ..$225.00

Wine cooler, yellow & white lg swirl, black trim, ca 1960, 7" dia $275.00

Griswold Cast-Iron Cooking Ware

Late in the 1800s, the Griswold company introduced a line of cast-iron cooking ware that was eventually distributed on a large scale nationwide. Today's collectors appreciate the variety of skillets, cornstick pans, Dutch ovens, and griddles available to them, and many still enjoy using them to cook with.

Several marks have been used; most contain the Griswold name, though some were marked simply 'Erie.'

If you intend to use your cast iron, you can clean it safely by using any commercial oven cleaner. (Be sure to re-season it before you cook in it.) A badly pitted, rusty piece may leave you with no other recourse than to remove what rust you can with a wire brush, paint the surface black, and find an alternate use for it around the house. For instance, you might use a kettle to hold a large floor plant or some magazines. A small griddle or skillet would be attractive as part of a wall display in a country kitchen. It should be noted that most of our prices are for pieces in excellent condition. Items that are cracked, chipped, pitted, or warped are worth substantially less or nothing at all, depending on rarity.

Note: The letters PIN in the following listings indicate Product Identification Numbers; TM indicates trademark, and FM full writing.

Breadstick pan, #23, EX...$35.00

Breadstick pan, #24, PIN 957, G.............................$150.00

Brownie cake pan, #9, EX......................................$60.00

Cake mold, Santa..$445.00

Casserole, #845, w/lid, EX.....................................$75.00

Corn bread pan, #21, EX.......................................$50.00

Cornstick pan, #22, ERIE, PIN 954, EX, from $55 to........$75.00

Cornstick pan, #28, EX $195.00

Cornstick pan, #262, ERIE USA, EX........................$20.00

Cornstick pan, #262, EX, from $55 to $75.00

Cornstick pan, #272, EX..$70.00

Cornstick pan, #273, 7 sticks, EX...........................$35.00

Cornstick pan, #282, from $150.00 to $165.00.

Cornstick pan, #283, EX $90.00

Dutch oven, #6, G..$95.00

Family grill, #18, G...$60.00

Gem pan, #1, VG..$40.00

Gem pan, #2, w/pattern number, EX..........................$165.00

Gem pan, #3, PIN 942, variation #3, EX $60.00

Gem pan, #14, rectangular, variation #4, G................$425.00

Gem pan, #947, EX..$100.00

Golf ball pan, #19, EX...................................$375.00
Griddle, #7, ERIE, PIN 607, EX.......................**$55.00**
Griddle, #9, New England, EX..........................$75.00
Kettle ashtray, #32, EX $40.00
Lard press, 4-qt, EX.....................................**$125.00**
Muffin pan, #7, w/pattern number, EX $200.00
Muffin pan, #17, G.......................................$70.00
Patty bowl, PIN 871, G $40.00
Roaster, #5, Slant/ERIE, PINs 2627 & 2630, oval, VG/EX.**$180.00**
Skillet, #2, Block TM, smooth bottom, EX $260.00
Skillet, #2, Slant/Erie, smoke ring, EX $350.00
Skillet, #3, Block TM, VG $20.00
Skillet, #3, flat bottom, EX $28.00
Skillet, #4, Slant/ERIE, PIN 702, EX $60.00
Skillet, #5, Erie, PIN 3348, G.........................$400.00
Skillet, #6, sm logo, EX $25.00
Skillet, #6, Victor, fully marked, EX $160.00
Skillet, #8, extra deep, Block TM, no heat ring, self-basting lid, EX ..**$90.00**
Skillet, #8, hinged, EX $68.00
Skillet, #8, Victor, fully marked, EX $35.00
Skillet, #8, w/self-basting lid, EX $80.00
Skillet, #9, Slant/ERIE, PIN 727, wooden handle, VG/EX .$20.00
Skillet, #12, Mountain, EX $130.00
Skillet, #13, Block TM, G...............................$900.00
Skillet, #13, Slant/ERIE, G-.........................$1,250.00
Skillet, #14, bailed handle, G.......................$1,100.00
Skillet, #43, Chef, G $40.00
Skillet, #663, Colonial Breakfast, EX $80.00
Skillet, fish; #15, PN 1013, oval, EX $200.00
Skillet grill, #250...$30.00
Skillet lid, #4, high dome, smooth top, EX.......$300.00
Skillet lid, #6, low dome, FM, G $100.00
Skillet lid, #11, low dome, smooth top, EX $310.00

**Trivet, Classic, 6x4½", from
$70.00 to $90.00.**

Vienna bread pan, #26, EX...............................$80.00
Waffle iron, #18, Hearts & Star, EX $135.00

Guardian Ware

The Guardian Service Company was in business from 1935 until 1955. They produced a very successful line of hammered aluminum that's just as popular today as it ever was. (Before 1935 Century Metalcraft made similar ware under the name SilverSeal, you'll occasionally see examples of it as well.) Guardian Service was sold through the home party plan, and special hostess gifts were offered as incentives. Until 1940 metal lids were used, but during the war when the government restricted the supply of available aluminum, glass lids were introduced. The cookware was very versatile, and one of their selling points was top-of-the-stove baking and roasting — 'no need to light the oven.' Many items had more than one use. For instance, their large turkey roaster came with racks and could be used for canning as well. The kettle oven used for stovetop baking also came with canning racks. Their Economy Trio set featured three triangular roasters that fit together on a round tray, making it possible to cook three foods at once on only one burner; for even further fuel economy, the casserole tureen could be stacked on top of that. Projections on the sides of the pans accommodated two styles of handles, a standard detachable utility handle as well as black 'mouse ear' handles for serving.

The company's logo is a knight with crossed weapons, and if you find a piece with a trademark that includes the words 'Patent Pending,' you'll know you have one of the earlier pieces.

In 1955 National Presto purchased the company and tried to convince housewives that the new stainless steel pans were superior to their tried-and-true Guardian aluminum, but the ladies would have none of it. In 1980 Tad and Suzie Kohara bought the rights to the Guardian Service name as well as the original molds. The new company is based in California, and is presently producing eight of the original pieces, canning racks, pressure cooker parts, serving handles, and replacement glass lids. Quoting their literature: 'Due to the age of the GS glass molds, we are unable to provide perfect glass covers. The covers may appear to have cracks or breaks on the surface. They are not breaks but mold marks and should be as durable as the originals.' They go on to say: 'These glass covers are not oven proof.' These mold marks may be a good way to distinguish the old glass lids from the new, and collectors tell us that the original lids have a green hue to the glass. The new company has also reproduced three cookbooks, one that shows the line with the original metal covers. If you want to obtain replacements, see the Directory for Guardian Service Cookware.

Be sure to judge condition when evaluating Guardian Service. Wear, baked-on grease, scratches, and obvious signs of use devaluate its worth. Our prices range from pieces in average to exceptional condition. To be graded exceptional, the interior of the pan must have no pitting and the surface must be bright and clean. An item with a metal lid is worth approximately 25% more than the same piece with a glass lid. To most successfully clean your grungy garage-sale finds, put them in a self-cleaning oven, then wash them in soap and water. Never touch them with anything but a perfectly clean hotpad while they're hot, and make sure they're completely cooled before you put them in water. Abrasive cleansers only scratch the surface.

Advisor: Dennis S. McAdams (See the Directory, Guardian Service Cookware)

Ashtray, glass, w/knight & white stars logo, hostess gift, from $10 to **$15.00**
Bacon fryer, rectangular, 9x13", w/bacon press **$135.00**

Beverage urn, w/lid (no screen or dripper), common, from $15 to...**$20.00**

Beverage urn (coffeepot), glass lid, complete w/screen & dripper, 15", from $50 to..**$60.00**

Can of cleaner, unopened...**$15.00**

Casserole, all glass, Alumiglass Ovenware, w/lid, very rare, 3½x8" dia..**$550.00**

Coasters, glass w/knight logo, 6 in upright metal carrier......**$35.00**

Condiment bowl, glass lid, Deco handles, 1 from condiment set, from $40 to **$50.00**

Condiment set, 3 glass-lidded containers in 3-legged wire frame w/wooded knob finial, from $175 to...........................**$225.00**

Cookbook, Century Metal Crafts, 1st edition, metal lids shown .**$35.00**

Cookbooks, Guardian Ware, metal lids shown, intact, 72 pages, 5½x8½", from $25 to...**$35.00**

Dome cooker, Tom Thumb, glass lid, w/handles, 3½x4⅞" dia, from $25 to **$35.00**

Dome cooker, 1-qt, glass lid, w/handles, 6¾" dia, from $30 to ..**$45.00**

Dome cooker, 1-qt, metal lid, w/handles, 6¾" dia, from $35 to..**$45.00**

Dome cooker, 2-qt, glass lid, w/handles, 4½x10½" dia, from $35 to **$50.00**

Dome cooker, 4-qt, glass lid, w/handles, 6½x10½" dia, from $35 to **$55.00**

Double boiler, 2 pcs w/handles, glass lid, 12x9¾" overall **$75.00**

Fryer, breakfast; glass lid, 10", from $35 to.........................**$50.00**

Fryer, chicken; glass lid, 12", from $60 to.........................**$80.00**

Gravy boat, w/undertray, from $25 to...............................**$40.00**

Griddle broiler, octagonal, w/handles, polished center, 16½" dia, from $35 to **$40.00**

Griddle/tray, w/handles, 12½" dia cooking area, 17" wide, from $20 to **$30.00**

Handle, clamp-on style, from $15 to **$20.00**

Handles, slip-on style, Bakelite, pr, from $20 to **$30.00**

Ice bucke (silver-tone) & 8 glasses (w/knight & shield), in chrome stand, hostess gift...**$75.00**

Ice bucket, glass lid, liner & tongs, 9", from $50 to.............**$75.00**

Kettle oven, glass lid, bail handle, w/rack, 6-qt, 11" dia, from $150 to **$185.00**

Kettle oven, glass lid, bail handle, w/rack, 8x12" dia, from $100 to **$125.00**

Lid, glass, triangular, from $15 to **$20.00**

Lid, glass, 7" dia, from $15 to...**$18.00**

Lid, glass, 8½" dia, from $20 to..**$25.00**

Lid, glass, 10" dia...**$30.00**

Lid, glass, 12" dia...**$35.00**

Omelet pan, hinged in center, black handle on ea half, from $60 to **$75.00**

Pitcher, metal, bulb jug w/recessed disk in ea side, hostess gift, 8x10", minimum value **$275.00**

Pot, triangular, w/glass lid, 7" to top of finial, 11" L, from $30 to...**$40.00**

Potato ricer, w/wood pestle, complete, 11"........................**$125.00**

Pots, triangular, ea w/glass lid, 7" to top of final, 11" L, ea from $25 to **$35.00**

Pressure cooker, minimum value **$100.00**

Roaster, metal lid, 4x12½" L, from $60 to..........................**$80.00**

Roaster, turkey; glass lid, no rack, 16½" L, from $100 to ..**$125.00**

Roaster, turkey; glass lid, 15" L, +metal serving tray/lid, 3-pc set **$275.00**

Roaster, turkey; metal lid, w/rack, 16½" L, from $175 to..**$225.00**

Salt & pepper shakers, metal, chef figures, hostess gift, 3½", pr from $40 to **$50.00**

Salt & pepper shakers, teapot forms, metal tops, pressed glass bottoms, hostess gift, pr, from $30 to **$45.00**

Service kit, w/3 cleaners, 1 brush, 1 cookbook, 1 clamp-on handle, pr of slip-on handles, steel wool, from $125 to...........**$150.00**

Steak servers, well & tree bottom, oval, set of 4 ....**$60.00**

Travel bar, 4 aluminum tumblers, tray, 2 jiggers & stirrer in fitted carrying case...**$85.00**

Tray, serving; hammered center, w/handles, 13" dia, from $20 to..**$30.00**

Tray, serving; hammered center, w/handles, 15" dia, from $25 to..**$35.00**

Tray/platter, w/handles, hammered surface, also used as roaster cover for stacking, 10x15" L, from $25 to **$35.00**

Trivet, expanding, chrome plated, adjusts from 10⅜" L to 13½x8" **$80.00**

Trivet, for Economy Trio set, 11¾" dia, from $35 to...........**$45.00**

Tumblers, glassware, stylized knight & shield in silver, & coasters w/embossed head of knight, 4 of ea in metal rack.........**$80.00**

Tumblers & ashtray/coasters, glassware w/Guardian logo, white stars & gold trim, hostess gift, 6 of ea, from $275 to.........**$325.00**

Tureen, bottom; glass lid, from $40 to...............................**$65.00**

Tureen, casserole; glass lid, from $65 to **$90.00**

Tureen, top; glass lid, from $30 to **$45.00**

Roaster, glass lid, 4x15", from $65.00 to $90.00.

Gurley Candle Company

Gurley candles were cute little wax figures designed to celebrate holidays and special occasions. They are all marked Gurley on the bottom. They were made so well and had so much great detail that people decided to keep them year after year to decorate with instead of burning them. Woolworth's and other five-and-dime stores sold them from about 1940 until the 1970s. They're still plentiful today and inexpensive.

Tavern Novelty Candles were actually owned by Gurley. They were similar to the Gurley candles but not quite as detailed. All are marked Tavern on the bottom. Prices listed here are for unburned candles with no fading.

Buyers should note that some of these candles are being reproduced. The Vermont Country Store Fall 2006 catalog has several Halloween, Thanksgiving, and Christmas candles. The listing describes them as reproductions of the 1950s. The candles pictured are witch, ghost, jack-o'-lantern, Indians (two sizes), Pilgrims (two sizes), turkey, angel, Santa, choir boy, and choir girl. At this time it is unknown if these new items are marked.

Advisor: Debbie Coe (See Directory, Cape Cod)

Christmas, A Night Before Christmas, boy & girl (2¾") w/sm dog & fireplace (3¼x5") w/stockings, MIB **$215.00**
Christmas, angel girl praying, blond hair, blue wings, 3" **$30.00**
Christmas, angel looking down on baby Jesus in manger, star shining above, 6" **$27.50**
Christmas, angel w/gold glitter, 4¾", pr **$15.00**

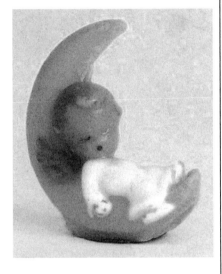

Christmas, baby angel sleeping on crescent moon, 3", $6.00.

Christmas, baby angel on half moon, marked Gurley, 2½" **$6.00**
Christmas, Black caroler man w/red clothes, 3" **$9.50**
Christmas, caroler man w/red clothes, 7" **$8.50**
Christmas, choir boy, maroon, 7", pr **$24.00**
Christmas, choir boy or girl, 2¾", ea **$3.50**
Christmas, choir boy or girl (Black), 2¾", pr **$20.00**
Christmas, evergreen tree, 3¼" **$6.00**
Christmas, lamppost, 12½", EXIB **$16.00**
Christmas, man playing violin, lady caroler & street lamp, EX on starry cardboard scene, missing cellophane wrapper **$12.50**
Christmas, Nativity, 2½" Mary, 3" Joseph, 2" Baby Jesus, 2½" lambs & 3½" star, MIP **$35.00**
Christmas, pine cone w/red spiral candle on top, 4" **$9.50**
Christmas, reindeer, marked Tavern, 3½" **$2.50**
Christmas, Rudolph w/red nose, 3" **$3.50**
Christmas, Santa Claus boots, red, 1940s, 3" **$6.50**
Christmas, Santa's head (hollow), candle behind lights face, EX... **$20.00**
Christmas, Santa standing, 7½" **$15.00**
Christmas, Santa waving, 5½" **$15.00**

Christmas, scenic candle w/lg tree towering at left of snowy scene w/evergreens & cottage on snow base, MIB **$45.00**
Christmas, snowman running w/red hat, 3" **$7.50**
Christmas, snowman w/fawn, 4" **$8.00**
Christmas, snowman w/red pipe & green hat, 5" **$6.00**
Christmas, spiral candle on pine cone, red & green w/gold glitter, 4" **$8.00**
Christmas, star & angel in blue sky over Baby Jesus, 6" **$30.00**
Christmas teddy bear, white w/red & green stocking cap, holly-trimmed scarf, 5½", MIB **$17.50**
Christmas, white church w/choirboy inside, 6" **$14.50**
Christmas, 3" deer standing in front of candle, 5" **$7.50**
Easter, birdhouse, pink w/yellow bird, 3" **$7.50**
Easter, calla lilies (10 of 12), MIB **$30.00**
Easter, chick, pink or yellow, 3" **$6.00**
Easter, chick (yellow) hatching from pink egg, chocolate inside ..**$20.00**
Easter, cross, pink on green grassy base, angel & rabbit at foot, 3" **$25.00**
Easter, cross w/lilies on pastel shape of stained-glass window, angel & lamb at base, 5½" **$30.00**
Easter, duck, white w/orange beaks & feet, black spot on tail feathers, Socony, 2½", set of 4, MIB **$30.00**
Easter, duck, yellow w/purple bow, 5" **$9.50**
Easter, egg, pink w/bunny inside, 3" **$10.00**
Easter, egg, pink w/squirrel inside, 3" **$12.00**
Easter, rabbit, pink, winking & holding carrot, 3¼" **$6.00**
Easter, rabbit, pink on green stump w/yellow tulips, MIB ... **$22.00**
Easter, rabbit, pink or yellow, 3" **$4.50**
Easter, rabbit (yellow) in green basket w/lg draping pink bow . **$25.00**
Easter, rabbit boy & girl: white w/lavender coat & hat, white w/yellow dress, lavender ear tips, 3½", 3¼", pr **$55.00**
Easter, tulip (head only), pink or yellow **$4.50**
Easter, white lily w/blue lip & green candle, 3" **$4.50**
Halloween, black cat (4") w/orange candlestick beside it **$22.50**
Halloween, Frankenstein, later issue but harder to find, 6" ..**$24.00**
Halloween, ghost, orange, 5", from $18 to **$10.00**
Halloween, ghost, white, 5" **$20.00**
Halloween, ghost in haunted house, 6" **$45.00**
Halloween, ghost w/trick-or-treat bag, 6", MIB **$24.00**
Halloween, jack-o'-lantern, orange w/green stem, round eyes & mouth, triangular nose, 3⅜" **$17.50**
Halloween, jack-o'-lantern, orange w/green stem, w/smiling mouth, 3⅝" **$24.00**
Halloween, jack-o'-lantern, painted features, tall black hat, 4". **$15.00**
Halloween, jack-o-lantern man, green outfit, brown hat, painted features, 1960s, 3", pr **$15.00**
Halloween, owl, black on orange stump, 3½" **$10.00**
Halloween, pumpkin w/black cat, 2½" **$9.00**
Halloween, pumpkin-face scarecrow, 5" **$14.00**
Halloween, skeleton, 8½" **$35.00**
Halloween, skull, pink w/black, 7" **$28.00**
Halloween, witch, black, 8" **$22.50**
Halloween, witch in cauldron, 6" **$28.00**
Halloween, witch's head, 5½" **$24.00**
Halloween, witch w/black cape, 3½" **$9.50**
Halloween, witching holding jack-o'-lantern, broom at side, orange & black, 8¾" **$25.00**

Halloween, 4" cut-out orange owl w/7½" black candle behind it **$24.00**

Halloween, 5 orange jack-o'-lanterns w/white candles, 1950s, unused, NMIB (sealed) **$50.00**

Other holidays, birthday boy, marked Tavern, 3" **$5.00**

Other holidays, birthday tugboats, red & blue, set of 4, MIP. **$25.00**

Other holidays, bride & groom, 4½", ea............................**$12.50**

Other holidays, Eskimo & igloo, marked Tavern, 2-pc **$12.50**

Other holidays, St Patrick's Day elf, light green, 1950s, 3½" ..**$24.00**

Other holidays, Western girl or boy, 3", ea............................**$8.00**

Thanksgiving, acorns & leaves, 3½" **$5.00**

Thanksgiving, gold sailing ship, 7½" **$12.50**

Thanksgiving, Indian boy & girl, brown & green clothes, 5", pr... **$24.00**

Thanksgiving, Pilgrim boy & girl, 5¼", 5½", pr **$15.00**

Thanksgiving, Pilgrim girl & boy, 2½", pr............................**$7.00**

Thanksgiving, Pilgrims (3 boys & 1 girl) & turkey, 3⅜", 3", 3¼x2", 5-pc set, MIB..**$18.00**

Thanksgiving, sailing ship, orange & yellow-brown, 3½", from $20 to **$18.00**

Thanksgiving, turkey, 2½" **$2.50**

Thanksgiving, turkey, 5¾", $10.00.

Thanksgiving, turkey, 6¼" **$12.00**

Hadley, M. A.

Since 1940, the M.A. Hadley Pottery (Louisville, Kentucky) has been producing handmade dinnerware and decorative items painted freehand in a folksy style with barnyard animals, baskets, whales, and sailing ships in a soft pastel palette of predominately blues and greens. Each piece is signed by hand with the first two initials and last name of artist-turned-potter Mary Alice Hadley, who has personally inspired each design. Some items may carry an amusing message in the bottom — for instance, 'Please Fill Me' in a canister or 'The End' in a coffee cup! Examples of this ware are beginning to turn up on the secondary market, and it's being snapped up not only by collectors who have to 'have it all' but by those who enjoy adding a decorative touch to a country-style room with only a few pieces of this unique pottery.

Horses and pigs seem to be popular subject matter; unusual pieces and the older, heavier examples command the higher prices.

Advisor: Lisa Sanders (See Directory, Hadley, M.A.)

Bank, cow figural, 5x3x6½", $20.00. (Photo courtesy Michael Sessman)

Bean pot, cow & pig, pitcher form w/spout, w/lid, 7" **$50.00**

Bowl, cow, oval, 1½x11x7" **$40.00**

Bowl, duck, oval, 8¼x7½", from $32 to **$28.00**

Bowl, farmer & wife, 3x11", from $35 to **$45.00**

Bowl, mixing; rooster, 4x8½" **$40.00**

Bowl, My Dog & bone, 2½x7¾" **$25.00**

Bowl, pears & grapes, 3x8" **$15.00**

Bowl, soup; skier, 7" **$15.00**

Butter dish, cow, rectangular, 2x7½" **$30.00**

Candleholder, angel w/harp & shamrock, 2" halo for candle, 10", ea **$25.00**

Canister, Coffee, Please Fill Me inside, 5½x5¾" **$40.00**

Canister, Dog Treats, Please Fill Me inside, 5½x5¾" **$40.00**

Canister, Goodies, Please Fill Me inside, 7x6½"...................**$45.00**

Canisters, set of four, $125.00. (Photo courtesy Michael Sessman)

Casserole, Bouquet, sm handles, 5x12" **$40.00**

Casserole, pig & cow, The End inside, w/lid, 3x10½" **$45.00**

Child's place setting, duck, plate, cup & bowl $27.50
Clock, barn, runs on battery, 9" dia $37.00
Cookie jar, Goodies & flower, 6x5" dia $40.00
Creamer & sugar bowl, cow & pig, miniature, 2x3½" $15.00
Creamer & sugar bowl, frog, w/lid, 2½" $30.00
Cup & saucer, demitasse; pear & grape, 2¼", 4¼", set of 8 ..... $55.00
Cup & saucer, jumbo; Dad, The End inside cup $25.00
Dispenser, Hand Soap $25.00
Flowerpot, turtle, 5x5" $25.00
Gravy boat, cow, 3x7" $30.00
Jar, jam/jelly; Sweets to the Sweet, slot in lid $20.00
Knob, farm/animal pattern, 1¼" dia, set of 11 .... $85.00
Mug, dog, flared sides, 12-oz $15.00
Mug, lamb, flared sides, 12-oz, 4¾" $15.00
Mug, turtle, 3¾" $13.00
Pet dish, Dog & 2 bones, 4x6½" $20.00
Pie plate, sailboat $35.00
Pitcher, cow, 6" $30.00
Pitcher, cow & tree, 8x5" $40.00
Pitcher, pig, 7¾" $30.00
Pitcher, ship & whale, 28-oz, 5¼x5" $27.50
Pitcher, syrup; 3½" $20.00
Place setting, donkey, mug, 5" bowl, 7" breakfast plate, 9" luncheon
    plate & 11" dinner plate, 5-pc set $57.50
Plate, cowboy stands w/rope, 11" $20.00
Plate, girl, 11" $20.00
Plate, horse, 11" $20.00
Plate, turtle, 7½" $15.00
Platter, bouquet of flowers, 13½x9" $30.00
Platter, cow, 11½x7¼" $38.00
Platter, farmer & wife, 13" dia $30.00
Platter, horse, 13" $60.00
Platter, rabbit, 13¾x9" $30.00
Salt & pepper shakers, lighthouse, 4½x2½", pr $25.00
Salt box, Salt, 5¼" $40.00
Teapot, Christmas tree, 1-qt $40.00
Teapot, house, 6½" $25.00
Vase, rooster figural, 5 holes in back, old signature, 9" $150.00
Wall pocket, flowers, conical, 8x7½x3½" $45.00
Water cooler, horse, brass spout, w/lid, 12" $150.00

Hagen-Renaker

This California-based company is one of the few surviving US Potteries from the 1940s and 1950s. Hagen-Renaker started out in 1945 in a garage in Culver City, California. In 1946 they moved to Monrovia, California, where they made mostly dishes with hand-painted fruit and animal designs. By 1948 they started producing realistic miniature animals, which are still their bestselling line. In 1952 they introduced Designers Workshop, a line of larger, very life-like animal figurines. The company is particularly famous for their beautiful horses, and many of their molds were leased to Breyer, who used them to make their famous plastic horses. In the late 1950s, Hagen-Renaker made gorgeous Disney figurines. Walt Disney was particularly impressed with these pieces, saying that Hagen-Renaker made the finest three-dimensional figurines he had ever seen.

In the late 1950s and early 1960s, Hagen-Renaker produced several new lines in an attempt to compete with cheaply made Japanese imports. Some of the lines they produced during that time were Millesan Drews Pixies, Rock Wall Plaques and Trays decorated with primitive animals similar to cave drawings, a grotesque miniature line called Little Horribles, and Black Bisque animals. They also experimented with cold paint called Aurasperse. This paint was used on miniature animals and a rare group of larger whimsical animals called Zany Zoo. Generally, Aurasperse-painted pieces are more valuable than normally fired items because they were made for such a short time, and the Aurasperse paint tends to wash off. Even with these new lines, the company was forced to shut down for a few months. Shortly after reopening, they moved to San Dimas, California, where they are still operating today.

From 1980 to 1986 Hagen-Renaker operated a second factory that specialized in the larger Designers Workshop figurines. Located in San Marcos, California, it had previously been Freeman-McFarlin. Hagen-Renaker added new designs and colors, but continued to make the Freeman-McFarlin line as well. In some cases it is impossible to tell which of the two companies made a particular piece. Hagen-Renaker also resurrected figurines from its Designers Workshop line of the '50s and '60s. These San Marcos-era pieces are becoming quite desiarble, particularly the horses.

In the late '80s Hagen-Renaker introduced new Stoneware and Speciality lines which are generally larger than the miniatures and smaller than the Designers Workshop pieces. The Stoneware line was quickly discontinued, but they still make the Specialty pieces. The current Hagen-Renaker line consists of 50 Specialty pieces and 200 miniatures. In addition, they intermittently release limited edition larger horses. Some are new molds, while others are reissues of the Designers Workshop line. There are currently five of these larger horses available in various colors with more to come. Some of these Designers Workshop horses are only available throught the Hagen-Renaker Collector's Club.

Advisors: Ed and Sheri Alcorn (See Directory, Hagen-Renaker)

Newsletter: The Hagen-Renaker Collector's Club Newsletter
c/o Debra Kerr
2055 Hammock Moss Drive
Orlando, FL 32820
Subscription rate: $24 per year

Black Bisque, cat head (cocked), black & white, 1959, 4⅞"..$105.00
Black Bisque, Feather Duster (bird), black & green, 1959, 5" . $65.00
Black Bisque, fox, black & green, 1959, 3¾" $100.00
Butter pat, apple design, #610, 1946-49, 3½" $35.00
Designers Workshop figurine, Abu Farwa, Arabian horse, turned
    head, 1955-57, 6" $550.00
Designers Workshop figurine, Arthur (chick), head down, 1955-67,
    1½" $75.00
Designers Workshop figurine, Beanbag, dachshund sitting, 1959-70,
    2" $35.00
Designers Workshop figurine, Bedouin on horse (gray) w/rifle,
    1956-58, 9½" $1,200.00

Designers Workshop figurine, Bucking Foal Peggy Lou, 1959, 4", $500.00. (Photo courtesy Ed and Sheri Alcorn)

Designers Workshop figurine, Cape buffalo, 1955 only, 4¾" . **$450.00**

Designers Workshop figurine, Frog Prince in hat, green, 1981-83, 3½"...**$150.00**

Designers Workshop figurine, giraffe baby, 1952-54, 5" **$125.00**

Designers Workshop figurine, grizzly bear on rock, 1961-81, 7¾"..**$300.00**

Designers Workshop figurine, Holstein cow, 1983-86, 5"..**$125.00**

Designers Workshop figurine, Honora (sm), American Saddlebred horse, brown matt, 1962-84, 6¾".................................**$375.00**

Designers Workshop figurine, Jamboree, Appaloosa horse, tan, 1993-94, 5" **$275.00**

Designers Workshop figurine, Lady, Fireside dalmatian, 1956-62, 10"..**$500.00**

Designers Workshop figurine, Life-Size Lying Cat, gray gloss, 1985 – 1986, 7" tall, $350.00. (Photo courtesy Ed and Sheri Alcorn)

Designers Workshop figurine, Little Red Hen, wearing apron, holding spoon & bread, 1986, 6½" **$250.00**

Designers Workshop figurine, Madame Fluff, Persian cat, 1954-55, 5"...**$125.00**

Designers Workshop figurine, Metalchex, quarter horse (lg), buckskin gloss, 1981-86, 11¾" **$500.00**

Designers Workshop figurine, Nubian goat doe, 1984-86, 5". **$125.00**

Designers Workshop figurine, Patience, recumbent doe, 1954-86, 4"...**$40.00**

Designers Workshop figurine, Pip Emma, cocker spaniel, black & white spotted, rare color, 1954-55, 2½".......................**$350.00**

Designers Workshop figurine, Puff, Persian kitten, 1954-55, 2½" **$100.00**

Designers Workshop figurine, Puss in Boots, 1984-86, 6½"..**$150.00**

Designers Workshop figurine, Tommy tortoise, 1955, 1½"..**$250.00**

Disney lg size, Bambi, 1956-57, 3½".................................**$300.00**

Disney lg size, Dumbo cookie jar, rare, 1956, 10" **$1,200.00**

Disney miniature, Bacchus from Fantasia, 1982, 2¾"........**$150.00**

Disney miniature, Flora from Sleeping Beauty, 1959-60, 2³⁄₁₆".**$160.00**

Disney miniature, John from Peter Pan, 1957-60, 2⅛"......**$400.00**

Disney miniature, Lady from Lady & the Tramp, 1955-59, 1¾" **$30.00**

Disney miniature, Mad Hatter, Alice in Wonderland, 1956, 1¼"..**$275.00**

Little Horribles miniature, Cave, 1959-60, 3½" **$100.00**

Little Horribles miniature, Eye (spider), #386, 1958-59, ⅞"..... **$50.00**

Little Horribles miniature, FHA, 1959, 1⅜" **$125.00**

Little Horribles miniature, Peeping Tom, 1959, 1⅝" **$140.00**

Miniature, alley cat, gray tabby, A-464, 1959-76, ¾" **$15.00**

Miniature, Appaloosa mare & foal on base, A-2011/2010, current, 2¼" **$10.00**

Miniature, Australian shepherd, A-2052, 1989-90, 1¾" **$35.00**

Miniature, ballerinas, 1958 – 1959, 2½" to 2¾", $125.00 each. (Photo courtesy Ed and Sheri Alcorn)

Miniature, banana bunch, A-1312A, 1956-80, ⅜" **$12.00**

Miniature, bear mama w/umbrella, A-1, 1949-50, 2" **$20.00**

Miniature, buzzard on branch, A-3374, 1999-2000, 2" **$15.00**

Miniature, Charlie, Cairn terrier, A-3290, current, 1¼" **$8.00**

Miniature, chihuahua seated, A-078, 1966-67, 1½" **$25.00**

Miniature, circus dog w/collar begging, A-270, 1955-56, 2"..**$55.00**

Miniature, crow on rock, A-889, 1987 ....**$25.00**

Miniature, dog dish, A-2008, 1988-92, ⅜"...........................**$8.00**

Miniature, flat fish, orange & black Aurasperse, A-123, 1960, rare, 1"..**$100.00**

Miniature, flat fish, pink & black, A-123, 1960-76, 1"........**$20.00**

Miniature, Flukes whale, A-887, 1987, ¾" **$25.00**

Miniature, German shepherd w/frisbee, A-2073, 1990-99, 2½" **$15.00**

Miniature, goat kid w/head up, A-3121, 1994-95, 1" **$10.00**

Miniature, guinea pig, A-3221, 1996-97, 1" **$15.00**

Miniature, Hereford bull, A-357, 1957-65, 1½" **$40.00**

Miniature, hippo baby, A-3193, 1996-98, ¾" **$8.00**

Miniature, horse rearing, glossy buckskin, A-234, 1950s, 3½" ..**$135.00**

Miniature, kitten, playful, white, A-075, 1950, 1" **$35.00**

Miniature, mallard duck w/wings spread, A-134, 1951-52, 2½" **$20.00**

Miniature, Monarch butterfly, A-99, 1950-51, rare, 2¾" ...**$225.00**

Miniature, Morgan mare, chestnut, A-388, 1959-70, 2¾" **$225.00**

Miniature, mouse crouching, A-180, 1953-current, ⅜" **$3.00**

Miniature, Native Dancer, race horse, A-012, 1961-66, 3" **$160.00**

Miniature, ostrich mama, A-43, 1959-87, 2½" **$20.00**

Miniature, Persian (papa) cat on pillow, white, A-353, 1968, 2⅛" **$75.00**

Miniature, Saddlebred horse, brown, A-458, 1959-69, 3" ..**$150.00**

Miniature, Scotch Fold kitten, gray, A-2043, 1989-90, ⅞" ..**$25.00**

Miniature, Scotch Fold kitten, spotted, A-2043, 1989-90, ⅞".. **$45.00**

Miniature, Swan Lake w/swans, A-380A, 1976-77, 5" **$85.00**

Miniature, zebra baby, A-174, 1983-86, 1" **$25.00**

Miniature, zebra mama, A-173, 1983-86, 1½" **$35.00**

Shadow box, Victorian lady, signed HR Calif, 1946-49, 4x5" **$50.00**

Specialty figurine, Canada geese on pond, #3030, 1991-94, 3⅛" **$55.00**

Specialty figurine, cat on pillow, #3108, 1993-94, 2⅝" **$40.00**

Specialty figurine, chimpanzee pr on base, #3148, 1994-96, 2" **$30.00**

Specialty figurine, frog playing banjo, #3180, 1995-current, 2¼" **$18.00**

Specialty figurine, hen & chick, #3327, 2000-05, 3½" **$25.00**

Specialty figurine, Orion, Appaloosa stallion, #32667, 1998-2000, 3⅛" **$45.00**

Specialty figurine, Wrangler, Shetland pony, #3345, 2001-05, 3¼" **$25.00**

Wall plaque, buck, 1959, 16" **$250.00**

Wall plaque on wood, geisha, 1959, 22x10½" **$230.00**

Zany Zoo, walrus w/monocle, gray Aurasperse finish, 1960 only, 3⅛" **$200.00**

Hall China Company

Hall China is still in production in East Liverpool, Ohio, where they have been located since around the turn of the century. They have produced literally hundreds of lines of kitchen and dinnerware items for both home and commercial use. Many of these have become very collectible.

They're especially famous for their teapots, some of which were shaped like automobiles, basketballs, doughnuts, etc. Each teapot was made in an assortment of colors, often trimmed in gold. Many were decaled to match their dinnerware lines. Some are quite rare, and collecting them all would be a real challenge.

During the 1950s, Eva Zeisel designed dinnerware shapes with a streamlined, ultra-modern look. Her lines, Classic and Century, were used with various decals as the basis for several of Hall's dinnerware patterns. She also designed kitchenware lines with the same modern styling. They were called Casual Living and Tri-Tone. All her designs are very popular with today's collectors, especially those with an interest in the movement referred to as "50s modern.'

Although some of the old kitchenware shapes and teapots are being produced today, you'll be able to tell them from the old pieces by the backstamp. To identify these new issues, Hall marks them with the shaped rectangular 'Hall' trademark they've used since the early 1970s.

For more information we recommend *Collector's Encyclopedia of Hall China, Third Edition,* by Margaret and Kenn Whitmyer (Collector Books).

Club/Newsletter: *Hall China Collector's Club newsletter*
P.O. Box 360488, Cleveland, OH 44136
Subscription: $13 per year

Acacia, bowl, Radiance, 6", from $18 to **$22.00**

Acacia, casserole, Medallion, from $40 to **$50.00**

Acacia, salt & pepper shakers, handled, pr from $40 to **$48.00**

Blue Blossom, baker, rectangular, from $225 to **$250.00**

Blue Blossom, custard, Thick Rim, from $25 to **$28.00**

Blue Blossom, jug, Donut, from $250 to **$300.00**

Blue Blossom, teapot, New York, from $300 to **$375.00**

Blue Garden, donut jug, from $1,200.00 to $1,400.00.
(Photo courtesy Margaret and Kenn Whitmyer)

Cactus, batter bowl, Five Band, from $20 to **$25.00**

Cactus, creamer, New York, from $30 to **$35.00**

Cactus, syrup, Five Band, from $95 to **$125.00**

Cameo Rose, bowl, cereal; tab handles, 6¼", from $16 to ... **$18.00**

Cameo Rose, creamer, from $9 to **$11.00**

Cameo Rose, plate, 8", from $8 to **$9.50**

Cameo Rose, platter, oval, 15½", from $25 to **$30.00**

Century Fern, bowl, soup/cereal; 8", from $7.50 to **$8.50**

Century Fern, jug, from $30 to **$35.00**

Century Fern, ladle, from $18 to **$22.00**

Century Fern, platter, 13¾", from $24 to **$28.00**

Century Fern, teapot, 6-cup, from $150 to **$185.00**

Christmas Tree & Holly, bowl, oval, from $55 to **$60.00**

Christmas Tree & Holly, bowl, plum pudding; 4½", from $25 to **$30.00**

Christmas Tree & Holly, platter, 15½", from $55 to........... **$65.00**

Fantasy, casserole, Sundial #4, from $55.00 to $65.00. (Photo courtesy Margaret and Kenn Whitmyer)

Game Bird, bowl, Thick Rim, 6", from $25 to..................**$30.00**
Game Bird, cup, from $22 to...**$27.00**
Game Bird, platter, oval, 13¼", from $70 to **$80.00**
Game bird, teapot, Windshield, from $255 to **$315.00**
Heather Rose, bowl, flat soup; 8", from $10 to....................**$12.00**
Heather Rose, creamer, from $9 to......................................**$11.00**
Heather Rose, gravy boat & underplate, from $30 to **$35.00**
Heather Rose, pie baker, from $25 to **$27.00**
Heather Rose, platter, oval, 11¼", from $16 to....................**$18.00**
Meadow Flower, ball jug, #2, from $160 to **$195.00**
Meadow Flower, casserole, Radiance, from $60 to **$70.00**
Meadow Flower, cookie jar, Five Band, from $280 to **$320.00**
Meadow Flower, teapot, Streamline, from $750 to.............**$900.00**
Medallion, casserole, Lettuce, from $35 to...........................**$40.00**
Medallion, drip jar, Chinese Red, from $45 to......................**$55.00**
Medallion, teapot, colors other than Lettuce or Chinese Red, 40-oz, from $195 to **$250.00**
Prairie Grass, bowl, oval, 9¼", from $22 to **$25.00**
Prairie Grass, plate, 9¼", from $8.50 to...............................**$11.00**
Prairie Grass, tidbit, 3-tier, from $65 to...............................**$75.00**
Primrose, ashtray, from $8 to...**$10.00**
Primrose, bowl, salad; 9", from $16 to................................**$18.00**
Primrose, jug, Rayed, from $18 to **$22.00**
Primrose, plate, 9¼", from $7 to **$8.50**
Radiance, bowl, ivory, #2, 5¼", from $5 to **$6.50**
Radiance, canister, colors other than red, cobalt or ivory, 2-qt, from $190 to **$210.00**
Radiance, casserole, red or cobalt, from $50 to **$60.00**
Ribbed, baker, Russett, diagonal ribs, 12-oz, from $8 to......**$10.00**
Ribbed, casserole, Chinese Red, 9", from $35 to **$45.00**
Ribbed, ramekin, Russet, 2- to 2¾-oz, from $4 to.................**$5.50**
Sears' Arlington, bowl, vegetable; w/lid, from $35 to...........**$40.00**
Sears' Arlington, gravy boat & underplate, from $25 to.......**$27.00**
Sears' Arlington, platter, oval, 13¼", from $18 to................**$22.00**
Sears' Arlington, sugar bowl, w/lid, from $16 to..................**$18.00**
Sears' Fairfax, bowl, fruit; 5¼", from $3.50 to......................**$4.50**
Sears' Fairfax, plate, 6½", from $2.50 to...............................**$3.50**
Sears' Fairfax, plate, 9¼", from $6.50 to...............................**$7.50**
Sears' Monticello, bowl, cream soup; 5", from $80 to..........**$90.00**
Sears' Monticello, cup, from $5 to **$6.00**
Sears' Monticello, plate, 9¼", from $8 to..............................**$9.00**

Sears' Mount Vernon, bowl, oval, 9¼", from $22 to............**$25.00**
Sears' Mount Vernon, casserole, w/lid, from $40 to.............**$45.00**
Sears' Mount Vernon, plate, 9¼", from $6.50 to...................**$8.50**
Sears' Mount Vernon, sugar bowl, w/lid, from $20 to.........**$22.00**
Sears' Richmond/Brown-Eyed Susan, bowl, vegetable; 9", from $22 to **$25.00**
Sears' Richmond/Brown-Eyed Susan, creamer, from $7 to.....**$9.00**
Sears' Richmond/Brown-Eyed Susan, jug, Rayed, from $16 to. **$19.00**
Sears' Richmond/Brown-Eyed Susan, plate, 10", from $7 to..**$9.00**
Serenade, ball jug, #3, from $125 to **$150.00**
Serenade, bowl, fruit; 5½", from $4.50 to **$5.50**
Serenade, pie baker, from $40 to..**$45.00**
Serenade, plate, 9", from $9 to..**$11.00**
Serenade, teapot, New York, from $120 to........................**$150.00**
Shaggy Tulip, bowl, Radiance, 7½", from $27 to.................**$32.00**
Shaggy Tulip, drip coffeepot, all china, Kadota, from $95 to .. **$115.00**
Shaggy Tulip, pretzel jar, from $175 to **$195.00**
Silhouette, bowl, Radiance, 9", from $20 to.........................**$22.00**
Silhouette, creamer, Modern, from $18 to............................**$22.00**
Silhouette, gravy boat, from $30 to.....................................**$35.00**
Silhouette, plate, 8¼", from $7 to...**$8.50**
Silhouette, teapot, Streamline, from $250 to.......................**$285.00**
Sundial, batter jug, red or cobalt, from $170 to.................**$210.00**
Sundial, casserole, red or cobalt, #4, 8", from $35 to..........**$40.00**
Sundial, teapot, red or cobalt, 6-cup, from $185 to **$225.00**
Sunglow, bowl, salad; 11¾", from $28 to.............................**$32.00**
Sunglow, casserole, from $55 to...**$60.00**
Sunglow, plate, 8", from $7.50 to...**$9.50**
Sunglow, relish, 4-part, from $35 to....................................**$42.00**
Sunglow, sugar bowl, w/lid, from $20 to.............................**$25.00**

Tea-For-Two, Cadet Blue with gold Illinois decoration, from $120.00 to $140.00. (Photo courtesy Margaret and Ken Whitmyer)

Teapot, Airflow, Cadet, from $65 to **$75.00**
Teapot, Airflow, Orchid, from $250 to **$300.00**
Teapot, Aladdin, Emerald, from $75 to **$85.00**
Teapot, Aladdin, pink w/standard gold, from $80 to **$90.00**
Teapot, Albany, black w/standard gold, from $50 to...........**$60.00**
Teapot, Albany, ivory w/standard gold, from $45 to...........**$55.00**
Teapot, Albany, turquoise, from $45 to...............................**$55.00**
Teapot, Automobile, cobalt, from $550 to **$600.00**
Teapot, Baltimore, black w/standard gold, from $45 to **$55.00**

Teapot, Baltimore, Warm Yellow, from $55 to **$65.00**

Teapot, Baltimore, Warm Yellow w/Minuet decal, from $200 to.. **$225.00**

Teapot, Baseball, Warm Yellow w/standard gold, from $520 to **$570.00**

Teapot, Basket, Emerald w/standard gold, from $160 to....**$195.00**

Teapot, Birdcage, maroon, from $300 to **$350.00**

Teapot, Boston, black, 4- to 8-cup, from $20 to **$25.00**

Teapot, Boston, Dresden, from $30 to................................. **$35.00**

Teapot, Boston, rose w/standard gold, from $50 to............. **$55.00**

Teapot, Damascus, green, from $190 to........................... **$210.00**

Teapot, Danielle, maroon, from $185 to......................... **$200.00**

Teapot, French, Canary w/standard gold, 1- to 3-cup, from $30 to **$35.00**

Teapot, French, pink w/gold label, 10- to 12-cup, from $65 to **$75.00**

Teapot, French, turquoise w/standard gold, 4- to 8-cup, from $45 to **$60.00**

Teapot, Globe, Marine w/standard gold, from $100 to...... **$125.00**

Teapot, Hollywood, stock brown or green, ea from $30 to .. **$40.00**

Teapot, Hook Cover, Chinese Red, from $200 to **$225.00**

Teapot, Hook Cover, Warm Yellow, from $60 to **$70.00**

Teapot, Los Angeles, Canary w/standard gold, 6-cup, from $50 to **$55.00**

Teapot, Los Angeles, Warm Yellow w/standard gold, 6-cup, from $40 to **$50.00**

Teapot, Moderne, Cadet w/standard gold, from $60 to **$70.00**

Teapot, Moderne, pink, from $45 to................................. **$55.00**

Teapot, New York, Addison, 1- to 4-cup, from $25 to......... **$30.00**

Teapot, New York, black w/standard gold, 6- to 8-cup, from $27 to **$32.00**

Teapot, New York, turquoise w/standard gold, 1- to 4-cup, from $45 to **$55.00**

Teapot, New York, Warm Yellow w/standard gold, 6- to 8-cup, from $45 to **$55.00**

Teapot, Parade, Chinese Red, from $300 to **$350.00**

Teapot, Philadelphia, Emerald w/standard gold, 1- to 4-cup, from $40 to **$45.00**

Teapot, Philadelphia, Indian Red, 10-cup, from $215 to ... **$230.00**

Teapot, Star, Canary, from $100 to **$115.00**

Teapot, Surfside, cobalt w/standard gold, from $210 to..... **$230.00**

Tomorrow's Classic Arizona, candlestick, 4½", ea from $28 to . **$32.00**

Tomorrow's Classic Arizona, onion soup, w/lid, from $35 to.... **$37.00**

Tomorrow's Classic Arizona, platter, 17", from $34 to......... **$38.00**

Tomorrow's Classic Arizona, vinegar bottle, from $80 to **$85.00**

Tomorrow's Classic Bouquet, bowl, coupe soup; 9", from $14 to....**$16.00**

Tomorrow's Classic Bouquet, egg cup, from $55 to **$60.00**

Tomorrow's Classic Bouquet, marmite, w/lid, from $37 to .. **$40.00**

Tomorrow's Classic Bouquet, vase, from $80 to **$95.00**

Tomorrow's Classic Buckingham, bowl, open baker; 11-oz, from $20 to **$24.00**

Tomorrow's Classic Buckingham, gravy boat, from $40 to...**$45.00**

Tomorrow's Classic Buckingham, vase, from $80 to............. **$95.00**

Tomorrow's Classic Caprice, bowl, vegetable; sq, 8¾", from $22 to **$25.00**

Tomorrow's Classic Caprice, cup, from $8 to...................... **$10.00**

Tomorrow's Classic Caprice, platter, 12¼", from $20 to....... **$22.00**

Tomorrow's Classic Caprice, sugar bowl, w/lid, from $20 to..... **$22.00**

Tomorrow's Classic Fantast, creamer, AD; from $11 to........ **$13.00**

Tomorrow's Classic Fantasy, bowl, open baker, 11-oz, from $18 to **$22.00**

Tomorrow's Classic Fantasy, coffeepot, 6-cup, from $80 to **$100.00**

Tomorrow's Classic Fantasy, ladle, from $18 to.................... **$22.00**

Tomorrow's Classic Fantasy, salt & pepper shakers, pr from $28 to **$32.00**

Tomorrow's Classic Frost Flowers, butter dish, from $140 to.. **$160.00**

Tomorrow's Classic Frost Flowers, casserole, 2-qt, from $45 to. **$55.00**

Tomorrow's Classic Frost Flowers, gravy boat, from $35 to..**$40.00**

Tomorrow's Classic Frost Flowers, platter, 17", from $34 to **$38.00**

Tomorrow's Classic Mulberry, bowl, salad; 14½", from $35 to. **$45.00**

Tomorrow's Classic Mulberry, candlestick, 4½", ea from $28 to.. **$32.00**

Tomorrow's Classic Mulberry, creamer, from $14 to **$16.00**

Tomorrow's Classic Mulberry, teapot, 6-cup, from $195 to..... **$210.00**

Tomorrow's Classic Pine Cone, ashtray, from $7.50 to.......... **$9.00**

Tomorrow's Classic Pine Cone, butter dish, from $140 to .**$180.00**

Tomorrow's Classic Pine Cone, egg cup, from $42 to **$45.00**

Tomorrow's Classic Pine Cone, gravy boat, from $32 to...... **$35.00**

Tomorrow's Classic Pine Cone, vase, from $70 to **$80.00**

Tulip, bowl, flat soup; 8½", from $18 to **$22.00**

Tulip, bowl, Thick Rim, 6", from $16 to........................... **$18.00**

Tulip, plate, 9", from $11 to **$13.00**

Tulip, stack set, Radiance, from $95 to **$110.00**

Tulip, tidbit, 3-tier, from $60 to **$70.00**

Wildfire, bowl, oval, from $27 to..................................... **$30.00**

Wildfire, platter, oval, 13¼", from $28 to......................... **$30.00**

Wildfire, salt & pepper shakers, Teardrop, pr from $36 to...**$44.00**

Wild Poppy, oval casserole, #101, 9½", from $90.00 to $110.00.
(Photo courtesy Margaret and Kenn Whitmyer)

Yellow Rose, bowl, cereal; 6", from $12 to.......................... **$14.00**

Yellow Rose, bowl, salad; 9", from $22 to **$27.00**

Yellow Rose, coffeepot, Kadota bottom, from $55 to........... **$65.00**

Yellow Rose, cup & saucer, from $10 to............................. **$12.00**

Yellow Rose, custard, from $16 to **$18.00**

Yellow Rose, teapot, New York, from $150 to.................... **$200.00**

Hallmark Ornaments

Since the early 1970s when Hallmark first introduced their glass ball and yarn doll ornaments, many lines and themes have been developed to the delight of collectors. Many early ornaments are now valued at several times their original price. This is especially true of the first one issued in a particular series.

Barbie Solo in the Spotlight, QX1504-9, 1995, MIB........... **$15.00**

Batmobile, QX573-9, 1995, MIB **$22.50**

Christmas Visitors: St Nicholas, QX508-7, 1995, MIB **$22.50**

Classic American Car, 1957 Corvette, 1st in series, 1991, MIB... **$80.00**

Cycling Santa, QX435-5, 1982, MIB **$32.50**

Deep Space Nine, QX-6065, 1001, MIB **$17.50**

Elfin Antics, QX142-1, 1980, MIB **$85.00**

Friendly Greetings, QX504-1, 1992, MIB **$12.50**

Frosty Friends, Eskimo child & Husky pup in igloo, #800QX4335, 2nd in series, 1981, MIB **$210.00**

Frosty Friends, Eskimo child & polar bear cub on ice cube, 1st in series, 1980, MIB, from $295 to................. **$335.00**

Frosty Friends, North Pole, #QX403-1, 1988, MIB............. **$27.50**

Frosty Friends, QX482-2, 1985, MIB......................... **$47.50**

Holiday Heirloom Toys & Bell, QXC460-5, 1989, MIB..... **$30.00**

Horse Weathervane, WX4632, 1989, MIB **$15.00**

It's Christmas Eve, Hallmark Club Exclusive, 2005, MIB.... **$30.00**

Kermit the Frog (on skis), QX495-6, 1982, MIB **$42.00**

Mailbox Kitten, QX415-7, 1983, MIB **$32.00**

Mother Goose, QX498-4, 1992, MIB **$30.00**

Nostalgia Locomotive, QX222-1, 1976, MIB................. **$32.00**

Nostalgic Houses, Drugstore, QX528-6, 1994, MIB **$12.50**

Ornament Express, QX580-5, 1989, MIB **$25.00**

Outdoor Fun, QX150-7, 1979, MIB........................... **$32.50**

Popeye, WX525-7, 1995, MIB **$24.00**

Rocking Horse, QX422-2, 1st in series, 1981, MIB, from $250 to... **$285.00**

Rocking Horse (pinto), WX493-2, 1985, MIB................. **$17.50**

Santa's Flight, QX138-1, 1980, MIB **$65.00**

Santa's Ski Trip, QX496-2, 1985, MIB **$22.00**

S. Claus Free Delivery Truck, sixth in the series, 1984, MIB, $30.00.

Secret Pal, QX542-4, 1992, MIB........................... **$12.50**

Skating Snowman, QX139-9, 1979, MIB.................... **$28.00**

Spirit of Christmas, QX452-6, 1982, MIB **$22.50**

St Nicholas, WX446-2, 1981, MIB **$32.00**

Star Trek: Shuttlecraft Gallileo, WLX733-1, 1992, MIB...... **$15.00**

Superman, QLX730-9, 1995, MIB............................ **$30.00**

Sweet Slumber, QXM566-3, 1991, miniature, MIB **$25.00**

Tin Locomotive, WX403-6, red & yellow, 1986, MIB **$45.00**

Twirl-About Angel, QX171-1, 1976,l MIB................... **$40.00**

Victorian Dollhouse, QX448-1, 1984, MIB **$70.00**

Wizard of Oz: Tin Man, QX544-3, 1994, MIB................. **$32.50**

Yesteryears Santa, QX182-1, 1976, MIB, from $25 to......... **$45.00**

Yesteryears Train, QX181-1, 1976, MIB **$32.00**

Shaq O'Neal, Hoop Star series, 1995, MIB, $12.00.

Halloween

Halloween is now the second biggest money-making holiday of the year, and more candy is sold at this time than for any other holiday. Folk artists are making new items to satisfy the demands of collectors and celebrators that can't get enough of the old items. Over 100 years of celebrating this magical holiday has built a social history strata by strata, and wonderful and exciting finds can be made in all periods! From one dollar to thousands, there is something to excite collectors in every price range, with new collectibles being born every year. For further information we recommend *Collectible Halloween; More Halloween Collectibles; Halloween: Collectible Decorations & Games; Salem Witchcraft and Souvenirs; Postmarked Yesterday, Art of the Holiday Postcard;* and *The Tastes & Smells of Halloween*; also see *Around Swanzey* and *The Armenians of Worcester* (Arcadia). The author of these books is Pamela E. Apkarian-Russell (Halloween Queen™), a free-lancer who also writes an ephemera column for *Unravel the Gavel*.

Advisor: Pamela E. Apkarian-Russell (See Directory, Halloween)

Newsletter: *Trick or Treat Trader*
577 Boggs Run Rd., Benwood, WV 26031-1002
Castle Halloween Museum
halloweenqueen@castlehalloween.com
www.castlehalloween.com
Subscription: $15 per year in USA ($20 foreign) for 4 issues

Bell, black cat, jack-o'-lantern & moon, black & orange tin litho, wooden handle, 1930s, 6", EX **$45.00**

Bowl, Dracula flipping out red cape (forming bowl), Fitz & Floyd, ca 1987, M **$150.00**

Candelabra, haunted tree w/lizard, pumpkins, ghost & buzzard, 3-light, Fitz & Floyd, 1988, 12¼x7", M.........................**$150.00**

Candy container, black cat, papier-maché, original tin hole cover in bottom, USA, 7½x4", VG+ **$150.00**

Candy container, jack-o'-lantern, painted pulp w/original inserts, bail handle, marked Pulp Reproduction Co, EX..........**$20.00**

Candy container, jack-o'-lantern, painted tin, whistle in nose, Trick or Treats printed at bottom, 1950s, 6", EX...................**$95.00**

Candy container, snowman, orange plastic w/black details, opening at back, NM **$45.00**

Candy container, witch on motorcycle, yellow & black plastic, 6¾" L, EX **$200.00**

Candy container, witch on rocket ship, orange & black plastic, held suckers in tail, 4", EX **$95.00**

Candy container/nodder, black cat, papier-maché, opens in middle, West Germany, EX **$92.50**

Candy container/pull toy, boy in black, white & orange on 4-wheeled base holds jack-o'-lantern, Rosbro, EX..........**$200.00**

Candy container/pull toy, jack-o'-lantern on wheels, sm witch & black cat ea side, orange & green plastic, 1950s, EX.....**$40.00**

Candy container/pull toy, witch wearing mask & holding jack-o'-lantern on 4-wheeled base, Rosbro, 1960s, 5x4", NM.................**$135.00**

Candy container/pull toy, Zook clown (name on hat), orange plastic w/black paint, 1950s, EX, from $70 to.........................**$65.00**

Costume, Bart Simpson, Ben Cooper, 1989, EXIB..............**$20.00**

Costume, Darth Vader, Ben Cooper, 1977, NMIB..............**$25.00**

Costume, Dr. Doom, Ben Cooper, 1967, NM in 8x10" window-display box, $50.00. (Photo courtesy Bill Bruegman)

Costume, Herman Munster, Ben Cooper, 1964, NMIB **$110.00**

Costume, King Kong, Ben Cooper, 1976, EXIB.................**$85.00**

Decoration, black cat on jack-o'-lantern, die-cut cardboard, pin holes, 12x12", NM **$40.00**

Decoration, cat pulling witch in wagon, orange & black, celluloid, 1930s, 1½x3½", NM **$110.00**

Decoration, jack-o'-lantern, die-cut cardboard, M USA, 12x17", EX **$85.00**

Decoration, owl, die-cut cardboard, Germany, 1930s, 15½", EX **$40.00**

Decoration, witch flying on broom w/moon before her, die-cut cardboard, ca 1930s, Germany, 9x11", G..........................**$45.00**

Game, Cat & Witch, pin the tail on black cat, 24 tails included, Whitman #3016, 1930s, NMIB **$50.00**

Game, Halloween Crystal Fortunes, spinner game, cardboard litho, HE Luhrs, 1940, EX...**$55.00**

Halloween mask, Paul McCartney, Ben Cooper, VG **$50.00**

Jack-o'-lantern, glass & tin, uses 2 C batteries, Made in Japan, MIB marked Pumpkin Lantern **$62.50**

Jack-o'-lantern, pulp, metal bail handle, metal candleholder inside, Germany, 2¾" (+handle), NM **$70.00**

Lantern, devil's face, heavy red cardboard w/paper inset, wire bail, EX **$150.00**

Lantern, skull, white molded glass w/black details, switch at jaw, uses 2 C batteries, Hong Kong, 1950s, 5x3½", MIB **$100.00**

Light, haunted house, orange plastic w/black details, 17½", EX..**$50.00**

Magazine, Dennison's Bogie Book, #12, 1924, EX **$135.00**

Magazine, Halloween Party Book, Dell, 20 pages, 1955, EX..**$125.00**

Mask, Frankenstein (Boris Karloff), Universal Studios Famous Movie Monsters line, latex, covers head completely, M.**$25.00**

Ornament, cat w/top hat holding jack-o'-lantern, orange & black plastic, E Rosen, 1950s, 3⅛", NM **$46.00**

Sparkler, Old Witch, 1950s, MIP, $125.00. (Photo courtesy Dunbar Gallery)

Squeak toy, jack-o'-lantern cardboard face w/paper accordian between, Japan, 2¾" dia, EX **$125.00**

Tablecloth, ghosts, goblins, black cats, jack-o'-lanterns on white crepe paper, 1930s, unopened, NM **$85.00**

Tambourine, jack-o'-lantern & dancing figures, tin litho, US Metal Toy Mfg Co, 1955, 6½" dia, EX **$125.00**

Tambourine, jack-o'-lantern & figures in orange on black, Chein USA, 7" dia, NM..**$125.00**

Tambourine, 2 black cats on orange, Chein USA, 7" dia, EX. **$150.00**

Handkerchiefs

Though ladies no longer carry handkerchiefs as they did in the days before disposable tissues, these mementos of an earlier and perhaps a more genteel era are today being collected by those who find in them a certain charm. Some are delicate works of art with lace and embroidery, while others are souvenirs or represent a particular event or theme. For more information, we recommend *Handkerchiefs,*

A Collector's Guide, Vol. 1 and *Vol. II*, by Helene Guarnaccia and Barbara Guggenheim (Collector Books).

Arthur Murray...in a Hurry, from $40.00 to $45.00. (Photo courtesy Helene Guarnaccia and Barbara Guggenheim)

Betty Boop, white w/various scenes in ea corner, from $30 to .. **$35.00**

Black cocker spaniel on light brown, dark brown border, from $15 to **$20.00**

Blue bumblebees on red background w/blue border, from $10 to **$15.00**

Boy Scouts, beige w/Boy Scout in ea corner, logo in center, from $15 to **$20.00**

Clarabell holding yellow balloon on blue, from $40 to **$50.00**

Congratulations written in sky, stork w/bundle flies over couple's silhouette in beige house, gold label, from $20 to **$25.00**

Courting scenes in pink & green on ivory, Put On Your Old Grey Bonnet w/the Blue Ribbons on It, from $25 to **$30.00**

Donkey w/rope draped around neck on light blue background, Doerig, from $8 to... **$12.00**

Hearts attached by red & black ribbons to red key in middle, round, from $15 to **$20.00**

Hello, Dolly! in green w/blue train, Dolly on back, Faith Austin, from $30 to **$35.00**

Howdy Doody on red & white background w/blue rope trim, from $35 to **$40.00**

Kangaroos in each corner, multicolored on white, Heil, from $10 to **$15.00**

Noah's Ark in pink & yellow on gray background, Tammis Keffe, from $25 to **$30.00**

Pink & gray pussy willows, 1950s, from $12 to................... **$15.00**

Puppy in rocket flying through space, blue, ivory, red & yellow w/ blue border, from $10 to.. **$15.00**

Roulette scene on light blue, white border w/red trim, from $30 to.. **$35.00**

Scenic view of Florida on light blue w/floral border, round, from $10 to **$15.00**

Silhouettes of ladies on horses, black & green background, from $30 to **$40.00**

Spider web w/various hearts, Caught in red, scalloped edge, from $30 to **$35.00**

Swissair yodeler, multicolored on green, paper label, from $20 to .. **$15.00**

Thank You written in different scripts on blue w/2 lg pink roses in center, Tammis Keefe, from $20 to **$25.00**

Umbrella shape, couple silhouette, blue trim on yellow, from $30 to.. **$40.00**

U.S. Marines, from $15.00 to $20.00. (Photo courtesy Helene Guarnaccia and Barbara Guggenheim)

Violets on white, Best Wishes, scalloped edges, from $6 to.. **$10.00**

White bird silhouette (in flight) on red, Givenchy, from $10 to.......**$15.00**

Harker Pottery

Harker was one of the oldest potteries in the country. Their history can be traced back to the 1840s. In the 1930s, a new plant was built in Chester, West Virginia, and the company began manufacturing kitchen and dinnerware lines, eventually employing as many as 300 workers.

Several of these lines are popular with collectors today. One of the most easily recognized is Cameoware. It is usually found in pink or blue decorated with white silhouettes of flowers, though other designs were made as well. Colonial Lady, Red Apple, Amy, Mallow, and Pansy are some of their better-known lines that are fairly easy to find and reassemble into sets.

If you'd like to learn more about Harker, we recommend *The Collector's Encyclopedia of American Dinnerware* by Jo Cunningham, published by Collector Books.

Amy, bowl, 9" **$18.00**

Amy, creamer **$17.50**

Amy, cup & saucer, footed **$15.00**

Amy II, jug creamer, paneled, 4".................................... **$35.00**

Cameo Rose, batter jug, w/lid... **$35.00**

Cameo Rose, casserole, w/lid, base: 6¾x6¾" **$50.00**

Cameo Rose, cup & saucer **$12.50**

Cameo Rose, mixing bowls, 6", 7", 8" & 9", set of 4 for..... **$60.00**
Cameo Rose, salt & pepper shakers, 4¾", pr from $45 to ... **$55.00**
Chesterson, soup bowl **$15.00**
Colonial Lady, plate, luncheon; 9¼"............................ **$7.50**
Corinthian, gravy boat & liner, from $15 to **$18.00**
Corinthian, plate, salad; 8¼" **$9.00**
Deco Dahlia, canister, yellow & black, Hot Oven decal, 5x6".. **$70.00**
Deco Dahlia, flour scoop, orange-red w/black, 6" **$65.00**

Deco Dahlia, set of six individual casseroles in wire holder, from $35.00 to $45.00.

Deco Dahlia, syrup pitcher **$45.00**
Gadroon, dessert set, 10½" cake plate & 6 6¼" dessert plates .. **$35.00**
Ivy Wreath, bowl, divided vegetable; 10½" **$30.00**
Ivy Wreath, bowl, vegetable; w/lid.................................... **$40.00**
Ivy Wreath, plate, salad; 7¼" **$5.00**
Ivy Wreath, platter, oval, 16x12" **$18.00**
Mallow, bowl, utility; 4¼x9".. **$17.50**
Mallow, cake plate, Deco shape, 12" **$50.00**
Mallow, pie plate & server, 1½x9", 9" **$75.00**
Mallow, rolling pin, 15", from $65 to **$75.00**

Mallow, salt and pepper shakers, 4½", $25.00 for the pair.
(Photo courtesy Jo Cunningham)

Modern Tulip, bowl, coupe cereal; 6⅛" **$9.00**
Modern Tulip, cup & saucer, flat **$16.00**
Modern Tulip, plate, luncheon; 9½" **$10.00**
Oriental Poppy, bowl, pedestal foot, 2¾x6" **$40.00**
Pate sur Pate, luncheon set, dark blue-green w/cream, service for 4 (8 pcs) **$50.00**
Petit Point, bowl, 2⅞x5⅞"... **$12.00**
Petit Point, casserole, w/lid, 1½-qt **$35.00**

Petit Point, chip & dip set, 2-pc.. **$27.50**
Petit Point, creamer **$15.00**
Petit Point, plate, dinner; Bakerite, 10¼" **$15.00**
Petit Point, salt & pepper shakers, 5½", pr **$22.00**
Petit Point, teapot, 5½".. **$35.00**
Petite Rose, tea set, teapot w/creamer & sugar bowl............ **$50.00**
Rockingham, Daniel Boone mug, 4½" **$25.00**
Rockingham, Jolly Roger mug, 4½"................................... **$20.00**
Snow Leaf Cameo Ware, cup & saucer w/7¼" plate **$18.00**
Souvenir plate, Gettysburg PA, 6¼", from $15 to **$18.00**
Wild Rose, cup & saucer, flat **$16.00**
Wild Rose, plate, salad **$8.00**
Wild Rose, tidbit, 2-tiered **$30.00**

Hartland Plastics, Inc.

The Hartland company was located in Hartland, Wisconsin, where during the '50s and '60s they made several lines of plastic figures: Western and Historic Horsemen, Miniature Western Series, and the Hartland Sport Series of Famous Baseball Stars. Football and bowling figures and religious statues were made as well. The plastic, virgin acetate, was very durable and the figures were hand painted with careful attention to detail. They're often marked.

Though prices have come down from their high of a few years ago, rare figures and horses are still in high demand. Dealers using this guide should take these factors into consideration when pricing their items: values listed here are for the figure, horse (unless they're standing gunfighters), hat, guns, and all other accessories for that particular figure in near-mint condition (unless another condition is specified) with no rubs and all original parts. All parts were made exclusively for a special figure, so a hat is not just a hat — each one belongs to a specific figure! Many people do not realize this, and it is important for the collector to be knowledgeable. An excellent source of information is *Hartland Horses and Riders* by Gail Fitch.

In our listings for sports figures, mint to near-mint condition values are for figures that are white or near-white in color; excellent values are for those that are off-white or cream-colored. These values are representative of traditional retail prices asked by dealers; Internet values for Hartlands, as is so often the case nowadays, seem to be in a constant state of flux. Be aware that Hartland is producing all 18 of the original figures for the last time. Their plans are to release three per month until the series is completed.

See also *Schroeder's Collectible Toys, Antique to Modern* (Collector Books).

Gunfighters

Bat Masterson, NMIB.. **$500.00**
Bret Maverick, NM... **$350.00**
Chris Colt, NM **$150.00**
Clay Holister, NM **$200.00**
Dan Troop, NM... **$600.00**
Jim Hardy, NM.. **$150.00**
Johnny McKay, NM **$800.00**
Paladin, NM **$400.00**

Vint Bonner, NMIB...$850.00

Wyatt Earp, NM, $150.00. (Photo courtesy Ellen and Jerry Harnish)

Horseman

Lone Ranger, NM, $150.00. (Photo courtesy Shirley Bertrand)

Alpine Ike, NM...$150.00
Annie Oakley, NM...$275.00
Bat Masterson, NM $250.00
Bill Longley, NM...$600.00
Brave Eagle, NM...$200.00
Bret Maverick, miniature series $75.00
Bret Maverick, w/gray horse, rare, NM $600.00
Bullet, w/tag, NM..$150.00
Champ Cowgirl, very rare, NM $275.00
Cheyenne, miniature series, NM.........................$190.00
Chief Thunderbird, rare shield, NM $150.00
Cochise, NM $150.00
Commanche Kid, NM.......................................$150.00
Dale Evans, blue, rare, NM $500.00
Dale Evans, green, NM.....................................$175.00

Dale Evans, purple, NM $250.00
Davy Crockett, NM..$500.00
General Custer, NM $150.00
General Custer, NMIB.......................................$350.00
General George Washington, NM........................$125.00
General George Washington, NMIB.....................$175.00
General Robert E Lee, NMIB $175.00
Gil Favor, prancing, very rare, NM $1,100.00
Gil Favor, semi-rearing, NM $550.00
Hoby Gillman, NM...$250.00
Jim Bowie, w/tag, NM.......................................$250.00
Jim Hardy, EX+ $200.00
Jim Hardy, NMIB...$300.00
Jockey, NM $150.00
Josh Randle, NM $650.00
Lone Ranger, Champ version, w/chaps, black breast collar, NM $125.00
Lone Ranger, miniature series, NM......................$75.00
Lone Ranger, rearing, NMIB $300.00
Matt Dillon, w/tag, NMIB $300.00
Paladin, NMIB..$350.00
Rebel, miniature series, NM...............................$125.00
Rebel, NM $250.00
Rebel, NMIB $1,200.00
Rifleman, miniature series, EX $75.00
Rifleman, NMIB...$350.00

Ronald MacKenzie, NM, $1,200.00.

Roy Rogers, semi-rearing, NMIB $600.00
Roy Rogers, walking, NMIB..............................$300.00
Seth Adams, NM $275.00
Sgt Lance O'Rourke, NMIB...............................$300.00
Sgt Preston, NM..$650.00
Tom Jeffords, NM..$175.00
Tonto, miniature series, NM...............................$75.00
Tonto, NM...$150.00
Tonto, semi-rearing, rare, NM $650.00

Warpaint Thunderbird, w/shield, NMIB $350.00
Wyatt Earp, NMIB $250.00

Sports Figures

Babe Ruth, NM, from $175 to $225.00
Batboy, 25th Anniversary, NM.................................... $50.00
Dick Groat, w/bat, NM, minimum value $1,000.00
Dick Groat, 25th Anniversary, MIB............................ $40.00
Don Drysdale, EX, from $275 to................................ $350.00
Duke Snyder, EX+ $360.00
Eddie Matthews, NM $150.00
Ernie Banks, NM, from $200 to.................................. $250.00
Ernie Banks, 25th Anniversary, MIB, from $30 to.............. $40.00
Hank Aaron, EX... $250.00
Hank Aaron, M $350.00
Hank Aaron, 25th Anniversary, MIB $35.00
Harmon Killebrew, NM, from $400 to........................... $500.00
Harmon Killebrew, 25th Anniversary, MIB..................... $45.00
Little Leaguer, 4", EX, from $50 to.............................. $75.00
Luis Aparicio, NM, from $250 to $300.00
Luis Aparicio, 25th Anniversary, MIB........................... $32.00
Mickey Mantle, MIB $535.00
Mickey Mantle, NM, from $285 to $320.00
Mickey Mantle, 25th Anniversary, MIB......................... $50.00
Nellie Fox, EX, from $135 to..................................... $165.00
Nellie Fox, MIB, from $285 to $300.00
Rocky Colavito, NM, from $600 to.............................. $700.00
Roger Maris, NM, from $325 to $375.00
Stan Musial, NM $235.00
Ted Williams, NM $300.00
Ted Williams, 25th Anniversary, MIP........................... $50.00
Washington Redskins, running back, NM, minimum value .. $500.00

Willie Mays, NM, from $250.00 to $285.00.

Willie Mays, 25th Anniversary, MIB.............................. $50.00
Yogi Berra, no mask, NM, from $100 to $150.00

Yogi Berra, w/mask, NM, from $165 to........................... $200.00
Yogi Berra, w/mask, 25th Anniversary, M (NM box) $38.00

Head Vases

Fun to collect, vases modeled as heads of lovely ladies, delightful children, famous people, clowns — even some animals — were once popular as flower containers. Today they represent a growing area of collector interest. Most of them were imported from Japan, although some American potteries produced a few as well.

If you'd like to learn more about them, we recommend *Head Vases, 2nd edition,* by Kathleen Cole; *Collecting Head Vases* by David Baron; and *The World of Head Vase Planters* by Mike Posgay and Ian Warner.

Advisor: Larry G. Pogue (See Directory, Head Vases)

Newsletter: *Head Hunters Newsletter*
Maddy Gordon
P.O. Box 83H, Scarsdale, NY 10583
914-472-0200
Subscription: $24 per year for 4 issues; also holds convention

Jackie Kennedy, Inarco #E-1852, 1964, 6", $995.00. (Photo courtesy Larry Pogue)

Animal, poodle head in bonnet w/neck bow, pink w/gold trim, #38, 6"... $65.00
Baby, blond, sucking finger, Relpo #495B, 5"..................... $65.00
Baby, light brown hair, blanket over head, holding kitten, unmarked, 6".. $65.00
Baby girl w/kitten, bow in hair, Enesco, 5½" $55.00
Boy, blond, head bowed & hands folded in prayer, Inarco #E1575, 5¾"... $85.00
Boy, blond, in fireman uniform, Inarco, 5" $75.00
Boy, blond w/blue cap, Hummel-like, Relpo #K1018A, 8" $225.00
Clown, red nose & mouth, green hat, ruffled collar, Napcoware #3321, 6".. $75.00

Girl, blond, winking, flowered hat, lg bow at neck, unmarked, 5" $75.00

Girl, polka dot scarf, Little Miss Dream #113005, rare, 6"...$350.00

Girl w/flowers in hair, Wales Reg...Japan foil label, 6" $145.00

Girl w/umbrella, blond in aqua plaid, 3½"+umbrella $250.00

Lady, Art Deco, white w/brown hair, yellow hat, pearls, unmarked, 7½" $110.00

Lady, blond, hat, sleeveless bodice, hands to face, Lefton's #2900, 6" $125.00

Lady, blond w/long hair, sm hat, pearls, Kelvin label, #P529, 6" $215.00

Lady, Colonial, white curls, gold trim, eyes open, Relpo #K1633, 7¼" $320.00

Lady, frosted hair w/lg white bow, pearls, blue bodice, Relpo #K1695, 7" $315.00

Lady, Mary Lou, black hat, yellow ruffled bodice, thick lashes, 5½" $250.00

Madonna & Child, long lashes, Hull #26, 7" $55.00

Man, black hair, winking, green hat & jacket, bow tie, unmarked, 4½" $45.00

Man, white scarf over black hair, 1 gold earing, Royal Copley, 7¾" $65.00

Nun w/Bible, thick lashes, Inarco #E188/M, 1961, 6" $60.00

Oriental lady, w/ornate headdress, pastels w/gold, Japan, 5" $50.00

Teen girl, blond w/sunglasses & ponytails, unmarked, 7½" ...$450.00

Teen girl, brown updo, pearls, ruffled collar, Caffco #E3142, 7"...$300.00

Teen girl, glasses on top of head, 2 ponytail, unmarked, 7½" . $375.00

Uncle Sam, allover green, unmarked, 6½" $45.00

Heisey Glass

From just before the turn of the century until 1957, the Heisey Glass Company of Newark, Ohio, was one of the largest, most successful manufacturers of quality tableware in the world. Though the market is well established, many pieces are still reasonably priced; and if you're drawn to the lovely patterns and colors that Heisey made, you're investment should be sound.

After 1901 much of their glassware was marked with their familiar trademark, the 'Diamond H' (an H in a diamond) or a paper label. Blown pieces are often marked on the stem instead of the bowl or foot.

Numbers in the listings are catalog reference numbers assigned by the company to indicate variations in shape or stem style. Collectors use them, especially when they buy and sell by mail, for the same purpose. Many catalog pages (showing these numbers) are contained in *The Collector's Encyclopedia of Heisey Glass, 1925 – 1938*, by Neila and Tom Bredehoft. This book and *Elegant Glassware of the Depression Era* by Gene and Cathy Florence are both excellent references for further study. If you're especially interested in the many varieties of glass figures Heisey produced, you'll want to get *Glass Animals* by Dick and Pat Spencer (Collector Books).

See also Glass Animals and Related Items.

Newsletter: *The Heisey News*
Heisey Collectors of America
169 W Church St., Newark, OH 43055; 740-345-2932

Charter Oak, Hawthorne, coaster, oak leaf, #10 ....$35.00

Charter Oak, Hawthorne, sherbet, low foot, #3362, 6-oz....$50.00

Chintz, crystal, bowl, Nasturtium, 7½" $20.00

Chintz, crystal, cordial, Duquesne, #3389, 1-oz.................$100.00

Chintz, crystal, cup $15.00

Chintz, Sahara, compote, oval, 7" $85.00

Chintz, Sahara, creamer, individual....................................$30.00

Chintz, Sahara, vase, dolphin foot, 9" $185.00

Classic, crystal, cup, #8869 ....$75.00

Crystolite, crystal, ashtray, w/book match holder, 5"..........$45.00

Crystolite, crystal, bowl, dessert; 5½" $14.00

Crystolite, crystal, coaster, 4" $12.00

Crystolite, crystal, cocktail shaker, w/#1 strainer, #86 stopper, 1-qt...$325.00

Crystolite, crystal, plate, sandwich; 14"..............................$55.00

Crystolite, crystal, puff box, 4¾" $75.00

Crystolite, crystal, tumbler, blown, 8-oz.............................$35.00

Empress, Alexandrite, plate, 6"...$40.00

Empress, Alexandrite, salt & pepper shakers, pr.................$450.00

Empress, Flamingo, bowl, cream soup $30.00

Empress, Flamingo, tray, celery; 13" $30.00

Empress, Moongleam, ice tub, dolphin foot, metal handles..$350.00

Empress, Moongleam, plate, sandwich; handles, 12" $60.00

Empress, Sahara, bowl, jelly; footed, handles, 6" $25.00

Empress, Sahara, sugar bowl, dolphin foot, 3-handled $45.00

Greek Key, crystal, bowl, banana split; flat, 9" $45.00

Greek Key, crystal, coaster...$20.00

Greek Key, crystal, jar, horseradish; w/lg lid $140.00

Greek Key, crystal, water bottle..$220.00

Ipswich, cobalt, bowl, floral, footed, 11" $450.00

Ipswich, crystal, plate, sq, 8" $35.00

Ipswich, Flamingo, candy jar, w/lid, ½-lb............................$325.00

Ipswich, green, candlestick centerpiece, $450.00. (Photo courtesy Gene and Cathy Florence)

Ipswich, Moongleam, oil cruet, footed, w/#86 stopper, 2-oz... **$300.00**

Ipswich, Sahara, pitcher, ½-gal $550.00

Kalonyal, crystal, bottle, molasses; 13-oz $185.00

Kalonyal, crystal, butter dish, domed lid $150.00

Kalonyal, crystal, egg cup, 9½-oz $75.00

Kalonyal, crystal, pitcher, ½-gal $350.00

Kalonyal, crystal, toothpick holder $425.00

Lariat, crystal, basket, bonbon; 7½" $100.00

Lariat, crystal, oil cruet, handled, w/#133 stopper, 4-oz $180.00

Lariat, crystal, platter, oval, 15" $60.00

Lariat, crystal, tumbler, juice; footed, 5-oz $22.00

Lariat, crystal, vase, fan; footed, 7" $30.00

Lariat, crystal, wine, pressed, 3½-oz $22.00

Minuet, crystal, bell, dinner; #3408 ....$75.00

Minuet, crystal, cocktail icer, w/liner, #3304 Universal $125.00

Minuet, crystal, plate, service; 10½" $190.00

New Era, crystal, bottle, rye; w/stopper $140.00

New Era, crystal, goblet, tall foot, 10-oz $20.00

New Era, crystal, pilsner, 12-oz $45.00

New Era, crystal, sugar bowl $37.50

New Era, crystal, tumbler, soda; footed, 12-oz $20.00

Octagon, crystal, bowl, mint; #1229, 6" $10.00

Octagon, Flamingo, basket, #500, 5" $300.00

Octagon, Hawthorne, tray, celery; 12" $50.00

Octagon, Marigold, ice tub, #500 ....$150.00

Octagon, Moongleam, sugar bowl, #500 ....$35.00

Octagon, Sahara, plate, muffin; sides up, #1229, 10" $30.00

Old Colony, Sahara, bouillon cup, handles, footed $25.00

Old Colony, Sahara, bowl, jelly; handles, footed, 6" $30.00

Old Colony, Sahara, creamer, dolphin foot $45.00

Old Colony, Sahara, flagon, #3390, 12-oz $100.00

Old Colony, Sahara, plate, muffin; sq, handles, 13" $50.00

Old Colony, Sahara, salt & pepper shakers, pr $125.00

Old Colony, Sahara, tray, hors d'oeuvres; handles, 13" $75.00

Old Colony, Sahara, tumbler, bar; footed, #3380, 5-oz $16.00

Old Sandwich, cobalt, decanter, w/#98 stopper, 1-pt $500.00

Old Sandwich, crystal, compote, 6" $60.00

Old Sandwich, Flamingo, mug, beer; 18-oz $400.00

Old Sandwich, Moongleam, parfait, 4½-oz $60.00

Old Sandwich, Sahara, creamer, oval $85.00

Pleat & Panel, crystal, bowl, chow-chow; 4" $6.00

Pleat & Panel, crystal, pitcher, 3-pt $45.00

Pleat & Panel, crystal, plate, 6" $4.00

Pleat & Panel, Flamingo, cheese & cracker set, tray w/compote, 10½" $75.00

Pleat & Panel, Flamingo, marmalade, 4¾" $30.00

Pleat & Panel, Flamingo, vase, 8" $80.00

Pleat & Panel, Moongleam, creamer, hotel $30.00

Pleat & Panel, Moongleam, platter, oval, 12" $47.50

Pleat & Panel, Moongleam, saucer $5.00

Provincial, crystal, candy box, footed, 5½" $85.00

Provincial, crystal, cup, punch $10.00

Provincial, crystal, plate, buffet; 18" $70.00

Provincial, crystal, sugar bowl, footed $25.00

Provincial, crystal, tray, celery; oval, 13" $22.00

Provincial, crystal, tumbler, juice; footed, 5-oz $14.00

Provincial, crystal, vase, sweet pea; 6" $45.00

Provincial, Limelight Green, bowl, relish; 4-part, 10" $150.00

Provincial, Limelight Green, mayonnaise set, w/plate, ladle & bowl, 7" $150.00

Provincial, Limelight Green, nappy, 5½" $40.00

Provincial, Limelight Green, plate, buffet; 18" $175.00

Provincial, Limelight Green, plate, luncheon; 8" $50.00

Provincial, Limelight Green, tumbler, footed, 9-oz ..$80.00

Provincial, Limelight Green, vase, violet; 3½" $95.00

Queen Ann, crystal, jug, footed, 3-pt $100.00

Queen Ann, crystal, marmalade, w/lid, dolphin foot $60.00

Queen Ann, crystal, plate, hors d'oeuvres; handles, 13" $60.00

Queen Ann, crystal, sugar bowl and creamer with dolphin feet, $60.00 for the set. (Photo courtesy Neila and Tom Bredehoft)

Queen Ann, crystal, tray, buffet relish; 4-part, 16" $35.00

Ridgeleigh, crystal, ashtray, round $14.00

Ridgeleigh, crystal, bottle, rock & rye; w/#104 stopper $240.00

Ridgeleigh, crystal, candle vase, 6" $35.00

Ridgeleigh, crystal, decanter, w/#95 stopper, 1-pt ..$210.00

Ridgeleigh, crystal, pitcher, ball shape, ½-gal $380.00

Ridgeleigh, crystal, sherry, blown, 2-oz $90.00

Ridgeleigh, crystal, tray, celery & olive; divided, 12" $50.00

Ridgeleigh, crystal, tumbler, old-fashioned; pressed, 8-oz $40.00

Saturn, crystal, bottle, bitters; w/short tube, blown $75.00

Saturn, crystal, bowl, salad; 11" $40.00

Saturn, crystal, mustard, w/lid & paddle $60.00

Saturn, crystal, sugar shaker $80.00

Saturn, crystal, vase, straight, 8½" $55.00

Saturn, Limelight or Zircon, bowl, baked apple $100.00

Saturn, Limelight or Zircon, nappy, 5" $90.00

Saturn, Limelight or Zircon, pitcher, juice $500.00

Saturn, Limelight or Zircon, salt & pepper shakers, pr $600.00

Saturn, Limelight or Zircon, tumbler, soda, 12-oz ..$85.00

Saturn, Zircon, sugar bowl and creamer, $360.00 for the set. (Photo courtesy Neila and Tom Bredhoft)

255

Stanhope, crystal, bowl, floral; handles, 11" $75.00
Stanhope, crystal, candelabra, 2-light, w/bobeche & prisms, ea.. $225.00
Stanhope, crystal, plate, 7" $25.00
Stanhope, crystal, pressed cocktail, 3½-oz $25.00
Stanhope, crystal, vase, ball shape, 7" $100.00
Twist, Alexandrite, bowl, nasturtium; round, 8" $450.00
Twist, Alexandrite, ice bucket, w/metal handles $300.00
Twist, crystal, nappy, ground bottom, 8" $20.00
Twist, crystal, plate, Kraft cheese; 8" $20.00
Twist, Flamingo, bonbon, handles, 6" $25.00
Twist, Flamingo, platter, 12" $50.00
Twist, Marigold, baker, oval, 9" $60.00
Twist, Marigold, tray, pickle; ground bottom, 7" $45.00
Twist, Moongleam, bottle, French dressing $110.00
Twist, Moongleam, tumbler, iced tea; flat bottom, 12-oz..... $60.00
Twist, Sahara, bowl, mint; handles, 6" $20.00
Twist, Sahara, salt & pepper shakers, footed, pr $140.00

Waverly, crystal, candlestick, two-light, $40.00.
(Photo courtesy Neila and Tom Bredhoft)

Yeoman, crystal, bowl, vegetable; handles, w/lid, 9".............$35.00
Yeoman, crystal, champagne, 6-oz..$6.00
Yeoman, crystal, cup $5.00
Yeoman, crystal, tray, celery; 13"..$20.00
Yeoman, Flamingo, bowl, berry; handles, 8½" $22.00
Yeoman, Flamingo, creamer, #1001 ....$60.00
Yeoman, Flamingo, finger bowl...$11.00
Yeoman, Flamingo, pitcher, qt..$130.00
Yeoman, Flamingo, plate, cream soup underliner..................$7.00
Yeoman, Flamingo, vase, #516-2, 6" $50.00
Yeoman, Hawthorne, compote, w/lid, #3350......................$110.00
Yeoman, Hawthorne, egg cup $60.00
Yeoman, Hawthorne, plate, 7" $17.00
Yeoman, Hawthorne, saucer, after dinner............................$10.00
Yeoman, Marigold, bowl, pickle/olive; rectangular, 8"..........$35.00
Yeoman, Marigold, oil cruet, 2-oz.......................................$85.00
Yeoman, Marigold, parfait, 5-oz..$35.00
Yeoman, Marigold, plate, cheese; handles............................$25.00
Yeoman, Moongleam, bowl, floral; low, 12".........................$45.00
Yeoman, Moongleam, gravy boat/dressing, w/underliner $45.00
Yeoman, Moongleam, puff box w/insert...............................$175.00
Yeoman, Moongleam, sugar bowl, w/lid, #1189 ....$55.00
Yeoman, Sahara, ashtray, bow-tie handle, 4" $22.00

Yeoman, Sahara, bottle, cologne; w/stopper $160.00
Yeoman, Sahara, sherbet, 5-oz...$10.00
Yeoman, Sahara, tray, hors d'oeuvre; w/covered center, 13".. $52.00

Holt Howard

Now's the time to pick up the kitchenware (cruets, salt and peppers, condiments, etc.), novelty banks, ashtrays, and planters marked Holt Howard. They're not only marked but dated as well; you'll find production dates from the 1950s through the 1970s. (Beware of unmarked copy-cat lines!) There's a wide variety of items and decorative themes; those you're most likely to find will be from the rooster (done in golden brown, yellow, and orange), white cat (called Kozy Kitten), and Christmas lines. Not as easily found, the Pixies are by far the most collectible of all, and in general, Pixie prices continue to climb, particularly for the harder-to-find items. Watch for a new 'generation' of Pixies that are now showing up on eBay. They're marked GHA for Grant Howard associates.

Internet auctions have affected this market with the 'more supply, less demand' principal (more exposure, therefore in some cases lower prices), but all in all, the market has remained sound. Only the very common pieces have suffered.

Our values are for mint condition, factory-first examples. If any flaws are present, you must reduce the price accordingly.

Christmas

Ashtray, starry-eyed Santa...$35.00
Bowl, white bag tied w/gold rope, 3¼x3¾" $20.00
Candle climbers, Santa, 1958, pr $25.00
Candle set, 2 mice climbers & 2 Santa candleholders, 1958,
   MIB..$38.00
Candleholder, angel, 4", ea..$25.00
Candleholder, boy dressed as 1 of 3 Kings, 1960, ea............$20.00
Candleholder, double branch, holly w/Santa sitting in middle
   branch, 1960, ea $20.00
Candleholder, evergreen tree, 15 holes w/colored cellophane, candle
   goes inside, 1959, 6", ea..$20.00
Candleholder, 3 Santas holding presents, Merry Christmas on front,
   NM, ea $40.00
Candleholders, holly w/leaves, set of 4, MIB.......................$25.00
Candleholders, Santa w/bags, w/label, 1958, pr $32.00
Candy dish, Santa head, beard forms dish, 1959, 7x4" $35.00
Cheese crock, white w/holly decoration, Cheese on lid w/Mr & Mrs
   Santa, #17/382, 4½"..$40.00
Figurine, angel, 'spaghetti' trim at bottom of dress, gold details,
   1958, 4¼", pr..$24.00
Figurine, boy holding candle & bell, holly around neck, 3". $45.00
Figurine, girl holding Christmas tree in left hand, 5½"........$30.00
Head vase, Christmas decor, 1959, 4" $60.00
Lamp, oil; Holly Girl, unused wick, 7" $60.00
Mug, Santa..$40.00
Napkin holder, Santa head $18.00
Planter, Santa Express, Santa riding train, 6x7½"................$30.00
Planter, 3 comical carolers hold song book w/Noel on cover,
   #PX3122, 5x5"...$25.00

Punch set, Santa, 6x7¾" boxl, 8 mugs (4 winking) & ladle.... **$235.00**
Salt & pepper shakers, angels, 1 w/bell, other w/hands in muff, 1959, pr..**$25.00**
Salt & pepper shakers, girl Christmas trees, holly in hair, #6216, 4¼", pr..**$35.00**
Salt & pepper shakers, Rudolph & Clarisse heads, #6181, 1950s, 3¾", 3½", pr..**$50.00**

Salt and pepper shakers, Santa, $22.00 for the pair. (Photo courtesy Helene Guarnaccia)

Salt & pepper shakers, Santa winking, w/label, pr................**$30.00**
Tray, Santa's head, beard forms tray, 1959 ....**$17.50**

Kozy Kitten

Ashtray, green & white pillow w/brass match holder, 1958..**$85.00**
Ashtray, plaid kitten standing & holding a match in center, sq, 4½"..**$100.00**
Butter dish, 2 kittens peek from under lid, 7", from $90 to....**$110.00**
Cheese crock, Stinky Cheese on side, 2 kissing cats on lid, 1958 .**$60.00**
Cleanser shaker, full figure, 1958, rare, 6½", from $140 to.....**$165.00**
Cookie jar, head form **$40.00**
Cottage cheese dish, 2 kissing cats atop lid **$45.00**
Creamer & sugar bowl, stackable, head is sugar bowl, body is creamer w/tail handle, from $125 to **$150.00**
Creamer & sugar bowl, white cylinders, plaid rim & kitten finial on sugar bowl lid, cat handle on creamer, minimum........**$600.00**
Grocery clip, Kitty Catch, 1958, from $125 to...................**$150.00**
Match holder, Match Dandy, 1959, 6", from $85 to **$110.00**
Memo Minder, flat cat w/Memo Minder on collar, 7", from $60 to..**$75.00**
Mug, cat on side, w/squeaker, 8-oz, from $35 to **$45.00**
Napkin holder, wireware coil centers, salt shaker on 1 end, pepper shaker on other, 7¾"..**$45.00**
Oil bottle, slender sitting cat, 7½", from $100 to **$140.00**
Pin box, cat on top w/tape-measure tongue, 1958 ....**$50.00**
Pitcher, white w/kitten, 1960, 7½", from $100 to **$120.00**
Salt & pepper shakers, heads only, male in cap, pr from $25 to ...**$35.00**
Salt & pepper shakers, kitten in basket, 1 winking, rubber stoppers, 2½", pr from $75 to **$95.00**
Salt & pepper shakers, 1 w/pink bow tie, 2nd w/blue noisemaker, 1958, pr..**$28.00**
Spice set, 4 cat faces hang on vertical wire w/hooks, 11" overall..**$150.00**
Spoon rest/recipe holder, cats on handle w/Hold Recipes Here, fish decor on bowl, 1959, 2½x8x3½"................................**$80.00**

String holder, $40.00.

Sugar shaker, cat in apron holding sugar can w/cork stopper, 1958 ....**$85.00**
Vase, full-bodied cat, male or female, 6½", ea from $65 to..**$80.00**
Wall pocket, full-bodied cat w/hook tail, 7x3", from $45 to **$60.00**

Pixie Ware

Bottle topper, 300 Proof..**$300.00**
Cherries jar, black-haired cross-eyed spoon finial, from $145 to...**$185.00**
Cocktail Onions jar, green-striped onion finial on spoon...**$150.00**
Honey jar, winking yellow-head spoon finial, rare, minimum value **$500.00**
Hors d'oeuvres, boy w/tall green hat in center, 7½x5¾", minimum **$200.00**
Instant coffee jar, girl w/blond hair & blue ribbon spoon finial, from $200 to **$245.00**

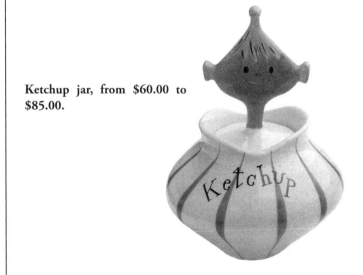

Ketchup jar, from $60.00 to $85.00.

Lil Sugar & cream crock, winking auburn-haired Pixie finial on sugar lid; no Pixie on creamer, from $120 to **$140.00**
Marmalade, 5½", very rare, minimum value.....................**$600.00**
Mayonnaise jar, winking brown-haired head spoon finial, from $200 to **$235.00**

Mustard jar, scowling yellow head spoon finial, from 85 to ... **$110.00**

Olives jar, green winking head spoon finial, from $100 to . **$125.00**

Onions jar, onion head spoon finial, from $125 to **$140.00**

Relish, crabby green head spoon finial, 1959, from $200 to ... **$250.00**

Salt & pepper shakers, Salty & Peppy, wooden side handles, pr from $125 to **$150.00**

Spoons, set of 4 .... **$700.00**

Towel hook, orange-haired Pixie, minimum **$165.00**

Rooster

Cigarette holder, wooden, 11¾", $30.00; recipe box, $30.00; pitcher, no handle (recessed hand holds), $40.00. (Photo courtesy Pat and Ann Duncan)

Ashtray, rooster form, body is receptacle, 3¾x3¾x2½", from $12 to **$15.00**

Bowl, cereal; 6" **$6.00**

Butter dish, embossed rooster, ¼-lb, from $35 to **$45.00**

Chocolate pot, white w/embossed rooster, flaring sides, plain handle, from $40 to **$50.00**

Coffeepot, white w/rooster decoration, electric, 1960, from $45 to **$55.00**

Cookie jar, embossed rooster, from $55 to **$65.00**

Creamer, embossed rooster, tail handle, 3½" **$20.00**

Cutting board, 15x8½", from $85 to **$95.00**

Egg cup, double, from $9 to **$12.00**

Jam 'n Jelly, embossed rooster, from $30 to.................... **$35.00**

Jam jar, rooster finial, from $25 to **$35.00**

Mug, embossed (3 sizes), ea from $6 to **$9.00**

Mustard jar, embossed rooster, from $25 to **$35.00**

Napkin holder, 6", from $20 to **$30.00**

Pitcher, milk; embossed rooster, slim, plain handle, 7" **$20.00**

Pitcher, water; embossed rooster, tail handle **$45.00**

Salt & pepper shakers, figural, 4¾", pr **$25.00**

Sugar bowl, white w/red bottom, rooster finial, 1960, 5x4" dia, from $25 to **$35.00**

Tray, flat rooster form, 4¾x3¾" **$9.00**

Vase, figural, 6¼", from $25 to **$35.00**

Miscellaneous

Bank, Coin Kitty, head nodder, from $175 to **$200.00**

Bowl, cantalope form, green w/yellow interior, 2½x6¼", 8 for. **$55.00**

Candleholder, girl praying, 1960, ea **$10.00**

Candleholders, horse w/red hearts & flowers, 1964, 4¼", pr.... **$50.00**

Candleholders/flower frogs, Peepin' Tom & Tweetie, pr **$30.00**

Creamer, Hummel-type boy on spout, 5½" **$35.00**

Cups, tomato w/leaf-shaped handle, 6 for **$24.00**

Italian dressing, whimsical ethnic face stopper, 1959......... **$225.00**

Pickled onions jar, crying onion **$18.00**

Pitcher, juice; orange painted on white, slim, 1962, 7⅞" **$60.00**

Russian dressing bottle, whimsical ethnic face stopper, 1959 . **$225.00**

Salt & pepper shakers, Chattercoons, squeakers, 4", pr........ **$25.00**

Salt & pepper shakers, chick on egg cup, 1959, 3¾", 4-pc set.. **$42.50**

Salt & pepper shakers, mouse figural, old noismakers in bottom, 1958, 4¼", pr **$35.00**

Smoker ashtray, fisherman, vents in mouth and ears, 1960s, 5¼", $35.00. (Photo courtesy Pat and Ann Duncan)

Snack set, lettuce leaf plate & tomato cup, 8-pc, serves 4..... **$35.00**

Tea bag holders, teapot shape, set of 4 in metal rack **$35.00**

Wall pocket, anthropomorphic sunflower, lg **$35.00**

Wall pocket, anthropomorphic sunflower, sm **$25.00**

Homer Laughlin China Co.

Since the first pottery rolled out of the kiln in 1873, the Homer Laughlin China Company has produced a vast quantity of dinnerware, toiletry items, art ware, and various sundry items. In all probability Mr. Homer Laughlin and his brother Shakespeare Laughlin had no idea of the scope and magnitude their pottery would have on the entire world, as the Homer Laughlin China Company has produced an estimated 15,000 different patterns on approximately 150 different shapes during the past 101 years. In 1877, Homer Laughlin purchased his brother's interest and carried on alone until he sold the business to the Aaron and Wells families in 1898. Today the pottery is still owned by the Wells family and continues to produce reintroduced Fiesta, restaurant ware, and various kitchenware items.

For further information see *The Collector's Encyclopedia of Homer Laughlin China* by Joanne Jasper (Collector Books). Also recommended is *Homer Laughlin China 1940's and 1950's*, and *Homer Laughlin, A Giant Among Dishes*, both by Jo Cunningham (Schiffer), and *Homer Laughlin China Identification Guide to Shapes and Patterns* by Jo Cunningham and Darlene Nossaman (Schiffer). *The Collector's Encyclopedia of Fiesta, Tenth Edition,* by Sharon and Bob Huxford (Collector Books), has photographs and prices of several of the more collectible lines such as listed here.

See also Fiesta.

Advisor: Darlene Nossaman (See Directory, Dinnerware)

Club/Newsletter: Homer Laughlin China Collector's Association (HLCCA)
P.O. Box 26021
Crystal City, VA 22215-6021
Dues $25.00 single; $40.00 couple or family, includes *The Dish* magazine (a 16-page quarterly), free classifieds
www.hlcca.org

American Beauty Shape, 1898

Some patterns are Pansy, Primrose, Petite Alpine Rose, Crab Apple, and Trinity Rose.

Baker, from $15 to	**$20.00**
Bowl, fruit; lg, from $35 to	**$40.00**
Bowl, oatmeal; from $12 to	**$16.00**
Butter dish, from $35 to	**$45.00**
Casserole, w/lid, from $35 to	**$45.00**

Celery tray, pansy decoration, from $25.00 to $35.00. (Photo courtesy Darlene Nossaman)

Compote, from $45 to	**$55.00**
Creamer, from $15 to	**$18.00**

Cup, from $10 to	**$15.00**
Jug, lg, from $35 to	**$45.00**
Plate, 7", from $8 to	**$12.00**
Plate, 10", from $12 to	**$16.00**
Platter, lg, from $20 to	**$25.00**
Saucer, from $6 to	**$8.00**
Sugar bowl, w/lid, from $25 to	**$30.00**
Teapot, from $50 to	**$60.00**

Charm House Shape

This hollow ware shape was introduced in 1950 and was used with other flatware shapes (such as Rhythm) in dinnerware lines such as Lotus Hai, Lyric, Ming Glory, Cinnamon Tree, and Pink Magnolia. These prices are for hollowware only:

Bowl, cereal/soup; from $10 to	**$15.00**
Casserole, w/lid, from $20 to	**$25.00**
Creamer, from $10 to	**$15.00**
Nappy, 8", from $12 to	**$15.00**
Salt & pepper shakers, pr from $15 to	**$20.00**
Sauceboat, from $14 to	**$18.00**
Teapot, from $35 to	**$40.00**

Coronet Shape

Some patterns are Greenbriar, Petit Point, June Rose, Chintz, and Nova.

Baker, from $10 to	**$14.00**
Bowl, 5", from $5 to	**$7.00**
Casserole, w/lid, from $20 to	**$30.00**
Creamer, from $8 to	**$12.00**
Cup, from $8 to	**$10.00**
Plate, 7", from $6 to	**$8.00**
Plate, 10", from $8 to	**$10.00**
Platter, 13", from $14 to	**$16.00**
Sauceboat, from $10 to	**$12.00**
Saucer, from $3 to	**$5.00**
Sugar bowl, w/lid, from $15 to	**$18.00**

Decorated Skytone on Jubilee Shape

Most often found in solid sky blue with white handles and finials, Decorated Skytone on Jubilee shapes was introduced in 1950. It was also produced in patterns, some of which are Dogwood, Morning Bloom, Stardust, White Thistle, and Blue Mist.

Bowl, coupe soup; from $6 to	**$8.00**
Bowl, fruit; 5½", from $5 to	**$7.00**
Casserole, w/lid, from $20 to	**$25.00**
Coffeepot, from $20 to	**$25.00**
Creamer, from $8 to	**$10.00**
Cup, from $7 to	**$10.00**
Egg cup, from $15 to	**$18.00**
Plate, 7", from $6 to	**$8.00**
Plate, 10", from $10 to	**$12.00**

Platter, 13", from $14 to $18.00
Salt & pepper shakers, pr from $14 to $18.00
Sauceboat, fast stand, from $12 to $15.00
Sugar bowl, w/lid, from $12 to $16.00
Teapot, from $30 to $35.00

Theme Shape

Some patterns are Cameo, Regency, Surrey, Della Robbia, and Stratford.

Baker, from $10 to...$14.00
Casserole, w/lid, from $18 to..$24.00
Creamer, from $10 to...$15.00
Cup, from $8 to...$12.00
Plate, 7", from $5 to...$8.00

Plate, Surrey decal, 10", from $8.00 to $12.00. (Photo courtesy Darlene Nossaman)

Platter, 11", from $12 to..$15.00
Salt & pepper shakers, pr from $18 to.................................$25.00
Sauceboat, from $15 to...$18.00
Saucer, from $4 to...$6.00
Sugar bowl, w/lid, from $15 to..$20.00
Teapot, from $35 to...$45.00

Horton Ceramics

Following the end of WWII, Mr. Horace Horton and his wife, Geri, returned to Mr. Horton's hometown, Eastland, Texas. In 1947 they started a ceramics company utilizing the clays of the area, with Geri doing the modeling and art work, while Horace oversaw the business. The small shop grew into a successful business and the company branched out from beginning with small novelty items to large outdoor planters and serving pieces. The trademark 'horton ceramics' in small letter script is incised on the bottom of each piece, so Horton Ceramics is easly recognizable. Mr. and Mrs. Horton

sold their ceramic business in 1961. (The number refers to the mold number incised on the bottom of each piece.)

Advisor: Darlene Nossaman (See Directory, Horton Ceramics)

Animal, dog, natural color, D2, 8", from $15 to..................$18.00
Animal, elephant, gray, E1, 8", from $15 to $18.00
Animal, giraffe, yellow & brown, G1, 9½", from $15 to $18.00
Animal, penguin, black & white, P1, 7", from $15 to.........$18.00
Kitchenware, bean pot, yellow, brown or green, BQPB, 3", from $10 to $12.00
Kitchenware, canister, yellow, brown or green, C6, 6x4½", from $12 to $16.00
Kitchenware, grease jar, yellow, brown or green, C8, 6", from $10 to $12.00
Kitchenware, pitcher, yellow, brown or green, P5, 1-qt, from $12 to $14.00
Novelty planter, baby shoe, white only, 6x3", from $10 to...$14.00
Novelty planter, Gingham Cat, mixed colors, from $18 to ..$22.00
Novelty planter, Gingham Dog, mixed colors, from $18 to .$22.00
Novelty planter, girl's head, neutral only, #454, 4x6", from $15 to..$18.00

Nut bowl, #H4, $15.00. (Photo courtesy Darlene Nossaman)

Vase/planter, #1418, blue or white, 18x5", from $15 to $18.00
Vase/planter, #805, 2-tone white, green or mustard, 7x3", from $12 to $15.00
Vase/planter, football player, natural color, B9, 10", from $16 to.$18.00
Vase/planter, P75, white, black, lime, blue or sand, 7x5", from $12 to $15.00
Vase/planter, V955, white, blue, green or pink, 9x5½", from $14 to $16.00

Hull

Hull has a look of its own. Many lines were made in soft, pastel matt glazes and modeled with flowers and ribbons, and as a result, they have a very feminine appeal.

The company operated in Crooksville (near Zanesville), Ohio, from just after the turn of the century until they closed in 1985. From the 1930s until the plant was destroyed by fire in 1950, they preferred the soft matt glazes so popular with today's collectors, though a few high gloss lines were made as well. When the plant was rebuilt, modern equipment was installed which they soon found did not lend itself to the duplication of the matt glazes, so they began to concentrate on the production of glossy wares, novelties, and figurines.

During the '40s and '50s, they produced a line of kitchenware items modeled after Little Red Riding Hood. Original pieces are expensive today and most are reproduced by persons other than Hull. (See also Little Red Riding Hood.)

Hull's Mirror Brown dinnerware line made from 1960 until they closed in 1985 was very successful for them and was made in large quantities. Its glossy brown glaze was enhanced with a band of ivory foam, and today's collectors are finding its rich colors and basic, strong shapes just as attractive now as they were back then. In addition to table service, there are novelty trays shaped like gingerbread men and fish, canisters and cookie jars, covered casseroles with ducks and hens as lids, vases, ashtrays, and mixing bowls. It's easy to find, and though you may have to pay 'near book' prices at co-ops and antique malls, bargains are out there. It may be marked Hull, Crooksville, O; HPCo; or Crestone.

If you'd like to learn more about this subject, we recommend *The Collector's Encyclopedia of Hull Pottery* and *The Ultimate Encyclopedia of Hull Pottery*, both by Brenda Roberts; and *Collector's Guide to Hull Pottery, The Dinnerware Lines*, by Barbara Loveless Gick-Burke.

Advisor: Brenda Roberts (See Directory, Hull)

Bow-Knot, candleholder, #B-17, 4", ea from $140 to........**$175.00**
Bow-Knot, vase, #B-3, 6½", from $200 to **$245.00**
Calla-Lily, bowl, console; #590/32, 13", from $175 to **$225.00**
Calla-Lily, ewer, #506, 10", from $380 to..........................**$480.00**

Calla-Lily, vase, #560/33, 13", from $500.00 to $600.00.

Camellia, sugar bowl, #112, 5", from $125 to **$150.00**
Camellia, teapot, #110, 8½", from $350 to **$425.00**
Cinderella Kitchenware, Blossom, creamer, #28, 4¼", from $45 to..**$70.00**
Cinderella Kitchenware, Bouquet, pitcher, #28, 32-oz, from $25 to..**$35.00**

Dogwood, basket, #501, 7½", from $295 to **$350.00**
Dogwood, teapot, #507, 6½", from $300 to **$400.00**
Dogwood, vase, #516, 4¾", from $75 to...........................**$95.00**

Ebb Tide, pitcher, 14", from $210.00 to $295.00.

Iris, candleholder, #411, 5", ea from $125 to....................**$155.00**
Iris, vase, #405, 8½", from $210 to **$250.00**
Magnolia, gloss, candleholder, #H-24, 4", ea from $50 to ...**$65.00**
Magnolia, gloss, double cornucopia, #H-15, 12", from $150 to...**$200.00**
Magnolia, glossy, teapot, #H-20, 6½", from $175 to.........**$225.00**
Magnolia, matt, bowl, console; #26, 12", from $200 to.....**$250.00**
Magnolia, matt, creamer, #24, 3¾", from $55 to................**$80.00**
Magnolia, matt, ewer, #14, 4¾", from $75 to....................**$105.00**

Magnolia, matt, vase, #3, 8½", from $155.00 to $200.00.

Magnolia, matt, vase, #4, 6¼", from $70 to **$90.00**
Mardi Gras/Granada, basket, #65, 8", from $100 to..........**$145.00**
Mardi Gras/Granada, teapot, #33, 5½", from $235 to.......**$310.00**

Novelty, peacock vase, #73, 1951, 10½", from $35 to **$50.00**
Novelty, planter, clover-shaped, #121, 4½", from $20 to **$28.00**
Novelty, planter, flying duck, #104, from $75 to **$105.00**
Novelty, rooster planter, #54, 1953, 7½", from $115 to **$150.00**
Novelty, swan ashtray/planter, #70, 4", 1951, from $14 to ..**$20.00**
Novelty, wall pocket, flying goose, #67, 6", from $55 to......**$75.00**
Orchid, bulb bowl, #312, 7", from $150 to.....................**$200.00**
Orchid, jardiniere, #310, 6", from $225 to.....................**$265.00**
Orchid, vase, bud; #306, 6¾", from $175 to...................**$225.00**

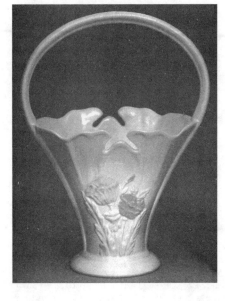

Poppy, basket, #601, 12", from $1,300.00 to $1,600.00.

Poppy, bowl, low, #602, 6½", from $225 to **$275.00**
Poppy, ewer, #610, 4¾", from $165 to **$200.00**
Poppy, wall pocket, #609, 9", from $310 to...................**$410.00**
Rosella, basket, #R-12, 7", from $260 to......................**$310.00**
Rosella, sugar bowl, w/lid, #R-4, 5½", from $150 to........**$170.00**
Rosella, wall pocket, #R-10, 6½", from $150 to...............**$175.00**
Sunglow, basket, #84, 6¼", from $95 to.........................**$145.00**
Sunglow, bowl, mixing; #50, 7½", from $25 to..................**$35.00**
Sunglow, cornucopia, #96, 8½", from $75 to **$110.00**
Sunglow, grease jar, #53, 5¼", from $50 to **$75.00**
Thistle, vase, #54, 6½", from $90 to **$125.00**
Tulip, jardiniere, #115-33, 7", from $295 to....................**$345.00**
Tulip, vase, bud; #104-33, 6", from $140 to....................**$165.00**
Water Lily, candleholder, #L-22, 4½", ea from $85 to **$125.00**
Water Lily, ewer, #L-17, 13½", from $525 to **$650.00**
Water Lily, jardiniere, #L-24, 8½", from $365 to **$425.00**
Water Lily, sugar bowl, w/lid, #L-20, 5", from $80 to **$110.00**
Water Lily, vase, #L-1, 5½", from $55 to.........................**$80.00**
Wildflower, basket, #W-16, 10½", from $375 to.............**$425.00**
Wildflower, basket, laced handle, #W-16, 10½", from $375 to.**$425.00**
Wildflower, candleholder, #W-22, 2½", ea from $60 to **$85.00**
Wildflower, ewer, #W-2, 5½", from $105 to **$140.00**
Wildflower, vase, #W-1, 5½", from $65 to **$90.00**
Wildflower, vase, #W-20, 15½", from $450 to **$600.00**
Wildflower (# series), bonbon, handled, #65, 7", from $375 to...**$475.00**
Wildflower (# series), creamer, #73, 4¾", from $240 to **$275.00**
Wildflower (# series), teapot, #72, 8", from $850 to.......**$1,150.00**
Wildflower (# series), vase, #62, 6¼", from $140 to..........**$165.00**

Woodland, ewer, #W-6, 6½", from $180 to **$240.00**
Woodland, planter, #W-19, 10½", from $175 to..............**$235.00**

Dinnerware

Avocado, bowl, soup/salad; 6½", from $4 to.....................**$6.00**
Avocado, creamer, 4½", from $15 to................................**$22.00**
Avocado, mug, 3½", from $5 to **$7.00**
Avocado, pitcher, 7½", from $25 to.................................**$40.00**
Avocado, plate, dinner; 10¼", from $8 to........................**$10.00**
Avocado, teapot, 6½", from $40 to..................................**$65.00**
Country Belle, pie plate, 11", from $25 to.......................**$35.00**
Country Belle, pitcher, 3½", from $25 to **$35.00**
Country Belle, plate, luncheon; 8½", from $8 to..............**$10.00**
Country Belle, platter, oval, 12", from $15 to...................**$22.00**
Country Squire, bean pot, 6½", from $30 to.....................**$40.00**
Country Squire, bowl, mixing; 8¼", from $20 to...............**$30.00**
Country Squire, cookie jar, 9", from $50 to.....................**$85.00**
Country Squire, mug, 4", from $4 to................................**$5.00**
Country Squire, plate, dinner; 10¼", from $8 to...............**$10.00**
Crestone, bowl, 10", from $20 to **$25.00**
Crestone, cup, 7-oz, from $4 to **$7.00**
Crestone, pitcher, 38-oz, from $25 to **$35.00**
Crestone, plate, dinner; 10½", from $8 to.......................**$10.00**
Crestone, plate, luncheon; 9⅜", from $6 to.......................**$8.00**
Crestone, saucer, 5⅞", from $2 to.....................................**$3.00**
Crestone, sugar bowl, w/lid, 4¼", from $20 to **$25.00**
Gingerbread Man, butter dish, gray or sand, 7½", from $20 to.......**$30.00**
Gingerbread Man, cookie jar, sand, 12", from $450 to **$650.00**
Gingerbread Man, teapot, gray, 6½", from $40 to **$60.00**
Heartland, bowl, fruit; from $8 to **$10.00**
Heartland, cookie jar, 9", from $100 to.........................**$125.00**
Heartland, creamer, 4¾", from $25 to **$35.00**
Heartland, mug, 5", from $12 to **$16.00**
Heartland, pitcher, 4", from $25 to **$35.00**
Heartland, pitcher, 9", from $75 to **$100.00**
Heartland, plate, salad; 6½", from $8 to..........................**$10.00**
Heartland, salt shaker, 6", from $20 to **$25.00**
Mirror Almond, bowl, vegetable; oval, 11", from $20 to **$30.00**
Mirror Almond, creamer, 4½", from $15 to **$20.00**
Mirror Almond, cruet, vinegar; 5¾", from $15 to **$20.00**
Mirror Almond, pepper shaker, 3¾", from $10 to **$12.00**
Mirror Almond, plate, salad; 6½", from $2 to **$3.00**
Mirror Almond, saucer, 6¾", from $2 to **$3.00**
Mirror Brown, baker, sq, 9½", from $20 to **$35.00**
Mirror Brown, bean pot, 6½", from $30 to **$40.00**
Mirror Brown, bowl, salad; oval, incised rooster, 1968-72, 6½",
    from $75 to **$100.00**
Mirror Brown, casserole, French handle, 11¾", from $50 to...**$75.00**
Mirror Brown, cookie jar, 1960-85, 9", from $50 to...........**$85.00**
Mirror Brown, cruet, vinegar; 6½", from $30 to.................**$40.00**
Mirror Brown, duck planter, #F69, 10", from $30 to **$40.00**
Mirror Brown, mug, coffee; 3", from $4 to........................**$6.00**
Mirror Brown, pepper shaker, 1978-83, 3¾", from $10 to ..**$15.00**
Mirror Brown, plate, dinner; 10½", from $8 to...................**$10.00**
Mirror Brown, salt shaker, 3¾", ea from $8 to....................**$12.00**
Mirror Brown, spoon rest, 1978-83, 6½", from $40 to **$50.00**

Mirror Brown, teapot, 6", from $25 to **$35.00**
Mirror Brown, vase, cylindrical, 9", from $35 to **$45.00**
Provincial, bean pot, 6½", from $40 to................................**$50.00**
Provincial, bowl, fruit; 5¼", from $4 to **$5.00**
Provincial, bowl, mixing; 5¼", from $10 to.........................**$15.00**
Provincial, creamer, 4¼", from $16 to.................................**$22.00**
Provincial, mug, 4", from $3 to **$5.00**
Provincial, pitcher, 7½", from $22 to...................................**$30.00**
Provincial, pitcher, 9", from $40 to......................................**$60.00**
Provincial, plate, salad; 6½", from $4 to **$5.00**
Provincial, sugar bowl, w/lid, 3½", from $16 to **$22.00**
Rainbow, pitcher, 9", from $40 to...**$60.00**
Rainbow, plate, dinner; 10½", from $8 to **$10.00**
Rainbow, vase, bud; #F90, 6½", from $15 to **$20.00**
Tangerine, ashtray, 8", from $25 to.......................................**$35.00**
Tangerine, butter dish, 7½", from $20 to **$30.00**
Tangerine, creamer, 4½", from $15 to...................................**$22.00**
Tangerine, dish, chip 'n dip; 15", from $45 to **$65.00**
Tangerine, dish, leaf-shaped, 7", from $15 to.......................**$22.00**
Tangerine, gravy boat, 6", from $45 to **$65.00**
Tangerine, mug, coffee; 3", from $4 to **$6.00**
Tangerine, teapot, 6½", from $15 to......................................**$22.00**
Tangerine, tidbit server, 10", from $50 to **$75.00**

Imperial Glass

Organized in 1901 in Bellaire, Ohio, the Imperial Glass Company made carnival glass, stretch glass, a line called NuCut (made in imitation of cut glass), and a limited amount of art glass within the first decade of the century. In the mid-'30s, they designed one of their most famous patterns (and one of their most popular with today's collectors), Candlewick. Within a few years, milk glass had become their leading product.

During the '50s they reintroduced their NuCut line in crystal as well as colors, marketing it as 'Collector's Crystal.' In the late '50s they bought molds from both Heisey and Cambridge. Most of the glassware they reissued from these old molds was marked 'IG,' one letter superimposed over the other. When Imperial was bought by Lenox in 1973, an 'L' was added to the mark. The ALIG logo was added in 1981 when the company was purchased by Arthur Lorch. In 1982 the factory was sold to Robert Stahl of Minneapolis. Chapter 11 bankruptcy was filled in October that year. A plant resurgence continued production. Many Heisey by Imperial animals done in color were made at this time. A new mark, the NI for New Imperial, was used on a few items. In November of 1984 the plant closed forever and the assets were sold at liquidation. This was the end of the 'Big I.'

Numbers in the listings were assigned by the company and appeared on their catalog pages. They were used to indicate differences in shapes and stems, for instance. Collectors still use them.

For more information on Imperial we recommend *Imperial Glass* by Margaret and Douglas Archer; *Elegant Glassware of the Depression Era* by Gene and Cathy Florence; and *Imperial Glass Encyclopedia, Vol. I, A to Cane, Vol. II, Cane to M,* and *Vol. III, M to Z,* edited by James Measell. To research Imperial's glass figurines refer to *Glass Animals* by Dick and Pat Spencer (Collector Books).

See also Candlewick.

Note: To determine values for Cape Cod in colors, add 100% to prices suggested for crystal for Ritz Blue and Ruby. Amber, Antique Blue, Azalea, Evergreen, Verde, black, and milk glass are 50% higher than crystal.

Club: National Imperial Glass Collectors' Society, Inc.
P.O. Box 534, Bellaire, OH 43906
Dues: $18 per year (+$3 for each additional member of household), quarterly newsletter: *Glasszette,* convention every June
www.imperialglass.org

Cape Cod, ashtray, #160/134, 4" **$14.00**
Cape Cod, bottle, cologne; w/stopper, #1601 ....**$60.00**
Cape Cod, bowl, fruit; #160/23B, 5½" **$10.00**
Cape Cod, carafe, wine; #160/185, 26-oz..........................**$225.00**
Cape Cod, cordial, #1602, 1½-oz **$6.00**
Cape Cod, cruet, w/stopper, #160/70, 5-oz **$30.00**
Cape Cod, decanter, bourbon; #160/260............................**$100.00**
Cape Cod, egg cup, #160/225 ....**$30.00**
Cape Cod, finger bowl, #1602, 4" **$12.00**
Cape Cod, ice bucket, #160/63, 6½".................................**$195.00**

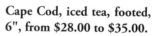
Cape Cod, iced tea, footed, 6", from $28.00 to $35.00.

Cape Cod, ladle, marmalade; #160/130.............................**$10.00**
Cape Cod, nappy, #160/5F, 7"..**$22.00**
Cape Cod, pitcher, milk; #160/240, 1-pt.............................**$55.00**
Cape Cod, plate, bread & butter; #160/1D, 6½" **$7.00**
Cape Cod, plate, salad; #160/5D, 8" **$9.00**
Cape Cod, platter, oval, #160/124D, 13½" **$80.00**
Cape Cod, punch bowl, #160/20B, 12".................................**$65.00**
Cape Cod, saucer, coffee; #160/37...**$2.00**
Cape Cod, teacup, #160/35 ....**$6.00**
Cape Cod, tumbler, juice; footed, #1602, 6-oz **$5.00**
Cape Cod, vase, footed, #160/22, 6¼" **$35.00**
Crocheted Crystal, basket, 12" **$85.00**
Crocheted Crystal, bowl, mayonnaise; flat or footed, 5¼", ea...**$12.50**
Crocheted Crystal, bowl, narcissus; 7" **$40.00**
Crocheted Crystal, bowl, salad; 10½" **$30.00**
Crocheted Crystal, cake stand, footed, 12" **$40.00**

Crocheted Crystal, candleholder, double, high, 4½", ea.......**$14.00**
Crocheted Crystal, cheese & cracker dish, footed, plate: 12" **$40.00**
Crocheted Crystal, creamer, footed **$20.00**
Crocheted Crystal, epergne, footed bowl, center vase, 11" .**$130.00**
Crocheted Crystal, mayonnaise ladle......................................**$5.00**
Crocheted Crystal, plate, mayonnaise; 7½"..........................**$7.50**
Crocheted Crystal, plate, 9½"...**$12.50**
Crocheted Crystal, plate, 14" **$25.00**
Crocheted Crystal, punch bowl, 14" **$65.00**
Crocheted Crystal, relish, 4-part, 11½".................................**$25.00**

Crocheted Crystal, sugar bowl and creamer, $37.50 each. (Photo courtesy Gene and Cathy Florence)

Crocheted Crystal, sugar bowl, footed..................................**$20.00**
Crocheted Crystal, tumbler, fruit juice; footed, 6-oz, 6" **$25.00**
Crocheted Crystal, vase, 8" **$35.00**
Crocheted Crystal, water goblet, 9-oz, 7⅛"..........................**$30.00**
Crocheted Crystal, wine goblet, 4½-oz, 5½".........................**$32.00**

Indiana Glass

In 1971 the Indiana Glass Co. introduced a line of new carnival glass, much of which was embossed with grape clusters and detailed leaves using their Harvest molds. It was first introduced in blue, and later gold and lime green were added. Prior to 1971 the Harvest molds had been used to produce a snowy white milk glass; blue and green satin or frosted glass; ruby red flashed glass; and plain glass in various shades of blue, amber, and green. Because this line was mass produced (machine-made) carnival, there are still large quantities available to collectors.

They also produced a line of handmade carnival called Heritage, which they made in amethyst and Sunset (amberina). Because it was handmade as opposed to being machine made, production was limited, and it is not as readily available to today's collectors as is the Harvest pattern carnival. There is a significant amount of interest in both lines today. Now that these lines are 30 years old, Grandmother, Mother, and Aunt are leaving a piece or two to the next generation. The younger generation is off and running to complete Granny's collection via the Internet. This has caused a revival of interest in Indiana carnival glass as a collectible.

The company also produced a series of four Bicentennial commemorative plates made in blue and gold carnival: American Eagle, Independence Hall, Liberty Bell, and Spirit of '76. These are valued at $15.00 to $18.00 each (unboxed). A large Liberty Bell cookie jar and a small Liberty Bell bank were also made in gold carnival. Today

the cookie jars are valued at around $20.00 while the banks generally sell for $10.00 or less..

This glass is a little difficult to evaluate, since you see it in malls and flea markets with such a wide range of 'asking' prices. On one hand, you have sellers who themselves are not exactly sure what it is they have but since it's 'carnival' assume it should be fairly pricey. On the other hand, you have those who just 'cleaned house' and want to get rid of it. They may have bought it new themselves and know it's not very old and wasn't expensive to start with. (The Harvest Princess Punch Set sold for $5.98 in 1971.) So take heart, there are still bargains to be found, though they're becoming rarer with each passing year. The best buys on Indiana carnival glass are found at garage and estate sales.

In addition to the iridescent lines, Indiana Glass produced a line called Ruby Band Diamond Point, a clear, diamond-faceted pattern with a wide ruby-flashed rim band; some items from this line are listed below. Our values are for examples with the ruby flashing in excellent condition.

See also King's Crown; Tiara.

Iridescent Amethyst Carnival Glass (Heritage)

Basket, footed, 9x5x7", from $60 to **$75.00**
Butter dish, 5x7½" dia, from $50 to....................................**$65.00**
Candleholders, 5½", pr from $45 to.....................................**$60.00**
Center bowl, 4¾x8½", from $50 to......................................**$60.00**
Goblet, 8-oz, from $15 to..**$22.00**
Pitcher, 8¼", from $50 to...**$70.00**
Punch set, 10" bowl, 8 cups, no pedestal, from $150 to **$185.00**
Punch set, 10" bowl & pedestal, 8 cups, ladle, 11-pc, from $200 ....**$235.00**
Swung vase, slender & footed w/irregular rim, 11x3", from $50 to..**$60.00**

Iridescent Blue Carnival Glass

Basket, Canterbury, waffled pattern, flared sides drawn in at handle, 11x8x12", from $50 to **$65.00**
Basket, Monticello, allover faceted embossed diamonds, 7x6" sq, from $25 to **$35.00**
Bowl, Harvest, embossed grapes, scalloped rim, paneled sides, 2¼x6¼" **$60.00**

Butter dish, Harvest, embossed grapes, 8" long, from $25.00 to $35.00.

Candleholders, Harvest, embossed grapes, compote shape, 4", pr from $20 to **$30.00**

Candy box, embossed ribs, rectangle w/lacy edge, footed, w/lid, 7x7" L, from $30 to **$40.00**

Candy box, Harvest, embossed grapes w/lace edge, w/lid, 6½", from $35 to **$45.00**

Candy box, Princess, diamond-point bands, pointed faceted finial, 6x6" dia, from $18 to **$22.00**

Canister/Candy jar, Harvest, embossed grapes, 7", from $30 to .. **$45.00**

Canister/Cookie jar, Harvest, embossed grapes, 9", from $125 to ..**$175.00**

Canister/Snack jar, Harvest, embossed grapes, 8", from $120 to..**$150.00**

Center bowl, Harvest, embossed grapes w/paneled sides, 4-footed, 4½x8½x12", common, from $25 to **$35.00**

Compote, Harvest, embossed grapes, scalloped rim on bowl, w/lid, 10", from $25 to..**$35.00**

Cooler (iced tea tumbler), Harvest, embossed grapes, 14-oz, 5⅞", from $9 to **$12.00**

Creamer & sugar bowl on tray, Harvest, embossed grapes, 3-pc, from $30 to **$35.00**

Egg/Hors d'oeuvres tray, sectioned w/off-side holder for 8 eggs, 12¾" dia, from $32 to...**$42.00**

Garland bowl (comport), paneled, 7½x8½" dia, from $15 to .. **$20.00**

Goblet, Harvest, embossed grapes, 9-oz, from $9 to **$12.00**

Hen on nest, from $18 to **$25.00**

Pitcher, Harvest, embossed grapes, 10½", common, from $35 to..**$50.00**

Plate, Bicentennial; American Eagle, from $15 to **$18.00**

Plate, hostess; Canterbury, allover diamond facets, flared crimped rim, 10", from $18 to **$22.00**

Punch set, Princess, complete w/ladle & hooks, 26-pc, from $95 to...**$115.00**

Punch set, Princess, 12 cups, no ladle or hooks, from $65 to.... **$85.00**

Tidbit, allover embossed diamond points, shallow w/flared sides, 6½"...**$12.00**

Wedding bowl (sm compote), Thumbprint, footed, 5x5", from $10 to **$12.00**

Iridescent Gold Carnival Glass

Hen on nest, from $18.00 to $25.00.

Basket, Canterbury, waffle pattern, flaring sides drawn in at handle terminals, 9½x11x8½", from $35 to...........................**$55.00**

Basket, Monticello, lg faceted allover diamonds, sq, 7x6", from $25 to **$30.00**

Candleholders, Harvest, embossed grapes, footed compote form, 4x4½", pr **$22.50**

Candy box, Harvest, embossed grapes, lace edge, footed, 6½x5¾", from $20 to **$30.00**

Canister/Candy jar, Harvest, embossed grapes, 7", from $15 to .**$25.00**

Canister/Cookie jar, Harvest, embossed grapes, 9", from $60 to.**$80.00**

Canister/Snack jar, Harvest, embossed grapes, 8", from $40 to. **$50.00**

Center bowl, Harvest, oval w/embossed grapes & paneled sides, 4½x8½x12", from $12 to...**$15.00**

Console set, Wild Rose, wide naturalistic petals form sides, 9" bowl w/pr 4½" bowl-type candleholders, 3-pc, $25 to **$30.00**

Cooler (iced tea tumbler), Harvest, embossed grapes, 14-oz, from $8 to **$12.00**

Egg plate, 11", from $18 to **$25.00**

Goblet, Harvest, embossed grapes, 9-oz, from $10 to **$14.00**

Pitcher, Harvest, embossed grapes, 10½", from $30 to **$35.00**

Plate, hostess; diamond embossing, shallow w/crimped & flared sides, 10", from $15 to **$20.00**

Punch bowl, Princess, w/12 cups & ladle (no hooks) **$55.00**

Punch set, Princess, complete w/ladle & hooks, 26-pc, from $100 to **$125.00**

Relish tray, Vintage, 6 sections, 9x12¾", from $16 to **$22.00**

Salad set, Vintage, embossed fruit, apple-shaped rim w/applied stem, 13", w/fork & spoon, 3-pc, from $15 to......................**$20.00**

Snack plate, 8x10", w/2⅞" cup, from $20 to **$25.00**

Tumbler, Harvest, embossed grapes, 4", from $7 to **$10.00**

Wedding bowl, Harvest, embossed grapes, pedestal foot, 8½x8", from $20 to **$25.00**

Wedding bowl (sm compote), 5x5", from $9 to...................**$12.00**

Iridescent Lime Carnival Glass

Lime green examples are harder to find than either the gold or the blue.

Candleholders, Harvest, compote shape, 4x4½", pr from $45 to **$60.00**

Candy box, Harvest, embossed grapes w/lace edge, w/lid, 6½", from $25 to **$30.00**

Canister/Candy jar, Harvest, embossed grapes, 7", from $20 to.. **$30.00**

Canister/Cookie jar, Harvest, embossed grapes, 9", from $75 to. **$90.00**

Canister/Snack jar, Harvest, embossed grapes, 8", from $50 to . **$60.00**

Center bowl, Harvest, embossed grapes, paneled sides, 4-footed, 4½x8½x12", from $25 to...**$30.00**

Compote, Harvest, embossed grapes, 7x6", from $15 to......**$20.00**

Console bowl, Harvest, embossed grapes, stemmed foot, 7½x10"...**$45.00**

Console set, Harvest, embossed grapes, 10" bowl w/compote-shaped candleholders, 3-pc, from $55 to **$75.00**

Cooler (iced tea tumbler), Harvest, embossed grapes, 14-oz, rare, from $18 to **$25.00**

Creamer & sugar bowl on tray, Harvest, embossed grapes, 3-pc, from $25 to **$30.00**

Egg plate, 11", from $18 to **$25.00**

Goblet, Harvest, embossed grapes, 9-oz, from $10 to **$12.00**

Hen on nest, from $15 to **$22.00**

Pitcher, Harvest, embossed grapes, 10½", from $35 to **$45.00**

Plate, hostess; allover diamond points, flared crimped sides, 10", from $15 to **$22.00**

Punch bowl, Princess, w/12 cups (no ladle or hooks) **$65.00**

Punch set, Princess, complete w/ladle & hooks, 26-pc, from $100 to **$125.00**

Salad set, Vintage, embossed fruit, apple-shaped rim w/applied stem, 13", w/fork & spoon, 3-pc, from $18 to.......................**$25.00**

Snack set, Harvest, embossed grapes, 4 cups & 4 plates, 8-pc, from $80 to **$100.00**

Iridescent Sunset (Amberina) Carnival Glass (Heritage)

Basket, footed, 9x5x7", from $30 to **$45.00**

Basket, 9½x7½" sq, from $40 to **$55.00**

Bowl, crimped, 3¾x10", from $32 to **$40.00**

Bowl, 3½x8½", from $25 to...**$30.00**

Bowl, 4½x6", $30.00.

Butter dish, 5x7½" dia, from $40 to...................................**$50.00**

Center bowl, 4¾x8½", from $30 to......................................**$40.00**

Creamer & sugar bowl, from $30 to **$40.00**

Dessert set, 8½" bowl, 12" plate, 2-pc, from $40 to **$45.00**

Goblet, 8-oz, from $35 to...**$40.00**

Pitcher, 7¼", from $35 to..**$45.00**

Pitcher, 8¼", from $45 to..**$50.00**

Plate, 12", from $30 to **$40.00**

Plate, 14", from $40 to **$50.00**

Punch set, 10" bowl, pedestal, 8 cups, & ladle, 11-pc, from $125 to **$175.00**

Rose bowl, 4½x6½", from $25 to..**$30.00**

Swung vase, slender, footed, w/irregular rim, 11x3", from $50 to **$60.00**

Tumbler, 3½", from $15 to..**$18.00**

Patterns

Canterbury, basket, waffle pattern, Lime, Sunset, or Horizon Blue, 5½x12", from $35 to..**$45.00**

Fruit, tray, gold, 5-compartment, from $25 to **$28.00**

Lily Pons, bowl, gold, 2¾x7¼", from $18 to.......................**$22.50**

Lily Pons, tray, gold, oval, 9½" L **$10.00**

Loganberry, bowl, gold, triangular, 2x7¼", from $12 to **$15.00**

Monticello, basket, lg faceted diamonds overall, Lemon, Lime, Sunset, or Horizon Blue, sq, 7x6", from $25 to...........**$35.00**

Monticello, basket, lg faceted diamonds overall, Lemon, Lime, Sunset, or Horizon Blue, 8¾x10½", from $35 to.........**$50.00**

Monticello, candy box, lg faceted overall diamonds, w/lid, Lemon, Lime, Sunset, or Horizon Blue, 5¼x6", from $15 to **$20.00**

Pretzel, celery dish, gold, elongated oval................................**$8.00**

Ruby Band Diamond Point, butter dish, from $20.00 to $25.00.

Ruby Band Diamond Point, cake stand, 5x12", from $22 to.... **$25.00**

Ruby Band Diamond Point, candy dish, footed, w/lid, 12x6", from $15 to **$18.00**

Ruby Band Diamond Point, chip 'n dip set, 13" dia, from $20 to...**$25.00**

Ruby Band Diamond Point, compote, w/lid, 16x5½", from $25 to...**$30.00**

Ruby Band Diamond Point, cooler (iced tea tumbler), 15-oz, from $5 to **$8.00**

Ruby Band Diamond Point, creamer & sugar bowl, 4½", from $10 to...**$15.00**

Ruby Band Diamond Point, creamer & sugar bowl, 4¾", on 6x9" tray, from $15 to..**$20.00**

Ruby Band Diamond Point, decanter, 24-oz.......................**$20.00**

Ruby Band Diamond Point, goblet, 12-oz, from $9 to **$10.00**

Ruby Band Diamond Point, On-the-Rocks, 9-oz, from $4 to ... **$6.00**

Ruby Band Diamond Point, pitcher, 8", from $15 to **$20.00**

Ruby Band Diamond Point, plate, dinner; 10", from $60 to....**$75.00**

Ruby Band Diamond Point, plate, hostess; 12", from $18 to ...**$25.00**

Ruby Band Diamond Point, salt & pepper shakers, 4", pr...**$25.00**

Ruby Band Diamond Point, toothpick holder, metal top band, 3".**$35.00**

Ruby Band Diamond Point, tumbler, 5¾", from $7 to........**$10.00**

Teardrop Garland, compote, blue, 7½x8½".........................**$27.50**

Indianapolis 500 Racing Collectibles

You don't have to be a Hoosier to know that unless the weather interfers, this famous 500-mile race is held in Indianapolis every

Memorial day and has been since 1911. Collectors of Indy memorabilia have a plethora of race-related items to draw from and can zero in on one area or many, enabling them to build extensive and interesting collections. Some of the special areas of interest they pursue are autographs, photographs, or other memorabilia related to the drivers; pit badges; race programs and yearbooks; books and magazines; decanters and souvenir tumblers; model race cars; and tickets.

Advisor: Eric Jungnickel (See Directory, Indy 500 Memorabilia)

Advertisment, Mobiloil, Winner Indianapolis 500, Jimmy Bryant photo, 1958, 14x10", EX...**$15.00**

Ashtray, AJ Foyt Rides w/a Tiger in His Tank..., 1964, 7" dia, M **$35.00**

Badge, pit pass; Camaro w/Chevy emblem & checkered flag, 1982, EX **$40.00**

Badge, pit pass; old main gate, 1956, bronze, EX **$85.00**

Badge, pit pass; view of track, 1974, EX **$50.00**

Badge, pit pass; 50th Anniversary, 1961, EX......................**$120.00**

Badge, pit; 1953, helmet shape, bronze, EX........................**$95.00**

Belt buckle, 1991, resembles pit pass, bronzed pewter, M....**$15.00**

Book, The Race, Angelo Aneglopolous, 70 pages, w/sleeve, EX **$50.00**

Book, 500 Mile Race Record Book, 1988 Edition, Al Unser Sr cover art, 150+ pages, EX..**$12.00**

Booklet, 1960 500 Festival, 500 Queen in center cover, EX **$20.00**

Brick, from original brick track, EX....................................**$30.00**

Coaster set, glass inserts in tin, Indianapolis 500 & race car, set of 6, EX **$15.00**

Dash pass, for maintenance workers, 2001-2002, EX **$15.00**

Desktop accessory, vintage car, plaster cast, May 30, 1931, on reverse, 7½" long, VG+, $215.00.

Flag, Indianapolis Motor Speedway & race car on black & white checks, 1972, cloth w/wooden standard, 18x16", EX ...**$25.00**

Glass, Collins; 1911-72 winners list w/Tony Hulman signature & Indy logo, Libbey, 12-oz, set of 6, M (G box)..............**$30.00**

Glass, whiskey; 1965 Indianapolis 500 w/winners list, w/gold rim, 3⅛", M..**$10.00**

Hat pin, enameled logo, 1998, 1⅜", M **$25.00**

Key chain, logo inside clear acrylic, 83rd 500, 1999, 1½x2¼", EX **$7.00**

Pennant, Souvenir of Indianapolis Speedway, 1950s-style car, 12x30", EX **$50.00**

Photo, 1954 Pace Lap, M...**$20.00**

Plate, logo w/1911-1990 winners list, blue crystal, 13¼" dia, NM **$75.00**

Postcard, 1950, Jimmy Bryant in race car, 6x9", EX **$20.00**

Program, Official; The 40th 500, 1956, EX.........................**$20.00**

Program, Official; The 47th 500, w/4-page starting position insert, 1963, EX **$12.00**

Program, Official; The 55th 500, 1971, EX.........................**$15.00**

Record, Great Moments From The Indy 500, w/info & interviews, 33⅓ rpm, M (shrink wrapped) **$25.00**

Salt & pepper shakers, 1 as race car, 2nd as state of Indiana, pr **$30.00**

Telephone, commemorating 1986 500, GTE, EX................**$50.00**

Ticket, 1983, 1982 winner Gordon Johncock on back, EX .**$45.00**

Tickets, Bleacher & Grounds Admission, 1959, EX, pr.......**$20.00**

Tie bar, race car in gold-plated metal, 1940s, EX................**$40.00**

View-Master set, Indianapolis Motor Speedway, 1973, 3 reels & cover envelope, EX..**$17.50**

Yearbook, Carl Hungness Presents the Indianapolis 500 Vol XVII, 1989, 208 pages, 11x8½", NM **$22.50**

Yearbook, Official Floyd Cramer's; 1958, EX......................**$45.00**

Jacket, leather, limited edition, NM, $1,300.00. (Photo courtesy BJ Summers)

Italian Glass

Throughout the century, the island of Murano has been recognized a one of the major glassmaking centers of the world. Companies including Venini, Barovier, Aureliano Toso, Barvini, Vistosi, AVEM, Cenedese, Cappellin, Seguso, and Archimede Seguso have produced very fine art glass, examples of which today often bring several thousand dollars on the secondary market — superior examples much more. Such items are rarely seen at the garage sale and flea market level, but what you will be seeing are the more generic glass clowns, birds, ashtrays, and animals, generally referred to simply as Murano glass. Their values are determined by the techniques used in their making more than size alone. For instance, an item with gold inclusions, controlled bubbles, fused glass patches, or layers of colors is more desirable than one that has none of these elements, even though it may be larger. For more information concerning the specific companies mentioned above, see *Schroeder's Antiques Price Guide* (Collector Books).

Vase, black with copper inclusions, Maestri Vetrai label, 15", from $100.00 to $125.00.

Bell, pink ribbon spirals w/white crosshatch bands in clear, gold flecks, 4¼x3" $48.00

Bowl, aqua encased in clear w/white bottom, ruffled & folded rim, Murano, 2½x7¼" $45.00

Bowl, brown w/gold aventurine over white cased in clear, 3 folds at rim, Murano, 3¼x7" $45.00

Bowl, clear w/controlled bubbles & gold flecks, scalloped rim, 6x6½" $75.00

Bowl, green w/pink interior, thin white line between & at rim, resembles watermelon, spout at side, Murano label, 7" L $110.00

Bowl, latticinio ribbons, pink & white in clear, ruffled rim, flared foot, unmarked, 2¼x6½" $75.00

Bowl, soft aqua opalescent w/gold spirals in clear, Murano, 2½x7¾" $185.00

Candy dish, bright blue w/hand-painted gold florals, w/lid, Made in Italy label, 6x6" $65.00

Decanter, bright yellow w/sloped shoulders on sq body, teardrop stopper, unmarked, 1940s, 12¾x3¼x3¼" $60.00

Decanter, turquoise opaque w/blue flecks, fluted, tall teardrop stopper, Rossini foil label, 26¼x5½" dia $135.00

Lamp, spiraling gold & white stripes, 6 lobes in gold wire frame, hangs from chain, 12½x8½" $300.00

Lamp, vertical ribbing, clear w/controlled bubbles & gold flecking, Murano, 21", 36½" overall $365.00

Ornament, singer from barbershop quartet, applied blown straw hat, multicolor, 1950s, 5½" $75.00

Sculpture, bird w/slender wings up, clear w/gray head, Seguso AV mark, 15½x5½x3" $165.00

Sculpture, Black clown w/multicolor outfit, holding closed umbrella, Murano, 7" $75.00

Sculpture, clown holding latticinio ball, red hat, multicolor outfit & black shoes, Murano foil label, 10¼" $60.00

Sculpture, clown juggler, resting on chest, 1 leg up & 2nd leg down, ea w/ball, multicolor, Venetian, 9¾x7½" $175.00

Sculpture, clown w/accordion, orange hair, multicolor body, black shoes, 1950s, 8" $125.00

Sculpture, dachshund, cranberry encased in yellow vaseline, Murano sticker, 5½x5" $60.00

Sculpture, dancing lady, blue & white cased w/applied clear glass w/gold flecks, Barovier & Toso, 1950s, 14¼" $175.00

Sculpture, dove, pink opalescent, Murano foil label, 2¼x3¾x12½" $85.00

Sculpture, fish, clear w/2 wide white stripes, Seguso AV, 6½x8".......$70.00

Sculpture, owl, amber to red at wing tips, millefiori eyes, Salviati, 1950s, 7½x3½" $145.00

Sculpture, peacock glancing back, multicolor w/gold flecks in plumage, Murano label, 17" $195.00

Sculpture, ram, white cased in clear w/bubbles, white curling horns, 6½x3¾" $75.00

Sculpture, Siamese cat, cappuccino w/gold dust, clear cased, Murano, 5¼" $135.00

Sculpture, toucan, cut crystal w/black eyes & yellow beak, Kristal Color Made in Italy label, 1970s, 4¾x3x1¾" $30.00

Stem, orange swirls in clear in conical bowl, rooster encased w/in stem, orange & clear foot, Bimini, 4¾" $100.00

Toothpick holder, pink & white latticinio ribbons encased in clear, scalloped rim, 2⅛" $60.00

Vase, bluish purple w/creamy white streak & pink-violet accents, Seguso AV on base, ca 1985, 15½" $250.00

Vase, Bullicante series, green cased in clear w/controlled bubbles & gold flecks, 4 lobes, 1930s, 2⅝x2¾" $75.00

Vase, clear w/controlled bubbles & gold flecks, scalloped rim, Murano gold foil label, 10x6" $135.00

Vase, lg multicolor millefiori, bulbous body, short neck, rim-to-hip ornate handles, 3½" $175.00

Vase, rainbow swirls in clear w/bright blue handkerchief-like rim, 13x9" $135.00

Vase, red, white & tan swirls in clear, footed, Murano, 6¼x7"..$90.00

Vase, red interior over white to clear cased, 6 pulls at rim, Murano, 6x10" $60.00

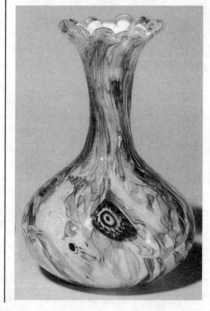

Vase, trails of aventurine, twisted canes and millefiori florets under crystal layer, all above white layer with silver mica, Murano, 10", $500.00. (Photo courtesy Cincinnati Art Galleries)

Jade-ite Glassware

For the past few years, Jade-ite has been one of the fastest-moving types of collectible glassware on the market. It was produced by several companies from the 1940s through 1965. Many of Anchor Hocking's Fire-King lines were available in the soft opaque green Jade-ite, and Jeannette Glass as well as McKee produced their own versions.

It was always very inexpensive glass, and it was made in abundance. Dinnerware for the home as well as restaurants and a vast array of kitchenware items literally flooded the country for many years. Though a few rare pieces have become fairly expensive, most are still reasonably priced, and there are still bargains to be had.

For more information we recommend *Anchor Hocking's Fire-King & More, Kitchen Glassware of the Depression Years*, and *Collectible Glassware of the 40s, 50s, and 60s,* all by Gene and Cathy Florence.

Alice, cup	$7.00
Alice, plate, 9½"	$26.00
Alice, saucer	$3.00
Beaded Edge, bowl, mixing; 6", from $22 to	$25.00
Charm, bowl, dessert; 4¾"	$18.00
Charm, creamer	$20.00
Charm, plate, dinner; 9¼"	$30.00
Charm, sugar bowl	$20.00
Colonial Kitchen, bowl, mixing; 6", from $70 to	$75.00
Colonial Kitchen, bowl, mixing; 8¾", from $80 to	$90.00

Fire-King, egg plate, 10x13", from $65.00 to $75.00.

Jane Ray, bowl, oatmeal; 5⅞"	$16.00
Jane Ray, cup, demitasse; Anchor Hocking	$30.00
Jane Ray, plate, salad; Anchor Hocking, 7¾"	$10.00
Restaurant Ware, bowl, deep, 10-oz	$25.00
Restaurant Ware, cup, narrow rim, 7-oz	$12.00
Restaurant Ware, plate, pie/salad; 6¾"	$10.00
Restaurant Ware, plate, 5-compartment, 9⅝"	$40.00
Restaurant Ware, platter, oval, 11½"	$35.00
Ribbed, bowl, mixing; 4¾", from $60 to	$70.00
Shell, bowl, dessert; 4¾"	$14.00
Shell, bowl, vegetable; 8½"	$28.00

Shell, cup, 8-oz	$10.00
Shell, platter, oval, 13x9½"	$48.00
Shell, sugar bowl, w/lid	$70.00
Swirl, cup, 8-oz	$30.00
Swirl, plate, dinner; 9⅛"	$65.00
Swirl, saucer, 5¾"	$22.00
Three Bands, bowl, vegetable; 8¼"	$85.00
Three Bands, cup, 8-oz	$50.00
Three Bands, plate, dinner; 9⅛"	$500.00
1700 Line, bowl, cereal; 5⅞"	$30.00
1700 Line, cup, Ransom, 9-oz	$14.00
1700 Line, platter, oval, 12x9"	$28.00
1700 Line, saucer, 5¾"	$3.00

Swirl, pitcher, Anchor Hocking, 80-ounce, from $1,500.00 to $2,000.00. (Photo courtesy Gene and Cathy Florence)

Miscellaneous

Bonbon, ruffled rim, diamond bottom, 6½", from $30 to	$35.00
Bowl, batter; w/Anchor Hocking label, from $50 to	$60.00
Bowl, bulb; draped, 5¼", from $20 to	$25.00
Bowl, mixing; Splash Proof, flower decals, 6¾", 1-qt, from $550 to	$600.00
Bowl, mixing; Splash Proof, 6¾", 1-qt, from $250 to	$300.00
Compote, footed, scalloped rim, 6", from $70 to	$75.00
Flowerpot, smooth top, 3⅝", from $18 to	$20.00
Grease jar, embossed ribs, screw-on lid, from $65 to	$75.00
Pitcher, plain ball form, 8-oz, from $500 to	$600.00
Shell dish, from $18 to	$20.00

Japan Ceramics

This category is narrowed down to the inexpensive novelty items produced in Japan from 1921 to 1941 and again from 1947 until the present. Though Japanese ceramics marked Nippon, Noritake, and Occupied Japan have long been collected, some of the newest fun-type collectibles on today's market are the figural ashtrays, pincushions, wall pockets, toothbrush holders, etc., that are marked 'Made in Japan' or simply 'Japan.' In her book, *Collector's Encyclopedia of*

Made in Japan Ceramics, Carole Bess White explains the pitfalls you will encounter when you try to determine production dates. Collectors refer to anything produced before WWII as 'old' and anything made after 1952 as 'new.' Backstamps are inconsistent as to wording and color, and styles are eclectic. Generally, items with applied devices are old, and they are heavier and thicker. Often they were more colorful than the newer items, since fewer colors mean less expense to the manufacturer. Lustre glazes are usually indicative of older pieces, especially the deep solid colors. When lustre was used after the war, it was often mottled with contrasting hues and was usually thinner.

Imaginative styling and strong colors are what give these Japanese ceramics their charm, and they also are factors to consider when you make your purchases. You'll find all you need to know to be a wise shopper in the books we've recommended.

See also Blue Willow; Cat Collectibles; Condiment Sets; Flower Frogs; Geisha Girl; Holt Howard; Kreiss; Lamps; Lefton; Napkin Dolls; Occupied Japan Collectibles; Powder Jars; Toothbrush Holders; Wall Pockets.

Advisor: Carole Bess White (See Directory, Japan Ceramics)

Newsletter: *Made in Japan Info Letter*
Carole Bess White
2225 NE 33rd
Portland, OR 97212-5116; fax: 503-281-2817
CBESSW@aol.com
Send SASE for information; no appraisals given.

Candy dish, abstract floral, 7½", from $60.00 to $80.00. (Photo courtesy Carole Bess White)

Ashtray, camel figural, opening in back, multicolor lustre & shiny glazes, black mark, 4¼" W, from $20 to $35.00
Basket, flowers at ends of handle, multicolor lustre, black mark, 4", from $20 to $30.00
Biscuit jar, pink flowers w/green leaves, much gold, 3 jewels, 4-legged, Hand Painted Japan mark, 6½x6½" **$40.00**
Bookends, Dutch boy & girl lean against book, pencil holder behind, multicolor, 3½x3x3" $24.00

Bookends, golfer swinging, standing on & beside books, gold mark, 6", from $30 to..$40.00
Bookends, poodle seated on book, pencil holder on back, black w/ gold trim, 6⅛" $28.00
Bowl, vegetable; Imari-like floral pattern, w/lid, unmarked Saji, 3½x11¾x5¾" $50.00
Candle climber, clown, multicolor, black mark, 3½", from $12 to..$18.00
Cleanser shaker, Cleanser Miss from Miss Cutie Pie series, Napco, marked A3905/BL, 5" $60.00
Coffeepot, platinum wheat on white w/gold trim, Fine China Japan, 8"..$40.00
Cracker jar, Little Bo Peep figural, Napco, 1957, NM $50.00
Creamer, moose figural, realistic, pours from mouth, tail handle, IWA Japan, 1950s-60s, 5x7" $42.50
Creamer & sugar bowl, floral on cream w/beige trim, w/lid, Mahuron Ware Hand Painted Japan mark, 3½", 4¾" ..$25.00
Cruets, anthropomorphic lemons, conjoined w/branch spouts, PY, 4½" $45.00
Decoration, bluebird w/metal clip, Vcago, 6x2½" $18.00
Figurine, boy hockey player, Hummel type, Miyoshi Collection Created in Japan label, 5¾" $30.00
Figurine, colonial man w/dog & lady w/bird & cage, Classic Gallery collection, Napco C6639, 8", pr...................................$50.00
Figurine, dachshund pup seated, brown w/white front paws, Napco, #C6537, 2¾x4" $20.00
Figurine, English spaniel, brown tones, Ucagco, 4½"..........$18.00
Figurine, foo dogs, blue w/multicolor accents on gray base, Andrea by Sadek, 7½x4x2¾", pr..$90.00
Figurine, fox hunter on horse about to jump over hedge, wreath mark, 8¼x7¾x2" $25.00
Figurine, girl w/duck, Hummel-like, red mark, 3" $12.50
Figurine, Goofy playing cello, Walt Disney Productions Japan mark, 3"..$20.00
Figurine, lady devil in dance pose, dressed in red w/feather skirt, Empress Made in Japan label, 6½" $70.00
Figurine, poodle in playful pose, brown w/much spaghetti, 2x5" $22.00
Figurine, rooster sitting, yellow, green & brown w/red waddle & comb, #W587D, 7x7" $50.00
Figurine, Windswept Girl, blowing flowered sundress, Napco Sticker, 8" $40.00
Figurines, bride & groom kissing, Napco, S488A & S488B, 5½", NM, pr $42.50
Honey pot, hive form w/Deco triangles & multicolor lustre, gold bees, 4x3½" $55.00
Mug, Miss Cutie Pie, Japan A3511/YP mark, 4" $40.00
Nodder, hula girl w/swinging grass skirt, Aloha on base, KN mark, 1940s-50s, 7" $55.00
Pincushion, calico rabbit beside green cushion, red mark, 2¾", from $18 to $28.00
Pitcher, pony's head, pink & blue details, Hand Painted mark, 4" $35.00
Planter, baby wrapped in flowered blanket hanging from handle of umbrella, blue & white, Napco, A5049, 5¼x5" $42.50
Planter, collie seated before container marked Buddy, brown tones, 5¾x4½" $25.00

Planter, girl w/poodle, spaghetti trim, AX2752B mark, 7x5x3½" **$60.00**

Planter, horse & foal, naturalistic colors, Relpo, 5⅞x5⅜" **$35.00**

Planter, horse head, black w/white star, brown eyes & gold bridle, Rublens Originals, 1960s................................**$35.00**

Planter, Indian boy beside tepee, Napco, 1950s-60s, 5½" **$15.00**

Planter, Mary Had a Little Lamb, girl w/school things & lamb following, marked S1493B Napco, 4¼"............................**$55.00**

Planter, pixie dressed in green stands before hollow stump, Ucago, 1940s-50s, 5¼x3" **$32.00**

Planter, squirrel sitting by tree stump, browns & greens, 3¼x4¼" **$20.00**

Plate, anthropomorphic lady apple, PY, 9⅝", NM..............**$45.00**

Teapot, camel w/ornate howdah on back, original wrapped handle, flower decor w/gold, 8½" L **$65.00**

Vase, Art Deco-style flowers w/yellow lustre, low handles, footed, Royal Trico, 7¼x5¼" **$35.00**

Vase, cobalt blue drips on deep yellow, classic form, Jwaji mark, 7", from $40 to **$50.00**

Vase, facing hands w/painted nails, pink roses along wrist, gold trim, 5x3x2" **$30.00**

Vase, gold & white stripes w/gray, silver, gold & brown hot-air balloons, Noritake Bone China...Japan, 11x3" **$45.00**

Vase, running gray, orange & brown, gourd shape, handles, 12", from $80 to **$120.00**

Wall pocket, cardinal on flowering branch, multicolor lustre, 1930s, 9"...**$80.00**

Wall pocket/planter, Santa's face, Napco, 6x5" **$72.50**

Pitcher, rooster in bright lustre glazes, 3½", from $15.00 to $25.00. (Photo courtesy Carole Bess White)

Jewel Tea Company

At the turn of the century, there was stiff competition among door-to-door tea-and-coffee companies, and most of them tried to snag the customer by doling out coupons that could eventually be traded in for premiums. But the thing that set the Jewel Tea people apart from the others was that their premiums were awarded to the customer first, then 'earned' through the purchases that followed. This set the tone of their business dealings which obviously contributed to their success, and very soon in addition to the basic products

they started out with, the company entered the food-manufacturing field. They eventually became one of the country's largest retailers. Today their products, containers, premiums, and advertising ephemera are all very collectible.

Advisors: Bill and Judy Vroman (See Directory, Jewel Tea)

Moth Jinx, orange spray can with dark blue and white graphics, from $15.00 to $22.00. (Photo courtesy Bill and Judy Vroman)

Baking powder, Jewel, cylindrical tin w/script logo & white lettering, 1950s-60s, 1-lb, from $20 to **$30.00**

Cake decorator set, late 1940s, from $50 to........................**$65.00**

Candy, Jewel Mints, round green tin, 1920s, 1-lb, from $30 to.......**$40.00**

Candy, Jewel Tea Spice Jelly Drops, orange box w/orange & white lettering, from $20 to **$30.00**

Cereal, Jewel Quick Oats, cylindrical box w/white & orange lettering **$40.00**

Cocoa, Jewel or Jewel Tea, various boxes, ea from $25 to.....**$45.00**

Coffee, Jewel Blend, orange & gold w/white lettering & logo, paper label **$40.00**

Coffee, Jewel Private Blend, brown & white lettering, 1-lb, from $15 to **$25.00**

Coffee, Jewel Special Blend, brown stripes on white, white & orange lettering on brown circle, 2-lb, from $15 to.................**$25.00**

Coffee, Royal Jewel, yellow, brown & white, 1-lb, from $20 to ..**$35.00**

Coffee, West Coast, orange & brown w/white lettering, bell at top of center, 1960s, 2-lb, from $25 to **$35.00**

Dishes, Melmac, 8 place settings, from $150 to.................**$170.00**

Extract, Jewel Imitation Vanilla, brown box w/orange & white lettering, 1960s, 4-oz **$20.00**

Extract, Jewel Lemon, orange, blue & white, 1916-19, from $40 to..**$50.00**

Flour sifter, litho metal, EX...**$485.00**

Garment bag, 1950s, MIP, from $25 to **$30.00**

Laundry, Daintiflakes, pink & blue box marked Soft Feather Flakes of Pure Mild Soap, from $25 to...................................**$30.00**

Laundry, Daybreak Laundry Set, from $15 to.....................**$20.00**

Laundry, Grano Granulated Soap, blue & white box marked Made for General Cleaning, 2-lb, from $25 to **$30.00**

Laundry, Pure Gloss Starch, teal & white box, from $25 to . **$30.00**
Malted milk mixer, Jewel-T, from $40 to **$50.00**
Mix, Jewel Subrite Mix, Mason jar w/paper label & metal screw lid, 1960s, 26-oz, from $15 to **$25.00**
Mix, Jewel Tea Coconut Dessert, round tan tin w/brown & white logo & lettering, 1930s, 14-oz, from $30 to **$40.00**
Mix, Jewel Tea Prepared Tapioca, tall sq orange & brown striped tin w/logo & brown lettering, 1930s, from $25 to **$35.00**
Mixer, Mary Dunbar, electric stand w/bowl & original hang tag, white... **$100.00**
Mixer, Mary Dunbar, hand-held, w/stand, 1940, from $40 to . **$50.00**
Napkins, paper w/printed pattern, box of 200 .... **$25.00**
Nuts, Jewel Mixed Nuts, round brown-striped tin w/orange & brown lettering, 1960s, 1-lb, from $15 to..................... **$20.00**
Peanut Butter, Jewel Tea, glass jar w/paper label & screw lid, 1930s, 1-lb, from $30 to **$40.00**
Pickle fork, Jewel-T, from $20 to **$25.00**
Razor blades, Jewel-T **$5.00**
Scales, Jewel-T, from $45 to... **$55.00**
Sweeper, Jewel, gold lettering on black, 1930s-40s, from $80 to ..**$100.00**
Sweeper, Jewel Little Bissell, from $40 to **$50.00**
Sweeper, Jewel Suction Sweeper, early 1900s, lg **$150.00**
Sweeper, Jewel Suction Sweeper, 1930s-40s, from $60 to...**$100.00**

Tea, Orange Pekoe and Pekoe Black Tea, from $20.00 to $25.00. (Photo courtesy Bill and Judy Vroman)

Tea bags, Jewel Tea, dragon logo, gold & brown, 1948........**$65.00**

Jewelry

Today's costume jewelry collectors may range from nine to ninety and have tastes as varied as their ages, but one thing they all have in common is their love of these distinctive items of jewelry, some originally purchased at the corner five-&-dimes, others from department stores and boutiques.

Costume jewelry became popular, simply because it was easily affordable for all women. Today jewelry made before 1954 is considered to be 'antique,' while the term 'collectible' jewelry generally refers to those pieces made after that time. Costume jewelry was federally recognized as an American art form in 1954, and the copyright law was passed to protect the artists' designs. The copyright mark © found on the back of a piece identifies a post-1954 'collectible.'

Quality should always be the primary consideration when shopping for these treasures. Remember that pieces with colored rhinestones bring the higher prices. (Note: A 'rhinestone' is a clear, foil-backed, leaded glass crystal — unless it is a 'colored rhinestone' — while a 'stone' is not foiled.) A complete set (called a parure) increases in value by 20% over the total of its components. Check for a manufacturer's mark, since a signed piece is worth 20% more than one of comparable quality, but not signed. Some of the best designers are Miriam Haskell, Eisenberg, Trifari, Hollycraft, and Joseff.

Early plastic pieces (Lucite, Bakelite, and celluloid, for example) are very collectible. Some Lucite is used in combination with wood, and the figural designs are especially desirable.

There are several excellent reference books available if you'd like more information. Look for *Unsigned Beauties of Costume Jewelry; Signed Beauties of Costume Jewelry, Vols. I* and *II; Coro Jewelry;* and *Rhinestone Jewelry: Figurals, Animals, Whimsicals* by our advisor Marcia Brown. Lillian Baker has written several, including *Fifty Years of Collectible Fashion Jewelry,* and *100 Years of Collectible Jewelry.* Books by other authors include *Collectible Silver Jewelry* and *Costume Jewelry* by Fred Rezazadeh; *Collectible Costume Jewelry* by Cherri Simonds; *Collecting Costume Jewelry 101* and *202* by Julia C. Carroll; *Inside the Jewelry Box* by Ann Mitchell Pittman; *Brillant Rhinestones* and *20th Century Costume Jewelry, 1900 – 1980,* by Ronna Lee Aikins; and video books *Hidden Treasures Series* by Christie Romero and Marcia Brown. All are available through Collector Books. The videos may be purchased by contacting Marcia Brown.

See also Christmas Tree Pins

Advisor: Marcia Brown (See Directory, Jewelry)

Club/Newsletter: *Vintage Fashion and Costume Jewelry Newsletter Club*
P.O. Box 265, Glen Oaks, NY 11004
Membership: $20 in US; www.lizjewel.com/vf/

Bracelet, Bakelite, hearts on rainbow shapes, 15½", $275.00.

Bracelet, bangle; Bakelite, butterscotch, carved, 1935, from $100 to..**$150.00**
Bracelet, bangle; Lucite, white w/scattered rhinestones, 1935, from $75 to... **$85.00**
Bracelet, Charel, thermoset cabochons, 2 in each of 5 metal links, from $45 to **$55.00**
Bracelet, Eisenberg, rhinestones in double row, bar design w/2 chatons between **$145.00**
Bracelet, Hobè, faux jade cabochon w/gold-plated leaves **$85.00**
Bracelet, Judy Lee, 4 scarab inserts (red, purple, & green) in gold-tone links **$25.00**
Bracelet, Kenneth Jay Lane, good-luck dragon (2 heads), green enameling, faux turquoise lower jaws, diamanté rhinestones ..**$110.00**

Bracelet, Monet, gold-tone strips link white enamel links, w/safety chain, 7⅛x1" **$25.00**

Bracelet, Trifari, expansion type w/distinct wave pattern, 1" W **$35.00**

Bracelet, Trifari, 8 Nouveau-style silver-tone links w/clear rhinestones **$45.00**

Bracelet, unsigned, blue-green crystal dangling stones cover expansion-type metal base **$50.00**

Bracelet, unsigned, pastel green clamshells between gold-tone leaves, 7¾x1¼" **$28.00**

Bracelet, unsigned, pear-shaped & round prong-set rhinestones in rhodium metal, 7¼x½" **$40.00**

Bracelet, unsigned, polished multicolor stones secured to silver-plated metal links, 1960s **$28.00**

Bracelet, unsigned, sq cut clear rhinestones set in gold-tone metal, ca 1960, 7x¼" **$26.00**

Bracelet, unsigned, topaz rhinestone ovals in gold-tone metal filigree links, fold-over clasp, 1950s, 7¼x¾" **$45.00**

Bracelet, unsigned, 2 strands of smoky aurora borealis beads, silver-tone clasp w/rhinestone center **$30.00**

Brooch, Bakelite, Scottie dog, green w/painted features, 1935, from $95 to **$125.00**

Brooch, Castlecliff, butterfly trembler hovers above gold leaf, pavé rhinestone wings, 2" **$125.00**

Brooch, Castlecliff, sterling crown w/3 pearls at top, ruby-red rhinestones w/diamanté accents, 2x1¾" **$225.00**

Brooch, Coco Chanel, 3 enameled flowers, white w/blue veins, rhinestones centers, intertwined leaves **$450.00**

Brooch, Hollycraft, golden rhinestone spray **$70.00**

Brooch, Kenneth Jay Lane, kissing fish, imitation jade bodies, gold-tone fins, rhinestone heads **$65.00**

Brooch, Marcel Boucher, butterfly w/faux diamonds, rubies, sapphires & emeralds, turquoise stone used in body **$145.00**

Brooch, Marcel Boucher, lyre bird, gold-plated metal w/pavé breast & head on branch w/faux pearls **$475.00**

Brooch, Schiaparelli, gold & brown rhinestones w/3 drops. **$195.00**

Brooch, Star Novelty, diamantè rhinestone silver-plated branch. **$175.00**

Brooch, unsigned Austria, multicolor rhinestone floral nosegay. **$75.00**

Brooch, unsigned, vermeil pink-gold wash over sterling lily, pavé diamanté leaves, and ribs of blossom, lavender rhinestones top the stamens, $225.00.
(Photo courtesy Marcia Brown)

Brooch & earrings, Kenneth Jay Lane, gold-plated bow w/pavé diamanté rhinestones **$98.00**

Brooch & earrings, La Roco, gold & ornate snowflake forms ... **$80.00**

Brooch & earrings, Lisner, gold-plated flowers w/pink aurora borealis rhinestones **$68.00**

Brooch & earrings, Marcel Boucher, pastel blue plastic & silver plate, marked Marboux **$135.00**

Buckle, Bakelite, transparent butterscotch w/carved-out leaves & rhinestones, 1-pc **$78.00**

Earrings, Joan Rivers, multicolor cabochons set in gold-tone rope frames in Byzantine style, 1" dia **$45.00**

Earrings, Judy Lee, amber, olivene & caramel prong-set rhinestones form spray, 1" central reverse-carved stone **$28.00**

Earrings, Kenneth Jay Lane, imitation jade & opal shoulder dusters w/diamanté rhinestones **$235.00**

Earrings, Marcel Boucher, pink moonstones w/pavé diamanté leaves **$60.00**

Earrings, Taxco, abalone inlay & sterling leaves, 1½x1" **$40.00**

Earrings, unsigned, aurora borealis half-moon shapes w/silver-tone backing, clip backs **$35.00**

Earrings, unsigned, aurora borealis rhinestone cluster **$38.00**

Earrings, unsigned, gold-tone basketweave button type, ⅞" dia.. **$30.00**

Earrings, unsigned, red teardrop glass stone w/surrounding black chaton-cut Swarovski crystals, 1940s **$48.00**

Earrings, unsigned, 4mm cultured pearls in silver fluted cups, screwbacks, ¼" **$25.00**

Fur clip, Star Novelty, emerald-cut rhinestones, silver plated.. **$280.00**

Necklace, ART, butterfly pendant in pastel enamels on gold-tone metal, 2¼" on 24" gold-tone chain **$45.00**

Necklace, Coro, white thermo-set leaves w/clear rhinestones form links, adjusts to 18" **$38.00**

Necklace, Florenza, turquoise & gold-tone butterfly clasp secures 5 pearl strands **$125.00**

Necklace, Germany, amethyst faceted crystals set in brass bezels on chain w/faux pearls, on clasps, 57" **$110.00**

Necklace, Hobè, white plastic beads in 2 strands, gold-tone metal clasp & earrings resembling cameo **$65.00**

Necklace, Hollycraft, diamanté rhinestones, $185.00.
(Photo courtesy Marcia Brown)

Necklace, Japan, 5 strands of pink beads shading from light 12" strand to darkest: 16" **$28.00**

Necklace, Kenneth Jay Lane, faux pearls, 3-strand, initials on clasp **$110.00**

Necklace, Marvella, double strand of faux pearls, ca 1980, choker length **$25.00**

Necklace, Miriam Haskell, crystal beads w/silver turban spacers **$85.00**

Necklace, Napier, bright gold-tone metal w/crystal chaton rhinestones forming links, adjusts up to 18½" **$25.00**

Necklace, Trifari, ivory-colored pumpkin like beads separated by sm gold-tone beads, 18" **$35.00**

Necklace, unsigned, gold-tone Nouveau leaves w/faux pearl drops.. **$60.00**

Necklace, unsigned, light pink faux pearls (⁵⁄₁₆" dia), no clasp, 38" **$15.00**

Necklace, unsigned, 5 links w/blue moonstone beads & smaller sapphire chaton rhinestones on silver-tone chain **$35.00**

Necklace, Weiss, amethyst & fuchsia rhinestone clusters in alternating pattern on gold-plate, chain extender.................... **$110.00**

Necklace & bracelet, unsigned, pink emerald-cut rhinestones & clear rhinestone chatons, prong set, 1940s-50s.............. **$55.00**

Necklace & earrings, Hattie Carnegie, tourmaline rhinestones in crescent form **$275.00**

Necklace & earrings, Trifari, gold-tone & ivory-painted links form fringe look w/white ball dangles, ca 1970s **$55.00**

Necklace & earrings, Trifari, gold-tone chain choker w/6 white beads & pink enameled flower pendant, flower earrings......... **$95.00**

Parure, Christian Dior, triple strand earthtone beads (necklace & bracelet), matching earrings w/3 lg & 3 sm beads....... **$650.00**

Parure, Sara Coventry, faux pearls & rhinestones on gold-tone, necklace, wide bracelet & dangle earrings **$80.00**

Ring, amethyst (approximately 6mm) dia w/6 sm diamonds on ea side set in 14k yellow gold, ca 1920s **$200.00**

Ring, bloodstone oval cabochon in 14k gold mount........... **$95.00**

Ring, brown moonstone 14x10mm oval cabochon set sideways in 14kt rose gold-filled wire **$45.00**

Ring, carnelian octagon stone w/marcasite accents, marked Sterling **$115.00**

Ring, opalene clusters on gold plate **$45.00**

Ring, pink rose quartz 10mm round stone set in 14k gold-filled wire.. **$40.00**

Johnson Bros.

There is a definite renewal of interest in dinnerware collecting right now, and just about any antique shop or mall you visit will offer a few nice examples of the wares made by this Staffordshire company. They've been in business since well before the turn of the century and have targeted the American market to such an extent that during the 1960s and 1970s, as much as 70% of their dinnerware was sold to distributors in this country. They made many scenic patterns as well as florals, and with the interest today's collectors have been demonstrating in Chintz, dealers tell me that Johnson Brothers' Rose Chintz and Chintz (Victorian) sell very well for them, especially the latter. In addition to their polychrome designs, they made several patterns in both blue and pink transferware.

Though some of their lines, Old Britain Castles, Friendly Village, His Majesty, and Rose Chintz, for instance, are still being produced, most are no longer as extensive as they once were, so the secondary market is being tapped to replace broken items that are not available anywhere else.

In her book *Johnson Brothers Dinnerware Pattern Directory and Price Guide* author Mary Finegan breaks pricing down into three groups: Base Price, One Star, and Two Star. About 90% of Johnson Brothers patterns have proven to be popular sellers and have been made in an extensive range of pieces (with the possible exception of buffet plates and 20" turkey platters, which were produced primarily in holiday patterns only). Some of the patterns you are most likely to encounter and are thus included in the Base Price group are Bird of Paradise, Mount Vernon, Castle on the Lake, Old Bradbury, Day in June, Nordic, Devon Sprays, Old Mill (The), Empire Grape, Pastorale, Haddon Hall, Pomona, Harvest Time, Road Home (The), Indian Tree, Vintage (older version), Melody, and Windsor Fruit. (Also included in this value range are any other patterns not mentioned below.)

One-Star patterns include Autumn's Delight, Coaching Scenes, Devonshire, Fish, Friendly Village, Gamebirds, Garden Bouquet, Hearts and Flowers, Heritage Hall, Indies, Millstream, Olde English Countryside, Rose Bouquet, Sheraton, Tulip Time, and Winchester. Two Star patterns include Barnyard King, Century of Progress, Chintz — Victorian, Dorchester, English Chippendale, Harvest Fruit, His Majesty, Historic America, Merry Christmas, Old Britain Castles, Persian Tulip, Rose Chintz, Strawberry Fair, Tally Ho, Twelve Days of Christmas, and Wild Turkeys.

Our prices pertain to older pieces only, usually recognizable by the crown in the backstamp. Newer pieces from the 1990s to the present do not carry this crown and are available in any number of retail and outlet stores today. New prices are much lower — while a complete place setting of Old Britain Castles is normally priced at about $50.00, in some outlets you may be able to purchase it for half of that.

In the listings that follow, values apply only to the patterns in the base price group. One and Two Star patterns are in high demand and hard to find, and so command higher prices. They sell for as much as 20% to 50% over the base values. Not all pieces are available in all patterns. In addition to their company logo, much of the dinnerware is also stamped with the pattern name. Today Johnson Brothers is part of the Wedgwood group.

Advisor: Gerry Monroe (See Directory, Johnson Brothers)

Devon Sprays, platter, base price group.

Bowl, cereal/soup; round, sq or lug, ea from $10 to.............**$20.00**
Bowl, soup; round or sq, 7", from $12 to **$25.00**
Bowl, vegetable; oval, from $20 to upwards of....................**$50.00**
Butter dish, from $50 to **$80.00**
Chop/cake plate, from $50 to **$80.00**
Coffee mug, from $20 to upwards of..................................**$25.00**
Coffeepot, from $90 to upwards of...................................**$100.00**
Demitasse set, 2-pc, from $20 to **$30.00**
Egg cup, from $15 to..**$30.00**
Pitcher/jug, from $45 to upwards of **$55.00**
Plate, dinner; from $14 to...**$30.00**
Plate, salad; round or sq, from $10 to upwards of..............**$18.00**
Platter, med, 12-14", ea from $45 to upwards of **$55.00**
Salt & pepper shakers, pr from $40 to upwards of..............**$48.00**
Sauceboat/gravy, from 40 to upwards of.............................**$48.00**
Sugar bowl, open, from $30 to **$40.00**
Teacup & saucer, from $15 to upwards of...........................**$30.00**
Teapot, from $90 to upwards of..**$100.00**
Turkey platter, 20½", from $200 to upwards of................**$300.00**

Harvest Time, platter, base price group.

Josef Originals

Figurines of lovely ladies, charming girls, and whimsical animals marked Josef Originals were designed by Muriel Joseph George of Arcadia, California, from 1945 to 1985. Until 1960 they were produced in California, but production costs were high, and copies of her work were being made in Japan. To remain competitive, she and her partner, George Good, found a company in Japan to build a factory and produce her designs to her satisfaction. Muriel retired in 1982; however, Mr. Good continued production of her work and made some design changes on some of the figurines. The company was sold in late 1985. The name is currently owned by Dakin/Applause, and a limited number of figurines with the Josef Originals name are being made. Those made during the ownership of Muriel are the most collectible. They can be recognized by these characteristics: the girls have a high-gloss finish, black eyes, and most are signed on the bottom. As of the 1970s

a bisque finish was making its way into the lineup, and by 1980 glossy girls were fairly scarce in the product line. Brown-eyed figures date from 1982 through 1985; Applause uses a red-brown eye, although they are starting to release copies of early pieces that are signed Josef Originals by Applause or by Dakin. The animals were nearly always made with a matt finish and bore paper labels only. In the mid-1970s they introduced a line of animals with fuzzy flocked coats and glass eyes. Our advisors, Jim and Kaye Whitaker have three books which we recommend for further study: *Josef Originals, Charming Figurines (Revised Edition); Josef Originals, A Second Look;* and *Josef Originals, Figurines of Muriel Joseph George.* These are all currently available, and each has no repeats of items shown in the other books.

Please note: All figurines have black eyes unless specified otherwise. As with so many collectibles, values have been impacted to a measurable extent since the advent of the Internet.

See also Birthday Angels.

Advisors: Jim and Kaye Whitaker (See Directory, Josef Originals; no appraisal requests please)

Alley Cat Family, various poses, 5 in series, Japan, 3-4", ea..**$16.00**
Angel, Birthday Girl, 1-12, various sizes, Japan, ea from $30 to..**$45.00**
Angel, Crystal Wing Horoscope, 12 months, CA, 4", ea **$50.00**
Angel, Horoscope, series of 12 months, Japan, 4", ea...........**$45.00**
Belle Series, skirt is bell, 6 in series, CA, 3½", ea **$35.00**
Belle Series, skirt is bell, 6 in series, Japan, 4", ea.................**$35.00**
Bicentennial music box, God Bless America, 1976, Japan, 6",
    ea **$65.00**
Birthstone Doll of the Month, 12 decorated w/birthstones, CA,
    3¼", ea...**$55.00**
Birthstone Doll of the Month, 12 holding birthstone bouquet,
    Japan, 3¾", ea...**$20.00**
Camel baby, recumbent, Japan, 2½" **$35.00**
Camel standing, Japan, 6¼"...**$60.00**
Cherry Blossom & Autumn Leaf, Oriental girls w/fans, CA, 5",
    ea...**$40.00**
Cho Cho & Sakura, Oriental lady, various colors w/fans, CA, 10¾",
    ea **$95.00**

Colonial Day Series, Jeanne in lavender gown, 10", $115.00. (Photo courtesy Jim and Kaye Whitaker)

Colonial Days, Louise, Maria, Pamela, Adelade, Caroline, Japan, 9", ea... **$115.00**
Colonial Days, series of 6 girls doing chores, Japan, 5", ea.. **$50.00**
Curtain Call Ladies, half doll, Marietta, Nanette, Villa, 2 colors ea, CA, 5½", ea.. **$45.00**

Doll of the Month, January and August, 1967, each $40.00. (Photo courtesy Jim & Kaye Whitaker)

Doll of the Month, 1974 debut, 12 months, Japan, 4", ea... **$40.00**
Ecology Girls, 1974 debut, 6 in series, Japan, 4", ea........... **$40.00**
Elephant Family, Papa, Mama, babies, various sizes, Japan, from $25 to **$30.00**
Farmer's Daughter, series of 6, Japan, 5", ea....................... **$35.00**
Flower Girls Series, girls holding bouquets, Japan, 5½", ea.. **$65.00**
Hedy & Teddy, boy & girl, CA, 4½", ea................................ **$35.00**
Hippo Family, various poses, Japan, 2-2½", ea.................... **$14.00**
Kandy, various colors, CA, 4", ea....................................... **$45.00**
Kennel Klub series, 6 breeds, Japan, 4", ea........................ **$15.00**
Little Gourmets, girls w/recipes holding food, Japan, 3¾", ea... **$35.00**
Little Internationals, 32 countries represented, Japan, 4½", ea **$45.00**
Love Story series, courtship to wedding, 6 in series, Japan, 8", ea.. **$95.00**
Mama, 3 poses in 2 colors, CA, 7¼", ea **$75.00**
Mary Ann, 3 poses in 2 colors, matches Mama, CA, 3½", ea... **$40.00**
Missy, various colors, CA, 4", ea **$45.00**
Mouse Village, series of mice dressed in various poses, Japan, ½-2", ea **$8.00**
Music Box Girls, 4 in series, ceramic bases, Japan, 1974, 9", ea ... **$70.00**
Nursery Rhyme Music Box series, Japan, 6", ea **$70.00**
Nursery Rhyme Series, 6 in series, Japan, 4", ea................. **$50.00**
Party Cake Toppers, 6 in series, Japan, 3½", ea.................. **$40.00**
Penny, girl sitting, various colors, CA, 4½", ea.................... **$65.00**
Persian cats, various poses, Japan, 2½-4", ea...................... **$18.00**
Santa Claus Is Coming to Town Music Box, Japan, 7", ea ... **$45.00**
Siamese cats, various poses, Japan, 2½-4", ea **$18.00**
Special Occasions Series, 6 in series, Japan, 4½", ea.............. **$50.00**
Watusi Luau Series, hunter in pot, natives, Japan, 5", ea...... **$55.00**
Wee Ling & Wee Ching, Oriental girl & boy, CA, 5", ea **$40.00**
Zodiac Girls Series, series of 12, Japan, 4¾", ea.................. **$55.00**

Kaye of Hollywood

This was one of the smaller pottery studios that operated in California during the 1940s — interesting in that people tend to confuse the name with Kay Finch. Kay (Schueftan) worked for Hedi Schoop before striking out on her own; because her work was so similar to that of her former employer's, a successful lawsuit was brought against her, and it was at this point that the mark was changed from Kaye of Hollywood to Kim Ward.

Figurine, girl w/sm vase of flowers in left hand, flower in right palm, flaring apron & skirt, Kim Ward/#46, 8", $35 to **$40.00**
Figurine, lady in off-shoulder gown & bonnet carrying basket in front of her, Kaye #2126, 10¼", EX............................. **$45.00**
Figurine, lady singer w/book in hand, unmarked, 10" **$45.00**
Flower holder, Dutch boy w/2 flower baskets, pink & green, Kaye #3173, 9¾"... **$50.00**
Flower holder, Dutch girl w/flower baskets, pink & green, Kaye #3132, 7½"... **$55.00**
Flower holder, lady, draped flower cup on ea hip, #3125, 9".. **$45.00**
Flower holder, lady w/blue hat w/pink bow, white flowered dress, holds pot in right hand, #113, 9½", from $50 to **$60.00**
Flower holder, lady w/2 open bowls held by resting on hips, pink, white & green, ruffled bodice, Kaye #336, 10¼x8"...... **$40.00**

Flower holder lady, #302, 9", $50.00.

Lamp, dancing girl w/lace trim on dress, 10" figure on metal base, vintage pink shade, 20".. **$150.00**
Planter, lady leaning & resting on 11" W basket, #351, 10". **$85.00**
Vase, Hawaiian hula girl, topless w/lei covering breast, cala lily bud holders, 11", NM... **$165.00**
Wall pocket, lady in hoop skirt w/tassels & rickrack, #201, 9". **$65.00**
Wall pocket, Oriental lady w/green headdress w/flowers, #345, 7x5¼" **$55.00**

Keeler, Brad

California pottery is becoming quite popular among collectors, and Brad Keeler is one of the better known designers. After studying art for a time, he opened his own studio in 1939 where he created naturalistic studies of birds and animals. Sold through giftware stores, the figures were decorated by airbrushing with hand-painted details. Brad Keeler is remembered for his popular flamingo figures and his Chinese Modern Housewares. Keeler died of a heart attack in 1952, and the pottery closed soon thereafter. For more information, we recommend *Collector's Encyclopedia of California Pottery, 2nd Edition* and *California Pottery Scrapbook*, by Jack Chipman.

Bone dish, fish figural, teal green to tan, #151, 8" **$35.00**

Bowl, Lobster Ware, lettuce leaves, lg red lobster on dome lid, #825, 11" L **$85.00**

Box, duck figural, brown & green w/white band at neck, 4½x5½", from $25 to **$35.00**

Butter dish, Lobster Ware, lobster finial, ladle for melted butter, 6" L, NM **$38.00**

Dish, 2 red radishes resting on green leaf, #863, 7x6½", from $15 to **$20.00**

Figurine, Asian peafowl, 1940s, 6x16x3¼", NM **$195.00**

Figurine, Asian peafowl standing on 1 foot, #22, 7" **$75.00**

Figurine, bird, peach & blue, long scissors-like tail, wings up, #716, 10¾" **$200.00**

Figurine, bluebird on stump, #718, 5¼" **$35.00**

Figurine, bunny scratching, #981, 3" **$30.00**

Figurine, canary, yellow & black on brown stump, 6", from $15 to **$20.00**

Figurine, cockatoo, yellow, green, & white tones, #35, 8½"..**$55.00**

Figurine, cockatoo, yellow & green tones, #34, 6x7½", from $35 to **$50.00**

Figurine, duck standing on oval vase, #50, 4½x6", from $50 to ..**$60.00**

Figurine, duck w/wings folded, multicolor, #930, 5x6", from $48 to **$60.00**

Figurine, eagle w/wings wide, #28, 9½" **$275.00**

Figurine, exotic pheasant, #21, 6½", $40.00.

Figurine, flamingo in tall grasses, #2, 10", from $70 to **$90.00**

Figurine, flamingo on grassy base w/head down, 7¼" **$60.00**

Figurine, flamingo w/wings folded, grassy base, Brad Keeler G mark, 11⅞", from $80 to..**$100.00**

Figurine, flamingo w/wings half, grassy base, Ceramics by B Keeler, 8½", from $85 to...**$100.00**

Figurine, flamingo w/wings up (wings spanning 4¼") head up, #47, 10¼", from $140 to..**$160.00**

Figurine, hen w/head up, multicolor, #936, 4½x3¾" **$30.00**

Figurine, peahen, multicolor pastels, head up, #717, 10½" ...**$200.00**

Figurine, peahen, multicolor pastels, head up, 6x7½" **$80.00**

Figurine, pheasant, long plumed tail, #9-38A, 7x11", from $75 to...**$100.00**

Figurine, rooster, black w/green accents, head down, tail up, 8x9½"...**$45.00**

Figurine, Siamese cat on red pillow, #944, 2½x3".............**$45.00**

Figurine, Siamese cat playing w/ball of yarn, 6x15", from $140 to...**$165.00**

Figurine, Siamese cat stainding w/head turned left, 12", from $125 to...**$140.00**

Figurine, Siamese cat standing w/head turned to right, 7¼x9" .**$85.00**

Figurine, squirrel, brown tones, #627, 2¼x4x3½" **$15.00**

Figurine, swan w/wings stretched upward, white w/black detail, #705, 14½", from $175 to **$225.00**

Figurines, Siamese kittens (2), 1 about to pounce, 2nd on back, 5", 3", pr...**$70.00**

Planter, Santa waving from sled, #909, 7½x8½x4½" **$30.00**

Plate, lobed leaf shape, green, to use w/Lobster Ware, 13" ...**$30.00**

Plate, lobed leaf shape w/tendril handle, green, 8", from $18 to **$22.00**

Shelf sitters, Siamese cats (2), 1 standing & 2nd w/paw reaching down, #798/#760, 7", 10", pr **$80.00**

Tray, lobster, #868, 9", $28.00.

Tray, lobster between 2 green leaves, 12x7"...........................**$52.50**

Tureen, Lobster Ware, lobster on lettuce leaf lid, #761, 6¾x8½" **$50.00**

Tureen, Lobster Ware, lobster on lettuce leaf lid, #971, 7x9", w/leaf undertray **$65.00**

Tureen, Lobster Ware, lobster on lettuce leaf lid, no #, 4½x5¾" **$35.00**

Kentucky Derby Glasses

Since the the late 1930s, every running of the Kentucky Derby has been commemorated with a special glass tumbler. Each year at

Churchill Downs on Derby day you can buy them filled with mint juleps. In the early days this was the only place where these glasses could be purchased. Many collections were started when folks carried the glasses home from the track and then continued to add one for each successive year as they attended the Derby.

The first glass appeared in 1938, but examples from then until 1945 are extremely scarce and are worth thousands — when they can be found. Because of this, many collectors begin with the 1945 glasses. There are three: the tall version, the short regular-size glass, and a jigger. Some years, for instance 1948, 1956, 1958, 1974, 1986, and 2003, have slightly different variations, so often there is more than one to collect. To date a glass, simply add one year to the last date on the winners' list found on the back.

Each year many companies put out commemorative Derby glasses. Collectors call them 'bar' glasses (as many bars sold their own versions filled with mint juleps). Because of this, collectors need to be educated as to what the official Kentucky Derby glass looks like.

These prices are for pristine, mint-condition glasses with no chips or flaws. All colors must be bright and show no signs of fading. Lettering must be perfect and intact, even the list of past winners on the back. If gold trim has been used, it must show no wear. If any of these problems exist, reduce our values by 50% to 75%, depending on the glass and the problem. Many more Kentucky Derby shot glasses, jiggers, cordials, boreals, and shooters in various colors and sizes were produced — too many to list here. But be aware that these may present themselves along the collecting trail.

Advisor: Betty L. Hornback (See Directory, Kentucky Derby and Horse Racing)

1940, aluminum $1,000.00
1940, French Lick, aluminum.......................................$1,000.00
1941-1944, plastic Beetleware, ea, from $2,500 to $4,000.00
1945, jigger, green horse head, I Have Seen Them All $1,000.00
1945, regular, green horse head facing right, horseshoe...$1,600.00
1945, tall, green horse head facing right, horseshoe $450.00
1946-47, clear frosted w/frosted bottom, L in circle, ea $100.00
1948, clear bottom, green horsehead in horseshoe & horse on other side $225.00
1948, frosted bottom, green horse head in horseshoe & horse on other side $250.00
1949, He Has Seen Them All, Matt Winn, green on frost.$225.00
1950, green horses running on track, Churchill Downs behind. $450.00
1951, green winnner's circle, Where Turf Champions Are Crowned $650.00
1952, Gold Derby Trophy, Kentucky Derby Gold Cup $225.00
1953, black horse facing left, rose garland.........................$200.00
1954, green twin spires $225.00
1955, green & yellow horses, The Fastest Runners.............$175.00
1956, 1 star, 2 tails, brown horses, twin spires $275.00
1956, 1 star, 3 tails, brown horses, twin spires $400.00
1956, 2 stars, 2 tails, brown horses, twin spires..................$200.00
1956, 2 stars, 3 tails, brown horses, twin spires..................$250.00
1957, gold & black, horse & jockey facing right................$125.00
1958, Gold Bar, solid gold insignia w/horse, jockey & 1 spire ...$175.00
1958, Iron Liege, same as 1957 w/'Iron Leige' added.........$225.00
1959-60, both black & gold, ea $100.00

1961, black horses on track, jockey in red, gold winners....**$110.00**
1962, Churchill Downs, red, gold & black **$70.00**
1963, brown horse, jockey #7, gold lettering **$70.00**
1964, brown horse head, gold lettering................................**$55.00**
1965, brown twin spires & horses, red lettering..................**$85.00**
1966-68, black, black & blue respectively, ea **$60.00**
1969, green jockey in horseshoe, red lettering.....................**$65.00**

1970, green shield, gold lettering, $70.00.

1971, green twin spires, horses at bottom, red lettering **$55.00**
1972, 2 black horses, orange & green print.........................**$55.00**
1973, white, black twin spires, red & green lettering **$60.00**
1974, Federal, regular or mistake, brown & gold, ea..........**$200.00**
1974, mistake (Canonero in 1971 listing on back), Libbey..**$18.00**
1974, regular (Canonero II in 1971 listing on back)............**$16.00**
1975...**$12.00**
1976, plastic tumbler or regular glass, ea.............................**$16.00**
1977...**$14.00**
1978...**$16.00**

1979, racing scene, $16.00.

1980..**$22.00**

1981-82, ea	$15.00
1983-85, ea	$12.00
1986	$14.00
1986 ('85 copy)	$20.00
1987-89, ea	$12.00
1990-92, ea	$10.00
1993-95, ea	$9.00
1996-98, ea	$8.00
1999-2000, ea	$6.00
2001-2002, ea	$5.00
2003, mistake	$6.00
2003 to 2006	$4.00

Bluegrass Stakes Glasses, Keeneland, Lexington, KY

1996	$15.00
1997	$13.00
1998-99, ea	$12.00
2001-02, ea	$10.00
2003	$8.00
2004, discontinued at this time	

Breeders' Cup Glasses

1985, Aqueduct, not many produced	$300.00
1988, Churchill Downs	$40.00

1989, Gulfstream Park, $65.00.
(Photo courtesy Betty Hornback/ Photographer Dean Langdon)

1990, Bellmont Park	$45.00
1991, Churchill Downs	$15.00
1992, Gulfstream Park	$30.00
1993, Santa Anita	$35.00
1993, Santa Anita, 10th Running, gold	$40.00
1994, Churchill Downs	$15.00
1995, Belmont Park	$20.00
1996, Woodbine, Canada	$30.00
1997, Hollywood Park	$20.00
1998, Churchill Downs	$10.00

1999, Gulfstream Park	$10.00
2000, Churchill Downs	$9.00
2001, Belmont Park, or 2002, Arlington Park	$8.00
2003, Santa Anita	$8.00
2004, Lone Star Park	$8.00
2005, Belmont Park	$7.00
2006, Churchill Downs	$7.00

Festival Glasses

1968	$95.00
1984	$20.00
1985-86, no glass made	
1987-88, ea	$12.00
1989-90, ea	$12.00
1991-92, ea	$10.00
1993, very few produced	$75.00
1994-95, ea	$8.00
1996-98, ea	$7.00
1999-2000, ea	$7.00
2001-03, fewer produced, ea	$12.00
2004-2006	$10.00

Jim Beam/Spiral Stakes Glasses

1980, 6"	$350.00
1981, 7"	$300.00
1982	$275.00
1983	$50.00
1984	$35.00
1985-86, ea	$25.00
1987-88, ea	$20.00
1988	$16.00

1990, $16.00. (Photo courtesy Betty Hornback/Photographer Dean Langdon)

1991-95, ea	$14.00
1996-2000, ea	$12.00
2001-2006, ea	$10.00

Shot Glasses

1987, 1½-oz., red or black (black version shown), $350.00. (Photo courtesy Betty Hornback/Photographer Dean Langdon)

1987, 3-oz, black/gold lettering	$700.00
1987, 3-oz, red & gold	$1,500.00
1988, 1½-oz	$45.00
1988, 3-oz	$60.00
1989, 3-oz	$45.00
1989-91, 1½-oz, ea	$35.00
1991, 3-oz	$40.00
1992, 1½-oz	$25.00
1992, 3-oz	$30.00
1993, 1½-oz or 3-oz, ea	$20.00
1994, 1½-oz or 3-oz, ea	$14.00
1995, 1½-oz or 3-oz, ea	$14.00
1996, 1½-oz or 3-oz, ea	$12.00
1997, 1½-oz or 3-oz, ea	$12.00
1998, 1½-oz or 3-oz, ea	$10.00
1999, fluted whiskey, 1½-oz	$10.00
2000-2002, fluted whiskey, 1½, 2-oz, ea	$8.00
2003-06, jigger, ea	$7.00

WAMZ Radio KY Derby Bar Glass, Sponsored by Jim Beam

1991	$35.00
1992	$32.00
1993-94, ea	$20.00
1995-96	$15.00
1997-99, ea	$12.00
2000	$10.00
2001, discontinued	

Kindell, Dorothy

Yet another California artist that worked during the prolific years of the '40s and '50s, Dorothy Kindell produced a variety of household items and giftware, but today she's best known for her sensual nudes. One of her most popular lines consisted of mugs, a pitcher, salt and pepper shakers, a wall pocket, bowls, a creamer and sugar set, and champagne glasses, featuring a lady in various stages of undress, modeled as handles or stems (on the champagnes). In the set of six mugs, she progresses from wearing her glamorous strapless evening gown to ultimately climbing nude, head-first into the last mug. These are relatively common but always marketable. Except for these and the salt and pepper shakers, the other items from the nude line are scarce and rather pricey.

Collectors also vie for her island girls, generally seminude and very sensuous.

Ashtray, Beachcombers, 2 sets of nude legs stick out from under lg sombrero, 6x4½", from $60 to	$70.00
Ashtray, Hawaiian hula girl in 7" dia black ashtray, 4½"	$530.00
Champagne glass, black glass goblet w/gold nude on side, 6"	$235.00
Champagne glass, nude at stem, 6", from $125 to	$150.00
Creamer & sugar bowl, nude handles, 3½x3"	$300.00
Dresser box, Hawaiian girl finial, 5x4x6½", from $400 to	$500.00
Dresser box, nude seated on jar shaped as stacked disks, 10¾"	$500.00
Dresser box, topless Hawaiian girl finial, 5½x4x3"	$320.00
Dresser box, turtle lying on back, 7x5"	$80.00
Figurine, Airedale, seated, marbled glaze, 6"	$45.00
Figurine, foal, white mane & tail, 5¾"	$45.00
Figurine, horse, Registered California sticker, 6½"	$45.00
Figurine, lady dancing in long dark green strapless dress, arms at side, 9"	$295.00
Figurine, nude w/flowers in hair, legs in air, 9x9", from $175 to	$235.00
Figurine, seated nude, red scarf across left arm & behind head, 11½x4½", from $250 to	$300.00
Head vase, Black native girl, red lips & necklace, 5"	$65.00
Head vase, Black native girl w/separate blue ceramic necklace, red lips & black hair, 6"	$75.00
Head vase, brunette head & shoulders, green eyeliner & earrings, 5¼"	$80.00

Head vase, 6¼", $95.00. (Photo courtesy David Barron)

Ice bucket, nude handle on ea side, 11x4½"	$150.00

Lamp bases (no hardware), kneeling seminude Oriental (man & woman), exotic headgear, 13½", pr..............**$450.00**

Mug, Boy Scout insignia on bark pattern w/axe handle, 1953, 3½" **$85.00**

Mug, horse head embossed on 1 side w/Pop on other, nude handle, 4⅛", from $30 to......................**$40.00**

Mug, nude handle, 6 in series, ea from $40 to **$50.00**

Mug, nude w/red ballerina shoes as handle **$175.00**

Pitcher, water; nude handle..**$320.00**

Salt & pepper shakers, barrel shape w/nude at side, 3", pr...**$50.00**

Shelf sitter, nude w/red turban & red towel on lap, 12".....**$250.00**

Wall pocket, nude from mug series, rare **$295.00**

King's Crown, Thumbprint

Back in the late 1800s, this pattern was called Thumbprint. It was first made by the U.S. Glass Company and Tiffin, one of several companies who were a part of the US conglomerate, through the 1940s. U.S. Glass closed in the late 1950s, but Tiffin reopened in 1963 and reissued it. Indiana Glass bought the molds, made some minor changes, and during the 1970s, they made this line as well. Confusing, to say the least! Gene and Cathy Florence's *Collectible Glassware of the 40s, 50s, and 60s,* explains that originally the thumbprints were oval, but at some point Indiana changed theirs to circles. And Tiffin's tumblers were flared at the top, while Indiana's were straight. Our values are for the later issues of both companies, with the ruby flashing in excellent condition.

Bowl, divided mayonnaise; 5" **$50.00**

Bowl, flower floater, 12½" **$80.00**

Bowl, salad; 9¼" **$85.00**

Bowl, 5¾" **$20.00**

Candy box, flat, 6" **$65.00**

Cheese stand **$35.00**

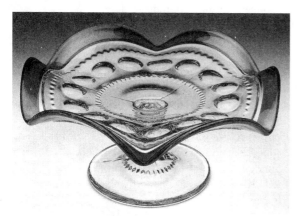

Compote, footed, crimped, 7½x12", $140.00. (Photo courtesy Gene and Cathy Florence)

Cup **$8.00**

Goblet, water; 9-oz...**$12.00**

Oyster cocktail, 4-oz **$7.00**

Pitcher...**$215.00**

Plate, dinner; 10" **$42.00**

Plate, snack; w/indent, 9¾" **$12.50**

Punch bowl foot..**$150.00**

Punch set, w/foot, 15-pc...**$1,275.00**

Saucer **$6.00**

Sugar bowl **$20.00**

Tumbler, iced tea; footed, 12-ounce, $20.00; Tumbler, iced tea; 11-ounce, $14.00. (Photo courtesy Gene and Cathy Florence)

Vase, bud; 12¼" **$135.00**

Wedding bowl, 10½x6" **$100.00**

Kitchen Collectibles

If you've never paid much attention to old kitchen appliances, now is the time to do just that. Check in Grandma's basement — or your mother's kitchen cabinets, for that matter. As styles in home decorating changed, so did the styles of appliances. Some have wonderful Art Deco lines, while others border on the primitive. Most of those you'll find still work, and with a thorough cleaning you'll be able to restore them to their original 'like-new' appearance. Missing parts may be impossible to replace, but if it's just a cord that's gone, you can usually find what you need at any hardware store.

Even larger appliances are collectible and are often used to add the finishing touch to a period kitchen. Please note that prices listed here are for appliances that are free of rust, pitting, or dents and in excellent working condition.

During the nineteenth century, cast-iron apple peelers, cherry pitters, and food choppers were patented by the hundreds, and because they're practically indestructible, they're still around today. Unless parts are missing, they're still usable and most are very efficient at the task they were designed to perform.

A lot of good vintage kitchen glassware is still around and can generally be bought at reasonable prices. Pieces vary widely from custard cups and refrigerator dishes to canister sets and cookie jars. There are also several books available for further information and study. If this area of collecting interests you, you'll enjoy *300 Years of Kitchen Collectibles* by Linda Campbell, and *Kitchen Antiques, 1790 – 1940,* by Kathryn McNerney. Other books include: *Kitchen Glassware of the Depression Years* and *Anchor Hocking's Fire-King & More* by Gene and Cathy Florence; and *Collector's Encyclopedia of Fry Glassware* by H.C. Fry Glass Society.

See also Anchor Hocking; Aluminum; Clothes Sprinkler Bottles;

Glass Knives; Griswold; Jade-ite; Kitchen Prayer Ladies; Porcelier; Pyrex; Reamers.

Appliances

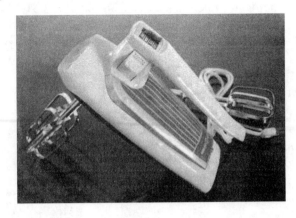

Hand mixer, General Electric, pink, three-speed, two sets of beaters, from $25.00 to $30.00. (Photo courtesy Lori Kalal/on eBay: dlkunited)

Blender, Continental De Luxe '57, General Electric, copper beehive type, glass pitcher, EX.....................**$45.00**

Blender, Hamilton Beach, chrome & black plastic, 5-cup clear glass pitcher, 7-speed, NM.......................**$60.00**

Blender, Hitachi, red & white base, 2-speed, EX **$45.00**

Blender, Hollywood Liquefier Model 41, blue & white base, clear & frosted glass container, EX **$200.00**

Blender, Oster #432 Standard, chrome beehive type w/4-cup glass pitcher, rubber lid, 2-speed, EX **$55.00**

Blender, Southern Comfort, K&M logo on plastic lid, cream base, glass canister, 16½", EX......................**$150.00**

Blender, Vita-Mix Mark 20, stainless steel w/black Bakelite, ca 1965 (dated receipt), MIB **$75.00**

Blender, Vita-Mix Super 3600, stainless steel, MIB...........**$200.00**

Blender, Waring Blendor (sic), aqua green w/gray trim, NM ...**$75.00**

Blender, Waring Blendor (sic), pink & gray, EX..................**$50.00**

Can opener/ice crusher, Oster Touch-A-Matic #565, 8½x9x5", EX......................................**$65.00**

Coffee mill/grinder, KitchenAid, glass hopper, green base, 14", EX **$110.00**

Cooker/deep fryer, Creative Chef, removable stoneware insert, cooks from 150 to 350 degrees, 9x10" dia, EX+ **$35.00**

Cooker/deep fryer, Sunbeam, chrome w/black label & base, black Bakelite handles, NM **$45.00**

Crepe maker/fryer, Sunbeam, variable settings, black handle, 8" dia, EX **$12.50**

Crock pot, Rival #3150, removable crock insert w/brown Pyrex lid, 3½-qt, EX **$35.00**

Egg cooker, Oster Automatic Model 581, beige lid, cooks up to 8 eggs at a time, MIB, from $40 to...................**$50.00**

Egg cooker, Perfect Automatic Egg Timer & Mfg Co, 4 cooking slots w/egg holders, set for 1-14 minutes, EX **$115.00**

Egg cooker/grill, Presto Eggs Every Way, ca late 1970s, MIB.... **$30.00**

Fryer, Flavo-Rite Automatic, chrome w/black base, ca 1948, NMIB.....................................**$65.00**

Grill, Sunbeam Party Grill, chrome w/black handle, temperature control on hinged lid, rectangular, EX **$40.00**

Grill/panini sandwich maker, Hamilton Beach, chrome w/black handles, non-stick surface, 5x15x12", EX **$25.00**

Grill/slow cooker, West Bend, brown enameled pot w/glass lid, sits on non-stick base, w/wire rack, 1980s, NM..................**$55.00**

Hot plate, Atlantic Precision Works Model 101, 38 watts, 7¾" dia, EX **$15.00**

Hot plate, GS&SM Works, ceramic element, silver-painted metal, ca mid-1930s, 6¾" dia, EX........................**$15.00**

Hot plate/tabletop stove, Montgomery Ward, 2-burner, metal base, cloth cord, 4x16x8", EX........................**$12.50**

Ice cream freezer, Richmond Cedar Works, wooden basket, electric, makes 5 qts, EX **$45.00**

Juicer, Champion, avocado green, ⅓-horsepower motor, NMIB .**$85.00**

Juicer, Proctor Silex Juicit Juicer #85102, black & off-white, EX .**$40.00**

Juicer, Rival Juice-o-Mat, red & chrome metal, 8½x6x6", EX.. **$35.00**

Juicer, Sunkist Juicit, white glass reamer top, 9½", EX.........**$35.00**

Mixer, Kenmore Model #8276, pink, portable, 6" L, MIB ..**$65.00**

Mixer, KitchenAid by Hobart, stainless steel, very heavy, w/glass bowl, NM...............................**$265.00**

Mixer, Sunbeam, aqua blue w/black, complete w/beaters & glass bowls, EX.....................................**$165.00**

Mixer, Sunbeam Mixmaster, chrome w/black, 12-speed, 3 clear glass bowls, EX.....................................**$125.00**

Mixer, Sunbeam Mixmaster, turquoise, 10-speed, w/turquoise glass bowls, 1950s, EX....................................**$80.00**

Percolator, Camfield Manufacturing, stainless steel w/Bakelite handle, 3 settings, 8-cup, EXIB **$50.00**

Percolator, Oster Coffeemaker, avocado green w/tinted see-through middle, M in worn box........................**$65.00**

Percolator, Universal #15P50, tapered chrome body w/gold bands, black handle, makes 4 to 10 cups, EX......................**$70.00**

Percolator, Universal: Landers, Frary & Clark, copper & brass w/ glass top, 15½x10".......................**$55.00**

Percolator, West Bend, turquoise, waisted style, 10-cup, NMIB... **$35.00**

Popcorn popper, Mirro, aluminum w/glass lid, NM **$50.00**

Popcorn popper, West Bend, aluminum w/red finish, black handles & feet, EX **$30.00**

Popcorn popper, West Bend Poppery II, hot-air type, EX....**$25.00**

Popcorn popper, West Bend Stir Crazy, removable metal rack, 6-qt, EX **$35.00**

Salad shooter, w/2 slicing, ripple cutter & shredding cones, funnel guide, Presto Salad Shooter, MIB.................................**$45.00**

Skillet, Farberware #310-A, stainless steel w/black handles & knob, 12" dia, EX **$36.00**

Skillet, Sunbeam X Model FP-10A, chrome w/black handle, sq, 10½", EX.......................................**$40.00**

Skillet/fry pan, Saladmaster #7256, oil core, 12", NM.......**$195.00**

Skillet/fry pan, Sunbeam #S31L, completely immersible, 11½" sq, black handle, EX................................**$36.00**

Slow cooker, West Bend Lazy Day, brown enamel pot, black handles, w/book, NM, from $75 to................**$85.00**

Toaster, General Electric #139T82, chrome w/black handles, 2-slice, EX **$55.00**

Toaster/oven, General Electric #35T83, chrome w/dual controls, long slot in top, removable tray below, 12x10x6½", EX............. **$35.00**

Vacuum cleaner, Electra, compact canister, beige & white, EX .. **$165.00**

Vacuum cleaner, Electrolux #1205, turquoise canister w/power nozzle & accessories, NM **$215.00**

Vacuum cleaner, General Electric Roll-Easy R1, turquoise canister, w/attachments & extra bags, EXIB **$365.00**

Vacuum cleaner, Kenmore #2299, w/attached tote & accessories, NM......................**$195.00**

Vacuum cleaner, Kirby Model 516, complete w/attachments including floor polisher, EXIB **$525.00**

Waffle iron, General Electric #A6G44T, chrome w/Teflon coated grids, black handles, EX **$80.00**

Waffle iron, Manning-Bowman Twin-O-Matic, chrome w/Bakelite, cloth cord, EX......................**$65.00**

Waffle iron, Royal Rochester, chrome w/ceramic insert (unknown floral pattern) in lid, makes 7½" waffle, 1930s, EX **$60.00**

Waffle iron, Royal Rochester/Fraunfelter China, Golden Pheasant pattern, EX **$85.00**

Waffle iron, Sunbeam, chrome w/black handles, 11x11" sq, EX......**$40.00**

Toaster, Sunbeam T-1-C, $75.00. (Photo courtesy Jim Barker)

Glassware

Baker, Cameo, white on gray, sq, Glasbake, 9"....................**$22.00**

Baker, crystal, Pyrex, 8-oz............................**$5.00**

Baker, pudding; crystal, Fry, 2⅛x6⅜" **$40.00**

Baker, Queen Anne, crystal, ring mold, Glasbake **$9.50**

Baker, Turquoise, round, w/clear lid, Pyrex, 1½-qt, 8¼" **$25.00**

Batter jug, black, metal top, McKee, from $150 to **$160.00**

Batter jug, green, Paden City, from $100 to......................**$110.00**

Bean pot, crystal, w/lid, Pyrex, 1920s, 2-qt......................**$22.00**

Bottle, water; CrissCross, green, Hazel-Atlas, 64-oz, from $165 to......................**$175.00**

Bowl, dessert; Clover Blossom, purple floral on milk glass, Federal, 4⅞"......................**$3.50**

Bowl, mixing; Blossom, crystal, Federal, #248, 9"................**$10.00**

Bowl, serving; crystal, oval, 8-sided, w/metal frame, Fry, 6½x9" ..**$50.00**

Butter dish, CrissCross, blue, Hazel-Atlas, 1-lb, from $135 to **$145.00**

Cake pan, angel food; crystal, Glasbake **$15.00**

Cake pan, Safe Bake Heart, crystal, heart-shape w/arrow, Glasbake, w/label **$25.00**

Cake plate, crystal, round, Fry, 9"......................**$35.00**

Canister, Chalaine Blue, Tea in black lettering, press-on lid, from $475 to **$500.00**

Canister, Coffee in black lettering on custard, McKee, from $165 to **$185.00**

Canister, Red Dots on Custard, screw-on lid, round, McKee, 48-oz, from $225 to **$275.00**

Canister, Wild Rose on white, w/lid, Glasbake, 48-oz..........**$65.00**

Canisters with rooster finials, fired-on red, from $25.00 to $50.00.

Casserole, Cameo w/Urn, white on blue, Glasbake, 2-qt **$25.00**

Casserole, crystal, oval, w/lid & metal frame, engraved, Fry, 8". **$55.00**

Casserole, crystal w/red-orange handles & finial on lid, Art Deco, Glasbake, 10"......................**$30.00**

Casserole, Maple Leaves, green & brown leaves on white, Federal, 1½-qt......................**$12.00**

Ice bucket, amber, etched grapes designs, Cambridge, from $55 to......................**$60.00**

Ice tub, Peacock Blue, from $40 to **$45.00**

Ladle, amberina, Cambridge, from $50 to **$55.00**

Ladle, pink, Cambridge, from $25 to **$28.00**

Loaf pan, Currier & Ives, gray-blue on white, Glasbake, 1½-qt ... **$22.00**

Measuring cup, crystal, Glasbake, 1-cup, 8-oz, 3½" **$15.00**

Measuring cup, Jennyware, crystal, ½-cup, Jeannette, from $40 to..**$45.00**

Measuring cup, Jennyware, pink, Jeanette, 1-cup, from $70 to. **$75.00**

Measuring pitcher, crystal, Hazel-Atlas, 4-cup, from $28 to.**$30.00**

Measuring pitcher, green fired-on color, McKee, 2-cup, from $50 to **$55.00**

Pie plate, crystal, w/metal frame, Fry, 10" **$45.00**

Pie plate, Sealtest, crystal, Glasbake, 9¼"......................**$7.50**

Pitcher, Dots on White, McKee, 2-cup, from $55 to **$60.00**

Pitcher, green, CrissCross, Hazel-Atlas, 54-oz, from $150 to ..**$175.00**

Pitcher, milk; cobalt, Hazel-Atlas, from $85 to **$95.00**

Platter, fish; crystal, engraved, Fry, 17"......................**$85.00**

Ramekin, Lime or Pearl, Fry, 2½"......................**$25.00**

Refrigerator dish, Delphite, McKee, 4x5", from $50 to **$55.00**

Refrigerator dish, yellow, sq, McKee, 7¼", from $45 to......**$50.00**

Roaster, crystal, lg, w/lid, Glasbake **$60.00**

Salt & pepper shakers, Delphite Blue, Jeannette, 8-oz, pr from $50 to **$55.00**

Salt & pepper shakers, Jennyware, pink, footed, Jeannette, ea from $30 to **$35.00**

Saucepan, crystal, handled, Glasbake, 10⅛" **$20.00**

Sugar shaker, green, Jeannette, from $135 to **$145.00**

Sugar shaker, Red Dots on Custard, McKee, from $110 to..... **$115.00**

Syrup pitcher, pink, metal top, Paden City, from $65 to...... **$75.00**

Syrup pitcher, pink, New Martinsville, from $75 to............. **$85.00**

Teakettle, white w/brown handle, Glasbake, from $40 to **$45.00**

Utility pan, Cameo w/Urn, Glasbake, 2½-qt, 13⅞x8¹⁄₁₆"..... **$25.00**

Measuring cup, pearl ovenware, one-spout, #1933, Fry, $55.00.

Miscellaneous Gadgets

Apple peeler, cast iron, clamps to table, crank handle, White Mountain, 9x6", EX **$30.00**

Apple peeler, cast iron, clamps to table, Reading Hardware #78, 11½x6¼", EX.. **$30.00**

Apple peeler, painted cast iron, crank handle, Made in the United States of America #76, 12x7½", EX.............................. **$45.00**

Apple peeler, turquoise painted cast iron, peels, cores & slices in 1 step, crank handle, Goodell Improved, EX **$115.00**

Bread box, aluminum, aqua trim, Kromex, 1940s-50s, EX+ .**$70.00**

Bread box, brushed aluminum lid w/black plastic knob, unmarked Kromex, EX... **$45.00**

Bread-slicing guide, color-coded slots, tilted design, Presto, EX. **$15.00**

Cake/candy mold, chicken sitting on nest, crescent moon mark #L103, 2-pc, 7x9x6" **$80.00**

Canisters, aluminum, pink plastic lids w/black knobs, tall Flour & Sugar, stacking Tea & Coffee, unmarked, set of 4, NM..... **$55.00**

Cheese/butter dish, aluminum, wood finial on lid, West Bend, 4x7½" dia **$35.00**

Chopper/grinder, Universal Model, 3 cutting heads, crank handle, MIB.. **$35.00**

Clock, black & white w/black & red hands, red center, metal frame, Sentinel Wafer, Ingraham Clock Co, 1950s, 7¼", EX ..**$55.00**

Clock, green porcelain w/black & white face, 6-sided w/flowers at ea corner, Miller, 1920s, 10½", EX.................................... **$75.00**

Clock, Plexiglas bubble over aqua circle, hours/minutes marked w/bars, Telechron, 1940s-50s, 8½" dia, EX **$75.00**

Clock, Plexiglas bubble over face, green plastic rectangular frame, Telecron Model 2H29, 1940s-50s, EX........................... **$52.50**

Colander, cream enamel on metal, green trim, triangular w/3 oval feet (sm chips), 3x10½x8¼" **$40.00**

Crimper, butterscotch plastic, ca 1950s, 5", VG **$30.00**

Crimper, tin wheel, wooden handle, unmarked, 6", EX....... **$15.00**

Crimper/measuring cups, white plastic, ¼-cup (1 side) & ⅓-cup (other), Tupper Ware, 1960s, 4¼" handle....................... **$5.00**

Cutlery set, wall/drawer holder w/4 knives: carver, slicer, chef's & butcher's, brown marbleized handles, Cutco, NM **$75.00**

Dipper/ladle, aluminum w/green painted wood handle, 14" 4"..**$12.50**

Egg beater, cast iron, double-geared, Cyclone, Patent 1901, 14" **$45.00**

Egg beater, cast-iron top, wire whisk attached to crank & wheel, wooden handle, Silvers Brooklyn, 13", EX.................... **$75.00**

Egg beater, metal w/heart-shaped beaters, Henderson Corporation Seattle, 1930 Patent, 11¾", EX **$75.00**

Egg beater, tin box shape, footed, crank handle on side, Hodges, 8¼x5¼x5¼", EX... **$60.00**

Garlic press, metal, pliers type, EX..................................... **$10.00**

Juicer/processor, aluminum, Foley Food Mill, 4x7" dia+6" handle, EX, from $15 to **$20.00**

Knife holder, white painted wood w/red flower trim, holds 5, wall hanging, Good Housekeeping seal, copyright 1939, EX .. **$35.00**

Lemon squeezer, cast iron & wood, hinged hand-held press, Pearl, 7¼" (closed), EX **$22.50**

Lemon squeezer, heavy metal, hinged, 11x11", EX............. **$27.50**

Lemon squeezer, metal w/porcelain insert, Arcade #2, EX ...**$30.00**

Lemon squeezer, wooden w/metal hinge, EX patina, 10½x2" .. **$25.00**

Mayonnaise maker, J. Hutchinson, trademark S&S Long Island, from $125.00 to $150.00. (Photo courtesy Gene and Cathy Florence)

Pastry blender, curved wires attached to red wooden handle, Androck, 1940s, EX.. **$10.00**

Pitcher, aluminum, 1-qt under pouring lip, Wagner Sidney O, 6½" **$80.00**

Popcorn popper, bottom stirring system, works on stove top, Whirley, 6-quart, EX **$50.00**

Potato masher, cobalt blue, KitchenAid, scarce, MOC........ **$20.00**

284

Potato masher, stainless steel coils form 7x5½" masher, 28" stainless handle (for deep pans), NM...**$10.00**

Potato masher, stainless steel 5½" head, 18" wooden handle ... **$10.00**

Potato ricer, hinged metal basket type w/red handles, 1940s, 11" L, EX **$12.50**

Roaster, aluminum, w/insert & lid, Wagner Ware #4265, oval, 12½" L...**$125.00**

Rolling pin, aluminum, holds ice water, red Bakelite handles, in cardboard tube...**$30.00**

Rolling pin, milk glass w/wooden handles, 18"....................**$50.00**

Rolling pin, turned wood w/green painted handles, made in 3 pieces, EX, from $10 to **$15.00**

Rolling pin, white ceramic w/blue advertising; Pekin Coal... Nebraska..., wooden handles, EX...............................**$60.00**

Salt & pepper shakers, aluminum w/5 embossed bands near top, glass base, 4x2", pr...**$20.00**

Scales, tin pan hangs from 3 chains, green paint, American Family, 60-lb capacity, 1930s, EX **$60.00**

Sifter, Androck Handi Sift, three-screen, 5½", EX, from $40.00 to $55.00.

Sifter, tin, painted red starbursts on white, 3 screens, Androck, NM **$25.00**

Sifter, tin, red apples & green leaves on white, Bromwell, 5¾", EX **$12.50**

Sifter, tin, red stripes & cherries on white, 5¾", EX **$30.00**

Sifter, tin, Tower-Hubbard Lumber Co...Wis advertising in blue on white, EX...**$40.00**

Sifter, tin, tulip & advertising for Polson MT store, sq sides, EX **$35.00**

Spice jars, brushed aluminum w/embossed name of spice, black plastic lid, Kromex, 3¾", set of 8 on rack.....................**$50.00**

Strainer, aluminum, punched circles, 5½x10⅜" (handle to handle) **$8.00**

Strainer, tin, nasturtiums on white w/yellow checked borders, 1940s, EX **$40.00**

Teakettle, aluminum w/textured surface, black Bakelite grip on bail handle, Lifetime USA, lg, EX **$22.00**

Teapot, aluminum, ball form w/red plastic stick handle & ball ball finial, Pure Aluminum Made in USA, 5½", EX...........**$30.00**

Thermometer, print on white enamel, Good Housekeeping advertising, shows up to 500 degrees, 5¼" on 3" base.............**$22.00**

Kitchen Prayer Ladies

The Enesco importing company of Elk Grove, Illinois, distributed a line of kitchen novelties during the 1960s that they originally called 'Mother in the Kitchen.' Today's collectors refer to them as 'Kitchen Prayer Ladies.' The line was fairly extensive — some pieces are common, others are very scarce. All are designed around the figure of 'Mother' who is wearing a long white apron inscribed with a prayer. The more common Enesco Prayer Lady is pink. She is also found in blue and white or white with blue trim. The white lady with blue trim is the most difficult to find, so to evaluate items in this color combination, use the high end of our range of values.

Advisor: Judy Foreman (See Directory, Kitchen Prayer Ladies)

Sprinkler bottle, any color, minimum value $600.00. (Photo courtesy Pat and Ann Duncan)

Air freshener, E-5200, 5", from $100 to **$175.00**

Bank, Mother's Pin Money, 5½", from $85 to **$120.00**

Bell, E-2825, 4½", from $75 to **$85.00**

Candleholders, rare, 4", pr from $300 to **$375.00**

Canister, Flour, Sugar, Tea, Coffee; rare, ea from $250 to ..**$400.00**

Cookie jar, blue, 10", from $275 to **$350.00**

Cookie jar, pink, 10", from $150 to **$225.00**

Creamer, pink, 4", from $55 to...**$75.00**

Crumb tray & brush, 8½", from $125 to **$155.00**

Egg timer, E-4810, 5¾", from $50 to **$70.00**

Jar, Instant Coffee, blue, 6", from $130 to.......................**$165.00**

Jar, Instant Coffee, pink, 6", from $95 to **$115.00**

Napkin holder, blue, E-2826, 6¼", from $15 to................**$25.00**

Napkin holder, pink, E-2826, 6¼", from $10 to **$18.00**

Napkin holder, white, E-2826, 6¼", from $20 to..............**$30.00**

Picture frame, E-4809, 6", minimum value **$350.00**

Planter, E-2826, rare, 6¼", from $75 to.............................**$150.00**

Ring holder, E-4247 (red paint on crown often gone, many found w/gold & white crown), 5¾", from $75 to.................**$110.00**

Salt & pepper shakers, blue, pr from $10 to **$20.00**

Salt & pepper shakers, pink, pr from $5 to.......................**$15.00**

Salt & pepper shakers, white, pr from $15 to **$25.00**

Scouring pad/soap dish, blue (tray has 3 styles), E-4246, 5½", from $50 to **$70.00**

Scouring pad/soap dish, pink (tray has 3 styles), E-4246, 5½", from $35 to **$55.00**

Spoon rest, pink, E-3347, 5¾", from $15 to **$25.00**

Spoon storage/holder, pink, upright, E-4811, 6", from $25 to . **$40.00**

String holder, 6", from $85 to **$125.00**

Sugar bowl, pink, 4", from $55 to **$75.00**

Teapot, blue, 6", from $90 to... **$125.00**

Teapot, pink, 6", from $75 to **$100.00**

Toothpick holder, blue, E-5199, 4½", from $12 to............. **$18.00**

Toothpick holder, pink, E-5199, 4½", from $8 to **$15.00**

Toothpick holder, white, E-5199, 4½", from $15 to........... **$20.00**

Vase, bud; rare, from $150 to.. **$175.00**

Wall plaque, full figure, E-3349, 7½", from $35 to **$70.00**

Kreiss & Co.

Collectors are hot on the trail of figural ceramics, and one area of interest are those unique figurines, napkin dolls, planters, mugs, etc., imported from Japan during the 1950s by the Kreiss company, located in California. Though much of their early production was run of the mill, in the late 1950s, the company introduced unique new lines — all bizarre, off the wall, politically incorrect, and very irreverent — and today it's these items that are attracting the interest of collectors. There are several lines. One is a totally zany group of caricatures called Psycho-Ceramics. There's a Beatnick series, Nudies, and Elegant Heirs (all of which are strange little creatures), as well as some that are very well done and tasteful. Several will be inset with with colored 'jewels.' Many are marked either with an ink stamp or an in-mold trademark (some are dated), so you'll need to start turning likely looking items over to check for the Kreiss name.

There is a very helpful book on the market. For some great photos and helpful information, we recommend *The World of Kreiss Ceramics* by Pat and Larry Aikins (L-W Book Sales).

Prices are drastically lower than those we saw for Kreiss figures a few years ago, affected no doubt by Internet trading which has made them so much more accessible. Our values are based on actual online sales.

See also Napkin Ladies.

Ashtray, angry pink creature w/sword through his head, red rhinestone eyes, Japan sticker, 5x4½x3½", NM **$45.00**

Ashtray, guy w/lg saucer-like eyes waving right hand at side, Psycho Ceramics, 5¼" **$58.00**

Ashtray, winking creature w/blue-green rhinestone eye, pink hat forms tray, Psycho-Ceramics, 5x3½"............................. **$65.00**

Ashtray, yellow creature w/blue tray on his back, gold rhinestone eyes, 5", NM.. **$40.00**

Bank, Beatnik, Dad I'm Waiting for the world to go PFFT!, 7" .. **$65.00**

Bank, pig reclining in bikini, Our Vacation on tummy, 3¾x6" **$68.00**

Bank, pig w/graduation cap, My Savings Are Growing..., 6¾" ...**$65.00**

Bank, Poodle Bank, pink & white poodle bust w/blue rhinestone eyes, 7" **$65.00**

Christmas card holder, Santa by receiver marked Christmas Cards, 1950s, 6½x8" **$35.00**

Figurine, creature w/4 blue rhinestone eyes, yellow tones w/blue hat, Japan sticker, 5" **$50.00**

Figurine, guy w/worried expression chewing fingernails, Psycho Ceramics, 5" **$65.00**

Figurine, guy w/4 saucer-like eyes, sm blue hat, Psycho Ceramics, 5¼" **$65.00**

Figurine, Happy Birthday, hobo (bum), waving right hand, multi-color attire, 5½" **$35.00**

Figurine, Hi Ya, hobo (bum) dressed in red, green & black, 5½" ..**$35.00**

Figurine, hobo (bum), dressed in red & green, 6½" **$40.00**

Figurine, Little Champ, blond boy w/boxing gloves raised over head, 6½" **$32.00**

Figurine, poodle seated, white w/pink hat & multicolor jewels, 5¼" **$35.00**

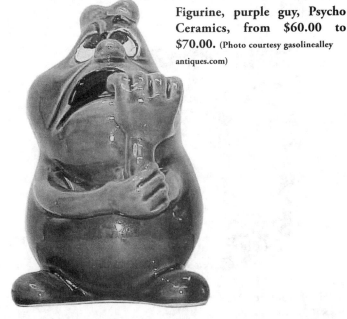

Figurine, purple guy, Psycho Ceramics, from $60.00 to $70.00. (Photo courtesy gasolinealley antiques.com)

Figurine, Robin Hood, dressed in green, 7" **$65.00**

Figurine, vulture, yellow, brown & black w/green eyes, 4½"... **$140.00**

Figurines, skunks (3), mother w/2 babies attached w/chains, 5" & 2½" **$32.50**

Mug, angry monster face, purple w/blue eyes, plugs in ears . **$45.00**

Mug, guy w/cave-man like apperance, Psycho Ceramics, 4¾". **$35.00**

Mug, lady w/1 tooth, green bow in blond hair, Psycho Ceramics, 4¾" **$48.00**

Salt & pepper shakers, hippos, gray & pink, 4¼", pr.......... **$55.00**

Salt & pepper shakers, Lil' Red Devils (cute), 1955, Japan sticker, 4x2", pr.. **$40.00**

Lamps

Aladdin Electric Lamps

Aladdin lamps have been made continually since 1908 by the Mantle Lamp Company of America, now Aladdin Mantle Lamp

Company in Clarksville, Tennessee. Their famous kerosene lamps are highly collectible, and some are quite valuable. Many were relegated to the storage shelf or thrown away after electric lines came through the country. Today many people keep them on hand for emergency light.

Few know that Aladdin Industries, Inc. was one of the largest manufacturers of electric lamps from 1930 to 1956. They created new designs, colorful glass, and unique paper shades. These are not only collectible but are still used in many homes today. Many Aladdin lamps, kerosene as well as electric, can be found at garage sales, antique shops, and flea markets. You can learn more about them in the books *Aladdin Electric Lamps* and *Aladdin — The Magic Name in Lamps, Revised Edition,* written by J.W. Courter, who also periodically issues updated price guides for both kerosene and electric Aladdins. A free eight-page history of Aladdin lamps is available by writing the author.

Advisor: J.W. Courter (See Directory, Lamps)

Newsletter: *Mystic Lights of the Aladdin Knights*
J.W. Courter
3935 Kelley Rd., Kevil, KY 42053
Subscription: $25 (6 issues, postpaid 1st class) per year with current buy-sell-trade information. Send SASE for information about other publications.

Bed, #832 SS, Whip-o-lite pleated shade	**$175.00**
Bedroom, P-071, ceramic, from $25 to	**$35.00**
Boudoir, E-410, glass, early	**$50.00**
Boudoir, G-49, Alacite, from $40 to	**$50.00**
Bridge, #2051	**$225.00**
Figurine, G-16, lady, crystal, etched, EX, from $600 to	**$700.00**
Figurine, G-163, double nudes, NM, from $2,500 to	**$3,000.00**
Floor, #3334, reflector	**$175.00**
Pinup, G-352, Panel & Scroll, Alacite	**$100.00**
Ranch House, G-378C, Bullet, Alacite, lit/decaled urn, EX, from $325 to	**$375.00**
Table, G-140, Moonstone	**$80.00**
Table, G-331, Alacite, illuminated base, from $60 to	**$80.00**
Table, G-98, Moonstone, from $100 to	**$125.00**
Table, M-463, ivory ceramic w/black iron base, from $30 to	**$40.00**
TV, M-384, shell, ceramic, from $50 to	**$60.00**
TV, MT-520, cherry & brass, base, NM, from $400 to	**$500.00**

Motion Lamps

Though some were made as early as 1920 and as late as the 1970s, motion lamps were most popular during the 1950s. Most are cylindrical with scenes such as waterfalls and forest fires and attain a sense of motion through the action of an inner cylinder that rotates with the heat of the bulb. Prices below are for lamps with original parts in good condition with no cracks, splits, dents, or holes. Any damage greatly decreases the value. As a rule of thumb, the oval lamps are worth a little more than their round counterparts. **Caution:** Some lamps are being reproduced (indicated in our listings by '+'). Currently in production are Antique Autos, Trains, Old Mill, Ships in a Storm, Fish, and three Psychedelic lamps. The color on the

scenic lamps is much bluer, and they are in plastic stands with plastic tops. There are quite a few small motion lamps in production that are not copies of the 1950s lamps.

Advisors: Jim and Kaye Whitaker (See Directory, Lamps)

Antique Autos, Econolite, 1957, 11" (+)	**$110.00**

Butterflies #753, brass base, Econolite, 11", $150.00. (Photo courtesy Jim and Kaye Whitaker)

Cover Girls #754, Elvgren, Econolite, 14"	**$295.00**
Elvgrin Pinup Girls	**$375.00**
Fish, Fresh Water, Econolite, 11"	**$125.00**
Fish, Tropical, Econolite, 11" (+)	**$110.00**
Flames, Scene in Action, 10"	**$125.00**
Forest Fire, Scene in Action, 10"	**$110.00**
Forest Fire #FF, Roto-Vue Jr, Econolite, 10"	**$90.00**
Forest Fire #761, Econolite, 11"	**$100.00**
Forest Fire #2003, LA Goodman, 11"	**$75.00**
Fountain of Youth, Roto-Vue Jr, Econolite, 10"	**$120.00**
Hawaiian Scene #701, Econolite, 11"	**$135.00**
Lighthouse/Sailing Ship, LA Goodman, 11"	**$100.00**
Marine Scene, ship/lighthouse, Scene in Action, 10"	**$125.00**
Niagara Falls, Scene in Action, 10"	**$100.00**
Niagara Falls #NF, Roto-Vue Jr, Econolite, 10"	**$65.00**
Niagara Falls #762, Econolite, 11"	**$75.00**
Niagara Falls #2007, LA Goodman, 11"	**$55.00**
Niagara Falls Rainbow, Econolite, 11"	**$135.00**
Old Mill #764, Econolite, 11" (+)	**$100.00**
Oriental Garden #702, Econolite, 11"	**$135.00**
Sailing Ships #772, Econolite, 11" (+)	**$115.00**
Snow scene #766 & #767 (2 scenes), Econolite, 11"	**$135.00**
Steamboats #764, Econolite, 11"	**$120.00**
Train #763, Econolite, 11"	**$120.00**
Waterfall - Campfire, LA Goodman, 11"	**$90.00**

TV Lamps

By the 1950s, TV was commonplace in just about every home in the country but still fresh enough to have our undivided attention. Families gathered around the set and for the rest of the evening delighted in being entertained by Ed Sullivan or stumped by the $64,000 Question. Pottery producers catered to this scenario by producing TV lamps by the score, and with the popularity of anything from the 1950s being what it is today, these lamps are making appearances at flea markets and co-ops everywhere.

For more information we recommend *TV Lamps to Light the World* by John A. Shuman (Collector Books). See also Maddux of California; Morton Potteries, Royal Haeger.

Afghan dog, brown shading to cream & white, Lane & Co, 1958, 12x12" **$120.00**
Angelfish (2), black gloss w/white speckles, Gilner, 10½x8½" .. **$55.00**
Bowl-like shape formed by leaves, brown tones, 7½x11x7¼". **$55.00**
Boy & girl w/rickshaw, cold painted, 8½" (to top of pottery), 13½" L **$70.00**
Cocker spaniel, recumbent, flocked finish, Model #2500 Pat Pending, AN Brooks...Chicago, EX+ **$100.00**
Comedy & Tragedy masks, green, holds 2 bulbs, 1950s, 7x11" **$65.00**
Covered wagon w/scenic laced shade, made from cactus wood, EX **$48.00**
Deco-style dog stands beside golden globe, painted chalkware, 1930s, 15½" **$95.00**
Flamingos (2) on green pool-like base, Lane & Co, 1957, 14". **$135.00**
Flower form, Deco-style, deep green, 9½x6½", NM............**$35.00**
Horse on swirling planter base, brown tones, 9x9", NM......**$55.00**
Horse w/Trojan-like mane, green on platform base, 1950s...**$95.00**

Horses, gold on black, unmarked, $35.00.

Horses' heads (2) facing right, black gloss **$75.00**
Horses racing (2), chartreuse on black & light green base, Royal Haeger, 11x17" **$100.00**
Hula girl surrounded by palm fronds, painted chalkware, red backing in center shields light, 1940s, EX+........................**$395.00**
Mallard duck w/2 ducklings, Royal Copley, 12" L, (babies 5¾" ea)...**$65.00**
Oriental boy & girl w/instruments sit in arbor beside a well, 1950s...**$60.00**

Owl w/wings wide, brown tones, light shines through eyes, Kron, 11½"...**$40.00**
Panther (facing left) on planter base, green, unmarked, 1950s, 4¾x11x4½" **$50.00**
Panther at waterfall, Ebony Cascade (black w/white speckles & accents), Royal Haeger, 1962 ....**$125.00**

Poodle and pug, glass eyes, Kron, 13", from $70.00 to $80.00.

Poodle pulling flower cart, bulb in back of cart (hides behind flowers, 5½x11½" **$45.00**
Poodles (2), gray, standing w/1 looking back at other, Lane & Co, 10x14", NM **$95.00**
Pup w/ball in his mouth, brown w/black ears, 6x7x4½" **$70.00**
Sailing ship on base of waves, lustreware, 1940s-40s, 9x8⅞" ... **$60.00**
Sea horses (2/white) at sides of lg green shell, Beauceware, 9½x8¼x4" **$120.00**
Siamese cat w/paw raised, blue-point coloring, eyes glow, Made in California USA, 11½", EX **$120.00**
Siamese mother & kitten, brown tones, Kron, 12½x8½x4". **$90.00**

L.E. Smith

Originating just after the turn of the century, the L.E. Smith company continues to operate in Mt. Pleasant, Pennsylvania, at the present time. In the 1920s they introduced a line of black glass that they are famous for today. Some pieces were decorated with silver overlay or enameling. Using their own original molds, they made a line of bird and animal figures in crystal as well as in colors. The company is currently producing these figures, many in two sizes. They were one of the main producers of the popular Moon and Star pattern which has been featured in their catalogs since the 1960s in a variety of shapes and colors.

If you'd like to learn more about their bird and animal figures, *Glass Animals* by Dick and Pat Spencer shows many made by L.E. Smith.

See also Kitchen Collectibles, Glassware; Moon and Star.

Bonbon/tidbit, black glass, center handle, 1930s, 6½" dia...**$25.00**

Bookends, rearing horses, amber, ca 1925, pr **$45.00**

Bowl/candy dish, Mt Pleasant Double Shield, black amethyst, 3-footed, 6"..**$35.00**

Candleholder, Daisy & Button, milk glass, Heritage Line, 1950s, 2¾x3¼", ea **$7.50**

Candleholder, milk glass, #200 Square Optic, 1½x4½", ea....**$8.00**

Candleholder, Wig Wam, green, 2¾", $25.00 each.
(Photo courtesy Gene and Cathy Florence)

Candleholders, black amethyst, 1940s, 3½x4¼", pr **$28.00**

Candleholders, milk glass, embossed grapes, 4½", pr..........**$16.00**

Candy dish, Daisy & Button, blue opal, footed, w/lid, 7½x5½" **$38.00**

Canoe, Daisy & Button, amber **$15.00**

Compote, amber w/4 pinwheels in bowl, scalloped rim, zipper-patterned stem, ca 1971, 5¾x4½" **$15.00**

Covered dish, bunny on nest, pink, 4x4½" **$35.00**

Covered dish, fighting cock (rooster), milk glass, 9x9½"......**$65.00**

Covered dish, turkey, crystal, 7½" **$40.00**

Covered dish, turkey, crystal carnival, 7½" **$55.00**

Covered dish, turkey, emerald green, 1970s, 7½" **$55.00**

Covered salt dish, hen on nest, amber, 2½" L **$20.00**

Figurine, Goose Girl, Flame, 6x3¾", from $20 to **$28.00**

Figurine, Scottie dog, milk glass, 5x6½", NM **$38.00**

Flower block, vaseline, Greek Key pattern at top, clear yellow flower holder, painted flowers on front, 3½x4¼" **$38.00**

Lefton China

China, porcelain, and ceramic items with that now familiar mark, Lefton, have been around since the early 1940s and are highly sought after by collectors in the secondary marketplace today. The company was founded by Mr. George Zoltan Lefton, an immigrant from Hungary. In the 1930s he was a designer and manufacturer of sportswear, but eventually his hobby of collecting fine china and por-

celain led him to initiate his own ceramic business. When the bombing of Pearl Harbor occurred on December 7, 1941, Mr. Lefton came to the aid of a Japanese-American friend and helped him protect his property from anti-Japanese groups. Later, Mr. Lefton was introduced to a Japanese factory owned by Kowa Koki KK. He contracted with them to produce ceramic items to his specifications, and until 1980 they made thousands of pieces that were marketed by the Lefton company, marked with the initials KW preceding the item number. Figurines and animals plus many of the whimsical pieces such as Bluebirds, Dainty Miss, Miss Priss, Cabbage Cutie, Elf Head, Mr. Toodles, and Dutch Girl are eagerly collected today. As with any antique or collectible, prices vary depending on location, condition, and availability.

See also Birthday Angels.

Advisor: Loretta DeLozier.

Ashtray, Miss Priss, #1524, 6", from $50 to **$60.00**

Bank, Miss Priss, #4916, from $250 to **$300.00**

Bank, purse marked Pin Money, applied roses & flowers, 4x6", NM **$48.00**

Biscuit jar, Green Heritage, #6131, 7x5".............................**$80.00**

Bookends, dogs, #7484, 4¾", from $40.00 to $45.00. (Photo courtesy Loretta DeLozier)

Bowl, salad; Sweet Violets, #2870, 10", from $50 to **$60.00**

Bowl, vegetable; Americana Rose, oval, w/lid, 5x10" L **$72.50**

Butter dish, Bluebird...**$60.00**

Butter dish, Daisy, rectangular **$50.00**

Butter dish, Miss Priss..**$125.00**

Candleholder, Pixie Girl, 3 variations, #7047, 3½", ea from $8 to **$12.00**

Candy box, White Christmas, #1342, from $20 to..............**$30.00**

Cigarette set, French Rose, 7-pc, from $35 to **$45.00**

Coffee set, Heavenly Rose, pot w/creamer & sugar bowl, 3-pc ..**$100.00**

Coffeepot, Brown Heritage, #NE1866, 8⅞" **$55.00**

Coffeepot, Heavenly Rose, foil label, 9" **$65.00**

Compartment dish, Dainty Miss, figural center handle, skirt forms tray, 10" **$185.00**

Cookie jar, Bloomer Girl, #3966...**$275.00**

Cookie jar, Bluebird, from $125 to **$150.00**

Cookie jar, Green Holly, 7", from $40 to............................**$50.00**

Creamer & sugar bowl, Bluebird, w/lid, #7170 & #6161, 5"...**$65.00**

Creamer & sugar bowl, Floral Chintz, #8034, from $45 to . **$65.00**

Creamer & sugar bowl, Green Heritage, w/lid **$65.00**

Creamer & sugar bowl, Heavenly Rose, w/lid **$42.50**

Creamer & sugar bowl, Thumbelina, w/lid **$35.00**

Egg cup, Miss Priss, from $40 to **$50.00**

Figurine, angel children riding on candy cane, #626, 3¼x10½", MIB **$85.00**

Figurine, angel w/musical instrument, #2543, 4", from $15 to... **$25.00**

Figurine, colonial man & lady, #568, 8", pr from $140 to **$160.00**

Figurine, Colonial Village Station, w/station master, lights from back, #5822, 1986, 7x7¼x5½", MIB **$75.00**

Figurine, horse, tan w/white mane & tail, #4066, 5½x7" **$85.00**

Figurine, Hot Cross Buns, grandmother & grandaughter w/basket of buns, matt coloring, sticker **$70.00**

Figurine, Humpty Dumpty, #1250 .... **$72.50**

Figurine, lady w/2 lg flower baskets, pastel colors, KW4047, 8" .. **$70.00**

Figurine, policeman, #538, 8¼", from $45 to..................... **$55.00**

Figurine, tabby cat, #6364, 4½", from $12 to **$14.00**

Figurine, white rabbit, Easter, #880, from $25 to **$35.00**

Figurines, Boy Blue & Pinkie, 8", pr................................. **$50.00**

Figurines, Green Holly reindeer, from $50.00 to $60.00 for the pair.

Gravy boat, Pink Clover, #2505, 8½", from $18 to............. **$28.00**

Jam jar, Cuddles, #1451, from $25 to................................ **$35.00**

Jam jar, Miss Priss, #1515, from $95 to **$110.00**

Lamp, hurricane; Green Holly, #4229, 5½", from $40 to.... **$45.00**

Nightlight, mouse w/mushroom, #7920, 6", from $22 to ... **$28.00**

Pitcher, Bluebird, #287, 4½", from $75 to **$95.00**

Pitcher, Poinsettia, #4389, 6¼", from $125 to................... **$150.00**

Pitcher, water; Green Heritage, #NE796, 6½" **$65.00**

Pitcher & saucer, Green Holly, 7" **$45.00**

Planter, blond lady in pastel blue w/embossed flowers, holds parasol, 6½" **$45.00**

Planter, blond lady in pink w/flower basket, #2587, 6½" **$45.00**

Planter, blond lady w/white w/flowers cascading down front of gown, #6640, 7½" **$48.00**

Planter, Bluebird, rhinestone eyes, #288............................ **$55.00**

Planter, clown's head, #4498, 4", from $45 to.................... **$55.00**

Planter, Priscella, white headscarf & apron w/brown lace, yellow dress, holds spade & basket, #1685C, 6" **$50.00**

Plate, cake; Green Heritage, #719, from $38 to.................. **$42.00**

Plate, salad; Heavenly Rose, 6¾" **$18.00**

Salt & pepper shakers, Bluebird, pr.................................... **$50.00**

Salt & pepper shakers, Mammy & Chef, #2046, 3¼", pr from $30 to **$35.00**

Silent butler, Green Heritage.. **$100.00**

Tea bag holder, Miss Priss face on teapot shape, $65 to **$85.00**

Tea set, Lefton Rose, pot w/stacking creamer & sugar bowl. **$1,220.00**

Tea set, Violet Chintz, stacking pot w/creamer & sugar bowl . **$100.00**

Teapot, Bluebird, 1950s, 6x8¼" **$150.00**

Teapot, Dutch Girl **$85.00**

Teapot, Green Heritage, #792, from $65 to **$75.00**

Teapot, honey bee, #1278, from $85 to **$110.00**

Teapot, Mr Toodles, 7½" **$150.00**

Teapot, Regal Rose, flower finial, individual **$110.00**

Tray, Miss Priss in center of 2 trays, #1507 .... **$85.00**

Vase, bud; cherub w/guitar & bird at base, gold trim, 5½x4½x3". **$75.00**

Vase, lady's hand holding shoe, 7" **$90.00**

Wall plaques, facing mermaids w/brown hair riding sea horses, 7", pr **$150.00**

Wall plaques, red & blue parrot mother & 2 babies, she: 9x4", 3-pc set **$175.00**

Wall pocket, Bluebird w/top hat **$120.00**

Wall pocket, Dainty Miss.. **$37.50**

Wall pocket, Miss Priss, #1509, from $125 to **$150.00**

Wall pocket, Puppy Pal **$95.00**

Lamp, clown #3867, 8", $50.00. (Photo courtesy David Barron)

L.G. Wright

Until closing in mid-1990, the L.G. Wright Glass Company was located in New Martinsville, West Virginia. Mr. Wright started his business as a glass jobber and then began buying molds from defunct glass companies. He never made his own glass, instead many companies pressed his wares, among them Fenton, Imperial, Viking, and Westmoreland. Much of L.G. Wright's glass was reproductions of Colonial and Victorian glass and lamps. Many items were made from the original molds, but the designs of some were slightly changed. His company flourished in the 1960s and 1970s. For more information we recommend *The L.G. Wright Glass Company* by James Measell and W.C. 'Red' Roetteis (Glass Press).

Bowl, Daisy and Button, vaseline opalescent, oval, 5½" long, from $25.00 to $30.00.

Bowl, Paneled Grape, iced green carnival, oval, 6x12" $25.00
Bowl, Paneled Grape, light blue, tall stem, disk foot, 6½x6½" . $15.00
Cake plate, Holly, custard glass, 12" $75.00
Candy dish, Daisy & Button, amberina, footed, w/lid, 7x5¼" . $20.00
Candy dish, Westward Ho, clear & frosted, figural finial, 10x4½" $35.00
Canister, Daisy & Button, turquoise, 11½x5¾" $35.00
Canoe, Daisy & Button, blue, 12" $25.00
Covered dish, cow (recumbent) on basketweave base, blue slag, 5½" $70.00
Covered dish, hen on nest, amethyst carnival, 7" $50.00
Covered dish, owl (head) on basket base, blue slag, 5½" dia $95.00
Covered dish, rabbit w/ears back, amber, 6½" L $48.00
Covered dish, turkey, amber carnival, 8½" $95.00
Covered dish, turkey on basket base, purple slag, 5½" $50.00
Covered dish, turkey on basket base, sapphire blue, 5½" $25.00
Covered dish, turtle, milk glass, 4x6" $250.00
Fairy lamp, Embossed Rose, green, 4-pc $48.00

Fairy lamp, Eyewinker, green, 5½", from $40.00 to $45.00.

Goblet, Daisy & Button, amethyst, 10-oz, 6" $22.50
Goblet, Grasshopper w/Insect, amber, 6x3" $25.00
Goblet, Grasshopper w/Insect, blue, 6x3½" $35.00
Goblet, wine; Embossed Rose, pink, 5-oz, 6 for $35.00
Jar/canister, Daisy & Button, green, 11½x5¾" $30.00
Lamp, kerosene; Daisy & Fern, blue opalescent, clear globe, 13" .$500.00
Mustard jar, bull's head, purple slag, 4½" $55.00
Open salt, frog, amber carnival, 3½" $30.00
Open salt, frog, blue slag, 3½" $15.00
Open salt, frog, purple carnival, 3½" $30.00
Pitcher, Cherry, red slag, lg $30.00
Pitcher, water; Westward Ho, clear & frosted, flat, 4" $110.00
Pitcher, Wreathed Cherry, pink, 4¾" $25.00
Spice jars, custard glass, plastic shaker tops, set of 6 in 13¾" rack .. $40.00
Toothpick holder, Daisy & Button, canary, 2¾x2" $12.00
Tumbler, Westward Ho, log cabin, buffalo & deer, clear & frosted, flat, 4" $35.00
Vase, Mary Dugan, vaseline, 10 scallops, angle handles, 6¼" $35.00

Liberty Blue

'Take home a piece of American history!,' stated an ad from the 1970s for this dinnerware made in Staffordshire, England. Blue and white depictions of George Washington at Valley Forge, Paul Revere, Independence Hall — 14 historic scenes in all — were offered on different place-setting pieces. The ad goes on to describe this 'unique... truly unusual..museum-quality...future family heirloom.'

For every five dollars spent on groceries you could purchase a basic piece (dinner plate, bread and butter plate, cup, saucer, or dessert dish) for 59 cents on alternate weeks of the promotion. During the promotion, completer pieces could also be purchased. The soup tureen was the most expensive item, originally selling for $24.99. Nineteen completer pieces in all were offered along with a five-year open stock guarantee.

Beware of 18" and 20" platters. These are part of a line of recent imports and are not authentic Liberty Blue. For more information we recommend Jo Cunningham's book, *The Best of Collectible Dinnerware* (Schiffer).

Advisor: Gary Beegle (See Directory, Dinnerware)

Bowl, cereal; 6½" $10.00
Bowl, flat soup; 8¾", from $18 to $20.00
Bowl, fruit; 5" $2.50
Bowl, vegetable; oval, from $30 to $35.00
Bowl, vegetable; round $30.00
Butter dish, ¼-lb $45.00
Casserole, w/lid, from $115 to $135.00
Coaster (4 in set, ea w/different scene), ea $8.50
Creamer, from $15 to $18.00
Creamer & sugar bowl, w/lid, original box $60.00
Cup & saucer $3.50
Gravy boat $40.00
Gravy boat liner $18.00
Mug $9.50
Pitcher, 7½", from $85 to $95.00

Plate, bread & butter; 6" **$2.00**
Plate, dinner; 10", from $5 to **$7.00**
Plate, luncheon; scarce, 8¾" **$20.00**
Plate, 7" **$9.00**
Platter, 12", from $35 to **$45.00**

Platter, 14", from $65.00 to $85.00.

Salt & pepper shakers, pr **$35.00**
Soup ladle, plain white, no decal, from $30 to............**$35.00**
Soup tureen, w/lid...**$245.00**
Sugar bowl, no lid **$5.00**
Sugar bowl, w/lid **$24.00**
Teapot, w/lid, from $85 to.................................**$95.00**

License Plates

Some of the early porcelain license plates are valued at more than $500.00. First-year plates are especially desirable. Steel plates with the aluminum 'state seal' attached range in value from $150.00 (for those from 1915 to 1920) down to $20.00 (for those from the early 1940s to 1950). Even some modern plates are desirable to collectors who like those with special graphics and messages.

Our values are given for examples in good or better condition, unless noted otherwise. For further information see *License Plate Values* distributed by L-W Book Sales.

Advisor: Richard Diehl (See Directory, License Plates)

Newsletter: *Automobile License Plate Collectors Association*
Richard Dragon
P.O. Box 8400, Warwick, RI 02888-0400
www.alpca.org

Magazine: *License Plate Collectors Hobby Magazine*
Drew Steitz, Editor
P.O. Box 222
East Texas, PA 18046; phone or fax: 610-791-7979
PL8Seditor@aol.com or RVGZ60A@prodigy.com
www.PL8S.com

Issued bimonthly; $18 per year (1st class, USA). Send $2 for sample copy

1915, New Hampshire, green lettering on white, EX+, $65.00.

1923, New Jersey **$15.50**
1926, Colorado **$35.00**
1934, Nebraska **$15.50**
1936, South Dakota..**$20.00**
1938, Florida **$25.00**
1941, Kansas **$15.50**
1941, Maine..**$20.00**
1941, Minnesota...**$12.50**
1946, Illinois, Soybean **$15.50**
1954, Michigan...**$10.50**
1956, Wisconsin **$1.00**

1957, Oklahoma Semi-Centennial, red lettering on white, NM, $25.00.

1957, Rhode Island..**$9.50**
1963, Washington..**$6.50**
1964, Oklahoma **$8.50**
1966, Iowa **$4.00**
1967, Montana **$5.50**
1967, Utah..**$5.50**
1969, Virginia...**$3.50**
1970, Alabama **$5.50**
1971, Maryland **$5.50**
1971, Ohio..**$3.50**
1972, Missouri **$2.50**
1975, North Carolina, First in Freedom **$8.50**
1976, Alaska, Bear **$25.00**
1977, Washington, DC, Inauguration...................**$7.50**
1984, California, blue **$5.50**
1984, Nevada, blue **$4.50**
1985, Pennsylvania...**$4.50**
1986, Idaho...**$3.50**

1987, Arizona **$5.50**
1987, North Dakota, Teddy **$9.50**
1988, Louisiana, World's Fair **$12.50**
1989, Tennessee **$3.50**
1990, South Carolina............................. **$3.00**
1994, Indiana, Enviroment **$20.00**
1996, Vermont.................................... **$10.50**
1997, Mississippi.................................. **$5.50**
1998, Hawaii, Rainbow **$3.50**
1999, New Mexico, Cactus **$2.50**
2000, Kentucky...................................... **$6.50**
2002, Connecticut **$10.50**
2003, Georgia, Peach **$2.50**
2004, Oregon, Tree **$4.50**
2005, Wyoming, Devil's Head **$6.50**

Linens

As early as the 1880s, thrifty farm wives were putting cloth feed sacks to a second use around the home as dishcloths, diapers for the babies, even simple articles of clothing. Soon manufacturers were catering to the ladies by printing the feed sacks in colorful designs better suited for making dresses, curtains, pillow cases, and the like. During the Depression when times were especially hard, literally millions of American ladies and their children were wearing feed sack garments. Besides those with allover designs, some sacks were offered with printed-on patterns for cloth dolls, aprons, or pillowcases. By the late 1940s fabric feed sacks were phased out in favor of those made of heavy paper. Today, these early fabric sacks are coveted collectibles. Especially interesting are those printed with Disney characters, nursery rhyme figures, and those signed by a famous designer.

Tablecloths and dishtowels from the 1940s and 1950s add a cheerful note to any kitchen, and collectors will pay a pretty penny for good examples with vibrant flowers and fruit, classic Dutch boys and girls, sailboats, Mexican motifs, cottages, and the like — all fun types that depict America at a happier, more carefree time. Souvenir linens representing states or particular sites are especially sought after. If they are signed by a well-known illustrator/designer, as is true in other fields of collecting, those signatures serve to drive the prices up even more.

Holiday-related items are hot, but reproductions are out there. Buyers beware! Reproduction colors are off and do not show up as much on the back due to less color saturation. They also have plastic-type tags that are sewn in. Old linens feature fabric labels or homemade tags. Close examination of a reproduction shows a looser weave that is less heavy and has fewer details, made by printing rather than the silkscreening process.

When evaluating vintage linens, condition is an important factor — watch for fading, stains, holes, and other signs of wear. Our values are for examples that are in nearly new, very clean spot-free condition unless noted otherwise.

Advisor: Darrell Thomas

Dish towel, appliquéd Mammy face w/embroidered details on white huck, red stripes down sides, 1950s, 28x16" **$75.00**

Dish towel, embroidered Southern belle walking dog on white cotton, tagged, 22x16" **$25.00**
Dish towel, embroidered table setting on white cotton, black & yellow trim along edge, 28x17" **$22.50**
Dish towel, printed cornucopia & fruits on white cotton w/red border, 30x16" **$45.00**
Dish towel, printed floral trellis (vivid colors) on white cotton, cotton crocheted border, 1940s, 28x16" **$45.00**
Dish towel, printed lady & tomato plants on white cotton w/red border, 26x16" **$65.00**
Dish towel, printed Niagara Falls attractions on green cotton, Made in Czechoslovakia, 29x16" **$35.00**
Dish towel, printed pineapples & tropical fruit on white cotton, 27x17" **$45.00**

Feed sack, boxes and flowers, 37x46", $36.00. (Photo courtesy dewittco.com - vintage textiles & ephemera)

Feed sack, blue & white swirls in quilt-like repeating pattern, opened, 39x36".................... **$35.00**
Feed sack, floral (poinsettias?) & abstracts on white, opened, 39x36", minimum value.................... **$60.00**
Feed sack, flower wreaths join checked squares, yellow, blue & white, opened, ca 1925, 45x36" **$40.00**
Feed sack, palm trees, sailboats, grass huts, multicolor on white, opened, 1940s, 38x32" **$50.00**
Napkins, printed bridge (card game) theme on white cotton, hand-drawn hem, 1950s, 10½x10½", set of 4 .... **$15.00**
Napkins, printed fruit in corner on white cotton w/blue border, 11x11", set of 4 .... **$10.00**
Napkins, printed red roses & green leaves on white cotton, 17x15", set of 4.................... **$25.00**
Tablecloth, embroidered child in red & blue on white cotton, 1940s, 34x33".................... **$55.00**
Tablecloth, embroidered flower wreath center w/sprays in ea corner on cream cotton, 33x35" **$30.00**
Tablecloth, printed Black man w/banjo singing on white cotton, souvenir of New Orleans, 27x16", minimum value **$100.00**
Tablecloth, printed blue flowers w/brown leaves along edge w/blue check border, 1950s, 58x45".................... **$32.50**

Tablecloth, printed chef/barmaid/waiter/etc among pots & pans in black & red on white cotton, 54x49" **$65.00**

Tablecloth, printed chrysanthemums on white cotton, ca 1960, 52x52", w/coordinating gold 17½" sq napkins **$40.00**

Tablecloth, printed evergreens/candy canes/pine cones/wreaths on cream cotton/rayon blend, 1940s, 66x48" **$85.00**

Tablecloth, printed flowers & plaid on textured cotton, chartreuse border, tiny repair, 50x48" **$30.00**

Tablecloth, printed flowers/fruits on white cotton, 1940s, 49x48" w/4 matching 16x15" napkins **$90.00**

Tablecloth, printed holly, berries & bows on white cotton w/gold flocking, 1950s, 62x52" **$85.00**

Tablecloth, printed Mexican theme w/bright colors on white, 1950s, 64x50" **$45.00**

Tablecloth, printed mixed flowers on white cotton, pinks, oranges & greens dominating colors, 64x54" **$48.00**

Tablecloth, printed pink clover bouquets w/green ribbons & bows on white cotton w/green border, 59x49" **$60.00**

Tablecloth, printed pink flowers & pussy willows on turquoise blue cotton, Calaprint label, 1950s, 65x53" **$65.00**

Tablecloth, printed poinsettias/candles w/metallic gold holders/etc on white cotton, 76x60", minimum value **$85.00**

Tablecloth, printed red & white tropical flowers on white cotton w/red & white borders, 52x48" **$75.00**

Tablecloth, printed red roses w/green leaves & stems on heavy white cotton, 50x46" **$65.00**

Tablecloth, printed vegetables on white cotton, dark red border, 52x48" **$95.00**

Tablecloth, printed Wisconsin landmarks on white cactus cloth, bright colors, 38x32" **$45.00**

Tablecloth, ribbons and clover blossoms, textured cotton, 59x49", $60.00. (Photo courtesy www.retro-redheads. com)

Tablecloth, white cotton w/blue & yellow stripes forming border, 1950s, 51x51".. **$30.00**

Tablecloth, woven-in red & white check linen, Belgium, 1940s, 67x52", w/6 12" sq napkins... **$75.00**

Tablecloth, woven-in red floral & grapes border, Simtex label, 50x47½" **$35.00**

Little Red Riding Hood

This line of novelty cookie jars, canisters, mugs, teapots, and other kitchenware items was made by both Regal China and Hull. Today any piece is expensive.

The complete line is covered in *The Collector's Encyclopedia of Hull Pottery* by Brenda Roberts (Collector Books).

Planter, wall mount, 9x6", from $400.00 to $500.00.

Bank, standing, 7", from $900 to **$1,350.00**
Butter dish, from $350 to **$400.00**
Canister, cereal **$1,375.00**
Canister, coffee, sugar or flour; ea from $600 to **$700.00**
Canister, salt... **$1,100.00**
Canister, tea **$700.00**
Casserole, red w/embossed wolf, Red Riding Hood, Grandma & axe man, 11¾", from $1,800 to.. **$2,500.00**
Cookie jar, closed basket, from $450 to **$650.00**
Cookie jar, full skirt, from $750 to **$850.00**
Cookie jar, open basket, from $400 to.............................. **$500.00**
Cracker jar, unmarked, from $600 to................................ **$750.00**
Creamer, side pour, from $150 to **$225.00**
Creamer, top pour, no tab handle, from $400 to **$425.00**
Creamer, top pour, tab handle, from $350 to.................... **$375.00**
Dresser jar, 8¾", from $450 to **$575.00**
Lamp, from $2,000 to.. **$2,650.00**
Match holder, wall hanging, from $400 to........................ **$650.00**
Mustard jar, w/original spoon, from $375 to **$460.00**
Pitcher, 7", from $450 to **$675.00**
Pitcher, 8", from $550 to **$850.00**
Salt & pepper shakers, Pat design 135889, med size, pr (+) from $800 to **$900.00**
Salt & pepper shakers, 3¼", pr from $95 to **$140.00**
Salt & pepper shakers, 5½", pr from $180 to **$235.00**
Spice jar, sq base, ea from $650 to **$750.00**
String holder, from $1,800 to **$2,500.00**
Sugar bowl, crawling, no lid, from $300 to........................ **$450.00**
Sugar bowl, standing, no lid, from $175 to........................ **$225.00**
Sugar bowl, w/lid, from $350 to **$425.00**
Sugar bowl lid, minimum value **$175.00**
Teapot, from $400 to... **$450.00**
Wolf jar, red base, from $925 to **$1,000.00**
Wolf jar, yellow base, from $750 to.................................. **$850.00**

Little Tikes

For more than 25 years, this company (a division of Rubbermaid) has produced an extensive line of toys and playtime equipment, all made of heavy-gauge plastic, sturdily built and able to stand up to the rowdiest children and the most inclement weather. As children usually outgrow these items well before they're worn out, you'll often see them at garage sales, priced at a fraction of their original cost. We've listed a few below, along with what we feel would be a high average for an example in the stated condition. Since there is no established secondary market pricing system, though, you can expect to see a wide range of asking prices.

Activity Garden Playset, EX....................................**$150.00**
Castle, built-in slide, NM, from $225 to **$300.00**
Country Cottage Toddler Bed, NM, from $150 to **$175.00**
Country Kitchen, EX, from $125 to................................**$150.00**
Cozy Cottage Toddler Bed, EX **$165.00**
Football Toy Chest, 31x28x20", NM..............................**$165.00**

Imagine Sounds playhouse, EX, from $175.00 to $200.00.

Log Cabin, EX, from $165 to..**$185.00**
Noah's Ark Bed, EX **$185.00**
Octopus Merry-Go-Round, seats 3 children, NM..............**$165.00**
Patio Playhouse, NM **$325.00**
Pirate Ship Climber, w/cannon sprinkler & slide, NM **$225.00**
Snooze & Cruise Toddler Car Bed, NM **$225.00**
Treehouse Playset, NM **$165.00**
Tropical Playground, w/2 slides, NM, from $350 to..........**$400.00**
Twin Race Car Bed, red w/black & white tires, 103" L, NM, from $225 to..**$285.00**
Variety Climber w/Swing Set extension, 2 slides & climbing net, EX **$350.00**
Wave Climber Slide Gym, NM, from $150 to....................**$175.00**
Workshop, w/smaller bench, chair, phone, tools & accessories, NM **$175.00**
Young Explorer Computer Desk, NM, from $350 to **$375.00**

5-in-1 Super Sports Bouncer, NM **$275.00**
8-in-1 Adjustable Playground, NM, from $250 to............**$325.00**

Lladro Porcelains

Lovely studies of children and animals in subtle colors are characteristic of the Lladro porcelains produced in Labernes Blanques, Spain. Their retired and limited editions are popular with today's collectors.

Shepherd Boy With Dog, #4659, 1969 – 1985, 7½", from $165.00 to $200.00. (Photo courtesy Jackson's International Auctioneers & Appraisers of Fine Art & Antiques)

Angel playing violin, 1997, 5" **$135.00**
Awakening, #4870, 1974-99, 8½" **$95.00**
Bird Watcher, #4730, retired..**$350.00**
Boy Blowing, 1970s, 7¾" **$80.00**
Boy w/Dog, #4522M, 1970-1991, 7½"............................**$95.00**
Boy w/Drum, #14616, 1969-79, 4¼" **$365.00**
Caress & Rest, #1246G, 1972-1989, 8¼" **$260.00**
Christmas Bell, satin ribbon, 1988, MIB **$22.50**
Dancer, #5050, 11½"..**$175.00**
Dog & Cat, #5032, 1979-1997 ....**$275.00**
Donkey in Love, #4524, ca 1972 ....**$375.00**
Feeding the Ducks, 1963-1995, 9" L................................**$175.00**
Girl w/Child, 1960s-1979, 7¾" **$185.00**
Girl w/Doll, #1211, retired in 1984..................................**$575.00**
Girl w/Duckling, 12x6" **$135.00**
Girl w/Milk Pail & Duck, #4682, 2003-2004, 9½" **$185.00**
Girl w/Piglet, #1011, 7" **$135.00**
Girl w/Piglets, 1969-1985, 10½x7½" **$335.00**
Girl w/Umbrella & Geese, #4510, 1969-1993...................**$175.00**
Golden Wedding, #4937, retired 1981, 14¼"....................**$800.00**
Good Night, #5449, 1987, 8¼" **$300.00**
Hawaiian Flower Vendor, 1985, 10½" **$335.00**
Mother & Child, #4575, ca 1972, 13" **$335.00**
Nude Torso, 1969-85, 12" **$370.00**
Pretending, #564, retired 1996, 6¼" **$60.00**
Pretty Pickings, #5222, 1985-2006, 7" **$125.00**
Roaring Twenties, 1980s, 13"...**$235.00**
Summer Stroll, #7611, MIB **$375.00**

Sweet Scent, #5221G, 6½" **$95.00**
Thinking, #4539, 1969-2004 ....**$75.00**
Wheelbarrow w/Flowers, #1283, 9.............................**$450.00**
Wind, The; boy & girl shielding puppy, #1279, 1974-1992, 14¼" **$750.00**

Longaberger Baskets

In the early 1900s in the small Ohio town of Dresden, John Wendell ('J.W.') Longaberger developed a love for hand-woven baskets. In 1973 J.W. and his fifth child, Dave, began to teach others how to weave baskets. J.W. passed away during that year, but the quality and attention to detail found in his baskets were kept alive by Dave through the Longaberger Company.

Each basket is hand-woven, using hardwood maple splints. Since 1978 each basket has been dated and signed by the weaver upon completion. In 1982 the practice of burning the Longaberger name and logo into the bottom of each basket began, guaranteeing its authenticity as a Longaberger basket.

New baskets can be obtained only through sales consultants, usually at a basket home party. Collector and speciality baskets are available only for a limited time throughout the year. For example, the 1992 Christmas Collection Basket was offered only from September through December 1992. After this, the basket was no longer available from Longaberger. Once an item is discontinued or retired, it can only be obtained on the secondary market.

This information is from *The 2006 – 2007 Edition Bentley Collection Guide*. See the Directory for ordering information or call 1-800-837-4394.

Note: Values are for baskets only, unless accessories such as liners and protectors are mentioned in the description. Sizes may vary as much as one-half inch. All dimensions are given in length x width x height.

Advisor: Jill S. Rindfuss (See Directory, Longaberger Baskets)

Medium Easter Basket, swinging handle, from $50.00 to $75.00. (Photo courtesy Nancy McDaniel)

1979-93, Retired Mini Cradle™ (basket only), sm rectangular, no color trim or weave, no handles, wood rockers, $45 to .**$90.00**

1983, JW Medium Market® (basket only), rectangular, blue weave & trim, 1 stationary handle, brass tag: Longaberger - JW Medium Market, from $910 to **$1,257.00**

1984-90, Booking/Promo Candle™ (basket only), rectangular, no color trim or weave, 1 stationary handle, ⅜" weave, from $30 to **$70.00**

1988-2003, MBA™, Classic stain, no color weave or trim strip, attached lid, given to consultants promoted to management bound associate status, from $55 to **$85.00**

1990, Mother's Day Small Oval™ (basket only), pink weave & trim strip, 2 leather handles, from $51 to **$86.00**

1990-2001, Heartland Bakery™ (basket only), rectangular, Heartland Blue shoestring weave, 2 leather ears, Heartland logo burned on bottom, from $37 to...**$60.00**

1990-92, Hostess Remembrance™ (basket only), rectangular, no color trim or weave, 2 swinging handles, woven attached lid, from $125 to **$175.00**

1991, JW Corn® (basket only), round, blue trim & accent weave, 2 leather handles, brass tag: Longaberger — JW Corn, from $200 to **$273.00**

1991, Mother's Day Small Purse™ (basket only), rectangular, pink trim & accent weave, 1 swinging handle, from $55 to..**$80.00**

1992, All-American Small Market™ (basket only), rectangular, red trim w/red & blue accent weave, 2 swinging handles, from $43 to **$65.00**

1992, Father's Day Paper™ (basket only), rectangular, higher in the back than in the front, Dresden blue & burgundy trim, no handles, from $70 to..**$95.00**

1993, All-Star Trio™ (w/liner & protector), rectangular, red & blue weave & trim, 2 leather ears, from $38 to **$54.00**

1993, Christmas Bayberry™ (basket only), sq, red or green trim & accent weave, 2 swinging handles, ⅜" weave, from $42 to **$69.00**

1993, Crisco® Baking™ (basket only), oval, red & blue weave & trim, 2 leather ears, burned-in Crisco® logo, from $50 to **$107.00**

1994, Father's Day Tall Tissue™ (basket only), Classic stain, burgundy & dark green trim strip, WoodCrafts lid available separately, from $44 to **$60.00**

1994, Holiday Hostess Sleigh Bell™ (basket only), round top, rectangular bottom, red or green trim w/red & green accent weave, 2 swinging handles, from $160 to...............................**$185.00**

1994, Shades of Autumn Recipe™ (basket only), rectangular w/higher back, green, rust & deep blue weave w/rust trim, Woodcrafts lid, set of recipe cards included, from $54 to **$77.00**

1995-97, Woven Traditions Spring® (basket only), sq, red, blue & green shoestring weave, 1 stationary handle, from $51 to **$65.00**

1996, Sweetheart Bouquet™ (basket only), red weave & trim strip, 1 swinging handle, from $49 to **$75.00**

1997, JW Collection Miniature Waste Basket™ (basket only), blue trim strip, ⅛" blue weave, 2nd in series of reproductions woven by JW Longaberger, brass tag: Longaberger - JW Miniature Waste, available only to collectors club members, from $110 to.......**$185.00**

1998, Bee™ (basket only), available to consultants who attended Bee 98, blue & red weave & trim strip, brass tag reads: Join Our Celebration, from $42 to **$50.00**

1998, Perfect Attendance™ (basket only), red weave & trim strip, 1 swinging handle, brass tag/box, given to company employees for perfect attendance July 1, 1997 to June 20, 1998, from $405 to ...**$425.00**

1999, Lots of Luck™ (basket only), sq, green chain link weave & trim, ⅜" weave, 1 stationary handle, no tag, special burned-in logo, from $50 to..**$100.00**

1999, May Series Daisy™ (basket only), round, blue weave & trim, 1 swinging handle, ⅜" weave, board bottom, $49 to **$93.00**

1999, Traditions® Generosity™ (basket only), oval, green trim & accent weave, 2 swinging handles, no box, brass tag, from $119 to **$131.00**

2000, Autumn Reflections Small Harvest Blessings™ (basket only), rectangular, sage, brown & burgundy accent weave, 2 leather ears, from $50 to **$79.00**

2000, Cheers™ (basket only), oval, stained, periwinkle & purple double trim, 1 stationary handle, board bottom w/burned-in logo, commemorative silver tag, from $50 to................**$71.00**

2000, Frosty™ (basket only), green & red trim strip, works w/Small Wrought Iron Snowman, same shape & size as Darning Basket, available September 1 to December 31, 2000, from $47 to.**$54.00**

2001, Collectors Club Whistle Stop™ (basket only), tall, rectangular, blue trim, red shoestring weave, star-shaped tacks, 1 swinging handle, commemorative tag, collectors club logo burned on bottom, w/box, from $100 to **$115.00**

2001, Pumpkin Patch™, shape resembles pumpkin, ⅜" weave in center of basket & ³⁄₁₆" weave at top & woven reinforced bottom, 1 swinging handle, woven from collapsible form, from $82 to **$110.00**

2001, Special Events Inaugural™ (basket only), rectangular, blue trim w/pewter star studs, red shoestring accent weave, 1 swinging handle, from $53 to **$79.00**

2002, Horizon of Hope™ (basket only), classic stain or white-wash w/2-tone pink color weave & trim, round top/sq bottom, 1 swinging handle, ⅜" weave, 8th edition of series, American Cancer Society logo burned into bottom of basket, from $38 to **$79.00**

2002, Small Easter™ (basket only), oval, classic or white-washed stain w/pink, green or yellow trim & accent weave, 1 stationary handle, reinforced board bottom, from $55 to.............**$68.00**

2002, Tour Golf Basket™ (basket only), classic stain w/dark blue upsplints & trim, 1 swinging handle, woven bottom, brass tag, from $74 to **$75.00**

2003, Entertaining w/Longaberger Book, features 115 recipes, 38 projects, helpful hints for 14 celebrations, includes creative ways to use Longaberger baskets & pottery, full-color photos..............**$30.00**

1997, Snowflake, 7x9x10", from $73.00 to $90.00. (Basket, no lid, from $58.00 to $88.00.) (Photo courtesy Nancy McDaniel)

Miscellaneous

1990, Father Christmas Cookie Mold™ First Casting, brown pottery, inscription on back: Longaberger Pottery - First Casting - Christmas 1990, w/box, from $32 to **$36.00**

1990-91, Roseville Grandma Bonnie's Apple Pie Plate™, pottery, blue accents, embossing on bottom: Roseville Ohio, w/box, from $35 to **$51.00**

1992-95, Booking/Promo Potpourri Sachet™, Herbal Garden™ or Garden Splendor™ fabrics, from $13 to **$15.00**

1999, Fruit Medley Pottery - Pitcher™, Vitrified China, hand-painted fruit designs, logo on bottom, w/box, from $69 to.........**$113.00**

2002, Pottery Falling Leaves Vase™, Vitrified China, round opening, butternut color w/sage lip, Longaberger Pottery emblem, w/box, from $41 to...**$65.00**

2002, Pottery Shamrock Ramekin™, Vitrified China, 3-leaf clover shape, Woven Traditions Heritage Green, box, $24 to ..**$33.00**

Lu Ray Pastels

This was one of Taylor, Smith, and Taylor's most popular lines of dinnerware. It was made from the late 1930s until sometime in the early 1950s in five pastel colors: Windsor Blue, Persian Cream, Sharon Pink, Surf Green, and Chatham Gray.

Bowl, coupe soup; flat	**$18.00**
Bowl, cream soup	**$70.00**
Bowl, fruit; Chatham Gray, 5"	**$16.00**
Bowl, fruit; 5"	**$6.00**
Bowl, lug soup; tab handled	**$24.00**
Bowl, mixing; 10¼"	**$150.00**
Bowl, mixing; 5½", 7", or 8¾", ea	**$125.00**
Bowl, salad; colors other than yellow	**$65.00**
Bowl, salad; yellow	**$55.00**
Bowl, vegetable; oval, 9½" L	**$25.00**
Bowl, 36s oatmeal	**$60.00**
Bud vase	**$400.00**

Butter dish, colors other than Chatham Gray, $60.00; Chatham Gray, $90.00.

Calendar plate, 8", 9", or 10", ea	**$40.00**
Casserole	**$140.00**
Chocolate cup, AD; straight sides	**$80.00**
Chocolate pot, AD; straight sides	**$400.00**
Coaster/nut dish	**$65.00**

Coffee cup, AD $22.50
Coffeepot, AD $200.00
Creamer $10.00
Creamer, AD; from chocolate set, individual.....$92.00
Creamer, AD; ind $40.00
Egg cup, double $30.00
Epergne $125.00
Jug, water; footed $150.00
Muffin cover $140.00
Muffin cover, w/8" underplate $165.00
Nappy, vegetable; round, 8½" $25.00
Pickle tray $28.00
Pitcher, bulbous w/flat bottom, colors other than yellow ...$125.00
Pitcher, bulbous w/flat bottom, yellow..............$95.00
Pitcher, juice $200.00
Plate, cake $70.00
Plate, chop; 15" $38.00
Plate, grill; 3-compartment $35.00
Plate, 6" $3.00
Plate, 7" $12.00
Plate, 8" $25.00
Plate, 9" $10.00
Plate, 10" $25.00
Platter, 11½" $20.00
Platter, 13" $24.00

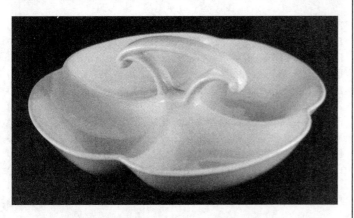

Relish dish, four-part, $125.00.

Salt & pepper shakers, pr $18.00
Sauce boat, fixed stand, yellow $27.50
Sauceboat...$28.00
Saucer $2.00
Saucer, coffee; AD $12.50
Saucer, coffee/chocolate $30.00
Saucer, for cream soup $28.00
Sugar bowl, AD; w/lid $40.00
Sugar bowl, AD; w/lid, from chocolate set..........$92.00
Sugar bowl, w/lid $15.00
Teacup..$8.00
Teapot, curved spout.......................................$125.00
Teapot, flat spout $160.00
Tumbler, juice $50.00
Tumbler, water $80.00

Lucy and Me

Lucy and Me bears are designed by Seattle artist Lucy Rigg for Enesco. These darling bisque porcelain teddy bears range from 2½" to 3" tall. All feature delightful outfits. The bears are all marked and dated. Besides figurines, there is also matching giftware.

Advisors: Debbie and Randy Coe (See Directory, Cape Cod)

Figurine, baby in highchair, 1986, 2½"..................................**$6.50**
Figurine, bowler w/red outfit, 1982, 3¼" **$7.50**
Figurine, carpenter holding hammer & saw, 1984, 3¼" **$8.50**
Figurine, child in sailor outfit holding sailboat, 1984, 3¼"....**$7.50**
Figurine, clown in polka-dot outfit, 1985, 3¼" **$6.50**
Figurine, cowboy w/blue shirt holding lasso, 1984, 3" **$9.50**
Figurine, gardener holding shovel & plant, 1980 ....**$9.50**
Figurine, jogger in blue & white outfit, 1985, 3¼" **$8.50**
Figurine, policeman directing traffic, 1984, 3¼"..................**$8.50**

Music box, wedding couple, $14.50. (Photo courtesy Debbie and Randy Coe)

Lunch Boxes

Character lunch boxes made of metal have been very collectible for several years, but now even those made of plastic and vinyl are coming into their own.

The first lunch box of this type ever produced featured Hopalong Cassidy. Made by the Aladdin company, it was constructed of steel and decorated with decals. But the first fully lithographed steel lunch box and matching Thermos bottle was made a few years later (in 1953) by American Thermos. Roy Rogers was its featured character. Since then hundreds have been made, and just as is true in other areas of character-related collectibles, the more desirable lunch boxes are those with easily recognizable, well-known subjects — western heroes; TV, Disney, and cartoon characters; and famous entertainers like the Bee Gees and the Beatles.

Learn to grade your lunch boxes carefully. Values hinge on

condition. We have given a range of values. Use the low side to evaluate a box in excellent condition, the high side for one mint or nearly so. A grade of 'excellent' for metal boxes means that you will notice only very minor defects and less than normal wear. Plastic boxes may have a few scratches and some minor wear on the sides, but the graphics must be completely undamaged. Vinyls must retain their original shape; brass parts may be tarnished, and the hinge may show signs of beginning splits. If the box you're trying to evaluate is in any worse condition than we've described, to be realistic, you must cut these prices drastically. Values for metal lunch boxes do not include the Thermos; those are listed separately. Prices for vinyl and plastic boxes, however, are for those complete with their original Thermos bottle.

If you would like to learn more, we recommend *Schroeder's Collectible Toys, Antique to Modern*, published by Collector Books.

Note: Watch for reproductions marked 'China.'

Metal

A-Team, 1980s, from $25 to $40.00
A-Team, 1980s, plastic bottle, from $8 to $12.00

Addams Family, 1970s, from $75.00 to $125.00. (Photo courtesy Larry Doucet)

Addams Family, 1970s, plastic bottle, from $15 to $20.00
Annie, 1980s, from $30 to..$40.00
Annie, 1980s, plastic bottle, from $5 to.............................$10.00
Apple's Way, 1970s, from $50 to...$75.00
Apple's Way, 1970s, plastic bottle, from $15 to...................$25.00
Astronauts, 1960, dome, from $85 to.................................$150.00
Astronauts, 1960, metal bottle, from $30 to.......................$50.00
Astronauts, 1969, from $75 to...$125.00
Astronauts, 1969, plastic bottle, from $20 to.....................$50.00
Atom Ant, 1960s, from $75 to...$175.00
Atom Ant, 1960s, metal bottle, from $35 to........................$65.00
Batman & Robin, 1960s, from $150 to..............................$200.00
Batman & Robin, 1960s, metal bottle, from $50 to $75.00
Battle of the Planets, 1970s, from $50 to............................$75.00
Battle of the Planets, 1970s, plastic bottle, from $15 to.......$20.00
Beatles, 1960s, from $450 to $600.00
Beatles, 1960s, metal bottle, from $125 to........................$225.00

Berenstain Bears, 1980s, from $50 to....................................$75.00
Berenstain Bears, 1980s, plastic bottle, from $10 to............$20.00
Beverly Hillbillies, 1960s, from $100 to.............................$150.00
Beverly Hillbillies, 1960s, metal bottle, from $50 to............$75.00
Black Hole, 1970s, from $30 to..$60.00
Black Hole, 1970s, plastic bottle, from $10 TO...................$20.00
Bonanza, 1960s, 3 versions, ea from $100 to......................$175.00
Bonanza, 1960s, 3 versions, metal bottle, ea from $50 to $75.00
Brave Eagle, 1950s, from $150 ....$200.00
Brave Eagle, 1950s, metal bottle, from $50 to $100.00
Buck Rogers, 1970s, from $25 to..$50.00
Buck Rogers, 1970s, plastic bottle, from $15 to...................$25.00
Bullwinkle & Rocky, 1960s, from $500 to.........................$750.00
Bullwinkle & Rocky, 1960s, metal bottle, from $175 to....$275.00
Campbell Kids, 1970s, from $125 to..................................$175.00
Campbell Kids, 1970s, metal bottle, from $30 to $60.00
Care Bears, 1980s, from $25 to..$50.00
Care Bears, 1980s, plastic bottle, from $5 to.......................$10.00
Cartoon Zoo Lunch Chest, 1960s, from $200 to $275.00
Cartoon Zoo Lunch Chest, 1960s, metal bottle, from $65 to.......$115.00
Charlie's Angels, plastic bottle, from $10 to $20.00
Charlies Angels, 1970s, from $50 to...................................$100.00
Chitty Chitty Bang Bang, 1960s, from $75 to...................$125.00
Chitty Chitty Bang Bang, 1960s, metal bottle, from $20 to $40.00
Close Encounters of the Third Kind, 1970s, from $50 to..$100.00
Close Encounters of the Third Kind, 1970s, plastic bottle, from $10 to $20.00
Daniel Boone, Aladdin, 1960s, from $125 to $175.00
Davy Crockett, 1955, At the Alamo, from $250 to $350.00
Davy Crockett, 1955, At the Alamo, metal bottle, from $400 to . $600.00
Dick Tracy, 1960s, from $125 to $175.00
Dick Tracy, 1960s, metal bottle, from $25 to......................$50.00
Disney on Parade, 1970s, from $30 to.................................$60.00
Disney on Parade, 1970s, plastic bottle, from $15 to...........$25.00
Disneyland, 1950s-60s, from $150 to.................................$200.00
Disneyland, 1950s-60s, metal bottle, from $20 to $60.00
Doctor Dolittle, 1960s, from $75 to..................................$125.00
Doctor Dolittle, 1960s, metal bottle, from $20 to $40.00
Double-Deckers, 1970s, from $50 to...................................$75.00
Double-Deckers, 1970s, plastic bottle, from $15 to.............$30.00
Dudley Do-Right, 1960s, from $500 to..............................$800.00
Dudley Do-Right, 1960s, metal bottle, from $225 to........$325.00
Dyno Mutt, 1970s, from $35 to...$55.00
Dyno Mutt, 1970s, plastic bottle, from $10 to $20.00
Emergency!, 1973, from $50 to..$75.00
Emergency!, 1973, plastic bottle, from $20 to.....................$40.00
ET, 1980s, from $25 to...$50.00
ET, 1980s, plastic bottle, from $5 to...................................$10.00
Family Affair, 1960s, from $45 to..$90.00
Family Affair, 1960s, metal bottle, from $20 to $40.00
Flipper, 1960s, from $100 to..$150.00
Flipper, 1960s, metal bottle, from $20 to............................$40.00
Gene Autry Melody Ranch, 1950s, from $175 to..............$275.00
Gene Autry Melody Ranch, 1950s, metal bottle, from $50 to..$100.00
Get Smart, 1960s, from $125 to $175.00
Get Smart, 1960s, metal bottle, from $25 to $50.00
Gomer Pyle, 1960s, from $100 to......................................$150.00

Grizzly Adams, 1970s, dome, from $50 to $75.00

Grizzly Adams, 1970s, plastic bottle, from $15 to..............$30.00

Gunsmoke, 1972, from $75 to $125.00

Gunsmoke, 1972, plastic bottle, from $30 to $60.00

Happy Days, 1970s, 2 versions, ea from $50 to..................$75.00

Happy Days, 1970s, 2 versions, plastic bottle, ea from $10 to.. $20.00

Harlem Globetrotters, 1970s, from $30 to.........................$60.00

Harlem Globetrotters, 1970s, metal bottle, from $15 to......$25.00

Hogan's Heroes, 1960s, dome, from $200 to $300.00

Hogan's Heroes, 1960s, metal bottle, from $30 to $75.00

HR Pufnstuf, 1970s, from $100 to $150.00

HR Pufnstuf, 1970s, plastic bottle, from $20 to $40.00

Huckleberry Hound & Friends, 1960s, from $100 to........$175.00

Huckleberry Hound & Friends, 1960s, metal bottle, from $20 to ..$40.00

Indiana Jones, 1980s, from $20 to $40.00

Indiana Jones, 1980s, plastic bottle, from $5 to $15.00

Jet Patrol, 1950s, from $200 to.......................................$300.00

Jet Patrol, 1950s, metal bottle, from $50 to $100.00

Julia, 1960s, from $50 to $100.00

Julia, 1960s, metal bottle, from $15 to $40.00

Knight Rider, 1980s, from $20 to $40.00

Knight Rider, 1980s, plastic bottle, from $5 to $15.00

Kung Fu, 1970s, from $40 to $80.00

Kung Fu, 1970s, plastic bottle, from $5 to $15.00

Land of the Giants, 1960s, from $100 to...........................$160.00

Land of the Giants, 1960s, plastic bottle, from $20 to........$40.00

Laugh-In, 1971, from $75 to $150.00

Laugh-In, 1971, plastic bottle, from $15 to $30.00

Lost in Space, 1960s, dome, from $350 to..........................$450.00

Lost in Space, 1960s, metal bottle, from $30 to..................$60.00

Man From UNCLE, 1960s, from $100 to $150.00

Man From UNCLE, 1960s, metal bottle, from $20 to $40.00

Mickey Mouse Club, 1960s, from $65 to $100.00

Mickey Mouse Club, 1960s, metal bottle, from $15 to........$30.00

Mr Merlin, 1980s, from $20 to $35.00

Mr Merlin, 1980s, plastic bottle, from $5 to.......................$15.00

Munsters, 1960s, from $200 to...$375.00

Munsters, 1960s, metal bottle, from $75 to $125.00

Nancy Drew Mysteries, 1970s, from $30 to.........................$60.00

Nancy Drew Mysteries, 1970s, plastic, from $10 to.............$20.00

Osmonds, 1970s, from $50 to $75.00

Osmonds, 1970s, plastic bottle, from $15 to $25.00

Pac-Man, 1980s, from $20 to $35.00

Pac-Man, 1980s, plastic bottle, from $5 to $10.00

Peanuts, 1973, from $25 to...$50.00

Peanuts, 1973, plastic bottle, from $5 to............................$15.00

Pebbles & Bamm Bamm, 1970s, from $40 to.....................$80.00

Pebbles & Bamm Bamm, 1970s, plastic bottle, from $15 to ...$30.00

Popeye, 1980, from $40 to..$80.00

Popeye, 1980, plastic bottle, from $10 to...........................$20.00

Raggedy Ann & Andy, 1970s, from $20 to.........................$40.00

Raggedy Ann & Andy, 1970s, plastic bottle, from $10 to....$20.00

Rescuers, 1970s, from $25 to..$50.00

Resuers, 1970s, plastic bottle, from $15 to........................$25.00

Ronald McDonald, 1980s, from $15 to..............................$30.00

Ronald McDonald, 1980s, plastic bottle, from $6 to..........$12.00

Sesame Street, 1980s, from $20 to.....................................$40.00

Sesame Street, 1980s, plastic bottle, from $5 to $10.00

Snoopy, 1969, dome, from $50 to $100.00

Snoopy, 1969, metal bottle, from $15 to $25.00

Sport Goofy, 1980s, from $20 to $40.00

Sport Goofy, 1980s, plastic bottle, from $5 to $15.00

Star Trek The Motion Picture, from $100 to.....................$200.00

Star Trek The Motion Picture, plastic bottle, from $20 to....$30.00

Strawberry Shortcake, 1980s, from $20 to $40.00

Strawberry Shortcake, 1980s, plastic bottle, from $5 to $10.00

Super Friends, 1970s, from $40 to.....................................$80.00

Super Friends, 1970s, plastic bottle, from $10 to................$20.00

Superman, 1960s, from $100 to $175.00

Superman, 1960s, metal bottle, from $50 to......................$75.00

Tarzan, 1960s, from $100 to...$150.00

Tarzan, 1960s, metal bottle, from $20 to $40.00

Thundercats, 1980s, from $25 to.......................................$50.00

Thundercats, 1980s, plastic bottle, from $5 to $10.00

UFO, 1970s, from $50 to $85.00

UFO, 1970s, plastic bottle, from $15 to $30.00

Voyage to the Bottom of the Sea, 1960s, from $175 to......$250.00

Voyage to the Bottom of the Sea, 1960s, metal bottle, from $50 to ..$75.00

Waltons, 1970s, from $50 to $75.00

Waltons, 1970s, plastic bottle, from $15 to........................$30.00

Winnie the Pooh, 1970s, from $150 to $200.00

Winnie the Pooh, 1970s, plastic bottle, from $25 to...........$50.00

Yellow Submarine, Beatles, 1960s, from $250.00 to $500.00; Thermos, from $75.00 to $150.00.

Yogi Bear & Friends, 1960s, from $85 to............................$135.00

Yogi Bear & Friends, 1960s, metal bottle, from $20 to........$40.00

Zorro, 1950s or 1960s, ea from $100 to $200.00

Zorro, 1950s-60s, metal bottles, ea from $20 to $75.00

Plastic

Values are for boxes complete with their original Thermos, and range from low indicating excellent condition to high for a mint example.

A-Team, 1980s, from $15 to..$20.00

Astrokids, 1980s, from $15 to..$25.00

Barney Baby Bop, 1990s, from $5 to $10.00

Casper the Friendly Ghost, 1990s, from $8 to $15.00

Chip 'n Dale, 1980s, from $5 to..$10.00

CHiPs, 1970, dome, from $40 to $60.00

Dick Tracy, 1990s, red, from $10 to....................................$15.00

Dr Seuss, 1990s, from $20 to $25.00

Fat Albert, 1970s, from $20 to..$30.00

Flintstones (A Day at the Zoo), Denny's logo, 1989, from $20
    to..$30.00

Hello Kitty, Sanrio, 1990s, $15.00. (Photo courtesy Larry Doucet)

Holly Hobby, 1989, from $20 to $25.00

Hot Wheels, 1990s, from $15 to $20.00

Jabberjaw, 1970s, from $30 to $40.00

Jurassic Park, 1990s, w/recalled bottle, from $25 to.............$30.00

Keebler Cookies, 1980s, from $30 to $50.00

Little Orphan Annie, 1970s, dome, from $35 to $45.00

Mickey Mouse & Donald Duck, 1980s, from $10 to $15.00

Minnie Mouse, 1980s, head form, from $30 to $40.00

Muppet Babies, 1980s, from $15 to.....................................$25.00

Muppets, 1990s, from $10 to $18.00

New Kids on the Block, 1990s, from $15 to.........................$25.00

Nosey Bears, 1990s, from $10 to $20.00

Pepsi, 1980s, from $30 to $40.00

Rap It Up, 1990s, from $20 to $25.00

Rocky & Bullwinkle, 1990s, from $75 to $125.00

Rover Dangerfield, 1990s, from $20 to................................$30.00

Shadow, 1990s, from $10 to $20.00

Snoopy & Woodstock, 1970s, dome, from $20 to..............$30.00

Star Trek (TNG), 1970s, from $10 to $20.00

Sunnie Miss, 1970s, from $50 to $75.00

SWAT, 1970s, dome, from $30 to $40.00

Train Engine #7, 1990s, from $15 to...................................$25.00

Vinyl

Values are for boxes complete with their original Thermos, and range from low indicating excellent condition to high for a mint example.

Annie, 1980s, from $50 to..$75.00

Barbarino (Welcome Back Kotter), 1970s, from $125 to ...$150.00

Barbie, 1970s, from $65 to $85.00

Barbie Lunch Kit, 1960s, from $300 to $400.00

Batman, 1990s, from $15 to $25.00

Casper the Friendly Ghost, 1960s, from $400 to $500.00

Denim, 1970s, from $45 to $65.00

Deputy Dawg, 1960s, from $325 to $375.00

Donny & Marie, 1970, from $80 to....................................$120.00

Fire Station Engine Co #1, 1970s, from $115 to $135.00

Holly Hobbie, 1970s, from $50 to $75.00

Jr Deb, 1960s, from $100 to...$150.00

Li'l Jodie, 1980s, from $50 to $75.00

Lion in the Van, 1970s, from $50 to....................................$75.00

Little Old Schoolhouse, 1970s, from $50 to $75.00

Mardi Gras, 1970s, from $50 to $110.00

Mary Poppins, 1970s, from $75 to $100.00

Monkees, 1960s, from $300 to $350.00

Pac Man, 1980s, from $40 to $60.00

Pepsi-Cola, 1980s, yellow, from $50 to................................$75.00

Pink Panther, 1980s, from $75 to $100.00

Psychedelic Blue, 1970s, from $40 to...................................$60.00

Ringling Bros & Barnum & Bailey Circus, 1970s, from $125
    to $175.00

Ronald McDonald, 1980s, lunch bag, from $75 to...........$125.00

Snoopy, 1970s, brunch bag, from $75 to $125.00

Snoopy at Mailbox, 1969, red, from $65 to........................$85.00

Soupy Sales, 1960s, from $300 to $375.00

Speedy Turtle, 1970s, drawstring bag, from $15 to $25.00

Strawberry Shortcake, 1980, from $75 to $135.00

The Sophisticate, 1970s, drawstring bag, from $50 to $75.00

Tic-Tac-Toe, 1970s, from $50 to $75.00

Wonder Woman, 1970s, from $100 to $150.00

World of Barbie, 1971, from $50 to $75.00

Ziggy, 1979, from $50 to...$75.00

MAD Collectibles

MAD, a hotly controversial and satirical publication that was first established in 1953, spoofed everything from advertising and politics to the latest movies and TV shows. Content pivoted around a unique mix of lofty creativity, liberalism, and the ridiculous. A cult-like following has developed over the years. Eagerly sought are items relating to characters that were developed by the comic magazine such as Alfred E. Neuman or Spy vs Spy.

Book, Golden Trashery of Mad, introduction by Sid Caesar, EC
    Publications, 1960, EX $55.00

Book, paperback; Spy Vs Spy, Prohias, VG $12.00

Bust, Alfred E Neuman, white porcelain, Contemporary Ceramics,
    ca 1961, 4x2"..$110.00

Button, Watch Out! I'm MAD, Alfred E Neuman, plastic, 2⅛" .$110.00

Cookie jar, Alfred E Neuman, Clay Art, 2000, 14", from $60 to $75.00

Cuff links, Alfred E Neuman, gold plated, ⅞", MIB...........$75.00

Doll, Alfred E Neuman, 12", MIB......................................$35.00

Game Spy vs Spy, game board, EXIB $22.50

Magazine, 1955, July, EX, from $70 to.................................$80.00

Magazine, 1956, September, EX $50.00

Magazine, 1958, The Worst From MAD Magazine, w/stickers, EX $78.00

Magazine, 1959, March, valentine cover, EX $40.00

Magazine, 1977, Lighter Side of Corruption Special Edition, EX $38.00

Magnet, Wheaties box form w/Alfred E Neuman on front, magnetized rubber, 3x2" $55.00

Model kit, Alfred E Neuman, Revell, MIB $35.00

Model kit, Alfred E Neuman, unassembled, Aurora, 1965, NM in EX box..$80.00

Portrait, Alfred E Neuman, printed paper, 9x7" $40.00

Record, Musically Mad, Bernie Green, RCA Victor, Alfred E Neuman cover, 1959 LP, EX, from $25 to....................$35.00

Record, 33⅓ rpm, 1962, original sleeve, VG, $50.00.

Statuette, Alfred E Neuman, Warner Bros Studio Store, 1994, 14" $80.00

Tie, Spy vs Spy, printed silk, EC Publications, 1992, NM ...$18.00

Maddux of California

Founded in Los Angeles in 1938, Maddux not only produced ceramics but imported and distributed them as well. They supplied chain stores nationwide with well-designed figural planters, TV lamps, novelty and giftware items, and during the mid-1960s their merchandise was listed in every major stamp catalog. Because of an increasing amount of foreign imports and an economic slowdown in our own country, the company was forced to sell out in 1976. Under the new management, manufacturing was abandoned, and the company was converted solely to distribution. Collectors have only recently discovered this line, and prices right now are affordable though increasing.

Ashtray, green oval w/3 rests in center along bottom, 1½x10½x4½"..$10.00

Ashtray, red w/black speckles, swirling free-form shape, #701 ......$8.00

Figurine, flamngo, wings up, #103, 7" $85.00

Figurines, cockatoos on perch, 2 w/wings wide perched high, 2 w/ closed wings below, pink to white, 10½x10" $80.00

Luncheon/bridge set, 6 white shell #3021 bowls & lg covered #3037 bowl...$45.00

Planter, angelfish (3) rise above base, multicolor pastels, 1959, from $25 to $35.00

Planter, bluebird on planter base, #536, 1959.....................$22.50

Planter, cockatoo w/crest erect & foot lifted, pink & white, 10¼x8½"..$65.00

Planter, flamingo, 9½", from $45.00 to $60.00.

Planter, flamingos back-to-back, pink tones, 5¼x6¾" $40.00

Planter, swan, pink & cream, #510, 11" $15.00

Tidbit tray, 3 joined shells, white w/center handle, #3042, ca 1940, from $22 to $28.00

TV lamp, egret, pearly white, #33509, 10x6x2", from $30 to ..$40.00

TV lamp, horse, pearly white, 12¼x11x6¼", from $30 to...$40.00

TV lamp, mallard duck in w/wings wide over grassy base (no planter), realistic colors, 14x9x9½", from $55 to..................$65.00

TV lamp/planter, white swan w/wings up, from $35 to.......$40.00

Vase, horse head, brown woodgrain, #225, 1959, 12½x4½", from $40 to $48.00

Vase, swan w/tall feathers together forming vase, white, #2321, 12¼"...$25.00

Magazines

There are lots of magazines around today, but unless they're in fine condition (clean, no missing or clipped pages, and very little other damage); have interesting features (cover illustrations, good advertising, or special-interest stories); or deal with sports greats, famous entertainers, or world-renowned personalities, they're worth very little. Issues printed prior to 1950 generally have value, and pre-1900 examples are now considered antique paper. Our values are for magazines in excellent condition with no label. Address labels on the fronts are acceptable, but if your magazine has one, follow these guidelines. Subtract 5% to 10% when the label is not intruding on the face of the cover. Deduct 20% if the label is on the face of an important cover and 30% to 40% if on the face of an important illustrator cover, thus ruining framing quality. For further information see *The Masters Price & Identification Guide to Old Magazines* (5th edition), *Life Magazines, 1898 to 1994; Saturday Evening Post, 1899 – 1965; Old Movie, TV, Radio Magazines, 1st edition* and several other up-to-the-minute guides covering specific magazine titles — all by Denis C. Jackson (See Directory, Magazines). We also recommend *Old Magazines Identification and Value Guide* by Richard E. Clear (Collector Books). See also TV Guides.

Online Publication: *The Illustrator Collector's News* Free web-use site, free classifieds
Denis C. Jackson, Editor
P.O. Box 6433
Kingman, AZ 86401
www.olypen.com/ticn

Argosy, 1939, January/February, Synthetic Men of Mars, from $100 to $200.00
Argosy, 1950, January - December, ea from $2.50 to $5.00
Automotive Digest, 1942-50, ea from $7.50 to $15.00
Best Western Magazine, 1935-57, w/Louis L'Amour story, ea from $15 to $30.00
Bride's Magazine, 1970 to present, from $5 to $10.00
Click Photo - Parade, 1938-44, ea from $10 to $15.00
Collier's The National Weekly, 1940-57, w/Arthur Conan Doyle story, from $50 to $300.00
Down Beat, 1934-59, from $15 to.......................................$22.00
Ebony, 1950-59, from $18 to $28.00
Esquire, 1960s-70s, from $25 to $30.00
Family Circle, 1940-1959, from $2.50 to $5.00
Fantastic Universe, 1953-1960, from $3.50 to $7.00
Farm Journal, 1939-1952, from $2.50 to...............................$5.00
Field & Stream, 1950-69, from $5 to $10.00
Film World, 1953-59, from $3 to $6.00
Fortune, 1950-59, from $7.50 to...$15.00
Frontier Stories, 1926-1953, ea from $10 to.......................$30.00
Girl From UNCLE Magazine, 1966-67, ea from $8 to........$14.00
Good Housekeeping, 1960 to present, ea from $2.50 to........$5.00

Grooves, 1979, December, Rolling Stones cover, with fan club poster inside, NM, $25.00. (Photo courtesy gasolinealleyantiques.com)

Hollywood Detective, 1943-50, ea from $25 to...................$50.00
Hot Rod Magazine, 1949, ea from $15 to $22.00

House Beautiful, 1940-59, from $7 to................................$12.00
Ladies' Home Journal, 1930-39, ea from $10 to $25.00
Ladies' Home Journal, 1940-49, ea from $5 to....................$20.00
Ladies' Home Journal, 1970 to present, ea from $1 to..........$8.00

Life, 1954, November 1, Dorothy Dandridge cover, EX, from $35.00 to $45.00. (Photo courtsy P.J. Gibbs)

Life, 1950-59, from $5 to...$10.00
Life, 1960-72, ea from $2.50 to..$5.00
Look, 1950-59, ea from $5 to..$10.00
Look, 1960-71, ea from $2.50 to...$5.00
Master Detective, 1940-50, ea from $5 to $10.00
McCall's Magazine, 1950-59, ea from $3.50 to.....................$7.00
McCall's Magazine, 1960 to present, ea from $1.50 to $3.00
Metropolitan a Monthly Review, 1935-59, ea from $2.50 to.$5.00
Motor Life, 1960-69, ea from $3.50 to..................................$7.00
Motor Trend, 1957-69, ea from $5 to..................................$10.00
Movie Mirror, 1940-43, ea from $15 to...............................$30.00
Movie Radio Guide, 1940-43, ea from $8 to $10.00
Movie Stars Parade, 1950-58, ea from $3.50 to $7.00
National Geographic, 1920-29, ea from $6 to $12.00
National Geographic, 1930-49, ea from $3 to $6.00
National Geographic, 1950 to present, ea from $1 to............$2.00
New Yorker, 1940-49, ea from $5 to....................................$10.00
New Yorker, 1950-59, ea from $2.50 to $5.00
New Yorker, 1960 to present, ea from $1 to...........................$2.00
Newsweek, 1950-59, ea from $2.50 to $5.00
Newsweek, 1960 to present, ea from $1 to $2.00
Outdoor Life, 1940-59, ea from $2.50 to $5.00
Photoplay, 1960-69, ea from $3.50 to $7.00
Photoplay, 1970 to present, ea from $1.50 to........................$3.00
Playboy, 1954, Volume 2, from $250 to $500.00
Playboy, 1955, Betty Page issue, from $200 to...................$400.00
Playboy, 1958-70, ea from $6 to $12.00
Playboy, 1980 to present, ea from $1 to $2.00
Popular Mechanics, 1940-59, ea from $2.50 to $5.00
Prairie Farmer, 1940-59, ea from $2.50 to $5.00
Radio Mirror, 1945-48, ea from $2.50 to $5.00
Saddle & Bridle, 1940-59, ea from $2.50 to $5.00
Saturday Evening Post, 1920-39, ea from $15 to $30.00

Saturday Evening Post, 1940-49, ea from $7.50 to **$15.00**
Saturday Evening Post, 1950-59, ea from $3.50 to **$7.00**
Saturday Evening Post, 1960 to present, ea from $1.50 to **$3.00**
Seventeen, 1950-59, ea from $5 to **$10.00**
Seventeen, 1960 to present, ea from $2.50 to **$5.00**
Silver Screen, 1940-49, ea from $10 to **$20.00**
Silver Screen, 1950-54, ea from $5 to **$10.00**

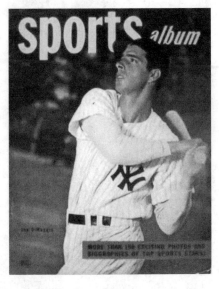

Sports Album, 1948, Joe DiMaggio cover, EX, $125.00. (Photo courtesy gasolinealleyantiques.com)

Sports Illustrated, 1955-79, ea from $5 to **$10.00**
Stocking Parade, 1937-43, ea from $15 to **$30.00**
Time, 1946-49, ea from $5 to... **$10.00**
Time, 1950-59, ea from $2.50 to... **$5.00**
Time, 1960 to present, ea from $1 to **$2.00**
Travel, 1940-59, ea from $5 to **$10.00**
Travel, 1960 to present, from $2.50 to.................................... **$5.00**
US News & World Report, 1948-59, ea from $2.50 to **$5.00**
Variety, 1940-49, ea from $3 to **$6.00**
Vogue, 1950-59, ea from $3.50 to **$7.00**
Vogue, 1960 to present, ea from $1.50 to............................... **$3.00**
Woman's Home Companion, 1940-57, ea from $3.50 to **$7.00**

Marbles

There are three broad categories of collectible marbles, the antique variety, machine-made, and contemporary marbles. Under those broad divisions are many classifications. Everett Grist delves into all three categories in his books called *Big Book of Marbles* and *Antique and Collectible Marbles* (Collector Books).

Sulfide marbles have figures (generally animals or birds) encased in the center. The glass is nearly always clear; a common example in excellent condition may run as low as $100.00, while those with an unusual subject or made of colored glass may go for more than $1,000.00. Many machine-made marbles are very reasonable, but if the colors are especially well placed and selected, good examples sell in excess of $50.00. Peltier comic character marbles often bring prices of $100.00 and up with Betty Boop, Moon Mullins, and Kayo being the rarest and most valuable (in that order). Watch for reproductions. New comic character marbles have the design printed on a large area of plain white glass with color swirled through the back and sides.

No matter where your interests lie, remember that condition is extremely important. From the nature of their use, mint-condition marbles are very rare and may be worth as much as three to five times more than one that is near-mint. Chipped and cracked marbles may be worth half or less, and some will be worthless. Polishing detracts considerably.

When no size is given, assume our values are for average-size marbles from ½" to 1" in excellent condition.

See also Akro Agate.

China, hand-painted design over glaze prior to 2nd firing, ⅝"...... **$100.00**
Christensen Agate, green Peewee... **$10.00**
Christensen Agate, green slag, ¾" **$10.00**
Christensen Agate, orange & yellow swirl, ¾" **$25.00**
Christensen Agate, red & yellow flames on green opaque core..**$200.00**
Christensen Agate, royal blue slag, ¹¹⁄₁₆" **$10.00**
Indian swirl, black glass w/colored swirls in earth tones, ⅝".... **$150.00**
Limeade corkscrew **$30.00**
Lutz type, blue opaque, gold swirl w/white borders & thin white swirls, ⅝" **$350.00**
Lutz type, clear w/gold-color surface swirls, blue & white borders, ⅝"...**$125.00**
Marble King, Cat-Eye Hybrid, shooter size........................... **$4.00**
Marble King, Cub Scout blue & yellow.................................. **$6.00**
Marble King, multicolor Rainbow **$4.00**
Marble King, Wasp, orange & black **$6.00**
Peppermint swirl, red, white & blue, ⅝"................................ **$100.00**
Sulfide, #1, 1¾" **$400.00**
Sulfide, child w/hammer, EX details, 1¾".............................. **$600.00**
Sulfide, crucifix, crudely made, 1¾" **$650.00**
Sulfide, eagle, 1¾", average value.. **$200.00**
Sulfide, owl w/spread wings, detailed feathers, 1¾" **$350.00**
Transparent swirl, double swirl ribbon core of red, yellow, light & dark blue & pink, ⅝" **$200.00**
Transparent swirl w/red core, blue & white outer lines, yellow threads, ⅝" **$60.00**

Transparent swirl, yellow latticino core, outer bands of red and white, ⅝", $325.00. (Photo courtesy Everett Grist)

Vitro Agate, prominent V, ea from $2 to **$10.00**
Vitro Agate, red, white & blue swirls, faded-looking colors ..... **$.50**

Mar-Crest Stoneware

The Western Stoneware Company of Monmouth, Illinois, made products for Marshall Burns, a Division of Technicolor (a distributor from Chicago), with the Marshall Burns trademark, 'Mar-Crest.' The most collectible of these wares is a line of old-fashioned oven-proof stoneware in the Warm Colorado Brown glaze. The pattern is called Daisy and Dot, though it is also referred to as Pennsylvania Dutch.

Bean pot, Daisy & Dot, shouldered, w/handles, lg, from $20 to **$30.00**
Bean pot, Daisy & Dot, shouldered, w/handles, 2½" **$20.00**
Bowl, cereal; Daisy & Dot on dark brown, from $7 to **$9.00**
Bowl, Daisy & Dot, sq, scarce, 3x6" **$85.00**
Bowl, Daisy & Dot, 10" **$17.50**
Bowl, divided vegetable; Daisy & Dot, from $16 to **$20.00**
Bowl, divided; pink w/embossed rings, 10x8", from $30 to . **$45.00**
Bowl, lug soup; Daisy & Dot, 2¼x4¾"+handle.................... **$8.00**
Bowl, mixing; Daisy & Dot, 8" **$15.00**
Bowl, mixing; Daisy & Dot, 9¾" **$22.50**
Carafe, Daisy & Dot, from $20 to....................................... **$25.00**
Casserole, Daisy & Dot, w/lid, 8".......................................**$28.00**
Casserole, Daisy & Dot, w/lid, 8", +warming stand, from $40 to .**$45.00**
Casserole, Nordic Mint, w/lid, 5½x8½" **$30.00**
Chip & dip set, Daisy & Dot, 12" plate & 5⅜" bowl **$78.00**
Cookie jar, Daisy & Dot, 7½x6", from $22 to **$30.00**

Cookie jar, Daisy and Dot, 11", $35.00.

Creamer & sugar bowl, Daisy & Dot, w/lid, from $25 to ...**$38.00**
Cup & saucer, Daisy & Dot, 3½x3¼", 6", from $6 to **$9.00**
Fondue pot, geometric bands on dark brown, w/lid & metal stand..**$85.00**
Lazy Susan, Daisy & Dot, 3-compartment, on stand, 11" dia, from $160 to **$185.00**
Mug, coffee; Daisy & Dot on dark brown, 3½" **$5.00**
Pie plate, Nordic Mint, 10" **$18.00**
Pitcher, Daisy & Dot, cylindrical, 6", from $12 to **$15.00**
Pitcher, Daisy & Dot, rounded form (not cylindrical), rare shape, 7" **$135.00**
Pitcher, pink ball form w/4 embossed rings, ice lip, 8" **$30.00**
Plate, Daisy & Dot, 3-compartment, 11" **$35.00**
Plate, Daisy & Dot, 9½", from $7 to **$12.00**
Plate, dinner; Nordic Mint, 9"..**$7.50**
Plate, salad; Nordic Mint, 7½" **$5.00**
Platter, Nordic Mint, 12" dia **$18.00**

Relish, Daisy & Dot, 6 wedge-shaped compartments, center handle, w/stand **$175.00**
Relish, Nordic Mint, oblong...**$20.00**
Salt & pepper shakers, Daisy & Dot, pr from $15 to **$20.00**
Snack set, Daisy & Dot, 9¾" plate w/inset for mug & 3¼x3½" mug **$45.00**
Teapot, Nordic Mint, multicolor leaf pattern on white **$45.00**
Teapot, pink ball sahpe w/4 stepped rings, 6x7½" **$40.00**

Pitcher, Daisy and Dot, 8", $30.00.

Max, Peter

Born in Germany in 1937, Peter Max came to the United States in 1953 where he later studied art in New York City. His work is colorful and his genre psychedelic. He is a prolific artist, best known for his designs from the '60s and '70s that typified the 'hippie' movement. In addition to his artwork, he has also designed housewares, clothing, toys, linens, etc. In the 1970s, commissioned by Iroquois China, he developed several lines of dinnerware in his own distinctive style. Today, many of those who were the youth of the hippie generation are active collectors of his work.

Ashtray, psychedelic figure on green in center on white ceramic, 3 rests, 5⅜" dia **$20.00**
Ashtray, white w/butterfly design, Iroquois China, 1x5" **$30.00**
Ashtray, white w/Dove in red & a white dove w/floral design, Iroquois China, 1¼x10" dia **$25.00**
Beach towel, planet w/stars & mushrooms, fringed edge, 1960s, EX **$60.00**
Belt buckle, LOVE, silver-tone metal, 1960s **$135.00**
Binder, 3-ring; butterfly design, 1960s, EX..........................**$25.00**
Book, Peter Max Poster Book, 24 full-color 11x16" prints, 1970 edition, EX...**$125.00**
Bowl, multicolored bubbles, flowers & mushrooms, 2x10½" ... **$85.00**
Catalog, JC Penney's Special Edition, artwork cover & throughout pages, 1969, 11x8", EX **$60.00**
Clock, ladies w/rainbow colors around heads on black background, red hands, General Electric, 1960s, 9" dia **$60.00**
Clock, psychedelic floral design, General Electric Model 8504, 1968, 9" dia, EX..**$100.00**
Cookie jar, Zero, Sigma, 1989, from $175 to **$250.00**

Cup, coffee; geometric design w/gold on rim, marked Bon Appetit, 4½" **$28.50**

Eyeglass case, smiling lips design **$70.00**

Fondue pot, green w/floral design, pot w/lid, stand & bottom plate, 1970s **$150.00**

Hat, visor style w/open top, stretchy strap fits around head, creased brim, bright colors, 7-Up advertising print, EX **$22.50**

Ice cream cooler, Borden Yogurt, zipper top w/plastic removeable liner, 1970s, 10x½x10½", EX+ **$150.00**

Jigsaw puzzle, Drummer, Life Magazine, Shisgall Enterprises Inc, 1970, 500 pcs, 20x13", EXIB **$40.00**

Jigsaw puzzle, Umbrella man, 550 pcs, 1999, 20x20", MIB (sealed) **$15.00**

Magazine, Life, Peter Max on cover, September 5, 1969, EX, from $10 to **$15.00**

Patch, Peace sign w/2 people & doves, 3x4" **$25.00**

Pillow, butterfly, inflatable vinyl, 1968-70, 16x16" **$45.00**

Pillow, running figure & world on red, inflatable vinyl, 16x16", from $35 to **$50.00**

Pin-back button, peace symbol w/doves & running figures, 2½" .. **$80.00**

Plaque, Brown Lady, painted porcelain, Franklin Mint, 1992, 16x13½" **$110.00**

Plate, bull's-eye design on glass, 9¼" **$60.00**

Plate, screened flower on smoked glass, ca 1980s?, 9½" **$90.00**

Poster, Bill Clinton Inaugural, An American Reunion, portrait before flag, 1993, 36x24"+mat & frame **$135.00**

Poster, Glove, authorized reprint, image: 14⅝x10", 16x11⅛" .. **$22.00**

Poster, Love, Peter Max Poster Corp, 1968, 36x24", EX.... **$215.00**

Poster, Man on the Moon, quote from R Goddard (1st space scientist), 36x24" **$60.00**

Poster, Nutriment Number Two, taken from poster book, 1970, 13³⁄₁₆x16" **$25.00**

Poster, NYC Marathon, runners, 1995, 33x21" **$120.00**

Poster, Pan Am, authorized reprint, image: 15½x10¼", 16x11⅛" .. **$22.00**

Poster, Peace, running figures & doves interact w/lg blue peace sign, 1970, 36x24" **$425.00**

Poster, Self Portrait, psychedelic imagery, marked Peter Max Poster Corp 1968, 36x24", from $300 to............................. **$400.00**

Poster, The Coach w/the 6 Insides, ca 1970, 36x26½", EX.... **$135.00**

Poster, 1994 World Cup Soccer, 36x24" **$60.00**

Poster book, contains 24 posters, 1970, 16x11", EX......... **$160.00**

Print, Profile w/Hat, plate #177 from book: The Art of Peter Max, double mat, in 17x15" frame **$175.00**

Saucepan, floral decor on red enamelware, wooden handle, w/lid.. **$40.00**

Scarf, butterfly design on green, silk, 21x21" **$40.00**

Scarf, figures floating in landscape, intact label, 14x42" **$55.00**

Scarf, Love, silk, 26x26"... **$55.00**

Scarf, Stars & Planet, red, white & blue, 22x21" **$40.00**

Scarf, Zodiac signs w/in circle on green, acetate, Made in Italy RM 3988 Peter Max, 1960s, 26x26", from $35 to............... **$50.00**

Sheet set, Tastemaker, blue w/doves & flowers, fitted & flat sheet+ 2 pillowcases, 1970s, MIP... **$160.00**

Shirt, multicolor cotton knit, Derail from Mondrian, 1986 c Peter Max 1988 Signature Series, Neomax, ¾-sleeves, NM.... **$38.00**

Stamps, Expo 74 World's Fair issue, 1974, full sheet of 40... **$95.00**

T-shirt, Dale Earnhardt, Takin' It to the Max print on black, cotton, adult's size **$17.50**

T-shirt, World Cup '94, socker player **$25.00**

Tote bag, LOVE design, vinyl, 15½x12½" dia.................... **$50.00**

Tray, LOVE design, enameled metal, 1¼x12¾", EX........... **$35.00**

Tray, tri-face w/Happy on head, enameled metal, 13", EX... **$30.00**

Wristwatch, Save the Rain Forests, black plastic band, white acrylic 2⅛" dia face, ca 1988, NM **$90.00**

Book, *Paper Airplane Book*, May, 1971, EX+, **$20.00**. (Photo courtesy Richard Synchef)

McCoy Pottery

This is probably the best-known of all American potteries, due to the wide variety of goods they produced from 1910 until the pottery finally closed only a few years ago.

They were located in Roseville, Ohio, the pottery center of the United States. They're most famous for their cookie jars, made in several hundred styles and variations. (For a listing of these, see the section entitled Cookie Jars.) McCoy is also well known for their figural planters, novelty kitchenware, and dinnerware.

They used a variety of marks over the years, but with little consistency, since it was a common practice to discontinue an item for awhile and then bring it out again decorated in a manner that would be in sync with current tastes. All of McCoy's marks were 'in the mold.' None were ink stamped, so very often the in-mold mark remained as it was when the mold was originally created. Most marks contain the McCoy name, though some of the early pieces were simply signed 'NM' for Nelson McCoy (Sanitary and Stoneware Company, the company's original title). Early stoneware pieces were sometimes impressed with a shield containing a number. If you have a piece with the Lancaster Colony Company mark (three curved lines — the left one beginning as a vertical and terminating as a horizontal, the other two formed as 'C's contained in the curve of the first), you'll know that your piece was made after the mid-'70s when McCoy was owned by that group. Today even these later pieces are becoming collectible.

If you'd like to learn more about this company, we recommend *McCoy Pottery, Volumes 1, 2,* and *3,* by Bob and Margaret Hanson and Craig Nissen. All are published by Collector Books.

A note regarding cookie jars: beware of *new* cookie jars marked McCoy. It seems that the original McCoy pottery never registered their trademark, and for several years it was legally used by a small company in Rockwood, Tennessee. Not only did they use the original mark, but they reproduced some of the original jars as well. If you're not an experienced collector, you may have trouble distinguishing the new from the old. Some (but not all) are dated #93, the '#' one last attempt to fool the novice, but there are differences to watch for. The new ones are slightly smaller in size, and the finish is often flawed. He has also used the McCoy mark on jars never produced by the original company, such as Little Red Riding Hood and the Luzianne mammy. Only lately did it become known that the last owners of the McCoy pottery actually did register the trademark; so, having to drop McCoy, he has since worked his way through two other marks: Brush-McCoy and and BJ Hull.

See Also Cookie Jars.

Advisor: Bob Hanson

Newsletter: *NM Xpress*
Carol Seman, Editor
8934 Brecksville Rd., Suite #406, Brecksville, OH 44141-2518
440-526-2094 (voice and fax)
McCjs@aol.com; http://members.aol.com/nmXpress

Figurine, angelfish, white or green, no mark, 1940s, 6", from $300.00 to $400.00. (Photo courtesy Margaret and Bob Hansen and Craig Nissen)

Ashtray, Zane's Truce Commemoration, McCoy mark, from $40 to **$50.00**

Bank, cats at the barrel, red, white, blue or yellow, NCP mark, from $70 to **$90.00**

Bank, Metz Premium Beer, barrel form, 6¼", from $35 to .. **$45.00**

Bank, Woodsy Owl, Give a Hoot...Don't Pollute, multicolor, 1974, from $100 to **$125.00**

Birdbath, blue or white speckled, 3 metal legs, 1950s-60s, 18x13", from $175 to **$200.00**

Bookends, lily, green w/multicolor decoration, 1948, 5½x5", from $125 to **$150.00**

Console set, Starburst Line, bowl & candleholders, marked MCP, 1972, 3-pc, from $80 to **$100.00**

Flower holder, Hands of Friendship, white w/hand-painted flowers, NM mark, 1930s-40s, 3x4", from $75 to **$150.00**

Flowerpot, Butterfly, various pastels, 1940s, 5", from $50 to.. **$75.00**

Flowerpot, embossed ribs, attached base, NM mark, 1940s, 3¾", from $25 to **$35.00**

Jardiniere, Butterfly, various pastels, 1940s, 7½", from $100 to **$150.00**

Jardiniere, swallows in relief on brown gloss, 7", from $90 to . **$125.00**

Jardiniere & pedestal, leaves & berries embossed on white, 10½", 18½", from $650 to....................................**$750.00**

Lamp base, Blossomtime, pink flowers & green leaves on white, ornate handles, 1946, 7", from $175 to.....................**$225.00**

Lamp base, brown onyx, handles, 1930s, from $175 to **$200.00**

Lazy Susan, green and brown glazes, 1970s, 12", $40.00. (Photo courtesy Margaret and Bob Hansen and Craig Nissen)

Oil jar, cobalt, NM mark, 1930s, 12", from $125 to.........**$200.00**

Oil jar, white w/blue interior, NM mark, 1940s, 12", from $125 to..**$200.00**

Pitcher, Butterfly, embossed decor on yellow, NM mark, 10", from $125 to **$200.00**

Pitcher, Hobnail, turquoise, pink or blue, ball form, early 1940s, 6", from $100 to **$150.00**

Pitcher, Hobnail, white, 1940s, 10", from $110 to...........**$160.00**

Pitcher, pig, green, 1940s, 5", from $700 to **$800.00**

Pitcher vase, parrot, green or brown spray, 1952, 7", from $175 to **$225.00**

Planter, baby crib, pink or blue, 1954, from $60 to............**$75.00**

Planter, bird dog pointing, white w/black spray, 1959, 7¼", from $135 to **$185.00**

Planter, donkey, brown, black & white (airbrushed), Floraline, 8x10¼", from $40 to..**$50.00**

Planter, Dutch shoe, bird on branches, Floraline, 8" L, from $18 to..**$25.00**

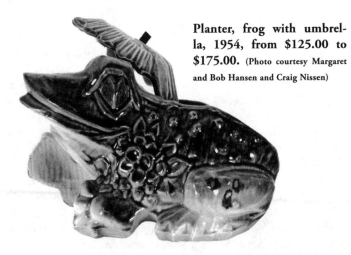

Planter, frog with umbrella, 1954, from $125.00 to $175.00. (Photo courtesy Margaret and Bob Hansen and Craig Nissen)

Planter, kitten w/ball of yarn, #3026, 7x5½", from $80 to **$100.00**

Planter, lamb, black gloss, NM mark, 1940s, 4½x6x3", from $40 to **$50.00**

Planter, Mammy sitting on scoop, 1953, 7½", from $150 to **$200.00**

Planter, orange resting on green leaves, from $50 to **$70.00**

Planter, panther, chartreuse, 1950, from $70 to **$90.00**

Planter, Plow Boy, figure on horse, brown & green blended, 1955, 7x8", from $100 to **$150.00**

Planter, swan, Antique Rose, brown on white, 7½", from $50 to....**$60.00**

Planter, turtle, green or chartreuse drip, McCoy mark, 1955, 12½x9", from $150 to **$200.00**

Planter, yellow ball shape w/Garden Club sticker, 1950s-60s, 5¾x4¾", from $25 to... **$35.00**

Planter, zebra & baby, black & white stripes, McCoy mark, 1956, 6½x8½", from $650 to **$800.00**

Planters/bookends, violin, white, turquoise or black matt, 1959, 10", from $100 to **$150.00**

Salt & pepper shakers, cucumber & bell pepper, 1954, pr from $75 to **$100.00**

Soup & sandwich set, turquoise, yellow, beige or oatmeal, cup & rectangular tray, 1963, from $35 to **$45.00**

Stretch animal, lion, cobalt, 1940s, 4x5¼", from $250 to....... **$350.00**

Teapot, leaves & berries embossed on pastel green, 1920s-30s, from $75 to **$100.00**

TV lamp/planter, rocking chair, green, 8½x5½", from $60 to.. **$80.00**

Vase, Blossomtime, pink flower & green leaves on yellow, urn form w/low handles, 1946, 6½", $50 to............................... **$65.00**

Vase, Butterfly, various pastels, handles, 1940s, 10", from $150 to.. **$225.00**

Vase, double tulips, yellow w/green leaves, late 1940s, 8", from $75 to **$100.00**

Vase, feather form, red or green, 1954, 8½", from $40 to....**$50.00**

Vase, flared cylinder w/embossed ribs, green or white, 1950s, 10", from $60 to **$70.00**

Vase, heart form w/embossed flowers, green matt, 1940s-50s, 6", from $60 to **$100.00**

Vase, Hobnail, green, V-shaped rim, NM mark, 9", from $125 to.. **$150.00**

Vase, ivy, green & brown on cream, twig handles, McCoy mark, 1953, 9", from $100 to....................................... **$150.00**

Vase, ivy, green on yellow, 1950s, 6", from $400 to.......... **$500.00**

Vase, pastel gloss, 4 sm scrolls at rim, flared foot, 1940s, 9", from $50 to **$90.00**

Vase, Sunburst Gold, ornate handles, flared foot, 6", from $30 to..**$40.00**

Vase, Swirl Line, orchid, flared foot, 1950s-60s, 8", from $25 to...**$30.00**

Violet pot, Tudor Rose, 1965, 2½", from $10 to................. **$15.00**

Wall pocket, bananas resting on leaves, yellow & green, 1950s, 7x6", from $125 to **$150.00**

Wall pocket, lady w/bonnet, standard decoration, 1940s, 8", from $200 to **$350.00**

Wall pocket, violin shape, brown, McCoy mark, mid-1950s, 10½", from $100 to **$130.00**

Melmac Dinnerware

The postwar era gave way to many new technologies in manufacturing. With the discovery that thermoplastics could be formed by the interaction of melamine and formaldehyde, Melmac was born. This colorful and decorative product found an eager market due to its style and affordability. Another attractive feature was its resistance to breakage. Who doesn't recall the sound it made as it bounced off the floor when you'd accidentally drop a piece.

Popularity began to wane: the dinnerware was found to fade with repeated washings, the edges could chip, and the surfaces could be scratched, stained, or burned. Melmac fell from favor in the late '60s and early '70s. At that time, it was restyled to imitate china that had become popular due to increased imports.

As always, demand and availability determine price. Our values are for items in mint condition only; pieces with scratches, chips, or stains have no value. Lines of similar value are grouped together. As there are many more manufacturers other than those listed, for a more thorough study of the subject we recommend *Melmac Dinnerware* by Gregory R. Zimmer and Alvin Daigle Jr.

See also Russel Wright.

Advisor: Gregory R. Zimmer (See Directory, Melmac)

Internet Information: Melmac Dinnerware Discussion List: www.egroups.com; search for Melmac Dinnerware

Aztec, Debonaire, Flite-Lane, Mar-Crest, Restraware, Rivieraware, Stetson, Westinghouse

Bowl, cereal; from $2 to..**$3.00**

Bowl, serving; from $4 to...**$5.00**

Creamer, from $1 to...**$2.00**

Gravy boat, from $5 to...**$6.00**

Salt & pepper shakers, pr from $4 to...................................**$5.00**

Tumbler, 6-oz, from $6 to..**$7.00**

Boontoon, Branchell, Brookpark, Harmony House, Prolon, Watertown Lifetime Ware

Bowl, soup; w/lid, from $5 to..**$6.00**

Creamer, from $5 to...**$6.00**

Gravy boat, from $6 to...**$8.00**

Jug, w/lid, from $20 to...**$25.00**

Plate, compartment; from $10 to...$12.00
Salad tongs, from $12 to...$15.00
Tumbler, 10-oz, from $12 to..$15.00

Branchell, divided serving bowl, from $8.00 to $10.00; butter dish, from $5.00 to $7.00; salt and pepper shakers, from $6.00 to $8.00 for the pair. (Photo courtesy Gregory R. Zimmer and Alvin Daigle Jr.)

Fostoria, Lucent

Fostoria, butter dish, from $15.00 to $18.00; sugar bowl, with lid, from $12.00 to $15.00; creamer, from $8.00 to $10.00. (Photo courtesy Gregory R. Zimmer and Alvin Daigle Jr.)

Bowl, serving; from $15 to..$18.00
Plate, bread; from $3 to..$4.00
Plate, dinner; from $6 to...$8.00
Relish tray, from $15 to..$18.00

Metlox Pottery

Founded in the late 1920s in Manhattan Beach, California, this company initially produced tile and commercial advertising signs. By the early '30s, their business in these areas had dwindled, and they began to concentrate their efforts on the manufacture of dinnerware, artware, and kitchenware. Carl Gibbs has authored

Collector's Encyclopedia of Metlox Potteries, which we recommend for more information.

Carl Romanelli was the designer responsible for modeling many of the figural pieces they made during the late '30s and early '40s. These items are usually imprinted with his signature and are very collectible today. Coming on strong is their line of 'Poppets,' made from the mid-'60s through the mid-'70s. There were 88 in all, whimsical, comical, sometimes grotesque. They represented characters ranging from the seven-piece Salvation Army Group to royalty, religious figures, policemen, and professionals. Many came with a name tag, some had paper labels, others backstamps. If you question a piece whose label is missing, a good clue to look for is pierced facial features.

Poppytrail and Vernonware were the trade names for their dinnerware lines. Among their more popular patterns were California Ivy, California Provincial, Red Rooster, Homestead Provincial, and the later embossed patterns, Sculptured Grape, Sculptured Zinnia, and Sculptured Daisy.

Some of their lines can be confusing. There are two 'rooster' lines, Red Rooster (red, orange, and brown) and California Provincial (this one is in dark green and burgundy), and three 'homestead' lines, Colonial Homestead (red, orange, and brown like the Red Rooster line) Homestead Provincial (dark green and burgundy like California Provincial), and Provincial Blue. See also Cookie Jars.

Advisor: Carl Gibbs, Jr. (See Directory, Metlox)

California Aztec, coffee carafe, w/stopper, 8" $200.00
California Aztec, bowl, lug soup; from $42 to $45.00
California Aztec, celery dish, from $75 to...........................$80.00
California Aztec, cup, juice; from $60 to $65.00
California Aztec, pitcher, water; from $275 to $300.00
California Ivy, butter dish, from $60 to $65.00
California Ivy, cup & saucer, 6-oz, 6", from $16 to $18.00
California Ivy, egg cup, from $35 to $38.00

California Ivy, salt and pepper shakers, large, from $20.00 to $25.00 for the pair.

California Ivy, salt & pepper shakers, sm, pr from $28 to....$30.00
California Ivy, tray, 2-tier, from $50 to $55.00
California Provincial, bowl, vegetable; 10", from $55 to......$60.00
California Provincial, coffeepot, 7-cup, from $125 to........$135.00
California Provincial, cruet set, 5-pc, complete, from $200 to ..$215.00

California Provincial, plate, luncheon; 9", from $28 to........**$30.00**
California Provincial, saucer, 6⅛", from $5 to......................**$6.00**
Colorstax, bowl, mixing; sm, 16-oz, from $30 to................**$35.00**
Colorstax, butter dish, from $50 to............................**$55.00**
Colorstax, cup, lg, 16-oz, from $22 to **$25.00**
Colorstax, flowerpot, 7", from $35 to **$40.00**
Colorstax, mug, 9-oz, from $16 to **$18.00**
Colorstax, plate, salad; 7¾", from $11 to.....................**$12.00**
Colorstax, salt & pepper shakers, sm, pr from $26 to **$28.00**

Della Robbia, cup and saucer, from $14.00 to $16.00; platter, 11", from $45.00 to $50.00; fast-stand gravy boat, from $35.00 to $40.00. (Photo courtesy Carl Gibbs, Jr.)

Homestead Provincial, cup & saucer, 6-oz, 6½", from $18 to .. **$20.00**
Homestead Provincial, gravy boat, 1-pt, from $45 to..........**$50.00**
Homestead Provincial, plate, luncheon; 7½", from $14 to...**$15.00**
Homestead Provincial, salt & pepper shakers, pr from $30 to .. **$32.00**
Homestead Provincial, soup tureen, w/lid, from $475 to...**$500.00**
Homestead Provincial, teapot, 7-cup, from $135 to..........**$145.00**
Provincial Blue, butter dish, from $75 to **$80.00**
Provincial Blue, pepper mill, from $55 to **$60.00**
Provincial Blue, pitcher, 1-qt, from $75 to......................**$85.00**
Provincial Blue, plate, dinner; 10", from $18 to.................**$20.00**
Provincial Blue, sprinkling can, from $95 to....................**$105.00**
Provincial Blue, tumbler, 11-oz, from $45 to **$50.00**
Provincial Blue, turkey platter, 22½", from $300 to **$325.00**
Red Rooster, bowl, salad; 11⅛", from $80 to....................**$85.00**
Red Rooster, buffet server, 12½", from $65 to...................**$70.00**
Red Rooster, butter dish, from $60 to.............................**$65.00**
Red Rooster, cookie jar, from $100 to............................**$110.00**
Red Rooster, gravy boat, 2-pt, from $35 to **$40.00**
Red Rooster, pitcher, 1½-pt, from $40 to **$50.00**
Sculptured Grape, coffeepot, 8-cup, from $100 to.............**$110.00**
Sculptured Grape, compote, footed, 8½", from $75 to........**$80.00**
Sculptured Grape, creamer, 10-oz, from $28 to **$30.00**
Sculptured Grape, plate, dinner; 10½", from $16 to...........**$18.00**
Sculptured grape, sugar bowl, w/lid, from $32 to **$35.00**
Woodland Gold, baker, oval, 11", from $45 to **$50.00**
Woodland Gold, bowl, fruit; 5⅜", from $12 to....................**$14.00**
Woodland Gold, plate, salad; 8", from $9 to **$10.00**
Woodland Gold, platter, oval, 11", from $35 to **$40.00**
Woodland Gold, salt & pepper shakers, pr from $24 to **$26.00**

Miscellaneous

Celadon, ashtray, gunmetal base, from $30 to...................**$35.00**
Celadon, bowl, 4½x7", from $65 to **$70.00**
Celadon, vase, 4½x5½", from $45 to **$50.00**
Disney figurine, Dumbo, sm, from $150 to....................**$175.00**
Disney figurine, Grumpy, Happy, or Sneezy, from $200 to **$250.00**
Disney figurine, Gus from Cinderella, from $225 to **$250.00**
Disney figurine, Pinocchio, from $400 to.........................**$450.00**
Giftware, Cabbage, chip & dip, green, 1980s, 12", from $65 to..**$75.00**
Giftware, Cabbage, soup bowl, 1980s, 8", from $18 to **$20.00**
Giftware, Cat platter, 1980s, from $85 to..........................**$95.00**
Giftware, Chicken individual server, w/lid, from $80 to **$85.00**
Giftware, Humpty Dumpty child's plate, 1980s, from $30 to .. **$35.00**
Giftware, Loveland clock, 1980s, from $90 to **$100.00**
Leaves of Enchantment, banana leaf, 24", from $45 to........**$50.00**
Leaves of Enchantment, lotus leaf, 11½", from $25 to **$30.00**
Miniature, bird, wings folded, from $80 to.......................**$130.00**
Miniature, Dodo bird, 6", from $100 to...........................**$140.00**
Miniature, elephant, 3½" L, from $75 to...........................**$125.00**
Miniature, otter, from $125 to......................................**$175.00**
Miniature, penguin, 2½", from $40 to **$60.00**
Modern Masterpiece, Confucious incense burner, 6", from $275
    to..**$285.00**
Modern Masterpiece, fan vase, 9", from $325 to...............**$375.00**
Modern Masterpiece, High Life mug, from $100 to **$125.00**
Nostalgia, Chevrolet, from $75 to...................................**$85.00**
Nostalgia, coachman, from $65 to **$70.00**
Nostalgia, drum table, from $40 to **$45.00**
Nostalgia, fire wagon, from $90 to.................................**$100.00**
Nostalgia, piano & lid, from $75 to.................................**$80.00**
Poppet, Angelina, angel, 7⅝", from $75 to........................**$85.00**

Poppet, Colleen, 7", from $45.00 to $55.00. (Photo courtesy Jeannie Fedock)

Poppet, Mickey, choir boy #1, from $40 to........................**$50.00**
Poppet, Sarah, choral lady #1, 7¾", from $75 to.................**$85.00**
Poppet, Tina, costumed girl, 8½", from $55 to...................**$65.00**

Topper, Skipper, sailor boy, from $70 to $80.00
Toppet, Ann, girl w/flowers, from $70 to..........................$80.00
Toppet, Arthur, knight, from $70 to.................................$80.00

Milk Bottles

Between the turn of the century and the 1950s, milk was bought and sold in glass bottles. Until the 1920s, the name and location of the dairy was embossed in the glass. After that it became commonplace to pyro-glaze (paint and fire) the lettering onto the surface. Farmers sometimes added a cow or some other graphic that represented the product or related to the name of the dairy.

Because so many of these glass bottles were destroyed when paper and plastic cartons became popular, they've become a scarce commodity, and today's collectors have begun to take notice of them. It's fun to see just how many you can find from your home state — or try getting one from every state in the union!

What makes for a good milk bottle? Collectors normally find the pyro-glaze decorations more desirable, since they're more visual. Bottles from dairies in their home state hold more interest for them, so naturally New Jersey bottles sell better there than they would in California, for instance. Green glass examples are unusual and often go for a premium; so do those with the embossed baby faces. (Watch for reproductions here!) Those with a 'Buy War Bonds' slogan or a patriotic message are always popular, and cream-tops are good as well. As the round pyro bottles from the 1930s and 1940s have become rarer and more costly, many newer collectors have turned their attention to the more common and much less expensive square quarts from the 1950s and 1960s.

Some collectors enjoy adding 'go-alongs' to enhance their collections, so the paper pull tops, advertising items that feature dairy bottles, and those old cream-top spoons will also interest them. The spoons usually sell for about $10.00 to $18.00 each.

Newsletter: *The Milk Route*
National Association of Milk Bottle Collectors, Inc.
PO Box 105, Blooming Grove, NY 10914
milkroute@yahoo.com

Newsletter: *Creamers*
Lloyd Bindscheattle
P.O. Box 11, Lake Villa, IL 60046-0011
Subscription: $5 per year

Bayer Milk Company, New Britain CT, black pyro, tall round qt .$85.00
Bessemer Creamery, Bessemer MI, blue pyro, round qt $110.00
Blakeney Dairy Grade A, Poplar Bluff MO, baby w/bottle, black pyro, round pt $100.00
Borden's Condensed Milk Company, eagle & Borden's embossed on clear, round qt...$45.00
Buy War Bonds, Windfield KS, red pyro, round pt $72.50
Clover Leaf Dairy, Ohio, policeman, boy & microscope, green pyro, cream top, qt...$55.00
Dairyland Health in Every Drop, Des Moines IA, red pyro, cream top, round qt...$110.00
Druley's Clarified Milk, Eaton OH, red pyro, tall round qt. $90.00

EM Dwyer Dairy, Weymouth, red pyro, baby-face cream top, sq qt...$40.00
Everett Milk & Ice Cream Co, Everett PA, orange pyro, sq ½-pt $55.00
Garden City Dairies, Missoula MT, brown & orange pyro, tall round qt $55.00
Gillespie's Dairy, Fort Bragg CA, brown pyro, 1946, tall round qt...$110.00
Grove's Dairy, Dallastown PA embossed on clear, round ½-pt .. $52.50
Joseph's Dairy, Harbeson DE, brown pyro, round qt $130.00
Longhorn Creamery, Abilene TX, longhorn, red pyro, round qt $60.00
Maid of California, Vallejo CA, embossed letters on clear, tall round qt...$48.00
McGill Dairy, McGregor IA, boy & dog, green pyro, tall round qt...$68.00
Meadow Gold, It Whips, red pyro, cream top, round pt......$42.50
Meadow Gold, red, gold & black pyro, round pt.................$80.00
Merced Dairy & Ice Co, Merced CA, black pyro, tall round qt..$55.00
Muller's Dairy, Caldwell ID, red pyro, round qt, EX $130.00
Muller's Rockford's Pioneer Dairy, black pyro, round qt $110.00
Mumper's Dairy, Elizabeth Town PA, cow w/piece of alfalfa, red & green pyro, tall sq qt $70.00
North Star, blue pyro, wide mouth pt..............................$75.00

O.H. Hoffmire & Son Dairy, Trumansburg, New York, red pyro child and Scottie dog, from $75.00 to $125.00. (Photo courtesy Candace Sten Davis and Patricia J. Baugh)

Old Health way, Fredericktown MO, red pyro, tall round qt .. $55.00
Orrco Farms, Liberty IN, red pyro, round ½-pt..................$40.00
People's Milk Co 70-78 E Ferry St, embossed letters on amber, round qt...$45.00
PJ Meyer, Dudley MA, embossed letters on clear, tall round qt ..$50.00
Ringsted Co-Op Creamery, Ringsted IA, red pyro, round qt....$88.00
Roosevelt Diary, Mesa AZ, red pyro, sq qt..........................$40.00
Sardis Creamer, V & plane on back, Sardis MS, green pyro, round qt $110.00
Trail's End, Shinglehouse PA, red pyro, tall round qt..........$80.00

Zimmerman's Dairy, Lehighton PA, embossed letters on clear, round pt **$50.00**

Miller Studios

Imported chalkware items began appearing in local variety stores in the early 1950s. Cheerfully painted hot pad holders, thermometers, wall plaques, and many other items offered lots of decorator appeal. While not all examples will be marked Miller Studios, good indications of that manufacturer are the holes on the back where stapled-on cardboard packaging has been torn away — thus leaving small holes. There should also be a looped wire hanger on the back, although a missing hanger does not seem to affect price. Copyright dates are often found on the sides. Miller Studios, located in New Philadelphia, Pennsylvania, are the only existing American firm that makes hand-finished wall plaques yet today. Although they had over 300 employees during the 1960s and 1970s, they presently have approximately 75. Because these items are made from material that often tends to chip, our values are suggested for examples in near mint condition. Collectors aware of this, however, generally accept interesting pieces without discounting values to any great extent. If the item you're evaluating is truly mint, you should add from 20% to 30% to our prices.

Bathometer, fish, green w/pink face & red lips, 1977 .... **$12.50**
Bathometer, poodle in tub, 1973 .... **$10.00**
Bathometer, skunk, 1954, 6½x8" **$30.00**
Memo holder, owl w/note pad & pencil, 7x6¾" **$10.00**
Plaque, boy in blue pajamas kneeling in prayer, 1984, 6x2½" . **$12.50**
Plaque, mushrooms (2 joined), yellow, dark orange & white, 1976, 6½x6" **$15.00**
Plaque, mushrooms (4) in cluster, yellow, white & green, 1978, 5" **$12.50**
Plaque, Recipes on brown box among vegetables & wooden spoon, 1981 .... **$17.50**
Plaque, sea horse, bright yellow & dark green, no date, 8½x4¾" .. **$15.00**
Plaque, swan, black & gold w/detailed wings, 1968, 8x10" ... **$12.50**
Plaques, baskets of daisies, brown & yellow w/green leaves, 5½x5½", pr **$15.00**
Plaques, bluebirds, blue & yellow, 1960, 4½x3", 3-pc set **$25.00**
Plaques, bluebirds on dogwood branch, 1970, 5x4", pr **$20.00**
Plaques, boy & girl, ea holding ear of corn, 1955, 5¼x5¾", pr .. **$25.00**
Plaques, dachshund heads, brown tones, 1961, 3¾x4⅛", pr .. **$17.50**
Plaques, Dutch boy & girl, 1958, 5¾", pr **$17.50**
Plaques, fruit, yellow, brown & green tones, 1970, 8x11½", 5¾x6¼", 5x6¼", 3-pc **$25.00**
Plaques, goldfish, pink, 1954, 5½x5½", pr **$12.50**
Plaques, kittens, pink & gray w/lg black eyes, 6⅛x4", pr **$20.00**
Plaques, No Matter Where I Serve My Guests It Seems They Like My Kitchen Best (in 2 parts), 1977, 8½x5½", pr **$12.50**
Plaques, palomino horse heads, 1961, 5¾x5", pr **$17.50**
Plaques, palomino horses on black textured background, 1967, 4½x8½", pr **$28.00**
Plaques, parrots on branches, bright multicolors, 1974, 14", 13", pr **$150.00**
Plaques, roosters w/ornate tail feathers, 1965, 12¼x5¾", 10x7½", pr **$15.00**

Plaques, swans in oval, blue tail feathers, 1965, 7x3½", pr... **$50.00**
Plaques, wine jug & fruit, 1967, 5½x5½", pr **$17.50**
Thermometer, fruit & Cheer Up! We All Have our Ups & Downs, 1978, 7x5½" **$10.00**
Thermometer, rooster weathervane, coppery brown tones, 1969 . **$22.50**

Thermometer, wishing well, brown, 1966, 7x6", $15.00.

Thermometer, woodpecker on side of tree, 1959, 7⅛x5½" .. **$28.00**

Model Kits

By far the majority of model kits were vehicular, and though worth collecting, especially when you can find them still mint in the box, the really big news are the figure kits. Most were made by Aurora during the 1960s. Especially hot are the movie monsters, though TV and comic strip character kits are popular with collectors too. As a rule of thumb, assembled kits are valued at about half as much as conservatively priced mint-in-box kits. The condition of the box is just as important as the contents, and top collectors will usually pay an additional 15% (sometimes even more) for a box that retains the factory plastic wrap still intact. *Schroeder's Toys, Antique to Modern* (Collector Books), contains prices and descriptions of hundreds of models by a variety of manufacturers.

Adams, Hawk Missile Battery, 1958, MIB **$70.00**
Addar, Evel Knievel, 1974, MIB **$50.00**
Addar, Planet of the Apes, 1974, Dr Zaius, MIB **$40.00**
Airfix, Sam-2 Missile, 1973, MIB **$40.00**
AMT, Flintstones Rock Crusher, 1974, MIB **$75.00**
AMT, Wackie Woodie Krazy Kar, 1960s, MIB **$85.00**
AMT/Ertl, Peterbilt 359 Truck, MIB **$35.00**
Aurora, Archie's Car, 1969, MIB **$100.00**
Aurora, Bloodthirsty Pirates, 1965, Blackbeard, MIB **$225.00**
Aurora, Chitty Chitty Bang Bang, 1965, assembled, EX **$40.00**
Aurora, Creature From the Black Lagoon, 1969, glow-in-the-dark, MIB **$200.00**
Aurora, Dracula, 1962, MIB **$300.00**
Aurora, Invaders, 1975, UFO, MIB **$75.00**
Aurora, Superman, 1963, assembled, EX **$45.00**
Aurora, Tonto, 1974, Comic Scenes, MIB **$75.00**
Bachmann, Fisher Boy, 1962, MIB **$80.00**

Bandai, Godzilla, 1984, MIB $50.00
Billiken, Frankenstein, 1988, MIB $150.00
Dark Horse, King Kong, 1992, vinyl, MIB $75.00
Eldon, Pink Panther, 1970s, MIB $75.00
Geometric Design, Lon Chaney Jr as the Wolfman, MIB $50.00
Hawk, Cherokee Sports Roadster, 1962, MIB $35.00
Hawk, Cobra II, 1950s, MIB $75.00
Horizon, Invisible Man, NMIB $50.00
Horizon, Marvel Universe, 1991 Dr Doom, MIB $45.00
Imai, Orguss, 1990 Incredible Hulk, MIB $45.00
Imai, Orguss, 1994, Cable, MIB $40.00
ITC, Dog Champions, 1959, German Shepherd, MIB $35.00
Life-Like, Corythosaurus, 1970s, MIB $20.00
Life-Like, Roman Chariot, 1970s, MIB $20.00
Lunar Models, Angry Red Planet, Giant Amoeba, MIB $100.00
Lunar Models, Lost in Space, Space Pod, MIB $125.00
Monogram, Blue Thunder Helicopter, 1984, MIB $30.00
Monogram, Sand Crab, 1969, MIB $50.00
MPC, Alien, 1979, MIB (sealed) $100.00
MPC, Batman, 1984, MIB (sealed) $40.00

MPC, Sweathogs Dream Machine, 1976, MIB, $50.00.

Pyro, Peacemaker 45, 1960, MIB (sealed) $100.00
Pyro, Surf's Up!, 1970, MIB $40.00
Revell, Alien Invader, 1979, w/lights, MIB (sealed) $50.00
Revell, Love Bug, 1970s, MIB $50.00
Revell, Penny Pincher VW Bug, 1980, MIB $35.00
Revell, US Army Nike Hercules, 1958, MIB $60.00
Screamin', Mars Attacks, Target Earth, assembled, NM $30.00
Screamin', Werewolf, MIB $100.00
Toy Biz, Thing, 1996, MIB $20.00
Tsukada, Ghostbusters, Stay Puft Man (sm), 1984, MIB $40.00
Tsukuda, Metaluna Mutant, MIB $100.00

Modern Mechanical Banks

The most popular (and expensive) type of bank with today's collectors are the mechanicals, so called because of the antics they perfrom when a coin is deposited. Over 300 models were pro-duced between the Civil War period and the first World War. On some, arms wave, legs kick, or mouths open to swallow up the coin — amusing nonsense intended by the inventor to encourage and reward thriftiness. Some of these original banks have been known to sell for as much as $20,000.00 — well out of the price range most of us can afford! So many opt for some of the modern mechanicals that are available on the collectibles market, including Book of Knowledge and James D. Capron, which are reproductions marked to indicate that they are indeed replicas. But beware — unmarked modern reproductions are common.

Advisor: Dan Iannotti (See Directory, Banks)

Always Did 'Spise a Mule, Boy on Bench, Book of Knowledge.. $175.00
Artillery Bank, Book of Knowledge, NM $225.00
Artillery Bank, NM $225.00
Bad Accident, James Capron, M $700.00
Boy on Trapeze, Book of Knowledge $295.00
Butting Buffalo, Book of Knowledge, M $250.00
Cat & Mouse, Book of Knowledge, NM $200.00
Clown on Globe, James Capron, M $650.00
Cow (kicking), Book of Knowledge, NM $250.00
Creedmore Bank, Book of Knowledge, M $250.00
Dentist Bank, Book of Knowledge, EX $125.00
Eagle & Eaglets, Book of Knowledge, M $225.00
Elephant, James Capron, M $225.00
Humpty Dumpty, Book of Knowledge, M $175.00
Indian & Bear, Book of Knowledge, M $225.00
Jonah & the Whale, Book of Knowledge, M $175.00
Leap Frog, Book of Knowledge, NM $225.00

Lion and Monkeys, James Capron, M, $700.00. (Photo courtesy Dan Iannotti)

Monkey, James Capron, MIB $200.00
Organ Bank (Boy & Girl), Book of Knowledge, NM $195.00
Owl (turns head), Book of Knowledge, NM $175.00
Paddy & the Pig, Book of Knowledge, NM $195.00
Professor Pug Frog's Great Bicycle Feat, James Capron, M $850.00
Punch & Judy, Book of Knowledge, NM $175.00
Tammany Bank, Book of Knowledge, NMIB $200.00

Teddy & the Bear, Book of Knowledge, NM $175.00
Trick Dog, James Capron, NM............................. $400.00
Uncle Remus, Book of Knowledge, M $195.00
US & Spain, Book of Knowledge, M $175.00
William Tell, Book of Knowledge, M $195.00

Mood Indigo by Inarco

This line of Japanase-made ceramics probably came out in the 1960s, and enough of it was produced that a considerable amount has reached the secondary market. Because of the interest today's collectors are exhibiting in items from the '60s and '70s, it's beginning to show up in malls and co-ops, and the displays are surprisingly attractive. The color of the glaze is an electric blue, and each piece is modeled as though it were built from stacks of various fruits. It was imported by Inarco (Cleveland, Ohio) and often bears that company's foil label.

Collectors are sticklers for condition (damaged items are worth very little, even if they are rare) and prefer pieces with a deep, rich blue color and dark numbers on the bottom that are very legible. All pieces carry a number, and most collectors use these to keep track of their acquisitions. In addition to the items described and evaluated below, here is a partial listing of other known pieces.

E-2373 — Oblong Pitcher, 3" x 6"
E-2374 — Covered Candy Dish, 9"
E-2719 — Relish Tray
E-3095 — Fluted Vase, 7¾"
E-3145 — Pitcher, 6"
E-3445 — Plate, 9½"
E-3462 — Pedestal Cake Plate, 9½"
E-4011 — Butter Dish, 7½"

These pieces can be bought for as little as $5.00 to as much as $75.00. Prices vary widely, and bargains can still be had at many flea markets and garage sales.

Ashtray, rest in ea corner, E-4283, 9" $25.00
Bell, 5" $15.00
Bowl, fruit; E-3870, 5x11x6½" $30.00
Bud vase, E-3096, 8", from $20 to $22.50
Cake plate, footed, E-3462, 2¾x9⅜" $50.00
Candleholders, goblet shape, 4½", pr.................................... $28.00
Candleholders, owl figural, E-4612, 6", pr............................... $20.00
Candy dish, molded as 2 curved leaves w/fruit to side, 8".... $20.00
Candy jar, cylindrical, footed, w/lid, 9½" $45.00
Centerpiece, stacked-up fruit on ribbed incurvate base, 12x6" $25.00
Cigarette lighter, E-3100, 3¾" $22.00
Coffee cup, E-2431, 4", from $4 to $6.00
Cookie jar/canister, E-2374, 8" $18.00
Creamer & sugar bowl, w/lid, from $10 to $12.00
Cruet, E-3098, 7½" $28.00
Dish, footed, w/lid, E-2375, 6".. $15.00
Dish, oval, E-2376, 8½x5¾" $18.00
Figurine, E-2883, cat seated, rare, 14½" $75.00
Gravy boat, E-2373, 6½" $15.00
Jar, cylindrical, w/lid, 6½" $15.00
Ladle, 9¾" $25.00

Lavabo, 2-pc: handled covered vase (11") over ½-bowl shape, 5x9", from $35 to $45.00
.... $12.00
Mug, E-4489, 5".. $25.00
Oil lamp, E-3267, frosted shade, 9½" $15.00
Pitcher, E-2853, footed, 6" $15.00
Pitcher, E-5240, 4", w/saucer undertray............................. $18.00
Pitcher, footed, E-2429, 6½" $18.00
Planter, donkey pulling cart, 6x7¾" $12.00
Planter, hexagonal foot, #3097, 4½x5" $30.00
Plate, hanging; allover fruit, E-2432, 10" $45.00
Platter, 15x10" $12.00
Salt & pepper shakers, E-2371, 3½", pr............................. $22.00
Soap dish, cherub sits on side of shell, E-4656, 4¾" $22.00
Teapot, E-2430, 8"... $30.00
Tray, divided, E-2728, 12x6" $40.00
Tray, shell shape, 3-compartment, E-4555 .... $10.00
Trivet, 6" dia...

Tureen/covered dish, E-3379, $30.00.

Moon and Star

Moon and Star (originally called Palace) was first produced in the 1880s by John Adams & Company of Pittsburgh. But because the glassware was so heavy to transport, it was made for only a few years. In the 1960s, Joseph Weishar of Wheeling, West Virginia, owner of Island Mould & Machine Company, reproduced some of the original molds and incorporated the pattern into approximately 40 new and different items. Two of the largest distributors of this line were L.E. Smith of Mt. Pleasant, Pennsylvania, who pressed their own glass, and L.G. Wright of New Martinsville, West Virginia, who had theirs pressed by Fostoria and Fenton. Both companies carried a large and varied assortment of shapes and colors. Several other companies were involved in its manufacture as well, especially of the smaller items. All in all, there may be as many as 100 different pieces, plenty to keep you involved and excited as you do your searching.

The glassware is already collectible, even though it is still being made on a limited basis. Colors you'll see most often are amberina (yellow shading to orange-red), green, amber, crystal, light blue, and ruby. Pieces in ruby and light blue are most popular and harder to find than the other colors, which seem to be abundant. Purple, pink, cobalt, amethyst, tan slag, and light green and blue opalescent were made, too, but on a lesser scale.

Current L.E. Smith catalogs contain a dozen or so pieces that are still available in crystal, pink, cobalt (lighter than the old shade), and these colors with an iridized finish. A new color was introduced in 1992, teal green, and the water set in sapphire blue opalescent was pressed in 1993 by Weishar Enterprises. They are now producing limited editions in various colors and shapes, but they are marking their glassware 'Weishar,' to distinguish it from the old line. Cranberry Ice (light transparent pink) was introduced in 1994.

Values are given with a wide range, reflecting not only the color preferences of collectors but also supply and demand. Use the high end to evaluate ruby and light blue; amber and green are represented by the lower end of the range, and amberina values fall near mid-range.

Ashtray, allover pattern, moons form scallops along rim, 4 rests, 8" dia, from $16 to..$25.00
Ashtray, moons at rim, star in base, 6-sided, 5½", from $18 to..$28.00
Ashtray, moons at rim, star in base, 6-sided, 8½", from $24 to..$32.00
Banana boat, allover pattern, moons form scallops along rim, 12", from $30 to..$45.00
Basket, allover pattern, moons form scallops along rim, solid handle, 5", from $30 to..$45.00
Basket, allover pattern, moons form scallops along rim, solid handle, 6", from $30 to..$40.00
Basket, allover pattern, moons form scallops along rim, solid handle, 9", from $40 to..$55.00
Basket, allover pattern, moons form scallops along rim, split handle, 9x6", from $90 to..$125.00
Bowl, allover pattern, footed, crimped rim, 7½", from $20 to....$30.00
Bowl, allover pattern, footed, scalloped rim, 3x5", from $18 to ...$25.00
Bowl, allover pattern, footed, scalloped rim, 5x9½", from $30 to..$45.00
Bud vase, 6½", from $16 to..$25.00
Butter dish, allover pattern, stars form scallops along rim of base, star finial, oval, ¼-lb, 8½", from $55 to..$75.00
Butter/cheese dish, patterned lid, plain base, 7" dia, from $45 to..$65.00
Cake salver, allover pattern w/scalloped rim, raised foot w/scalloped edge, 5x12" dia, from $50 to..$65.00
Cake stand, allover pattern, plate removes from standard, 2-pc, 11" dia, from $70 to..$90.00
Candle lamp, patterned shade, clear base & cup, 7¾x4½", from $30 to..$45.00
Candle lamp, patterned shade & base, plain insert, 9", from $45 to..$60.00
Candleholder, allover pattern, bowl style w/ring handle, 2x5½", ea from $12 to..$18.00
Candleholders, allover pattern, flared base, 4½", pr from $20 to . $35.00
Candy dish, allover pattern on base & lid, footed ball shape, 6", from $25 to..$45.00
Canister, allover pattern, 1-lb or 2-lb, from $10 to $20.00
Canister, allover pattern, 3½-lb or 5-lb, from $30 to...........$40.00
Chandelier, ruffled dome shape w/allover pattern, amber, 10", from $60 to..$70.00
Cheese dish, patterned base, clear plain lid, 9½", from $50 to.. $65.00

Compote, allover pattern, raised foot, patterned lid & finial, 7½x6", from $25 to..$35.00
Compote, allover pattern, raised foot on stem, patterned lid & finial, 10x6", from $45 to..$55.00
Compote, allover pattern, scalloped foot on stem, patterned lid & finial, 8x4", from $25 to..$38.00
Compote, allover pattern, scalloped rim, footed, 5x6½", from $10 to..$20.00
Compote, allover pattern, scalloped rim, footed, 7x10", from $25 to..$40.00

Compote, crimped rim, 7¾x6½", from $22.00 to $30.00.

Console bowl, allover pattern, scalloped rim, flared foot w/flat edge, 8", from $20 to..$35.00
Creamer & sugar bowl (open), disk foot, sm, from $15 to .. $30.00
Cruet, vinegar; 6¾", from $50 to $65.00
Egg plate, from $35 to..$55.00
Epergne, allover pattern, 2-pc, 9", from $75 to.................$120.00

Fairy lamp, cylindrical dome-top shade, 6", $25.00.

Goblet, water; plain rim & foot, 5¾", from $12 to $16.00

Jardiniere/cracker jar, allover pattern, patterned lid & finial, 7¼", from $60 to **$100.00**

Jelly dish, patterned body w/plain flat rim & disk foot, patterned lid & finial, 6¾x3½", from $25 to **$35.00**

Lamp, miniature; amber, from $100 to.............................**$125.00**

Lamp, miniature; blue, from $165 to...................................**$190.00**

Lamp, miniature; red, from $175 to **$200.00**

Lamp, oil or electric; allover pattern, all original, red or light blue, 24", minimum value...........................**$300.00**

Lamp, oil; patterned hurricane shade, oval base w/handle, 12", from $45 to **$65.00**

Nappy, allover pattern, crimped rim, 2¾x6", from $18 to ...**$28.00**

Pitcher, straight sides, 1-qt, 7½", from $45 to **$85.00**

Plate, patterned body & center, smooth rim, 8", from $30 to .. **$60.00**

Relish bowl, 6 lg scallops form allover pattern, 1½x8" L, from $25 to **$40.00**

Relish tray, patterned moons form scalloped rim, star in base, rectangular, 8", from $30 to **$50.00**

Rose bowl, allover pattern, scalloped incurvate rim, 3x4½", from $35 to **$50.00**

Soap dish, allover pattern, oval, 2x6", from $9 to **$12.00**

Spooner, allover pattern, footed, 5½x4", from $60 to..........**$75.00**

Sugar bowl, allover pattern, straight sides, patterned lid & finial, scalloped foot, 8x4½", from $35 to **$50.00**

Sugar/cheese shaker, allover pattern, chrome lid, 4½", from $30 to...**$45.00**

Syrup pitcher, allover pattern, metal lid, 4½x3½", from $45 to... **$65.00**

Tumbler, juice; no pattern at rim or on disk foot, 5-oz, 3½", from $10 to...**$18.00**

Tumbler, no pattern at rim or on disk foot, 6½", from $20 to . **$28.00**

Vase, pattern near top, ruffled rim, disk foot, 6", from $22 to ..**$30.00**

Mortens Studios

During the 1940s, a Swedish sculptor by the name of Oscar Mortens left his native country and moved to the United States, settling in Arizona. Along with his partner, Gunnar Thelin, they founded the Mortens Studios, a firm that specialized in the manufacture of animal figurines. Though he preferred dogs of all breeds, horses, cats, and wild animals were made, too, but on a much smaller scale.

The material he used was a plaster-like composition molded over a wire framework for support and reinforcement. Crazing is common, and our values reflect pieces with a moderate amount, but be sure to check for more serious damage before you buy. Most pieces are marked with either an ink stamp or a paper label.

Bay pup, recumbent, unclipped ears, 5½" L **$65.00**

Bedlington terrier, standing, 3½x5" **$165.00**

Black Labrador retriever, standing, 6¾", from $70 to **$85.00**

Bookends, playful bears, #305, 5½x4½", from $75 to.......**$100.00**

Boston terrier, seated, 3¾x3½" **$55.00**

Boxer (male) dog, standing, 5½" **$85.00**

Boxer dog seated, brown tones w/black muzzle, 6½x5" **$68.00**

Chihuahua, standing, golden brown, 5½x6½" **$75.00**

Chihuahua head, plaque, Mortens 3-D Head Studios, 5½x6"..**$120.00**

Cocker spaniel, standing, golden brown, 5½x7¼" **$65.00**

Cocker spaniel pup, seated, 2¾x3¼" **$30.00**

Collie, recumbent, 5¼x5¼" **$80.00**

English bulldog, standing, 3½x6", from $65 to **$75.00**

German shepherd puppy, seated, 3½x2¼" **$75.00**

Horse, black w/white socks, striding, 7½", from $70 to **$85.00**

Horse, palomino, left foreleg extended, head up, Royal Design decal, 5", from $80 to **$95.00**

Horse, wild stallion, on base, #718, 9½", from $95 to **$110.00**

Irish setter plaque, 7x8½" **$100.00**

Lion, striding, 12" L, from $95 to **$120.00**

Panther, slightly rearing, 12½" L, from $120 to.................**$145.00**

Pekingese, lying on belly, 2½" L, from $45 to.....................**$55.00**

Pekingese, standing, brown tones, 3x4½" **$60.00**

Pug dog, w/label, 4½x5½" **$65.00**

Saint Bernard, standing, 6¾" **$75.00**

Wire-Haired Terrier, standing, 5¼x6½" **$60.00**

Boxer, seated, fairly common, 6", $75.00.

Morton Pottery

Six different potteries operated in Morton, Illinois, during a period of 99 years. The first pottery, established by six Rapp brothers who had immigrated from Germany in the mid-1870s, was named Morton Pottery Works. It was in operation from 1877 to 1915 when it was reorganized and renamed Morton Earthenware Company. Its operation, 1915 – 1917, was curtailed by World War I. Cliftwood Art Potteries, Inc. was the second pottery to be established. It operated from 1920 until 1940 when it was sold and renamed Midwest Potteries, Inc. In March 1944 the pottery burned and was never rebuilt. Morton Pottery Company was the longest running of Morton's potteries. It was in operation from 1922 until 1976. The last pottery to open was the American Art Potteries. It was in production from 1947 until 1961.

All of Morton's potteries were spin-offs from the original Rapp brothers. Second, third, and fourth generation Rapps followed the tradition of their ancestors to produce a wide variety of pottery. Rockingham and yellow ware to Art Deco, giftwares, and novelties were produced by Morton's potteries.

To learn more about these companies, we recommend *Morton Potteries: 99 Years, Vol. II,* by Doris and Burdell Hall.

Advisors: Doris and Burdell Hall (See Directory, Morton Pottery)

Morton Pottery Works — Morton Earthenware Company, 1877 – 1917

Bank, acorn shape, cobalt, 3¼" $65.00
Bowl, rice nappy, yellow ware, fluted, 8" $80.00
Chamber pot, yellow ware, miniature $50.00
Coffeepot, dripolator, brown Rockingham, sm infuser, 10-cup....$90.00
Crock, brown Rockingham, marked, 2-gal...............$60.00
Cuspidor, brown, 7"...$50.00
Marble, brown, Rockingham, 4¼" $35.00
Marble, cobalt, 4¼" $45.00
Miniature, creamer, brown Rockingham, 1¾" $45.00
Miniature, milk jug, cobalt, 4½".............................$60.00
Teapot, Rebecca at the Well, brown Rockingham, 8½-pt...$150.00

Cliftwood Art Potteries, Inc., 1920 – 1940

Bean pot, Old Rose, individual $10.00
Bowl, deep bulb, blue/gray, 6" $24.00
Bowl, sweetmeat; yellow/green drip, w/lid, 2x4¾x4¾" $40.00
Candlesticks, cobalt semi-lustre, 7", pr...................$50.00
Cardholder, elephant w/side pockets, cobalt, 5¾x4x5" $90.00
Figurine, American eagle, natural colors spray glaze, 8½" ..$150.00
Figurine, cat, reclining, brown drip, 6½" $45.00
Figurine, lion, gold/brown, miniature, 1¾x4"...........$50.00
Flower frog, Lorelei, blue/Mulberry drip, 6½" $75.00
Flower frog, turtle, blue/Mulberry drip, 5½" $30.00
Lamp, bulb w/embossed lovebirds, jade green, w/harp, 20"....$60.00
Planter, police dog, open back, white matt, 5" $30.00
Salt & pepper shakers, range; yellow & green drip over white, 5", pr...$30.00
Vase, peacock feather w/twig handles, turquoise matt, 15½" ...$55.00
Wall pocket, conical, blue & mulberry, #123, 6x2¾" $55.00
Wall pocket, tree trunk w/3 openings, chocolate drip, 8½"..$80.00

Midwest Potteries, Inc., 1940 – 1944

Figurine, sailfish, airbrushed blue and yellow, 9", $45.00.
(Photo courtesy Doris and Burdell Hall)

Candleholder, Jack-be-nimble type, lime green, w/handle, 7", ea $24.00
Creamer, cow figural, brown drip w/yellow handle, 5".........$30.00
Figurine, camel, tan, 8½"..$30.00
Figurine, cockatoo, yellow w/green drip, on pedestal, 6"......$24.00
Figurine, Irish setter, brown drip, green base, 4½" $35.00
Figurine, sunfish, airbrushed brown & yellow, 11" $50.00
Figurine, tiger, yellow w/brown stripes, 6x10".....................$40.00
Miniature, polar bear, white, 2½x1¾" $20.00
Pitcher, cow, tail handle, white w/gold, 4½" $25.00
Pitcher, duck figural w/cattail handle, brown & gray spray, 10" ...$50.00
Planter, elephant, blue & yellow drip, 5½x6¾" $20.00
Plaque, African native, male, black glossy, 9" $50.00

Morton Pottery Company, 1922 – 1976

Ashtray, hexagon, red, Nixon, 3¾" $40.00
Ashtray, teardrop, Rival Crock Pot, 6" $20.00
Bank, kitten reclining, gray, 4x6" $25.00
Bank, pig, wall hanger, blue $40.00
Bank, Scottie dog, black, 7" $22.00
Christmas planter, Santa's boot, red & white, #676 ....$24.00
Cookie jar, clown, straw hat lid................................$75.00
Cookie jar, fruit basket, natural-color fruit in green basket ..$55.00
Figurine, fawn, brown spray, 7x5x2".........................$15.00
Grass grower, GI, HI Buddy $25.00
Honey jug, underglaze flowers & bee, Herm's Honey $50.00
Lamp, teddy bear $45.00

Planter, sleigh, white with hand-painted holly and berries, #3015, $24.00. (Photo courtesy Doris and Burdell Hall)

Stein, barrel form, brown Rockingham, advertising embossed on side $24.00
Water fountain figure, fish, pink $40.00

American Art Potteries, 1947 – 1963

Bottle, crown shape, yellow & gray spray, 6" $24.00
Candlestick, free-form, green, w/3 cups, #141, 8x9", ea $40.00
Creamer, bird figural, tail forms handle, spray glaze, 4".......$24.00
Doll parts, head, arms & legs, hand painted, 3½", 6" dia....$72.00
Figurine, Afghan hounds, cobalt, 15", pr...........................$55.00

Figurine, Hampshire hog, natural colors, 5½", $50.00. (Photo courtesy Doris and Burdell Hall)

Figurine, horse rearing, brown w/green spray, #501, 11½" .. **$30.00**
Flower bowl, bullet form, black & gray spray, 3½x12" **$20.00**
Flower frog, titmouse on raised disk, mauve/yellow spray, 8" . **$30.00**
Honey jug, 14k gold, #50G, 5½" **$25.00**
Lamp, TV; panther, black **$40.00**
Lamp, TV; 2 afghan hounds, cobalt, 15" **$75.00**
Planter, deer reclining by stump, green w/brown spray **$24.00**
Planter, quail, natural colors... **$45.00**
Planter, teddy bear on 3 building blocks, white, pink & blue, 12x4x4" **$30.00**
Vase, ewer form, pink, 14" **$20.00**
Vase, swan w/elongated neck, green & yellow spray w/gold, 11" **$25.00**
Vase, 4 elephant tusks, gray & white spray, #215, 12½" **$40.00**

Moss Rose

Though a Moss Rose pattern has been produced by Staffordshire and American pottery companies alike since the mid-1800s, the ware we're dealing with here has a much different appearance. The pattern consists of a pink briar rose with dark green mossy leaves on stark white glaze. Very often it is trimmed in gold. In addition to dinnerware, many accessories and novelties were also made. It was a popular product of Japanese manufacturers from the 1950s on, and even today giftware catalogs show a few Moss Rose items.

Refer to *Schroeder's Antiques Price Guide* (Collector Books) for information on the early Moss Rose pattern. All the items listed below were produced in Japan unless noted otherwise.

Bell, heart finial w/gold trim, Golden Crown, Made in England... **$15.00**
Bottle, perfume; w/stopper & tray, Made in Japan, 5½", 5½" dia **$30.00**
Bowl, dessert; Royal Rose, 5½" **$5.00**
Bowl, Johann Haviland, 3x8½" **$40.00**
Bowl, scalloped rim w/5 reticulated areas, Rosenthal, 1½x7¾" **$35.00**
Bowl, soup; Johann Havilind, 7½", set of 4, MIB **$27.50**

Bowl, vegetable; pierced handles, Pompadour, Rosenthal, 8⅝" . **$27.50**
Bowl, vegetable; w/lid, Pompadour, Rosenthal, 1-qt **$70.00**

Bowl, vegetable; with lid, Rosenthal, 7x9x4", $75.00.

Butter dish, rectangular, gold trim, 2½x6x3" **$22.50**
Candleholders, cornucopia shape, unmarked, 1940s, 3¼x3¼", pr.. **$45.00**
Candy dish, 2-compartment, tab handles, gold trim, unmarked Japan, 7½" **$18.00**
Coffeepot, demitasse; silver base, Rosenthal **$65.00**
Coffeepot, gold trim, Johann Haviland, 11" **$65.00**
Coffeepot, Pompadour shape, Rosenthal, 10¾", from $65 to... **$80.00**
Condiment dish, w/lid, spoon & underplate, Japan mark, 4½", 5¼" dia... **$45.00**
Condiment dish, w/lid & spoon, unmarked Japan, 4½" **$24.00**
Creamer & sugar bowl, gold trim, ornate handles, gold trim, unmarked Japan, 5¼", 5" **$18.00**
Creamer & sugar bowl, gold trim, simple handle, SM-41 mark on ea **$15.00**
Creamer & sugar bowl, w/lid, Ucagco **$15.00**
Cup & saucer, demitasse; footed, blue Japan sticker, 2½x3¼", 5½" **$28.00**
Cup & saucer, demitasse; gold trim, ornate handle, unmarked. **$12.50**
Cup & saucer, demitasse; Sealy China Made in Japan.......... **$15.00**
Cup & saucer, unmarked Japan, 1940s, 2¼x3¾", 5½", 6b for **$75.00**
Egg coddler, w/lid, unmarked Japan, 4" **$20.00**
Egg cup, gold scalloped edge, footed, unmarked, 1960s, 2¼" ... **$9.00**
Gravy boat, attached underplate, Pompadour, Rosenthal, 5x9"... **$30.00**
Gravy boat, attached underplate, Thames China Japan, 7½x7½"... **$22.50**
Gravy boat, separate undertray, Johann Haviland, 5x9½x4"... **$22.50**
Oil lamp, Aladdin style, gold trim, Japan, 8" w/glass shade... **$35.00**
Oil lamp, Aladdin style, milk glass shade, Japan, 7x5¼" **$50.00**
Plate, dinner; gold trim, Sango Japan, 10" **$15.00**
Plate, dinner; Johann Haviland, 10", 4 for........................ **$40.00**
Plate, salad; Johann Haviland, 8", 4 for **$25.00**
Platter, Johann Haviland, 12¾x9½" **$27.50**
Platter, scalloped rim, gold trim, Ucagco China, 14¼x10¼".. **$40.00**
Powder box, rectangular, gold trim, unmarked Japan, 4½" long.. **$20.00**
Relish tray, 3-part w/center handle, Gold Castle, 1950s, 7" dia .. **$80.00**
Salt & pepper shakers, bulbous base, silver top & base, Rosenthal, 5½x2¼" dia, pr... **$52.50**

318

Salt & pepper shakers, Johann Haviland, 4½", pr................$25.00
Salt cellar, silver foot, Rosenthal, 1¾", w/3" spoon $40.00
Smoke set, 4 trays in rectangular holder, Gold Bond China ..$35.00
Snack set, plate w/indent & cup, gold trim, Ucagco Japan, 8",
    2x3½" $15.00
Tea bag holder, I'll Hold the Bag on teapot shape, Japan, 8 for...$30.00
Tea service, Gold Coast China Japan, serves 6, 46-pc set $65.00
Teapot, electric, Japan, 1960s, 7" $25.00
Teapot, ornate mold & handles, Pompadour, Rosenthal,
    7x10"... $200.00
Teapot, pearl lustre w/gold trim, individual $15.00
Teapot, Royal Sealy, 8½" $20.00
Teapot, Ucagco, 7½" $24.00
Tidbit tray, 2-tier, Johann Haviland, 6¼" & 10" plates $35.00
Tureen, w/handles & lid, Johann Haviland, 7x9"................$50.00
Vase, ruffled rim w/gold trim, handles, sm foot, 5¾x5¼"....$45.00

Motion Clocks (Electric)

Novelty clocks with some type of motion or animation were popular in spring-powered or wind-up form for hundreds of years. Today they bring thousands of dollars when sold. Electric-powered or motor-driven clocks first appeared in the late 1930s and were produced until quartz clocks became the standard, with the 1950s being the era during which they reached the height of their production.

Four companies led their field. They were Mastercrafters, United, Haddon, and Spartus in order of productivity. Mastercrafters was the earliest and longest-lived, making clocks from the late '40s until the late '80s. (They did, however, drop out of business several times during this long period.) United began making clocks in the early '50s and continued until the early '60s. Haddon followed in the same time frame, and Spartus was in production from the late '50s until the mid-'60s.

These clocks are well represented in the listings that follow; prices are for examples in excellent condition and working. With an average age of 40 years, many now need repair. Dried-out grease and dirt easily cause movements and motions not to function. The other nemesis of many motion clocks is deterioration of the fiber gears. Originally intended to keep the clocks quiet, fiber gears have not held up like their metal counterparts. For fully restored clocks, add $50.00 to $75.00 to our values. (Full restoration includes complete cleaning of motor and movement, repair of same; cleaning and polishing face and bezel; cleaning and polishing case and repairing if necessary; and installing new line cord, plug, and light bulb if needed.) Brown is the most common case color for plastic clocks. Add 10% to 20% or more for cases in onyx (mint green) or any light shade. If any parts noted below are missing, value can drop one-third to one-half. We must stress that 'as is' clocks will not bring these prices. Deteriorated, nonworking clocks may be worth less than half of these values.

This is one of many areas of collecting that has been greatly affected by Internet trading. Dealers report that the selling price of many motion clocks is much lower than a few years ago, and right now at least, the market is very volatile. We have tried to be realistic with our suggested values but concede that values to a large extent are fluctuating.

Note: When original names are not known, names have been assigned.

Advisors: Sam and Anna Samuelian (See Directory, Motion Clocks)

Haddon

Based in Chicago, Illinois, Haddon produced an attractive line of clocks. They used composition cases that were hand painted, and sturdy Hansen movements and motions. This is the only clock line for which new replacement motors are still available.

Children on seesaw (Teeter Totter), from $100 to.............$150.00
Cowboy on horse (Ranch-O), composition, 7x12", from $100 to.$150.00
Granny rocking on porch (Home Sweet Home), 7½x12½x4", from
    $75 to $100.00
Ship on waves (Ship Ahoy), from $175 to $225.00

Lux

This clockmaker was originally called The Lux Clock Company; it was founded 1914 in Waterbury, Pennsylvania. They made a large assortment of novelty clocks including a shoeshine boy, beer drinkers, organ grinder, cat faces, and Li'l Abner's schmoo.

Boy Scout waves semaphore flags, green tent, campfire & pot along
    edge, 5x4", EX...$700.00
Cat, pendulum causes cat's eyes to roll back & forth, 7½x4¼".$145.00

Clown with seals, from $135.00 to $150.00.

Dixie Boy, blinking eyes, tie pendulum, 8½x4½" $65.00
Mary Had a Little Lamb, pendulum, 6¼x4⅛", EX $365.00
Old Codger, clock in trunk of body, 6¾", EX $400.00
Puppy peeking his head over top of clock, 7¾" w/pendulum,
    EX $185.00
Waiter, modeled after figural corkscrew, 6", EX $375.00
Windmill, pressed wood w/painted scene, 1930s, 10¼", EX ..$145.00

Mastercrafters

Based in Chicago, Illinois, this company produced many of the most appealing and popular collectible motion clocks on today's market. Cases were made of plastic, with earlier examples being a sturdy urea plastic that imparted quality, depth, and shine to their finishes. Clock movements were relatively simple and often supplied by Sessions Clock Company, who also made many of their own clocks.

Church w/bell ringer, from $50 to $75.00

Fireplace with mantel, marbleized plastic, 10¾", from $60.00 to $90.00. (Photo courtesy Sam and Anna Samuelian)

Golfer practicing putting, from $50 to.................................$85.00
Swinging boy & girl (Swing Playmates), 11x8x4", from $100 to $125.00
Swinging girl (Cottage Swing), from $200 to....................$250.00
Toaster, toast pops up & down as clock rotates, Model #362, from $75 to $125.00
Waterfall w/campfire, w/trees & bushes border below clock, 11x8", from $60 to $90.00

Spartus

This company made clocks well into the '80s, but most later clocks were not animated. Cases were usually plastic, and most clocks featured animals.

Cat, black, moving eyes & tail, long slender neck, 13" (+8" tail) . $65.00
Mill w/turning water wheel, plastic, 9x10½", from $45 to ..$50.00
Panda Bear, eyes move back & forth, from $25 to $35.00
Tiger, orange w/black stripes & white cheeks, eyes & tail move, 13" (+8" tail) $65.00

United

Based in Brooklyn, New York, United made mostly cast-metal cases finished in gold or bronze. Their movements were somewhat more complex than Mastercrafters'. Some of their clocks contained

musical movements, which while pleasing can be annoying when continuously run.

Ballerina inside gold-draped case w/clock at side, she turns w/music, wooden, #870, 10x13", from $75 to............................$85.00
Children on swing, heart-shaped opening, 12", from $80 to ... $90.00
Chuck wagon pulled by 4 horses, whip moves in driver's hand, #550, 9x20" $100.00
Couple watch sailboats move across lake w/lighthouse on side, from $150 to $200.00
Cowboy & saddle horse w/clock in between, lasso on clock moves, 11½x20", from $135 to...$185.00
Davy Crockett, metal, 10", from $450 to $500.00
English horse cab, driver's hand moves w/whip & lamppost lights up, #701, 13x16x4", from $60 to $70.00
Fireplace w/mantel, light-up roller makes fire burn, clock at side, 1950s, 8½x10", from $60 to $70.00
Fish move in underwater scene, clock in marine steering wheel, 1950s, from $75 to...$100.00
Huck Finn, fishing pole & fish move, from $100 to..........$125.00
Hula girl moves her hips as boy beats drum, 13½", from $250 to $350.00
Owl on branch, eyes move back & forth, 11", from $75 to. $90.00

Motorcycle Collectibles

At some point in nearly everyone's life, they've experienced at least a brief love affair with a motorcycle. What could be more exhilarating than the open road — the wind in your hair, the sun on your back, and no thought for the cares of today or what tomorrow might bring. For some, the passion never diminished. For most of us, it's a fond memory. Regardless of which description best fits you personally, you will probably enjoy the old advertising and sales literature, books and magazines, posters, photographs, banners, etc., showing the old Harleys and Indians, and the club pins, dealership jewelry and clothing, and scores of other items of memorabilia such as collectors are now beginning to show considerable interest in. For more information and lots of color photographs, we recommend *Motorcycle Collectibles With Values* by Leila Dunbar (Schiffer). See also License Plates.

Advisor: Bob 'Sprocket' Eckardt (See Directory, Motorcycles)

Ashtray, Harley-Davidson, amber glass w/black logo in bottom, 5" dia...$12.00
Bank, Harley-Davidson motorcycle w/side car, die cast, Harley-Davidson limited edition $100.00
Bank, mechanical; Harley-Davidson motorcycle near garage, cast iron, Franklin Mint..$110.00
Belt, black leather w/3 chrome & red reflectors on center back, marked Stimsonite, EX $40.00
Brochure, Indian parts list, 1916-22, VG...........................$75.00
Brochure, Suzuki Savage MX TS-250, 2-sided sheet, 1960s, EX $110.00
Catalog, Triumph/Tri-Cor Motorcycle accessories, black & white pictures, 31 glossy pages, 1959, EX $55.00

Cigarette case, Harley-Davidson logo etched on silver, holds 1 pack, NM..$50.00

Decal, orange, white and blue, 1950s, 4x4", $60.00.
(Photo courtesy Dunbar Gallery)

Hat, Harley-Davidson, black silk-like cloth w/white bill, emblem on front, Kant-Krak in side brim, EX...............................$85.00
Helmet, Buco Guardian racing type, 1950s-60s, EX............$85.00
Jacket, black leather, fringe down arms, zippers from elbows to wrist, belt-studded waist, quilted lining, EX.........................$65.00
License plate, Tenn 1965, yellow w/black lettering, EX......$135.00
Magazine, Custom Bike, April 1980, 82 pages, EX..............$14.00
Magazine, Hot Bike, Hulk Hogan Vs Golden Goose, 1992, EX...$18.00
Marble, black glass w/Harley-Devidson logo, ¹⁵⁄₁₆".................$7.50
Memo note pad, Indian Motorcycles, speed charts, gear ratios, much more, ca 1940, 4½x2½", EX.................................$110.00
Mittens black leather, flared cuff, 13" L, EX.......................$27.50
Patch, Indian Motorcycles, chief & wings, embroidered cotton, 5x11½", EX..$38.00
Pencil, mechanical, Harley-Davidson Motor Cycles, black & yellow, EX..$50.00
Pennant, Langhorne PA Motorcycle Races printed on red felt, 1940s-50s, 26½" L, VG...$595.00
Pin-back button, Indian Motorcycle, Springfield MA, Indian portrait, Whitehead & Hoag, ⅞", EX.............................$70.00
Postcard, Harley-Davidson Motorcycles advertising, 1935, 3¼x5½", VG..$60.00

Poster, cardboard, 14x11", $70.00.
(Photo courtesy Wm. Morford Auctions)

Poster, Cumberland Raceway Motorcycle Races, racing scene, multicolor, ca 1952, 22x14", EX..$100.00
Poster, Motorcycle Hill Climb, Mt Garfield, Muskegon MI, 1953, race scene, multicolor, 1-sheet, EX.............................$50.00

Siren, rear wheel mounted, foot operated, Sterling Fire Alarm Co, Rochester NY, EX..$110.00
Suspenders, Harley-Davidson, red logo on black, unused....$25.00
T-shirt, Harley-Davidson emblem on white cotton, sleeveless style, unused...$20.00
Wrench, adjustable, Wakefield Wrench No 17... & on bottom: Indian Motorcycles Hendee Mfg..., EX.......................$55.00

Movie Posters and Lobby Cards

Although many sizes of movie posters were made and all are collectible, the preferred size today is still the one-sheet, 27" wide and 41" long. Movie-memorabilia collecting is as diverse as films themselves. Popular areas include specific films such as *Gone With the Wind, Wizard of Oz*, and others; specific stars — from the greats to character actors; directors such as Hitchcock, Ford, Spielberg, and others; specific film types such as B-Westerns, all-Black casts, sports related, Noir, '50s teen, '60s beach, musicals, crime, silent, radio characters, cartoons, and serials; specific characters such as Tarzan, Superman, Ellery Queen, Blondie, Ma and Pa Kettle, Whistler, and Nancy Drew; specific artists like Rockwell, Davis, Frazetta, Flagg, and others; specific art themes, for instance, policeman, firemen, horses, attorneys, doctors, or nurses (this list is endless). And some collectors just collect posters they like. In the past twenty years, movie memorabilia has steadily increased in value. Movie memorabilia is a new field for collectors. In the past, only a few people knew where to find posters. Recently, auctions on the east and west coasts have created much publicity, attracting scores of new collectors. Many posters are still moderately priced, and the market is expanding, allowing even new collectors to see the value of their collections increase.

Adventures of Huck Finn, Eddie Hodges, Tony Randall, Archie Moore, 1960, 14x22", NM.......................................$40.00
Alice Doesn't Live Here Anymore, Ellen Burstyn & Kris Kristofferson, 1975, 40x27", EX...$60.00
Annie Hall, Woody Allen & Diane Keaton, black & white, 1977, 41x27', NM..$225.00
Calamity Jane, Doris Day & Howard Keel, Doris w/whip, 1953, 22x28", EX...$35.00

Cat on a Hot Tin Roof, 1958, Elizabeth Taylor, Paul Newman, and Burl Ives, 41x27", NM, from $150.00 to $200.00.

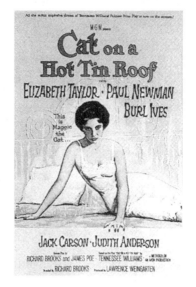

Chase, Charlie Sheen & Kristy Swanson, 1994, 40x27", NM .. **$75.00**

Coma, Michael Douglas, Genevieve Bujold & Richard Widmark, 1977, 41x27", NM **$55.00**

Devil's Widow, Ava Gardner, 1972, 41x27", EX **$40.00**

Dragonslayer, Peter MacNicol, Ralph Richardson & Caitlin Clarke, 1981, 41x27", NM **$50.00**

Durango Kid, Two-Fisted Stranger, Charles Starrett & Smiley Burnette, 1940s, 41½x27¼", EX.................**$125.00**

Easy Rider, Peter Fonda, black light type, 1971, 22x24", EX... **$55.00**

Eye of the Needle, Donald Sutherland, Kate Nelligan, black, white & red, 1981, 36x14", EX..................**$45.00**

Fast Times at Ridgemont High, Sean Penn & Jennifer Jason Leigh, 1982, 41x27", NM **$85.00**

Flashdance, Jennifer Beals seated, 1983, 41x27", EX **$55.00**

Gone With the Wind, Clark Gable & Vivien Leigh, 1998 re-release, 20x14", M **$85.00**

Great Escape, Steve McQueen on motorcycle, black & white, 1963, 17x11", EX..................**$17.50**

Honeymoon in Vegas, Nicolas Cage, Sarah Jessica Parker & James Caan, 1992, NM **$55.00**

Jaws 2, Roy Scheider, Lorraine Gary, shark about to attack surfer, 1979, 41x27", NM..................**$85.00**

Junior G-Men of the Air, 1942, Dead End Kids and Little Tough Guys, lobby card, 14x11", G, $275.00; EX, $375.00.

(Photo courtesy Harry and Judy Whitworth)

Knights of the Round Table, Robert Taylor, Eva Gardner & Mel Ferrer, 1953, 81x41", VG **$60.00**

Last of the Mohicans, Daniel Day-Lewis & Madeleine Stowe, 1992, 30x13", NM **$60.00**

Meet the Parents, Robert DeNiro giving Ben Stiller lie detector test, 40x27", NM **$15.00**

Mirage, Gregory Peck & Diane Baker kissing, 1967, 22x28", EX **$150.00**

My Foolish Heart, Susan Hayward & Dana Andrews in embrace, 1959, 41x27", EX..................**$300.00**

O Brother Where Art Thou? George Clooney, John Turturro, Tim Blake Nelson, John Goodman, 2-sided, 2001, 40x27", M............**$55.00**

Octopussy, Roger Moore & Maud Adams, 1983, 41x27", NM .**$85.00**

Patriot, Mel Gibson (closeup of face), 2000, 40x27", NM...**$40.00**

Pearl Harbor, Ben Affleck, Kate Beckinsale & Josh Hartnet, planes in cloudy sky, double sided, 2001, 40x27", NM..........**$60.00**

Pirates of the Caribbean Curse of the Black Pearl, Elizabeth Swann portrait, reprint, 2003, 37x27", M....................**$17.50**

Pollyanna, Haley Mills, portraits of 9 other characters on yellow, Walt Disney, 1960, 22x14", EX....................**$50.00**

Popeye, Robin Williams & Shelley Duval, 1980, 41x27", NM ..**$50.00**

Saturday Night Fever, John Travolta, dance scene, 1977, 41x27", G **$150.00**

South Sea Sinner, Shelley Winters & MacDonald Carey, 1949, 17x14", EX....................**$35.00**

Spy Who Came In From the Cold, Richard Burton, Claire Bloom, black & white, 1965, 41x27", NM....................**$50.00**

Staircase, Richard Burton & Rex Harrison, 1969, 22x28", NM.**$40.00**

Strawberry Roan, Gene Autry w/Champion, 2-color, 41½x27¼", EX **$175.00**

Superfly, Ron O'Neal, Curtis Mayfield in bottom right-hand corner, 1980s, 41x27", VG **$50.00**

Swamp Thing, Adrienne Barbeau & Louis Jourdan, 1982, 41x27", NM....................**$165.00**

Sword of Sherwood Forest, Richard Green & Peter Cushing, 1960, 30x14"+frame **$60.00**

Timber Tramps, Claude Akins, Tab Hunter & Joseph Cotton, 17x14", EX....................**$40.00**

Titanic, Leonardo DiCaprio & Kate Winslet in embrace, 33x23", NM....................**$12.50**

Wanderers of the West, Monogram Pictures, 1941, 41x78", $430.00. (Photo courtesy Jackson's International Auctioneers & Appraisers of Fine Art & Antiques)

Where the Boys Are, Lisa Hartman, Russell Todd, Lorna Luft, others in beach scene, 1984, 60x40", EX **$45.00**

Wizard of Oz, Judy Garland & characters from movie, 1967 limited edition of original 1939 lithograph, 20x28", NM........**$65.00**

Napkin Dolls

Cocktail, luncheon, or dinner..., paper, cotton, or damask..., solid, patterned, or plaid — regardless of size, color, or material, there's always been a place for napkins. In the late 1940s and early 1950s, buffet-style meals were gaining popularity. One accessory common to many of these buffets is now one of today's hot collectibles — the napkin doll. While most of the ceramic and wooden examples found today date from this period, many homemade napkin dolls were produced in ceramic classes of the 1960s and 1970s.

For information on napkin dolls as well as egg timers, string holders, children's whistle cups, baby feeder dishes, razor blade banks, pie birds, laundry sprinkler bottles, and other unique collectibles from the same era, we recommend *Collectibles for the Kitchen, Bath and Beyond*; for ordering information see our advisor's listing in the Directory.

Advisor: Bobbie Zucker Bryson (See Directory, Napkin Dolls)

Betson's yellow colonial lady, bell clapper, marked Hand Painted, 9", from $55 to **$75.00**

Byron Molds, pink & white lady w/arms crossed holding a bouquet, bow on top of head, 8½", from $65 to **$85.00**

California Ceramic mold, yellow & purple lady w/candleholder in top of hat, 12½", from $60 to **$75.00**

California Originals, holding toothpick basket aloft, $60.00. (Photo courtesy Bobbie Zucker Bryson)

California Originals, Miss Versatility Cocktail Girl, 13", from $50 to **$75.00**

California Originals, pink & white, Spanish dancer, slits on back only, foil label, 15", from $95 to.................................**$125.00**

Can Can, ceramic figure of blue & gold girl holding skirt open to expose legs, 9½", from $125 to...................................**$150.00**

Enesco, Genie at Your Service, holding lantern, paper label, 8", from $100 to **$135.00**

German, metal silhouette of Art Deco woman, black & gold w/wire bottom, marked E Kosta DBGM 1744970, EX, from $95 to .**$135.00**

Goebel, half doll holding a rose on wire frame, marked Goebel, W Germany, ca 1957, 8¼", from $175 to **$250.00**

Hachiya Bros, lady holding yoke w/bucket salt & pepper shakers, hat conceals candleholder, from $125 to............................**$150.00**

Holland Mold, Daisy, No 514, 7¼", from $50 to...............**$75.00**

Holland Mold, lady holding hat behind her back, red & white, 6¾", from $85 to **$100.00**

Holland Mold, Rebecca No H-265, wearing white dress w/tiers of napkin slits, 10½", from $150 to...............................**$195.00**

Holland Mold, Rosie, No H-132, 10⅞", from $45 to.........**$75.00**

Holt Howard, pink Sunbonnet Miss, marked Holt Howard, 1958, 5", from $125 to...**$150.00**

Holt Howard, yellow Sunbonnet Miss, marked Holt Howard, 1959, 5", from $125 to...**$150.00**

Holt Howard-style baker w/towel & tray of rolls, ceramic & metal, holes at top for toothpicks, #2026, 9", from $95 to ...**$110.00**

Japan, angel, pink, holding flowers, slits in shoulders so napkins form wings, 5⅜", from $100 to...................................**$135.00**

Japan, girl in yellow colonial-style dress, brown hair, holds tureen toothpick tray, 9¾", from $55 to.................................**$75.00**

Japan, Holt Howard style, wooden doll w/outstretched arms on wooden base, 11¼", from $30 to...................................**$40.00**

Japan, lady in blue w/pink umbrella, bell clapper, unmarked, 9", from $50 to **$75.00**

Japan, lady in pink dress w/blue shawl & yellow hat, 8½", from $60 to **$85.00**

Japan, Santa, marked Chess, 1957, 6¾", from $95 to........**$135.00**

Kreiss & Co, angel, candleholder in halo, holding a Christmas tree, 11", from $100 to **$110.00**

Kreiss & Co, green doll w/gold trim holding muff, jeweled eyes, candleholder in hat, marked, 10¼", from $95 to........**$125.00**

Kreiss & Co, green doll w/poodle, jeweled eyes, necklace & ring, candleholder behind hat, marked, 10¾", from $100 to **$125.00**

Kreiss & Co, yellow lady w/fan, candleholder behind fan, marked, 10½", from $50 to...**$65.00**

Lefton, white birds w/gold trim, wires in tail for napkins, heads (salt & peppers) lift off, 4⅜", from $25 to **$35.00**

Mallory Ceramics Studio, Christine, blue dress w/purple flower trim, blond hair, 9", from $135 to.............................**$150.00**

Marcia of California, woman w/molded apron, 1 hand holding bowl on her head, blue iridescent finish, 13", from $95 to..**$150.00**

Marybell, mold P71, Southern lady holding hat, 9¾", from $150 to **$195.00**

Paris Art, Black native, metal w/gold cap, earrings & trim, bold felt bikini-type top, 8", from $100 to **$135.00**

Plastic, half doll w/red hair, green satin decorated bodice, ca 1959, 11", from $30 to...**$50.00**

Rooster, black w/red & yellow trim, slits in sides for napkins, w/ matching salt & pepper shakers, from $50 to **$65.00**

Servy Etta, wood, gray w/marble base, marked USD Patent No 159,005, 11½", from $35 to **$45.00**

Swedish doll, wooden, marked Patent No 113861, 10", from $20 to **$35.00**

Viking Japan, man (bartender), green & white, holding tray w/ candleholder, 8¾", from $85 to...................................**$100.00**

Willoughby Studio, golden yellow lady w/brown applied trim holding tilted pitcher, 12", from $100 to.........................**$125.00**

Wooden, do-do bird w/pointed beak & long neck, slits in body for napkins, 7", from $25 to...**$35.00**

Wooden, pink & blue doll w/red strawberry toothpick holder on head, 8", from $60 to **$75.00**

Wooden, umbrella, marked Reg Prop No 382.649, Reproduction Prohibited, Industria Argentina, 8⅜", from $25 to.......**$35.00**

Wooden Jamaican lady, movable arms, paper label: Ave 13 Nov 743, A Sinfonia, Tel 2350 Petropolis, 6", from $50 to **$75.00**

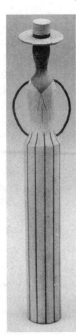

Finland, wooden lady with wire arms, 10¼", from $40.00 to $50.00. (Photo courtesy Bobbie Zucker Bryson)

NASCAR Collectibles

Over the past decade, interest in NASCAR racing has increased to the point that the related collectibles industry has mushroomed into a multi-billion dollar business. Posters, magazines, soda pop bottles, and model kits are only a few examples of hundreds of items produced with the sole intention of attracting racing fans. Also included as a part of this field of collecting are items such as race-worn apparel — even parts from the racing cars themselves — and these, though not devised as such, are the collectibles that command the highest prices!

Autograph, Richard Petty, signed photo, $15.00. (Photo courtesy Racing Collectibles Price Guide)

Banner, Dale Earnhardt Jr & #8 Chevrolet Monte Carlo, from 2005 Brickyard 400, 20' L, EX **$70.00**

Book, Brickyard 400, celebrates 1st 1994 race, leather cover w/winner Jeff Gordon, UMI limited edition, 158 pages, NM **$15.00**

Book, Winston Cup 25th Anniversary, leather covered, 1995, NM **$15.00**

Camping chair, Dale Earnhardt Jr, Budweiser, folding type w/carrying case, NM **$30.00**

Cards, Maxx Race Cards, 1991, box of 36, unopened, MIB .. **$35.00**

Chair, folding; Dale Earnhardt Sr signature & 3 on navy cloth, built-in cup holder, NM in cloth case w/shoulder strap **$22.50**

Cigarette lighter, Dale Earnhardt #3, gold-tone metal, butane, EX **$22.00**

Clock, Dale Earnhardt Sr portrait on black, Jebcote gloss finish, Jebco, 23x11"...**$55.00**

Game, Champions, Jeff Gordon & Dale Earnhardt on box, board game, missing poster, VGIB.....................................**$12.50**

Grille cover, Dale Earnhardt Jr #8, red, white & black, flannel-backed vinyl, EX...**$30.00**

Hat, Dale Earnhardt, Peter Max, GM Goodwrench Service Plus, pastel colors on the car, unused....................................**$60.00**

Lamp, Dale Earnhardt #8 simulated signature, checkerboard shade, 18"...**$40.00**

Lamp, table; Dale Earnhardt Jr, translucent plastic cylinder glows from inside, 3-way switch, 17", EX.........................**$50.00**

Light switch cover, Mark Martin #6, MIP **$8.00**

Medallion, Jeff Gordon, 1995 Winston Cup Champion, $50.00.

Mug, helmet form, plastic, yellow w/black eye shield, NASCAR emblem on side, Sherwood Brands, China, 2003 ....**$18.00**

Patch, 50th Anniversary, embroidered cloth, 3x3¾", M.......**$35.00**

Pepsi bottle, Richard Petty series, marked No Refill, 12-oz ..**$12.00**

Pez dispenser, #20 Tony Stewart pull-&-go action car, press bumper to dispense candy, MIB w/3 packages of Pez candy.......**$12.50**

Pin, NASCAR International, enamel on silver-tone metal, screw-on back, 1959, ⅝" wide...**$75.00**

Plush gorilla, Bristol Motor Speedway, in bright blue jersey, 7", EX **$18.00**

Postcard, Fireball Roberts, Young Ford, 1964, 5x7", EX....**$125.00**

Poster, Earnhardt vs Earnhardt, father & son side by side, 2001, 27x19", NM **$38.00**

Program, Food City 500, 2003, softcover, EX.....................**$15.00**

Puzzle, #21 Elliot Sadler Motorcraft Ford Taurus, 1001, 100-pieces, 12x9", MIB **$10.00**

Puzzle, jigsaw; Crisco Racing, features Brett Bodine, 17x11", EXIB..**$20.00**

Rug, welcome mat; Tony Stewart, woven polyester w/foam backing, 20x30", NM **$25.00**

Safety glasses, Dale Earnhardt Jr #8, clear, NASCAR Officially Licensed, Encon Safety, scratch resistant coating..........**$12.00**

Shirt, crew; Rusty Wallace #2, Miller Lite advertising in blue, Winston cup patch, EX **$125.00**

Shirt, Dale Jr embroidery on jersey knit baseball style, Chase, NM **$45.00**

Soda bottle, Sun-Drop Citrus Soda, Dale Earnhardt 1980 Winston Cup, green glass, 12-oz, unopened....................**$18.00**

T-shirt, Skoal Bandit, multicolor graphics on white, unused....**$35.00**

Tire cover, Dale Jarrett #88 & UPS, M in bag.....................**$17.50**

Toy car, Darrel Waltrip #66 Ford Taurus w/Route 66 Victory Tour theme, diecast, 1999, 1/64 scale, MIP **$15.00**

Toy car, Dub City #3 1971 SS Chevelle, Dale Earnheadt Sr, Wheaties logos, hood & trunk open, 1:24 scale, NM **$40.00**

Yearbook, Winston Cup, champion Bill Elliot featured, UMI, 1988, 136 pages, EX w/jacket..........................**$210.00**

New Martinsville

Located in a West Virginia town by the same name, the New Martinsville Glass Company was founded in 1901 and until it was purchased by Viking in 1944 produced quality tableware in various patterns and colors that collectors admire today. They also made a line of glass animals which Viking continued to produce until they closed in 1986. In 1987 the factory was bought by Mr. Kenneth Dalzell who reopened the company under the title Dalzell-Viking. He used the old molds to reissue his own line of animals, which he marked 'Dalzell' with an acid stamp.

See also Glass Animals and Related Items.

Janice, blue or red, basket, oval, 10x12"..............**$265.00**

Janice, blue or red, bowl, flared rim, 11"..............**$65.00**

Janice, blue or red, candlestick, single, #4554, 5½x5", ea **$50.00**

Janice, blue or red, candy box, #4541-SJ Swan, 5½" **$155.00**

Janice, blue or red, ice pail, w/handle, #4589, 10" **$595.00**

Janice, blue or red, plate, handles, 12".............**$55.00**

Janice, blue or red, plate, mayonnaise; 6"............**$12.50**

Janice, blue or red, platter, oval, #4588, 13" **$90.00**

Janice, blue or red, sugar bowl, flat, #4532, individual.........**$22.00**

Janice, blue or red, vase, cupped, 3-toed, 8"...........**$115.00**

Janice, crystal, ball form, 9" **$55.00**

Janice, crystal, basket, #4552, 11".....................**$75.00**

Janice, crystal, basket, 4-toed, 9x6½"..................**$75.00**

Janice, crystal, bowl, cupped, footed, 11"................**$45.00**

Janice, crystal, ice tub, footed, #4584, 6"...............**$115.00**

Janice, crystal, plate, rolled edge, footed, 14" **$40.00**

Janice, crystal, saucer, #4580 ....**$2.00**

Janice, crystal, syrup, w/drip-cut top **$85.00**

Kalonyal, crystal, celery tray, 12" **$65.00**

Kalonyal, crystal, spoon tray **$60.00**

Kalonyal, crystal, toothpick holder........................**$425.00**

Lions, amber or crystal, bowl, cream soup; handles, #34 Addie ..**$20.00**

Lions, amber or crystal, candleholder, #37 Moondrops, ea ..**$25.00**

Lions, amber or crystal, creamer, #37 Moondrops **$15.00**

Lions, amber or crystal, sugar bowl, #37 Moondrops...........**$15.00**

Lions, black, candy dish, w/lid.........................**$110.00**

Lions, black, compote, cheese **$35.00**

Lions, black, plate, 8" **$30.00**

Lions, black, saucer, #34 Addie **$35.00**

Lions, pink or green, candy dish, w/lid..........................**$75.00**

Lions, pink or green, compote, cheese...........................**$25.00**

Lions, pink or green, cup, #34 Addie **$25.00**

Lions, pink or green, plate, cracker; 12"..........................**$30.00**

Lions, pink or green, sugar bowl, #34 Addie **$25.00**

Meadow Wreath, crystal, bowl, flared rim, footed, #4265/26, 11"..........................**$45.00**

Meadow Wreath, crystal, bowl, punch; #4221/26, 5 qt......**$140.00**

Meadow Wreath, crystal, candlestick, 2-light, ea **$42.50**

Meadow Wreath, crystal, compote, #421826, 10"..............**$35.00**

Meadow Wreath, crystal, cup, punch; tab handle, 4-oz..........**$9.00**

Meadow Wreath, crystal, plate, 11"..........................**$35.00**

Meadow Wreath, crystal, relish, 3-part, #4223/26, 7".........**$18.00**

Meadow Wreath, crystal, salver, footed, #42/26, 12" **$40.00**

Meadow Wreath, crystal, tray, creamer & sugar bowl; oval, #42/26..........................**$15.00**

Meadow Wreath, crystal, vase, flared, #42/26, 10"...............**$55.00**

Meadow Wreath, crystal, vase, 10", from $60.00 to $70.00.

Radiance, amber, bowl, crimped rim, 12" **$35.00**

Radiance, amber, bowl, relish; 3-part, 8"............................**$35.00**

Radiance, amber, candlesticks, 8", pr **$95.00**

Radiance, amber, condiment set, 4-pc w/tray....................**$175.00**

Radiance, amber, cup, punch **$7.00**

Radiance, amber, plate, luncheon; 8" **$10.00**

Radiance, amber, vase, flared or crimped, 10"..........................**$75.00**

Radiance, ice or cobalt blue, bowl, bonbon, 6" **$33.00**

Radiance, ice or cobalt blue, bowl, crimped, 10" **$55.00**

Radiance, ice or cobalt blue, compote, 6" **$35.00**

Radiance, ice or cobalt blue, creamer **$27.50**

Radiance, ice or cobalt blue, lamp, 12" **$125.00**

Radiance, ice or cobalt blue, salt & pepper shakers, pr.........**$95.00**

Radiance, red, bowl, bonbon, w/lid, 6"..........................**$115.00**

Radiance, red, butter dish **$465.00**

Radiance, red, compote, 5" **$35.00**

Radiance, red, decanter, w/handle & stopper $225.00
Radiance, red, tray, oval $45.00

Nichols, Betty Lou

This California artist/potter is probably best known for her head vases, which display her talents and strict attention to detail to full advantage. Many of her ladies were dressed in stylish clothing and hats that were often decorated with applied lace, ruffles, and bows; the signature long eyelashes are apparent on nearly every model she made. Because these applications are delicate and susceptible to damage, mint-condition examples are rare and very valuable. The few figures she made without applied components generally sell for under $100.00, though some may go higher. Most of her head vases and figurines carry not only her name but the name of the subject as well.

Bobble-head nodder, Percy, hands behind back, 7½" $75.00
Decanter, bartender w/white tux, Victor Reisel on front, Merry Christmas from Bartender's Union..., 8½", NM $400.00
Figure vase, Melanie Ann, white jacket w/olive green print, olive green skirt & hat, carrying basket, 4¾", NM $40.00

Figurine, B'Lou, 6", $375.00.
(Photo courtesy David Barron)

Figurine, Frieda, lady w/swirling skirt & yellow head scarf stands w/bowl on head, 10½" $65.00
Figurine, Nora, blond lady in pink bodice, yellow & black skirt, 9½", EX $55.00
Figurine, Rosalyn, flowered gown w/ruffles at neck & elbows, 9" $755.00
Figurine, Santa, left hand w/palm up, right pointing upward, 'spaghetti' fur, 10x12", NM $450.00
Figurines, Santa & Mrs Claus, Santa w/black bag over shoulder & Mrs w/black bag in front, 1950, 9½", EX, pr $150.00
Head vase, Bella, plaid dress & hat, 7", EX+ $540.00
Head vase, Centennial Sue, blond curled hair, floral brown dress, flat hat, 8" $550.00
Head vase, Demi - Dorable, pink hearts on white bodice, 3½" . $100.00
Head vase, Ermyn-trude, dressed in green, brown tube curls, thick black lashes, 6" $200.00

Head vase, Ermyn-trude, white dress w/black double V neckline, tilted hat, 9" $640.00
Head vase, Flora-Belle, green & yellow plaid hat & bodice, thick black lashes, 11" $1,000.00
Head vase, Linda, pink & black hat, blond w/thick black lashes, ruffled bodice, 8" $600.00
Head vase, Lita, low-cut dress, wide-brim hat, 6½", EX+ $1,070.00
Head vase, Louisa, crimped ribbon, ruffle trim, pink & cream polka dots on brown dress, thick eyelashes, 6½" $350.00

Head vase, Luanne, 9", minimum value, $1,000.00. (Photo courtesy David Barron)

Head vase, Mary Lou, black multicolored floral dress, 6" .. $360.00
Head vase, Mary Lou, blond w/thick black lashes, ruffled bodice, 6½" $375.00
Head vase, Nancy, blond w/thick lashes, lavender dress & ruffles, black hat, 6½", EX $265.00
Head vase, Nancy Lou, rolled curls high (near hat), pink & black bodice, thick black lashes, 8¾" $550.00
Head vase, Nellie, ruffle over 1 shoulder, slanted hat, 9" $600.00
Head vase, Valerie, thick lashes & black hair, yellow dress & hat w/plaid ribbon, 5¾", NM $375.00
Head vase, Vicki, green dress w/white decoration, feathers at collar, 8¼" $600.00
Planter/centerpiece, sleigh form, white w/red sides, 7½x11", EX $90.00

Niloak Pottery

The Niloak Pottery company was the continuation of a quarter-century-old family business in Benton, Arkansas. Known as the Eagle Pottery in the early twentieth century, its owner was Charles Dean Hyten who continued in his father's footsteps making utilitarian wares for local and state markets. In 1909 Arthur Dovey, an experienced potter formerly from the Rookwood Pottery of Ohio and the Arkansas-Missouri based Ouachita Pottery companies, came to Benton and created America's most unusual art pottery. Introduced in 1910 as Niloak (kaolin spelled backwards), Dovey and Hyten produced art pottery pieces from swirling clays with a wide range of artificially created colors including red, blue, cream, brown, gray, and later green. Connected to the Arts & Crafts Movement by 1913, the pottery was labeled as Missionware (probably due to its seeming simplicity in the making). Missionware (or swirl) production continued alongside utilitarian ware manufacturing until the 1930s when economic factors led to the making of another type of art pottery and later to (molded) industrial castware. In 1931 Niloak Pottery introduced Hywood Art Pottery (marked as such), consisting of regular glaze techniques including overspray, mottling, and drips of two colors on vases and bowls that were primarily hand thrown. It was short-lived and soon replaced with the Hywood by Niloak (or Hywood) line to increase marketing potential through the use of the well-recognized Niloak name. Experienced potters, designers, and ceramists were involved at Niloak; among them were Frank Long, Paul Cox, Stoin M. Stoin, Howard Lewis, and Rudy Ganz. Many local families with long ties to the pottery included the McNeills, Rowlands, and Alleys. Experiencing tremendous financial woes by the mid-1930s, Niloak came under new management which was led by Hardy L. Winburn of Little Rock. To maximize efficiency and stay competetive, they focused primarily on industrial castware such as vases, bowls, figurines, animals, and planters. Niloak survived into the late 1940s when it became known as the Winburn Tile Company of North Little Rock; it still exists today.

Virtually all of Niloak Missionware/swirl pottery is marked with die stamps. The exceptions are generally fan vases, wall pockets, lamp bases, and whiskey jugs. The terms '1st' and '2nd art marks' used in the listings refer to specific die-stamped trademarks. The earlier mark was used from 1910 to 1925, followed by the second, very similar mark used from then until the end of Mission Ware production. Letters with curving raised outlines were characteristic of both; the most obvious difference between the two was that on the first, the final upright line of the 'N' was thin with a solid club-like terminal Be careful when you buy unmarked swirl pottery — it is usually Evans pottery (made in Missouri) which generally has either no interior glaze or is chocolate brown inside. Moreover, Evans made swirl wall pockets, lamp bases, and even hanging baskets that find their way on to today's market and are sold as Niloak. Niloak stickers are often placed on these unmarked Evans pieces — closely examine the condition of the sticker to determine if it is damaged or mutilated from the transfer process.

For more information, we recommend *Collector's Encyclopedia of Niloak Pottery* (Collector Books) by David Edwin Gifford, a historian of Arkansas pottery.

Ashtray, frog figural w/open mouth, block letters, 3½" **$36.00**

Ashtray, Mission, 1 rest, 2nd art mark, individual, 3" dia **$57.00**

Bowl, Mission, incurvate rim, 1st art mark, 1½x6¼" **$98.00**

Bowl, Peter Pan on edge, impressed mark, 7½", from $25 to ... **$30.00**

Candlestick, Mission, attached self-liner, 2nd art mark, 4", ea. **$165.00**

Candlestick, Mission, flared foot, 1st art mark, 10⅛", ea... **$150.00**

Cookie jar, tab handles, matt, impressed mark, 11" **$125.00**

Cornucopia vase, almost upright, semigloss, impressed mark, 7½" **$25.00**

Cup, punch; Mission, 2½" **$90.00**

Ewer, green-brown tobacco spit, graceful arc handle, impressed mark **$22.50**

Ewer, Ozark Blue Glaze by Lewis, Peterson design, Niloak in low relief mark, 11", from $75.00 to $100.00; pitcher, same glaze, no mark, 9", from $75.00 to $100.00. (Photo courtesy David Edwin Gifford)

Figurine, dog, brown flecked matt, 2½" **$135.00**

Figurine, Southern Belle, Ozark Blue or Ozark Dawn, mark in relief, 10" **$185.00**

Figurine, Trojan horse, matt, 2nd art mark, 8½" **$180.00**

Flower frog, Mission, unmarked, 1¼x3¼" **$55.00**

Humidor, Mission, indent for sponge, dark colors, 1st art mk, 6" **$585.00**

Jar, cigarette; Mission, initials embossed on brass lid, 2nd art mark, 4½x3½" **$275.00**

Mug, Bouquet dinnerware line, impressed mark, 3½", from $5 to **$10.00**

Paperweight, brick shape, matt, Niloak top mark, 1¾x6x3" ... **$175.00**

Pitcher, lemonade; Mission; bulbous, 1st art mark, 7x6½" **$950.00**

Pitcher, maroon, graceful handle, straight sides, 2nd art mark, 3" **$20.00**

Planter, bulldog w/spiked collar, prone, 2½x6" **$95.00**

Planter, kangaroo boxing, matt, block letters, 5½" **$38.00**

Planter, pouter pigeon, ivory, impressed mark, 9" **$185.00**

Planter, seal w/cold-painted features, 4¼" **$35.00**

Salt & pepper shakers, fat penguin, unmarked, 2½", pr from $24 to **$40.00**

Shot glass, Mission, 2nd art mark, 2", from $65 to............ **$110.00**

Stein, Mission, straight sides, flared base, thumb rest on handle, 2nd art mark, 6¼" **$165.00**

Teapot, Fox Red, Aladdin lamp style, unmarked, 6½" **$95.00**

Tumbler, Mission, flared rim, Patent Pending, 5" **$200.00**

Vase, flamingo & palm trees embossed, rope-like handles, block letter mark, 7½" **$130.00**

Vase, Mirror Black, high sloping shoulders w/2 tiny handles, 1st Hywood mark, 9" **$165.00**

Vase, Mission, classic shape w/flared rim, 1st art mark, 5½" **$95.00**

Vase, Mission, conical w/flared foot, 1st art mark, 6".........**$175.00**

Vase, Mission, cylindrical, no rim, 2nd art mark, 6".........**$130.00**

Vase, Mission, cylindrical w/flared base, 9" **$295.00**

Vase, Mission, fan form w/flared pedestal foot, 2nd art mark, 6¾" **$195.00**

Vase, Mission, teardrop w/narrow neck opening, 1st art mark, 9½" $265.00
Vase, Winged Victory handles, Ozark Dawn, 4½-6", from $15 to $30.00
Wall pocket, rolled rim, browns & blues, unmarked, 9" $310.00

Vase, Mission, 10", $550.00.

(Photo courtesy Treadway Gallery Inc.)

Noritake

Before the government restricted the use of the Nippon mark in 1921, all porcelain exported from Japan (even that made by the Noritake Company) carried the Nippon mark. The company that became Noritake had its beginning in 1904 and over the years experienced several changes in name and organization. Until 1941 (at the onset of WWII) they continued to export large amounts of their products to America. (During the occupation, when chinaware production was resumed, all exports were to have been marked 'Occupied Japan,' though because of the natural resentment on the part of the Japanese, much of it was not.)

Many variations will be found in their marks, but nearly all contain the Noritake name. Reproductions abound; be very careful.

Newsletter: *Noritake News*
David H. Spain
1237 Federal Ave. E, Seattle, WA 98102; 206-323-8102

Azalea

The Azalea pattern was produced exclusively for the Larkin Company, who offered it to their customers as premiums from 1916 until the 1930s. It met with much success, and even today locating pieces to fill in your collection is not at all difficult. The earlier pieces carry the Noritake M-in-wreath mark. Later the ware was marked Noritake, Azalea, Hand Painted, Japan.

Bonbon, #184, 6¼" $60.00
Bowl, fruit; #9, 5¼" $8.00
Bowl, oatmeal; #55, 5½" $25.00
Bowl, vegetable; oval, #172, 9¼" $42.00

Butter tub with insert, #54, $42.00. (Photo courtesy Linda Williams)

Casserole, gold finial, w/lid, #372 ....$395.00
Cheese/butter dish, #314 ....$125.00
Compote, glass...$95.00
Creamer & sugar bowl, demitasse; open, #123 ....$125.00
Cup & saucer, bouillon; #124, 3½" $26.00
Gravy boat, #40 ....$40.00
Mustard jar, #191, 3-pc $48.00
Olive dish, #194 ....$25.00
Plate, breakfast/luncheon; #98 ....$18.00
Plate, salad; sq, 7⅝" $65.00
Relish, 2-part, loop handle, #450......................................$295.00
Teapot, #15...$110.00
Whipped cream/mayonnaise set, #3, 3-pc...........................$38.50

Tree in the Meadow

Made by the Noritake China Company during the 1920s and 1930s, this pattern of dinnerware is beginning to show up more and more at the larger flea markets and antique malls. It's easy to spot; the pattern is hand painted, so there are variations, but the color scheme is always browns, gold-yellows, and orange-rust, and the design features a large dark tree in the foreground, growing near a lake. There is usually a cottage in the distance.

Teapot, $95.00. (Photo courtesy Linda Williams)

Basket, Dolly Varden..$95.00
Bowl, oval, 9½" $48.00

Bowl, soup $38.00
Butter pat $25.00
Candy dish, octagonal, w/lid, 5½" $395.00
Cheese dish $95.00
Coffeepot, demitasse $250.00
Creamer & sugar bowl, berry $110.00
Creamer & sugar bowl, demitasse $125.00
Egg cup $30.00
Lemon dish $15.00
Plate, dinner; 9¾" $75.00
Platter, 10" $110.00
Relish, divided $30.00
Vase, fan form $95.00

Various Dinnerware Patterns

So many lines of dinnerware have been produced by the Noritake company that to list them all would require a volume in itself. More than 800 patterns have been recorded, and while many had specific names, others simply carried identification numbers. We are listing some of the more popular lines; most were produced from the 1950s through the 1980s.

Anniversary #1979, cup & saucer, footed $30.00
Anniversary #1979, plate, dinner; 10½" $32.00
Anniversary #1979, platter, oval, 14⅛", from $80 to $95.00
Anniversary #1979, sugar bowl, w/lid $37.50
Asian Dream #2502, bowl, vegetable; w/lid, from $80 to .. $100.00
Asian Dream #2502, creamer, 4" $28.00
Asian Dream #2502, cup & saucer, footed $27.50
Asian Dream #2502, plate, salad; 8" $8.00
Astor Rose #6515, bowl, divided vegetable; 10" $40.00
Astor Rose #6515, plate, salad; 8" $8.00
Astor Rose #6515, salt & pepper shakers, pr $38.00
Astor Rose #6515, teapot, 3-cup, from $100 to $135.00
Carrie #2864, plate, dinner; 10½" $20.00
Carrie #2864, platter, oval, 15", from $60 to $80.00
Carrie #2864, salt & pepper shakers, pr $27.99
Carrie #2864, tureen, w/lid, from $100 to $135.00
Denise #5508, cup & saucer, flat $10.00
Denise #5508, plate, bread & butter; 6½" $5.00
Denise #5508, platter, 14" $30.00
Denise #5508, sugar bowl, w/lid $15.00
Flirtation #7227, plate, dinner; 10½" $12.00
Flirtation #7227, cup & saucer, footed, 3⅛" $12.00
Flirtation #7227, sugar bowl, w/lid $15.00
Georgian #6440, bowl, fruit/dessert; 5½" $10.00
Georgian #6440, bowl, vegetable; oval, 10" $27.50
Georgian #6440, plate, salad; 8" $8.00
Georgian #6440, platter, oval, 13⅜" $55.00
Larkspur #7048, bowl, vegetable; 8½" $25.00
Larkspur #7048, creamer, 12-oz $12.00
Larkspur #7048, cup & saucer, footed, 3¼" $14.00
Larkspur #7048, plate, dinner; 10", from $32 to $38.00
Madeleine #2251, bowl, coupe soup; 7⅜" $12.00
Madeleine #2251, bowl, vegetable; oval, 9½" $35.00
Madeleine #2251, platter, oval, 16", from $50 to $60.00

Madeleine #2251, teapot, 4-cup $60.00
Maywood #5154, bowl, fruit/dessert; 5½" $6.00
Maywood #5154, bowl, rimmed soup; 8" $7.00

Maywood #5154, cup, gold edge, 1950s, $12.00. (Photo courtesy Aimee Neff Alden)

Maywood #5154, plate, dinner; 10" $15.00
Maywood #5154, platter, oval, 16½" $48.00
Maywood #5154, sugar bowl, w/lid, 3⅛" $25.00
Natalie #5815, bowl, fruit/dessert; 5½" $5.00
Natalie #5815, creamer, 8-oz $12.00
Natalie #5815, cup & saucer, flat, 1⅞" $8.00
Natalie #5815, gravy boat w/attached undertray $37.50
Oriental #6341, coffeepot, 3-cup $35.00
Oriental #6341, plate, bread butter; 5½" $5.00
Oriental #6341, plate, salad; 8" $8.00
Oriental #6341, platter, oval, 11½" $15.00
Painted Desert #8603, bowl, vegetable; 8" $27.50
Painted Desert #8603, creamer, 14-oz $8.00
Painted Desert #8603, plate, dinner; 10½" $25.00
Painted Desert #8603, tea/coffeepot, 7-cup $32.50
Remembrance #5146, bowl, rimmed soup; 8¼" $8.00
Remembrance #5146, bowl, vegetable; oval, 10⅝" $35.00
Remembrance #5146, cup & saucer, footed, 2⅛", from $16 to . $20.00
Remembrance #5146, plate, dinner; 10" $16.00
Running Free #B968, bowl, cereal; 6½" $27.00
Running Free #B968, cup & saucer, 3⅛" $12.00
Running Free #B968, plate, dinner; 10½" $32.00
Running Free #B968, salad; 8" $20.00
Summer Bloom #901, percolator, 9-cup $55.00
Summer Bloom #901, teapot, 5-cup $45.00
Vicki #2214, bowl, vegetable; oval, 9¾" $30.00
Vicki #2214, candleholders, pr $28.00
Vicki #2214, cup & saucer $12.50
Vicki #2214, plate, dinner; 10½" $14.00

Miscellaneous

Ashtray, pipe sits on club shape, M-in-wreath mark, 5¼" .. $140.00
Basket vase, gold o/l on cobalt, mk, 8¾" $350.00
Bowl, floral rim w/cobalt on white, gold handles, M-in-wreath mark, 8" $70.00
Bowl, parrot on branch, black rim, M-in-wreath mark, 10". $85.00

Cake plate, exotic birds, pink border w/gold, M-in-wreath mark, 8¼" $70.00

Candlesticks, floral/exotic bird reserve on lustre, M-in-wreath mark, 9¼", pr $240.00

Cheese dish, yellow band w/Deco flowers on white, slant lid, M-in-wreath mark, 8" L $125.00

Cigarette holder, floral on bell shape, bird finial, M-in-wreath mark, 5" $200.00

Dresser tray, scenic reserves in gold band on burgundy, marked, 13" L $120.00

Egg cup, windmill & river scenic, earth tones, M-in-wreath mark, 3½" $40.00

Humidor, lion killing python in relief on red, M-in-wreath mark, 6¾" $850.00

Match holder, horses' heads on brown bell shape, M-in-wreath mark, 3½" $150.00

Napkin ring, multicolor roses, M-in-wreath mark, 2¼" wide .. $45.00

Sauce dish, roses on tan w/orange lustre, M-in-wreath mark, 5", +ladle & tray $85.00

Shaving mug, river scenic, earth tones w/gold, M-in-wreath mark, 3¾" $120.00

Snack set, floral on cream w/yellow border, M-in-wreath mark, cup+7½" tray $65.00

Vase, geometric band on orange lustre, waisted, M-in-wreath mark, 8¾" $145.00

Vase, peacock feathers on tan, ruffled rim, slim, marked, 8", pr. $180.00

Vase, red mark, 5½", from $70.00 to $85.00. (Photo courtesy Joan Van Patten)

Vase, tulip figural, purple & green, M-in-wreath mark, 5¼" .. $300.00

Novelty Radios

Novelty radios come in an unimaginable variety of shapes and sizes from advertising and product shapes to character forms, vehicles, and anything else the manufacturer might dream up. For information on these new, fun collectibles read *Schroeder's Collectible Toys, Antique to Modern* (Collector Books).

Batman & Robin, clips to belt, FM only, DC Comics, Kenner, 1997, MIP $60.00

Beer barrel, brown plastic, AM only, Made in Japan, EX $30.00

Big Bird sitting on nest, transistors, Sesame Street, Concept 2000, NMIB $15.00

Cabbage Patch Kid (boy or girl) on green base, transistors, EX. $15.00

Champion Spark Plug, gray & white, 15x5", EX $65.00

Cookie Monster leaning against a cathedral radio, AM, Sesame Street, MIB $40.00

Dekalb sign (ear of corn logo) lights up, green plastic base forms body, EX $125.00

Globe, hard plastic, 6 transistors, Peerless, 1970s, 8½", NM .. $55.00

Harley-Davidson Junior Rider, AM/FM, comes with cassette player and stereo headphones, 9x15", from $50.00 to $75.00. (Photo courtesy Bunis and Breed)

Hopalong Cassidy, red plastic case, lasso antenna, 4½x8x4", NM $995.00

Huckeberry Hound (head only), blue plastic w/enameling, British Hong Kong, ca 1960, MIB $32.50

Jem roadster, pink & yellow plastic, FM, Hasbro, 1980s, EX ... $50.00

Knight standing & holding sword, plastic, transistors, EX ... $25.00

Ladybug, Sonnet, AM, Made in Hong Kong, 1960s-70s, 4¾x3¼", MIB $55.00

Little Orphan Annie & Sandy above Annie (in red letters), plastic, transistors, Hong Kong, 1981, MIB $50.00

Mickey Mouse face on blue sq, ears are dials, eyes light up, appears to wink when tuning, Disney, National R-81, NM $38.00

Mickey Mouse in red car, AM only, Concept 2000, Walt Disney Productions #181, Hong Kong, NM $40.00

Owl figural, cream & gold hard plastic, knobs are eyes, transistors, Japan, 7" $75.00

Panapet R-60S ball on chain, Panasonic, 1970s, EX $50.00

Pinocchio, AM only, Walt Disney Productions, Philgee International, 6¾x6", EX $35.00

Radio Shack, red plastic lettering, AM only, Tandy Corporation, 1979, 4x6¾x1¾", EX $38.00

Radio spelled out w/white letters, red speaker inside letter 'O,' transistors, Isis Model #20, EX $40.00

Rolls Royce car, side-mounted spare tires are on/off switch & dial, plastic, Hong Kong, EX $28.00

Sinclair Dino Supreme gas pump, gallon indicator is dial numbers, 6 transistors, w/case & ear phones, MIB $55.00

Sinclair Gas Pump, Dino logo, AM only, 1960s, EX **$40.00**

Skin So Soft bath oil bottle, AM/FM, Hong Kong, 1990, EXIB. **$30.00**

Soft drink shape, McDonald's 30th Anniversary, transistors, sun faded, 1985, 4¾x2⅝" dia, EX **$125.00**

Spider-Man climbing building (radio dial), AM/FM, 1993, EX.**$50.00**

Sputnik shape, red & white plastic, Japan, 1950s, 4½x2", EX.. **$45.00**

Suntory Whisky bottle, AM, transistors, Japan, 1960, MIB **$35.00**

TAZ, AM/FM radio/alarm clock, Toshiba, MIB **$35.00**

Tuna-Tiger, yellow tiger w/sweet face, plastic, AM only, Hong Kong, MIB **$20.00**

Winnie the Pooh's head, yellow plastic, transistors, takes 9 volt battery, 6x5¼x1", MIB **$45.00**

Zany perfume bottle, AM, Avon, Hong Kong, 1979, EX **$40.00**

Oatmeal Creme Pies, story of founder on back, $55.00. (Photo courtesy Bunis and Breed)

Novelty Telephones

Novelty telephones modeled after products or advertising items are popular with collectors — so are those that are character related. For further information we recommend *Schroeder's Collectible Toys, Antique to Modern* (Collector Books).

Airplane, yellow plastic w/acrylic propeller w/centered rotary dial, receiver forms wings, 1970s, 6x9x8", EX **$135.00**

Alf holds burnt-orange handset w/touch-tone key pad, 1970, 12x12x10", EX, from $65 to **$80.00**

Buzz Lightyear, rocket flame lights up, Disney, Brooktel, 1996, 16", MIB **$60.00**

Gaffer, Tetley (tea) on base, multicolor plastic, blue is dominate color, EX.. **$60.00**

Goofy reclining asleep, wakes up & talks when phone rings, Disney, 10", EX/NM, from $65 to.. **$85.00**

Goofy standing w/tangled phone cord, animated talker w/cordless receiver, MIB **$55.00**

Kermit the Frog seated in chair, yellow receiver rests on leg, touch-tone key pad, 12x10x9", EX, from $60 to **$85.00**

Lips, red plastic, upper lip is receiver, push-button dial inside bottom lip, TeleMania, Made in China, NM **$85.00**

Mickey Mouse standing & holding yellow receiver, Disney, 1976.**$45.00**

Mickey Mouse stands by red receiver, AT&T, 1990, 14½x10". **$38.00**

Occa the killer whale on wave stand, touch-tone pad, makes whale sounds as ringer, 10½", EX... **$35.00**

Opus the penguin, head turns to side when receiver is picked up, touch-tone dial, Tyco, EX **$65.00**

Pluto holding black receiver in mouth, rotary dial, wags tail & wimpers as Mickey gives commands, Telemania, NM **$35.00**

Punchy (Hawaiian Punch) character, Would You Like a..., plastic, EX **$55.00**

Rolling Stones lips & tongue, red plastic, Tristar, 1983, EX.... **$80.00**

Ronald McDonald seated on base holding receiver, 1970s-80s, 14x9½x10¼", EX, from $145 to **$165.00**

Snoopy, 50th Aniversary, w/saxophone, plays tune when phone rings, taps foot, Woodstock spins around, NMIB **$35.00**

Snoopy stands & holds yellow receiver, Woodstock stands beside him, rotary dial, AT&T, 1977, EX, from $25 to **$50.00**

Stars and Stripes, 1973, 12", $50.00.

7-Up Spot, stands & holds white receiver, EX, from $35 to **$50.00**

Occupied Japan Collectibles

Some items produced in Japan during the period from the end of WWII until the occupation ended in 1952 were marked Occupied Japan. No doubt much of the ware from this era was marked simply Japan, since obviously the 'Occupied' term caused considerable resentment among the Japanese people, and they were understandably reluctant to use the mark. So even though you may find identical items marked simply Japan or Made in Japan, only those with the more limited Occupied Japan mark are evaluated here.

Assume that the items described below are ceramic unless another material is mentioned. For more information, we recommend *Collector's Encyclopedia of Occupied Japan* by Gene and Cathy Florence (Collector Books).

Newsletter: *The Upside Down World of an O.J. Collector*
The Occupied Japan Club
c/o Florence Archambault
29 Freeborn St., Newport, RI 02840-1821
Published bimonthly. Information requires SASE

Planter, bird on floral branch, from $50.00 to $65.00. (Photo courtesy Gene and Cathy Florence)

Ashtray, baseball glove, metal $15.00
Ashtray, Georgia, shape of state, from $12.50 to $15.00
Bank, elephant trumpeting, white w/floral decor $35.00
Bell, chef w/rolling pin, 3" $35.00
Bookends, penguins, 4"....................................$25.00
Bowl, oval w/open latticework, floral center, gold trim $15.00
Box, peacock on red background, embossed w/flag, CKS in emblem, metal...$20.00
Butter dish, basket weave, rectangular $20.00
Christmas decoration, reindeer, celluloid, 7x7½", from $12.00 to.$15.00
Cookie jar, cottage shape, T-in-circle mark.............$75.00
Crumb pan, metal, embossed NY scene, from $10 to..........$20.00
Cup & saucer, chintz-like floral on white, Merit.................$20.00
Cup & saucer, demitasse; floral on white, from $10 to $12.00
Cup & saucer, house scene, lustre $15.00
Dinnerware, complete set for 4, w/3 sizes of plates, creamer & sugar bowl, cereal/soup bowls................................$200.00
Dinnerware, complete set for 6, same as for 4+gravy boat & platter...$250.00
Dinnerware, complete set for 8, same as for 6+sm platter $350.00
Dinnerware, complete set for 12, same as for 4+3 platters & serving bowl...$500.00
Doll, celluloid, Betty Boop type, under 8" $50.00
Figurine, angelic trio in robes playing instruments, 5¾", ea..$30.00
Figurine, Black shoeshine boy, 5½", from $50 to..................$55.00
Figurine, bride & groom on base, bisque, 6⅛" $50.00
Figurine, colonial couple at piano, 4"....................$22.50
Figurine, cowboy w/rope, 6½" $20.00
Figurine, dog pushing 2 puppies in basket-like buggy, 3" $15.00
Figurine, fisher boy w/basket & pole, Ucagco, 7" $40.00
Figurine, girl w/teddy bear in basket, 5⅜" $25.00
Figurine, horses jumping, brown pr on base, 5", from $35 to..$45.00
Figurine, Hummel-type boy & girl standing under umbrella on base, 6"...$45.00
Figurine, Hummel-type gardening boy & girl on base, Paulux, 5½"..$60.00
Figurine, man beside lady playing cello, Maruyama, 3½" $25.00
Figurine, Mexican on donkey, 8¼" $30.00
Figurine, spaniel-type dog, seated, 4⅜", from $20 to...........$25.00
Figurine, villain in black w/captive lady, blue mark, 7½" $65.00
Ice bucket, lacquerware, 7⅜", from $50 to $60.00
Incense burner, Oriental figure, 4¼" $20.00

Lamp base, colonial couple, Chikuoa, 10¼" to top of socket .. $40.00
Leaf dish, fruit decal, multicolor on white, gold trim...........$17.50
Match holder, coal hod, white w/colonial couple scene, gold trim $15.00
Pencil holder, dog figure.....................................$10.00
Pitcher, chicken figural, white w/red, black & brown accents ... $25.00
Planter, couple w/rabbits sit before planter, bisque, multicolor, 5¼x7¼"..$150.00
Planter, duck w/cart, 3x5", from $6 to......................$7.50
Planter, elf w/tulip pot $20.00
Planter, lady standing beside lg open flower, bisque, Paulux, 6". $75.00
Plaque, mallard in flight, wings wide, 6½"......................$25.00
Salt & pepper shakers, Dutch windmill form, blue & white, pr from $20 to $25.00
Salt & pepper shakers, penguin figural, metal, pr................$20.00
Shelf sitter, boy w/horn, 3¾" $15.00
Teapot, ribbed stoneware ball form w/bamboo handle.........$30.00
Teapot, windmill shape $50.00
Vase, snake charmer couple stand before vase, 5½" $30.00

Wall pocket, man and lady in alcoves lower baskets, 7x5", from $40.00 to $45.00. (Photo courtesy Gene and Cathy Florence)

Wall pocket, peacock on branch decor $30.00

Old MacDonald's Farm

This is a wonderful line of novelty kitchenware items fashioned as the family and the animals that live on Old MacDonald's Farm. It's been popular with collectors for quite some time, and prices are astronomical, though they seem to have stabilized, at least for now.

These things were made by the Regal China Company, who also made some of the Little Red Riding Hood items that are so collectible, as well as figural cookie jars, 'hugger' salt and pepper shakers, and decanters.

Advisor: Rick Spencer (See Directory, Regal China)

Butter dish, cow's head..$135.00
Canister, flour, cereal, or coffee; med, ea from $225 to $245.00

Canister, pretzels, peanuts, popcorn, chips or tidbits; lg, ea from $270 to **$315.00**

Canister, salt, sugar, or tea; med, ea from $110 to.............**$135.00**

Canister, soap, or cookies; lg, ea from $315 to **$375.00**

Cookie jar, barn **$175.00**

Creamer, from $65.00 to $75.00; sugar bowl, $85.00.

Grease jar, pig, from $110 to..**$135.00**

Pitcher, milk; from $180 to...**$200.00**

Salt & pepper shakers, boy & girl, pr...................................**$75.00**

Salt & pepper shakers, churn, gold trim, pr **$80.00**

Salt & pepper shakers, feed sacks w/sheep, pr from $80 to..**$110.00**

Spice jar, assorted lids, sm, ea from $110 to.......................**$135.00**

Teapot, duck's head **$200.00**

Paper Dolls

One of the earliest producers of paper dolls was Raphael Tuck of England, who distributed many of their dolls in the United States in the late 1800s. Advertising companies used them to promote their products, and some were often included in the pages of leading ladies' magazines.

But over the years, the most common paper dolls have been those printed on the covers of a book containing their clothes on the inside pages. These were initiated during the 1920s and because they were inexpensive retained their popularity even during the Depression years. They peaked in the 1940s, but with the advent of television in the 1950s, children began to loose interest. Be sure to check old boxes and trunks in your attic; you just may find some!

But what's really exciting right now are those from more recent years — celebrity dolls from television shows like 'The Brady Bunch' or 'The Waltons,' the skinny English model Twiggy, and movie stars like Rock Hudson and Debbie Reynolds. Unless otherwise noted, our values are for paper dolls in mint, uncut, original condition. Just remember that cut sets (even if all original components are still there) are worth only about half as much. Damaged sets or those with missing pieces should be priced accordingly.

If you'd like to learn more about them, we recommend *20th Century Paper Dolls, Price Guide to Lowe & Whitman Paper Dolls,* and *Price Guide to Saalfield and Merrill Paper Dolls* by Mary Young.

Other references: *Schroeder's Collectible Toys, Antique to Modern,* and *Paper Dolls of the 1960s, 1970s, and 1980s* by Carol Nichols.

Advisor: Mary Young (See Directory, Paper Dolls)

Airline Stewardess, Lowe #4913, 1957 ....**$45.00**

Annette in Hawaii, Whitman #1969, 1961, used, VG+.......**$30.00**

Archies, Whitman #1987, 1969 ....**$50.00**

Baby First Step, Whitman #1997, 1965...............................**$35.00**

Baby Sparkle Plenty, Saalfield #2500, 1948........................**$50.00**

Betty, Jane & Dick, Lowe #130, 1943 ....**$22.00**

Betty Buttercup, Lowe #2754, 1964 ....**$15.00**

Big & Little Sister, Whitman #4411, 1962 ....**$25.00**

Bride & Groom, Lowe #2493, 1959 ....**$50.00**

Career Girls, Lowe #958, 1950 ....**$35.00**

Cheerleaders, Lowe #2741, 1962 ....**$25.00**

Coke Crowd, Merrill #3445, 1946 ....**$100.00**

Cuddles & Rags, Lowe #1283, 1950 ....**$50.00**

Dolls of Many Lands, Whitman #3046, 1931, MIB............**$85.00**

Dotty Dimple, Lowe #2711, 1957.......................................**$15.00**

Elizabeth Taylor, Whitman #2057, 1957 ....**$150.00**

Family Dolls, Whitman #4574, 1960 ....**$40.00**

Farmyard, Lowe #1254, 1943, standups **$10.00**

Flintstones, Whitman #4796, 1962 ....**$50.00**

Glamour Girl, Whitman #973, 1942....................................**$50.00**

Gloria's Make-Up, Lowe #2585, 1952 ....**$50.00**

Good Neighbor, Saalfield #2487, 1944................................**$40.00**

Gretchen, Whitman #4613, 1966 ....**$15.00**

Henry & Henrietta, Saalfield #2189, 1938 ....**$25.00**

Honey Hill Bunch, Whitman/ Western/Mattel #1976-1, 1977, from $10.00 to $18.00. (Photo courtesy Carol Nichols)

It's a Date, Whitman #1976, 1956......................................**$40.00**

Janet Leigh, Lowe #2405, 1957 ....**$75.00**

Janet Lennon, Whitman #4613, 1962 ....**$50.00**

Julia, Saalfield #6055, 1970 ....**$50.00**

Lennon Sisters, Whitman #1979, 1958 ....**$75.00**

Little Brothers & Sisters, Whitman #971, 1953...................**$25.00**

Little Women, Artcraft #5127, from $30 to.........................**$40.00**

Magic Stay-On Doll, Whitman #4618, 1963 ....**$20.00**

Me & Mimi, Lowe #L144, 1942 ....**$40.00**

Mickey & Minnie Steppin' Out, Whitman #1979, 1977.....**$25.00**
Miss America, Whitman #7410D, 1980, from $12 to.........**$15.00**
Mother & Daughter, Lowe #1860, 1963 ....**$18.00**

My Fair Lady, Ottenheimer, 1965, $75.00. (Photo courtesy Mary Young)

My Baby Book, Whitman #1011, 1942...............................**$50.00**
National Velvet, Whitman #1958, 1961 ....**$65.00**
One Hundred & One Dalmatians, Whitman #1993, 1960 ...**$60.00**
Patti Page, Lowe #2488, 1958...**$75.00**
Pink Prom Twins, Merrill #2583, from $55 to....................**$65.00**
Pixie Doll & Pup, Lowe #2764...**$25.00**
Sally, Sue & Sherry, Lowe #2785, 1969 ....**$10.00**
Sheree North, Saalfield #4420, 1957................................**$90.00**
Soldiers & Sailors, Lowe #2573, 1943, standups.............**$40.00**
Sonny & Sue, Lowe #522, 1940 ....**$35.00**
Strawberry Sue, Whitman #1976-2, 1979.........................**$10.00**

Three High Fashion Models, Magic Wand Corporation #201, $30.00. (Photo courtesy Mary Young)

Teen Queens, Lowe #2710, 1957......................................**$20.00**
Three Little Sisters, Whitman #996, 1943 ....**$75.00**
Tom the Aviator, Lowe #1074, 1941.................................**$75.00**
Tropical Barbie, Golden #1523-1, 1986, from $12 to..........**$15.00**
Twins Bob & Jean, Lowe #128, 1944 ....**$30.00**
Umbrella Girls, Merrill #2562, 1956 ....**$75.00**
Vera Miles, Whitman #2086, 1957....................................**$125.00**
Waltons, Whitman #4334, 1974, boxed set.......................**$30.00**
Wonderful World of Brothers Grimm, Saalfield #1336, 1963, from $35 to **$50.00**

Pencil Sharpeners

The whittling process of sharpening pencils with pocketknives was replaced by mechanical means in the 1880s. By the turn of the century, many ingenious desk-type sharpeners had been developed. Small pencil sharpeners designed for the purse or pocket were produced in the 1890s. The typical design consisted of a small steel tube containing a cutting blade which could be adjusted by screws. Mass-produced novelty pencil sharpeners became popular in the late 1920s. The most detailed figurals were made in Germany. These German sharpeners that originally sold for less than a dollar are now considered highly collectible!

Disney and other character pencil sharpeners have been produced in Catalin, plastic, ceramic, and rubber. Novelty battery-operated pencil sharpeners can also be found. For over 50 years pencil sharpeners have been used as advertising giveaways — from Baker's Chocolates and Coca-Cola's metal figurals to the plastic 'Marshmallow Man' distributed by McDonald's. As long as we have pencils, new pencil sharpeners will be produced, much to the delight of collectors.

Advisors: Phil Helley; Martha Hughes (See Directory, Pencil Sharpeners)

Bakelite, Casey Jr., Walt Disney, 1¾", $35.00.

Bakelite, Charlie McCarthy decal on red figural, 1¾x1¼"...**$55.00**
Bakelite, chick figural, green w/yellow eye, from $35 to.......**$35.00**
Bakelite, Donald duck decal on butterscotch, Walt Disney, 1" dia **$75.00**
Bakelite, Dumbo decal on cream-colored rectangle, 1¼x⅞".**$40.00**
Bakelite, Dumbo decal on pale green elephant form **$45.00**
Bakelite, Ferdinand the Bull decal on red, WD Ent, 1¾", from $50 to **$75.00**
Bakelite, Jiminy Cricket decal on red figural shape, Plastic Novelties of NY, 1940s, from $60 to...............................**$75.00**
Bakelite, mantle clock form, green **$40.00**
Bakelite, Mickey Mouse decal on on round red shape, 1930s.**$85.00**
Bakelite, Mickey Mouse riding train engine, 1940s, 1⅜x1¼".**$65.00**
Bakelite, military tank, sm star sticker................................**$40.00**
Bakelite, NY World's Fair, metal appliqué of Trylon & Perisphere, 1" dia...**$65.00**
Bakelite, pistol w/G Man decal, multicolor mottle, 2" L......**$40.00**
Bakelite, Pluto decal on red, 1" dia **$50.00**
Bakelite, Popeye decal on figural shape, butterscotch, King Features Syndicate, 1929 ....**$90.00**
Bakelite, Scottie dog figural, bright green, 1½x1⅝" **$25.00**
Bakelite, Scottie dog figural, Souvenir of Washington DC on base, 1½"..**$40.00**

Bakelite, Scottie dog, red, 1½" long, $35.00.

Bakelite, Spanky photo covered w/round plastic lens, Hal Roach Our Gang Comedies below photo **$85.00**

Bakelite, US Army airplane, green.............................**$55.00**

Bakelite, Walt Disney's Bambi decal, 1x2¾x½" **$50.00**

Bakelite, We Can Will Must Win, swirling multicolor **$45.00**

Celluloid, elephant on base, white, Made in Japan.............**$165.00**

Celluloid, pelican, white w/orange beak, Made in Japan **$145.00**

Celluloid, penguin on metal base, Made in Japan **$135.00**

Celluloid, traffic light signal, metal sharpener in base of pole, 3½", EX **$250.00**

Metal, Coca-Cola bottle, old paint...........................**$25.00**

Metal, Coca-Cola can shape.................................**$25.00**

Metal, male ballet dancer on sharpener base, Hong Kong, 3¼" ..**$35.00**

Metal, milk bottle, blue & white w/Drink Milk on label, 1⅜". **$25.00**

Metal, National cash register, hand crank, Contado of Spain..**$25.00**

Metal, old-style fold-out camera, black paint, Hong Kong, 1960s, 2½" **$10.00**

Metal, pistol, gold paint, ring on bottom pulls out & holds eraser, marked Germany **$25.00**

Metal, pistol, metallic green paint, metal piece on top hinged to empty, marked Germany, 2½" L.............................**$35.00**

Metal, roadster, black paint, 2x3"...........................**$10.00**

Metal, ship's wheel, 1960s, 3¼" **$10.00**

Metal, stagecoach, black paint, Made in Hong Kong, 1960s, 1¾x2½". **$10.00**

Metal, vending cart, crank handle **$60.00**

Metal, Victrola, hand crank, record & needle move, 1960s, 2½". **$10.00**

Metal, 1902 Mercedes, copper paint, Hong Kong, 1⅛x2¾x1⅛"..**$15.00**

Plastic, continents in bas relief, Commonwealth Plastic Corporation, 2", EX..**$75.00**

Plastic, dog, yellow w/red cap & black nose, sad blue eyes, Hasbro, 1976 ....**$25.00**

Plastic, gnome w/lantern, multicolor paint....................**$25.00**

Plastic, Mummy's head, green, ABC Products...NY, 2¾" **$10.00**

Plastic, rocking horse, black & white w/red saddle & green runners, Made in Hong Kong, 2¾" **$10.00**

Plastic, seal w/ball on nose, front flippers rest on yellow Bakelite sharpener **$40.00**

Plastic, Wolfman's head, ABC Products...NY, 2¾"...........**$10.00**

Tin, globe on stand, multicolor litho, Germany, 2" **$35.00**

Tin & lead, Atlas holding globe, silver paint.................**$55.00**

Pennsbury Pottery

From the 1950s throughout the 1960s, this pottery was sold in gift stores and souvenir shops along the Pennsylvania Turnpike. It was produced in Morrisville, Pennsylvania, by Henry and Lee Below. Much of the ware was hand painted in multicolor on caramel backgrounds, though some pieces were made in blue and white. Most of the time, themes centered around Amish people, barbershop singers, roosters, hex signs, and folksy mottos.

Much of the ware is marked, and if you're in the Pennsylvania/New Jersey area, you'll find lots of it. It's fairly prevalent in the Midwest as well and can still sometimes be found at bargain prices.

Advisor: Shirley Graff (See Directory, Pennsbury)

Ashtray, Hex, 5", from $15.00 to $20.00; matching items: creamer (2⅝") and sugar bowl (3"), from $25.00 to $30.00; salt and pepper shakers, from $20.00 to $25.00 for the pair.

Ashtray, Pennsbury Inn, 8" **$45.00**

Bowl, Amish, motto, 9"....................................**$60.00**

Bowl, divided vegetable; Rooster, 9½x6¼" **$50.00**

Bowl, Hex, 3x11¼" **$40.00**

Bowl, pretzel; Eagle, 12x8"................................**$85.00**

Bowl, two-part; Rooster, 9½x6¼", $50.00.

Butter dish, Rooster, ¼-lb, from $45 to **$50.00**

Candleholders, Rooster, saucer type, pr.....................**$60.00**

Candy dish, Hex, heart shape...............................**$35.00**

Canister, Rooster, Sugar, 7½"..............................**$110.00**

Casserole, Hex, w/lid, 6½".................................**$65.00**

Chip & dip, holly & berries................................**$40.00**

Chip & dip, Rooster, 11".....................................$85.00
Compote, holly & berries, 5"..............................$25.00
Creamer & sugar bowl, Amish............................$30.00
Cruets, Amish, pr..$75.00
Cruets, rooster finials, pr..................................$50.00
Desk basket, Two Women Under Tree, 5"............$50.00
Egg cup, Folkart..$16.00
Figurine, Magnolia Warbler $150.00
Figurines, rooster & hen, various colors, 12", pr...............$450.00
Mug, beer; eagle & flag......................................$20.00
Mug, coffee; Amish, 3¼".....................................$22.00
Mug, coffee; Gay Nineties, from $15 to.................$22.00
Mug, Irish coffee; horse w/gold trim $40.00
Pie plate, Amish boy & girl, romantic verse, 9", from $80 to ... $95.00
Pie plate, Rooster, 9"..$40.00
Pitcher, E Pluribus Unum & eagle in blue, 6¼".................$45.00
Pitcher, Gay Ninety, 7¼"...................................$125.00
Pitcher, Hex, 6¼"...$65.00

Pitcher, Red Barn, 6", $30.00.

Pitcher, Yellow Daisy, ca 1959, 4".......................$32.00
Plaque, Amish Sayings, 7x5"...............................$25.00
Plaque, Baltimore & Ohio Railroad, Lafayette (train), rectangular...$45.00
Plaque, horse & carriage, 6"................................$50.00
Plaque, Mercury Dime, 8" dia..............................$65.00
Plaque, Outen the Light, 4¼"..............................$24.00
Plaque, Pennsylvania Railroad 1857, Tiger Locomotive, 8x5⅝" .$48.00
Plate, Amish, 09"..$40.00
Plate, Amish, 11¼"..$65.00
Plate, Family Wagon, 8".....................................$30.00
Plate, Peahen Over Heart, 11" $85.00
Plate, Red Rooster, dinner size $32.00
Platter, fish, 17x10¼" $225.00
Tea tile, skunk, Why Be Disagreeable, 6"................$40.00
Tray, Rooster, 7½x5"...$30.00
Wall pocket, cowboy, from $75 to $95.00
Wall pocket, floral in heart shape w/blue border, 6½"..........$50.00

Pepsi-Cola

People have been enjoying Pepsi-Cola since before the turn of the century. Various logos have been registered over the years; the familiar oval was first used in the early 1940s. At about the same time, the two 'dots' between the words Pepsi and Cola became one,

though more recent items may carry the double-dot logo as well, especially when they're designed to be reminiscent of the old ones. The bottle cap logo came along in 1943 and with variations was used through the early 1960s.

Though there are expensive rarities, most items are still reasonable, since collectors are just now beginning to discover how fascinating this line of advertising memorabilia can be. There are three books in the series called *Pepsi-Cola Collectibles*, written by Bill Vehling and Michael Hunt, which we highly recommend. Another good reference is *Introduction to Pepsi Collecting* by Bob Stoddard. For more information we recommend *Antique and Collectible Advertising Memorabilia* and *Collecting Soda Pop Memorabilia* by B.J. Summers (Collector Books).

Note: In the descriptions that follow, the double-dot logo is represented by the equal sign.

Advisor: Craig Stifter (See Directory, Pepsi-Cola)

Newsletter: *Pepsi-Cola Collectors Club Express*
Bob Stoddard, Editor
P.O. Box 817
Claremont, CA 91711
Send SASE for information

Ashtray, chrome bowl w/painted bottle cap, Pepsi-Cola Montreal, 1956, EX $90.00
Bank, Drink...The Original Pure Food Drinks, vending machine form, plastic, NM......................................$32.00
Bottle, Iowa Bowl 1978 commemorative, unopened, 16-oz..$15.00
Bottle, red & white label on twist body, 8-oz, 8⅞" $5.00
Bottle carrier, wood, 6-pack, triangular w/cut-out handle, 1930s, EX+ $150.00
Bottle opener, solid brass w/banner logo, Muddler, 1940s-50s, 5¼x2½", EX..$42.50
Calendar, Famous American Paintings, complete, 1943, 23", VG...$60.00
Carrier, cardboard, blue w/white stripes, w/6 full 12-oz bottles, NM...$50.00
Carrier, painted metal, double-dot logo in red, WE Co Atlanta, 1947, EX $60.00
Carrier, wood, double-dot logo in red & blue stenciling, holds 6 bottles, ca 1940, 10¾x8½x5¾", EX...........$135.00
Cigarette lighter, bottle cap & Pepsi on can form, VG.........$35.00
Clock, Be Sociable Have a Pepsi, lights up, sq, 15¾", EX....$75.00
Clock, Say Pepsi Please, lights up, 1970s, 22x16", EX........$30.00
Clock, The Light Refreshment, plastic, lights up, 1950s, G..$350.00
Clock, Time for Pepsi=Cola, red, white & electric blue, sq, Sessions, 14½", VG...$75.00
Door push, Drink Pepsi & bottle cap on yellow, wrought-iron look, fits 30" to 40" door, EX...............................$125.00
Door push, Enjoy Pepsi-Cola Iced, red & white w/yellow on porcelain, 3¼x32", EX.......................................$115.99
Fountain glass, red, white & blue painted-on label on clear, 4½" .$15.00
Menu board, Enjoy..., yellow tin w/blackboard bottom, 27x19", EX..$165.00
Menu board, Have a..., bottle cap logo, self-framed tin, 1950s, 30x19½", VG.....................................$120.00

Menu board, plastic light-up, modern logo/menu slots, 21x54x8", G **$25.00**

Menu board, self-framed tin, bottle cap, 30x19½", EX, $185.00. (Photo courtesy B.J. Summers)

Pitcher, stained-glass window-style logo in red & blue on clear glass, 8¼" **$32.00**

Rack, wire w/die-cut cap logo, 3-tiered, 1940s, 42x22", VG . **$185.00**

Radio, plastic bottle form w/Pepsi=Cola logo, 23", EX **$400.00**

Sign, bottle cap, painted metal, 1950s, 31", NM **$200.00**

Sign, bottle-cap die cut, red, whtie & blue, Stout Sign Co, ca 1965, 30", EX...**$175.00**

Sign, It's Got a Lot To Give, couple w/bottle, cardboard in metal frame, 25½x37¼", EX..**$135.00**

Sign, Listen to Country-Spy..., paper, 8x19", NM **$85.00**

Sign, Santa in long johns, cardboard die-cut standup, 20x16", EX..**$55.00**

Sign, Say Pepsi Please, bottle cap, self-framed metal, single-sided, 11½x31", VG **$110.00**

Sign, Say Pepsi Please, embossed tin, bottle & cap on yellow, ca 1956, 47x16½", EX..**$155.00**

Straws, each reads 'Drink Pepsi-Cola' in red and blue, 11x4x4", $200.00. (Photo courtesy Pettigrew Auctions)

Thermometer, bottle cap at top on red painted tin, 1950s, 27x8½", VG..**$115.00**

Thermometer, bottle cap at top on yellow painted tin, 1950s-60s, 27x8", EX, from $125 to..**$160.00**

Thermometer, More Bounce to the Ounce on white painted tin, 27", EX..**$325.00**

Thermometer, Say Pepsi Please, self-framing tin litho, scale-type bar, 28x7½", VG **$90.00**

Toy dispenser, Pepsi-Cola Logo, white plastic, 10", EXIB **$85.00**

Tray, Bigger & Better, stylized flowers, 1940, 11x14", EX ...**$50.00**

Tray, modern reproduction of 1909 Gibson girl, Fabcraft of Frenchtown New Jersey, NM **$20.00**

Whistle, plastic twin bottles, 3x1½", EX..............................**$20.00**

Perfume Bottles

Here's an area of bottle collecting that has come into its own. Commercial bottles, as you can see from our listings, are very popular. Their values are based on several factors. For instance, when you assess a bottle, you'll need to note: is it sealed or full, does it have its original label, and is the original package or box present.

Figural bottles are interesting as well, especially the ceramic ones with tiny regal crowns as their stoppers.

See also Czechoslovakia.

Advisors: Monsen & Baer (See Directory, Perfume Bottles)

Club: International Perfume Bottle Association (IPBA)
Susan Arthur, Membership Secretary
295 E. Swedsford Rd. PMB 185
Wayne, PA 19087
susanarthur@comcast.net; www.perfumebottles.org
Membership: $45 USA or $50 Canada

Aucoin Perfume Co, Vitivert, clear w/frosted ground glass stopper, 2¾x1¾", from $40 to...**$60.00**

Avon, Golden Promise Sachet, paper label on clear, ca 1947, 2¾x1½", from $20 to...**$25.00**

Bab's Creations, Gay Whirl, Art Deco step-up bottle w/Bakelite ballerina stopper, 1940, 6¾", from $100 to **$150.00**

Bacorn, Azura, 3¾x2", from $65.00 to $95.00. (Photo courtesy Jane Flanagan)

Bacorn, Azura, frosted green w/green & gold label, 3¼x2", from $65 to **$95.00**

Bacorn, Crabapple, red & gold label on clear, ground stopper, 4x1⅜", from $60 to **$80.00**

Bacorn, Lilas Lore, pale green frosted w/carved diagonal lines, green & gold label, 4", from $75 to **$95.00**

Blanchard, Evening Star, embossed label w/gold, oversized ground stopper, 1951, 2½x¾", from $30 to................................ **$50.00**

Bourjois, Courage, clear w/blue stopper, half full, 3¾", NMIB.. **$125.00**

Caron, French Cancan, embossed rings, ruffle at white cap, 3", w/box **$200.00**

Caron, golden cylinder, refillable, held Nuit de Noel or Fleurs de Rocaille, ca 1960s, 5", ea from $25 to **$35.00**

Caron, Nuit de Noel, black w/gold label, button stopper, 4⅜", MIB.. **$200.00**

Ciro, Acclaim, crystal w/arrow design, ground stopper, 1950, 4¼x2", from $50 to **$80.00**

Corday, Kay Sang, black w/multicolor Oriental design, resembles inkwell, 3" **$660.00**

Coty, L'Origan, clear w/dark green cap, 1940s, from $40 to... **$50.00**

Crown top, dachshund, red-brown w/painted features, Germany, 3" **$80.00**

Crown top, goggle-eyed clown (face), painted milk glass, Germany, 2¼" **$165.00**

Dana, Tabu, clear w/ground stopper, embossed Dana Made in France on base, 1932, from $25 to **$35.00**

De Vilbiss, amber w/black reverse paint, abstract gold long stem, disk foot, metal atomizer, original bulb, 7" **$150.00**

De Vilbiss, cranberry swirl, gold enamel stopper w/dauber, 6¼" .**$415.00**

De Vilbiss, crystal thistle intaglio on hexagon bell form, metal atomizer, black bulb, 4½" **$100.00**

De Vilbiss, orange enamel on clear w/black butterflies, metal atomizer, replaced bulb, 6¾" **$115.00**

Diva, Ungaro, 1980s, from $50.00 to $60.00.

(Photo courtesy Jane Flanagan)

Elizabeth Taylor, amethyst, 1987, refillable purse size w/satin pouch w/mink collar, 3⅛", MIB, from $75 to **$100.00**

Estèe Lauder, Private Collection, frosted crystal, Made in France, 1972, 3½", w/pouch & presentation box, $50 to **$75.00**

Estèe Lauder, White Linen, clear shouldered form w/glass stopper, 1978, 2x1⅝", from $50 to.................................... **$75.00**

Evyan, Most Precious, lay-down type, heart shape w/gold screw-on cap, ca 1947-present, 2¼", from $25 to **$35.00**

Fabergé, Babe, circular bottle w/glass stopper, 1977, 2¼x1¼", in presentation case, from $50 to **$750.00**

Germaine Monteil, Champagne, black w/crystal stopper w/sm embossed star, 1983, 2½x1½", from $35 to **$50.00**

Giorgio of Beverly Hills, Giorgio, crystal w/gold lettering, 1981, from $55 to **$75.00**

Guerlain, Chamade, inverted heart shape, acid-etched mark on bottom, 1969, 6x1⅛", from $55 to **$75.00**

Guerlain, Shalimar, clear shouldered form w/cream & gold label, fan-shaped black stopper w/gold lettering, 3⅛x2⅛" **$150.00**

Guerlain, Shalimar eue de toilette spray, blue & white print, refillable, marked 1968, 3-oz, 6½", from $25 to............... **$35.00**

Helena Rubenstein, Heaven Scent, baby angel, metal cap, mini, 2⅜" **$75.00**

Houbigant, Chantilly, sq shoulders, paper label, disk-like stopper, 1950s, in presentation case, from $50 to **$100.00**

HP signature of Pouchet et du Courval, crystal w/Deco-style stepped shoulders, 1960s, 3x1⅜", from $75 to **$85.00**

Hudnut, Yankee Clover, clear w/flower-design frosted stopper, long dauber, 3", from $35 to **$65.00**

IW Rice, lavender frosted inverted fan shape w/ground glass stopper, Taiwan, 1950s, 4¼x1¾", from $50 to **$90.00**

Jean D'Albret, Casaque, urn form, 1957, ¼-oz, 3¼", from $40 to... **$60.00**

Jean D'Albret, Ecussion, paper label on shield shape w/screw-on cap, 1952, 1½", w/plastic case, from $50 to **$75.00**

Jean Patou, Joy, crystal Baccarat bottle w/JP etched into stopper, ca 1934, 2⅛x2⅛", from $55 to **$75.00**

Lander, Apple Blossom, squat & shouldered, ornate tiara-like cap w/flower design, 3⅞x1", from $35 to **$50.00**

Lander, Little Miss Pixie, paper heart-shaped label, pink screw-on cap, 3½x1⅛", from $25 to **$30.00**

Lander, Rose in gold at neck, pixie trademark on gold label, 3½x¾", from $55 to **$75.00**

Lander, Spice Bouquet, squat base, Bakelite fan-type cap w/nudes, ca 1940, 3⅞, from $80 to **$100.00**

Langlois, Cara Nome, clear shouldered form w/multicolor label, flat stopper, 2⅛x2", from $75 to.................................... **$100.00**

Lanvin, My Sin, gold foil label on sq shape, black plastic cap, 1960s, 4x1¼", from $20 to **$30.00**

Lubin, L'Ocean Bleu, 2 dolphins w/hole in center, Baccarat, 6⅛" **$330.00**

Lucien Lelong, clear jar to hold perfume nips (sm vials), screw-on top, 4¼x2" dia.. **$35.00**

Marie Earle, green cylinder w/flat shoulders, Bakelite cap, 1940s, 4⅜x1½", from $55 to.. **$70.00**

Matchabelli, Beloved, crown shape, screw-on cap, 1950s, 2x1⅞", from $20 to **$25.00**

New Martinsville, crystal w/stepped shoulders, fan-like stopper, 1930s, 4½x2¾", from $50 to **$75.00**

Nina Ricci, L'Air Du Temps, swirling shape w/dove top, Lalique, 1948, 3½", from $75 to **$150.00**

NM, made for Neiman Marcus, triangular w/gold NM, crystal stopper, ca 1950, 2½x1½", from $75 to..............................**$100.00**

Oscar De La Renta, Ruffles, half-moon shape, w/tall glass stopper, signed HP, 1983, 2½", from $30 to...............................**$50.00**

Prince Matchabelli, Albano, clear w/crown-like shoulders, gold metal cap, 3⅛x1" dia, from $20 to **$25.00**

Prince Matchabelli, Chimere, simple clear bottle w/C-shaped stopper, 1979, ¼-oz, 3", from $50 to **$75.00**

Prince Matchabelli, Royal Gardenia, frosted crown, 3¾" ...**$200.00**

Prince Obolenski, Credo, sq column form w/3 steps, gold crown screw-on cap, ca 1937, 5⅝x1⅞", from $80 to **$100.00**

Rochas, Byzance, blue disk shape w/circular plaque ea side covering solid center, blue stopper, 1987, ½-oz, $50 to...............**$60.00**

Samsara, Guerlain, 1989, from $25.00 to $35.00.

Schiaparelli, Shocking, purse/travel type, 1937, 3", from $75 to.**$95.00**

Schiaparelli, Shocking, S label, cube stopper, half full, 3¾", w/box..**$45.00**

Shulton, Friendship Garden, embossed crown on green onion shape, 2-oz, 4⅛", from $20 to...**$30.00**

Unknown, aqua lyre shape, inward rolled mouth, pontil scar, 5½" .**$80.00**

Unknown, ball form w/embossed waves, glass fish top w/cork stopper, ca 1942, from $75 to **$150.00**

Unknown, dark grape amethyst, 12-sided w/sloped shoulders, smooth base, rolled mouth, 4⅛".................................**$140.00**

Unknown, dark green, corseted, original glass stopper, 6"....**$75.00**

Unknown, med pinkish amethyst, 12-sided, smooth base, rolled mouth, 6½" **$110.00**

Unknown, pale green cello form, green plastic screw-on top, 1940s-50s, from $25 to **$35.00**

Wrisley, Gold Tassel, clear tassel shape w/cream enameled ball top, 1942, 5⅜x2½", from $45 to.......................................**$55.00**

Wrisley, Muguet, paper label on crystal shell shape, white cap, from $50 to **$60.00**

Pez Candy Dispensers

Though Pez candy has been around since the late 1920s, the dispensers that we all remember as children weren't introduced until the 1950s. Each had the head of a certain character — a Mexican, a doctor, Santa Claus, an animal, or perhaps a comic book hero. It's hard to determine the age of some of these, but if yours have tabs or 'feet' on the bottom so they can stand up, they were made in the last ten years. Though early on, collectors focused on this feature to evaluate their finds, now it's simply the character's head that's important to them. Some have variations in color and design, both of which can greatly affect value.

Condition is important; watch out for broken or missing parts. If a Pez is not in mint condition, most are worthless. Original packaging can add to the value, particularly if it is one that came out on a blister card. If the card has special graphics or information, this is especially true. Early figures were sometimes sold in boxes, but these are hard to find. Nowadays you'll see them offered 'mint in package,' sometimes at premium prices. But most intense Pez collectors say that those cellophane bags add very little if any to the value.

For more information, refer to _A Pictorial Guide to Plastic Candy Dispensers Featuring Pez_ by David Welch; _Schroeder's Collectible Toys, Antique to Modern_ (Collector Books); and _Collecting Toys #10_ by Richard O'Brien.

Advisor: Richard Belyski (See Directory, Pez)

Newsletter: _Pez Collector's News_
Richard Belyski, Editor
P.O. Box 14956
Surfside Beach, SC 29587
peznews@juno.com;
www.pezcollectorsnews.com
Subscription: $19 for 6 issues; Next annual convention to be held in the spring of 2005 in Stamford, CT

Jiminy Cricket, from $180.00 to $200.00.

Aardvark, w/feet..**$5.00**
Baloo, w/feet...**$20.00**
Barney Bear, no feet...**$40.00**
Batman, w/feet, blue or black, ea from $3 to **$5.00**
Boy, brown hair, w/feet..**$3.00**
Bubble Man, w/feet...**$3.00**

Candy Shooter, red & white, w/candy & gun license, unused ..$125.00
Captain Hook, no feet $75.00
Chicago Cubs 2000, Charlie Brown in package w/commemorative
    card..$30.00
Clown, whistle head, w/feet $6.00
Daffy Duck, no feet $15.00
Dino, purple, w/feet, from $1 to $3.00
Donald Duck's Nephew, no feet..$30.00
Droopy Dog (A), plastic w/swivel ears, no feet.....................$25.00
Eerie Spectres, Air Spirit, Diabolic or Zombie (no feet), ea...$185.00
Football Player $175.00
Frog, whistle head, w/feet..$40.00
Gargamel, w/feet $5.00
Gorilla, black head, no feet $80.00
Henry Hawk, no feet $75.00
Indian brave, reddish, no feet..$125.00
Inspector Clouseau, w/feet $5.00
Jerry Mouse, painted face, w/feet $6.00
Kermit the Frog, red, w/feet, from $1 to................................$3.00
Lamb, no feet $15.00
Lazy Garfield, w/feet...$5.00
Merry Melody Makers, rhino, donkey, panda, parrot, clown, tiger or
    penguin, w/feet, MOC, ea $6.00
Mickey Mouse, w/feet, from $1 to..$3.00
Monkey sailor, w/white cap, no feet......................................$50.00
Nermal, gray, w/feet $3.00
Odie, w/feet...$5.00
Penguin (Batman), soft head, no feet $175.00
Pilgrim, no feet $125.00
Raven, yellow beak, no feet..$6.00
Ringmaster, no feet $350.00
Rooster, white or yellow head, w/feet, ea...............................$30.00
Sheik, no feet $55.00
Smurfette, w/feet...$5.00
Space Trooper Robot, full body, no feet $300.00
Spike, w/feet..$6.00
Thor, no feet..$300.00

Tom, $35.00.

Truck, many mariations, ea, minimum value $1.00
Uncle Sam, no feet...$175.00
Witch, no feet, 3-pc...$15.00
Yappy dog, orange or green, no feet, ea.................................$80.00

Pfaltzgraff Pottery

Pfaltzgraff has operated in Pennsylvania since the early 1800s making redware at first, then stoneware crocks and jugs, yellow ware and spongeware in the '20s, artware and kitchenware in the '30s, and stoneware kitchen items through the hard years of the '40s. In 1950 they developed their first line of dinnerware, called Gourmet Royale (known in later years as simply Gourmet). It was a high-gloss line of solid color accented at the rims with a band of frothy white, similar to lines made later by McCoy, Hull, Harker, and many other companies. Although it also came in pink, it was the dark brown that became so popular. Today these brown stoneware lines have captured the interest of young collectors as well as the more seasoned, and they all contain more than enough unusual items to make the hunt a bit of a challenge and loads of fun.

The success of Gourmet was just the inspiration that was needed to initiate the production of the many dinnerware lines that have become the backbone of the Pfaltzgraff company.

A giftware line called Muggsy was designed in the late 1940s. It consisted of items such as comic character mugs, ashtrays, bottle stoppers, children's dishes, a pretzel jar, a cookie jar, etc. All of the characters were given names. It was very successful and continued in production until 1960. The older versions have protruding features, while the later ones were simply painted on.

Village, an almond-glazed line with a folksy, brown stenciled tulip decoration, is now discontinued (though a few pieces are being made now and then for collectors). It's a varied line with many wonderful, useful pieces, and besides the dinnerware itself, the company catalogs carried illustrations of matching glassware, metal items, copper accessories, and linens.

Several dinnerware lines are featured in our listings. To calculate the values of Yorktowne, Heritage, and Folk Art items not listed below, use Village prices.

For further information, we recommend *Pfaltzgraff, America's Potter,* by David A. Walsh and Polly Stetler, published in conjunction with the Historical Society of York County, York, Pennsylvania.

Note: Pfaltzgraff dinnerware prices have been tremendously affected by eBay. Because it is still so readily available on the secondary market, eBay always has hundreds of items up for auction, and many times they are sold at no reserve. This plus the fact that the dinnerware is heavy and shipping charges can mount up fast has caused values to decline, though interest is still evident.

Christmas Heritage, bowl, salad; 1½x8½" $15.00
Christmas Heritage, bowl, soup/cereal; #009, 5½", from $6 to ...$8.00
Christmas Heritage, bowl, vegetable; 12-sided oval, 11x8¼"..$18.00
Christmas Heritage, butter tub, from $25 to........................$35.00
Christmas Heritage, cake plate, pedestal foot, 12" $25.00
Christmas Heritage, casserole, w/lid, 2-qt $40.00
Christmas Heritage, cheese tray, #533, 10½x7½" $9.00
Christmas Heritage, coffee carafe, thermal, 13" $22.50
Christmas Heritage, coffee cup, 4"..$5.00
Christmas Heritage, cookie jar, from $28 to $35.00
Christmas Heritage, dish, oblong w/lobed rim, 8¼x6" $20.00
Christmas Heritage, gravy boat & undertray........................$20.00
Christmas Heritage, lamp, green shade, 14".........................$30.00
Christmas Heritage, ornament, angel, 1987, MIB, from $22 to.$30.00

Christmas Heritage, pedestal mug, #290, 10-oz......................**$5.00**

Christmas Heritage, pie plate, 9" **$22.00**

Christmas Heritage, pitcher, tankard, 7½" **$25.00**

Christmas Heritage, pitcher, 5¾" **$20.00**

Christmas Heritage, plate, dinner; #004, 10", from $6 to....**$10.00**

Christmas Heritage, platter, 16¼x12" **$25.00**

Christmas Heritage, salt & pepper shakers, lighthouse form, pr..**$15.00**

Christmas Heritage, star dish, tree & toy train, 1994, 10½",
MIB **$32.00**

Christmas Heritage, teapot, lighthouse shape, 8½" **$15.00**

Christmas Heritage, tumbler, glass w/red & green decor, 5½", set of
10 ....**$35.00**

Christmas Heritage, 2-tier dish, 10" & 8" plates, MIB **$20.00**

Gourmet Royale, ashtray, #AT32, skillet shape, 9", from $10 to.**$12.00**

Gourmet Royale, ashtray, #069, 10" **$15.00**

Gourmet Royale, ashtray, #321, 7¾", from $9 to **$12.00**

Gourmet Royale, ashtray, #618, 10" **$25.00**

Gourmet Royale, baker, #321, oval, 7½", from $8 to **$10.00**

Gourmet Royale, baker, #323, 9½", from $12 to **$15.00**

Gourmet Royale, baking dish, 12x7" **$35.00**

Gourmet Royale, bean pot, #11-1, 1-qt, from $10 to **$12.00**

Gourmet Royale, bean pot, #11-2, 2-qt, from $15 to **$20.00**

Gourmet Royale, bean pot, #11-3, 3-qt **$25.00**

Gourmet Royale, bean pot, #11-4, 4-qt **$35.00**

Gourmet Royale, bean pot, w/lid, #30, lg, from $30 to **$40.00**

Gourmet Royale, bean pot warming stand **$10.00**

Gourmet Royale, bowl, berry; 4⅝" **$5.00**

Gourmet Royale, bowl, cereal; #934SR, 5½" **$5.00**

Gourmet Royale, bowl, mixing; 6", from $8 to.................**$12.00**

Gourmet Royale, bowl, mixing; 8", from $10 to...............**$15.00**

Gourmet Royale, bowl, mixing; 10", from $20 to..............**$25.00**

Gourmet Royale, bowl, mixing; 14", from $70 to..............**$70.00**

Gourmet Royale, bowl, oval, #241, 7x10", from $10 to **$12.00**

Gourmet Royale, bowl, salad; tapered sides, 10", from $10 to..**$14.00**

Gourmet Royale, bowl, soup; 2¼x7¼", from $6 to **$9.00**

Gourmet Royale, bowl, spaghetti; shallow, #219, 14", from $15
to **$20.00**

Gourmet Royale, bowl, vegetable; divided, #341 ....**$14.00**

Gourmet Royale, bowl, vegetable; 8⅛" **$12.50**

Gourmet Royale, butter dish, stick type, #394, ¼-lb, from $9 to..**$12.00**

Gourmet Royale, butter warmer, stick handle, double spout, #301,
9-oz, w/stand, from $12 to **$14.00**

Gourmet Royale, candleholders, saucer type w/finger ring, pr...**$20.00**

Gourmet Royale, candleholders, tall, w/finger ring, 6", pr from $35
to **$45.00**

Gourmet Royale, canister set, 4-pc, from $50 to.................**$60.00**

Gourmet Royale, casserole, hen on nest, 2-qt, from $50 to..**$60.00**

Gourmet Royale, casserole, stick handle, #399, individual, 12-oz,
from $7 to **$8.50**

Gourmet Royale, casserole, stick handle, 1-qt, from $9 to ...**$12.00**

Gourmet Royale, casserole, stick handle, 2-qt, from $12 to ..**$15.00**

Gourmet Royale, casserole, stick handle, 3-qt, from $15 to..**$20.00**

Gourmet Royale, casserole, stick handle, 4-qt, from $25 to..**$35.00**

Gourmet Royale, casserole-warming stand **$7.00**

Gourmet Royale, chafing dish, w/handles, lid & stand, 8x9", from
$25 to **$30.00**

Gourmet Royale, cheese shaker, bulbous, 5¾", from $12 to .**$15.00**

Gourmet Royale, chip 'n dip, #306, 2-pc set, w/stand, from $22
to **$25.00**

Gourmet Royale, chip 'n dip, #311, molded in 1 pc, 12"..**$20.00**

Gourmet Royale, coffeepot, 9"..............................**$25.00**

Gourmet Royale, cookie jar, bean-pot shape, w/handles,
6½x7½" **$40.00**

Gourmet Royale, corn dish, 3x8½", from $6 to................**$8.00**

Gourmet Royale, creamer, #382.............................**$4.00**

Gourmet Royale, cruet, coffeepot shape, fill through spout, 4", from
$12 to **$15.00**

Gourmet Royale, cup & saucer **$5.00**

Gourmet Royale, cup & saucer, demitasse **$18.00**

Gourmet Royale, egg plate, center handle, 8x12"............**$20.00**

Gourmet Royale, egg/relish tray, 15" L **$30.00**

Gourmet Royale, goblet, 5¼".............................**$9.00**

Gourmet Royale, gravy boat, w/stick handle, 2-spout, from $8
to **$12.00**

Gourmet Royale, gravy boat, 2-spout, #426, lg, +underplate, from
$9 to **$14.00**

Gourmet Royale, jug, #384, 32-oz, from $18 to...............**$25.00**

Gourmet Royale, jug, #385, 48-oz, from $20 to...............**$25.00**

Gourmet Royale, jug, ice lip, #386, from $25 to **$32.00**

Gourmet Royale, ladle, sm, from $12 to **$15.00**

Gourmet Royale, ladle, 3½" dia bowl, w/11" handle, from $18
to **$20.00**

Gourmet Royale, lazy Susan, 3 sections w/center bowl, #308, 14",
from $22 to **$30.00**

Gourmet Royale, lazy Susan, 5-part, molded in 1 pc, #220, 11",
from $15 to **$20.00**

Gourmet Royale, mug, #286, 18-oz.........................**$20.00**

Gourmet Royale, mug, #391, 12-oz.........................**$7.00**

Gourmet Royale, mug, #392, 16-oz.........................**$12.00**

Gourmet Royale, pie plate, #7016, 9½", from $10 to.........**$15.00**

Gourmet Royale, pitcher (9½") & bowl (3x12") **$35.00**

Gourmet Royale, plate, bread; #528, 12" L..................**$20.00**

Gourmet Royale, plate, dinner; #88R, from $7 to **$10.00**

Gourmet Royale, plate, egg; holds 12 halves, center metal handle,
7¾x12½", from $15 to..................................**$20.00**

Gourmet Royale, plate, Give Us This Day..., 10" **$45.00**

Gourmet Royale, plate, grill; 3-section, #87, 11", from $9 to ...**$12.00**

Gourmet Royale, plate, luncheon; 8½", from $6 to..............**$8.00**

Gourmet Royale, plate, salad; 6¾", from $2 to................**$4.00**

Gourmet Royale, plate, steak; 12", from $10 to................**$15.00**

Gourmet Royale, platter, #16, 14" **$25.00**

Gourmet Royale, platter, #17, 16" **$35.00**

Gourmet Royale, platter, #20, 14" **$25.00**

Gourmet Royale, rarebit, #330, w/lug handles, oval, 11" **$9.00**

Gourmet Royale, relish dish, #265, 5x10", from $12 to **$15.00**

Gourmet Royale, roaster, oval, #325, 14", from $18 to........**$25.00**

Gourmet Royale, roaster, oval, #326, 16", from $25 to........**$32.00**

Gourmet Royale, salt & pepper shakers, #317/#318, 4½", pr **$7.00**

Gourmet Royale, salt & pepper shakers, bell shape, pr from $15
to **$20.00**

Gourmet Royale, scoop, any size, from $8 to.................**$12.00**

Gourmet Royale, shirred egg dish, #360, 6", from $7 to......**$10.00**

Gourmet Royale, souffle dish, #393, 5-qt, +underplate, from $50
to **$60.00**

Gourmet Royale, soup & sandwich, rectangular 12" tray w/cup well, +soup cup, from $12 to $18.00

Gourmet Royale, spoon rest, coffeepot shape, $9.00.

Gourmet Royale, sugar bowl, handles $6.00
Gourmet Royale, teapot, #381, 6-cup, from $18 to $22.00
Gourmet Royale, teapot, #701, 6x10" $25.00
Gourmet Royale, toby mug, 6¼", from $30 to....................$38.00
Gourmet Royale, tray, serving; round, 4-section, center handle, #397, from $15 to $18.00

Gourmet Royale, tray, three-part, 15½" long, $20.00.

Gourmet Royale, tray, tidbit; 2-tier, from $10 to $14.00
Heritage, bowl, batter; 3-qt $24.00
Heritage, bowl, soup; wide rim, 8½", from $8 to $10.00
Heritage, butter dish, #002-028...$6.00
Heritage, butter tub, w/lid, #065, 3x5½"............................$30.00
Heritage, cake plate, pedestal, 6½x12½"..............................$75.00
Heritage, cake/serving plate, #002-529, 11¼" dia.................$9.00
Heritage, canisters, set of 4, from $55 to.............................$60.00
Heritage, casserole, straight sides, glass lid, 3-qt, 9¾" $28.00
Heritage, coffee/teapot, 13½" $40.00
Heritage, condiment server, 3 cups in wood wire stand........$30.00
Heritage, cookie jar, canister shape, 9½" $30.00
Heritage, corn dish, 8¼" L..$5.00

Heritage, cup & saucer, #002-002, 9-oz.................................$3.00
Heritage, fondue pot w/handle, #522H, +7x11½", +warmer stand...$32.00
Heritage, gravy boat, w/undertray.......................................$22.00
Heritage, honey pot, w/lid & drizzler...................................$40.00
Heritage, ice bucket, dome lid, #650 ....$50.00
Heritage, lazy Susan, 4-pc, wooden base, from $55 to $75.00
Heritage, mug, footed $7.00
Heritage, napkin rings, set of 4, MIB...................................$22.00
Heritage, pitcher, water; 10¼" $35.00
Heritage, pitcher, 5"..$17.50
Heritage, pitcher, 5", w/#772 bowl $25.00
Heritage, plate, chop; 12½" $25.00
Heritage, plate, dinner; 10¼", from $7 to.............................$8.00
Heritage, plate, egg; holds 12, 12½" L, from $40 to...........$50.00
Heritage, plate, salad; 7", from $3 to $4.00
Heritage, platter, oval, 14¼" $16.00
Heritage, punch bowl, 6 cups & ladle...................................$75.00
Heritage, quiche dish, 1¾x9"...$25.00
Heritage, salt & pepper shakers, w/handle, 5", pr from $20 to ...$30.00
Heritage, salt crock jar, #560..$35.00
Heritage, soup tureen, #002-160, 3½-qt, w/ladle & underplate, from $35 to $45.00
Heritage, soup tureen, #150, 3½-qt, w/ladle & underplate, from $35 to $40.00
Heritage, teapot, lighthouse shape, 8" $32.00
Heritage, tidbit, 3-tier $35.00
Heritage, vase, bud; 6½" $18.00
Heritage, water jug, 10" $38.00
Muggsy, ashtray...$125.00
Muggsy, bottle stopper, head, ball shape.............................$85.00
Muggsy, canape holder, Carrie, lift-off head pierced for toothpicks, from $125 to $150.00
Muggsy, cigarette server...$95.00
Muggsy, clothes sprinkler bottle, Myrtle, Black, from $275 to $375.00
Muggsy, clothes sprinkler bottle, Myrtle, white, from $250 to...$295.00

Muggsy, cookie jar, character face, minimum value, $250.00.

Muggsy, cookie jar, character face, minimum value............**$250.00**

Muggsy, mug, action figure (golfer, fisherman, etc), any, from $65 to......................................**$85.00**

Muggsy, mug, Black action figure **$125.00**

Muggsy, mug, character face....................................**$38.00**

Muggsy, shot mug, character face, ea from $40 to...............**$50.00**

Muggsy, tumbler **$60.00**

Muggsy, utility jar, Handy Harry, hat w/short bill as flat lid ..**$150.00**

Planter, donkey, brown drip, common, 10", from $15 to **$20.00**

Planter, elephant, brown drip, scarce, from $90 to.............**$100.00**

Village, baker, oval, #024, 10¼", from $7 to **$9.00**

Village, baker, oval, #240, 7¾", from $6 to **$8.00**

Village, baker, oval, #241, 10" **$10.00**

Village, baker, rectangular, tab handles, #236, 2-qt, from $10 to . **$14.00**

Village, baker, sq, tab handles, #237, 9", from $10 to..........**$14.00**

Village, bean pot, 2½-quart, $28.00.

Village, beverage server, #490, from $18 to..........................**$22.00**

Village, bowl, batter; w/spout & handle, 8", from $32 to....**$40.00**

Village, bowl, dough; #462, 8-qt, 7x13", from $40 to **$55.00**

Village, bowl, fruit; #008, 5"..**$3.00**

Village, bowl, Kitty **$45.00**

Village, bowl, mixing; #453, 1-qt, 2-qt, & 3-qt, 3-pc set, from $45 to **$50.00**

Village, bowl, mixing; enamelware, set of 4 w/lids **$50.00**

Village, bowl, onion soup; stick handle................................**$8.00**

Village, bowl, oval, handles, 12" **$26.00**

Village, bowl, pasta; 12" **$50.00**

Village, bowl, rim soup; #012, 8½", from $6 to **$8.00**

Village, bowl, serving; #010, 7", from $8 to **$12.00**

Village, bowl, serving; basketweave sides, 2½x9", from $25 to **$35.00**

Village, bowl, soup/cereal; #009, 6"..................................**$4.00**

Village, bowl, vegetable; #011, 8¾"..................................**$12.00**

Village, bowl, vegetable; 2-part, 13x8½" **$25.00**

Village, bowl, vegetable; 3-part, 1½x12x7½" **$30.00**

Village, bread tray, 12"..**$15.00**

Village, butter dish, #028..**$10.00**

Village, candlesticks, pr **$25.00**

Village, candy dish, rabbit figural....................................**$60.00**

Village, canister, Treats..**$45.00**

Village, canisters, #520, 4-pc set, from $45 to **$55.00**

Village, canisters, wooden w/ceramic oval, sq, set of 4, minimum value **$200.00**

Village, casserole, w/lid, #315, 2-qt, from $18 to................**$22.00**

Village, cheese tray, glass dome, round plate, on oval wooden tray, 10x14", from $40 to **$50.00**

Village, chip & dip set, 2-pc, from $20 to **$30.00**

Village, clock (plate)..**$35.00**

Village, coffee mug, #89F, 10-oz, from $5 to **$8.00**

Village, coffeepot, lighthouse shape, 48-oz, from $20 to......**$25.00**

Village, colander, enamel on metal, footed..........................**$30.00**

Village, cookie jar, #540, 3-qt **$20.00**

Village, cookie jar, glass w/ceramic lid, 10½", from $30 to..**$35.00**

Village, cooler/drink dispenser, spigot on front, 10x7", from $50 to..**$65.00**

Village, creamer & sugar bowl, #020, from $9 to **$12.00**

Village, cruets, vinegar & oil; pr, from $30 to......................**$40.00**

Village, cup, punch **$5.00**

Village, cup & saucer, #001 & #002................................**$3.50**

Village, flatware, Oneida, service for 4, 20 pcs, from $125 to ...**$175.00**

Village, flowerpot, 4½", from $12 to **$15.00**

Village, garlic keeper, 5x4½", from $35 to **$45.00**

Village, gravy boat & saucer, #443, 16-oz, from $12 to.......**$15.00**

Village, ice bucket, metal liner **$55.00**

Village, ice bucket, wood & copper, 8¾x7½" sq................**$50.00**

Village, lazy Susan, 5-pc..**$45.00**

Village, measuring cups, ceramic, 4 on hanging rack **$40.00**

Village, measuring cups, copper, 4 on wooden rack w/pierced copper insert, EX **$40.00**

Village, mold, heart shape..**$42.50**

Village, mug, 10-oz **$12.00**

Village, onion soup crock, #295, stick handle, sm, from $7 to **$9.00**

Village, pedestal mug, #90F, 10-oz..................................**$10.00**

Village, picture frame, 3½x5"..**$38.00**

Village, pie plate, 9½"..**$20.00**

Village, piggy bank..**$25.00**

Village, pitcher, #416, 2-qt, from $20 to **$25.00**

Village, plate, dinner; #004, 10¼", from $3 to **$4.00**

Village, plate, snack; w/indent for cup, 9x12"....................**$15.00**

Village, plate, teddy-bear shape **$55.00**

Village, plate, You Are Special Today, 10½" **$70.00**

Village, platter, #016, 14", from $12 to **$18.00**

Village, potpourri jar, 4¾", from $10 to **$12.00**

Village, quiche, 9" **$16.00**

Village, refrigerator magnet picture frame, 2" **$15.00**

Village, salt & pepper shakers, pr from $10 to....................**$15.00**

Village, salt box, punched copper w/wooden top **$45.00**

Village, scouring pad holder, high back, 5" W **$32.00**

Village, seafood baker, fish shape, 10½"............................**$45.00**

Village, seafood server, fish shape, w/sauce cup **$45.00**

Village, shell, #243, 3x11x11, +6 sm shells, #242, 7-pc set..**$75.00**

Village, soap dish..**$42.00**

Village, soap dispenser, 6" $28.00
Village, soup tureen, #160, w/lid & ladle, 3½-qt, from $40 to ...$45.00
Village, Sun Tea jar (like drink dispenser w/spigot), glass.....$35.00
Village, table light, clear glass chimney on candleholder base, #620, from $12 to $14.00
Village, tape dispenser........................$85.00
Village, teakettle, 3-qt $35.00
Village, teapot, ball shape w/C handles, 6x11", from $80 to..$100.00
Village, teapot, individual, 16-oz......................$10.00
Village, vase, bud; 5" $12.00
Village, vase, cylindrical, 7½"...................$45.00
Village, welcome plaque, oval, 4¾x6¾" $30.00

Yorktown, soup tureen, with lid and ladle, 3½-quart, from $40.00 to $45.00.

Pie Birds

Pie birds are hollow, china, or ceramic kitchen utensils. They date to the 1800s in England, where they were known as pie vents or pie funnels. They are designed to support the upper crust and keep it flaky. They also serve as a steam vent to prevent spill over.

Most have arches on the base and they have one, and *only* one, vent hole on or near the top. There are many new pie birds on both the US and British markets. These are hand painted rather than air-brushed like the older ones.

The Pearl China Co. of East Liverpool, Ohio, first gave pie birds their 'wings.' Prior to the introduction in the late 1920s of an S-neck rooster shape, pie vents were non-figural. They resembled inverted funnels. Funnels which contain certain advertising are the most sought after.

The first bird-shaped pie vent produced in England was designed in 1933 by Clarice Cliff, a blackbird with an orange beak on a white base. The front of the base is imprinted with registry numbers. The bird later carried the name Newport Pottery; more recently it has been marked Midwinter Pottery.

Advisor: Linda Fields (See Directory, Pie Birds)

Newsletter: Pie Birds Unlimited
For subscription information, contact:

John LoBello
qps1@earthlink.net
541-994-3007

Benny the Baker, holds pie crimper & cake tester, Cardinal China Co, ca 1950, 5¼" $75.00
Bird, multicolor, Morton Pottery, 5¼".................$40.00
Bird, thin neck, Scotland, 1972, 4¼", from $75 to $90.00
Bird, white w/green wings, pink beak & base, Shawnee, 1950s..$50.00
Bird on nest, Artesian Galleries, copyright mark, 1950s, from $450 to $300.00
Black chef, blue apron, white hat, spoon, 4½" $140.00
Blackbird, TG Green, 4", MIB $50.00
Blackbird, yellow beak & eyes, 4½" $85.00

Bluebird, blue and yellow, American Pottery Co., ceramic, 4½", $50.00 to $65.00.

Bugs Bunny, California, 5"..................$35.00
Clown, white w/green cap, painted closed eyes w/long lashes, white w/brown painted-on buttons, 4".................$110.00
Cutie Pie, Josef (or Lorrie Design), hen in bonnet, from $125 to..................$150.00
Donald Duck, identified on side, c Walt Disney...............$825.00
Duck w/long neck, pink w/gray, yellow beak, 5", from $115 to..$125.00
Dutch girl, multipurpose kitchen tool, from $75 to...........$100.00
Eagle, marked Sunglow, golden color, from $75 to $85.00
Elephant, head turned & trunk up, Nutbrown Pie Funnel Made in England $95.00
Elephant on drum, solid pink base, CCC, from $150 to ...$185.00
Funnel, aluminum, England $25.00
Funnel, terra cotta, marked Wales.....................$35.00
Funnel, white, Nutbrown Pie Funnel Co, 1940s, 3"...........$35.00
Great Blue Heron, Carmack, 4"........................$40.00
Homepride Fred the Flour Grader, 1978 ....$70.00
Mammy, designed to hold measuring spoons & cups (missing), 4½"..................$90.00
Pie Boy, white w/green sombrero $400.00
Rooster, multicolor, marked Cleminson or Cb....................$50.00

V & Keep 'em Flying w/airplane at top, red, white & blue, WWII era, NM **$28.00**

Vote Betty Crocker, red, white & blue, General Mills, 1940s-50s, 1⅛", EX **$10.00**

Wichita River Festival May 7-16, 1982, Admit One, windwagon silhouette in black, 2¼", NM **$18.00**

Worcester Salt, celluloid over metal, blue, cream, and black, 1½", $30.00.

Yankees, We're No 1, baseball & Uncle Sam's Hat, red, white & blue, 1970s, 3½" **$12.50**

1993 Hawyard Musky Fest, Muskellunge (lg fish) on blue, black, white, green & blue, NM **$22.50**

Kellogg's Pep Pins

Chances are if you're over 50, you remember Kellogg's Pep Pin's — one in each box of PEP (Kellogg's wheat-flake cereal that was among the first to be vitamin fortified). There were 86 in all, each carrying the full-color image of a character from one of the popular cartoon strips of the day — Maggie and Jiggs, the Winkles, Dagwood and Blondie, Superman, Dick Tracy, and many others. Very few of these cartoons are still in print.

The pins were issued in five sets, the first in 1945, three in 1946, and the last in 1947. They were made in Connecticut by the Crown Bottle Cap Company, and they're marked PEP on the back. You could wear them on your cap, shirt, coat, or the official PEP pin beanie, an orange and white cloth cap made for just that purpose. The Superman pin — he was the only D.C. Comics Inc. character in the group — was included in each set.

Compared to the value of pin in near mint condition, those that are foxed or faded can be worth as much as 75% less, depending on the extent of the problem

Advisor: Michael McQuillen (See Directory, Pin-Back Buttons)

Andy Gump, EX **$12.00**
BO Plenty, NM **$30.00**
Corky, NM **$16.00**
Dagwood, NM **$30.00**
Dick Tracy, NM **$30.00**
Don Winslow, MIP **$20.00**
Fat Stuff, NM **$15.00**
Felix the Cat **$40.00**
Flash Gordon, NM **$25.00**
Flat Top, NM **$23.00**

Goofy, NM **$10.00**
Gravel Gertie, NM **$15.00**

Harold Teen, NM, $15.00.

Inspector, NM **$12.50**
Jiggs, NM **$25.00**
Judy, NM **$10.00**
Kayo, NM **$12.00**
Little King, NM **$15.00**
Little Moose, NM **$15.00**
Maggie, NM **$25.00**
Mama De Stross, NM **$30.00**
Mama Katzenjammer, NM **$25.00**
Mamie, NM **$15.00**
Moon Mullins, NM **$10.00**
Olive Oyle, NM **$18.00**
Orphan Annie, NM **$25.00**
Pat Patton, NM **$10.00**
Perry Winkle, NM **$15.00**
Phantom, NM **$60.00**
Pop Jenkins, NM **$15.00**
Popeye, NM **$30.00**
Rip Winkle, NM **$20.00**
Skeezix, NM **$15.00**
Smokey Stover, EX **$10.00**
Superman, NM **$25.00**
Toots, NM **$15.00**
Uncle Avery, EX **$20.00**
Uncle Walt, NM **$20.00**
Uncle Willie, NM **$12.50**
Wimpy, NM **$20.00**
Winkle Twins, NM **$25.00**
Winnie Winkle, NM **$15.00**

Pinup Art

Some of the more well-known artists in this field are Vargas, Petty, DeVorss, Elvgren, Moran, Ballantyne, Armstrong, and Phillips, and some enthusiasts pick a favorite and concentrate their collections on only his work. From the mid-'30s until well into the '50s, pinup art was extremely popular. As the adage goes, 'Sex sells.' And well it did. You'll find calendars, playing cards, magazines, advertising, and merchandise of all types that depict these unrealistically perfect ladies. Though not all items will be signed, most of these artists have a distinctive, easily identifiable style that you'll soon be able to recognize.

Along with hundreds of other types of collectibles, eBay has lowered the value of pinup art by as much as 50% to 70% on many but not all items. Unless noted otherwise, values listed below are for items in at least near-mint condition.

Advisor: Denis Jackson (See Directory, Pinup Art)

Online Newsletter: *The Illustrator Collector's News*
Denis Jackson, Editor
www.olypen.com/ticn
ticn@olypen.com

Blotter, All American, blond on back holding ball w/feet, Enoch Bolles, ca 1939, M......**$50.00**
Book, Playboys Vargas Girls, 1972, EX......**$90.00**
Calendar, A Pleasing Discovery, Elvgren girl on scale w/dog, Gil Elvgren, full pad, 1946, 10½x6"......**$25.00**
Calendar, different girl ea month, Layne art, complete, 1950, 14¾x7⅛", VG......**$100.00**
Calendar, different girl ea month, Vargas, Esquire, 1946, 12x8½", in envelope......**$145.00**
Calendar, different girl ea month, Vargas, verses by Phil Stack, Esquire, 1944, complete......**$78.00**
Calendar, Enchantment, Zoe Mozert, 1952, complete, 14¼x11", EX......**$185.00**

Calendar, Vargas, Esquire, 1946, 8½x12", EX, $200.00.

Calendar, Let's Be Friends, brunette w/back exposed, Rolf Armstrong, 12 sheets, 1949, 17¼x10", EX......**$55.00**
Calendar, Petty, split-spiral bound, 1948, 12x8⅞", EX, from $45 to......**$50.00**
Calendar, True Magazine, Petty, spiral bound, 1948, complete w/ original envelope, 12x9"......**$60.00**
Calendar print, lady holding orchids, DeVorss, 1930s, 9½x8", EX (watch for repros)......**$70.00**
Centerfold, girl in swimsuit, 4-fold pull-out w/12 girls on back, Vargas, Esquire, 1946, 40x13", EX......**$80.00**
Cigarette lighter, sexy girl in black on telephone, Petty, Zippo, 1999......**$30.00**

Cigarette lighter, Zippo Salutes Pinup Girls, 4 girls representing seasons of the year, 1996, MIB......**$115.00**
Clock, Sundrop Golden Cola, girl in coffee cup, lights up, sq, Pam, 1959, 15", EX......**$100.00**
Date book, Vargas girls & movie-star pinups, for GIs in war, spiral bound, Esquire, 1945, 102 pages, 7x5", EX......**$55.00**
Hot water bottle, girl figural, soft plastic, hat unscrews, Pioynter Products Inc, Cincinnati Ohio 1957, 22½x8", EX......**$65.00**
Lithograph, Adorable, lady in revealing gown leans against rail, hat in hand, blue background, 22x16", +mat & frame......**$125.00**
Lithograph, girl in cut-off bib overalls w/fishing pole & can of worms, 26x18", +frame......**$150.00**
Lithograph, girl in see-through black outfit & ballet slippers, Vargas, Esquire, copyright 1987, 26x35" +mat & frame......**$365.00**
Movie poster, Behave Yourself, Vargas image of Shelley Winters, 1951, 1-sheet, EX......**$125.00**
Mutoscope card, Bird's Eye View, penguin at feet of girl, Follies Girl, 1940s, 5¼x3¼", EX......**$45.00**
Original art, Phantom Lady, pens, colored markers & pencils on Bristol board, Robin Bielefeld, 14x11"......**$165.00**
Painting, Kelly Burke (Playboy centerfold) nude on blanket w/white dog, copied from 1966 centerfold, unsigned, 22x28"...**$165.00**
Photo, Mamie Van Doren, in shorts outfit, w/poodle dog, black & white glossy, heavy paper, 13½x10½", EX......**$115.00**
Photograph, Betty Page in sexy lingerie beside bed, black & white, 1950s, 3½x5", EX......**$130.00**
Photograph, Natalie Wood in corset w/garters & black hose, black & white glossy, 10x8"......**$100.00**
Playing cards, Anything Goes, various pinups, 1 on ea card, Vargas, double deck, EXIB......**$110.00**
Playing cards, Top Hat, pinup girls, Gil Elvgren, EXIB......**$60.00**
Playing cards, Winning Aces, Vargas girls, double deck, 1 w/cowgirl in red, other w/blond, blond w/4 aces on box, EXIB....**$55.00**
Playing cards, 53 Pinups, Vargas, Western World Playing Cards, poker-size deck, MIB......**$100.00**
Pocketknife, September 1945 calendar girl on side, 2-blade, 1950s?, opens to 7", EX......**$45.00**
Print, Alluring, full-figure nude, signed by Earl Moran, 25x20⅝"......**$100.00**
Print, Gorgeous, blond in white fur coat, Erbit, Thomas D Murphy Co, 1939, 8¼x6¼"......**$110.00**
Print, Happy Landing, DeVorss, blonde skiing, 15½x11", EX. **$40.00**
Print, Jeanne, girl w/white flowers, in white sheet, Vargas, American Classics, 36x24"......**$45.00**
Print, No Time To Lose, girl w/groceries putting coin into meter, panties at ankles, Art Frahm, 1951, 14x12"......**$50.00**
Print, Pistol Packin' Mama, Vargas, 1944, 17½x13", EX......**$40.00**
Print, Temptation, draped brunette reclining, Vargas, American Classics, 24x36"......**$45.00**
Tray, girl taking break from her gardening, Elvgren, Mobil giveaway, 1950s, 1¼x6x5"......**$50.00**

Playing Cards

Here is another collectible that is inexpensive, easy to display (especially single cards), and very diversified. Among the endless variations are backs that are printed with reproductions of famous paintings and pinup art, carry advertising of all types, and picture tourist attractions and world's fair scenes. Early decks are scarce, but those from the '40s on are usually more attractive anyway, so pick an area that interests you most and have fun! Though they're usually not dated, you may find some clues that will help you to determine an approximate date. Telephone numbers, zip codes, advertising slogans, and patriotic messages are always helpful. For more information we recommend *Collecting Playing Cards* by Mark Pickvet (Collector Books).

See also Pinup Art.

Club/Newsletter: American Antique Deck Collectors
52 Plus Joker Club
Clear the Decks, quarterly publication
Wally Mach, Auctioneer
waltermach@hotmail.com

Homes of Longfellow and Emerson, double deck, VG, $15.00.

Air Force One, Ronald Reagan, blue backs, double deck, MIB (sealed)..$80.00
Alabama Crimson Tide 1972, portrait aces, 54 cards, EX in poor box..$110.00
American Saddlebred Stars of the Past, Congress, NM in hinged box..$28.00
Automobile Back, Bicycle #808, US Playing Card Co, 52 complete, no jokers or box, VG $38.00
Budweiser King of Beers, premium deck, USPC, M in wrapper.$10.00
Catalina Island Steamship Line, Congress, 1940s, EXIB......$45.00
Chippendales, sexy men backs, 1982, MIP $27.50
Cocker spaniel portrait (2 different) on blue, double deck, Duratone, EXIB..$25.00
Discover Lighthouses, 52 different photo-image backs, 52+2 jokers+extra card, EXIB $35.00
Eden big-eyed girl (2 different) backs, double deck, MIB (sealed)..$55.00
Famous Cities, Happy Families Game, Piatnik, ca 1952, complete, EX $40.00
Golden Lights Quality Playing Cards, resembles cigarette package, 1970s, MIP..$16.00
Golden Nugget Inc 2nd & Fremont Las Vegas Nevada, rose back, 1960s?, MIP (sealed)...$35.00

Great Northern Railway, Indian girl w/Indian baby doll, advertising on ace of spades, Brown & Bigelow, 53 complete, EXIB $130.00
Great Seal of State of Florida among orange blossoms, scenic cards, 53 bridge size cards, ca 1930s, EXIB....................$85.00
Greyhound Scenicruiser Service, bus on blue backs, single deck, M (sealed)..$40.00
Hillbilly backs, Highland Builders Supply Co, Paul Webb art, 1950s, EXIB..$12.50
Historical Facts About Texas, mid-1960s, complete, M (sealed)..$25.00
Horse head, black & white, double deck, Congress, MIB....$45.00
Jeep w/3 soldiers wearing M-17A1 helmets, Congress Hamilton Card Co, WWII era, unopened, MIB.........................$38.00
KEM, Arrow Poker design, all plastic, regular, 2 decks, MIB..$25.00
KEM, maple leaf backs (black & red), all plastic, double deck, MIB..$28.00
Lady w/dogs, double deck, Congress, 54 cards, MIB w/instructions $27.50
London & North Eastern Railway, Scarboro, scenic backs, 54 cards, EXIB..$75.00
Marlboro Texan #45 Poker Cards, star backs, copyright 1984, MIB..$48.00
Oliver Finest in Farm Machinery, double deck, red & green backs, NMIB..$180.00
Playing cards, Pabst Brewing Co, Ahead of All, girl riding bike, 52 complete, EX $45.00
Port scenes by Lionel Barrymore, double deck, Brown & Bigelow, 1960s, M $45.00
Sailing ships in oval on red or blue, double deck, Kem, MIB....$60.00
Santa Fe train (2 scenes) backs, Cel-U-Tone finish, Congress, double deck, EXIB $30.00
Siamese kittens (2) on green grass, all plastic, Astor Playing Card Co, double deck, M (sealed)..............................$67.50
Southern the Big Airline That's Small Enough To Care, blue & white backs, single deck, MIB (sealed)....................$32.50
Space Shuttle, Kennedy Space Center souvenir, 1980s, EXIB...$8.00
Spaniel dogs, Stardust Plastic Coated w/Nu-Vue Tint, double deck, Congress, bridge size, MIB $22.50
Springer spaniel & Irish setter backs, double deck w/4 jokers, EXIB w/REX logo $32.50
Transarctic Expedition 1958, 2 men shaking hands in snowy landscape, double deck, EXIB $110.00
Trip or Trap, drug info, WR Spence MD, Spenco, 1960, 54 cards, MIB..$35.00
US Bicentennial Society, eagles in oval w/13 stars, plastic, Kem, MIB..$35.00
US Capitol building, linen, 10¢ tax stamp, 53 cards, EXIB ..$25.00
Wabash Railroad Serving the Heart of America, maroon backs, 52+joker+1945 calendar, EX...$50.00
Walt Disney's Epcot Center, 1970s souvenir, M (in clear plastic case) $7.50

Political Memorabilia

Political collecting is one of today's fastest-growing hobbies. Between campaign buttons, glassware, paper, and other items, collectors are scrambling to acquire these little pieces of history. Before the turn of the century and the advent of the modern political button, candidates produced ribbons, ferrotypes, stickpins, banners, and many household items to promote their cause. In 1896 the first celluloid (or cello) buttons were used. Cello refers to a process where a paper disc carrying a design is crimped under a piece of celluloid (now acetate) and fastened to a metal button back. In the 1920s the use of lithographed (or litho) buttons was introduced.

Campaigns of the 1930s through today have used both types of buttons. In today's media-hyped world, it is amazing that in addition to TV and radio commercials, candidates still use some of their funding to produce buttons. Bumper stickers, flyers, and novelty items also still abound. Reproductions are sometimes encountered by collectors. Practice and experience are the best tools in order to be aware.

One important factor to remember when pricing buttons is that condition is everything. Buttons with any cracks, stains, or other damage will only sell for a fraction of our suggested values. Listed below are some of the items one is likely to find when scrutinizing today's sales.

For more information about this hobby, we recommend you read Michael McQuillen's monthly column 'Political Parade' in *Antique Week* newspaper.

Advisor: Michael McQuillen (See Directory, Political)

Club: A.P.I.C. (American Political Items Collectors) of Indiana
Michael McQuillen
P.O. Box 50022
Indianapolis, IN 46250-0022
michael@politicalparade.com www.politicalparade.com
National organization serving needs of political enthusiasts; send SASE for more information

Badge, Democratic Convention Delegate, Chicago, 1932, EX ...**$45.00**
Badge, 1944 IN Republican State Convention, plastic, EX+ ..**$20.00**
Book, Barry Goldwater, Mr Conservative, 1974, 150 pages, EX .**$12.50**
Book, Just a Country Lawyer (Sam Ervin), 1974, EX **$15.00**
Lapel pin, IKE, metal letters, 1953, ¾x¾", MOC **$12.00**
Lapel pin, IKE, silver-tone metal, ⅞" L, EX **$5.00**
License plate, For President Roosevelt, red on white, VG.....**$65.00**

License plate, Forward With Roosevelt, 1936, EX, $150.00.

License plate, Reagan Inaugural, 1981, NM **$30.00**
Magazine, Meet LBJ, Tatler Publishing, 1964, EX...............**$24.00**
Magazine, Time, Thomas P O'Neill on cover, February 1974, EX..**$12.00**
Mug, Vote 72, Uncle Sam pointing finger, lists Young Democrats running for office, milk glass, Federal Glass..................**$35.00**

Neck tie, Wallace on blue, clips on, EX...............................**$25.00**
Paper doll, Ronald Reagan, w/clothes from movie roles & as president, Tom Tierney, 1984, uncut, NM...........................**$16.00**
Pennant, Our 36th President Lyndon B Johnson, portrait on shield, multicolor on white felt, NM **$15.00**
Pin, elephant head & 2 horseshoes, gold-plated metal, ¾", M..**$12.00**
Pin, GOP spelled out in clear rhinestones, prong-set on silver-tone, 1950s, ⅞x1¾", M..**$25.00**
Pin-back button, Betty Ford First Lady, black & white portrait w/red border, celluloid, 1976, 2½", EX **$15.00**
Pin-back button, Bill Clinton for President, red, white & blue, M **$4.00**
Pin-back button, Clinton & Gore Deserve Four More, black & white portraits, M...**$2.00**
Pin-back button, Clinton & Gore Inauguration Day, A New Beginning, 1993, M...**$7.50**
Pin-back button, Ford for President, black & white portrait w/red lettering, sm, M **$4.00**
Pin-back button, Humphrey for President, red, white & blue, 1967, 2¼", M **$7.50**
Pin-back button, I'm For Nixon/portrait flasher, 2¼", EX...**$10.00**
Pin-back button, I Signed the Perot Petition Have YOU?, red, white & blue, M...**$2.00**
Pin-back button, Independent FDR Voter, red, white & blue, EX **$15.00**
Pin-back button, John Kennedy, smiling portrait, black & white, M **$16.00**
Pin-back button, Johnsons w/their dogs, donkey & suitcases, Goldwater & wife on elephant, EX...............................**$25.00**

Pin-back, Kennedy/Johnson, either one, $60.00; Jacqueline Kennedy, $55.00.

Pin-back button, McGovern, orange & yellow, 1972, M **$4.00**
Pin-back button, Nixon/Agnew flasher, 2½", EX.................**$12.50**
Pin-back button, Read My Lips...Perot, flag behind name, red, white & blue, M...**$2.00**
Pin-back button, Roosevelt for Humanity, red, white & blue, sm, VG...**$10.00**
Pin-back button, Students for Dukakis '88, black, white, blue & red, M **$3.00**
Pin-back button, Wallace for President, red, white & blue, 1", M ..**$6.00**
Pin-back button, WIN (Whip Inflation Now), red & white, lg, M **$2.00**
Pin-back button, Wings for Willkie America, plane, multicolor, EX **$28.00**
Plate, President & Mrs John F Kennedy, unmarked, 9", M .**$15.00**
Plate, Rosalynn Carter portrait on white porcelain, American Treasury Special Edition, 8¼", M **$10.00**

Postcard, Nixon's the One, w/photo, 1968, unused, EX.........**$6.00**

Postcard, Ronald Reagan as cowboy, black & white photo, unused, EX **$10.00**

Postcard, Ronald Reagan as surgeon, Abolish Waist & Reduce Inflation (represented by figure on table), 1982, EX.......**$5.00**

Poster, Back Ike's Team, red & blue on white, 1946, 44x28", VG .**$55.00**

Poster, I Pledge Allegiance..., African American w/face painted to resemble flag, 1970, 28x22", EX.....................................**$15.00**

Poster, Kennedy, Robert Kennedy portrait, Nebraska primary, black & white, 1968, 19x12", M......................................**$42.50**

Poster, LBJ for the USA, portrait & map, black, white & red, vinyl, 24x17½", EX..**$27.50**

Poster, Nixon & Agnew as cartoon bikers, black & white, 22x34", EX **$100.00**

Poster, Reagan-Bush '84, Bringing America Back, color portraits on white, 1984, 21½x16", EX **$32.50**

Poster, Vermont Republican Rally, 1956, black print on yellow, 22x14", EX...**$25.00**

Poster, Vice President Spiro Agnew dressed as Hippie, 30x21", VG...**$30.00**

Record, Richard M Nixon, vinyl on paper, 33⅓ rpm, EX....**$15.00**

Record album, JF Kennedy on civil rights, 7 speeches, EX ..**$35.00**

Sheet music, Dear Old Boston, dedicated to Mayor James M Curley, 1923, EX **$24.00**

Sheet music, Hail Prosperity, FD Roosevelt portrait cover, 1936, EX **$40.00**

Souvenir, Jimmy Carter & How He Won, Peterson Publishing, 1976, EX **$28.00**

Tapestry, Martin Luther King, John & Robert Kennedy, late 1960s, 19x37", EX **$40.00**

Thermometer, Richard J Daley for Mayor, tin litho, 1955, 6⅜", EX **$50.00**

Wristwatch, Spiro Agnew, copyright Sheffield Watch, leather band, NM...**$25.00**

Porcelier China

The Porcelier Manufacturing Company was founded in East Liverpool, Ohio, in 1926. They moved to Greensburg, Pennsylvania, in 1930, where they continued to operate until closing in 1954. They're best known for their extensive line of vitrified china kitchenware, but it should also be noted that they made innumerable lighting fixtures.

The company used many different methods of marking their ware. Each mark included the name Porcelier, usually written in script. The mark can be an ink stamp in black, blue, brown, or green; engraved into the metal bottom plate (as on electrical pieces); on a paper label (as found on lighting fixtures); incised block letters; or raised block letters. With the exception of sugar bowls and creamers, most pieces are marked.

Our advisor for this category, Susan Grindberg, has written the *Collector's Guide to Porcelier China, Identification and Values.*

Advisor: Susan (Grindberg) Lynn (See Directory, Porcelier)

Appliance coasters, apple green or white, 6-sided, set of 4, lg...**$20.00**

Boiler, Oriental Deco, 6-cup or 8-cup, ea **$65.00**

Casserole, Basketweave Cameo, w/lid, 8½" **$85.00**

Coffeepot, Beehive Floral Spray, 6-cup..............................**$30.00**

Coffeepot, Colonial Silhouette, 6-cup, double **$125.00**

Coffeepot, Dainty Rose, 4-cup..**$40.00**

Coffeepot, Diamond Leaf, 2-cup **$32.00**

Coffeepot, French drip; Autumn Leaves, 6-cup..................**$30.00**

Coffeepot, French drip; Cameo Silhouette, 6-cup **$35.00**

Coffeepot, Geometric Wheat, 6-cup or 8-cup....................**$25.00**

Coffeepot, Rose & Wheat, 4-cup or 6-cup..........................**$25.00**

Coffeepot, Scalloped Wild Flowers, 6-cup..........................**$45.00**

Coffeepot, Serv-All Line, platinum, non-electric................**$60.00**

Coffeepot, Sunken Panel, 2-cup **$32.00**

Creamer, Beehive Floral Spray..**$10.00**

Creamer, Tree Trunk..**$25.00**

Creamer & sugar bowl, Golden Fuchsia Platinum, ea..........**$30.00**

Creamer & sugar bowl, Nautical, ea....................................**$20.00**

Mug, pheasant, sailfish, dog or horse head, gold trim, ea **$40.00**

Percolator, Antique Rose Deco...**$65.00**

Percolator, Cattail..**$400.00**

Percolator, Leaf & Shadow, short handle **$125.00**

Pitcher, batter; Barock-Colonial, ivory, red or blue, #2014 ..**$70.00**

Pitcher, batter; Serv-All Line, gold or red/black..................**$40.00**

Pitcher, hexagonal form, Field Flowers or Flower Pot, ea **$45.00**

Pretzel jar, Barock-Colonial, gold **$150.00**

Salt & pepper shakers, #3020, any, ea................................**$15.00**

Sugar bowl, Flamingo **$8.00**

Sugar bowl, Medallion...**$10.00**

Teapot, Daisy Teardrop, gold trim, 4-cup..........................**$150.00**

Teapot, Dogwood II, black, 4-cup **$85.00**

Teapot, Dutch boy and girl, 7x9", from $35.00 to $45.00.

Toaster, Scalloped Wild Flowers, from $900 to..............**$1,100.00**

Toaster, Serv-All Line, gold or red/black, #3002, from $1,1000 to **$1,200.00**

Urn, Reversed Field Flowers Hostess or Platinum, ea...........**$90.00**

Urn, Silhouette Hostess...**$95.00**

Waffle iron, Silhouette, from $125 to **$170.00**

Wall sconce, floral decal, w/fluted shade **$47.00**

Powder Jars

Ceramic Powder Jars

With figural ceramics becoming increasingly popular, powder jars are desired collectibles. Found in various subjects and having great eye appeal, they make interesting collections. For more information we recommend *Collector's Encyclopedia of Made in Japan Ceramics* by Carole Bess White (Collector Books).

Advisor: Carole Bess White (See Directory, Japan Ceramics)

Cherubs in white rococo reserve on cobalt w/gold trim, Dresden type, 3x5¾" dia **$30.00**
Chinese man seated figural, Andre Francois, Limoges, 7½x5¾x4¾" **$265.00**

Colonial lady, Japan, 7", from $125.00 to $165.00.

(Photo courtsy Carole Bess White)

Deco girl w/mirror in hand figural, signed G Granger, Edmund Etling, 7½x4½" **$360.00**
Flapper girl w/bouquet figural, multicolor, #5482, 5½" **$55.00**
Fruit (peaches, grapes & cherries) hand painted on lid, signed D Jones, Aynsley England, 4¼" **$18.00**
Lady figural, dressed in yellow, Germany, Germany, 4½" **$80.00**
Lady figural, dressed in yellow, parrot resting on arm, Germany, #4457, 4", NM **$115.00**
Lady figural, holding hat, gold trim, marked Limoges in gold, 6" **$25.00**
Lady figural, holds fan, dressed in pink, Noritake mark **$400.00**
Lady figural, long hoop skirt, bandeau bodice, Deco, Carlton Ware, England, ca 1930s, 5½" **$120.00**
Lady figural, pink dress, Germany, illegible mold number, 5¼" .. **$65.00**
Lady figural, purple gown & parasol, pink hat, Germany, #14791, 5" **$75.00**
Lady finial, seated on box decorated w/tassels & butterflies, Germany, #13357, 5½x5¼" **$120.00**
Madam Pompadour figural, holding green dress side, E&R Germany, 5x4" **$72.50**
Pierrette figural, painted bisque, Germany, #3658, 5" **$85.00**
Pierrot down on 1 knee on lid, white w/red & black details, #2820, 6¼" **$85.00**

Roses/gold hand painted on white, signed Bertha Moore, Limoges Pickard, 5½" dia **$25.00**

Glass Powder Jars

Glassware items such as powder jars, trays, lamps, vanity sets, towel bars, and soap dishes were produced in large quantities during the Depression era by many glasshouses who were simply trying to stay afloat. They used many of the same colors as they had in the making of their colored Depression glass dinnerware that has been so popular with collectors for more than 30 years.

Some of their most imaginative work went into designing powder jars. Subjects ranging from birds and animals to Deco nudes and Cinderella's coach can be found today, and this diversity coupled with the fact that many were made in several colors provides collectors with more than enough variations to keep them interested and challenged.

Advisor: Sharon Thoerner (See Directory, Powder Jars)

Amethyst glass, very plain, New Martinsville, 4½" dia **$35.00**
Annabella, pink **$175.00**
Annette, green frost **$120.00**
Annette, pink frost **$200.00**
Ballerina, pink frost **$185.00**

Bambi, marigold carnival, Jeannette Glass Co., $32.00.

Camellia (nude), pink frost, sq, 8x4¾", NM **$175.00**
Cleopatra II, crystal, shallow base, deep lid, 4¾" **$95.00**
Colonial Lady, light blue opaque, Akro Agate, from $100 to .. **$125.00**
Crinoline Girl, green frost, off-the-shoulder gown, flowers in right hand, embossed bows on skirt **$100.00**
Curtsy, pink frost **$140.00**
Dancing Girl, pink frost, US Glass, 6x5" **$85.00**
Deco lady w/2 dogs, clear w/peach flashing **$125.00**
Deco lady w/2 dogs on lid, pink frost **$125.00**
Dolly Sisters, green frost **$175.00**
Elephant (trunk back, head up), crystal **$30.00**
Elephant (trunk down), green frost, lg **$85.00**
Elephants battling, green frost, 4½x4½" **$120.00**
Elephants battling, pink frost **$125.00**

Horse & Coach, pink frost, round $350.00

Jackie, pink frost $160.00

Judy, green, New Martinsville $75.00

Lillian VII, pink frost, cone-shaped base $195.00

Lovebirds, pink frost, 4½x4½" $90.00

Martha Washington, green frost $150.00

Mexican man w/sombrero tipped forward & man by cactus embossed on sides, sombrero lid, brown & white swirl, Akro Agate .. $85.00

Minnie (flapper) sitting w/legs extended on lid, green frost, ca 1930, 4x3" dia $120.00

Minstrel, crystal $50.00

Modernistic, pink satin, New Martinsville, original sticker label. $115.00

Nude finial, embossed nudes along sides, clear frosted, 4x4"..... $65.00

Obelisk, green frost, flat, no feet $85.00

Pandora (draped nude) finial, pink frost, 6x6" L, NM $265.00

Parakeets, crystal frost $100.00

Poodle, iridescent, Jeannette..........................$40.00

Puppy Love, boy & dog on lid, milk glass, 2-compartment $450.00

Rapunzel, milk glass, 6½x4½" $350.00

Rose Blossom, milk glass, 3½x4¼", NM $110.00

Roxana, green frost..$135.00

Scottie, light blue opaque, Akro Agate $125.00

Scottie, milk glass, Made in USA, 7x4"............$60.00

Southern Belle, green frost $125.00

Sphinx, pink frost..$110.00

Spike (bulldog), green frost, 4½" $65.00

Square Penguins, pink frost, 5¼x4" $250.00

Swan finial, green frost, Jeannette, 1950s-60s.....$35.00

Three Birds, green or pink frost, ea $85.00

Tramp, green frost, flapper's head forms finial....$155.00

Tramp, pink frost, flapper's head forms finial $120.00

Victorian lady, blue frost, Germany, 1930s, 5x4" dia $265.00

Wendy, fully painted, 4½x5½x4", $145.00. (Photo courtesy Sharon Thorner)

Precious Moments

Precious Moments is a line consisting of figurines, picture frames, dolls, plates, and other items, all with inspirational messages. They were created by Samuel J. Butcher and are produced by Enesco Inc. in the Orient. You'll find these in almost every gift store in the country, and some of the earlier, discontinued figurines are becoming very collectible. For more information, we recommend *Collector's Value Guide to Precious Moments by Enesco* (CheckerBee Publishing)

and *The Official Precious Moments® Collector's Guide to Figurines* by John and Malinda Bomm (Collector Books).

Autumn's Praise, #12084, olive branch mark, MIB **$50.00**

Blessed Are the Pure in Heart, E-3104, hourglass mark, MIB... **$25.00**

Blessings From My House to Yours, E-0503, fish mark, MIB... **$45.00**

Bundles of Joy, E-2374, hourglass mark, MIB **$80.00**

Cheers to the Leader, #104035, cedar tree mark, MIB.........**$55.00**

Come Let Us Adore Him, E-2395, flower mark, MIB.........**$40.00**

Eggs Over Easy, E-3118, flower mark, MIB.......................**$25.00**

God Understands, E-1379B, fish mark, MIB......................**$38.00**

Hallelujah Country, #105821, flower mark, MIB **$35.00**

Happy Birthday Little Lamb, #15946, dove mark, MIB......**$24.00**

His Eye Is on the Sparrow, E-0530, fish mark, MIB **$75.00**

His Sheep Am I, E-7161, flower mark, MIB.......................**$35.00**

I Get a Bang Out of You, #12262, dove mark, MIB...........**$60.00**

I'll Play My Drum for Him, E-2356, fish mark, MIB..........**$40.00**

Keep Looking Up, #15997, dove mark, MIB.....................**$24.00**

Love Beareth All Things, E-7158, flower mark, MIB...........**$30.00**

Love Is Kind, E-5377, cedar tree mark, MIB **$38.00**

Love Lifted Me, E-1375A, fish mark, MIB **$45.00**

Love Lifted Me, E-5201, hourglass mark, MIB **$50.00**

Loving Is Sharing, E-3110G, hourglass mark, MIB **$25.00**

Make Me a Blessing, #100102, cedar tree mark, MIB.........**$50.00**

Nobody's Perfect, E-9268, fish mark, MIB **$42.50**

Praise the Lord Anyhow, E-9254, G clef mark, MIB **$45.00**

Puppy Love Is From Above, #106798, cedar tree mark, MIB... **$65.00**

Seek Ye the Lord, E-9261, fish mark, MIB **$35.00**

Sharing our Joy Together, E-2834, olive branch mark.........**$45.00**

Wishing You a Season Filled w/Joy, E-2805, dove mark, MIB.. **$42.50**

You Can Fly, #12335, olive branch mark, MIB..................**$50.00**

You Can't Run Away From God, E-0525, fish mark, MIB...**$40.00**

Princess House Company

The home party plan of Princess House was started in Massachusetts in 1963 by Charlie Collis. His idea was to give women an opportunity to have their own business by being a princess in their house, thus the name for this company. The founder wanted every woman to be able to afford fine glassware. Originally the company purchased glass from other manufacturers; but as they grew, the need developed to make their own. In 1972 they bought the Louis Glass Company of West Virginia.

In 1987 Collis sold his company to Colgate-Palmolive. It became a division of that company but was still allowed to operate under its own name. In 1994 a group of investors bought Princess House from Colgate-Polmolive; they own the company yet today. In order to better focus on the home party plan which had been its primary goal, the company sold the glassmaking division to Glass Works WV in 2000. This company will continue to make glass for Princess House but will also allow the facility to develop a new and greater glass market.

Most Princess House pieces are not marked in the glass — they carry a paper label. The original line of Pets also carries the Princess House label, but animals from the Wonders of the Wild and Crystal Treasures lines are all marked with a PH embossed on the glass itself.

This new PH mark will make it easy to identify these pieces on the secondary market.

Heritage is a crystal, cut floral pattern. It was introduced not long after the company started in business. Fantasia is a crystal pressed floral pattern, introduced about 1980. Both lines continue today; new pieces are being added, and old items are continually discontinued.

Advisor: Debbie and Randy Coe (See Directory, Cape Cod)

Animals, Birds, and Fish

African elephant, Wonders of the Wild, #874, 5½" $60.00
Bear, Bernie, #813, Pets collection, 3½" $12.00
Bull, Wonders of the Wild, #770 .... $60.00
Cocker spaniel, Cassie, #820, Pets collection, 3½" $14.00
Cougar, Wonders of the Wild, 5¼x6½" $65.00
Dinosaur, Danny, 2½x4", from $20 to $25.00
Frog, Freddie, #849, Pets collection, 2¾" $14.00
Giraffe, Wonders of the Wild, #41, 3¾", MIB $60.00
Grizzly bear, Wonders of the Wild, #996, 4½" $60.00
Kitten, Katrina, #811, Pets collection, 3¼" $12.00
Large-Mouth Bass, Wonders of the Wild, #989, 6" $50.00
Lion, Wonders of the Wild, #881, 4½x7" $60.00
Moose, Wonders of the Wild, 7½x7½" $55.00
Mouse, Millicent, #882, Pets collection, 3" $16.00
Owl, Wonders of the Wild, 8x9" $55.00
Pony, Sophia, #939, Pets collection, 3" $16.00

Sea Lion, Wonders of the Wild, 3x5", $55.00.

Tiger, Wonders of the Wild $65.00
Trout, Wonders of the Wild, MIB, from $40 to $48.00
Wild Mustang, recumbent, #935, Wonders of the Wild, 7½" .. $58.00
Wolf, Wonders of the Wild $48.00

Fantasia

Baker, #588, 3¼x12¾x8¾", MIB, from $35 to $45.00
Baker, w/lid, 4¼x12x8½" $28.00
Bowl, salad; #567, 10¾" $24.50

Butter dish, rectangular, #527, ¼-lb, 8" $14.50
Cake plate, domed lid, invert to make punch bowl & pedestal . $85.00
Canister set, #5212, 7"; #4213, 8¼"; #5214, 9½"; 3 for $42.50
Casserole, #529, w/lid, 3-qt, 5x11x8¼" $30.00
Compote, dessert; footed, #575, 10-oz $7.00
Cookie jar, #569, 10" $30.00
Cup & saucer, #515 .... $5.00
Deviled egg plate, #591, 10" $24.00
Dish, lasagna; crystal handles, #535, 3½x12½x8¼", from $45 to . $55.00
Goblet, water; #519, 10½-oz, 7", from $8 to $9.00
Mug, #523 .... $8.00
Pie plate, 9" $18.00

Plate, 9", $12.00.

Plate, bread & butter; #512, 6" $4.50
Plate, dinner; #511, 10" $12.00
Plate, luncheon; #437, 8" $8.00
Punch set, 4-qt bowl, +12 cups & ladle $60.00
Relish, 3-part, #534, 12¼x7" $18.00
Salt & pepper shakers, #542, 4", pr $12.50
Tumbler, #545, 12-oz, from $8 to $10.00

Heritage

Basket, #033, hostess booking gift, 10x7¾", $45.00.
(Photo courtesy Randy and Debbie Coe)

Bowl, salad; #441, 5½x10" $24.50
Bowl, trifle; #021, MIB $40.00

Bowls, nesting, set of 4 ranging from 1-qt to 4-qt, smallest: 4½x6⅛",
    largest: 6⅛x9⅞", MIB **$100.00**
Butter dish, domed lid, #461, 4¾x4½" **$9.50**
Cake pan, sculptured tube, #6127, hostess gift, 10"............**$45.00**
Cake plate, domed lid, #076, hostess booking gift, 8½x9½" **$65.00**
Chip & dip, #41, 11¼" **$19.50**
Goblet, bridal flute; #431, 7½-oz, 10" **$12.50**
Goblet, margarita; #479, 16-oz...**$9.50**
Goblet, martini; #435, 7-oz..**$10.00**
Goblet, tulip champagne; #432, 7-oz..................................**$9.50**
Goblet, water; #418, 11-oz...**$8.50**
Goblet, wine; #420, 6½-oz...**$8.50**
Hurricane lamp, #428, 2-pc, 11¾" **$12.50**
Ice bucket, #522, 5½"...**$12.50**
Lamp, Romance, electric, #971, 1989, 11", MIB..................**$45.00**
Mayonnaise, 2½x5", +6" underplate **$10.00**
Mug, cappuccino; #580, 14-oz...**$9.50**
Mug, coffee; footed, #504, 10-oz, 5½" **$7.50**
Pie server, dome lid, #054, 10½" dia, MIB.........................**$48.00**
Pitcher, chiller; bell shape, center unit holds ice to chill drinks,
    domed lid, 12½", from $75 to....................................**$85.00**
Punch bowl set, #584, brandy snifter-shaped bowl, +12 cups ..**$65.00**
Roaster, w/lid, #041, 13½" L, from $60 to........................**$75.00**
Salt & pepper shakers, #471, 4", pr....................................**$9.50**
Skillet, aluminum w/etched glass lid, #6451, 2¼x12", from $45
    to...**$55.00**
Straw dispenser, metal lid, 10½" **$70.00**
Teapot, #050, hostess gift...**$60.00**
Tray, #292, hostess gift, 15x12½" **$45.00**
Tray, 3-part, 8", 17x8½" **$45.00**
Tumbler, cooler, #4672, 6¼" **$10.00**
Tumbler, pilsner, footed, #442, 9-oz, 7½", from $8 to........**$10.00**
Tumbler, roly poly, 2¼" **$6.00**
Vase, #475, 11½"...**$19.50**
Vase, bud; 4", from $5 to..**$7.00**

Purinton Pottery

With its bold colors, prominent design elements, and unusual shapes, Purinton Pottery is much admired by today's dinnerware collectors.

The company operated in Ohio before it relocated to Pennsylvania in 1941. It was founded by Bernard Purington, but it was William H. Blair, brother of Bernard's wife Dorothy, who was responsible for designing most of Purinton's early patterns, in particular Peasant Ware and two of the company's most recognizable patterns, Apple and Intaglio. Peasant Ware was enormously successful; as a result, Purinton was encouraged to expand the pottery. This was accomplished by building a new plant in Shippenville, Pennsylvania. About this time, Bill Blair left Purinton to open his own pottery. Dorothy Purinton assumed the role of designer, and took on the task of training new decorators. However, she was never a paid employee. Once operational in Shippenville, Purinton started full production on their many dinnerware lines.

Purinton's signature pattern was Apple. It features a bold red apple with accents of yellow and brown and two-tone green leaves.

Apple (a Blair design) became their bestselling line and was produced throughout the entire life of the pottery. Another top-selling pattern (designed by Dorothy Purinton) was Pennsylvania Dutch featuring stylized hearts and tulips. Other long-term patterns followed, among them the Plaids (Heather — Red, and Normandy — Green) and the Intaglios (Brown, Turquoise, and Caramel). Several short-lived patterns were also produced: Chartreuse, Maywood, Ming Tree, Mountain Rose, Peasant Garden, Petals (made exclusively for Sears, Roebuck & Co.), Provincial Fruit, Saraband, and Tea Rose. One of the most exclusive patterns, Palm Tree, was developed for sale at a Fort Myers, Florida, souvenir store that was owned by a son of Bernard and Dorothy Purinton.

In addition to Purinton's main dinnerware lines, they also produced a line of floral ware such as planters. Contract work was done for Esmond Industries and RUBEL as well. Both of these companies were distributors based in New York City. Taylor Smith & Taylor contracted Purinton to make the Howdy Doody cookie jar and bust bank, both of which have become highly collectible.

But today it is the items painted by Dorothy Purinton that are the most collectible. Dorothy made special one-of-a-kind plates for weddings, anniversaries, holidays, and local festivals. She also made Amish- and Pennsylvania Dutch-inspired blessing plates with prayers such as 'Bless this House' and 'Give us this Day Our Daily Bread.' Dorothy generally signed these special plates on the back. They are avidly sought after by collectors and command premium prices.

The pottery was sold to Taylor Smith & Taylor in 1958 and closed in 1959, due to heavy competition from foreign imports.

The majority of the dinnerware produced by Purinton was not marked, but its unusual shapes are easily recognized. A small number of items were stamped 'Purinton Slip Ware' in ink, and some of the early Wellsville, Ohio, pieces were signed 'Purinton Pottery.' A limited number of Dorothy's items, including Blessing and Anniversary plates, have been found bearing her signature 'Dorothy Purinton' or 'D. Purinton.' Also several Wellsville, Ohio, items have emerged that were painted by Mr. William H. Blair and are signed on the back with his signature 'Wm. H. Blair' or simply 'Blair.' Such pieces are rare and command premium prices.

Advisor: Joe McManus (See Directory, Dinnerware)

Club/Newsletter: Purinton News and Views
c/o Joe McManus, Editor
PO Box 153, Connellsville, PA 15425
Subscription: $16 per year

Apple, baker, 7" **$30.00**
Apple, bottles, oil & vinegar; 1-pt, 9½", pr **$75.00**
Apple, bowl, salad; 11" **$50.00**
Apple, candy dish, divided, w/pottery handle, 6¼"............**$50.00**
Apple, coffeepot, flaring sides, 10".....................................**$350.00**
Apple, coffeepot, 8-cup, 8" **$90.00**
Apple, mug, beer; 16-oz, 4¾" **$55.00**
Apple, planter, rum jug shape, 6½".....................................**$55.00**
Apple, plate, dinner; 9¾" **$15.00**
Apple, platter, meat; 12" **$45.00**
Apple, wall pocket, 3½" **$40.00**
Blue Pansy, basket planter, 6¼" **$65.00**

Cactus, plate, breakfast; desert scene, 8½" $95.00
Cactus Flower, teapot, 2-cup.........................$125.00
Chartreuse, bowl, vegetable; 8½" $30.00
Chartreuse, juice mug, 6-oz, 2½" $25.00
Desert Scene, plate, 8½" $75.00
Fruit, bowl, range; red trim, w/lid, 5½" $45.00
Fruit, cookie jar, red trim, oval, 9" $60.00
Fruit, plate, chop; 12" $35.00
Fruit, sugar bowl, w/lid, 4" $25.00
Grapes, bowl, range; w/lid, 5½" $45.00
Grapes, bowl, unusual mold, 4½x5½" $45.00
Heather Plaid, jug, 5-pt, 8" $75.00

Heather Plaid, Kent jug, 4½", $30.00.

Heather Plaid, teapot, 6-cup, 6" $65.00
Intaglio, bean pot, w/lid, 3¾" $50.00
Intaglio, bowl, vegetable; divided, 10½" $30.00
Intaglio, plate, dinner; 9¾" $15.00
Intaglio, saucer, 5½" $3.00
Intaglio, teapot, 6-cup, 6½" $65.00

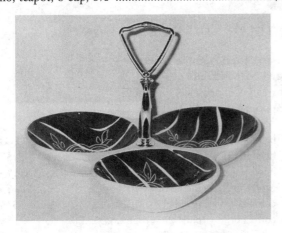

Intaglio, three-part relish tray, 10" diameter, $45.00.

Ivy (red), cornucopia vase, 6" $25.00
Ivy (red), salt & pepper shakers, jug style, 2½", pr.........................$20.00
Leaves, jardiniere, 5" $25.00

Maywood, baker, 7" $25.00
Maywood, cup & saucer, 2½" & 5½" $15.00
Maywood, teapot, 6-cup, 6½" $45.00
Ming Tree, cup & saucer.........................$30.00
Ming Tree, planter, 5" $25.00
Mountain Rose, bean pot, 4½" $65.00

Mountain Rose, chop plate, 12", $95.00.

Mountain Rose, decanter, 5" $45.00
Mountain Rose, wall pocket, 3½" $65.00
Normandy Plaid, bowl, fruit; 12" $35.00
Normandy Plaid, cookie jar, oval, 9½" $60.00
Palm Tree, basket planter, 6¼" $100.00
Palm Tree, vase, 5" $75.00
Saraband, cookie jar; oval, w/lid, 9½" $100.00
Saraband, teapot, 6-cup, 6½" $25.00
Seafoam, salt & pepper shakers, 3", pr.........................$55.00
Tea Rose, bowl, vegetable; open, 8½" $40.00
Tea Rose, platter, meat; 12" $50.00
Windflower, jardiniere, 5".........................$30.00
Woodflowers, pitcher, 6½".........................$65.00
Woodflowers, relish tray, 8" $45.00

Purses

By definition a purse is a small bag or pouch for carrying money or personal articles, but collectors know that a lady's purse is so much more! Created in a myriad of wonderful materials reflecting different lifestyles and personalities, purses have become popular collectibles. Lucite examples and those decorated with rhinestones from the 1940s and 1950s are 'hot' items. So are the beautifully jeweled Enid Collins bags of the 1950s and 1960s. Tooled leather is a wonderful look as well as straw, silk, and suede. Look for fine craftsmanship and designer names.

For more information we recommend *100 Years of Purses, 1880s to 1980s,* by Ronna Lee Aikens (Collector Books).

Chanel, black leather w/embossed logo on front flap, sm pocket inside, 6¼x4⅞"+leather & metal chain strap **$200.00**

Chanel, black patent leather, CC logo on 1 side, Chanel on other, strap handle, 10x11½x3½" **$225.00**

Coach, bucket, ivory/bone leather, 13x14x6"+adjustable 40" strap **$185.00**

Coach, Duffle, white leather, nickel hardware, #1452, 11x11"+adjustable strap **$235.00**

Coach, Gallery Tote, chocolate leather, 4 metal feet, #7585, 10x14x6"+adjustable straps **$265.00**

Coach, Gallery Tote, signature on green fabric w/white leather zebra stripes, silver hardware, #FS1862 .... **$225.00**

Coach, Hobo, khaki, inside zip pocket, zip top closure w/tassle, mini signature, #2158, 10½x14½x4⅛"+strap **$300.00**

Coach, Market Tote, khaki signature w/dark brown leather trim, #6042, 9x14x6"+adjustable straps **$275.00**

Coach, Med Carryall, khaki signature w/white leather trim, nickel hardware, 8x12x4"+17" handles **$260.00**

Coach, Pocket Flap Handbag, dark brown leather, #F05S-3653, 7½x12x4½"+strap **$245.00**

Coach, Resort Tote, off-white signature canvas w/lilac suede stripe, 11½x14x5"+straps **$250.00**

Coach, Soho Hobo, black leather, #6266SV/BK, 6½x11x3"+strap, w/matching black #6017 wallet **$290.00**

Coach, Tote, lime green leather w/silver hardware, signature nylon lining, #9780, 10x15x4"+adjustable strap, EX **$285.00**

Coblentz, Mod Bucket, ivory canvas w/black leather trim, open circles, w/clutch, 1960s, 9½x9x6¾" dia+handle, EX **$150.00**

Dooney & Bourke, Bana Bag, Vintage Leather collection, black w/black hardware, med size **$140.00**

Dooney & Bourke, Sling/Belt Bag, black w/burnt cedar trim, clip-on shoulder straps, brass hardware, 5½x7x2" **$65.00**

Dooney & Bourke, Wallet Purse, green & tan leather, magnetic snap, 3 zip pockets, 2 ID holders, 5 slots, on 25" strap **$110.00**

Enid Collins, Bird Watcher II, cat & bird in bush on ivory w/brown leather trim, 8½x12½"+handles **$215.00**

Enid Collins, Collinsiana, 7 popular designs on ivory linen w/cream leather trim, 10½x13" **$350.00**

Enid Collins, Gift Horse, box type, triple ball latch, 1967, 8¾x8¾"+leather handle, VG+ **$100.00**

Enid Collins, Grows on Trees, bird on floral branch on white linen, many jewels, 9x14" (including handles) **$375.00**

Enid Collins, Money Tree, bird resting on lg tree w/11 coins & rhinestone jewels, 9x12"+handles **$265.00**

Enid Collins, Night Owls, jeweled owls on black painted wooden box shape, brass clasp, 3¼x8½x4¼", NMIB **$135.00**

Enid Collins, Owl & Pussycat, box type w/olive green stain, 1966, 5⅞x11¼x2¾" **$160.00**

Enid Collins, Pavan, peacocks (2) & jeweled flower, 8½x7¼x4¾"+handle **$115.00**

Enid Collins, Road Runner 11, multicolor on black Irish linen, black leather handles & trim, 10x16" (including handles) ... **$235.00**

Gucci, Doctor's Handbag, brown GG fabric w/red & green stripe, brown leather trim, 7x11x5", EX **$315.00**

Gucci, Half Moon, beige GG monogram w/ivory leather trim, gold metal hardware, 16x11"+adjustable strap **$315.00**

Gucci, Tote, GG jacquard denim w/brown leather trim, silver hardware, 8x10½x5½"+straps **$250.00**

Judith Leiber, white patent leather, taffeta lining, gold-tone clasp, chain strap, 6¾x9½x2" **$85.00**

Lesco, dark brown alligator, brushed gold-color hardware, 4 gold-colored feet, 2 leather handles, 9x12x3", NM **$195.00**

Louis Vuitton, 6½x11½x2", EX, $150.00.

Louis Vuitton, Bucket, dark brown monogram w/dark brown suede trim, drawstring opening, 12x11x8", EX **$215.00**

Louis Vuitton, Doctor Bag Speedy 30, dark brown w/leather handles, 8x12x7", EX **$200.00**

Louis Vuitton, Epi Trocadero, red leather, #M51276, 6x9"+adjustable leather strap, EX **$165.00**

Louis Vuitton, pink monogram patent leather w/tan adjustable strap, flap closure, med size **$315.00**

Louis Vuitton, Shoulder, dark brown w/light brown leather trim, 9x11x3"+adjustable leather strap, EX **$165.00**

Majestic, black Lucite w/lace pattern, beveled edge, handle attached to hinged lid, 7x7¾x4¾" **$215.00**

MW Handbags, brown Lucite & metal w/engraved flowers on lid, picnic basket shape, 3¼x4"+handle **$165.00**

Patricia of Miami, black Lucite picnic basket form, clear top w/geometric lines, swing handles, 5" L **$240.00**

Ranhill, tortoise-shell Lucite, mirror in lid, from $125.00 to $150.00.

Rhinestones (prong-set) cover body of bag, ornate bezel-set rhinestone frame, wrist strap, 4x5" **$125.00**

Robert Bastien, white ostrich skin w/orange-brown marbled Lucite frame, front flap w/brass clasp, 6½x9x4", EX **$200.00**

Roberta Di Camerino, navy cut velvet, leather lined, sm strap handle, 6x11" **$175.99**

Rynor, brown alligator leather w/plastic tortoise frame, leather lining, 7x11x6"+leather strap **$150.00**

Spain, red Lucite, fabric lined, red Lucite chain handle, 5x6¾x3½" **$175.00**

Unmarked, gold Lucite w/confetti threads & stars, floral carvings on barrel form, hinged lid w/handle, 5½x11" **$215.00**

Unmarked, silver filigree w/black Bakelite oval-shaped lid, clear Lucite handle **$200.00**

Unmarked, white Lucite w/rhinestones outlining the front, opens for money clip & mirror & compact on other side, 5x3x1".. **$120.00**

Wilardy, black Lucite w/crisscross pattern & gold flakes, 2-compartment, brass hardware, 3x9¼x4", EX **$225.00**

Wilardy, brown marbleized Lucite, lunch-shape shape w/starburst patterned ends, 5¼x8x4¼"+Lucite handle **$175.00**

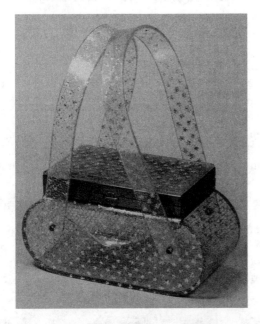

Wilardy, clear Lucite imbedded with gold tulle and sparkles, fitted interior, 3¾x7x3¼", from $250.00 to $350.00. (Photo courtesy Roselyn Gerson)

Wilardy, marbleized brown Lucite w/gold to copper shimmers throughout, gold rope-twist handle, 4¼x7¼x3¾" **$245.00**

Wilardy, marbleized silver Lucite, 2 Lucite handles, 5¾x8¼x3¼"+handles **$135.00**

Wilardy (attributed), plaid ribbon-like pattern w/silver streaks, clutch style, 1960s, 4x7x1⅝" **$235.00**

Puzzles

The first children's puzzle was actually developed as a learning aid by an English map maker, trying to encourage the study of geography. Most nineteenth-century puzzles were made of wood, rather boring, and very expensive. But by the Victorian era, nursery rhymes and other light-hearted themes became popular. The industrial revolution and the inception of color lithography combined to produce a stunning variety of themes ranging from technical advancements, historical scenarios, and fairy tales. Power saws made production more cost effective, and wood was replaced with less expensive cardboard.

As early as the 1920s and 1930s, American manufacturers began to favor character-related puzzles, the market already influenced by radio and the movies. Some of these were advertising premiums. Diecutters had replaced jigsaws, cardboard became thinner, and now everyone could afford puzzles. During the Depression they were a cheap form of entertainment, and no family get-together was complete without a puzzle spread out on the card table for all to enjoy.

Television and movies caused a lull in puzzle making during the 1950s, but advancements in printing and improvements in quality brought them back strongly in the 1960s. Unusual shapes, the use of fine art prints, and more challenging designs caused sales to increase.

If you're going to collect puzzles, you'll need to remember that unless all the pieces are there, they're not of much value, especially those from the twentieth century. The condition of the box is important as well. Right now there's a lot of interest in puzzles from the '50s through the '70s that feature popular TV shows and characters from that era. Remember, though a frame-tray puzzle still sealed in its original wrapping may be worth $10.00 or more, depending on the subject matter and its age, a well used example may well be worthless as a collectible.

To learn more about the subject, we recommend *Schroeder's Toys, Antique to Modern* (Collector Books). *Toys of the Sixties, A Pictorial Guide*, by Bill Bruegman (Cap'n Penny Productions) is another good source of information.

Flipper, Whitman, 1967, 99-piece, MIB, $15.00. (Photo courtesy Greg Davis and Bill Morgan)

Angela Cartwright — America's Little Darling on TV — The Danny Thomas Show, frame-tray, Saalfield #7030, 1962, EX .. **$40.00**

Aristocats, frame-tray, image around chair, 1970s or 1980s, MIP, N2 .... **$15.00**

Blondie, jigsaw, Dagwood's in Trouble, Jaymar, 1960s, NMIB ... **$15.00**

Bozo the Clown, jigsaw, Bozo walking the high wire, Whitman, 1969, NMIB...........$15.00

Broken Arrow, jigsaw, white man & Indian talking w/group of Indians on horseback, Built-Rite, 1958, NMIB...........$30.00

Captain Kangaroo, jigsaw, Fairchild #4430, 1970s, EXIB....$18.00

Charlie's Angels in Action, jigsaw, 1977, EXIB, N2.............$35.00

Cheyenne Puzzle Set, jigsaw, Milton Bradley #4705-2, set of 3, NMIB.................$50.00

Deputy Dawg, jigsaw, Deputy Dawg on bucking rocking horse, Whitman, 1972, NM................$15.00

Donald Duck, frame-tray, Donald dancing w/senorita, 1960, EX.................$15.00

Donald Duck, frame-tray (2-sided), Hornet's Nest, 1985, EX..$10.00

Flash Gordon, frame-tray, Milton Bradley, 1951, set of 3, EXIB .$65.00

Flintstones, frame-tray, Pebbles on top of stuffed Dino, Whitman, 1963, NM................$18.00

Flipper, jigsaw, Flipper & Porter Ricks playing in water, Whitman, 1965, NMIB.................$20.00

GI, jigsaw, Battle 1 or Battle 2, 1985, EXIB, ea..................$15.00

Gulliver's Travels, jigsaw, Saalfield, 1930s, set of 2, EXIB...$100.00

Gulliver's Travels Picture Puzzles Set, jigsaw, Saalfield/Paramount, 1939, 2 different, EXIB $100.00

H.R. Puffenstuff, Whitman, frame tray, 1970, from $40.00 to $45.00. (Photo courtesy Greg Davis and Bill Morgan)

Hoppity Hooper, frame-tray, Whitman, 1965, EX+.............$15.00

Howdy Doody, frame-tray, Clarabell getting haircut from Flub-A-Dub, Whitman, 1954, EX+..................$8.00

James Bond 007/Goldfinger, jigsaw, James Bond w/Goldfinger & Golden Girl, Milton Bradley, 1965, NMIB..................$60.00

Jungle Book, frame-tray, Golden, 8x11", EX $5.00

Katzenjammer Kids, jigsaw, Featured Funnies, 1930s, 14x10", EXIB.................$80.00

Land of the Giants, jigsaw, gang being attacked by giant kitty (cartoon art), round, Whitman, 1969, NMIB..................$40.00

Laverne & Shirley, jigsaw, HG Toys, 1976, 3 different, 150 pcs, unused, MIB, ea..................$15.00

Linus the Lion-Hearted, frame-tray, Linus & Sugar Bear watching stage play, Whitman, 1966, EX..................$25.00

Lone Ranger, frame-tray, Jaymar, 1947, Lone Ranger & Tonto escorting stage to town, NM..................$25.00

Looney Tune Characters, frame-tray (2-sided), 1985, EX, N2..$10.00

Love Boat, HG Toys, 1978, from $20.00 to $25.00. (Photo courtesy Greg Davis and Bill Morgan)

Marlin Perkins Wild Kingdom, jigsaw, Sparrow Hawk, 1971, VGIB, N2.................$15.00

Marx Bros, jigsaw, The Late Show, 1970s, NMIB................$12.00

Mary Poppins, frame-tray, kids sliding down banister, Whitman, 1966, VG+.................$10.00

Mister Bug, frame-tray, Milton Bradley, 1955, EX..............$20.00

Monkees, jigsaw, Speed Boat, Fairchild, 1967, NMIB.........$50.00

Mr Jinks, frame-tray, Mr Jinks w/Pixie & Dixie on high wire, Whitman, 1961, EX+.................$15.00

Munsters, jigsaw, family in laboratory, Whitman, 1965, VG+.$40.00

Our Gang, jigsaw, Saalfield #912, set of 3, EX (G+ window box) $100.00

Perils of Penelope Pitstop, frame-tray, Silvester Sneekly giving Penelope a flower, Whitman, 1969, EX $8.00

Pinocchio Picture Puzzles, Whitman, 1939, set of 2, 10x8½", NMIB.................$50.00

Pitfall Harry, jigsaw, Playskool, 1983, EXIB, N2 ....$20.00

Popeye in 4 Picture Puzzles, jigsaw, Saalfield/KFS #908, few pcs missing, VGIB $65.00

Raggedy Ann & Andy, frame-tray, picnic scene, Milton Bradley, 1955, EX+.................$15.00

Rin-Tin-Tin, frame-tray, Indians chasing Rin-Tin-Tin w/glove in mouth, Whitman, 1956, VG $6.00

Robert Louis Stevenson Puzzle Box, Saalfield #575, 1930s, 7 complete puzzles, EXIB $65.00

Rocketeer, frame-tray, #4510F-51, 1991, MIP.....................$5.00

Rootie (Kazootie) Wins the Soap Box Race..., frame-tray, Fairchild Corp, 1940s, 10x14", EX, P6 ....$30.00

Rootie Kazootie, frame-tray, EE Fairchild, 1950s, set of 3, VGIB.................$30.00

Santa, frame-tray, Santa entertaining children by Christmas Tree, Milton Bradley, 1910, NM.................$200.00

Santa's Workshop, Santa standing next to ice 'North Pole' w/reindeer, 1950s, EX+.................$30.00

Shotgun Slade, jigsaw, Milton Bradley, 1960, NMIB..........$30.00

Sleeping Beauty, frame-tray, 3 fairies blessing Sleeping Beauty, Whitman, 1958, NM $15.00

Smurfs, jigsaw, camping scene, Peyo, 1988, EXIB.................$8.00

Smurfs, Papa Smurf at table, Milton Bradley #4190-5, 1987, NMIB...$10.00

Snagglepuss, jigsaw, Snagglepuss having tea w/Yakky Doodle & Chopper, Whitman, 1962, NMIB...............................$30.00

Super Six, jigsaw, Whitman, 1969, NMIB.........................$30.00

Superman, jigsaw, Superman rescuing Lois & Jimmy in submarine, Whitman, 1965, NMIB...$30.00

Superman, jigsaw, Superman roaring into space after spaceship, Whitman, 1966, NMIB...$30.00

Superman Saves a Life, jigsaw, Saalfield, 1940s, 500 pcs, EX+IB..$300.00

Superman the Man of Tomorrow, jigsaw, Saalfield, 1940, 300 pcs, EX+IB..$200.00

Sword in the Stone, frame-tray, Whitman #4456, 1963, G+ . $10.00

Tennesse Tuxedo, jigsaw, Fairchild, 1971, NMIB.................$40.00

WackyRaces, frame-tray, car on 'One Way' street, Whitman, 1969, EX $25.00

Welcome Back Kotter, frame-tray, Mr Kotter (closeup) or TV cast, unused, M (sealed), ea $15.00

Wild Bill Hickok, jigsaw, HG Toys, 1976, several different, 150 pcs, unused, MIB, ea $30.00

Wizard of Oz, frame-tray, photo image, 1988, EX, N2........$15.00

Woody Woodpecker, frame-tray, Woody climbing cliff w/baby eagles harassing him, Whitman, 1976, NM..............................$10.00

101 Dalmatians, frame-tray, dalmatian family around TV watching dog on screen, Jamar, 1960, NM+................................$18.00

101 Dalmatians, frame-tray, puppies in kitchen w/cook, Jaymar, 1960, NM $15.00

Pyrex

Though the history of this heat-proof glassware goes back to the early years of the twentieth century, the Pyrex that we tend to remember best is more than likely those mixing bowl sets, casseroles, pie plates, and baking dishes that were so popular in kitchens all across America from the late 1940s right on through the 1960s. Patterned Pyrex became commonplace by the late 1950s; if you were a new bride, you could be assured that your bridal shower would produce at least one of the 'Cinderella' bowl sets or an 'Oven, Refrigerator, Freezer' set in whatever pattern happened to be the most popular that year. Among the most recognizable patterns you'll see today are Gooseberry, Snowflake, Daisy, and Butterprint (roosters, the farmer and his wife, and wheat sheaves). There was also a line with various solid colors on the exteriors. You'll seldom if ever find a piece that doesn't carry the familiar logo somewhere. To learn more about Pyrex, we recommend *Kitchen Glassware of the Depression Years, 6th Edition*, by Gene and Cathy Florence (Collector Books).

Bottle, clear, w/stopper, 4½" $12.00

Bottle, nursing; clear, 8-oz, MIB.......................................$20.00

Bowl, child's; white w/red Christmas decoration, 8-oz.........$30.00

Bowl, mixing; blue, green, red or yellow fired-on, 2½-qt $12.50

Bowl, mixing; Balloon-Print Cinderella, 4-qt....................$15.00

Bowl, mixing; blue, green, yellow or red fired-on, 1½-pt .. $10.00

Bowl, mixing; blue, green red or yellow fired-on, 4-qt $20.00

Bowl, mixing; Butter-Print Cinderella, 8¼".....................$16.00

Bowl, mixing; Delphite Blue, 8½" $35.00

Bowl, mixing, primary colors: Yellow, 9½", $12.00; Blue, 6½", $6.00; Red, 7½", $10.00; Green, 8½", $10.00. (Photo courtesy Gene and Cathy Florence)

Bowl, mixing; pink, 4-qt..$35.00

Butter dish, Butterfly Gold on white, ¼-lb $12.00

Butter dish, Spring Blossom on white, #72, ¼-lb $12.00

Cake dish, clear, round, w/handles, 8⅝" $12.00

Cake dish, Tulip-Print, #222, 8½" sq..............................$75.00

Carafe, juice; clear w/yellow lemons, yellow top..................$15.00

Casserole, clear, Windmill & Dutch Girl embossed on lid... $45.00

Casserole, lime, round, w/lid, 1½-qt $20.00

Custard cups, clear, boxed set of 8 ....$60.00

Divided dish, oval, Daisy-Print Cinderella, w/clear lid, 1½-qt, MIB $22.00

Loaf pan, clear..$10.00

Measuring cup, crystal, 1-cup $10.00

Measuring cup, dry; no spout, 1-cup $20.00

Measuring cup, red, 2-cup $100.00

Mug, gold eagle w/shield on brown, 10-oz...........................$8.00

Mug, Terra-Print, white interior, 12 oz..............................$5.00

Oven-refrigerator dish, brown, w/clear lid, 1½ cup.............$10.00

Oven-refrigerator dish, Woodland, white floral on green, 1½-pt . $10.00

Pie plate, clear, hexagonal, #1203, 9⅞"..........................$15.00

Ramekin, blue, green, red or yellow, 7-oz............................$8.00

Refrigerator dish, American Heritage, brown on white, 1½-pt.. $10.00

Refrigerator dish, Butter-Print, w/lid, 1½-qt $18.00

Salt & pepper shakers, Garland, blue on clear, pr..................$8.00

Salt & pepper shakers, Spring Blossom, green floral on white, pr $8.00

Utility dish, Butterfly Gold, 3-qt $18.00

Quilts

Quilting is appreciated as an art form, and beautiful handmade quilts have always found a ready market. The finer examples can easily bring in excess of $1,000.00 when offered at auction. There are many types of construction. Though most are pieced or appliqued; others are made in the trapunto style, which involves padding being inserted between layers quilted together in a decorative pattern. Still another type is the crazy quilt, made by stitching pieces of various sizes and shapes together following no orderly design. Amish quilts are known for their bold geometrics and bright colors.

When evaluating a quilt, condition is important, as is intricacy of pattern, good color composition, and craftsmanship. These factors are of prime concern whether evaluating vintage quilts or those by contemporary artists. For more invormation we recommend *Vintage Quilts, Identifing, Collecting, Dating, Preserving & Valuing* by Bobbie Aug, Sharon Newman & Gerald Roy (Collector Books).

Appliquéd

Dogwood chains, pink & green on white, handmade from kit, ca 1960-70, 90x76" **$295.00**

Floral bouquets (5) joined by ribbon, multicolor on white, hand quilted, made from kit, dated 1997, 90x76" **$225.00**

Floral cornucopias, multicolor on white, fancy quilting, sm stains, recent, 74x93 ....**$525.00**

Flower Basket, multicolor on white w/pink border, made from kit, ca 1970, full size, EX **$195.00**

Flower baskets, green, red & yellow on white, tulip border, 82x80", EX **$375.00**

Irish bouquet center w/iris sprays on white, 1940s, 92x79", EX.. **$350.00**

Ribbons & Roses, multicolor on white, made from kit, fine hand quilting, 1960s-70s, 93x82", unused..................**$495.00**

Roses on vine, yellow, orange & green on white, hand quilted, made from kit, 1960s, full size, unused **$400.00**

Spread eagle in center w/vining tulips etc, 1930s, light stains, 100x82" **$1,350.00**

Trailing Ivy, yellow-green, green & white w/green binding, hand quilted, PA origins, 1940s, 72x88" **$900.00**

Tulip, yellow & green on white, hand sewn, fine hand quilting, 72x84", EX **$300.00**

Pieced

Lone Star, red and white, 71x76", $400.00. (Photo courtesy Garth's Auctions)

Baskets, purple & white, machine pieced w/feather hand quilting, ca 1940, 84x86", EX.......................................**$800.00**

Bow Tie, bold printed florals & stripes w/solids, 1930s, 89x72", EX **$125.00**

Double Wedding Ring, multicolor prints on white, 1930s, 90x70" **$400.00**

Dresden Plate, green borders & grid, ca 1980s, 84x90" **$100.00**

Dresden Plate, pastels & white w/red binding, 1930s, 78x90", EX **$295.00**

Fan, multicolor prints & solids on white, hand quilted w/red binding, 1930s-40s, 83x68" **$250.00**

Flower Garden, bright multicolor w/green binding, hand sewn & quilted, 1940s, 88x10", EX.......................................**$400.00**

Flower Garden, pastel prints & solids, 1930s, 70x88", VG .**$225.00**

Friendship, Cozy Corner, multicolor calicos on white, ca 1947, 76x84", EX **$450.00**

Geometrics, multicolor prints on pink cotton, fine hand quilting, 78x78" **$275.00**

Grandmother's Flower Garden, multicolor & white w/yellow border, 1940s, 98x84", EX.......................................**$300.00**

Irish Double Chain, brown & white cottons, fancy quilting, 1930s, 87x70" **$425.00**

Irish Double Chain, dark red & bleached muslin, 1930s, 80x90", EX **$350.00**

Lone Star, bright pastels & solids, peach binding, 84x94"...**$375.00**

Patchwork Sofa, pink & white, EX hand quilting, 1930s, 72x70", EX **$295.00**

Postage Stamp, browns, white & dark blues, ca 1930, 85x77". **$400.00**

Sawtooth diamond & border, red on ivory, feather quilting, 20th Century, 102" sq...**$475.00**

Shoo-Fly, multicolor on white, ca 1930-50 (some blocks much older), 84x68"...**$255.00**

Snail's Trail, yellow & blue on white, hand sewn & quilted, 1940s-50s, sm stains, full size.......................................**$240.00**

Snowball, pastel prints & bleached muslin w/green binding, 1930s, 66x75", EX **$300.00**

Star, red & white w/burgundy prints, 1940s, 65x66".........**$250.00**

Stars (5), red, white & blue w/red border, hand quilted, 1950s, 80x89" **$275.00**

Streak of Lightning, multicolor prints, machine pieced & hand-quilted, ca 1950, 64x74", EX.......................................**$650.00**

Sunshine & Shadow, multicolor wools & knits, Amish origins, ca 1930, 80x80", VG **$350.00**

Triple Irish Chain, multicolor on white, ca 1950, 94x64"..**$350.00**

Wedding Ring, pastels, yellow & bleached muslin, hand-sewn, 1930s, 68x82", EX...**$300.00**

Yo-yo, solids & prints, 1930s, 78x76".......................................**$250.00**

4-Pointed Star, multicolor & white w/green border, patterned quilting, ca 1930-50, 80x66", EX **$295.00**

Railroad Collectibles

It is estimated that almost 200 different railway companies once operated in this country, so to try to collect just one item representative of each would be a challenge. Supply and demand is the rule governing all pricing, so naturally an item with a marking from a long-defunct, less prominent railroad generally carries the higher price tag.

Railroadiana is basically divided into two main categories, paper and hardware, with both having many subdivisions. Some collectors tend to specialize in only one area — locks, lanterns, ticket punches, dinnerware, or timetables, for example. Many times estate sales and garage sales are good sources for finding these items, since retired railroad employees often kept such memorabilia as keepsakes. Because many of these items are unique, you need to get to know as much as possible about railroad artifacts in order to be able to recognize and evaluate a good piece.

Advisors: Lila Shrader; John White, Grandpa's Depot (See Directory Railroadiana)

Dinnerware

Ashtray, Chesapeake & Ohio 'Chessie' pattern, Syracuse, 1955 – 1962, no backstamp, from $85.00 to $100.00. (Photo courtesy Barbara Conroy)

Ashtray, C&O, George Washington, 3x7" **$110.00**
Bowl, oatmeal/salad; N&W, Yellow Bird, no back stamp, 6½". **$40.00**
Bowl, soup; SP, Sunset, flat, top mark & bottom stamped, 8¾" **$45.00**
Butter pat, ATSF, Santa Fe, California Poppy, no back stamp, 3½", from $16 to **$36.00**
Butter pat, John H Murphy, Scarab-Pinstripes, top logo, 3⅜". **$50.00**
Butter pat, Washington Terminal pattern, top logo, 3⅜" **$50.00**
Chocolate pot, ATSF, California Poppy, no bottom stamp, 5½", from $130 to **$145.00**
Compote, Louisville & Nashville, Green Leaf, pedestal foot, no back stamp, 3⅛x6" **$60.00**
Creamer, Fred Harvey, Trend, handle, no back stamp, individual, 3¾" **$30.00**
Creamer, Pullman, Indian Tree, no handle, side logo, no bottom stamp, individual **$46.00**
Cup, bouillon; UP, Winged Streamliner, Sterling, 4½" dia...**$30.00**
Cup & saucer, bouillon; STL&SF, Denmark, handles, stock pattern, no back stamp..**$35.00**
Cup & saucer, KSC Southern, Roxbury, stock pattern, no back stamp, demitasse **$25.00**
Egg cup, UP, Winged Streamliner, sm pedestal, Scammell's Trenton, 2¼" **$40.00**
Pitcher, NYC, Hyde Park pattern, back stamp, Limoges, 5½". **$60.00**

Plate, Burlington & Quincy 'Violets and Daisies' pattern, railroad backstamp, 1919 – 1971, from $60.00 to $75.00. (With no backstamp, from $24.00 to $30.00.) (Photo courtesy Barbara Conroy)

Plate, GN, Spokane, no bottom stamp, 8½"......................**$35.00**
Plate, L&N, Regent, stock pattern, no bottom mark, 1946, 9¾".. **$135.00**
Plate, service; MP, State Flowers w/steam engine, no back stamp, 10½"..**$140.00**
Platter, GN, Glory of the West, back stamp, 9¾x8" **$225.00**
Sherbet, UP, Columbine, pedestal foot, full back stamp, 3⅛" **$550.00**
Teapot, B&O, Centenary, bottom mark, Shenango **$110.00**
Teapot, WP, cobalt, side logo, no back stamp, 4½"............**$130.00**

Glassware

Ashtray, B&O, top logo in blue pyro, 2 rests, heavy, 5½"....**$55.00**
Ashtray, PRR, enameled Keystone logo, 6" sq.....................**$17.00**
Beer goblet, GN, white pyro GN Rocky side logo, stemmed, 6½"..**$27.00**
Bottle, milk; CMStP&P, 3 Forks Dairy, side logo in red pyro, ½-pt **$75.00**
Bottle, milk; MP embossed buzz-saw logo, qt....................**$47.00**
Bottle, oil; SP logo embossed+label: Return Bottle to Stationary Store, 5"..**$30.00**
Carafe, wine; SP, etched side logo, 9½"...........................**$50.00**
Cocktail, ATSF, side logo acid-etched script Santa Fe, 4½"..**$55.00**
Cordial/liquor stem, DL&W, Phoebe Snow image cut side logo, 4" **$175.00**
Martini pitcher, UP, pyro UP shield side logo, 5¼" **$22.50**
Tumbler, ATSF, white pyro Santa Fe script side logo, 5¾" ...**$22.50**
Tumbler, CRI&P, white pyro wreath side logo, 4½" **$38.00**
Tumbler, DL&W, lavender pyro Phoebe Snow cursive signature side logo, 4¾" **$28.00**
Tumbler, juice; ATSF, Santa Fe enamel & script, 3¾".........**$12.50**
Tumbler, juice; IC, diamond-shaped pyro side logo, 4-oz, 3½" **$22.00**
Wine stem, ATSF, white pyro Santa Fe script side logo, 5½". **$25.00**

Silver Plate

Bread tray, NP, oval, International, bottom marked, 10½x4¾". **$80.00**

Butter pat, Pullman, Ribbon & Reed, bottom stamped, International, 3½" sq **$50.00**

Creamer, IC, hinged lid, International or Reed & Barton, bottom stamped, 7-oz...**$85.00**

Fork, dinner; Erie, Grecian, top marked, International, 7"...**$75.00**

Fork, dinner; SAL, Cromwell, International, top marked, 7½"..**$28.00**

Fork, seafood cocktail; UP Salt Lake Route, Westfield, top logo, International **$38.00**

Hot water pot, SP, Ball & Wing finial/hinged lid, bottom stamped, International, 5" **$100.00**

Jam holder, SP, lever-controlled slotted lid, w/insert, side logo, Reed & Barton, 6x6"...................................**$410.00**

Ladle, condiment; NYC, Century, bottom marked, 5¾" **$35.00**

Plate, NP, YPL top logo, 5"..**$100.00**

Spoon, condiment; NYC, Century, International, top mark, 4¼".**$36.00**

Spoon, iced tea; NYC, Century, back stamped, International, 7¾".**$42.50**

Sugar bowl, NP, handles, open, YPL side logo, 4½"............**$80.00**

Syrup, PRR, hinged lid, SM keystone logo, bottom stamped, 6" **$260.00**

Teapot, ATSF, Santa Fe side mark, Art Deco, hinged lid, thermal, 7½"..**$280.00**

Teaspoon, Erie, Grecian, top marked, International, 6" **$95.00**

Teaspoon, SP, Grecian, bottom mark, 6"..............................**$8.00**

Tray, MKT, Wallace, bottom mark, 6" dia **$140.00**

Vase, bud; UP RR, Winged Streamliner top mark, bottom marked, International, 8" **$320.00**

Miscellaneous

Calendar, Great Northern, December 1944 sheet and complete 1945 pad, 33x15½", NM, $300.00.
(Photo courtesy Buffalo Bay Auction Company)

Ashtray, SL&SW, Cotton Belt Route, bronze-tone metal, 3 rests, 3½", from $20 to......................................**$40.00**

Badge, cap; B&Me Agent, gold finish, curved top, 3⅝" **$75.00**

Badge, hat; CMStP&SSM Railway Conductor, silver-tone metal, 3½x¾" **$120.00**

Badge, hat; Penn Central Conductor, anodized brass, dome top.**$45.00**

Blanket, CMStP&P, beige/brown checked wool, Greek key border, 84x60", EX..**$150.00**

Blotter, IC, green diamond logo, St Louis to Chicago, 4x9". **$38.00**

Blotter, T&P, The Eagles, 1947 calendar, unused, 3¾x8½". **$24.00**

Book, Railroads of Hawaii, Narrow & Standard Gauge, 1979..**$75.00**

Book, Virginian Railroad, Reid, hardback w/embossed cover, 208 pages **$210.00**

Booklet, Kansas City, Mexico & Orient Railway, text & map, pre-1900 ....**$160.00**

Brochure, SP, 4 Gateways...Pacific Coast, 15 pages, 1917, 4½x8½" **$80.00**

Calendar, Burlington Route, NB Zephyr illustrations, 1949, 25½x18"...**$125.00**

Calendar, Dynamic Progress, Pennsylvania RR, 11/55-10/56, 28½" **$60.00**

Calendar, Pennsylvania RR, 1951, complete, 28½x28½".....**$20.00**

Cap badge, conductor's; Chicago Great Western, nickel-plated, 1½x2⅝"..**$45.00**

Hat, conductor's; CN, black wool w/CNR & brass hat badge.**$55.00**

Headrest cover, Lehigh Valley w/red diamond logo on white, RBH, 19x14"..**$20.00**

Headrest cover, SR w/green-on-white logo at 1 end, RBH, 19x15" **$6.00**

Magazine, employee; B&O, October, 1952, 48-page, 8½x11".**$32.00**

Menu, ATSF Monument Valley, CW Love cover, 1951 ....**$22.00**

Menu, dinner; Golden State Ltd, Carriso Gorge cover, 1923, 6x9"..**$80.00**

Napkin, CRI&P, center RI logo, white on white damask, 22x128"...**$37.50**

Napkin, UP, pink damask w/UPRR embroidered in border, 18" sq **$22.00**

Playing cards, Monon, Hoosier Line, scenic, unopened slip case, double deck **$235.00**

Postcard, Doland SD Railroad yards & depot, NM **$12.00**

Poster, Santa Fe logo lower corner, California, ocean & palms scene, 18x24"...**$475.00**

Stool, passenger step; GN, embossed side mark, metal.......**$390.00**

Tablecloth, CRI&P, white on white damask logo w/edge of oak leaves, unused, 54x36"..................................**$68.00**

Tablecloth, SAL, Through the Heart of the South, white on white damask, 54x47" **$55.00**

Timetable, employee; Nevada Northern Railway, 1-sheet, 1/5/47, 10½x14"...**$130.00**

Timetable, employee; SP, Coast Division, #152, 1944 ....**$85.00**

Timetable, employee; WP, system includes Sacramento to Northern, 1982 ....**$20.00**

Timetable, public; Puget Sound Electric, cardstock, 1930s, 3x4½" **$80.00**

Razor Blade Banks

Razor blade banks are receptacles designed to safely store used razor blades. While the double-edged disposable razor blades date back to as early as 1904, ceramic and figural razor blade safes most likely were not produced until the early 1940s. The development of the electric razor and the later disposable razors did away with the need for these items, and their production ended in the 1960s.

Shapes include barber chairs, barbers, animals, and barber poles, which were very popular. Listerine produced a white donkey and elephant in 1936 with political overtones. They also made a white ceramic frog. These were used as promotional items for shaving cream. Suggested values are based on availability and apply to items in near-mint to excellent condition. Note that regional pricing could vary.

Advisor: Deborah Gillham (See Directory, Razor Blade Banks)

Barber bust, handlebar mustache (no tie), Lipper & Mann, from $75.00 to $95.00.
(Photo courtesy Debbie Gillham)

Barber, bust only, white shirt w/black sleeves, mustache & hair, unmarked, 5½".................................**$75.00**
Barber, wood w/Gay Blade bottom, unscrews, Woodcraft, 1950, 6", from $65 to **$75.00**
Barber, wood w/key & metal holders for razor & brush, 9", from $60 to **$80.00**
Barber chair, sm, from $100 to **$125.00**
Barber head, different colors on collar, Cleminson, from $25 to..**$35.00**
Barber holding pole, marked Blades on back, Occupied Japan, 4", from 65 to **$75.00**
Barber holding pole, Occupied Japan, 4", from $50 to........**$60.00**
Barber pole, red & white, w/ or w/out attachments & various titles, from $20 to **$25.00**
Barber pole, red & white stripes, Royal Copley sticker, 6½"...**$30.00**

Barber pole, barber head and derby hat, from $40.00 to $60.00. (Photo courtesy Debbie Gillham)

Barber pole w/face, red & white, from $30 to.....................**$40.00**
Barber standing in blue coat & stroking chin, from $65 to..**$85.00**
Barber w/buggy eyes, pudgy full body, Gleason look-alike, from $65 to **$75.00**
Barbershop quartet, 4 singing barber heads, from $95 to...**$125.00**
Bell, white w/man shaving, California Cleminsons, 3½" **$25.00**
Box w/policeman holding up hand, metal, Used Blades, from $75 to **$100.00**
Dandy Dans, plastic w/brush holders, from $25 to.............**$35.00**
Friar Tuck, Razor Blade Holder (on back), Goebel............**$300.00**
Frog, green, For Used Blades, from $60 to **$70.00**
Grinding stone, For Dull Ones, from $80 to **$100.00**
Half barber pole, hangs on wall, may be personalized w/name, from $40 to **$60.00**
Half shaving cup, hangs on wall, Gay Blades w/floral design, from $75 to **$100.00**
Half shaving cup, hangs on wall, Gay Old Blade w/quartet, from $65 to **$75.00**
Indian head, porcelain, Japan, 4" **$25.00**
Listerine donkey, from $20 to **$30.00**
Listerine elephant, from $25 to **$35.00**
Listerine frog, from $15 to **$25.00**
Looie, right- or left-hand version, from $85 to **$110.00**
Man shaving, mushroom shape, Cleminson, from $25 to....**$35.00**
Man shaving, mushroom shape, Cleminson, personalized, from $45 to **$55.00**
Razor Bum, from $85 to **$100.00**
Safe, green, Blade Safe on front, from $40 to.....................**$60.00**
Shaving brush, white w/red Blades on front & red bottom, brown bristles, 5½" **$40.00**
Shaving brush, wide style w/decal, from $45 to **$65.00**
Souvenir, wood-burned outhouse, For Gay Old Blades, by Crosby, found w/names of several states, from $35 to **$45.00**
Specialist in Used Blades in bottom of white outhouse, from $75 to **$90.00**
Tony the Barber, Ceramic Arts Studio, from $85 to............**$95.00**

Reamers

Reamers were a European invention of the late 1700s, devised as a tool for extracting liquid from citrus fruits, which was often used as a medicinal remedy. Eventually the concept of freshly squeezed juice worked its way across the oceans. Many early U.S. patents (mostly for wood reamers) were filed in the mid-1880s, and thanks to the 1916 Sunkist 'Drink An Orange' advertising campaign, the reamer soon became a permanent fixture in the well-equipped American kitchen. Most of the major U.S. glass companies and pottery manufacturers included juicers as part of their kitchenware lines. However, some of the most beautiful and unique reamers are ceramic figures and hand-painted, elegant china and porcelain examples. The invention of frozen and bottled citrus juice relegated many a reamer to the kitchen shelf. However, the current trend for a healthier diet has garnered renewed interest for the manual juice squeezer.

Most of the German and English reamers listed here can be attributed to the 1920s and 1930s. Most of the Japanese imports are from the 1940s.

Advisor: Bobbie Zucker Bryson (See Directory, Reamers)

Newsletter:

National Reamer Collectors Association

www.reamers.org

Ceramics

Anthropomorphic peach w/smiling face, #1K3358, ca 1950s, 4¾" **$35.00**

Beige w/yellow flowers, green leaves, tan & yellow honey bees, Japan, 4½x6" **$30.00**

Cat face, pink, blue & black, yellow hat forms reamer, side handle, 5¾", NM **$50.00**

Clown, green & white w/black eyes & buttons, seated, unmarked Japan **$95.00**

Clown, green & yellow hat, blue & white pants, seated, Mikori Ware Made in Japan, 7¾" **$110.00**

Clown, Japan, black mark, 6½", from $65.00 to $75.00; lotus, Japan, red mark, from $50.00 to $65.00. (Photo courtesy Carole Bess White)

Duck, duck figural, white w/tail handle, reamer on back, 3½x6" **$15.00**

Duck, yellow w/black iris on white, orange beak & wing feathers, reamer on back, Maison...NY/Made in Japan label, NM . **$45.00**

Girl's face on white teapot form, reamer top, Marutomo Ware, 4½", NM **$55.00**

House w/thatched roof, reamer lid, hand painted, Japan, 5⅛x4½" dia. **$45.00**

Lemons & green leaves on white, reamer top, Germany #2887, 2-pc, 3x3" **$55.00**

Majolica grapevines & brown wooden fence on ivory, sq pitcher form w/reamer top, Made in Japan, 7¼" **$225.00**

Pear, speckled yellow w/green leaves forming finial, Japan, 3-pc, 5" **$55.00**

Pig down on tummy, kerchief around neck, reamer on back, white, Japan, 3¼x6½" **$20.00**

Reamer, white pitcher w/reamer top, 2-pc, 4½" **$15.00**

Swan figural, hand-painted roses on cream, reamer on back, Marutomo Ware, 4½x7¼" **$65.00**

Toucan figural, white lustre w/multicolor details, reamer on back, unmarked Japan **$95.00**

Glassware

Amber, handled, spout opposite, Indiana Glass, from $275 to ..**$300.00**

Crystal, elephant-decorated base, Fenton, 2-pc, from $110 to ...**$125.00**

Crystal, embossed Tcheco-Schovaquie on handle, from $25 to...**$30.00**

Crystal, horizontal handle, Indiana Glass, from $20 to **$25.00**

Crystal, LE Smith, 2-pc in metal frame, from $75 to..........**$95.00**

Crystal, RADNT, from $125 to...**$135.00**

Custard w/red trim, embossed McK, 6", from $35 to **$40.00**

Fired-on red, Hazel-Atlas, 2-pc, from $65 to **$70.00**

French Ivory, Sunkist, from $$5 to **$55.00**

Frosted crystal, no decor, Westmoreland, 2-pc, from $75 to...**$95.00**

Green, Anchor Hocking, 2-cup pitcher w/reamer top, from $65 to **$70.00**

Green, Anchor Hocking, 2-cup ribbed pitcher w/reamer top, from $70 to **$80.00**

Green, Crisscross, Hazel-Atlas, from $35 to **$40.00**

Green, Hex Optic, bucket style, from $60 to **$65.00**

Green, marked A&J, Hazel-Atlas, 4-cup pitcher+reamer top, from $55 to **$65.00**

Green, metal handle, insert near top of cup, graduated measurments on side, US Glass, from $60 to.................................**$65.00**

Green, pointed cone, Federal Glass, from $25 to **$28.00**

Green, 6-sided cone, vertical handle, Indiana Glass, from $70 to **$75.00**

Green w/silver Rockwell decoration, Cambridge, from $225 to.**$250.00**

Jade-ite, embossed Saunders, from $1,600.00 to $1,700.00. (Photo courtesy Gene and Cathy Florence)

Jadite (dark), unembossed Sunkist, from $150 to..............**$165.00**

Light green, straight sides, Fry, from $40 to........................**$45.00**

Pearl, fluted sides, Fry, from $75 to....................................**$85.00**

Pearl opalescent, straight sides, Pearl opalescent, from $40 to.**$45.00**

Pink, embossed Lindsay on side, from $450 to **$500.00**

Pink, Jennyware, from $110 to **$125.00**

Pink, Party Line, 4-cup pitcher w/reamer top, from $135 to.**$145.00**

Pink, ribbed, loop handle, Federal Glass Company, from $45 to **$50.00**

Pink, Westmoreland, 2-pc, from $225 to **$245.00**

Seville Yellow, McKee, grapefruit size, from $225 to **$250.00**

White w/embossed Fleur-de-Lis, from $60 to **$65.00**

White w/embossed Valencia, from $135 to **$150.00**

Yellow-amber, tab handle, Federal Glass, from $300 to......**$325.00**

Records

Records are still plentiful at flea markets and some antique malls, but albums (rock, jazz, and country) from the 1950s and

1960s are harder to find in collectible condition (very good or better). Garage sales are sometimes a great place to buy old records, since most of what you'll find there have been stored more carefully by their original owners.

There are two schools of thought concerning what is a collectible record. While some collectors prefer the rarities — those made in limited quantities by an unknown who later became famous, or those aimed at a specific segment of music lovers — others like the vintage top-10 recordings. With the increasing use of Internet auctions, which gives amateur sellers access to a world-wide market, many records described as or even believed to be 'scarce' or 'rare' are offered with some frequency. A majority of records offered receive no bids; only truly scarce, unusual, or exceptionally choice records inspire competition. So most records, even if listed in price guides, may be unsaleable, except as garage sale items. Now that they're so often being replaced with CDs, we realize that even though we take them for granted, the possibility of their becoming a thing of the past may be reality tomorrow.

Whatever the slant your collection takes, learn to visually inspect records before you buy them. Condition is one of the most important factors to consider when assessing value. Our values are for records in near-mint to mint condition. To be judged as mint, a record may have been played but must have no visual or audible deterioration — no loss of gloss to the finish, no stickers or writing on the label, no holes, no skips when it is played. If any of these are apparent, at best it is considered to be excellent, and its value is up to 90% lower than a mint example. Many records that seem to you to be in wonderful shape would be judged only very good, excellent at the most, by a knowledgeable dealer. Sleeves with no tape, stickers, tears, or obvious damage at best would be excellent; mint condition sleeves are impossible to find unless you've found old store stock.

LPs must be in their jackets, which must be in at least excellent condition. Be on the lookout for colored vinyl or picture discs, as some of these command higher prices; in fact, older Vogue picture discs commonly sell in the $25.00 to $75.00 range, some even higher. It's not too uncommon to find old radio station discards. These records will say either 'Not for Sale' or 'Audition Copy.' These 'DJ copies' may be worth more than their commercial counterparts, especially where records of 'hot' artists such as the Beatles, Elvis Presley, and the Beach Boys are involved.

If you'd like more information, we recommend *American Premium Record Guide* by L.R. Docks.

Advisor: L.R. Docks (See Directory, Records)

45 rpm

As Other Lovers Are, The Debonaires, Combo 129, from $40 to **$50.00**
Birddoggin', Billy Crash Craddock, Colonial 721, from $10 to.**$15.00**
Blue Velvet, The Clovers, Atlantic 1052, from $7 to............**$10.00**
Buttercup, Vince Everett, Towne 1964, from $8 to.............**$12.00**
Cheatin', Fats Domino, Imperial 5220, red plastic, from $40 to **$60.00**
Crying Over You, The Hornets, Flash 125, from $15 to......**$20.00**
Danny Boy, Slim Whitman, Imperial 8201, from $7 to.......**$10.00**
Darling I'm Sorry, The Ambassadors, Timely 1001, from $8 to.**$10.00**

Dreamy Eyes, Squires, Aladdin 3360, from $15 to **$20.00**
Gotta Go, Louis Jordan, Aladdin 3295, from $8 to............**$12.00**
Great Pretender, The Platters, Mercury 70753, maroon label, from $7 to **$10.00**
Guess Who, Miller Sisters, Ember 1004, from $7 to...........**$10.00**
How You Lied, The Cuff Links, Dootone 413, from $15 to.**$20.00**

I Feel So Worried, Sammy Lewis, Sun BMI-146, from $80.00 to $95.00. (Photo courtesy Rick Towndsend)

I Had a Dream Last Night, The Aladdins, Aladdin 3298, from $20 to **$30.00**
I'll Hide My Tears, Flames, GM 2110, from $20 to **$30.00**
I Love My Baby, Tokens, Melba 104, from $15 to...............**$20.00**
I'm a Boogie Man, Johnny Lee, De Luxe 6009, from $15 to..**$20.00**
I'm a Honky Tonk Girl, Loretta Lynn, Zero 107, from $35 to.**$50.00**
I'm Lookin' for Some Lovin', Lee Bonds, Decca 29338, from $5 to **$8.00**
It's Heaven, Four Dots, Freedom 44002, from $10 to **$15.00**
Knock Knock Rattle, Rex Allen, Decca 30674, from $7 to..**$10.00**
Laura Lee, Neil Sedaka, Decca 30520, from $10 to.............**$15.00**
Let's Call It a Day, The Belmonts, Sabina #513, from $8 to...**$12.00**
Little Dream Girl, The Cashmeres, Herald 474, from $10 to.**$15.00**
Moonlight, Young Lads, Neil 100, from $15 to...................**$20.00**
My Baby Walks All Over Me, Waylon Jennings, Ramco 1989, from $7 to **$10.00**
My Love, Heartbreakers, Vik 0299, from $25 to **$30.00**
Night Life, Willie Nelson, Bellair 107, red plastic, from $15 to.**$20.00**
Our First Kiss, The Aquatones, Fargo 1003, from $7 to......**$10.00**
Party Pooper, Bobby Lord, Columbia 41352, from $8 to **$12.00**
Pistol Packin' Mama Has Laid Her Pistol Down, Charlie Adams, Columbia 231445, from $7 to.....................................**$10.00**
Searching for a New Love, Majestics, Pixie 6901, from $10 to.**$15.00**
Shake It Up, Conway Twitty, Mercury 71148, from $15 to.**$20.00**
Since I Fell For You, The Buckeyes, De Luxe 6110, from $20 to **$30.00**
Speedo, The Cadillacs, Josie 785, from $5 to.......................**$8.00**
Surfin', The Beach Boys, Candix 331, from $30 to.............**$50.00**
Sweet Georgia Brown, The Beatles, Atco 6302, from $7 to .**$10.00**
Take All of Me, Five Royales, Apollo 443, from $15 to **$20.00**
Tell Me What's on Your Mind, The Blenders, Decca 31284, from $15 to **$20.00**
That's My Baby, Jimmy Breedlove, Atco 6094, from $7 to ..**$10.00**
That's Where I Want To Be, Bobby Bare, Fraternity 861, from $5 to **$8.00**
To Keep Our Love, Penguins, Dooto 451, from $10 to.......**$15.00**

Too Late for Tears, Lloyd Price, KRC 483, from $5 to **$8.00**

Turn Around Look at Me, Glen Campbell, Crest 1087, from $7 to **$10.00**

Valley of Tears, Mickey Gilley, Sabra 518, from $10 to........ **$15.00**

White Christmas, Ravens, Mercury 70505, from $15 to **$25.00**

You Baby You, The Cleftones, Gee 1000, from $8 to.......... **$12.00**

You Belong to Me, The Duprees, Coed 569, from $5 to **$8.00**

You Can't Catch Me, Chuck Berry, Chess 1645, from $5 to.. **$8.00**

78 rpm

Are You Really Mine?, Jimmie Rodgers, Roulette 4070, from $10 to **$15.00**

Baby Baby, Dale Hawkins, Checker 876, from $15 to......... **$20.00**

Book of Love, Monotones, Argo 5290, from $15 to **$20.00**

Charlie Brown, The Coasters, Atco 6132, from $20 to........ **$30.00**

Church Bells May Ring, The Diamonds, Mercury 70835, from $7 to **$10.00**

Confidential, Sonny Knight, Dot 15507, from $10 to......... **$15.00**

Diana, Paul Anka, ABC Paramount 9831, from $15 to....... **$20.00**

First Date, First Kiss, First Love; Sonny James, Capitol 3674, from $7 to **$10.00**

For Your Precious Love, Jerry Butler & the Impressions, Abner 1013, from $15 to **$20.00**

Headin' for the Poorhouse, Silhouettes, Ember 1032, from $7 to **$10.00**

I Walk the Line, Johnny Cash, Sun 241, from $10 to.......... **$15.00**

It's Shameful, Jimmy Bowen, Roulette 4023, from $10 to ... **$15.00**

La Dee Dah, Billy & Lilly, Swan 4002, from $15 to............ **$20.00**

Mr Lee, The Bobbettes, Atlantic 1144, from $10 to **$15.00**

Queen of the Hop, Bobby Darin & the Jaybirds, Atco 6127, from $15 to **$20.00**

Raunchy, Ernie Freeman, Imperial 5474, from $7 to **$10.00**

Rumble, Link Wray & His Wraymen, Cadence 1347, from $10 to **$15.00**

Short Fat Fannie, Larry Williams, Specialty 608, from $10 to .. **$15.00**

Silhouettes, Rays, Cameo 117, from $15 to **$20.00**

Stood Up, Ricky Nelson, Imperial 5483, from $15 to **$20.00**

Think It Over, The Crickets (w/Buddy Holly), Brunswick 55072, from $50 to **$75.00**

This Could Be Magic, The Dubs, Gone 5011, from $15 to . **$20.00**

LP Albums

Alan Freed Rock & Roll Show, Alan Freed, Brunswick 54043, from $40 to **$60.00**

Blues Ballads, Laverne Baker, Atlantic 8007, from $30 to.... **$40.00**

Bobby's Biggest Hits, Bobby Rydell, Cameo 1009, from $20 to.**$30.00**

Campus Party, Rivieras, Rivera 701, from $40 to................ **$60.00**

Come Rock w/Me, Johnny Preston, Mercury 20609, from $25 to **$40.00**

Cookin' w/the Miracles, Miracles, Tamla 223, from $50 to . **$75.00**

Crazy Little Mama, El Dorados, Vee Jay 1001, black label, from $15 to **$20.00**

Deck of Cards, Wink Martindale, Dot 3245, from $15 to .. **$20.00**

Delta Rhythm Boys Sing, Delta Rhythm Boys, Elektra 138, from $15 to **$20.00**

Found Love, Jimmy Reed, Vee Jay 1022, from $20 to **$30.00**

Goodnight It's Time To Go, Spaniels, Vee Jay 1002, black label, from $50 to **$75.00**

Hank Snow Salutes Jimmy Rodgers, Hank Snow, RCA 3131, from $20 to **$30.00**

Joy Ride, Four Lovers, RCA 1317, from $150 to.............. **$200.00**

Just Rollin' w/Johnny Olenn, Johnny Olenn, Liberty 3029, from $50 to **$75.00**

Lift Up Your Voice, Red Foley, Decca 5338, 10", from $15 to. **$20.00**

Marvin & Johnny, Marvin & Johnny, Crown 5381, from $15 to **$25.00**

Mood Music, Charles Brown, Aladdin 702, black vinyl, 10", from $100 to **$150.00**

One Dozen Berrys, Chuck Berry, Chess 1432, from $30 to.**$50.00**

Original Sun Sound of Johnny Cash, Johnny Cash, Sun 1275, from $15 to **$20.00**

Pachuka Hop, Chuck Higgins, Combo 300, from $80 to..**$120.00**

Party Time, Julia Lee, Capitol H-288, from $30 to.............. **$40.00**

Rock w/Bill Haley & the Comets, Bill Haley & the Comets, Essex 202, from $100 to **$150.00**

Rockin & Driftin', The Drifters, Atlantic 8059, from $20 to. **$30.00**

Rockin w/Wanda, Wanda Jackson, Capitol 1384, from $75 to .**$100.00**

Sentimentally Yours, Patsy Cline, Decca 4282, from $20 to . **$30.00**

Surfer's Choice, Dick Dale & the Del-Tones, Deltone 1001, from $50 to **$75.00**

T Bone Blues, T-Bone Walker, Atlantic 8020, from $25 to..**$35.00**

Teddy Bears Sing!, Teddy Bears, Imperial 9067, from $50 to . **$75.00**

The Moonglows Meet the Flamingos, The Moonglows, Vee Jay 1052, from $15 to **$20.00**

This Is Bobby Darin, Bobby Darin, Atco 115, from $15 to . **$20.00**

Danny Bonaduce, Partridge Family, Lion Records, 1973, from $35.00 to $45.00. (Photo courtesy Greg Davis and Bill Morgan)

Red Wing

For almost a century, Red Wing, Minnesota, was the center of a great pottery industry. In the early 1900s several local companies merged to form the Red Wing Stoneware Company. Until they introduced their dinnerware lines in 1935, most of their production centered around stoneware jugs, crocks, flowerpots, and other utilitarian items. To reflect the changes made in 1935, the name was changed to Red Wing Potteries Inc. In addition to scores of lovely dinnerware lines, they also made vases, planters, flowerpots, etc., some with exceptional shapes and decoration.

Some of their more recognizable lines of dinnerware and those you'll most often find are Bob White (decorated in blue and brown brush strokes with quail), Tampico (featuring a collage of fruit including watermelon), Random Harvest (simple pink and brown leaves and flowers), and Village Green (or Brown, solid-color pieces introduced in the '50s). Often you'll find complete or nearly complete sets, and when you do, the lot price is usually a real bargain.

If you'd like to learn more about the subject, we recommend *Red Wing Stoneware, An Identification and Value Guide,* and *Red Wing Collectibles,* both by Dan and Gail DePasquale and Larry Peterson.

Club/Newsletter: *Red Wing Collectors Newsletter*
Red Wing Collectors Society, Inc.
Doug Podpeskar, membership information
624 Jones St., Eveleth, MN 55734-1631
218-744-4854; www.redwingcollectors.org
Please include SASE when requesting information.

Artware

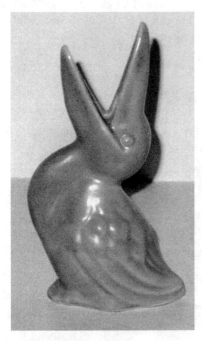

Ash receiver, pelican, from $125.00 to $150.00.

Bowl, brown w/orange interior, flat, #414, 7" $38.00
Bowl, centerpiece; Renaissance, ivory/brown wipe, #526, 12", from $45 to $60.00
Bowl, hat shape; Hyacinth semi-matt, #670, 1960s, 5x6", from $20 to $26.00
Bowl, shell; Blue Nile FLeck, #M1567, 9" $50.00
Bowl, Zephyr Pink Fleck, curled edge, #M1463, 12" $45.00
Candleholder, English Garden, ivory/brown wipe, #1190, 6", ea from $22 to $28.00
Candleholder, Hyacinth, tapered, #678, 6", ea $30.00

Candleholders, Magnolia, double, Eggshell Ivory w/brown wash, pr $110.00
Candleholders, Sylvan, ivory/brown wipe, 2-socket, #397, 1½", pr from $44 to $56.00
Compote, white, pedestal, brass handles, #M1598, 8" $55.00
Compote, white semi-matt, med pedestal, #M1597, 1950s-60s, 7", from $22 to $28.00
Dish, marmalade; aqua, pear shape, 4½" $18.00
Jardiniere, flecked pink, scalloped top, #M1610, 6" $22.00
Juicer, yellow, pedestal, #256 ....$150.00
Pitcher, urn; Vintage, semi-matt ivory-brown wipe, #616, 11", from $75 to $110.00
Pitcher vase, Zephyr Pink Fleck, #1559, 1950s-60s, 9½", from $32 to $40.00
Planter, gray w/coral interior, sq, #1378, 5½" $40.00
Planter, Magnolia, Eggshell Ivory w/brown wash, 1940, 3⅞x14⅛x4" $95.00
Planter, viloin shape, black semi-matt, #1484, 1950s-60s, 13", from $48 to $58.00
Planter/wall pocket, violin form, turquoise, #M1484 ....$120.00
Teapot, yellow, chicken shape, #257 ....$125.00
Vase, Bird of Paradise Tropicana, bronze, 8⅛x7" $47.00
Vase, contempory shape, burnt orange gloss w/green interior, #B-1425, 1950s-60s, 8", from $26 to $32.00
Vase, gloss gray w/coral interior, #B1397, 7" $35.00
Vase, Mandarin type, white w/green interior, #1553, 1950s-60s, 6½", from $26 to $32.00

Vase, orange, pelican handles, 10", $50.00.

Vase, swirl, yellow gloss, #1590, 10" $50.00

Dinnerware

Blossom Time, bowl, cream soup; w/lid $12.00
Blossom Time, relish dish $18.00
Bob White, bowl, salad; individual, 5½" $10.00
Bob White, casserole, w/handles & lid, 13" L $50.00
Bob White, cocktail tray, rectangular, 9x5", from $90 to ...$110.00
Bob White, cup & saucer $12.00
Bob White, gravy boat, stick handle, w/lid $38.00

Bob White, hors d'oeuvres, bird figural, 8½" **$40.00**
Bob White, pitcher, slim, 7" **$35.00**
Bob White, pitcher, water; 12", from $40 to **$50.00**
Bob White, plate, dinner **$15.00**
Bob White, plate, salad **$8.00**
Bob White, platter, 13¾x8¾" **$35.00**
Bob White, platter, 19½" L, from $65 to **$80.00**
Bob White, salt & pepper shakers, pr **$25.00**
Bob White, teapot **$50.00**
Brittany, beverage server, w/lid **$70.00**
Brittany, teapot **$75.00**
Capistrano, bowl, cereal **$14.00**
Capistrano, bread tray **$28.00**
Capistrano, cup & saucer, tea **$12.00**
Capistrano, nappy **$18.00**
Capistrano, platter, 13" **$20.00**
Capistrano, teapot, w/lid **$70.00**
Capistrano, tureen, soup; w/lid **$110.00**
Crocus, bowl, vegetable **$24.00**
Desert Sun, bean pot, w/lid, 1½-qt **$40.00**
Desert Sun, bowl, fruit **$10.00**
Desert Sun, bread tray **$50.00**
Desert Sun, pitcher, water; 1½-qt **$55.00**
Desert Sun, platter, 13" **$20.00**
Desert Sun, salt & pepper shakers, pr **$20.00**
Frontenac, platter, 13" **$22.50**
Iris, celery dish **$18.00**
Lexington, bowl, soup; sa, 7½" **$7.00**
Lexington, casserole, stick handle, w/lid, 1¼-qt **$28.00**
Lexington, coffee cup **$10.00**
Lexington, creamer **$9.00**
Lexington, dinner plate **$12.00**
Lexington, nappy **$14.00**
Lexington, relish dish **$12.00**
Lexington, supper tray **$14.00**
Lexington, teapot, 11" W **$55.00**
Lotus, bowl, divided, 6½x11" **$35.00**
Lotus, creamer **$10.00**
Lotus, cup, coffee **$10.00**
Lotus, dish, sauce/fruit **$6.00**
Lotus, plate, chop **$30.00**
Lotus, plate, dinner; 10½" **$12.00**
Lotus, plate, salad; 7½", from $8 to **$10.00**
Lute Song, bowl, vegetable **$22.00**
Lute Song, bread tray **$28.00**
Lute Song, casserole, w/lid **$40.00**
Lute Song, creamer **$12.00**
Lute Song, platter, sm **$24.00**
Lute Song, salt & pepper shakers, pr **$16.00**
Lute Song, teapot **$135.00**
Magnolia, beverage server, w/lid **$50.00**
Magnolia, bowl, berry; sm **$5.00**
Magnolia, bowl, cereal **$8.00**
Magnolia, celery dish **$16.00**
Magnolia, coffee cup **$12.00**
Magnolia, gravy boat, w/tray **$22.00**
Magnolia, platter, 13" L **$25.00**

Orleans, French casserole, 12" long, $45.00.

Orleans, plate, 7" **$12.00**
Orleans, teacup & saucer **$20.00**
Pepe, bowl, serving; 4½x10½" **$110.00**

Pepe, bread tray, $30.00; bean pot, $38.00. (Photo courtesy B.L. and R.L. Dolan)

Pepe, creamer, 5" **$10.00**
Pepe, cup & saucer, from $7 to **$9.00**
Pepe, dish, vegetable; divided, 12½" L **$45.00**
Pepe, pitcher, lg, 13" **$115.00**
Pepe, platter, 15" **$65.00**
Plum Blossom, bowl, cereal **$12.00**
Plum Blossom, dish, fruit **$12.00**
Plum Blossom, plate, 6½" **$8.00**
Provincial Oomph, casserole, w/lid, 7" **$25.00**
Provincial Oomph, pitcher, 8" **$30.00**
Random Harvest, bowl, serving; 9x8" **$38.00**
Random Harvest, chip & dip **$30.00**
Random Harvest, coffeepot **$65.00**
Random Harvest, creamer **$38.00**
Random Harvest, cup & saucer **$10.00**
Random Harvest, dish, vegetable; divided **$24.00**
Random Harvest, plate, dinner **$12.00**
Random Harvest, plate, salad/dessert; 7" **$9.00**
Round-Up, cocktail tray **$50.00**
Smart Set, casserole, tab handles, 15" **$55.00**
Smart set, coffee/teapot **$135.00**
Smart Set, cup & saucer, from $12 to **$15.00**
Smart Set, pitcher, 14" **$65.00**
Smart Set, tray, 24" L **$50.00**
Tampico, bowl, rim soup **$18.00**
Tampico, coffeepot **$75.00**

Tampico, creamer...$18.00
Tampico, mug, coffee...$22.00
Tampico, nappy $22.00
Tampico, plate, 8½"..$16.00
Tampico, teapot, w/lid $65.00
Tampico, trivet, 4 sm feet, 8¾"............................$65.00
Town & Country, bowl, batter.............................$150.00
Town & Country, bowl, cereal; 5¾", from $50 to.............$60.00
Town & Country, bowl, mixing; 9".......................$80.00
Town & Country, creamer, from $35 to...................$40.00
Town & Country, marmite, tab handle, w/lid, 5½x7".........$65.00
Town & country, pitcher, 2-pt, 6½", from $90 to...........$120.00
Town & Country, pitcher, 3-pt, 8", from $90 to.............$120.00
Town & Country, plate, 8"....................................$20.00
Town & Country, platter, 15", from $80 to.....................$90.00
Town & Country, spoon rest $45.00
Town & Country, sugar bowl, w/lid, from $45 to.............$55.00
Town & Country, syrup jug, from $80 to...................$95.00
Town & Country, teapot, Dusk Blue.....................$275.00
Village Green, dish, vegetable...............................$30.00
Village Green, mug, beverage/coffee.....................$15.00
Zinnia, teapot $85.00

Roundup, platter, 13", $90.00; pitcher, 11½", from $110.00 to $125.00.

Regal China

Perhaps best known for their Beam whiskey decanters, the Regal China company (of Antioch, Illinois) also produced some exceptionally well-modeled ceramic novelties, among them their 'hugger' salt and pepper shakers, designed by artist Ruth Van Tellingen Bendel. (Of all pieces about 15% are Bendel and 85% are Van Tellingen.) Facing pairs made to 'lock' together arm-in-arm, some huggies are signed Bendel while others bear the Van Tellingen mark. Another popular design is her Peek-a-Boo Bunny line, depicting the coy little bunny in the red and white 'jammies' who's just about to pop his buttons. (The cookie jar has been reproduced.)

See also Cookie Jars; Old MacDonald's Farm.

Advisor: Judy Posner (See Directory Black Americana)

Bank, monkey scratching head, marked C Miller, 12", from $110.00 to $120.00. (Photo courtesy Jim and Beverly Mangus)

Bowl, salad; Caesar Salad recipe in center, blue decor on white, 12", EX $22.50
Salt & pepper shakers, A Nod to Abe, 3-pc nodder, from $200 to......$250.00
Salt & pepper shakers, Bendel, bears, white w/pink & brown trim, pr......$75.00
Salt & pepper shakers, Bendel, bunnies, white w/black & pink trim, pr......$75.00
Salt & pepper shakers, Bendel, love bugs, burgundy, lg, pr.$125.00
Salt & pepper shakers, Bendel, love bugs, green, sm, pr.......$75.00
Salt & pepper shakers, Bendel, pigs kissing, gray w/pink trim, lg, pr from $250 to $275.00
Salt & pepper shakers, cat sitting w/eyes closed, white w/hat & gold bow, pr......$225.00
Salt & pepper shakers, clown, pr.........................$250.00
Salt & pepper shakers, Dutch girl, pr from $200 to..........$225.00
Salt & pepper shakers, Fifi, pr.............................$250.00
Salt & pepper shakers, fish, marked C Miller, 1-pc.............$55.00
Salt & pepper shakers, French chef, white w/gold trim, pr.$250.00
Salt & pepper shakers, Humpty Dumpty, pr.......................$75.00
Salt & pepper shakers, Peek-a-Boo, red dots, lg (have been reproduced), pr from $350 to $400.00
Salt & pepper shakers, Peek-a-Boo, red dots, sm, pr from $125 to......$150.00
Salt & pepper shakers, Peek-a-Boo, solid white, sm, pr......$175.00
Salt & pepper shakers, pig, pink, marked C Miller, 1-pc $75.00
Salt & pepper shakers, tulip, pr.............................$35.00
Salt & pepper shakers, Van Tellingen, bears, brown, pr from $25 to $28.00
Salt & pepper shakers, Van Tellingen, boy & dog, Black, pr .$75.00
Salt & pepper shakers, Van Tellingen, boy & dog, white, pr .$65.00
Salt & pepper shakers, Van Tellingen, bunnies, solid colors, pr from $28 to......$32.00
Salt & pepper shakers, Van Tellingen, Dutch boy & girl, pr from $45 to $50.00

Salt and pepper shakers, Van Tellingen, ducks, $25.00 for the pair.

Salt & pepper shakers, Van Tellingen, Mary & lamb, pr from $40 to **$50.00**

Salt & pepper shakers, Van Tellingen, sailor & mermaid, pr from $100 to **$125.00**

Restaurant China

Restaurant china, also commonly called cafe ware, diner china, hotelware, or commercial china, is specifically designed for use in commercial food service. In addition to restaurants, it is used on board airplanes, ships, and trains, as well as in the dining areas of hotels, railroad stations, airports, government offices, military facilities, corporations, schools, hospitals, department and drug stores, amusement and sports parks, churches, clubs, and the like. Though most hotelware produced in America before 1900 has a heavy gauge nonvitrified body, vitrified commercial china made post-1910 includes some of the finest quality ware ever produced, far surpassing that of nonvitrified household products. A break- and chip-resistant rolled or welted edge is characteristic of American restaurant ware produced from the 1920s through the 1970s and is still frequently used, though no longer a concern on the very durable high alumina content bodies introduced in the 1960s. In addition, commercial tableware is also made of porcelain, glass-ceramic, glass laminate, glass, melamine, pewter-like metal, and silver plate. Airlines use fine gauge china in first class, due to space and weight factors. And beginning in the late 1970s, fine gauge porcelain and bone china became a popular choice of upscale restaurants, hotels, and country clubs. To reduce loss from wear, most decoration is applied to bisque, then glazed and glaze fired (i.e. underglaze) or to glaze-fired ware, then fired into the glaze (i.e. in-glaze). Until the 1970s many restaurants regularly ordered custom-decorated white, deep tan, blue, or pink-bodied patterns. However, it is estimated that more than 90% of today's commercial ware is plain or embossed white. For decades collectors have searched for railroad and ship china. Interest in airline china is on the rise. (Note: Most airlines discontinued the use of china after 9/11.) Attractive standard (stock) patterns are now also sought by many. Western motifs and airbrushed stencil designs are especially treasured. The popularity of high quality American-made Asian designs has increased. Most prefer traditional medium-heavy gauge American vitrified china, though fine china collectors no doubt favor the restaurant china products of Pickard or Royal Doulton. While some find it difficult to pass up any dining concern or transportation system topmarked piece, others seek ware that is decorated with a military logo or department store, casino, or amusement park name. Some collect only creamers, others butters or teapots. Some look for ware made by a particular manufacturer (e.g. Tepco), others specific patterns such as Willow or Indian Tree, or pink, blue, or tan body colors. It is currently considered fashionable to serve home-cooked meals on mismatched topmarked hotelware. Reminiscent of days gone by, restaurant or railroad china made before 1960 brings to mind pre-freeway cross-country vacations by car or rail when dining out was an event, unlike the quick stops at today's fast-food and family-style restaurants. For a more thorough study of the subject, we recommend *Restaurant China, Identification & Value Guide for Restaurant, Airline, Ship & Railroad Dinnerware, Volume 1* and *Volume 2,* by Barbara Conroy (Collector Books); her website, which has detailed descriptions of her books, contains even more information on additional restaurant china. The URL is listed below.

In the lines below, TM indicates topmarked or side-marked with name or logo. Please note: Commercial food service china is neither advertising nor souvenir china, since it is not meant to be removed from the restaurant premises.

See also Railroadiana.

Advisor: Barbara Conroy (See Special Interests, Dinnerware)

Restaurant and Transportation China Online Forum:
http://groups.yahoo.com/group/Restaurant_China/

Clearman's North Woods Inn embossed flagon, Hall, #588 (number not marked), 12-ounce, ca. 1980s, $24.00. (Photo courtesy Barbara Conroy)

Antola's platter, Wallace, 1960s, 11½" L **$25.00**

Aurelio's Pizza (IL, IN, MN chain) mug, Jackson, 1980 date code **$20.00**

Bergoff (Chicago IL) embossed tankard, Hall 3592 (# not marked), 1960s, 14-oz **$30.00**

Bowater Steamship Co Alice Bowater pattern plate (BOW-1a), Maddock, ca 1940s, 8" **$50.00**

Burger Pit (sm CA chain), platter, Tepco, ca 1950s - early 1960s, 13¼" L **$40.00**

Burger Pit (sm CA chain) mug, Sterling, 1968 date code.....**$40.00**

BWIA International Airways Golden Ibis pattern casserole (BWA-1a), metallic gold logo, Pfaltzgraff, 1980s **$12.50**

Casa Montero plate, Syracuse, 1977 date code, 6½" **$12.50**

Commodore Hotel (New York NY) match stand (NYC-1.1), Lenox, ca 1930s...**$42.00**

Court of Two Sisters (New Orleans LA) Irish Coffee mug, Hall #1272, 1960s, 8-oz..**$15.00**

Foster's (San Francisco CA) plate, Shenango, 1957 date code, 11" **$40.00**

Golfcrest Country Club (Pearland, Texas) plate, Shenango, 1981 date code, 10½", $24.00.

Hobo Joe's Family Restaurant mug (Irish coffee), Hall #1272 backstamp, 1960s, 8-oz...**$28.00**

Hotel Richmond (Richmond VA) service plate, Maddock (England), ca 1910s, 9¾"...**$50.00**

Howard Johnson's Ice Cream Shoppes & Restaurants scenic-border plate, Mayer, 1951 date code, 9".....................**$42.00**

Jackie Jensen's Bow & Bell (sports-related, Oakland CA) plate, Homer Laughlin, 1965 date code, 5½" **$24.00**

King's Coffee (Cambridge England) plate, Rocklite backstamp, 1970s, 6½"..**$15.00**

Liggetts (East Coast drug store chain) plate, Warwick, 1920s-40s, 7"..**$30.00**

Neptune's Palace (San Francisco CA) plate, Jackson, 1980 date code, 6½"...**$15.00**

New Britain Masonic Hall Association (New Britain CT) plate, Scammell's Trenton backstamp, 1930s, 9"...................**$18.00**

New Ebbitt Hotel (Washington DC) cake plate, Mayflower shape, Syracuse, 1906 date code, 10¼" **$125.00**

Ocean Spray Cranberry House bouillon, Walker, 1965 date code...**$15.00**

Palace Hotel (San Francisco CA) cup & saucer, Shenango, 1945 & 1952 date codes...**$25.00**

Palmer House (Chicago IL), candlestick, teal w/gold band, Hall #604 (# not marked), Palmer House backstamp, 1930s-40s.. **$30.00**

Quantas Alice Springs pattern butter plate, Wedgwood, Quantas backstamp, 1960s-85 ....**$22.00**

Restaurant Lombard (San Francisco CA) cream pitcher, pink on white, Sterling inlay, 1940s, 3¼" **$32.00**

Southland Hotel (Norfolk VA) service plate, Scammell's Lamberton backstamp, 1920s, 11"...............................**$85.00**

Standard Sandwich Shop plate, Shenango, ca 1930s, 8" **$65.00**

Stuart Anderson's Black Angus Restaurant (CA) platter, Laughlin, 1993 date code, 16" L **$50.00**

Surfside Hotel (Miami Beach FL) service plate, Iroquois, ca 1930s-40s, 10¾" **$50.00**

The Velvet Turtle (West Coast) plate, Mayer, 1971 date code, 6¾" **$18.00**

Trans-Europe Express (railroad) Inverted TEE pattern ashtray (TEE-2), Largenthal, dated 1976..**$30.00**

University of California (Davis CA) plate, Syracuse, 1961 date code, 5½" **$14.00**

Veteran Administration mug, Inter-American Brasil backstamp, 1977-mid-1980s **$15.00**

Wardman Park Inn (Washington DC) guest room toothbrush holder, Lamberton backstamp, 1911-23 ....**$45.00**

Westbury Hotel (Brussels, Germany) tray, Maastricht, 1960s, 4¼" **$6.50**

Stock Patterns

Air New Zealand Tasman Empire pattern plate, Air New Zealand backstamp, Noritake, 1980s, 5¾"...............................**$15.00**

Ambassador Red pattern cream pitcher, Homer Laughlin, 1982 date code **$7.50**

Athol Marone pattern plate, Steelite backstamp, Royal Doulton, early 1980s, 7¾", from $8.00. (Photo courtesy Barbara Conroy)

Black leaves transfer-printed, lined & banded plate, Duraline Grindley Hotel backstamp, 1961 date code, 5½" **$8.00**

Bountiful pattern mug, Rego, 1980s-90s **$9.00**

Brown glaze w/lustre teapot, unmarked Fraunfelter, 1930s ..**$20.00**

Brown transfer-printed compartment plate, Iroquois Puerto Rico backstamp, 1949 date code, 9½" **$18.00**

Buvico shape blue-bodied mug, Victor, 1960s **$20.00**

Decor (pattern) grapefruit, WH Grindley Alpha 27 backstamp, 1970s.. **$6.00**

Deep teal transfer-printed plate, Iroquois Puerto Rico backstamp, 1948 date code, 7¼".................................... **$8.00**

Delmar pattern compartment plate, Mayer, 1930s-40s **$20.00**

Doughnut jug, maroon, Hall #1335 backstamp, late 1930s-60s, 7¼".. **$65.00**

Eva Air Eva Leaves pattern cup & saucer, Eva Air backstamp, Narumi, early 1990s **$30.00**

Flowered decals & gold lines teapot, Maddock (Entland) Ultra Vitrified backstamp, 1974 date code............................ **$24.00**

Glen Usk Hotel, Indian Tree pattern tray, sq, Dunn Bennett Rocklite backstamp, 1970s... **$15.00**

Greek key transfer-printed, lined & banded creamer, Grindley Hotel Ware backstamp, 1926 date code................................. **$10.00**

Green Mill pattern sauceboat, Hutchenreuther Black Knight backstamp, 1930s... **$20.00**

Hand-lined, banded & detailed ice cream shell, Grindley Hotel Ware backstamp, 1908-20s **$10.00**

Jasper Ware ashtray, light brown & white, Dudson Jasper Ware backstamp, 1947-65, 4½" **$35.00**

Lisa pattern plate, Jackson's Royal Jackson backstamp, 1985-86, 6½" **$8.00**

London-shaped teapot, yellow, Hall #82 backstamp, 1980s, 16-oz.. **$22.00**

Marilyn pattern sauceboat, Mayer, ca 1930s **$18.00**

Pink & shite stencil airbrushed (referred to as fishbowl pattern) fruit, Jackson, 1977 date code.. **$30.00**

Red transfer-printed plate, Maddock (England) Ultra Vitrified backstamp, ca 1970s, 6½"... **$15.00**

Sculptura shape sauceboat, Mayer, Sculptura backstamp, 1970 date code **$12.00**

Tricolor flower stencil airbrushed plate (as used in Kapok Tree Inn, Clearwater FL), Jackson, 1968 date code, 5½" **$15.00**

Tricolor leaves stencil airbrushed pattern plate, Jackson, 1965 date code, 7½" **$12.00**

Webster pattern on American shape cream pitcher, Syracuse Syralite backstamp, 1974 date code... **$10.00**

Robinson Ransbottom Pottery Company

A contemporary of McCoy, this company was the result of a union between Frank Ransbottom, one of Roseville, Ohio's, most successful producers of stoneware pots and jars, and the Robinson Clay Products Company, who until the merger in 1920 made mostly brick and tile. Over the years they expanded their products to include an extensive line of cookie jars, giftware, pet feeders, birdbaths, and gardenware, which collectors are beginning to take note of today. In addition to their cookie jars, some of the more collectible items to watch for are their jardinieres and pedestals, their kitchenware, and their large vases. Though very reminiscent of earlier examples made in the area, the green and brown jardineres, pedestals, floor vases, and flowerpots were made circa 1960s

through the 1980s. Many have been unwittingly purchased for old Roseville pottery, since the mark is 'RRPCO, Roseville, Ohio.' (Just remember, the Roseville Pottery Company was located in nearby Zanesville, Ohio, not Roseville.) Today, though, they're collectible in their own right. The jardinere and pedestal has an embossed wild rose branch and was made from a mold that was purchased from the Weller Pottery when it closed. It was also produced with solid background colors of white, yellow, blue, pink, and green with contrasting flowers. Be sure to watch for their blue-sponged stoneware items, as these are gaining in popularity with those who enjoy the country look in home decor. The things we mention here are those most commonly found at garage sales and flea markets, but today, nearly all their wares are collectible, at least to some extent. For more information we recommend *The Sanford's Guide to the Robinson Ransbottom Pottery Co.* by Sharon and Larry Skillman (published by Adelmore Press).

Bowl, console; Tionesta, brown tones, #157, USA, 4¾x8½" .. **$45.00**

Canisters, blue spongeware, 2-qt, 1-qt, 1-pt, +salt & pepper shakers **$40.00**

Crock, bl spongeware, 3¼x4½"...................................... **$15.00**

Crock, Robinson Ransbottom Pottery Est 1900..., cobalt on creamy tan, 7¾x7¾" **$85.00**

Flowerpot, brown w/mottled turquoise drip at top, 3½"...... **$15.00**

Flowerpot, embossed sunbursts on brown shading to green, 5" . **$32.00**

Jardiniere, embossed wild roses, multicolor on pink, made from Weller mold, 8" **$90.00**

Jardiniere, Luxor, unglazed brushed ware w/gr glazed interior, 1920s, 5¼x7¾" **$50.00**

Jardiniere & pedestal, embossed wild roses, brown to green blend, #421, 22" overall **$165.00**

Lawn ornament, turtle, multicolor airbrushing, #1104/GR, ca 1956, 5½x12½x8½" **$55.00**

Pie plate, blue spongeware w/blue wheat sprig in center, 2x9½" .**$17.50**

Pie plate, embossed pattern on yellow, 1⅝x9¾" **$38.00**

Pitcher, green & white spongeware, 9"................................. **$30.00**

Vase, embossed foliate designs on white matt, 1930s, 15"....**$70.00**

Vase, embossed leaves on creamy white, 10½x6¼".................. **$32.00**

Washbowl & pitcher, bl spongeware, 3x11¾", 9x8½"..........**$55.00**

Rock 'n Roll Memorabilia

Ticket stubs and souvenirs issued at rock concerts, posters of artists that have reached celebrity status, and merchandise such as dolls, games, clothing, etc., that was sold through retail stores during the heights of their careers are just the things that interest collectors of rock 'n roll memorabilia. Some original, one-of-a-kind examples — for instance, their instruments, concert costumes, and personal items — often sell at the large auction galleries in the east where they've realized very high-dollar prices. For more information we recommend *A Price Guide to Rock and Roll Collectibles* by Greg Moore, which is distributed by L-W Book Sales.

Note: Most posters sell in the range of $5.00 to $10.00; those listed below are the higher-end examples in excellent or better condition.

See also Beatles Collectibles; Elvis Presley Memorabilia; Magazines; Movie Posters; Pin-Back Buttons; Records.

Advisor: Bojo/Bob Gottuso (See Directory, Character and Personality Collectibles)

Aerosmith, belt buckle, Aerosmith in red on blue w/gold metal border, Pacifica, 1976, EX......................**$35.00**

Aerosmith, blanket, Get Your Wings tour, woven, fan club exclusive, 50x71", EX......................**$200.00**

Aerosmith, concert banner, Toys in the Attic, 1977, 5¾x43½", EX......................**$30.00**

Aerosmith, denim jacket, Get a Grip World tour 1993, Student Union (brand) 1990, EX......................**$65.00**

Aerosmith, guitar pick, pearlescent, Nine Lives tour, Joe Perry faux signature w/batwings on back, EX......................**$45.00**

Aerosmith, hockey jersey, Nine Lives tour, red w/black stripe, EX......................**$70.00**

Aerosmith, standee, caricature of the band w/Draw the Line & logo, 25x18", EX......................**$90.00**

Aerosmith, T-shirt, 1984-85 Back in the Saddle tour, w/band members names, gray w/black sleeves, EX......................**$40.00**

Bay City Rollers, pendant, letters spell name, silvered metal, 1970s, EX......................**$20.00**

Bobby Darin, sheet music, Dream Lover, EX......................**$20.00**

Cowsills, fan club postcard, members on house, 1968, 5x9", EX......................**$90.00**

Culture Club, T-shirt, Boy George in V Westwood squiggle shirt, 1983, EX......................**$20.00**

David Cassidy, three-ring binder, Westab, 1972, NM, from $40.00 to $50.00. (Photo courtesy Greg Davis and Bill Morgan)

Doors, poster, Jim Morrison's arrest in New Haven CN, 1967, reproduction, 11x14", NM......................**$15.00**

Joey Romone, bobblehead, w/microphone, NECA, NMIB.......**$20.00**

John Bon Jovi, calendar, Official, 1991, unused, M.............**$25.00**

KISS, belt buckle, photo of band, Pacifica, 1978, EX..........**$60.00**

KISS, game, KISS on Tour, late 1970s, EXIB......................**$60.00**

KISS, goblet, hand-blown glass w/Gene Simmons pewter base, 1998, 9", MIB......................**$45.00**

KISS, inflatable chair, adult size, 1990s, MIP (sealed)..........**$85.00**

KISS, model kit, KISS Custom Chevy Van, AMT, 1977, MIB (sealed)......................**$170.00**

KISS, necklace, Paul Stanley in gold script on gold chain, 1978, Aucoin, MIP......................**$250.00**

KISS, pencils, set of 4, Wallace Pencil Company, 1978, MIP.**$75.00**

KISS, poster, 1977 KISS Alive II tour, 58x42", M (sealed)...**$300.00**

KISS, puzzle, Peter Criss w/2 black panthers on chains, Milton Bradley #4990, 1978, M (EX box)......................**$55.00**

KISS, radio, box shape w/KISS members photo, 1977, NMIB.**$250.00**

KISS, songbook, Double Platinum, EX......................**$30.00**

KISS, stickpin, Gene Simmons in gold script, Aucoin, 1978, MOC......................**$235.00**

KISS, stuffed animal, Peter Criss, The Dynasty Collection, 18", MIB......................**$100.00**

KISS, tour book, KISS on Tour, 1976, EX, from $130 to..**$160.00**

KISS, trash can, photos, P&K Products Company Inc, 1978, EX......................**$180.00**

Michael Jackson, magazine, Michael, souvenir edition, Volume 1, issue 1, photo cover, 1984, 13x11", NM......................**$17.50**

Michael Jackson, T-shirt, Bad tour, portrait on white, cotton-polyester, 1987, NM......................**$25.00**

Monkees, paint by number set, unused, complete, EX, $140.00. (Photo courtesy Bojo/Bob Gottuso)

Neil Young, concert poster, w/Booker T & The MG's, 8/12/93, 17x11", EX......................**$15.00**

Pink Floyd, concert program, The Wall, 1980 American tour, EX......................**$45.00**

Pink Floyd/Animals, poster flag, smoky cityscape printed on silk-like material, 42x30", NM......................**$20.00**

Queen, song book, 12 songs for piano, vocals & guitar, EX..**$20.00**

Ricky Nelson, concert program, Orpheum Theater, Seattle WA, 20 pages, 9x12", EX......................**$35.00**

Ricky Nelson, sheet music, Hello Mary Lou, photo cover, ca 1961, EX......................**$10.00**

Rolling Stones, pin-back, tongue logo, gold glitter, MIP......**$15.00**

Rolling Stones, poster, American tour 1972, 36x24", EX.....**$45.00**

Rolling Stones, poster, nude w/flowing hair, Sticky Fingers tour, 35x23", EX......................**$35.00**

Rolling Stones, program, 1972 tour, Jagger w/arms raised, EX.**$35.00**

Rolling Stones, program, 20 pages, 1966, 11½x10½", EX...**$30.00**

Supremes, tour program, Japan, 1974, EX......................**$25.00**

Rookwood

Although this company was established in 1879, it continued to produce commercial artware until it closed in 1967. Located in Cincinnati, Ohio, Rookwood is recognized today as the largest producer of high-quality art pottery ever to operate in the United States.

Most of the pieces listed here are from the later years of production, but we've included some early pieces as well. With few exceptions, all early Ohio art pottery companies produced an artist-decorated brown-glaze line — Rookwood's was called Standard. Among their other early lines were Sea Green, Iris, Jewel Porcelain, Wax Matt, and Vellum.

Virtually all of Rookwood's pieces are marked. The most familiar mark is the 'reverse R'-P monogram. It was first used in 1886, and until 1900 a flame point was added above it to represent each passing year. After the turn of the century, a Roman numeral below the monogram was used to indicate the current year. In addition to the dating mark, a die-stamped number was used to identify the shape.

The Cincinnati Art Galleries routinely hold large and important cataloged auctions. The full-color catalogs sometime contain company history and listings of artists and designers with their monograms (as well as company codes and trademarks). Collectors now regard them as an excellent source for information and study.

Ashtray, #2457, 1954, drama mask, gray and ivory mottle, marked Romulus-Remus, 3¾x6", $200.00. (Photo courtesy David Rago/Craftsman Auctions)

Ashtray, #6500, 1945, fish at side, Chinese Turquoise, X, 6". **$125.00**
Bookend, #2446, 1927, child on park bench, blue matt, 5½", ea...**$650.00**
Bookend, #6259, 1931, sunfish pr, celadon gloss, 6", ea.**$1,000.00**
Bookend, #6261, 1931, seated elephant, ivory matt, 5¼", EX, single...**$375.00**
Bookends, #2446, 1940, child on park bench, ivory matt, 5½", EX...**$325.00**
Bookends, #6158, 1930, Indian head, mottled orange matt, repair, 5¾"...**$3,600.00**
Bookends, 1941, water lilies embossed on rose matt, 3¾x5¼". **$230.00**
Bowl, #354, 1923, aqua matt, 3-handle, 3" **$150.00**
Bowl, #2145, 1924, leaves & flowers on yellow matt, 7½". **$125.00**
Bowl, #2147, 1928, stylized decor, pink matt, 8" **$225.00**
Bowl, #6424, 1951, blossom form, turquoise matt, 2⅞x8", NM...**$80.00**
Bud vase, 1929, ivory matt w/green interior, 7" **$150.00**
Figurine, #6405, 1936, rook, blue matt, 4½" **$375.00**
Figurine, #6899, 1948, Madonna & Child, white gloss, 7¼". **$250.00**
Figurine, 36484, 1965, polar bear seated, L Abel, striated blue, 6½"...**$1,000.00**

Ginger jar, #1321-E, 1929, pink matt, cutouts on lid, 3-pc, 4".**$200.00**
Inkwell, #2022, 1921, maple leaves on green over blue, w/lid, 2¾x4½"...**$365.00**
Paperweight, #1623, 1924, rook, brown matt, 4½" W **$550.00**
Planter, #1159, Faience, floral/fruit wreaths on gray crackle, 10", EX **$300.00**
Trivet, #1794, 1929, rook among lattice, multicolor, 5¾" sq, NM **$225.00**
Trivet, #3077, 1921, parrot among flowers, 6-color, 5½" sq.**$225.00**
Trivet, #6774, 1940, man in medieval garb w/falcon, turquoise gloss, 5¾"...**$325.00**
Vase, #1090, 1950, leaves on coral/pink, 4½"....................**$75.00**
Vase, #1322, 1920, footed, cut-out lid, tan matt, 5½".......**$275.00**
Vase, #1825, 1923, diamond-accented panels, light blue matt, 5"...**$160.00**
Vase, #1907, 1928, floral panels, pink & green matt, 5½" ...**$200.00**
Vase, #2088, 1928, berries, purple matt, 5¼" **$250.00**
Vase, #2090, 1938, embossed leaves on ivory matt, 4½" **$75.00**
Vase, #2110, 1928, Deco berries & lace embossed on honey matt, 7¼"...**$300.00**
Vase, #2123, 1925, maple leaves, brown matt, 5½"...........**$250.00**
Vase, #2413, 1931, floral, turquoise matt, 7½"................**$400.00**
Vase, #2488, 1921, leaves on dark blue matt, X, 10½"......**$250.00**
Vase, #2584, 1924, floral, 6-sided, 9½" **$250.00**
Vase, #2971, 1928, overlapping leaves on light blue matt, 3¼".**$170.00**
Vase, #5432, 1946, floral on Blue de Roi, 4" **$75.00**
Vase, #6031, 1928, carved roses, turquoise matt, 7" **$400.00**
Vase, #6147, 1948, flowers & berries on Celadon.............**$150.00**
Vase, #6410, 1932, Glaze Effect, oatmeal crystalline w/tan & purple, 5"...**$250.00**
Vase, #6762, 1946, Mexicans on burros embossed on yellow gloss, 5½"...**$70.00**

Vase, #6762, 1954, embossed Southwestern village, green gloss, 5½", $275.00. (Photo courtesy David Rago/Craftsman Auctions)

Wall pocket, #2957, 1928, faceted form, green mottled matt, 6½"...**$225.00**

Rooster and Roses

Back in the 1940s, newlyweds might conceivably have received some of this imported Japanese-made kitchenware as a housewarming gift. They'd no doubt be stunned to see the prices it's now bringing! Rooster and Roses (Ucagco called it Early Provincial) is one of those lines of novelty ceramics from the '40s and '50s that are among today's hottest collectibles. Ucagco was only one of several importers whose label you'll find on this pattern; among other are Py, ACSON, Norcrest, and Lefton. The design is easy to spot — there's the rooster, yellow breast with black crosshatching, brown head and, of course, the red crest and waddle, large full-blown roses with green leaves and vines, and a trimming of yellow borders punctuated by groups of brown lines. (You'll find another line having blue flowers among the roses, and one with a rooster with a green head and a green border. These are not considered Rooster and Roses by purist collectors, though there is a market for them as well.) The line is fun to collect, since shapes are so diversified. Even though there has been relatively little networking among collectors, more than 100 items have been reported and no doubt more will surface.

Advisor: Jacki Elliott (See Directory, Rooster and Roses)

Ashtray, rectangular, part of set, 3x2" **$9.50**
Ashtray, round or sq, sm, from $15 to **$25.00**
Ashtray, round w/4-lobed well centered by hand-painted rooster, rests between lobes, 6" **$65.00**
Ashtray, sq, lg, from $35 to........................ **$45.00**
Basket, flared sides, 6", from $45 to................. **$55.00**
Bell, from $45 to................................. **$75.00**
Bell, rooster & chicken on opposing sides, rare, from $95 to . **$125.00**
Bonbon dish, pedestal base, minimum value................ **$55.00**
Bowl, cereal; from $14 to........................... **$18.00**
Bowl, rice; on saucer, from $25 to **$35.00**
Bowl, 8", from $45 to.............................. **$55.00**
Box, trinket; w/lid, round, from $25 to **$35.00**
Box, 4½x3½", from $25 to........................... **$35.00**
Butter dish, ¼-lb, from $20 to...................... **$25.00**
Candle warmer (for tea & coffeepots), from $25 to............ **$35.00**
Candy dish, flat chicken-shaped tray w/3-dimensional chicken head, made in 3 sizes, from $35 to................ **$65.00**
Candy dish, w/3-dimensional leaf handle, from $25 to........ **$35.00**
Canister, cylindrical, wooden lid, 7x5", from $160 to........ **$195.00**
Canister set, round, 4-pc, from $150 to................ **$175.00**
Canister set, sq, 4-pc, from $150 to.................. **$175.00**
Canister set, stacking, rare, minimum value................ **$150.00**
Canister set, tea & coffee stack amid lg sugar & flour, fits in wooden cabinet w/D-curved front, rare, 7x11x3", $275 to...... **$300.00**
Carafe, no handle, w/stopper lid, 8", from $65 to **$85.00**
Carafe, w/handle & stopper lid, 8", from $75 to **$100.00**
Casserole dish, w/lid, from $65 to.................... **$85.00**
Castor set in revolving wire rack, 2 cruets, mustard jar & salt & pepper shakers, rare, from $125 to **$150.00**
Chamberstick, saucer base, ring handle, 3x6" dia, from $35 to. **$50.00**
Cheese dish, slant lid, from $40 to.................... **$55.00**
Cigarette box w/2 trays, hard to find, from $60 to **$70.00**
Coaster, ceramic disk embedded in round wooden tray, rare, minimum value................................. **$45.00**
Coffee grinder, rare, minimum value.................... **$150.00**
Coffeepot, 'Coffee' in neck band, w/creamer & sugar bowl, both w/ appropriately lettered neck bands, 3 pcs from $75 to...... **$85.00**

Coffeepot, new tankard shape, 8" **$50.00**
Condiment set, 2 cruets, salt & pepper shakers w/mustard jar atop wire & wood holder, 4 spice canisters below, $150 to. **$175.00**
Condiment set, 2 cruets, salt & pepper shakers w/mustard jar on tray, miniature, from $50 to........................ **$75.00**
Condiment set, 2 sq shakers over 2 cruets, 4 sq shakers on bottom row, in wooden frame **$60.00**
Cookie jar, ceramic handles, 7x6½", minimum value **$175.00**
Cookie/cracker jar, cylindrical w/rattan handle, 5x6", from $55 to.. **$75.00**
Creamer & sugar bowl, w/lid, 4", from $40 to **$50.00**
Creamer & sugar bowl on rectangular tray, from $55 to...... **$70.00**
Cruets, bottle shape, bulbous bottom, lg handle, pr........... **$145.00**
Cruets, cojoined w/twisted necks, sm................... **$45.00**
Cruets, oil & vinegar, flared bases, pr from $50 to.............. **$60.00**
Cruets, oil & vinegar, sq, lg, pr from $30 to **$45.00**
Cruets, oil & vinegar, w/salt & pepper shakers in shadow box, from $55 to **$75.00**
Cup & saucer.. **$25.00**
Demitasse pot, elongated ovoid, long handle & spout, 7½", minimum value **$90.00**
Demitasse pot, w/4 cups & saucers, minimum value **$150.00**
Demitasse pot, w/6 cups & saucers, minimum value **$175.00**
Deviled egg plate, 12 indents, patterned center, 10", from $35 to.. **$50.00**
Egg cup, from $20 to................................. **$25.00**
Egg cup on tray, from $35 to......................... **$45.00**
Flowerpot, buttress handles, 5", from $35 to **$45.00**
Hamburger press, wood w/embedded ceramic tray, round, minimum value................................. **$24.00**
Instant coffee jar, no attached spoon holder on side, minimum value **$55.00**
Instant coffee jar, spoon-holder tube on side, rare............ **$45.00**
Jam & jelly containers, cojoined, w/lids & spoons, from $45 to **$60.00**
Jam & jelly containers, cojoined, w/lids & spoons, w/loop handles & lids, very rare **$85.00**
Jam jar, attached underplate, from $35 to **$45.00**
Ketchup or mustard jar, flared cylinder w/lettered label, ea from $25 to.. **$30.00**
Lamp, pinup; made from either a match holder or a salt box, ea from $75 to.. **$100.00**
Lazy Susan on wood pedestal, round covered box at center, 4 sections around outside (2 w/lids), from $150 to..................... **$250.00**
Marmalade, round base w/tab handles, w/lid & spoon, minimum value, from $35 to **$50.00**
Match holder, wall mount, from $50 to................... **$75.00**
Measuring cup set, 4-pc w/matching ceramic rack, from $45 to. **$65.00**
Measuring spoons on 8" ceramic spoon-shaped rack, from $40 to.. **$55.00**
Mug, rounded bottom, med, from $25 to................... **$30.00**
Mug, straight upright bar handle, lg, from $25 to............... **$35.00**
Napkin holder, from $30 to.......................... **$40.00**
Pipe holder/ashtray, from $30 to...................... **$50.00**
Pitcher, bulbous, 5", from $25 to...................... **$30.00**
Pitcher, lettered Milk on neck band, 8", from $28 to **$35.00**
Pitcher, tankard shape, 3"............................ **$28.00**

Planter, rolling pin shape, rare, minimum value...................$50.00
Plate, bread; from $15 to...$20.00
Plate, dinner; from $30 to..$40.00
Plate, luncheon; from $15 to......................................$25.00

Plate, side salad; crescent shape, hard to find, from $50.00 to $60.00. (Photo courtesy Jacki Elliott)

Platter, 12", from $50 to...$60.00
Recipe box, w/salt & pepper shakers; part of shadow-box set, from $40 to..$50.00
Relish tray, 2 round wells w/center handle, 12", from $35 to....$40.00
Relish tray, 3 wells w/center handle, from $55 to.................$65.00
Rolling pin, minimum value..$50.00
Salad fork, spoon, 2 shakers, funnel, oil & vinegar bottles, tea bag jar in wood frame w/4 spice drawers, EX, $65 to................$85.00
Salad fork, spoon & salt & pepper shakers w/wooden handles, on ceramic wall rack, minimum value.................................$55.00
Salad fork & spoon w/wooden handles on ceramic wall-mount rack, from $45 to...$65.00
Salt & pepper shakers, drum shape w/long horizontal ceramic handle, lg, pr from $30 to...$40.00
Salt & pepper shakers, w/applied rose, sq, pr....................$23.00
Salt & pepper shakers, w/handle, pr from $15 to..................$20.00
Salt & pepper shakers, w/lettered neck band, pr..................$25.00
Salt & pepper shakers, wall hanging, 3¾", pr +2½x6" hanger w/scalloped top, from $25 to...$45.00
Salt & pepper shakers, 4", pr from $15 to.........................$20.00
Salt box, wooden lid, from $45 to.................................$60.00
Salt canister, sq, 6x4"...$50.00
Shaker, cheese or sugar, 4".......................................$35.00
Slipper, 3-dimensional rose on toe, rare, from $85 to............$125.00
Snack tray w/cup, oval, 2-pc, minimum value......................$65.00
Snack tray w/cup, rectangular, 2-pc, from $50 to.................$60.00
Spice rack, 2 rows of 3 curved-front containers, together forming half-cylinder shape w/flat back, from $75 to.......................$85.00
Spice rack, 3 rows of 2 curved-front containers, together forming half-cylinder shape w/flat back....................................$85.00
Spice set, 9 sq containers in wood frame w/pull-out ceramic tray in base, from $75 to...$95.00
Spoon holder, w/lg salt shaker in well on side extension, from $20 to..$25.00
Stacking tea set, teapot, creamer & sugar bowl...................$125.00

Syrup pitcher, w/2 sm graduated pitchers on tray, minimum value...$75.00
Tazza (footed tray), 3¼x7½" dia, from $45 to.....................$55.00
Tazza (footed tray), 3x6" dia.....................................$45.00
Tea bags jar, bulbous w/lettering, no crosshatching, w/lid, 6"...$60.00
Teapot, 6x9", from $45 to...$60.00
Toast holder, rare, minimum value.................................$75.00
Tray, closed tab handles ea end, 11", from $25 to................$30.00
Tray, round w/chamberstick-type handle on 1 side, 5½", from $15 to..$20.00
Tumbler..$18.00
Vase, round w/flat sides, 6", from $20 to.........................$30.00
Wall hanger, teapot shape, pr.....................................$90.00

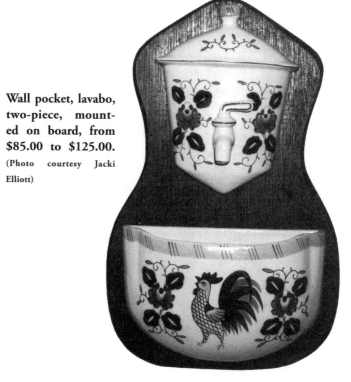

Wall pocket, lavabo, two-piece, mounted on board, from $85.00 to $125.00. (Photo courtesy Jacki Elliott)

Wall pocket, scalloped top, bulbous bottom, from $55 to....$65.00
Wall pocket, teapots, facing ea other, pr, minimum value....$90.00
Watering can, from $25 to..$35.00

Roselane Sparklers

Beginning as a husband and wife operation in the late 1930s, the Roselane Pottery Company of Pasadena, California, expanded their inventory from the figurines they originally sold to local florists to include a complete line of decorative items that eventually were shipped to Alaska, South America, and all parts of the United States.

One of their lines was the Roselane Sparklers. Popular in the '50s, these small animal and bird figures were airbrush decorated and had rhinestone eyes. They're fun to look for, and though prices are rising steadily, they're still not terribly expensive.

If you'd like to learn more, there's a chapter on Roselane in

Collector's Encyclopedia of California Pottery, Second Edition, and *California Pottery Scrapbook* by Jack Chipman.

Advisor: Lee Garmon (See Directory, Advertising, Reddy Kilowatt)

Angelfish, 4½", from $20 to	**$25.00**
Basset hound, sitting, 4", from $15 to	**$18.00**
Basset hound pup, 2", from $12 to	**$15.00**
Basset hound puppies (2), 1 sitting & 1 recumbent, marked #99 & #98, pr	**$50.00**
Bulldog, fierce expression, looking up & right, jeweled collar, 3½", from $22 to	**$25.00**
Bulldog puppy, blue eyes seated, 1¾"	**$12.00**

Cat: 5½", from $25.00 to $30.00; chihuahua, 7½", $28.00; Siamese, 6½", $35.00.

Cat, recumbent, head turned right, tail & paws tucked under body, from $20 to	**$25.00**
Cat, Siamese looking straight ahead, no collar, 5"	**$45.00**
Cat, Siamese lying down, head turned right & resting on left paw, tail lying over back, jeweled collar, 5½" L	**$45.00**
Cat, Siamese sitting, looking straight ahead, jeweled collar, 7", from $40 to	**$50.00**
Cat, Siamese sitting, 3⅞""	**$30.00**
Cat, Siamese standing, head turned left, jeweled collar, 4"	**$32.00**
Cat mama holding babies, 5", from $40 to	**$45.00**
Cat sitting, head turned right, tail out behind, from $25 to	**$28.00**
Cat standing, head turned right, tail arched over back, jeweled collar, 5½", from $25 to	**$30.00**
Cats, Siamese mother & 2 babies, blue eyes, 9½", 3¾"	**$75.00**
Chihuahua sitting, left paw raised, looking straight ahead, 7"	**$28.00**
Cocker spaniel, 4½", from $15 to	**$20.00**
Deer standing, head turned right, looking downward, 5½"	**$25.00**
Deer w/antlers, standing, jeweled collar, 4½", from $22 to	**$28.00**
Donkey standing, lg ears, pink eyes	**$35.00**
Elephant sitting on hind quarters, 6", from $35 to	**$40.00**
Elephant striding, trunk raised, jeweled headpiece, 6", from $35 to	**$40.00**
Fawn, legs folded under body, 4x3½"	**$25.00**
Fawn, upturned head, 4x3½"	**$20.00**

Fawn, 4½x1½"	**$20.00**
Kangaroo mama holding babies, 4½", from $40 to	**$45.00**
Kitten sitting, 1¾"	**$12.00**
Owl, very stylized, lg round eyes, teardrop-shaped body, lg	**$25.00**
Owl, 3½"	**$15.00**
Owl, 5¼"	**$25.00**
Owl, 7"	**$30.00**
Owl baby, 2¼", from $12 to	**$15.00**
Pheasants, 1 (pink, 3¾"), 1 (blue, 5"), looking back, pr from $30 to	**$35.00**
Pig, lg	**$25.00**
Pouter pigeon, 3½"	**$20.00**
Raccoon standing, 4½", from $20 to	**$25.00**
Road runner, 8½" L, from $30 to	**$45.00**
Squirrel eating nut, lg bushy tail, blue & brown highlights, 4"	**$30.00**
Whippet sitting, 7½", from $25 to	**$28.00**

Rosemeade Pottery

The Wahpeton Pottery Company of Wahpeton, North Dakota, chose the trade name Rosemeade for a line of bird and animal figurines, novelty salt and pepper shakers, bells, and many other items which were sold from the 1940s to the 1960s through gift stores and souvenir shops in that part of the country. They were marked with either a paper label or an ink stamp; the name Prairie Rose was also used.

Advisor: Bryce Farnsworth (See Directory, Rosemeade)

Club: North Dakota Pottery Collectors Society
Sandy Short, Membership Chairperson
Box 14, Beach, ND 58621
701-872-3236 or csshortnd@mcn.net
www.ndpcs.org
Annual dues: $15; sponsors annual convention and includes four newsletters

Bell, peacock, with label, 5", from $140.00 to $165.00.

Advertising, dealer sign, pink, rare, 3¾x7", minimum value.	**$1,500.00**
Ashtray, fish, pink, 6¼", from $100 to	**$125.00**

Ashtray, pheasant & fish figures on back of bowl form, 1940s, rare, 7"...**$1,880.00**

Bank, bear, aqua, 3¾x6", minimum value **$400.00**

Basket, blue, twisted handle, 3x2¾", from $100 to...........**$125.00**

Basket, white w/rose handle, 5x5¼", from $100 to...........**$125.00**

Candleholders, pink w/white, heart shape, 3", pr from $100 to **$125.00**

Cigarette box, embossed horse, 5", from $250 to.............**$300.00**

Creamer & sugar bowl, white ducks, from $125 to **$150.00**

Figurine, circus horse, red & yellow, solid, 4¼x4¼", from $350 to..**$400.00**

Figurine, frog, green w/black spots, 1¼", from $100 to.....**$125.00**

Figurine, potato, 1½x2½", from $100 to.........................**$125.00**

Figurine, walrus, marked 'as sold in November 1944,' rare, 4¼x6½"...**$500.00**

Lamp, brown horse on green grass, rare, 9½x8¾", minimum value..**$800.00**

Mug, Prairie Rose, 3¾", from $65 to................................**$85.00**

Pin, blackbird, 2¼", minimum value.............................**$1,000.00**

Pin, mallard drake, 2", minimum value.........................**$1,000.00**

Pitcher, Prairie Rose, 6", from $75 to.............................**$100.00**

Planter, sleigh, pink, 4x5¼", from $75 to **$125.00**

Plaque, walleye decal on round tile, 6", from $75 to.........**$125.00**

Salt & pepper shakers, black Angus, 1¾", pr from $300 to..**$350.00**

Salt and pepper shakers, chihuahua, from $75.00 to $100.00 for the pair. (Photo courtesy Darlene Hurst Dommel)

Salt & pepper shakers, hen & rooster, 2", 3¼", pr from $85 to.**$100.00**

Salt & pepper shakers, red potato, ¾", 1½", w/3" tray, set from $400 to **$450.00**

Spoon rest, Prairie Rose, 8½", from $75 to.....................**$100.00**

Spoon rest, white dogwood, rare, 3½", minimum value.....**$300.00**

Toothpick holder, rooster strutting, 3¾x2¾", from $100 to...**$125.00**

Vase, black/blue crackle glaze, hand thrown, 5", from $150 to ..**$200.00**

Vase, blue to pink, hand thrown, North Dakota mark, 3½", minimum value **$250.00**

Vase, wheat on green, 5⅞", from $65 to **$85.00**

Vases, horses running (3), Harvest Gold, 7", rare, minimum value **$350.00**

Wall pocket, deer, aqua, 5", from $40 to............................**$60.00**

Roseville Pottery

This company took its name from the city in Ohio where they operated for a few years before moving to Zanesville in the late 1890s. They're recognized as one of the giants in the industry, having produced many lines of the finest in art pottery from the beginning to the end of their operations. Even when machinery took over many of the procedures once carefully done by hand, the pottery they produced continued to reflect the artistic merit and high standards of quality the company had always insisted upon.

Several marks were used over the years as well as some paper labels. The very early art lines often carried an applied ceramic seal with the name of the line (Royal, Egypto, Mongol, Mara, or Woodland) under a circle containing the words Rozane Ware. From 1910 until 1928 an Rv mark was used, the 'v' being contained in the upper loop of the 'R.' Paper labels were common from 1914 until 1937. From 1932 until they closed in 1952, the mark was Roseville in script, or R USA. Pieces marked RRP Co Roseville, Ohio, were not made by the Roseville Pottery but by Robinson Ransbotton of Roseville, Ohio. Don't be confused. There are many jardinieres and pedestals in a brown and green blended glaze that are being sold at flea markets and antique malls as Roseville that were actually made by Robinson Ransbottom as late as the 1970s and 1980s. That isn't to say they don't have some worth of their own, but don't buy them for old Roseville.

Most of the listings here are for items produced from the 1930s on — things you'll be more likely to encounter today. If you'd like to learn more about the subject, we recommend *The Collector's Encyclopedia of Roseville Pottery, Vols. 1* and *2* (revised editions, 2001 pricing by Mike Nickel) and *Roseville Pottery Price Guide* by Sharon and Bob Huxford (Collector Books); *A Price Guide to Roseville Pottery by the Numbers* by John Humphries (L&W Book Sales); *Roseville in All Its Splendor* by Jack and Nancy Bomm (L&W Book Sales); and *Collector's Compendium of Roseville Pottery, Vols. 1* and *2*, by R.B. Monsen (Monsen & Baer).

Advisor: Mike Nickel (See the Directory, Roseville)

Newsletter: *Rosevilles of the Past*
Nancy Bomm, Editor
P.O. Box 656
Clarcona, FL 32710-0656
Subscription: $19.95 per year for 6 to 12 newsletters

Apple Blossom, bowl, blue, #326-6, 2½x6½", from $175 to.**$200.00**

Apple Blossom, vase, pink or green, #390-12, 12½", from $350 to **$400.00**

Artcraft, jardiniere, tan, 4", from $200 to **$250.00**

Artwood, planter, #1054-8½, 6½x8½", from $85 to **$95.00**

Autumn, jardiniere, 9½", from $600 to **$700.00**

Autumn, toothbrush holder, 5", from $275 to...................**$325.00**

Aztec, vase, shouldered, long neck, 9½", from $400 to......**$500.00**

Aztec, vase, 9½", from $400 to **$500.00**

Azurean, candlestick, floral, signed V Adams, 9", ea from $900 to...**$1,000.00**

Bank, buffalo, 3x6½", from $350 to **$400.00**

Bank, dog, 4", from $450 to..**$500.00**

Bank, eagle, 2½", from $400 to **$450.00**

Bank, pig, 2½x5", from $175 to **$200.00**

Bittersweet, cornucopia, #857-4, 4½", from $100 to........**$125.00**

Bittersweet, planter, #828-10, 10½", from $150 to **$175.00**

Blackberry, jardiniere, 4", from $300 to **$350.00**

Blackberry, vase, 6", from $400 to **$450.00**

Blackberry, wall pocket, 8½", from $1,500 to................**$1,700.00**

Bleeding Heart, candlesticks, blue, #1139-4½, 5", pr from $225 to **$275.00**

Bleeding Heart, vase, pink or green, #964-6, 6½", from $125 to **$150.00**

Blended Glaze, jardiniere & pedestal, pine cones, 12" overall, from $200 to **$250.00**

Bushberry, vase, blue, #34-8, 8", from $250 to **$275.00**

Bushberry, vase, green, #157-8, 8", from $225 to **$250.00**

Cameo II, flowerpot, 5½", from $200 to **$250.00**

Cameo II, jardiniere, 8", from $375 to **$450.00**

Cameo II, vase, double bud; 4x7½", from $200 to **$250.00**

Capri, leaf, #532-16, 16", from $35 to **$45.00**

Capri, vase, #582-9, 9", from $50 to **$60.00**

Carnelian I, fan vase, 6", from $70 to **$80.00**

Carnelian I, flower frog, 4½", from $75 to **$85.00**

Carnelian I, vase, 10", from $200 to **$250.00**

Carnelian I, wall pocket, 8", from $200 to **$250.00**

Carnelian II, basket, 4x10", from $225 to **$275.00**

Carnelian II, ewer, 12½", from $800 to **$900.00**

Carnelian II, planter, 3x8", from $125 to **$150.00**

Carnelian II, vase, 10", from $225 to **$275.00**

Carnelian II, vase, 14", from $800 to **$900.00**

Carnelian II, wall pocket, 8", from $350 to **$400.00**

Cherry Blossom, hanging basket, #350, 8": brown, from $400.00 to $500.00; pink and blue, from $2,000.00 to $2,250.00.

Chloron, bowl, 3", from $250 to **$300.00**

Chloron, jardiniere, #487, 5½", from $400 to **$450.00**

Clemana, flower frog, tan, #23, 4", from $150 to **$175.00**

Clemana, vase, green, #754, 8½", from $450 to **$500.00**

Clematis, bowl, center; blue, #458-10, 14", from $200 to .**$250.00**

Columbine, cornucopia, blue or tan, #149-6, 5½", from $150 to **$175.00**

Corinthian, wall pocket, #1232, 8", from $200 to **$250.00**

Cornelian, jardiniere, Our Leader, #119, 6½", from $100 to .**$125.00**

Cornelian, pitcher, 4", from $50 to **$60.00**

Cosmos, vase, blue, #950-8, 8", from $350 to **$400.00**

Creamware, mug, FOE, Liberty, Truth, Justice, Equality, 5", from $125 to **$150.00**

Creamware, ring tree, Forget-Me-Not, 3½", from $125 to ..**$150.00**

Creamware, tumbler, Holly, 4", from $250 to **$300.00**

Cremona, vase, fan form, #73, 5", from $125 to **$150.00**

Crocus, letter receiver, 3½", from $400 to **$450.00**

Crocus, vase, 7", from $650 to **$750.00**

Crocus, vase, 9", from $750 to **$850.00**

Dahlrose, hanging basket, #343, 7½", from $250 to **$300.00**

Dahlrose, vase, #418, 6", from $150 to **$175.00**

Dahlrose, wall pocket, 10", from $300 to **$350.00**

Dahlrose, window box, takes ceramic liner, #375-10, 6x11½", from $325 to **$375.00**

Dawn, vase, green, #833-12, 12", from $350 to **$400.00**

Dogwood I, vase, double bud; 8", from $175 to **$200.00**

Dogwood I, wall pocket, 9", from $350 to **$400.00**

Dogwood I, wall pocket, 10", from $375 to **$425.00**

Dogwood II, hanging basket, #340, 5", from $250 to **$300.00**

Dogwood II, jardiniere, #608, 8", from $250 to **$300.00**

Dogwood II, vase, #301, 7", from $200 to **$250.00**

Donatella, creamer, Forget-Me-Not, from $60 to **$70.00**

Donatella, sugar bowl, Seascape, w/lid, from $70 to **$80.00**

Donatello, ashtray, 3", from $125 to **$150.00**

Donatello, basket, 7½", from $300 to **$350.00**

Donatello, bowl, 3x8", from $100 to **$125.00**

Donatello, powder jar, 2x5", from $400 to **$450.00**

Dutch, pitcher, 7½", from $225 to **$275.00**

Dutch, shaving mug, 4", from $125 to **$150.00**

Dutch, tankard, 11½", from $175 to **$200.00**

Dutch, toothbrush holder, 4", from $100 to **$125.00**

Earlam, planter, #89, 5½x10½", from $400 to **$450.00**

Early Pitcher, Landscape, 7½", from $150 to **$175.00**

Early Pitcher, Poppy, #11, 9", from $350 to **$400.00**

Early Pitcher, The Bridge, 6", from $150 to **$175.00**

Falline, vase, blue, #647, 7½", from $800 to **$900.00**

Falline, vase, tan, #650, 6", from $600 to **$700.00**

Ferella, vase, tan, #499, 6", from $400 to **$450.00**

Florane, bowl, 10", from $30 to **$35.00**

Florane, jar, 8", from $90 to **$115.00**

Florane, vase, double bud; 5", from $100 to **$125.00**

Florane, vase, 12½", from $200 to **$250.00**

Florane, wall pocket, 9", from $175 to **$225.00**

Florentine, ashtray, #17-3, 5", from $125 to **$150.00**

Florentine, bowl, #125-6, 7", from $85 to **$100.00**

Florentine, vase, #254-7, 7", from $175 to **$225.00**

Florentine, wall pocket, 12½", from $300 to **$350.00**

Forget-Me-Not, creamer, 1½", from $100 to **$125.00**

Foxglove, tray, green/pink, #419, 8½", from $200 to **$225.00**

Foxglove, vase, pink, #47-8, 8½", from $225 to **$275.00**

Freesia, flowerpot w/saucer, green, #670-5, 5½", from $175 to .**$200.00**

Freesia, vase, green, #124-9, 9", from $185 to **$210.00**

Fuchsia, vase, blue, #898-8, 8", from $475 to **$525.00**

Futura, vase, #432, 10", from $700 to **$800.00**

Gardenia, #666-8, 9½", from $300 to **$350.00**

Gardenia, tray, #631-14, 15", from $200 to **$250.00**

Gardenia, vase, #685-10, 10", from $175 to **$225.00**

Holland, mug, 4", from $60 to **$75.00**

Holland, powder jar, 3", from $125 to **$150.00**

Holly, chamberstick, 7", from $600 to **$700.00**

Holly, creamer, 3", from $200 to **$225.00**

Holly, tumbler, creamware, 4", from $250 to **$300.00**

Imperial I, basket, #7, 9", from $200 to **$250.00**

Imperial I, compote, 6½", from $175 to **$225.00**

Imperial I, planter, 14x16", from $300 to **$350.00**

Imperial I, vase, 10", from $250 to **$300.00**

Imperial II, bowl, #198, 4½", from $350 to **$400.00**

Imperial II, vase, #478, 8", from $550 to.......................... **$650.00**

Iris, vase, blue, #647-3, 3½", from $125 to **$150.00**

Iris, vase, pink or tan, #917-6, 6½", from $150 to **$175.00**

Ivory II, cornucopia, #2, 5½x12", from $75 to................... **$95.00**

Ivory II, shelf, #8, 5½", from $125 to.............................. **$175.00**

Ixia, basket, hanging, 7", from $200 to............................ **$250.00**

Jonquil, jardiniere, #621, 4", from $200 to...................... **$250.00**

Jonquil, vase, #93, 4½", from $375 to.............................. **$425.00**

Jonquil, vase, #529, 8", from $450 to **$500.00**

Juvenile, creamer, Sad Puppy, 3½", from $500 to **$600.00**

Juvenile, cup & saucer, Rabbit, 2", 5", from $200 to........ **$250.00**

Juvenile, custard, Goose, 2½", from $600 to **$650.00**

Juvenile, mug, Fat Puppy, 3½", from $500 to.................... **$600.00**

Juvenile, mug, Rabbit, 3", from $175 to............................ **$200.00**

Juvenile, plate, Chicks, sm rolled edge, 7", from $100 to... **$125.00**

Juvenile, plate, Skinny Puppy, 8", from $125 to **$150.00**

La Rose, vase, #236, 4", from $125 to **$150.00**

La Rose, vase, #238, 6", from $150 to **$175.00**

La Rose, wall pocket, #1233, 9", from $300 to.................. **$350.00**

Lombardy, jardiniere, 6½", from $150 to **$200.00**

Lotus, bowl, #L6-9, 3x9", from $150 to **$175.00**

Lotus, planter, #L9-4, 3½x4", from $100 to **$125.00**

Lotus, vase, pillow form, #L4-10, 10½", from $275 to...... **$325.00**

Luffa, candlesticks, #1097, 5", pr from $500 to................ **$600.00**

Lustre, candlestick, 5½", ea from $45 to........................... **$55.00**

Magnolia, conch shell, brown or green, #453-6, 6½", from $95
    to **$110.00**

Magnolia, cornucopia, brown or green, #184, 6", from $85 to. **$95.00**

Matt Green, wall pocket, 11", from $350 to **$400.00**

Mayfair, jardiniere, #1109-4, 4", from $60 to..................... **$75.00**

Mayfair, vase, #1106-12, 12½", from $90 to **$110.00**

Ming Tree, ashtray, #599, 6", from $75 to **$85.00**

Ming Tree, bowl, #526-9, 4x11½", from $95 to............... **$110.00**

Mock Orange, vase, #985-12, 13", from $350 to **$450.00**

Mock Orange, window box, #956-8, 4½x8½", from $100 to. **$125.00**

Moderne, candleholder, triple, #1112, 6", ea from $250 to .**$275.00**

Moderne, compote, #295, 5", from $225 to **$250.00**

Morning Glory, pillow vase, ivory, #120, 7", from $275 to ..**$325.00**

Moss, pillow vase, #781, 8": pink and green or orange and green, from $350.00 to $400.00; blue, from $300.00 to $350.00. (Photo courtesy Treadway Gallery Inc.)

Moss, wall pocket, #1278-8, 8", from $550 to.................. **$650.00**

Mostique, bowl, 5½", from $100 to **$125.00**

Mostique, compote, 7", from $300 to............................... **$350.00**

Mostique, jardiniere, 8", from $225 to **$250.00**

Normandy, hanging basket, 7", from $250 to................... **$300.00**

Orian, candleholders, red, #1108, 4½", pr from $375 to...**$425.00**

Orian, vase, tan, #733, 6", from $200 to **$225.00**

Orian, vase, tan, #740, 10½", from $325 to **$375.00**

Pasadena, planter, #L-17, 3½x9", from $40 to.................... **$45.00**

Pasadena, planter, #L-35, 3½x10½", from $65 to.............. **$75.00**

Peony, bookends, #11, 5½", pr from $200 to **$250.00**

Peony, candleholders, double; #115-3, 5", pr from $200 to..**$250.00**

Persian, creamer, stylized crocus on creamware, 3", from $75 to. **$100.00**

Persian, jardiniere, 8", from $450 to **$500.00**

Pine Cone, bowl, green, #320-5, 4½", from $150 to........ **$175.00**

Pine Cone, pitcher, blue, #485-10, 10½", from $850 to ..**$950.00**

Pine Cone, vase, green, #908-8, 8", from $200 to **$225.00**

Poppy, bowl, pink, #336-10, 12", from $225 to **$275.00**

Poppy, vase, gray/green, #872-9, 9", from $225 to **$275.00**

Primrose, vase, #760-6, 7", from $125 to **$150.00**

Primrose, vase, tan, #761-6, 6½", from $125 to **$150.00**

Raymor, bowl, vegetable; #160, 9", from $30 to.................**$40.00**

Raymor, corn server, #162, individual, 12½", from $45 to..**$50.00**

Raymor, gravy boat, #190, 9½", from $30 to **$35.00**

Rosecraft Black, compote, 4x11", from $125 to.............. **$150.00**

Rosecraft Black, vase, 9", from $175 to........................... **$200.00**

Rosecraft Blended, vase, stick neck, 12½", from $150 to...**$175.00**

Rosecraft Blended, vase, 6", from $90 to **$110.00**

Rosecraft Hexagon, bowl, green, 7½", from $275 to **$300.00**

Rosecraft Hexagon, candlestick, brown, 8", ea from $375 to..**$425.00**

Rosecraft Hexagon, vase, blue, 8", from $575 to **$625.00**

Rosecraft Panel, window box, brown, 6x12", from $450 to..**$500.00**

Rosecraft Vintage, vase, 12", from $500 to **$550.00**

Rosecraft Vintage, window box, 6x11½", from $500 to **$550.00**

Rozane, letter holder, floral, C Neff, 3½", from $250 to....**$275.00**

Rozane, vase, #872, 5½", from $150 to **$175.00**

Rozane, vase, floral, angle handles, #7, 12", from $375 to.**$425.00**

Rozane Light, mug, grapes, signed Pillsbury, 5", from $300 to.**$350.00**

Rozane Light, vase, floral, signed W Myers, 8½", from $450
    to **$550.00**

Rozane Pattern, vase, #5-8, 8½", from $200 to.................. **$225.00**

Rozane 1917, bowl, 5", from $125 to.............................. **$150.00**

Russco, triple cornucopia, heavy crystals, #111, 2½x8", from $300
    to **$350.00**

Russco, vase, #699, 9½", from $150 to............................ **$175.00**

Russco, vase, double bud; #101, 8½", from $100 to......... **$125.00**

Russco, vase, heavy crystals, #108, 7", from $200 to......... **$225.00**

Silhouette, box, #740, 4½", from $150 to **$175.00**

Silhouette, vase, #784-8, 8", from $100 to...................... **$125.00**

Snowberry, vase, blue or pink, #1UR-8, 8½", from $225 to .. **$250.00**

Snowberry, vase, green, #1UR-8, 8½", from $175 to......... **$200.00**

Stein, Better Late Than Never, 5", from $250 to **$300.00**

Sunflower, bowl, center; 3x12½", from $800 to **$900.00**

Sunflower, bowl, 4", from $450 to.................................. **$500.00**

Sylvan, vase, 9½", from $600 to **$700.00**

Teasel, vase, dark blue or rust, #888-12, 12", from $300 to .**$350.00**

Thorn Apple, vase, #816-8, 8½", from $250 to **$300.00**

Thorn Apple, vase, #820-9, 9½", from $275 to **$325.00**

Topeo, candlesticks, double; red, 5", pr from $300 to........**$350.00**
Topeo, vase, red, 6", from $250 to.....................**$300.00**
Tuscany, flower arranger, gray/light blue, #66, 5", from $75 to. **$100.00**
Tuscany, vase, pink, #349, 12", from $300 to **$350.00**
Tuscany, vase, pink, #68, 4", from $100 to **$125.00**
Tutura, vase, #382, 7", from $325 to **$375.00**
Velmoss, vase, green, #719, 9½", from $275 to **$325.00**
Velmoss, vase, red, #718, 8", from $350 to.......................**$400.00**
Velmoss Scroll, vase, bowl, 3", from $100 to **$125.00**
Velmoss Scroll, vase, 5", from $125 to **$150.00**
Velmoss Scroll, vase, 10", from $200 to........................**$225.00**
Velmoss Scroll, wall pocket, 11", from $375 to...............**$450.00**
Venetian, bake pan, 7", from $50 to **$60.00**
Venetian, pudding crock, from $40 to **$50.00**
Victorian Art Pottery, vase, #257, 7", from $500 to..........**$550.00**
Vista, basket, 9½", from $900 to **$1,000.00**
Volpato, vase, 9", from $100 to **$125.00**
Water Lily, candlesticks, brown, #1155-4½, 5", pr from $125 to...**$175.00**
Water Lily, vase, brown, #78-9, 9", from $200 to **$250.00**

Water Lily, vase, #84, 16": brown, from $500.00 to $550.00; blue, from $600.00 to $650.00; rose with green, from $650.00 to $700.00.
(Photo courtesy David Rago Auctions)

White Rose, basket, #362-8, 7½", from $200 to **$250.00**
White Rose, vase, double bud; #148, 4½", from $85 to **$95.00**
Wincraft, basket, #210-12, 12", from $450 to...................**$500.00**
Wincraft, vase, #288-15, 16", from $325 to **$375.00**
Windsor, bowl, center; rust, 3½x10½", from $350 to **$400.00**
Windsor, lamp base, rust, #551, 7", from $700 to.............**$800.00**
Wisteria, bowl vase, blue, #632, 5", from $450 to **$500.00**
Wisteria, vase, tan, #682, 10", from $750 to **$850.00**
Woodland, vase, 6", from $450 to **$500.00**
Zephyr Lily, fan vase, blue, #205-6, 6½", from $175 to **$200.00**
Zephyr Lily, vase, blue, #202-8, 8½", from $250 to **$275.00**

Royal China

The dinnerware and kitchenware lines made by Royal China of Sebring, Ohio (1934 – 1986), have become very collectible, those cataloged here in particular. The most sought after today have their origins in supermarket and gas station promotions; some were given away, and others distributed by stamp companies. They were also retailed through major outlet stores such as Montgomery Ward, Sears Roebuck, and W.T. Grant.

The Royal China Company is credited with revolutionizing the dinnerware industry through the introduction of Kenneth Doyle's stamping machine in 1948. Prior to this innovative technique, transfers were laboriously applied by hand.

Veteran collectors find that the number of shapes and patterns produced by Royal seems almost endless, and many can turn up in unexpected colors. For example, Blue Willow is not restricted to blue but on rare occasions can be found in pink, black, and even multi-colorations. To simplify pattern identification, focus on the pattern's border which will nearly always be consistent. Memory Lane features a border of oak leaves and acorns. Bucks County, an exclusive of W.T. Grant, sports a gold Pennsylvania Dutch tulip-motif garland. Fair Oaks has magnolia blossoms surrounded by periwinkle edging. The Willows (Blue Willow, Pink Willow, Yellow, etc.) speak for themselves. Colonial Homestead and Old Curiosity Shop are typically found in green and are often mistaken one for the other. Here's how to tell the difference: Old Curiosity Shop's border depicts metal hinges and pulls, while Colonial Homestead's features wooden boards with pegged joints. Most Currier & Ives dinnerware pieces regardless of color will have the famous scroll border designed by art director Gordon Parker. Note that our prices are for items in the blue pattern. This line was made on a very limited basis in pink as well. To evaluate that color, you'll have to double our values.

Our advisors are happy to answer any questions on American clay products from figurines to dinnerware via e-mail. For further reading on this subject with an emphasis on Currier & Ives, we highly recommend *A Collector's Guide for Currier & Ives Dinnerware by the Royal China Company* by Elden R. Aupperle (with 2001 Price Guide, 112 pages, soft cover) as well as the club listed below.

Club/Newsletter: *Currier and Ives China by Royal*
c/o Jack and Treva Hamlin
145 Township Rd. 1088, Proctorville, OH 45669; 740-886-7644

Club: C&I Dinnerware Collectors
E.R. Aupperle, Treasurer
29470 Saxon Road
Toulon, IL 61483-9205
309-896-3331; fax: 309-856-6005; www.royalchinaclub.com

Blue Heaven, bowl, fruit nappy; 5½" **$3.00**
Blue Heaven, bowl, vegetable; 10" **$22.00**
Blue Heaven, butter dish, ¼-lb, from $20 to................**$25.00**
Blue Heaven, creamer **$8.00**
Blue Heaven, cup & saucer **$5.00**
Blue Heaven, gravy boat, w/tray...............................**$32.00**
Blue Heaven, pitcher, ice lip, 8½" **$30.00**
Blue Heaven, plate, dinner; 10", from $6 to **$8.00**
Blue Heaven, platter, tab handles, 10½" **$20.00**
Blue Heaven, sugar bowl...**$12.00**
Blue Willow, ashtray, 5½", from $8 to........................**$12.00**
Blue Willow, bowl, cereal; 6¼" **$15.00**
Blue Willow, bowl, fruit nappy; 5½" **$6.50**

Blue Willow, bowl, soup; 8¼" $15.00
Blue Willow, bowl, vegetable; 10" $28.00
Blue Willow, butter dish, ¼-lb $45.00
Blue Willow, casserole, w/lid $95.00
Blue Willow, creamer $6.00
Blue Willow, cup & saucer $6.00
Blue Willow, gravy boat, double spout $28.00
Blue Willow, pie plate, 10" $30.00
Blue Willow, plate, bread & butter; 6¼" $3.00
Blue Willow, plate, dinner; 10" $8.00
Blue Willow, plate, salad; rare, 7¼" $7.00
Blue Willow, platter, oval, 13" $32.00
Blue Willow, platter, serving; tab handles, 10½" ... $20.00

Blue Willow, platter, tab handles, 10½", $20.00. (Photo courtesy Mary Frank Gaston)

Blue Willow, salt & pepper shakers, pr $25.00
Blue Willow, sugar bowl, w/lid $15.00
Blue Willow, teapot $135.00
Blue Willow, tray, tidbit; 2-tier $95.00
Buck's County, ashtray, 5½" $15.00
Buck's County, bowl, soup; 8½" $18.00
Buck's County, bowl, vegetable; 10" $28.00
Buck's County, casserole, w/lid $125.00
Buck's County, creamer $8.00
Buck's County, cup & saucer $8.00
Buck's County, gravy boat, double spout $35.00
Buck's County, plate, bread & butter; 6¼" $4.00
Buck's County, plate, dinner; 10" $12.00
Buck's County, platter, oval, 13" $45.00
Buck's County, platter, serving; tab handles, 10½" .. $25.00
Buck's County, salt & pepper shakers, pr $35.00
Buck's County, sugar bowl, w/lid $18.00
Buck's County, teapot $145.00
Colonial Homestead, bowl, cereal; 6¼" $15.00
Colonial Homestead, bowl, fruit nappy; 5½" $5.00
Colonial Homestead, bowl, soup; 8¼" $12.00
Colonial Homestead, bowl, vegetable; 10" $24.00
Colonial Homestead, casserole, angled handles, w/lid .. $75.00
Colonial Homestead, chop plate, 12" $18.00
Colonial Homestead, creamer $5.00
Colonial Homestead, cup & saucer $5.00

Colonial Homestead, gravy boat, double spout $15.00
Colonial Homestead, pie plate $25.00
Colonial Homestead, plate, bread & butter; 6" $3.00
Colonial Homestead, plate, dinner; 10" $8.00
Colonial Homestead, plate, salad; rare, 7¼" $8.00
Colonial Homestead, platter, oval, 13" $28.00
Colonial Homestead, platter, serving; tab handles, 10½" ... $15.00
Colonial Homestead, salt & pepper shakers, pr $18.00
Colonial Homestead, sugar bowl, w/lid $15.00
Colonial Homestead, teapot $95.00
Currier & Ives, ashtray, 5½" $15.00
Currier & Ives, bowl, cereal; round $15.00
Currier & Ives, bowl, dip; from Hostess set, 4⅜" ... $40.00
Currier & Ives, bowl, fruit nappy; 5½" $6.00
Currier & Ives, bowl, soup; 8½" $10.00
Currier & Ives, bowl, vegetable; deep, 10" $30.00
Currier & Ives, bowl, vegetable; 9" $20.00
Currier & Ives, butter dish, summer scene, ¼-lb ... $45.00
Currier & Ives, butter dish, winter scene, ¼-lb $35.00
Currier & Ives, cake plate, flat, 10" $45.00
Currier & Ives, cake plate, footed, 10" $200.00
Currier & Ives, casserole, angled handles, w/lid $100.00
Currier & Ives, casserole, angled handles, all white lid .. $175.00

Currier & Ives, casserole, tab handles, with lid, $200.00. (Photo courtesy Jack and Treva Hamlin)

Currier & Ives, creamer, angled handle $8.00
Currier & Ives, creamer, round handle, tall, rare $75.00
Currier & Ives, cup & saucer $6.00
Currier & Ives, deviled egg tray, from Hostess set .. $250.00
Currier & Ives, gravy boat, double spout $20.00
Currier & Ives, gravy boat, tab handles, w/liner (like 7" plate). $150.00
Currier & Ives, lamp, candle; w/globe $375.00
Currier & Ives, pie baker, from Hostess set, 11" ... $60.00
Currier & Ives, pie baker, 10", (depending on print) from $25 to $45.00
Currier & Ives, plate, bread & butter; 6⅜", from $3 to ... $5.00
Currier & Ives, plate, calendar; ca 1969-86 .... $20.00
Currier & Ives, plate, chop; Getting Ice, 11½" $35.00
Currier & Ives, plate, dinner; 10" $5.00
Currier & Ives, plate, luncheon; very rare, 9" $20.00
Currier & Ives, plate, salad; rare, 7" $15.00
Currier & Ives, platter, oval, 13" $35.00

Currier & Ives, platter, Rocky Mountains, tab handles, 10½" dia $20.00

Currier & Ives, salt & pepper shakers, pr, from $30 to $35.00

Currier & Ives, sugar bowl, angled handles, from $15 to $18.00

Currier & Ives, sugar bowl, no handles, flare top, w/lid $65.00

Currier & Ives, sugar bowl, no handles, straight sides, w/lid ..$35.00

Currier & Ives, teapot, 8 different styles & stampings, from $125 to $245.00

Currier & Ives, tidbit tray, 3-tier $30.00

Currier & Ives, tumbler, iced-tea; glass, 12-oz, 5½" $15.00

Currier & Ives, tumbler, juice; glass, 5-oz, 3½" $15.00

Currier & Ives, tumbler, old-fashioned; glass, 3¼" $15.00

Currier & Ives, tumbler, water; glass, 4¾" $15.00

Fair Oaks, bowl, divided vegetable $45.00

Fair Oaks, bowl, soup $15.00

Fair Oaks, bowl, vegetable; 9" $30.00

Fair Oaks, butter dish $45.00

Fair Oaks, casserole, w/lid $95.00

Fair Oaks, creamer $12.00

Fair Oaks, cup & saucer $8.00

Fair Oaks, gravy boat, w/underplate $25.00

Fair Oaks, plate, bread and butter; 6½", $12.00.

Fair Oaks, plate, dinner; 10" $12.00

Fair Oaks, platter, tab handles, 10½" $25.00

Fair Oaks, platter, 13" L $20.00

Fair Oaks, salt & pepper shakers, pr $25.00

Fair Oaks, sugar bowl, w/lid $18.00

Fair Oaks, teapot $145.00

Memory Lane, bowl, cereal; 6¼" $15.00

Memory Lane, bowl, fruit nappy; 5½" $6.00

Memory Lane, bowl, soup; 8½" $8.00

Memory Lane, bowl, vegetable; 10" $28.00

Memory Lane, butter dish, ¼-lb $35.00

Memory Lane, casserole, w/lid $85.00

Memory Lane, creamer $8.00

Memory Lane, cup & saucer $5.00

Memory Lane, gravy boat, double spout $24.00

Memory Lane, gravy boat liner, from $12 to $15.00

Memory Lane, plate, bread & butter; 6⅜" $3.00

Memory Lane, plate, chop; 12" $25.00

Memory Lane, plate, chop; 13" $35.00

Memory Lane, plate, dinner $12.00

Memory Lane, plate, luncheon; rare, 9¼" $18.00

Memory Lane, plate, salad; rare, 7" $12.00

Memory Lane, platter, oval, 13" $38.00

Memory Lane, platter, tab handles, 10½" $22.00

Memory Lane, salt & pepper shakers, pr $25.00

Memory Lane, sugar bowl, w/lid $15.00

Memory Lane, teapot $85.00

Memory Lane, tumbler, iced tea; glass $18.00

Memory Lane, tumbler, juice; glass $9.00

Old Curiosity Shop, ashtray, 5½" dia $15.00

Old Curiosity Shop, bowl, fruit nappy; 5½" $5.00

Old Curiosity Shop, bowl, soup/cereal; 6½" $15.00

Old Curiosity Shop, bowl, vegetable; 09" $25.00

Old Curiosity Shop, bowl, vegetable; 10" $28.00

Old Curiosity Shop, butter dish, ¼-lb $45.00

Old Curiosity Shop, casserole, w/lid $90.00

Old Curiosity Shop, creamer $8.00

Old Curiosity Shop, cup & saucer $5.00

Old Curiosity Shop, pie plate, 10" $32.00

Old Curiosity Shop, plate, bread & butter; 6⅜" $3.00

Old Curiosity Shop, plate, dinner; 10" $8.00

Old Curiosity Shop, plate, luncheon; rare, 9" $12.00

Old Curiosity Shop, plate, salad; rare, 7" $10.00

Old Curiosity Shop, platter, oval, 13" $35.00

Old Curiosity Shop, platter, tab handles, 10½" $22.00

Old Curiosity Shop, salt & pepper shakers, pr $22.00

Old Curiosity Shop, sugar bowl, w/lid $15.00

Old Curiosity Shop, teapot $115.00

Old Curiosity Shop, tidbit, 3-tier, center handle, from $35 to $45.00

Plain (goes w/any pattern), ladle, white..............................$50.00

Royal Copley

This is a line of planters, wall pockets, vases, and other novelty items, most of which are modeled as appealing animals, birds, or human figures. They were made by the Spaulding China Company of Sebring, Ohio, from 1942 until 1957. The decoration is under-glazed and airbrushed, and some pieces are trimmed in gold (which can add 25% to 50% to their values). Not every piece is marked, but they all have a style that is distinctive. Some items are ink stamped; others have (or have had) labels. (In the listings below, 'paper label only' indicates a piece that never was produced with an ink stamp.)

Royal Copley is really not hard to find, and unmarked items may sometimes be had at bargain prices. The more common pieces seem to have stabilized, but the rare and hard-to-find examples are showing a steady increase. Your collection can go in several directions; for instance, some people choose a particular animal to collect. If you're a cat lover, they were made in an extensive assortment of styles and sizes. Teddy bears are also popular; you'll find them licking a lollipop, playing a mandolin, or modeled as a bank, and they come in various colors as well. Wildlife lovers can collect deer, pheasants, fish, and gazelles, and there's also a wide array of songbirds.

If you'd like more information, we recommend *Collector's Guide to Royal Copley Plus Royal Windsor & Spaulding, Books I* and *II,* by Joe Devine.

Advisor: Joe Devine (See Directory, Royal Copley)

Ashtray, bird on perch, embossed inside, USA mark, 5½x6"..**$40.00**
Bank, rooster, marked Chicken Feed..., 8", from $75 to **$85.00**
Figurine, canary, paper label, hard to find, 5½", from $65 to.**$75.00**
Figurine, cockatoo, full bodied, 7¼", from $40 to **$45.00**
Figurine, flycatcher, tail down, paper label only, 8", from $40 to **$45.00**
Figurine, gull, wing molded to base, paper label only, 8", from $40 to **$45.00**
Figurine, hen, 5½", from $35 to..................................**$45.00**
Figurine, lark, paper label only, 5", from $15 to **$20.00**
Figurine, wren, tail up, paper label, 6¼", from $20 to **$25.00**
Figurines, pheasants, ring around necks, 12x6¾", 9x10½", pr from $40 to **$50.00**
Lamp, child praying, paper label only, 7¾", from $75 to.....**$85.00**
Lamp, Oriental boy (or girl) figural, 7½", from $75 to........**$85.00**
Pitcher, Floral Beauty, colors other than cobalt, green stamp or embossed mark, 8", from $55 to...............................**$60.00**

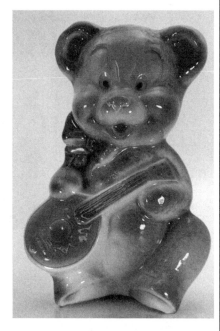

Planter, bear with banjo, 6½", from $65.00 to $75.00.

Planter, coach, green stamp or embossed mark, 3¼x6", from $20 to **$30.00**
Planter, dog in picnic basket, paper label only, hard to find, 7¾", from $90 to **$100.00**
Planter, duck & mail box, paper label only, rare, 6¾", from $85 to **$100.00**
Planter, Dutch boy (or girl) w/bucket, paper label only, 6", from $25 to **$35.00**
Planter, elephant w/ball, 7½", from $40 to **$60.00**
Planter, hat w/flowers along band, made to hang or rest on table, embossed mark, 7", from $45 to...................................**$50.00**
Planter, Indian boy & drum, easy to find, 6½", from $25 to .**$30.00**
Planter, Madonna praying, Royal Windsor, embossed mark, 8½", from $40 to **$45.00**

Planter, Oriental boy (or girl) w/lg basket on back, paper label only, scarce, 8", from $45 to..**$50.00**
Planter, poodle resting, dark gray w/red collar, Royal Windsor, 6½", from $75 to **$80.00**
Planter, ram's head, paper label only, 6½", from $25 to **$30.00**
Planter, rooster, low tail, common, paper label only, 7⅛", from $30 to **$35.00**
Planter, teddy bear, med brown, paper label only, 6¼", from $40 to.**$45.00**
Planter/wall pocket, girl w/wide-brim hat, right hand under right cheek, embossed mark, 7½", from $40 to....................**$45.00**
Vase, bud; warbler on stump, green stamp or embossed mark, 5", from $20 to **$25.00**
Vase, floral decal, handles, gold stamp, 6¼", from $10 to....**$14.00**
Vase/planter, nuthatch on stump, paper label only, 5½", from $30 to **$35.00**

Planter, colonial old man, 8", from $50.00 to $60.00. (Photo courtesy Bill and Betty Newbound)

Royal Haeger, Haeger

Many generations of the Haeger family have been associated with the ceramic industry. Starting out as a brickyard in 1871, the Haeger Company (Dundee, Illinois) progressed to include artware in their production as early as 1914. That was only the beginning. In the '30s they began to make a line of commercial artware so successful that as a result a plant was built in Macomb, Illinois, devoted exclusively to its production.

Royal Haeger was their premium line. Its chief designer in the 1940s was Royal Arden Hickman, a talented artist and sculptor who also worked in mediums other than pottery. For Haeger he designed a line of wonderfully stylized animals and birds, high-style vases, and human figures and masks with extremely fine details.

Paper labels were used extensively before the mid-'30s. Royal Haeger ware has an in-mold script mark, and their Flower Ware line (1954 – 1963) is marked 'RG' (Royal Garden).

Collectors need to be aware that certain glazes can bring two to three times more than others. For those wanting to learn more about this pottery, we recommend *Haeger Potteries Through the Years* by David D. Dilley (L-W Book Sales).

Advisor: David D. Dilley (See Directory, Royal Haeger)

Club: Haeger Pottery Collectors of America
Lanette Clarke
5021 Toyon Way
Antioch, CA 94509, 925-776-7784
Monthly newsletter available

Compote, gold lava glaze, wood finial, 10¾", $65.00.

Ashtray, Douglas, R-1096, 7".................................$15.00
Ashtray, Earth Graphic Wrap, brown, #2058X, 6¾"...........$15.00
Ashtray, elephant at side, blue, 1934 A Century of Progress label, 1⅞x4½x3¼", minimum value.......................................$50.00
Ashtray, Fern Agate Earth Graphic Wrap, #2125X, 1970s, 1¾x7¾" dia, minimum value...$10.00
Ashtray, Green Agate, free-form, molded mark: Royal Haeger R-873 USA, minimum value...$15.00
Basket, Rose of Sharon, chartreuse w/red flowers, R-575, 7" dia.. $75.00
Bookends, panther, ebony, embossed Royal Haeger R-638 USA, 4x5¼x7¾", minimum value..$150.00
Bowl, cloudy blue w/applied white flowers, R-373, unmarked, 1950s, 6½x19x6", minimum value..............................$75.00
Bowl, conch shell, R-329, 7"....................................$45.00
Bowl, Daisy, chartreuse, R-224, 2x11¾"......................$40.00
Bowl, Dutch Cup, Green Agate, R-370, 18½" L................$40.00
Bowl, lilac, foil label: Handcrafted Royal Haeger, marked Royal Haeger R-333 c USA, 4½x16¼x7", minimum value....$20.00
Bowl, Modern; chartreuse & ebony, paper label, R-1338, 3½x13¼x6½", minimum value.................................$20.00
Bowl, peasant, Gold Tweed, #329-H, 21¼" L.................$40.00
Bowl, w/fruit clusters, footed, R-421, 7x14½" L..............$50.00
Candleholder, Peach Agate, twisted stem, #243, no marks, ca 1927, 7½x4¼", ea, minimum value.................................$50.00
Candleholder/planter, leaves, Silver Spray, oval foil label: Haeger Made in USA, 7¼x8x4¾", minimum value.................$15.00
Candleholders, blue crackle, marked Haeger #004, 1⅜x5¾x3¼", pr, minimum value...$15.00
Candleholders, boat shaped, lilac, R-1746, 6" L, pr............$20.00

Candleholders, lily form, turquoise & blue, Royal Haeger foil label, R-1285, 5x5½x3¼", pr, minimum value.....................$15.00
Candy box, Hawaiian, round, 2-pc, R-590, 8"..................$50.00
Candy dish, triple shell w/fish finial, blue, R-459, 8½" L....$50.00
Cigarette lighter, Marigold Agate, insert marked Japan, #813-H, 10½x4" dia, minimum value...$15.00
Compote, Green Gold Tweed, sq, footed, Royal Haeger Green Gold Tweed USA RT63, ca 1960, 7x4x4", minimum value ..$15.00
Figurine, baby booties on sq base, light blue, foil label: 75th Anniversary, 3x4⅝x4", minimum value $10.00
Figurine, cock pheasant, Mauve Agate, R-435, unmarked, 12x13", minimum value..$50.00
Figurine, fighting cock, left, R-790, 11½" $75.00
Figurine, panther, ebony, foil crown label: Royal Haeger - Dundee Illinois, #495, 5½x24½x4¾", minimum value $40.00
Figurine, pheasant hen, R-164, 6" $85.00
Figurine, rooster, Burnt Sienna, #612, ca 1973, 11x8½x4", minimum value...$50.00
Figurine, wild goose, white matt, #F-17, unmarked, ca 1941, 6½x6¼x2", minimum value...$15.00
Figurne, tigress, amber, R-314, Royal Haeger USA, 11x10¼x4¼", minimum value...$75.00

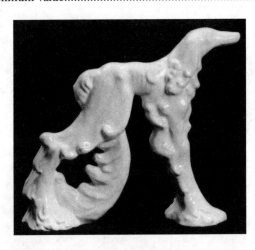

Figurine, Whippet, R-319, 8½", $135.00.

Flower frog, nude bathing, white, #77, unmarked, ca 1927, 7x5" dia, minimum value..$75.00
Flowerpot, double tulip, R-525, 10" $16.00
Lamp, stallions's head, oxblood & white mottle, #6204, 18" base, 36" allover, minimum value......................................$250.00
Planter, colonial girl, chartreuse, #3318, 9"..................$20.00
Planter, fish, R-752, 8½" $24.00
Planter, gondolier, Green Agate, R-657, 19" L................$75.00
Planter, greyhound, R-1331, 12"................................$50.00
Planter, oblong, w/stand, R-1416, 14".........................$40.00
Toe Tapper, Bennington Brown Foam, #8296, 9¼", from $40 to...$50.00
Triple candleholder dish, brown w/white accents, #3068, 12" dia .$45.00
Vase, butterfly, R-1221, 7½"...................................$24.00
Vase, Earth Graphic Wrap, brown, #4233-X, 11" $30.00
Vase, pillow; chartreuse & Silver Spray, R-476, 15" L.........$25.00
Vase, relief design, Briar Agate, #257, 9¼"...................$15.00

Vase, Sculpted, Cotton White w/turquoise interior, Royal Haeger c 489 USA, 14⅛x4", minimum value $50.00

RumRill

RumRill-marked pottery was actually made by other companies who simply provided the merchandise that George Rumrill marketed from 1933 until his death in 1942. Rumrill designed his own lines, and the potteries who filled the orders were the Red Wing Stoneware Company, Red Wing Potteries, Shawnee (but they were involved for only a few months), Florence, and Gonder. Many of the designs were produced by more than one compnay. Examples may be marked RumRill or with the name of the specific pottery.

Advisors: Wendy and Leo Frese, Three Rivers Collectibles (See Directory, RumRill)

Ball jug, #50, orange, w/cap, 6¼x8" $45.00
Bowl, #E19, deep blue, flower form, 2x6½" $30.00
Ewer vase, #184, stippled Dutch Blue, 7" $60.00
Pitcher, #547, green, tilted ball form, 7" $70.00
Pitcher, #547, green w/brown overspray, tilted ball form, 7" .. $35.00
Pitcher, #549, orange-red & brown matt, tilted ball form, 1930s, 7" $110.00
Planter, #F40, green w/embossed leaves, 2x7x6¼", NM $35.00
Planter, #H39, gray-blue, basket-like appearance $32.00

Planter, swan, white matt, #259, 6", $45.00. (Photo courtesy B.L. and R.L. Dollen)

Vase, #H54, blue w/embossed drips at top, low handles, 9". $65.00
Vase, #J26, white, ornate handles, 11½" $95.00
Vase, #195, Magnolia, light pink wash, w/partial sticker, 9". $140.00
Vase, #274, green to pink, swirled rim, sm scroll handles, 5x7" .. $55.00
Vase, #290, Nile Green w/Suntan interior, offset handles, 9½". $48.00
Vase, #302, peach orange peel to green, bulbous, rim-to-hip handles, 5½x6" $55.00
Vase, #356, creamy tan, embossed ribs, sm handles, 7" $35.00
Vase, #420, Florentine, brown over green, 4-handle, 9½" .. $120.00

Vase, #500, Classic, semi-matt blue and white stippled, 5½", from $75.00 to $90.00. (Photo courtesy B.L. and R.L. Dollen)

Vase, #507, 3 pine cones, blue, green & tan-brown shaded, 8½x9", NM $60.00
Vase, #591, floral vines embossed on white, handles, 7½" ... $38.00
Vase, #601, Athenian Line, Suntan w/green interior, 3 (¼" dia) holes for arranging flowers, 5¾" dia $60.00
Vase, #637, white, low upturned handles, 7¾x5⅛" $40.00
Vase, green to pink w/pink interior, 2 swan's head handles, 4½x6" $35.00
Vase, Neo-Classic, Art Deco fan w/5 graduated balls along sides, blue, 7x7¾" $75.00

Russel Wright Dinnerware

One of the country's foremost industrial designers, Russel Wright, was also responsible for several lines of dinnerware, glassware, and spun aluminum that have become very collectible. American Modern, produced by the Steubenville Pottery Company (1939 – 1959) is his best known dinnerware and the most popular today. It had simple, sweeping lines that appealed to tastes of that period, and it was made in a variety of solid colors. Iroquois China made his Casual line, and because it was so serviceable, it's relatively easy to find today. It will be marked with both Wright's signature and 'China by Iroquois.' His spun aluminum is highly valued as well, even though it wasn't so eagerly accepted in its day, due to the fact that it was so easily damaged.

Note: Values are given for solid color dinnerware unless a pattern is specifically mentioned.

American Modern

The most desirable colors are Cantaloupe, Glacier Blue, Bean Brown, and White; add 50% to our values for these colors. Chartreuse is represented by the low end of our range; Cedar, Black Chutney, and Seafoam by the high end; and Coral and Gray near the middle. To evaluate patterned items, deduct 25%.

Bowl, baker; from $40 to $50.00
Bowl, salad; from $100 to $115.00
Butter dish, w/lid, from $200 to $250.00
Celery dish, from $38 to $45.00
Child's plate, from $50 to $75.00
Creamer, from $15 to $20.00
Pickle dish, from $20 to $25.00
Plate, chop; from $45 to $55.00
Plate, dinner; 10", from $18 to $20.00

Salad spoon, from $85 to...**$95.00**
Sugar bowl, from $20 to..**$25.00**

Teapot, chartreuse, from $125.00 to $150.00.

Vegetable dish, open, 36-oz, 8⅛", from $20 to...................**$25.00**

Highlight

Cup, from $40 to...**$55.00**
Plate, bread & butter; from $12 to **$15.00**
Platter, sm, oval, from $50 to...**$75.00**
Sugar bowl, from $65 to..**$75.00**

Iroquois Casual

To price Brick Red, Aqua, and Cantaloupe Casual, double our values; for Avocado, use the low end of the range. Oyster, White, and Charcoal are at the high end.

The high end of the range should be used to evaluate solid-color examples.

Bowl, fruit; 9½-oz, 5½", from $12 to **$14.00**
Bowl, vegetable; 36-oz, 8⅛", from $25 to..........................**$30.00**
Carafe, wine/coffee; from $200 to....................................**$225.00**
Casserole, 2-qt, 8", from $35 to.......................................**$45.00**
Coffeepot, w/lid, from $150 to..**$175.00**
Cup/saucer, coffee; from $18 to.......................................**$22.00**
Mug, 13-oz, from $75 to..**$95.00**
Plate, salad; 7½", from $12 to **$15.00**
Platter, oval, 12¾", from $35 to.......................................**$45.00**
Salt & pepper shakers, stacking, pr from $30 to **$40.00**

Knowles

Bowl, vegetable; divided, from $55 to.................................**$75.00**
Creamer, from $35 to **$45.00**
Cup, from $8 to..**$10.00**
Plate, bread & butter; 6", from $6 to **$8.00**
Platter, oval, 13", from $45 to...**$55.00**
Teapot, from $250 to..**$300.00**

Plastics

These values apply to Home Decorator, Residential, and Flair (which is at the high end of the range). Copper Penny and Black

Velvet items command 50% more. Meladur items are all hard to find in good condition, and values can be basically computed using the following guidelines (except for the fruit bowl, which in Meladur is slightly higher.

Bowl, fruit; #707, from $15 to...**$18.00**
Bowl, lug soup; #706, from $10 to **$12.00**
Bowl, vegetable; divided, #714, from $20 to.......................**$25.00**
Bowl, vegetable; oval, deep, #709, from $15 to...................**$18.00**
Bowl, vegetable; oval, shallow, $708, from $15 to **$20.00**
Creamer, #711, from $8 to...**$10.00**
Cup, #701, from $6 to...**$8.00**
Onion soup, w/lid, #716, ea pc, from $18 to.......................**$20.00**
Plate, bread & butter; #705, from $6 to **$8.00**
Plate, dinner; #703, from $8 to.......................................**$10.00**
Plate, salad; #704, from $8 to...**$10.00**
Platter, #710, from $25 to..**$28.00**
Sugar bowl, #712, w/lid, from $12 to **$15.00**
Tumbler, #715, from $15 to..**$18.00**

Spun Aluminum

Bowl, from $75 to...**$95.00**

Bun warmer, 10", EX, $75.00.

Cheese board, from $75 to...**$100.00**
Flower ring, from $125 to...**$150.00**
Ice bucket, from $75 to..**$100.00**
Pitcher, sherry; from $250 to..**$275.00**
Tea set, from $500 to..**$700.00**
Tidbit, double, from $150 to...**$200.00**

Sterling

Values are given for undecorated examples.

Ashtray, from $75 to **$100.00**
Bowl, soup; 6½-oz, from $18 to.......................................**$22.00**
Pitcher, water; 2-qt, from $125 to....................................**$150.00**

Plate, dinner; 10¼", from $10 to......................................**$15.00**
Plate, salad; 7½", from $10 to **$12.00**
Platter, oval, 13⅝", from $30 to **$32.00**
Sugar bowl, w/lid, 10-oz, from $22 to **$25.00**
Teapot, 10-oz, from $125 to **$150.00**

White Clover (for Harker)

Ashtray, Clover decorated, from $40 to...........................**$45.00**
Creamer, Clover decorated, from $25 to **$35.00**
Cup, from $12 to...**$15.00**
Plate, bread & butter; color only, 6", from $10 to **$15.00**
Plate, salad; Clover only, 7⅝", from $18 to.....................**$20.00**
Salt & pepper shakers, either size, pr from $30 to............**$35.00**

Salt Shakers

Probably the most common type of souvenir shop merchandise from the 1920 through the 1960s, salt and pepper shakers can be spotted at any antique mall or flea market today by the dozens. Most were made in Japan and imported by various companies, though American manufacturers made their fair share as well. When even new shakers retail for $10.00 and up, don't be surprised to see dealers tagging the better vintage varieties with some hefty prices.

'Miniature shakers' are hard to find, and their prices have risen faster than any others'. They were all made by Arcadia Ceramics (probably an American company). They're usually less than 2" tall, some so small they had no space to accommodate a cork. Instead they came with instructions to 'use Scotch tape to cover the hole.'

Advertising sets and premiums are always good, since they appeal to a cross section of collectors. If you have a chance to buy them on the primary market, do so. Many of these are listed in the Advertising Character Collectibles section of this guide.

Recent sales have shown a rise in price for some shakers that were in the past considered low end. Some attract people who are not really salt shaker collectors but have a connection to the theme or topic that is represented, i.e. doctors will buy medical-related shakers, etc. Fish shakers are on the rise, especially specific breed fish. Some high-end shakers are getting soft. Many of the rare vintage sets are being reproduced and redesigned so collectors can own a set at a more reasonable cost.

We highly recommend *Florences' Big Book of Salt & Pepper Shakers* by Gene and Cathy Florence (Collector Books) to help you stay informed.

See also Advertising Character Collectibles; Breweriana; Condiment Sets; Holt Howard; Occupied Japan; Regal China; Rosemeade; Shawnee; Vandor; and other specific companies.

Note: Sets having both the salt and pepper shaker modeled identically (will be indicated with pr), while '2-pc' will indicate that they are only complementary, for instance, Paul Bunyan and Babe the Blue Ox.

Advisor: Judy Posner (See Directory, Salt and Pepper Shakers)

Club: Novelty Salt and Pepper Shakers Club
c/o Louise Davis, Membership Coordinator

P.O. Box 416
Gladstone, OR 97027-0416
http://members.aol.com/spclub1234/index.htm
Publishes quarterly newsletter and annual roster. Annual dues: $30 in USA, Canada, and Mexico; $35 US funds in other countries; second membership at same address $5 per year.

Advertising

Ballantine Ale can, cardboard w/metal lid, 2⅜", M in carry pack **$20.00**

Bud Man, Ceramarte, Brazil, 1991, 3½", from $35.00 to $45.00.

Calvert Daiquiri, whiskey bottle, green glass, American Airlines mark, 4¼", pr...**$12.50**
Chicken of the Sea, fish (1 blue, 2nd yellow), ceramic, 2x2⅞", pr...**$24.00**
Coca Cola, delivery guy & hand truck w/cases of Coke, copyright Coca-Cola Company 1996, 2-pc set.........................**$30.00**
Conoco, gas pump, plastic w/decal, 2¾", pr, MIB..............**$55.00**
Dairy Queen, blond girl, ceramic, multicolor, flat backs, marked tm Dairy Queen, Japan, 4", pr...**$125.00**

Dooley and Shultz (Utica Beer), from $95.00 to $100.00.
(Photo courtesy Judy Posner)

Goetz Country Club, amber glass w/applied label, 4½", pr .**$35.00**
Grain Belt Beer, bottle, paper label on brown glass, 4", pr ...**$55.00**
Greyhound bus, pottery, multicolor, Japan paper label on bottom, 1960s, 1½x3¼", pr..**$45.00**
Hamm's Beer, bear seated & holding sign, ceramic, 4", pr ...**$85.00**
Heinz Ketchup, bottle, red plastic w/paper label, white plastic top, Hong Kong, 4¼", pr..**$20.00**
Homepride Flour, Flour Fred, hard plastic, 4¼", pr............**$35.00**
Kentucky Fried Chicken, Colonel & Mrs Sanders bust, white molded plastic, Magardt Corp, 1972, 4", 2-pc set **$75.00**

Koppitz beer bottle, amber glass w/decal label, metal top, 3⅜", pr ..**$35.00**

Lennox Furnaces, Lennie Lennox, pottery w/decals on front, 1950, 5", pr **$125.00**

M&Ms, red & yellow guy, plastic, Mars Inc Copyright 1991, red: 3¾", 2-pc set **$28.00**

Magic Chef, chef, pottery, black & white, 1940s, 5", pr **$75.00**

Mason Ball jar, clear glass w/screw-on lids, 2⅞", pr **$24.00**

McWilliams Wine, Moselle monk, ceramic, Japan, 3½", pr.**$75.00**

Nugget Casino, Nugget Sam, ceramic, Japan, 1950s, 4", pr.**$35.00**

Old Cliff House Restaurant, seal, pottery, unglazed bottom, 3¾", pr **$25.00**

Phillips 66, gas pump, hard plastic, Avsco, pr **$35.00**

Rice-a-Roni, cable car (made up of 2 pcs), ceramic, 1970s, 2-pc set..**$32.00**

Rosie's Diner, diner (separates), ceramic, multicolor, 1994, 2½x6¼", 2-pc set **$45.00**

Royal Canadian Whiskey, amber glass bottle w/metal screw-on lid, 1950s, 4¼", pr.................................**$22.00**

Schmidt's Beer, mini 6-pack of salt shakers, heavy cardboard w/plastic tops & bottoms, 1½", 6 in original case, NM **$20.00**

Sourdough Jake & burro, ceramic, copyright Kelvin SP-40, 1950s-60s, 2-pc set **$55.00**

Speedy Flame Gas, anthropomorphic flame, ceramic, ca 1950s, 4⅜", pr **$85.00**

Texaco, gas pump, plastic, EXIB **$35.00**

Thomas Moore Possom Hollow Whiskey, clear glass flask w/metal screw-on lid, 3¾", pr **$20.00**

Vess Soda, bottle, clear (& green) glass w/applied decal, plastic top, pr **$45.00**

Volkswagen van, pottery w/plastic stoppers & VW on fronts, 1¼x3¾", pr **$55.00**

White Satin Gin, bottle, green glass w/paper label, metal top, 4⅞", pr..**$24.00**

Yenems Cigarette pack & match pack, ceramic, multicolor, unmarked, 1950s, 3¾", 2⅞", 2-pc set **$20.00**

Anthropomorphic

Corn on cob & broccoli people, Clay Art, 2-pc set..............**$35.00**

Corn people, from $20.00 to $30.00. (Photo courtesy Helene Guarnaccia)

Dustpan girl holding broom, ceramic, 1950s, pr, minimum value **$165.00**

Feet w/smiling faces, ceramic, multicolor, Japan paper label, 1950s, 3½", pr **$22.00**

Fork & spoon dancing couple, ceramic, 5", 2-pc set...........**$45.00**

Ladybug w/leaf head, ceramic, multicolor, 1950s, Japan mark, 3½", pr **$28.00**

Lamb w/glasses, pottery, multicolor copyright MS, Japan mark, 1950s, 4½", pr..**$35.00**

Lion w/monocle seated on ball, pottery, multicolor, Japan, 1950s, 4⅝", pr **$40.00**

Onion-head girl, ceramic, PY Miyao, 3¾", pr **$65.00**

Pear & orange, ceramic, crudely painted, unmarked Japan, 2-pc set **$20.00**

Plum couple, ceramic, PY, 2-pc, NM................................**$35.00**

Telephone-faced girl, ceramic, Japan, 1950s, pr, MIB, minimum value **$150.00**

Character

Mammy and Pappy Yokum, characters by Al Capp, from $100.00 to $125.00. (Photo courtesy Helene Guarnaccia)

Aladdin & lamp, ceramic, brown & white, Made in Japan, ca 1960s, 4¼", 2¾x5¾", 2-pc set..............................**$30.00**

Aladdin & lamp, ceramic, chartreuse, flat unglazed bottoms, unmarked USA, 1950s, 2", 2-pc set...........................**$24.00**

Babar Elephant, ceramic, multicolor, Japan, 1950s, 4⅞", stacking 2-pc set **$70.00**

Bahama Policeman, ceramic, multicolor, 1960s, 4⅜", pr **$28.00**

Betty Boop (carhop) & Bimbo in car, ceramic, multicolor, Vandor, 1898, Betty: 4¾", 2-pc set...........................**$30.00**

Betty Boop & Bimbo, ceramic, multicolor, sitting in wooden 3½x5" boat, Vandor, 1981, 3-pc set **$65.00**

Bonzo, ceramic, gold & white, flat unglazed bottom, unmarked, 1930s, 3", pr **$28.00**

Buddha, ceramic, gold paint, Made in Japan, 3¾", pr **$22.00**

Buddha, ceramic, tan, Japan, 1950s, 3½", pr......................**$30.00**

Dandy & Preacher Crow from Dumbo, ceramic, 3", 4", 2-pc set **$80.00**

Donald Duck, ceramic, multicolor, Dan Brechner, 1961, 4⅞", pr..**$95.00**

Donald Duck w/pipe (2nd w/flowers), ceramic, multicolor, Carey & Tomkins, Japan marks, 1940s-50s, 2¾", pr **$28.00**

Felix the Cat, ceramic, 1 black, 2nd white, Benjamin-Medwin, 1991, 4", pr, MIB **$25.00**

Gingham Dog & Cat, ceramic, multicolor, 1950s, 4½", 2-pc set .**$30.00**

Goofy & cake, ceramic, multicolor, New England Collector Society, Disney, Taiwan, 2-pc set **$45.00**

Jack Spratt & wife, ceramic, he: 3½", 2-pc set **$52.50**

Little Mermaid on rock, ceramic, Disney China, 5¼", stacking 2-pc set **$30.00**

Ludwig & Donald Duck, ceramic, multicolor, Disney, 1961, 5¼", 2-pc set **$95.00**

Marvin the Martian & spaceship, ceramic, Warner Bros, 1996, 2-pc set, MIB **$55.00**

Mickey & Minnie Mouse in chef's caps, ceramic, multicolor, Walt Disney, Hoan Ltd, Made in Taiwan, 4¼", 2-pc set **$30.00**

Miss Muffet & spider, ceramic, multicolor, Poinsettia Studios, she: 2½", 2-pc set **$65.00**

Mother Goose, ceramic, multicolor, Josef Originals, 3⅝", pr .**$40.00**

Old Mother Hubbard & dog, ceramic, multicolor w/gold trim, Poinsettia Studio, she: 3½", 2-pc set **$75.00**

Peanut w/lg smile & shoes (representing Jimmy Carter), ceramic, brown tones, Made in Japan, #693, 3½", pr **$34.00**

Pebbles & Bamm-Bamm, ceramic, multicolor, Harry Hames, 4", 2-pc set **$40.00**

Peter Pumpkin Eater, bone china, multicolor, mini, Peter: 2½", 2-pc set **$55.00**

Pink Panther, seated & hugging knees, ceramic, pr, minimum value **$160.00**

Pinocchio & girlfriend, porcelain, multicolor w/hand-painted features, Made in Japan, 1940s, he: 4⅞", 2-pc set **$95.00**

Queen of Hearts & jester, ceramic, multicolor, Japan mark, 4⅜", 2-pc set **$45.00**

Raggedy Ann, ceramic, multicolor pastels, unmarked, 4", pr .**$40.00**

Robin Hood sitting on rock, ceramic, multicolor, Japan, 1950s, stacking 2-pc set **$28.00**

Sylvester the Cat, ceramic, Warner Bros, 1970s, 4¼", pr **$75.00**

White Rabbit from Alice in Wonderland, ceramic, multicolor, Japan mark, stacking 2-pc set **$75.00**

Winnie the Pooh & Hunny pot, ceramic, multicolor, New England Collector Society, Pooh: 3", 2-pc set **$40.00**

Winnie the Pooh & Rabbit, ceramic, Disney, Enesco, 1960s, 3½", 4", 2-pc set **$65.00**

Yoda, ceramic, Sigma, 1983, 4", pr **$195.00**

Yosemite Sam, ceramic, multicolor, Warner Brothers, Lego paper label, 1960s, 4", pr **$75.00**

Holidays and Special Occasions

Christmas, candle w/holly (or bow), ceramic, multicolor, Lefton, 4⅜", pr **$18.00**

Christmas, Santa & Mrs Claus hugging (interlocking type), ceramic, multicolor, 1960s, 3¼", 2-pc set **$18.00**

Christmas, Santa & sack of toys, ceramic, multicolor, unmarked, 1950s, 3½", 2-pc set **$18.00**

Christmas, Santa going down chimney & snowy evergreen, ceramic, multicolor, Japan sticker, 3½", 2-pc set **$22.00**

Christmas, Santa holding Merry (Christmas), ceramic, multicolor, Japan, 4½", pr **$20.00**

Christmas, Santa on bell, ceramic, multicolor, Napcoware X6047, 1950s, 3½", pr **$22.00**

Christmas, Santa w/horn & dalmatian howling, ceramic, multicolor, Otagiri, 2-pc set from $18 to **$22.00**

Christmas, snowman w/cane (2nd shaker), ceramic, white w/black & red details, 2-pc set from $18 to **$22.00**

Thanksgiving, pilgrim and turkey, Japan paper label, #20032, 5¼", from $12.00 to $15.00. (Photo courtesy Gene and Cathy Florence)

Thanksgiving, roast turkey in pan, ceramic, multicolor, unmarked, 2½", 2-pc set from $12 to **$15.00**

Thanksgiving, turkey gobbler & hen, ceramic, multicolor, japan paper label, 3", 2-pc set, from $10 to **$12.00**

Thanksgiving, turkeys in full strut, ceramic, multicolor, 1991, 4", pr from $12 to **$15.00**

People

Clowns, Japan, 5", from $30.00 to $35.00. (Photo courtesy Gene and Cathy Florence)

Alcatraz prison inmate bust, ceramic, multicolor, Japan import, 4½", pr **$45.00**

Army & Navy men, ceramic, multicolor, 1940s-50s, 2¾", 2-pc set **$28.00**

Baby w/lollipop & baby crying, ceramic, multicolor, Clay Art, 3½", 2-pc set **$25.00**

Bellhop w/2 suitcases (shakers), ceramic, Japan, 1950s, 4", 3-pc set **$55.00**

Black boy w/shoeshine box, ceramic, Japan, he: 3", 2-pc set ..**$65.00**

Bride & groom, ceramic w/gold, red Japan mark, 1950s, 4⅛", pr...**$25.00**

Chef bust (winking), ceramic, multicolor, Japan paper label, 1950s, 3¼", pr...**$20.00**

Choir boy, ceramic, 1 in red, 2nd in blue, Japan, 1950s, 4¾", pr...**$22.00**

Comical man & pregnant lady, Good Bye Cruel World, Watermelon Seed? Hell! on bases, ceramic, multicolor, Japan, 2-pc set...**$38.00**

Drunk & lamppost, ceramic, Maruri...Japan, 1950s, 3-pc set.**$22.50**

Eskimo & igloo, ceramic, multicolor, Japan, 1950s, figure: 4½", 2-pc set...**$24.00**

Grandma and Grandpa Turnabouts, frowning/ smiling 4¾", from $15.00 to $18.00. (Photo courtesy Gene and Cathy Florence)

Indian boy & girl, ceramic, multicolor, 1962, 4⅜", 2-pc set ..**$22.00**

Indian on horse (2nd shaker), ceramic, Japan, 4¾" overall, 2-pc set...**$55.00**

Jogger w/hat pulled down in running suit, ceramic, multicolor, Enesco foil label, 1978, 4⅛", pr.................................**$35.00**

Kissing boy & girl, From Little Things Happiness Springs on bases, ceramic, multicolor, 4¼", 2-pc set..........................**$24.00**

Lady (bare breasted) & naughty man, ceramic, multicolor, Empress Made in Japan sticker, 1950s, 4½", 2-pc set **$60.00**

Lyndon B Johnson portrait on monument-like shape, ceramic, multicolor on white, 2⅜", pr...**$20.00**

Maid & chef, I'm Salt & I'm Pep on caps, ceramic, multicolor, Japan, 1950s, 3", 2-pc set...**$20.00**

Mammy w/mixing bowl, bisque, LAG NO 1977 Taiwan, pr.**$32.00**

Man & lady (interlocking type w/exaggerated features), ceramic, multicolor, 1950s, 5⅜", 2-pc set.............................**$45.00**

Man in toilet, Good-bye Cruel World, ceramic, multicolor, Japan, 1950s, 2-pc set...**$35.00**

Mexican man w/fruit cart, shakers w/raised fruit tops sit in cart, ceramic, multicolor, Japan, 1950s, 3-pc set..................**$23.00**

Moon man & rocket ship, ceramic, multicolor, Enesco, 1950s, spaceship: 4¼", 2-pc set...**$45.00**

Native, wooden head & wire body, drum shakers, Japan, 1950s, 3-pc set...**$40.00**

Oriental man & lady, bisque, hand-painted details, 1950s, 5¼", 2-pc set...**$30.00**

Pirate & treasure chest, ceramic, green & brown, unmarked, 1950s, he: 3½", 2-pc set...**$22.00**

Scottish boy & girl saluting, ceramic, multicolor traditional attire, Josef Originals, 4½", 2-pc set...**$38.00**

Zodiac boy & girl, ceramic, multicolor, red Japan mark, 4½", 2-pc set...**$35.00**

Souvenir

Baseball player, ceramic, multicolor, Copalis Beach WA, 1950s, 3½", pr...**$75.00**

Basket of clothes & iron, Souvenir of Ohio Turnpike, ceramic, multicolor, Made in Japan labels, 1960s, 2-pc set **$24.00**

Battleship Texas & San Jacinto, roadside souvenir, ceramic, white, 1960s-70s, monument: 4", 2-pc set....................**$32.00**

Cactus, Yuma Arizona, ceramic, green & white, 4⅛", pr from $8 to **$10.00**

Car, metal, w/gold-tone metal tray, Movieland Wax Museum Buena Park Calif, Japan, 3-pc set....................................**$28.00**

Cars, gold-painted metal on chromolitho tray, Pike's Peak or Bust, Enco Japan, 1950s, tray: 4¼x3¼", 3-pc set **$35.00**

Coffeepot, Williamsburg VA, painted wood, 2½", pr from $5 to **$7.00**

Covered wagon, Abiline Kansas, ceramic, white w/gold trim, Japan paper label, 2", pr from $6 to **$8.00**

Dolphin, Marineland Pacific, ceramic, multicolor, EW Japan foil label, 2¼x5¼", pr...**$28.00**

Eagle (patriotic), painted chalkware, Denver souvenir sticker, 2⅝", pr...**$35.00**

Feet, Ozarks Gully Jumper, ceramic, white w/red toenails & black lettering, unmarked, 2½" L, pr from $6 to **$8.00**

Guitar, Grand Ole Opry Nashville TN, ceramic, multicolor, 3¾", pr from $5 to **$7.00**

Knotts Berry Farm, embossed prospector, covered wagon & train on copper-tone metal w/blue enameling, 2", pr **$22.00**

Man w/Her towel & brushing teeth, lady w/His towel & brushing hair, ceramic, multicolor, 1950s, 2-pc set.....................**$38.00**

Pipe, Wolf Creek Dam KY, ceramic, 2 rest on base, 2¾", 3-pc set from $8 to **$10.00**

Potty & window, Colorado souvenir, ceramic, unmarked, 1¼", 2¾", 2-pc set...**$24.00**

Ship going through lock, Eisenhower Lock, St Lawrence Seaway, ceramic, multicolor, Japan label, 1⅜x4⅞x2½", 2-pc..**$29.00**

Singing Tower, Lake Wales Fla, silver-tone metal, 3½", pr...**$35.00**

Stein, view of Prospect Point, Niagara Falls, ceramic, multicolor, MS products, 4", pr from $12 to...**$15.00**

Miscellaneous

Alligator, redware, brown tones, EX details, Mexico, 1x5", pr .**$20.00**

Bass fish, ceramic, Made in Japan label, 2x5½", pr **$25.00**

Blue gill fish, ceramic, realistic, Enesco, 2x4", pr **$25.00**

Brush w/comb & mirror, ceramic, Arcadia, mini, 2-pc set...**$35.00**

Coffee mill & graniteware coffeepot, ceramic, Arcadia, mini, 2-pc set...**$20.00**

Cookbook, Bride's Cook Book, The Way to His Heart, ceramic, white w/multicolor, Poinsettia Studios, 2⅝", pr............**$35.00**

Dinosaur w/tail up, pottery, plastic stopper, unmarked, 1970s, 3", pr...**$28.00**

Fish, hole in mouth, ceramic, multicolor, Arcadia, mini, 1⅛", pr...**$20.00**

Flying saucer, ceramic, white w/red & green, marked Coventry, 1950s, 2¼x2½x3", pr **$40.00**

Flying saucer, saucer shape w/wings, ceramic, white w/blue, black lettering, 1950s, 2¼x3¼", pr **$28.00**

Jack-in-the-box, ceramic, multicolor, unmarked, 1950s, 4", pr. **$28.00**

Koala bear, bone china, multicolor, unmarked Japan, 1960s-70s, 2⅛", pr **$20.00**

Leopard, ceramic, Victoria Ceramics...Japan, 4", 2½x4¼", pr. **$35.00**

Orangutan, pair in wire cage, from $10.00 to $15.00. (Photo courtesy Helene Guarnaccia)

Penguin in formal attire, pottery, ca 1984, 3½", pr **$18.00**

Phonograph (crank style), ceramic, multicolor, Napco Originals by Giftcraft, 1950s, 3¼", pr **$24.00**

Pixie riding rocket ship, ceramic, multicolor w/gold, unmarked, 1950s, 2¾x3½", pr **$45.00**

Purple cow, pottery, Made in Japan by Thames, 1950s, 4", pr. **$22.00**

SS Loveboat, ceramic, white & black, Enesco, 1979, 1⅝x3", pr **$30.00**

Statue of Liberty, ceramic, blue-green w/gold torch, 5 & Dime Co (division of Sarsaparilla), 1992, 5⅜", pr **$28.00**

Wanted poster on cactus, references to Salty McCoon & Pepper O'shay, ceramic, multicolor, unmarked, 1950s, 3⅜", pr.. **$22.00**

Sango Dinnerware

This company is located in Indonesia and has for decades been that country's leading producer of dinnerware. They have successfully marketed their wares through many of this country's larger chain stores. Patterns range from simple solid or two-tone colors to holiday themes, abstracts, and florals. You'll often find nice pieces on your garage sale rounds, and collectors are now searching for items to replace those that have been broken or to add accessories that are no longer available through retail outlets.

Black Lilies, bowl, coupe soup; Quadrille shape, 7½" **$7.50**

Black Lilies, cup & saucer, Quadrille shape, footed, 3½" **$8.00**

Black Lilies, gravy boat w/attached underplate, Quadrille shape . **$22.50**

Black Lilies, potpourri jar, Quadrille shape, w/lid **$14.00**

Black Lilies, tumbler, old-fashioned; 10-oz, 5¼" **$7.00**

Cabaret, bowl, vegetable; 9⅝" **$50.00**

Cabaret, cheese plate, footed, w/glass dome **$25.00**

Cabaret, plate, salad; 8⅜" **$12.50**

Cabaret, tidbit tray, center handle **$30.00**

Calligraphy II, cup & saucer, 3⅛" **$7.50**

Calligraphy II, plate, salad; 8⅜" **$5.00**

Calligraphy II, plate, serving; handles **$17.50**

Calligraphy II, tidbit tray, center handle, 8⅜" **$20.00**

Country Cottage, cake stand, metal pedestal **$27.50**

Country Cottage, cup & saucer, footed **$8.00**

Country Cottage, plate, dinner; 10⅝" **$8.00**

Country Cottage, sugar bowl, w/lid **$12.50**

Fanciful Fruit, cheese plate, footed, glass dome **$22.50**

Fanciful Fruit, plate, dinner; 10¾" **$20.00**

Fanciful Fruit, sugar bowl, w/lid **$20.00**

Fanciful Fruit, tidbit tray, 2-tier **$32.50**

Fortune, bowl, coupe soupe; 7¼" **$7.00**

Fortune, cup & saucer, flat, 3½" **$10.00**

Fortune, plate, salad; 7½" **$6.50**

Home for Christmas, bowl, rimmed soup; pink trim, 9¼" .. **$22.00**

Home for Christmas, butter dish, pink trim, ¼-lb **$17.50**

Home for Christmas, cup & saucer, pink trim, 2⅜" **$8.00**

Home for Christmas, sugar bowl, pink trim, w/lid, 2⅞" **$22.00**

Home for Christmas, teapot, six-cup, $40.00.

Nova, creamer, black, 10-oz **$15.00**

Nova, cup & saucer, black, 3½" **$12.00**

Nova, plate, dinner; black, 10¾" **$8.00**

Nova, sugar bowl, black, w/lid **$20.00**

Orbit, bowl, vegetable; blue rings, 9¼" **$22.00**

Orbit, creamer, blue rings **$10.00**

Orbit, cup & saucer, blue rings, 3⅜" **$8.00**

Orbit, plate, chop; blue rings, 12¼" **$32.50**

Primrose #621, candleholders, pr **$30.00**

Primrose #621, creamer, 3½" **$12.00**

Primrose #621, plate, dinner; 10⅝" **$10.00**

Primrose #621, platter, oval, 14⅛" **$30.00**

Primrose #621, sugar bowl, w/lid, 3¼" **$15.00**

Rosetta, bowl, divided vegetable, 11⅝" **$30.00**

Rosetta, cup & saucer, footed, 2¼" **$12.00**

Rosetta, plate, dinner; 10⅝" **$16.00**

Rosetta, platter, oval, 12⅜" **$20.00**

Spanish Lace, bowl, fruit; 5½" **$6.00**
Spanish Lace, gravy boat w/attached undertray **$60.00**
Spanish Lace, platter, oval, 14⅛" **$35.00**
Spranish Lace, plate, dinner; 10⅝" **$22.00**

Schoop, Hedi

One of the most successful California ceramic studios was founded in Hollywood by Hedi Schoop, who had been educated in the arts in Germany. She had studied not only painting but sculpture, architecture, and fashion design as well. Fleeing Nazi Germany with her husband, the famous composer Frederick Holander, Hedi settled in California in 1933 and only a few years later became involved in producing novelty giftware items so popular that they were soon widely copied by other California companies. She designed many animated human figures, some in matched pairs, some that doubled as flower containers. All were hand painted and many were decorated with applied ribbons, sgraffito work, and gold trim. To a lesser extent, she modeled animal figures as well. Until fire leveled the plant in 1958, the business was very productive. Nearly everything she made was marked.

If you'd like to learn more about her work, we recommend *The Collector's Encyclopedia of California Pottery, Second Edition,* and *California Pottery Scrapbook* by Jack Chipman (Collector Books).

**Figurine, Josephine, 13",
from $100.00 to $125.00.**

Bowl, console; 3-hand-painted butterflies on light gray, 3½x11x7½" **$40.00**
Butterfly dish, shaded green w/gold sponging, 1¼x8½x7", NM . **$25.00**
Candleholder, lady w/head back holds lg urn in front, 8", ea from $50 to **$60.00**
Candleholder, Madonna praying, green dress w/brown decor, 11¼" **$85.00**

Candleholder/bowl, duck form, raspberry sherbet w/sponged gold, 5x8" **$65.00**
Console bowl/candleholders, double duck head w/candleholders in ea head, white w/gold sponging, 6¾x13" **$95.00**
Figurine, Chinese boy playing golden horn, green & gold, Young China line, 1946, 11" **$70.00**
Figurine, Dutch girl w/head tilted to left, basket in right hand, 11" **$55.00**
Figurine, lady in blue dress w/floral decor, lg hat, holding basket, 11" **$75.00**
Figurine, lady in pink w/floral trim reading book w/2 vases behind, 9" **$60.00**
Figurine, lady w/basket on right arm walking collie, 10" ... **$175.00**
Figurine, lady w/lg bowl resting in right hand & on right shoulder, white dress, yellow apron w/multicolor flowers, 11" **$45.00**
Figurine, Oriental man w/black & white shirt & white pants, lg hat, 12½" **$60.00**
Figurine, Siamese dancers, pale green outfit, black base, 14½", pr, NM **$135.00**
Figurine, Tyrolean girl holds dress out as planter, 11" **$80.00**
Figurines, Oriental boy & girl carrying buckets, 12", pr **$165.00**
Flower holder, girl kneeling, opening in apron, brown hair, brown, yellow & white outfit, ruffled neck/sleeves, 8¼" **$35.00**
Flower holder, lady w/basket on head, lavender bodice & flowers on white skirt, skirt held wide, 12½" **$85.00**
Flower holders, dancing blond ladies w/swirling skirts, ea holding apron in opposite hand, aqua & white, 7¾", pr, NM ... **$45.00**
Flower holders, Dutch boy & girl, she w/lg vase in right hand, he w/hands in pockets, light blue, 11", 9½", pr **$85.00**
Flower holders, Oriental boy & girl, he w/pot, she w/fan in hands, green & white, 12", 11¼", pr **$65.00**
Flower holders, Pfantasy ladies w/flowers, green gowns w/much gold, 12¼", 12", pr **$200.00**
Planter, skunk w/hands folded together, 6" **$55.00**
Tray, butterfly, rose colored w/gold trim **$40.00**
Vase, fancy feathers hand painted in blue on gray, aqua interior, marked, 12x4" **$60.00**

Scouting Collectibles

Collecting scouting memorabilia has long been a popular pastime for many. Through the years, millions of boys and girls have been a part of this worthy organization founded in England in 1907 by retired Major-General Lord Robert Baden-Powell. Scouting has served to establish goals in young people and help them to develop leadership skills, physical strength, and mental alertness. Through scouting, they learn basic fundamentals of survival. The scouting movement came to the United States in 1910, and the first World Scout Jamboree was held in 1911 in England.

Advisor: R.J. Sayers (See Directory, Scouting Collectibles)

Boy Scouts

Award, Silver Beaver sterling pendant on blue & white ribbon, 1968, EX **$125.00**

Belt buckle, conestoga wagon w/BSA on side, 1953 National Jamboree, Irvine Ranch CA, Max Sibler, bronze, EX..**$150.00**

Belt buckle, Daniel Webster Council, New Hampshire, Old Man in the Mountains, bronze, Max Sibler, 1950s, EX...........**$190.00**

Belt buckle (wood badge award), axe in log, brass, 1950s, 2x2¾", EX **$30.00**

Book, Handbook for Boys, paperback, 568 pages, 1948, EX .**$20.00**

Book, program; 1953 3rd National Jamboree, Irvine Ranch CA, 12x9", EX..**$20.00**

Bookends, logo w/Be Prepared banner, cast iron, 1940s, 6x4x6", EX, pr **$70.00**

Bugle, Rexcraft Official, brass & chrome, mouthpiece attached to sm chain, EX **$90.00**

Bus token, Camp Alexander, Colorado Springs, 1967, EX...**$20.00**

Compass, plastic case w/emblem & Be Prepared, #1075 Bar Needle Compass, Tayler Instruments, EXIB **$45.00**

Cuff links, yellow emblem w/black ribbon w/Be Prepared, enameled, EX, pr **$20.00**

Firemaking equipment, Official; complete, EXIB **$45.00**

Flag, Explorer; I Proved I Believe in Exploring, I Organized a New Post Personally, Full ⅓ Award, 108x144", EX.........**$35.00**

Flag pole top, emblem on ball, brass & aluminum, EX........**$25.00**

Flashlight, right angle, Scout Master's, EXIB **$35.00**

Flint & steel set, Official; complete, 1946, EXIB................**$40.00**

Handbook, revised first edition, 1942, EX, $22.00.

Hat, Scout Master campaign; w/logo on band, 1958, EXIB...**$85.00**

Hatchet head, emblem on side, Genuine Plumb, EX...........**$35.00**

Neckerchief slide, Broad Creek, 10 Years, 1957, wooden w/bark edge, 3¾x1½", NM...**$20.00**

Neckerchief slide, 1957 BSA National Jamboree, Valley Forge, Onward for God & My Country, 2¼" dia, EX............**$15.00**

Neckerchief slide, 1957 National Jamboree, Medical/1st Aid Staff, EX **$180.00**

Patch, Achievement; 2nd Canadian BS Jamboree, Ottawa, 1953, 5" dia, EX...**$25.00**

Patch, Division Commissioner, gold emblem w/wreath on red, EX..**$35.00**

Patch, Fall Fellowship, Canyon Camp, Order of the Arrow, 1967, EX **$25.00**

Patch, jacket; 1953 National Jamboree, Irvine Ranch Calif, chuck wagon scene, 5¾" dia, NM.......................................**$150.00**

Patch, Miami Valley Council, 1916-1991, 75 Years of Service, 4½", EX **$20.00**

Patch, Pheasant Council, Honor Camper, Camp Iyataka, 1960s, 3", EX **$20.00**

Patch, Philadelphia, Cradle of Liberty, 1950s, 3x4⅝", EX ...**$10.00**

Patch, shoulder; Heart of America Council, 1985 National Jamboree, KS-MO, 5½", EX...**$90.00**

Patch, 1979 Pow Wow, Alaska Royal Rangers, EX **$25.00**

Patch, 1985 National Jamboree Contingent, Penn Mountains Council, 5½", NM..**$20.00**

Pin, Eagle Scout, Be Prepared on banner w/red, white & blue ribbon w/eagle pendant, 1950s, EXIB...............................**$110.00**

Pin, Sea Scouts emblem in silver w/blue enameled ring, ¾", EX.**$50.00**

Pin-back, Boy Scout War Bond Salesman, ⅞" dia, EX.........**$60.00**

Plaque, George Washington bust, bronze on wood, 1950 National Jamboree PA/NH, EX...**$75.00**

Plate, Can't Wait, Scout saluting w/dog at side, Norman Rockwell, 1981, 8½" dia, EX **$29.00**

Pocketknife, Leader's, #1043, bone handle, 2 blades, NM (plastic case).**$50.00**

Poster, Hey! Register & Vote, 3 Scouts ringing bells, 1952, 13x11", EX **$50.00**

Sandwich maker, Toas-Tite Sandwich Grill, emblem on face, EX... **$55.00**

Tent, Official Voyageur, #1414-200, canvas, c 1962, 84x103x72", VG+ (in drawstring duffle bag).................................**$130.00**

Utensil set, fork, spoon & knife, logo on leather pouch, EX...**$45.00**

Patch, Region Seven, 1940, letters on canoe, $600.00; mid to late 1940s, no letters, $200.00. (Photo courtesy Don and R.C. Raycraft)

Girl Scouts

Bank, Juliette Low bust, brass, 6", EX+.............................**$145.00**

Book, How Girls Can Help Their Country, Juliette Low, 144 pages, 1972 reprint, EX..**$10.00**

Book, Junior, GS Handbook, original plastic cover, 1963, EX .**$15.00**

Book, Trefoil Around the World, 20 pages w/maps & info of girls from around the world, 1958, EX+..............................**$20.00**

Bracelet, emblem w/sq chain links, 1950s, 6", EX **$25.00**

Camera, Official GS 920, George Herbert Co, box style, EX.**$25.00**

Catalog, GS Equipment, Fall 1967-Spring 1968, 23 pages, EX.**$20.00**

Catalog, GS equipment, Spring 1952, 40th Anniversary, EX+ .**$50.00**

Compass, green plastic case, Taylor #11-358, EXIB.............**$30.00**

Cookbook, Cooking Out-Of-Door, spiral bound, 200 pages, 5½x8½", EX...**$25.00**

Doll, complete, Terri Lee Sales Corp #11-955, MIB.........**$165.00**

Doll, Madame Alexander #317, complete w/wrist tag, EXIB .**$90.00**

Doll, Official Cadette, Effanbee, vinyl, 11", MIB **$200.00**

Doll, paper; GS, DeJournette #11-949, 29 uncut pages, 1960s, NMIB..**$55.00**

Doll, Patsy Ann, in Brownie dress w/pantaloons & cap, Effanbee, 1959, 15", EX..**$60.00**

Doll outfit, Dress Uniform, 8" doll size, 1950s, M (NM box). **$120.00**

Golden Eaglet, made in 3 sizes, ½x½" - 1½x1", ea **$400.00**

Hand puppet, white w/black lines made to color over & over again, 1998-2000, 19", NM **$25.00**

Hat, Beanie, w/2 original bows, #2-153, 1950s, EX+ (G box) . **$15.00**

Mess kit, plate, skillet, cup & pot w/lid, plaid carrying bag, 1950s, EXIB..**$20.00**

Patch, Central Maryland Council, state image w/trees, round, EX **$10.00**

Patch, Northern Oakland County GS Council, rainbow graphics, NM..**$10.00**

Patch, Whispering Oaks GSC, The Beginning, 1986, acorn center, brown on blue, EX **$10.00**

Pin, Brownie holding cat, Bakelite, 2"..............................**$25.00**

Pin, GS Volunteer, 15-year pin, 1960s, 1x½", EX...............**$20.00**

Pin, 50th Anniversary, GS on center trefoil, GS of the USA, 1912-1962, EX **$15.00**

Pocketknife, Brownie/Be Wise Beware Use Me With Care, 1-blade, 1960s, 3⅛" closed, NM..**$39.00**

Poster, Smokey Bear w/GS, Pals...Working Together - Help Prevent Forest Fires, 1956, 14x10¼", EX..................................**$95.00**

Sewing kit, complete w/needle & thread spools, blue case w/gold emblem, 1960s, EX **$30.00**

Utensil set, fork, spoon, knife w/can opener, w/leather pouch, Schrade, EX..**$70.00**

Whistle, plastic, 1950s – 1960s, $25.00. (Photo courtesy Don and R.C. Raycraft)

Wristwatch, GS emblem on face, blue plastic band, Timex, EX..**$25.00**

Sears Kitchen Ware

During the 1970s the Sears Company sold several lines of novelty kitchen ware, including Country Kitchen, Merry Mushrooms, and Neil the Frog. These lines, especially Merry Mushrooms, are coming on strong as the collectibles of tomorrow. There's a lot of it around and unless you're buying it from someone who's already aware of its potential value, you can get it at very low prices. It was made in Japan. Besides the ceramic items, you'll find woodenware, enamelware, linens, and plastics.

Country Kitchen

Bread box, w/drawers, enamel ware, 16x12x18"..................**$75.00**

Butter dish **$15.00**

Canisters, set of 4..**$40.00**

Creamer, 4¼"..**$9.00**

Napkin holder, 4½x5¾" **$15.00**

Salt & pepper shakers, cylindrical, 4¾", pr **$15.00**

Spoon rest, rectangular, 4 rests **$10.00**

Merry Mushrooms

Ashtray, mushroom shape, rests on side, 6x5" **$85.00**

Bowl, salad; w/original wooden fork & spoon, rare............**$60.00**

Butter dish, from $20 to **$25.00**

Canister set, basketweave background, 4-pc, from $55 to **$65.00**

Canister set, mushroom shape, 4-pc, from $40 to **$50.00**

Canister set, plastic, brown lids, 4-pc **$32.00**

Canister set, smooth background, cylindrical, w/wooden lids, 4-pc, from $40 to **$50.00**

Casserole, Corning Ware, glass lid, 1¾-qt **$35.00**

Casserole, Corning Ware, glass lid, 2½-qt, from $40 to **$50.00**

Clock, wall mount, battery-operated, from $25 to **$30.00**

Coffee mug, textured background, 10-oz **$9.00**

Coffee mug, thermo-plastic..**$16.00**

Coffee mugs, textured background, 4 on scrolling metal tree . **$45.00**

Coffeepot, Corning ware, 6-cup..**$70.00**

Coffeepot, yellow enamelware, clear glass lid, black handle..**$35.00**

Coffeepot, 9½" **$25.00**

Cookie jar/lg canister **$18.00**

Corn dishes, mushroom at end of corn tray, set of 4, MIB ..**$60.00**

Creamer & sugar bowl, w/lid..**$35.00**

Curtain valance, 12x66", from $35 to................................**$45.00**

Curtains, 68x24", pr, MIP **$45.00**

Cutlery set, consists of carving knife, fillet knife, bread knive & meat fork **$32.50**

Dutch oven, enamel ware, $30.00.

Fondue set, 2-qt, MIB..**$35.00**

Gravy boat, 5½", w/7" undertray...$30.00
Lamp shade, ceiling mount, glass & metal, hexagonal $60.00
Lazy Susan canister, 4 units fit together to form lg mushroom, 1 lid covers all, 11½x10½"..$125.00
Mail holder/letter sorter, wooden, 3-pocket, 8x6x2" $40.00
Measuring cups, pitcher form, set of 4 ....$95.00
Mold, 3 mushrooms on white, 2½x9½x7½", from $35 to ..$45.00
Napkin holder, from $20 to $25.00
Napkin rings, set of 4...$25.00
Paper towel holder, wooden, w/shelf above, 20" L $60.00
Place mats, mushrooms on quilted white fabric w/brown corded edge, set of 4 w/4 orange napkins, from $40 to $60.00
Planter, textured background on brown undertray $35.00
Plaque, mushrooms in relief on oval, 9½x7½"....................$60.00
Salt & pepper shakers, 5", pr, from $16 to...........................$22.00
Soup mug, hard to find, 3x4¾" $25.00
Spice jar, paper label identifies contents, sm......................$5.00
Spice rack, 2-tier, 2 drawers in base, w/12 spice jars, minimum value $65.00
Spoon rest, 2 indents at bottom, 7½x5", MIB....................$30.00
Tea light holder, mushroom shape, dated 1981, 7¾" $30.00
Teapot, 7"...$22.50
Timer, dial in mushroom shape..$35.00
Toaster cover, printed cloth, from $15 to $20.00
Toaster cover, vinyl...$20.00
Tureen, w/underplate & ladle, 2½-qt $58.00
Utensil holder, w/original utensils $100.00
Wall pocket, pitcher & bowl shape $35.00

Neil the Frog

Bank, frog leaning on elbow, from $35 to.............................$45.00
Bell, frog on yellow lily pad in relief on white, 1978, 4¾", from $60 to $75.00

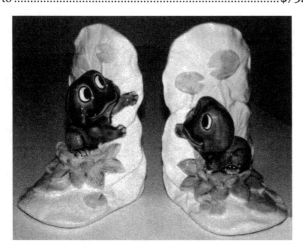

Bookends, $45.00 for the pair.

Bowl, water lily leaves on sides, 2 3-D frogs play on rim, 3¾x7" . $60.00
Canister set, plastic w/green lids, 4-pc, from $16 to.............$20.00
Canister set, 4-pc, from $60 to $80.00
Clock, lotus leaf shape, wall mount, battery-operated, 7½x7", from $35 to $45.00

Coffee mug, from $6 to $8.00
Coffee mugs, set of 4 on scrolling metal tree, from $25 to...$35.00
Cookie jar, frog finial, 10½" $35.00
Cookie jar, lg seated frog, from $50 to $60.00
Creamer & sugar bowl, from $20 to $25.00
Cruets, oil & vinegar, 5", pr...$30.00
Figurines, 1 holding yellow flower, 2nd w/umbrella, 1¾", 1⅝", pr...$45.00
Kitchen towel, frogs playing among mushrooms, 24x15½" ...$9.00
Mustard jar, slot in lid for spoon (present), from $30 to $40.00
Napkin holder, frog on lily pad, from $15 to $20.00
Pitcher, frog figural, mouth is spout, 6½", from $45 to $50.00
Place mats, frog on white lily pad, 4 for $25.00
Salt & pepper shakers, frog & lily pad, 2-pc set $20.00
Salt & pepper shakers, frog & sunflower, pr.........................$20.00
Salt & pepper shakers, range; cylindrical w/embossed frog, 5", pr..$18.00
Saucepan, enamelware, green lid, 6½" dia.............................$25.00
Soap dish, frog w/scrub brush in hand submerged in tub of white bubbles, 7" L $75.00
Spice rack, white painted wood 2-tier shelf w/12 spice shakers . $85.00
Spoon rest, frog at side of 2 lily pads....................................$20.00
Teapot, 2-cup, 5¾" $95.00
Trivet, cast iron w/ceramic insert..$40.00

Sebastians

These tiny figures were first made in 1938 by Preston W. Baston and sold through gift stores, primarily in the New England area. When he retired in 1976, the Lance Corporation chose 100 designs which they continued to produce under Baston's supervision. Since then, the discontinued figures have become very collectible.

Baston died in 1984, but his son, P.W. Baston, Jr., continues the tradition.

The figures are marked with an imprinted signature and a paper label. Early labels (before 1977) were green and silver foil shaped like an artist's palette; these are referred to as 'Marblehead' labels (Marblehead, Massachusetts, being the location of the factory) and figures that carry one of these are becoming hard to find and are highly valued by collectors.

America Remembers, Family Sing, 3½" $45.00
Becky Thatcher, 1946 ....$70.00
Ben Franklin $65.00
Christmas Sleigh Ride $30.00
Colonial Kitchen, 1952..$78.00
Colonial Watchman, Marblehead label $60.00
Coronado & Senora, 1960, 3"...$35.00
Cow Jumped Over the Moon...$250.00
Cranberry Picker, 1950 ....$28.00
Croquet, 1982 ....$35.00
Eagle Boy Scout $110.00
Family Picnic $40.00
Fisherman, 1947, 3"...$35.00
Fisherman's Wife $95.00
Headless Horseman, 1950..$60.00

Howard Johnson Pieman $200.00
In the Candy Store, 1947..$47.00
Jimmy Jund, 1984..$25.00
John Hancock..$85.00
Juliet $35.00
Mrs Beacon Hill, Marblehead era, MIB $45.00
Nativity..$70.00
Now's the Time For Jell-O, 1952, 3¾" $325.00
Oliver Twist & the Beadle..$30.00
Parade Rest, 1978 ....$24.00
Plymouth Plantation..$125.00

Rx Obocell, $50.00.

Scotsman, limited edition $175.00
Shoemaker $70.00
St Joan of Arc..$225.00
Uncle Sam, 1967..$45.00
Will Rogers, 2¾" $40.00
Williamsburg Couple, MIB $35.00

Sewing Collectibles

Ladies whose lot it has been to sew for their families have used a variety of tools — some were strictly utilitarian, while others were whimsical. Seamstresses are few and far between these days, but collectors search for the figural tape measures, sewing baskets, pincushions, and thimbles like grandma once used.

If you're interested in learning more about the subject, we recommend *Sewing Tools & Trinkets* by Helen Lester Thompson (Collector Books). In the listings that follow, unless noted otherwise, values are for examples in at least near-mint condition.

Advisor: Kathy Goldsworthy (See Directory, Sewing)

Basket, wooden barrel w/divider, on 3 wooden legs, hinged lid, handle, 19½x13" dia..$95.00
Basket, woven cords on wood frame, red braided trim, hinged lid, Sears, 1950s, 6x10x7"..$100.00

Book, Simplicity Unit of Sewing, softcover, 142 pages, 1957, EX $7.50
Book, Singer Instructions for Art Embroidery & Lace Work, softbound, 225 pages, 1931, 10¾x7¾", EX.....................$40.00
Book, Singer Sewing Book, Mary Brooks Picken, pictures & diagrams, copyright 1949, EX $35.00
Box, wooden, ea side pulls out to form 3 layers of drawers, center handle, 1960s, 7x12x7", EX $55.00
Buttonhole attachment kit, Kenmore, complete w/booklet, NMIB $16.00

Charms, sterling from $6.00 to $10.00 each. (Photo courtesy Glenda Thomas)

Darner, ebony egg w/embossed grapes on silver handle marked Sterling, 6¼"..$70.00
Darner, silver glove type w/repoussé flowers, marked Sterling, 4"..$50.00
Darner, turned wood, pine (?) w/dark finish, 2½" ball end, 10", EX..$15.00
Darner, wooden egg form, solid, Germany, 7" $35.00
Dress pattern, Vogue, sexy halter dress, flared skirt, in-seam pockets, 1950s, M in VG package $24.00
Emery, Miss Dinah, Black lady's head, w/poem on lid of box, MIB $140.00
Manual, Aprons & Caps, Woman's Institute of Domestic Arts & Sciences, Scranton PA, 1920s, 9x6", EX $20.00
Manual, Sears 222K Featherweight sewing machine, VG.....$40.00
Pincushion, ceramic, bird & mushroom (cushion on mushroom top), cold painted, Made in Japan, 3½x3" $20.00
Pincushion, ceramic, dog w/Bonzo-like appearance by yellow top hat w/cushion top, Japan $65.00
Pincushion, ceramic, frog w/flowers applied along open back w/ cushion top, Japan, 1¾x3½x2¼" $10.00
Pincushion, ceramic, German shepherd dog lying atop velvet pillow, 1930s, 1½x2¼" $65.00
Pincushion, ceramic, girl w/basket, cushion in basket, Japan, 5x3" $45.00
Pincushion, ceramic, pelican, multicolor w/lustre, cushion on back, Japan...$40.00
Pincushion, ceramic, poodle w/spaghetti sits on velvet cushion, wears scissors eyeglasses, 7½" $45.00
Pincushion, ceramic, potbellied stove, door front pulls for tape measure, cushion top, 1950s $15.00
Pincushion, metal, rat/mouse, cushion back, 3" $50.00

Pincushion, metal, shoe w/pointed toe, 1893 World's Fair, minor wear **$45.00**

Pincushion, porcelain, poodle sitting on green suede-like pillow, 4x3¼" **$45.00**

Pincushion, silver, turtle w/cushion on back, Sterling, 1x2". **$40.00**

Scissors, lady's leg handles, Capitol Cutlery Co Germany, 5⅜". **$10.00**

Scissors, silver, orchids & flowering tendrils on handles, marked F&B Germany, 4½x2" **$65.00**

Scissors, stork figural, Rochester Cutlery Co, 3½", EX, from $20 to **$35.00**

Scissors, stork figural w/engraved flowers, WH Morley & Sons Germany, 4" **$30.00**

Scissors, stork standing, baby dangles from finger ring, gilt metal, 3⅝+1¾" beak (blades) **$125.00**

Tape measure, brass, shoe, Three Feet in One Shoe on front, 1½x2¼" **$95.00**

Tape measure, celluloid, alligator, cloth tape removes from lower jaw, EX **$185.00**

Tape measure, celluloid, baseball player, tape removes from back, Made in Japan, NM **$250.00**

Tape measure, celluloid, Billiken w/lg smile, measure in side, 2½x¼", VG **$40.00**

Tape measure, celluloid, chick on base w/measure, 2⅝", EX. **$60.00**

Tape measure, celluloid, clown's head, sm black cap on head is pull for tape, Germany, EX+ **$200.00**

Tape measure, celluloid, deer w/spots on its back, Japan, 1950s, EX **$65.00**

Tape measure, celluloid, flamingo on base, multicolor, original 29¢ price tag, 2⅝" **$75.00**

Tape measure, celluloid, Indian boy w/headdress, red pants, tan shirt, EX **$135.00**

Tape measure, celluloid, kangaroo, pull Joey for tape, 2¾x2⅜", EX **$80.00**

Tape measure, celluloid, pheasant sitting on wall w/2 chicks, measure in wall, Japan, NM **$165.00**

Tape measure, celluloid, pig w/red hat, pulls out from under tail, Japan, 1¼x2½", EX **$55.00**

Tape measure, celluloid, sailing ship, EX details, cloth tape, Japan, EX **$110.00**

Tape measure, celluloid flower basket, lady bug pulls out tape w/inches & centimeters, 1½x1⅞", EX+ **$110.00**

Tape measure, gold-tone metal, clamshell, measures inches & metric, EX **$25.00**

Tape measure, metal, egg w/all-over yellow enamel, fly on top is pull, 2½" L, EX **$100.00**

Tape measure, petit point on silk, metal tape coiled inside, Germany, ½x1¾" dia **$38.00**

Tape measure, plastic, Hoover vacuum cleaner, pull at top, EX. **$45.00**

Tape measure, plastic, red apple w/green metal leaf that pulls for measure, 2½x1¾" dia **$45.00**

Tape measure, porcelain, girl kneelings & holds bunch of flowers in ea hand, tape in base, Germany **$185.00**

Tape measure, Singer Machines, A Century of Sewing Service 1851-1951, blue disk form, EX **$65.00**

Tatting shuttle, mother-of-pearl, 2⅝", EX **$35.00**

Thimble, silver, basketweave, 3 daisy chain bands, narrow, Webster USA **$30.00**

Thimble, silver, Christmas bells & holly, Sterling **$60.00**

Thimble, silver, church embossed on border, Sterling **$50.00**

Thimble, silver w/plain gold band, sm fan design above rim, Simons & Co **$15.00**

Thimble, silver w/red stone cap, plain band, Italy **$75.00**

Thimble, steel core w/silver coating, leafy band, Dorcas, Pat 10 .**$50.00**

Thimble, sterling w/14k gold decorative band, Ketcham & McDougall **$80.00**

Thimble, 14k gold, clamshell design, cartouch w/monogram, lg **$150.00**

**Wastebasket, tin, 13",
$15.00.** (Photo courtesy Glenda Thomas)

Shawnee Pottery

In 1937 a company was formed in Zanesville, Ohio, on the suspected site of a Shawnee Indian village. They took the tribe's name to represent their company, recognizing the Indians to be the first to use the rich clay from the banks of the Muskingum River to make pottery there. Their venture was very successful, and until they closed in 1961, they produced many lines of kitchenware, planters, vases, lamps, and cookie jars that are very collectible today.

They specialized in figural items. There were 'Winnie' and 'Smiley' pig cookie jars and salt and pepper shakers; 'Bo Peep,' 'Puss 'n Boots,' 'Boy Blue,' and 'Charlie Chicken' pitchers; Dutch children; lobsters; and two lines of dinnerware modeled as ears of corn.

Values sometimes hinge on the extent of an item's decoration. Most items will increase by 100% to 200% when heavily decorated with decals and gold trimmed.

Not all of their ware was marked Shawnee; many pieces were simply marked U.S.A. (If periods are not present, it is not Shawnee) with a three- or four-digit mold number. If you'd like to learn more about this subject, we recommend *Shawnee Pottery, The Full Encyclopedia,* by Pam Curran; *The Collector's Guide to Shawnee Pottery* by Duane and Janice Vanderbilt; and *Shawnee Pottery, Identification & Value Guide,* by Jim and Bev Mangus.

See Also Cookie Jars.

Advisors: Jim and Beverly Mangus (See Directory, Shawnee)

Club: Shawnee Pottery Collectors' Club
P.O. Box 713
New Smyrna Beach, FL 32170-0713
Monthly nationwide newsletter. SASE (c/o Pamela Curran) required when requesting information. Optional: $3 for sample of current newsletter

Corn Ware

Bowl, cereal; King or Queen, Shawnee 94, from $45 to **$50.00**
Bowl, fruit; King or Queen, Shawnee 92, 6", from $40 to... **$45.00**
Bowl, mixing; King, Shawnee 8, 8", from $40 to................ **$45.00**
Bowl, mixing; Queen, Shawnee 8, 8", from $30 to............. **$35.00**
Bowl, vegetable; King or Queen, Shawnee 95, 9", from $50 to.. **$55.00**
Casserole, King or Queen, Shawnee 73, individual, from $125 to... **$150.00**
Casserole, Queen, Shawnee 74, lg, from $45 to.................. **$50.00**
Cookie jar, King or Queen, Shawnee 66, from $300 to **$350.00**
Corn roast set, Queen, from $165 to **$175.00**
Cup, Queen, 90, from $28 to **$30.00**
Mug, King or Queen, Shawnee 69, from $45 to.................. **$50.00**
Plate, Queen, Shawnee 68, 10", from $35 to **$40.00**
Plate, salad; Queen, Shawnee 93, 8", from $28 to **$32.00**
Salt & pepper shakers, King or Queen, 3¼", pr from $26 to ... **$28.00**
Saucer, Queen, 91, from $15 to **$18.00**
Shawnee, Queen, sugar bowl, Shawnee 78, from $30 to......**$35.00**

Kitchenware

Salt and pepper shakers, Jack and Jill, blue trim, from $45.00 to $55.00 for the pair.

Bowl, batter; Snowflake, from $20 to.................................. **$25.00**
Canister, Dutch decal, USA, 2-qt, from $45 to................... **$50.00**
Canister, Puss 'n Boots, USA 85, from $100 to **$125.00**
Canister, Snowflake, 2-qt, from $45 to **$55.00**
Creamer, Flower & Fern, from $18 to **$22.00**
Creamer, Puss 'n Boots, USA 85, from $100 to................ **$125.00**
Creamer, Smiley the Pig w/gold trim & cloverbud, patented Smiley USA, from $150 to.. **$165.00**
Creamer, Sunflower, USA, from $50 to **$55.00**
Creamer, Tulip, USA, from $75 to....................................... **$80.00**
Grease jar, Sahara, Kenwood USA 977, from $50 to........... **$55.00**
Pitcher, Bo Peep, USA Pat Bo Peep, 40-oz, from $85 to **$90.00**
Pitcher, Chanticleer w/gold & decal, Patented Chanticleer USA, from $350 to **$400.00**

Pitcher, Fern, octagonal, 1½-pt, from $60 to **$70.00**
Pitcher, Flower & Fern, 4-cup, from $22 to........................ **$24.00**
Pitcher, Laurel Wreath, USA, from $22 to **$24.00**
Pitcher, Smiley the Pig, gold trim & embossed flowers, Pat Smiley USA, from $175 to.. **$200.00**
Salt & pepper shakers, chanticleer, pr from $45 to **$50.00**
Salt & pepper shakers, duck, sm, pr from $25 to................ **$30.00**
Salt & pepper shakers, fruit, lg, pr from $35 to **$40.00**
Salt & pepper shakers, milk can, pr from $30 to **$35.00**
Salt & pepper shakers, Muggsy, gold trim, lg, pr from $200 to .**$225.00**
Salt & pepper shakers, Puss 'n Boots, pr from $30 to **$35.00**
Salt & pepper shakers, Smiley & Winnie the Pig, w/clover buds, pr from $200 to **$235.00**
Salt & pepper shakers, Smiley & Winnie the Pig, w/gold trim, pr from $70 to **$90.00**
Salt & pepper shakers, Smiley the Pig, green neckerchief, pr from $125 to **$135.00**
Salt & pepper shakers, Smiley w/gold & decals, lg, pr from $185 to **$200.00**
Salt & pepper shakers, wheelbarrow, sm, pr from $24 to **$26.00**
Sugar bowl, Sunflower, w/lid, USA, from $50 to **$55.00**
Sugar bowl/utility jar, Cloverbud, USA, from $50 to........... **$55.00**
Teapot, Criss Cross, USA, 5-cup, from $30 to **$35.00**
Teapot, Fern, octagonal, 6-cup, from $75 to....................... **$85.00**
Teapot, Granny Ann, gold trim, Patented Granny Ann USA, 7-cup, minimum value.. **$200.00**
Teapot, Horseshoe, USA, 8-cup, from $40 to **$45.00**
Teapot, Pennsylvania Dutch, USA, 30-oz, from $200 to....**$225.00**
Teapot, Tom the Piper's Son, gold trim, Patented Tom the Pipers Son USA, 5-cup, from $150 to... **$160.00**

Lobster Ware

Bowl, batter; w/handle, 928, from $50 to **$55.00**
Casserole, French; 900, 10-oz, from $18 to **$21.00**
Creamer, 921, from $45 to **$50.00**
Hors d'oeuvres holder, lobster figural, USA, 7¼", from $250 to **$275.00**
Plate, compartment; claw shape, USA 912, from $75 to....**$100.00**
Salt & pepper shakers, claw shape, USA, pr from $35 to.....**$40.00**
Salt & pepper shakers, jug style, USA, from $100 to.........**$110.00**
Snack jar/bean pot, Kenwood USA 925, 40-oz, from $750 to. **$775.00**

Valencia

Ashtray, from $16 to **$18.00**
Bowl, nappy, unmarked, 8½", from $20 to.......................... **$22.00**
Candleholder, bulb style, ea from $20 to **$22.00**
Casserole, 7½", from $55 to **$60.00**
Cup & saucer, AD; unmarked, from $22 to **$25.00**
Egg cup, from $18 to.. **$20.00**
Fork, from $40 to **$45.00**
Marmite, 4½", from $25 to **$30.00**
Plate, chop; unmarked, 13", from $20 to............................. **$25.00**
Plate, 6½" or 7¾", ea from $10 to....................................... **$12.00**
Plate, 9¾", from $12 to **$14.00**
Punch bowl, 12", from $45 to **$55.00**

Spoon, from $40 to...$45.00
Teacup & saucer, unmarked, from $20 to..................$22.00
Teapot, regular, from $55 to $65.00

Pitcher, ice; from $30.00 to $35.00.

Miscellaneous

Ashtray, Hostess line, triangular free-form, USA 201, 5", from $12 to $14.00
Ashtray, shell form, USA 204, from $20 to...............$25.00
Bowl, console; Flax Blue w/embossed ribs, oval, USA, 4x10", from $18 to $20.00
Candleholders, dark blue w/embossed leaves, 3¼", pr from $22 to $24.00
Figurine, lamb, flowers around neck, bow on tail, unmarked, 6½", from $25 to $30.00
Figurine, Scottie dog, USA, 7½", from $25 to.............$30.00
Flowerpot, embossed diamonds, USA 484, 4", from $10 to ..$12.00
Flowerpot & saucer, embossed flowers & diamonds, USA 454, 3", from $10 to $12.00
Jardiniere, tulips embossed on blue, USA, 5", from $8 to $10.00
Lamp base, ballerina figural (sitting on base), unmarked, from $65 to $75.00
Lamp base, Oriental girl w/mandolin, high base, unmarked, from $30 to $35.00
Miniature, baby buggy, USA, from $18 to...............$20.00
Miniature, swan vase, USA, from $18 to $20.00
Miniature, watering can, USA, from $24 to...............$26.00
Pitcher, Stars & Stripes, USA, from $16 to $18.00
Planter, Chinese figures (2) w/basket, USA 537, from $10 to .$12.00
Planter, clown w/pot, USA 619, from $12 to...............$15.00
Planter, donkey & cart, USA, from $10 to $12.00
Planter, elephant w/trunk up, gold trim, USA 759, from $24 to.$26.00
Planter, fawn & stump, unmarked, from $16 to.................$18.00
Planter, girl w/umbrella, USA 560, from $26 to.................$28.00
Planter, highchair, USA 727, from $60 to...................$65.00
Planter, hound dog, USA, from $10 to $12.00
Planter, kitten & basket, Shawnee USA 2026, from $30 to .$32.00
Planter, lovebirds, USA, from $10 to $12.00
Planter, pony, Shawnee 506, from $35 to $40.00
Planter, poodle & carriage, USA 704, from $32 to $35.00
Planter, squirrel & nut, USA 713, from $30 to.................$35.00

Planter, tractor & trailor, Shawnee 680 & 681, pr from $60 to..$70.00
Vase, bud; organic form, USA 705, 5", from $12 to...........$14.00
Vase, cornucopia; USA, 3½", from $12 to.....................$14.00
Vase, double; organic form, Shawnee USA, 5", from $16 to.$18.00
Vase, hand holding vase, ivory w/red fingernails, USA, 8", from $16 to $18.00
Vase, philodendrons in gold on yellow, handles, #805, 6½", from $35 to $40.00
Vase, swirled body, USA, 5", from $12 to.....................$14.00
Wall pocket, bow w/gold trim, USA 434, from $30 to $35.00

Sheet Music

Flea markets are a good source for buying old sheet music, and prices are usually very reasonable. Most examples can be bought for less than $5.00. More often than not, it is collected for reasons other than content. Some of the cover art was done by well-known illustrators like Rockwell, Christy, Barbelle, and Starmer, and some collectors like to zero in on their particular favorite, often framing some of the more attractive examples. Black Americana collectors can find many good examples with Black entertainers featured on the covers and the music reflecting an ethnic theme.

You may want to concentrate on music by a particularly renowned composer, for instance George M. Cohan or Irving Berlin. Or you may find you enjoy covers featuring famous entertainers and movie stars from the '40s through the '60s, for instance. At any rate, be critical of condition when you buy or sell sheet music. As is true with any item of paper, tears, dog ears, or soil will greatly reduce its value.

If you'd like a more thorough listing of sheet music and prices, we recommend *The Sheet Music Reference and Price Guide* by Anna Marie Guiheen and Marie-Reine A. Pafik (Collector Books), and *The Collector's Guide to Sheet Music* by Debbie Dillon.

If You Are But a Dream, Moe Jaffe, Jack Fulton, and Nat Bonx, Frank Sinatra photo, 1941, $17.00. (Photo courtesy Anna Marie Guiheen and Marie-Reine A. Pafik)

Adios, Eddie Woods & Enrico Madriguera, 1931 ....$5.00
Adorable, George Marion Jr & Richard Whiting, Movie: Adorable, Janet Gaynor photo, 1933 ....$10.00
Along the Santa Fe Trail, Dubin, Coolidge & Groz, Movie: Along The Santa Fe Trail, 1940..$8.00

America Calling, Meredith Wilson, 1941 .... $5.00

Bad & the Beautiful, The; Raskin, Movie: The Bad & the Beautiful, Kirk Douglas & Lana Turner photo, 1953 .... $6.00

Bibbidi-Bobbidi-Boo, Mack David, Al Hoffman & Jerry Livingston, Movie: Cinderella (Disney), 1949 .... $15.00

Boulevard of Memories, Edward Lane & John Jacob Loeb, 1947 .... $3.00

Bring Back the Thrill, Ruth Poll & Peter Rugolo, Eddie Fisher photo, 1950 .... $5.00

C'est Si Bon, Jerry Seelen & Henri Betti, 1950 .... $2.00

Careless Hands, Bob Hilliard & Carl Sigman, John Laurenz photo, 1949 .... $3.00

Christmas Song, Mel Tormé & Robert Wells, 1946 .... $3.00

Color My World, James Pankow, 1970 .... $3.00

Dream a Little Dream of Me, Gus Kahn, W Schwandt & F Andree, Dinah Shore photo, 1931 .... $5.00

Eastbound Train, The; Nick Manaloff, Winnie, Lou & Sally photo, Lou Kummel & Transportation cover, 1935 .... $10.00

Ev'ry Day of My Life, Jimmie Crane & Al Jacobs, Bobby Vinton photo, 1953 .... $3.00

Eyes of Blue, Stone & Young, Movie: Shane, Alan Ladd, Jean Arthur & Van Heflin photo, 1953 .... $5.00

Faithful Forever, Leo Robin & Ralph Rainger, Movie: Gulliver's Travels, 1939 .... $8.00

First Time I Saw Your Face, The; Ewan MacColl, 1972 .... $3.00

Five Minutes w/Mr Thornhill, Claude Thornhill, 1942 .... $5.00

Forever Darling, Cahn & Kaper, Movie: Forever Darling, Lucille Ball, Desi Arnaz & James Mason photo, 1955 .... $8.00

Galveston, Webb, Glen Campbell photo, 1968 .... $5.00

Gigi, Alan J Lerner & Frederick Loewe, Movie: Gigi, 1958 ... $5.00

Give a Little Whistle, Carolyn Leigh & Cy Coleman, Movie: Wildcat, 1960 .... $5.00

Have I Told You Lately That I Love You, Scott Wiseman, Bing Crosby & Andrew Sisters photo, 1946 .... $10.00

Heaven Is a Raft on a River, Robert & Helen Thomas, Jane Pickens photo, 1954 .... $5.00

Holiday for Strings, David Rose, 1943 .... $5.00

Hundred Million Miracles, A; Richard Rodgers & Oscar Hammerstein II, Movie: Flower Drum Song, 1961 .... $8.00

I Am Ashamed That Women Are So Simple, Cole Porter, Musical: Kiss Me Kate, 1948 .... $6.00

I Believe in Miracles, Barry Mason & Les Reed, Engelbert Humperdinck photo, 1976 .... $3.00

I'd Be Lost Without You, Sunny Skylar, George Paxton photo, 1946 .... $4.00

I'd Like To Teach The World To Sing, B Backer, B Davis, R Cook & R Greenaway, 1971 .... $3.00

If You'll Say 'Yes' Cherie, Ray Noble, 1934 .... $3.00

Jean, Rod McKuen, Movie: Prime of Miss Jean Brodie, Oliver photo, 1969 .... $5.00

Jesse James, Jerry Livingston, Eileen Barton photo, 1954 .... $5.00

Jubilee, Stanley Adams & Hoagy Carmichael, Movie: Every Day's a Holiday, Mae West caricature, 1937 .... $10.00

Just Because You're You, Cliff Friend, 1932 .... $3.00

Kansas City, Richard Rodgers & Oscar Hammerstein II, 1943 .... $3.00

Last Night I Had That Dream Again, Oliver Wallace, 1944 .. $3.00

Leaving on a Jet Plane, John Denver, Peter, Paul & Mary photo, 1969 .... $5.00

Let It Snow!, Sammy Cahn & Jule Styne, Griff Williams photo, 1945 .... $4.00

Love Song From the Buccaneer, David & Bernstein, Yul Brynner & Charlton Heston photo, 1958 .... $6.00

Lover, The; Albert Hay Malotte, 1938 .... $3.00

Malaguena, Marian Banks and Ernesto Le Cuona, Connie Francis photo, 1954, $8.00. (Photo courtesy Anna Marie Guiheen and Marie-Reine A. Pafik)

May I Never Love Again, Sano Marco & Jack Erickson, 1940 . $5.00

Maybe It's the Moon, Richard A Whiting, 1931' $5.00

Memory Lane, Jess Williams & Lester Palmer, 1936 .... $3.00

Michelle, John Lennon & Paul McCartney, Paul McCartney & The Beatles, 1965 .... $15.00

Misfits, The; North, Movie: The Misfits, Marilyn Monroe, Clark Gable & Montgomery Clift photo, 1960 .... $10.00

Mobile, Bob Wells & David Holt, Julius LaRosa photo, 1954 .... $3.00

Moon River, Johnny Mercer & Henry Mancini, Movie: Breakfast at Tiffany's, Audrey Hepburn photo, 1961 .... $8.00

Nice To Be Around, Williams & Williams, Movie: Cinderella Liberty, James Caan & Marsha Mason photo, 1973 .... $4.00

Nickel for a Memory, A; Perry Alexander, Bob Hilliard & Ann Beardsley, 1941 .... $3.00

No Two People, Frank Loesser, Movie: Hans Christian Andersen, Danny Kaye photo $10.00

Noon at Midnight, Lou Holzer & Harry Kogen, 1935 .... $5.00

Off Shore, Steve Graham & Leo Diamond, Russ Morgan signed photo, 1953 .... $3.00

Oh Gee! Oh Joy!, PG Wodehouse & George & Ira Gershwin, 1949 .... $5.00

On the Atchison, Topeka & the Santa Fe, J Mercer & H Warren, Movie: The Harvey Girls, Judy Garland photo, 1934 ... $16.00

One Last Kiss, Lee Adams & Charles Strause, Movie: Bye, Bye Birdie, 1960 .... $3.00

Oops!, Mercer & Warren, Movie: The Belle of New York, Fred Astaire & Vera Ellen photo, 1952 .... $10.00

Pretty Kitty Blue Eyes, Mann Curtis & Vic Mizzy, 1944 .... $3.00

Put That Ring on My Finger, Sunny Skylar & Randy Ryan, 1945 .... $3.00

Put Your Head on My Shoulder, Paul Anka, 1958 .... $5.00

Que Sera, Sera, Whatever Will Be, Will Be; Jay Livingston & Ray Evans, Mary Hopkins photo, 1955 .... **$3.00**

Quentin's Theme, Robert Cobert, 1969 .... **$2.00**

Quicksilver, Irving Taylor, George Wyle & Eddie Pola, Bing Crosby photo, 1949 .... **$4.00**

Rainbow at Midnight, Lost John Miller, Lost John Miller photo, 1946 .... **$3.00**

Red River Valley, Harold Potter, Movie: Red River Valley, Gene Autry photo, 1935 .... **$6.00**

Red Silk Stockings & Green Perfume, Dick Sanford, Sammy Mysels & Bob Hilliard, 1947 .... **$3.00**

Remember Me I'm the One Who Loves You, Stuart Hamblen, 1950 .... **$3.00**

Rhapsody in Blue, George Gershwin, 1939 .... **$3.00**

Rolling Home, Cole Porter, Movie: Born To Dance, Eleanor Powell photo, 1936 .... **$6.00**

Rum & Coca Cola, Morey Amsterdam, Jeri Sullivan & Paul Baron, Andrews Sisters photo (WWII), 1944 .... **$12.00**

Salt Water Cowboys, Redd Evans, 1944 .... **$4.00**

Sandman, Ralph Freed & Bonnie Lake, 1934 .... **$3.00**

Seal It With a Kiss, Edward Heyman & Arthur Schwartz, Movie: That Girl From Paris, Lily Pons photo, 1936 .... **$5.00**

Secret Love, Paul Francis Webster & Sammy Fain, Movie: Calamity Jane, Doris Day & Howard Keel photo, 1953 .... **$5.00**

Sentimental Journey, Bud Green, Les Brown & Ben Homer, Les Brown photo, 1944 .... **$3.00**

Sew the Buttons On, John Jennings, Musical: Riverwind, 1963 .... **$3.00**

Shadows of the Night, Charles Crean & Robert Cobert, 1969. **$3.00**

So in Love, Cole Porter, Musical: Kiss Me Kate, 1948 .... **$3.00**

Somewhere My Love, Paul Francis Webster & Maurice Jarre, Movie: Doctor Zhivago, Ray Conniff photo, 1965 .... **$4.00**

Sweet & Low, Joseph Barnby & Alfred Tennyson, Starr Sisters photo, 1935 .... **$5.00**

Talking to Myself About You, Alex Stordahl, Paul Weston & Irving Taylor, Peggy Lee photo, 1948 .... **$5.00**

Tell Me Why, Al Alberts & Marty Gold, The Four Aces photo, 1951 .... **$5.00**

Ten Pins in the Sky, Joseph McCarthy & Milton Ager, Movie: Listen Darling, 1938 .... **$5.00**

Thanks a Million, Arthur Johnston & Gus Kahn, Movie: Thanks a Million, Dick Powell photo, 1948 .... **$5.00**

That Shenandoah Sally of Mine, Lacy L Leonard, 1938 .... **$3.00**

There Goes My Dreams, David Heneker, 1940 .... **$5.00**

To You Sweetheart, Aloha, Harry Owens, 1936 .... **$3.00**

To-Morrow, Roy Turk & Vee Lawnhurst, 1933 .... **$5.00**

Under the Bridges of Paris, Dorcas Cochran & Vincent Scotto, 1953 .... **$3.00**

Until Today, Benny Davis, J Fred Coots & Oscar Levant, 1936. **$3.00**

Valentine Candy, Sherman & Sherman, Movie: The Happiest Millionaire, Leslie Ann Warren photo, 1966 .... **$3.00**

Velvet Moon, Edgar De Lange & J Myrow, Freddy Martin photo, Holley cover, 1942 .... **$3.00**

Volare, Mitchell Parish & Domenico Modugno, McGuire Sisters photo, 1958 .... **$3.00**

Wait Till Tomorrow, Lloyd & DePaul, Movie: The Ballad of Josie, Doris Day & Peter Graves photo, 1967 .... **$5.00**

Wait Until Dark, Livingston, Evans & Mancini, Movie: Wait Until Dark, Audrey Hepburn photo, 1967 .... **$10.00**

Warsaw Concerto, Richard Addinsell, 1942 .... **$5.00**

We Sat Beneath the Maple on the Hill, Gussie L Davis, 1935.. **$5.00**

You Are My Sunshine, Jimmie Davis & Charles Mitchell, Jimmie Davis photo, 1940 .... **$4.00**

You're Here My Love, Burke & Lilley, Movie: The Seven Little Foys, Bob Hope photo, 1955 .... **$3.00**

You've Got Me This Way, Johnny Mercer & Jimmy McHugh, Movie: You'll Find Out, 1940 .... **$6.00**

Zigeuner, Noel Coward, 1941 .... **$5.00**

Zip-A-Dee-Doo-Dah, Allie Wrubel & Ray Gilbert, Movie: Song Of the South (Disney), 1946 .... **$15.00**

Shell Pink Glassware

This beautiful soft pink, opaque glassware was made for only a short time in the late 1950s by the Jeannette Glass Company. Though a few pieces are commanding prices of more than $200.00 (the Anniversary cake plate, the cigarette box with the butterfly finial, and the lazy Susan tray with the base), most pieces carry modest price tags, and the ware, though not as easy to find as it was a few years ago, is still available for the collector who is willing to do something. Refer to *Collectible Glassware from the 40s, 50s, and 60s,* by Gene and Cathy Florence (Collector Books) for photos and more information.

Ashtray, butterfly shape **$25.00**
Base, for lazy Susan, w/ball bearings **$160.00**
Bowl, Florentine, footed, 10" **$30.00**
Bowl, Holiday, footed, 10½" **$45.00**
Bowl, Lombardi, design in center, 4-footed, 11" **$42.00**
Bowl, Pheasant, footed, 8", from $40 to **$50.00**
Bowl, wedding; w/lid, 6½" **$20.00**
Cake plate, Anniversary **$275.00**
Cake stand, Harp, 10" **$45.00**

Candleholder, Pheasant, Jeannette Co., 2½x6⅜", $250.00.
(Photo courtesy Gene and Cathy Florence)

Candleholders, Eagle, 3-footed, pr **$70.00**
Candy dish, Floragold, 4-footed, 5¼" **$20.00**
Candy dish, sq, w/lid, 6½" H **$30.00**
Celery/relish, 3-part, 12½" **$40.00**
Cigarette box, butterfly finial, from $185 to **$210.00**

Compote, Windsor, 6" $22.50
Cookie jar, w/lid, 6½" $125.00
Honey jar, beehive shape, notched lid, from $50 to $60.00
Powder jar, w/lid, 4¾" $45.00
Punch bowl, 7½-qt $125.00
Punch cup, 5-oz (also fits snack tray) $4.00
Relish, Vineyard, octagonal, 4-part, 12" $40.00
Stem, water goblet; Thumbprint, 8-oz $12.50
Sugar bowl, Baltimore Pear, footed, w/lid $20.00
Tray, Harp, 2-handled, 12½x9¾" $60.00
Tray, lazy Susan, 5-part, 13½" $60.00
Tray, Venetian, 6-part, 16½" $35.00
Tray, 5-part, 2-handle, 15¾" $85.00
Tumbler, juice; Thumbprint, footed, 5-oz $8.00
Vase, 7" $35.00

Shirley Temple

Born April 23, 1928, Shirley Jane Temple danced and smiled her way into the hearts of America in the movie *Stand Up and Cheer*. Many successful roles followed and by the time Shirley was eight years old, she was #1 at box offices around the country. Her picture appeared in publications almost daily, and any news about her was news indeed. Mothers dressed their little daughters in clothing copied after hers and coiffed them with Shirley hairdos.

The extent of her success was mirrored in the unbelievable assortment of merchandise that saturated the retail market. Dolls, coloring books, children's clothing and jewelry, fountain pens, paper dolls, stationery, and playing cards are just a few examples of the hundreds of items that were available. Shirley's face was a common sight on the covers of magazines as well as in the advertisements they contained, and she was the focus of scores of magazine articles.

Though she had been retired from the movies for nearly a decade, she had two successful TV series in the late '50s, *The Shirley Temple Story-Book* and *The Shirley Temple Show*. Her reappearance caused new interest in some of the items that had been so popular during her childhood, and many were reissued.

Always interested in charity and community service, Shirley became actively involved in a political career in the late 1960s, serving at both the state and national levels.

If you're interested in learning more about her, we recommend *The Complete Guide to Shirley Temple Dolls and Collectibles* by Tonya Berraldi-Camaretta and *Shirley in the Magazines* by Gen Jones.

Newsletter: *Lollipop News*
P.O. Box 6203
Oxnard, CA 93031
Dues: $18 per year

Newsletter: *The Shirley Temple Collectors News*
8811 Colonial Rd.
Brooklyn, NY 11209; Dues: $20 per year; checks payable to Rita Dubas

Advertisement, The Little Princess meeting Queen Victoria, Saturday
    Evening Post page, 1939, 14x11", EX...........................**$15.00**

Bank, portrait of Shirley Temple on top of sq form, 1930s ..**$35.00**
Beauty set, 4 pc: bubble bath, cologne, hand lotion & talc, Gabriel,
    #340, MIB...**$50.00**
Book, Heidi, Shirley cover, Random House, 1950s, VG w/dust
    jacket **$40.00**
Book, Now I Am Eight, black & white illustrations, color cover,
    Saalfield, #1766, 1937, 10x9½" paperback, VG **$40.00**
Book, Rebecca of Sunnybrook Farm, KD Wiggin, Random House,
    1950s, EX w/G- dust jacket.......................................**$35.00**
Book, Shirley Temple American Princess, Anne Edwards, copyright
    1988, 444 pages, EX w/dust jacket..............................**$30.00**
Book, Shirley Temple in Heidi, Saalfield, hardcover, 1930s,
    VG **$20.00**
Book, Shirley Temple Little Star, Saalfield, softcover, #1762, 1936,
    EX **$50.00**
Book, Shirley Temple's Favorite Poems, Saalfield Authorized Edition,
    Brueggeman illustrations, 1936, EX............................**$30.00**
Book, Shirley Temple 21st Birthday Album, Dell, softcover, April
    1949, VG..**$20.00**
Book, Susannah of the Mounties, Muriel Denison, Random House,
    1950s, VG w/dust jacket..**$30.00**
Book, The Story of My Life, Shirley Temple, softcover, Fox Film
    Corp, 1934, EX **$50.00**
Bowl, cereal; portrait on cobalt glass, Hexagon pattern, scalloped
    edge, Hazel-Atlas, 6½"...**$60.00**
Charm bracelet, 10 charms on gold bracelet, Danbury Mint, 1990-
    2000 ....**$75.00**
Coloring book, Shirley Temple Crosses the Country, Saalfield,
    #1779, softcover, 1939, EX..**$40.00**
Cup, plastic, red w/white cameo of Shirley, 1950s, EX **$20.00**
Doll, bisque, Curly Top outfit, Germany, EX.....................**$50.00**
Doll, composition, cream satin dress w/high collar, Japanese, 6",
    EX **$100.00**

Doll, composition, Ideal, EX, 20", $1,100.00; Baby buggy, 27" handle height, $900.00. (Photo courtesy McMasters Harris Auctions)

Doll, composition, original dress & wig, 1930s, 13", VG+ .**$285.00**
Doll, hard plastic shoulder head w/compo arms & legs, cloth body,
    Little Colonel outfit, 1940s, 29", EX...........................**$395.00**

Doll, plastic, cotton sailor dress, original shoes & socks, Ideal, 1972-73, 16", EX..**$50.00**

Doll, porcelain, Poor Little Rich Girl, military outfit, 25", EX ..**$300.00**

Doll, porcelain, Stand Up & Cheer, Shirley w/white rabbit, hinged box, Susan Wakeen, 2001 ....**$125.00**

Doll, vinyl, Bo Peep, sleep eyes, 4 upper teeth, dimples, Ideal, 1962, 15"...**$250.00**

Doll, vinyl, cowgirl outfit, Western-style black shirt & skirt w/white fringe, black hat & white boots, #9718, 12", EX........**$265.00**

Doll, vinyl, flowered pinafore, all original, Ideal, 1960, 12" .**$235.00**

Doll, vinyl, Heidi, #9722, Ideal, 12", EX **$175.00**

Doll, vinyl, Heidi, German costume & wooden shoes, Ideal, 1982, MIB...**$40.00**

Doll, vinyl, Little Colonel, fully jointed, Ideal, 1984, 36", NRFB **$345.00**

Doll, vinyl, original blue playsuit, shoes & socks, Ideal, 1962, 12", NM...**$195.00**

Doll, vinyl, Poor Little Rich Girl, all original, Ideal, 1983, 8". **$40.00**

Doll, vinyl, Rebecca of Sunnybrook Farm, all original, Ideal, 1950s, 17"..**$185.00**

Doll, vinyl, red felt jumper w/Scottie dog on front, white shirt & purse, #9714, Ideal, 12", EX....................**$200.00**

Doll, vinyl, Stowaway, turquoise blouse & black pants, Ideal, 1982, MIB...**$40.00**

Doll outfit, red & white gingham shirt w/horse head appliquè & red shorts, #9750, Ideal, 1961, MIB..........**$150.00**

Doll pattern, Simplicity #3217, fits 17" doll, NMIP **$25.00**

Drawing set, 3 pc: coloring book, crayons & watercolors, Saalfield, #1738, 1935, MIB..........................**$100.00**

Fan, Shirley holding teddy bear, Italy, 1930s, EX.................**$60.00**

Figurine, Poor Little Rich Girl, porcelain, Nostalgia Collection Limited Edition, MIB....................................**$65.00**

Figurine, Shirley standing w/hands on hips, ceramic, 6" **$20.00**

Jewelry set, imitation pearl necklace & bracelet, Shirley w/tiara on package, MIP, minimum value.....................**$200.00**

Jewelry set, Snap-on, Gabriel, #302, late 1950s, rare, minimum value **$100.00**

Mug, portrait on cobalt, Hazel-Atlas, 1935-36, 3¾"............**$40.00**

Music box, Little Miss Broadway scene on lid, Danbury Mint, 1990s...**$20.00**

Paper dolls, Authorized Edition of Shirley Temple Dolls & Dresses, 8 uncut pages, Saalfield #280, 1934.........................**$145.00**

Paper dolls, Dover Publications, 16 plates, 3 color dolls, 1986, ea nearly 21" **$15.00**

Paper dolls, Shirley Temple & Her Playhouse, Saalfield, #1780, 1935, MIB...**$100.00**

Paper dolls, Shirley...Paper Doll Cutouts, Whitman #7409, 1976, uncut, MIB...**$40.00**

Paper dolls, Snap-on Paper Doll, #299, Gabriel, 1959, MIP ..**$80.00**

Photo, Shirley in uniform saluting (pre-adolescent), black & white, 8x10", EX...**$25.00**

Photo postcard, Shirley in lg bonnet w/satin bow, black & white, divided back, 1930s-40s, EX..........................**$25.00**

Pin-back button, Be My Friend Shirley Temple, black & white portrait (teenager), red border, ca 1980, 1½" **$8.00**

Pin-back button, black & white portrait of Shirley w/her dog, green border, ca 1980, 1¾" dia **$10.00**

Pin-back button, STK in white on blue background, Shirley Temple Klub in gold border, Czechoslovakia, 1930s.................**$30.00**

Pin-back button, The World's Darling...An Ideal Doll, celluloid, 1¼", EX...**$55.00**

Pitcher, black & white portrait on cobalt glass, Hazel-Atlas, 1930s, 4½", from $35 to **$45.00**

Plate, Ambassador of Smiles, Donald Zolan, Danbury Mint, 1995, MIB...**$30.00**

Plate, Baby Take a Bow, Danbury Mint, 2002, 12", MIB, from $30 to **$40.00**

Postcard, linen, Shirley portrait reserve & Her Hollywood Home, divided back, 1940s, unused **$15.00**

Postcard, Shirley caricature, 1930s **$15.00**

Record, Shirley narrating Dumbo, RCA, 1960 ....**$20.00**

Sheet Music, Curly Top's Birthday, Shirley holding birthday cake on cover, 1937, Movietone, rare...........................**$50.00**

Sheet music, On the Good Ship Lollipop, Shirley's face on pink & blue cover, 1934...**$10.00**

Sheet music, Poor Little Rich Girl, portrait cover, 1936, EX **$10.00**

Stamps, Shirley in 6 different poses, 1947...........................**$20.00**

Stationery, Shirley reading book on cover of box, WT & S Corp, 1930s...**$50.00**

Tea set, pink and white plastic, Ideal, late 1950s – early 1960s, MIB, $300.00. (Per piece, $20.00.) (Photo courtesy Tonya Bervaldi-Camaratta)

Writing set, 2 pens w/Shirley Temple stamped on barrel, 1930s, MIB...**$150.00**

Shot Glasses

Shot glasses are small articles of glass that generally hold an ounce or two of liquid; they measure about 2" to 4" in height. They've been around since the 1830s have been made in nearly every conceivable type of glass.

Shot glass collectors are usually quantity collectors often boasting of hundreds or even a thousand glasses! The most desirable to collectors are whiskey sample or advertising glasses from the Pre-Prohibition era. Most carry etched white lettering that comprises messages relating to a distiller, company, proprietor, or other alcohol-related advertising. Shot glasses like these sell for around $75.00 to $100.00, but recently many rare examples have been auctioned off at prices in excess of $300.00.

These values are only estimates and should be used as a general guide. Many one-of-a-kind items or oddities are a bit harder to classify, especially sample glasses. Often this may depend on the elaborateness of the design as opposed to simple lettering. For more information, we recommend *Shot Glasses* (Schiffer Publishers) and *The Shot Glass Encyclopedia*, both by Mark Pickvet.

Note: Values for shot glasses in good condition are represented by the low end of our ranges, while the high end reflects estimated values for examples in mint condition.

Advisor: Mark Pickvet (See Directory, Shot Glasses)

Sports (professional team), from $5.00 to $7.50.

Barrel shaped, from $5 to	**$7.50**
Black porcelain replica, from $3 to	**$5.00**
Carnival colors, plain or fluted, from $100 to	**$150.00**
Carnival colors, w/patterns, from $125 to	**$175.00**
Culver 22k gold, from $6 to	**$8.00**
Depression, colors, from $10 to	**$12.50**
Depression, colors w/patterns or etching, from $17 to	**$25.00**
Depression, tall, general designs, from $10 to	**$12.50**
Depression, tall, tourist, from $5 to	**$7.50**
European design, rounded w/gold rim, from $4 to	**$6.00**
Frosted w/gold designs, from $6 to	**$8.00**
General, advertising, from $4 to	**$6.00**
General, enameled design, from $3 to	**$4.00**
General, etched design, from $5 to	**$7.50**
General, frosted design, from $3 to	**$5.00**
General, gold design, from $6 to	**$8.00**
General, porcelain, from $4 to	**$6.00**
Inside eyes, from $6 to	**$8.00**
Iridized silver, from $5 to	**$7.50**
Mary Gregory or Anchor Hocking Ships, from $150 to	**$200.00**
Nude, from $25 to	**$35.00**
Plain, w/or w/out flutes, from 50¢ to	**$.75**
Planet Hollywood/Hard Rock Cafe, from $10 to	**$12.50**
Pop or soda advertising, from $12 to	**$15.00**

Ruby flashed, from $35 to	**$50.00**
Sayings & toasts (1940s & 1950s), from $5 to	**$7.50**
Square, general, from $6 to	**$8.00**
Square, w/etching, from $10 to	**$12.50**
Square, w/pewter, from $12.50 to	**$15.00**
Square, w/2-tone bronze & pewter, from $15 to	**$17.50**
Standard glass w/pewter, from $7 to	**$10.00**
Steuben or Lalique crystal, from $150 to	**$200.00**
Tiffany, Galle or fancy art, from $600 to	**$8.00**
Tourist, colored glass, from $4 to	**$6.00**
Tourist, general, from $3 to	**$4.00**
Tourist, porcelain, from $3 to	**$5.00**
Tourist, Taiwan, from $2 to	**$3.00**
Tourist, turquoise & gold, from $6 to	**$8.00**
Whiskey or beer advertising, modern, from $5 to	**$7.50**
Whiskey sample, good condition, from $50 to	**$100.00**
Whiskey sample, M, from $75 to	**$350.00**
19th-century cut patterns, from $35 to	**$50.00**

Silhouette Pictures

These novelty pictures are familiar to everyone. Even today a good number of them are still around, and you'll often see them at flea markets and co-ops. They were very popular in their day and never expensive, and because they were made for so many years (the '20s through the '50s), many variations are available. Though the glass in some is flat, in others it is curved. Backgrounds may be foil, a scenic print, hand tinted, or plain. Sometimes dried flowers were added as accents. But the characteristic common to them all is that the subject matter is reverse painted on the glass. People (even complicated groups), scenes, ships, and animals were popular themes. Though quite often the silhouette was done in solid black to create a look similar to the nineteenth-century cut silhouettes, colors were sometimes used as well.

In the '20s, making tinsel art pictures became a popular pastime. Ladies would paint the outline of their subjects on the back of the glass and use crumpled tinfoil as a background. Sometimes they would tint certain areas of the glass, making the foil appear to be colored. This type is popular with with collectors of folk art.

If you'd like to learn more about this subject, we recommend *The Encyclopedia of Silhouette Collectibles on Glass; 1996 – 97 Price Guide for Encyclopedia of Silhouette Collectibles on Glass;* and *Vintage Silhouettes on Glass and Reverse Paintings* (copyright 2000, all new items pictured) by Shirley Mace. These books show examples of Benton Glass pictures with frames made of metal, wood, plaster, and plastic. The metal frames with the stripes are most favored by collectors as long as they are in good condition. Wood frames were actually considered deluxe when silhouettes were originally sold. Recently some convex glass silhouettes from Canada have been found, nearly identical to the ones made by Benton Glass except for their brown tape frames. Backgrounds seem to be slightly different as well. Among the flat glass silhouettes, the ones signed by Diefenbach are the most expensive. The wildflower pictures, especially ones with fine lines and good detail, are becoming popular with collectors.

The alphanumeric codes in the listings that follow indicate the maker (i.e., FI is Fisher, BG is Benton Glass), the next two numbers indicate the size (68 is 6" x 8"), and the number after the dash is an item number assigned by the author of the book we reference above.

Advisor: Shirley Mace (See Directory, Silhouette Pictures)

Convex Glass

Boy & his dog fishing, FI 44-2, dried wildflowers, marked Fisher **$30.00**

Boy stands beside girl in pumpkin, BG 45-233, Benton Glass . **$50.00**

Boy w/dog showing mother the fish he caught, BG 45-109, Benton Glass **$35.00**

Couple dancing in interior scene, she in ruffled gown, BG 68-264, Benton Glass...**$40.00**

Couple in cottage scene, BG 45-81, Benton Glass **$35.00**

Courting couple dancing in outdoor scene, BG 45-245, Benton Glass **$35.00**

Fence & tree, courting couple airbrushed background, Sandre, BG 68-407, Benton Glass **$30.00**

Indian maiden w/bow, colorful rocky Western scenic background (lithographic print), BG 68-347, Benton Glass.............**$65.00**

Lady & child w/cat, dark blue, BG 68-7B, Benton Glass.....**$60.00**

Lady looks upon well on hill, BG 45-182, Benton Glass **$30.00**

Snowland Splendor, deer watches man w/team of sled dogs, BA 45-2, advertising, Baco Glass Plaque, 1950 ....**$32.00**

Venetian gondola, colorful street scene background (lithographic print), BG 68-313, Benton Glass..................................**$45.00**

Woman shoots bow & arrow while man looks on, BG 45-77, Benton Glass..**$30.00**

Flat Glass

Couple before lake and cottage, Benton Glass, 5x4", $45.00.
(Photo courtesy Shirley and Ray Mace)

Beau Brummel, man in tails w/top hat & cane, RE 57-125, clear cellophane behind glass, Reliance Products **$18.00**

Boy & girl feeding ducks, AP 3 1/2 5-204, Art Publishing Co . **$40.00**

Child says prayers at bedtime w/dog, MF 34-37, unknown manufacturer **$20.00**

Elfin Music, RI 57-760, C&A Richards............................**$140.00**

Family scene before fireplace, NE 68-11, Newton...............**$28.00**

Girl chasing dog w/stolen doll, FL 44-1, Flowercraft **$30.00**

Goldilocks & the Three Bears, RE 711-3, Reliance Picture Frame Co...**$75.00**

Happy Bride, lady adjust veil for bride, BB 46-50, Buckbee-Brehm **$40.00**

My Mother, lady rocking, California wildflowers make up background, FI 68-22, Fisher Studios **$55.00**

Nude about to dive into water, LM 58-3, Lee Mero **$50.00**

Swan Pond, RE 711-2, Reliance Products **$30.00**

Terriers playing tug-of-war, RE-57-74, unmarked (Reliance Products)..**$18.00**

Silver-Plated and Sterling Flatware

The secondary market is being tapped more and more as the only source for those replacement pieces needed to augment family heirloom sets, and there are many collectors who admire the vintage flatware simply because they appreciate its beauty, quality, and affordability. Several factors influence pricing. For instance, a popular pattern though plentiful may be more expensive than a scarce one that might be passed over because it very likely would be difficult to collect. When you buy silverplate, condition is very important, since replating can be expensive.

Pieces with no monograms are preferred; in fact, newer monogrammed sterling is very hard to sell. Monograms seem to be better accepted on pieces over 100 years old. To evaluate monogrammed items, deduct 15% from fancy or rare examples; 30% from common, plain items; and 50% to 70% if they are worn.

Interest in silverplated flatware from the 1950s and 1960s is on the increase as the older patterns are becoming harder to find in excellent condition. As a result, prices are climbing.

Dinner knives range in size from 9⅜" to 10"; dinner forks from 7⅜" to 7¾". Luncheon knives are approximately 8½" to 8¾", while luncheon forks are about 6¾" to 7". Place knives measure 8⅞" to 9¼", and place forks 7⅛" to 7¼".

Our values are given for flatware in excellent condition. Matching services often advertise in various trade papers and can be very helpful in locating the items you're looking for.

If you'd like to learn more about the subject, we recommend *Silverplated Flatware* by Tere Hagan (Collector Books).

Advisor: Rick Spencer (See Directory, Regal)

Silver Plate

Adam, dinner knife, French handle, Community, 9¾" **$8.00**

Adam, fruit knife, Community **$9.50**

Adam, seafood fork, Community **$8.25**

Adam, tablespoon, Community **$7.00**

Ambassador, dinner knife, blunt, 1847 Rogers.....................**$8.00**

Ambassador, gumbo cream soup, 1847 Rogers, 7" **$8.50**

Bird of Paradise, dinner fork, Community, 7½"....................$5.00
Bird of Paradise, meat fork, Community, 8½" $12.00
Bird of Paradise, salad fork, Community $5.00
Bird of Paradise, sugar spoon, Community $2.75
Charter Oak, grapefruit spoon, 1847 Rogers $26.50
Charter Oak, luncheon fork, 1847 Rogers, 7" $14.50
Charter Oak, teaspoon, 1847 Rogers $13.00
Distinction, butter spreader, flat handle, Prestige $7.00
Distinction, meat fork, Prestige...$15.50
Distinction, oval soup, Prestige, 6¼" $8.25
Distinction, sugar spoon, Prestige $4.50
First Love, dinner fork, modern handle, 1847 Rogers, 9¼" .$12.00
First Love, iced teaspoon, 1947 Rogers $12.00
First Love, oval soup spoon, 1847 Rogers $6.00
First Love, tablespoon, 1847 Rogers...................................$7.25
Grosvenor, curved baby spoon, Community $10.00
Grosvenor, dinner knife, modern handle, Community, 9¼" .$6.00
Grosvenor, grill fork, Community.......................................$4.00
Grosvenor, salad fork, Community $6.00
Heritage, dinner fork, 1847 Rogers, 7½" $12.00
Heritage, dinner knife, modern handle, 1847 Rogers, 9¼"..$12.00
Heritage, master butter knife, 1847 Rogers..........................$4.75
Lady Hamilton, dinner fork, Community, 7½" $6.00
Lady Hamilton, grill knife, French handle, Community........$4.75
Lady Hamilton, iced teaspoon, Community $7.25
Marquise, dinner knife, French handle, 1847 Rogers, 9½" ..$10.00
Marquise, grill knife, modern handle, 1847 Rogers..............$9.50
Marquise, master butter knife, 1847 Rogers..........................$5.00
Marquise, salad fork, 1847 Rogers $10.50
Morning Star, grill fork, Community...................................$8.50
Morning Star, oval soup spoon, Community $6.00
Morning Star, salad/dessert fork, Community, 6¼" $7.25
Nobless, dinner fork, Community, 7½" $7.25
Nobless, dinner knife, French handle, Community, 9½" $8.50
Nobless, grill fork, Community $6.00
Nobless, tablespoon, Community $12.00
Patrician, dinner fork, Community, 7¾" $6.00
Patrician, gravy ladle, Community.....................................$18.00
Patrician, master butter knife, Community...........................$4.75
Patrician, teaspoon, Community $2.50
Queen Bess 1946, dinner fork, Oneida, 7½" $4.75
Queen Bess 1946, dinner knife, Oneida, 9½".......................$6.00
Queen Bess 1946, tablespoon, Oneida..................................$6.00
Queen Bess 1946, teaspoon, Oneida....................................$1.50
Remembrance, grill fork, 1847 Rogers, 7½" $11.00
Remembrance, iced teaspoon, 1847 Rogers $8.50
Remembrance, master butter knife, 1847 Rogers...................$2.50
Remembrance, roast carving set, 1847 Rogers, 2-pc............$90.00
Remembrance, sugar spoon, 1847 Rogers $3.75
Silhouette, dinner fork, 1847 Rogers, 7½"............................$6.00
Silhouette, grill fork, 1847 Rogers......................................$4.75
Silhouette, master butter spreader, 1847 Rogers....................$3.50
Silhouette, salad fork, 1847 Rogers $6.00
Tiger Lily, dinner knife, French handle, Reed & Barton, 9".$13.00
Tiger Lily, luncheon fork, Reed & Barton, 7" $11.00
Tiger Lily, meat fork, Reed & Barton..................................$27.50
Tiger Lily, salad fork, Reed & Barton..................................$13.00

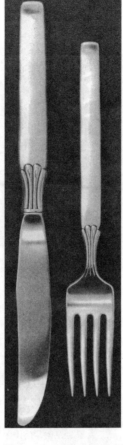

Twilight, Community, 1958: dinner knife, from $8.00 to $12.00; dinner fork, from $8.00 to $12.00. (Photo courtesy Francis Bones and Lee Roy Fisher)

Vintage, cream soup, 1847 Rogers $28.00
Vintage, dinner knife, hollow handle, 1847 Rogers.............$30.00
Vintage, luncheon knife, hollow handle, 1847 Rogers, 8½" ...$24.00
Vintage, table serving spoon, 1847 Rogers..........................$18.00
Vintage, teaspoon, 1847 Rogers...$11.00
White Orchid, cream soup, Community, 7" $8.50
White Orchid, demitasse spoon, Community.........................$5.00
White Orchid, meat fork, Community $20.00
White Orchid, teaspoon, Community $3.50
Wildwood, bouillon soup, Reliance Plate, 5½" $12.00
Wildwood, fruit knife, flat handle, Reliance Plate...............$12.00
Wildwood, fruit knife, hollow handle, Reliance Plate $18.00
Wildwood, melon spoon, round pointed bowl, Reliance Plate . $14.50
Wildwood, sauce ladle, Reliance Plate................................$24.00
Wildwood, seafood fork, Reliance Plate $14.50
Wind Song, butter spreader, flat handle, Nobility.................$8.50
Wind Song, demitasse spoon, Nobility $7.25
Wind Song, gravy ladle, Nobility.......................................$19.00
Wind Song, master butter Spreader, Nobility........................$6.00
Wind Song, seafood fork, Nobility......................................$8.50
Wind Song, sugar spoon, Nobility.......................................$3.75

Sterling

Afterglow, cream soup, Oneida $19.50
Afterglow, gravy ladle, Oneida...$34.50
Afterglow, tablespoon, Oneida $27.00
Afterlow, butter spreader, flat handle, Oneida $15.00
Alexandra, cocktail fork, Lunt..$25.00

Alexandra, place fork, Lunt, 7⅜" $25.00

Alexandra, sugar spoon, Lunt $21.00

Alexandra, teaspoon, Lunt $21.00

Andante, iced teaspoon, Gorham $35.00

Andante, salad fork, Gorham $34.00

Andante, teaspoon, Gorham $18.50

Angelique, butter knife, hollow handle, International $17.25

Angelique, place fork, International $24.00

Angelique, teaspoon, International $16.00

Angelique, youth knife, International $18.50

Autumn Leaves, iced teaspoon, Reed & Barton $26.50

Autumn Leaves, pie server, Reed & Barton $27.50

Autumn Leaves, place spoon, Reed & Barton $25.50

Autumn Leaves, teaspoon, Reed & Barton $15.00

Autumnn Leaves, sugar spoon, Reed & Barton $17.25

Bridal Rose, cold meat fork, 7⅝" $155.00

Bridal Rose, grapefruit spoon, Alvin $37.00

Bridal Rose, salad fork, Alvin, 5⅞" $125.00

Bridal Rose, serving fork, 7½" $250.00

Camellia, butter spreader, flat handle, Gorham $14.00

Camellia, dessert spoon, Gorham, 6¾" $36.00

Camellia, pickle fork, Gorham $18.50

Camellia, sugar spoon, Gorham $16.00

Chantilly, bonbon, Gorham $37.00

Chantilly, butter spreader, flat handle, Gorham $27.50

Chantilly, salad fork, Gorham, 6½" $27.50

Chapel Bells, bouillon spoon, Alvin $26.50

Chapel Bells, butter knife, flat handle, Alvin $17.00

Chapel Bells, iced teaspoon, Alvin $12.50

Chapel Bells, salad fork, Alvin $17.00

Chateau Rose, dinner fork, Alvin, 7⅞" $31.00

Chateau Rose, gravy ladle, Alvin $48.00

Chateau Rose, luncheon fork, Alvin $24.00

Chateau Rose, teaspoon, Alvin $13.75

Damask Rose, cold meat fork, Oneida, 8⅛" $40.00

Damask Rose, luncheon fork, Oneida, 7¼" $23.00

Damask Rose, luncheon knife, modern handle, Oneida, 8¾" . $20.00

Damask Rose, salad fork, Oneida $23.00

Damask Rose, tablespoon, Oneida $37.00

Devonshire, dinner fork, International, 7¾" $27.50

Devonshire, gumbo spoon, International, 7" $22.00

Devonshire, teaspoon, International, 5¾" $10.00

El Grande, butter knife, hollow handle, Towle $23.00

El Grande, sugar spoon, Towle $29.00

El Grande, tablespoon, Towle $67.00

El Grande, teaspoon, Towle $21.00

Enchantress, dinner fork, International, 7⅞" $29.00

Enchantress, gravy ladle, Internationsl $35.00

Enchantress, luncheon fork, International, 7¼" $26.50

Fontana, cold meat fork, Towle, 9⅛" $48.50

Fontana, gravy ladle, Towle $42.00

Fontana, place fork, Towle $25.00

Fontana, sugar spoon, Towle $15.00

Georgian Rose, iced teaspoon, Reed & Barton $23.00

Georgian Rose, salad fork, Reed & Barton $20.00

Georgian Rose, teaspoon, Reed & Barton $15.00

Griswold, butter spreader, flat handle, Gorham $12.50

Griswold, tablespoon, Gorham $30.00

Griswold, teaspoon, Gorham, 5⅜" $8.50

King Cedric, butter spreader, flat handle, Oneida $14.00

King Cedric, cold meat fork, Oneida, 8" $34.00

King Cedric, teaspoon, Oneida $15.00

Lady Diana, demitasse spoon, Towle $7.00

Lady Diana, dessert spoon, Towle, 7" $30.00

Lady Diana, salad fork, Towle $18.50

Lady Diana, sugar tongs, Towle $27.50

Lasting Spring, cream soup spoon, Oneida, 6½" $18.50

Lasting Spring, luncheon fork, Oneida, 7⅛" $22.00

Lasting Spring, sugar spoon, Oneida $15.00

Madeira, cocktail fork, Towle $16.00

Madeira, lemon fork, Towle $17.00

Madeira, place fork, Towle $18.50

Madeira, sugar spoon, Towle $15.00

Mary Chilton, dessert spoon, Towle, 7⅜" $29.00

Mary Chilton, gravy ladle, Towle $37.00

Mary Chilton, teaspoon, Towle, 5¾" $10.00

Mt Vernon, cream ladle, Lunt $31.00

Mt Vernon, salad fork, Lunt, 6⅛" $22.00

Mt Vernon, teaspoon, Lunt, 5¾" $14.00

Old Mirror, oval spoon, Towle, 6¾" $40.00

Old Mirror, salad fork, Towle $22.00

Old Mirror, tablespoon, Towle $44.00

Rambler Rose, cocktail fork, Towle $11.50

Rambler Rose, cream soup, Towle $20.00

Rambler Rose, grapefruit spoon, Towle $20.00

Rambler Rose, tablespoon, Towle $38.50

Rondo, butter knife, hollow handle, Gorham $24.00

Rondo, cold meat fork, Gorham $57.00

Rondo, knife, modern handle, Gorham, 8¾" $23.00

Rondo, place spoon, Gorham, 6¾" $32.00

Silver Flutes, iced tea spoon, Towle $21.00

Silver Flutes, luncheon knife, Towle $24.00

Silver Flutes, sugar spoon, Towle $15.00

Southwind, gravy ladle, Towle $34.50

Southwind, place fork, Towle, 7½" $24.00

Southwind, sugar spoon, Towle $15.00

Sweetheart Rose, butter spreader, flat handle, Lunt $11.50

Sweetheart Rose, place fork, Lunt, 7¼" $22.00

Sweetheart Rose, tablespoon, Lunt $46.00

Waltz of Spring, cold meat fork, Wallace $62.50

Waltz of Spring, place knife, Wallace $31.00

Waltz of Spring, teaspoon, Wallace $18.50

Waltz of Spring, salad fork, Wallace $31.00

Skookum Indian Dolls

The Skookums Apple Packers Association of Wenatchee, Washington, had a doll made for their trademark. Skookum figures were designed and registered by a Montana woman, Mary McAboy, in 1917. Although she always made note of the Skookums name, she also used the 'Bully Good' trademark along with other information to inform the buyer that 'Bully Good' translated is 'Skookums.' McAboy had an article published in the March 1920 issue of *Playthings* magazine explaining the history of Skookum dolls. Anyone interested can obtain this information on microfilm from any large library.

In 1920 the Arrow Novelty Company held the contract to make the dolls, but by 1929 the H.H. Tammen Company had taken over their production. Skookums were designed with life-like facial characteristics. The dried apple heads of the earliest dolls did not last, and they were soon replaced with heads made of a composition material. Wool blankets formed the bodies that were then stuffed with dried twigs, leaves, and grass. The remainder of the body was cloth and felt.

Skookum dolls with wooden legs and felt-covered wooden feet were made between 1917 and 1949. After 1949 the legs and feet were made of plastic. The newest dolls have plastic heads. A 'Skookums Bully Good Indians' paper label was placed on one foot of each early doll. Exact dating of a Skookum is very difficult. McAboy designed many different tribes of dolls simply by using different blanket styles, beading, and backboards (for carrying the papoose). The eyes are almost always looking to the right. The store display dolls, 36" and larger, are the most valuable of the Skookums. Prices range from $1,000.00 to $1,500.00 per doll or $2,500.00 to $3,000.00 for the pair. Beware of imitations, they are not not as desirable or valuable as the originals.

Advisor: Jo Ann Palmieri (See Directory Skookum Dolls)

Child, plastic legs, 6" to 8", from $25 to **$35.00**
Child, plastic legs, 8" to 10", from $35 to **$50.00**
Child, wooden legs, 6½", from $50 to................................**$60.00**
Female, wooden legs, 13½", from $150 to......................**$200.00**
Female, wooden legs, 16", from $200 to..........................**$300.00**
Female w/papoose, wooden legs, 8" to 10", from $50 to **$75.00**
Female w/papoose, wooden legs, 10" to 12", from $75 to .**$100.00**
Female w/papoose, wooden legs, 14" to 16", from $175 to..**$200.00**

Male, wooden legs, 14", $175.00; Male, wooden legs, 12", $150.00.

Male, wooden legs, 8" to 10", from $75 to.......................**$100.00**

Male, wooden legs, 10 to 12", from $100 to.....................**$125.00**
Male, wooden legs, 14" to 16", from $175 to...................**$300.00**

Smiley Face

The Smiley Face was designed in 1963 by Harvey Ball, a commercial artist that had been commissioned by an insurance company to design a 'happy' logo to use on office supplies and pin-back buttons — seems spirits were low due to unpopular company policies, and the office manager was looking for something that would cheer up employees. 'Operation Smile' was a huge success. Who would have thought that such a simple concept — tiny eyes with a curving line to represent a big smile in black on a bright yellow background — would have become the enduring icon that it did. Mr. Ball was paid a mere $45.00 for his efforts, and no one even bothered to obtain a trademark for Smiley! Over the years, many companies have designed scores of products featuring the happy face. The McCoy Pottery Company was one of them; they made a line of cookie jars, mugs, banks, and planters. No matter if you collect Smiley or McCoy, you'll want to watch for those!

Today, the Smiley face is enjoying renewed popularity. You'll find 'new' examples in nearly any specialty catalog. But if you buy the vintage Smileys, expect to pay several times their original retail price.

Advisor: Pam Speidel (See Directory, Smiley Face)

Mug, Anchor Hocking, Fire-King, from $50.00 to $60.00.

Bank, yellow, McCoy, 6", metal stopper................................**$35.00**
Bank, 2 Smiley figures holding yellow Smiley heart, ceramic, yellow w/black details, 1990s repro...**$22.50**
Ceiling lamp fixture, white w/yellow & orange faces, 1970s, 14" dia, EX **$25.00**
Clock, alarm; face in dial, wind-up, Westclox **$25.00**
Clock, yellow w/Have a Happy Day in black, electric, Emdeko, 7" dia, EX...**$17.50**
Cookie jar, yellow w/Have a Happy Day on base, marked McCoy 235 USA, 1970s, 11", from $50 to............................**$100.00**
Cuff links, yellow w/black features, pr...................................**$30.00**
Dashboard hula dancer, Smiley figure in grass skirt, 5", MIB.**$20.00**
Lamp, swag; yellow plastic, 1990s, 140" chain, 13" dia **$50.00**
Lighter, Scripto-Vu, yellow face on white.............................**$80.00**
Mug, ceramic, w/Happy Birthday on hat lid, Teleflora, 1990s .**$20.00**

Mug, green & black faces on milk glass, unmarked............... $7.50

Mug, white w/red eyes & mouth (same mold as yellow mug), McCoy, 1970s, 4".. $16.00

Mugs, yellow, McCoy USA, 1970s, 4⅞", set of 4 .... $65.00

Napkin holder, yellow plastic w/gold glitter, notched for napkins on sides, EX.. $40.00

Patio light set, 3 white, 2 yellow & 2 red ones, all w/green eyes, 1970s, 7" dia (ea), EX................................ $14.00

Planter/flowerpot, attached saucer, McCoy, #0386, 1970s, 4¼" . $20.00

Spoon rest, Have a Happy Day below smiling bowl, Treasure Craft copyright USA, 1970s................................ $30.00

Tennis shoes, white w/overall faces, Jantzen, 1970s, EX, pr.. $15.00

Tumblers, plastic, 1970s, 5½", set of 8 .... $20.00

Snow Domes

Snow dome collectors buy them all, old and new. The older ones (from the '30s and '40s) are made in two pieces, the round glass globe that sits on a separate base. They were made here as well as in Italy, and today this type is being imported from Austria and the Orient.

During the '50s, plastic snow domes made in West Germany were popular as souvenirs and Christmas toys. Some were half-domes with blue backs; others were made in bottle shapes or simple geometric forms.

There were two styles produced in the seventies. Both were made of plastic. The first were designed as large domes with a plastic figure of an animal, a mermaid, or some other character draped over the top. In the other style, the snow dome itself was made in an unusual shape.

Christmas tree, 1976, $25.00.

Balto promotional, from Universal animated film, 1995, MIB. $95.00

Beauty & the Beast's Belle, Disney Store, 7x7".................... $60.00

Busch Stadium in glass globe on wooden base, plays Take Me Out to the Ball Game, 6" $42.50

Charlie Brown & Snoopy standing by Christmas tree, musical, 6", MIB.. $35.00

Dallas landmarks on glass dome, plays Yellow Rose of Texas, Saks 5th Avenue, 6½x4½" dia................................ $50.00

Elephant pr w/trunks up, glass dome, Endangered Species on ceramic base w/2 elephants, plays How Great Thou Art $45.00

Goofy riding carousel horse playing banjo, musical, EX...... $20.00

Jiminy Cricket, glass globe on wooden base, NE The First Limited Edition Disney Crystal Snow Globe Collection, 4" $65.00

Lone Ranger Round-Up, Lone Ranger w/lasso (dexterity game), Driss Co, copyright TLR Inc, 4" $165.00

Mickey Mouse seated w/globe between legs, marked Walt Disney Productions, 5", EX+ $30.00

Phantom of the Opera, San Francisco Music Box & Gift Co, China... $45.00

Phantom of the Opera Music of the Night sheet music w/rose & mask in globe, stage base, San Francisco Music Box Co, MIB... $60.00

Santa, figural w/dome in belly, plastic, 6", EX $17.50

Santa & Mrs Claus on red brick fireplace, red & white plastic, dome in base, Made in Hong Kong, #8827, 5x4" $12.50

Santa w/deer across his shoulders, dome in belly, plastic, Hong Kong, #758, 1960s, 5¼"................................... $18.00

Souvenir, Crystal Cave, PA, plastic, 2¼" $14.00

Souvenir, Paris buildings, plastic, Made in France, 2¼x3" ... $20.00

Souvenir, 2 Mexican men sleeping on seesaw, Mexico, plastic, Made in Hong Kong No 354-V, 1970s, 2¾x4"..................... $22.00

Wicked Witch from Oz, holds w/Dorothy & Toto inside, Warner Bros, 8"... $75.00

50 Years of Leadership American Household Storage 1903-1953, glass globe on black plastic base, 4x3x3"................. $85.00

Soda-Pop Memorabilia

A specialty area of the advertising field, soft-drink memorabilia is a favorite of many collectors. Now that vintage Coca-Cola items have become rather expensive, interest is expanding to include some of the less widely exploited sodas — Grapette, Hires Root Beer, and Dr. Pepper, for instance.

For further information we recommend *Collectible Soda Pop Memorabilia* by B.J. Summers (Collector Books). In the listings that follow, values are given for items in at least near-mint condition.

See also Coca-Cola; Pepsi-Cola.

Advisor: Craig Stifter (See Directory, Soda-Pop Collectibles)

Club: National Pop Can Collectors

Newsletter: Can-O-Gram
Bruce Mobley, Director
P.O. Box 163
Macon, MO 63552-0163
http://members.tripod.com/sodacans/

A&W Root Beer, mug, Snoopy serving mug, multicolor enameling on clear glass, United Feature Syndicate, 6"................. $85.00

A&W Root Beer, sign, porcelain over steel, 12" dia, EX......**$35.00**

Bireley's, bottle cap, Drink Bireley's Grapefruit Flavor, cork lined, EX **$27.50**

Bireley's, thermometer, tin litho, bottle of orange soda on white, 16x6", VG **$55.00**

Bubble Up, sign, tin litho, green & white, 1960s, 12x30" .**$130.00**

Bubble Up, sign, tin litho, red & white lettering & bubbles on green, Press Sign Co, 12x28", EX..........................**$110.00**

Bubble Up, thermometer, green painted metal, 17x5", EX ..**$75.00**

Canada Dry, picnic cooler, painted metal w/embossed logo on front & back, tray inside, 14x20x10½" **$50.00**

Canada Dry, sign, tin, Drink Canada Dry, yellow & white lettering on green, 12x30", EX **$65.00**

Canada Dry, sign, tin die-cut shield & crown, 1950s, 14⅜x14¾", EX **$40.00**

Canada Dry, thermometer, convex glass front, aluminum frame, Made in USA, 1950s, 12" dia..........................**$165.00**

Cliquoit Club Pale Ginger Ale, thermometer, tin litho, 1950s, 13½x5¾", EX..**$140.00**

Dad's Root Beer, bottle topper, cardboard litho, winking boy, 11¾x7½" **$32.00**

Dad's Root Beer, crate, wooden w/printing on side, metal strapping, 10¼x18x13", EX **$22.50**

Dad's Root Beer, star, tin, Fastest Straw in the West, 6 points, EX **$12.00**

Dad's Root Beer, thermometer, tin litho, Just Right for Dad's, ca 1951, 26", EX..**$135.00**

Dad's Root Beer, tin sign, You'll Love Dad's..., bottle-cap shape, 29" dia..**$110.00**

Diet-Rite Cola, sign, tin litho, bottle at left of Diet-Rite cola (lower case) on yellow, 12x32", EX..........................**$160.00**

Diet-Rite Cola, sign, tin litho, Enjoy Sugar Free..., rectangular, 1961, 12x32", EX..**$80.00**

Dog 'n Suds Root Beer, clock, dog serving hot dog & frosty mug, aluminum case, convex glass front, round, NM..........**$350.00**

Donald Duck Cola, sign, cardboard standup, Tops For Flavour, 1950s, 26", NM, from $165.00 to $185.00.

Double Cola, clock, convex glass in black frame, Ingraham, 1953, 8½" dia, EX..**$95.00**

Double Cola, sign, tin flange, Enjoy..., 22x18", EX..........**$415.00**

Double Cola, sign, tin litho, A Great Drink... w/in sunburst & a Mighty Flavor, 1937, 18x40", EX..........................**$195.00**

Double Cola, sign, tin litho, Drink Double Cola in oval, red, white & light blue, 11¾x31¾", EX **$165.00**

Dr Pepper, bottle opener, metal wall-mount type, 3x2", VG **$62.50**

Dr Pepper, bullet pencil/bottle opener, EX..........................**$65.00**

Dr Pepper, clock, double bubble, Dr Pepper Co limited edition, 15" dia, NMIB..**$225.00**

Dr Pepper, clock, glass front, diamond shape, Pam, 1950s, 15", EX..**$215.00**

Dr Pepper, cooler, metal w/plastic handles, red lettering on green, Progress Refrigerator Co, 1950s?, 13x22", EX **$165.00**

Dr Pepper, ice chest, wood w/rope handles, red lettering, 1885-1985, EX..**$50.00**

Dr Pepper, mug, Serve Dr Pepper Hot, red lettering on white glass, Fire-King..**$55.00**

Dr Pepper, sign, porcelain, resembles brick wall, 1940s, 10½x26⅛", EX **$215.00**

Dr Pepper, sign, tin litho, bottle, 10-2-4 on yellow, 55x18", G **$110.00**

Dr Pepper, thermometer, glass front, red & blue on white, Pam, 1960s, 12" dia..**$285.00**

Dr Pepper, thermometer, Hot or Cold, Pam, 18" dia........**$240.00**

Dr Pepper, thermometer, tin litho, Hot or Cola, red & white, 1970s, 12x7" **$145.00**

Frostie Root Beer, menu board, tin & blackboard, 1950s, 30x19½", EX **$95.00**

Frostie Root Beer, mug, lettering on clear glass, 5½" **$18.00**

Frostie Root Beer, sign, embossed metal, Frosty showing carved log, 1950s, 13½x19½", EX **$175.00**

Frostie Root Beer, sign, plastic, figure holding sign, 1950s, 12x13" **$120.00**

Frostie Root Beer, thermometer, convex glass front w/metal frame, 12" dia, EX..**$110.00**

Frostie Root Beer, thermometer, tin litho, The Family Favorite & mug on white, 1950s, 12x3¼"..........................**$145.00**

Frostie Root Beer, thermometer, tin litho w/bottle cap on white, 1980s, Stout Sign Co, 30x7", EX+ **$80.00**

Grapette, bank, clear glass cat figural, clown lid w/slot, 6¼".**$48.00**

Grapette, bottle, clown figural, holds concentrated syrup, slot in lid for use as bank, 1950s, EX+..........................**$35.00**

Grapette, bottle carrier, cardboard litho, holds 6-pack of 6-oz bottles, 1950s, EX..**$25.00**

Grapette, sidewalk marker, solid brass, 1930s, 4"..............**$30.00**

Grapette, sign, cardboard, lady at pool's edge, bottle before her, aluminum frame, 1940s, 23x34½", EX..........................**$110.00**

Grapette, sign, tin litho, black & white w/red border, oval, 1956, 10x17" **$355.00**

Grapette, thermometer, tin litho, bottle on white, 1960s, 16x6", EX **$125.00**

Grapette, thermometer, tin litho, Thirsty or Not, 1950s, 14⅞x5⅞" **$100.00**

Grapette Soda, cardboard, girl in wedding dress, 20x31½", EX **$165.00**

Hires, menu board, tin litho top, 29x15", EX....................**$175.00**

Hires, sign, tin litho, Drink...in Bottles on blue & white stripes, bottle cap form, 35" dia, EX..........................**$285.00**

Hires, sign, tin litho, Enjoy..., girl in red cap on blue, 1930s, 10x28", EX..**$220.00**

Hires, sign, tin, 24" diameter, EX, $150.00.

Hires Root Beer, thermometer, bubble glass front, 2½x12" dia...$98.00

Hires Root Beer, thermometer, tin litho, multicolor on white, 1950s, 27x8¼", EX...$225.00

Hires Root Beer, thermometer, tin litho bottle shape, 28½x7½".$85.00

Kist Beverages, clock, convex glass front, diamond shape, Pam, 1961, 15", EX..$135.00

Kist Beverages, clock, diamond shape, Pam, 1961, 15½", EX. $165.00

Kist Beverages, clock, It's Kist Time, bubble glass front, 16" dia, EX...$250.00

Kist Beverages, mirror, Refreshing Anytime & lips, 12x12". $65.00

Kist Beverages, sign, porcelain over metal w/flange, 14x18", VG... $250.00

Kist Beverages, soda can, Kist Orange Soda, heavy steel, open flat top, 1950s, 12 fluid oz, EX...$17.50

Kist Orange Soda, thermometer, tin litho, multicolor on black, 16x6", EX..$90.00

Mission Orange of California, sign, tin litho, embossed bottles & lettering, 12x30", EX...$110.00

Mountain Dew, soda jerk hat, hillbilly, red, white & green, 1960s...$30.00

Moxie, hand fan, cardboard litho, Moxie boy & boy on rocking horse w/letters TNT on boy's hat, copyright 1922, EX.$40.00

Moxie, sign, tin litho, Drink Moxie Distinctively Different, Donaldson, 19x27", EX...$215.99

Nehi, bottle opener, metal, wall mount, Starr Patd X Reg, early, EX.. $110.00

Nehi, menu board, embossed tin litho top, 1950s, 27½x19¾", EX... $95.00

Nehi, sign, cardboard litho, Nehi Square Deal Service, lady's legs & bottle, 8x9½", VG...$35.00

Nehi, sign, paper litho, girl rowing boat, 1938, 18½x11¼", EX. $165.00

Nehi, sign, tin litho, Drink Genuine..., bottle at left of lady's leg's, 11¼x16¾", EX...$35.00

Nehi, tray, girl in red swimsuit in ocean wave & bottle, rectangular, 1920s, VG $110.00

Nesbitt's, thermometer, Don't Say Orange Say..., professor & lg soda bottle at top, 22½"...$165.00

Nesbitt's, thermometer, tin litho, orange bottle on white (left side), 16x6", EX..$115.00

NuGrape, clock, bottle & logo, round convex glass face, lights up, Telechron, 1950s, EX...$150.00

NuGrape, clock, NuGrape Soda on white, 2¾x9" dia.........$85.00

NuGrape, sign, paper die-cut, girl standing in boat w/bottle in hand, 1930s, 31½x21", EX $185.00

NuGrape, thermometer, Have Fun w/(NuGrape bottle) on white, Made in USA, 12" dia, EX...$75.00

NuGrape, thermometer, tin litho, Have Fun w/... & bottle on white, 1960s, 12" dia, NM...$135.00

NuGrape, tray, tin litho, hand holding bottle on green, American Art Works, rim chips, VG...$45.00

NuGrape soda, tray, tin litho, hand holding bottle, American Art Works, 1920s, 13¼x10½", EX.....................................$27.50

Orange-Crush, bottle opener, metal, wall mount, Made in USA, Starr, Patd Apr 1925, EX...$40.00

Orange-Crush, menu board, tin litho top, 26½" L, EX.......$60.00

Orange-Crush, sign, steel & iron, shows ribbed bottle, F Robertson, 1927, 35x9", VG...$275.00

Orange-Crush, sign, tin bottle cap form, mounts to wall, 39" dia, EX...$665.00

Orange-Crush, thermometer, bubble glass front, Pam, 12" dia, NM...$295.00

Orange-Crush, thermometer, metal bottle form, 28".........$185.00

Orange-Crush, thermometer, tin litho, bottle cap at top on green, 14½x5½"...$135.00

Orange-Crush, thermometer, tin litho, bottle cap at top on green, 14½x5½", EX...$95.00

Quiky, thermometer, tin litho, Grapefruit Kissed w/Lemon..., 14x5"...$165.00

Royal Crown Cola, clock, convex glass front, Best by Taste Test, 15" dia, EX...$425.00

Royal Crown Cola, clock, Drink..., glass front, wooden frame, sq, 16x16", EX...$385.00

Royal Crown Cola, clock, glass front, diamond shape, Pam, 1963 ....$185.00

Royal Crown Cola, cooler, metal, red letters embossed on yellow, bail handle, tray inside, 15¾x18x8⅞", EX.........................$85.00

Royal Crown Cola, cooler, painted metal, red lettering on yellow, VG...$85.00

Royal Crown Cola, menu board, embossed tin top, red, white & blue, 28x19¾", EX...$75.00

Royal Crown Cola, sign, embossed tin litho, Best by Taste-Test on red, 22x52", EX...$875.00

Royal Crown Cola, sign, tin litho bottle shape, Donaldson, 1953, 58½" H, G...$165.00

Royal Crown Cola, thermometer, tin litho, Best by Taste-Test, ca 1947, 25½x9½", EX...$155.00

Royal Crown Cola, thermometer, tin litho, bottle at right on yellow, 1930s, 13½x5¾", EX.....................................$195.00

Royal Crown Cola, thermometer, tin litho, Enjoy RC on white, minor rust, 26x10", VG...$48.00

Royal Crown Cola, thermometer, tin litho, red & cream, Donasco, 1957, 25½x10", EX...$85.00

Seven-Up, clock, glass front, wooden frame, sq, 4½x16x16", EX. $175.00

Seven-Up, clock, You Like It..., glass front in sq oak frame, 1950s, EX...$115.00

Seven-Up, door push, painted aluminum, EX....................$175.00

Seven-Up, menu board, hand pouring bottle above blackboard, 1950s, 27½x19½"...$165.00

Seven-Up, sign, tin litho, Fresh Up, 1956, 13x6½", NM...$200.00

Seven-Up, sign, tin litho, Fresh Up w/7-Up & bubbles on oval, 40x30", EX...$300.00

Seven-Up, sign, tin litho, tilted logo on white, 12x14", EX+..**$165.00**

Seven-Up, sign, tin litho, Uncola & rainbow, 12x24", EX..**$155.00**

Seven-Up, sign, tin litho, 7-Up! Likes You, triangular (resembles pennant), 8¼x10½", EX............................**$70.00**

Seven-Up, thermometer, convex glass w/aluminum frame, black & red on white, round, VG **$60.00**

Seven-Up, thermometer, tin litho, lg green bottle on right, 15x6", EX **$150.00**

Seven-Up, thermometer, tin litho, logo on black, 20x5", EX..**$100.00**

Sprite, thermometer, green plastic, light fading, 18x7", EX..**$35.00**

Squirt, cooler, metal, red lettering on yellow, Progress Refrigerator, 1950s, 14½x19½x10", EX.......................**$360.00**

Squirt, cooler, tin, red lettering embossed on yellow, w/original sandwich tray, 18½x19x13", EX **$135.00**

Squirt, menu board, boy & bottle on yellow above blackboard, 23¾x19½", EX.......................................**$90.00**

Squirt, menu board, 1950, 28x20", EX, $150.00.

Squirt, sign, tin flange, Switch to Squirt on yellow, 1955, 13½x17½", EX **$250.00**

Squirt, sign, tin litho, character boy showing bottle, multicolor, 1959, 10½x14", G.................................**$75.00**

Squirt, thermometer, tin litho, bottle & name on white (no boy shown), 1977, 13½x5¾", EX **$70.00**

Squirt, thermometer, tin litho, boy & bottle on white, ca 1960s, 13½x5¾", EX.......................................**$90.00**

Squirt, thermometer, tin litho, red, white, yellow & green, 1961, 13½x5¾"...**$385.00**

Sun Crest, bottle topper, cardboard litho, 1950s, 7½x9½" ..**$37.50**

Sun Crest, clock, blue & white lettering on orange, convex glass, 8" dia, G...**$60.00**

Vernor's Ginger Ale, sign, tin litho, man in round reserve, 6x18", EX **$70.00**

Whistle, door push, painted metal, adjusts from 30" to 36" in length, EX...**$130.00**

Whistle, sign, cardboard die-cut bottle, 1951, 30x11" **$250.00**

Whistle, sign, cardboard litho, girl between 2 lg bottles, 1940s, 26x34", EX...**$155.00**

Whistle, sign, metal bottle cap, Thirsty Just Whistle, red, white & blue, 3x28" dia **$150.00**

Whistle, sign, tin litho, blue & white lettering on orange, 1948, 4x21½", NM...**$220.00**

Whistle, thermometer, elf pushing cart holding bottle, Pam, 12" dia, EX **$400.00**

Wink, thermometer, tin litho, bottle at right, 26½x9", EX..**$95.00**

Soda Bottles With Painted Labels

The earliest type of soda bottles were made by soda producers and sold in the immediate vicinity of the bottling company. Many had pontil scars, left by a rod that was used to manipulate the bottle as it was blown. They had a flat bottom rather than a 'kick-up,' so for transport, they were laid on their side and arranged in layers. This served to keep the cork moist, which kept it expanded, tight, and in place. Upright the cork would dry out, shrink, and expel itself with a 'pop,' hence the name 'soda pop.'

Until the '30s, the name of the product or the bottler was embossed in the glass or printed on a paper label (sometimes pasted over reused returnable bottles). Though a few paper labels were used as late as the '60s, nearly all bottles produced from the mid-'30s on had painted-on (pyro-glazed) lettering, and logos and pictures were often added. Imaginations ran rampant. Bottlers waged a fierce competition to make their soda logos eye-catching and sales inspiring. Anything went! Girls, airplanes, patriotic designs, slogans proclaiming amazing health benefits, even cowboys and Indians became popular advertising ploys. This is the type you'll encounter most often today, and collector interest is on the increase. Look for interesting, multicolored labels, rare examples from small-town bottlers, and those made from glass in colors other than clear or green.

Ace UP, green glass, 2 dice, Ft Wayne IN, 1952, 12-oz........**$25.00**

Amber glass, ca. 1954 – 1965, any shown, $125.00. (Photo courtesy Thomas Marsh)

Beehive Beverages, clear glass, Bringham City UT, 1970s, 10-oz..**$27.50**

Big Chief Soda Water, clear glass, McAllen TX, 1950s, 9-oz ..**$30.00**

Bubble Up, green glass, 8.45-oz **$15.00**

Canada Dry Ginger Ale, green glass, Worland WY, 1955, 1-pt 12-oz (rare size) $65.00

Canada Dry Ginger Ale, Worland WY, green glass, 1-pt 12-oz $65.00

Canada Dry Pale Ginger Ale, green glass, w/gold foil, 12-oz ..$35.00

Cleo Soda, Cleopatra on green, dated 1935, 12-oz $185.00

Clicquot Club, green glass, Leverenz Bottling, w/cap, qt......$75.00

Col Albert Lea, clear glass, 7½-oz...$20.00

Country Club, clear glass, golfing scene, Daytona Beach FL, 1963, 7-oz..$27.50

Crush, clear glass, 1956, 10-oz...$12.00

Cub Beverages, clear glass, bear cub, 1947, 7-oz $40.00

Dad's Root Beer, brown glass, Junior on neck, 10-oz $10.00

Dad's Root Beer, brown glass, w/cap, 1-qt, 10".....................$22.00

Donald Duck Cola, clear glass, w/cap, 1950s, 7-oz..............$28.00

Double Line Cola, clear glass, 10-oz $8.00

Dr Pepper, slant bottle cap design on clear glass, 1955, unopened $145.00

Flambeau Beverages, clear glass, Indian in canoe, 7⅞" $40.00

Fox Valley Beverage Co, clear glass, red fox, 7-oz $40.00

Fudgy, amber glass, Marby's Beverage Co, 1956, 6-oz..........$65.00

Hamilton, clear glass, 1490s, 12-oz......................................$32.00

Kist Beverages, green glass, 28-oz...$15.00

Lemon Cola, clear glass, boy making drink, 1940, 7-oz.......$20.00

Lincoln, green glass, Duraglas, 1951, 7-oz $120.00

Mason's Old Fashioned Root Beer, amber glass, 10-oz $7.50

Milky's Party Time Sparkling Beverages, clear glass, Twin Pines, 10-oz...$22.50

Mission Beverages, green glass, Keystone Bottling Co, 1-qt, 12" .$28.00

Nehi, clear glass, 10-oz...$15.00

Orange-Crush, amber glass w/embossed ribs, unopened, 7-oz $25.00

Orange-Crush, Crushie on back, amber glass, 30-oz..........$675.00

Roxo, clear glass, 12-oz $20.00

Sno-Top, clear glass, 7-oz $12.50

Sprite, green glass, 7-oz $10.00

Sun-Drop Citrus, Dale Ernhardt, 1980 Winston Cup Champion, green glass, 12-oz..$18.00

Uppity Up, green glass, 12-oz $260.00

Whistle, clear glass, Brownies, Vess Dry Co, 1959, 12-oz $15.00

21, green glass, playing cards, Duraglas, 1949, 7-oz............$37.50

4%, green glass, Grand Rapids Bottling Co, 1952, 7-oz $25.00

7-Up, French version, green glass, 7-oz $15.00

Sporting Goods

Catalogs and various ephemera distributed by sporting good manufacturers, ammunition boxes, and just about any other item used for hunting and fishing purposes are collectible. In fact, there are auctions devoted entirely to collectors with these interests.

One of the best known companies specializing in merchandise of this kind was the gun manufacturer, The Winchester Repeating Arms Company. After 1931, their mark was changed from Winchester Trademark USA to Winchester-Western. Remington, Ithaca, Peters, and Dupont are other manufacturers whose goods are especially sought after.

Advisor: Kevin R. Bowman (See Directory, Sports Collectibles)

Barrel, DuPont 30 Calibre Smoking Rifle Powder, litho label w/eagle & flags, 1-lb size, 3¾x3¼", EX..............................$75.00

Boat, camouflage vinyl PVC, inflatable w/grab lines & oar locks, 75x45", EX...$35.00

Book, A History of the Colt Revolver, CT Haven & FA Belden, Wm Morrow & Co 1st edition, 1940, EX....................$175.00

Book, Book of Fish & Fishing, Lewis Rhead, hardback, Charles Scribner's Sons, 1922, 306 pages, EX...........................$50.00

Book, Upland Game Hunters Bible, Dan Holland, 1961, 192 pages, EX $15.00

Box, Red Head shotgun shells, goose graphics, 2x2½".......$325.00

Box, Remington UMC Nitro Club Game Loads, 12-Gauge Snipe Load, 2-pc, 4¼x4x2½", EX......................................$200.00

Box, Western 16 Gauge Xpert Mark 5 shotgun shells (empty), EX $10.00

Box, Winchester Leader Staynless Lacquered 12-gauge shotgun shells, 4x4x2½", EX..$60.00

Brochure, Remington UMC Kleanbore Hi-Speed .22s, folds out to 3¼x10", EX..$70.00

Bullet board, Nosler Do-It-Yourself, solid oak frame, 1991 ..$320.00

Calendar, The Spirit of '46, Hercules Black Powder, NC Wyeth, EX $190.00

Calendar, Western World Champion Ammunition, Bird Scents, dog sniffing hunter's clothes, 1931, 28x15", EX...............$750.00

Call, crow; JC Higgins, walnut, 4¼"....................................$25.00

Call, duck, FA Allen, Monmouth IL, NP brass section, 5" ..$50.00

Call, duck; Perfectone 2126 Iowa St Davenport IA in gold letters on side of barrel, 4¾" $15.00

Call, turkey; Ben Lee, striker & trough, signed, 1975, EX.$200.00

Call, turkey; ML Lynch #102, 1958 ....$210.00

Cartridge case, The Peters Cartridge Co., wood with red and black lettering, 9⅛x14½x9½", EX, $65.00.

Catalog, Smith & Wesson, Catalog D, Revolvers & Pistols, 1917-19, EX $150.00

Catalog, Weatherby Rifles, 1956-57, 8th edition, EX........$190.00

Catalog, Winchester #79, 1914, 224 pages, VG................$160.00

Crate, Winchester 410 Shells stenciled on dovetailed wood, 5x14x6½", EX..$32.00

Creel, woven basket type, sliding wooden lid, leather shoulder strap, ca 1940, 6x13x7", EX.....................$120.00

Creel, woven basketry, wooden slid lid, handle on back, 1930s-40s, 7x12x5", NM $100.00

Jacket, red & black plaid wool w/plain red sleeves, zipper front, waist length...............................$55.00

Net, fishing; bamboo w/brass fittings, 2-pc handle, ca 1930, 16x19" net opening, 68" L, EX.........................$120.00

Patch, Michigan's Living Resources, Badger, 1980-81 ....$140.00

Patch, Successful Deer Hunter, man dragging deer graphics, 1975, half-moon shape, EX $150.00

Patch, Working Together for Wildlife, PA Game Commission, river otter graphics, 1983, EX.....................$150.00

Pin-back, Western Shot Gun Shells - Metallic Cartridges, celluloid, ⅝".............................$170.00

Poster, Marlin Big Game Rifles, Danger Ahead, man on horse, F Remington, cardboard easel-back, 1960s, 30x20", EX+ .$275.00

Reel, bait caster; Meek #30, EX $250.00

Reel, fly fishing; National Sportsman model, Horrocks Ibbotson of Utica NY, 1930s-40s, 3⅜" dia, MIB.........$100.00

Reel, fly fishing; solid brass, original wooden knob, English, 1920-30, 2½" dia, 2½" reel foot, EX.................$140.00

Reel, Heddon Pal Model 25, MIB $590.00

Rod, fly fishing; bamboo, w/3 tips, converts to 64" casting rods, unmarked, EX..........................$125.00

Rod, fly; Heddon #17 Black Beauty, 3-pc, 108 ", EX+ $320.00

Rod, Shakespeare Wonderrod Model #1487M, 2-pc white fiberglas w/gold wraps, 84", M in plastic sock & tube.............$100.00

Scale, streamside; solid brass, marked Feb 1912, C in side diamond trademark, weighs up to 15 lbs, 6½" L, EX................$100.00

Shot shell box, Winchester Leader 12 gauge, 4x4x2½", EX+, $190.00. (Photo courtesy Wm. Morford Auctions)

Ski poles, bamboo w/leather hand grips, 55", pr.................$50.00

Skis, bird's-eye maple w/leather bindings, 70x3½", EX, pr ...$120.00

Skis, solid birch, pointed tips w/incising, marked Northland, ca 1900-20, 7' long, pr.........................$130.00

Snow shoes, old leather boot harnesses, restrung w/new cat gut, Big Chief by Bastien Bros, 41¾x13½", pr $110.00

Tin, powder; Curtiss & Harvey #6, diamond label on black, 4½x5½x1½", EX.............................$150.00

Tin, powder; Falcon Sporting Powder, Oriental Powder Mills, oval, EX $225.00

Tin, powder; Indian Rifle Powder, Indian graphics, oval, 6x4", EX..............................$170.00

Watch fob, American Powder Works Dead Shop, celluloid insert e/enameled game bird falling, 1½" dia, EX................$150.00

Sports Collectibles

When the baseball card craze began sweeping the country well over a decade ago, memorabilia relating to many types of sports began to interest sports fans. Today ticket stubs, autographed baseballs, sports magazines, and game-used bats and uniforms are prized by baseball fans, and some items, depending on their age or the notoriety of the player or team they represent, may be very valuable. Baseball and golfing seem to be the two sports most collectors prefer, but hockey and auto racing are gaining ground. Game-used equipment is sought out by collectors, and where once they preferred only items used by professionals, now the sports market has expanded, and collectors have taken great interest in the youth equipment endorsed by many star players now enshrined in their respective halls of fame. Some youth equipment was given away as advertising premiums and bear that company's name or logo. Such items are now very desirable.

See also Autographs; Indianapolis 500 Memorabilia; Magazines; Motorcycle Memorabilia; Pin-Back Buttons; Puzzles.

Advisors: Don and Anne Kier (See Directory, Sports Collectibles)

Badge, 1966 Masters at Augusta National Golf Club, EX..$300.00

Baseball shoes, Wilson's Nellie Fox's, size 9½, EXIB $85.00

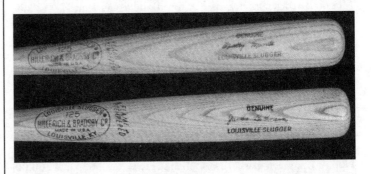

Bats, store model, Louisville Slugger #125, 35": Mickey Mantle or Jackie Robinson, NM, from $100.00 to $125.00 each.

Book, Nat Fleischer's All-Time Ring (Boxing) Record Book, 548 pages, 1941, EX..........................$450.00

Charm, 1969-70 Bobby Hull All-Star Charm, NHL All-Star w/ crossed hockey sticks & star, NM $75.00

Media guide, University of Alabama, Bear Bryant article, 1970, EX...................................$40.00

Media guide, 1963 Houston Colt 45s, Press/Radio/Television, 76 pages, NM $95.00

Megaphone, Go With the Eagles, NFL logo, green, 1950s, 7", EX...................................$80.00

Pennant, World Football League, mid-1970s, EX $95.00

Pennant, 1955 World Series, Yankees vs Dodgers, EX........$360.00

Pennant, 1961 World Series Champions NY Yankees, team photo, 12x30", NM $165.00

Pennant, 1968 Detroit Tigers, Sock It To 'Em, 29½", EX ... **$80.00**

Pin set, Coca Cola 1984 Official Olympic International Flag Pin Series, 150 flag pins, framed under glass, NMIB **$75.00**

Pin-back, Boston Red Sox, crossed bats w/red socks on yellow, ⅞" dia, EX **$40.00**

Pocketknife, baseball shape w/faux signature of Babe Ruth, Camillus, EX **$75.00**

Press book, 1967-68 LA Lakers, Official Guide & Records, EX .. **$70.00**

Press pin, 13th World Series, St Louis, w/stadium, 1982, EX. **$75.00**

Press pin, 1971 World Series, Pittsburg vs Baltimore, pirate head over stadium, EX **$165.00**

Press pin, 1973 Oakland A's, made by Jostens, M **$95.00**

Program, Buffalo Bills vs NY Jets, 68 pages, 1968, EX **$70.00**

Program, Buffalo Bills vs NY Titans, American Football League, 1962, EX **$95.00**

Program, Fight of the Champions, Muhammad Ali vs Joe Frazier, Madison Square Gardens, 1961, EX **$110.00**

Program, Joe Frazier vs Dave Zyglewicz, Title Fight, 4/22/69, EX **$130.00**

Program, Larry Holmes vs Ernie Shavers, 10/28/79, EX...... **$95.00**

Program, Memphis Pros vs NY Nets, American Basketball Association, 1970, EX+ **$85.00**

Program, Oregon State Beavers vs USC Trojans, 38 pages, 11/11/67, EX **$85.00**

Program, San Diego Chargers vs Boston Patriots, 1965, 58 pages, EX **$95.00**

Program, Super Bowl XI, Oakland Raiders vs Minnesota Vikings, 1977, NM **$275.00**

Program, 1951 NFL World's Championship, Cleveland Browns vs Detroit Lions, NM **$365.00**

Program, 1952 NCAA Basketball Final Four, EX **$290.00**

Program, 1955 World Series, New York Yankees & Brooklyn Dodgers, complete, NM+ **$500.00**

Program, 1959 NFL Championship Game, Baltimore Colts vs NY Giants, EX **$190.00**

Program, 1960 Baseball All-Star Game, Municipal Stadium, Kansas City MO, EX **$110.00**

Program, 1962 All-Star Game, DC Stadium, EX................. **$85.00**

Program, 1966 World Championship Game, Packers vs Browns, EX **$160.00**

Program, 1967 World Championship Game, AFL vs NFL, 1st Super Bowl, EX **$300.00**

Program, 1968 World Series, Detriot Tigers vs St Louis Cardinals, Tiger Stadium, EX **$110.00**

Program, 1971 National League Championship, Giants vs Pirates at Candlestick Park, rare, EX **$275.00**

Program, 1974 Final Four, EX **$100.00**

Program, 1974 NCAA Final Four, w/scorecard insert, EX. **$100.00**

Program, 4th Annual Cracker Jack Old-Timers Baseball Classic, 1985, EX **$90.00**

Schedule, TV; MN Twins, Hamm's Brings You 50 TV Games, 1962, EX **$75.00**

Schedule, 1953 NY Yankees, Brooklyn Dodgers & NY Giants, home games, EX **$100.00**

Ticket, Leon Spinks vs Muhammad Ali, unused, 9/15/78, NM+ **$185.00**

Ticket, Rain Check, Cincinnati Reds, 1947, EX............... **$115.00**

Ticket, Super Bowl XI, 1977, NM...................................... **$70.00**

Tickets, 2002 World Heavyweight Championship, Mike Tyson vs Lennox Lewis, unused, EX, pr **$180.00**

Yearbook, 1955 Cincinnati Reds, EX+............................... **$90.00**

Yearbook, 1956 Brooklyn Dodgers, EX............................. **$110.00**

Yearbook, 1958 San Francisco Giants, EX........................ **$105.00**

Yearbook, 1962 New York National League Baseball Club, Mets, EX **$435.00**

Yearbook, 1963 NY Mets, EX.. **$95.00**

Yearbook, 1964 Green Bay Packers, Bart Starr cover, EX ... **$105.00**

Yearbook, 1964 Green Bay Packers, Vince Lombardi cover, 175 pages, EX **$105.00**

Pennant, Detroit Tigers, orange felt, ca. 1960s, 27" long, $50.00.

St. Clair Glass

Since 1941, the St. Clair family has operated a small glasshouse in Elwood, Indiana. They're most famous for their lamps, though they've also produced many styles of toothpick holders, paperweights, and various miniatures as well. Though the paperweights are usually stamped and dated, smaller items may not be marked at all. In addition to various colors of iridescent glass, they've also made many articles in slag glass (both caramel and pink) and custard.

At the present, rose weights are in demand, especially the rare pedestal roses; so are sulfides, in particular those with etching or windows. Pieces signed by Ed and Paul are rare, as these brothers signed only items they made during their breaks or lunch time. Sulfides and lamps made by Maude and Bob are in demand as well, and three- and four-ball lamps by Joe are highly sought after by today's collectors. Items signed by Mike Mitchell, who once worked for Bob St. Clair, are scarce and usually bring very good prices. For more information, we recommend *St. Clair Glass Collector's Book, Vol. II,* by our advisor, Ted Pruitt (see Directory, St. Clair).

Advisor: Ted Pruitt (See Directory, St. Clair)

Animal dish, reclining colt, cobalt custard, from $135 to .. **$160.00**

Bell, flowers, from $75 to... **$100.00**

Bowl, fluted & scalloped rim, from $225 to **$250.00**

Bowl, pink slag, pedestal foot, from $150 to..................... **$175.00**

Box, wheelbarrow, w/lid, from $115 to **$125.00**

Covered dish, dolphin, from $100 to.................................$125.00
Creamer & sugar bowl, Paneled Grape, from $60 to...........$65.00
Dish, dolphin, w/lid, from $100 to.....................................$125.00
Doorstop, duck, from $750 to...$800.00
Figurine, fish, blue, handmade (blown), from $225 to.......$250.00

Figurine, Scottie dog, blue carnival, marked R.M. St. Clair, ca. 1979, from $150.00 to $200.00.

Figurine, Southern Belle, various colors, from $75 to........$100.00
Fruit, pear, carnival, from $95 to......................................$100.00
Goblet, Rose in Snow, from $40 to.....................................$50.00
Goblet, Thistle, from $40 to...$50.00
Insulator, carnival, from $100 to.......................................$125.00
Novelty, piano, from $115 to...$125.00
Paperweight, bear, windowed & etched, from $225 to.......$250.00
Paperweight, cameo, dove, from $175 to...........................$200.00
Pen holder, handmade, from $65 to....................................$75.00
Pen holder, signed Paul St Clair..$350.00
Pitcher, Hollyband, caramel slag, from $90 to....................$95.00
Plate, Mt St Helens, from $20 to..$25.00
Plate, Reagan - Bush, from $25 to......................................$30.00
Salt dip, swan, white carnival, from $125 to......................$150.00
Sugar bowl, Hollyband, white carnival or amber Tiffany, ea from $85
   to...$100.00
Toothpick holder, Daisy & Button, from $25 to..................$30.00
Toothpick holder, flowers, blue, ruffled rim, from $65 to....$95.00
Tumbler, Cactus, various colors, from $30 to......................$35.00
Wine glass, Paneled Grape, from $35 to..............................$45.00

Stanford Corn

Teapots, cookie jars, salt and pepper shakers, and other kitchen and dinnerware items modeled as ears of yellow corn with green husks were made by the Stanford company, who marked most of their ware. The Shawnee company made two very similar corn lines; just check the marks to verify the manufacturer.

Butter dish $45.00
Casserole, 8" L...$40.00
Corn dish (holds ear)...$22.00
Creamer & sugar bowl, w/lid...$45.00

Cup $15.00
Grease jar, 6½"...$45.00
Marmalade jar...$25.00
Mustard jar...$25.00
Pitcher, 6½"...$35.00
Pitcher, 7½"...$45.00
Plate, 9" L...$25.00
Relish tray..$35.00
Salt & pepper shakers, sm, pr...$20.00
Salt & pepper shakers, 4", pr $25.00
Snack set, cup & plate w/indent, #709 ....$65.00
Spoon rest..$25.00
Sugar bowl...$20.00
Teapot..$60.00
Tumbler $25.00

Cookie jar, from $75.00 to $100.00.

Stangl

The Stangl company's roots sprang from the old Sam Hill Pottery (1814), making it one of the longest-existing potteries in the United States. It became known as Fulper ca 1860, when its output focused mainly on art pottery. Martin Stangl became president in 1928, and although their products began to carry the Stangl name, it was not until 1955 that the name change became official. After Stangl's death in 1972, the firm was purchased by Wheaton Industries; all operations ceased in 1978. For more information see *Collector's Encyclopedia of Stangl Artware, Lamps, and Birds* by Robert Runge, Jr. (Collector Books).

Advisor: Popkorn Antiques (See Directory, Stangl)

Club: Stangl/Fulper Collectors Club
P.O. Box 538
Flemington, NJ 08822; www.stanglpottery.org

Birds

In 1940, the company introduced a line of ceramic birds in order to fullfill the needs of a market no longer able to access foreign imports, due to the onset of WWII. These bird figures immediately attracted a great deal of attention. At the height of their productivity, 60 decorators were employed to hand paint the birds at the plant, and the overflow was contracted out and decorated in private homes. After WWII, inexpensive imported figurines once again saturated the market, and for the most part, Stangl curtailed their own production, though the birds were made on a very limited basis until as late as 1978.

Nearly all the birds were marked. A four-digit number was used to identify the species, and most pieces were signed by the decorator. An 'F' indicates a bird that was decorated at the Flemington plant.

#3250A, Duck standing, 3¼" $100.00
#3250B, Duck preening, 3¼" $75.00
#3250D, Duck grazing, 3¾" $75.00
#3250F, Duck quacking, 3¼" $75.00
#3273, Rooster, hollow, 5¾", from $550 to..................$650.00
#3274, Penguin, 6" $400.00
#3275, Turkey, 3½" $350.00
#3276D, Bluebirds (pr), 8½" $150.00
#3285, Rooster, early, 4½" $100.00
#3286, Hen, late, 3¼" $50.00
#3401, Wren, dark brown, revised, 3½" $40.00
#3401D, Wrens (pr), old version $450.00
#3401D, Wrens (pr), revised version..................................$90.00
#3402, Oriole, beak down, old style, 3½"..................$125.00
#3402, Oriole, revised, 3¼" $45.00
#3402D, Orioles (pr), revised, w/leaves, 5½" $100.00
#3404D, Lovebirds (pr) kissing, old version, 4½" $375.00
#3405, Cockatoo, 6" $50.00
#3405D, Cockatoos (pr), revised, 9½"..................................$100.00
#3406, Kingfisher, teal, 3½" $75.00
#3406D, Kingfishers (pr), blue, 5" $150.00
#3407, Owl, 5½x2½" $350.00
#3408, Bird of Paradise, 5½" $80.00
#3432, Duck running, brown $500.00
#3443, Duck flying, gray, 9" $225.00
#3444, Cardinal, female..................................$150.00
#3444, Cardinal, glossy pink, revised, 7" $65.00
#3445, Rooster, gray, 10" $175.00
#3446, Hen, yellow, 7" $120.00
#3447, Yellow Warbler..................................$45.00
#3448, Blue-Headed Vireo, 4¼" $60.00
#3449, Paroquet, 5½" $165.00
#3450, Passenger Pigeon, 9x18"..................................$1,700.00
#3452, Painted Bunting, 5" $85.00
#3454, Key West Quail Dove, single wing up, 10" $225.00
#3455, Shoveler Duck, 12¼x14" $1,250.00
#3458, Quail, 7½" $1,800.00
#3490D, Redstarts (pr), 9" $150.00
#3491, Hen Pheasant, 6¼x11" $150.00
#3492, Cock Pheasant $165.00
#3580, Cockatoo, med, 8⅞" $125.00
#3581, Chickadees, brown/white, group of 3, 5½x8½" $150.00
#3582D, Parakeets (pr), blue, 7"..................................$250.00
#3582D, Parakeets (pr), green, 7"..................................$200.00
#3583, Parula Warbler, 4¼" $35.00

#3584, Cockatoo, signed Jacob, lg, 11⅜" $225.00
#3584, Cockatoo, white matt, lg..................................$1,000.00
#3585, Rufous Hummingbird, 3" $70.00
#3586, Pheasant (Della Ware), natural colors..................$1,800.00
#3586, Pheasant (Della Ware), Terra Rose, green $500.00
#3590, Carolina Wren, 4½" $150.00
#3591, Brewster's Blackbird, 3½" $150.00
#3592, Titmouse, 3" $45.00
#3593, Nuthatch, 2½" $50.00
#3595, Bobolink, 4¾" $150.00
#3596, Gray Cardinal, 5" $60.00
#3597, Wilson Warbler, yellow & black, 3" $40.00
#3598, Kentucky Warbler, 3" $45.00
#3626, Broadtail Hummingbird, blue flower $150.00
#3627, Rivoli Hummingbird, pink flower, 6" $150.00
#3628, Rieffer's Hummingbird $125.00
#3629, Broadbill Hummingbird, 4½" $125.00
#3634, Allen Hummingbird, 3½" $100.00
#3635, Gold Finches (group) $175.00
#3715, Blue Jay, w/peanut, 10¼"..................................$600.00

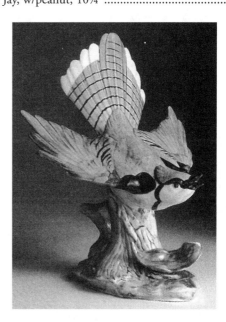

#3716, Blue Jay, with leaf, 10½", $550.00. (Photo courtesy David Rago Auctions)

#3746, Canary (right), rose flower, 6¼"..................$225.00
#3747, Canary (left), blue flower, 6¼"..................$225.00
#3750, Scarlet Tanager, 8½" $350.00
#3751, Red-Headed Woodpecker, glossy pink, 6¼"..........$300.00
#3754D, White-Wing Crossbills (pr), glossy pink, 9x8" $450.00
#3758, Magpie-Jay, 10¾" $1,250.00
#3811, Chestnut Chicadee, 5" $125.00
#3812, Chestnut Warbler, 4½" $125.00
#3813, Crested Goldfinch, 5" $150.00
#3814, Townsend Warbler, 3" $150.00
#3815, Western Bluebird, 7" $400.00
#3848, Golden-Crowned Kinglet, 4¼" $90.00
#3850, Western Warbler, 4" $125.00

#3852, Cliff Swallow, 3½" $125.00
#3868, Summer Tanager, 4" $650.00
#3924, Yellow Throat, 6" $600.00

Dinnerware

Stangl introduced their first line of dinnerware in the 1920s. By 1954, 90% of their production centered around their dinnerware lines. Until 1942 the clay they used was white. Although most of the dinnerware made before WWII had solid-color glazes, they also did many hand-painted (but not carved) patterns in the 1930s and early 1940s. In 1942, however, the first of the red-clay lines that have become synonymous with the Stangl name was created. Designs were hand carved into the greenware, then hand painted. More than 100 different patterns have been cataloged. From 1974 until 1978, a few lines previously discontinued on the red clay were reintroduced with a white clay body. Soon after '78, the factory closed.

Amber-Glo #3899, bowl, salad; 12", from $35 to...............$50.00
Amber-Glo #3899, casserole dish, skillet shape, 8", from $15 to $20.00
Amber-Glo #3899, coffeepot, 4-cup, from $70 to $85.00
Amber-Glo #3899, plate, chop; 12½", from $25 to.............$40.00
Blueberry #3770, butter dish, from $50 to $60.00
Blueberry #3770, egg cup, from $20 to $25.00
Blueberry #3770, saucer, from $7 to $8.00
Chicory #3809, creamer, individual, from $25 to $30.00
Chicory #3809, pickle dish, from $20 to $25.00
Colonial #1388, candy jar, from $45 to $55.00
Colonial #1388, pitcher, 6-oz, from $15 to $20.00
Colonial #1388, ramekin, 4", from $12 to $15.00
Country Garden #3943, bowl, fruit; from $12 to...............$15.00
Country Garden #3943, plate, grill; 9", from $40 to $50.00
Festival #5072, cruet, w/stopper, from $35 to.....................$45.00
Florette #5073, gravy boat, from $15 to $20.00
Florette #5073, salt & pepper shakers, ea from $8 to..........$10.00
Florette #5073, teapot, from $75 to.................................$85.00
Garland #4067, cake stand, from $20 to...........................$25.00
Garland #4067, coffeepot, 8-cup, from $95 to $125.00
Holly #3869, coffee mug, 2-cup $50.00
Holly #3869, punch cup, from $40 to..................................$50.00
Mediterranean #5186, casserole, w/lid, 8", from $75 to.......$90.00
Mediterranean #5186, sugar bowl, from $10 to...................$15.00
Mediterranean #5186, tidbit, 2-tier, from $20 to.................$25.00
Newport #3333, ashtray, from $20 to $30.00
Newport #3333, creamer, from $35 to................................$40.00
Orchard Song #5110, bowl, mixing; #5150, 12", from $50 to. $60.00
Orchard Song #5110, sauceboat, from $20 to......................$25.00
Pink Lily #3888, relish dish, from $15 to $20.00
Pink Lily #3888, salt & pepper shakers, pr from $16 to $20.00
Sculptured Fruit #5179, comport, 6", from $10 to..............$15.00
Sculptured Fruit #5179, plate, picnic; 10" $5.00
Town & Country #5287, baking dish, blue, 9x14", from $75 to $100.00
Town & Country #5287, chamber pot, green, handled, from $40 to $50.00

**Verna, fruit bowl, $20.00; lug soup, $25.00; chop plate, 12",
$90.00; plate, 8", $20.00.** (Photo courtesy Robert C. Runge, Jr.)

Windfall #3930, bread tray, from $20 to $25.00
Yellow Tulip #3637, gravy boat, from $25 to $30.00
Yellow Tulip #3637, teapot, from $85 to.............................$95.00

Miscellaneous

Air freshener, long-eared rabbit, made for Airwick, solid blue, #3109, 1937-38, 7½", from $125 to $175.00
Ashtray, Apple Blossom, sq, #3666, 1964, 4½", from $15 to. $20.00
Ashtray, pansy form, flat, 6", from $45 to..........................$60.00
Ashtray, sailfish leaping, white engobe, obal, Kay Hackett design, #3926, 1960-65, from $35 to.....................................$50.00
Bank, pig, jeweled decoration, #1076, early 1960s, 4", from $200 to $250.00
Basket, pink blossoms, #3621, 1974, 5½", from $45 to $55.00
Birdhouse, gray roof, 1972-74, 7½x7", from $25 to...........$30.00
Bowl, Cosmos, Terra Rose, #1869, 1940s, 12", from $50 to.. $60.00
Bowl, Tropical Ware, blue & yellow, 3-footed, #2023, 1935-36, 7", from $170 to $195.00
Cache pot, Rosebud, bowl shape, 1975 only, 6½", from $20 to.$30.00
Candleholders, Rainbow Artware, double handles, #3184, 1939, 4x2½", pr from $80 to $125.00
Candy jar, Terra Rose, #1388, 1940s, 5x5", from $80 to...$100.00
Chamberstick, Town & Country, blue, #5287, 1974-78, ea from $40 to $50.00
Christmas card, Christmas Tree, business, from $100 to....$125.00
Christmas card, Gold Bells & Holly, business, from $150 to..$175.00
Christmas card, Poinsettia, business, from $150 to $175.00
Christmas card, Spaniel, personal, from $190 to...............$225.00
Cigarette box, Caribbean, flat top, #3630, 1968-70, 4½x5½", from $60 to $75.00
Cigarette box, Mediterranean, flat top, #3630, 4½x5½", from $75 to $95.00
Cigarette box, Mountain Laurel, #3630, 1946-48, from $65 to .. $80.00
Coaster ashtray, Aztec, #A-3630, 1963-65, 5", from $15 to. $20.00
Figurine, buffalo, natural colors, #3246, 2½", from $250 to .. $300.00
Figurine, cat sitting, Mandarin Red, 9", from $400 to.......$500.00
Figurine, draft horse, natural colors, #3244, 3", from $125 to ...$150.00
Figurine, elephant, Granada Gold, #5281, 1973-75, 5", from $75 to $125.00

Figurine, gazelle, natural colors, #3247, 3¾", from $200 to.**$250.00**
Figurine, wire-haired dog, natural colors, #3243, 3¼", from $200 to **$250.00**
Flowerpot, Pennsylvania Artware, scalloped top, #1643, 4", from $20 to **$25.00**
Flowerpot, Sunburst, handmade, attached saucer, #1550L, 1929-34, 8", from $120 to..**$145.00**
Flowerpot, Yellow Tulip, hand carved, #3661, 1953-65, 4", from $20 to..**$25.00**
Leaf dish, Antique French Crackle, #5146, 8x7¾", from $10 to **$15.00**
Mug, Franklin D Roosevelt, #1647-1, from $145 to **$165.00**
Pitcher, Appliqué, #4060, 1964-65, 5¼", from $15 to **$20.00**
Pitcher, Pompeii, #4056, 1971, 8¾", from $25 to..............**$30.00**
Plate, Jersey Shore, Angelfish, 1947-48, 11", from $400 to ..**$500.00**
Sand jar, Swirl, Sunburst, #1590, 1932-34, 22", from $1,000 to **$1,200.00**
Tray, vanity; Patrician, #5328-626, 1978, 7½", from $20 to ..**$25.00**
Vase, Amber-Glo, cylindrical, 1954-78, 10", from $30 to....**$40.00**
Vase, Antique French Crackle, milk can shape, #3688, 7", from $25 to **$35.00**
Vase, bud; Aztec, #A-5093, 1963-65, 5¾", from $20 to......**$25.00**
Vase, Cosmos, Terra Rose Mauve, #3413, 1940-50s, 7", from $30 to **$40.00**
Vase, Pebblestone, Rose Herbeck design, #5274, 1972-73, 8½", from $45 to **$55.00**

Vase, Tangerine, #1764, bulbous with five dimples, 1933 – 1935, from $100.00 to $125.00. (Photo courtesy Robert C. Runge, Jr.)

Vase, Terra Rose, #3117, 1946-52, 5½", from $20 to..........**$30.00**
Vase, Windfall, cylindrical, #3592, 1956-59, 8", from $30 to...**$40.00**
Wall pocket, Town & Country, green, brown or yellow, 1974-78, from $40 to **$50.00**

Star Trek Memorabilia

Trekkies, as fans are often referred to, number nearly 40,000 today, hold national conventions, and compete with each other for choice items of Star Trek memorabilia, some of which may go for hundreds of dollars.

The Star Trek concept was introduced to the public in the mid-1960s through a TV series which continued for many years in syndication. An animated cartoon series (1977), the success of 'Star Trek: The Next Generation' (Fox network, 1987), the great 'Enterprise' series broadcast in syndication, and the release of what now amounts to 10 major motion pictures (1979 through 2002), have all served as a bridge to join two generations of loyal fans.

Its success has resulted in the sale of vast amounts of merchandise, both licensed and unlicensed, such as clothing, promotional items of many sorts, books and comics, toys and games, records and tapes, school supplies, and party goods. Many of these are still available at flea markets around the country. An item that is 'mint in box' is worth at least twice as much as one in excellent condition but without its original packaging. For more information, refer to *Schroeder's Collectible Toys, Antique to Modern* (published by Collector Books).

Bank, Spock, plastic, Play Pal, 1975, 12", MIB **$60.00**
Book, Star Trek, Pop-Up, Motion Picture, 1977, EX..........**$25.00**
Bop Bag, Spock, 1975, MIB **$80.00**

Communicators, blue plastic, Mego, 1979, MIB, $175.00.

Figure, Galoob, Star Trek Next Generation, Antican, Ferengi, Q, or Selay, (M, $30 ea), MOC, ea **$65.00**
Figure, Galoob, Star Trek Next Generation, Data, blue face, (M, $50), MOC **$75.00**
Figure, Galoob, Star Trek Next Generation, Data, brown face, (M, $25), MOC **$50.00**
Figure, Galoob, Star Trek Next Generation, Data, flesh face, (M, $15), MOC **$25.00**
Figure, Galoob, Star Trek Next Generation, Data, spotted Face, (M, $18), MOC **$32.00**
Figure, Galoob, Star Trek Next Generation, Lt Worf, Picard, or Riker, (M, $6 ea), MOC, ea **$18.00**
Figure, Galoob, Star Trek Next Generation, Tasha Yar, (M, $12), MOC..**$24.00**
Figure, Galoob, Star Trek V, any character, 1989, (M, $12), MOC **$28.00**
Figure, Mego, 12", Arcturian, 1979, (M, $65), MIP **$130.00**
Figure, Mego, 12", Capt Kirk, 1979, (M, $40), MIP **$80.00**

Figure, Mego, 12", Decker, 1979, (M, $60), MIP **$120.00**
Figure, Mego, 12", Ilia, 1979, (M, $40), MIP **$80.00**
Figure, Mego, 12", Klingon, 1979, (M, $60), MIP............**$120.00**
Figure, Mego, 12", Mr Spock, 1979, (M, $40), MIP...........**$80.00**
Figure, Mego, 3¾", Acturian, Betelgeusian, Klingon, Magarite or Zatanite, Series 2, (M, $50 ea), MOC, ea....................**$125.00**
Figure, Mego, 3¾", Capt Kirk, Decker, Dr McCoy, Illia, Mr Spock or Mr Scott, Series 1, (M, $10 ea), MOC, ea **$30.00**
Figure, Mego, 8", Andorian, 1970s, (M, $300), MOC......**$600.00**
Figure, Mego, 8", Capt Kirk, 1970s, (M, $30), MOC.........**$60.00**
Figure, Mego, 8", Cheron, 1970s, (M, $75), MOC...........**$150.00**
Figure, Mego, 8", Dr McCoy, 1970s, (M, $75), MOC.......**$150.00**
Figure, Mego, 8", Gorn, 1970s, (M, $95), MOC..............**$175.00**
Figure, Mego, 8", Klingon, 1970s, (M, $25), MOC............**$50.00**
Figure, Mego, 8", Lt Uhura, 1970s, (M, $65), MOC........**$130.00**
Figure, Mego, 8", Mr Scott, 1970s, (M, $40), MOC **$90.00**
Figure, Mego, 8", Mr Spock, 1970s, (M, $30), MOC **$60.00**
Figure, Mego, 8", Mugato, 1970s, (M, $300), MOC **$550.00**
Figure, Mego, 8", Neptunian, 1970s, (M, $125), MOC....**$200.00**
Figure, Mego, 8", Romulan, 1970s, (M, $800), MOC ...**$1,200.00**
Figure, Mego, 8", Talos, 1970s, (M, $300), MOC............**$525.00**
Figure, Mego, 8", The Keeper, 1970s, (M, $80), MOC.....**$160.00**
Figure, Playmates, DS9, Chief O'Brien, Commander Sisko, Major Nerys, Morn, Odo or Quark, 1994, (M, $5 ea), MIP, ea..**$10.00**
Figure, Playmates, DS9, Dr Julian Bashir, 1994, (M, $10), MOC...**$20.00**
Figure, Playmates, DS9, Lt Jadzia Dax, 1994, (M, $6), MIP..**$15.00**
Figure, Playmates, First Contact, 5", Borg, Dr Crusher, Lily or Picard, 1996, (M, $10 ea), MOC, ea............................**$16.00**
Figure, Playmates, First Contact, 5", Data, Troi, La Forge, Picard, Riker, Worf or Cochrane, 1996, (M, $8 ea), MOC, ea.**$14.00**
Figure, Playmates, First Contact, 9", Capt Picard in 21st century outfit or Cochrane, 1996, (M, $20), MIP, ea................**$26.00**
Figure, Playmates, First Contact, 9", Data, Picard or Riker, 1996, (M, $15 ea), MIP, ea...**$20.00**
Figure, Playmates, Insurrection, 9", any character, 1998, (M, $8 ea), MIP, ea..**$15.00**
Figure, Playmates, Insurrection, 12", any character, 1998, (M, $8 ea), MIP, ea..**$15.00**
Figure, Playmates, Star Trek Next Generation, 1st Series, Borg, Data, Picard, Riker or Worf, 1992, (M, $12 ea), MOC, ea....**$22.00**
Figure, Playmates, Star Trek Next Generation, 1st Series, Deanna Troi or Romulan, 1992, (M, $20 ea), MOC.................**$35.00**
Figure, Playmates, Star Trek Next Generation, 1st Series, Ferengui, Gowron or La Forge, (M, $15 ea), MOC, ea................**$30.00**
Figure, Playmates, Star Trek Next Generation, 2nd Series, any character, 1993, (M, $10 ea), MOC, ea **$18.00**
Figure, Playmates, Star Trek Next Generation, 3rd Series, any except Data or Esoqq, (M, $5-$10), MOC, ea from $15 to....**$25.00**
Figure, Playmates, Star Trek Next Generation, 3rd Series, Data in red suit, 1994, (M, $80), MOC...**$275.00**
Figure, Playmates, Star Trek Next Generation, 4th or 5th series, any, 1995, (M, from $8 to $12 ea), MOC, ea from $12 to..**$22.00**
Figure, Playmates, Voyager, any except Chakotay the Maquis, Doctor or Harry Kim, 5", (M, $10 ea), MIP, ea **$18.00**
Figure, Playmates, Voyager, Janeway or Lt B'Elanna Torres, 5", (M, $18 ea), MOC, ea...**$30.00**

Figure, Star Trek Next Generation, 3rd Series, any character except, Esoqq or Data in red suit, 1994, M, from $6 to..........**$12.00**
Pennant, Spock Lives, black, red & yellow on white, Image Products, 1982, 30", M..**$15.00**
Playset, Command Communications Console, Mego, 1976, MIB, from $125 to **$150.00**
Playset, Engineering, Generation Movie, Playmates, MIB....**$35.00**
Playset, Mission to Gamma VI, Mego, 1975, rare, MIB....**$400.00**
Playset, Telescreen Console, Mego, 1975, MIB..................**$125.00**
Playset, Transporter Room, Mego, 1975, MIB..................**$125.00**
Playset, USS Enterprise Bridge, Mego, 1975, complete w/3 figures, EX **$80.00**
Puzzle book, Wanderer Books, 1986, unused, NM+ **$8.00**
Trading cards, 25th Anniversary, Series 1, Impel, 1991, complete set of 160 different cards, NM+ **$15.00**
Vehicle, Ferengi Fighter, Star Trek Next Generation, Galoob, 1989, NRFB...**$75.00**
Vehicle, Klingon Cruiser, Mego, 1980, 8" L, MIB..............**$70.00**
Vehicle, Romulan Warbird, Playmates, MIB **$50.00**
Vehicle, USS Enterprise B, Motion Picture, Playmates, M...**$65.00**

Vehicle, USS Enterprise NCC-1701-E, Playmates, 1996, NMIB, from $50.00 to $60.00.

Wastebasket, Motion Picture, M **$35.00**

Star Wars

In the late '70s, the movie 'Star Wars' became a box office hit, most notably for its fantastic special effects and its ever-popular theme of space adventure. Two more movies followed, 'The Empire Strikes Back' in 1980 and 'Return of the Jedi' in 1983. After the first movie, an enormous amount of related merchandise was released. A large percentage of these items was action figures, made by the Kenner company who used the logo of the 20th Century Fox studios (under whom they were licensed) on everything they made until 1980. Just before the second movie, Star Wars creator, George Lucas, regained control of the merchandising rights, and items inspired by the films can be identified by his own Lucasfilm logo. Since 1987, Lucasfilm Ltd. has operated shops in conjunction with the Star Tours at Disneyland theme. The most current movies are Episode I through III, and each has spawned a new burst of collector-aimed merchandise.

What to collect? First and foremost, buy what you yourself enjoy. But remember that condition is all-important. Look for items still mint in the box. Using that as a basis, if the box is missing, deduct at least half from its mint-in-box value. If a major accessory or part is gone, the item is basically worthless. Learn to recognize the most desirable, most valuable items. There are lots of Star Wars bargains yet to be had!

Original packaging helps date a toy, since the package or card design was updated as each new movie was released. Naturally, items representing the older movies are more valuable than later issues. For more coverage of this subject, refer to *Schroeder's Collectible Toys, Antique to Modern* and *Star Wars Super Collector's Wish Book* by Geoffery T. Carlton (Collector Books).

Bank, Chewbacca (kneeling), Sigma, M **$45.00**
Bop Bag, Darth Vader, Kenner, MIB **$125.00**
Bop Bag, Jawa, Kenner, MIB **$225.00**
Card game, Return of the Jedi - Play for Power, Parker Bros, 1983, MIB **$15.00**
Case, Darth Vader, EX **$15.00**
Coloring book, Ewoks, Kenner #18240, 1985, unused, NM+ . **$12.00**

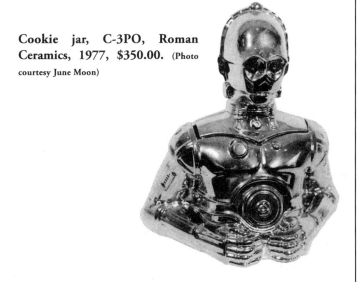

Cookie jar, C-3PO, Roman Ceramics, 1977, $350.00. (Photo courtesy June Moon)

Eraser & sharpener, Ewok, 1983, MOC **$15.00**
Figure, A-Wing Pilot, Droids, M..................................... **$50.00**
Figure, Anakin Skywalker, Power of the Force, M **$35.00**
Figure, Ben (Obi-Wan) Kenobi, Empire Strikes Back, gray hair, M **$15.00**
Figure, Ben (Obi-Wan) Kenobi, Return of the Jedi, white hair, M **$10.00**
Figure, Ben (Obi-Wan) Kenobi, Star Wars, MOC (21-back). **$190.00**
Figure, Biker Scout, Return of the Jedi, M.......................... **$18.00**
Figure, Boba Fett, Droids, M **$25.00**
Figure, Boba Fett, Empire Strikes Back, 12", MIB **$625.00**
Figure, C-3PO, Power of the Force, removable limbs, M..... **$15.00**
Figure, C-3PO, Star Wars, MOC (21-back)....................... **$125.00**
Figure, Chewbacca, Empire Strikes Back, MOC................ **$275.00**
Figure, Chewbacca, Power of the Force, M **$20.00**
Figure, Chewbacca, Star Wars, 12", MIB **$235.00**
Figure, Chief Chirpa, Return of the Jedi, MOC **$50.00**

Figure, Cloud Car Pilot, Empire Strikes Back, MOC **$130.00**
Figure, Cloud Car Pilot, Return of the Jedi, MOC..............**$75.00**
Figure, Darth Vader, Return of the Jedi, light saber drawn, MOC..**$65.00**
Figure, Darth Vader, Star Wars, 12", MIB **$270.00**
Figure, Death Squad Commander, Star Wars, M **$15.00**
Figure, Death Star Droid, Return of the Jedi, MOC..........**$125.00**
Figure, Dengar, Empire Strikes Back, M **$10.00**
Figure, Dulok Scout, Ewoks, M.....................................**$10.00**
Figure, Dulok Shaman, Ewoks, MOC **$35.00**
Figure, Emperor, Power of the Force, MOC **$105.00**
Figure, Emperor's Royal Guard, Return of the Jedi, M **$11.00**
Figure, General Madine, Return of the Jedi, M..................**$8.00**
Figure, Greedo, Star Wars, M.......................................**$15.00**
Figure, Hammerhead, Empire Strikes Back, MOC **$150.00**
Figure, Hammerhead, Star Wars, M.................................**$12.00**
Figure, Han Solo, Empire Strikes Back, MOC...................**$250.00**
Figure, Han Solo, Power of the Force, Carbonite Chamber, M .**$115.00**
Figure, Han Solo, Return of the Jedi, MOC (tri-logo).......**$125.00**
Figure, Han Solo, Star Wars, 12", MIB...........................**$595.00**
Figure, Imperial Commander, Return of the Jedi, M **$10.00**
Figure, Imperial Dignitary, Power of the Force, M..............**$35.00**

Figure, Imperial Dignitary, POTF, MOC, $110.00.

Figure, Imperial Gunner, Power of the Force, M.................**$95.00**
Figure, Jann Tosh, Droids, M..**$25.00**
Figure, Jawa, Empire Strikes Back, MOC **$125.00**
Figure, Jawa, Star Wars, MOC (21-back).........................**$200.00**
Figure, Jord Dusat, Droids, M **$22.00**
Figure, Kea Moll, Droids, M...**$26.00**
Figure, King Gorneesh, Ewoks, MOC **$35.00**
Figure, Klaatu, Return of the Jedi, Skiff outfit, M..............**$12.00**
Figure, Lady Ugrah Gorneesh, Ewoks, MOC **$35.00**
Figure, Lando Calrissian, Empire Strikes Back, no teeth, M ...**$15.00**
Figure, Lando Calrissian, Return of the Jedi, Skiff outfit, M ..**$19.00**
Figure, Lobot, Return of the Jedi, M................................**$10.00**
Figure, Logray, Ewoks, MOC..**$25.00**
Figure, Luke Skywalker, Empire Strikes Back, Bespin fatigues, blond hair, M **$24.00**

Figure, Luke Skywalker, Empire Strikes Back, brown hair, MOC $325.00
Figure, Luke Skywalker, Power of the Force, battle poncho, M. $10.00
Figure, Luke Skywalker, Power of the Force, Stormtrooper outfit, M.. $235.00
Figure, Luke Skywalker, Return of the Jedi, blue light saber, M ... $65.00
Figure, Luke Skywalker, Return of the Jedi, brown hair, M..$26.00
Figure, Luke Skywalker, Return of the Jedi, X-Wing Pilot, M . $15.00
Figure, Luke Skywalker, Star Wars, blond hair, MOC (21-back) ..$265.00
Figure, Lumat, Power of the Force, M $22.00
Figure, Nien Nunb, Return of the Jedi, M........................ $10.00
Figure, Nikto, Return of the Jedi, M................................ $15.00
Figure, Paploo, Power of the Force, M $20.00
Figure, Paploo, Power of the Force, MOC $125.00
Figure, Power Droid, Empire Strikes Back, MOC............. $200.00
Figure, Power Droid, Star Wars, M $12.00
Figure, Princess Leia, Empire Strikes Back, Bespin crew neck, M $22.00
Figure, Princess Leia, Return of the Jedi, Hoth outfit, MOC.. $100.00
Figure, Princess Leia, Star Wars, 12", MIB........................ $285.00
Figure, Rancor Keeper, Return of the Jedi, MOC.............. $55.00
Figure, Rebel Commander, Empire Strikes Back, MOC $115.00
Figure, Rebel Commando, Return of the Jedi, MOC $65.00
Figure, Rebel Soldier, Empire Strikes Back, MOC............. $90.00
Figure, Rebel Soldier, Return of the Jedi, M $10.00
Figure, Romba, Power of the Force, M $25.00
Figure, R2-D2, Droids, MOC $150.00
Figure, R2-D2, Power of the Force, w/pop-up light saber, MOC $225.00
Figure, R2-D2, Return of the Jedi, w/sensorscope, MOC.... $50.00
Figure, R5-D4, Empire Strikes Back, MOC...................... $150.00
Figure, Sandpeople, Empire Strikes Back, MOC............... $145.00
Figure, Sandpeople, Star Wars, MOC, (12-back) $375.00
Figure, Stormtrooper, Star Wars, 12", M.......................... $145.00
Figure, Yoda, Empire Strikes Back, orange snake, MOC.... $250.00
Game, Destroy Death Star, Kenner, MIB........................... $55.00
Game, Laser Battle, Star Wars, Kenner, MIB $85.00
Magnets, Return of the Jedi, set of 4, MOC....................... $25.00
Nightlight, Yoda, Return of the Jedi, 1980s, MOC............. $12.00
Playset, Cloud City, Empire Strikes Back, complete, EX.... $135.00
Playset, Dagobah, Darth Vadar & Luke Battle, Empire Strikes Back, complete, EX $25.00
Playset, Droid Factory, Star Wars, MIB............................ $145.00
Playset, Ewok Village, Return of the Jedi, complete, EX...... $35.00
Playset, Jabba the Hut, Return of the Jedi, complete, EX..... $20.00
Playset, Land of the Jawas, Star Wars, Complete, EX........... $55.00
Puppet, Yoda, Kenner, hollow vinyl, 1981, 10", EX............ $25.00
Radio watch, Lucasfilm/Bradley, R2-D2 & C-3PO on face, 1982, MIB... $50.00
Scissors, Return of the Jedi, MOC.................................... $10.00
Sit 'N Spin, Ewoks, MIB $80.00
Speaker phone, Darth Vader, MIB.................................... $95.00
Stickers, Return of the Jedi, 12-pc, 1983, MOC................. $10.00
Talking telephone, Ewoks, MIB.. $50.00
Vehicle, B-Wing Fighter, Return of the Jedi, complete, EX.. $65.00
Vehicle, Captivator (CAP-2), Empire Strikes Back, mini-rig, MIB.. $35.00

Vehicle, Darth Vader's TIE Fighter, Star Wars, complete, EX . $55.00
Vehicle, Ewok Battle Wagon, Power of the Force, complete, EX.. $60.00

Vehicle, Imperial Cruiser, ESB, MIB, $150.00.

Vehicle, Imperial Sniper, Power of the Force, MIB............. $110.00
Vehicle, Millennium Falcon, Empire Strikes Back, MIB $255.00
Vehicle, One-Man Sand Skimmer, Power of the Force, MIB.. $100.00
Vehicle, Sandcrawler, radio-controlled, complete, EX......... $175.00
Vehicle, Scout Walker (AT-ST), complete, EX $35.00
Vehicle, Side Gunner, Droids, complete, EX...................... $25.00
Vehicle, TIE Fighter (Battle Damage), Return of the Jedi, MIB.$135.00
Vehicle, X-Wing Fighter, Star Wars, MIB.......................... $425.00
Vehicle, Y-Wing Fighter, Return of the Jedi, MIB $225.00
Vehicles, All Terrain Attack Transport, complete, EX.......... $90.00
Yo-yo, Darth Vader, Dairy Queen promo, Humphrey, 1970s, rare, NM.. $25.00

Stauffer, Erich

From a distance, these child-like figures closely resemble Hummel figurines. They're marked 'Designed by Erich Stauffer' in blue script, often with a pair of crossed arrows or a crown. They always carry a number, sometimes with the letter S or U before it. As an added bonus, you may find a paper label bearing the title of the featured subject. Arnart Imports Inc imported Erich Stauffer figurines from Japan from the late 1950s through the 1980s. Some of these pieces may be found with original Arnart blue and gold stickers.

Figurines range in size from 4½" up to 12½" tall. The most common is the single figure, but some may have two or three children on a single base. The most interesting are those that include accessories or animals to complete their theme. Note that Arnart Imports also made a similar line, but those pieces are smaller and not of the same quality.

Note: The majority of the listings that follow were gleaned from Internet auction sales. They indicate not only the winning bid but also include postage, insurance, and occasionally handling charges as well, since those costs must be added to the winning bid to arrive at an accurate reflection of the final costs.

Advisor: Joan Oates (See Directory, Erich Stauffer Figurines)

#S8386N, planter, bricked, boy sits on top & holds beets & shovel, 5x4½x2" $18.00

#S8520, planter, sq box w/boy standing at side, lower right leg is bandaged, 5¼x4½x3" **$18.00**

#U8561, April Showers, boy w/umbrella, 7½" **$15.00**

#U8561, Sandy Shoes, girl cleaning shoe, 7½" **$15.00**

#1538, Visiting, boy before short fence holds a 2-tier wrapped present, 4½" **$10.00**

#22/619, Arnart's 'Little Sport,' boy w/baseball glove, 5⅜" .. **$12.00**

#2619, Arnart's 'Little Sport,' boy w/baseball glove, 2 geese at feet, 5⅜" **$12.00**

#44/173, Play Time, boy stands & holds baseball bat, 5¾" . **$16.00**

#44/175, Play Time, girl holding boy doll in her right hand, 4½" **$12.00**

#55/475, Pray Every Day, girl stands & prays by milk can, 5½" **$18.00**

#55/723, Napkins, napkin holder, boy w/towel over arm & hands folded as if praying, pineapple at his feet, 6" **$20.00**

#55/723, Napkins, napkin holder w/boy wearing chef's hat & holding 2 bottles of milk, towel over arm, 6" **$18.00**

#55/971, soap dish, boy seated on one end, 3x4½", rare, $35.00; bathroom tumbler, 3¾" boy as handle, 3½", rare, $25.00. (Photo courtesy Joan Oates)

#55/971, toothbrush holder w/3 holes, rare, 5¾x3¼" dia.... **$45.00**

#8349, boy sititng before fence playing flute, dog at his side, 4¼" **$15.00**

#8395, By the Old Apple Tree, boy playing violin beside tree, goose at his side, 5" **$18.00**

Steiff Animals

These stuffed animals originated in Germany around the turn of the century. They were created by Margaret Steiff, whose company continues to operate to the present day. They are identified by the button inside the ear and the identification tag (which often carries the name of the animal) on their chest. Over the years, variations in tags and buttons help collectors determine approximate dates of manufacture.

Teddy bear collectors regard Steiff bears as some of the most valuable on the market. When assessing the worth of a bear, they use some general guidelines as a starting basis, though other features can come into play as well. For instance, bears made prior to 1912 that have long gold mohair fur start at a minimum of $75.00 per inch. If the bear has dark brown or curly white mohair fur instead, that figure may go as high as $135.00. From the 1920 to 1930 era, the rule of thumb would be about $50.00 minimum per inch. A bear (or any other animal) on cast-iron or wooden wheels starts at $75.00 per inch; but if the tires are hard rubber, the value is much lower, more like $27.00 per inch.

For more information see Cynthia Powell's *Collector's Guide to Miniature Teddy Bears.*

Newsletter/Club: *Collector's Life*
The World's Foremost Publication for Steiff Enthusiasts
Beth Savino, Editor
Westgate Village, 3301 West Central Ave.
Toledo, OH 43606; 1-800-862-8697; www.toystore.net
Quarterly, $15 per year; club pin

Eric Bat, mohair, with tag, 1960s, rare, EX, minimum value, $675.00.

Alligator, mohair, w/button & tag, 1950s, 13½", M.......... **$165.00**

Baboon, Coco, wool & felt, glass eyes, red collar, no ID, ca 1970, 6", EX **$38.00**

Bear, Baby Ophelia, white mohair, black stitched nose & mouth, lace tutu, bow at neck, ear button, 1986 repro, 12", NM **$265.00**

Bear, Jackie, honey-colored mohair w/pink bow, all ID, 1994 replica of 1953 bear, 5½", NM **$110.00**

Bear, Preppy, dressed in Polo Ralph Lauren clothing, blond mohair, fully jointed, growler, ear button, 14", NM **$265.00**

Bear, tan mohair w/clipped muzzle, glass eyes, original button & tag, ca 1963-90s, 14", NM.. **$150.00**

Bear, 1907 replica, brown mohair, fully jointed, growler, all ID, 27", MIB **$365.00**

Camel, Trotty, light tan mohair, glass eyes, w/button & tags, 6x6", EX **$115.00**

Cat, Ginger, tabby w/red bow, green eyes, ear button, ca 1945-91, 9x13½" (w/tail), EX **$135.00**

Cat, Kitty, striped mohair, velveteen muzzle, 1940s, all ID, ca 1950, 4x4¼"+tail, NM **$295.00**

Cat, Snurry, white mohair w/brown markings, curled position, swivel head, 1964-66 only, ear button, 6" H, NM...... **$325.00**

Cat, Susi, striped mohair, original red bow, pink floss nose & mouth, chest tag, 8", EX **$220.00**

Chick, yellow wool, w/tag, 1940s, 1x1⅝", EX..................... **$40.00**

Chimp, Jocko, cinnamon mohair, wool stuffed, glass eyes, felt ears, jointed, squeaker, button in ear, 1930s, 12", VG **$280.00**

Dachshund, Waldi, long mohair, green outfit, ear button & chest tag, 1950-57, 9", NM..$625.00

Fox, Xorry, honey gold w/cream & black, amber glass eyes, chest tag/ear button, 10x18", EX...$265.00

Frog, green plush w/tan tummy, button eyes, button on left foot, 1975, 4" L, NM $110.00

German shepherd, Arco, brown tones, all ID, 1960s, 5½x10½", NM...$140.00

Goat, Zicky, tan mohair, all ID, 1950s, 6x6½", EX.............$70.00

Goose, Tulla, white w/orange bill & feet, w/button & label, 5", EX..$85.00

Hedgehog, Mecki, dressed as hobo, no ID, 6¾", EX..........$55.00

Horse, Cosy Ferdy, brown & white w/fluffy creamy white mane, w/button & tag, 1986-90, 8", NM.............................$45.00

Lamb, Lamby, white mohair, glass eyes, squeaker (silent), no ID, 12x12", EX...$75.00

Lynx, Luxy, bright mohair, working squeaker, 1963 only, chest tag & ear button, 10", NM......................................$325.00

Mountain goat, Rocky, wool & felt w/green glass eyes, no ID, 3¼", EX...$30.00

Owl, plush w/white fur around face, chest tag & ear tag, 5", EX.$35.00

Parakeet, Hansi, yellow & green velvet, felt & rubber, silver button, 1978, 8", EX..$65.00

Pekingese, Pekey, long brown hair, black muzzle w/brown accents, w/bow, button & tag, ca 1965-67, 6¼x6", NM $100.00

Pig, Good Luck Happy Pig, pink woven mohair, w/button, tag & hang tag, 2000, 5x8", M.....................................$95.00

Pony on wheels, brown w/orange glass eyes, red wheels marked Steiff 125, ca 1970, 20½x26½x12", EX.............................$285.00

Ram, cream & black mohair, w/button & tags, 1950s, 5x5", M..$125.00

Rhinocerous, brown mohair, glass eyes, no ID, 6", EX........$45.00

Rooster, Gallo, plush multicolors, brass button, old style flag & chest tag, 6", NM $60.00

Seal, Robby, brown mohair, w/button & tag, 4½", NM......$30.00

Spidy Spider, mohair, script button on leg, 7" (from top of head to bottom of torso), scarce, paper tag missing, from $700.00 to $1,000.00. (Photo courtesy McMaster's Harris Auction Company)

Squirrel, brown mohair, felt acorn, w/button & tag, 1950s, 6x6½", EX $145.00

Tiger, striped mohair, paper tag but no button, 1950s, 8½", VG . $135.00

Weasel, Minky, cream mohair w/shaded tan & brown, white felt feet, glass eyes, chest tag/ear button, 7x18", EX..............$265.00

String Holders

Today we admire string holders for their decorative nature. They are much sought after by collectors. However, in the 1800s, they were strictly utilitarian, serving as dispensers of string used to wrap food and packages. The earliest were made of cast iron. Later, advertising string holders appeared in general stores. They were made of tin or cast iron and were provided by companies pedaling such products as shoes, laundry supplies, and food. These advertising string holders command the highest prices.

These days we take cellophane tape for granted. Before it was invented, string was used to tie up packages. String holders became a staple item in the home kitchen. To add a whimsical touch, in the late 1920s and 1930s, many string holders were presented as human shapes, faces, animals, and fruits. Most of these novelty string holders were made of chalkware (plaster of Paris), ceramics, or wood fiber. If you were lucky, you might have won a plaster of Paris 'Super Hero' or comic character string holder at your local carnival. These prizes were known as 'carnival chalkware.' The Indian string holder was a popular giveaway, so was Betty Boop and Superman.

Our values are for examples in excellent condition.

Advisor: Larry G. Pogue (See Directory, String Holders)

Acorn, painted chalkware, 8½" $185.00

Anthropomorphic tomato face, painted chalkware, 5½" $175.00

Aunt Jemima (head only), painted chalkware, 1940s-50s, 7¾".. $395.00

Bananas, painted chalkware, ca 1980s, 5¾" $85.00

Batman (head only), painted chalkware, Copyright DC Comics, 8¾"..$325.00

Black boy riding alligator, painted chalkware, Copyright 1948, 9" $345.00

Black children (2) eating watermelon slice, painted chalkware, 1950s, 4¾"..$295.00

Black girl (face only), sad, painted chalkware, 1950s, 7½".. $395.00

Black porter (face only), black skin tones, ceramic, Fredericksburg Art Pottery USA, 6½"..$425.00

Bonzo, full figure, painted chalkware, 6½" $185.00

Bozo the Clown (head only), painted chalkware, 1950s, 7½".. $285.00

Buddha, sits on countertop, ceramic, Japan, 1940s, 5¾" ...$145.00

Campbell Soup Kid, painted ceramic, Copyright Campbell, 1950s, 6¾"..$395.00

Cat (face only) w/bow, scissors holder, ceramic, gray & white w/pink details, 5¾"..$60.00

Cat face w/pink polka-dot bow, w/scissors holder, ceramic, Japan sticker, 5⅜"..$145.00

Cat w/ball of twine, ceramic, 5½"......................................$95.00

Cat w/ball of twine & bow, painted chalkware, 6½".........$105.00

Chipmunk (head only) w/bow tie, ceramic, 5½" $135.00

Clown w/string tied to his tooth, painted chalkware, 1950s, 7".$250.00

Conovers Chef, painted chalkware, Conovers Original 1945, 6x6"..$245.00

Corn (single ear), painted chalkware, 9" $225.00

Corn (3 ears), painted chalkware, 5½" $175.00

Dagwood (head only), painted chalkware, Copyright Chic Young, 8"..$325.00

Dog (face only), ceramic, Made in England by Arther Wood, 4½". **$155.00**

Dutch boy (head only), match holder in top of hat, painted chalkware, 6½" **$375.00**

Elmer the Bull (head only), painted chalkware, 1950s, 7½". **$425.00**

Indian chief (head only), painted chalkware, 1950s, 8¾" ... **$275.00**

Mammy, black skin tones, ceramic, Made in Japan, 6½" ... **$235.00**

Mammy (big busted) w/apron, painted chalkware, 1940s, 7¾". **$365.00**

Mammy (face only) w/bow at top (w/slot for razor blade), painted chalkware, 6½" **$395.00**

Mammy w/arms out, half figure made for cloth skirt (to hold string) ceramic, 4½" **$145.00**

Mickey Mouse (head facing left), painted chalkware, Copyright WDE, 1940s, 8x9½" **$595.00**

Monkey on ball of twine, painted chalkware, 7½" **$245.00**

Mr. Peanut, painted chalkware, incised with 'Registered Mr. Peanut,' 6", $450.00. (Photo courtesy Larry Pogue)

Mutt dog (face only), painted chalkware, 1950s-60s, 6½". **$185.00**

Pear w/plums, painted chalkware, 7¾" **$85.00**

Rooster (head & neck only), painted chalkware, 8½" **$225.00**

Rooster (head only), painted chalkware, 1950s, 9" **$275.00**

Rose, painted chalkware, 8" **$175.00**

Sailor boy (head only), painted chalkware, 8" **$225.00**

Santa (head only), painted chalkware, 9¼" **$245.00**

Smokey Bear (head only), painted chalkware, Copyright 1957 NM, 6½" **$425.00**

Squash, yellow crook-neck type, painted chalkware, Ellis Studios, 7½" **$135.00**

String Along w/Me on heart shape, painted chalkware, 5½". **$135.00**

Superman (head only), painted chalkware, Copyright DC Comics, 7½" **$325.00**

Westie dog (head only), painted chalkware, 9" **$195.00**

Woody Woodpecker (head only), painted chalkware, Copyright Walter Lantz, 9½" **$345.00**

Swanky Swigs

These glasses, ranging in size from 3⅛" to 5⅝", were originally distributed by the Kraft company who filled them with their cheese spread. They were introduced in the 1930s and until 1976 were decorated with various colorful designs. Though no one has ever been able to document the actual number of variations available, our advisor tells us that in her own collection, she has cataloged more than 230.

Patterns range from sailboats, animals, and flowers to bands, dots, stars, checks, etc.

In 1951 Kraft came out with the first small clear glass with indented designs while still producing the color silkscreen Kraft Cheese Spread Swanky Swig designs such as Bustlin' Betsy, Antique No. 1, Bachelor Button, and Kiddie Kup. Some of the indented patterns were Crystal Petal, Hostess Design, and Coin Design.

By 1976 Kraft had dropped making the color-decorated Swanky Swigs and began using only clear glasses with indented designs — Colonial in 1976 and Petal Star in 1978. (The latter was used for their 50th anniversary; these were dated 1933 – 1983 in the glass itself.) Even today, you can buy Kraft Cheese spread in these clear small glasses.

After 27 years, Kraft resumed the production of a few color-decorated Swanky Swigs. There were eight of them, two of which were brought out in 2003 — one with dark blue hearts and red apples, the second with dark blue stars and red hearts. Six more came out in 2004, one with the word Greetings and the image of a passenger car and another with the word Holiday and the image of a train engine. The other four new to the market that year featured NASCAR drivers Mark Martin #6, Matt Kenseth #17, Kurt Busch #97, and Michael Waltrip #15.

In 1999 a few Kraft Swanky Swigs from Australia began to surface. They have been verified as such through Kraft magazine ads. We now have identified Swanky Swigs from three countries: the United States, Canada, and Australia.

Here is a listing of some of the harder-to-find examples: In the small (Canadian) size (about 3¹⁄₁₆" to 3¼") look for Band No. 5 (two red and two black bands); Galleon (two ships on each example, made in five colors — black, blue, green, red, and yellow); Checkers (made in four color combinations — black and red, black and yellow, black and orange, and black and white, all having a top row of black checks); and Fleur-De-Lis (black fleur-de-lis with a bright red filigree motif).

In the regular size (about 3⅜" to 3⅞") look for Dots Forming Diamonds (diamonds made up of small red dots); Lattice and Vine (white lattice with flowers in these combinations — white and blue, white and green, and white and red); Texas Centennial (a cowboy and horse in these colors — black, blue, green, and red); three special issues with dates of 1936, 1938, and 1942; and Tulip No. 2 (available in black, blue, green, and red).

In the large (Canadian) size (about 4³⁄₁₆" to 5⅝"), you'll find Circles and Dot (circles with a small dot in the middle, in black, blue, green, and red); Star No. 1 (small scattered stars, made in black, blue, green, and red); Cornflower No. 2 (in dark blue, light blue, red, and yellow); Provencial Crest (made only in red and burgundy with maple leaves).

Even the lids are collectible and are valued at a minimum of $3.00, depending on condition and the advertising message they convey.

For more information we recommend *Swanky Swigs* by Ian Warner; *Swanky Swigs* by Mark Moore; and *Collectible Glassware of the 40s, 50s, and 60s* and *The Collector's Encyclopedia of Depression Glass*, both by Gene and Cathy Florence.

Note: In the following listings, all descriptions are for American issues unless noted Canadian.

Advisor: Joyce Jackson (See the Directory, Swanky Swigs)

Antique #1, black, blue, brown, green, orange or red, Canadian, 1954, 4¾", ea **$20.00**

Antique #1, black, blue, brown, green, orange or red, Canadian, 3¼", ea **$8.00**

Antique #1, black, blue, brown, green, orange or red, 1954, 3¾", ea **$4.00**

Antique #2, lime green, deep red, orange, blue or black, Canadian, 1974, 4⅝", ea **$20.00**

Bachelor Button, red, green & white, 1955, 3¾" **$3.00**

Bachelor Button, red, white & green, Canadian, 1955, 3¼" .. **$6.00**

Bachelor Button, red, white & green, Canadian, 1955, 4¾" .. **$15.00**

Band #1, red & black, 1933, 3⅜" **$3.00**

Band #2, black & red, Canadian, 1933, 4¾" **$20.00**

Band #2, black & red, 1933, 3⅜" **$3.00**

Band #3, white & blue, 1933, 3⅜" **$3.00**

Band #4, blue, 1933, 3⅜" **$3.00**

Bicentennial Tulip, green, red or yellow, 1975, 3¾", ea **$15.00**

Blue hearts & red apples, US, 2003 .... **$5.00**

Blue stars & red hearts, US, 2003 .... **$5.00**

Blue Tulips, 1937, 4¼" **$20.00**

Bustlin' Betsy, brown, green, orange, red, or yellow, 1953: 3¾", $4.00 each; Canadian, 3¼", $8.00. (Photo courtesy Gene and Cathy Florence)

Bustlin' Betty, blue, brown, green, orange, red or yellow, Canadian, 1953, 4¾", ea **$20.00**

Carnival, blue, green, red or yellow, 1939, 3½", ea **$9.00**

Checkerboard, white w/blue, green or red, Canadian, 1936, 4¾", ea **$20.00**

Checkerboard, white w/blue, green or red, 1936, 3½", ea ... **$20.00**

Circles & Dot, any color, 1934, 3½", ea **$7.00**

Circles & Dot, black, blue, green or red, Canadian, 1934, 4¾", ea **$20.00**

Coin, clear & plain w/indented coin decor around base, Canadian, 1968, 3⅛" or 3¼", ea **$2.00**

Coin, clear & plain w/indented coin decor around base, 1968, 3¾". **$1.00**

Colonial, clear w/indented waffle design around middle & base, 1976, 3¾", ea .... **$.50**

Colonial, clear w/indented waffle design around middle & base, 1976, 4⅜", ea **$1.00**

Cornflower #1, light blue & green, Canadian, 1941, 4⅝", ea . **$20.00**

Cornflower #1, light blue & green, Canadian, 3¼", ea **$8.00**

Cornflower #1, light blue & green, 1941, 3½", ea **$4.00**

Cornflower #2, dark blue, light blue, red or yellow, Canadian, 1947, 3¼", ea **$8.00**

Cornflower #2, dark blue, light blue, red or yellow, Canadian, 1947, 4¼", ea **$30.00**

Cornflower #2, dark blue, light blue, red or yellow, 1947, 3½", ea. **$4.00**

Crystal Petal, clear & plain w/fluted base, 1951, 3½", ea **$2.00**

Dots Forming Diamonds, any color, 1935, 3½", ea **$50.00**

Ethnic Series, lime green, royal blue, burgundy, poppy red or yellow, Canadian, 1974, 4⅝", ea **$20.00**

Forget-Me-Not, dark blue, light blue, red or yellow, Canadian, 3¼", ea **$8.00**

Forget-Me-Not, dark blue, light blue, red or yellow, 1948, 3½", ea **$4.00**

Galleon, black, blue, green, red or yellow, Canadian, 1936, 3⅛", ea **$30.00**

Hostess, clear & plain w/indented groove base, Canadian, 1960, 3⅛" or 3¼", ea **$2.00**

Hostess, clear & plain w/indented groove base, Canadian, 1960, 5⅝", ea **$5.00**

Hostess, clear & plain w/indented groove base, 1960, 3¾", ea. **$1.00**

Jonquil (Posy Pattern), yellow & green, Canadian, 1941, 3¼" . **$8.00**

Jonquil (Posy Pattern), yellow & green, Canadian, 1941, 4⅝", ea **$20.00**

Jonquil (Posy Pattern), yellow & green, 1941, 3½", ea **$4.00**

Kiddie Kup, black, blue, brown, green, orange or red, Canadian, 1956, 3¼", ea **$6.00**

Kiddie Kup, black, blue, brown, green, orange or red, Canadian, 1956, 4¾", ea **$20.00**

Kiddie Kup, black, blue, brown, green, orange or red, 1956, 3¾", ea **$3.00**

Lattice & Vine, white w/blue, green or red, 1936, 3½", ea .. **$100.00**

NASCAR driver, No 1 Mark Martin #6, No 2 Matt Kinseth #17, US, 2004, ea **$10.00**

NASCAR driver, No 3 Kurt Busch #97, No 4 Michael Waltrip #15, ea **$10.00**

Petal Star, clear, 50th Anniversary of Kraft Cheese Spreads, 1933-1983, ca 1983, 3¾", ea **$2.00**

Petal Star, clear w/indented star base, Canadian, 1978, 3¼", ea ... **$2.00**

Petal Star, clear w/indented star base, 1978, 3¾", ea .... **$.50**

Plain, clear, like Tulip #1 w/out design, 1940, 3½", ea **$4.00**

Plain, clear, like Tulip #3 w/out design, 1951, 3⅞", ea **$5.00**

Provencial Crest, red & burgundy, Canadian, 1974, 4⅝", ea . **$25.00**

Sailboat #1, blue, 1936, 3½", ea **$12.00**

Sailboat #2, blue, green, light green or red, 1936, 3½", ea ... **$12.00**

Special Issue, Cornflower #1, light blue flowers/green leaves, Greetings From Kraft, etc, 1941, 3½" **$410.00**

Special Issue, Lewis-Pacific Dairyman's Assoc, Kraft Foods, Sept 13, 1947, Chehalis WA, 3½" **$100.00**

Special Issue, Posy Pattern Tulip, red tulip w/green leaves, Greetings From Kraft, CA Retail Assoc, etc, 1940, 3½" **$350.00**

Special Issue, Posy Pattern Violet, Greetings From Kraft, CA Retail Assoc, Grocers Merchants, Del Monte, 1942, 3½" **$350.00**

Special Issue, Sailboat #1, blue, Greetings From Kraft, CA Retail Assoc, Grocers Merchants, Del Monte, 1936, 3½" **$350.00**

Special Issue, Tulip #1, red, Greetings From Kraft, CA Retail Assoc, Grocers Merchants, Del Monte, 1938, 3½"................**$350.00**

Special Issue, 4-H Club, clear glass w/3 green parallel lines top/bottom, 2 clovers, Farewell Luncheon, 27th National 4-H Club Congress, Guest of JL Kraft, Dec 2, 1948 ....**$300.00**

Sportsmen Series, red hockey, blue skiing, red football, red baseball or green soccer, Canadian, 1976, 4⅝", ea **$20.00**

Stars #1, black, blue, green, red or yellow, Canadian, 1934, 4¾", ea **$20.00**

Stars #1, black, blue, green or red, 1935, 3½", ea **$7.00**

Stars #1, yellow, 1935, 3½", ea **$25.00**

Stars #2, clear w/orange stars, Canadian, 1971, 4⅝", ea **$5.00**

Texas Centennial, black, blue, green or red, 1936, 3½", ea..**$30.00**

Train, passenger car, Greetings, blue, 2005...........................**$5.00**

Train engine, Holiday, wine, 2004 ....**$5.00**

Tulip (Posy Pattern), red & green, Canadian, 1941, 3¼", ea .**$8.00**

Tulip (Posy Pattern), red & green, Canadian, 1941, 4⅝", ea **$20.00**

Tulip (Posy Pattern), red & green, 1941, 3½", ea **$4.00**

Tulip #1, black, blue, green, red or yellow, Canadian, 3¼", ea.....**$8.00**

Tulip #1, black, blue, green, red or yellow, 1937, 3½", ea......**$4.00**

Tulip #1, black, blue, green or red, Canadian, 1937, 4⅝", ea ...**$20.00**

Tulip #2, black, blue, green or red, 1938, 3½", ea **$25.00**

Tulip #3, dark blue, light blue, red or yellow, Canadian, 1950, 4¾", ea **$20.00**

Tulip #3, dark blue, light blue, red or yellow, Canadian, 3¼", ea **$8.00**

Tulip #3, dark blue, light blue, red or yellow, 1950, 3⅞", ea .**$4.00**

Violet (Posy Pattern), blue and green, 1941: 3½", $4.00; Canadian, 4⅝", $20.00; 3½" with label, $16.00; Canadian, 3¼", $8.00. (Photo courtesy Gene and Cathy Florence)

Wildlife Series, black bear, Canadian goose, moose or red fox, Canadian, 1975, 4⅝", ea **$20.00**

Syroco

Syroco Inc. originated in New York in 1890 when a group of European wood carvers banded together to produce original hand carvings for fashionable homes of the area. Their products were also used in public buildings throughout upstate New York, including the state capitol. Demand for those products led to the develop-

ment of the original Syroco reproduction process that allowed them to copy original carvings with no loss of detail. They later developed exclusive hand-applied color finishes to further enhance the product, which they continued to improve and refine over 90 years.

Syroco's master carvers use tools and skills handed down from father to son through many generations. Woods used, depending on the effect called for, include Swiss pear wood, oak, mahogany, and wormy chestnut. When a design is completed, it is transformed into a metal cast through their molding and tooling process. A compression mold system using wood fiber was employed from the early 1940s to the 1960s. Since 1962 a process has been in use in which pellets of resin are injected into a press, heated to the melting point, and then injected into the mold. Because the resin is liquid, it fills every crevice, thus producing an exact copy of the carver's art. It is then cooled, cleaned, and finished.

Other companies have produced similar items, among them are Multi Products, now of Erie, Pennsylvania. It was incorporated in Chicago in 1941 but in 1976 was purchased by John Hronas. Multi Products hired a staff of artists, made some wood originals and developed a tooling process for forms. They used a styrene-based material, heavily loaded with talc or calcium carbonate. A hydraulic press was used to remove excess material from the forms. Shapes were dried in kilns for 72 hours, then finished and, if the design required it, trimmed in gold. Their products included bears, memo pads, thermometers, brush holders, trays, plaques, nut bowls, napkin holders, etc., which were sold mainly as souvenirs. The large clocks and mirrors were made before the 1940s and may sell for as much as $100.00 and more, depending on condition. Syroco used gold trim, but any other painted decoration you might encounter was very likely done by an outside firm. Some collectors prefer the painted examples and tend to pay a little more to get them. You may also find similar products stamped 'Ornawood,' 'Decor-A-Wood,' and 'Swank'; these are collectible as well.

Cigarette box and ashtray, glass insert missing, marked, 8" long, $20.00.

Bookends, cowboy saddle, hat & boots, brown tones, 7x5½", pr.. **$30.00**

Bookends, eagle in relief, metal base, 5½x5¼", pr **$30.00**

Bookends, sailing ship & sea gulls in relief, brown stain, 7x5x2½" **$38.00**

Bookends, terrier dog, brown stain, 1950s, 7x4⅝", pr **$37.50**

Bottle opener, horse head figural, 4⅛x5x2⅛" **$70.00**

Brush, laughing man figural handle **$215.00**

Brush holder, dog w/glass eyes, red tongue pulls out to reveal wooden clothes brush, 3½x6" **$45.00**

Brush set, polo player on horse on holder that contains matching mahogany 7⅜" brushes, paper label **$55.00**

Business card holder, sailing ships in relief at ea end, brown tones, foil label, 3¾x7" **$25.00**

Candleholders, flower form, 1¼x4" dia, pr **$30.00**

Candleholders, 2-light, gold swirling Nouveau design, 19x8", pr **$110.00**

Clock, eagle crest, gold paint, gold hour & minute hands, key-wind, #5080, 16" **$45.00**

Clock, gold sunburst, gold Roman numerals on face, 8-day jeweled movement, 23" dia, VG **$40.00**

Clock, swirls, feathers & scrolls w/openwork form frame, antique gold paint, 8-day movement, w/key, 19" dia **$50.00**

Corkscrew, bulldog figural, walnut stain, 5¾" **$100.00**

Corkscrew, Indian chief standing, 8½" **$650.00**

Corkscrew, monk standing, brown tones, 8" **$650.00**

Corkscrew, Scottie head figural handle, VG paint **$35.00**

Corkscrew, Senator Volstad Codger (aka Old Codger), 1930s, 8½" **$160.00**

Corkscrew, waiter figural, multicolor paint w/slight wear, sharp helix, EX, from $85 to **$95.00**

Doorstop, bulldog w/glass eyes, brown w/green collar, ca 1930s-40s, 6½x7x4" **$55.00**

Doorstop, cat, recumbent w/tail curled to body, white w/yellow eyes, 1970s **$25.00**

Doorstop, cocker spaniel, brown tones, 5x9" **$65.00**

Figurine, Dagwood Bumstead, marked 1944 KFS, 5" **$35.00**

Figurines, peacock male & female, gold paint, 1960s, 13", 8" .. **$35.00**

Ice bucket, grapes in relief, bail handle, brown stain **$30.00**

Mirror, acorns along border, 4-lobe shape, 29x25½" **$90.00**

Mirror, eagle crest (w/gold paint) atop brown Federal-style frame, convex mirror, #4010, 1960, 29x16" **$55.00**

Mirror, ornate foliate openwork, gold paint, oval, 29x18" . **$110.00**

Mirror, ornate roses & leaves, beveled glass, easel back, 18x14½" .. **$65.00**

Mirror, ornately carved & reticulated medallions & scrolls, gold paint, #4715, 1950s, 33x17¾" **$70.00**

Mirror, streaming bows & flowers, creamy white paint, easel back, 14x11" **$100.00**

Mirror, Victorian scrolls w/4 scallops framing inset mirror, 3 scrolled candle arms, white paint, 26x14" **$40.00**

Mirror, 8-sided filigree frame, black paint w/gold accents, 22½x9½" **$55.00**

Pipe stand, acorns & leaves, brown stain, holds 3 pipes, 2½x6¾x4½" **$36.00**

Plaque, American bald eagle, black & gold label, 1947, 47" W **$140.00**

Plaque, Confederate bald eagle w/Confederate flat in talons, 30". **$55.00**

Plaque, key, ornate w/rearing lion standing on top of bar, swirls/scallops, gold paint, #3661-B, 7½x18" **$20.00**

Plaque, lady w/basket on head stands before palm tree, cactus at sides, 6" dia **$50.00**

Plaques, basket overflowing w/flowers, 12¼x11¾", pr **$20.00**

Plaques, Canadian geese, 1967, 16½x20½", 15½x20½", pr .. **$40.00**

Plaques, fruit swag, bronze-like paint, Copyright MCMLXXIV, 41x14", pr **$55.00**

Plaques, Roman helmets (pr) & sword, multicolor paint w/much detail, 1959, helmets: 16x17x3", sword: 36x11½" **$45.00**

Plaques, roosters, openwork along curling tail feathers, copper finish, 1960s, 14x12", 12½x12½", pr **$25.00**

Plaques, roses & rosebuds, chrysanthemums in cluster, ivory & gold paint, 1962, 18x12", pr **$40.00**

Plaques, sailing ships, multicolor paint, 21x28", 13x17", pr .. **$55.00**

Plaques, sea gulls (3, 2 joined at wing), w/gilt, marked MCMLXVII... USA, joined pr: 46" L, single: 13x28½" **$42.50**

Sconce, ornate ribbon swag w/roses & wildflowers, 6 ornate candleholders extend across swag, 25x39" **$50.00**

Sconces, ornate scrolls, gold paint, ea holds single candle, 1965, 13¼", pr **$20.00**

Shelf, rose & flowers amidst scrolls, white w/gold wash, #6202, 1965, 7x19x8" **$40.00**

Shelves, dogwood flowers w/openwork, 2-shelf, 1950s, 13x5¼", pr **$20.00**

Shelves, organic shape somewhat resembling bundle of wheat, gold washed, 13" w/11" dia top, 1930s, pr **$55.00**

Shoe brush holder, terrier dog & luggage w/golf clubs & bag, wood tones, gold metal & leather top on brush, 5½", VG+ ... **$25.00**

Tie rack, Scottie head above rack w/8 folding hooks, 7x9" .. **$40.00**

Taylor, Smith and Taylor

Though this company is most famous for their pastel dinnerware line, Lu Ray, they made many other patterns, and some of them are very collectible in their own right. Located in the East Liverpool area of West Virginia, the 'dinnerware capitol' of the world, their answer to HLC's very successful Fiesta line was Vistosa. It was made in four primary colors, and though quite attractive, the line was never developed to include any more than 20 items.

See also LuRay Pastels.

Autumn Harvest, plate, dinner; 10" **$8.00**

Autumn Harvest, platter, oval, 13½" **$25.00**

Boutonniere, bowl, berry; lg **$15.00**

Boutonniere, butter dish **$25.00**

Boutonniere, coffee mug **$15.00**

Boutonniere, cup & saucer, from $10 to **$15.00**

Boutonniere, plate, bread/dessert; 6¾" **$5.00**

Boutonniere, tumbler, juice; decal on clear glass, 3¾" **$15.00**

Bride's Bouquet, creamer & sugar bowl, w/lid **$35.00**

Bride's Bouquet, cup & saucer **$15.00**

Bride's Bouquet, plate, bread & butter; 6½" **$7.00**

Bride's Bouquet, plate, dinner; 10" **$15.00**

Bride's Bouquet, plate, salad; 7½" **$8.00**

Brocatelle, coffeepot, 10" **$40.00**

Brocatelle, creamer, 4" **$8.00**

Brocatelle, plate, dinner; 10" **$9.00**

Brocatelle, sugar bowl, wooden lid w/brass finial, 3½".........**$20.00**
Cathay, butter dish, rectangular, from $32 to......................**$36.00**
Cathay, creamer & sugar bowl, w/lid **$37.50**
Cathay, gravy boat, from $25 to.......................................**$32.00**
Cathay, tidbit tray, 2-tier, from $35 to **$45.00**

Coffee Tree, plate, dinner; $8.50.

Conversation, plate, dinner **$8.00**
Conversation, platter, 13½x10"..**$20.00**
Corinthian, creamer, blue interior, 4" **$10.00**
English Abbey, creamer & sugar bowl, w/lid......................**$25.00**
English Abbey, platter, 11x8", from $20 to **$25.00**
Golden Button, platter, 13½x10" **$10.00**
Leaf O' Gold, plate, dinner; 10", from $10 to **$12.00**
Morning Glory, plate, bread & butter; gold trim, 6½" **$6.00**
Morning Glory, plate, dinner; 10¼" **$10.00**
Pastoral, plate, bread & butter; 6½", from $5 to................**$6.00**
Pebbleford, bowl, serving; 9"...**$15.00**
Pebbleford, chop plate, from $20 to................................**$25.00**
Pebbleford, coffeepot, from $28 to..................................**$38.00**
Pebbleford, creamer..**$10.00**
Pebbleford, cup & saucer **$10.00**
Pebbleford, plate, dinner; 10", from $10 to **$12.00**
Pink Castle, bowl, vegetable; 9", from $25 to **$32.00**
Pink Castle, plate, luncheon; 8", from $8 to **$10.00**
Pink Dogwood, bowl, vegetable; w/lid, from $30 to...........**$35.00**
Pink Dogwood, salt & pepper shakers, pr from $20 to........**$25.00**
Plate, calendar; 1962, gold decor, Dutch windmill scene, 10"...**$20.00**
Reveille Rooster, bowl, soup/cereal; 6½", from $5 to.............**$7.00**
Reveille Rooster, cup & saucer **$6.00**
Reveille Rooster, plate, bread & butter; 6½" **$5.00**
Reveille Rooster, plate, dinner; 10" **$9.00**
Shasta Daisy, plate, salad; 8¼" **$8.00**
Summer Rose, bowl, serving; platinum trim, 2½x9"...........**$15.00**
Summer Rose, platter, platinum trim, oval, 13½" **$16.00**
Summer Rose, platter, platinum trim, 10½" **$14.00**
Tea Rose, bowl, serving, tab handles, 2⅝x8¾"...................**$16.00**
Tea Rose, creamer & sugar bowl, w/lid, from $28 to **$38.00**

Tea Rose, cup & saucer **$10.00**
Tulip, pitcher, 7½"...**$24.00**
Verona, bowl, serving; w/handles & lid, 3x11" L...............**$17.50**
Verona, platter, oval, 18x12½"...**$25.00**
Wildflower, platter, oval, 11½x8½"...................................**$15.00**
Wildflower, sugar bowl, w/lid **$9.00**

Tea Bag Holders

Whimsical yet functional, these little trays designed to hold a used tea bag can be found in many shapes. The most common is the teapot, but you'll be amazed at the variety of form and design you may find. They're small, so they take up very little space — a perfect collectible for apartment dwellers or anyone who simply finds them cheerful and fun.

Be an Angel & Let Me Hold the Tea Bag, girl kneeling & holding tray, ceramic, Japan label, 3" **$22.50**
Cat's face on teapot form, multicolor pastels, ceramic, #CT-12, 4½"..**$38.00**
Cherry w/smiling face, red w/green leaves at top, ceramic, Enesco **$20.00**
Doll-face flower w/arms & legs, multicolor, ceramic, Japan N-in-circle mark, 5" **$20.00**
I Will Hold the Teabag on teapot form, ceramic, set of 4 in frame **$35.00**
Miss Cutie-Pie, girl's face on teapot form, ceramic, Napco label **$16.00**
Pineapple w/face on teapot shape, multicolor, ceramic, 1950s, 4¼x4¼" **$10.00**
Smiling face on lemon shape, yellow & green, ceramic, Enesco, #-0307, 3¾"...**$15.00**
Smiling face on teapot shape, multicolor, ceramic, Davar Originals Japan, set of 4 in metal frame **$20.00**
Strawberry, red & green, ceramic, 3¾", set of 4 in 5x4¾x2½" wrought-iron frame..**$25.00**

Teapot form, Let Me Hold the Bag, Cleminson, $15.00. (Photo courtesy Rosemary Nichols)

Teapot shape w/red & green roses w/gold, ceramic, Lefton, 3¼x4¾" **$6.00**

Teapots

The continued popularity of teatime and tea-related items has created a tighter market for collectors on the lookout for teapots. Vintage and finer quality teapots have become harder to find, with those from the 1890s and 1920s reflecting age with three and four digit prices.

Most collectors begin with a general collection of varied teapots until they decide upon the specific category that most appeals to them. Collecting categories include miniatures, doll or toy sets, those made by a certain manufacturer, figurals, or a particular style. While teapots made in Japan have waned in collectibility, collectors have begun to realize many detailed and delicate examples are available.

Anniversary Rose, lg red rose on white swirled body w/gold trim, ceramic, Myott, 6-cup...$80.00

Apples in relief on green barrel-like form, brown handle, Japan, 7"...$15.00

Art Deco geometric design w/flowers & multicolor lustre, rectangular ceramic body, Japan $25.00

Blue Tulip, blue on blue, ceramic, Cronin Pottery, 6-cup.....$40.00

Camel kneeling w/orange-draped gold-encrusted box on back, multicolor, he w/allover gold motifs, wrapped handle, Japan..$180.00

Cherry blossoms & leaves on branches on trunk-like form, majolica style, Japan..$18.00

Chocolate brown speckled w/creamy white polka dots, Price Bros Made in England, ca 1934-61, NM............................$35.00

Cottage & flower garden on white, ceramic, Sadler, Staffordshire England, sm...$25.00

Dogwood on white w/gold trim, ceramic, Japan Oven-Detergent Proof, 10", w/candle warmer base $75.00

Duck figural, blue & whtie, ceramic, copper handle, Made in Thailand by Sigma, 4¾" $55.00

Elephant, brown with enamel details, Japan, ca. 1930s, 7½x9½", from $50.00 to $65.00.

Elephant w/howdah, trunk up, multicolor lustre, ceramic, Japan, 6x10" $75.00

Fern & Bamboo, green & white majolica, Wardle & Co Hanley England, 7½"...$275.00

Floral, gray/black w/touches of pink, green & yellow on white, Arthur Wood England, 5½" $35.00

Floral chintz w/gold trim, bone china, Adderley Lawley England, 7½"...$125.00

Floral reserves w/cobalt & gold trim, squat, Nippon mark, 4½", NM..$135.00

Fruit forms body, predominately green, ceramic, Japan, C-1725, 8"...$26.00

Golden Laurel, hand-painted pattern on white swirled body, ceramic, Lefton, 32426, NM $36.00

Intaglio Annet, ceramic, Mikasa CAC20...........................$65.00

Lady figural, crinoline skirt forms pot, Ye Daintee Ladyee Teapot Regd No 824571 Made in England, 7x7"................$135.00

Lotus blossoms on green w/gold trim, ceramic, Occupied Japan, 2-cup...$75.00

Macaw parrot figural, extended wing & tail, pastels on black, Fitz & Floyd, 1989, 7¼"..$195.00

Paisley Chintz, Ovolo Gibsons England PT NO 773128 RG No 735583, 3¾x6"..$95.00

Pansies on swirled white body, ceramic, Cauldon-Vale, 8" ...$35.00

Peggotty (head only), light brown hair & beard, black hat, rope handle, Beswick #1116, 6"...................................$47.50

Pink floral on white w/gold trim, ceramic, Royal Park China, 4¾" $22.00

Pink rose (lg) embossed on white ribbed body, ceramic, USA mark, 4½x6"...$25.00

Pink rose figural w/bud finial, green handle & spout, ceramic, Japan, PY21929...$45.00

Pink roses in dotted pattern on white w/gold trim, M Nasco Fine China, 4¼"...$28.00

Poppies on white basketweave pattern, ceramic, Arthur Wood, ca 1940, 7½"..$30.00

Rabbit figural, brown shading to white w/multicolor details, ceramic, Shafford, 7"...$95.00

Roses decal on white w/gold, Ellgreave, 1950s, 5" $42.50

Rusticana, red transfer ware, Villeroy & Boch....................$150.00

Teapot, painted dot decoration on dark brown w/gold, ceramic, Japan, 3¾"...$17.50

Tomato form w/green spout & handle, ceramic, Japan, 4¼"..$50.00

Wild duck figural, brown w/gold accents, gold bow at neck, redware, wire handle, 4½x10".......................................$20.00

Windmill figural, blue roof, brown blades, ceramic, Japan, 5" $32.00

Tiara Exclusives

Tiara Exclusives was the dream of a determined man named Roger Jewett. With much hard work and planning and the involvement of Jim Hooffstetter of Indiana Glass, Tiara home party plan operations were initialized in July of 1970. Tiara Exclusives was a subsidiary of Indiana Glass, which is a division of Lancaster Colony. Tiara did not manufacture the glassware it sold. Several companies were involved in producing the glassware, among them Indiana Glass, Fenton, Fostoria, Dalzell Viking, and L.E. Smith. The Tiara Exclusives direct selling organization closed in 1998.

In 1999 and 2000, Home Interiors offered a small selection of Tiara Sandwich Glass dinnerware in an attractive transparent purple color called Plum. They have also marketed Tiara's square honey box and children's dish set.

Advisor: Mandi Birkinbine (See Directory, Tiara)

Crown Dinnerware

In the mid-1980s Tiara made Crown Dinnerware in Imperial Blue. This is the pattern most collectors know as King's Crown Thumbprint. The color is a rich medium blue, brighter than cobalt.

Bowl, 2⅛x4¼", from $5 to	$7.00
Bowl, 4x9¼", from $12 to	$15.00
Cup	$3.00
Goblet, stemmed, 8-oz, from $3 to	$5.00
Pitcher, 8¾", from $25 to	$30.00
Plate, bread; 8"	$5.00
Plate, dinner; 10"	$7.00
Saucer	$2.00

Honey Boxes

One of Tiara's more popular items was the honey box or honey dish. It is square with tiny tab feet and an embossed allover pattern of bees and hives. The dish measures 6" tall with the lid and was made in many different colors, usually ranging in value from $15.00 up to $45.00, depending on the color. Unusual colors may have greater values.

Amber, from $15 to	$25.00
Black, from $25 to	$35.00
Chantilly (pale) Green, from $25 to	$40.00
Clear, from $35 to	$45.00
Cobalt blue, from $35 to	$45.00
Light blue, from $20 to	$40.00

Milk glass, from $45.00 to $65.00.

Peach, from $35 to	$40.00
Spruce (teal) Green, from $15 to	$25.00

Sandwich Pattern

Among the many lovely glass patterns sold by Tiara, the Sandwich pattern was the most popular. Tiara's Sandwich line reintroduced Indiana Glass and Duncan & Miller Glass designs from the 1920s and 1930s alongside items designed specifically for Tiara. Tiara Sandwich Glass has been made in Crystal, Amber, Ruby, Chantilly (light green), Spruce (teal), Peach, and other colors in limited quantities. The dark blue color named Bicentennial Blue was introduced in 1976 in observance of America's Bicentennial. According to the Tiara brochure, Bicentennial Blue Sandwich glass (sometimes also called Anniversary or Midnight Blue by collectors) was approved for a production of 15,000 sets. The only Tiara Sandwich items produced in pink were a dinner bell and a 'glo lamp' (fairy lamp). All other pink-toned Tiara Sandwich is actually peach. We've listed a few pieces of Tiara's Sandwich below, and though the market is somewhat unstable and tends to vary from region to region, our estimates will serve to offer an indication of current asking prices. Because this glass is not rare and is relatively new, collectors tend to purchase only items in perfect condition. Chips or scratches will decrease value significantly.

With most items, the quickest way to tell Anchor Hocking's Sandwich from Tiara and Indiana Sandwich is by looking at the flower in the pattern. The Tiara/Indiana flower is outlined with a single line and has convex petals. Anchor Hocking's flower is made with double lines, so has a more complex appearance, and the convex area in each petal is tiny. Tiara's Chantilly Green Sandwich is a pale green color that resembles the light green glass made by Indiana Glass during the Depression era. Use of a black light can help determine the age of pale green Sandwich Glass. The green Sandwich made by Indiana Glass during the Depression will fluoresce yellow-green under a black light. Tiara's Chantilly Green reflects the purple color of the black light bulb, but does not fluoresce yellow-green. To learn more about the two lines, we recommend *Collectible Glassware from the 40s, 50s, and 60s,* by Gene and Cathy Florence (Collector Books). Also available is *Tiara Exclusives Glass: The Sandwich Pattern* by our advisor, Mandi Birkinbine. (See the Directory for ordering information.)

Ashtray, Amber, 1¼x7½", from $8 to	$10.00
Basket, Amber, tall & slender, 10¾x4¾", from $40 to	$50.00
Basket, Chantilly Green, 7¾x5x6½", from $65 to	$85.00
Basket, Ruby, 10¾x4¾", from $50 to	$65.00
Bell, dinner; Pink, 6", from $12 to	$15.00
Bowl, Amber, slant sides, 1¾x4¾", from $4 to	$5.50
Bowl, Amber, 6-sided, 1¼x6¼", from $8 to	$12.00
Bowl, console; Amber, footed, flared rim, 3⅞x11", from $25 to	$30.00
Bowl, salad; Amber, crimped, 4¾x10", from $15 to	$18.00
Bowl, salad; Amber, slant sides, 3x8⅜", from $10 to	$15.00
Bowl, salad; Chantilly Green, slant sides, 3x8⅜", from $15 to	$20.00
Butter dish, Amber, domed lid, 6" H, from $20 to	$25.00
Butter dish, Bicentennial Blue, domed lid, 6" H, from $25 to	$35.00
Butter dish, Chantilly Green, domed lid, 6" H, from $20 to	$30.00
Butter dish, dark Teal Green, domed lid, 6" H, from $25 to	$35.00
Cake plate, Chantilly Green, footed, 4x10", from $60 to	$75.00
Candleholders, Amber, flared foot, 3¾", pr from $10 to	$12.00
Candleholders, Sea Mist (light), 8½", pr from $35 to	$45.00

Candy box, Amber, w/lid, 7½", from $65 to **$80.00**

Canister, Amber, 26-oz, 5⅝", from $12 to **$20.00**

Canister, Amber, 38-oz, 7½", from $12 to **$20.00**

Canister, Amber, 52-oz, 8⅞", from $18 to **$26.00**

Celery tray/oblong relish, Amber, 10⅜x4⅜", from $16 to..**$22.00**

Celery tray/oblong relish, Bicentennial Blue, 10⅜x4⅜", from $15 to **$20.00**

Clock, Amber, wall hanging, 12" dia, from $12 to **$18.00**

Clock, Amber, wall hanging, 16" dia, from $45 to **$55.00**

Clock, Peach, wall hanging, 12" dia, from $12 to **$18.00**

Clock, Spruce, wall hanging, 12" dia, from $12 to **$18.00**

Coaster, Amber, from $3 to.. **$5.00**

Compote, Amber, 8", from $18 to....................................... **$25.00**

Creamer & sugar bowl, Bicentennial Blue, round, flat, pr from $20 to **$25.00**

Cup, coffee; Amber, 9-oz, from $3 to **$4.00**

Cup, snack/punch; & saucer, crystal, 2⅝x3⅜", from $3 to....**$5.00**

Cup, snack/punch; Amber, from $2 to..................................... **$3.00**

Dish, club, heart, diamond or spade shape, Amber, 4", ea from $3 to **$5.00**

Dish, club, heart, diamond or spade shape, clear, 4", ea........ **$3.00**

Fairy (Glo) lamp, Amber, egg shape, pedestal foot, 2-pc, 5¾", from $8 to **$12.00**

Fairy (Glo) lamp, Chantilly Green (light), from $20 to **$25.00**

Fairy (Glo) lamp, Hazel Brown (med brown w/purple cast), 2-pc, 5¾", from $12 to **$18.00**

Fairy (Glo) lamp, Horizon (bright) Blue, 2-pc, 5¾", from $20 to **$25.00**

Fairy (Glo) lamp, Peach, 2-pc, 5¾", from $12 to................. **$15.00**

Fairy (Glo) lamp, Pine Green (dark), 2-pc; 5¾", from $12 to **$18.00**

Goblet, table wine; Amber, 8½-oz, 5½", from $6 to............. **$8.00**

Goblet, water; Amber, 8-oz, 5¼", from $6 to **$8.00**

Goblet, water; Bicentennial Blue, 8-oz, 5¼", from $10 to ... **$12.00**

Goblet, water; clear, 5¼", from $6 to **$9.00**

Goblet, water; Spruce Green, 8-oz, 5¼", from $5 to............. **$7.00**

Gravy boat, Amber, 3⅛x7⅜", from $35 to.......................... **$45.00**

Mug, Amber, footed, 5½", from $6 to **$8.00**

Napkin holder, Amber, 4x7½", from $15.00 to $20.00. (Photo courtesy Mandi Birkinbine)

Napkin holder, Spruce Green, footed fan shape, 4x7½", from $30 to **$45.00**

Pitcher, Amber, 8¼", from $25 to....................................... **$35.00**

Pitcher, Peach, 8½", from $20 to.. **$30.00**

Plate, dinner; Amber, 10", from $9 to.................................. **$15.00**

Plate, dinner; Chantilly Green, 10", from $8 to.................... **$12.00**

Plate, salad; Amber, 8", from $5 to **$8.00**

Plate, salad; Chantilly Green, 8¼", from $4 to **$8.00**

Platter, Amber, sawtooth rim, 12", from $8.50 to................ **$12.00**

Puff box, Amber, 3⅝" dia, from $10 to **$15.00**

Puff box, Horizon Blue, 3⅝" dia, from $12 to..................... **$15.00**

Salt & pepper shakers, Amber, 4¾", pr, from $18 to **$25.00**

Saucer, Amber **$2.00**

Sherbet, Amber, 3x3⅝"... **$5.00**

Tray, Amber, footed, 1¾x12¾", from $20 to **$35.00**

Tray, Chantilly Green, 3-part, 12" **$19.00**

Tray, divided relish; Amber, 4-compartment, 10", from $15 to ..**$20.00**

Tray, egg; Amber, 12", from $15 to **$20.00**

Tray, egg; Peach, 12", from $20 to **$35.00**

Tray, egg; Spruce Green, 12", from $15 to **$18.00**

Tray, oval snack; Crystal (goes w/punch cup), 8⅜x6¾" **$3.00**

Tray, tidbit; Horizon Blue, center silver-colored metal handle, 8¼" dia, from $12 to **$15.00**

Tumbler, juice; Amber, footed, 3", from $10 to **$12.00**

Tumbler, juice; Amber, 8-oz, 4", from $12 to **$14.00**

Tumbler, water; Amber, 10-oz, 6½" **$8.00**

Vase, Amber, ruffled, footed, 3¼x6½", from $13 to **$15.00**

Vase, bud; Amber, 3⅝", from $15 to **$20.00**

Wine set, Amber, decanter & tray w/8 goblets, from $30 to.**$40.00**

Wine set, Chantilly, decanter & tray w/6 goblets, from $45 to **$65.00**

Wine set, clear, decanter & tray w/8 goblets, from $45 to **$60.00**

Tire Ashtrays

Manufacturers of tires issued miniature versions containing ashtray inserts that they usually embossed with advertising messages. Others were used as souvenirs from World's Fairs. The earlier styles were made of glass or glass and metal, but by the early 1920s, they were replaced by the more familiar rubber-tired variety. The inserts were often made of clear glass, but colors were also used, and once in awhile you'll find a tin one. The tires themselves were usually black; other colors are rarely found. Hundreds have been produced over the years; in fact, the larger tire companies still issue them occasionally, but you no longer see the details or colors that are evident in the pre-WWII ashtrays. Although the common ones bring modest prices, rare examples sometimes sell for up to several hundred dollars, and eBay has only served to exacerbate this situation. For ladies or non-smokers, some miniature tires were made as pin trays.

For more information we recommend *Tire Ashtray Collector's Guide* by Jeff McVey.

Advisor: Jeff McVey (See Directory, Tire Ashtrays)

Allstate Cargo Lug, Sears Allstate Truck Tires in red lettering on white in center of clear glass insert, 1960s **$20.00**

BF Goodrich Silvertown, milk glass insert, 6½".................**$32.00**

BF Goodrich Silvertown 770, blue & white advertising on clear insert... **$30.00**

BF Goodrich Silvertown...Tubeless, blue & white logo & advertising on clear insert, 5¾"...**$26.00**

Bridgestone D-Lug 37.23-35 36PR Tubeless, 8½", MIB **$85.00**

Continental, clear glass insert w/3 rests, 8" **$215.00**

Continental Titan, clear glass insert, 7"...........................**$110.00**

Dominion Royal Master 7.50-16, green tire w/amber insert, 6½" **$415.00**

Dunlop Fort 5.00-16, Dunlop embossed on clear glass insert, 6".. **$110.00**

Firestone, black plastic w/red plastic ashtray insert, 1⅞x6" dia.. **$22.00**

Firestone Champion 6.00-16 Safety-Lock Cord, cobalt insert (rare color) **$575.00**

Firestone Great Lakes Exposition etched on amber glas insert, dated 1936 ....**$60.00**

Firestone Gum Dipped Balloon, amber glass insert, 5½" **$62.50**

Firestone Phoenix Lichtenfeld, red logo on clear glass insert w/2 rests, 6" **$130.00**

Firestone The Spirit of 76 (tractor tire), red, white & blue on clear insert, 6¾"...**$20.00**

Firestone Tractor R-1 All Traction Field & Road F151 Shock Fortified Gum Dipped, frosted letters on clear insert....**$25.00**

Firestone Transport 100 F Tubeless, clear glass insert **$69.00**

Fisk embossed on clear glass insert, crackling along tire, 6½" . **$215.00**

Gillette Super Traction, Gillette & bear going through tire embossed on clear insert, 7"..**$95.00**

Goodyear Custom Power Cushion Polyglass, decal & logo on glass insert in center, 6"...**$20.00**

Goodyear Eagle VR50, clear glass insert, 6" **$30.00**

Goodyear Wrangler Radials Light Trucks/ Rv's, 6½", $25.00.

Kelly Springfield Tires embossed on clear glass insert, 1904, 1915, 1916, & 1918 patent dates on tire, 4½", VG **$110.00**

US Royal Tempered Rubber Heavy Duty Six 6.70-18 4 Ply, embossed clear glass insert, 7"...................................**$110.00**

Tobacco Collectibles

Until lately, the tobacco industry spent staggering sums advertising their products, and scores of retail companies turned out many types of smoking accessories such as pipes, humidors, lighters, and ashtrays. Even though the smoking habit isn't particularly popular nowadays, collecting tobacco-related memorabilia is!

See also Advertising Character Collectibles, Joe Camel; Ashtrays; Cigarette Lighters.

Club/Newsletter: *Tobacco Jar*
Society of Tobacco Jar Collectors
1705 Chanticleer Drive
Cherry Hill, NJ 08003
www.tobaccojarsociety.com

Sign, Kool Cigarettes, embossed painted tin, 10½x25", $50.00. (Photo courtesy B.J. Summers)

Ash stand, brass colored metal over cast iron, amber 5¾" glass tray in top, ca 1940s-50s, 27x8" dia **$35.00**

Ashtray/cigar cutter; brass w/embossed decor, guillotine type w/cutter at lion's mouth, 6x4", EX **$90.00**

Bag, Mail Pouch Ribbon Cut Chewing Tobacco, printed paper, holds 1¾-oz tobacco, a/ad for brass spittoon on back, 3x5"........**$5.00**

Box, cigar; Bances & Suarez La Carolina, original factory scscene, Cuban lady on inside label, 1930s, EX **$45.00**

Box, cigar; Par Buster, golfing scene on wood, copyright 1934, VG **$22.50**

Cigar store figure, Indian chief, painted composition, 1920s-30s, for countertop, 18x4x4", EX **$875.00**

Cigarette paper, Top Wheat Straw, RJ Reynolds, 100 in package. **$10.00**

Cutter, Brown's Mule, CI w/embossed lettering, 7x18", VG **$50.00**

Cutter, Enterprise, cast iron, 7x19", EX.............................**$70.00**

Humidor, glass w/silver-plated Deco-style lid, pipe finial, unmarked..**$45.00**

Humidor, La Palina Cigars, clear glass, Congress Cigar Co, 7½x5¾" dia..**$32.00**

Humidor, wood w/felt lining, Decatur Industries, 3x11x7¾".**$20.00**

Label, Chief Joseph, portrait & scenes, Petre Schmidt & Bergmann Litho NY, 6x10" **$120.00**

Label, crate; Harlequin, man in tights holding sword, A Hoen & Co Richmond VA, 13x7", EX **$40.00**

Label, crate; Zadie, classical lady w/dove, Petersburg USA, 13¾x7" **$40.00**

Lighter, cigar; brass eagle figural, tail lever, 8x4½x3½", EX ..**$100.00**

Lighter, cigar; Punch figural, brass, w/attachment for gas line, 7x2¾", EX...**$100.00**

Lighter, cigarette; Chesterfield Cigarettes, Ritepoint, EX **$45.00**

Lighter, cigarette; chromium, Ronson Standard, ca 1935, 2x1⅝" **$70.00**

Lighter, cigarette; Marlboro logo w/bull's head, Zippo, 1989, M..**$65.00**

Lighter, cigarette; metal ladybug, squeeze antennas to open, 1940s **$50.00**

Lighter, cigarette; Minerva, floral on porcelain, Ronson, ca 1953, 3"...**$50.00**

Lighter, cigarette; Philip Morris Cigarettes, Zippo, 1960s, NM ..**$40.00**

Lighter, cigarette; Winston Filter Cigarettes, red & white enameling, 1970s, unused..**$20.00**

Lighter, Punch figural, cast iron w/gilt finish, hat tilts back to fill w/kerosene, 6x3½", EX..............................**$70.00**

Match holder, Punch figural, brass, hat tips back, 6x4"......**$110.00**

Matchbook, various businesses, ca 1940s, unused, ea from $3 to **$10.00**

Pack, Home Run Cigarettes, baseball scene, brittle but unopened w/1910 tax stamp, EX **$230.00**

Pack, Lucky Strike Cigarettes, red & black logo, MIP (sealed)..**$45.00**

Pipe, Black Forest, bear, EX details, 3⅜x2½x3¼".............**$115.00**

Pipe, briarwood, carved matador, Spain, ca 1950.................**$50.00**

Pipe, Dunhill FE Root Briar, Vulcanite mouthpiece, 1959...**$200.00**

Pipe, Dunhill Root Briar #250FT, 1958, EX **$75.00**

Pipe, Dunhill Root Briar #5213, 6¾", EX.........................**$115.00**

Pipe, Dunhill Shell Briar #315FT, 1966, EX **$120.00**

Pipe, Dunhill Shell Briar #475, cherry wood, 5½"............**$135.00**

Pipe, Tanshell, Dunhill #4032, EX.....................................**$125.00**

Pipe rest, dachshund, cold-painted, ceramic, unmarked, 3x5" ..**$30.00**

Pipe tamper, pick & scraper blades that attached to faux tortoise handle, marked Corona **$5.00**

Pipe tamper/pen knive, Dunhill, 2 tamper blades+pen knife & spoon shaped blades, 2⅞".........................**$110.00**

Pipe tool, Kleen Reem, WJ Young Co Peabody, M in case...**$12.00**

Postcard, Stag Tobacco, stag in woods, built-in vinyl record, 3⅝x5⅝", EX..**$50.00**

Scissors, cigar cutter; folding pocket type, 2⅛x1⅝" **$15.00**

Tin, Bagdad Short Cut Pipe Smoking, Middle-Eastern man's portrait amid 2 flags, 3½x3¾x1", EX......................**$50.00**

Tin, Bagley's Old Colony Mixture Smoking Tobacco, pocket size, unopened, $375.00. (Photo courtesy B.J. Summers)

Tin, Bagley's Sweet Tips Smoking, black label on gold-tone, oval variation, 4x2½x1⅜", EX+ **$70.00**

Tin, Edgeworth Ready-Rubbed Extra High Grade, America's Finest Pipe Tobacco, vertical stripes, 4⅜x3⅛x1", EX **$160.00**

Tin, High Plane, single-engine plane, Larus Bros, tax stamp remnants, 4⅜x3x⅞", EX..**$220.00**

Tin, Honey Moon Tobacco, couple seated in moon crest, John Igelstroem litho, 9¾x6¾", NM **$800.00**

Tin, Lucky Strike Roll Cut Tobacco, 4½x3", VG..............**$115.00**

Tin, Patterson's Tuxedo Tobacco, man's portrait reserve on green, concave tin litho, vertical, sample size, 2¾", VG **$100.00**

Tin, Philip Morris Revelation Smoking Mixture, red, black & cream, pocket size, 4x3¼", EX................................**$10.00**

Tobacco silk, lady w/Red Cross flag, Nebo Cigarette Co, 5x3" **$15.00**

Tools

Mass-produced tools have been with us for many years. Some have found their way to the secondary market. Quality tools are a favorite among bargain hunters. Factors important in evaluating tools are scarcity, usefulness, portability, age, and condition. Modern manufactured tools found with the manufacturer's mark are generally worth more than unmarked items. Look for items marked Stanley, Lufkin, Defiance, or Craftsman to name a few.

Hand drills, Keen Kutter: wooden handle with removable top to hold twist bits, 3½" gear wheel, from $75.00 to $125.00; hollow brass handle with drill compartment, 3⅛" gear wheel, from $75.00 to $125.00. (Photo courtesy Jerry and Elaine Heuring)

Adze, carpenter's; Diamond A, 4½" W, 32" handle, EX.......**$50.00**

Auger, fore; AA Wood & Sons, steel yoke, cuts 1¼" dia tenon w/ tapered shoulder, EX...................................**$185.00**

Auger, hollow; AA Wood & Sons, adjusts from ¼" to 1¼" dia, repainted & cleaned, VG **$100.00**

Bevel, sliding T; Stanley No 25, embossed gold lettering on rosewood handle, Made in USA, 6", NM **$30.00**

Bit, countersink; J Askham, old-style tang w/notch, VG........**$8.00**

Bit, screwdriver; Stanley No 26, Made in USA, ⁵⁄₁₆", M.........**$8.00**

Brace, Stanley No 923-10, 10" sweep, Made in USA logo, drills from ⅛" to ½" dia, NM.......................................**$30.00**

Chisel, butt; Stanley No 750, ¼" bevel edge, marked blade, USA on socket, 9", EX+ **$50.00**

Chisel, socket firmer; Buck Bros, ⅜", cast steel, 5¼" blade, 13", EX **$30.00**

Chisel, socket firmer; DR Barton, ⅛", rosewood handle, 5" blade, 11½", VG..**$50.00**

Chisel, socket firmer; Shapleigh Hardware, Diamond Edge, ⅜" bevel edge, VG..**$25.00**

Chisel, socket mortise; Winstead Edge Tool Works, ¼", 15½", EX...**$40.00**

Cutter, plug; Hargrave (on tang), ⅝", EX............................**$15.00**

Divider, angle; Stanley No 31, script logo on blade, rosewood body, VG..**$175.00**

Drill, hand; North Bros Yankee No 1530A, 3-jaw chuck w/³⁄₁₆" capacity, VG...**$50.00**

Gauge, marking & mortising; Stanley No 98, Sweetheart logo, EX..**$35.00**

Gauge, marking; Stanley No 72, Sweetheart logo, 1930s, NM. **$50.00**

Gouge, deep sweep; Buck Brothers No 11, ⁵⁄₁₆", VG............**$30.00**

Hammer, claw; Plumb, 7-oz, EX......................................**$25.00**

Knife, draw; AJ Wilkinson, folding handles, laminated blade, Patented July 16 1895, VG.............................**$80.00**

Knife, draw; Greenlee, maple handles, 10", NM................**$35.00**

Knife, patternmaker's draw; Sargent, black egg-shaped handles, 4", VG..**$35.00**

Level, Goodell Pratt, sq ends, orange paint on cast iron, 6", EX... **$150.00**

Level, Standard Tool, pitch adjuster on side, cast iron, Pat May 11 1897, 6", VG...**$300.00**

Nippers, W Schollhorn, Bernard's Patent Oct 24 1899, VG... **$20.00**

Plane, block; Stanley No 18 Type 10, adjustable throat, nickeled trim, VG...**$45.00**

Plane, block; Stanley No 9½, adjustable throat & cutter, notched rectangle mark, ca 1940s, EX..................**$60.00**

Plane, carriage maker's rabbet; Stanley No 10 Type II, Bailey patent mark, rosewood handle, EX...................**$750.00**

Plane, circular; Ohio No 020, VG **$165.00**

Plane, duplex rabbet & filletster; Stanley No 78, Sweetheart logo, 1930s, EX...**$65.00**

Plane, fore; Stanley No 6C type 11, T trademark, dark rosewood handle, EX...**$125.00**

Plane, jack; Stanley Bedrock No 604, Sweetheart logo, rosewood handle, later model, VG..........................**$175.00**

Plane, jack; Stanley No 5C, Sweetheart logo, early keyhole slot, rosewood handle, VG...............................**$85.00**

Plane, jointer; Stanley No 8, USA trademark, rosewood handle, ca 1950, NM **$225.00**

Plane, jointer; Union Mfg Co No X-8 (size 8), adjustment lever, mahogany handle, scarce, EX....................**$300.00**

Plane, low angle block; Craftsman #732, gray enamel & nickel plate, EX **$40.00**

Plane, rabbet; Stanley #191, 1¼", USA trademark, EX........**$50.00**

Plane, scrub; Stanley No 40½, Sweetheart logo, beech handle, VG..**$125.00**

Plane, smooth; Millers Falls No 9 (#4 size), NMIB.............**$85.00**

Plane, smooth; Stanley No 3, notched rectangle logo, rosewood handle, ca 1950, VG...**$70.00**

Plane, smooth; Stanley No 4½, notched rectangle logo, rosewood handle, MIB **$190.00**

Plane, smooth; Stanley No 4C, notched rectangle logo, rosewood handle, EX...**$75.00**

Plane, smooth; Stanley No 4, notched rectangle logo, rosewood handle, 1950s, EX..**$85.00**

Plane, smooth; Union Mfg Co No 22, wood bottom, 8", EX. **$70.00**

Plane, Stanley Bedrock #604, Pat 7-24-88/B Pat'd Apr 2-95, $80.00.

Pointer, spoke; Sterns No 1, adjustable graduated tang, points up to 1⅞" dia, VG...**$40.00**

Rule, zigzag; Lufkin No 1206, aluminum, EX.....................**$35.00**

Rule, zigzag; Stanley No 856, 6-ft, EX...............................**$20.00**

Saw, crosscut; Simonds No 8, 10 teeth per inch, Pat Dec 27 1887, maple handle, 26", G.......................................**$25.00**

Saw, docking; Disston No 498, 4½ teeth per inch crosscut, iron handle, 30", EX...**$65.00**

Saw, rip; Henry Disston & Sons D-8, 5½ teeth per inch, applewood handle, 26", VG.....................................**$50.00**

Saw set, Stanley No 442 Pistol-Grip, 18 gauge or thinner, 10 teeth per inch or less, marked Patent Pend, VG...................**$32.50**

Scraper, cabinet; Stanley No 80, Sweetheart logo on crossbar, USA logo on cutter, EX.......................................**$40.00**

Screwdriver, offset ratchet; Stanley Yankee No 3400, right-or left-hand action, 4", EX.....................................**$18.00**

Screwdriver, spiral ratchet; North Bros Yankee No 131A, quick return (spring) type, w/3 bits, 25", NMIB...................**$75.00**

Spoke shave, Stanley No 54, adjustable throat, T trademark, ca 1910s, VG **$35.00**

Spoke shave, Stanley No 64, USA logo on cutter, G............**$20.00**

Square, bevel; Marshall Wells, lg logo in frame, Pat Oct 29 '07, 6", EX **$35.00**

Square, combo; Fitchburg Tool Co, w/level & scribe, 12", EX. **$20.00**

Square, try & miter; Stanley No 1, Sweetheart logo on blade, VG..**$25.00**

Square, try; Henry Disston & Sons, English & Metric measurements, brass-plated rosewood handle, 10", EX.............**$50.00**

Vise, North Bros Yankee No 1993, swivel base, cam-action lock, 1915 patent date, EX.......................................**$45.00**

Wrench, buggy; Diamond Wrench Co, Pat Nov 2 80, 12", VG.**$35.00**

Wrench, monkey; Gower & Lyon GEM, 4½", VG.............**$35.00**

Wrench, pipe; Eaton Cole & Burnham, Franklin patent, July 20 1886, VG..**$120.00**

Wrench; quick-adjust monkey; H&H Co Balto MD, 6", EX .. **$85.00**

Toothbrush Holders

Novelty toothbrush holders have been modeled as animals of all types, in human forms, and in the likenesses of many storybook personalities. Today all are very collectible, especially those representing popular Disney characters. Most of these are made of bisque and are decorated over the glaze. Condition of the paint is an important consideration when trying to arrive at an evaluation.

For more information, refer to *Pictorial Guide to Toothbrush Holders* by Marilyn Cooper. Plate numbers in some of our descriptions correspond with this book.

Advisor: Marilyn Cooper (See Directory, Toothbrush Holders)

Bear, shaded brown, 1 hole, no tray, Germany, plate #167, 5¾", from $85 to **$100.00**

Bellhop w/flowers, 1 hole, Japan, plate #21, 5¼", from $75 to...**$85.00**

Bonzo, multicolor lustre, 2 holes, Japan, plate #22, 5¾", from $75 to **$85.00**

Bonzo w/side tray, mouth holds brush, multicolor lustre, Germany, plate #23, 3⅝", from $145 to **$155.00**

Boy in knickers, multicolor, 2 holes, stands, no tray, plate #223, 4¾", from $75 to...**$95.00**

Boy w/violin, 2 holes, Japan (Goldcastle), plate #30, 5½", from $80 to **$95.00**

Calico cat, tray at feet, 2 holes, Japan, plate #37, 5½", from $100 to **$120.00**

Circus elephant, bright multicolors, 1 hole, tray at feet, Japan, plate #56, 5⅜", from $85 to **$100.00**

Clown, multicolor paint on cast iron, arms hold brush, plate #175, 3¾", from $225 to...**$250.00**

Dog w/basket, multicolor, hole in basket, tray at feet, Japan, plate #72, 5¾", from $95 to **$100.00**

Dog w/basket on back, multicolor lustre, 2 holes, stands w/tray, Japan (Goldcastle), plate #201, 6", from $100 to **$120.00**

Donald Duck, bisque, 2 holes, tray at feet, WDE, plate #83, 5¼", from $285 to **$315.00**

Duckling, painted chalkware, 2 holes, no tray, plate #181, 4¾", from $40 to **$50.00**

Ducky Dandy, multicolor, 2 holes, tray at feet, Japan, plate #84, 4¼", from $175 to...**$200.00**

Dumbo, multicolor details on gray, 3 holes, c WDP, plate #182, 3", from $360 to **$400.00**

Dutch boy w/hands on hips, 3 holes (2 at pockets), tray at feet, Japan, plate #87, 5¼", from $70 to **$75.00**

Dutch girl w/lg hat, 1 hole, stands w/tray, plate #207, 5½", from $110 to **$135.00**

Elephant w/tusk (facing right), multicolor, 1-hole, tray at feet, Japan, plate #95, 5½", from $80 to **$95.00**

Fawn, Brush Teeth Daily, 3 holes, Japan, plate #12, 4", from $100 to **$115.00**

Giraffe, multicolor, 3 holes, tray at feet, Japan, plate #97, 6", from

$130 to **$145.00**

Girl w/umbrella, multicolor, 2 holes, tray at feet, Japan, plate #45, 4½", from $75 to **$80.00**

Girl washing boy's face, multicolor, 2 holes, tray at feet, copyright GB, plate #104, 5", from $80 to...................................**$95.00**

Henry & Henrietta, multicolor bisque, 2 holes, tray at feet, c 1934 CA-Japan, plate #112, 4½", from $535 to.................**$565.00**

Indian chief, multicolor, 2 holes, tray across chest, Japan, plate #115, 4½", from $265 to...**$285.00**

Mandolin player, multicolor, 1 hole, stands, no tray, #231, 4⅛", from $110 to **$135.00**

Mary Poppins w/purse & umbrella, multicolor, 2 holes tray at base, plate #119, 5¾", from $145 to......................................**$175.00**

Mother Hubbard, dog at her feet, Germany, plate #3, 6¼", from $400 to **$430.00**

Old Woman in Shoe, multicolor w/brown shoe, 3 holes, tray at base, Japan, plate #126, 4½", from $80 to **$95.00**

Peter Rabbit, name on overalls, 2 holes, tray at feet, plate #130, 5½", from $100 to **$135.00**

Popeye, multicolor paint on bisque, 1 hole, stands, no tray, Japan, plate #244, 5", from $525 to **$575.00**

Sailors on anchor, multicolor on white, 2 holes, tray at base, Japan, plate #145, 5½", from $70 to **$75.00**

Soldier with sash, two holes, plate #149, 6", $100.00. (Photo courtesy Marilyn Cooper)

Three Bears, multicolor, 2 holes, tray at feet, Japan, plate #153, 5", from $85 to **$100.00**

Uncle Willie, multicolor, 2 holes, tray at feet, FAS Japan, plate #157, 5⅛", from $95 to...**$110.00**

Toys

Toy collecting has long been an area of very strong activity, but over the past decade it has literally exploded. Many of the larger auction galleries have cataloged toy auctions, and it isn't uncommon for scarce nineteenth-century toys in good condition go for $5,000.00 to $10,000.00 and up. Toy shows are popular, and there are clubs, newsletters, and magazines that cater only to the needs and wants of toy collectors. Though once buyers ignored toys less than 30 years old, in more recent years, even some toys from the '80s are sought after.

Condition has more bearing on the value of a toy than any other factor. A used toy in good condition with no major flaws will still be worth only about half (in some cases much less) as much as one in mint (like new) condition. Those mint and in their original boxes will be worth considerably more than the same toy without its box.

There are many good toy guides on the market today including: *Collecting Toys* and *Collecting Toy Trains* by Richard O'Brien; *Schroeder's Collectible Toys, Antique to Modern; Elmer's Price Guide to Toys* by Elmer Duellman and *Occupied Japan Toys With Prices* by David C. Gould and Donna Crevar-Donaldson. More books are listed in the subcategory narratives that follow.

See also Advertising Character Collectibles; Breyer Horses; Bubble Bath Containers; Character Collectibles; Disney Collectibles; Dolls; Fisher-Price; Halloween; Hartland Plastics Inc.; Model Kits; Paper Dolls; Games; Puzzles; Star Wars; Steiff Animals.

Action Figures and Accessories

Back in 1964, Barbie dolls were sweeping the feminine side of the toy market by storm. Hasbro took a risky step in an attempt to capture the interest of the male segment of the population. Their answer to the Barbie craze was GI Joe. Since no self-respecting boy would admit to playing with dolls, Hasbro called their boy dolls 'action figures,' and to the surprise of many, they were phenomenally successful. Today action figures generate just as much enthusiasm among toy collectors as they ever did among little boys.

Action figures are simply dolls with poseable bodies. Some — the original GI Joes, for instance, were 12" tall, while others were 6" to 9"in height. In recent years, the 3¾" figure has been favored. GI Joe was introduced in the 3¾" size in the '80s and proved to be unprecedented in action figure sales. (See also GI Joe.)

In addition to the figures themselves, each company added a full line of accessories such as clothing, vehicles, play sets, weapons, etc. — all are avidly collected. Be aware of condition! Original packaging is extremely important. In fact, when it comes to the recent issues, loose, played-with examples are seldom worth more than a few dollars.

Club: The Mego Adventurers Club
Old Forest Press, Inc.
PMB 195, 223 Wall St.
Huntington, NY 11743; Membership: $18.95 per year ($30 foreign);
Includes 6 issues of *Mego Head,* the official club newsletter

A-Team, accessory, Combat Headquarters, (w/4 figures), Galoob, MIB, from $45 to **$55.00**

A-Team, accessory, Corvette (w/Face figure), Galoob, M **$35.00**

A-Team, figure, Amy Allen, Galoob, 6½", MOC, from $28 to **$32.00**

A-Team, figure, BA Baracus, Galoob, 6½", MOC, from $32 to **$36.00**

Action Jackson, accessory, Campmobile, Mego, MIB **$75.00**

Action Jackson, accessory, Jungle House, Mego, MIB **$75.00**

Aliens, accessory, Power Loader or Stinger XT-37, MIP, ea from $15 to **$18.00**

Aliens, figure, Series 3, Arachnid Alien, Clan Leader, Predator, King Alien or Swarm Alien, Kenner, MOC, ea from $18 to..**$22.00**

Aliens, figure, Series 3, Cracked Tusk Predator, Kill Krab or Lava Predator, Kenner, MOC, ea from $10 to **$15.00**

American West, figure, Buffalo Bill Cody or Cochise, Mego, MOC, from $80 to **$90.00**

American West, figure, Davy Crockett, Mego, MIB, from $90 to **$100.00**

American West, figure, Sitting Bull, Mego, MIB, from $75 to . **$85.00**

American West, figure, Sitting Bull, Wild Bill Hickok or Wyatt Earp, Mego, MOC, ea from $100 to **$115.00**

American West, figure, Wild Bill Hickok or Wyatt Earp, Mego, MIB, ea from $65 to..**$75.00**

American West, horse, Shadow, Mego, MIB, from $125 to..**$135.00**

American West, playset, Dodge City, Mego, MIB, from $150 to **$175.00**

Archies, figure, any, Marx, NM, ea from $12 to **$18.00**

Avengers, figure, any figure from any series, Toy Biz, MIP, from $6 to **$10.00**

Batman (Animated), accessory, Batcave, Kenner, MIP, from $100 to **$130.00**

Batman (Animated), accessory, Street Jet or Turbo Batplane, Kenner, MIP, ea from $18 to..**$26.00**

Batman (Animated), figure, Bola Trap Robin or Sky Dive Batman, Kenner, MOC, ea from $8 to **$12.00**

Batman (Dark Knight), accessory, Joker Cycle, Kenner, MIP, from $20 to **$25.00**

Batman (Dark Knight), figure, Bruce Wayne, Kenner, MOC, from $18 to **$22.00**

Batman & Robin, figure, Aerial Combat Batman or Mr Freeze (Jet Wing w/Ring), Kenner, MIP, ea from $18 to...............**$22.00**

Battlestar Galactica, accessory, Colonial Scarab, Mattel, MIB, from $65 to **$70.00**

Battlestar Galactica, figure, 1st Series, any character, Mattel, 3¾", MOC, ea from $30 to **$35.00**

Battlestar Galatica, figure, 2nd Series, Baltar, Noray, Cylon Commander or Lucifer, Mattel, 3¾", MOC, ea from $80 to.............**$115.00**

Bionic Woman, accessory, House Playset, Kenner, MIP, from $25 to **$50.00**

Bionic Woman, figure, Jaime Sommers (w/Mission Purse), Kenner, MIB, from $160 to **$180.00**

Blackstar, accessory, Warlock, Galoob, MIB, from $45 to **$55.00**

Blackstar, figure, Gargo (w/Laser Light), Galoob, MIB, from $30 to **$40.00**

Buck Rogers, accessory, Draconian Marauder, Mego, MIP, from $35 to **$45.00**

Buck Rogers, figure, Adrella or Killer Kane, Mego, 3¾", MOC, from $14 to **$18.00**

Captain Action, accessory, Anti-Gravitational Power Pack, Ideal, MIB, from $200 to **$275.00**

Captain Action, figure, Action Boy, Ideal, M, from $225 to.**$250.00**

Captain Action, figure, Dr Evil, Ideal, M (from photo box), from $225 to **$275.00**

Captain Action, outfit, Steve Canyon (w/ring), Ideal, M, from $175 to **$200.00**

Charlie's Angels (Movie), figure, any, Jakks Pacific, MIB, ea...**$40.00**

Charon, figure, Charon, Mattel, M, from $25 to **$28.00**

CHiPs, accessory, motorcycle w/ramp (for 3¾" figures), Mego, MIP, from $45 to **$55.00**

CHiPs, figure, Sarge, Mego, 3¾", MOC, from $22 to **$28.00**

CHiPs, figure, Sarge, Mego, 8", MOC..................................**$52.00**

Comic Action Heroes, figure, Robin, Superman or Wonder Woman, Mego, MIP, ea from $60 to......................................**$70.00**

Commando (Schwarzenegger), figure, any except Matrix, Diamond Toymakers, 8", M, ea from $12 to..............................**$18.00**

Dukes of Hazzard, accessory, Jeep w/Daisy figure or General Lee w/Bo & Luke figures, Mego, 3¾", MIP, ea from $45 to...........**$55.00**

Dukes of Hazzard, figure, Bo, Mego, 3¾", MOC, from $12 to.**$16.00**

Dukes of Hazzard, figure, Bo or Luke, Mego, 8", M, ea from $12 to..**$16.00**

Dukes of Hazzard, figure, Boss Hogg, Mego, 3¾", MOC, from $18 to..**$22.00**

Dukes of Hazzard, figure, Boss Hogg, Mego, 8", M, from $18 to..**$22.00**

Dukes of Hazzard, figure, Cletus, Cooter, Coy, Rosco, Jesse or Vance, 3¾", MOC, ea from $28 to **$32.00**

Dukes of Hazzard, figure, Daisy, Mego, 3¾", M, from $10 to.**$12.00**

Dukes of Hazzard, figure, Daisy, Mego, 8", MOC, from $48 to **$52.00**

Dukes of Hazzard, figure, Uncle Jesse, 3¾", MOC, from $14.00 to $18.00.

Emergency, accessory, Rescue Truck, LJN, MIP, from $225 to..**$250.00**

Evel Knievel, figure, Evel Knievel, Ideal, 1973-74, MIP, from $40 to **$60.00**

Flash Gordon, figure, Dr Zarkov, Mego, MOC, from $90 to.**$110.00**

Flash Gordon, figure, Ming the Merciless, Mego, MOC, from $80 to **$90.00**

Hulk Hogan, figure, Hasbro, M, from $12 to......................**$15.00**

Indiana Jones & the Temple of Doom, figure, Giant Thugee or Mola Ram, LJN, MOC, ea from $65 to **$75.00**

Indiana Jones & the Temple of Doom, figure, Indiana, LJN, M, from $60 to **$70.00**

Indiana Jones in Raiders of the Lost Ark, accessory, Convoy Truck, Kenner, 4", MIB, from $145 to **$165.00**

Indiana Jones in Raiders of the Lost Ark, figure, Indiana w/whip, Kenner, 4", M, from $75 to...**$85.00**

Indiana Jones in Raiders of the Lost Ark, figure, Sallah, Kenner, 4", M, from $25 to..**$35.00**

James Bond, figure, Bond (Pierce Brosnan), Medicom, MIB..**$85.00**

James Bond (Moonraker), figure, Bond, Mego, MIB, from $140 to **$160.00**

Legend of the Lone Ranger, accessory, Western Town, Gabriel, MIB, from $75 to **$100.00**

Legend of the Lone Ranger, figure, Lone Ranger, Gabriel, M, from $15 to **$20.00**

Lone Ranger Rides Again, accessory, Carson City Bank Robbery, Gabriel, M, from $25 to..**$30.00**

Lone Ranger Rides Again, accessory, Red River Flood Waters, M, from $15 to **$20.00**

Lone Ranger Rides Again, accessory, Tribal Teepee and Prairie Wagon, MIB, from $25.00 to $30.00 each.

Lord of the Rings, figure, any, Toy Vault, 1998-99, MOC, ea from $12 to..**$18.00**

Lost in Space, accessory, Bubble Fighter, Trendmasters, M, from $25 to **$30.00**

Lost in Space, figure, (Classic) Will Robinson, Trendmasters, 9", MIP, from $28 to..**$32.00**

Lost in Space, figure, Cyclops, Trendmasters, M, from $25 to ..**$30.00**

Lost in Space, figure, Don West (Battle Armor), Trendmasters, M, from $4 to **$6.00**

M*A*S*H, figure, BJ, Hawkeye or Hot Lips, Tri-Star, 8", MOC, ea from $55 to **$65.00**

M*A*S*H, figure, Hot Lips, Tri-Star, 3¾", MOC, from $20 to..**$25.00**

Major Matt Mason, figure, Captain Lazer, Mattel, M, from $125 to **$135.00**

Major Matt Mason, figure, Jeff Long, Mattel, M, from $150 to **$175.00**

Man From UNCLE, accessory, Arsenal Set #1 or #2, Gilbert, MIP, from $35 to **$45.00**

Marvel Super Heroes, (Secret Wars), figure, Hobgoblin, Mattel, MOC, from $55 to..**$60.00**

Marvel Super Heroes, figure, Daredevil, Toy Biz, M, from $18 to $20.00

Marvel Super Heroes, figure, Green Goblin (back lever) or Thor (back lever), Toy Biz, MOC, ea from $38 to.................$42.00

Marvel Super Heroes, figure, Invisible Woman (catapult), Toy Biz, MOC, from $15 to......................................$18.00

Marvel Super Heroes, figure, Venom or Tongue-Flicking Venom, Toy Biz, MOC, ea from $18 to $22.00

Marvel Super Heroes (Secret Wars), accessory, Doom Cycle, Mattel, MIP, from $18 to $22.00

Masters of the Universe, accessory, He-Man & Wind Raider, Mattel, MIP, from $22 to...$28.00

Masters of the Universe, accessory, Jet Sled, Mattel, MIP, from $12 to $18.00

Masters of the Universe, figure, Battle Armor He-Man or Battle Armor Skeletor, Mattel, MOC, ea from $38 to $42.00

Masters of the Universe, figure, Evil-Lyn, Mattel, MOC, from $48 to $52.00

Masters of the Universe, figure, Grizzlor (black), Mattel, MOC, from $145 to $155.00

Masters of the Universe, figure, Leech, Mattel, MOC, from $30 to $35.00

Masters of the Universe, figure, Man-At-Arms, Mattel, MOC, from $38 to $42.00

Micronauts, accessory, Battle Cruiser, Mego, MIB, from $55 to.. $65.00

Micronauts, accessory, Hornetroid, Mego, MIB, from $45 to .. $50.00

Micronauts, figure, Centaurus, Mego, MOC, from $150 to... $175.00

Micronauts, figure, Force Commander, Mego, MIB, from $25 to..$30.00

Micronauts, figure, Nemesis Robot, Mego, MIB, from $12 to. $18.00

One Million BC, figure, Grok, Mada, Orm, Trag or Zon, Mego, MOC, ea from $45 to $55.00

One Million BC, figure, Tyrannosaur creature, Mego, MIB, from $250 to $275.00

Planet of the Apes, accessory, Action Stallion, remote-controlled, Mego, 1970s, MIB, from $75 to.............................$110.00

Planet of the Apes, accessory, Catapult & Wagon, Mego, 1970s, MIB, from $125 to..$165.00

Planet of the Apes, figure, any, Hasbro, 1999, 7", MIP, ea from $5 to $8.00

Pocket Super Heroes, accessory, Spider-Car (w/Spider-Man & the Hulk), Mego, MIB, from $75 to $100.00

Pocket Super Heroes, figure, Batman, Mego, MOC (red card), ea from $65 to $75.00

Pocket Super Heroes, figure, Gen Zod, Mego, MOC (red card), from $20 to $30.00

Pocket Super Heroes, figure, Jor-El or Lex Luthor, MOC (red card), from $18 to $22.00

Pocket Super Heroes, figure, Spider-Man, Mego, MOC (red card), from $45 to $55.00

Pocket Super Heroes, figure, Wonder Woman, Mego, MOC (white card), from $70 to...$80.00

Power Lords, figure, any, MOC, ea from $20 to $30.00

Rambo, accessory, .50 Caliber Anti-Aircraft Gun or .50 Caliber Machine Gun, Coleco, MIP, ea from $10 to.................$15.00

Rambo, accessory, SAVAGE Strike Cycle, Coleco, MIB, from $18 to $22.00

Rambo, figure, Dr Hyde, Snakebite, TD Jackson or X-ray, Coleco, MOC, ea from $18 to $22.00

Rambo, figure, Sgt Havoc, Turbo or White Dragon, Coleco, MOC, ea from $8 to $15.00

Robotech, accessory, Gladiator, Invid Scout Ship, Invid Shock Trooper or Raider X, Matchbox, MIB, ea from $30 to .$45.00

Robotech, accessory, Spartan, Tactical Battle Pod or Veritech Fighter, Matchbox, MIB, ea from $30 to...................................$45.00

Robotech, figure, Miriya (black), Matchbox, 3¾", MOC, from $60 to $70.00

Rococop (Ultra Police), figure, any, Kenner, 1988-90, MOC, ea from $15 to $25.00

Rookies, figure, Chris, Mike, Terry or Willie, LJN, MOC, ea from $25 to $30.00

Six Million Dollar Man, accessory, Mission Control Center, Kenner, MIB, from $65 to..$75.00

Six Million Dollar Man, figure, Maskatron, Kenner, MIB, from $145 to $155.00

Spider-Man, figure, any, Toy Biz, 5", MOC, ea from $5 to ...$8.00

Star Gate, figure, any, Hasbro, MOC, ea from $4 to $6.00

Starsky & Hutch, accessory, car, Mego, MIB, from $150 to.$175.00

Super Heroes, figure, Aquaman, Mego, 8", M, from $55 to.$60.00

Super Heroes, figure, Batgirl (Bend 'n Flex), Mego, 5", MOC, from $100 to $125.00

Super Heroes, figure, Captain America (Bend 'n Flex), Mego, 5", MOC, from $90 to...$100.00

Super Heroes, figure, Flacon, Mego, 8", MIB, from $125 to..$150.00

Super Heroes, figure, Human Torch, Mego, 8", MOC, from $45 to $55.00

Super Heroes, figure, Incredible Hulk, Mego, 8", MOC, from $45 to $55.00

Super Heroes, figure, Isis, Mego, 8", M, from $70 to $80.00

Super Heroes, figure, Joker, Mego, 8", M, from $55 to $65.00

Super Heroes, figure, Mr Fantastic, Mego, 8", MOC, from $55 to $60.00

Super Heroes, figure, Robin (painted mask), Mego, 8", M, from $65 to $75.00

Super Heroes, figure, Tarzan (Bend 'n Flex), Mego, 5", MOC, from $55 to $65.00

Super Heroes, figure, Wonder Woman (Bend 'n Flex), Mego, 5", MOC, from $75 to..$100.00

Super Naturals, accessory, Ghost Finder, Tonka, 1986, MIB, from $25 to $30.00

Super Naturals, accessory, Lionwings Battle Creature, Tonka, 1986, MIB, from $15 to...$20.00

Super Naturals, figure, any Warrior, Tonka, MOC, from $8 to ..$10.00

Super Powers, accessory, Delta Probe One, Kenner, 1984, MIB, from $30 to $35.00

Super Powers, accessory, Hall of Justice, Kenner, MIB, from $100 to $150.00

Super Powers, figure, Aquaman, Kenner, MOC, from $45 to .. $50.00

Super Powers, figure, Batman, Kenner, M, from $38 to.......$42.00

Super Powers, figure, Brainiac, Kenner, M, from $18 to......$20.00

Super Powers, figure, Clark Kent, Kenner, M (mail-in), from $60 to $65.00

Super Powers, figure, Cyborg, Kenner, M, from $155 to ...$160.00

Teen Titans, figure, Aqualad, Mego, M, from $175 to.......$200.00

Teen Titans, figure, Wondergirl, Mego, M, from $150 to ..**$175.00**

Waltons, accessory, barn or country store, Mego, MIB, ea from $75 to **$100.00**

Wizard of Oz, accessory, Wizard of Oz & His Emerald City (for 4" figures), Mego, MIB, from $100 to **$125.00**

Wizard of Oz, figure, Wicked Witch, Mego, 8", MIB, from $90 to **$115.00**

WWF, figure, Akeem, Hasbro, M, from $16 to **$18.00**

WWF, figure, Animal (Shotgun Sat Night #1), Jakks, MOC, from $8 to **$10.00**

WWF, figure, Bret Hart (Superstars #1), Jakks, MOC, from $18 to **$22.00**

WWF, figure, Dusty Rhodes, Hasbro, M, from $65 to........**$70.00**

WWF, figure, Greg The Hammer Valentine, Hasbro, MOC, from $12 to **$15.00**

WWF, figure, Jake The Snake Roberts, Hasbro, MOC, from $8 to **$12.00**

WWF, figure, Rowdy Roddy Piper, Hasbro, MOC, from $28 to **$32.00**

WWF, figure, Undertaker, Hasbro, MOC, from $24 to.......**$26.00**

X-Men/X-Force, figure, Bridge or Brood, Toy Biz, MOC, ea from $12 to **$16.00**

X-Men/X-Force, figure, Cannonball (purple), Toy Biz, MOC, from $18 to **$22.00**

X-Men/X-Force, figure, Gideon or Grizzly, Toy Biz, MOC, ea from $16 to **$18.00**

X-Men/X-Force, figure, Sabretooth I or Sabretooth II, Toy Biz, MOC, ea from $16 to **$18.00**

Zorro (Cartoon Series), figure, Captain Ramon or Sgt Gonzales, M, ea from $5 to **$8.00**

Zorro (Cartoon Series), figure, Tempest or Picaro, Gabriel, M, ea from $8 to **$10.00**

Zorro (Cartoon Series), figure, Zorro or Amigo, Gabriel, M, ea from $6 to **$8.00**

Battery-Operated

It is estimated that approximately 95% of the battery-operated toys that were so popular from the '40s through the '60s came from Japan. (The remaining 5% were made in the United States.) To market these toys in America, many distributorships were organized. Some of the largest were Cragstan, Linemar, and Rosko. But even American toy makers such as Marx, Ideal, Hubley, and Daisy sold them under their own names, so the trademarks you'll find on Japanese battery-operated toys are not necessarily that of the manufacturer, and it's sometimes just about impossible to determine the specific company that actually did made them. After peaking in the '60s, the Japanese toy industry began a decline, bowing out to competition from the cheaper diecast and plastic toy makers.

Remember that it is rare to find one of these complex toys that has survived in good, collectible condition. Batteries caused corrosion, lubricants dried out, cycles were interrupted and mechanisms ruined, rubber hoses and bellows aged and cracked, so the mortality rate was extremely high. A toy rated good, that is showing signs of wear but well taken care of, is generally worth about half as much as the same toy in mint (like new) condition. Besides condition, battery-operated toys are rated on scarcity, desirability, and the number

of 'actions' they perform. A 'major' toy is one that has three or more actions, while one that has only one or two is considered 'minor.' The latter, of course, are worth much less.

In addition to the books we referenced in the beginning narrative to the toy category, you'll find more information in *Collecting Battery Toys* by Don Hultzman (Books Americana).

Accordion Bear, Alps, remote-controlled microphone, 1950s, 10½", NMIB...**$725.00**

Accordion Player Hobo (w/Monkey), Alps, sealed hobo plays accordion while monkey plays cymbals, 1950s, NMIB.......**$350.00**

Acrobatic Umbrella, lady in cloth outfit holding litho tin umbrella, 10", GIB...**$110.00**

Air Control Tower (w/Airplane & Helicopter), Bandai, 1960s, 10½", EXIB..**$250.00**

Answer Game Machine (Robot), Ichida, 1960s, 15", NMIB..**$450.00**

Antique Gooney Car, Alps, litho tin w/vinyl-headed figure, 1960s, 9", EX...**$75.00**

Army Seachlight Truck, Daisy, plastic & tin, 11½", MIB **$75.00**

Baby & Carriage Pony Tail Girl, Rosko/S&E, girl w/ponytail, in cloth dress, pushing carriage, 1950s, 8", EXIB...........**$175.00**

Baby Carriage, TN, litho tin carriage w/plastic baby, 1950s, 13", EXIB..**$120.00**

Barber Bear, TN, plush, tin base, 1950s, nonworking, 10", G...**$150.00**

Barney Bear the Drummer, Cragston, NM+IB, $200.00.

Bartender, TN, white-haired gent in red jacket standing behind litho tin bar, 1960s, 12", EXIB **$30.00**

Bear the Xylophone Player, Y, plush & tin, remote-controlled, 1950s, 10", EX..**$275.00**

Big Ring Circus (Circus Parade), MT, tin litho circus truck, 1950s, 13", EXIB..**$200.00**

Big Wheel Ice Cream Truck, Taiyo, 1970s, 10", EX..........**$100.00**

Bimbo the Drumming Clown, Cragstan, remote-controlled, 1950s, 11", EXIB..**$220.00**

Birdwatcher Bear, MT, plush, seated w/bird on paw, 10", VG. **$440.00**

Blushing Gunfighter, Y, litho tin w/cloth shirt, 1950s, 11", NMIB.. **$250.00**

Blushing Willie, Y, white-haired gent pouring himself a drink, 1960s, 10", EXIB..**$75.00**

Boil Over Car (Automoball), MT, 1950s, 10", EXIB.........**$150.00**

Bubble Blowing Boy, Y, litho tin, boy seated on base blowing bubbles, 1950s, 8", EXIB...**$230.00**

Bubble Blowing Washing Bear, Y, plush bear in cloth dress standing at wash tub on litho tin base, 1950s, 8", EXIB...........**$375.00**

Bubble Lion, MT, litho tin, 1950s, 7", EXIB...................**$125.00**

Bumper Automatic Control Bus, Bandai, 15", EXIB.........**$225.00**

Burger Chef, Y, plush & litho tin, 1950s, 9", EXIB..........**$175.00**

Busy Secretary, Linemar, 1950s, 7½", EXIB **$250.00**

Calypso Joe, Linemar, remote-controlled, 1950s, 10", EX .**$350.00**

Cement Mixer #25, Masaduya, 1950s, 10", NMIB **$200.00**

Central Cable Streamliner, TN, litho tin train engine & car, 13½", EXIB...**$85.00**

Champion Weight Lifter, YM, plush dressed monkey w/lg barbell, 1960s, 10", EXIB...**$115.00**

Chap the Obedient Dog, Rosko, 1960s, MIB....................**$150.00**

Chef Cook, Y, 1960s, 9", EXIB **$130.00**

Chimpy the Jolly Drummer, Alps, plush monkey seated at drum w/cymbals, 9", EXIB...**$50.00**

Cindy the Meowing Cat, Tomiyama, 1950s, 12", EX..........**$75.00**

Circus Fire Engine, MT, litho tin & plastic, 1960s, 11", EX ..**$200.00**

Circus Lion, Rock Valley, plush, seated atop drum roaring, w/whip & flannel carpet, 1950s, 10", VG+IB **$430.00**

Clown the Violinist, Alps, clown w/plastic head, cloth costume seated on litho tin barrel lying on its side, 10½", EX....**$85.00**

Clucking Clara, CK, 1950s, NM **$130.00**

Coffeetime Bear, TN, plush & tin, 1960s, 10", EX **$150.00**

Coffeetime Bear, TN, plush & tin, 1960s, 10", EXIB........**$250.00**

College Jalopy, Linemar, 10", NMIB **$375.00**

Collie, Alps, barks & begs, eyes light up, plush, remote-controlled, 1950s, EXIB **$75.00**

Communication Truck, MT, friction, battery-operated lights, 1950s, 12", NMIB **$250.00**

Cragstan Melody Band (Daisy the Jolly Drummer Duck), Alps, plush & litho tin, eyes light up, 1950s, 9", EXIB **$275.00**

Cragstan Tootin'-Chuggin' Locomotive w/Mystery Action (Santa Fe), litho tin, 24", EXIB **$100.00**

Cymbal Playin' Monkey, light brown plush w/pointed hat, metal cymbals, remote-controlled, 12", VGIB **$40.00**

Dalmatian (The Jolly Drumming Dog), Cragstan, plush, 9", EXIB **$150.00**

Dancing Dan (w/His Mystery Mike), Bell Prod, 1950s, 16", EXIB **$170.00**

Dandy Turtle, DSK, 1950s, 8", M...................................**$150.00**

Dentist Bear, S&E, plush & tin, 1950s, 10", MIB............**$500.00**

Dixie the Dog (Dachshund), Linemar, remote-controlled, 10" (at head), EXIB **$75.00**

Dream Boat (Rock 'n Roll Hot Rod), TN, tin, 7", EX **$225.00**

Drinking Captain, S&E, cloth outfit, 12", MIB **$125.00**

Drinking Dog, Y, plush & tin, NM+IB **$110.00**

Drumming Bunny, white plush w/red nose, standing beating drum, 12", EXIB **$65.00**

Electro Matic Filling Station & Car, Distler, litho tin station (battery box) w/plastic car, 6½" L station, EXIB......................**$200.00**

Electronic Periscope-Firing Range, Cragstan, 1950s, VGIB ..**$100.00**

Farm Truck (John's Truck), TN, 1950s, 9", MIB **$350.00**

Father Bear, MT, plush, seated in rocking chair reading & drinking, 1950s, EXIB **$170.00**

Fido the Xylophone Player, Alps, plush, 1950s, 9", EXIB ..**$130.00**

Fighter F-50 Jet Plane, KO, chunky plastic plane w/pilot under clear dome, 9", VGIB..**$140.00**

Fire Chief Car, litho tin, open car w/2 figures, siren by windshield, simulated spoke wheels, 10" L, EXIB **$135.00**

Fishing Bear (Lighted Eyes), Alps, plush & tin, 1950s, 11", EXIB...**$220.00**

Fishing Panda Bear (Lighted Eyes), Alps, plush & tin, 1950s, 11", EXIB...**$275.00**

Ford Mustang Fastback 2x2, plastic, light blue, 16", EXIB (box marked 2x2 Cool & Pow!) **$165.00**

Frankenstein (Mod Monster — Blushing Frankenstein), TN, standing on litho tin base w/name, 1960s, 13", EXIB.........**$175.00**

Frankie the Roller Skating Monkey, Alps, plush w/cloth outfit, remote-controlled, 1950s, 12", VGIB **$115.00**

Friendly Joco My Favorite Pet, Alps, dressed monkey, remote-controlled, 1950s, 10", EXIB **$125.00**

Friendly Puppy Barking & Begging, Alps, plush, remote-controlled, 1950s, 8", EXIB..**$35.00**

Funland Cup Ride, Sansco, 1960s, 7", NM+IB **$350.00**

Furure Fire Car, TN, 1950s, 9", VG **$225.00**

Galloping Horse & Rider, Cragstan, 12", EXIB................**$230.00**

Genie Bottle, Hobby Craft/Hong Kong, plastic, 12", NM+IB .**$65.00**

GM Coach Bus, Y, litho tin, bump-&-go action, doors open to passengers disembarking, 1950s, 16", EXIB, A................**$300.00**

Green Caterpillar, Daiya, tin & fabric, 10" L, NMIB **$200.00**

Handy-Hank Mystery Tractor w/Light, TN, 1950s, 11", EXIB ..**$88.00**

Happy 'n Sad Magic Face Clown, Y, cloth costume, remote-controlled, 1950s, 11", EXIB **$385.00**

Happy Naughty Chimp, Saishin, 1960s, 10", M **$50.00**

Happy Santa, Alps, plush outfit, walking w/drum, remote-controlled, 1950s, 11", VGIB..**$160.00**

Highway Patrol Car, Okuma, black & white Oldsmobile, remote-controlled, 11½", EXIB..**$150.00**

Home Washing Machine, Y, 1950s, 6", MIB....................**$100.00**

Hong Kong Rickshaw, PMC, 1960s, 9", EXIB..................**$90.00**

Hoop Zing Girl, Linemar, 1950s, 12", MIB.....................**$375.00**

Hungry Hound Dog, Y, 1950s, 10", M **$400.00**

Indian Signal Choo-Choo, Kanto Toys, 1960s, 10", EXIB ..**$55.00**

Indianapolis 500 Racer, Sears/TN, 1950s, 15", NMIB......**$450.00**

Jaguar Champ O' Raver, ASC, remote-controlled, tin, w/driver, 8", NM+IB...**$100.00**

Jeep (Tipping Action), Linemar, duck driver, litho tin, 8" L, EXIB...**$180.00**

Jig-Saw Magic, Z Co, 1950s, 7x5x9", MIB.....................**$100.00**

Jolly Daddy the Smoking Elephant, Marusan, plush in cloth outfit, remote-controlled, 1950s, 9", VGIB **$150.00**

Jolly Peanut Vendor, Cragstan, plush bear pushing peanut cart, 9", EXIB...**$330.00**

Jumbo the Bubble-Blowing Elephant, Y, 1950s, 7", GIB ...**$125.00**

Kissing Couple, Ichido, 1950s, 11", MIB **$350.00**

Knitting Grandma (Lighted Eyes), TN, plush bear, 1950s, 9", VGIB...**$170.00**

Lady Carrying Jug (On Head), China, cloth outfit, 9", VGIB. **$130.00**

Laughing Clown (Robot), Waco, multicolored plastic, 14", NM+IB **$200.00**

Light-A-Wheel Lincoln, Rosko, bump-&-go action, 1950s, 10½", NM..**$150.00**

Lite-O-Wheel Go-Kart, Rosko, 1950s, 11", EXIB **$175.00**

Loop the Loop Clown, TN, cloth costume, litho tin base, 1960s, 12", EXIB **$85.00**

Magic Action Bulldozer, TN, 1950s, 10", MIB..................**$250.00**

Magic Beetle, Linemar, 7", EXIB **$55.00**

Magic Man (Clown), Marusan, puffs smoke, remote-controlled, 1950s, 12", EXIB...**$250.00**

Magic Snow Man, MT, holding broom, 1950s, 11", EXIB..**$140.00**

Major Tooty (Drum Major), Alps, tin, 11", NM+IB **$125.00**

Marshal Wild Bill, Y, cloth outfit, remote-controlled, 1950s, 10½", VGIB **$185.00**

Mercedes Benz 250SL Convertible, Bandai, w/vinyl driver, 10", NM+...**$150.00**

Mew-Mew the Walking Cat, MT, plush, remote-controlled, 1950s, 7", VGIB **$85.00**

Mexicali Pete the Drum Player, Alps, cloth-dressed figure seated & playing drum, 1950s, 10", EXIB **$175.00**

Mischief (Mischievous Monkey), MT, 1950s, 13", EX+IB.**$250.00**

Mobile Loudspeaker (Truck), Remco, 1950s, 22", NMIB .**$125.00**

Monorail Set, Haji, 1950s, complete, EXIB......................**$175.00**

Mother Bear (Sitting & Knitting in Her Old Rocking Chair), MT, plush, 1950s, 10", EXIB **$150.00**

Mr Al-E-Gator (The Amazing), Alps, remote-controlled, 1950s, 13" L, NMIB **$200.00**

Mr McPooch Taking a Walk & Smoking His Pipe, SAN, plush dog in cloth outfit, remote-controlled, 1950s, 8", EXIB....**$150.00**

Mumbo Jumbo Hawaiian Drummer, Alps, 1960s, 10", VG...**$150.00**

Musical Comic Jumping Jeep, Alps, 12", M......................**$175.00**

Mystery Action Tractor, Japan, 1950s, 7", MIB **$150.00**

Naughty Dog & Busy Bee, MT, plush pup & bee, 10", EXIB.**$65.00**

Old Fashioned Car, SH, jalopy w/driver, 1950s, 9", EXIB...**$65.00**

Over Land Express Locomotive #3140, MT, 1950s, 15", NMIB **$30.00**

Pa Pa Bear, Marusan, plush w/cloth outfit, tin shoes, standing smoking pipe, remote-controlled, 9", NMIB **$90.00**

Passenger Bus, Y, working headlights, opening & closing door, 1950s, 16", EXIB...**$250.00**

Peppermint Twist Doll, Haji, 1950s, 12", EXIB **$245.00**

Pesky Pup the Shoe Stealer, Y, 1950s, 8", M **$110.00**

Pete the Talking Parrot, TN, 1950s, 18", M.....................**$250.00**

Picnic Bear (It Drinks), Alps, plush, 1950s, 12", EXIB......**$100.00**

Playing Monkey, S&E, 9½", NM+IB **$150.00**

Police Dept Jeep, Japan, white litho tin, w/2 officers, 11", VG+.**$125.00**

Popcorn Vendor (Duck), TN, 1950s, 8", EX **$300.00**

Power Construction Truck, Alps, 12" L, NMIB..................**$235.00**

Racer #7, Marusan, litho tin, silver w/red number & trim, driver w/white helmet, 10", nonworking, G+ **$85.00**

Railroad Hand Car, KDP, litho tin, 1950s, 6" L, EXIB **$75.00**

Return Tram, MT, 1950s, rare, 30", NM...........................**$350.00**

Rex Doghouse, Tel-E-Toy, 1950s, 5", M...........................**$130.00**

Ricky the Begging Poodle, Rosko, plush, remote-controlled, 1950s, 8", VGIB **$45.00**

River Steam Boat (With Whistle & Smoke), MT, litho tin, 14", VG+IB...**$75.00**

Roaring Gorilla Shooting Gallery, MT, 1950s, 9", VG+IB.**$125.00**

Roof-O-Matic Charger (Car), TN, litho tin, 15", NM+IB .**$150.00**

Roulette Man, dressed man standing at roulette table, complete w/chips & plastic cloth, 9", EXIB........................**$220.00**

Sammy Wong the Tea Totaler, Rosko/TN, 1950s, 10", EXIB.**$385.00**

Santa Bank, Trim-A-Tree/Noel Decorations, plush figure seated on top of house, 11", EXIB **$150.00**

Santa Claus #M-750 (Eyes Light Up/Sitting on House), HTC, plush, 1950s, EXIB...**$65.00**

Santa Fe Train Set, TN, litho tin, 1950s, 22", EXIB...........**$55.00**

Scotch Watch (Lighted Eyes), Flare, plush Scottie dog w/plaid neck bow, remote-controlled, 8", VGIB **$65.00**

Showdown Sam Robot Target Game, figure w/pistol in ea hand, 10", complete, EXIB **$115.00**

Shuttling Dog Train, Japan, complete, nonworking, 15" L, VG+IB...**$85.00**

Shuttling Train & Freight Yard, Alps, litho tin, 1950s, 16", EXIB...**$100.00**

Sight Seeing Bus, Bandai, tin w/figure under clear roof dome, passengers lithoed on side windows, 15", NM+IB **$200.00**

Sleeping Baby Bear, Linemar, litho tin w/cloth outfit & bedding, 9½", VGIB **$220.00**

Sloppy Pup, V, plush, white w/black spots, remote-controlled, 1950s, 10", VGIB..**$30.00**

Smoking & Shoe Shining Panda Bear, Alps, plush, 1950s, 10", EXIB...**$250.00**

Smoking Grandpa (in Rocking Chair), SAN, 1950s, 8½", NM+IB...**$300.00**

Smoky Bear, SAN, plush cloth outfit, remote-controlled, 1950s, 9", EXIB...**$350.00**

Space Patrol (Snoopy), MT, litho tin, Snoopy in rocketship, 1960s, 11½" L, EXIB..**$200.00**

Squirmy Hermy the Snake, HTC, remote-controlled, tin, 12", NMIB...**$225.00**

Strutting My Fair Dancer, Haji, figure on round base, 1950s, 9", EXIB...**$285.00**

Stunt Car, 1969, Japan, MIB, $175.00.

Super Coach (Transcontinental Bus), TN, w/horn noise, 16", NMIB...**$100.00**

Suzette the Eating Monkey, Linemar, 1950s, 9", EXIB......**$350.00**
Swimming Fish, Koshibe, 1950s, 11", NM.......................**$125.00**

Switchboard Operator, Lineman, 1950s, 7½x7", EXIB, $825.00. (Photo courtesy Bertoia Auction)

Taxi, Linemar, working light-up sign on top, remote-controlled, 7½", NMIB **$85.00**
Teddy Bear Swing, TN, plush bear on trapeze, 1950s, 14", EXIB...**$550.00**
Teddy the Artist, Electro Toy/Y, plush bear in cloth outfit seated at desk, 1950s, 10", EXIB..............................**$450.00**
Telephone Bear, Linemar, plush bear in cloth overalls seated in straight chair w/phone, 19590s, 9", EXIB **$160.00**
Telephone Rabbit (Ringing & Talking in Her Old Rocking Chair), MT, white plush, pink overalls, 1950s, 10", EXIB......**$175.00**
Tom & Jerry Comic Car, Rico Co/Spain, tin auto w/Tom driving, 13" L, EX+IB....................................**$350.00**
Tractor on Platform, TN, tin w/rubber treads, 1950s, 9" L, NM+IB...**$130.00**
Tractor T-27, Amico, 1950s, 12", rare, M........................**$125.00**
Transport Express (Overland), MT, litho tin cabover semi, 17", EXIB..**$150.00**
Traveler Bear, K, plush bear carrying tin suitcase, remote-controlled, 1950s, nonworking, 8", VG..................**$120.00**
Trolly Bus, roof extends over open cab w/driver, passengers lithoed on windows, 13", EX..........................**$45.00**
Tugboat (w/Realistic Noises & Puffs of Real Smoke...), SAN/Cragstan, litho tin, 1950s, 13", EXIB..................**$175.00**
Tuggy the Tugboat, Japan, litho tin, 13", EXIB **$125.00**
Tumbling Bozo the Clown, Sonsco, 1970s, 8", M.............**$160.00**
Tumbling Monkey, brown plush w/vinyl face, ears, hands & feet, red & white striped outfit, 7", VGIB.................**$80.00**
TV Broadcasting (VW) Van, Gakken Toy/Japan, 1960s, 8", EXIB.**$325.00**
Twirly Whirly Rocket Ride, Alps, litho tin, 1950s, 13", VGIB ..**$550.00**
Two-Gun Sheriff, Cragstan, cloth outfit, plastic hat, remote-controlled, 10", EXIB......................................**$200.00**
Unmarked Secret Agents Car, Spesco, bump-&-go action, 14½", NM+IB...**$225.00**
Vertol AirPort Service Helicopter, Alps, 1950s, 13", NMIB.**$250.00**
Wagon Master, MT, 1960s, 18" L, NM..........................**$150.00**
Walking Bear, brown plush, realistic, walking on all fours, remote-controlled, 6" L, VGIB **$65.00**

Walking Bear w/Xylophone, Linemar, plush w/tin shoes & xylophone, 1950s, 10", EXIB...........................**$350.00**
Walking Elephant, Linemar, plush w/red back blanket, remote-controlled, 1950s, 9", VGIB.......................**$85.00**
Walking Elephant (Carrying Free Flying Ball), MT, plush, remote-controlled, 1590s, 9", EXIB.................**$110.00**
Walking Gorilla, Linemar, plush, eyes light, has voice, remote-controlled, 6½", NMIB...........................**$275.00**
Walking Horse (Cowboy Rider), Linemar, litho tin, remote-controlled, 1950s, 7", EXIB **$350.00**
Wee Little Baby Bear (Reading Bear/Lighted Eyes), Alps, plush, 10", EXIB...**$375.00**
Windy the Juggling Elephant, TN, plush elephant on tin drum balancing umbrella on nose, 1950s, 10", G+IB **$200.00**
Worried Mother Duck & Baby, TN, 1950s, 7", MIB........**$250.00**
Xylophone, Ace, 1950s, 6" L, NM.....................................**$60.00**

Guns

One of the bestselling kinds of toys ever made, toy guns were first patented in the late 1850s. Until WWII most were made of cast iron, though other materials were used on a lesser scale. After the war, cast iron became cost prohibitive, and steel and diecast zinc were used. By 1950 most were made of either diecast material or plastic. Hundreds of names can be found embossed on these little guns, a custom which continues to the present time. Because of their tremendous popularity and durability, today's collectors can find a diversity of models and styles, and prices are still fairly affordable.

Leslie-Henry, Range Rider Gun and Holster Set, 1950s, MIB, $350.00.

Agent Zero Radio-Rifle, Mattel, 1964, NMIB.....................**$80.00**
American Cap Pistol, Kilgore, 1st version, flying eagle on ivory-colored grips, 1940s, 9", EX...................................**$325.00**
Automatic Repeater Paper Pop Pistol, Marx, 1930, 7", NM+IB..**$75.00**
Batman Freeze Ray Gun, Baravelli/Italy, plastic, battery-operated, NMIB...**$200.00**
Bronco Six-Shooter Cap Pistol, Kilgore, short-barrel version w/mountain lion engraving, white grip, 1950s, 8", NMIB.........**$135.00**
Buck Rogers Pop Gun, Daisy, pressed steel, name inscribed on handle, 10", EX **$200.00**

Champion Cap Pistol, Hubley, lever opening, nickel-plated w/horse heads embossed on white grips, 1940s, 9", EX **$85.00**

Crack Shot Dart Pistol, Wyandotte, 8", complete, VGIB..... **$65.00**

Davy Crockett, Frontier Rifle, Marx/WDP, metal, 34", NMIB. **$175.00**

Detective Shoulder Hoster (w/Gun), Rayline #36, plastic & vinyl, 1950s, complete w/wallet, bullets, etc, EXOC **$125.00**

Dick Tracy Jr Click Pistol, #78, Marx, 1930s, aluminum, EX+ ... **$65.00**

Dixie Cap Pistol, Kenton, nickel plate, checkered patterns on on black grips, red jewels, 1930s, 6½", G+ **$85.00**

Duck Hunt Set, Japan, litho tin, 1960s, 18" L, missing darts otherwise EXIB **$45.00**

Foxhole Tommy Gun Space Rifle, TN, litho tin, battery-operated, 1950s, 17", NMIB.. **$250.00**

G-Man Automatic Gun, Marx, pressed steel, windup, 4", EX+ ... **$80.00**

Gene Autry Cap Pistol, Kenton, short barrel, white signature grips, 1950s, 6½", VG.. **$100.00**

Hopalong Cassidy Cap Pistol, Schmidt, black grip w/embossed white silhouette bust image, 9½", NM+ **$275.00**

James Bond 007 Harpoon Gun, Lone Star, 1960s, EXIB ..**$100.00**

James Bond 007 Hideaway Pistol, Coibel, 1985, NMIB...... **$75.00**

Little Burp Gurrilla Machine Gun, Mattel, NMIB **$125.00**

Lone Ranger Sparkling Pop Pistol, Marx, metal, 1938, 7½", EXIB... **$165.00**

Long Tom Cap Pistol, Kilgore, 2nd version w/2-pc revolving cylinder, ivory-colored grips, 1940s, 10½", EXIB **$500.00**

Mirror Man Double Barrel Pop Gun, Takatoku, tin & plastic, 21", NMIB...**$100.00**

Mountie Repeating Cap Pistol, Hubley, nickel plate w/engraved grip, 1960s, 7", NM+IB **$45.00**

Multi-Pistol 09, Topper Toys, NM+ (in case)...................... **$95.00**

Padlock Cap Gun, Hubley, barrel extends & fires when key is turned, silver finish, 1950s, NM+.............................. **$75.00**

Persuader Revolving Cap Pistol, Kenton, nickel-plated cast iron w/crisscross detail on grips, 6½", EX **$100.00**

Red Ranger Jr Cap Pistol, Wyandotte, nickel-plated w/horse heads & star medallion on white grips, 7½", NMIB **$75.00**

Ric-O-Shay .45 Cap Pistol, Hubley, revolving cylinder, nickel-plated w/slick black grips, 1950s, 12", NM **$125.00**

Sheriff Repeating Cap Pistol, J&E Stevens, nickel-plated, black horse head grips w/red jewels, 1940s, 8", NMIB.................. **$200.00**

Shootin' Shell Scout Rifle, Mattel, MIB................... **$350.00**

Silver Eagle Tracer Machine Gun, w/automatice crank action, 21", EX+IB.. **$140.00**

Stallion .32 Six Shooter, Nichols, nickel-plated, 8", NM+IB...... **$125.00**

Tom Corbett Cadet Space Gun, Marx, litho tin, 10", NMIB (box reads Official Space Patrol) **$300.00**

Wild Bill Hickock Double Gun & Holster Set, 2-tone brown leather w/name in relief, 44 cap pistols, 11", EX.................... **$450.00**

Zorro Cap Pistol, flintlock style, NM **$100.00**

49-er Cap Pistol, J&E Stevens, gold-tone finish, white grips, 1940s, 9", VG **$125.00**

Ramp Walkers

Though ramp-walking figures were made as early as the 1870s, ours date from about 1935 on. They were made in Czechoslovakia from the 1920s through the 1940s and in this country during the 1950s and 1960s by Marx, who made theirs of plastic. John Wilson of Watsontown, Pennsylvania, sold his worldwide. They were known as 'Wilson Walkies' and stood about 4½" high. But the majority has been imported from Hong Kong.

Advisor: Randy Welch (See Directory, Toys)

Ankylosaurus w/clown, Marx **$40.00**

Astro **$150.00**

Astro & George Jetson **$75.00**

Astro & Rosey **$75.00**

Baby Walk-A-Way, lg...**$40.00**

Bear, plastic **$20.00**

Big Bad Wolf & Mason Pig **$50.00**

Big Bad Wolf & Three Little Pigs **$150.00**

Bison w/native, Marx **$40.00**

Bonnie Braids' Nursemaid...**$50.00**

Boy & girl dancing, plastic **$45.00**

Brontosaurus w/monkey, Marx **$40.00**

Bull, plastic **$20.00**

Bunnies carring carrot, plastic **$35.00**

Bunny on back of dog, plastic **$50.00**

Bunny pushing cart, plastic **$60.00**

Camel w/2 humps, head bobs, plastic **$20.00**

Chicks carrying Easter egg, plastic..**$35.00**

Chilly Willy, penguin on sled pulled by parent **$25.00**

Chinese man w/duck in basket, plastic **$30.00**

Chipmunks carrying acorns, plastic..**$35.00**

Chipmunks Marching Band w/drum & horn, plastic **$35.00**

Clown, Wilson **$30.00**

Cow, metal legs, sm, plastic **$20.00**

Cowboy on horse, plastic w/metal legs, sm **$30.00**

Dachshund...**$20.00**

Dairy cow **$20.00**

Dog, plastic Pluto look-alike w/metal legs, sm **$20.00**

Donald Duck & Goofy riding go-cart **$40.00**

Donald Duck pulling nephews in wagon **$35.00**

Donald Duck pushing wheelbarrow, all plastic.....................**$25.00**

Donald Duck pushing wheelbarrow, plastic w/metal legs, sm. **$25.00**

Double Walking Doll, boy behind girl, plastic, lg **$60.00**

Duck, plastic **$20.00**

Dutch boy & girl, plastic **$40.00**

Elephant, plastic...**$20.00**

Elephant, plastic w/metal legs, lg..**$30.00**

Eskimo, Wilson..**$100.00**

Farmer pushing wheelbarrow, plastic.....................................**$30.00**

Fiddler & Fifer Pigs..**$50.00**

Figaro the Cat w/ball...**$30.00**

Fireman, plastic..**$35.00**

Fred & Wilma Flintstone on Dino..**$60.00**

Fred Flintstone & Barney Rubble **$40.00**

Fred Flintstone on Dino...**$75.00**

Goat, plastic...**$20.00**

Goofy riding hippo **$45.00**

Hap & Hop Soldiers **$25.00**

Hippo w/native, Marx..**$40.00**

Horse, circus style, plastic **$20.00**

Horse, plastic, lg	$30.00
Horse, plastic, yellow w/rubber ears & string tail, lg	$30.00
Horse w/English rider, plastic, lg	$50.00
Indian Chief, Wilson	$70.00
Indian pulling baby on travois, plastic	$95.00
Jiminy Cricket w/cello	$30.00
Kangaroo w/baby in pouch, plastic	$30.00
Lion w/clown, Marx	$40.00
Little King & Guard	$60.00
Little Red Riding Hood, Wilson	$40.00
Mad Hatter w/March Hare	$50.00
Mama Duck w/3 ducklings, plastic	$35.00
Mammy, Wilson	$40.00
Marty's Market Lady pushing shopping cart	$65.00
Mexican cowboy on horse, plastic w/metal legs, sm	$30.00
Mickey Mouse & Donald Duck riding alligator	$40.00
Mickey Mouse & Minnie, plastic w/metal legs, sm	$40.00
Mickey Mouse & Pluto hunting	$40.00
Mickey Mouse pushing lawn roller	$35.00
Milking cow, plastic, lg	$40.00
Minnie Mouse pushing baby stroller	$35.00
Monkeys carrying bananas	$60.00
Mother Goose	$45.00
Mother Goose, plastic	$45.00
Nurse, Wilson	$30.00
Nursemaid pushing baby stroller, plastic	$20.00
Olive Oyl, Wilson	$175.00
Pebbles on Dino	$75.00
Penguin, Wilson	$25.00
Pig, plastic	$20.00
Pig, Wilson	$40.00
Pigs, 2 carrying 1 in basket, plastic	$40.00

Pinocchio; $200.00; elephant, $30.00; Donald Duck, $175.00 (all manufactured by Wilson). (Photo courtesy Randy and Adrien Welch)

Pluto, plastic w/metal legs, sm	$35.00
Popeye, Irwin, celluloid, lg	$60.00
Popeye, Wilson	$200.00
Popeye & Wimpy, heads on strings, MIB	$85.00
Popeye pushing spinach can wheelbarrow	$30.00
Rabbit, Wilson	$75.00
Reindeer, plastic	$45.00
Sailor, Wilson	$30.00

Sailors SS Shoreleave, plastic	$25.00
Santa & Mrs Claus, faces on both sides	$50.00
Santa & snowman, faces on both sides	$50.00
Santa Claus, Wilson	$90.00
Santa w/gold sack	$45.00
Santa w/white sack	$40.00
Santa w/yellow sack	$40.00
Sheriff facing outlaw	$65.00
Sheriff facing outlaw, plastic	$65.00
Slugger the Walking Bat Boy, w/ramp box, plastic	$250.00
Soldier, Wilson	$30.00
Spark Plug	$200.00
Stegosaurus w/Black caveman, Marx	$40.00
Teeny Toddler, walking baby girl, plastic, Dolls Inc, lg	$40.00
Tin Man Robot pushing cart, plastic	$150.00
Top Cat & Benny	$65.00
Triceratops w/native, Marx	$40.00
Walking baby, plastic w/moving eyes & cloth dress, lg	$40.00
Walking baby in Canadian Mountie uniform, plastic, lg	$50.00
Wimpy, Wilson	$175.00
Wiz Walker Milking Cow, plastic, Charmore, lg	$40.00
Yogi Bear & Huckleberry Hound	$50.00
Zebra w/native, Marx	$40.00

Pumpkin Head Man and Woman, faces on both sides of head, $100.00. (Photo courtesy Randy and Adrien Welch)

Rings

Toy rings are a fairly new interest in the collecting world. Earlier radio and TV mail-order premiums have been popular for some time but have increased in value considerably over the past few years. Now there is a growing interest in other types of rings as well — those from gumball machines, World's Fairs souvenirs, movie and TV show promotions, and any depicting celebrities. They may be metal or plastic; most have adjustable shanks. New rings are already being sought out as future collectibles.

Note: All rings listed here are considered to be in fine to very fine condition. Wear, damage, and missing parts will devaluate them considerably.

Annie, face, NM+	$100.00
Annie, secret message, EX	$250.00
Batman, Nestlè, M	$90.00
Captain Midnight, secret compartment, EX	$140.00
Captain Video, photo, EX	$325.00
Davy Crockett, compass w/expansion band, EX	$175.00

Davy Crockett, TV flicker, M $150.00
Flash Gordon, Post Toasties, MIP $75.00

Frank Buck, black leopard, bronze, NM, $3,200.00.

Gabby Hayes, cannon, EX $250.00

Green Hornet, Seal, gold-colored metal with glow-in-the-dark secret compartment, 1947, NM, from $850.00 to $950.00.

Hopalong Cassidy, hat/compass, EX $275.00
Howdy Doody, Clarabelle horn, EX $385.00
Lassie, Friendship, EX $150.00
Lone Ranger, Six Shooter, 1947, EX $150.00
Melvin Pervis, Jr G-Men Corps, EX......................$85.00
Phantom, skull, brass w/red eyes, 1950s, EX............$800.00
Rin-Tin-Tin, magic, w/pencil, EX $550.00
Roy Rogers, microscope, EX $125.00
Roy Rogers, saddle, silver, EX $350.00
Shadow, Diamond Co, EX................................$200.00
Sky King, radar, EX $125.00
Superman, Crusader, EX.................................$235.00
Tom Corbett, face, EX...................................$125.00
Tom Mix, Straight Shooter, EX..........................$100.00
Wonder Woman, Nestlè, 1977, EX.......................$110.00
Woody Woodpecker, Club Stamp, EX $150.00
Zorro, silver plastic w/logo on black top, EX $60.00

Robots and Space Toys

Japanese toy manufacturers introduced their robots and space toys as early as 1948. Some of the best examples were made in the '50s, during the 'golden age' of battery-operated toys. They became more and more complex, and today some of these in excellent condition may bring well over $1,000.00. By the '60s, more and more plastic was used in their production, and the toys became inferior.

Apollo Space Craft, Masudaya, battery-operated, astronaut circles above craft, 11" L, EXIB...............................$225.00
Atomic Reactor, Linemar, battery-operated & steam-powered, metal, 10x12", EXIB $410.00
Battery-Operated Tractor w/Robot Driver, tin, rubber treads, pistons light & fan spins, 10", NMIB.........................$450.00
Blast-Off Space Game, Replogle Globe-Chicago, 1953, NMIB. $675.00
Circus Car #8, ATC, friction, litho tin, robot driving sports car, 8" L, VG $500.00
Driving Robot/Flying Man, SY, windup, litho tin, 5½", NMIB $350.00
Dux Astroman, West Germany, battery-operated, plastic, nonworking otherwise NMIB..................................$400.00
Fire Bird #308 Space Rocket, Masudaya, friction, litho tin, 12½", VG+IB $150.00
Flying Saucer w/Space Pilot, KO, battery-operated, litho tin, 7½" dia, NM+IB $225.00
Ground Zero Robot, ST, wind-up, litho tin w/vinyl head, 9½", NMIB $175.00
ICBM Launching Station, Horikawa, crank action, litho tin, 19" L, EXIB..$250.00
Interceptor #230, S&E, battery-operated, litho tin & plastic, 14½", EXIB, ...$355.00
Journey to the Moon From Space Station to the Moon, Mego, battery-operated, 36" L, EX+IB $275.00
Jupiter Rocket, Japan, friction, litho tin, multicolored, 9", EXIB $100.00
Kamen Rider, Bullmark, friction, tin, vinyl & plastic, advances on feet or stomach, 1960s, 7", NMIB.....................$400.00
Krome Dome, Y, battery-operated, plastic, 9½", NM+IB .. $350.00
Lunar Loop, Japan, battery-operated, plastic, Space Craft vehicle travels loop, 14", GIB $75.00
Man From Mars (Shooting), Irwin, windup, plastic figure in red suit, clear bubble helmet, 11", EXIB $300.00
Martin the Martian, Y, battery-operated, plastic, 15", NM+IB .. $450.00
Missile Savings Bank, Japan, missile shoots coin into moon, litho tin, 7" L, NMIB..$525.00
Orbit Explorer (w/Airborne Satellite), KO, windup, litho tin, 8½" L, NMIB..$400.00
Planet Robot, KO, remote-controlled, tin, nonworking, 9", EX. $300.00
Robert the Robot, Ideal, remote-controlled, tin, skirted bottom, 16", EXIB..$220.00
Robot (Directional), Y, battery-operated, litho tin, skirted bottom, red light atop head, 1960s, 11", VG $440.00
Robot Torpedo, Marusan, crank action, tin, 11½", NM....$475.00
Rocket Patrol Target Game, American Toy Prod, 1950s, EX+... $75.00
Satellite, Japan, battery-operated, 3 red plastic rockets encircling litho tin globe on wire supports, 10", EXIB...............$430.00
See-Thru Robot, Hong Kong, battery-operated, plastic, 12", VGIB $475.00
Sonicon Rocket, MT, litho tin, 13" L, NMIB.................$675.00
Space Controlled Tractor, Hong Kong, battery-operated, plastic, bulldozer w/robot driver, 12", EXIB $425.00

Space Man, Linemar, windup, tin & plastic, 6", EX **$225.00**

Spinaround Planet Bank, Vacumet, die-cast & plastic, planets on disk around sun bank, 8" dia, NMIB **$65.00**

Tetsujin 28 #3, TN, windup, tin w/rubber nose, walks w/engine noise, 10", EX+ **$890.00**

Two-Stage Earth Satelite, Linemar, crank-operated, litho tin, 9" L, EX+IB **$350.00**

Two-Stage Rocket Launching Pad, TN, battery-operated, 8x7x4", NMIB **$650.00**

Universe Teleboat #7, China, battery-operated, litho tin & plastic, astronaut w/camera seated in rocket, 15" L, EX **$50.00**

V-3 Rocket, Cragston, friction, litho tin, 1950s, 3", NM **$75.00**

Vureiza (Blazer), Bullmark, windup, tin w/vinyl head, walks as arms move, 8½", NM+IB (Japanese box) **$450.00**

Winner #23 Rocket Vehicle, KDP, battery-operated, litho tin, 1960s, 5½", EX. **$115.00**

Zabitan, TT, windup, tin w/vinyl head, 9", NMIB, (Japanese box) **$225.00**

Zero of Space Robot, Hong Kong, plastic, battery-operated, 1970s, NM+IB **$375.00**

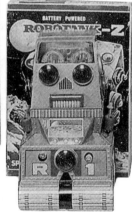

Robotank-Z, Japan, 10½": metallic brown version, NMIB, $350.00; metallic violet version, NMIB, $500.00.

Slot Car Racers

Slot cars first became popular in the early 1960s. Electric raceways set up in storefront windows were commonplace. Huge commercial tracks with eight and ten lanes were located in hobby stores and raceways throughout the United States. Large corporations such as Aurora, Revell, Monogram, and Cox, many of which were already manufacturing toys and hobby items, jumped on the bandwagon to produce slot cars and race sets. By the end of the early 1970s, people were losing interest in slot racing, and its popularity diminished. Today the same baby boomers that raced slot cars in earlier days are revitalizing the sport. As you would expect, slot cars were generally well used, so finding vintage cars and race sets in like-new or mint condition is difficult. Slot cars replicating the 'muscle' cars from the '60s and '70s are extremely sought after.

Advisor: Gary Pollastro (See Directory, Toys)

Car, Tomy, Camaro GT #88 Auto Tech, M, from $10.00 to $20.00.

Accessory, Aurora, Home Raceway by Sears, #79N9513C, VG **$225.00**

Accessory, Aurora AFX, Devil's Ditch Set, EX **$40.00**

Accessory, Cox, Ontario 8, #3070, w/Eagle & McLaren, GIB.. **$75.00**

Accessory, Eldon, Raceway Set #24, 1/24th scale, VG **$75.00**

Accessory, Ideal, Mini-Motorific Set, #4939-5, EX **$85.00**

Accessory, Motorific, GTO Torture Track, lg, EXIB **$100.00**

Accessory, Revell, HiBank Raceway Set #49-9503, w/Cougar GTE & Pontiac Firebird, EXIB **$150.00**

Accessory, Strombecker, Thunderbolt Monza, Montgomery Ward, VGIB **$150.00**

Car, Aurora, Thunderjet, Dune Buggy, white w/red striped roof, EX **$30.00**

Car, Aurora AFX, Autoworld McLaren XIR, #1752, blue & white, EX **$14.00**

Car, Aurora AFX, Autoworld Porsche #5, white w/blue stripes, EX **$12.00**

Car, Aurora AFX, BMW 3201 Turbo, #1980, yellow & orange, EX **$20.00**

Car, Aurora AFX, Chevy Nomad, #1760, orange, EX.......... **$20.00**

Car, Aurora AFX, Dodge Challenger, #1773, lime & blue, NM . **$35.00**

Car, Aurora AFX, Dodge Charger Stock Car, #1910, white w/black hood, EXIB.. **$25.00**

Car, Aurora AFX, Ferrari #2, #1763, red & white or white & blue, EX, ea **$10.00**

Car, Aurora AFX, Jeep CJ-7 Flamethrower, #1987, orange & red, NM **$18.00**

Car, Aurora AFX, Monza GT, #1948, white & green, EX ... **$15.00**

Car, Aurora AFX, Pontiac Grand Am, #10-191, red, white & blue, EX **$15.00**

Car, Aurora AFX, Porsche 917-10, #1747, white, red & blue, EX **$12.00**

Car, Aurora AFX, Speed Beamer, red, white & blue stripe, VG ... **$10.00**

Car, Aurora Cigarbox, Dino Ferrari, red, EX **$20.00**

Car, Aurora G-Plus, Amrac Can Am, yellow & black w/white stripe, EX **$15.00**

Car, Aurora G-Plus, Indy Valvoline, black, VG **$12.00**

Car, Aurora Thunderjet, Cobra #1375, yellow w/black stripe, VG+ **$30.00**

Car, Aurora Thunderjet, Ford Car, #1382, white & blue, VG .. **$25.00**

Car, Aurora Thunderjet, Lola GT, #1378, turquoise & white w/blue stripe, VG $25.00

Car, Aurora Thunderjet, Thunderbird Sports Roadster, #1355, EX $45.00

Car, TCR, Maintenance Van, red & white, EX $15.00

Car, Tyco, '40 Ford Coupe, #8534, black w/flames, EX $20.00

Car, Tyco, Autoworld Carrera, white & red w/blue stripe, G.. $10.00

Car, Tyco, Caterpillar #96, black & yellow, EX $20.00

Car, Tyco, Corvette #12, white & red w/blue stripes, EX $12.00

Car, Tyco, Firebird, #6914, cream & red, VG $12.00

Car, Tyco, Highway Patrol #56, black & white, w/sound, EX .. $16.00

Car, Tyco, Lamborghini, red, VG............................ $12.00

Car, Tyco, Military Police, #45, white & blue, EX.............. $30.00

Car, Tyco, Pinto Funny Car Goodyear, red & yellow, EX $20.00

Vehicles

These are the types of toys that are intensely dear to the heart of many a collector. Having a beautiful car is part of the American dream, and over the past 80 years, just about as many models, makes, and variations have been made as toys for children as the real vehicles for adults. Novices and advanced collectors alike are easily able to find something to suit their tastes as well as their budgets.

One area that is especially volatile includes those 1950s and 1960s tin scale-model autos by foreign manufacturers — Japan, U.S. Zone Germany, and English toy makers. Since these are relatively modern, you'll still be able to find some at yard sales and flea markets at reasonable prices.

There are several good references for these toys: *Hot Wheels, The Ultimate Redline Guide, Second Edition* and *Vol. 2,* by Jack Clark and Robert P. Wicker; *Collector's Guide to Tonka Trucks, 1947 – 1963,* by Don and Barb deSalle; *Matchbox Toys, 1947 to 2003, The Other Matchbox Toys,* and *Toy Car Collector's Guide* by Dana Johnson.

Newsletter: *Matchbox USA*
Charles Mack
62 Saw Mill Rd., Durham, CT 06422; 203-349-1655
MTCHBOXUSA@aol.com; www.charliemackonline.com

Ahi, Alfa Romeo Giuletta Sprint, from $20 to $25.00

Ahi, Rolls Royce Silver Wraith, from $25 to $30.00

Bandai, Buick (1958), friction, 8", VG $75.00

Bandai, Chevy Impala (1963), friction, working headlights, 18", NMIB $300.00

Bandai, Ford T-Bird (1959), friction, 8", M $260.00

Bandai, Jaguar XKE, 1960s, battery-operated, 10", EXIB .. $275.00

Bandai, Mercedes-Benz (Gullwing), remote-controlled, engine sound, opening doors, 8", VG+IB $200.00

Bandai, Plymouth Fury Convertible (1959), friction, 8½", NMIB $400.00

Bandai, Pontiac Firebird (1967), battery-operated, w/windshield wipers, 9½", EXIB $125.00

Bandai, Subaru 360 (1960s), friction, 7", VG+ $150.00

Barclay, Mack Pickup Truck, 3½", from $30 to $35.00

Barclay, Searchlight Truck, from $145 to $160.00

Buddy L, Air Force Supply Truck, blue w/cloth topper, BRT, 1950s, 15", G+, A $185.00

Buddy L, Boat Hauler, light blue w/white grille, WWT, 2 red & white plastic boats, 1960s, 27", VG $190.00

Buddy L, Dump Truck, enclosed cab w/curved dump bed, black wooden wheels (4), 1940s, 17", VG $110.00

Buddy L, Emergency Auto Wrecker, yellow w/red boom, nickel-plated grille, 1940s, 15", VG+ $230.00

Buddy L, Fast Freight Semi, open U-shaped trailer w/chain across open back, 6-wheeled, 1940s, 20", NMIB $650.00

Buddy L, Flivver Coupe, 1920s, black, MSW, 11", EX+, A .$715.00

Buddy L, Greyhound Bus, automatic door, ringing bell, battery-operated lights, blue & white, 16", G+, A $275.00

Buddy L, Hydraulic Dumper, turquoise, BRT, 6 wheels, 1961, 20", VG $110.00

Buddy L, Machinery Truck, green w/light yellow bed, BRT, 6-wheeled, 1950s, 23", VG+ $250.00

Buddy L, Merry-Go-Round Truck, 1960s, 13", NM $330.00

Buddy L, Motor Market Truck, 20", G $600.00

Buddy L, Repair-It Service Truck, red cab w/white dump bed, w/accessories, 1950s, 21", EXIB $440.00

Buddy L, Scoop & Dump Truck, 4 wheels 1950s, 18", G ... $75.00

Buddy L, Shell Fuel Oils Tanker, 1938 International, yellow w/diagonal red on nose, 21", VG+ $260.00

Buddy L, Super Market Delivery Truck, white, BRT, w/accessories, 1940s, 13", G $85.00

Buddy L, Telephone & Maintenance Truck, #450, 2-tone green, no accessories, 1940s $80.00

Buddy L, Utilities Service Truck, GMC, orange w/lg black crane, 1950s, 15", EX $385.00

Buddy L, Van Freight Carriers Semi, trailer w/removable roof, 6-wheeled, 1940s, 20", VG $90.00

Buddy L, Wrecking Truck, red, black & gray w/black boom, silver-painted grille, embossed lettering, 1940s, 17", VG $65.00

Chein, Fancy Groceries Truck, 6", EX............................. $300.00

Chein, Fire Pumper Truck, open seat, 18", G, A $200.00

Chein, Greyhound Coast-to-Coast Bus, disk wheels, 9", VG.. $225.00

Chein, Ice Truck, #600, 20", VG $600.00

Chein, Junior Truck, 8", EX $350.00

Chein, Limousine, 1930s, 6", EX $275.00

Chein, Motor Express Truck, 1928, 19", G $450.00

Chein, Oil Truck, 9", G $225.00

Chein, Railway Express Agency Truck, 20", G+ $425.00

Chein, Roadster, #221, 1920s, 8", EX $325.00

Chein, Royal Blue Line Bus, mid-1920s, 18", G $700.00

Chein, Sedan, yellow w/red & green trim, disk wheels, 7", EX, A $600.00

Chein, Tow Truck, 18", VG $600.00

Chein, Yellow Taxi (Main 7570), 1930s, 7", NMIB........... $425.00

Corgi, #50, Massey-Ferguson 50B Tractor, from $60 to....... $75.00

Corgi, #55, Fordson Power Major Tractor, from $100 to... $125.00

Corgi, #58, Beast Carrier, from $50 to $65.00

Corgi, #60, Fordson Power Major Tractor, from $90 to..... $120.00

Corgi, #154, Ferrari Formula I, from $45 to..................... $60.00

Corgi, #158, Tyrrell-Ford Elf, from $40 to $55.00

Corgi, #161, Quartermaster Dragster, from $35 to.............. $50.00

Corgi, #200, Ford Consul, solid colors, from $150 to $175.00

Corgi, #201, Saint's Volvo, from $175 to $200.00

Corgi, #217, Fiat 1800, from $70 to $85.00

Corgi, #219, Plymouth Suburban, from $90 to $110.00

Corgi, #221, Chevrolet Impala Taxi, from $100 to $125.00

Corgi, #224, Bentley Continental, from $100 to $125.00

Corgi, #231, Triumph Herald, from $100 to $125.00

Corgi, #245, Buick Riviera, from $85 to $100.00

Corgi, #247, Mercedes Benz 600 Pullman, from $75 to $90.00

Corgi, #337, Chevrolet Sting Ray, from $60 to $80.00

Corgi, #393, Mercedes Benz 350 SL, metallic green, from $100 to $125.00

Corgi, #406, Land Rover Pickup, from $75 to....................$95.00

Corgi, #510, Citroen Tour De France, from $125 to.........$150.00

Corgi, #906, German Rocket Launcher, from $80 to $95.00

Dinky, #102, MG Midget, from $225 to $260.00

Dinky, #109, Gabriel Model T Ford, from $150 to $175.00

Dinky, #123, Princess 2200 HL, from $170 to $190.00

Dinky, #136, Vauxhall Viva, from $140 to $165.00

Dinky, #154, Ford Taurus 17M, from $160 to $195.00

Dinky, #156, Saab 96, from $150 to..............................$200.00

Dinky, #169, Ford Corsair, from $135 to $165.00

Dinky, #175, Hillman Minx, from $180 to $210.00

Dinky, #189, Lamborghini Marzal, from $145 to.............$185.00

Dinky, #197, Morris Mini Traveller, lime green, from $250 to ..$325.00

Dinky, #202, Fiat Abarth 2000, from $45 to $65.00

Dinky, #213, Ford Capri, from $110 to...........................$140.00

Dinky, #221, Corvette Stingray, from $140 to $165.00

Dinky, #228, Super Sprinter, from $115 to $130.00

Dinky, #243, Volvo Police Racer, from $120 to $140.00

Dinky, #255, Ford Zodiac Police Car, from $100 to.........$130.00

Dinky, #265, Plymouth Taxi, from $195 to $225.00

Dinky, #279, Aveling Barford Diesel Roller, from $120 to ...$145.00

Dinky, #360, Eagle Freighter, from $225 to.....................$250.00

Dinky, #410, Bedford Van, Royal Mail, from $115 to.......$140.00

Dinky, #572, Dump Truck, Berleit, from $225 to $250.00

Dinky, #696, Leopard Anti-Aircraft Tank, from $175 to ...$200.00

Dinky, #822, M3 Half-Track, from $240 to $265.00

Dinky, #977, Shovel Dozer, from $200 to $225.00

Goodee, Ford Fuel Truck (1955), 3", from $12 to $16.00

Goodee, Studebaker Coupe (1953), 3", from $20 to $24.00

Haji, DeSoto Sedan (1958), friction, 8", NM..................$275.00

Haji, Ford Fairlane (1960), opening hood, 11", NM+IB. $350.00

Hot Wheels, Alive '55 Chevrolet Station Wagon, redline, plum, 1973, EX+ $200.00

Hot Wheels, Blown Camaro, black walls, turquoise, 1980s, MOC...$10.00

Hot Wheels, Classic '57 T-Bird, redline, metallic red w/cream interior, 1969, EX+ $35.00

Hot Wheels, Double Vision, redline, light green, 1973, NM+...$180.00

Hot Wheels, El Rey Special, redline, dark blue, 1974, NM+ .. $315.00

Hot Wheels, Ferrari 312P, redline, red, 1970, M $45.00

Hot Wheels, Formula Fever, black walls, yellow, 1983, MIP.. $8.00

Hot Wheels, Gremlin Grinder, redline, green, 1975, NM+ .$45.00

Hot Wheels, Heavyweight Dump Truck, redline, blue, 1970, M $50.00

Hot Wheels, Incredible Hulk, black walls, yellow w/multicolored tampo, 2 rear windows, 1979, NM...............................$22.00

Hot Wheels, Jet Threat, redline, metallic yellow, 1971, M...$90.00

Hot Wheels, Lotus Turbine, redline, orange, 1969, NM+....$27.00

Hot Wheels, Mantis, redline, metallic green, 1970, NM $35.00

Hot Wheels, Nitty Gritty Kitty, redline, metallic blue, 1970, complete, EX+ $28.00

Hot Wheels, Paramedic, redline, yellow w/red tampo, 1975, MIP $65.00

Hot Wheels, Rip Cord, blue, original lime driver w/white full-face helmet, training wheels, 1973, M (on EX card) $375.00

Hot Wheels, Shadow Jet, yellow w/maroon accents, MIP $10.00

Hot Wheels, Thrill Drivers Torino, black walls, white, 1977, NM ..$95.00

Hot Wheels, Volkswagon Bug, redline, orange w/black, yellow & green tampo, 1974, M $80.00

Hubley, Packard Sedan (1939-40), 5½", from $75 to..........$90.00

Joal, Chrysler 150, from $35 to....................................$45.00

Johnny Lightning, Custom XKE, doors open, 1969 ....$125.00

Kirk, Chevrolet Monza GT, from $65 to $75.00

Lledo, Delivery Van, 1983, from $15 to $20.00

Lone Star, Cadillac Coupe de Ville, white & blue, from $80 to. $100.00

Marx, Aero Oil Co Tanker, tin, 5½", VG+ $215.00

Marx, Contractor's Truck, front loader, spring-loaded dumping action, 20", EX $200.00

Marx, Dump Truck, DUMP lettered on sides of bed, 12", EX. $90.00

Marx, Fire Chief Car, windup, w/siren, red, 14", G+.........$190.00

Marx, Inter City Delivery Service Stake Truck, red, blue & yellow lithoed detail, 4 wheels, 1940s, 18", VG....................$120.00

Marx, Lumar Construction End Loader, 1950s, 16", EX.....$35.00

Marx, Meadow Farm Dairy Truck, 13", VG $150.00

Marx, Polar Ice Co Stake Truck, 4 covered wheels, 13", EX3", EX...$275.00

Marx, Sears Roebuck & Co Semi, opening rear doors, 2-tone green, 25", VG...$225.00

Marx, Toy Town Express Van Lines, box van, 4 covered wheels, 1950s, 12", G...$130.00

Marx, US Army Stake Truck, dark blue w/light blue detail, marked USA 41573147, 4 wheels, 14", EX...............................$85.00

Marx, US Navy Jeep & Searchlight Trailer, 23" overall, VG+IB.$400.00

Marx, Willy's Jeep, 13", VG+IB $200.00

Matchbox, Aston Martin DB2 Saloon, #53, metallic light green w/gray plastic wheels, 1958, MIP, from $65 to.............$85.00

Matchbox, Bedford Wreck Truck, #13 (cast into base), tan w/gray plastic wheels, 1958, MIP, from $80 to......................$110.00

Matchbox, Commer Pickup, #50, light or dark tan w/metal or plastic wheels, 1958, MIP, ea from $75 to $90.00

Matchbox, DeTomaso Pantera, #8, white w/blue base, 1975, MIP, from $10 to $15.00

Matchbox, Ergomatic Horse Box (AEC), #17, Super Fast, 1970, MIP, from $25 to $40.00

Matchbox, Ford Capri, #54, 1971, MIP, from $12 to..........$18.00

Matchbox, Gruesome Twosome, #4, gold w/amber windows, 1971, MIP, from $12 to...$16.00

Matchbox, Honda ATC, #23, red, 1985, MIP, from $10 to...$12.00

Matchbox, Iron Fairy Crane, #42, 1969, MIP, from $45 to.$75.00

Matchbox, Jeep Hot Rod, #2, pink or red, 1971, MIP, from $16 to $20.00

Matchbox, Land Rover Fire Truck, #57, Super Fast, 1970, MIP, from $50 to...$65.00

Matchbox, Safair Land Rover, #12, gold w/tan luggage, 1965, MIP, from $85 to $100.00

Matchbox, Toyota Mini Pickup Camper, #22, 1983, MIP, from $6 to **$8.00**

Matchbox, Wells Fargo Armored Truck, #69, red w/clear windows, 1978, MIP, from $35 to **$50.00**

Renwal, Ford Sunliner Convertible, from $40 to **$55.00**

Renwal, Pontiac Convertible, from $125 to **$140.00**

Rextoys, Ford Coupe (1935), from $35 to **$45.00**

Solido, #1512, 1987 Bentley Continental, M, $15.00. (Photo courtesy Dana Johnson)

Tonka, Allied Van Lines, red cab-over w/aluminum trailer, 1950s, 24", VG **$140.00**

Tonka, Cement Truck, 10 wheels, 1960s, 16", EX **$85.00**

Tonka, Farms Stake Truck, 1960s, 14", G **$75.00**

Tonka, Grain Hauler, 1940s, 22", VG **$120.00**

Tonka, Log Truck, w/chains & logs, 16 wheels, 1940s, 21", EX **$140.00**

Tonka, Motor Transport, 1950s, 28", VG **$100.00**

Tonka, Rescue Squad, 1960s, 13", VG+ **$120.00**

Tonka, Thunderbird Express Semi, white w/red & black decals, BRT, 14 wheels, 24", EX+ **$275.00**

Tootsietoy, Auto Carrier, Mack C-style cab & trailer w/MDW, 1 sedan & 2 coupes, 8½" overall, VG+ **$200.00**

Tootsietoy, Boat Fleet Set, includes 12 warships, EX (EX 15x10" box) **$250.00**

Tootsietoy, Kayo Ice Truck, 3", VG+ **$260.00**

Tootsietoy, Mack Auto Transport, 1930s, w/4 cars, 11", G ... **$220.00**

Tootsietoy, Railway Express Truck w/Wrigley's Gum Advertising, WRT, 4", EX **$400.00**

Tootsietoy, Smitty Delivery Cycle, side car has opening lid, 3", VG+ **$275.00**

Tootsietoy, Uncle Walt Roadster (Gasoline Alley), 3", VG+ .. **$330.00**

Windup Toys

Windup toys, especially comic character or personality related, are greatly in demand by collectors today. Though most were made from the '30s through the '50s, they carry their own weight against much earlier toys and are considered very worthwhile investments. Mechanisms vary; some are key wound while others depended on lever action to tighten the mainspring and release the action of the toy. Tin and celluloid were used in their manufacture, and although it is sometimes possible to repair a tin windup, experts advise against putting your money into a celluloid toy whose mechanism is not working, since the material may be too fragile to tolerate the repair.

Air Carousel (Kiddie City Amusement Park, litho tin, AHI, 7", NM+IB **$175.00**

Artie the Clown in Crazy Car, litho tin, Unique Art, 7" L, G. **$250.00**

Babes in Toyland Soldier, Chein, 1961, lithographed tin, 6", EX, from $300.00 to $350.00. (Photo courtesy Scott Smiles)

Banjo Player, plush in cloth outfit, Japan, 6", EXIB **$50.00**

Billiard Table, litho tin, Ranger Steel Prod, 2 men at table w/cues, 13½" L, EX+IB **$350.00**

Black Smith Teddy, plush, Japan, 6", EXIB **$180.00**

Bubble Blowing Bear, tin, plush & plastic, Alps, 8", EX+ .. **$150.00**

Capitol Hill Racer, litho tin, Unique Art, 11" L, EXIB **$135.00**

Carousel, litho tin, red, white & blue w/circus theme, Wolverine, 12" dia, VG **$300.00**

Chef on Roller Skates, Black litho tin figure w/articulated arms, TPS, 6", G **$300.00**

Circus Boy, litho tin, Japan, 6", EXIB **$150.00**

Circus Plane, litho tin, clown pilot, Japan, 4" W, EXIB **$100.00**

Clown on Roller Skates, litho tin, Japan, 7", VG+IB **$300.00**

Cowboy on Rocking Horse, litho tin, white horse w/red rocker, Cragstan, 7" L, EXIB **$245.00**

Cragstan Police Car Chase, litho tin, Japan, 9" L, VG+IB ... **$75.00**

Dancing Senorita, plastic, Irwin, 10", EXIB **$75.00**

Doing the Howdy Doody, litho tin, Unique Art, 8" L, EXIB. **$825.00**

Donald (Duck) the Driver, litho tin, drives car w/iamges of other Disney characters, Linemar, 7", EXIB **$650.00**

Donald Duck Hand Car, composition Donald behind doghouse w/Pluto figure, Lionel, 11" L, VG **$425.00**

Donkey, stands upright & smokes pipe, plush w/cloth outfit, 10", EXIB **$125.00**

Drum Major, litho tin, Wolverine, 14", EX **$275.00**

Ferdinand the Bull, litho tin, Linemar, 6", VG **$125.00**

Fire Engine, litho tin, Chad Valley, 8", EX **$150.00**

Fishing Boy, Linemar, 5", NMIB **$450.00**

GI Joe & His Jouncing Jeep, litho tin, Unique Art, 7", EXIB. **$275.00**

Go-Round Tram Car, litho tin, Yonezawa, 5½" sq, NMIB. **$150.00**

Happy Bunny, litho tin rabbit in lithoed outfit beats on drums while standing, Nomura, 8", EX+IB **$520.00**

Howdy Doody Cart, litho tin, Ny-Lint, 9", VG **$300.00**

Humphrey Mobile, litho tin, Wyandotte, 9", G **$200.00**

Jazzbo Jim (Banjo Player), litho tin, Unique Art, 10", EXIB... **$500.00**

Jet Roller Coaster, pressed steel & litho tin, Wolverine, 12" L, EXIB..**$175.00**

Jungle Pete the Mechanical Alligator, litho tin, Automatic Toy, 15" L, VGIB...**$150.00**

Lester the Jester, celluloid & tin clown in cloth costume twirls cane, Alps, 9½", NMIB **$250.00**

Li'l Abner & His Dogpatch Band, litho tin, Unique Art, 8½", VG+IB...**$700.00**

Lincoln Tunnel, litho tin, Unique Art, 24" L, complete, EXIB..**$350.00**

Loop the Loop, litho tin, w/auto, McDowell, 13" L, VGIB .**$250.00**

Man on the Flying Trapeze, litho tin, Wyandotte, 9", VG+IB....**$100.00**

Merry Tourist Land, litho tin, K, 6" sq, NMIB.................**$100.00**

Mickey Mouse Whirling Tale, litho tin, Linemar, 6½", EXIB. **$600.00**

Monkey Carousel, litho tin, 4 monkeys spin & flip, 6", EX+IB ... **$110.00**

Mr Machine, multicolor plastic, Ideal, VGIB.....................**$200.00**

Nautilus Submarine, green tin, from Disney's 20,000 Leagues Under the Sea, 9½", NMIB **$200.00**

Pluto the Band Leader, litho tin, Linemar, 6", G **$175.00**

Popeye Walker Carrying 2 Parrot Cages, litho tin, 8½", VG.**$275.00**

Rocky (Fred Flintstone look-a-like), litho tin, Japan, 4", EXIB ..**$165.00**

Singing Warbler, litho tin bird w/realistic detail, Japan, 5", EXIB..**$175.00**

Skeeter-Bug Bumper Car, litho tin couple in painted steel car, Lindstrom, 1940s, 9½", EXIB **$425.00**

Steam Roller, litho tin, Lindstrom, 11½" L, VG+IB **$200.00**

Super Sonic Race Car #36, litho tin, MT, 9", EX+IB **$275.00**

Tambourine Clown, in cloth costume w/tambourine, TN, 6", EXIB..**$50.00**

Taxi, tin litho, Minic, 4", EXIB **$230.00**

Train Set, litho tin, Unique Art, 4-pc w/10" L locomotive w/tender, boxcar & caboose, w/tracks, NMIB **$300.00**

GI Joe and His Jouncing Jeep, Unique Art, 1941, NM, $225.00. (Photo courtesy Scott Smiles)

Transistor Radios

Introduced during the Christmas shopping season of 1954, transistor radios were at the cutting edge of futuristic design and miniaturization. Among the most desirable is the 1954 four-transistor Regency TR-1 which is valued at a minimum of $750.00 in jade green. Black may go for as much as $300.00, other colors from $350.00 to $400.00. The TR-1 'Mike Todd' version in the 'Around the World in Eighty Days' leather book-look presentation case goes for $4,000.00 and up! Some of the early Toshiba models sell for $250.00 to $350.00, some of the Sonys even higher — their TR-33 books at a minimum of $1,000.00, their TR-55 at $1,500.00 and up! Certain pre-1960 models by Hoffman and Admiral represented the earliest practical use of solar technology and are also highly valued. Early collectible transistor radios all have civil defense triangle markings at 640 and 1240 on the frequency dial and nine or fewer transistors. Very few desirable sets were made after 1963.

Values in our listings are for radios in at least very good condition — not necessarily working, but complete and requiring very little effort to restore them to working order. Cases may show minor wear. All radios are battery-operated unless noted otherwise.

Admiral Y2307GPS, brown plastic, vertical, 6 transistors, perforated grille, AM, 1963, from $20 to **$30.00**

Admiral Y821 Holiday, coral & white horizontal w/clock, 8 transistors, lattice grille, AM, 1960, from $10 to **$15.00**

Airline, GTI_1234A, horizontal, vertical 4-band slide rule dial, perforated grille, handle, AM/FM, 1963, from $15 to.......**$20.00**

Airline GEN-1202A, horizontal w/vertically divided front, 6 transistors, left grille, AM, 1962, from $25 to **$35.00**

Amico Boy's, plastic horizontal/desk set, 2 transistors, checkered grille, pen holder, AM, Japan, from $35 to **$45.00**

Arvin #61435, ice blue plastic, vertical, 7 transistors, perforated grille, AM, Made in USA, 1961, 4⅛", from $20 to......**$30.00**

Arvin #66R78, horizontal, 10 transistors, 3 switches, perforated grille, handle, AM/FM, 1967, from $15 to...................**$20.00**

Bradford #TR-1626, plastic, vertical, 6 transistors, metal perforated grille, AM, 1963, from $55 to **$75.00**

Bulova #870, plastic, AM, 3x2x1", $30.00. (Photo courtesy Marty and Sue Bunis)

Candle #PTR-85C, plastic, vertical, 8 transistors, step-down top, perforated grille, AM, Japan, 1963, from $40 to...........**$60.00**

Columbia #400R, red, vertical, 4 transistors, circular grille w/vertical bars, AM, 1960, from $45 to.......................................**$55.00**

Commodore #YTR-601, plastic, vertical, 6 transistors, textured/perforated grille, AM, Japan, 3¾", from $35 to................**$45.00**

Crosley, #JM-8BK Enchantment, leather-covered book shape, 3 sub-miniature tubes & 2 transistors, AM, 1956, 7", $125 to. **$150.00**

Delmonico #7TA-2, horizontal, 7 transistors, lg perforated grille, AM, 1963, from $30 to **$40.00**

Emerson #849, plastic, horizontal, hourglass-shaped panel, checkered grille, AM, 1955, 5¾", from $150 to **$175.00**

General Electric #C2419A Mickey Mouse, yellow plastic, w/ clock, horizontal, 3-D Mickey on dial, AM, 10¾", from $50 to **$75.00**

General Electric #P797A, light beige leather, horizontal, plastic lattice grille, leather handle, AM, 1958, from $15 to **$20.00**

General Electric #P968A, leather, vertical, 10 transistors, perforated grille, AM, 1965, from $10 to **$15.00**

Grundig Transworld Ambassador, horizontal, lower grille, 2 antennas, AM/FM, from $25 to **$35.00**

Hitachi #KH-915, horizontal, 9 transistors, circular checkered grille, FM, 1963, from $20 to **$25.00**

Juliette #LR-57, plastic, lamp/radio combo, 7 transistors, w/original shade, AM, 1968, from $25 to **$35.00**

Linmark #T-71, vertical, 6 transistors, lower round perforated grille, AM, 1959, from $35 to **$45.00**

Magnavox #AM-22, plastic, horizontal, 6 transistors, metal perforated grille, AM, 4¼", from $35 to **$45.00**

Marvel #6YR-05, vertical, 6 transistors, round dial, lower perforated grille, AM, Japan, 1961, 3⅞", from $45 to **$55.00**

Mitsubishi #6X-145, plastic, vertical, 6 transistors, lower metal perforated grille, swing handle, AM, 3¾", $100 to..........**$125.00**

Motorola #X37E, black leather, vertical, 6 transistors, front perforated grille, AM, 1962, 4", from $20 to.........................**$25.00**

Motorola #8X26E Power 10, charcoal plastic, vertical, horizontal grille bars w/logo, swing handle, AM, 7", from $35 to .**$45.00**

Norelco #L4X95T, brown leatherette w/cream plastic front, horizontal, 7 push buttons, lower grille, AM, 1960, $25 to......**$35.00**

Panasonic #R-111 Tiny-Tote, vertical, right side thumbwheel tuning, lower round grille, AM, 2¾", from $40 to **$50.00**

Philco #NT-1004, leather, horizontal, 10 transistors, slide rule dial, checkered grille, AM/FM, 1965, from $10 to..............**$15.00**

Philips #L0X91T Fanette, plastic, horizontal, left lattice grille, AM, West Germany, 1963, from $30 to **$40.00**

RCA #4RG56, plastic, vertical, turquoise window dial, perforated grille w/horizontal lines, AM, 1963, 6½", $20 to **$30.00**

Realistic Hi-Fiver, plastic, horizontal, top thumbwheel, metal grille w/logo, AM, Japan, 5¼", from $60 to **$85.00**

Realtone, #TR-1948, vertical, 9 transistors, thumbwheel tuning, lower grille w/bars, AM, 1964, from $10 to **$15.00**

Ross #RE-101 Dynamic, plastic, vertical, 10 transistors, round dial knob, lower lattice grille, AM, 1964, from $15 to **$20.00**

Seminole #1101, horizontal, 11 transistors, step-down right side, metal perforated grille, AM, Japan, 5½", $35 to...........**$45.00**

Silvertone #206, vertical, 4 transistors, quarter-round window dial on right, V-shaped grille bars, AM, 1960, $20 to.........**$30.00**

Silvertone #4211, horizontal, 8 transistors, metal flip-up front, slide rule dial, metal grille, AM, 7¼", from $20 to **$30.00**

Sony #TR-1819, plastic cube shape, lg top round dial knob, perforated side grille, AM, from $20 to **$25.00**

Sony #TR-72, wood, horizontal, 7 transistors, metal textured grille, handle, AM, Japan, 7x10¼x3¼", from $200 to.........**$250.00**

Standard #SR-J100F, plastic, horizontal, 10 transistors, metal grille, AM/FM switch, AM, Japan, 8¾", from $25 to **$35.00**

Sylvania #7P12, plastic, vertical, 7 transistors, thumbwheel tuning, metal grille w/logo, AM, 1959, from $35 to **$45.00**

Tempest #HT-1251, plastic, vertical, 14 transistors, 2 oval metal grilles, AM, Japan, 4½", from $20 to.........................**$30.00**

Toshiba #6P-35, plastic, horizontal, 6 transistors, left metal grille, AM, Japan, 4⅛", from $25 to` **$35.00**

Trav-Ler #TR-286-B Power-Mite, red & ivory plastic, vertical, 6 transistors, round dial knob, metal grille, AM, 1958...**$100.00**

Universal #PTR-81B, plastic, vertical, thumbwheel dial, metal grille w/logo, AM, Japan, 1962, 4⅜", from $30 to **$40.00**

Vista #NTR-850, horizontal, 8 transistors, slide rule dial, oval grille, AM, 1963, from $20 to **$30.00**

Westinghouse #H-939P8GP, white plastic, vertical, 8 transistors, lower metal grille, AM, Japan, 4¼", from $10 to..........**$15.00**

Westinghouse #H621P6 Cordless, charcoal plastic, horizontal, 6 transistors, lattice grille, swing handle, 1958, $45 to.....**$55.00**

Zenith Royal 16, plastic outer case w/perforated front cover, vertical billfold style, AM, Japan, 5⅜", from $20 to **$25.00**

Zenith Royal 645, leatherette, horizontal, right dial knob over patterned grille, handle, AM, 1963, 7⅞", from $20 to......**$25.00**

Realtone, six transistors, aqua blue, 1950s, from $40.00 to $50.00. (Photo courtesy Marty and Sue Bunis)

Treasure Craft/Pottery Craft

Al Levin commissioned Cope Pottery of Laguna Beach to turn his designs into ceramic novelties in 1947. Their success with 1949's Lucky California Sprites led him to open plants in South Gate and Compton, shifting to wood-stained Latin Dancers, TV lamps, and Barrel kitchenware. Designers Tony Guerrero and Ray Murray (of Bauer fame) created hula dancers, fish, and leaf trays for their new Hawaiian plant in 1959, while wood-textured kitchenware led California production.

Levin's son Bruce transformed designer Robert Maxwell's ideas into Pottery Craft in 1973, the first nationally successful stoneware lines with studio styling. Along with cookie jars by Don Winton and others, these formed the basis for Treasure Craft's 1980s emergence as California's largest (and last) dinnerware maker. Purchased at their 1988 peak by Pfaltzgraff, the vast Compton plants were closed after the 1994 passage of NAFTA. Some molds were sent to Mexico and China; all production ceased a few years later.

Our advisor is George A. Higby, ISA, author of the book *Treasure Craft Pottery.* He is listed in the Directory under Treasure Craft.

See also Cookie Jars.

Dinnerware

Butterfly or Poppy, hermetic canister, from $10 to	**$12.00**
Butterfly or Poppy, plate, dinner; from $13 to	**$17.00**
Butterfly or Poppy, tureen/ladle, from $40 to	**$50.00**
Garden Party, canisters, set of 4, from $60 to	**$80.00**
Midnight Sun, chip & dip, from $55 to	**$65.00**
Mirage or Southwest, baking dish, from $35 to	**$40.00**
Mirage or Southwest, chop plate, lg, from $18 to	**$22.00**
Mirage or Southwest, soup mug, from $5 to	**$7.00**
Saratoga, teepee teapot, from $30 to	**$36.00**
Stitch in Time/Auntie Em, dealer's plaque, from $10 to	**$15.00**
Stitch in Time/Auntie Em, napkin holder, from $8 to	**$10.00**
Taos, batter bowl, from $40 to	**$45.00**
Taos, condiment/spoon, from $20 to	**$24.00**
Taos, relish, 3-part, from $35 to	**$40.00**
Taos, tortilla warmer, from $30 to	**$36.00**

Figurals

Sprite, vase, 8½", from $40.00 to $45.00.

Apple Seller boy, 1961, from $45 to	**$50.00**
California Leprechaun (various), 1948, MIB, from $40 to	**$45.00**
Calypso Dancers, pr from $100 to	**$120.00**
Harem Guard & Dancer, 8", pr from $75 to	**$95.00**
Horse heads (double), TV lamp, from $75 to	**$95.00**
Jolly the Clown, 1948 only, w/hang tag, from $50 to	**$60.00**
Man's face, bottle vase, Raul Coronel, 1970, from $150 to	**$200.00**
Sprite, cigarette box w/lid & trays, from $40 to	**$45.00**
Sprite, Lazy, w/lore, 1949, MIB, from $30 to	**$35.00**
Sprite, planter, 1907 Olds, red, from $45 to	**$50.00**
Sprite, vase, tree trunk, from $20 to	**$24.00**
Stallion, 8", from $45 to	**$50.00**

Hawaiian Wares

Coconut calabash, Ray Murray design, mini, from $15 to	**$18.00**
Dancers, Keiki girl & boy, 8", pr from $55 to	**$65.00**
Drummer boy, 1959, 11", from $60 to	**$70.00**
Hula dancer, Royal Hawaiian, grass skirt, from $60 to	**$70.00**
Menehune Greeting, island name, from $20 to	**$24.00**
Plate, Dole Kids, antique white, 7", from $12 to	**$14.00**
Tiki god, Ku, 11", from $85 to	**$100.00**
Tiki god, Lono, 12", from $110 to	**$125.00**
Tray, abstract fish, mini, from $14 to	**$18.00**
Tray, fish, flame glaze, 16", from $40 to	**$45.00**
Valet, Elemakule (old man), scarce, 8½", from $110 to	**$125.00**
Wall pocket, sea horse, from $24 to	**$28.00**

Kitchenware

Butter dish, Lucky Leprechaun line, from $18 to	**$22.00**
Canister, Barrel line, cookies, from $20 to	**$24.00**
Deviled egg tray, Cavalier line, lime green, 12", from $14 to	**$18.00**
Salt & pepper shakers, car & trailer, 1940s, pr from $24 to	**$28.00**
Salt & pepper shakers, dog & hydrant, 1940s, pr from $18 to	**$22.00**
Salt & pepper shakers, Indian in canoe, 1940s, pr from $24 to	**$28.00**
Tray, arches, Raul Coronel, 1970, 16", from $95 to	**$110.00**
Wall pocket, grapes, South Gate mark, from $32 to	**$40.00**

Pottery Craft

Botanica vase, intaglio design, 9", from $32 to	**$40.00**
Canister, Farm Fresh transfer, from $15 to	**$20.00**
Carafe/slant cups, Moonstone glaze, from $50 to	**$60.00**
Cat, Mitsuo design, Tierra glaze, from $29 to	**$35.00**
Clay Menagerie figure (various), sm, ea from $15 to	**$20.00**
Matsu sprouter, Tierra glaze, from $24 to	**$30.00**
Owl, Maxwell design, 11", from $65 to	**$75.00**
Vase, Masa Mami, corrugated, 15", from $65 to	**$75.00**
Vase, Maxwell design, bottle, early, 5", from $35 to	**$45.00**
Vase, Maxwell design, overlap glaze, scarce, 24", from $100 to	**$150.00**

Trolls

The legend of the Troll originated in Scandinavia. Nordic mythology described them as short, intelligent, essentially unpleasant, supernatural creatures who were doomed to forever live underground. During the '70s, a TV cartoon special and movie based on J.R.R. Tolkien's books, *The Hobbit* and *The Lord of the Rings,* caused an increase in Trolls' popularity. As a result, books, puzzles, posters, and dolls of all types were available on the retail market. In the early '80s, Broom Hilda and Irwin Troll were featured in a series of books as well as Saturday morning cartoons. Today trolls are enjoying a strong comeback.

Troll dolls of the '60s are primarily credited to Thomas Dam of Denmark. Many, using Dam molds, were produced in America by Royalty Des. of Florida and Wishnik. In Norway A/S Nyform created a different version. Some were also made in Hong Kong, Japan, and Korea, but those were of inferior plastic and design.

The larger trolls (approximately 12") are rare and very desirable to collectors. Troll animals by Dam, such as the giraffe, horse, cow, donkey, and lion, are bringing premium prices.

Unless otherwise noted, our values are for examples in at least near-mint condition.

Advisor: Pat Peterson (See Directory, Trolls)

Boy w/long brown hair, amber eyes, jointed body, original brown pants & white shirt, TH Dam c 1979, #806, 17".........**$75.00**
Boy w/white hair & amber eyes, green pants w/1 strap, red shirt, Dam Lykkentroll mark on foot, 9", EX **$215.00**
Boy w/white hair & amber eyes, pants w/1 strap, green shirt, Dam Likkentrold tag around neck, 1960s, 9"......................**$480.00**
Boy w/wooly straw-colored hair, amber eyes, jointed head & arms, original blue & white 1-pc outfit, Dam, 8" **$125.00**

Cow, Dam Thing, light-color body, blond hair, 4", EX, $35.00. (Photo courtesy Pat Peterson)

Cow, short brown hair, dark amber eyes, Thomas Dam, made in 1990 from 1960s mold, 7" **$65.00**
Cow standing, short yellow hair, amber eyes, leather collar, Dam Things Est 1964, 6½x7½"..**$82.50**
Donkey sitting, brown hair, c Dam Things Establishment 1964 on bottom, 3" **$465.00**
Donkey standing, short white hair, amber eyes, 1960s, 9", EX ..**$155.00**
Elephant, flesh color w/white hair, amber eyes, Dam, 6" ...**$185.00**
Elephant sitting up, pink hair, Dam Est 1964, 3⅛", EX......**$55.00**
Fire chief, dark hair, amber eyes, yellow rain slicker, red felt hat, Dam, 1977, 9", EX...**$35.00**
Giraffe, brown hair, Thomas Dam mark on foot, 1960s, 12" .**$65.00**
Girl that sucks thumb, long brown, amber eyes, original knit outfit & undies, TH Dam 1979, #806, 16" **$85.00**
Girl w/dark brown hair & amber eyes, dressed in plaid red & green dress, Dam Things Est 1964 on head & foot, 12" **$175.00**

Girl w/long dark hair, dark amber eyes, green shirt & red skirt, USA Foreign Patent Pending, Made in Denmark, 1960s, 9". **$60.00**
Girl w/long purple hair, paisley tie, patterned shirt, green cap & skirt, Thomas Dam, 1960s, 5½"................................**$80.00**
Girl w/long white hair, lg amber eyes, original polka-dot trimmed skirt & jacket, jointed, Dam c 1979, w/tag, 16"..........**$80.00**
Girl w/pale pink saran hair, blue spiral eyes, dressed in red & carrying American flag, white stap shoes, 3" **$110.00**
Girl w/poseable tail, original blue plaid dress, burlap apron, left arm moves, Thomas Dam 1977, w/tag, 10"......................**$95.00**
Groom, white hair, amber eyes, in black tux w/white tie, 9"...**$75.00**
Henry, white shaggy hair, bib overalls & striped shirt, TH Dam/Made in Denmark, 1979, 16"..**$70.00**
Horse, blond mane & tail, Dam Thing, 1964, 8½x8" **$95.00**
Horse, long brown mane & tail, Dam Things Est 1964 on bottom, 2½x2"..**$215.00**
Lion standing, brown mohair mane & tail, amber eyes, Thomas Dam, 1960s, 5x7"..**$70.00**
Livvy, white shaggy hair, yellow print dress, undies & bow in hair, TH Dam 1979, 16"...**$70.00**
Maid, original outfit w/cap & apron, M in clear plastic box w/original sticker..**$155.00**
Mermaid, pink mohair hair, purple spiral eyes, stuffed metallic white tail, 1960s, 2¾" **$65.00**
Monkey, light brown wooly hair, amber eyes, swivel neck, jointed shoulders, nude, Thomas Dam, 7½" **$80.00**
Mouse, brown hair, black shiny eyes, original blue felt dress w/black button, w/whiskers, Dam, 4x4" w/2½" tail **$80.00**
Playboy Bunny, pink hair & bunny ears, orange spiral eyes, original bunny suit w/pom-pom tail, 2½" **$55.00**
Reindeer, brown tones, amber eyes, white leather collar & bell, Dam, 1960s, 3x3", from $350 to...**$400.00**
Sailor boy, white hair, original costume, c Dam Things Establishment 1964, 12", EX+...**$200.00**
Santa, white hair & beard, amber eyes, original felt outfit, Dam Things Est 1964, 12½"...**$120.00**
Troll, black hair, amber eyes, burgundy & green outfit, pointed hat, Dam, 1977, 10"...**$55.00**
Viking, white mohair, silver metallic tunic, removable helmet, Thomas Dam 1977, w/tag, 9½" **$65.00**
2-headed, light blue hair w/black tips & orange hair, nude, Uneeda 19 c 65 on head, 2¾" **$225.00**
2-headed, peach-colored hair w/gold eyes, & blond w/orange eyes, re-dressed, white shoes, Uneeda 1965 on neck, 2½" ...**$175.00**

TV Guides

This publication goes back to the early 1950s. Granted, those early issues are very rare, but what an interesting, very visual way to chronicle the history of TV programming!

Values in our listings are for examples in fine to mint condition; be sure to reduce them significantly when damage of any type is present. For insight into *TV Guide* collecting, we recommend *The TV Guide Catalog* by Jeff Kadet, the *TV Guide* Specialist.

Advisor: Jeff Kadet (See Directory, *TV Guides*)

1953, September 25, George Reeves 'Superman,' EX, $135.00.

1954, April 23, Lucille Ball.................................$166.00

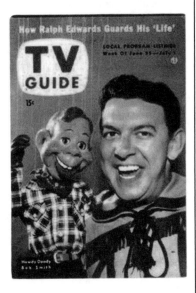

1954, June 25, Howdy Doody, Bob Smith, EX, $50.00.

1954, January 1, Bing Crosby.................................$61.00
1954, November 6, Burns & Allen $85.00
1955, December 17, Robert Montgomery $23.00
1955, January 22, Ed Sullivan...............................$39.00
1955, May 14, Perry Como $51.00
1956, April 21, Nanette Fabray...............................$25.00
1956, August 25, Esther Williams............................$30.00
1956, January 14, Loretta Young.............................$43.00
1956, November 17, Buddy Hackett $19.00
1957, April 27, Groucho Marx $30.00
1957, February 2, Jane Wyman................................$22.00
1957, June 8, Lassie $90.00
1958, March 15, James Arness & Amanda Blake..........$71.00
1958, May 3, Shirley Temple $68.00
1958, October 11, Fred Astaire & Barrie Chase............$26.00
1959, August 29, Dick Clark $35.00
1959, February 14, Alfred Hitchcock........................$63.00
1959, October 3, June Allyson................................$14.00

1960, April 9, Efrem Zimbalist, Jr $19.00
1960, January 2, cast of Gunsmoke $63.00
1961, January 21, Barbara Stanwyck........................$28.00
1961, July 1, The Flintstones...............................$150.00
1961, May 6, Donna Reed....................................$32.00
1962, August 11, Robert Stack $43.00
1962, December 8, Dick Van Dyke $41.00
1962, February 10, Mrs John F Kennedy....................$90.00
1963, August 17, Fred MacMurray $17.00
1963, January 19, cast of Car 54, Where Are You? $43.00
1964, December 19, Merry Christmas........................$27.00
1964, June 27, Mr & Mrs Johnny Carson $15.00
1964, March 21, cast of Andy Griffith Show $165.00
1965, April 24, Andy Griffith $78.00
1965, January 2, cast of The Munsters....................$195.00
1965, May 22, Julie Andrews $26.00
1966, August 20, Red Skelton...............................$26.00
1966, June 18, cast of Bewitched $50.00
1966, September 24, Barbara Eden of I Dream of Jeannie.$109.00
1967, December 2, Danny & Marlo Thomas $21.00
1967, July 22, cast of Bonanza..............................$82.00
1967, March 4, William Shatner & Leonard Nimoy of Star Trek......$225.00
1968, April 6, Barbara Anderson of Ironside................$25.00
1968, January 20, cast of High Chapparral $43.00
1968, October 12, Olympics Preview $15.00
1969, February 8, cast of Mission Impossible $35.00
1969, June 14, Glen Campbell $12.00
1969, November 22, I Dream of Jeannie Marriage $54.00
1969, October 4, Bill Cosby $19.00
1970, April 25, Raquel Welch & John Wayne $22.00
1970, January 24, Tom Jones.................................$20.00
1971, April 17, Paul Newman.................................$9.00
1971, February 13, Goldie Hawn $8.00
1971, May 29, cast of All In the Family....................$35.00
1971, October 2, Jimmy Stewart.............................$13.00
1972, April 22, Don Rickles $13.00
1972, September 16, cast of Anna & the King $9.00
1973, December 15, Katherine Hepburn......................$10.00
1973, February 24, cast of M*A*S*H.........................$48.00
1973, July 14, cast of the Waltons..........................$21.00
1974, August 31, Telly Savalas of Kojak.....................$18.00
1974, December 7, Michael Landon of Little House on the Prairie..........$33.00
1974, January 26, David Carradine of Kung Fu $18.00
1975, February 1, James Garner of Rockford Files............$14.00
1975, May 10, Muhammad Ali $10.00
1975, October 4, Lee Remick as Jennie $10.00
1976, March 27, Jack Palace of Bronk $9.00
1976, November 6, Gone With the Wind $15.00
1977, January 29, Wonder Woman.............................$52.00
1977, March 19, Last Mary Tyler Moore Show $29.00
1977, September 24, cast of Betty White Show $25.00
1978, January 7, cast of Happy Days.........................$28.00
1978, October 21, cast of WKRP In Cincinnati.................$25.00
1979, July 21, cast of BJ & the Bear $9.00
1979, March 3, Gary Coleman $31.00
1979, September 1, Miss America..............................$7.00

1980, April 19, cast of Alice.................................$12.00
1980, May 17, cast of the Jeffersons....................$16.00
1980, November 22, Pam Dawber of Mork & Mindy.........$12.00
1980, September 20, Priscilla Presley $16.00
1981, August 1, Miss Piggy................................$20.00
1981, January 10, David Hartman of Good Morning America...$8.00
1981, May 30, Dan Rather...................................$5.00
1982, August 21, Nell Carter of Gimme A Break $7.00
1982, March 27, Larry Hagman of Dallas $14.00
1983, February 5, Cheryl Ladd as Grace Kelly..........$14.00
1983, September 3, final All in the Family............$23.00
1984, January 28, Cybill Shepherd $13.00
1984, November 24, cast of Kate & Allie $7.00
1985, April 6, Richard Chamberlain $12.00
1985, January 5, Elvis Presley $29.00
1985, September 21, Michael J Fox $12.00
1986, April 5, cast of Family Ties........................$12.00
1986, August 30, Mystery of Bobby's Return.............$12.00
1986, June 14, Emmanuel Lewis of Webster.............$9.00
1987, April 19, Tony Danza of Who's The Boss.........$14.00
1987, January 31, cast of Golden Girls $22.00
1987, November 7, Jacqueline Bisset & Armand Assante of Napoleon $8.00
1988, March 5, Oprah Winfrey $6.00
1988, May 21, Charles & Diana $21.00
1988, October 22, The Aids Scare $8.00
1988, September 24, cast of Cosby Show $9.00
1989, June 10, Fred Savage $17.00
1989, March 4, Vanna White.................................$6.00
1989, May 27, Kirstie Alley of Cheers $14.00
1990, April 21, Arnold Schwartzenegger................$6.00
1990, January 20, Arsenio Hall & Dana Delaney..............$10.00
1991, April 20, Burt Reynolds & Marilu Henner..............$7.00
1991, January 5, Jane Pauley..............................$6.00
1992, December 19, Toon Boom $14.00
1992, February 1, Jessica Lange $6.00
1992, March 28, Disney's Beast/Oscars................$14.00
1992, September 5, Joan Lunden $5.00
1993, August 7, Full House's Mary Kate & Ashley Olsen....$19.00
1993, January 23, Fresh Prince Will Smith.............$14.00
1994, April 23, Jason Alexander of Seinfeld............$9.00
1994, August 20, Barbra Streisand by Hirschfeld.................$20.00
1994, October 22, Suzanne Somers & Jay Leno $12.00
1995, December 2, Tea Leoni $5.00
1995, March 11, David Duchovny & Gillian Anderson of X-Files $42.00
1995, September 23, cast of Friends $14.00
1996, August 31, Eagle's Ricky Watters.................$14.00
1996, July 6, Gillian Anderson of X-Files $21.00
1996, May 11, Tom Selleck & Coutney Cox $7.00
1997, April 12, Michael Jordan.............................$6.00
1997, August 2, Nascar's Jeff Gordon...................$14.00
1997, January 11, Dilbert..................................$5.00
1997, June 7, Leann Rimes $14.00
1998, March 28, cast of South Park...................$14.00
1999, July 31, John F Kennedy, Jr $8.00
1999, March 6, cast of 7th Heaven $5.00

Twin Winton

The genius behind the designs at Twin Winton was sculptor Don Winton. He and his twin, Ross, started the company while sill in high school in the mid-1930s. In 1952 older brother Bruce Winton bought the company from his two younger brothers and directed its development nationwide. They produced animal figures, cookie jars, and matching kitchenware and household items during this time. It is important to note that Bruce was an extremely shrewd business man, and if an order came in for a nonstandard color, he would generally accommodate the buyer — for an additional charge, of course. As a result, you may find a Mopsy (Raggedy Ann) cookie jar in a wood stain finish or some other unusual color, even though Mopsy was only offered in the Collector Series in the catalogs. This California company was active until it sold in 1976 to Roger Bowermeister, who continued to use the Twin Winton name. He experimented with different finishes. One of the most common is a light tan with a high gloss glaze. He owned the company only one year until it went bankrupt and was sold at auction. Al Levin of Treasure Craft bought the molds and used some of them in his line. Eventually, the molds were destroyed.

One of Twin Winton's most successful concepts was their Hillbilly line — mugs, pitchers, bowls, lamps, ashtrays, decanters, and novelty items molded after the mountain boys in Paul Webb's cartoon series. Don Winton was the company's only designer, though he free-lanced as well. He designed for Disney, Brush-McCoy, Revell Toys, The Grammy Awards, American Country Music Awards, Ronald Reagan Foundation, and numerous other companies and foundations. Some of Don's more prominent pieces of art are currently registered with the Smithsonian in Washington, D.C.

If you would like more information, read *A Collector's Guide to Don Winton Designs*, written by our advisor Mike Ellis. Other sources of information are *The Ultimate Collector's Encyclopedia of Cookie Jars* by Joyce and Fred Roerig.

See also Cookie Jars.

Advisor: Mike Ellis (See Directory, Twin Winton)

Club: Twin Winton Collector Club
Also Don Winton Designs (other than Twin Winton)
266 Rose Lane
Costa Mesa, CA 92627; 714-646-7112 or fax: 7414-645-4919
winwinton.com
ellis5@pacbell.net

Ashtray, Bambi, TW-205, 6x8".........................$100.00
Bank, Dutch girl, TW-418, 8".........................$50.00
Bank, elf, TW-408, 8".................................$50.00
Bank, Friar Tuck (Monk), TW-407, 8"................$40.00
Bank, nut, TW-416, 8"................................$50.00
Bank, pig, TW-401, 8" $50.00
Bank, teddy bear, TW-409, 8" $40.00
Bowl, salad; Artist Palette Line, 13", minimum value $250.00
Candleholder, Aladdin, TW-510, 6½x9½", ea...........$45.00
Candleholder, El Creco, short, TW-500S, 6x4½", ea...........$12.00
Candy jar, bear, TW-354, 8x10½" $85.00
Candy jar, nut, TW-353, 9x8" $75.00

Candy jar, Pot 'O Candy, TW-359, 8x10" $65.00
Candy jar, Sailor Elephant, TW-356, 9x6" $65.00
Canister, Coffee House, Canisterville, TW-103, 9x5" $95.00
Canister, Cookie Bucket, TW-59, 8x9" $60.00
Canister, Sugar Bucket, TW-61, 6x7" $40.00
Canister, Tea House, Canisterville, TW-104, 3x7" $50.00
Creamer, Artist Palette Line, 4" dia...................................$40.00
Decanter, pink elephants, 11x4" $500.00
Decanter, Russian Cossack w/bomb, Twin Winton Design, Pasadena CA, 10" $500.00
Expanimal, chipmunk bookends, TW-127, 7½" $125.00
Figurine, angel playing flute, 4" $35.00
Figurine, Asian boy holding frog, 5½" $150.00
Figurine, ballerina in blue, 3¾" $12.00

Figurine, BooBoo Bear, made for Idea Inc., 4", $75.00. (Photo courtesy Mike Ellis)

Figurine, boy standing by mailbox, T-8, 5½" $160.00
Figurine, boy wearing Mickey Mouse hat, w/plane & hot dog, T-1, 5½" $150.00
Figurine, collie, TW-602, 7½" $65.00
Figurine, girl playing dress-up, T-19, 5½" $200.00
Figurine, Mickey the Apprentice, bisque, 7" $75.00
Figurine, Snow White holding flowers, sm, 7⅛" $12.00
Figurine, Wally Gator, bisque, 6" $80.00
Lamp, monkey, TW-259, 13" $175.00
Miniature, blind mouse, #208, ¾" $6.00
Miniature, skunk sitting, #203, ¾" $5.00
Mug, bear, TW-504, 3¼" $85.00
Mug, coffee; Bergie, 5½" $40.00
Mug, elephant, 3½x5" $125.00
Mug, kitten face, TW-503, 3¼" $85.00
Mug, squirrel handle, 5" $100.00
Napkin holder, cow, TW-479, 6x7" $85.00
Napkin holder, Dobbin, TW-487, 7x5" $65.00
Napkin holder, Persian cat, TW-470, 5½x7" $75.00
Napkin holder, rabbit, TW-452, 6x4" $150.00

Napkin holder, Ranger Bear, TW-478, 9x4" $75.00
Planter, box; Merry Xmas, 4x15" $40.00
Planter, pipe, 5" $50.00
Planter, squirrel, TW-329, 8" $45.00
Plate, salad; Artist Palette Line, 8" $40.00
Plate, Santa face, 14" $50.00
Salt & pepper shakers, bucket, TW-65, pr $30.00
Salt & pepper shakers, churn, TW-171, pr $40.00
Salt & pepper shakers, dinosaur, TW-172, pr $100.00
Salt & pepper shakers, Dutch girl, TW-147, pr $35.00
Salt & pepper shakers, house, TW-140, pr.........................$60.00
Salt & pepper shakers, Pirate Fox, TW-146, pr..................$45.00
Spoon rest, Ranger Bear, TW-12, 10x5" $40.00
Teapot, rooster, 10" $125.00
Toothpick dispenser, pig w/floral decor, hind quarters up, 5" .$60.00
Tumbler, Artist Palette Line, 7".......................................$20.00
Vase, bud; Snoopy Bear, 3x4" $65.00
Wall planter, puppy head, TW-303, 5½" $100.00
Wall pocket, rabbit (head),TW-302, 5½" $100.00

Hillbilly Line

Men of the Mountain, candy dish, 5¼" dia $75.00
Men of the Mountain, cigarette box, outhouse, H-109, 7" ..$75.00
Men of the Mountain, ice bucket, man bathing finial, TW-31, 16x7½" $375.00
Men of the Mountain, ice bucket, suspenders, TW-30, 14x7½" ..$250.00
Men of the Mountain, ice bucket, w/jug, TW-33, 14x7½" .$350.00
Men of the Mountain, lamp, hillbilly on barrel, H-106, 27" .$350.00
Men of the Mountain, mug, H-102, 5" $30.00

Men of the Mountain, pitcher, 7½", $85.00. (Photo courtesy Mike Ellis)

Men of the Mountain, pouring spout, H-104, 6½" $25.00
Men of the Mountain, punch cup, H-111, 3" $15.00

Universal Dinnerware

This pottery incorporated in Cambridge, Ohio, in 1934, the outgrowth of several smaller companies in the area. They produced many lines of dinnerware and kitchenware items, most of which were marked. They're best known for their Ballerina dinnerware (simple modern shapes in a variety of solid colors) and Cat-Tail (see Cat-Tail Dinnerware). The company closed in 1960.

Ballerina, bowl, coupe soup; 7¾", from $8 to......................$12.00
Ballerina, bowl, mixing; 4½x6"......................................$10.00
Ballerina, bowl, serving; lg, from $12 to $15.00
Ballerina, cake plate, tab handles, from $25 to....................$30.00
Ballerina, coffee/teapot, slim, 11¼", from $30 to $40.00
Ballerina, pitcher, ice lip, ball form, from $25 to $35.00
Ballerina, plate, chop; 10½x11"...................................$18.00
Ballerina, plate, chop; 13", from $25 to..........................$30.00
Ballerina, plate, dinner; 10", from $8 to..........................$12.00
Ballerina, salt & pepper shakers, pr $20.00
Ballerina, sugar bowl, w/lid, from $18 to.........................$22.00
Bittersweet, casserole, w/lid, 2½-qt, 4¼x8¾".....................$65.00
Bittersweet, casserole, w/lid, 3⅜x6"..............................$45.00
Bittersweet, drippings jar, w/lid, from $30 to....................$35.00
Bittersweet, mixing bowls, 2x6½", 2½x6½", 3½x6½", set of 3, from $35 to $50.00
Bittersweet, pitcher, w/lid...$65.00
Bittersweet, salt & pepper shakers, egg shape, pr..................$25.00
Bittersweet, stack set, 3 pcs w/lid $50.00
Blue & white, canteen jug, rectangular, cork stopper, from $30 to...$40.00
Blue & white, pitcher, cylindrical, from $15 to....................$25.00
Blue & White, teapot, from $35 to.................................$45.00
Calico Fruit, bowl, custard; 2⅞x3⅜", from $15 to $18.00
Calico Fruit, bowl, sauce; 5", from $15 to $18.00
Calico Fruit, bowl, storage; w/lid, 4x5⅜", from $20 to........$25.00
Calico Fruit, bowl, vegetable; 9⅛", from $25 to $30.00
Calico Fruit, bowls, mixing; 3x6", 3½x7", pr.....................$35.00
Calico Fruit, casserole dish, w/lid, 4x8", from $20 to $25.00
Calico Fruit, cup & saucer, from $8 to $12.00
Calico Fruit, pie lifter, 9"..$50.00
Calico Fruit, pie plate, 10"...$40.00

Calico Fruit, pitcher, 5", from $15.00 to $20.00.

Calico Fruit, pitcher, milk; 4⅞".................................$25.00
Calico Fruit, pitcher, refrigerator; w/lid, 7½" $65.00
Calico Fruit, plate, bread & butter; 6¼", from $7 to...........$10.00
Calico Fruit, plate, dinner; 10", from $12 to $18.00

Calico Fruit, platter, 13", from $18 to $22.00
Calico Fruit, salt & pepper shakers, on wooden tray w/center handle, 3-pc set $90.00
Calico Fruit, salt & pepper shakers, pr from $20 to............$25.00
Calico Fruit, saucer $3.00
Calico Fruit, syrup pitcher, w/lid, 5¼", from $55 to...........$60.00
Holland Rose, pitcher, cylindrical, 6⅛x4½" $20.00
Hollyhocks, canteen jug..$30.00
Iris, bowl, deep, 4", from $15 to $18.00
Iris, bowl, mixing; 10½" $35.00
Iris, bowl, vegetable; oval; 9⅛".....................................$27.50
Iris, cake plate, tab handles, 13¼" $28.00
Iris, creamer, from $15 to...$18.00
Iris, gravy boat, from $25 to $32.00
Iris, pie serving plate, 10"...$30.00
Iris, pitcher, 32-oz, 7", from $25 to $35.00
Iris, plate, luncheon; 9", from $7 to $10.00
Iris, plate, 7¼" $6.00
Iris, platter, sq w/rounded corners, 11½" $25.00
Iris, salt & pepper shakers, 2¾", pr from $20 to.................$25.00

Mixed Fruit, refrigerator jar, with lid, 4", $15.00.

Poppy, creamer, from $18 to $22.00
Poppy, cup & saucer, flat, from $12 to............................$15.00
Poppy, plate, dinner; 10", from $12 to............................$15.00
Poppy, plate, luncheon; 9", from $9 to $12.50
Poppy, platter, oval, 13½", from $30 to $38.00
Rodeo, bowl, cereal; 6" $10.00
Rodeo, cake plate, rope edge, tab handles $23.00
Rodeo, plate, dinner..$14.00
Rose, bowl, coupe soup; 7¾" $10.00
Rose, bowl, vegetable; oval; 9" $25.00
Rose, chop plate, handles, 13" $35.00
Rose, cup & saucer, flat..$12.50
Rose, plate, bread & butter; 6¼" $4.00
Rose, plate, luncheon; 9" $8.00
Shasta Daisy, creamer...$15.00
Shasta Daisy, cup & saucer..$12.50

Shasta Daisy, plate, bread & butter; 6¼" **$4.00**
Shasta Daisy, plate, dinner; 10" **$12.50**
Shasta Daisy, platter, oval, 12" **$30.00**
Shasta Daisy, sugar bowl, w/lid **$17.50**
Thistle, bowl, coupe soup; 7¾" **$12.00**
Thistle, bowl, fruit/dessert; 5⅜" **$7.50**
Thistle, cup & saucer **$15.00**
Thistle, plate, dinner; 10" **$12.50**
Thistle, plate, salad; 7½" **$6.00**
Woodvine, bowl, salad; 9¾" **$45.00**
Woodvine, bowl, vegetable; oval, 9⅛" **$25.00**
Woodvine, cup & saucer, flat **$12.50**
Woodvine, gravy boat **$45.00**
Woodvine, plate, luncheon; 9⅜" **$7.50**

Valentines

As is true with all collectibles, values change constantly, and valentines are no different. Some valentines have sky rocketed, while others have gone down in value, due to the infiltration of cards coming out of attics, basements, etc., and immediately put up for sale on Internet auctions. Look at this as an opportunity to expand your collecting experience and venture into the eclectic side of valentine collecting, i.e. advertising, paper dolls, postcards, party favors, decorations, etc., No matter how prices on the Internet change, 'what to look for' when purchasing a card still remains constant: age, category, condition, size, manufacturer, artist signature, and scarcity. It is important to remember when selling cards on the Internet to always include the size of the card — width, height, and depth. This does play an important role when determining value. For more information we recommend *Valentines with Values, One Hundred Years of Valentines,* and *Valentines for the Eclectic Collector,* all by our advisor, Katherine Kreider. All books are available at her website: valentinesdirect.com. You may e-mail her at Katherinekreider@valentinesdirect.com. Unless noted otherwise, our values are for examples in excellent condition. In the listings below HCPP was used for honeycomb paper puff.

Advisor: Katherine Kreider (See Directory, Valentines)

Newsletter: *National Valentine Collectors Bulletin*
Evalene Pulati
P.O. Box 1404
Santa Ana, CA 92702; 714-547-1355

Dimensional, Big-Eyed Child in front of castle, Printed in Germany, 1920s, 5½x4x2¾" **$15.00**
Dimensional, 1D, cherub fishing, HCPP base, Printed in Germany, early 1900s, 5x4x4" **$5.00**
Dimensional, 1D, dirigible w/jumping horse, Printed in Germany, 1940s, 6x4x1½" **$25.00**
Dimensional, 1D, gazebo w/Dutch children, Printed in Germany, early 1900s, 9x4x4" **$20.00**
Dimensional, 1D, train, American Greetings, 1950s, 6x7x5". **$10.00**
Dimensional, 1D, train, Printed in Germany, early 1900s, 5¾x6x3" **$20.00**

Dimensional, 2D, girl w/spinning wheel, Printed in Germany, 1920s, 3¾x1½x3" **$10.00**
Dimensional, 2D, pansies & child, Printed in Germany, early 1940s, 4x3½x¾" **$5.00**
Dimensional, 3D, cowboy/cowgirl on pony, unsigned Drayton, 1930s, 9x6x3" **$40.00**
Dimensional, 3D, garden w/child, Printed in Germany, early 1900s, 4x6x4½" **$15.00**
Flat, African American chef, Norcross, 1930s, 7x4½" **$10.00**
Flat, Army man w/bullet, 1940s, 3½x2½" **$3.00**
Flat, Art Deco lady w/Scottie dog, Carrington Co, 1920s, 9½x5" **$6.00**
Flat, boy playing accordion, 1950s, 2¾x4" **$2.00**
Flat, bull mastiff w/dachshund, photochromatic, 1940s, 6x3". **$4.00**
Flat, children playing checkers, 1940s, 3x2¾" **$2.00**
Flat, crossword puzzle, USA, 1950s, 6¾x2½" **$6.00**

Flat, drummer girl, M.F. USA, 1940s, 6x5½", $3.00. (Photo courtesy Katherine Kreider)

Flat, girl troll, 1960s, 4x3½" **$4.00**
Flat, girl w/basket of flower, Gibson, unsigned JG Scott, 4x2½" .**$3.00**
Flat, letter P w/child, 1940s series, 4½x3" **$3.00**
Flat, Tin Man, Wizard of Oz, 1960s, 3½x2½" **$3.00**
Flat, Tom & Jerry, 1960s, 3½x5" **$4.00**
Flat, Yogi Bear, 1960s, 3½x5" **$4.00**
Folded-flat, Army man typing, 1940s, 3½x4" **$2.00**
Folded-flat, girl w/ruler, 1940s, 5x2½" **$2.00**
Greeting card, Fun 'n Laffs comic valentine booklet, Gibson, 1950s, 6x4½" **$4.00**
Greeting card, girl roller skating series, 1940s, 4½x3" **$2.00**
Greeting card, jar of honey (food series), 1940s, 5x5" (oversized)....**$3.00**
Greeting card, Jimmy Durante caricature, 1940s, 4½x4½" **$6.00**
Greeting card, Mary Jane paper doll, Hallmark, 1960s, 6½x4¼". **$6.00**
Greeting card, pig in top hat series, 1940s, 4½x3" **$2.00**
Greeting card, real photo of children w/pedal car, 1940s, 4x4". **$6.00**
HCPP, cherub sitting on flower, Printed in Germany, early 1900s, 7½x6x3" **$5.00**

HCPP, lamp, Printed in Germany, 1930s, 8x5x2¾" **$20.00**

HCPP, pedestal w/clown, 1920s, 5x5" **$3.00**

Mechanical-flat, Army men in woods, USA, 9½x7½" **$8.00**

Mechanical-flat, Art Deco airplane, Carrington Co, 1940s, 3½x5½" **$6.00**

Mechanical-flat, children reading books, Katz, USA, 1920s, 6¾x6¾" **$5.00**

Mechanical-flat, girl getting manicure, Twelvetrees, Printed in Germany, 1940s, 4x3" **$4.00**

Mechanical-flat, girl standing on dresser, Twelvetrees, Printed in Germany, 1940s, 6¾x4¾" **$5.00**

Mechanical-flat, girl with baby doll, easel back, by Edwin Boese, USA, 1919, 7x4", $15.00. (Photo courtesy Katherine Kreider)

Mechanical-flat, scissors, USA, 1930s, 4x4" **$4.00**

Mechanical-flat, St Bernard, Printed in Germany, 1920s, 5x4". **$4.00**

Mechanical-flat, tennis player, Printed in Germany, 1920s, 7½x3½" **$5.00**

Novelty, advertising, Fuller Brush Toilet Water bottle attached to card, 1950s, 5x2" **$25.00**

Novelty, candy container w/dimensional top, Philadelphia, 1925, ½x2" **$15.00**

Novelty, gift giving, pup w/hankie in original box, 1940s, 8x5½" **$25.00**

Novelty, HCPP basket, Beistle, USA, 1920s, 4x4", EX **$2.00**

Novelty, HCPP basket, Beistle, USA, 1920s, 8½x8" **$15.00**

Penny Dreadful, Big Business, USA, 1932, 5x6" **$2.00**

Penny Dreadful, Conceited, signed Hugh Chenoweth, USA, 1934, 11x8" **$8.00**

Penny Dreadful, Lawyer, USA, 1930s, 9½x6" **$5.00**

Penny Dreadful, Slow Suicide, initial H, 14½x9½" **$15.00**

Vandor

For more than 35 years, Vandor has operated out of Salt Lake City, Utah. They're not actually manufacturers but distributors of novelty ceramic items made overseas. Some pieces will be marked 'Made in Korea,' while others are marked 'Sri Lanka,' 'Taiwan,' or 'Japan.' Many of their best things have been made in the last few

years, and already collectors are finding them appealing. They have a line of kitchenware designed around 'Cowmen Mooranda' (an obvious take off on Carmen), another called 'Crocagator' (a darling crocodile modeled as a teapot, a bank, salt and pepper shakers, etc.), character-related items (Betty Boop and Howdy Doody, among others), and some really wonderful cookie jars reminiscent of '50s radios and jukeboxes.

See also Cat Collectibles; Elvis Presley Memorabilia.

Advisor: Lois Wildman (See Directory, Vandor)

Popeye, bank, 7¼", from $35.00 to $50.00. (Photo courtesy Jim and Beverly Mangus)

Beatles, bath set, Yellow Submarine, tumbler, toothbrush holder & soap dish, 1999, MIB **$25.00**

Beatles, lava lamp, Yellow Submarine, 1999, MIB **$75.00**

Beatles, lunch box, Yellow Submarine, tin litho, 1999, 7½x10x3", came w/out thermos, M w/tags **$25.00**

Beatles, salt & pepper shakers, Paul & Ringo form 1 shaker, John & Goerge form 2nd shaker, 2-pc set, MIB **$25.00**

Beatles, snow globe, Yellow Submarine, musical, MIB **$82.50**

Betty Boop, bathroom set, cup, toothbrush/toothpaste holder (shoe) & glove soap dish, 1995, MIB **$35.00**

Betty Boop, cup & saucer, 1997, mini, MIB **$17.50**

Betty Boop, music box, Betty on swing hung from top of crescent moon, 6x4" **$32.50**

Betty Boop, salt & pepper shakers, Betty in bikini, sits between shakers on base w/her name across top **$25.00**

Curious George, salt & pepper shakers, George in car, 1997, 2-pc set, NM **$38.00**

Dr Seuss, bookends, Wump divided by Dr Seuss books, riders on back, MIB **$32.00**

Flamingo, coffee mug, pink, figural handle & painted palms, 1986 .... **$18.00**

Flintstones, bank, Fred Flintstone, 1990, 9x7" **$25.00**

Howdy Doody, nodder, 1980s, 5", NM **$40.00**

I Love Lucy, cake plate, 50th Anniversary, 2001, 10", MIB. **$40.00**

I Love Lucy, lamp, characters on TV screen which lights up, 10½x9x4¾" **$55.00**

I Love Lucy, music box, television w/Lucy mashing grapes on screen, plays I Love Lucy Theme, MIB......................**$30.00**

I Love Lucy, teapot, Friends Forever, telephone shape, 5½x9x5¼", MIB **$30.00**

Marilyn Monroe, salt & pepper shakers, teapot & cup, 2-pc set, MIB **$22.50**

Peanuts, salt & pepper shakers, Charlie Brown & Snoopy on dog house, 2-pc set, MIB......................**$38.00**

Popeye, bank, head figural, 1980 ....**$18.00**

Popeye, box, Popeye sesated on spinach crate, 4¾x3¾", MIB ..**$25.00**

Popeye, mug, head figural, 1980 ....**$30.00**

Popeye, Swee' Pea egg cup, KFS 1980, 3½" **$25.00**

Scooby Doo, picture frame, seated beside 3x5" frame dividing sandwich, MIB **$20.00**

Vernon Kilns

Founded in Vernon, California, in 1931, this company produced many lines of dinnerware, souvenir plates, decorative pottery, and figurines. They employed several well-known artists whose designs no doubt contributed substantially to their success. Among them were Rockwell Kent, Royal Hickman, Don Blanding, and Walt Disney, all of whom were responsible for creating several of the lines most popular with collectors today.

In 1940 they signed a contract with Walt Disney to produce a line of figurines, vases, bowls, and several dinnerware patterns that were inspired by Disney's film *Fantasia*. The Disney items were made for a short time only and are now expensive.

The company closed in 1958, but Metlox purchased some of the molds and continued to produce some of their bestselling dinnerware lines through a specially established 'Vernonware' division.

Most of the ware is marked in some form or another with the company name and in most cases the name or number of the dinnerware pattern.

Advisor: Ray Vlach (See Directory, Dinnerware)

Anytime Shape

Frolic: salt and pepper shakers, from $12.00 to $20.00 for the pair; covered vegetable bowl, from $30.00 to $50.00; dinner plate, from $9.00 to $15.00; cup and saucer, from $10.00 to $15.00.

Bowl, vegetable; round, 7½", from $10 to **$15.00**

Casserole, w/lid, 8", from $30 to **$50.00**

Coffeepot, 8-cup, from $30 to **$50.00**

Gravy boat, from $18 to **$20.00**

Mug, 12-oz, from $15 to **$25.00**

Pitcher, 1-pt, 6⅛", from $18 to **$22.00**

Pitcher, 1-qt, 8", from $20 to **$30.00**

Plate, bread & butter; 6", from $4 to **$6.00**

Plate, chop; from $18 to **$25.00**

Plate, salad; 7½", from $7 to **$10.00**

Platter, 11", from $12 to **$20.00**

Syrup, Drip-cut top, from $45 to **$65.00**

Teacup & saucer, from $10 to **$15.00**

Tray, oval, ring handle, 6", from $40 to **$50.00**

Chatelaine Shape

This designer pattern by Sharon Merrill was made in four color combinations: Topaz, Bronze, Platinum, and Jade.

Bowl, chowder; topaz or bronze, 6", from $12 to **$15.00**

Bowl, salad; topaz or bronze, 12", from $45 to **$55.00**

Bowl, serving; decorated platinum or jade, 9", from $35 to.**$45.00**

Creamer, decorated platinum or jade, from $30 to **$35.00**

Cup & saucer, coffee; topaz or bronze, flat base, from $15 to .**$20.00**

Plate, bread & butter; topaz or bronze, 6½", from $8 to **$10.00**

Plate, chop; decorated platinum or jade, 14", from $50 to ..**$65.00**

Plate, dinner; decorated platinum or jade, leaf on 4 corners, 10½", from $25 to **$30.00**

Plate, salad; decorated platinum or jade, 7½", from $15 to .**$18.00**

Platter, topaz or bronze, 16", from $50 to......................**$65.00**

Salt & pepper shakers, decorated platinum or jade, pr from $25 to **$30.00**

Sugar bowl, w/lid, topaz or bronze, from $25 to **$30.00**

Teacup & saucer, pedestal foot, decorated platinum or jade, from $22 to **$25.00**

Teapot, decorated platinum or jade, from $250 to **$295.00**

Lotus and Pan American Lei Shape

Patterns on this shape include Lotus, Chinling, and Vintage. Pan American Lei was a variation with flatware from the San Marino line. To evaluate Lotus, use the low end of our range as the minimum value; the high end of values apply to Pan American Lei.

Ashtray, Pan American Lei, 5½", from $30 to **$35.00**

Bowl, fruit; Lotus, 5½", from $6 to **$10.00**

Bowl, mixing; Pan American Lei, 5", from $20 to **$30.00**

Bowl, mixing; Pan American Lei, 9", from $40 to **$50.00**

Bowl, salad; Lotus, 12½", from $30 to **$45.00**

Bowl, soup; coupe, Pan American Lei, 8½", from $18 to **$25.00**

Bowl, vegetable; round, Lotus, 9", from $18 to **$22.00**

Butter dish, Pan American Lei, oblong, from $60 to......................**$65.00**

Cup & saucer, tea; Lotus, from $10 to......................**$15.00**

Pitcher, jug, Pan American Lei, 2-qt, from $65 to **$85.00**

Plate, chop; coupe, Pan American Lei, 13", from $50 to **$60.00**

Plate, coupe, Pan American Lei, 10", from $20 to **$30.00**

Plate, offset; Lotus, 6½", from $6 to......................**$8.00**
Platter, coupe, Pan American Lei, 13½", from $50 to.........**$65.00**
Sugar bowl, Lotus, w/lid, from $15 to **$18.00**
Teapot, Pan American Lei, 8-cup, from $85 to **$95.00**
Tumbler, Lotus, #5, 14-oz, from $18 to..............................**$20.00**

Melinda Shape

Patterns found on this shape are Arcadia, Beverly, Blossom Time, Chintz, Cosmos, Dolores, Fruitdale, Hawaii (Lei Lani on Melinda is priced at two to three times base value), May Flower, Monterey, Native California, Philodendron. The more elaborate the pattern, the higher the value.

Bowl, salad; footed base, 12", from $45 to..........................**$75.00**
Butter dish, oblong, from $35 to **$75.00**

Susan: creamer, $18.00; coffeepot, minimum value, $85.00; sugar bowl, $25.00. (Photo courtesy Linda and Jerry Lakomek)

Cup & saucer, AD; from $15 to **$20.00**
Jam jar, from $65 to...**$75.00**
Pitcher, 2-qt, from $35 to **$50.00**
Plate, bread & butter; 6½", from $6 to.................................**$10.00**
Plate, luncheon; sq, 8½", from $15 to **$20.00**
Platter, 12", from $20 to **$30.00**
Teapot, 6-cup, from $45 to **$85.00**

Montecito Shape (and Coronado)

This was one of the company's more utilized shapes — well over 200 patterns have been documented. Among the most popular are the solid colors, plaids, the florals, westernware, and the Bird and Turnbull series. Bird, Turnbull, and Winchester 73 (Frontier Days) are two to four times base values. Disney hollow ware is seven to eight times base values. Plaids (except Calico), solid colors, and Brown-eyed Susan are represented by the lower range.

Ashtray, round, 5½", from $12 to..**$20.00**
Bowl, mixing; 7", from $22 to...**$30.00**
Bowl, salad; 13", from $40 to **$65.00**

Coffeepot, AD; 2-cup, scarce, from $75 to **$125.00**
Compote, scarce, 9½", from $50 to....................................**$75.00**
Muffin tray, tab handles, 9", w/dome lid, from $75 to **$95.00**
Mugs, bulbous bottom, clip handle, 8-oz, 3¾", from $18 to .**$25.00**
Pitcher, jug, bulbous bottom, 1-qt, from $45 to **$65.00**
Plate, salad; 7½", from $8 to **$15.00**
Platter, 10½", from $18 to..**$25.00**
Spoon holder, angular, open, from $45 to............................**$65.00**
Sugar bowl, angular, individual, from $18 to **$20.00**
Tumbler, #1, banded rim & base, 4½", from $20 to..........**$25.00**

San Clemente (Anytime)

Late research has determined the company name designated for this was San Clemente, previously named Anytime. Patterns you will find on this shape include Tickled Pink, Heavenly Days, Anytime, Imperial, Sherwood, Frolic, Young in Heart, Rose-A-Day, and Dis 'N Dot.

Bowl, fruit; 5½", from $5 to...**$8.00**
Bowl, vegetable; round, 7½", from $15 to **$20.00**
Creamer, from $8 to **$12.00**
Plate, chop; 13", from $18 to **$25.00**
Tumbler, 14-oz, from $15 to..**$25.00**

San Fernando Shape

Known patterns for this shape are Desert Bloom, Early Days, Hibiscus, R.F.D, Vernon's 1860, and Vernon Rose.

Bowl, fruit; 5½", from $6 to...**$10.00**
Bowl, mixing; 8", from $25 to...**$32.00**
Creamer, regular, from $12 to **$15.00**
Cup & saucer, AD; from $15 to **$20.00**
Mug, 9-oz, from $20 to **$25.00**
Pitcher, 1½-qt, from $25 to **$35.00**
Plate, bread & butter; 6½", from $6 to.................................**$10.00**
Plate, chop; 14", from $35 to **$50.00**
Platter, 12", from $20 to **$30.00**
Spoon holder, from $40 to **$50.00**
Sugar bowl, w/lid, from $15 to **$20.00**
Tumbler, Style #5, 14-oz, from $20 to **$25.00**

San Marino Shape

Known patterns for this shape are Barkwood, Bel Air, California Originals, Casual California, Gayety, Hawaiian Coral, Heyday, Lei Lani (two to three times base values), Mexicana, Pan American Lei (two to three times base values), Raffia, Shadow Leaf, Shantung, Sun Garden, and Trade Winds.

Bowl, chowder; 6", from $10 to..**$15.00**
Bowl, serving; divided, 10", from $18 to **$25.00**
Coaster, ridged, 3¾", from $12 to **$15.00**
Custard, 3", from $18 to...**$22.00**
Egg cup, double, from $15 to **$22.00**
Pitcher, 2-qt, from $30 to **$40.00**

Plate, dinner; 10", from $10 to...$17.00

Plate, salad; 7½", from $7 to...$12.00

Platter, 9½", from $12 to...$18.00

Sauceboat, from $17 to..$22.00

Transitional (Year 'Round) Shape

Late research has determined the company name designated for this shape was Transitional; it was previously named Year 'Round. Patterns on this shape include Blueberry Hill, Country Cousin, and Lollipop Tree.

Bowl, fruit; 5½", from $5 to..$7.00

Bowl, vegetable; round, from $12 to..................................$17.00

Casserole, w/lid, 8", from $25 to $45.00

Gravy boat, from $18 to $25.00

Plate, bread & butter; 6", from $4 to..................................$6.00

Plate, salad; 7½", from $6 to...$10.00

Platter, 11", from $12 to...$20.00

Salt & pepper shakers, pr from $12 to $15.00

Sugar bowl, w/lid, from $10 to $15.00

Teacup & saucer, from $8 to..$12.00

Ultra Shape

More than 50 patterns were issued on this shape. Nearly all the artist-designed lines (Rockwell Kent, Don Blanding, and Disney) utilized Ultra. The shape was developed by Gale Turnbull, and many of the elaborate flower and fruit patterns can be credited to him as well; use the high end of our range as a minimum value for his work. For Frederick Lunning, use the mid range. For other artist patterns, use these formulas based on the high end: Blanding — 2X (Aquarium 3X); Disney, 5 – 7X; Kent — Moby Dick, 2½X, Our America, 3½X, and Salamina, 5 – 7X.

Rosalie, coffeepot, signed G. T. (Turnbull), $125.00. (Photo courtesy Maxine Feek Nelson)

Bowl, chowder; open, 9", from $12 to $20.00

Bowl, mixing; 5", from $15 to..$25.00

Bowl, mixing; 6", from $20 to..$30.00

Bowl, mixing; 7", from $25 to..$35.00

Bowl, serving; round, 9", from $18 to $30.00

Coffeepot, AD; 2-cup, from $65 to $125.00

Compote, from $50 to...$75.00

Egg cup, from $18 to $25.00

Pitcher, open, 2-qt, from $45 to $75.00

Plate, chop; 14", from $40 to $60.00

Plate, salad; 7½", from $8 to..$12.00

Salt & pepper shakers, pr from $20 to $30.00

Teapot, 6-cup, from $45 to $100.00

Vietnam War Collectibles

In 1949 the French had military control over Vietnam. This was true until they suffered a sound defeat at Dienbienphu in 1954. This action resulted in the formation of the Geneva Peace Conference which allowed the French to make peace and withdraw, but left Vietnam divided into North Vietnam and South Vietnam. The agreement was to reunite the country in 1956 when the general elections took place. But this didn't happen because of South Vietnam's political objections. The strife continued and slowly America was drawn into the conflict from the time of the Eisenhower administration until the Paris Peace Agreement in 1973. The war itself lingered on until 1975 when communist forces invaded Saigon and crushed the South Vietnamese government there.

Items relating to this conflict from the 1960s and early 1970s are becoming collectible. Most reflect the unpopularity of this war. College marches and political unrest headlined the newspapers of those years. Posters, pin-back buttons, political cartoons, and many books from that period reflect the anti-war philosophy of the day and are reminders of turbulent times and political policies that cost the lives of many brave young men.

Beret, Green; 5th Special Forces flash sewn on, shaped & shaved, dated 1968, EX...$100.00

Binoculars, IR-M18 night vision type, requires 1 battery, EX optics, working, 8¼x5½", EX..................................$280.00

Book, Uniforms & Equipment of US Military Advisors in Vietnam, hardcover, w/dust jacket, M $55.00

Book, Vietnam Veteran, a Record of Service; AM Palmer, 1995, M w/jacket $60.00

Boots, jungle combat; Army, high top lace-ups, Bata, EX, from $85 to $100.00

Canteen, olive drab w/plastic collapsible bladder, 2-qt capacity, EX $130.00

Compass, field; US Army, magnetic Radiosotope H3, military green, Union Instrument Corp, 1968, EX w/pouch...............$55.00

Hat, boonie; MILSPEC-H-43577, green dominant camouflage, EX $145.00

Hat, boonie; US Special forces, tiger stripes, G...................$95.00

Hat, utility; USMC, olive-drab cloth w/bill, EX..................$60.00

Helmet, MP (military police), red & white stripes painted on olive green metal, sm dents, w/liner, VG $115.00

Helmet, pith; NVA Regular, olive drab cloth covered, original liner, leather chin strap, EX...$180.00

Helmet, pot; M1, steel, w/liner & camouflage cover, all straps & attachments, EX..$45.00

Jacket, field; M-65, olive drab, US Army over left pocket, EX. $125.00

Jacket, flak; body armor vest type, M-1952A, unused........**$300.00**

Jacket, flak; olive drab, Jay Dee Militaryware, EX **$40.00**

Jacket, flight; Type G-1, dark brown leather w/fur collar, zipper front, elastic at waist, 2-pocket front, EX.....................**$90.00**

Knife, pilot's survival; Camillus, pre-1968, 5⅞" blade, EX in leather sheath...**$50.00**

Knife, Smoky Mountain Ultra Lite on blade, Parker Cut Co, Surgical Steel Japan, 4⅞" blade, 9⅛", EX in scabbard................**$60.00**

Lighter, map of Viet Nam & engraved name along w/1964 - 1965, Zippo, MIB **$50.00**

Lighter, Viet Nam Quang Ngai at top, US Navy SEAL Team logo below, Zippo, 1968, EX...**$48.00**

Lighter, Zippo, engraved Sai Gon, 68 – 69, VG, from $185.00 to $200.00.

Manual, US Army Sniper Training, 196 pages, 1969, EX....**$30.00**

Pants, W/R Rip-Stop Poplin Class 2, 100% cotton, Crane Mfg, EX...**$78.00**

Patch, F III, USAF, $200.00.

Patch, 173rd Airborne Infantry Brigade, wing & knife, EX.**$35.00**

Patch, 4th Division, 4 star-like shapes on green diamond, 2⅝", EX **$27.50**

Patch, 71 Highland Medics Evacuation Hospital (SMBL), embroidered cloth, 4¾x3¾", NM **$55.00**

Pouch, ammo shoulder; olive-drab canvas, holds 30 rounds of 7.62mm ammo, EX **$78.00**

Rucksack, US Army issue, X-frame, nylon w/all straps, buckles, snaps & drawstring, ca 1968, EX................................**$265.00**

Scope, US pvs-2 night vision, 4AA battery adapter, w/eyecup, mounting block & daylight cover, EX **$200.00**

Shell, Howitzer cannon; brass, HOW M137 M57, 105mm, 1969, empty, 14¾" **$50.00**

Shirt, US Army, tiger stripe camouflage, long sleeves, missing some buttons otherwise EX...**$235.00**

Stove, US Army, gasoline fueled, Coleman, 1964, w/spare parts box & manual, NM...**$145.00**

Walkie talkies, internal batteries, telescoping antenna, instructions on side, #110H562/#11)H161, 14½x2½" sq, pr..........**$45.00**

View-Master Reels and Packets

William Gruber was the inventor who introduced the View-Master to the public at the New York World's Fair and the Golden Gate Exposition held in California in 1939. Thousands of reels and packets have been made since that time on every aspect of animal life, places of interest, and entertainment.

Over the years the company has changed ownership five times. It was originally Sawyer's View-Master, G.A.F (in the mid-'60s), View-Master International (1981), Ideal Toy and, most recently, Tyco Toy Company. The latter three companies produced them strictly as toys and issued only cartoons, making the earlier non-cartoon reels and the three-reel packets very collectible.

Sawyer made two cameras so that the public could take their own photo reels in 3-D. They made a projector as well, so that the homemade reels could be viewed on a large screen. 'Personal' or 'Mark II' cameras with their cases usually range in value from $100.00 to $200.00; rare viewers such as the blue 'Model B' start at about $100.00, and the 'Stereo-Matic 500' projector is worth $175.00 to $200.00. Most single reels range from $1.00 to $5.00, but some early Sawyer's and G.A.F's may bring as much as $35.00 each, character-related reels sometimes even more.

Adam-12, #B-592, 1964, MIP...**$25.00**

Addams Family, #B-486, w/booklet, 1965, MIP.................**$65.00**

Annie Oakley in Indian Waterhole, 1958, set of 3, EX in package **$30.00**

Astrix & Cleopatra, #B-457, MIP.......................................**$26.00**

Barbie's Around the World Trip, #B-500, MIP....................**$28.00**

Benji's Very Own Christmas, #J-51, MIP.............................**$10.00**

Bonanza, #BB-0487, MIP..**$22.00**

Captain Kangaroo, #B-560, MIP...**$10.00**

Danger Mouse, #BD-214, MIP **$20.00**

Dr Who, #BD-216, MIP...**$70.00**

Eight Is Enough, #K76, MIP...**$18.00**

Emergency, #B-597, MIP...**$10.00**

Ferdy, #BD-269, MIP..**$8.00**

Gunsmoke, #B-589, MIP **$26.00**

Happiest Homecoming on Earth, 50 Years of Disney Theme Parks, viewer & reels, MIP..**$25.00**

Here's Lucy, #B-588, MIP...**$45.00**

James Bond (Live & Let Die), #B-393, MIP **$18.00**

Julia, 3B-572, MIP..**$22.00**

Lassie Rides the Log Flume, #B-489, MIP..........................$14.00

Laverne & Shirley, The Slow Child, GAF #J20, 1978, from $15.00 to $20.00 (Photo courtesy Bill Morgan and Greg Davis)

Lost in Space, #B-482, MIP.....................................$55.00
Mickey Mouse Jubilee, #J-29, MIP $12.00
Munsters, #B-481, w/booklet, MIP $67.50
Partridge Family, #BB-5924, MIP.............................$18.00
Pluto, #B-529, MIP $12.00
Raggedy Ann & Andy, #B-406, MIP $12.00
Search, #B-591, MIP $18.00
Sesame Street Circus Fun, #4097, MIP........................$6.00
Silverhawks, #1058, MIP $6.00
Snow White, 3B-300, MIP $8.00
SWAT, #BB-453, MIP $10.00
Thriller, boxed set w/viewer & 3 disks, NM $28.00
Thunderbirds, #B-453, MIP $45.00
UFO, #B-417, MIP $40.00
Winnetou, #BB-731, MIP $22.00

Viking Glass

Located in the famous glassmaking area of West Virginia, this company has been in business since the 1950s; they're most famous for their glass animals and birds. Their Epic Line (circa 1950s and 1960s) was innovative in design and vibrant in color. Rich tomato-red, amberina, brilliant blues, strong greens, black, amber, and deep amethyst were among the rainbow hues in production at that time. During the 1980s the company's ownership changed hands, and the firm became known as Dalzell-Viking. Viking closed their doors in 1998.

Some of the Epic Line animals were reissued in crystal, crystal frosted, and black. If you're interested in learning more about these animals, refer to *Glass Animals* by Dick and Pat Spencer (Collector Books.)

Ashtray, butterfly shape, amber, ca 1940-50, 4¼x5½", from $25
to $30.00
Basket, Epic Line, avacodo w/ruffled & scalloped rim, clear handle, #6711, 7½x7½".....................................$35.00

Basket, Janice, crystal, #4552, 11" $75.00
Bowl, Epic Line, amber, spiked rim, #6900, 4½x10½"........$25.00
Bowl, Epic Line, avocado green, flower form w/spiked petals pointing upward, 4¼x6½".....................................$12.50
Bowl, Epic Line, bright blue, 6 ruffled scallops, footed pedestal, 6x9¾" $32.00
Bowl, salad; Janice, blue or red, scalloped top, 12" $85.00

Candleholder, Epic #1100 Line, red (orange), 1⅜x8⅝", $17.50. (Photo courtesy Gene and Cathy Florence)

Candlholder, owl, ruby, ca 1980s, 7", ea from $35 to $40.00
Candleholders, Bull's Eye, cobalt, cube form, 3½", 2½", pr.$70.00
Candy dish, amber, bird w/long tail finial, 12", $50 to........$75.00
Creamer, Janice, crystal, 6-oz $12.00
Cup, Janice, blue or red, #4580 ....$23.00
Decanter, Yesteryear, ruby, flat disk stopper, 11¼", +4 footed goblets $60.00
Fairy lamp, Diamond Point, green, 7" $18.00

Fairy lamp, potbellied stove, amberina, $45.00.
(Photo courtesy M.R. Miller)

Fairy lamp, owl figural, blue satin, 7¼" **$35.00**
Goblet, water; Georgian, red **$22.00**
Ice pail, Janice, crystal, w/handle, #4589, 10" **$295.00**
Jam jar, Janice, blue or red, #4577, w/lid, 6" **$45.00**
Lighter, ruby base, heavy, original label, 3½x3¼" **$50.00**
Paperweight, apple, dark amethyst **$40.00**
Paperweight, mushroom, amber, 3x4" **$30.00**
Paperweight, mushroom, cobalt, 2⅜x3" **$35.00**
Paperweight, mushroom, crystal, ca 1971, 3½", from $25 to. **$35.00**
Paperweight, mushroom, vaseline, Epic Line, 3x4⅛" **$45.00**
Pitcher, Epic Line, turquoise, tall spout, 1960s 13".............. **$32.00**
Pitcher, Georgian, red, 7x9½" **$38.00**
Plate, salad; Janice, crystal, #4579, 8½" **$10.00**
Platter, Janice, blue or red, #4588, oval, 13" **$90.00**
Rose bowl, amethyst w/clear Flowerlite flower frog, on stem w/disk foot, 7" **$85.00**
Rose bowl, clear w/gold enameled flowers, 3-footed, w/clear 11-hole flower frog that fit on rim **$55.00**
Rose bowl, cobalt w/silver orchid overlay, clear flower frog, footed, 3x4½" dia **$90.00**
Salt & pepper shakers, Janice, crystal, pr **$40.00**
Saucer, Janice, blue or red, #4580 .... **$4.50**
Sugar bowl, Janice, crystal, 6-oz **$12.00**
Tray, for cream/sugar, Janice, blue or red, oval, handles........ **$25.00**
Tumbler, Georgian, Ultra Blue, #6900, 4⅛" **$18.00**
Tumbler, luncheon; Janice, crystal, #4551/23 .... **$14.00**
Vase, avocado green w/silver overlay poppies, pear shape w/flared & ruffled rim, 6¾" **$40.00**
Vase, clear w/silver overlay poppies, trumpet shape w/low upturned handles, footed, 10½" **$50.00**
Vase, Epic Drape, Avocado Green, 31x7" **$65.00**
Vase, Epic Hexagon, red w/dark amber at foot, pulled rim, 31x7" **$65.00**
Vase, Janice, blue or red, ball shape, 9" **$135.00**
Vase, Janice, crystal, footed, 7" **$35.00**
Vase, royal blue, cylindrical w/slightly bulbous top & angled rim, 13x5½" **$55.00**
Vase, royal blue, 8 pulled points at rim, octagonal foot, foil sticker, 12" **$35.00**

Vistosa

Vistosa was produced from about 1938 through the early 1940s. It was Taylor, Smith, and Taylor's answer to the very successful Fiesta line of their nearby competitor, Homer Laughlin. Vistosa was made in four solid colors: mango red, cobalt blue, light green, and deep yellow. 'Pie crust' edges and a dainty five-petal flower molded into handles and lid finials made for a very attractive yet nevertheless commercially unsuccessful product.

Bowl, cereal; 6¾" **$22.00**
Bowl, cream soup **$25.00**
Bowl, fruit.. **$10.00**
Bowl, salad; footed, 12", from $185 to **$200.00**
Bowl, soup; lug handle, from $25 to........................ **$30.00**
Bowl, 3x9¼", from $32 to **$38.00**

Chop plate, 12" **$40.00**
Chop plate, 15", from $40 to **$50.00**
Coffee saucer, AD; from $10 to **$15.00**
Coffeepot, AD; from $80 to **$90.00**
Creamer, from $20 to **$25.00**
Egg cup, footed, from $50 to **$70.00**
Plate, 6" **$9.00**
Plate, 7", from $12 to **$15.00**
Plate, 9", from $15 to **$20.00**
Plate, 10", from $25 to **$35.00**

Platter, 13", from $40.00 to $45.00.

Salt & pepper shakers, 3¼", pr from $25 to **$30.00**
Sauceboat, from $175 to... **$200.00**
Sugar bowl, w/lid, from $25 to **$30.00**
Teacup & saucer, from $20 to.................................. **$30.00**
Teapot **$90.00**
Water jug, 2-qt, from $90 to................................... **$120.00**

W.S. George Dinnerware

From the turn of the century until the late 1950s, this East Palestine, Ohio, company produced many lines of dinnerware. Some were solid colors, but the vast majority were decaled. Most of the lines were marked. If you'd like more information, we recommend *Collector's Encyclopedia of American Dinnerware* by Jo Cunningham.

Apollo, bowl, vegetable; 9" **$20.00**
Apollo, cup & saucer, flat....................................... **$14.00**
Apollo, plate, luncheon; 9" **$7.50**
Apollo, platter, oval, 13⅝" **$28.00**
Apollo, relish, 9" **$12.00**
Blossoms, bowl, vegetable; 8⅞"............................... **$30.00**
Blossoms, cup & saucer, flat................................... **$15.00**
Blossoms, plate, luncheon; 9½" **$8.00**
Camellia, bowl, vegetable; 9" **$28.00**
Camellia, cake stand, metal pedestal foot **$24.00**
Camellia, chip & dip set, 2-pc **$28.00**
Camellia, plate, dinner; 10" **$14.00**
Cherokee, bowl, coupe soup; 8" **$8.00**
Cherokee, bowl, fruit/dessert................................. **$7.00**

Cherokee, bowl, vegetable; oval, 9½" $20.00
Cherokee, cup & saucer, flat $7.50
Cherokee, plate, salad; 7⅜" $5.00
Cherokee, platter, oval, 13⅜" $27.50
Peach Blossom, bowl, vegetable; 9" $22.50
Peach Blossom, candleholders, pr $28.00
Peach Blossom, plate, bread & butter; 6½" $3.00
Peach Blossom, plate, salad; 7" $4.50

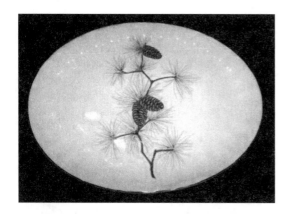

Pine Cone, platter, 11½", $15.00.

Pine Cone, salt & pepper shakers, 3¼", pr $32.00
Priscilla, bowl, vegetable; 9" $26.00
Priscilla, creamer $15.00
Priscilla, cup & saucer $12.00
Priscilla, relish, 9⅛" $12.00
Romance, bowl, coupe soup; 7¾" $9.50
Romance, bowl, fruit/dessert; 5" $7.00
Romance, candleholders, pr $28.00
Romance, plate, dinner; 10" $12.50
Romance, sugar bowl, w/lid $28.00
Tango, bowl, coupe soup; 8" $7.50
Tango, chip & dip set, 2-pc $20.00
Tango, cup & saucer $10.00
Tango, plate, bread & butter; 6" $3.00
Tango, plate, dinner; 10" $8.00
Tango, platter, oval, 13½" $27.50
Tango, tidbit, 2-tier $28.00

Wade Porcelain

If you've attended many flea markets, you're already very familiar with the tiny Wade figures, most of which are 2" and under. Wade made several lines of these miniatures, but the most common were made as premiums for the Red Rose Tea Company. Most of these sell for $3.50 to $7.00 or so, with a few exceptions such as the Gingerbread man. Wade also made a great number of larger figurines as well as tableware and advertising items.

The Wade Potteries began life in 1867 as Wade and Myatt when George Wade and a partner named Myatt opened a pottery in Burslem — the center for potteries in England. In 1882 George Wade bought out his partner, and the name of the pottery was changed to Wade and Sons. In 1919 the pottery underwent yet another change in name to George Wade & Son Ltd. Another Wade Pottery was established in 1891 — J & W Wade & Co., which in turn changed its name to A.J. Wade & Co. in 1927. At this time (1927) Wade Heath & Co. Ltd. was also formed.

These three potteries plus a new Irish pottery named Wade (Ireland) Ltd. were incorporated into one company in 1958 and given the name The Wade Group of Potteries. In 1990 the group was taken over by Beauford PLC and became Wade Ceramics Ltd. It sold again in early 1999 to Wade Management and is now a private company.

If you'd like to learn more, we recommend *The World of Wade, The World of Wade Book 2, Wade Price Trends — First Edition; The World of Wade — Figurines and Miniatures,* and *The World of Wade, Ireland,* by Ian Warner and Mike Posgay.

Advisor: Ian Warner (See Directory, Wade)

Club: The Official International Wade Collector's Club

Publication: *The Official Wade Club Magazine*
Wade Ceramics Ltd.
Royal Victoria Pottery Westport Rd., Burslem, Stoke-on-Trent, Staffordshire, ST6 4AP, England, UK
club@wade.co.uk; www.wade.co.uk

Animal figurine, calf, 1930s, 1¾x1¼" $170.00
Animal figurine, lion cub w/paw up, 1935-39, 8x5" $550.00
Animal figurine, Penny penguin, late 1940s-late 1950s, 2" . $230.00

Big Bad Wolf, musical pitcher, ca 1935, $950.00 (non-musical pitcher: $250.00).

Candleholder, Flowerlight, 1x4" dia, ea $14.00
Connoisseur's Collection, nuthatch, 5½" $400.00
Disney, Big Mama, 1981-87, 1¾" $68.00
Disney, Merlin as a hare, 1965, 2¼x1⅜" $210.00
Disney, Ring 'O Roses saucer, 1934-late 1950s, 4" $25.00
Disney, Sgt Tibbs, 1960-64, 2" $145.00
Disney Blo-Up, Si, Siamese cat, 1961-65, 5½x5" $250.00
Dogs & Puppies series, Alsatian puppy, 1968-82, 2¼" $16.00
Drum Box series, Clara, 1956-59, 2" $100.00

Drum Box series, Jem, 1956-59, 2" $100.00
Flower, anemone, Ajax bowl, earthenware...........................$35.00
Flower, posy basket, 1930-39, 3½" $100.00
Hanna-Barbera Character, Yogi Bear, 1959-60, 2½" $150.00
Happy Family series, rabbit baby, 1978-86, 1⅛" $18.00
Nursery Rhyme Character, Blynken, w/flowers, 2" $215.00
Nursery Rhyme Character, Butcher, 1949-58, 3⅛"...........$360.00
Nursery Rhyme Character, Tinker, 1949-58, 2½"..............$265.00
Red Rose Tea Promotion (Canada), Queen of Hearts, 1¾" .$16.00
Red Rose Tea Promotion (USA), beaver, 1985, 1¼" $6.00
Red Rose Tea promotion (USA), orangutan, 1985, 1¼"........$5.00
Souvenir dish, City of London, 4¼x4" $10.00
Whimsies, beagle, 1956, ¾x1" $78.00
Whimsies, bison, 1978, 1⅜x1¾" $15.00
Whimsies, crocodile, 1953-59, ¾x1⅝" $78.00
Whimsies, duck, 1972, 1¼x1½" $8.00
Whimsies, fox cub, 1955, 1⅜" $79.00
Whimsies, Golden Eagle, Land Series, 1984-88, 1⅛x1¾" ...$38.00
Whimsies, kitten, 1954, 1⅜" $95.00
Whimsies, leaping fawn, 1953-59, 1⅞" $48.00
Whimsies, spaniel, 1953, 2x2¾" $46.00
World of Dogs, poodle, 1990-91, 1½" $16.00
World of Survival series, American buffalo (cape buffalo) ..$500.00
World of Survival series, harp seal & pup, 1978-82, 3¾x9" .$600.00
World of Survival series, polar bear $400.00

Wall Pockets

A few years ago there were only a handful of avid wall pocket collectors, but today many are finding them intriguing. They were popular well before the turn of the century. Roseville and Weller included at least one and sometimes several in many of their successful lines of art pottery, and other American potteries made them as well. Many were imported from Germany, Czechoslovakia, China, and Japan. By the 1950s, they were passé.

Some of the most popular today are the figurals. Look for the more imaginative and buy the ones you especially like. If you're buying to resell, look for those designed as animals, large exotic birds, children, luscious fruits, or those that are particularly eye-catching. Appeal is everything. Examples with a potter's mark are usually more pricey (for instance Roseville, McCoy, Hull, etc.), because of the crossover interest in collecting their products. For more information refer to *Collector's Encyclopedia of Made in Japan Ceramics* by Carole Bess White and *Collector's Guide to Wall Pockets, Affordable and Others,* by Marvin and Joy Gibson.

Advisor: Carole Bess White (See Directory, Japan Ceramics)

Angel w/gold halo holding prayer book, God Bless Our Home, pedestal w/gold cross on bottom, foil label, 5¾x2¼" $45.00
Baby in pink gown & bonnet on blue scroll w/lamb, duck & dove, Congratulations in gold, Shafford #4176, 3⅝x5½" $18.00
Birdhouse, ivory w/red & green floral design, 2 sm bluebirds on front, 6"...$30.00
Birdhouse, yellow w/black bird on front, high gloss, 1940s, 4¾x4⅛x2¾" $50.00

Blue bird w/red breast, multicolored glossy glazes, majolica style, #73a, ½", from $45 to..$65.00
Book w/The Lord's Prayer on one side, flowers on the other, pink lustre ware, 4x4" $20.00
Boy & girl in blue kissing by wishing well, 2 bluebirds on side, 6x7¼"..$20.00
Butterfly in pink w/black accents, 1940s, 4½x5" $75.00
Carrots in a bunch held by yellow tie, Made in Italy #0278, 5¼x4¾"..$20.00
Crane in crescent moon swimming on water surrounded by water lilies, multicolored pastels, Made in Japan $25.00
Deer standing in front of bamboo plants, high gloss, 8x5¼"..$80.00
Fan w/embossed violets above bow w/gold accents, 4¼x8½" .$80.00
Fish w/pink fins & face & black body, ceramic, lg, 1950s....$30.00
Fox & son against blue background, both wearing white shirts & blue pants, 4⅝x4⅛"..$65.00

Geisha girl, moon style, Japan, 7¾", from $65.00 to $85.00.
(Photo courtesy Carole Bess White)

Hat w/wide brim, white w/wreath of blue flowers & green leaves over pink ribbon, high gloss, 1940s, 5¾x5¼" $20.00
Hydrangea, pink w/3 green leaves, high gloss, 6x6" $18.00
Iron, white w/vine design, hand painted, 1940s, 5x3¼" $30.00
Ladies in white Victorian dress w/gold trim, Made in Japan, 6½x2¼", pr..$48.00
Lady in blue dress w/red hair standing in front of brick wall, 1960s, Grant Crest Hand Painted Japan, 6x4½x3¼" $20.00
Man & lady standing behind wishing well, multicolored bisque, Made in Japan, 4½x4" $28.00
Nun in yellow, kneeling in prayer w/white cross behind her, glossy glazes, Napco #K1717, 5", from $20 to........................$30.00
Oriental girl wearing straw hat w/brown flowers surrounding head, high gloss, 6½", from $20 to $25.00
Owl standing on ivory half-moon, ca 1940s-50s, 7x5½" $85.00
Parrot in multicolored pastels on tree branch, 8x5x4¾".......$55.00
Shoes, yellow w/pink tulip on toe, Dutch-style, high gloss, 7½x2x½x3½", pr..$30.00

Skunk, black w/white striped tail, high gloss, Hand Painted Japan, 5⅛x3¼x1¾" **$60.00**

Stanford boy & girl, Sandy & Jean, green plaid striping w/orange bows, 7¼" **$45.00**

Stork carrying a bundle, white, high gloss, USA, 6½x4x2" .. **$28.00**

Strawberries w/brown bird perched on top, PY, 5⅞x4x3½" . **$46.00**

Swan on matt blue water w/gold lustre reeds behind, Germany #4019, 4x3" **$10.00**

Teapot, white w/lg red apple & blue flowers on front, high gloss, 1940s, 3¼x6⅜" **$45.00**

Umbrella, ivory w/red & yellow handle, majolica style, Goebel, 7x5" **$90.00**

Violin, ivory w/blue & pink floral, hand painted, Knox Imperial, 8¼", from $12 to **$15.00**

Violins, white w/applied pink roses & mint green leaves, hand painted, Napco, 8x3¾", pr **$60.00**

Watering can, white w/green, red & yellow rooster, 3½" **$15.00**

Zucchini & tomato, multicolored glossy glaze, #28, 4", from $20 to **$35.00**

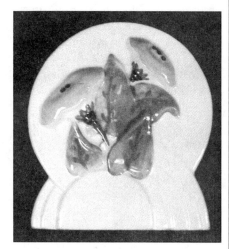

Morning glories, Block Pottery, 5¾", from $15.00 to $20.00. (Photo courtesy Bill and Betty Newbound)

Wallace China

This company operated in California from 1931 until 1964, producing many lines of dinnerware, the most popular of which today are those included in their Westward Ho assortment: Boots and Saddles, Rodeo, and Pioneer Trails. All of these lines were designed by artist Till Goodan, whose signature appears in the design. All are very heavy, their backgrounds are tan, and the designs are done in dark brown. The Rodeo pattern has accents of rust, green, and yellow. When dinnerware with a western theme became so popular a few years ago, Rodeo was reproduced, but the new trademark includes neither 'California' or 'Wallace China.'

Andy's (Restaurant), plate, dinner; 11¼" **$45.00**

Boots & Saddle, ashtray, 5½" **$35.00**

Boots & Saddle, bowl, cereal; 5¾" **$70.00**

Boots & Saddle, bowl, oval, 2½x9¼x12", from $120 to **$140.00**

Boots & Saddle, cup & saucer, from $65 to **$75.00**

Boots & Saddle, disk pitcher, 7½", from $225 to **$275.00**

Boots & Saddle, mug, 10-oz, 3½", from $45 to **$50.00**

Boots & Saddle, plate, chop; 13½" **$115.00**

Boots & Saddle, plate, 10½", from $75 to **$100.00**

Boots & Saddle, plate, 7", from $50 to **$65.00**

Boots and Saddle, salt shaker, 5¼", from $65.00 to $75.00 for the pair (one shown).

Boots & Saddle, sugar bowl, w/lid, 4¾x4⅝", from $90 to ... **$120.00**

Casa de Manana La Jolla, plate, dinner; 11¼" **$15.00**

Chuck Wagon, bowl, fruit; 5", from $28 to **$35.00**

Chuck Wagon, bowl, oval, 12x9" **$120.00**

Chuck Wagon, bowl, 2¼x4", from $35 to **$45.00**

Chuck Wagon, bowl, 6½" **$48.00**

Chuck Wagon, bowl, 10x7½", from $90 to **$100.00**

Chuck Wagon, butter pat, 3", from $45 to **$55.00**

Chuck Wagon, cup, soup; 2¼x3¾", from $35 to **$45.00**

Chuck Wagon, cup & saucer, from $50 to **$70.00**

Chuck Wagon, mustard jar, notch in lid, 3¾x3¼", from $150 to **$165.00**

Chuck Wagon, pitcher, water; 7½", from $135 to **$185.00**

Chuck Wagon, plate, dinner; 11" **$60.00**

Chuck Wagon, plate, 9⅛", from $35 to **$45.00**

Chuck Wagon, platter, 13" **$145.00**

Denny's Coffee Shop, plate, restaurant; 10½" **$40.00**

Desert Ware, cup, from $12 to **$15.00**

Desert Ware, grill plate **$18.00**

Desert Ware, Hill's Bros Coffee, saucer, 6¼" **$15.00**

Desert Ware, Mexican man decor, cup **$65.00**

Desert Ware, platter, 11½x7⅞" **$18.00**

El Rancho, bowl, chili; 2¼x5¾" **$75.00**

El Rancho, bowl, 1¼x6½", from $32 to **$48.00**

El Rancho, bowl, 1x4¾", from $25 to **$40.00**

El Rancho, bowl, 3½x8⅝" **$60.00**

El Rancho, creamer **$60.00**

El Rancho, drip jar, w/lid, 4¾x4¾" **$85.00**

El Rancho, mug, 3⅞", from $30 to **$38.00**

El Rancho, plate, Hitching Post, Cheyenne, 6" **$60.00**

El Rancho, plate, 5¾", from $35 to **$45.00**

El Rancho, plate, 7", from $35 to **$50.00**

El Rancho, plate, 9½", from $50 to **$60.00**

El Rancho, platter, oval, 9x6", from $65 to **$75.00**

El Rancho, platter, oval, 10½x7", from $75 to **$90.00**

El Rancho, platter, oval, 12½", from $90 to **$110.00**

El Rancho, sugar bowl, w/lid, 4" **$65.00**

Erawan Garden Hotel, plate, restaurant; scalloped edge, 7½". **$75.00**

Festival, cup, 2¾" **$8.00**

Hibiscus, bowl, 4½x8¾" **$90.00**

Hibiscus, plate, 10", from $40 to............................. **$55.00**

Kit Carson, ashtray, 4 rests, MIB **$90.00**

Little Buckaroo, bowl, cereal; 5¾", from $40 to **$50.00**

Little Buckaroo, plate, 9", from $45 to **$55.00**

Longhorn, bowl, cereal; 2x5", from $50 to **$70.00**

Longhorn, creamer, footed, 3¼x6¼", from $125 to **$135.00**

Longhorn, cup & saucer, from $150 to...................... **$165.00**

Longhorn, cup & saucer, jumbo **$270.00**

Longhorn, disk pitcher, 7", from $300 to **$325.00**

Longhorn, platter, oval, 15x13½" **$500.00**

Longhorn, saucer, 6⅝", from $50 to......................... **$60.00**

Pioneer Trails, ashtray, Davy Crockett portrait in center, 4 rests, 5½" dia.. **$110.00**

Pioneer Trails, ashtray, Will Rogers portrait, 4 rests, 5½" dia.. **$50.00**

Pioneer Trails, bowl, cereal; 2¼x5¾" **$80.00**

Pioneer Trails, creamer, 3¼", from $85 to............... **$95.00**

Pioneer Trails, cup & saucer, 3", 6", ... **$55.00**

Pioneer Trails, plate, chop; 13½", from $250 to **$270.00**

Pioneer Trails, plate, pioneer in center, 7", from $65 to **$75.00**

Pioneer Trails, plate, 7", from $50 to **$65.00**

Pioneer Trails, plate, 10", from $85 to **$110.00**

Pioneer Trails, platter, 12x6", from $150 to **$175.00**

Pioneer Trails, salt & pepper shakers, blue (rare color), cylindircal, 5", pr from $215 to **$225.00**

Pioneer Trails, sugar bowl, w/lid, 4½x4½" **$135.00**

Rod's Steak House, ashtray, from $22 to **$30.00**

Rod's Steak House, creamer, 3¾" **$35.00**

Rod's Steak House, cup & saucer **$40.00**

Rodeo, bowl, cereal; 2¼x5¾" **$55.00**

Rodeo, bowl, flared rim, 2⅛x4¾" **$60.00**

Rodeo, bowl, nesting; #2, 7", from $80 to............... **$100.00**

Rodeo, bowl, nesting; 5½x13", from $450 to **$475.00**

Rodeo, bowl, oval, 2⅜x9¼x11⅞", from $160 to **$180.00**

Rodeo, plate, chop; 13¼", from $140 to **$160.00**

Rodeo, plate, dinner; bronco rider, 1x10½", from $85 to.. **$110.00**

Rodeo, plate, 7¼", from $50 to............................. **$60.00**

Rodeo, plate, 9", from $70 to **$85.00**

Rodeo, platter, oval, 15¼x10⅜", from $150 to.................. **$175.00**

Rodeo, salt & pepper shakers, round, 5", pr from $85 to .. **$110.00**

Rodeo, shot glasses, set of 4, MIB............................ **$150.00**

Rodeo, sugar bowl, w/lid, 4½" **$125.00**

Shadow Leaf, bowl, fruit; green, 5" **$35.00**

Shadow Leaf, bowl, green, footed, 6¾" **$140.00**

Shadow Leaf, bowl, rare, 2¾x7", from $125 to.................. **$150.00**

Shadow Leaf, bowl, 2x4", from $12 to....................... **$18.00**

Shadow Leaf, butter pat, 3", from $20 to.................... **$25.00**

Shadow Leaf, creamer, 3", from $22 to...................... **$30.00**

Shadow Leaf, mug, coffee....................................... **$40.00**

Shadow Leaf, pitcher, green, 7½", from $125 to............. **$140.00**

Shadow Leaf, plate, chop; green, 13", from $100 to **$135.00**

Shadow Leaf, plate, dinner; 10½", from $65 to.............. **$80.00**

Shadow Leaf, platter, brown & white, oval, 2x19x12¾" **$400.00**

Shadow Leaf, platter, green, 12½", from $55 to.............. **$75.00**

Shadow Leaf, platter, green, 9", from $40 to................. **$60.00**

Snack Shop, plate, restaurant; white w/blue-gray border & logo, 10" **$30.00**

Storz, Your Favorite Brand, ashtray, 4 rests........................... **$60.00**

Texas-Southwestern Regional Restaurant Show, Dallas TX 1950, ashtray, 5⅜" **$20.00**

Watt Pottery

The Watt Pottery Company operated in Crooksville, Ohio, from 1922 until sometime in 1935. It appeals to collectors of country antiques, since the body is yellow ware and its decoration rather quaint.

Several patterns were made: Apple, Autumn Foliage, Cherry, Dutch Tulip, Morning-Glory, Pansy, Rooster, Tear Drop, Starflower, and Tulip among them. All were executed in bold brush strokes of primary colors. Some items you'll find will also carry a stenciled advertising message, made for retail companies as premiums for their customers.

For further study, we recommend *Watt Pottery* by Susan Morris-Snyder and Dave Morris.

Advisor: Sue Morris-Snyder (See Directory, Dinnerware)

Club/Newsletter:
Watt Collectors Association
1431 4th St. SW
PMB 221, Mason City, IA 50401

Rodeo, bowl, oval, 12" $220.00.

Rodeo, creamer, lg, 4¼" **$115.00**

Rodeo, creamer, 3¾", from $50 to............................. **$65.00**

Rodeo, cup & saucer, 3½", 6¾", from $50 to **$70.00**

Rodeo, nesting bowls, 6" to 11½", set of 5..................... **$1,875.00**

Rodeo, placemats, set of 8, 12x18", NM **$140.00**

Apple, baking dish, rectangular, 10"L **$1,500.00**

Apple, bean pot, handles, #76, 6½x7½" **$175.00**

Apple, bowl, cereal/salad; #52, 6½" **$50.00**

Apple, bowl, mixing; #5, 2¾x5" **$65.00**

Apple, bowl, mixing; #7, ribbed, 7" **$50.00**

Apple, bowl, mixing; #64, 5x7½" **$60.00**

Apple, bowl, oval, 5x6" **$200.00**

Apple, bowl, w/lid, #67, 6½x8½" $125.00
Apple, casserole, tab handles, #18, 4x5" $225.00
Apple, chip 'n dip set, 2 bowls w/metal rack, 5" & 8" $300.00
Apple, cookie jar, #503, 8¼x8¼" $450.00
Apple, fondue, 3x9" $900.00

Apple, jam and jelly dish, 5½" long, $45.00. (Photo courtesy
Susan Morris-Snyder)

Apple, mug, #61, 3x3¼" $500.00
Apple, oil & vinegar set, w/lids, 7", pr $1,800.00
Apple, pitcher, #15, 5½x5¾" $75.00
Apple, plate, dinner; #101, 10" $600.00
Apple, plate, dinner; no mark on bottom, 9½" $450.00
Apple, platter, #31, 15" $350.00
Apple, sugar bowl, w/lid, #98, 4½x5" $400.00
Apple, teapot, #112, 6" $1,500.00
Apple, tumbler, #56, 4½" $1,000.00
Apple (Double), bowl, #73, 4x9" $125.00
Apple (Double), creamer, #62, 4½x4½" $400.00
Autumn Foliage, creamer, #62, 4½" $1,000.00
Autumn Foliage, pie plate, #33, 1½x9" $125.00
Autumn Foliage, teapot, #505, 5¾x9" $1,600.00
Banded (Blue & White), bowl, mixing; 7" $25.00
Banded (Blue & White), pitcher, 7x7¾" $95.00
Banded (Brown), mug, #121, 3¾" $125.00
Banded (White), pitcher, 7" $85.00
Butterfly, bowl, #7, 7" $275.00
Cherry, bowl, berry; 5" $45.00
Cherry, bowl, mixing; #8, 4x8" $45.00
Cherry, pitcher, w/advertising, #15, 5½x5¾" $175.00
Cherry, salt shaker, barrel shape, 4x2½", ea. $90.00
Cut-Leaf Pansy, creamer & sugar bowl, pr $175.00
Cut-Leaf Pansy, Dutch oven, w/lid, 10½" $175.00
Cut-Leaf Pansy, pitcher, 6½x6¾" $175.00
Cut-Leaf Pansy, platter, 15" dia $110.00
Cut-Leaf Pansy, sugar & creamer $175.00
Dutch Tulip, bowl, w/lid, #5, 4x5" $250.00
Dutch Tulip, cheese crock, #80, 8½" $475.00
Eagle, bowl, cereal; #74, 2x5½" $85.00
Eagle, pitcher, w/ice lip, 8" $450.00
Esmond, platter, 15" $175.00
Kitch-N-Queen, bowl, mixing; plain sides, #14, 7x14" $60.00
Kitch-N-Queen, bowl, mixing; ribbed side, #5, 5" $45.00

Kitch-N-Queen, cookie jar, w/lid, #503, 8¼x8¼" $225.00
Morning Glory, casserole, w/lid, #94, 8½" $275.00
Morning Glory, creamer, #97, 4¼x4½" $500.00
Morning Glory, sugar bowl, #98, 4¼x5" $250.00
Old Pansy, bowl, spaghetti; #39, 13" $80.00
Old Pansy, casserole, #2/48, 4¼x7½" $75.00
Old Pansy, pitcher, #17, 8x8½" $225.00
Old Pansy, platter, #49, 12" dia $85.00
Raised Pansy, casserole, individual, French handle, 7½x3¾" .$225.00
Raised Pansy, pitcher, 7x7¾" $225.00
Rooster, canister set, flour, sugar, tea & coffee, 4-pc........$2,800.00
Rooster, ice bucket, unmarked, 7¼x7½" $275.00
Rooster, pitcher, #15, 5¾" $145.00

Rooster, pitcher, refrigerator; square, 8½", $550.00.

Rooster, sugar bowl, w/lid, #98, 4½x5" $500.00
Shaded Brown, mug, unmarked, 3x3¾" $10.00
Starflower, bowl, berry; 1½x5¾" $35.00
Starflower, ice bucket, w/lid, 7¼x7½" $185.00
Starflower, pie plate, #33, 1½x9" $200.00
Starflower, pitcher, w/ice lip, #17, 8x8½" $175.00
Starflower, tumbler, round-sided, #56, 4x3½" $275.00
Starflower (Green on Brown), bowl, mixing; #5, 2¾x5" $35.00
Starflower (Green on Brown), platter, #31, 15" $90.00
Starflower (Pink on Black), bowl, berry; 5" $45.00
Starflower (Pink on Black), casserole, w/lid, 4½x8¾" $125.00
Starflower (Pink on Green), plate, bread; 6½" dia. $35.00
Starflower (Red on Green), bowl, berry; 5¾" $35.00
Starflower (Red on Green), ice bucket, 7½" dia $185.00
Starflower (White on Green), bowl, #39, 3x13" $100.00
Starflower (White on Red), bowl, spaghetti; 12" $190.00
Tear Drop, bean server, #75, individual, 2¼x3½" $30.00
Tear Drop, casserole, sq, w/lid, 6x8" $850.00
Tear Drop, creamer, #62, 4¼x4½" $275.00
Tear Drop, salt & pepper shakers, 2½", pr $350.00
Tulip, creamer, #62, 4¼x4½" $225.00
Tulip, pitcher, #15, 5½" $550.00
White Daisy, plate, salad; marked Watt USA, 8½" $65.00

White Daisy, plate, salad; 8½" $65.00
Woodgrain, cookie jar, #617W, 11x8" $90.00
Woodgrain, pitcher, #615W, 9" $100.00

Wedding Cake Toppers

The popularity of all things 'wedding' has burst on the scene in recent years. With today's emphasis on the ceremony, the cake topper has come into its own as an untapped area of collectible Americana. The symbolic bride and groom can be traced back thousands of years to early Greece and Rome. Recent literature cites the writing of a slave in the Deep South around the time of the Civil War, 'a bride and groom atop a cake' is all that is given but it provides an intriguing glimpse into weddings 150 years ago.

By the 1890s European bakery chefs had mastered the art of molding marzipan and gum paste into human form. Tiny celluloid doll figures manufactured in Germany were dressed as brides and grooms.

The early twentieth century saw the introduction of bridal figures in plaster of Paris (chalkware), porcelain, and bisque. Germany and Japan, the two largest importers into the United States at the time, flooded the market with thousands of miniature bride and groom figures. Illustrations from commercial artists like Rose O'Neill and Grace Drayton were converted into three-dimensional form and used as toppers. 'Kewpie' and 'Diddums,' angelic and child-like respectively, were very popular.

The 'cutie,' a perfected celluloid figure, and the 'googlie' in bisque enjoyed their heyday in the 1930s. Both were noted for their molded curly hair and flirty eyes. Each was available in a variety of sizes and could be dressed to personalize one's wedding. The first plastic toppers debuted in the 1930s, but their time in the limelight was short-lived, due in part to stepped-up warfare production.

Cake toppers from the 1940s reflect the stark war years. Single flower stalks, cardboard, and chalkware replaced festooned arbors, porcelain, and bisque. Cake topper grooms exchanged tuxedos for military uniforms. Saltware and spelter toppers were produced primarily through the war years. They proved to be an inexpensive but delightful alternative to the conventional toppers of the past.

The 1950s ushered in the 'ceramic era' for cake toppers. These are most notable for 'trim' accents. Lighted cake toppers, with their hidden batteries, wires, and bulbs, were a brief fascination.

By the 1960s plastic had completely taken over the cake topper. Everything on it from the pedestal and base to the peak of the arbor was made of some form of plastic. The 1960s and 1970s saw a return of the military uniform on the groom but with an updated look and much more detailing.

Nostalgia struck in the 1980s. 'Heirlooms' and 'keepsakes' were the new buzzwords. Cake toppers reflected the trend. Cast resin, china, bisque, and glass were just some of the materials from which cake toppers were being manufactured.

'Specialty' toppers were used over the years as well: 'whimsies' — tiny, delicate china or bisque figures from the late 1800s and early 1900s; wax hands from the 1900s; bridal slippers from the 1930s; crepe paper and pipe cleaner figures from the same period; and doves from this early period and again in the 1970s.

Several key elements may help date a topper — materials used, plus period bridal fashions. As with any wonderful collectible, fakes and reproductions are always a possibility. Acquaint yourself thoroughly with all aspects of genuine old cake toppers, ie., cloth flowers, early plastics, fine netting, old crepe paper. Learn to recognize spelter, salt ware, plaster of Paris, parian, and celluloid. Study craftsmanship and attention to detail.

Values listed below are for cake toppers in very good to excellent condition.

1890s, porcelain whimsie, 2½" cherub holds gold heart in hands . $45.00
1900s, gum-paste couple on gum-paste base, bower of cloth flowers w/delicately painted centers $150.00
1900s pair of white wax hands (bride & groom), ea hand approximately 3" in length $75.00
1915 kewpie couple (bisque figures) on molded plaster base... $135.00
1920s bisque couple only, no base or pedestal, marked Germany & 4-digit number, 6" $85.00
1920s gum-paste couple on gum-paste base (bride wears wide collar, popular style for the period) $120.00
1930s bisque 'googlies' standing under 4-poster canopy atop molded cardboard steps, 6" overall.. $125.00
1930s bisque couple standing atop filigreed chalkware base & pedestal concealing key-wind music box, 11" overall........... $175.00
1930s celluloid Kewpie-type couple w/crepe-paper clothes, bride wears headband, ea figure 3" $50.00
1930s crepe-paper & pipe-cleaner bridal couple, 5" $45.00
1940s chalkware couple on chalkware base w/silver metal bell hanging from bower $45.00
1940s chalkware military couple stand arm-in-arm, no base or pedestal, 3¾" $60.00
1940s saltware couple, molded in 1 pc, 3½" $45.00
1950s chalkware couple, single mold, no base or pedestal, 4½" .. $25.00

1960s, plastic, two doves, each holding a silver metal ring, flank wedding couple, #51 printed on bottom, 9", $25.00. (Photo courtesy Jeannie Greenfield)

1970s bisque military couple, no base or pedestal, 3½" $50.00

Related Memorabilia

Related collectibles are becoming almost as popular as wedding cake toppers themselves. A marriage license, the bride's book, wedding favors, and decorations as well as invitations and announcements are just some of the selections available. These collectibles augment and enhance a topper collection.

Colorful and picturesque marriage licenses were popular from the mid-1800s to the late 1940s. Their average size measure 15" wide by 21" high. Values are in the $20.00 to $75.00 range, depending on age, size, condition, and graphics. The addition of tintypes (early photographs of the couple) increase the value. Bride's books were popular during the same time period as oversized marriage licenses. They offer insight into the personal moments of the bride's engagement and wedding. Most were 5" x 7" and usually held six to 12 plates for recording guest lists, gifts received, wedding attendants, and other details. Currently, values range from $5.00 to $40.00, depending on age, condition, and overall dimensions.

Jeannie Greenfield is our advisor for this category. See the Directory for information on her soon-to-be-released book *Wedding Cake Toppers, Memories and More*.

Advisor: Jeannie Greenfield (See Directory, Wedding Cake Toppers)

Book, bride's; artwork & poetry on subject of love, hardcover, 1920, 6 pages, 5x7" **$10.00**
Book, bride's; verious sections for bride to describe gown, trousseau, etc, hardcover, 1920s, 12 pages, 5x7", unused **$15.00**
Book, The Marriage Altar, JR Miller, hardcover, dated 1893, 33 pages **$5.00**

Bridal shower place card, heavy paper with silk ribbon, ca 1930s, 6", $35.00. (Photo courtesy Jeannie Greenfield)

Card, bridal shower; colorful graphics, 1950s, 4x4" **$1.00**
Card, bridal shower; heavy stock, 1930s, slightly smaller than modern postcard **$5.00**
Card, wedding; bride's bouquet embossed on white paper, silk ribbons hang & hold 2 metal rings, 1960s, 7x3½" **$2.00**
Marriage license, full-color graphics, dated April 24, 1918, 15x20" w/out frame **$40.00**

Napkin, bridal shower; printed paper, ca 1940s-50s...............**$2.00**
Place card (seating), handmade ring w/bride's profile in center, colorful graphics w/attached name card, 1930s, 6" **$20.00**
Salt & pepper shakers, bride & groom, he in black tux w/striped trousers, Japan sticker, 1950s, 4", pr **$10.00**

Weeping Gold

In the mid- to late 1950s, many American pottery companies produced lines of 'Weeping Gold.' Such items have a distinctive appearance; most appear to be covered with irregular droplets of lustrous gold, sometimes heavy, sometimes fine. On others the gold is in random swirls, or there may be a definite pattern developed on the surface. In fact, real gold was used; however, there is no known successful way of separating the gold from the pottery. You'll see similar pottery covered in 'Weeping Silver.' Very often, ceramic whiskey decanters made for Beam, McCormick, etc., will be trimmed in 'Weeping Gold.' Among the marks you'll find on these wares are 'McCoy,' 'Kingwood Ceramics,' and 'USA,' but most items are simply stamped '22k (or 24k) gold.'

Basket, organic swirling shape, slightly waisted, Elynor China, 8½" **$25.00**
Boot vase, unmarked, 7x6" **$40.00**
Coffee/teapot, pear shape w/curved handle, 24k Gold, Made in the USA, 8½" **$65.00**
Cup, demitasse; 2½" **$7.50**
Ewer vase, Elynor China 22k Weeping Gold, 13½x3¾" **$22.50**
Figurine, Art Deco nude w/draping scarf behind her on plinth, 8x5½" (4" dia base) **$50.00**
High-heeled shoe, 2x3x1" **$30.00**
Jar, vanity; Weeping bright Gold 22k USA, 6¾" dia...........**$25.00**
Planter, bird beside swirling open base, 8x8".....................**$45.00**
Planter, panther, allover gold (no black at base), 5½x9¼"....**$55.00**
Planter, panther, black base, 24k Gold, Made in USA, 5½x9½" . **$65.00**

Planter, sailfish, 9½x11", from $65.00 to $75.00.

Planter, telephone, black cradle, 24k Gold USA, 8¾x7½", from $100 to **$120.00**

Urn, tassel-shaped handles, w/domed lid, Decorated USA, 10" ... **$65.00**
Vase, fan form, chevron design at top, flared foot, 6½x6½". **$25.00**
Vase, scalloped rim, upturned handles, 9x6½" **$35.00**
Wall pocket, apple form, 24k Gold USA, 4¾x4½" **$25.00**
Wall pocket, fan form, unmarked, 8½" W **$25.00**
Wall pocket, washbowl & pitcher, 7¼x7" **$30.00**

Weil Ware

Though the Weil company made dinnerware and some kitchenware, their figural pieces are attracting the most collector interest. They were in business from the 1940s until the mid-1950s, another of the small but very successful California companies whose work has become so popular today. They dressed their 'girls' in beautiful gowns of vivid rose, light dusty pink, turquoise blue, and other lovely colors enhanced with enameled 'lace work' and flowers, sgraffito, sometimes even with tiny applied blossoms. Both paper labels and ink stamps were used to mark them, but as you study their features, you'll soon learn to recognize even those that have lost their labels over the years. Four-number codes and decorators' initials are usually written on their bases.

Bowl, aqua w/coral interior, incurvate rim, 2⅞x6½" **$20.00**
Bowl, divided vegetable; Brentwood, 8x11½" **$45.00**
Bowl, lug soup; Yellow Rose, 5⅛x6", set of 6 .... **$90.00**
Bowl, Ming Tree, 3¼x5½" **$20.00**
Butter dish, Malay Blossom, 2½x7¾" **$30.00**
Candleholder, Angel Pie on label, long hair, ruffled collar, 6x5½".. **$50.00**
Candlesticks, Malay Bamboo, sq bottom, 2¼x4", pr **$40.00**
Canister, Ming Tree, sq, w/lid, 5x5½" **$25.00**
Canister, Ming Tree, sq, w/lid, 8x5½" **$40.00**
Coffeepot, Malay Bamboo, pink, 8½" **$45.00**
Coffeepot, Mango, gray, 8¼" **$40.00**

Creamer and sugar bowl, Rose, from $20.00 to $25.00.

Cup & saucer, Malay Bamboo, from $9 to **$12.00**
Cup & saucer, Malay Blossom, sq, from $8 to **$10.00**
Dish, Malay Blossom, sq, 3x8x8" **$30.00**
Figurine, lady w/hands in muff, hat held w/scarf, floral dress, #4031, 10¾" **$55.00**
Flower holder, lady in pink, brown hair & blue scarf, flowers along apron, holds 2 white conical baskets, 9¾" **$55.00**

Flower holder, lady w/brown hair, dressed in yellow & green, flowers in hand & vase at left side, #4030 .... **$60.00**
Flower holder, lady w/right hand resting on holder, left behind back, scarf in hair, 10" **$50.00**
Flower holder, lady w/scarf in hair stands between 2 sq holders, #4027, 10¾" **$60.00**
Flower holder, Oriental lady w/flowers in hair, on 1 knee w/right arm around holder, #4021, 10½" **$50.00**
Flower holder, senorita w/bouquet of flowers in arms at chest, tree stump behind, 9¼", from $65 to **$80.00**
Plate, Malay Bamboo, 6¼" dia, from $9 to **$12.00**
Plate, Malay Blossom, sq, 6" **$8.00**
Plate, Malay Blossom, sq, 10" **$20.00**
Relish, Malay Blossom, 3-part, sq, 6x9½" **$28.00**
Shelf sitters, Oriental girls w/vases on ea side, 1 in hat, other w/flowers in hair, #4013 & #4046, 10", pr **$85.00**
Teapot, Malay Bamboo, 6¼" **$35.00**
Teapot, Malay Blossom, 7" **$40.00**
Tidbit, Malay Bamboo, 3-tiered, metal handle **$30.00**
Tray, Malay Blossom, 13x9" **$25.00**
Vase, cornucopia shell form, turquoise w/green interior, #719, 7x7" **$35.00**
Vase, Ming Tree, #953, 5" **$30.00**
Vase, Ming Tree, slanted top, 9½x3½", from $40 to **$50.00**

Wall pocket, little girl rests elbow on pocket, #9714, 9¾", $50.00.

Weller Pottery

Though the Weller Pottery has been closed since 1948, they were so prolific that you'll be sure to see several pieces anytime you're 'antiquing.' They were one of the largest of the art pottery giants that located in the Zanesville, Ohio, area, using locally dug clays to produce their wares. In the early years, they made hand-decorated vases, jardinieres, lamps, and other useful and decorative items for the home, many of which were signed by notable artists such as Fredrick Rhead, John Lessell, Virginia Adams, Anthony Dunlavy, Dorothy England, Albert Haubrich, Hester Pillsbury, E.L. Pickens, and Jacques Sicard, to name only a few. Some of their early lines were First and Second Dickens, Eocean, Sicardo, Etna, Louwelsa, Turada, and Aurelian. Portraits of Indians, animals of all types, lady golfers, nudes, and scenes of Dickens stories were popular themes, and some items were overlaid with silver filigree. These lines are rather hard to find at this point in time, and prices are generally high; but there's plenty of their later production still around, and some pieces are relatively inexpensive.

If you'd like to learn more, we recommend *The Collector's Encyclopedia of Weller Pottery* by Sharon and Bob Huxford.

Advisor: Hardy Hudson

Ardsley, candleholders, flower form, 3", pr..........................$85.00
Blue Drapery, planter, 4"...$75.00
Blue Ware, compote, 5½"..$275.00
Brighton, parrot on perch, 7½"...$750.00
Brighton, woodpecker, unmarked, 5".................................$250.00
Burntwood, vase, squat, unmarked, 3½"............................$100.00
Candis, basket, hanging, 5½"...$125.00
Classic, window box, Classic Ware paper label, 4"...........$85.00
Claywood, vase, spider's web, cylindrical, unmarked, 5½"..$110.00

Coppertone, figurine, two fish, 8", $3,250.00. (Photo courtesy Treadway Gallery Inc.)

Dickens Ware 3rd Line, vase, Wilkins Micawber, David Copperfield,
    signed LS, cylindrical, 10½"...$950.00
Eocean, basket, unmarked, 6½"..$550.00
Eocean (late line), vase, bud; unmarked, 6½".................$1,350.00
Etna, vase, frog near rim, snake near foot, 6½".................$950.00
Etna, vase, lg flowers, handles, 9"..$500.00
Evergreen, triple candleholder, 7½", ea..............................$115.00
Flemish, tub, handles, 4"..$115.00
Fleron, vase, 4½"..$125.00
Floretta, vase, embossed grapes, slim, 17".........................$350.00
Forest, pitcher, glossy, unmarked, 5½"................................$250.00
Glendale, vase, bird in landscape, 6"..................................$400.00
Hudson, vase, iris, signed Axline, 8½".................................$550.00
Hudson, wall pocket, white & decorated, 8".....................$600.00
Hudson-Perfecto, vase, floral, sgn C Leffler, 9½".............$950.00
Hudson-Perfecto, vase, floral, 5½".......................................$400.00
Ivory (Clinton Ivory), window planter, 6x15½"................$225.00

Jap Birdimal, vase, crane on gray, cylindrical, unmarked, 7".$450.00
L'Art Nouveau, bank, car of corn, unmarked, 8"...............$600.00
La Sa, vase, scenic, signed, 6"...$400.00
La Sa, vase, tree scene, unmarked, 7".................................$500.00
Lonhuda, vase, trumpet neck, signed S Reid McLaughlin, 5½".$350.00
Louwelsa, vase, cylindrical w/round shoulders, 12" ark, 12".$600.00
Lustre, candlestick, 8", ea...$75.00
Malvern, jardiniere & pedestal, 34"....................................$950.00
Marbleized, jardiniere, 10"...$450.00
Marbleized, vase, 4½"..$95.00
Melrose, vase, handles, 8½"..$125.00
Mirror Black, wall vase, 6"...$125.00
Muskota, figurine, boy fishing, unmarked, 6½"................$375.00
Muskota, girl w/watering can, unmarked, 7".....................$500.00
Paragon, vase, 7½"...$350.00
Parian, wall pocket, unmarked, 10".....................................$250.00
Roma, candleholder, flared foot, unmarked, 10½", ea.......$135.00
Roma, vase, bud; unmarked, 6½"..$75.00

Roma, vase, #R-20, from $125.00 to $150.00.

Rosemont, jardiniere, 4½"...$150.00
Sabrinian, window box, shell form, 3½x9"..........................$225.00
Sicardo, mug, unmarked, 3½"...$599.99
Woodcraft, basket, acorn shape, 9½"...................................$500.00
Woodcraft, bowl, unmarked, 3½"..$175.00

Xenia, vase, stylized floral, 8½", $850.00.

Zona, platter, unmarked, 12"...$85.00

West Coast Pottery

This was a small company operating in the 1940s and 1950s in Burbank, California. The founders were Lee and Bonnie Wollard; they produced decorative pottery such as is listed here.

Basket, leaves form body, shaded brown to yellow, lighter yellow inside, 9¼" $35.00
Basket, organic form, celery green, #209, 9¼x6¼x3¼" $40.00
Basket, swirling organic form, brown to yellow, #201, 9x6" . $40.00
Console set, white centerpiece w/candle at ea end, statuette of Virgin Mary in center, #513 & #303, 14" L, 10¾" $40.00

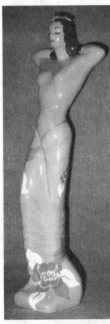

Figurine, Hawaiian lady, 17", $275.00.

(Photo courtesy Pat and Kris Secor)

Flower frog, tall bird perched on log w/sm holes, white, #903, 10½x5x4" $40.00
Pitcher, pink, tall & slim, marked Made in USA, 10" $20.00
Planter, swirling form that somewhat resembles Aladdin's lamp, mauve to gray, #217, 5½x12½" $35.00
Vase, cornucopia; turquoise to lavender, 7x5¾" $20.00
Vase, leaves embossed on body also form rim, green, #117, 6⅛". $38.00
Vase, organic form, blue to brown, #712, 7½x5" $55.00
Vase, pink to turquoise w/embossed leaves, sq, 7½x5x5" $40.00
Vase, scalloped shell form, light green to pink, #222, 5½x7⅜x3½" $12.50
Vase, shell-shaped fan form, deep green, #904, 7½" $16.00
Vase, white matt organic form w/uneven rim (somewhat petal-like) & flared foot, 9" $15.00
Wall pocket, bow shape, light green to rose, #451, 8x5½" ... $15.00
Wall pocket, curling feathers form, ivory, #306, 8½x6" $35.00
Wall pocket, lady's hat w/multicolor flowers along blue ribbon band, 9x6¼x2¾" $35.00

Western Collectibles

Although the Wild West era ended over 100 years ago, today cowboy gear is a hot area of collecting. These historic collectibles are not just found out west. Some of the most exceptional pieces have come from the East Coast states and the Midwest. But that should come as no surprise when you consider that the largest manufacturer of bits and spurs was the August Buemann Co. of Newark, New Jersey (1868 – 1926).

For more information refer to *Old West Cowboy Collectibles Auction Update & Price Guide*, which lists auction-realized prices of more than 650 lots, with complete descriptions and numerous photos. You can obtain a copy from our advisor, Dan Hutchins. He is also the author of *Wheels Across America* (Tempo International Publishing Co.). Unless otherwise noted, our values are for examples in at least excellent condition.

Advisor: Dan Hutchins (See Directory, Western Collectibles)

Belt buckle, Montana, Indian & cowboy embossed on solid brass, ca 1975-85, 3x3¾" $27.50
Bit, basic port-mouth, from $40 to $65.00
Bit, black steel w/copper inlay & hand-engraved silver overlay, 5" H port $42.50
Bit, cast iron, formed as ladies' bodies, original chin strap . $125.00
Bit, hackamore gag; 8" shanks w/5" wide mouthpiece, twisted sweet-iron mouth w/stainless-steel shanks, laced nosepiece $32.50
Bit, jointed mouth w/twist, from $15 to $20.00
Bit, tooled silver, 5" across inside mouthpiece, 3¼" dia conchos, 8¾" L $155.00
Book, Book of Indians, HC Hollings, hardcover, Platt & Munk, 1925, 125 pages $60.00
Book, Trail Driving Days, Dee Brown w/MF Schmitt, 125 photos, ca 1974, 8x5¼" $10.00
Boots, Trail Ridge, black leather, 1⅝" slanted heel, composite sole, man's, G $25.00
Bridle, bitless; Dr Robert Cook, Beta material, headstall only $85.00

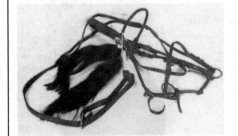

Bridle, leather head stall with horse rosettes, horsehair suspensions and snaffle bit, ca. 1920s, 35x7", $140.00.

Chaps, blue suede w/white leather buckstitching & fringe, metal zippers w/reinforced thighs, fits up to 50" waist, EX $75.00
Chaps, Woods Western Wear, cream ultra suede, scalloped edge, lightweight, lady's, 44" L $75.00
Hat, Double S (Houston Collection), black wool felt, w/simple black band & 3-pc buckle $35.00
Hat, tan wool, Bradford Western by Resistol, XX Premium Wool, in hard case $110.00
Headstall, Sedona, scalloped browband & cheek pieces w/turquoise crosses, rawhide wrapped, engraved buckles $27.50
Jacket, brown suede, fringed yoke, sleeves & pockets, leather buttons, fully lined, EX $70.00
Lariat, Predator, ⅜" dia, 31-35' L $15.00

Postcard, Saddling a Western Outlaw, cowboys breaking wild horse (photo), copyright 1910..$15.00

Saddle, Crates Western Trail, basketweave design, full quarter tree, 17" seat..$650.00

Saddle, Crates Youth Barrel, silver conchos, padded 13" seat, 7" gullet..$615.00

Saddle bags, leather w/buckles & straps, 1950s, 15½x8x2"..$50.00

Spurs, Buermann, CA style w/jingle bobs & chains, pr......$175.00

Spurs, silver inlay w/Greek key design, inlay fancy M on outside button, w/rowels, EX leather straps, 5½", pr....................$125.00

Spurs, silver-plated accents, sm spinners for spurs on blued steel, repaired leather, pr $110.00

Stirrups, carved wood, pr, from $45 to $75.00

Stirrups, oxbow; rawhide-covered leather, pr.......................$65.00

Westmoreland Glass

The Westmoreland Specialty Company was founded in 1889 in Grapeville, Pennsylvania. Their mainstay was a line of opalware (later called milk glass) which included such pieces as cream and sugar sets, novel tea jars (i.e., Teddy Roosevelt Bear Jar, Oriental Tea Jars, and Dutch Tea Jar), as well as a number of covered animal dishes such as hens and roosters on nests. All of these pieces were made as condiment containers and originally held baking soda and Westmoreland's own mustard recipe. By 1900 they had introduced a large variety of pressed tablewares in clear glass and opal, although their condiment containers were still very popular. By 1910 they were making a large line of opal souvenir novelties with hand-painted decorations of palm trees, Dutch scenes, etc. They also made a variety of decorative vases painted in the fashion of Rookwood Pottery, plus sprayed finishes with decorations of flowers, fruits, animals, and Indians. Westmoreland gained great popularity with their line of painted, hand-decorated wares. They also made many fancy-cut items.

These lines continued in production until 1939, when the Brainard family became full owners of the factory. The Brainards discontinued the majority of patterns made previously under the West management and introduced dinnerware lines, made primarily of milk glass, with limited production of black glass and blue milk glass. Colored glass was not put back into full production until 1964 when Westmoreland introduced Golden Sunset, Avocado, Brandywine Blue, and Ruby.

The company made only limited quantities of carnival glass in the early 1900s and then re-introduced it in 1972 when most of their carnival glass was made in limited editions for the Levay Distributing Company. J.H. Brainard, president of Westmoreland, sold the factory to Dave Grossman in 1981, and he, in turn, closed the factory in 1984. Westmoreland first used the stamped W over G logo in 1949 and continued using it until Dave Grossman bought the factory. Mr. Grossman changed the logo to a W with the word Westmoreland forming a circle around it.

Milk glass was always Westmoreland's main line of production. In the 1950s they became famous for their milk glass tableware in the #1881 'Paneled Grape' pattern. It was designed by Jess Billups, the company's mold maker. The first piece he made was the water goblet. Items were gradually added until a complete dinner service was available. It became their most successful dinnerware line, and

today it is highly collectible, primarily because of the excellence of the milk glass itself. No other company has been able to match Westmoreland's milk glass in color, texture, quality, or execution of design and pattern. Collectors need to know which colors were produced by Westmoreland and which were not. If you find a carnival piece be sure to check inside and on the bottom of the base. New carnival reproductions are not carnival on the inside and bottoms. Westmoreland always sprayed the carnival finish on the entire piece.

For more information see *Westmoreland Glass, The Popular Years 1940 – 1985,* by Lorraine Kovar (Collector Books).

Advisor: Cheryl Schafer (See Directory, Westmoreland)

Covered Animal Dishes

Camel, cobalt carnival..$175.00
Camel, emerald green carnival...$175.00
Camel, lilac mist $150.00
Camel, milk glass $100.00
Cat in boot, black $35.00
Cat on vertical rib base, apricot mist (+) $75.00
Cat on vertical rib base, milk glass (+)................................$50.00
Chick on egg pile on basketweave nest, brown, no details, 6¼" (+) $85.00
Chick on egg pile on basketweave nest, milk glass w/allover hand painting (+)..$175.00
Chick on oval 2-handled basket, Antique Blue (+)..............$70.00
Chick on oval 2-handled basket, white carnival (+) $35.00
Dog on vertical-rib base, Antique Blue, 5½".......................$90.00
Dog on vertical-rib base, milk glass, 5½" $75.00
Duck on oval rimmed base, Antique Blue, 8x6" $85.00
Duck on oval rimmed base, white or crystal carnival, 8x6".$100.00
Duck on oval vertical-rib or basketweave base, black carnival, 5" $135.00
Eagle w/spread wings, Antique Blue, 8x6" $150.00
Eagle w/spread wings, emerald green carnival, 8x6"..........$200.00
Fox on oval basket-weave or lacy base, milk glass, 7½" L...$125.00
Fox on oval basket-weave or lacy base, ruby marble (both pcs), 1982, 7½" L $250.00
Hen on basket-weave nest, black carnival, scarce, 5½" (+) .$100.00
Hen on basket-weave nest, milk glass, plain or hand-painted accents, 3½"..$20.00
Hen on basket-weave nest, milk glass (plain or hand-painted accents) or olive green, 5½" $30.00
Hen on basket-weave nest, ruby or black, 3½" $40.00
Hen on nest, Almond w/hand-painted red details, 7½" L (+). $100.00
Lamb on picket fence base, Antique Blue w/milk glass base, 5½" L $85.00
Lamb on picket fence base, milk glass (both pcs), 5½" L.....$50.00
Lamb on picket fence base, purple marble, 5½" L $150.00
Lion on basket-weave base, Antique Blue opaque, 6x8".....$175.00
Lion on basket-weave base, emerald green carnival, 6x8" ...$225.00
Lion on basket-weave base, milk glass w/hand-painted lion, 6x8"...$295.00
Lion on lacy base, milk glass plain, 6x8" $165.00
Lion on picket fence base, milk glass w/Antique Blue head, 6x8". $135.00

Lovebirds, almond or mint green, 5¼x6½"..........................$85.00

Lovebirds, Bermuda or Brandywine Blue, 5¼x6½" $75.00

Lovebirds, Golden Sunset, 5¼x6½".....................................$55.00

Lovebirds, olive green mist, 5¼x6½" $75.00

Mother eagle & babies on basketweave base, Antique Blue or milk glass w/hand painting, 8"..$150.00

Mother eagle & babies on basketweave base, milk glass, 8" ..$125.00

Rabbit on oval vertically ribbed base, black carnival, 5½"....$80.00

Rabbit on oval vertically ribbed base, milk glass, 5½" $50.00

Rabbit on oval vertically ribbed base, ruby carnival, 5½".....$75.00

Rabbit on picket fence, Antique Blue, 5½"........................$100.00

Rabbit on picket fence, caramel marble carnival or white carnival, 5½"...$145.00

Rabbit on picket base, milk glass, 5½", $60.00. (Photo courtesy Pat and Dick Spencer)

Rabbit w/eggs on oval base, milk glass, 8".......................$80.00

Rabbit w/eggs on oval base, milk glass w/hand-painted accents, 8"...$90.00

Rabbit w/eggs on oval base, purple slag carnival (150 made), 8". $190.00

Rabbit w/eggs on oval base, Ruby Marble, 8" $180.00

Rabbit w/eggs on oval base, white carnival (1,500 made), 8". $160.00

Robin on twig nest, Antique Blue, 6¼" $85.00

Robin on twig nest, blue pastel, 6¼" $70.00

Robin on twig nest, Laurel Green, 6¼" $100.00

Robin on twig nest, yellow mist, 6¼" $75.00

Robin on twig nest base, Almond, Coral, mint green or ruby carnival, 6¼" $95.00

Robin on twig nest base, green or light blue mist, olive green or olive green mist, or yellow mist, 6¼" $70.00

Robin on twig nest base, milk glass, 6¼" $50.00

Rooster on diamond base, Chocolate, 8" $190.00

Rooster on diamond base, crystal mist w/hand-painted accents, 8" $50.00

Rooster on diamond base, Electric Blue carnival (500 made), emerald green, or turquoise carnival, 8"...........................$225.00

Rooster on diamond base, milk glass, 8".............................$45.00

Rooster on diamond base, purple marble, 8" $150.00

Rooster on diamond base, ruby, 8" $95.00

Rooster on lacy base, milk glass...$45.00

Rooster on lacy base, milk glass, 8" $45.00

Rooster on lacy base, milk glass w/hand-painted accents, 8"...$50.00

Rooster on lacy base, white carnival (1,500 made), 8" $100.00

Rooster on oval vertical-ribbed base, purple marble, 5½" $75.00

Rooster on oval vertical-ribbed nest, milk glass w/Antique Blue head, 5½"..$65.00

Rooster on ribbed base, milk glass, 5½".............................$30.00

Rooster on ribbed base, ruby, caramel or purple marbled carnival, made for Levay, 1978 (500 made of ea), 5½" $100.00

Rooster standing, Antique Blue, Antique Blue w/milk glass head or black glass w/hand-painted accents, 8½" $95.00

Rooster standing, apricot mist, black, Brandywine Blue or Laurel Green, 8½" $85.00

Rooster standing, brown marble, purple marble or ruby marble, 8½" $95.00

Rooster standing, brown marble, 8½"..................................$85.00

Rooster standing, brown mist or crystal mist, ea w/hand-painted accents, 8½" $85.00

Rooster standing, milk glass, 8½" $30.00

Rooster standing, milk glass w/hand-painted accents, 8½" ..$35.00

Rooster standing, milk glass w/hand-painted details, 8½"....$85.00

Rooster standing, ruby marble, 8½".....................................$95.00

Swan (raised wing) on lacy base, black glass, cobalt carnival or purple marble, 6x9½"..$300.00

Swan (raised wing) on lacy base, cobalt, 6x9½" $340.00

Swan (raised wing) on lacy base, cobalt marble (both pcs), 6x9½"..$400.00

Swan (raised wing) on lacy base, emerald green, ice blue carnival or turquoise carnival, 6x9½" $225.00

Swan (raised wing) on lacy base, light blue or pink mist, 6x9½". $150.00

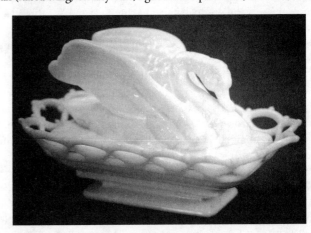

Swan (raised wing) on lacy base, milk glass, 6x9½", $150.00.

Swan (raised wing) on lacy base, milk glass mother-of-pearl, 6x9½" $190.00

Swan on diamond base, black carnival, 5½" $95.00

Swan on diamond base, caramel marble carnival, 5½".......$110.00

Swan on diamond base, milk glass, closed neck, 5½"...........$70.00

Swan on diamond base, milk glass, open neck, 5½" $50.00

Swan on diamond base, ruby carnival, 5½" $75.00

Toy chick on basket-weave base, milk glass or milk glass w/red accents, 2" $15.00

Toy chick on basket-weave base, milk glass w/any fired-on color, 2"..$20.00

Figurals and Novelties

Bird ashtray/pipe holder, any color marble...........................$30.00

Bird ashtray/pipe holder, any color mist or Moss Green.......$25.00

Bird w/feather on head, crystal..............................$15.00
Bulldog, Bermuda Blue or Coral, 3½"..................$35.00
Bulldog, milk glass or milk glass mist, 3½"...........$35.00
Bulldog, ruby or ruby carnival, 3½"......................$45.00
Bulldog doorstop, amber mist, 7-lb......................$350.00

Bulldog doorstop, Golden Sunset mist with green eyes, 8½", $400.00 (Photo courtesy Pat and Dick Spencer)

Bumblebee, Golden Sunset, size of a quarter, only shown in 1 undated catalog..............................$300.00
Bumblebee, Steel Blue or ruby lustre, size of a quarter, only shown in 1 undated catalog $400.00
Butterfly (lg), Almond or Mint Green.................$40.00
Butterfly (lg), Antique Blue, Antique Blue mist or Antique Green marble, ea $40.00
Butterfly (lg), apricot mist or yellow opaque $20.00
Butterfly (lg), on sq base perch, any combination, from $50 to..$55.00
Butterfly (lg) lilac $40.00
Butterfly (lg) vaseline $40.00
Cardinal, any mist color, solid glass....................$25.00
Cardinal, crystal, solid glass................................$15.00
Chick & egg pin tray, Electric Blue opalescent (+) $65.00
Chick & egg pin tray, milk glass (+).....................$15.00
Chick egg cup, milk glass $10.00
Chick egg cup, milk glass w/red hand-painted details $15.00
Chick mug, milk glass w/child's decal $50.00
Chick mug, Mint Green or Antique Green $30.00
Chick on oval 2-handled basket, apricot mist, 4" L (+)........$50.00
Dog house, match holder, milk glass....................$35.00
Dog house match holder, black............................$40.00
Duck salt dip/nut dish, black $30.00
Duck salt tip/nut dish, apricot or green mist.......$25.00
Eagle standing, crystal, 7½"...............................$250.00
Eagle standing, crystal mist, 7½"........................$350.00
Eagle standing, hand-painted details, 7½", minimum value .$500.00
Owl, toothpick holder, milk glass, #62, 3", from $20 to......$25.00
Owl bookends, pink mist, rare, minimum value $350.00
Owl on 2 stacked book, black or black mist, 3½"...............$30.00
Owl on 2 stacked books, Almond or Mint Green, 3½" $30.00
Owl on 2 stacked books, Brandywine Blue or brown, 3½" ..$22.50
Owl on 2 stacked books, milk glass or milk glass mist, 3½" ...$20.00
Owl on 2 stacked books, purple carnival or purple marble, 3½" .$35.00

Owl standing on tree stump, almond mist or Antique Blue, 5½" $40.00
Owl standing on tree stump, black carnival, 5½"...............$45.00
Owl standing on tree stump, Electric Blue carnival, 5½" $50.00
Owl standing on tree stump, ruby carnival or purple marble, 5½" $50.00
Owl standing on tree stump, Steele Blue lustre, 5½" $45.00
Penguin on ice floe, Bermuda Blue or blue $110.00
Penguin on ice floe, blue & blue mist or blue mist $125.00
Penguin on ice floe, Brandywine Blue mist, 1970s, 3¾", from $35 to $45.00
Penguin on ice floe, hand-painted black & white..............$145.00
Pouter pigeon, amethyst mist, #9, 2½", from $25 to..........$35.00
Pouter pigeon, apricot mist, 2¾" $35.00
Pouter pigeon, black, 2¾".....................................$42.50
Pouter pigeon, lilac or lilac mist, 2¾".................$40.00
Robin, Antique Blue or blue mist, sm.................$18.50
Robin, mint green, sm $25.00
Starfish candleholders, Almond, 5" wide, pr from $45 to $55.00
Swallow, Almond or Antique Blue, solid glass.....................$30.00
Swallow, crystal or green mist, wings down.......................$15.00
Swallow, Mint Green, solid glass $30.00
Wren, any opaque color, w/ or w/o pegs, solid glass............$32.50
Wren, milk glass, w/or w/out pegs, solid glass.....................$30.00
Wren on sq base perch, any color combination $55.00

Lamps

Please note that Americana with any decoration and a scroll base require a value of $20.00 more than those items without a scroll base.

Fairy, Wakefield, crystal with ruby stain, 6½", $75.00.

Americana, Country Floral, China Rose, green floral or yellow floral, smooth brass base, 13½"..............................$75.00
Americana, pink floral or Antique Fruit, smooth brass base, 13½" $85.00
Boudoir, English Hobnail/#555, milk glass, stick type w/flat base..$45.00
Candle, owl, red, on metal latticework base, #110, 4¼" $25.00

Candle, owl, yellow, on metal latticework base, #110, 4¼ ". **$25.00**

Child's electric mini, any child's decoration, wood base **$80.00**

Colonial, blue floral, scrolled brass base, 12¼" **$155.00**

Colonial, floral spray, green floral, or brown-beaded bouquet, scrolled brass base, 12¼"...**$125.00**

Colonial, pink floral or ruby floral, scrolled brass base, 12¼" . **$155.00**

Colonial, Wild Rose (blue or brown), scrolled brass base, 12¼" . **$135.00**

Colonial electric, any color or decoration, brass base w/scrollwork & glass shade...**$125.00**

Fairy, Wakefield, crystal w/silver trim, footed **$75.00**

Gone w/the-wind style, milk glass w/any beaded bouquet, w/shade, chimney & base **$1,500.00**

Gone-w/the-wind style, milk glass w/pink roses, w/shade, chimney & base **$1,500.00**

Gone-w/the-wind style, milk glass w/Roses & Bows, w/shade, chimney & base **$2,000.00**

Mini lite candle, Almond, mint green or ruby w/hand painting, w/shade **$45.00**

Mini lite candle, any mist w/out a decal, w/shade **$27.50**

Mini lite candle, crystal mist w/child's decal, w/shade.......... **$65.00**

Mini lite candle, crystal mist w/Roses & Bows, w/shade **$75.00**

Mini lite candle, milk glass w/child's decal, w/shade **$125.00**

Mini lite candle, milk glass w/Roses & Bows, w/shade....... **$135.00**

Tiffa, Almond w/Beaded Bouquet, scrolled brass base, ca 1978-79 ....**$140.00**

Tiffa, ruby w/hand-painted ruby floral, scrolled brass base, ca 1978-79 ....**$195.00**

Zodiac, blue mist or cased w/hand painting, cylinder shade.... **$250.00**

Modern Giftware

Ashtray, milk glass w/Roses & Bows, sq, 6½" **$45.00**

Banana bowl, ruby, Doric, $75.00. (Photo courtesy Lorraine Kovar)

Basket, Almond w/gold roses, 4" W **$55.00**

Basket, any color w/Beaded Bouquet, sm............................. **$35.00**

Basket, brown or dark blue mist w/daisy decal, flat, 4" dia .. **$30.00**

Basket, Cameo style, Mint Green w/Beaded Bouquet **$150.00**

Basket, Mary Gregory, crystal w/ruby stain, flat, sm, 4" dia. **$55.00**

Bell, Almond w/Almond Rose, ruffled rim, 6½" **$55.00**

Bell, brown mist w/daisy decal, plain rim, 5" **$22.50**

Bell, Mary Gregory, crystal w/ruby stain, plain rim, 5" **$30.00**

Bell, ruby w/Ruby Floral, ruffled rim.................................... **$45.00**

Bonbon, any color w/daisy decal, handles, flat, w/lid........... **$40.00**

Bonbon, milk glass w/Beaded Bouquet, handles, w/lid, flat. **$50.00**

Bonbon, ruby or ruby stain w/Ruby Floral, w/lid **$40.00**

Bottle, scent; milk glass w/purple Beaded Bouquet, w/stopper. **$125.00**

Bottle, scent; milk glass w/roses & Bows, w/stopper **$85.00**

Candlesticks, Crystal Velvet, skirted, 4", pr........................ **$45.00**

Candy dish, Colonial, any color w/Beaded Bouquet, w/lid.. **$45.00**

Candy dish, crystal mist w/Roses & Bows, footed, w/domed lid **$42.50**

Chocolate box, any mist color w/daisy decal, oval, w/lid....**$110.00**

Compote, Mary Gregory deer, dark blue mist, stemmed, w/ lid **$145.00**

Flowerpot, milk glass w/Beaded Bouquet, w/drip tray **$125.00**

Honey jar, Crystal Velvet, low foot, w/lid, 5"......................**$40.00**

Jardiniere, any mist color w/daisy decal, straight sides, footed, 5" **$30.00**

Plate, salad; Crystal Velvet, 8½" **$30.00**

Puff box/jelly, crystal mist w/Roses & Bows, w/lid, 4½" **$45.00**

Shell dish, milk glass w/Roses & Bows, 3-footed................**$47.50**

Straw jar, any color w/Beaded Bouquet, w/lid.....................**$80.00**

Sweetmeat, crystal mist w/Roses & Bows, footed, ruffled.....**$40.00**

Sweetmeat, Doric, Almond w/Almond Rose **$45.00**

Sweetmeat, Doric, ruby or ruby stain w/ruby floral.............**$55.00**

Tidbit tray, Crystal Velvet, center handle, 10½" dia.............**$40.00**

Trinket box, green or yellow mist w/daisy decal, egg shape, w/ lid..**$25.00**

Trinket box, Victorian, ruby or ruby stain w/Ruby Floral **$45.00**

Tumbler, any mist color w/daisy decal, plain, flat................**$65.00**

Tumbler, iced tea; milk glass w/Pastel Fruit, 12-oz, 6" **$35.00**

Vase, bud; any color w/Beaded Bouquet, crimped top, 6"....**$45.00**

Vase, bud; dark blue or green mist w/daisy decal, round foot, height varies..**$30.00**

Vase, Colonial, milk glass w/Beaded Bouquet, footed, lg ...**$350.00**

Vase, Mary Gregory, blue, ruffled top, flat bottom, (1,000 made)..**$95.00**

Vase, swung; milk glass w/Pastel Fruit, footed, slim, 14"......**$45.00**

Wedding bowl, milk glass w/Roses & Bows, w/lid, 8" **$80.00**

Tableware

Old Quilt, punch set, milk glass: bowl, cupped rim, $600.00; cup, $17.50; ladle, $75.00.

American Hobnail, basket, lilac opalescent, crimped & ruffled, 9½" W...**$100.00**

American Hobnail, bowl, milk glass, cupped, 8"..................**$40.00**

American Hobnail, compote, milk glass, footed, flared, 4x8" . **$20.00**

American Hobnail, compote, mint; Candlelight, crimped, 7½" **$40.00**

American Hobnail, cordial, crystal, 3⅜" **$22.50**

American Hobnail, egg cup, double; crystal **$12.50**

American Hobnail, goblet, water; Brandywine Blue, 8-oz **$30.00**

American Hobnail, salt & pepper shakers, milk glass, pr...... **$20.00**

American Hobnail, sherbet, milk glass or crystal, low foot... **$10.00**

American Hobnail, tumbler, iced tea; lilac, low foot, 11-oz, 6¼" **$40.00**

American Hobnail, tumbler, water; low foot, 7½-oz, 4¾".... **$15.00**

Asburton, goblet, claret/juice; any color, footed, 5⅜" **$12.50**

Ashburton, pitcher, any color, footed, lg **$60.00**

Beaded Edge, bowl, fruit; milk glass w/any child's decal, 5". **$50.00**

Beaded Edge, platter, milk glass w/fruit decal, oval, handles, 11¾" **$85.00**

Beaded Edge, salt & pepper shakers, milk glass w/red rim, pr... **$30.00**

Beaded Grape, ashtray, milk glass **$18.50**

Beaded Grape, candlesticks, Golden Sunset, 4", pr **$50.00**

Beaded Grape, cigarette box, crystal w/ruby stain **$65.00**

Beaded Grape, cup, milk glass **$20.00**

Beaded Grape, plate, dinner; milk glass, 10½" **$55.00**

Beaded Grape, plate, Golden Sunset, sq, 12½" **$45.00**

Beaded Grape, vase, milk glass, crimped rim, footed, 6" **$27.50**

Cherry, candlesticks, milk glass, 4", pr **$65.00**

Cherry, sugar bowl, milk glass, 3¾" **$20.00**

Colonial, goblet, water; Bermuda Blue or Laurel Green, footed... **$17.50**

Colonial, sherbet, brown or crystal **$7.50**

Colonial, tumbler, crystal, flat, 8-zo, 4" **$12.50**

Colonial, vase, green or light blue mist, footed, 12".............. **$25.00**

Della Robbia, basket, crystal w/any stain, oval, 12" **$250.00**

Della Robbia, basket, crystal w/any stain, 9"............... **$150.00**

Della Robbia, bowl, crystal w/any stain, 4½"................. **$27.50**

Della Robbia, compote, mint; crystal, footed, 6½" **$17.50**

Della Robbia, cup & saucer, crystal w/any stain................ **$25.00**

Della Robbia, finger bowl, crystal w/any stain, w/6" underplate .. **$40.00**

Della Robbia, goblet, water; crystal, 8-oz, 6" **$22.00**

Della Robbia, plate, dinner; crystal w/any stain, 10½".......**$150.00**

Della Robbia, sherbet, crystal w/any stain, low foot **$22.50**

English Hobnail, ashtray, crystal or milk glass, low hat form..... **$15.00**

English Hobnail, basket, cobalt, 9" **$100.00**

English Hobnail, bowl, cream soup; milk glass, handles, 5".**$17.50**

English Hobnail, bowl, crystal, rolled edge, 10¾"............. **$35.00**

English Hobnail, bowl, crystal or milk glass, oval, crimped edges, 11½x10" **$25.00**

English Hobnail, bowl, loving cup, crystal or milk glass, handles, hexagonal foot, 8" **$25.00**

English Hobnail, candlesticks, crystal or milk glass, 3½", pr .**$15.00**

English Hobnail, candy dish, crystal or milk glass, conical, w/lid, ½-lb **$20.00**

English Hobnail, coaster, crystal, 3" **$17.50**

English Hobnail, coaster, green or pink, 3" **$25.00**

English Hobnail, creamer, milk glass, hexagonal foot, 4½" .. **$10.00**

English Hobnail, cruet, milk glass, handle, 2-oz, 5" **$22.00**

English Hobnail, goblet, cocktail; milk glass, 3-oz, 4½" **$15.00**

English Hobnail, nut cup, amber, 4" **$15.00**

English Hobnail, rose bowl, crystal, crimped rim, 6" **$15.00**

English Hobnail, salt & pepper shakers, crystal, footed, pr .. **$25.00**

English Hobnail, sherbet, milk glass, footed........................ **$12.50**

English Hobnail, tumbler, iced tea; crystal w/black trim, 12½-oz, 6¼" **$25.00**

English Hobnail, tumbler, water; crystal, 9-oz, 6" **$15.00**

Lotus, candlesticks, Flame, ruffled, 3", pr **$50.00**

Lotus, compote, milk glass, footed, lipped, 5½" **$22.50**

Lotus, plate, mayonnaise; crystal w/ruby stain, 7" **$12.50**

Old Quilt, ashtray, milk glass, sq, 6½"........................ **$15.00**

Old Quilt, butter dish, milk glass, oblong, 1-lb **$30.00**

Old Quilt, candlesticks, milk glass, 4", pr **$25.00**

Old Quilt, cup, milk glass, flared **$20.00**

Old Quilt, goblet, water; Golden Sunset, footed, 8-oz........ **$15.00**

Old Quilt, plate, salad; milk glass, 8½" **$35.00**

Old Quilt, sugar bowl/candy jar, crystal or pink, w/lid, 6½" ..**$22.50**

Old Quilt, tumbler, juice; milk glass, flat, 5-oz **$27.50**

Old Quilt, tumbler, water; milk glass, flat, 9-oz **$12.50**

Old Quilt, vase, milk glass, bell shaped, footed, 9" ea........ **$75.00**

Paneled Grape, bowl, milk glass, shallow, 2x9" **$45.00**

Paneled Grape, canape set (3-pc), milk glass, 12½" dia tray, fruit cocktail & ladle..**$135.00**

Paneled Grape, candlesticks, milk glass, skirted, 4", pr........**$25.00**

Paneled Grape, chocolate box, milk glass, 6½" dia..............**$50.00**

Paneled Grape, compote, milk glass, ruffled edge, lipped, footed, 6"..**$45.00**

Paneled grape, creamer, Brandywine Blue or Laurel Green, footed, individual..**$17.50**

Paneled Grape, goblet, water; Brandywine Blue or Laurel Green, footed, 8-oz, 5⅞" **$25.00**

Paneled Grape, goblet, water; crystal or milk glass, footed, 8-oz, 5⅞"..**$17.50**

Paneled Grape, nut basket, milk glass, crimped edge, 5½" (reproduced)..**$35.00**

Paneled Grape, pitcher, crystal or milk glass, footed, 1-qt...**$40.00**

Paneled Grape, planter, milk glass w/22k gold trim, sq, footed, 4½"..**$40.00**

Paneled Grape, salt & pepper shakers, milk glass, footed, chrome lids, 4½", pr..**$20.00**

Paneled Grape, sauceboat w/oval underliner, milk glass, 2-pc.**$60.00**

Paneled Grape, scent bottle, milk glass, w/stopper, 5-oz.......**$75.00**

Paneled Grape, sugar bowl, milk glass, footed, tumbler-like.**$15.00**

Paneled Grape, sugar bowl, milk glass or crystal, footed, individual..**$12.50**

Princess Feather, Golden Sunset, water goblet, $15.00; sherbet, $12.50.

Thousand Eye, bowl, mayonnaise; crystal, footed, 4x5".......**$20.00**

Thousand Eye, candlesticks, crystal, amber, Golden Sunset, Laurel Green or brown, pr **$30.00**

Thousand Eye, candlesticks, purple marble, pr **$70.00**

Thousand Eye, decanter, crystal w/stain, w/stopper **$175.00**

Thousand Eye, plate, dinner; crystal, 10" **$45.00**

Thousand Eye, salt & pepper shakers, crystal w/stain, footed, pr . **$50.00**

Thousand Eye, sherbet, crystal, low foot, 4½" (+) **$12.50**

Thousand Eye, sugar bowl, crystal, low **$20.00**

Thousand Eye, tumbler, crystal, flat, 6-oz, 3¼" **$25.00**

Thousand Eye, turtle ashtray, black **$20.00**

Thousand Eye, vase, crystal w/stain, flat, 5¾" **$40.00**

Thousand Eye, whiskey/child's tumbler, crystal, 1½-oz (+) .. **$12.50**

Wexford

Wexford is a diverse line of glassware that Anchor Hocking has made since 1967. At one time, it was quite extensive, and a few pieces remain in production yet today. It's very likely you'll see it at any flea market you visit, and it's common to see a piece now and then on your garage sale rounds. It's not only very attractive but serviceable — nothing fragile about this heavy-gauge glassware! Right now, it's not only plentiful but inexpensive, so if you like its looks, now's a good time to begin your collection. Gene and Cathy Florence list 77 pieces in their book *Anchor Hocking's Fire-King and More* and say others will no doubt be reported as collectors become more familiar with the market.

Relish plate, five-section, large, $10.00.

Ashtray, 5½" **$4.00**

Ashtray, 8" **$12.00**

Bowl, dessert; 2½x5", from $3 to **$5.00**

Bowl, fruit; footed, 10" **$14.00**

Bowl, fruit; pedestal foot, 7x8" **$9.00**

Bowl, serving; 14" **$20.00**

Bowl, trifle; plain top, 8x8½" **$35.00**

Butter dish, ¼-lb **$18.00**

Candleholders, bowl shape, 5" dia, pr **$30.00**

Canister **$15.00**

Cigar/cigarette stand **$35.00**

Creamer, 8-oz **$4.00**

Cup & saucer **$3.00**

Decanter, bun bottom, 14" **$12.00**

Goblet, water; 9½-oz **$3.00**

Ice bucket, w/tongs, from $25 to **$30.00**

Jam & jelly set, chrome lids, spoons & stand, from $18 to .. **$22.00**

Jar, storage; hexagonal, 7x7½", from $15 to **$18.00**

Jar, storage; 4-sided, 9" **$20.00**

Lazy Susan, 9 pc: 14" tray, 5¼" bowl, six 4x5¾" inserts on swivel rack **$30.00**

Mug, 15-oz, from $8 to **$12.00**

Pitcher, ewer form, 11½" **$55.00**

Pitcher, 64-oz, 9¾", from $15 to **$20.00**

Plate, dessert; 6" **$6.00**

Plate, dinner; 9½" **$16.00**

Plate, serving; round, 14", from $18 to **$20.00**

Plate, snack; indent, 9½" **$6.00**

Platter, serving; round, 12" **$9.00**

Punch bowl, 12 cups & plastic hooks, w/plastic ladle & 9¾" base **$85.00**

Salad fork & spoon, pr **$20.00**

Salt & pepper shakers, 8-oz, pr **$8.00**

Saucer, 6" **$1.00**

Sherbet, stemmed, 7¼-oz **$2.50**

Shot glass **$6.00**

Sugar bowl, 8-oz **$4.00**

Tidbit, 2-tier, sectioned bottom plate, from $35 to **$45.00**

Tidbit, 3 scalloped 6" dishes in fold-up chrome base **$40.00**

Tidbit, 3-tier, from $45 to **$55.00**

Tidbit, 9½" plate **$15.00**

Tray, relish; 8½" **$14.00**

Tray, relish; 11" **$5.00**

Tumbler, iced tea; 6", from $6 to **$8.00**

Tumbler, rocks; 9½-oz **$4.00**

Tumbler, water; 5½" **$4.00**

Tumbler, wine/juice; 6-oz **$4.00**

Vase, bud; 9" **$7.00**

Vase, footed, 10½" **$12.50**

Wheaton

The Wheaton Company of Millville, New Jersey, has produced several series of bottles and flasks which are very collectible today. One of the most popular features portraits of our country's presidents. There was also a series of 21 Christmas bottles produced from 1971 through 1991, and because fewer were produced during the last few years, the newer ones can be hard to find and often bring good prices. Apollo bottles, those that feature movie stars, ink bottles and bitters bottles are among the other interesting examples. Many colors of glass have been used, including iridescents.

Benjamin Franklin, decanter, aqua, 1970, 8¼x3x1¾" **$22.00**

EC Booz's, miniature bottle, door & 3 windows w/Whiskey on back, 3x1¼x⅞" **$20.00**

Fisch's Bitters, amethyst, 7¾" **$33.00**

Golfer, ashtray, brass, 2½x7¼" **$28.00**

John F Kennedy, blue, 1967, w/original box, 8" **$18.00**

Liberty Bell, blue, 8x4¾" **$32.00**

Old Doc's Cure, corn shape, blue, w/cork stopper **$15.00**

Paul Revere Midnight Ride, plate, green iridescent, 8" **$22.00**

Poison, coffin shape, amethyst, RIP on wreath w/embossed nails all around, 5" **$15.00**

Poison, Liberty Bell, amethyst, 1953, 7½x4¾" **$13.00**

Poison, skull shape, amethyst, 5½" **$50.00**

Schoolhouse, ink bottle, red, Tuckahoe School 1891, 2½" ... **$15.00**

Ship sailing on seas, paperweight, signed M, 3½x3½" **$91.00**

Straubmuller's Elixir, green, w/cork stopper, 8¾" **$12.00**

TC Wheaton Co Manufacturing Building, bank, blue, 6x5" . **$18.00**

Thomas Jefferson, bottle, green, ca 1970s, 3⅛" **$12.00**

Uncle Sam, bank, blue, 6x4" **$12.00**

Violin, green, 7½" **$13.00**

Dwight D. Eisenhower, 'Peace With Justice...' on back, amethyst carnival, $15.00.

Will-George

This is a California-based company that began operations in the 1930s. It was headed by two brothers, William and George Climes, both of whom had extensive training in pottery science. They're most famous today for their lovely figurines of animals and birds, though they produced many human figures as well. For more information on this company as well as many others, we recommend *The Collector's Encyclopedia of California Pottery* by Jack Chipman (Collector Books).

Bowl, red onion, green stem finial on lid, 4x4¾" **$30.00**

Candleholders, petal shape, green w/pink interior, 6½", pr .. **$125.00**

Candleholders, upright blade leaves w/1 curled down, turquoise w/pink interior, 6¼x4¼x2", pr **$155.00**

Cordial, rooster stem w/clear bowl, 5" **$40.00**

Covered dish, reddish pink onion shape w/green top, 4½x4½" .. **$25.00**

Cup & saucer, red onion, onion shape saucer, EX **$25.00**

Figurine, ballerina, braided auburn hair, holding skirt w/both hands, dress up in back, 9" **$230.00**

Figurine, dachshund, black w/brown belly, 6x10" **$30.00**

Figurine, eagle on rock, white & brown, 10" **$150.00**

Figurine, flamingo, head down, wings closed, 4¼" **$55.00**

Figurine, flamingo, head down, wings closed, 6½", from $80 to .. **$100.00**

Figurine, flamingo, head up, wings closed, 7½" **$85.00**

Figurine, flamingo, head up, wings closed, 9½" **$125.00**

Figurine, flamingo, wings up, 8" **$200.00**

Figurine, flamingo, wings up, 16" **$400.00**

Figurine, flamingo in stride/preening, wings wide open, round base, 10" **$200.00**

Figurine, lady in dress w/white apron, flowered hat, #106, 1956, 5" **$110.00**

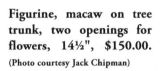

Figurine, macaw on tree trunk, two openings for flowers, 14½", $150.00.
(Photo courtesy Jack Chipman)

Figurine, monk, brown bisque, 4½" **$50.00**

Figurine, Pan w/forest creatures, 7" **$100.00**

Figurine, pheasant, 5¾x15" **$150.00**

Figurine, rooster, 4½" **$50.00**

Leaf dish w/parrot perched on side, 3¼x14½" **$90.00**

Martini glass, rooster stem, 5", set of 6 .... **$180.00**

Planter, Oriental man on knees w/sm basket held on left side of head & lg basket behind, 7½" **$35.00**

Planter, Swiss hiker, flower in left hand, basket (planter) on back, 16" **$50.00**

Plate, luncheon; red onion, 8½" **$15.00**

Plate, red onion, 10½" **$20.00**

Tray, flamingo pond, 14" L **$60.00**

Tumbler, chicken figure, multicolored, 4½" **$50.00**

Tumbler, rooster, formed by tall tail feathers, 4½" **$60.00**

Wilton Cake Pans

You've probably seen several of these as you make your garage sale rounds, but did you know that some are quite collectible? Especially good are the pans that depict cartoon, story book or movie characters. And, of course, condition is vital — examples with the insert, instructions, and accessory pieces bring the highest prices.

Wilton started mass merchandising the shaped pans in the early 1960s, and the company has been careful to keep up with trends in pop culture since then. Thus, many of the pans are of limited production which adds to the collectible factor. The company also makes all the items needed for cake decorating, including food dyes, frosting tips, and parchment triangles for making the frosting tubes. In addition, they train instructors in the Wilton Method and support the classes in the Wilton Method taught at craft stores such as Joann's and Michael's for people who want to learn to decorate. Most of the character and other shaped pans require simple decorating techniques which appeals to amateurs, while the simpler pans (for instance, the heart tiers or the grand piano) can call more more complex decorations, calling for those with professional level decorating skills.

Who knows if there will be a market for Teletubby pans 15 years from now? As with any collectible, future demand is impossible to predict. But since many Wilton pans can be found at garage sales and in thrift stores for $3.00 or less, right now it doesn't take a lot of money to start a collection.

Advisor: Cheryl Moody (See Directory, Wilton Cake Pans)

Alf, 1988, with insert and instructions, $20.00. (Photo courtesy whatacharacter.com)

Baby crawling, w/insert, EX	**$35.00**
Baseball glove w/ball, used, EX	**$42.50**
Batman emblem, #2105-9490, 1964, EX	**$40.00**
Bob the Builder, w/insert, 14x11½", M	**$30.00**
Boba Fett (Star Wars), w/insert, #502-1852, 1983, M, from $50 to	**$65.00**
C-3PO (Star Wars), w/insert, EX	**$55.00**
Care Bear, 2 pcs w/stand & clamps, w/instructions, 1984, EX	**$42.50**
Cookie Monster, w/insert & instructions, M	**$25.00**
Darth Vadar, w/insert, #2105-1278, 1980, EX, from $50 to	**$55.00**
Dumbo, #515-434, 1976, 6x9", EX, from $35 to	**$50.00**
Elephant, 1974, EX	**$40.00**
Elephant, 2-pc w/clamps, w/instructions, 1972, EX	**$52.50**

Football helmet, 1976, EX	**$45.00**
Frog, w/insert & instructions, #2105-2452, 1979, M, from $40 to	**$60.00**
Goofy, 1½x17x10", EX	**$45.00**
Grand piano, w/attachments, EX	**$50.00**
Grand Piano, 1970s, MIP	**$135.00**
Harley-Davidson, w/insert, 1999, EX	**$45.00**
Hexagon, 4-tier, 6", 9", 12" & 15" pans, EX	**$32.50**
Horse head in relief, 1975, EX	**$80.00**
Jiminy Cricket, 1976, EX	**$47.50**
Little Mermaid, w/insert, 15x11", NM, from $45 to	**$55.00**
My Little Pony, w/insert, #2105-2915, 1986, M, from $35 to	**$40.00**

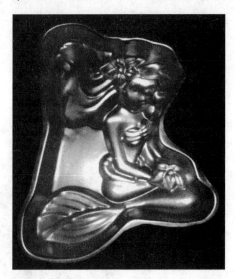

Little Mermaid, #2105-3400, pan only, EX, $45.00.

Little Mermaid, w/insert & lay-on, #2105-3400, EX	**$65.00**
Mystical Dragon, w/insert, #2105-1750, 1984, EX	**$70.00**
Pinocchio, 1976, EX	**$32.50**
Playboy Bunny, w/insert, EX	**$42.50**
Puffed heart, w/insert, #2105-172, 1999, EX, from $45 to	**$52.00**
R-2D2, 1980, EX, from $35 to	**$40.00**
Shell, w/insert, 1989, unused, 12½x11½", EX	**$37.50**
Snoopy on doghouse, w/insert & plastic face, EX	**$50.00**
Snoopy the Red Baron, #2105-1319, 1965, EX	**$42.50**
Super Heroes (Superman/Batman), w/insert, 1981, NM	**$20.00**
Super Mario Brothers, w/insert, Nintendo, 1989, M	**$40.00**
Thomas the Tank Engine, w/insert, M, from $30 to	**$40.00**
Winnie the Pooh, 2 pcs & core, made to stand up, w/instructions, EX	**$52.50**
Wizard, w/insert, 1984, 13x10", EX	**$50.00**
Wonder Woman, w/insert & plastic face, #502-7678, 1978, EX	**$65.00**

Winfield

The Winfield pottery first began operations in the late 1920s in Pasadena, California. In 1946 their entire line of artware and giftware items was licensed to the American Ceramic Products

Company, who continued to mark their semiporcelain dinnerware with the Winfield name. The original Winfield company changed their trademark to 'Gabriel.' Both companies closed during the early 1960s. For more information, see *The Collector's Encyclopedia of California Pottery* by Jack Chipman (Collector Books).

Bamboo, ashtray, 3¾" $3.00
Bamboo, bowl, 9" $18.00
Bamboo, charger, 11¼" $25.00
Bamboo, mug, 3½", from $15 to $20.00
Bamboo, mug, 5½" $35.00
Bamboo, pitcher, ice lip, 8" $65.00
Bamboo, plate, dinner $12.00
Bamboo, plate, salad; 7½" $7.50
Bamboo, teapot, cylindrical, 7¾" $52.50
Bird of Paradise, bowl, divided vegetable $16.00
Bird of Paradise, casserole, w/lid $30.00
Bird of Paradise, cup & saucer, from $9 to $11.00
Bird of Paradise, plate, dinner; 10", from $12 to $15.00
Bird of Paradise, platter, oval, 11¼" $30.00
Bird of Paradise, platter, rectangular, 11½", from $25 to $30.00
Bird of Paradise, tumbler, 3⅛" $22.50
Desert Dawn, bowl, divided vegetable; 13" L $22.00
Desert Dawn, casserole, w/lid, 1½-qt $25.00
Desert Dawn, coffeepot, 6½" $30.00
Desert Dawn, creamer & sugar bowl, w/lid $25.00
Desert Dawn, plate, dinner; 10" $28.00
Desert Dawn, platter, rectangular, 12x8" $22.00
Desert Dawn, sugar bowl, w/lid $25.00
Desert Dawn, tidbit, 2-tiered $37.50
Dragon Flower, butter dish $30.00
Dragon Flower, coffeepot $20.00
Dragon Flower, creamer $10.00
Dragon Flower, gravy boat, from $12 to $15.00
Dragon Flower, pitcher, water; 8", from $45 to $50.00
Dragon Flower, salt & pepper shakers, pr $25.00
Dragon Flower, teapot, ball form, 11" L, from $50 to $55.00
Passion Flower, ashtray, lg $15.00
Passion Flower, plate, dinner; 10" $16.00

Passion Flower, platter, 14", $35.00.

Pussy Willow, bowl, chowder $22.00
Pussy Willow, chip & dip set, 2-pc $25.00
Pussy Willow, cup & saucer $7.50
Pussy Willow, egg cup, double, 3½" $7.00
Pussy Willow, platter, rectangular, 15" $30.00
Pussy Willow, tray, vegetable; 3-compartment $32.50
Tiger Iris, plate, dinner $12.50
Wild Oats, plate, dinner; 10" $12.00
Wild Oats, platter, oval, 12" $30.00
Wild Oats, sugar bowl, w/lid $12.00
Wild Oats, tumbler, 14-oz $8.00

World's Fairs and Expositions

Souvenir items have been issued since the mid-1800s for every world's fair and exposition. Few fairgoers have left the grounds without purchasing at least one. Some of the older items were often manufactured right on the fairgrounds by glass or pottery companies who erected working kilns and furnaces just for the duration of the fair. Of course, the older items are usually more valuable, but even souvenirs from the past 50 years are worth hanging on to.

Advisor: Herbert Rolfes (See Directory, World's Fairs and Expositions)

Newsletter: *Fair News*
World's Fair Collectors' Society, Inc.
Michael R. Pender, Editor
P.O. Box 20806-3806
Sarasota, FL 34276; 941-923-2590, wfcs@aol.com; members.aol.com/Bbqprod/wfcs.html
Dues: $20 (6 issues) per year in USA; $25 in Canada; $30 for overseas members

Chicago, 1933

Ashtray, Chrysler Building, bronze, 3x3", M (EX box) $35.00
Ashtray, Fort Dearborn & Sky Ride, copper, 3½x3½" $30.00
Ashtray, orange w/black letters, personalized at Porcelain Enamel Institute Booth, 5½" dia $50.00
Badge, employee; #6167, Duck Co, Chicago, 2¼x2⅛", EX+... $80.00
Bank, log cabin, wood, slot in roof, 3x4¼x2¼", EX+ $70.00
Booklet, Arts & Crafts at the Swedish Chicago Expo, 93 pages, 8¼x5½", EX $40.00
Bottle opener, lady's head, pewter, 3½" $30.00
Bracelet, cuff style, skyline, zeppelin, logo, etc, silver-tone, ¾" W $25.00
Candy coin, Sear's Building, chocolate, 1½" dia $25.00
Cigarette case, turquoise w/Travel & Transportation Building, Hall of Science & Federal Building, 3¾x3⅜" $90.00
Cigarette lighter, camel shape, lighter in hump, silver-plated, Travel & Transportion Building, 2⅞x4", EX $75.00
Elongated cent, Ford Motor Company, 1½" L $20.00
Elongated cent, Goodyear Blimp, ¾x1½" $20.00
Letter opener, key shape, 1933 as teeth, 2-pc, EX $40.00
Medal, aerial view on front w/Travel & Transportation Building on back, 1¼" $35.00

Medallion, Jewish Day, bronze, 1¼" dia $55.00

Miniature, Fort Dearborn, metal, 2⅛x3½" $40.00

Nightlight, Transportation Building, plaster, 4x5" dia, EX+ . $225.00

Pamphlet, Chicago on Parade, photos of bread lines, people hunting food from garbage & sleeping in park, 10½x7", EX $10.00

Pillow sham, 9 building images, 18x16", EX $30.00

Pin-back button, 1933 Century of Progress, gold over blue, 1½" dia...$15.00

Poster, map; An Illustrated Map of Chicago..., Proud To Be Alive on border, Turzak & Chapman, 38x23", M (NM envelope) $375.00

Salad fork & spoon, Hall of Science, Bakelite, 8½", pr........$30.00

Tape measure, egg shape w/fly atop, logo in siver, M (NM box)... $190.00

Tapestry, Administration Building, 18x52", EX, from $50 to. $100.00

Tapestry, aerial view of the fair, 25x41", NM, $65.00.

Tea bag holder, bell shape w/8 perforated sides, saucer base, Japan, MIB $30.00

Ticket, Indiana State Fireman's Day, EX $35.00

Toy vehicle, Greyhound bus, Arcade, paint loss, VG, minimum value $100.00

Toy wagon, Radio Flyer, metal w/rubber wheels, 1¾x4x2", EX... $40.00

Treasure chest, wood-lined brass, sea horse decor on top, 2¾x3½x2¾", EX $35.00

Watch fob, baseball scorekeeper, leather strap, 1¾" dia $145.00

New York, 1939

Bank, Watch Your Savings Grow With Esso w/logo, 5¾x5¾" (4" thick), EX $45.00

Book, address; orange w/blue Trylon & Perisphere, ring-bound, 4x3", EX $22.50

Book, New York World's Fair in Pictures, Quality Art Novelty Co, 48 pages, 12x9½", EX $40.00

Book, Souvenir View Book of New York World's Fair, World of Tomorrow, Tichnor Bros, 68 pages, 10x6½", NM........$40.00

Booklet, Christian Science Building, 24 pages, 8x10", EX... $10.00

Booklet, Official World's Fair Pictorial Map, created by Tony Carg, 10 pages, 11x11", EX+ $40.00

Booklet, Sun Valley at World' Fair, 10-page pictorial, NM ..$40.00

Bookmark, Mr Peanut, Greetings From the World's Fair 1939, cardboard, 6½", EX...$25.00

Bookmark, Trylon & Perisphere, silk, American Silk Mfg Co, EX $65.00

Camera, New York World Fair on front, 127 film, Eastman Kodak, EX $125.00

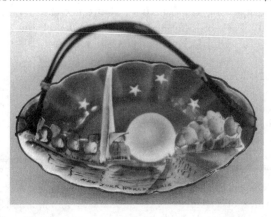

Candy dish, Japan, 7½", from $35.00 to $50.00. (Photo courtesy Carole Bess White)

Cane, wooden, carved Trylon & Perisphere on handle, sq, 34½" $35.00

Letter opener, cross shaped, New York World's Fair on blade, logo on ornate handle, metal, 4⅜x 1½" $35.00

Letter opener, sword shape, shield w/logo on blade near handle, stainless steel, Cutlass, 7" $20.00

License plate, black on yellow, VG $35.00

Money clip, metal w/enameled Trylon & Perisphere, ¾x2½" . $35.00

Paperweight, Trylon & Perisphere, metal, minor paint loss, 3¾", EX $55.00

Pennant, fair scene w/Souvenir of NY World's Fair 1939, white on blue, 18"L, EX...$20.00

Pennant, I Was There Closing Day, Oct 27, 1940, New York World's Fair, black on yellow, 3¼x9", EX.................................$15.00

Pin, man holds star w/flag behind, silver w/red enamel, Soviet Pavilion $40.00

Pin-back, airplane w/World's Fair USA Flight 1939 NX18973 on wings, brass...$25.00

Pin-back, hand holding coin w/logo, brass, 1½" $25.00

Pin-back, My World's Fair Guernsey's, Trylon & Perisphere in background, Whitehead & Hoag, 1¼" dia $28.00

Pin-back, Trylon & Perisphere, brass, 2x1½" $22.50

Planter, Trylon & Perisphere, white clay w/yellow gloss, Schweig & Sons, 5⅛" $100.00

Plate, George Washington, blue & white, Lamberton Scammel, 11"...$60.00

Postcard, aerial view of fair, Trylon & Perisphere pop-up inside, 6½x3¾" $50.00

Puzzle, jigsaw; fair map w/plastic Trylon & Perisphere in center, 8½x13", EXIB $60.00

Salt & pepper shakers, Trylon & Perisphere, marbleized plastic, 4", pr..$45.00

Spoon, Administration & Theme building on front w/Federal Building & Pylon on back, sterling silver, 5" $25.00

Swizzle stick, clear w/green striped & swirled design, Glass Pavilion, 5¾", M (in 6¼" glass tube) $35.00

Tape measure, tin lithograph of Trylon & Perisphere, USA, 48" L, 1½" dia, EX...$60.00

Thermometer, key shape, fair logo on front of handle w/eagle logo on back, 8½", EX $25.00
Thermometer, Trylon & Perisphere, Bakelite, NYWF in gold on base, EX $30.00
Toy train, cast iron w/tin roofs, greyhound jumping over Trylon & Perisphere, engine & 3 cars, Arcade, EX $350.00

Seattle, 1962

Ashtray, Mosaic tile w/Space Needle Seattle Washington in center, 5x5" $15.00
Badge, Century 21 Security Officer #161, eagle atop, NMOC .$150.00
Bolo tie, copper w/Space Needle & Century 21 logo, braided leather tie, EX $20.00
Book, Seattle World's Fair Century 21 Exposition Official Medals, contains 10 silver medals, complete $45.00
Coin, Official; Space Needle w/Century 21 logo on back, M. $20.00
Decanter, Jim Beam, Space Needle, 13½", EX $10.00
Glass set, frosted w/different buildings on ea, set of 8, 6½", EX $40.00
Horseshoe, silver-colored plastic w/rhinestones, Century 21 logo in center, EX $15.00
Lighter, table; Space Needle, bronze, 10½", EX $120.00
Money clip, MV Dominion Monarch, EX $15.00
Mug, coffee; embossed designs, Pacific Stoneware, EX $15.00
Pamphlet, Alweg Monorail, 10 pages, EX $10.00
Pin-back, Seattle World's Fair Construction Employee, EX.. $12.00

Plate, blue scenic vignettes on white, 10½", $12.00.

Plate, Seattle World's Fair 1962 w/Century 21 logo & caricature of fair scene, 10½" $15.00
Postcard, Seattle's World's Fair Gayway, unused $3.00
Scarf, white w/fair scene & Century 21 logos, rayon, 26x26", EX $20.00

Yona

Yona Lippin was a California ceramist who worked for Hedi Schoop in the early 1940s and later opened her own studio. Much of her work is similar to Schoop's. She signed her work with her first name. You'll also find items marked Yona that carry a 'Shafford, Made in Japan' label, suggesting a later affiliation with that importing company.

Cookie jar, circus clown on elephant, $400.00. (Photo courtesy Ermagene Westfall)

Creamer, Dutch girl forms handle, Tulip Tyme #8924Y, Shafford label $15.00
Figurine, angel reclining, Think No Evil on cloud supporting her, 1956, 4x5½", from $28 to $35.00
Figurine, clown w/sm umbrella & feet up in air, 5" $15.00
Figurine, Dutch girl, #29, 5" $14.00
Figurine, girl holding basket, #16, 8½" $45.00
Figurine, girl in strapless dress holds basket (w/opening), #43, 9" $60.00
Figurine, girl w/flowered dress holds basket (w/opening), #47, 7" $35.00
Figurine, Oriental girl in green stands w/basket (w/opening) on her head, 8¾" $35.00
Napkin holder, Country Club, chef's head atop $35.00
Ornament, angel w/golden wings, 4" $10.00
Salt & pepper shakers, chicken coop, #222, pr, NM $15.00
Salt & pepper shakers, Country Club, 5", pr $40.00
Salt & pepper shakers, Dutch boy & girl, #8976Y, Shafford label, pr $15.00
Straw holder, Country Club, 6½" $50.00
Sugar bowl, Dutch boy stands at side, w/lid, Tulip Tyme #8924Y, Shafford foil label $15.00
Vanity set, white w/black stripes, sq shapes, 4" ashtray, tumbler, powder box & 6" decanter, NM $30.00

Auction Houses

Many of the auction galleries we've listed here have appraisal services. Some, though not all, are free of charge. We suggest you contact them first by phone to discuss fees and requirements.

Aston Macek Auctions
2825 Country Club Rd.
Endwell, NY 13760-3349
607-756-1180
astonmacek@stny.rr.com
Specializing in and appraisers of Americana, folk art, other primitives, furniture, fine glassware and china

Bertoia Auctions
2141 DeMarco Dr.
Vineland, NJ 08360
856-692-1881; fax: 856-692-8697
www.bertoiaauctions.com
Online auctions: Bertoiaonline.com
Specializing in antique toys and collectibles

Buffalo Bay Auction Co.
825 Fox Run Trail
Edmond, OK 74034
405-285-8990
buffalobayauction@hotmail.com
www.buffalobayauction.com
Specializing in advertising, tins, and country store items

Cincinnati Art Galleries
225 E. Sixth St.
Cincinnati, OH 45202
513-381-2128; fax: 513-381-7527
www.cincinnatiartgalleries.com
Specializing in American art pottery, American and European fine paintings, watercolors

Craftsman Auctions
109 Main St.
Putnam, CT 06260
860-928-1966
jerry@craftsman-auctions.com
www.craftsman-auctions.com or
www.ragoarts.com
Color catalogs available

David Rago Auctions
Auction hall: 333 N. Main St.
Lambertville, NJ 08530
609-397-9374; fax: 609-397-9377
www.ragoarts.com
info@ragoarts.com

Gallery: 17 S Main St.
Lambertville, NJ 08530
Specializing in American art pottery and Arts & Crafts

Early Auction Co.
123 Main St.
Milford, OH 45150
513-831-4833; fax: 513-831-1441
www.earlyauctionco.com
info@earlyauctionco.com
Specializing in fine art glass, antique furniture and collectibles

Flying Deuce
14051 W. Chubbuck Rd.
Chubbuck ID 83202
208-237-2002; fax: 208-237-4544
www.flying2.com
flying2@ida.net
Specializing in vintage denim apparel; catalogs $10.00 for upcoming auctions; contact for details on consigning items

Garth's Auctions, Inc.
2690 Stratford Rd.
Box 369, Delaware, OH 43015
740-362-4771
www.garth's.com
info@garths.com

Jackson's International Auctioneers &
    Appraisers of Fine Art & Antiques
2229 Lincoln Street
Cedar Falls, IA 50613
319-277-2256; fax: 319-277-1252
jacksons@jacksonsauction.com
www.jacksonsauctions.com
Specializing in American and European art pottery and art glass, American and European paintings, decorative arts, toys and jewelry

James D. Julia Inc.
P.O. Box 830, Rt. 201
Skowhegan Rd.
Fairfield, ME 04937
207-453-7125; fax: 207-453-2502
www.juliaauctions.com
jjulia@juliaauctions.com

John Toomey Gallery
818 N. Blvd.
Oak Park, IL 60301-1302
708-838-5234; fax: 708-383-4828
info@johntoomeygallery.com
www.treadwaygallery.com
Specializing in furniture and decorative arts of the Arts & Crafts, Art Deco, and Modern Design movements; modern design expert: Richard Wright

Joy Luke Fine Art Brokers and Auctioneers
300 E. Grove St.
Bloomington, IL 61701-5290
309-828-5533; fax: 309-829-2266
robert@joyluke.com
www.joyluke.com

L.R. 'Les' Docks
Box 691035
San Antonio, TX 78269-1035
Providing occasional mail-order record auctions, rarely consigned (the only consignments considered are exceptionally scarce and unusual records)

Lloyd Ralston Gallery, Inc.
549 Howe Ave.
Shelton, CT 06484
203-924-5804; fax: 203-924-5834
www.lloydralstontoys.com
lrgallery@sbcglobal.net

Majolica Auctions
Strawser Auction Group
200 N. Main; P.O. Box 332
Wolcottville, IN 46795-0332
260-854-2859; fax: 260-854-3979
www.strawserauctions.com
info@strawserauctions.com
Issues colored catalog; also specializing in Fiestaware

Manion's International Auction House, Inc.
P.O. Box 12214
Kansas City, KS 66112
913-299-6692; fax: 913-299-6792
www.manions.com
collecting@manions.com

McMasters Harris Auction Company
P.O. Box 1755
5855 Glenn Highway
Cambridge, OH 43725-8768
740-432-7400; fax: 740-432-3191
800-842-3526
www.mcmastersharris.com
mark@mcmastersharris.com

Michael John Verlangieri
Calpots.com
PO Box 844,
Cambria, CA 93428
805-927-4428
michael1@calpots.com
www.calpots.com
Specializing in fine California pottery; cataloged auctions (video tapes available)

Monson & Baer, Annual Perfume Bottle
    Auction
Monsen, Randall; and Baer, Rod
Box 529
Vienna, VA 22183
703-938-2129; fax: 703-242-1357
Cataloged auctions of perfume bottles; will purchase, sell, and accept consignments; specializing in commercial, Czechoslovakian, Lalique, Baccarat, Victorian, crown top, factices, miniatures

Noel Barrett Antiques & Auctions
P.O. Box 300; 6183 Carversville Rd.
Carversville, PA 18913
215-297-5109; fax: 215-297-0457
www.noelbarrett.com
toys@noelbarrett.com

Perrault-Rago Gallery
333 N. Main St.
Lambertville, JN 08530
609-397-9374
www.ragoarts.com
Specializing in American art pottery, tiles, Arts & Crafts, Moderns, and Bucks County paintings

Richard Opfer Auctioneering, Inc.
1919 Greenspring Dr.
Timonium, MD 21093-4113
410-252-5035; fax: 410-252-5863
www.opferauction.com
info@opferauction.com

Skinner, Inc.
Auctioneers & Appraisers of Antiques and
    Fine Arts
The Heritage on the Garden
63 Park Plaza
Boston, MA 02116-3925
617-350-5400; fax: 617-350-5429
Second address: 357 Main St.
Bolton, MA 01740

978-779-6241; fax: 978-779-5144
www.skinnerinc.com

Smith & Jones, Inc.
12 Clark Lane
Sudbury, MA 01776
978-443-5517; fax: 978-443-8045
smithandjonesauctions.com
smithjnes@gis.net
Specializing in Dedham dinnerware, Buffalo china, and important American art pottery; full-color catalogs available

Treadway Gallery Inc.
2029 Madison Rd.
Cincinnati, OH 45208
513-321-6742; fax: 513-871-7722
www.treadwaygallery.com
info@treadwaygallery.com
Member: National Antique Dealers Association, American Art Pottery Association, International Society of Appraisers, and American Ceramic Arts Society

Vicki and Bruce Waasdorp
P.O. Box 434
10931 Main St.
Clarence, NY 14031
716-759-2361
www.antiques-stoneware.com
Specializing in decorated stoneware

Clubs and Newsletters

There are hundreds of clubs and newsletters mentioned throughout this book in their respective categories. There are many more available to collectors today; some are generalized and cover the entire realm of antiques and collectibles, while others are devoted to a specific interest such as toys, coin-operated machines, character collectibles, or railroadiana. We've listed several below. You can obtain a copy of most newsletters simply by requesting one. If you'd like to try placing a 'for-sale' ad or a mail bid in one of them, see the introduction for suggestions on how your ad should be composed.

Antique Advertising Association of America
   (AAAA)
P.O. Box 76
Petersburg, IL 62675
Also *Past Times* newsletter for collectors of popular and antique advertising. Subscription: $35 per year

Antique and Collectors Reproduction News
Mark Chervenka, Editor
PO Box 12130
Des Moines, IA 50312-9403
800-227-5531 (subscriptions only)
www.repronews.com; acrn@repronews.com
Monthly newsletter showing differences between old originals and new reproductions. Subscription: $32 per year

The Antique Trader Weekly
P.O. Box 1050 CB
Dubuque, IA 52003-1050
www.collect.com
collect@krause.com
Subscription: $38 (52 issues) per year

Autumn Leaf Newsletter
Bill Swanson, President
807 Roaring Springs Dr.
Allen, TX 75002-2112
972-727-5527
bescome@nalcc.org
www:nalcc.org

Butter Pat Patter Association
The Patter newsletter
265 Eagle Bend Drive
Bigfork, MT 59911-6235
Subscription to newsletter: $22 (payable to Mary Dessoie at above address), includes a Royal Doulton butter pat; Sample copies also available by sending $4 and LLSASE (60¢)

The Carnival Pump
International Carnival Glass Assoc., Inc.
Lee Markley, Secretary
Box 306
Mentone, IN 46359

CAS Collectors (Ceramic Arts Studio)
206 Grove Street
Rockton, IL 61072
Club website: www.cascollectors.com
Ceramic Arts Studio history website: www.ceramicartsstudio.com
Publishes quarterly newsletter; hosts annual convention. Family membership: $25 per year; information about the club and its activities a well as a complete illustrated CAS history is included in the book *Ceramic Arts Studio: The Legacy of Betty Harrington,* by Donald-Brian Johnson, Timothy J. Holthaus, and James E. Petzold (Schiffer Publishing 2003)

Cast Iron Collector's Club
Contact Dan Murphy Auctions
morphyauctions.com or 717-335-3455

Central Florida Insulator Collectors
3557 Nicklaus Dr.
Titusville, FL 32780-5356
407-267-9170
bluebellwt@aol.com
Dues $10 per year for single or family membership, includes *Newsnotes* newsletter, free advertising for members; send SASE for information

Chintz Connection newsletter
P.O. Box 222
Riverdale, MD 20738
Dedicated to helping collectors share information and find matchings; subscription four issues per year for $25

Coin-op online newsletter
Ken Durham, Publisher
909 26th St., NW; Suite 502
Washington, DC 20037
www.GameRoomAntiques.com
Free e-mail newsletter available; send your e-mail address to durham@GameRoomAntiques.com

Compact Collectors Club
Roselyn Gerson
PO Box 40, Lynbrook, NY 11563
516-593-8746; fax 516-593-0610
compactlady@aol.com
Publishes *Powder Puff* Newsletter, which contains articles covering all aspects of compact collecting, restoration, vintage ads, patents, history, and articles by members and prominent guest writers; Seeker and sellers column offered free to members

*Dorothy Kamm's Porcelain Collector's
   Companion*
P.O. Box 7460
Port St. Lucie, FL 34985-7460
561-465-4008; fax: 561-460-9050
dorothy.kamm@usa.net
Published bimonthly, Subscription: $30 per year

Early Typewriter Collectors Association
ETCetera Newsletter
Chuck Dilts/Rich Cincotta
PO Box 286
Southboro, MA 01772
etcetera@writeme.com
http://typewriter.rydia.net/etcetera.htm
Subscription: $25 in USA (4 issues)

Florence Ceramics Collectors Society
FlorenceCeramics@aol.com

International Cat Collector's Club
Contact: Peggy Way
CatCollectors@earthlink.net
www.CatCollectors.com

International Golliwog Collector Club
Beth Savino
The Toy Store/Collector's Gallery
3301 W. Central Ave.
Toledo, OH 43606
1-800-862-TOYS; fax: 419-531-2730
www.toystorenet.com
info@toystorenet.com

International Ivory Society
11109 Nicholas Dr.
Wheaton, MD 20902
301-649-4002
Membership is free

International Perfume Bottle Association
(IPBA)
Randall Monsen
P.O. 529
Vienna, VA 22183
Membership: $45 USA or $50 Canada

The Museum of the American Cocktail
Stephen Visakay, Founding Member
visakay@optonLine.net
www.MuseumOfTheAmericanCocktail.org

National Bicycle History Archive
Box 28242
Santa Ana, CA 92799
714-682-1949
Oldbicycle@aol.com
www.members.aol.com/oldbicycle
Resource for vintage and classic cycles from
1920 to 1970. Collection of over 1,000 classic bicycles. Over 30,000 original catalogs,
books, photos. Also over 100 original old
bicycle films 1930s – 1970s. Restoration
and purchase

Newspaper Collectors Society of America
517-887-1255
info@historybuff.com
www.historybuff.com
Publishes booklet with current values and
pertinent information

Nutcracker Collectors' Club
Susan Otto, Editor
11204 Fox Run Dr.
Chesterland, OH 44026
$15.00 annual dues, quarterly newsletters
sent to members, free classifieds

The Occupied Japan Club
c/o Florence Archambault
29 Freeborn St.
Newport, RI 02840-1821
florence@aiconnect.com
Publishes *Upside Down world of an O.J. Collector*, a bimonthly newsletter; information
requires SASE

Old Stuff
Donna and Ron Miller, Publishers
P.O. Box 1084
McMinnville, OR 97128
www.oldstuffnews.com
Published 6 times annually; Copies by mail:
$3.50 each; Annual subscription: $20

Pacific N. W. Fenton Association
P.O. Box 881
Tillamook, OR 97141
503-842-4815
Four newsletters a year, plus exclusive
Fenton glass animal; promotes spring & fall
shows and a convention in June, Membership: $35 per year

Paperweight Collectors Association, Inc.
P.O. Box 4153
Emerald Isle, NC 28594
info@paperweight.org

Peanut Pals
Judith Walthall Founder
P.O. Box 4465,
Huntsville, AL 35815
205-881-9198
Dues: $20 per year. For membership write:
246 Old Line Ave.
Laurel, MD 20724

Petroleum Collectibles Monthly
P.O. Box 556
LaGrange, OH 44050-0556
440-355-6608
Subscription: $35.95 per year in US

Restaurant China Online Forum:
http://groups.yahoo.com/group/Restaurant_China/

Southern Oregon Antiques and Collectibles
Club
P.O. Box 508
Talent, OR 97540
Meets 1st Wednesday of the month; Promotes 2 shows a year in Medford, OR
www.soacc.com
contact@soacc.com

Statue of Liberty Collectors' Club
Iris November
P.O. Box 535
Chautauqua, NY 14722
For membership information:
membership@statueoflibertyclub.com

Shine Express (Bimonthly) and clubs
Sunshine Chapter
Bill and Pat Poe, founders and current
officers
220 Dominica Circle, E.,
Niceville, FL 32578-4085
850-897-4163
BPoe220@cox.net

Thimble Collectors International
Jina Samulka, membership chairperson
6451 Leonard Ave.
Cocoa, FL 32927-4253
Membership: $25 U.S. ($30 international)
www.thimblecollectors.com

Three Rivers Depression Era Glass Society
Meetings held 1st Monday of each month at
Hoss's Restaurant, Canonsburg, PA
For more information call:
D. Hennen
3725 Sylvan Rd.
Bethel Park, PA 15102
412-835-1903
leasure@pulsenet.com
412-831-2702

Tiffin Glass Collectors
P.O. Box 554
Tiffin, OH 44883
Meetings at Seneca Cty. Museum on 2nd
Tuesday of each month
www.tiffinglass.org

The Wheelmen
Magazine: *Wheelmen Magazine*
63 Stonebridge Road
Allen Park, NJ 07042-1631
609-587-6487
membership@thewheelmen.org
www.thewheelmen.org
A club with about 800 members dedicated
to the enjoyment and preservation of our
bicycle heritage

World Airline Historical Society
Box 101
Covington, LA 70434
Quarterly magazine *Captain's Log,* Dues:
$25 annually

Directory of Contributors and Special Interests

In this section of the book we have listed dealers/collectors who specialize in many of the fields this price guide covers. Many of them have sent information, photographs, or advised us concerning current values and trends. This is a courtesy listing, and they are under no obligation to field questions from our readers, though some may be willing to do so. If you do write to any of them, don't expect a response unless you include an SASE (stamped self-addressed envelope) with your letter. If you have items to offer them for sale or are seeking information, describe the piece in question thoroughly and mention any marks. You can sometimes do a pencil rubbing to duplicate the mark exactly. Photographs are still worth a 'thousand words,' and photocopies are especially good for paper goods, patterned dinnerware, or even smaller three-dimensional items.

If you write to them, include your phone number as well as your e-mail address, since many people would rather respond with a call or an e-mail than a letter. If you're trying to reach someone by phone, always stop to consider the local time on the other end of your call.

With the exception of the Advertising, Books, Bottles, Character Collectibles, and Toys sections which we've alphabetized by character or type, buyers are listed alphabetically under bold topics. A line in italics indicates only the specialized interests of the particular buyer whose name immediately follows it. Recommended reference guides not available from Collector Books may be purchased directly from the authors whose addresses are given in this section.

Abingdon Pottery
Louise Dumont
318 Palo Verde Dr.
Leesburg, FL 34748-8811 (Summer: 103
Arnolds Neck Dr., Warwick, RI 02886);
LouiseD452@aol.com

Advertising *Aunt Jemima*
Judy Posner
P.O. Box 2194 SC
Englewood, FL 34295
www.judyposner.com
judyandjef@yahoo.com

Big Boy
Steve Soelberg
29126 Laro Dr.
Agoura Hills, CA 91301
818-889-9909

Jewel Tea products and tins
Bill and Judy Vroman
739 Eastern Ave.
Fostoria, OH 44830
419-435-5443

Mr. Peanut
Judith and Robert Walthall
P.O. Box 4465
Huntsville, AL 35815
205-881-9198
Also Old Crow memorabilia

Airline Memorabilia
Richard Wallin
P.O. Box 22
Rochester, IL 62563
217-498-9279
RRWALLIN@aol.com

Akro Agate
Author of book
Claudia and Roger Hardy
West End Antiques
10 Bailey St.
Clarksburg, WV 26301
304-624-7600 (days) or 304-624-4523
(evenings)
Closed Sundays & Mondays; Specializing
in furniture, glass, and Akro Authors of *The
Complete Line of Akro Agate Co.;* Specializing
in Akro Agate

Aluminum
Author of book
Dannie Woodard
P.O. Box 1346
Weatherford, TX 76086

Angels, Birthday
Author of books
Jim and Kaye Whitaker
Eclectic Antiques
PO Box 475, Dept GS
Lynnwood, WA 98046

Aprons
Darrell Thomas
PO Box 418
New London, WI 54961
woodenclockworks@msn.com

Architectural Antiques and Salvage
Second Chance
A 501 (c) (3) non-profit organization
1645 Warner St.
Baltimore, MD 21230
second-chance-inc@juno.com
Deconstruction, adaptive re-use, salvage, job
training, craftsmanship

Ashtrays
Author of book
Nancy Wanvig
Nancy's Collectibles
ashtrays@execpc.com

Tire ashtrays
Author of book ($12.95 postpaid)
Jeff McVey
1810 W State St., #427
Boise, ID 83702

Automobilia
Leonard Needham
P.O. Box 689
Bethel Island, CA 94511
925-684-9674
screensider@sbcgolbal.net

Autumn Leaf
Gwynneth Harrison
11566 River Heights Dr.
Riverside, CA 92505

Avon Collectibles
Author of book
Bud Hastin
P.O. Box 11530
Ft. Lauderdale, FL 33339

Banks
Modern mechanical banks
Dan Iannotti
212 W Hickory Grove Rd.
Bloomfield Hills, MI 48302-1127S
248-335-5042
modernbanks@prodigy.net

Barware
Especially cocktail shakers
Arlene Lederman Antiques
150 Main St.
Nyack, NY 10960

Specializing in vintage cocktail shakers
Author of book
Stephen Visakay
visakay@optonLine.net
Founding member of The Museum of the
American Cocktail
www.MuseumOfTheAmericanCocktail.org

Beanie Babies
Amy Sullivan
amysullivan@collectorbooks.com

Black Americana
Buy, sell, and trade
Judy Posner
P.O. Box 2194 SC
Englewood, FL 43295
www.judyposner.com
judyandjef@yahoo.com
Also toys, Disney, salt and pepper shakers,
general line

Black Cats
Author of book Peggy's Mews on Black Cats
Peggy Way
Parker, CO
Advanced cat collector specialing in black
cats from the 1950s
www.catcollectors.com
www.catladyauctions.com
To order book e-mail Glenna Moore at
mooremews@hawaiiantel.net
For identification or evaluation, e-mail photo
and request to Peggy: CatCollectors@earth-
link.net

Black Glass
Author of book
Marlena Toohey
703 S Pratt Pky.
Longmont, CO 80501
303-678-9726

Bookends
Author of book
Louis Kuritzky
4510 NW 17th Pl.
Gainesville, FL 32605
352-377-3193

Books
Big Little Books
Ron and Donna Donnelly
6302 Championship Dr.
Tuscaloosa, AL 35405

Bottle Openers
Charlie Reynolds
2836 Monroe St.
Falls Church, VA 22042
703-533-1322
reynoldstoys@erols.com

Boyd's Bears
Christine Cregar
Bearly Believable
218 Elizabeth Drive
Stephens City, VA 22655
Bearlybelievable@msn.com
www.wagglepop.com/stores/bearlybelievablegifts

Brastoff, Sascha
Lonnie Wells
Things from the Past
Doe Run, MO 63637
www.tias.com/stores/thingsfromthepast/
thingsfromthepast@tias.com

British Royal Commemoratives
Author of book, catalogs issued monthly, $5 each
Audrey Zeder
1320 SW 10th St.
North Bend, WA 98045
Specializing in British Royalty Commemo-
ratives from Queen Victoria's reign through
current royalty events

Brush-McCoy Pottery
Authors of book
Steve and Martha Sanford
230 Harrison Ave.
Campbell, CA 95008
408-978-8408

Bubble Bath Containers
Matt and Lisa Adams
8155 Brooks Drive
Jacksonville, FL 32244
904-772-6911
beatles@bellsouth.net
www.stores.ebay.com/tatonkatoys

California Perfume Company
Co-author of *Collector's Guide to Tammy, the*
Ideal Teen
Cindy Sabulis
P.O. Box 642
Shelton, CT 06484
toys4two@snet.net
www.dollsntoys.com

California Pottery
Specializing in California pottery and
porcelain; Orientalia
Marty Webster
6943 Suncrest Drive
Saline, MI 48176
313-944-1188

Editor of newsletter: The California Pottery Trader
Michael John Verlangieri Gallery
Calpots.com
P.O. Box 844
W Cambria, CA 93428-0844
805-927-4428
www.calpots.com
Specializing in fine California pottery; cata-
loged auctions (video tapes available)

Camark
Tony Freyaldenhoven
2200 Ada Ave., Ste. 305
Conway, AR 72034
501-730-3027 or 501-932-0352
tonyfrey@conwaycorp.net

Cameras
Classic, collectible, and usable
C.E. Cataldo
Gene's Cameras
4726 Panorama Dr. SE
Huntsville, Alabama 35801
256-536-6893
genecams@aol.com

Wooden, detective, and stereo
John A. Hess
P.O. Box 3062
Andover, MA 01810
Also old brass lenses

Candy Containers
Glass
Jeff Bradfield
90 Main St.
Dayton, VA 22821
540-879-9961
Also advertising, cast-iron and tin toys,
postcards, and Coca-Cola

Cape Cod by Avon
Debbie and Randy Coe
P.O. Box 173
Hillsboro, OR 97123
Also Elegant and Depression glass, art
pottery, Fenton, Golden Foliage by Libbey
Glass Company, and Liberty Blue dinner-
ware

Cast Iron
Door knockers, sprinklers, figural paperweights,
and marked cookware
Craig Dinner
P.O. Box 131
Warwick NY 10990
ferrouswheel123@yahoo.com

Cat Collectibles
Peggy Way
International Cat Collectors Club
CatCollectors@earthlink.net
www.CatCollectors.com

Ceramic Arts Studio
Donald-Brian Johnson
Author of numerous Schiffer Publishing Ltd.
books on collectibles
3329 South 56th Street, #611
Omaha, NE 68106
donaldbrian@webtv.net
Books include *Ceramic Arts Studio: The Leg-*
acy of Betty Harrington (in association with
Timothy J. Holthaus and James E. Petzold),
and (with co-author Leslie Piña), *Higgins:*
Adventures in Glass; Higgins: Poetry in Glass;
Moss Lamps: Lighting the '50s; Specs Appeal:
Extravagant 1950s and 1960s Eyewear; Whit-
ing & Davis Purses: The Perfect Mesh; Popular
Purses: It's in the Bag; and a four-volume
series on the chase Brass & Copper Co.

Character and Personality Collectibles
Any and all
Terri Ivers
Terri's Toys
114 Whitworth Ave.
Ponca City, OK 74601
580-762-8697 or 580-762-5174
toylady@cableone.net

Batman, Gumby, and Marilyn Monroe
Colleen Garmon Barnes
114 E Locust
Chatham, IL 62629

Beatles
Bojo
Bob Gottuso
P.O. Box 1403
Cranberry Twp., PA 16066-0403
phone or fax: 724-776-0621
bojo@zbzoom.net
www.bojoon.line.com
We do rock n' roll pricing for all of Schroeder's guides; specializing in Beatles, KISS,
Monkees, and Elvis original licensed memorabilia. Beatles sale catalogs are available 4
times a year at $3 a copy.

Disney, Western heroes, Gone With the Wind,
character watches ca 1930s to mid-1950s,
premiums and games
Ron and Donna Donnelly
6302 Championship Dr.
Tuscaloosa, AL 35405

Disney
Buy, sell and trade
Judy Posner
P.O. Box 2194 SC
Englewood, FL 34295
judyandjef@yahoo.com
www.judyposner.com

Elvis Presley
Lee Garmon
1529 Whittier St.
Springfield, IL 62704

Character and Promotional Drinking
Glasses
Authors of book; editors of Collector Glass
News
Mark Chase and Michael Kelly
P.O. Box 308
Slippery Rock, PA 16057
412-946-2838; fax: 724-946-9012
cgn@glassnews.com; www.glassnews.com

Character Clocks and Watches
Bill Campbell
1221 Littlebrook Ln.
Birmingham, AL 35235
205-853-8227; fax: 405-658-6986
acamp10720@aol.com
Also character collectibles, advertising
premiums

Character Nodders
Matt and Lisa Adams
8155 Brooks Dr.
Jacksonville, FL 32244

904-772-6911
beatles@bellsouth.net

Chintz
Mary Jane Hastings
310 West 1st South
Mt. Olive, IL 62069
phone or fax: 217-999-1222

Author of book
Joan Welsh
7015 Partridge Pl.
Hyattsville, MD 20782
301-779-6181

Christmas Collectibles
Especially from before 1920 and decorations
made in Germany
J.W. 'Bill' and Treva Courter
3935 Kelley Rd.
Kevil, KY 42053
270-488-2116

Clocks
All types
Bruce A. Austin
1 Hardwood Hill Rd.
Pittsford, NY 14534
716-387-9820
baagll@rit.edu

Clothes Sprinkler Bottles
Larry Pogue
L&J Antiques & Collectibles
8142 Ivan Court
Terrell, TX 75161
972-551-0221
LandJAntiques@netportusa.com
www.LandJAntiques.com
Also antique and estate jewelry, head vases,
egg timers, and string holders

Clothing and Accessories
Ken Weber
1119 Seminole Trail
Carrollton, TX 75007
cecilimose@aol.com
www.vintagemartini.com

Flying Deuce
1224 Yellowstone
Pocatello, ID 83201
208-237-2002; fax: 208-237-4544
flying2@nicoh.com

Coca-Cola

Also Pepsi-Cola and other brands of soda

Craig Stifter
218 S. Adams St.
Hinsdale, IL 60251
cstifter@collectica.com

Compacts

Unusual shapes, also vanities and accessories
Author of books

Roselyn Gerson
P.O. Box 40
Lynbrook, NY 11563
516-593-8746

Cookie Jars

Joe Devine
1411 3rd St.
Council Bluffs, IA 51503
712-328-7305

Buy, sell and trade

Judy Posner
P.O. Box 2194 SC
Englewood, FL 34295
judyandjef@yahoo.com
www.judyposner.com

Corkscrews

Author of books

Donald Bull
P.O. Box 596
Wirtz, VA 24184
540-721-1128
corkscrew@bullworks.net
www.corkscrewmuseum.com

Cracker Jack Items

Harriet Joyce
415 Soft Shadow Lane
DeBarry, FL 32713-2343

Author of books

Larry White
108 Central St.
Rowley, MA 01969-1317
978-948-8187
larrydw@erols.com

Crackle Glass

Authors of book

Stan and Arlene Weitman
101 Cypress St.
Massapequa Park, NY 11758
516-799-2619
www.crackleglass.com

scrackled@earthlink.net
Also specializing in Overshot

Cuff Links

Just Cuff Links
Eugene R. Klompus
P.O. Box 5970
Vernon Hills, IL 60061
phone: 847-816-0035; fax: 847-816-7466
genek@cufflinksrus.com
www.justcufflinks.com
Also related items

Cups and Saucers

Authors of books

Jim and Susan Harran
208 Hemlock Dr.
Neptune, NJ 07753
www.tias.com/stores/amit

Decanters

Roy Willis
Heartland of Kentucky Decanters and
    Steins
P.O. Box 428
Lebanon Jct., KY 40150
heartlandky@ka.net.
www.decantersandsteins.com
Huge selection of limited edition decanters
and beer steins — open showroom; include
large SASE (2 stamps) with correspondence;
fee for appraisals

deLee

Authors of book

Joanne and Ralph Schaefer
3182 Williams Rd.
Oroville, CA 95965-8300
530-893-2902 or 530-894-6263
jschaefer@sunset.net

Dinnerware

Blair

Joe McManus
P.O. Box 153
Connelsville, PA 15425
jmcmanus@hhs.net

Blue Danube

Lori Simnioniw
Auburn Main St. Antiques
120 E. Main St.
Auburn, WA 98002
253-804-8041
Specializing in glassware, china, jewelry, and
furniture

Blue Ridge

Author of several books

Bill and Betty Newbound
2206 Nob Hill Dr.
Sanford, NC 27330
Also milk glass, wall pockets, figural planters, collectible china and glass

Cat-Tail

Ken and Barbara Brooks
4121 Gladstone Ln.
Charlotte, NC 28205

Currier & Ives Dinnerware

Author of book

Eldon R. Bud Aupperle
29470 Saxon Road
Toulon, IL 61483
309-896-3331; fax: 309-856-6005

Fiesta, Franciscan, Bauer, Harlequin, Riviera,
    Lu Ray, Metlox, and Homer Laughlin

Fiesta Plus
Mick and Lorna Chase
380 Hawkins Crawford Rd.
Cookeville, TN 38501
931-372-8333
www.dishesoldandnew.com

Homer Laughlin China

Author of book

Darlene Nossaman
5419 Lake Charles
Waco, TX 76710

Liberty Blue

Gary Beegle
92 River St.
Montgomery, NY 12549
845-457-3623
Also most lines of collectible modern American dinnerware as well as Depression glass

Purinton Pottery

Joe McManus
P.O. Box 153
Connellsville, PA 15425
724-628-4409
jmcmanus@hhs.net
Also Blair

Restaurant China

Author of two restaurant china books

Barbara J. Conroy
http://restaurant-china.home.comcast.
net/home.htm
Details contents of *Restaurant China, Vol-*

ume 1 & 2,; information on restaurant china item names, reproductions, manufacturers' marks, related books, and so forth, with links to other restaurant china sites

Royal China
BA Wellman
P.O. Box 673
Westminster, MA 01473-0673
ba@dishinitout.com
Also Ceramic Arts Studio

Russel Wright, Eva Zeisel, Homer Laughlin
Charles Alexander
221 E 34th St.
Indianapolis, IN 46205
317-924-9665

Vernon Kilns
Ray Vlach
rayvlach@hotmail.com

Dollhouse Furniture and Accessories
Renwal, Ideal, Marx, etc.
Judith A. Mosholder
186 Pine Springs Camp Rd.
Boswell, PA 15531
814-629-9277
jlytwins@floodcity.net

Dolls
Dolls from the 1960s – 70s, including Liddle Kiddles, Dolly Darlings, Petal People, Tiny Teens, etc.
Author of book on Liddle Kiddles; must send SASE for info
Paris Langford
415 Dodge Ave.
Jefferson, LA 70121
504-733-0676
bbean415@aol.com

Liddle Kiddles and other small dolls from the late '60s and early '70s
Dawn Diaz
20460 Samual Dr.
Saugus, CA 91530-3812
661-263-8697
jamdiaz99@earthlink.net

Door Knockers
Craig Dinner
P.O. Box 184
Townshend, VT 05353
718-729-3850

Egg Cups
Author of book
Brenda Blake
Box 555
York Harbor, ME 03911
207-363-6566
301-652-1140
eggcentric@aol.com

Roselle Schleifman
16 Vincent Rd.
Spring Valley, NY 10977

Erich Stauffer Figurines
Joan Oates
1107 Deerfield Lane
Marshall, MI 49068
269-781-9791
koates120@earthlink.net
Also Phoenix Bird china

Fast Food Collectibles
Authors of several books
Joyce and Terry Losonsky
7506 Summer Leave Lane
Columbia, MD 21046-2455
McDonald's® Collector's Guide to Happy Meal® Boxes, Premiums and Promotions ($9 plus $2 postage). *McDonald's® Happy Meal® Toys in the USA* and *McDonald's ® Happy Meal® Toys Around the World* (both full color, $24.95 each plus $3 postage), and *Illustrated Collector's Guide to McDonald's® McCAPS®* ($4 plus $2 postage) are available from authors

Bill and Pat Poe
220 Dominica Cir. E
Niceville, FL 32578-4085
850-897-4163; fax: 850-897-2606
BPoe220@Cox.net or PatPoeToys@aol.com
Also cartoon and character glasses, Pez, Smurfs, and California Raisins

Fishing Collectibles
Publishes fixed-price catalog
Dave Hoover
1023 Skyview Dr.
New Albany, IN 47150
Also miniature boats and motors
lurejockey@aol.com

Fitz and Floyd
Susan Robson
516 Greenridge Drive
Coppell, TX 75019

Flashlights
Author of book; Editor of newsletter
Bill Utley
P.O. Box 4095
Tustin, CA 92781
714-730-1252
flashlight1@cox.net

Florence Ceramics
Jerry Kline
Florence Showcase
P.O. Box 468
Bennington, VT 05201
802-442-3336
sweetpea@sweetpea.net
floshow@sweetpea.net
www.sweetpea.net
Shop: 1265 South Route 7, Bennington (2 miles south of Downtown on US Rte 7), daily 10 – 6

Flower Frogs
Author of book
Bonnie Bull
Flower Frog Gazette Online
www.flowerfrog.com

Frankoma
Author of book
Phyllis Bess Boone
14535 E 13th St.
Tulsa, OK 74108

Fruit Jars
Especially old, odd, or colored jars
John Hathaway
3 Mills Rd.
Bryant Pond, ME 04219
207-665-2124
Also old jar lids and closures

Gas Station Collectibles
Scott Benjamin
Oil Co. Collectibles Inc.
Petroleum Collectibles Monthly Magazine
P.O. Box 556
LaGrange, OH 44050-0556
440-355-6608
Specializing in gas globes, signs and magazines

Gay Fad Glassware
Donna S. McGrady
P.O. Box 14, 301 E. Walnut St.
Waynetown, IN 47990
765-234-2187
dmcg@tctc.com

Geisha Girl China
Author of book
Elyce Litts
P.O. Box 394
Morris Plains, NJ 07950
happy-memories@worldnet.att.net
www.happy-memories.com
Also ladies' compacts

Gilner Potteries
Collector of Gilner Pottery
Carla Chilton
8351 Balboa Blvd #39
Northridge, CA 91325-4078
carlew1@earthlink.net

Carol Power
P.O. Box 528
Columbia, CA 95310
Also Pixie collectibles
PixieWatch@wyoming.com
www.rvingthegoldfields.com/PixieWatch/Index.htm

Glass Animals
Author of book
Spencer, Dick and Pat
Glass and More (Shows only)
1203 N. Yale
O'Fallon, IL 62269
618-632-9067
Specializing in Cambridge, FEnton, Fostoria, Heisey, etc.

Granite Ware
Author of books
Helen Greguire
864-848-0408
Also carnival glass and toasters

Guardian Service Cookware
Dennis S. McAdams
3258 E. Lancaster Rd.
Hayden Lake, ID 83835
HAYDENMAC4@adelphia.net

Guardian Service Cookware
2110 Harmony Woods Road
Owings Mills, MD 21117-1649
410-560-0777
http://members.aol.com/vettelvr93/

Hagen-Renaker
Hagen-Renaker Collector's Club
C/o Ed & Sheri Alcorn
14945 Harmon Dr.
Shady Hills, FL 34610
727-856-6762

horsenut@gate.net
US subscription rate: $24 a year
www.geocities.com/heartland/7456/index.html

Hadley, M.A.
Lisa Sanders
8900 Old State Rd.
Evansville, IN 47711-1326

Halloween
Author of books; autographed copies available from the author
Pamela E. Apkarian-Russell
The Halloween Queen™
577 Boggs Run Rd.
Benwood, WV 26031-1001
halloweenqueen@castlehalloween.com
www.castlehalloween.com
Lectures and tours available at Castle Halloween museum. Also interested in other holidays, postcards, and Joe Camel

Head Vases
Larry G. Pogue
L&J Antiques & Collectibles
8142 Ivan Court
Terrell, TX 75161-6921
972-551-0221
LandJAntiques@direcway.com
www.LandJAntiques.com (TIAS.com member); Also antique and estate jewelry, string holders, egg timers

Horton Ceramics
Darlene Nossaman
5419 Lake Charles
Waco, TX 76710

Indy 500 Memorabilia
Eric Jungnickel
P.O. Box 4674
Naperville, IL 60567-4674
630-983-8339; ericjungnickel@yahoo.com

Insulators
Jacqueline Linscott Barnes
3557 Nicklaus Dr.
Tutusville, FL 32780

Japan Ceramics
Author of books
Carole Bess White
2225 NE 33rd
Portland, OR 97212-5116

Jewel Tea
Products or boxes only; no dishes
Bill & Judy Vroman
739 Eastern Ave.
Fostoria, OH 44830
419-435-5443

Jewelry
Author, lecturer, and appraiser
Marcia Brown (Sparkles)
P.O. Box 2314
White City, OR 97503
541-826-3039; fax: 541-830-5385
Author of *Unsigned Beauties of Costume Jewelry* and *Signed Beauties of Costume Jewelry, Vols. I & II*; and *Coro Jewelry*; Co-author and host of seven *Hidden Treasure* book-on-tape videos; Antique shows: Robby/Don Miller appraisal clinics, Palmer Wirf shows, Calendar shows

Men's accessories and cuff links only; edits newsletter
The National Cuff Link Society
Eugene R. Klompus
P.O. Box 5970
Vernon Hills, IL 60061
847-816-0035; fax: 847-816-7466
genek@cufflinksrus.com
www.justcufflinks.com

Josef Originals
Authors of books
Jim and Kaye Whitaker
Eclectic Antiques
P.O. Box 475, Dept. GS
Lynnwood, WA 98046

Kay Finch
Co-authors of book, available from authors
Mike Nickel and Cynthia Horvath
P.O. Box 456
Portland, MI 48875
517-647-7646
Also fine Ohio art pottery

Kentucky Derby and Horse Racing
Betty L. Hornback
707 Sunrise Ln.
Elizabethtown, KY 42701
bettysantiques@kvnet.org
Inquiries require a SASE with fee expected for appraisals and/or identification of glasses. Booklet picturing Kentucky Derby, Preakness, Belmont and other racing glasses available for $15 ppd.

Kitchen Prayer Ladies
Judy Foreman
JudyForeman@alltel.net
www.SweetandForemost.com

Lamps
Aladdin
Author of books
J.W. Courter
3935 Kelley Rd.
Kevil, KY 42053
502-488-2116

Motion lamps
Eclectic Antiques
Jim and Kaye Whitaker
P.O. Box 475, Dept. GS
Lynwood, WA 98046

Authors of book
Sam and Anna Samuelian
P.O. Box 504
Edgemont, PA 19028-0504
610-566-7248
sms@bee.net
www.motionlamp.com
Also motion clocks, transistor and novelty radios

Letter Openers
Author of book
Everett Grist
P.O. Box 91375
Chattanooga, TN 37412-3955
423-510-8052

License Plates
Richard Diehl
5965 W Colgate Pl.
Denver, CO 80227

Linens
De Witt & Co.
402-683-2515 or 402-683-3455 (after hours)
michael@dewittco.com
www.dewittco.com
Carry a wide variety of vintage textiles and ephemera — fabric, needlework, feed sacks, sewing patterns; also vintage valentines, road maps, magazines, and postcards

Retro Redheads
www.retro-redheads.com
1-978-857-8898; on the web since 1997
An online catalog of vintage linens and housewares for the Modern Gal and Dapper Guy

Longaberger Baskets
Jill S. Rindfuss, editor of *The Bentley Collection Guide*®
597 Sunbury Rd.
Delaware, OH 43015
1-800-837-4394
infobg@bentleyguide.com
www.bentleyguide.com
The most accurate and reliable reference tool available for evaluating Longaberger Products. Full color with individual photographs of most baskets and products produced since 1979. Published once a year in June with a free six-month update being sent in January to keep the guide current for the entire year.

Holds exclusive auctions
Greg Michael
Craft & Michael Auction/Realty Inc.
P.O. Box 7
Camden, IN 46917
219-686-2615 or 219-967-4442
fax: 219-686-9100
gpmmgtco@netusal1.net

Lunch Boxes
Terri's Toys and Nostalgia
Terri Ivers
114 Whitworth Ave.
Ponca City, OK 74601-3438
580-762-8697 or 580-762-5174
toylady@cableone.net

Magazines
Issues price guides to illustrators, pinups, and old magazines of all kinds
Denis C. Jackson
Illustrator Collector's News
P.O. 6433
Kingman, AZ 86401
ticn@olypen.com

National Geographic
Author of guide
Don Smith's National Geographic Magazines
3930 Rankin St.
Louisville, KY 40214
502-366-7504

Marbles
Author of books
Everett Grist
P.O. Box 91375
Chattanooga, TN 37412-3955
423-510-8052

Block's Box is the longest continuously running absentee marble auction service in the country; catalogs issued
Stanley A. & Robert S. Block
P.O. Box 51
Trumbull, CT 06611
203-261-3223 or 203-926-8448
blockschip@aol.com

Match Safes
George Sparacio
P.O. Box 791
Malaga, NJ 08328
856-694-4167; fax: 856-694-4536
mrvesta1@aol.com

McCoy Pottery
Author of books
Robert Hanson
16517 121 Ave. NE
Bothell, WA 98011

Melmac Dinnerware
Co-author of book
Gregg Zimmer
4017 16th Ave. S
Minneapolis, MN 55407

Metlox
Author of book; available from author
Carl Gibbs, Jr.
c/o California Connection
1716 Westheimer Rd.
Houston, TX 77098
ccdinnerware.com

Morton Pottery
Authors of books
Doris and Burdell Hall
B&B Antiques
210 W Sassafrass Dr.
Morton, IL 61550-1245

Motion Clocks
Electric; buy, sell, trade and restore
Sam and Anna Samuelian
P.O. Box 504
Edgemont, PA 19028-0504
610-566-7248
sms@bee.net
www.motonlamp.com
Also motion lamps, transistor and novelty radios

Motorcycles and Motorcycle Memorabilia
Bob 'Sprocket' Eckardt
P.O. Box 172
Saratoga Springs, NY 12866
518-584-2405
sprocketBE@aol.com
Buying and trading; Also literature, posters, toys, trophies, medals, fobs, pennants, FAM – AMA & Gypsy Tour items, programs, photos, jerseys, clocks, advertising items, signs, showroom items, motorcycles, and parts

Napkin Dolls
Co-Author of book
Bobbie Zucker Bryson
634 Cypress Hills Drive
Bluffton, SC 29909
843-705-3820
napkindoll@aol.com
To order a copy of the second edition of *Collectibles for the Kitchen, Bath & Beyond* (featuring 500+ new items & updated pricing on napkin dolls, egg timers, string holders, children's whistle cups and baby feeder dishes, razor blade banks, pie birds, laundry sprinkler bottles, and other unique collectibles from the same era), contact Krause Publications, P.O. Box 5009, Iola, WI 54945-5009
1-800-258-0929

Occupied Japan Collectibles
Florence Archambault
29 Freeborn St.
Newport, RI 03850-1821
Publishes *The Upside Down World of an O.J. Collector,* published bimonthly; Information requires SASE

Paper Dolls
Author of books
Mary Young
P.O. Box 9244
Wright Bros. Branch
Dayton, OH 45409-9244

Pencil Sharpeners
Phil Helley
629 Indiana Ave.
Wisconsin Dells, WI 53965
608-254-8659

Pennsbury Pottery
Shirley Graff
4515 Graff Rd.
Brunswick, OH 44212

Pepsi-Cola
Craig Stifter
218 South Adams Street
Hinsdale, IL 60521
cstifter@collectica.com
Other soda-pop memorablia as well

Perfume Bottles
Especially commercial, Czechoslovakian, Lalique, Baccarat, Victorian, crown top, factices, miniatures; Buy, sell and accept consignments for auctions
Monsen and Baer
Box 529
Vienna, VA 22183
703-938-2129

Pez
Richard Belyski
P.O. Box 14956
Surfside Beach, SC 29587
peznews@juno.com
www.pezcollectorsnews.com

Pie Birds
Linda Fields
230 Beech Lane
Buchanan, TN 38222
731-644-2244
Fpiebird@compu.net.
Organizer of Pie Bird Collector's Convention and author of *Four & Twenty Blackbirds; Vols. I & II.* Specializing in pie birds, pie funnels and pie vents

Pierce, Howard
Author of books
Darlene Dommel
P.O. Box 22493
Minneapolis, MN 55422-0493
763-374-9645
Specializing in Howard Pierce and Dakota potteries

Pin-Back Buttons
Michael and Polly McQuillen
McQuillen's Collectibles
P.O. Box 50022
Indianapolis, IN 46250
317-845-1721
michael@politicalparade.com
www.politicalparade.com

Pinup Art
Issues price guides to pinups, illustrations, and old magazines
Denis C. Jackson
Illustrator Collector's News
P.O. Box 6433
Kingman, AZ 86401
ticn@olypen.com

Pixies
Collector of Pixies
Carla Chilton
8351 Balboa Blvd., #39
Northridge, CA 91325-4078
carlew1@earthlink.net

Author of CD for Pixie collectors
Carol Power
P.O. Box 528
Columbia, CA 95310
Also Gilner Pottery in general
PixieWatch@wyoming.com
www.rvingthegoldfields.com/PixieWatch/Index.htm

Political
Michael and Polly McQuillen
McQuillen's Collectibles
P.O. Box 50022
Indianapolis, IN 46250
317-845-1721
michael@politicalparade.com
www.politicalparade.com

Pins, banners, ribbons, etc.
Paul Longo Americana
Box 5510
Magnolia, MA 01930
978-525-2290

Poodle Collectibles
Author of book
Elaine Butler
233 S. Kingston Ave.
Rockwood, TN 37854

Porcelier
Author of book
Susan Grindberg Lynn
4038 Dustin Ave.
Las Vegas, NV 89120
702-898-7535

Postcards
Pamela E. Apkarian-Russell
The Halloween Queen Antiques™
577 Boggs Run Rd.
Benwood, WV 26031-1001

www.castlehalloween.com
halloweenqueen@castlehalloween.com
Also Halloween and other holidays

Powder Jars
Sharon Thoerner
15549 Ryon Ave.
Bellflower, CA 90706
562-866-1555
rthoerner@juno.com
Also slag glass

Puzzles
Wooden jigsaw type from before 1950
Bob Armstrong
15 Monadnock Rd.
Worcester, MA 01609
www.oldpuzzles.com

Radio Premiums
Bill Campbell
1221 Littlebrook Ln.
Birmingham, AL 35235
205-853-8227; fax: 405-658-6986

Railroadiana
*Also steamship and other transportation
   memorabilia*
Lila Shrader
Shrader Antiques
2025 Hwy. 199
Crescent City, CA 95531
707-458-3525
Also Buffalo, Shelley, Niloak and Hummels

*Any item; especially china and silver
   Catalogs available*
John White, 'Grandpa'
Grandpa's Depot
1616 17th St., Ste. 267
Denver, CO 80202
303-628-5590; fax: 303-628-5547
Also related items

Razor Blade Banks
Deborah Gillham
47 Midline Ct.
Gaithersburg, MD 20878
301-977-5727

Reamers
Co-author of book, ordering info under Napkin Dolls
Bobbie Zucker Bryson
634 Cypress Hills Drive
Bluffton, SC 29909
843-705-3820

napkindoll@aol.com
www.reamers.org

Picture and 78 rpm kiddie records
Peter Muldavin
173 W 78th St. Apt 5-F
New York, NY 10024
212-362-9606
kiddie78s@aol.com

Especially 78 rpms, author of book
L.R. 'Les' Docks
Box 691035
San Antonio, TX 78269-1035
docks@texas.net (no attachments please!)
Write for want list

Red Wing Artware
Holds cataloged auctions
Wendy and Leo Frese
Three Rivers Collectibles
P.O. Box 551542
Dallas, TX 75355
214-341-5165
rumrill@ix.netcom.com

Regal China
Rick Spencer
Salt Lake City, UT
801-973-0805
 Also Coors, Watt, silver plate (especially
grape patterns), sterling

Rooster and Roses
Jacki Elliott
9790 Twin Cities Rd.
Galt, CA 95632
209-745-3860

Rosemeade
NDSU research specialist
Bryce Farnsworth
1334 14 1/2 St. S
Fargo, ND 58103
701-237-3597

Roseville
Author of books
Mike Nickel
P.O. Box 456
Portland, MI, 48875
517-647-7646
Also Kay Finch, other Ohio art pottery

Royal Bayreuth
Don and Anne Kier
2022 Marengo St.
Toledo, OH 43614
d.a.k@worldnet.att.net

Royal Copley
Author of books
Joe Devine
1411 3rd St.
Council Bluffs, IA 51503
712-328-7305
Buys & sells; Also pie birds

Royal Haeger
Author of book
David D. Dilley
6125 Knyghton Rd.
Indianapolis, IN 46220
317-251-0575
glazebears@aol.com

RumRill
Holds cataloged auctions
Wendy and Leo Frese
Three Rivers Collectibles
P.O. Box 551542
Dallas, TX 75355
214-341-5165
rumrill@ix,netcom.com

Ruby Glass
Author of book
Naomi L. Over
8909 Sharon Ln.
Arvada, CO 80002
303-424-5922

Salt and Pepper Shakers
Figural or novelty
Buy, sell and trade
Judy Posner
P.O. Box 2194 SC
Englewood, FL 34295
judy&jef@yahoo.com

Scouting Collectibles
R.J. Sayers
P.O. Box 629
Brevard, NC 28712
Certified antiques appraiser; owner of
Southeastern Antiques & Collectibles,
305 N. Main St., Hendersonville, NC
28792

Sebastians
Jim Waite
308 S Main St.
Farmer City, IL 61842-0025
800-842-2593

Sewing
Kathy Goldsworthy
Past Glories
5302 234th St. E
Spanaway, WA 98387
pastglories@comcast.net

Sewing Machines
Toy only
Authors of book
Darryl and Roxana Matter
P.O. Box 65
Portis, KS 67474-0065

Shawnee
Authors of books
Beverly and Jim Mangus
4812 Sherman Church Ave SW
Canton, OH 44706-3958

Rick Spencer
Salt Lake City, UT
801-973-0805

Shot Glasses
Author of book
Mark Pickvet
Shot Glass Club of America
5071 Watson Dr.
Flint, MI 48506

Silhouette Pictures (20th Century)
Author of book
Shirley Mace
Shadow Enterprises
P.O. Box 1602
Mesilla Park, NM 88047
505-524-6717
silhouettes-us@yahoo.com
www.geocities.com/MadisonAvenue/Board
room/1631/

Silver-plated and Sterling Flatware
Rick Spencer
Salt Lake City, UT
801-973-0805
Also Coors and Watt

Skookum Indian Dolls
Jo Ann Palmieri
27 Pepper Rd.
Towaco, NJ 07082-1357

Smiley Face
Pam Speidel
84475 Hwy. 35
Norfolk, NE 68701
pam@smileycollector.com
www.smileycollector.com

Soda Fountain Collectibles
Harold and Joyce Screen
2804 Munster Rd.
Baltimore, MD 21234
410-661-6765
hscreen@home.com

Soda-Pop Memorabilia
Craig Stifter
218 South Adams St.
Hinsdale, IL 60521
cstifter@collectica.com

Sports Collectibles
Kevin R. Bowman
P.O. Box 4500
Joplin, MO 64803
showmequail@joplin.com

Equipment and player-used items
Don and Anne Kier
2022 Marengo St.
Toledo, OH 43614
d.a.k.@worldnet.att.net

St. Clair Glass
Ted Pruitt
3350 W 700 N
Anderson, IN 46011
Book available ($25)

Stangl
Birds, dinnerware, artware
Popkorn Antiques
Bob and Nancy Perzel
P.O. Box 1057
Flemington, NJ 08822
908-782-9631

String Holders
Larry G. Pogue
L&J Antiques & Collectibles
Terrell, TX 75161-6921
972-551-0221
LandJAntiques@direcway.com

www.LandJAntiques.com (TIAS.com member)
Also antique and estate jewelry, head vases,
string holders, and egg timers

Swanky Swigs
Joyce Jackson
817-441-8864
jjpick3@earthlink.net

Tiara Exclusives
Author of Books
Mandi Birkinbine
P.O. Box 121
Meridian, ID 83680-0121
info@shop4antiques.com
www.shop4antiques.com
Tiara Tiara Exclusives Glass: The Sandwich Pattern,
(Pictures and values of Tiara's Sandwich pattern
in over 20 different colors, $39.00+$2.75 postage
and handling in the continental US)

Tire Ashtrays
Author of book ($12.95 postpaid)
Jeff McVey
1810 W State St., #427
Boise, ID 83702-3955

Toothbrush Holders
Author of book
Marilyn Cooper
8408 Lofland Dr.
Houston, TX 77055-4811

Toys
Any and all
June Moon
143 Vine Ave.
Park Ridge, IL 60068
junmoonstr@aol.com
www.junemooncollectibles.com

Hot Wheels
D.W. (Steve) Stephenson
11117 NE 164th Pl.
Bothell, WA 98011-4003

Sand toys
Authors of book
Carole and Richard Smyth
Carole Smyth Antiques
P.O. Box 2068
Huntington, NY 11743

Slot race cars from 1960s-70s
Gary T. Pollastro
5047 84th Ave. SE
Mercer Island, WA 98040
206-232-3199

Transformers and Robots
David Kolodny-Nagy
Toy Hell
P.O. Box 75271
Los Angeles, CA 90075
toyhell@yahoo.com
www.toyhell.com

Walkers, ramp-walkers, and windups
Randy Welch
Raven'tiques
27965 Peach Orchard Rd.
Easton, MD 21601-8203
410-822-5441

Treasure Craft
Author of book
George A. Higby, ISA
Sutton Place #205
1221 Minor Ave.
Seattle, WA 98101
206-682-7288
geoahigby@hotmail.com

Trolls
Author of book
Pat Peterson
1105 6th Ave. SE
Hampton, IA 50441-2657
SASE for information

TV Guides
Giant illustrated 1948 – 1999 TV Guide
Catalog, $3.00; 2000+ catalog, $2.00
TV Guide Specialists
Jeff Kadet
P.O. Box 20
Macomb, IL 61455

Twin Winton
Author of book; now out of print
Mike Ellis
266 Rose Ln.
Costa Mesa, CA 92627
949-646-7112; fax: 949-645-4919

Valentines
Author of three books on subject; available
from author; Appraisal fee available upon
request. Please send self-addressed envelope
for any replies

Katherine Kreider
P.O. Box 7957
Lancaster, PA 17604-7957
717-892-3001
Katherinekreider@valentinesdirect.com
www.valentinesdirect.com

Vandor
Lois Wildman
175 E. Chick Rd.
Camano Island, WA 98282

Vernon Kilns
Author of book
Maxine Nelson
7657 E. Hazelwood St.
Scottscale, AZ 85251

Ray Vlach
rayvlach@hotmail.com

Wade
Author of book
Ian Warner
P.O. Box 93022
Brampton, Ontario
Canada L6Y 4V8
idwarner@rogers.com

Wedding Cake Toppers
Jeannie Greenfield
Author of book
310 Parker Rd.
Stoneboro, PA 16153-2810
724-376-2584
dlg3684@yahoo.com
25-year collector of wedding toppers and
memorabilia; author of *Wedding Cake*
Toppers, Memories and More (soon to be
released) with hundreds of color photos
and 76 bibliography sources, containing a
complete history of toppers and customs;
more than 500 toppers shown in more than
100 photos; tips on restoration, display,
storage, etc.

Weller Pottery
Hardy Hudson
1896 Wingfield Dr.
Longwood, FL 32779
447-404-9009 or 407-963-6093
todiefor@mindspring.com
Also Roseville, Grueby, Newcomb, Over-
beck, Pewabic, Ohr, Teco, Fulper, Clewell,
Tiffany, etc.

Western Collectibles
Author of book
Warren R. Anderson
American West Archives
P.O. Box 100
Cedar City, UT 84721
435-586-9497
Also documents, autographs, stocks and
bonds, and other ephemera

Western Heroes
Author of books, ardent researcher and guest
columnist
Robert W. Phillips
Phillips Archives of Western Memorabilia
1703 N Aster Pl.
Broken Arrow, OK 74012-1308
918-254-8205; fax: 918-252-9363

Westmoreland
Cheryl Schafer
RR 2, Box 37
Lancaster, MO 63548
660-457-3510
csch178@nemr.net
Winter address (November 1-May 1)
P.O. Box 1443
Webster, FL 33597
352-568-7383
chesch20@atlantic.net

Wilton Pans
Cheryl Moody
Hoosier Collectibles
607 N. Lafayette Blvd.
South Bend, IN 46601
www.rubylane.com/shops/hoosiercollectibles
www.goantiques.com (Dealer: Hoosier Collectibles)

World's Fairs and Expositions
Herbert Rolfes
Yesterday's World
P.O. Box 398
Mount Dora, FL 32756
352-735-3947
NY1939@aol.com

Index

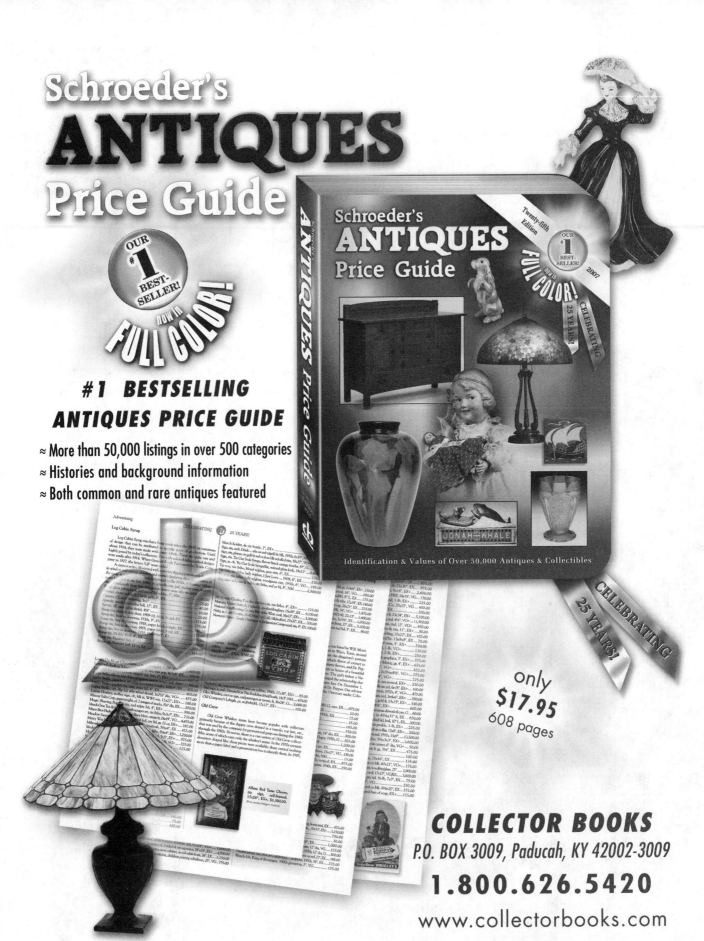